# GRAVEL-BED RIVERS

# GRAVEL-BED RIVERS: PROCESSES, TOOLS, ENVIRONMENTS

Edited by

**Michael Church**
*Department of Geography*
*The University of British Columbia*
*Vancouver, British Columbia, Canada*

**Pascale M. Biron**
*Department of Geography, Planning*
*and Environment, Concordia University*
*Montreal, Quebec, Canada*

**André G. Roy**
*Département de géographie*
*Université de Montréal*
*Montréal, Québec, Canada*

with Associate Editors

**Peter Ashmore**
*Department of Geography*
*University of Western Ontario*
*London, Ontario, Canada*

**Normand Bergeron**
*Institut National de la Recherche Scientifique,*
*Centre Eau-Terre-Environnement, St.Foy,*
*Québec, Canada*

**Thomas Buffin-Bélanger**
*Département de biologie, chimie et*
*géographie, Université de Québec*
*à Rimouski, Rimouski, Québec, Canada*

**Colin Rennie**
*Department of Civil Engineering*
*University of Ottawa*
*Ottawa, Ontario, Canada*

**WILEY-BLACKWELL**
A John Wiley & Sons, Ltd., Publication

This edition first published 2012 © 2012 by John Wiley & Sons, Ltd

Wiley-Blackwell is an imprint of John Wiley & Sons, formed by the merger of Wiley's global Scientific, Technical and Medical business with Blackwell Publishing.

*Registered office:*   John Wiley & Sons, Ltd, The Atrium, Southern Gate, Chichester, West Sussex, PO19 8SQ, UK

*Editorial offices:*   9600 Garsington Road, Oxford, OX4 2DQ, UK
                The Atrium, Southern Gate, Chichester, West Sussex, PO19 8SQ, UK
                111 River Street, Hoboken, NJ 07030-5774, USA

For details of our global editorial offices, for customer services and for information about how to apply for permission to reuse the copyright material in this book please see our website at www.wiley.com/wiley-blackwell.

*Library of Congress Cataloging-in-Publication Data*

Gravel bed rivers : processes, tools, environments / edited by Michael Church,
Pascale Biron, André G. Roy ; with associate editors Peter Ashmore . . . [et al.].
    p. cm.
  ISBN 978-0-470-68890-8 (cloth)
 1.  River channels.  I. Church, Michael Anthony, 1942- II. Biron, Pascale.
III. Roy, André G. IV. Ashmore, Peter.
   TC175.G765 2012
   551.48'3–dc23                                    2011025981

A catalogue record for this book is available from the British Library.

Wiley also publishes its books in a variety of electronic formats. Some content that appears in print may not be available in electronic books.

Set in 9.25/11pt Times New Roman by Thomson Digital, Noida, India

Printed and bound in Singapore by Markono Print Media Pte Ltd

First Impression 2012

# Contents

List of Contributing Authors . . . . . . . . . . . . . . . . . . . . . . . . . .   ix
Preface . . . . . . . . . . . . . . . . . . . . . . . . . . . . . . . . . . . .   xv

SECONDARY FLOWS IN RIVERS . . . . . . . . . . . . . . . . . . . . . .   1

 1  Secondary Flows in Rivers: Theoretical Framework, Recent Advances,
    and Current Challenges, *Vladimir Nikora and André G. Roy* . . . . . . . .   3
 2  Secondary Flows in Rivers: The Effect of Complex
    Geometry, *Bruce MacVicar* . . . . . . . . . . . . . . . . . . . . . . . .  23
 3  Aspects of Secondary Flow in Open Channels: A Critical Literature
    Review, *Athanasios (Thanos) N. Papanicolaou* . . . . . . . . . . . .  31

SEDIMENT TRANSPORT . . . . . . . . . . . . . . . . . . . . . . . . .  37

 4  Gravel Transport in Granular Perspective, *Philippe Frey*
    *and Michael Church* . . . . . . . . . . . . . . . . . . . . . . . . . . . .  39
 5  On Gravel Exchange in Natural Channels, *Judith K. Haschenburger* . . . .  56

MODELLING MORPHODYNAMICS . . . . . . . . . . . . . . . . . . . .  69

 6  Morphodynamics of Bars in Gravel-bed Rivers: Bridging Analytical
    Models and Field Observations, *Guido Zolezzi, Walter Bertoldi,*
    *and Marco Tubino* . . . . . . . . . . . . . . . . . . . . . . . . . . . . .  71
 7  Field Observations of Gravel-bed River Morphodynamics: Perspectives
    and Critical Issues for Testing of Models, *Nicola Surian* . . . . . . . .  90
 8  Morphodynamics of Bars in Gravel-bed Rivers: Coupling Hydraulic
    Geometry and Analytical Models, *Robert G. Millar* . . . . . . . . . . .  96
 9  Modelling Sediment Transport and Morphodynamics
    of Gravel-bed Rivers, *Erik Mosselman* . . . . . . . . . . . . . . . . . . 101
10  The Potential of using High-resolution Process Models to Inform
    Parameterizations of Morphodynamic Models, *Richard J. Hardy* . . . . . 116
11  The Importance of Off-channel Sediment Storage in 1-D
    Morphodynamic Modelling, *J. Wesley Lauer* . . . . . . . . . . . . . . . 123

RIVER RESTORATION AND REGULATION . . . . . . . . . . . . . . . 135

12  Stream Restoration in Gravel-bed Rivers, *Peter R. Wilcock* . . . . . . . 137

13  River Restoration: Widening Perspectives, *Nicholas J. Clifford* . . . . . .  150
14  Restoring Geomorphic Resilience in Streams, *Noah P. Snyder* . . . . . .  160
15  The Geomorphic Response of Gravel-bed Rivers to Dams: Perspectives
    and Prospects, *Gordon E. Grant* . . . . . . . . . . . . . . . . . .  165
16  Mitigating Downstream Effects of Dams, *David Gaeuman* . . . . . . .  182

ECOLOGICAL ASPECTS OF GRAVEL-BED RIVERS . . . . . . . . . . . . .  191

17  River Geomorphology and Salmonid Habitat: Some Examples
    Illustrating their Complex Association, from Redd to Riverscape
    Scales, *Michel Lapointe* . . . . . . . . . . . . . . . . . . . .  193
18  Incorporating Spatial Context into the Analysis of Salmonid–Habitat
    Relations, *Christian E. Torgersen, Colden V. Baxter, Joseph L. Ebersole,*
    *and Robert E. Gresswell* . . . . . . . . . . . . . . . . . . . .  216
19  Animals and the Geomorphology of Gravel-bed Rivers, *Stephen P. Rice,*
    *Matthew F. Johnson, and Ian Reid* . . . . . . . . . . . . . . . .  225
20  Geomorphology and Gravel-bed River Ecosystem Services: Workshop
    Outcomes, *Normand Bergeron and Joanna Eyquem* . . . . . . . . .  242

TOOLS FOR STUDY . . . . . . . . . . . . . . . . . . . . . . . . .  259

21  Remote Sensing of the Hydraulic Environment in Gravel-bed
    Rivers, *W. Andrew Marcus* . . . . . . . . . . . . . . . . . . . .  261
22  LiDAR and ADCP Use in Gravel-bed Rivers: Advances
    Since GBR6, *David J. Milan and George L. Heritage* . . . . . . . .  286
23  Remotely Sensed Topographic Change in Gravel Riverbeds with Flowing
    Channels, *D. Murray Hicks* . . . . . . . . . . . . . . . . . . .  303
24  Modern Digital Instruments and Techniques for Hydrodynamic
    and Morphologic Characterization of River Channels, *Marian Muste,*
    *Dongsu Kim, and Venkatesh Merwade* . . . . . . . . . . . . . . .  315
25  Mapping Water and Sediment Flux Distributions in Gravel-bed Rivers
    Using ADCPs, *Colin D. Rennie* . . . . . . . . . . . . . . . . . .  342

STEEP CHANNELS . . . . . . . . . . . . . . . . . . . . . . . . .  351

26  Recent Advances in the Dynamics of Steep Channels, *Francesco Comiti*
    *and Luca Mao* . . . . . . . . . . . . . . . . . . . . . . . . .  353
27  Examining Individual Step Stability within Step-pool
    Sequences, *Joanna Crowe Curran.* . . . . . . . . . . . . . . . .  378
28  Alluvial Steep Channels: Flow Resistance, Bedload Transport Prediction,
    and Transition to Debris Flows, *Dieter Rickenmann* . . . . . . . .  386

SEMI-ALLUVIAL CHANNELS . . . . . . . . . . . . . . . . . . . . .  399

29  Semi-alluvial Channels and Sediment-Flux-Driven Bedrock
    Erosion, *Jens M. Turowski* . . . . . . . . . . . . . . . . . . .  401
30  Transport Capacity, Bedrock Exposure, and Process
    Domains, *Thomas E. Lisle* . . . . . . . . . . . . . . . . . . .  419
31  Nomenclature, Complexity, Semi-alluvial Channels and
    Sediment-flux-driven Bedrock Erosion, *Lyubov V. Meshkova, Paul A. Carling,*
    *and Thomas Buffin-Bélanger* . . . . . . . . . . . . . . . . . .  424

## RIVER CHANNEL CHANGE . . . . . . . . . . . . . . . . . . . 433

32 Changes in Channel Morphology Over Human
Time Scales, *John M. Buffington* . . . . . . . . . . . 435

33 Channel Response and Recovery to Changes in Sediment
Supply, *Marwan A. Hassan and André E. Zimmermann* . . . . . . . . 464

34 Alluvial Landscape Evolution: What Do We Know About Metamorphosis
of Gravel-bed Meandering and Braided Streams?, *François Métivier
and Laurie Barrier* . . . . . . . . . . . . . . . . . 474

35 Differences in Sediment Supply to Braided and Single-Thread
River Channels: What Do the Data Tell Us?, *John Pitlick, Erich R. Mueller,
and Catalina Segura* . . . . . . . . . . . . . . . . 502

36 Can We Link Cause and Effect in Landscape Evolution?, *Thomas J. Coulthard
and Marco J. Van De Wiel* . . . . . . . . . . . . . . 512

## ICE IN GRAVEL-BED RIVERS . . . . . . . . . . . . . . . . . 523

37 River-Ice Effects on Gravel-Bed Channels, *Robert Ettema
and Edward W. Kempema* . . . . . . . . . . . . . . . 525

38 Is There a Northern Signature on Fluvial Form?, *James P. McNamara* . . . 541

39 Long-term and Large-scale River-ice Processes in Cold-region
Watersheds, *Etienne Boucher, Yves Bégin, Dominique Arseneault,
and Taha B.M.J. Ouarda* . . . . . . . . . . . . . . . 546

Index . . . . . . . . . . . . . . . . . . . . . . . . . 555

# List of Contributing Authors

*Note*: Bold names indicate the corresponding authors

*Dominique Arseneault*

Département de biologie, chimie et géographie, Université du Québec à Rimouski, Rimouski, Québec, Canada. *dominique_arseneault@uqar.qc.ca*

*Laurie Barrier*

Institut du Physique du Globe de Paris, Jussieu, Paris, France. *barrier@ipgp.fr*

*Colden V. Baxter*

Idaho State University, Pocatello, Idaho, USA. *baxtcold@isu.edu*

*Yves Bégin*

Institut National de la Recherche Scientifique, Centre Eau-Terre-Environnement, St.Foy, Québec, Canada. *yves.begin@ete.inrs.ca*

**Normand Bergeron**

Institut national de la recherche scientifique, Centre Eau-Terre-Environnement, Québec, Canada *normand.bergeron@ete.inrs.ca*

*Walter Bertoldi*

School of Geography, Queen Mary University of London, London, UK and Dipartimento di Ingegneria Civile e Ambientale, University of Trento, Trento Italy. *walter.bertoldi@ing.unitn.it*

**Pascale M. Biron**

Department of Geography, Planning and Environment, Concordia University, Montreal, Quebec, Canada

**Etienne Boucher**

CEREGE, Europole Mediterranéen de l'Arbois, Aix-en-Provence, France. *boucher.etienne@uqam.ca*

**Thomas Buffin-Bélanger**

Département de biologie, chimie et géographie, Université du Québec à Rimouski, Rimouski, Québec, Canada. *thomas_buffin-belanger@uqar.qc.ca*

**John M. Buffington**

USDA Forest Service, Rocky Mountain Research Station, Boise, Idaho, USA. *jbuffington@fs.fed.us*

**Paul A. Carling**

Geography and Environment, University of Southampton, Southampton, UK. *p.a.carling@soton.ac.uk*

Michael Church

Department of Geography, The University of British Columbia, Vancouver, British Columbia, Canada. *mchurch@geog.ubc.ca*

**Nicholas J. Clifford**

Department of Geography, King's College, London, UK. *nicholas.clifford@kcl.ac.uk*

**Francesco Comiti**

Faculty of Science and Technology, Free University of Bozen-Bolzano, Bolzano, Italy. *francesco.comiti@unibz.it*

**Thomas J. Coulthard**

Department of Geography, University of Hull, Hull, UK. *T.Coulthard@hull.ac.uk*

**Joanna Crowe Curran**

Department of Civil and Environmental Engineering, University of Virginia, Charlottesville, Virginia, USA. *curran@virginia.edu*

Joseph L. Ebersole

US Environmental Protection Agency, National Health and Environmental Effects Research Laboratory, Western Ecology Division, Corvallis, Oregon, USA. *ebersole.joe@epa.gov*

**Robert Ettema**

Civil and Architectural Engineering Department, University of Wyoming, Laramie, Wyoming USA. *rettema@uwyo.edu*

Joanna Eyquem

Parish Geomorphic Ltd., Mississauga, Ontario, Canada. *jeyquem@parishgeomorphic.com*

**Philippe Frey**

CEMAGREF, Unité de recherche Erosion Torrentielle, Neige et Avalanches, Saint-Martin-d'Hères, France. *phillipe.frey@cemagref.fr*

**David Gaeuman**

Trinity River Restoration Program, Weaverville California, USA. *dgaeuman@usbr.gov*

**Gordon E. Grant**

>   USDA Forest Service, Pacific Northwest Research Station, Corvalllis, Oregon, USA. *gordon.grant@oregonstate.edu*

*Robert E. Gresswell*

>   US Geological Survey, Northern Rocky Mountain Science Center, Bozeman, Montana, USA. *bgresswell@usgs.gov*

**Richard J. Hardy**

>   Department of Geography, Durham University, Durham, UK. *r.j.hardy@durham.ac.uk*

**Judith K. Haschenburger**

>   Department of Geological Sciences, University of Texas at San Antonio, San Antonio, Texas, USA. *judy.haschenburger@utsa.edu*

**Marwan A. Hassan**

>   Department of Geography, The University of British Columbia, Vancouver, British Columbia, Canada. *mhassan@geog.ubc.ca*

*George L. Heritage*

>   JBA Consulting, The Bank Quay House, Sankey St., Warrington, UK. *george.heritage@jbaconsulting.co.uk*

**D. Murray Hicks**

>   NIWA, Christchurch, New Zealand. *m.hicks@niwa.co.nz*

*Matthew F. Johnson*

>   Department of Geography, Loughborough University, Loughborough, Leicestershire, UK. *m.f.johnson@lboro.ac.uk*

*Edward W. Kempema*

>   Civil and Architectural Engineering Department, University of Wyoming, Laramie, Wyoming USA. *kempema@uwyo.edu*

*Dongsu Kim*

>   Department of Civil and Environmental Engineering, Dankook University, Kyunggido, Korea. *dongsu-kim@dankook.ac.kr*

**Michel Lapointe**

>   Department of Geography, McGill University, Montreal, Québec, Canada. *lapointe@geog.mcgill.ca*

**J. Wesley Lauer**

>   Department of Civil and Environmental Engineering, Seattle University, Seattle, Washington, USA. *lauerj@seattleu.edu*

**Thomas E. Lisle**

>   USDA Forest Service, Redwood Sciences Laboratory, Arcata, California, USA. *tel7001@humboldt.edu*

**Bruce MacVicar**

> Department of Civil and Environmental Engineering, University of Waterloo, Waterloo, Ontario, Canada. *bmacvicar@uwaterloo.ca*

*Luca Mao*

> Faculty of Science and Technology, Free University of Bozen-Bolzano, Bolzano, Italy. luca.mao@unibz.it

**W. Andrew Marcus**

> Department of Geography, University of Oregon, Eugene, Oregon, USA. *marcus@uoregon.edu*

**James P. McNamara**

> Department of Geosciences, Boise State University, Boise, Idaho, USA. *jmcnamar@boisestate.edu*

*Venkatesh Merwade*

> School of Civil Engineering, Purdue University, West Lafayette, Indiana, USA. *vmerwade@purdue.edu*

*Lyubov V. Meshkova*

> Geography and Environment, University of Southampton, Southampton, UK. *l.v.meshkova@soton.ac.uk*

**François Métivier**

> Institut du Physique du Globe de Paris, Jussieu, Paris, France. *metivier@ipgp.fr*

**David J. Milan**

> Department of Natural and Social Sciences, University of Gloucestershire, Cheltenham, Gloucestershire, UK. *dmilan@glos.ac.uk*

**Robert G. Millar**

> Department of Civil Engineering, The University of British Columbia, Vancouver, British Columbia, Canada. *millar@civil.ubc.ca*

**Erik Mosselman**

> Inland Water Systems Unit, Deltares and Faculty of Civil Engineering and Geosciences, Delft University of Technology, Delft, The Netherlands. *erik.mosselman@deltares.nl*

**Erich R. Mueller**

> Geography Department, University of Colorado, Boulder, Colorado, USA. *erich.mueller@colorado.edu*

**Marian Muste**

> IIHR-Hydroscience & Engineering and Civil & Environmental Engineering Department, The University of Iowa, Iowa City, Iowa, USA. *marian-muste@uiowa.edu*

*Vladimir Nikora*

School of Engineering, Kings College, Aberdeen, UK. *v.nikora@abdn.ac.uk*

*Taha B.M.J. Ouarda*

Institut National de la Recherche Scientifique, Centre Eau-Terre-Environnement, Québec, Canada. *taha_ouarda@ete.inrs.ca*

**Athanasios (Thanos) N. Papanicolaou**

IIHR-Hydroscience & Engineering and Civil & Environmental Engineering Department, The University of Iowa, Iowa City, Iowa, USA. *apapanic@engineering.uiowa.edu*

**John Pitlick**

Geography Department, University of Colorado, Boulder, Colorado, USA. *pitlick@colorado.edu*

*Ian Reid*

Department of Geography, Loughborough University, Loughborough, Leicestershire, UK. *ian.reid@lboro.ac.uk*

**Colin D. Rennie**

Department of Civil Engineering, University of Ottawa, Ottawa, Ontario, Canada. *crennie@genie.uottawa.ca*

**Stephen P. Rice**

Department of Geography, Loughborough University, Loughborough, Leicestershire, UK. *s.rice@lboro.ac.uk*

**Dieter Rickenmann**

Swiss Federal Research Institute WSL, Birmensdorf, Switzerland. *dieter.rickenmann@wsl.ch*

**André G. Roy**

Département de géographie, Université de Montréal, Montréal, Québec, Canada. *andre.roy@umontreal.ca*

*Catalina Segura*

Department of Forestry and Environmental Resources, North Carolina State University, Raleigh, North Carolina, USA. *csegura@ncsu.edu*

**Noah P. Snyder**

Department of Earth and Environmental Sciences, Boston College, Chestnut Hill, Massachusetts, USA. *noah.snyder@bc.edu*

**Nicola Surian**

Dipartimento di Geografia, Università di Padova, Padova, Italy. *nicola.surian@unipd.it*

*Christian E. Torgersen*

> US Geological Survey, Forest and Rangeland Ecosystem Science Center, Cascadia Field Station, University of Washington, School of Forest Resources, Seattle, Washington, USA. *ctorgersen@usgs.gov*

*Marco Tubino*

> Dipartimento di Ingegneria Civile e Ambientale, University of Trento, Trento Italy. *marco.tubino@ing.unitn.it*

**Jens M. Turowski**

> Swiss Federal Research Institute WSL, Birmensdorf, Switzerland. *jens.turowski@wsl.ch*

*Marco J. Van De Wiel*

> Department of Geography, University of Western Ontario, London, Ontario, Canada. *mvandew3@uwo.ca*

**Peter R. Wilcock**

> Department of Geography & Environmental Engineering, Johns Hopkins University, Baltimore Maryland, USA. *paintedrockwilcock@gmail.com*

*André E. Zimmermann*

> Northwest Hydraulics Consultants, Ltd., North Vancouver, British Columbia, Canada. *azimmermann@nhc-van.com*

**Guido Zolezzi**

> Dipartimento di Ingegneria Civile e Ambientale, University of Trento, Trento Italy. *guido.zolezzi@ing.unitn.it*

# Preface

The 7th International Gravel Bed Rivers Workshop was held in Canada at Tadoussac, Québec, between 6 and 10 September, 2010. Tadoussac, located on the north shore of the St Lawrence River at the mouth of the Saguenay Fjord, is the oldest settlement in British North America to have been continually occupied by European settlers and their descendents, dating from the establishment of a fur trading station by French colonists in 1600 (the site of a Basque whaling station, intermittently occupied in the late 16th century, is located immediately to the east of Tadoussac). It is still a relatively quiet village and so well fits the tradition of the Gravel Bed Rivers workshops to seek meeting places that permit concentrated discussion, some relaxation, and good meals.

In further keeping with that tradition, the workshop was designed to present an authoritative review of recent progress in understanding the morphology and processes in gravel bed rivers, a review that you have in your hands. Accordingly, the workshop was constructed around a series of invited keynote presentations that reviewed the principal themes selected for the meeting. The format of the workshop was, however, varied from that of past meetings to the extent that formal discussion papers were invited to accompany each keynote paper, the authors of which were the referees of the keynote paper to which they were invited to respond. Those discussions appear in the book as regular chapters.

The themes of the conference, reflected in the title of the book, were processes, tools, and environments. Processes, to provide for reviews of progress in fundamental understanding of gravel bed rivers; tools, to emphasize the important advances of recent years in observing and measuring instruments and methods – particularly advances in remote-sensing methods; environments, to emphasize the diverse conditions that give rise to rivers flowing over coarse-grained materials.

We have, however, introduced some new themes into this conference, in part in recognition of the meeting in Canada, a cold, northern country with abundant rock and fast-flowing rivers, and in part to address emerging topics of high interest. There was a session on ice in gravel bed rivers. Recognizing the importance of hydroelectric power in Canada, a keynote paper specifically considered dams on gravel bed rivers within the larger context of river channel regulation and restoration. In a session on riverine ecology, rivers as the environment for salmonid fishes – a major Canadian resource – was emphasized. Semi-alluvial channels, ones flowing partly on rock, were for the first time considered in a keynote session. At a more fundamental level, the opening theme session was dedicated to secondary flows, an important mediator of river morphology that has not previously been emphasized in the workshops (nor, indeed, sufficiently considered in the discipline). Numerical modelling of gravel bed river morphodynamics, a rapidly advancing art, was featured in another session. River channel change over extended periods was also given theme attention. Sessions on steep channels and on sediment transport – perhaps the most fundamental theme of all – rounded out the meeting.

Our traditional "practical" exercise was also different at this meeting. Always devoted to field work in the past, we felt a bit overwhelmed at the scale of Canadian rivers as a site for a part-day excursion (the St Lawrence opposite Tadoussac is actually a part of an inland sea that occupies a tectonic basin – not gumboot and measuring tape territory). Therefore, we remained in our comfortable hotel and conducted a workshop facilitated by Normand Bergeron and Joanna Eyquem on ecosystem services provided by gravel bed rivers. Again, a new topic for the workshops, but an important and timely one, reported as a full chapter in this volume.

In addition to the keynote and formal discussion papers presented in this book, the meeting attracted 75 poster presentations, many of them by the graduate student contingent, as usual a highly motivated and enthusiastic group. A selection of those posters has become a formal collection presented in a special edition of *Earth Surface Processes and Landforms*, edited by Peter Ashmore and Colin Rennie.

The meeting, as usual, featured field trips before and after the meeting. Thomas Buffin-Bélanger and André Roy conducted a three-day excursion before the meeting that commenced at Rimouski, on the south shore of the St Lawrence and spent two days investigating the rivers of the Gaspésie region – steep, gravel bed rivers significantly influenced by seasonal ice and subjected to a recent history of intensive log-drives to sawmills at the river mouths. On Saturday evening we made the 62 km crossing of the Gulf of St Lawrence between Matane, in Gaspésie, and Baie-Comeau on the north shore, where hydropower rivers were investigated on the third day. After the conference, Normand Bergeron and Michel Lapointe led a trip from Tadoussac to Québec City that examined river habitat in gravel bed salmon rivers, intensively investigated in recent years by members of the Centre Interuniversitaire de Recherche sur le Saumon Atlantique (CIRSA).

There are many people to thank for the success of the meeting. First, our sponsors, Hydro-Québec and Parish Geomorphic; GEOIDE, the Canadian Research Network of Excellence in Geomatics; Boréas, groupe de recherche sur les environnements nordiques; la Chaire de recherche du Canada en dynamique fluviale; Concordia University; l'Institut National de la Recherche Scientifique: Eau, Terre et Environnement (INRS-ETE); McGill University; The University of British Columbia; l'Université de Montréal; The University of Ottawa; l'Université du Québec à Rimouski (UQAR); The University of Western Ontario. Thanks to Laurence Therrien and Hélène Lamarre who greatly helped with the organization and management of the conference, Linda Lamarre who gave organizational and financial advice, the staff of the Tadoussac Hotel, especially Véronique Gaudreault, who delivered highly professional support through all stages of preparing and conducting the meeting. Maxime Boivin, Laurence Chaput-Desrosiers, Sylvio Demers, Geneviève Marquis, Taylor Olsen, and Michèle Tremblay prepared and helped to conduct the field trips and managed the poster sessions. Eric Leinberger, cartographer at the University of British Columbia Department of Geography, made heroic efforts to standardize the presentation of the figures in the book. Finally, the staff at John Wiley & Sons, especially Rachael Ballard and Fiona Woods have been wonderfully helpful in bringing to publication this most important aspect of the meeting – the permanent record. Finally, we must thank our four editorial associates, who have done so much to ensure the timely production of the book.

Thanks also to Professor Rob Ferguson, who entertained the meeting as its featured banquet speaker with the unofficial and nearly entirely correct history of GBR.

We trust that this book, like its predecessors, will become part of the authoritative record of advances in knowledge and understanding of gravel bed rivers. And we wish the hosts of the next meeting, GBR8, to be held in Japan, as much success as we have enjoyed.

Mike Church

# Secondary Flows in Rivers

# 1

# Secondary Flows in Rivers: Theoretical Framework, Recent Advances, and Current Challenges

### Vladimir Nikora and André G. Roy

## 1.1 INTRODUCTION

Water currents in rivers have fascinated and inspired researchers (and artists) for centuries, as reflected in numerous observations and paintings from ancient times (e.g., Rouse and Ince, 1963; Levi, 1995). Leonardo da Vinci's famous drawings are probably the most impressive and insightful examples of such observations. In his sketches and notes he highlighted a number of features of river flows whose signatures could be clearly observed at the water surface, especially behind obstacles and at stream confluences (Figure 1.1). 'Spiral' currents are particularly profound among these features and represent a key facet of nearly all of his water drawings. Using an analogy with curling hair, Leonardo summarized his observations as "Observe the motion of the surface of the water, how it resembles that of hair, which has two motions – one depends on the weight of the hair, the other on the direction of the curls; thus the water forms whirling eddies, one part following the impetus of the chief current, and the other following the incidental motion and return flow" (his written comment in Figure 1.1). It is fascinating how this description, given 500 years ago, is similar to a modern view of the mean flow structure as a superposition of the primary flow and the orthogonal secondary flows. Alternatively, Leonardo's comment may also be interpreted as the Reynolds decomposition of the instantaneous velocity into mean (i.e., time-averaged) and fluctuating turbulent components (Tsinober, 2009), although the first interpretation seems better justified.

Leonardo's astute comment on secondary flows was made well ahead of his time and it is nearly 400 years later that this phenomenon has been re-discovered by engineers and scientists working in hydraulics and theoretical fluid mechanics (e.g., Thomson, 1876; Francis, 1878; Wood, 1879; Cunningham, 1883; Stearns, 1883; Leliavski, 1894; Gibson, 1909; Joukowski, 1915). Their studies set up a background for the first fluid mechanical classification of the secondary flows proposed by Prandtl (1926). He suggested that "The phenomenon may be regarded as a combination of the main flow with a 'secondary flow' at right angles to it ..." and that this phenomenon combines two wide classes. The first class, known as Prandtl's secondary currents of the first kind, combines flow motions with streamwise mean (i.e., time-averaged) vorticity enhanced through vortex stretching. Secondary currents observed in curved pipe and river bends or meanders are typical examples provided by Prandtl to illustrate this type of secondary flow. Prandtl goes even further and proposes that the effect of secondary flows on sediment dynamics explains why "where they can, rivers always follow a winding course ('meandering')" (Prandtl, 1952, p. 147). The second class, often defined as Prandtl's secondary currents of the second kind, relates to secondary flows formed as a result of turbulence heterogeneity. These flows are often defined as turbulence-driven secondary currents and no channel curvature is required to generate them. Using rivers again as an example, Prandtl notes that "we may also mention the fact that small objects floating in rivers tend to move to the middle, which is explained by the existence of a surface current from the banks to the middle" (Prandtl, 1952, p. 148).

Typically, turbulence-generated longitudinal vorticity is much weaker than that in curved channels. However, even this seemingly mild three-dimensionality may introduce significant changes in the turbulence structure and should not be neglected. For instance, it is a common

*Gravel-bed Rivers: Processes, Tools, Environments*, First Edition. Edited by Michael Church, Pascale M. Biron and André G. Roy.
© 2012 John Wiley & Sons, Ltd. Published 2012 by John Wiley & Sons, Ltd.

**Figure 1.1** Leonardo da Vinci's Old Man with Water Studies (*c.* 1508–1509). Windsor, Royal Library, #12579.

claim in the experimental literature that the effects of the secondary flow on turbulence structure at the channel centreline are negligible, even in narrow channels. As a result, an assumption of a 2-D flow is often accepted based on the symmetry argument. This assumption ignores the cross-flow gradients of transverse velocities and turbulence parameters that may be (and often are) non-zero even at the channel centerline. Prandtl's secondary currents of the second kind typically occur at channel corners or at transverse bed roughness transitions. Recently, it has also been shown that this kind of secondary current may be formed in buoyancy-driven flows even in straight circular pipes (Hallez and Magnaudet, 2009), where normally this feature does not exist.

While turbulence acts to dissipate the secondary currents of the first kind, it represents a generating mechanism for the second kind of secondary currents. As a consequence, Prandtl's secondary currents of the second king are impossible in laminar flows, while Prandtl's first kind of secondary currents can be observed in both laminar and turbulent flows. Introduced rather intuitively, Prandtl's mechanism-based classification has survived extensive theoretical developments and is currently widely accepted as a starting point in considerations of secondary flows.

Prandtl's classification may additionally be supplemented with a topological classification that distinguishes two types of secondary flows: (1) non-helical cross-flows, and (2) helical flows (Bradshaw, 1987).

Combining Prandtl's and Bradshaw's classifications, it is possible to distinguish at least four types of secondary currents: (i) Prandtl's first kind of cross-flow (non-helical); (ii) Prandtl's second kind of cross-flow (non-helical); (iii) Prandtl's first kind of helical flow; and (iv) Prandtl's second kind of helical flow. It is likely that in real river configurations all four types of secondary flow may be observed, either superimposed or separated in space and/or in time (e.g., topology and mechanisms of secondary currents at low flow may differ from those at flood stage; see Rhoads and Kenworthy, 1998). In some cases, one of these types may dominate the flow topology (e.g., Prandtl's first kind of helical flow may be dominant in some meandering rivers), while in other cases all four types can be equally significant (e.g., in braided rivers).

Although the great significance of secondary flows for river processes has long been recognised, their origin, mechanics, effects, and inter-relations with the primary mean flow and turbulence are still a matter of debate and continue to attract close attention from hydrologists, geomorphologists, engineers, and, recently, stream ecologists. It is not surprising therefore that the literature related to secondary flows in open channels is extensive (Scopus shows over 600 journal papers since 1990) and includes frequently appearing reviews reflecting the progress and highlighting unsolved issues.

Prandtl's secondary currents of the first kind, particularly related to meandering rivers, have been extensively discussed in Ikeda and Parker (1989), Rhoads and

Welford (1991), Blanckaert and de Vriend (2004), Seminara (2006, 2010), Camporeale *et al.* (2007), Abad and Garcia (2009a, 2009b), Ikeda and McEwan (2009), and Gyr (2010), among others. In terms of mechanical engineering applications, a comprehensive review of this class of secondary flows has been given by Bradshaw 1987, covering 3-D boundary layers, vortex flows, and jets in cross-flows. Prandtl's secondary currents of the second kind have also attracted significant attention and their discussion has been even more controversial than that of secondary currents of the first kind. Bradshaw's (1987) popular review only slightly touched on this topic (mainly for 3-D free jets and wall jets), probably because a comprehensive treatment of duct flows had already been given in the review by Demuren and Rodi (1984). In relation to open-channel flows, Nezu and Nakagawa's (1993) review of the turbulence-driven secondary currents is still the most comprehensive source, and a recent update of this excellent review is available (Nezu, 2005). There are also a number of in-depth papers reviewing complex flow patterns at river confluences where both kinds of Prandtl's secondary flows are present and are interlinked in a multifaceted way (e.g., Rhoads and Kenworthy, 1998; Bradbrook *et al.*, 2000, 2001; Lane *et al.*, 2000; Rhoads and Sukhodolov, 2001; Sukhodolov and Rhoads, 2001; Szupiany *et al.*, 2009). The wide-ranging set of papers on this topic is also recorded in Rice *et al.* (2008), where extensive references and a thorough assessment of current and future research directions can be found.

The rapid development of measurement and numerical capabilities in recent years has brought new significant results and the authors feel that it may be useful to highlight recent progress in understanding secondary flows, as well as to identify research challenges and opportunities in studying this phenomenon, while keeping overlap with the previous reviews to the minimum. In particular, the focus of this chapter is on: (i) theoretical frameworks for studying secondary flows, (ii) interrelations between turbulence and secondary flows, and (iii) secondary flow effects on hydraulic resistance, sediment dynamics, and mixing. Examples from gravel-bed rivers will be presented. In addition to open-channel flows, some results related to conduits/ducts will also be considered as they are directly relevant to flows in ice-covered rivers (Ettema and Zabilansky, 2004; Buffin-Bélanger *et al.*, 2009).

## 1.2 THEORETICAL FRAMEWORK

Most theoretical and conceptual approaches in studying secondary flows in ducts and open channels have been based on: (i) the time-(ensemble)-averaged momentum equation, (ii) the energy balance equation for the mean flow, (iii) the energy balance equation for turbulence, and (iv) the mean (i.e., time-averaged) vorticity equation. These equations stem from the Navier–Stokes (momentum) equation for instantaneous velocities and pressure, representing its different forms and, thus, essentially containing the same information. However, in various equations this information is presented differently, highlighting particular facets of secondary flows. Most theoretical and experimental studies have been based on one or another equation, rarely involving joint consideration of two or more equations, thus reflecting authors' preferences, specific research questions, and/or data availability. Such a narrowly focused approach could be a reason for discrepancies in the identification and interpretation of the physical mechanisms creating and maintaining secondary flows in straight and curved channels (an example is given in Section 1.2.2). It is therefore instructive to provide a comparative overview of these equations, as well as to highlight other forms of the Navier–Stokes equations which could provide additional insight into the mechanics of secondary flows. In this review, we use Cartesian coordinates, although curvilinear coordinates (cylindrical or natural) have also been extensively used, especially in dealing with curved channels. For our purpose, however, Cartesian coordinates should be sufficient. Equations in the following sections are written using the Cartesian index notation, where $i = 1$ is for $x$ and velocity component $u$ (along the flow), $i = 2$ is for $y$ and velocity component $v$ (across the flow), and $i = 3$ is for $z$ and velocity component $w$ (orthogonal to the bed into the fluid). The repeated indices (known as dummy indices) mean summation.

### 1.2.1 Reynolds-Averaged Navier–Stokes (RANS) Equation

The time-(ensemble) averaged momentum equation, widely known as the Reynolds-Averaged Navier–Stokes (RANS) equation or just the Reynolds equation, is a logical starting point in the analysis of secondary flows and also a suitable platform to define them. For the benefit of readers who are not closely familiar with this topic, this equation is given below:

$$\underbrace{\frac{\partial \bar{u}_i}{\partial t} + \bar{u}_j \frac{\partial \bar{u}_i}{\partial x_j}}_{\substack{local \\ convective \\ accelerations}} = \underbrace{g_i}_{\substack{gravity \\ force}} - \underbrace{\frac{1}{\rho}\frac{\partial \bar{p}}{\partial x_i}}_{\substack{pressure \\ force}} - \underbrace{\frac{\partial \overline{u_i' u_j'}}{\partial x_j}}_{\substack{\text{``turbulent''} \\ force}} + \underbrace{\frac{\partial}{\partial x_j}\left(\nu \frac{\partial \bar{u}_i}{\partial x_j}\right)}_{\substack{viscous \\ shear \\ force}} \quad (1.1)$$

where $p$ is pressure, $\rho$ is water density, $\nu$ is viscosity, overbar denotes time-(ensemble)- averaging and prime denotes deviations of an instantaneous value of $f$ from its mean value in the Reynolds decomposition, i.e., $f = \bar{f} + f'$.

For straight, steady uniform *2-D* open-channel flow, the conditions $\bar{u}_2 = \bar{u}_3 = \overline{u'_1 u'_2} = \overline{u'_2 u'_3} = 0$ apply and all derivatives in Equation (1.1) along and across the flow are equal to zero. In this case, the flow is defined by the longitudinal velocity $\bar{u}_1$ and vertical momentum flux towards the bed $\tau/\rho = -\overline{u'_1 u'_3} + \nu \partial \bar{u}_1 / \partial x_3 \approx -\overline{u'_1 u'_3}$, while the vertical distribution of pressure may often be assumed to be hydrostatic (i.e., $g(H-z) \gg [\overline{u'_3 u'_3}(z_{ws}) - \overline{u'_3 u'_3}(z)]$, where $z_{ws}$ is the water surface elevation, $H$ is water depth, and S is bed slope). The velocity component $\bar{u}_1$ defines the overall mass flux through the channel cross-section and therefore is often called the primary flow velocity, with $\tau/\rho = -\overline{u'_1 u'_3}$ known as the primary Reynolds or turbulent stress. For a more general case of straight, steady uniform *3-D* open-channel flow, we have $\bar{u}_2, \bar{u}_3, \overline{u'_1 u'_2}, \overline{u'_2 u'_3} \neq 0$ in Equation (1.1), with the overall mass flux being still represented by the primary velocity $\bar{u}_1$ as the cross-sectionally averaged $\bar{u}_2$ and $\bar{u}_3$ are zero (i.e., there is no overall mass flux across the flow or in the vertical direction). For such an idealised 3-D mean open-channel flow, the velocity components $\bar{u}_2$ and $\bar{u}_3$ describe the helical water motions orthogonal to the primary flow and thus are often defined as helical secondary flow(s). For more complex flows in curved channels with irregular banks, the decomposition of the time-averaged water motion into primary flow and helical secondary flow(s) may not be as simple, since $\bar{u}_2$ and $\bar{u}_3$ can also include contributions from a variety of cross-flows which are not necessarily helical. This issue in relation to secondary flows at river confluences has been comprehensively discussed in Rhoads and Kenworthy (1998, 1999) and Lane *et al.* (1999, 2000), with practical field examples in Parsons *et al.* (2007) and Szupiany *et al.* (2009), among others..

The simplified versions of the time-averaged momentum Equation (1.1) have been extensively used for explanation of the origin and mechanics of secondary flows, and for their modelling (e.g., Gessner, 1973; Townsend, 1976; Demuren and Rodi (1984); Bradshaw 1987; Ikeda and Parker (1989);Rodi, 1993; Yang, 2005; Ikeda and McEwan (2009). It has been shown, for example, that it is likely that secondary flows in straight channels are generated by transverse pressure gradients

resulting from the turbulence anisotropy or turbulence heterogeneity observed for normal turbulent stresses $\overline{u'_2 u'_2}$ and $\overline{u'_3 u'_3}$ (e.g., Townsend, 1976). However, Equation (1.1), when used alone, may lead to potential misinterpretation of the secondary flow mechanisms and thus should ideally be supplemented with other flow dynamics equations. Examples of such misinterpretation are given, e.g., in Hinze (1967) and Gessner (1973), and one of them is highlighted in Section 1.2.2 below.

### 1.2.2 Energy Balance of the Mean Flow

In 1967, Hinze suggested that energy-based considerations are more suitable for analysing the secondary flow mechanics compared to the momentum equation and vorticity Equation (Hinze, 1967). His elegant analysis was mainly based on the turbulent energy balance and will be briefly described in the next subsection. As an alternative to the turbulent energy balance, Gessner (1973) proposed considering the mean flow energy balance. He deduced that the transverse gradients of the Reynolds shear stresses $\overline{u'_1 u'_2}$ and $\overline{u'_1 u'_3}$ are mostly responsible for the generation of secondary flows along channel corners, while the effects of the normal stresses $\overline{u'_2 u'_2}$ and $\overline{u'_3 u'_3}$ and the shear stress $\overline{u'_2 u'_3}$, highlighted by other researchers based on the momentum and vorticity equations, are of secondary importance. This conclusion, however, seems not to be universal, as follow-up analyses supported earlier findings about the significance of the normal stresses $\overline{u'_2 u'_2}$ and $\overline{u'_3 u'_3}$ (e.g., Demuren and Rodi (1984)). More recently, Yang and Lim (1997) used the mean flow energy balance to hypothesize that the surplus mean energy in any arbitrary flow volume will be transferred along the direction towards the nearest boundary. They applied this assumption to study the bed shear stress distribution in the presence of the secondary currents in uniform straight channels.

The potential of the mean energy balance for studying secondary flows is high and needs to be better explored. Below we propose an approach to how the mean energy balance can be utilized to look at possible energy fluxes between primary mean flow, secondary mean flow, and turbulence. The balance of the total mean kinetic energy (MKE) for an open-channel flow (and also for conduits/ducts) can be expressed as:

$$\underbrace{\frac{\partial}{\partial t}\left(\frac{\bar{u}_i^2}{2}\right) + \bar{u}_j \frac{\partial}{\partial x_j}\left(\frac{\bar{u}_i^2}{2}\right)}_{\text{rate of change of MKE}} = \underbrace{g_i \bar{u}_i}_{\substack{\text{energy income} \\ \text{from gravity}}} - \frac{\partial}{\partial x_j}\left[\underbrace{\frac{1}{\rho}\bar{u}_i \bar{p}}_{\substack{\text{pressure} \\ \text{transport}}} + \underbrace{\bar{u}_i \overline{u'_i u'_j}}_{\substack{\text{turbulent} \\ \text{transport}}} - \underbrace{\nu \frac{\partial}{\partial x_j}\left(\frac{\bar{u}_i^2}{2}\right)}_{\substack{\text{viscous} \\ \text{transport}}}\right] + \underbrace{\overline{u'_i u'_j}\frac{\partial \bar{u}_i}{\partial x_j}}_{\substack{\text{energy transfer} \\ \text{between mean} \\ \text{flow and turbulence}}} - \underbrace{\nu \left(\frac{\partial \bar{u}_i}{\partial x_j}\right)^2}_{\substack{\text{dissipation of} \\ \text{mean flow} \\ \text{energy}}} \quad (1.2)$$

This equation follows from the multiplication of Equation (1.1) by $\bar{u}_i$ and from some re-arrangements (e.g., Tennekes and Lumley, 1972). As already mentioned, simplified forms of Equation (1.2) have been used in Gessner (1973) and Yang and Lim (1997). However, for studying energy exchanges between the primary and secondary flows it is beneficial to decompose Equation (1.2) for the total MKE into two separate equations, i.e., for the primary flow MKE and for the secondary flow MKE. The first equation specifies the energy balance for the longitudinal velocity $\bar{u}_1$, while the second equation gives the combined energy balance for $\bar{u}_2$ and $\bar{u}_3$ (Equations (1.3) and (1.4), respectively):

$$\frac{\partial}{\partial t}\left(\frac{\bar{u}_1^2}{2}\right) + \bar{u}_j\frac{\partial}{\partial x_j}\left(\frac{\bar{u}_1^2}{2}\right) = g_1\bar{u}_1 - \bar{u}_1\frac{1}{\rho}\frac{\partial\bar{p}}{\partial x_1} - \frac{\partial\bar{u}_1\overline{u_1'u_j'}}{\partial x_j}$$
$$+ \nu\frac{\partial}{\partial x_j}\left(\frac{\partial}{\partial x_j}\frac{\bar{u}_1^2}{2}\right) + \overline{u_1'u_j'}\frac{\partial\bar{u}_1}{\partial x_j} - \nu\left(\frac{\partial\bar{u}_1}{\partial x_j}\right)^2 \qquad (1.3)$$

$$\frac{\partial}{\partial t}\frac{(\bar{u}_2^2 + \bar{u}_3^2)}{2} + \bar{u}_j\frac{\partial}{\partial x_j}\frac{(\bar{u}_2^2 + \bar{u}_3^2)}{2} = g_2\bar{u}_2 + g_3\bar{u}_3$$
$$- \bar{u}_2\frac{1}{\rho}\frac{\partial\bar{p}}{\partial x_2} - \bar{u}_3\frac{1}{\rho}\frac{\partial\bar{p}}{\partial x_3}$$
$$- \frac{\partial\bar{u}_2\overline{u_2'u_j'}}{\partial x_j} - \frac{\partial\bar{u}_3\overline{u_3'u_j'}}{\partial x_j} + \nu\frac{\partial}{\partial x_j}\left(\frac{\partial}{\partial x_j}\frac{(\bar{u}_2^2 + \bar{u}_3^2)}{2}\right)$$
$$+ \overline{u_2'u_j'}\frac{\partial\bar{u}_2}{\partial x_j} + \overline{u_3'u_j'}\frac{\partial\bar{u}_3}{\partial x_j} - \nu\left(\frac{\partial\bar{u}_2}{\partial x_j}\right)^2 - \nu\left(\frac{\partial\bar{u}_3}{\partial x_j}\right)^2 \qquad (1.4)$$

Applying Equations (1.3) and (1.4) for steady, uniform (straight) open-channel flow, ($\partial/\partial t = \partial p/\partial x_2 = \partial/\partial x_1 = 0$) with $g_1 = g\sin\alpha \approx gS$, $g_2 = 0$, $g_3 = -g\cos\alpha \approx -g$, and assuming the hydrostatic pressure distribution (i.e., $\rho g\cos\alpha + \partial\bar{p}/\partial x_3 \approx 0$), we obtain:

$$\bar{u}_2\frac{\partial}{\partial x_2}\left(\frac{\bar{u}_1^2}{2}\right) + \bar{u}_3\frac{\partial}{\partial x_3}\left(\frac{\bar{u}_1^2}{2}\right) = gS\bar{u}_1$$
$$- \left(\frac{\partial\bar{u}_1\overline{u_1'u_2'}}{\partial x_2} + \frac{\partial\bar{u}_1\overline{u_1'u_3'}}{\partial x_3}\right) + \left(\overline{u_1'u_2'}\frac{\partial\bar{u}_1}{\partial x_2} + \overline{u_1'u_3'}\frac{\partial\bar{u}_1}{\partial x_3}\right)$$
$$+ VT_1 + VD_1 \qquad (1.5)$$

$$\bar{u}_2\frac{\partial}{\partial x_2}\frac{1}{2}(\bar{u}_2^2 + \bar{u}_3^2) + \bar{u}_3\frac{\partial}{\partial x_3}\frac{1}{2}(\bar{u}_2^2 + \bar{u}_3^2)$$
$$= -\left(\frac{\partial\bar{u}_2\overline{u_2'u_2'}}{\partial x_2} + \frac{\partial\bar{u}_2\overline{u_2'u_3'}}{\partial x_3}\right) - \left(\frac{\partial\bar{u}_3\overline{u_3'u_2'}}{\partial x_2} + \frac{\partial\bar{u}_3\overline{u_3'u_3'}}{\partial x_3}\right)$$
$$+ \left(\overline{u_2'u_2'}\frac{\partial\bar{u}_2}{\partial x_2} + \overline{u_2'u_3'}\frac{\partial\bar{u}_2}{\partial x_3}\right) + \left(\overline{u_3'u_2'}\frac{\partial\bar{u}_3}{\partial x_2} + \overline{u_3'u_3'}\frac{\partial\bar{u}_3}{\partial x_3}\right)$$
$$+ VT_{2,3} + VD_{2,3} \qquad (1.6)$$

where viscous transport terms $VT_1$ and $VT_{2,3}$, and viscous dissipation terms $VD_1$ and $VD_{2,3}$ are:

$$VT_1 = \nu\frac{\partial}{\partial x_2}\left(\frac{\partial}{\partial x_2}\frac{\bar{u}_1^2}{2}\right) + \nu\frac{\partial}{\partial x_3}\left(\frac{\partial}{\partial x_3}\frac{\bar{u}_1^2}{2}\right),$$
$$VT_{2,3} = \nu\frac{\partial}{\partial x_2}\left(\frac{\partial}{\partial x_2}\frac{(\bar{u}_2^2 + \bar{u}_3^2)}{2}\right) + \nu\frac{\partial}{\partial x_3}\left(\frac{\partial}{\partial x_3}\frac{(\bar{u}_2^2 + \bar{u}_3^2)}{2}\right)$$
$$VD_1 = -\nu\left(\frac{\partial\bar{u}_1}{\partial x_2}\right)^2 - \nu\left(\frac{\partial\bar{u}_1}{\partial x_3}\right)^2,$$
$$VD_{2,3} = -\nu\left(\frac{\partial\bar{u}_2}{\partial x_2}\right)^2 - \nu\left(\frac{\partial\bar{u}_2}{\partial x_3}\right)^2 - \nu\left(\frac{\partial\bar{u}_3}{\partial x_2}\right)^2 - \nu\left(\frac{\partial\bar{u}_3}{\partial x_3}\right)^2$$

Equation (1.5) for the primary flow MKE and Equation (1.6) for the secondary flow MKE suggest that the following energy exchanges are likely to occur:

(1) For steady uniform (straight) open-channel flow, the external energy (i.e., potential gravity energy) is "pumped" into the mean kinetic energy of the primary flow only (term $gS\bar{u}_1$). This energy is then spatially redistributed by molecular and turbulent stresses, partly transferred to the turbulent kinetic energy, and partly dissipated into heat.

(2) The mean kinetic energy balance of the secondary flow Equation (1.6) does not explicitly include an external energy source, suggesting that the secondary flow should be fed only through coupling with the primary mean flow and/or turbulence. Equations (1.5) and (1.6) show that this coupling may occur through turbulent stresses $\overline{u_1'u_2'}$ and $\overline{u_1'u_3'}$ in (1.5) and $\overline{u_2'u_3'}$ in (1.6), as they have common velocity components between them and are involved in turbulent transport terms and in energy transfer between mean flow and turbulence (i.e., terms $\overline{u_i'u_j'}\partial\bar{u}_i/\partial x_j$). The latter terms are most probable candidates for the energy coupling between the primary and secondary flows as the transport terms $\partial\bar{u}_i\overline{u_i'u_j'}/\partial x_j$ in Equation (1.6) have to redistribute the already available energy of $\bar{u}_2$ and $\bar{u}_3$.

(3) Based on Equations (1.5) and (1.6) and some 3-D turbulence data (e.g., Nikora et al., 1998), the following energy pathway may be suggested: (i) the mean primary flow (PF) is fed by gravity through $gS\bar{u}_1$; (ii) PF transfers part of the received gravity energy to turbulent kinetic energy (TKE); (iii) TKE feeds mean secondary flow (SF) energy in particular flow regions through a subset of $-\overline{u_i'u_j'}\partial\bar{u}_i/\partial x_j$; and (iv) SF returns part of the received kinetic energy back to turbulence in particular flow regions through a different subset of $-\overline{u_i'u_j'}\partial\bar{u}_i/\partial x_j$. In other words, this analysis suggests that turbulence serves, very likely, as an energy link between the primary mean flow and secondary mean flow(s). Specifically, this link may occur through helical coherent structures and/or near-bed bursting processes (see Section 1.3 for more discussion).

To elaborate the proposed considerations for specific flow scenarios one would need detailed turbulence measurements involving estimates of velocity derivatives. This task will soon be realistic, even for field experiments.

Another interesting example of how the MKE balance may help in better understanding of secondary flows can also be derived from Equation (1.2), considering this time the total MKE balance. For steady uniform flow we may assume that there is a region in a flow where the combined effect of the transport terms and viscous dissipation in Equation (1.2) may be neglected, leading to:

$$\bar{u}_2 \frac{\partial}{\partial x_2}\left(\frac{\bar{u}_i^2}{2}\right) + \bar{u}_3 \frac{\partial}{\partial x_3}\left(\frac{\bar{u}_i^2}{2}\right) \approx gS\bar{u}_1 + \overline{u'_i u'_2}\frac{\partial \bar{u}_i}{\partial x_2} + \overline{u'_i u'_3}\frac{\partial \bar{u}_i}{\partial x_3}$$

(1.7)

Equation (1.7) explicitly shows that the secondary flows may be generated in flow regions with a significant imbalance between the energy income $gS\bar{u}_1$ and the energy loss $\overline{u'_i u'_j}\,\partial \bar{u}_i/\partial x_j$ (for turbulence generation), that provides a mechanism for the mean energy re-distribution. As in the previous example, however, this speculation requires support from data. Similar considerations can also be instrumental for flows in curved channels.

### 1.2.3 Turbulent Energy Balance

Another way to look at the inter-relations between the primary and secondary flows is to use the budget of the turbulent kinetic energy (TKE):

$$\underset{\substack{\text{rate of}\\\text{change}\\\text{of TKE}}}{\frac{\partial}{\partial t}\frac{\overline{u'_i u'_i}}{2}} + \underset{\substack{\text{convection of}\\\text{TKE by mean}\\\text{flow}}}{\bar{u}_j \frac{\partial}{\partial x_j}\frac{\overline{u'_i u'_i}}{2}} = \underset{\substack{\text{energy transfer}\\\text{between mean flow}\\\text{and turbulence}}}{-\overline{u'_i u'_j}\frac{\partial \bar{u}_i}{\partial x_j}} \underset{\substack{\text{pressure}\\\text{transport}}}{-\frac{\partial}{\partial x_j}\left[\frac{1}{\rho}\overline{p' u'_j}\right]} + \underset{\substack{\text{turbulent}\\\text{transport}}}{\frac{\overline{u'_i u'_i u'_j}}{2}} \underset{\substack{\text{viscous}\\\text{transport}}}{- \overline{\nu u'_i \left(\frac{\partial u'_i}{\partial x_j} + \frac{\partial u'_j}{\partial x_i}\right)}} \underset{\substack{\text{dissipation of}\\\text{turbulent energy}}}{- \frac{\nu}{2}\sum_{i,j}\overline{\left(\frac{\partial u'_i}{\partial x_j} + \frac{\partial u'_j}{\partial x_i}\right)^2}}$$

(1.8)

Equation (1.8) can be derived in a number of ways. For example, multiplying the Navier–Stokes equation by $u_i$, presenting $u_i$ and $p$ as $u_i = \bar{u}_i + u'_i$ and $p = \bar{p} + p'$, and then averaging, one may obtain the full kinetic energy equation. Subtraction of Equation (1.2) for MKE from this full equation will produce Equation (1.8) for TKE. Based on the available data for pipes, Hinze, 1967 suggested that for the flow regions away from the walls and the pipe centre, Equation (1.8) can be simplified, applying the boundary layer approximation, as:

$$\bar{u}_2 \frac{\partial}{\partial x_2}\frac{\overline{u'_i u'_i}}{2} + \bar{u}_3 \frac{\partial}{\partial x_3}\frac{\overline{u'_i u'_i}}{2} \approx -\overline{u'_1 u'_2}\frac{\partial \bar{u}_1}{\partial x_2} - \overline{u'_1 u'_3}\frac{\partial \bar{u}_1}{\partial x_3}$$
$$-\frac{\nu}{2}\sum_{i,j}\overline{\left(\frac{\partial u'_i}{\partial x_j} + \frac{\partial u'_j}{\partial x_i}\right)^2}$$

(1.9)

Hinze (1967) concluded that Equation (1.9) implies the following general rule: "when in a localised region, the production of turbulence energy is much greater (smaller) than the viscous dissipation, there must be a transport of turbulence-poor fluid into (out of) this region and a transport of turbulence-rich fluid outwards (into) the region." This rule is well supported by observations of the secondary flows formed at channel corners and at bed roughness transitions (Hinze, 1973). It is easy to see that Equation (1.7) proposed in the previous subsection has been inspired by Hinze's Equation (1.9). Summing up these two equations together we can obtain an equation for the simplified balance of the total kinetic energy, i.e.:

$$\bar{u}_2 \frac{\partial}{\partial x_2}\left(\frac{\bar{u}_i^2 + \overline{u'_i u'_i}}{2}\right) + \bar{u}_3 \frac{\partial}{\partial x_3}\left(\frac{\bar{u}_i^2 + \overline{u'_i u'_i}}{2}\right)$$
$$\approx gS\bar{u}_1 - \frac{\nu}{2}\sum_{i,j}\overline{\left(\frac{\partial u'_i}{\partial x_j} + \frac{\partial u'_j}{\partial x_i}\right)^2}$$

(1.10)

Equation (1.10) highlights a potentially more general rule for gravity-driven open-channel flows, i.e., the secondary flows are generated as a response to an imbalance in some flow regions between the external energy supply to the mean flow and the energy dissipation (viscous dissipation of the mean flow is neglected in Equations (1.7) and (1.10) as, in most cases, it is much smaller than the turbulent dissipation).

Equations (1.9) and (1.10) mainly relate to flows in straight channels. Detailed experimental analyses of the turbulent energy budget for secondary flows in a meandering channel have been reported in Blanckaert and de Vriend (2004, 2005a, 2005b). In their considerations, the authors combined the vorticity equation and the turbulent energy balance equation and showed that turbulence plays a minor role in the generation of the centre-region cell, which is mainly due to the centrifugal force. Another important observation made by these authors is that there are extensive flow regions within a channel bend where turbulent energy is transferred to the mean flow, playing a significant role in maintaining the outer-bank circulation cell. This observation provides some support to a suggested chain of energy transformations in an open-channel flow described in the previous subsection. The results of these authors will be considered in more detail in Section 1.3.

### 1.2.4 Mean Vorticity Equation

The idea of explaining the secondary flows in open channels using the mean vorticity equation was proposed by Einstein and Li (1958). The vorticity equation can be obtained by taking the curl of the momentum Equation (1.1) (or by its cross-differentiation). Einstein and Li (1958) focused on an equation for the streamwise vorticity component $\bar{\omega}_1$ that in the absence of the density stratification, and neglecting the Coriolis effect, can be expressed as:

term, representing vorticity "dissipation", i.e., damping. The last term in (1.12) is negligible except very close to the solid boundary. The 18-year-old text by Nezu and Nakagawa (1993) is still the most comprehensive work on Prandtl's second kind of secondary flows in straight open channels.

Interesting results for curved channels based on the vorticity equation in natural coordinates have been recently reported by Blanckaert and de Vriend (2004). Using high-quality laboratory data they performed a

$$\underbrace{\frac{\partial \bar{\omega}_1}{\partial t}}_{\substack{rate\ of\\change}} + \underbrace{\bar{u}_j \frac{\partial \bar{\omega}_1}{\partial x_j}}_{\substack{convection\\by\ mean\\flow}} = \underbrace{\bar{\omega}_j \frac{\partial \bar{u}_1}{\partial x_j}}_{\substack{vortex\\stretching\\and\ tilting}} + \underbrace{\frac{\partial^2}{\partial x_2 \partial x_3}\left(\overline{u'^2_3}-\overline{u'^2_2}\right)}_{\substack{stress\text{-}related\\vorticity\\\text{"generation"}}} + \underbrace{\left(\frac{\partial^2}{\partial x_3^2}-\frac{\partial^2}{\partial x_2^2}\right)\left(-\overline{u'_3 u'_2}\right)}_{\substack{stress\text{-}related\\vorticity\\\text{"dissipation"}}} + \underbrace{\frac{\partial}{\partial x_j}\left(\nu \frac{\partial \bar{\omega}_1}{\partial x_j}\right)}_{\substack{viscous\ \text{"dissipation"}\\of\ mean\ vorticity}}$$

$$+ \underbrace{\frac{\partial}{\partial x_1}\left(\frac{\partial -\overline{u'_1 u'_2}}{\partial x_3}-\frac{\partial -\overline{u'_1 u'_3}}{\partial x_2}\right)}_{\substack{vorticity\ change\ due\\to\ non\text{-}uniformity}} \qquad (1.11)$$

where the components of the mean vorticity vector $\bar{\omega}_j$ are defined as:

$$\bar{\omega}_1 = \frac{\partial \bar{u}_3}{\partial x_2}-\frac{\partial \bar{u}_2}{\partial x_3},\ \bar{\omega}_2 = \frac{\partial \bar{u}_1}{\partial x_3}-\frac{\partial \bar{u}_3}{\partial x_1},\ \bar{\omega}_3 = \frac{\partial \bar{u}_2}{\partial x_1}-\frac{\partial \bar{u}_1}{\partial x_2}$$

Nezu (2005) used Equation (1.11) as a basis for subdivision of secondary flows into Prandtl's first and second kinds. In flow configurations when the vortex stretching and tilting term in (1.11) is dominant, the first kind of secondary current is observed as, for example, in meandering channels. With channel curvature tending to zero (straight channels) this term disappears, as can be explicitly seen in the vorticity equation written in natural coordinates (Blanckaert and de Vriend, 2004). The second kind of secondary current occurs when turbulence terms in Equation (1.11) are dominant, i.e., due to turbulent stress anisotropy and heterogeneity. Of course, in real flow configurations superposition of both mechanisms has to be considered.

Nezu and Nakagawa (1993) reported a comprehensive study of Prandtl's second kind of secondary flows in straight channels, based on a simplified version of Equation (1.11) for steady, uniform open-channel flow:

$$\bar{u}_2 \frac{\partial \bar{\omega}_1}{\partial x_2} + \bar{u}_3 \frac{\partial \bar{\omega}_1}{\partial x_3} = \frac{\partial^2}{\partial x_2 \partial x_3}\left(\overline{u'_3}^2-\overline{u'_2}^2\right)$$
$$+ \left(\frac{\partial^2}{\partial x_3^2}-\frac{\partial^2}{\partial x_2^2}\right)\left(-\overline{u'_3 u'_2}\right) + \frac{\partial}{\partial x_j}\left(\nu \frac{\partial \bar{\omega}_1}{\partial x_j}\right) \qquad (1.12)$$

They concluded that secondary currents are generated as a result of differences between the first RHS term in (1.12), which is a production term, and the second RHS

combined analysis of the terms of the vorticity equation and the turbulent energy balance. The revealed complex structure of the secondary flow and associated turbulence properties were explained by the interplay of the effects of the centrifugal force and spatial distribution of the turbulent stresses (see also Section 1.3).

Although after Demuren and Rodi's (1984) and Nezu and Nakagawa's (1993) studies vorticity-related considerations are mainly based on Equations (1.11) and (1.12) for streamwise vorticity, it is worth noting that Gessner (1973) pointed out that two other equations, for the transverse and vertical components of the vorticity vector, can be even more important for explaining and predicting the secondary flows. This view, however, has not been properly explored yet.

### 1.2.5 Mean and Turbulent Enstrophy Balance Equations

The momentum, energy, and vorticity equations, briefly discussed above, have mainly been used for studying time-averaged secondary flows (i.e., mean streamwise vorticity). However, the time-averaged secondary flows are most likely a manifestation of frequently occurring instantaneous helical motions. The involvement of the fluctuating vorticity can be clearly seen if we use an alternative form of the vorticity Equation (1.11), i.e.:

$$\frac{\partial \bar{\omega}_i}{\partial t}+\bar{u}_j \frac{\partial \bar{\omega}_i}{\partial x_j}=\bar{\omega}_j \frac{\partial \bar{u}_i}{\partial x_j}-\underbrace{\frac{\partial}{\partial x_j}}_{\substack{turbulent\\convection}}\underbrace{\left(\overline{\omega'_i u'_j}-\overline{\omega'_j u'_i}\right)}_{\substack{turbulent\\stretching}}+\frac{\partial}{\partial x_j}\left(\nu \frac{\partial \bar{\omega}_i}{\partial x_j}\right)$$

$$(1.13)$$

where the Reynolds decomposition is used, i.e., $\omega_i = \bar{\omega}_i + \omega'_i$. The second RHS term represents effects of anisotropy and spatial heterogeneity of turbulent stresses expressed through correlations of fluctuating vorticity and velocity components. The derivative $\partial \overline{\omega'_j u'_i}/\partial x_j$ represents the gain (or loss) of mean vorticity due to stretching/tilting of the fluctuating vorticity by fluctuating strain rates, while the term $\partial \overline{\omega'_i u'_j}/\partial x_j$ represents vorticity transport in the $x_j$ direction (e.g., Tennekes and Lumley, 1972). Similar to the mean energy and turbulent energy, the coupling between the mean and fluctuating vorticities can be expressed using equations for $\bar{\omega}_i^2/2$ and $\overline{\omega'_i \omega'_i}/2$, which represent two components of the mean product $\overline{\omega_i \omega_i}/2 = \bar{\omega}_i^2/2 + \overline{\omega'_i \omega'_i}/2$, where $\omega_i \omega_i$ is known as enstrophy. Although there are some analogies between the MKE and mean enstrophy $\bar{\omega}_i^2/2$ (ME), and between the TKE and the turbulent enstrophy $\overline{\omega'_i \omega'_i}/2$ (TE), their physical nature is different, i.e., the enstrophy represents a measure of the density of the kinetic energy of helical motions rather than of all motions (e.g., Tsinober, 2009). As with Equation (1.2) for MKE, the mean enstrophy balance can be obtained by multiplying Equation (1.13) with $\bar{\omega}_i$, i.e.:

Equations (1.14) and (1.15) have been extensively studied in turbulence research with particular focus on their simplified versions for high-Reynolds-number flows with homogeneous turbulence. There have been no studies, to the writers' knowledge, involving these equations in the analysis of secondary flows. The main reason for this is probably the absence of experimental assessments of the terms of Equations (1.14) and (1.15). However, with recent advances in laboratory and field instrumentation it is quite likely that such experimental data will soon appear. In addition, recent progress in numerical simulation techniques and computing capabilities (e.g., Keylock et al., 2005; Lyn, 2008; Zeng et al., 2008; Constantinescu et al., 2009; van Balen et al., 2009; Stoesser et al., 2010) also encourages exploration of the potential of Equations (1.14) and (1.15) for studying secondary flows. Thus, the inclusion of the enstrophy balances in this review is justified, as it highlights a potentially fruitful theoretical framework for coupling mean and fluctuating vorticity fields, with the latter formed, most likely, by helical coherent structures. There may be several coupling mechanisms between these fields, with the gradient production term $\overline{u'_j \omega'_i} \partial \bar{\omega}_i/\partial x_j$ being the most obvious candidate as it is

$$\frac{\partial}{\partial t}\left(\frac{1}{2}\bar{\omega}_i^2\right) + \bar{u}_j\frac{\partial}{\partial x_j}\left(\frac{1}{2}\bar{\omega}_i^2\right) = \underbrace{-\frac{\partial}{\partial x_j}\bar{\omega}_i\overline{\omega'_i u'_j}}_{\substack{\text{transport of ME} \\ \text{by velocity-vorticity} \\ \text{interactions}}} + \underbrace{\overline{\omega'_i u'_j}\frac{\partial \bar{\omega}_i}{\partial x_j}}_{\substack{\text{gradient} \\ \text{production} \\ \text{of ME}}} + \underbrace{\bar{\omega}_i\bar{\omega}_j S_{ij}}_{\substack{\text{ME} \\ \text{stretching} \\ \text{by mean strain}}} + \underbrace{\bar{\omega}_i\overline{\omega'_j\frac{\partial u'_i}{\partial x_j}}}_{\substack{\text{ME stretching} \\ \text{by turbulent} \\ \text{strain}}}$$

$$\text{(rate of change of ME)} \quad \text{(convection of ME by mean flow)}$$

$$+ \underbrace{\nu\frac{\partial^2}{\partial x_j \partial x_j}\left(\frac{1}{2}\bar{\omega}_i^2\right)}_{\substack{\text{viscous} \\ \text{transport}}} - \underbrace{\nu\frac{\partial \bar{\omega}_i}{\partial x_j}\frac{\partial \bar{\omega}_i}{\partial x_j}}_{\substack{\text{dissipation of} \\ \text{mean enstrophy}}} \qquad (1.14)$$

where $S_{ij} = 0.5(\partial \bar{u}_i/\partial x_j + \partial \bar{u}_j/\partial x_i)$. The procedure for deriving the turbulent enstrophy balance is identical to that for the TKE balance (1.8), i.e., it involves multiplication of the equation for $\omega'_i$ by $\omega'_i$, and then subsequent time-(ensemble)-averaging (or, alternatively, subtraction of the mean enstrophy balance from the total enstrophy balance):

included in both Equations (1.14) and (1.15), similar to the TKE production term $\overline{u'_i u'_j} \partial \bar{u}_i/\partial x_j$ in Equations (1.2) and (1.8).

To summarise this brief overview of potential approaches for studying secondary flows, it should be noted that the recently achieved consensus among researchers is that there should be no preferred equation. Instead,

$$\frac{\partial}{\partial t}\left(\frac{\overline{\omega'_i\omega'_i}}{2}\right) + \bar{u}_j\frac{\partial}{\partial x_j}\left(\frac{\overline{\omega'_i\omega'_i}}{2}\right) = \underbrace{-\overline{u'_j\omega'_i}\frac{\partial \bar{\omega}_i}{\partial x_j}}_{\substack{\text{gradient} \\ \text{production of TE}}} - \underbrace{\frac{\partial}{\partial x_j}\frac{\overline{u'_j\omega'_i\omega'_i}}{2}}_{\substack{\text{turbulent} \\ \text{transport} \\ \text{of TE}}} + \underbrace{\overline{\omega'_i\omega'_j\frac{\partial u'_i}{\partial x_j}}}_{\substack{\text{TE production} \\ \text{by turbulent} \\ \text{stretching}}} + \underbrace{\overline{\omega'_i\omega'_j}\frac{\partial \bar{u}_i}{\partial x_j}}_{\substack{\text{change of} \\ \text{TE by} \\ \text{mean strain}}} + \underbrace{\bar{\omega}_j\overline{\omega'_i\frac{\partial u'_i}{\partial x_j}}}_{\substack{\text{"mixed"} \\ \text{production}}}$$

$$\text{(rate of change of TE)} \quad \text{(convection of TE by mean flow)}$$

$$\underbrace{\nu\frac{\partial^2}{\partial x_j \partial x_j}\left(\frac{\overline{\omega'_i\omega'_i}}{2}\right)}_{\text{viscous transport}} - \underbrace{\nu\frac{\overline{\partial \omega'_i}}{\partial x_j}\frac{\partial \omega'_i}{\partial x_j}}_{\text{viscous dissipation}} \qquad (1.15)$$

better understanding and predictions can only be achieved on the basis of combined approaches.

## 1.3 SECONDARY CURRENTS AND TURBULENCE

Although the importance of inter-relations between secondary currents and turbulence has been recognized since the beginning of the last century, knowledge concerning these inter-relations remains patchy and there are still significant gaps in our understanding of how they actually depend on each other. There are several conceptual frameworks in studying turbulence that represent different facets of turbulence. The most advanced among them are the Reynolds-averaging framework, the coherent structures concept, and the eddy cascade concept. The existing knowledge within these three directions is mostly related to 2-D (in a time-averaged sense) open-channel flows. The effects of mean flow three-dimensionality and secondary currents on turbulence are less understood and have been mainly studied in terms of bulk turbulence characteristics, with the most systematic and comprehensive work conducted by Nezu and his group for rectangular open-channel flows, as reviewed in Nezu (2005), and by Knight and his group for compound channels, as reviewed in Knight *et al.* (2009a).

The knowledge of these effects in more complex flows is much less complete although recent publications demonstrate some significant advances in studying flows in meandering channels (e.g., Blanckaert and de Vriend, 2004, 2005a, 2005b; Odgaard and Abad, 2008; Abad and Garcia, 2009a, 2009b; Blanckaert, 2009, 2010; Knight *et al.*, 2009a; Sanjou and Nezu, 2009; Gyr, 2010; Sukhodolov and Kaschtschejewa, 2010), riffle-pools (e.g., MacVicar and Roy, 2007a, 2007b), tidally-forced channels (e.g., Fong *et al.*, 2009), channel expansion-contractions (Papanicolaou *et al.*, 2007), at river confluences (e.g., Rhoads and Sukhodolov, 2001; Sukhodolov and Rhoads, 2001; Boyer *et al.*, 2006), and even in the complex situations of ice-covered rivers (Ettema, 2008). However, the relations between coherent structures, eddy cascade, and secondary currents remain poorly understood. Recent findings related to these inter-relations are briefly summarized below.

Within the *Reynolds-averaging framework*, turbulence is expressed with bulk parameters arising in the Reynolds-averaged equations for momentum, energy, and/or vorticity. Examples include turbulent energy, Reynolds stresses, absolute and relative turbulence intensities, velocity–vorticity correlations, enstrophy, and higher-order statistical moments such as skewness and kurtosis. The Reynolds-averaged equations represent both turbulence and secondary currents and therefore they seem to be a suitable platform for studying inter-

relations between them. In recent studies of secondary currents in straight open channels, the focus has been on flows over rough gravel beds, extending and complementing the well-established results of Nezu's group (Nezu, 2005) for smooth-bed open-channel flows. The major finding that has been independently reported by at least four groups is that secondary flow cells in rough-bed flows cover the whole channel cross-section evenly, even at width-to-depth ratios as high as 20 (Albayrak (2008); Rodriguez and Garcia, 2008; Belcher and Fox, 2009; Blanckaert *et al.* 2010). Figure 1.2 shows an example of the multicellular structures observed in an experiment with smooth side walls and a rough bed (Rodriguez and Garcia, 2008). This finding differs significantly from that for smooth-bed flows, where secondary currents disappear in the centre of the channel at aspect ratios larger than 5.

The most striking feature of the reported multicellular secondary currents is that their origin cannot be linked to sediment motion on the bed or to the transverse heterogeneity in bed roughness, as beds were not water-worked and no particle sorting or topographic variations were observed. Rodriguez and Garcia (2008) explain this phenomenon by the effect of the large gradient in roughness between the smooth glass walls and the gravel bed in their experiments, leading to an enhancement of near-wall cells and transverse transport of vorticity towards the centre of the channel. On the other hand, based on their extensive experiments in rectangular and trapezoidal channels Blanckaert *et al.* (2010) propose that the formation of secondary flow cells over the entre channel width is a result of hydrodynamic instability driven by near-bank secondary currents.

These observations can be supplemented with those of Cooper and Tait (2008) who reported the presence of high-speed longitudinal streaks in the time-averaged fields of streamwise velocity over water-worked gravel beds (no sediment motion was observed during the experiments). Interestingly, Cooper and Tait (2008) found no correlation between the time-averaged velocity streaks and bed topography, suggesting that their origin is not linked to variation in bed roughness or topography. Although the authors reject the presence of secondary currents as the possible explanation of the observed velocity streaks, their data are consistent with signatures of such currents and thus they should perhaps not be readily dismissed as the potential cause of the streaks.

Altogether, the results of these studies suggest that multicellular currents exhibit some form of self-organisation triggered by the pre-existing corner helical flows enhanced by bed roughness. Furthermore, Albayrak's (2008) study hints that the number of cells at a particular aspect ratio may depend on the properties of bed roughness. These observations shed new light on the old

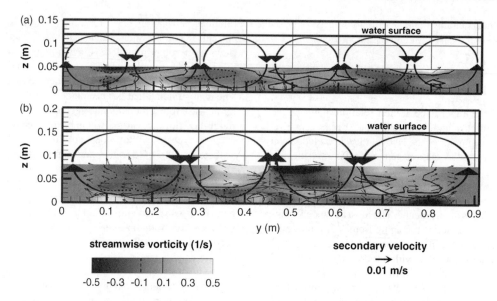

**Figure 1.2**    The results of a flume experiment with smooth walls and rough beds (Rodriguez and Garcia, 2008) at low flow (a) and high flow (b). The cells are delineated from the changes in direction in the streamwise vorticity and the directions of the secondary velocity. The cell size scales roughly with flow depth.

reports of longitudinal sediment ridges observed in some rivers (e.g., McLean, 1981; Nezu and Nakagawa, 1993) and may help in better formulations for channel morphodynamics. The physical origin of the observed multicellular structure is not yet clear and awaits a proper investigation.

Highlights of recent studies of the relation between secondary currents and turbulence in meandering channels include the detailed analysis of the spatial distribution of bulk turbulence properties by Blanckaert and de Vriend (2004, 2005a, 2005b). These authors performed comprehensive laboratory measurements of velocity vectors in a sharp open-channel bend, focusing on a bicellular pattern of secondary currents and its interrelations with turbulent energy, its production, dissipation, and transport. The revealed circulation pattern includes the classical centre-region helical cell and a weaker and smaller counter-rotating outer-bank cell (believed to play an important role in bank erosion processes). By analysing simultaneously the vorticity equation and the kinetic energy transfer between the mean flow and turbulence, the authors established that the centre-region cell is mainly formed due to the centrifugal force while the turbulence contribution is minor, as one could expect. The data also suggest that the origin of the outer cell can be explained by the interplay of the near-bank turbulence heterogeneity and channel curvature effects. This finding is somewhat consistent with laboratory and LES numerical studies of secondary circulation at the corners formed by a solid vertical wall

and flow free surface, i.e., at mixed-boundary corners (e.g., Grega et al., 2002; Broglia et al., 2003). However, in straight channels the mixed-boundary (inner) corner vortex rotates toward the solid wall at the water surface while in a curved channel the vortex rotation is opposite, probably reflecting additional effects of the centrifugal force and the associated centre-region cell. Blanckaert and de Vriend (2005b) proposed that the observed significant deviation of the turbulence structure in a curved channel from its straight channel counterpart is due to the streamline curvature effects. The transverse "stratification" of bulk turbulence properties is explained using an analogy with buoyancy-induced stratification and, therefore, can be quantified with the "curvature-flux-Richardson" number. The recent LES-based numerical study of van Balen et al. (2009, 2010) reproduces all key features observed in the laboratory experiments, additionally emphasizing the enhanced TKE and its production in the region of the outer near-bank cell.

Blanckaert and de Vriend's (2004, 2005a, 2005b) experiments covered an idealized situation of an isolated bend where the effects of adjacent bends were not present. A more realistic channel shape was used in recent experiments by Abad and Garcia (2009a, 2009b) who performed extensive velocity measurements in a unique five-bends facility known as the "Kinoshita channel" and reported detailed maps of mean velocity vectors, Reynolds stresses, and TKE. Both fixed-bed and mobile-bed scenarios were examined, particularly focusing on the effects of bend orientation, i.e., upstream or downstream. For a flat, smooth bed condition, the measurements revealed that at the bend apex the maximum velocity occurs near the inner bank for both upstream and downstream bend orientations. However, for the upstream-oriented bends, secondary flow was weaker compared to that in the downstream-oriented bends. Even more interesting, the hydraulic resistance factor appeared to depend on bend orientation, i.e., for the same channel sinuosity the resistance was higher for the downstream-skewed bends, probably reflecting stronger secondary currents. The laboratory data described above can be compared with comprehensive field turbulence measurements in a bend of the Spree River where the level of detail and measurement accuracy can compete with those in the laboratory set-ups (Sukhodolov and Kaschtschejewa, 2010). An example of a field study in a bend of the Tollense River near Lebbin (Germany) by Sukhodolov's group is shown in Figure 1.3.

These findings relate to the time-averaged structure and represent a significant step forward in our current understanding of secondary flows in straight and curved channels. However, the averaging procedures eliminate details on key agents forming this "time-averaged" structure. These agents are most likely coherent structures and eddy cascades, discussed below.

The concept of *coherent structures* is based on the recognition of some order in turbulence. A coherent structure (or eddy) can be broadly defined as a 3-D flow region over which at least one fundamental flow variable exhibits significant correlation with itself or with another variable over a range of space and/or time (e.g., Robinson, 1991; Roy *et al.*, 2004; Adrian, 2007). Many

kinds of coherent structures have been identified, depending on flow type and Reynolds number, and it has been shown that they play a significant role in mass and momentum transfer in rivers. The issue of identifying, detecting, and quantifying coherent structures remains a hot research topic in physics, engineering, and the earth sciences. It is likely that at least some secondary currents in river flows are formed by helical coherent structures, intermittently or quasi-periodically appearing in particular regions of the channel cross-sections (e.g., at corners). In addition (or independently), secondary flow cells can be partly controlled by the spatial distribution and intensity of near-bed bursting processes. These possibilities have been highlighted by works of Nakagawa and Nezu (1981), Gulliver and Halverson (1987), Nezu and Nakagawa (1993), Lane *et al.* (2000), Blankaert and de Vriend (2005b), Albayrak (2008), Sterling *et al.* (2008), Buffin-Bélanger *et al.* (2009), Miyawaki *et al.* (2009), and Pinelli *et al.* (2010). These mechanisms are also consistent with the analysis of the mean flow energy balance in Section 1.2.2, where it is proposed that secondary flows are fed by turbulence.

Pinelli *et al.* (2010) performed direct numerical simulations of smooth-wall turbulent flow in a straight square duct with a particular focus on the role of coherent structures in the generation and characterization of near-corner cells. They found that the buffer layer structures determine the distribution of mean streamwise vorticity, while the shape of the cells is influenced by larger-scale motions. Pinelli *et al.*'s (2010) paper is probably the first quantitative report that explicitly demonstrates close interconnections between near-corner secondary flows with both buffer-scale and duct-scale

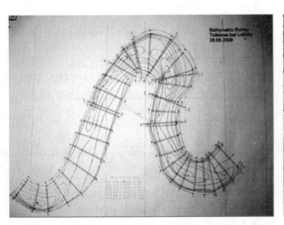 

**Figure 1.3**   Field experimental set-up in a bend of the Tollense River near Lebbin (2009) for studying secondary currents by the research group of A. Sukhodolov, Leibniz-Institute of Freshwater Ecology and Inland Fisheries, Berlin, Germany.

coherent structures. Although the range of Reynolds numbers was quite limited and flow configuration was very simplified, this study highlights potentially important effects that may be directly relevant to river flows. More realistic conditions of open-channel gravel bed flow have been studied by Albayrak (2008). Based on extensive experiments in a large, straight, gravel bed flume, Albayrak (2008) explored properties of prevailing coherent structures and their relation to the secondary flow cells. He found that Adrian's (2007) model of hairpin packets is applicable to the conditions of rough-bed open-channel flows, confirming earlier findings of Hurther et al. (2007). Furthermore, Albayrak (2008) showed that the vertical extension of the hairpin packets is significantly enhanced in upwelling zones of the secondary flow cells and reduced in downwelling zones. Albayrak's (2008) data also suggest that the time-averaged secondary flow cells represent effects of large instantaneous helical structures, similar to those observed by Gulliver and Halverson (1987).

Turbulent structures in a channel bend with well-documented secondary flow cells and bulk turbulence parameters were studied by Blankaert and de Vriend (2005b). These authors showed, for the first time, that velocity fluctuations within a bend can be considered as a superposition of large-scale structures occupying the whole channel cross-section and small-scale "background" turbulence. Large-scale width-coherent velocity fluctuations resemble wavelike motions and mainly contribute to the normal turbulent stresses, while the "background" turbulence is a main contributor to the shear stress generation. The origin of these two components and interrelations between them need further investigation.

A more intricate case of a meandering compound open-channel flow was examined by Sanjou and Nezu (2009) who employed a multilayer scanning PIV and revealed a strong connection between the horizontal vortices and secondary currents. Their phenomenological model is summarized in Figure 1.4. Buffin-Bélanger et al. (2009) and Demers et al. (2011) considered an even more complicated case of an ice-covered meandering flow and addressed the question of how coherent structures rising from the bed and ice boundaries interact and modify the overall structure of the flow. Based on laboratory and field studies, they compared an ice-covered flow and an ice-free flow in the same channel. They discovered that the flow field in the ice-covered condition is characterized by two counter-rotating helical cells at the bend entrance which evolve, further downstream, into one helical cell that rotates in the opposite direction compared to that without the ice cover. Turbulence properties are also significantly different for these two scenarios, showing low correlations between

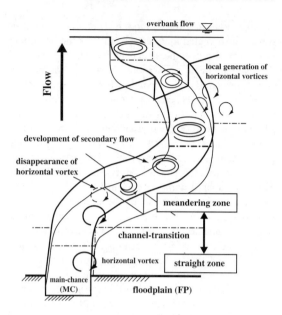

**Figure 1.4** Phenomenological flow model of horizontal vortices and secondary currents in meandering compound open-channel flow (Sanjuo and Nezu, 2009).

structures generated at the bed and at the ice cover, as if the two boundary layers were disconnected. How exactly these structures influence secondary flow cells in this most complicated set-up remains unclear.

The *eddy cascade concept* reflects the multiscale structure of turbulence. According to this concept, turbulence is initiated at an external scale of the flow (e.g., flow depth or width in a stream) as a result of hydrodynamic instability that transfers the energy from an external forcing to the largest eddies comparable to the external flow scale. These large eddies being unstable themselves then transfer their energy to smaller eddies and so on, until the eddy size reaches the so-called dissipative scale. At this scale, viscous forces overcome inertial forces and turbulence becomes suppressed by viscosity. The key analyses of this approach include velocity spectra, correlations, and structure functions (e.g., Tennekes and Lumley, 1972). In time-averaged 2-D open-channel flow over a flat bed, the eddy cascade is assumed to start with generation of large eddies (2–5 flow depths $H$ in length and 1–2 $H$ in width), which then will cascade their energy down to the dissipative scale. In this scenario, there is only one external scale and associated energy supply to turbulence from the mean flow. In rivers, of course, there may be several superimposed mechanisms of TKE production associated with multiscale bed forms. Altogether they represent different canals of energy transfer from the mean flow to turbulence (Nikora, 2008).

In addition to these mechanisms, the helical secondary flows may introduce a potentially important external scale and associated instability that may modify conventional transport of energy from gravity to the mean flow to the depth-scale eddies and through the eddy cascade to heat. Alternative scenarios are also possible. As has been highlighted in Section 1.2.2, it is quite likely that secondary flows in straight channels receive their energy from turbulence, suggesting the existence of an inverse energy cascade (i.e., flux of energy from smaller scales to larger scales to the mean flow) in particular regions of the flow. This conjecture is supported by Blanckaert and de Vriend's (2004) experiments. However, until now there have been no systematic studies of this aspect of secondary flow–turbulence interactions.

## 1.4 SECONDARY CURRENTS AND HYDRAULIC RESISTANCE

Although the effect of secondary currents on hydraulic resistance is widely recognized, its nature is not yet clear. Thus, its explicit incorporation into resistance equations is still an unsolved problem (e.g., Yen, 2002). In general, secondary currents modify the transverse distributions of mean velocities, fluid shear stresses, and bed shear stress. It is often assumed that these modifications increase the bulk friction factor $f = 8(u_*^2/U_o^2)$ compared to the case when secondary currents are absent ($u_*^2 = \tau_o/\rho$, $U_o$ is cross-section mean velocity, $\tau_o$ is a "reach-scale" bed shear stress). There are also indications that in some situations secondary flows do not affect the bulk friction factor, while significantly altering boundary shear stress and near-bank velocities (Kean et al., 2009). Indeed, since the bulk friction factor $f = 8(u_*^2/U_o^2)$ is a result of integration of the Reynolds-averaged momentum equation over the whole cross-section (or even over a river reach), the different resistance mechanisms are lumped together, making it difficult to unambiguously observe their individual contributions.

A more practical approach to account for the presence of secondary currents is to use the depth-averaged momentum equation and the local friction factor $f = 8(\tau_b/\rho U_d^2)$ defined at a particular vertical at the transverse coordinate $y$, where $\tau_b(y)$ is a "local" bed shear stress, and $U_d(y)$ is the depth-averaged velocity. This approach has been extensively developed and explored by Knight and his group (Knight et al. 2009a, 2009b, and references therein). Their work provides a thorough theoretical analysis, in-depth experimental support, and implementation in a range of analytical and computer models. The conceptual basis of the approach is the depth-averaged momentum equation expressed as (Knight et al. 2009a):

$$\underset{\substack{\text{gravity} \\ \text{term}}}{\rho g H S} + \underset{\substack{\text{transverse} \\ \text{stress term}}}{\frac{\partial}{\partial y}(H\hat{\tau}_{yx})} - \underset{\substack{\text{local bed} \\ \text{shear stress}}}{\tau_b\left(1 + \frac{1}{s^2}\right)^{1/2}} = \underset{\substack{\text{secondary} \\ \text{flow term}}}{\frac{\partial}{\partial y}(\rho H \bar{u}\bar{v})_d} \quad (1.16)$$

where $H$ is the flow depth, $\hat{\tau}_{yx}$ is the depth-averaged transverse shear stress, $s$ is the transverse bed slope (i.e., $dz_b/dy$), $\bar{u}$ and $\bar{v}$ are local time-averaged longitudinal and transverse velocities, and an index "$d$" in the secondary flow term indicates depth-averaging. The local friction factor $f = 8(\tau_b/\rho U_d^2)$ is involved in the parameterization of the transverse stress term and the bed shear stress term. Knight et al. (2009a) reviewed a range of closure models for the terms of Equation (1.16) and demonstrated their applicability for both straight and meandering compound channels, including those with vegetated floodplains. The reliability of the 2-D resistance models can be further strengthened if deeper understanding of the secondary flow mechanisms is developed and, based on this, more appropriate closures for the secondary flow term in Equation (1.16) are proposed (currently this term is often assumed to be a constant). The research in this direction is ongoing and can be well illustrated with recent results by Blanckaert (2009, and references therein), who proposed a set of relations describing different effects of secondary currents in meandering channels on the hydraulic resistance factor. The effect of bend orientation on hydraulic resistance, recently discovered by Abad and Garcia (2009a, 2009b) has already been mentioned in Section 1.3.

A potentially useful framework for assessment of secondary flow effects on hydraulic resistance has been recently suggested in Nikora (2009). Starting with the Reynolds-averaged momentum equation, he derived a relation for partitioning the bulk and local friction factors into constitutive components, accounting for the effects of: (i) viscous stress; (ii) turbulent stress; (iii) form-induced stress; (iv) flow unsteadiness and spatial heterogeneity of mean velocities (e.g., due to non-uniformity and/or secondary currents); (v) spatial heterogeneity of turbulence characteristics (e.g., due to secondary currents); and (vi) vertical heterogeneity of driving forces. These components of the friction factor account for the roughness geometry and highlight the significance of the Reynolds and form-induced stresses in the near-bed region, where their values are the largest. The suggested relation can guide better understanding of the resistance mechanisms and developing their parameterizations and models.

## 1.5 SECONDARY CURRENTS, SEDIMENTS AND MORPHODYNAMICS

Since the pioneering works of river navigation engineers, it is widely accepted that secondary flows play a significant role in channel deformation, bank stability, and sediment transport. One of the historically earliest explanations of secondary currents involved suspended sediments as a key factor of their generation (Vanoni, 1946). In his experiments, Vanoni (1946) noticed that the addition of a small amount of fine sediments in a clear-water open-channel flow led to the modification of the velocity distribution across the channel and formation of longitudinal streaks in the suspended sediment concentration field (three strong streaks at the channel centre and weaker streaks near the walls). Thus, Vanoni considered the effect of suspended sediment to be a cause of the observed secondary currents.

This experimentally guided conjecture was later replaced by the alternative idea that the observed suspended sediment streaks are generated by the pre-existing secondary currents. A recent study by Hallez and Magnaudet (2009), however, points out the possibility of generating secondary currents, even by weak density stratification, which could have been created in the Vanoni experiments by the addition of suspended sediments. In light of Hallez and Magnaudet's (2009) study, it is beneficial to reconsider Vanoni's (1946) abandoned hypothesis, which may well be correct, representing a specific form of Prandtl's second kind of secondary current.

The formation of sand ribbons on the beds of straight channels is another similar phenomenon that has been known for a long time and that is often explained by some kind of self-organization involving flow-bed sediment interactions (e.g., McLean, 1981; Nezu and Nakagawa, 1993; Garcia, 2008; Parker, 2008). Colombini (1993) and Colombini and Parker (1995) proposed an instability-based mechanistic explanation for these bed features, while McLelland *et al.* (1999) and Wang and Cheng (2006) provided the most systematic recent account on this topic, supported by extensive laboratory experiments with bimodal sediments and artificial bedforms.

Although bank erosion is often associated with secondary currents, detailed and reliable information on the mechanisms involved and their quantitative measures has become available only recently. Comprehensive reviews of various predictive engineering methods for bank erosion involving effects of secondary currents can be found in Pizzuto (2008) and Rinaldi and Darby (2008). These methods are often based on the depth-averaged Equation (1.16) and on parameterizations proposed by Knight and his group (e.g., Knight *et al.*, 2009a). Among recent works, special attention should be given to Papanicolaou *et al.*'s (2007) study, which combined detailed turbulence measurements in a gravel-bed stream (with cohesive banks) with extensive laboratory erosion tests. The 3-D and depth-averaged momentum equations, similar to Equations (1.1) and (1.16), were used by the authors as a framework for data analysis and interpretation. Papanicolaou *et al.* (2007) demonstrated that secondary currents increase the magnitude of the depth-averaged sidewall shear stress by a factor of at least 2.0, while the ratio of the maximum to the depth-averaged sidewall shear stress was found to be larger than 5. This finding suggests that the conventional approaches in morphodynamics based on the depth-averaged sidewall shear stress may not be a suitable approximation of the reality for natural channels with complex morphology involving contractions and expansions.

Another highlight of the influence of secondary flows on sediment transport is a study of bend orientation (curvature) effects on sediment dynamics and, through this, on morphodynamics (Abad and Garcia, 2009b). This study is complementary to the already mentioned set of experiments in the same facility with a fixed bed (Abad and Garcia 2009a). The experiments with mobile beds revealed significant differences in sediment dynamics between upstream- and downstream-oriented bends. In particular, downstream-oriented bends generated stronger secondary currents and more distinct bed forms, with higher shear stresses along the bed and banks. These hydrodynamic features may have significant morphological effects as they most likely produce higher erosion power and enhanced sediment transport rates leading to increased channel migration rates. In addition, this study provides qualitative and quantitative information on potential effects of secondary currents and flow non-uniformity on dune shape, sizes, and migration rates, knowledge of which is still very limited (Best, 2005). Consideration of Abad and Garcia's (2009b) study should be supplemented with laboratory experiments of Termini (2009) and Jamieson *et al.* (2010), which expand a range of Abad and Garcia's (2009b) scenarios in terms of bend shape and hydraulic conditions.

The more complicated case of braided channels involves a wide spectrum of secondary flow patterns that are the inherent component of nearly all morphodynamic processes occurring in this highly dynamic channel type. Specific examples can be found in a recent specialized volume on braided channels edited by Sambrook Smith *et al.* (2006). Although there have been some important advances in this area (e.g., Ashworth, 1996; De Serres *et al.* 1999; Richardson and Thorne, 2001), knowledge of secondary flows in braided channels remains fragmentary and rather qualitative. Quickly developing simulation methodologies such as DNS (direct numerical simulation) and LES (large eddy simulation) may soon appear to be of great help by complementing laboratory and field studies in clarifying details of secondary flows for typical elements of braided channel morphology such as confluences, bifurcations, islands, and anabranches (e.g., Keylock *et al.*, 2005; Lyn, 2008; Zeng *et al.*, 2010). A recent example of a successful application of the detached eddy simulation (DES) technique for studying flow structure at a river confluence is given in Miyawaki *et al.* (2009). This study convincingly shows that the time-averaged helical currents at the confluences are a result of frequently occurring helical coherent structures (Figure 1.5).

The most challenging scenarios for secondary currents and their roles in sediment transport and channel morphodynamics occur, not surprisingly, in ice-covered rivers. Due to the great technical difficulties of wintertime field work, the knowledge of secondary currents in ice-covered rivers is very fragmentary. Wide-ranging reviews of channel responses to ice cover are given in Ettema (2002, 2008), while unique data and their conceptualization are provided in Tsai and Ettema (1994), Ettema and Zabilansky (2004) and in the already discussed work of Buffin-Belanger *et al.* (2009) and Demers *et al.* (2011). Tsai and Ettema, 1994 studied the ice cover effect on the circulation pattern and its strength in a curved channel in a laboratory flume. The authors showed that the ice cover changes the topology of the secondary flow cells and dampens their strength. Ettema and Zabilansky (2004) reported unique wintertime fieldwork along the Fort Peck reach of the Missouri River. They documented, for the first time, how exactly ice cover can modify flow structures that trigger associated morphological responses, such as the migration of channel bends, transient scours, sediment deposition, and

cyclic shifts of the thalweg through sinuous-braided subreaches. All these changes reflect changes in secondary flow patterns accompanied by many other superimposed changes due to the ice cover.

## 1.6  SECONDARY CURRENTS AND MIXING PROCESSES

The presence of secondary currents may significantly modify vertical, transverse, and longitudinal mixing, as discussed in detail in Rutherford (1994). Depending on the specific flow configuration, secondary currents may either enhance or dampen mixing rates in all directions or selectively. For example, an increase in transverse mixing due to secondary currents may be associated with a reduction in longitudinal mixing. Progress in understanding the mixing processes when secondary currents are present depends on the depth of understanding of the overall hydrodynamics of secondary currents and of their inter-relations with turbulence.

In relation to straight channels, secondary flow effects on mixing in rectangular and one-sided compound channels have recently been considered by Kang and Choi (2009). Using the injection of dye into the compound channel, these authors found that the secondary flow cells move the location of the maximum dye concentration towards the floodplain, leading to a skewed distribution of the mean dye concentration in the spanwise direction. A similar but weaker effect was noted for rectangular channels. Kang and Choi (2009) also showed that the Reynolds fluxes reduce the concentration peak and thicken the tails of the mean dye concentration, while secondary currents affect the magnitude of the mean concentration over the entire channel width, moving the peak concentration in the flow direction.

These results can be supplemented with earlier experimental data obtained in a straight, smooth-bed channel that highlight particular features in the flow regions around the local symmetry $z$–$x$ planes between the helical secondary currents near side-walls and the central part of the flow (Nikora *et al.*, 1998). These regions are characterized by some anomalous properties:

(1)  Local minima in the longitudinal velocity which coincide with the local maxima in the vertical velocity, i.e., the minima in the longitudinal velocity occur in the upflow regions where the transverse velocity changes its sign.

(2)  Local minima in the transverse eddy diffusivity and in the turbulent energy generation term $-\overline{u'v'}\,d\bar{u}/dy$, surrounded by local maxima in these variables.

(3)  The transverse turbulent flux $-\overline{u'v'}$ in the near-bed layer is close to zero and changes its sign from

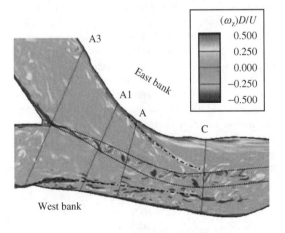

**Figure 1.5**  Instantaneous vorticity at the confluence visualized with the contours on the water surface (Miyawaki *et al.*, 2009). (See color version of this figure in color plate section.)

minus to plus (this means that transverse turbulent fluxes occur towards the boundary between each helical secondary current and the central flow).

(4) Fluid ejections are suppressed while fluid sweeps are increased, in agreement with the transverse distributions of velocity skewness and kurtosis.

Thus, the data suggest the existence of an interesting phenomenon – the suppression of transverse mixing in the narrow regions between the helical near-wall currents and the central flow. A qualitative confirmation of the suggested phenomenon can be found in aerial photographs from tracer experiments depicted on the cover of Rutherford's (1994) book. They clearly show suppressed mixing between stable dye strips near the banks and the central flow of the Waikato River in New Zealand. This could be explained by the near-bank helical currents, which suppress mixing between the near-bank flow region and the central flow region. However, this effect requires further investigation for a wider range of conditions.

In relation to curved channels, recent research on the effects of the mechanics of secondary flows on mixing processes has been reported by Boxall *et al.* (2003) and Marion and Zaramella (2006) for large laboratory self-formed channels, and by Rowinski *et al.* (2008) for the field sites. These authors show that channel curvature may have two effects on dispersion that tend to oppose each other. On one hand, curvature increases the longitudinal dispersion, reflecting an increase in the turbulence intensity. On the other hand, it reduces dispersion by enhancing transverse mixing. These results also show that the most efficient longitudinal dispersion occurs at the bend entrance, sharply decreasing beyond the meander apex. Theoretical and modelling aspects of the secondary flow effects on mixing and dispersion processes have been recently addressed by Czernuszenko and Rylov (2002), Albers and Steffler (2007), and Khosronejad *et al.* (2007), among others.

## 1.7 CONCLUSIONS

Twenty three years ago Bradshaw (1987) concluded that "Flows with strong skew-induced streamwise vorticity or flows dominated by stress-induced vorticity are particularly challenging, and the main conclusion of the present review is that we lack basic physical understanding of the effect of mean-flow three dimensionality on turbulence structure." His closing words were: "The step from 2-D to 3-D mean flow is as difficult in simulation as in experiment…" (Bradshaw 1987). Today, these conclusions remain largely valid, especially in relation to gravel bed rivers, where a complex combination of multiscale secondary currents is an inherent feature.

The present review shows that, although significant recent advances should be acknowledged in understanding the secondary flow mechanics and their inter-relations with other river processes, there are still many knowledge gaps that have to be addressed. In particular, these gaps relate to quantification and prediction of secondary flow effects on sediment transport, hydraulic resistance, mixing, and morphodynamics. Furthermore, the researcher's attention should be also extended to the identification of the role of secondary currents in the functioning of stream ecosystems. The profound effect of secondary currents on the mean velocities, turbulence, mixing, and sediment dynamics is likely to be reflected in ecosystem structure and functioning, but this effect remains to be understood and quantified. This focus area highlights the significance of secondary flows from a multidisciplinary perspective.

To achieve the goal of greater understanding, a number of theoretical, experimental, and conceptual issues should be resolved. In relation to theoretical analyses, a conceptual uncertainty related to the cause-and-effect relations between key processes and variables awaits to be resolved. This can only be achieved on the basis of combined approaches involving various forms of the Navier–Stokes equations, from the RANS to the enstrophy equations. There are also methodological issues that require urgent attention, with identification and quantification of secondary flow patterns in complex flows being among the most challenging. This task is particularly relevant to secondary flows in braided channels where partitioning into primary and secondary flows is, in most cases, unclear. The solution may be sought using analogies with the problem of coherent structure identification in turbulent flows, where a variety of invariant measures (i.e., independent of the coordinate system orientation) have been explored. Progress in this direction should advance the topological and mechanistic classification of secondary currents in river flows that, once developed, should help in a better coupling between channel morphology, flow structure, and sediment dynamics at multiple scales. In relation to the data base, laboratory studies, and quickly developing numerical simulation techniques need to be complemented by comprehensive field studies. Work in this direction is growing (e.g., Sukhodolov and Rhoads, 2001; Rhoads and Sukhodolov, 2001; Ettema and Zabilansky, 2004; Buffin-Belanger *et al.* 2009; Fong *et al.* 2009; Rowinski *et al.*, 2008; Sukhodolov and Kaschtschejewa, 2010).

## 1.8 ACKNOWLEDGEMENTS

VN acknowledges support from the Engineering and Physical Sciences Research Council, UK, Grant EP/ G056404/1 "High resolution numerical and experimental studies of turbulence-induced sediment erosion and near-bed transport" and from the Leverhulme Trust, UK, Grant F/00152/Z "Biophysics of flow-plants interactions in aquatic systems". AGR acknowledges financial support from the Natural Sciences and Engineering Research Council of Canada and the Canada Research Chair program. K. Blanckaert, G. Constantinescu, S. Cameron, N. Nikora, and M. Stewart provided useful comments on earlier versions of the manuscript. Reviews by Bruce MacVicar and Thanos Papanicolaou helped to sharpen the focus of this paper.

## 1.9 REFERENCES

Abad, J.D. and Garcia M.H. 2009a. Experiments in a high-amplitude Kinoshita meandering channel: 1. Implications of bend orientation on mean and turbulent flow structure. *Water Resources Research* **45**: W02401. doi:10.1029/2008 WR007016.

Abad, J.D. and Garcia M.H. 2009b. Experiments in a high amplitude Kinoshita meandering channel: 2. Implications of bend orientation on bed morphodynamics. *Water Resources Research* **45**: W02402. doi:10. 1029/2008 WR007017.

Adrian R.J. 2007. Hairpin vortex organization in wall turbulence. *Physics of Fluids* **19**: 041301.

Albayrak, I. 2008. *An experimental study of coherent structures, secondary currents and surface boils and their interrelation in open-channel flow*. Ph.D. Thesis, École Polytechnique Fédérale de Lausanne, no. 4112: 281pp. doi: 10. 5075/epfl-thesis- 4112.

Albers, C. and Steffler, P. 2007. Estimating transverse mixing in open channels due to secondary current-induced shear dispersion. *Journal of Hydraulic Engineering* **133**: 186–196.

Ashworth, P.J. 1996. Mid-Channel bar growth and its relationship to local flow strength and direction. *Earth Surface Processes and Landforms* **17**: 103–124.

Belcher, B.J. and Fox, J.F. 2009. Discussion of "Laboratory measurements of 3-D flow patterns and turbulence in straight open channel with rough bed" by Rodriguez, J.F. and Garcia, M. H. *Journal of Hydraulic Research* **47**: 685–688.

Best, J. 2005. The fluid dynamics of river dunes: A review and some future research directions. *Journal of Geophysical Research – Earth Surface* **110**: F04S02. doi: 10.1029/ 2004JF000218.

Blanckaert, K. 2009. Saturation of curvature induced secondary flow, energy losses and turbulence in sharp open-channel bends. Laboratory experiments, analysis and modelling. *Journal of Geophysical Research – Earth Surface* **114**: F03015. doi:10.1029/2008 JF001137.

Blanckaert, K. 2010. Topographic steering, flow recirculation, velocity redistribution and bed topography in sharp meander bends. *Water Resources Research* **46**: W09506. doi:10.1029/ 2009WR008303.

Blanckaert, K. and deVriend, H. J. 2004. Secondary flow in sharp open-channel bends. *Journal of Fluid Mechanics* **498**: 353–380.

Blanckaert, K. and deVriend, H. J. 2005a. Turbulence characteristics in sharp open-channel bends. *Physics of Fluids* **17**: 055102–055117.

Blanckaert, K. and de Vriend, H. J. 2005b. Turbulence structure in sharp open-channel bends. *Journal of Fluid Mechanics* **536**: 27–48.

Blanckaert, K., Duarte, A., and Schleiss, A.J. 2010. Influence of shallowness, bank inclination and bank roughness on the variability of flow patterns and boundary shear stress due to secondary currents in straight open channels. *Advances in Water Resources* **33**: 1062–1074. doi:10.1016/j. advwatres. 2010.06.012.

Boyer, C., Roy, A.G., and Best J.L. 2006. Dynamics of a river channel confluence with discordant beds: flow turbulence, bedload sediment transport and bed morphology. *Journal of Geophysical Research – Earth Surface* **111**: F04007. doi:10.1029/2005JF000458.

Boxall, J.B., Guymer, I., and Marion, A. 2003. Transverse mixing in sinuous natural open channel flows. *Journal of Hydraulic Research* **41**: 153–165.

Bradbrook, K.F., Lane, S.N., and Richards, K.S. 2000. Numerical simulation of time-averaged flow structure at river channel confluences. *Water Resources Research* **36**: 2731–2746.

Bradbrook, K. F., Lane, S.N., Richards, K.S., Biron, P.M., and Roy A.G. 2001. Flow structures and mixing at an asymmetrical open-channel confluence: a numerical study, *Journal of Hydraulic Engineering* **127**: 351–368.

Bradshaw, P. 1987. Turbulent secondary flows. *Annual Review of Fluid Mechanics* **19**: 53–74.

Broglia, R., Pascarelli, A., and Piomelli, U. 2003. Large-eddy simulations of ducts with a free surface. *Journal of Fluid Mechanics* **484**: 223–253.

Buffin-Belanger, T.K. Demers, S., and Roy, A. G. 2009. Macroturbulent coherent structures and helical cell motions in an ice-covered meander bend. American Geophysical Union, Fall Meeting 2009, San Francisco, CA. Abstract # EP23B-0629.

Camporeale, C., Perona, P., Porporato, A., and Ridolfi L. 2007. Hierarchy of models for meandering rivers and related morphodynamic processes. *Reviews of Geophysics* **45**: RG1001. doi:10.1029/2005RG000185.

Colombini, M. 1993. Turbulence-driven secondary flows and formation of sand ridges. *Journal of Fluid Mechanics* **254**: 701–719.

Colombini, M. and Parker, G. 1995. Longitudinal streaks. *Journal of Fluid Mechanics* **304**: 161–183.

Constantinescu, S.G., Sukhodolov, A., and McCoy, A. 2009. Mass exchange in a shallow channel flow with a series of groynes: LES study and comparison with laboratory and field experiments. *Environmental Fluid Mechanics* **9**: 587–615. doi: 10.1007/s10652-009-9155-2.

Cooper, J.R. and Tait, S.J. 2008. The spatial organisation of time-averaged velocity and its relationship with the bed surface topography of water-worked gravel beds. *Acta Geophysica*, **56**: 614-642. doi: 10.2478/s11600-008-0023-0.

Cunningham, A. 1883. Recent hydraulic experiments. *Institution of Civil Engineers, Minutes of Proceedings* **71**(Paper No. 1786): 1–36.

Czernuszenko, W. and Rylov, A. 2002. Modeling of three-dimensional velocity field in open channel flows. *Journal of Hydraulic Research* **40**: 135–143.

De Serres, B., Roy, A.G., Biron, P.M., and Best, J.L. 1999. Three-dimensional structure of flow at a confluence of river channels with discordant beds. *Geomorphology* **26**: 313–335.

Demers S., Buffin-Bélanger T., and Roy A.G. 2011. Helical cell motions in a small ice-covered meander river reach. *River Research and Applications* **27**. doi: 10.1002/rra. 1451.

Demuren, A.O. and Rodi, W. 1984. Calculation of turbulence-driven secondary motion in non-circular ducts. *Journal of Fluid Mechanics* **140**: 189–222.

Einstein, H.A. and Li, H. 1958. Secondary currents in straight channels. *American Geophysical Union Transactions* **39**: 1085–1088.

Ettema, R. 2002. Review of River-channel Responses to River Ice. *Journal of Cold Regions Engineering* **16**: 191–217.

Ettema, R. 2008. Ice effects on sediment transport in rivers. In Garcia, M., editor. *Sedimentation Engineering: Processes, Measurements, Modeling, and Practice*. American Society of Civil Engineers, Manuals and Reports on Engineering Practice 110, pp. 613–648.

Ettema, R. and Zabilansky, L. 2004. Ice influences on channel stability: Insights from Missouri's Fort Peck reach. *Journal of Hydraulic Engineering* **130**: 279–292.

Fong, D.A., Monismith, S.G., Stacey, M.T., and Burau, J.R. 2009. Turbulent stresses and secondary currents in a tidal-forced channel with significant curvature and asymmetric bed forms. *Journal of Hydraulic Engineering* **135**: 198–209.

Francis, J.B. 1878. On the cause of the maximum velocity of water flowing in open channels being below the surface. *Transactions of the American Society of Civil Engineers* **7**: 109–113.

Garcia, G. 2008. Sediment transport and morphodynamics. In Garcia, M., editor. *Sedimentation Engineering: Processes, Measurements, Modeling, and Practice*. American Society of Civil Engineers, Manuals and Reports on Engineering Practice 110, pp. 21–164.

Gessner, F.B. 1973. The origin of secondary flow in turbulent flow along a corner. *Journal of Fluid Mechanics* **58**: 1–25.

Gibson, A.H. 1909. On the depression of the filament of maximum velocity in a stream flowing through an open channel. *Proceedings of the Royal Society A. Mathematical and Physical Sciences* **82**: 149–159.

Grega, L.M., Hsu, T.Y., and Wei, T. 2002. Vorticity transport in a corner formed by a solid wall and a free surface. *Journal of Fluid Mechanics* **465**: 331–352.

Gulliver, M. and Halverson, M.J. 1987. Measurements of large streamwise vortices in an open channel-flow. *Water Resources Research* **23**: 115–123.

Gyr, A. 2010. The meander paradox – a topological view. *Applied Mechanics Reviews* **63**: 020801-1.

Hallez, Y. and Magnaudet, J. 2009. Turbulence-induced secondary motion in a buoyancy-driven flow in a circular pipe. *Physics of Fluids* **21**: 081704.

Hinze, J.O., 1967. Secondary currents in wall turbulence. *Physics of Fluids* **10**: S122–S125, doi:10.1063/1.1762429.

Hinze, J.O., 1973. Experimental investigation of secondary currents in the turbulent flow through a straight conduit. *Applied Science Research* **28**: 453–465.

Hurther, D., Lemmin, U., and Terray, E.A. 2007. Turbulent transport in the outer region of rough wall open-channel flows: the contribution of large coherent shear stress structures (LC3S). *Journal of Fluid Mechanics* **574**: 465–493.

Ikeda, S. and Parker, G.editors. 1989. *River Meandering*. American Geophysical Union, Washington, DC.

Ikeda, S. and McEwan, I.K.editors. 2009. *Flow and Sediment Transport in Compound Channels: The Experience of Japanese and UK Research*. International Association for Hydro-environment Engineering and Research (IAHR) Monograph Series. Rotterdam, Balkema.

Jamieson, E.C., Post, G., and Rennie, C.D. 2010. Spatial variability of three-dimensional Reynolds stresses in a developing channel bend. *Earth Surface Processes and Landforms* **35**: 1029–1043.

Joukowski, N.E. 1915. On the water flow at the river bend. *Mathematical Proceedings* **29**. Re-published in Joukowski,

N. E. 1937. *Full Collection of Papers*, vol. 4. Moscow-Leningrad, ONTI: 193–233 (in Russian).

Kang, H. and Choi, S.-U. 2009. Scalar flux modeling of solute transport in open channel flows: Numerical tests and effects of secondary currents. *Journal of Hydraulic Research* **47**: 643–655.

Kean, J.W., Kuhnle, R.A., Smith, J.D., Alonso, C.V., and Langendoen, E.J. 2009. Test of a method to calculate near-bank velocity and boundary shear stress. *Journal of Hydraulic Engineering* **135**: 591–601.

Keylock, C.J., Hardy, R.J., Parsons, D.R. *et al.* 2005. The theoretical foundations and potential for large-eddy simulation (LES) in fluvial geomorphic and sedimentological research. *Earth-Science Reviews* **71**: 271–304.

Khosronejad, A., Rennie, C.D., Salehi Neyshabouri, S.A.A., and Townsend, R.D. 2007. 3-D Numerical modeling of flow and sediment transport in laboratory channel bends. *Journal of Hydraulic Engineering* **133**: 1123–1134.

Knight, D.W., Aya, S., Ikeda, S., Nezu, I., and Shiono, K. 2009a. Flow structure. In Ikeda, S. and McEwan, I.K., editors. *Flow and Sediment Transport in Compound Channels: The Experience of Japanese and UK Research*. International Association for Hydro-environmenal Engineering and Research (IAHR) Monograph Series. Rotterdam, A.A.Balkema, pp. 5–113.

Knight, D.W., Ganey, C.M.C., Lamb, R., and Samuels, P.G. 2009b. *Practical Channel Hydraulics*. Amsterdam, Taylor and Francis.

3-DLane, S.N., Bradbrook, K.F., Richards, K.S., Biron, P.M., and Roy, A.G. 1999. Time-averaged flow structure in the central region of a stream confluence: a discussion. *Earth Surface Processes and Landforms* **24**: 361–367.

Lane, S.N., Bradbrook, K.F., Richards, K.S., Biron, P.M., and Roy, A.G. 2000. Secondary circulation in river channel confluences: Measurement myth or coherent flow structure? *Hydrological Processes* **14**: 2047–2471.

Leliavski, N.S. 1894. Currents in streams and the formation of stream beds. *6th International Congress on Navigation Proceedings*. The Hague, The Netherlands.

Levi, E. 1995. *The Science of Water. The Foundation of Modern Hydraulics*. New York, American Society of Civil Engineers Press.

Lyn, D.A. 2008. Turbulence models for sediment transport engineering. In Garcia, M., editor. *Sedimentation Engineering: Processes, Measurements, Modeling, and Practice*. American Society of Civil Engineers, Manuals and Reports on Engineering Practice 110, pp.763–826.

MacVicar, B.J. and Roy, A.G. 2007a. Hydrodynamics of a forced riffle pool in a gravel bed river: 1. Mean velocity and turbulence intensity. *Water Resources Research* **43**: W12401. doi: 10.1029/2006WR02572.

MacVicar, B.J. and Roy, A.G. 2007b. Hydrodynamics of a forced riffle pool in a gravel bed river: 2. Scale and structure of coherent turbulent events. *Water Resources Research* **43**: W12402. doi: 10.1029/2006WR005274.

Marion, A. and Zaramella, M. 2006. Effects of velocity gradients and secondary flow on the dispersion of solutes in curved channels. *Journal of Environmental Engineering* **132**, 1295–1302.

McLean, S.R. 1981. The role of non-uniform roughness in the formation of sand ribbons. *Marine Geology* **42**: 49–74.

McLelland, S.J., Ashworth, P., Best, J.L., and Livesey, J.R. 1999. Turbulence and secondary flow over sediment stripes in weakly bimodal bed material, *Journal of Hydraulic Engineering* **125**: 463–473.

Miyawaki, S., Constantinescu, G., Kirkil, G., Rhoads. B., and Sukhodolov, A. 2009. Numerical investigation of three-dimensional flow structure at a river confluence. *Proceedings of the 33rd IAHR Congress, 9–14 August, Vancouver, Canada (CD ROM)*. International Association for Hydro-environmenal Engineering and Research (IAHR).

Nakagawa, H. and Nezu, I. 1981. Structure of space-time correlations of bursting phenomena in an open-channel flow. *Journal of Fluid Mechanics* **104**: 1–43.

Nezu, I. 2005. Open-channel flow turbulence and its research prospect in the 21st century. *Journal of Hydraulic Engineering* **131**: 229–246.

Nezu, I. and Nakagawa, H. 1993. *Turbulence in Open-Channel Flows*. International Association for Hydraulic Research Monograph Series. Rotterdam, A.A.Balkema.

Nikora, V. 2008. Hydrodynamics of gravel-bed rivers: scale issues. In Habersack, H., Piégay, H. and Rinaldi, M. editors *Gravel-Bed Rivers, Vol. VI*, Amsterdam, Elsevier, Developments in Earth Surface Processes **11**: 61–81.

Nikora, V. 2009. Friction factor for rough-bed flows: interplay of fluid stresses, secondary currents, non-uniformity, and unsteadiness. *Proceedings of the 33rd IAHR Congress, 9–14 August, Vancouver, Canada (CD ROM)*. International Association for Hydro-environmenal Engineering and Research (IAHR).

Nikora V.I., Goring D.G., and Biggs B. *J. F.* 1998. Silverstream eco-hydraulics flume: hydraulic design and tests. *New Zealand Journal of Marine and Freshwater Research* **32**: 607–620.

Odgaard, A.J. and Abad, J.D. 2008. River meandering and channel stability. In Garcia, M., editor. *Sedimentation Engineering: Processes, Measurements, Modeling, and Practice*. American Society of Civil Engineers, Manuals and Reports on Engineering Practice **110**, pp. 439–460.

Papanicolaou, A.N., Elhakeem, M., and Hilldale, R. 2007. Secondary current effects on cohesive river bank erosion. *Water Resources Research* **43**: W12418, doi:10.1029/2006 WR005763.

Parker, G. 2008. Transport of gravel and sediment mixtures. In Garcia, M., editor. *Sedimentation Engineering: Processes, Measurements, Modeling, and Practice*. American Society of Civil Engineers, Manuals and Reports on Engineering Practice **110**, pp. 165–252.

Parsons, D.R., Best, J.L., Lane, S.N. *et al.* 2007. Form roughness and the absence of secondary flow in a large confluence-diffluence, Rio Parana, Argentina, *Earth Surface Processes and Landforms* **32**: 155–162. doi:10.1002/esp.1457.

Pinelli, A., Uhlmann, M., Sekimoto, A., and Kawahara, G. 2010. Reynolds number dependence of mean flow structure in square duct turbulence. *Journal of Fluid Mechanics* **644**: 107–122.

Pizzuto, J.E. 2008. Streambank erosion and river width adjustments. In Garcia, M., editor. *Sedimentation Engineering: Processes, Measurements, Modeling, and Practice*. American Society of Civil Engineers, Manuals and Reports on Engineering Practice **110**, 387–438.

Prandtl, L. 1926. Über die Ausgebildete Turbulenz. In Meissner, E., editor, *2e Internationaler Kongress der Technischen Mechanik, Verhandlung*. Füessli, Zürich, 62–75.

Prandtl, L. 1952. *Essentials of Fluid Mechanics*. London and Glasgow, Blackie & Son Ltd.

Rhoads, B. L. and Kenworthy, S.T. 1998. Time-averaged flow structure in the central region of a stream confluence. *Earth Surface Processes and Landforms* **23**: 171–191.

Rhoads, B. L. and Kenworthy, S.T. 1999. On secondary circulation, helical motion, and Rozovskii-based analysis of time-averaged 2-D velocity fields at confluences. *Earth Surface Processes and Landforms* **24**: 369–375.

Rhoads B.L. and Sukhodolov A. 2001. Field investigation of three-dimensional flow structure at stream confluences: Part I. Thermal mixing and time-averaged velocities. *Water Resources Research* **37**: 2393–2410.

Rhoads, B.L. and Welford, M.R. 1991. Initiation of river meandering. *Progress in Physical Geography* **15**: 127–156.

Rice, S.P., Roy, A.G., and Rhoads, B.L., editors. 2008. *River Confluences, Tributaries and the Fluvial Network*. Chichester, John Wiley & Sons, Ltd.

Richardson, W.R. and Thorne, C.R. 2001. Multiple thread flow and channel bifurcation in a braided river: Brahmaputra–Jamuna River, *Bangladesh. Geomorphology* **38**: 185–196.

Rinaldi, M. and Darby, S.E. 2008. Modelling river-bank erosion processes and mass failure mechanisms: progress towards fully coupled simulations. In Habersack, H., Piégay, H., and Rinaldi, M. editors. *Gravel-Bed Rivers VI*. Amsterdam, Elsevier, Developments in Earth Surface Processes **11**: 213–239.

Robinson S.K. 1991. Coherent motion in the turbulent boundary layer. *Annual Review of Fluid Mechanics* **23**: 601–639.

Rodi, W. 1993. *Turbulence Models and their Application in Hydraulics*. International Association for Hydro-environment Engineering and Research (IAHR) Monograph Series. Rotterdam, Balkema.

Rodriguez, J.F. and Garcia, M.H. 2008. Laboratory measurements of 3-D flow patterns and turbulence in straight open channel with rough bed. *Journal of Hydraulic Research* **46**: 454–465.

Rouse, H. and Ince, S. 1963. *History of Hydraulics*. New York, Dover Publications.

Rowiński P.M., Guymer I., and Kwiatkowski K. 2008. Response to the slug injection of a tracer – large scale experiment in a natural river. *Hydrological Sciences Journal* **53**: 1300–1309.

Roy, A.G., Buffin-Belanger, T., Lamarre, H., and Kirkbride, A. D. 2004. Size, shape, and dynamics of large-scale turbulent flow structures in a gravel-bed river. *Journal of Fluid Mechanics* **500**: 1–27.

Rutherford, J.C. 1994. *River Mixing*. Chichester, John Wiley & Sons, Ltd.

Sambrook Smith, G.H., Best, J., Bristow, C.S., and Petts, G.E. 2006. *Braided Rivers: Process, Deposits, Ecology and Management*. International Association of Sedimentologists, Special Publication 36. Chichester, John Wiley & Sons, Ltd.

Sanjou, M. and Nezu, I. 2009. Turbulence structure and coherent motion in meandering compound open-channel flows. *Journal of Hydraulic Research* **47**: 598–610.

Seminara, G. 2006. Meanders. *Journal of Fluid Mechanics* **554**: 271–297.

Seminara, G. 2010. Fluvial sedimentary patterns. *Annual Review of Fluid Mechanics* **42**: 43–66.

Stearns, F.P. 1883. On the current meter, together with a reason why the maximum velocity of water flowing in open channels is below the surface. *Transactions of the American Society of Civil Engineers* **12**: 331–338.

Sterling, M., Beaman, F., Morvan, H., and Wright, N. 2008. Bed shear stress characteristics of a simple, prismatic, rectangular channel. *Journal of Hydraulic Engineering* **134**: 1085–1094.

Stoesser, T., Ruether, N., and Olsen, N.R.B. 2010. Calculation of primary and secondary flow and boundary shear stresses in a meandering channel. *Advances in Water Resources* **33**: 158–170.

Sukhodolov, A. and Kaschtschejewa, E. 2010. Turbulent flow in a meander bend of a lowland river: Field measurements and preliminary results. In Dittrich, A., Koll, Ka., Aberle, J.,and Geisenhainer, P., editors. *River Flow 2010*. Bundesanstalt für Wasserbau, pp. 309–316.

Sukhodolov A. and Rhoads B. 2001. Field investigation of three-dimensional flow structure at stream confluences: Part II. *Turbulence. Water Resources Research* **37**: 2411–2424.

Szupiany, R.N., Amsler, M.L., Parsons, D.R., and Best, J.L. 2009. Morphology, flow structure, and suspended bed sediment transport at two large braid-bar confluences. *Water Resources Research* **45**: W05415. doi:10.1029/2008WR007428.

Tennekes, H. and Lumley, J.L. 1972. *A First Course in Turbulence*. Cambridge, MA, MIT Press.

Termini, D. 2009. Experimental observations of flow and bed processes in large-amplitude meandering flume. *Journal of Hydraulic Engineering* **135**: 575–587.

Thomson, J.J. 1876. On the origin of windings of rivers in alluvial plains, with remarks on the flow of water round bends in pipes. *Proceedings of the Royal Society of London* **25**: 5–8. Re-published in *Nature* **122**: 14 (1976).

Townsend, A.A. 1976. *The Structure of Turbulent Shear Flow*. Cambridge, Cambridge University Press.

Tsai, W.-F. and Ettema, R. 1994. Ice cover influence on transverse bed slopes in a curved alluvial channel. *Journal of Hydraulic Research* **32**: 561–582.

Tsinober, A. 2009. *An Informal Conceptual Introduction to Turbulence*. Dordrecht, Springer.

Van Balen, W., Uijttewaal, W.S.J., and Blanckaert, K. 2009. Large-eddy simulation of a mildly curved open-channel flow. *Journal of Fluid Mechanics* **630**: 413–442.

Van Balen, W., Blanckaert, K., and Uijttewaal, W.S.J. 2010. Analysis of the role of turbulence in curved open-channel flow at different water depths by means of experiments, LES and RANS. *Journal of Turbulence* **11**: Article no. 12. doi:10.1080/14685241003789404.

Vanoni, V.A. 1946. Transportation of suspended sediment by water. *Transactions of the American Society of Civil Engineers* **111**: 67–133.

Wang, Z-Q. and Cheng, N.-S. 2006. Time-mean structure of secondary flows in open channel with longitudinal bedforms. *Advances in Water Resources* **2**: 1634–1649.

Wood, D.V. 1879. On the flow of water in rivers. *Transactions of the American Society of Civil Engineers* **8**: 173–178.

Yang S.-Q., 2005. Interactions of boundary shear stress, secondary currents and velocity. *Fluid Dynamics Research* **36**: 121–136.

Yang, S.-Q. and Lim, S.-Y. 1997. Mechanism of energy transportation in a 3-D channel. *Journal of Hydraulic Engineering* **123**: 684–692.

Yen, B.C. 2002. Open channel flow resistance. *Journal of Hydraulic Engineering* **128**: 20–39.

Zeng, J., Constantinescu, G., Blanckaert, K., and Weber, L. 2008. Flow and bathymetry in sharp open-channel bends: Experiments and predictions. *Water Resources Research* **44**: W09401. doi:10.1029/2007 WR006303.

Zeng, J., Constantinescu, G., and Weber, L. 2010. 3-D calculations of equilibrium conditions in loose-bed open channels with significant suspended sediment load. *Journal of Hydraulic Engineering* **136**: 557–571.

## 1.10 DISCUSSION

### 1.10.1 Discussion by Tim Randle

Would the authors please comment on the potential for secondary currents of the second kind in straight channels (e.g. canals, straightened channels, perhaps meander cutoffs) to eventually evolve the channel platform to increased sinuosity and the development of secondary currents of the first kind?

### 1.10.2 Discussion by Gordon E. Grant

Is it possible to use our current understanding and ability to model secondary flows to establish a set of criteria (or even a set of hypotheses) about where such flows should and should not have morphodynamic significance? In other words, it's one thing to be able to identify that secondary flows, perhaps as stimulated by grain roughness or similar, should exist; it's another to argue that such flows should leave a discernible and measureable imprint on the channel morphology. For example, in very rough channels, any tendency for coherent secondary flow structures is likely to be suppressed by the turbulence set up by the form and large-scale grain roughness. It would help us better understand secondary flows and their role in channel morphology if we could identify, at least to first order, where we should expect to see coherent flow structures that could potentially modify channel form.

### 1.10.3 Reply by Vladimir Nikora and André G. Roy

T. Randle's question and G. Grant's comment highlight a potentially important role of secondary currents in generating instabilities in channels with erodible boundaries. For example, a time-averaged secondary cell in a straight channel can be viewed as a manifestation of the frequently occurring instantaneous helical motions, wandering, to a certain degree, across the channel and serving as large-scale perturbations leading to development of plane deformations of the channel. A similar situation may also occur in channels with more realistic and complex channel geometries, with different types of secondary currents. Recent achievements in this field suggest that soon we should have much better capabilities for predicting locations and strength of time-averaged secondary currents. However, it seems that the role of the mean secondary currents in channel morphodynamics is essentially defined by their instantaneous components (e.g., helical motions), regularly or intermittently occurring in the flow. We believe that the topology, intensity, and statistics of these instantaneous components of the time-averaged secondary currents, still practically unknown, will provide important knowledge to better understand many aspects of channel morphodynamics.

# 2

# Secondary Flows in Rivers:
# The Effect of Complex Geometry

## Bruce MacVicar

## 2.1 INTRODUCTION

Rivers are characterized by features such as bars, pools, and meanders that are defined by their complex or non-uniform geometry. While these features are known to be generated as part of feedback loops with the flow and sediment transport, understanding of the effect of complex geometry on turbulence and secondary flows in rivers is limited (Nezu, 2005; Nikora and Roy, Chapter 1, this volume). It is difficult to determine a general model to describe the role of turbulence and secondary currents in the formation of common non-uniform features of natural rivers due to the technical challenges that result from measuring during floods, and the uncertainty created by the particular geometry of a given study site.

As a companion to the review by Nikora and Roy on secondary flows in rivers, this chapter will review recent studies concerned with how secondary flow is affected by complex geometry. To limit the scope of this work, the reviewed studies are only those that have used a reductionist approach by modelling a complex natural form using simpler or more fundamental geometries. In practical terms, this means that the reviewed studies have isolated a particular aspect of channel non-uniformity and subjected it to intensive measurements and/or numerical simulations of 3-D flow and turbulence. It is hoped that such a review will encourage a range of field and laboratory experiments and allow the critical effect of channel non-uniformity to be included within the theoretical framework described by Nikora and Roy for secondary flows in rivers.

## 2.2 BACKGROUND

In his review of turbulence in open-channel flow, Nezu (2005) noted only two types of channel non-

uniformity: abrupt changes of roughness elements on the bed, such as dunes and steps, and side cavities or "wandos". These two examples are far from a complete list, however, and Nikora and Roy (Chapter 1, this volume) discussed a number of studies dealing with complex geometry. Prominent among those discussed were the studies in meandering channels by Blanckaert and deVriend (2004, 2005) and Abad and Garcia (2009a, 2009b), which used detailed measurements in physical models of meandering channels to investigate flow dynamics. To avoid overlapping subjects with Nikora and Roy and to focus this brief review, reviewed studies will be restricted to those that have reduced the dimensions of the geometry as much as possible, typically by working with a fixed bed and 2-D representations of 3-D forms. For example, the work of Blanckaert (2009) used a curved channel with straight side walls instead of a more natural asymmetric cross-section in the pool. This approach avoided the contamination of the data through the interaction of the flow with a mobile bed and simplified the results to the point that the secondary flow and turbulence patterns could be described with only the centreline measurements in the channel. In a similar fashion, the majority of the studies in this review have tried to isolate various non-uniformities, typically in experimental flumes and numerical simulations, but occasionally in controlled field experiments, in order to better understand the effect of the non-uniformity on turbulence and secondary flow.

To describe a consistent response of secondary flow to complex geometry and compare results between studies, it is necessary to first identify the types of non-uniformities in channels. Including the case of a curved channel and considering only the case of steady flow, five types of non-uniform channels were identified: (I) curved side walls; (II) non-uniform flow depth; (III) non-uniform channel width; (IV) non-uniform

*Gravel-bed Rivers: Processes, Tools, Environments*, First Edition. Edited by Michael Church, Pascale M. Biron and André G. Roy.
© 2012 John Wiley & Sons, Ltd. Published 2012 by John Wiley & Sons, Ltd.

shape of the cross-section; and (V) a local change of the width or depth (Figure 2.1).

Types I–IV can occur at different rates in the direction of flow. The channel depth, for example, can change suddenly at a step formed by a weir, or could experience a gradual increase in the depth over some distance. These two scenarios will produce very different effects on turbulence and secondary flow and have typically been studied separately due to the importance of flow separation in sudden geometrical changes. Type V is not strictly a unique type because it consists of a sudden lateral contraction followed by a short uniform section and a sudden lateral expansion. Nevertheless it is considered here as a separate type because it can be considered a point disturbance to the flow, whereas the other types have been studied as gradual changes to the geometry of the channel.

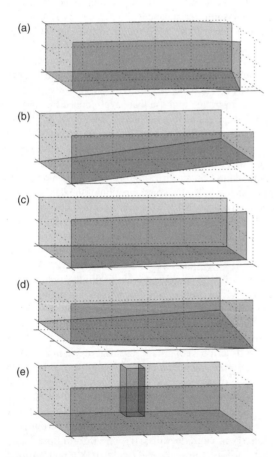

**Figure 2.1** Non-uniform geometries in an open channel: (a) curved side walls; (b) non-uniform flow depth; (c) non-uniform channel width; (d) non-uniform cross section; and (e) local lateral constriction.

To assist with the description of the reviewed studies, it is important to define the terms disturbance, recovery, transience and steady-state response in relation to patterns of flow in channels. In uniform channels, typical patterns of velocity and turbulence distribution develop as a force balance is found between the friction at the boundaries and gravity (Nezu and Nakagawa, 1993). The steady-state response of the flow in this case can be described by the classic log-law for the variation of streamwise flow with height above the bed of the channel. A point disturbance, such as a spur dike, or a step disturbance, such as a sudden narrowing of the channel width, will result in the disruption of typical patterns over a distance up- and downstream of the disturbance. This disruption is transient in the streamwise direction as the flow patterns will return to a uniform flow condition in a process called recovery (Blanckaert, 2009). In contrast with local disturbances to the flow in an otherwise uniform channel, gradual changes to the channel geometry produce a continuous disturbance due to the changing relation between the gravitational forces, which are a function of the water volume, and the frictional forces, which are a function of the contact area between the water volume and the surrounding surfaces. Despite the inability of these flows to return to a uniform condition, these systems will also tend to exhibit a transient-state response from which they recover to a steady-state or equilibrium response (Onitsuka *et al.*, 2009).

The objective of this review is to look at the five types of channel non-uniformity from the perspective of secondary flow. Mobile bed experiments will not be considered and any discussions of scour will be very limited. Instead, the review will concentrate on describing what is known about how specific aspects of non-uniformity in channels influence the development of helical and non-helical secondary flows driven by both vortex stretching, such as occurs in channel bends (Prandtl's first kind) and turbulence heterogeneity (Prandtl's second kind).

## 2.3 CHANNEL NON-UNIFORMITY AND SECONDARY FLOWS

### 2.3.1 Type I: Curved Channel

Curved channels have received considerable attention in recent years, primarily as a result of highly detailed laboratory experiments in mobile bed channels (Blanckaert and de Vriend, 2004, 2005; Abad and Garcia, 2009a, b; Jamieson *et al.*, 2010). It is clear, however, that there are many different variables to consider that are unique to curved channels, including the radius and skewness of curvature, the length of the curve and the asymmetry of the channel cross-section. In the interest of reducing the number of dimensions to the problems, a number of recent studies have adopted uniform channel sections to isolate the effect of channel curvature on flow dynamics (Booij, 2003; Blanckaert, 2009; Van Balen et al., 2009; Stoesser et al., 2010b; van Balen et al., 2010). Due to its importance for determining shear stress and erosion on the outside wall of the curved channel, these studies were particularly interested in understanding the formation of a second counter-rotating secondary flow cell in this location.

Booij (2003) measured the secondary flow in a mildly curved open channel bend (width of channel = 0.5 m, radius of curvature = 4.10 m). Measurements with an LDV system documented the occurrence of the outer bank cell. A comparison of Reynolds-averaged Navier–Stokes (RANS) and large eddy simulation (LES) models showed that the cell did not occur with the RANS model. The same curve was modeled by van Balen et al. (2009) again using an LES model of the channel. By considering the various terms of the streamwise vorticity equation written in spherical coordinates, it was shown that the secondary flow near the outer bank is driven by both vortex stretching and turbulence anisotropy (Prandtl's first and second kinds). This result indicates that RANS models using the standard $k - \varepsilon$ turbulence closure are not suitable for modelling situations where turbulence anisotropy drives the secondary currents.

Blanckaert (2009) used an acoustic Doppler vertical profiler (ADVP) to measure the secondary flow in a sharply curved open channel bend (width of channel = 1.3 m, radius of curvature = 1.7 m) with a flat horizontal bed. The purpose of this study was not to investigate the outer bank secondary cell, but to look at the effect of relative curvature, expressed as the ratio of the flow depth ($H$) to the radius of curvature ($R$), on secondary flow. By maintaining a constant bulk velocity in the channel, he was able to show that the relative curvature does not affect the induced secondary flow or energy losses in the curve and called this effect the "saturation" of curvature induced secondary flow. Blanckaert's results are also interesting because of their relevance for the description of disturbance and recovery in non-uniform channels. He noted a strong increase in the turbulent kinetic energy in the bend. Turbulence production in the frequency range less than 3 Hz increased rapidly in the upstream part of the bend and decreased as turbulence in the range between 3 and 7 Hz increased in the downstream portion of the bend. This result helps to describe the transient response of the flow to the disturbance of the bend. Numerical simulations of the sharp curve studied by Blanckaert (2009) were carried out by van Balen et al. (2010) using RANS and LES models. They found that the RANS model underestimated the main secondary flow cell and overestimated friction loss. Similar to van Balen et al. (2009), the

RANS model did not show an outer bank cell, while the LES model did. They conclude that, unlike straight channels where Prandtl's second kind of secondary flow is dominant, secondary flow in curved channels is the result of both Prandtl's first (centrifugal effects) and second kind (turbulence anisotropy).

In a numerical study using measurements from a rectangular channel with two linked curves (channel width = 0.25 m, radius of curvature = 1.0 m) Stoesser et al. (2010b) similarly compared LES and RANS models with experimental results. In contrast to what was observed by van Balen et al. (2009, 2010), Stoesser found that the RANS model was able to predict the generation of an outer bank cell. The mechanism by which it occurs in the second bend was found to be related to the residual flow from the first bend. Stoesser et al. (2010b) argue that, while the persistence of the outer bank secondary flow cell is the result of turbulence anisotropy (Prandtl's second kind), the generation of the cell is in fact the result of centrifugal effects (Prandtl's first kind).

### 2.3.2 Type II: Non-Uniform Flow Depth

Many authors have looked at the effect of non-uniform flow depth on the turbulent flow properties of the channel (Kironoto and Graf, 1995; Song and Chiew, 2001; Yang and Chow, 2008; Afzalimehr and Rennie, 2009; Afzalimehr, 2010). The non-uniform bed will induce convective acceleration and deceleration. For 2-D gradually varied flow, Yang et al. (2006) demonstrated, using the RANS equations, that there is a non-zero vertical velocity as a result of the difference in slope between the bed and the water surface. Defined normal to the bed slope, the vertical velocity component will be positive (away from the bed) in decelerating flow and negative (toward the bed) in accelerating flow. This net flow relative to the channel bed is non-helical secondary flow of Prandtl's first kind.

Similar to what is observed for curved channels, the secondary flow re-distributes the Reynolds stress on the bed and side walls of the channel. The Reynolds stress will deviate from a linear relation with the depth so that it is convex in shape in decelerating flow and concave in accelerating flow (Kironoto and Graf, 1995; Song and Chiew, 2001). Due to an additional momentum term that is the result of a non-zero value for the vertical velocity, the total stress can be written as:

$$-\frac{\overline{u'_1 u'_2} + \bar{u}_1 \bar{u}_2}{u_*^2} = \left(1 - \frac{z}{H}\right) + b\left(\frac{z}{H}\right) \qquad (2.1)$$

where $b$ is a coefficient that is positive in accelerating flow and negative in decelerating flow. In uniform flow the second term on the RHS disappears and the Reynolds stress distribution is a linear function of the relative depth. In convective acceleration and deceleration the sum of the two terms on the RHS of the equation also produce a linear distribution of the total stress.

There has been little consideration of the importance of the side walls in the case of a non-uniform flow depth. Yang and Lim (1997) used an order of magnitude analysis of the terms in the Reynolds equation to show that energy is transported towards the nearest boundary, creating triangular zones near the side walls of the channel, where the velocity gradient is a function of the distance from the side wall instead of the bed. As the channel deepens, the areal influence of the side walls should increase due to the change in the aspect ratio of the channel. Turbulence anisotropy and the generation of Prandtl's second kind of secondary flow are also likely to change in this region. Recent studies have attempted to test the effect of non-uniform depth in steady flow using flume experiments (MacVicar and Rennie, 2009) and LES numerical modelling (Stoesser et al., 2010a). Results showed that, even though flow separation does not occur, a high shear layer forms in the zone of flow deceleration near the bed. Measurements near the side wall indicated that turbulence generated in this area exceeds what is observed at the channel centreline (MacVicar and Rennie, 2009). Coherent structures near the side walls were predominantly oriented at an angle relative to the side walls of the flume as flow depth increased. Sweeps (fast flow moving towards the bed) tended to be oriented towards the side walls, while bursts (slow flow moving away from the bed) tended to be oriented towards the middle of the channel. This result demonstrates that flow is driven toward the centreline of the channel during convective flow deceleration. These secondary flows can be classified as non-helical flows of Prandtl's second kind. Both the measured and simulated results show that turbulent kinetic energy will initially increase in decelerating flow (MacVicar and Rennie, 2009; Stoesser et al., 2010a) in a manner similar to what was observed in a curved channel (Blanckaert, 2009).

An important study for the consideration of transitions from uniform to non-uniform sections of a channel was completed by Onitsuka et al. (2009). They measured velocity profiles downstream of changes to channel geometry in order to document the distance required for steady-state conditions to develop. Steady-state conditions in this case were defined by the shape of the streamwise velocity profile in the outer flow region, which was assessed using Coles' wake parameter ($\Pi$). The experiments in a decelerating flow show that a transient flow region begins at the transition from uniform to non-uniform flow and lasts for a streamwise distance of 12 times the water depth upstream of the transition. The wake parameter ($\Pi$) was found to asymptotically approach its final value.

### 2.3.3 Types III and IV: Non-Uniform Flow Width and Changes in Cross-Section Shape

Types III and IV of channel non-uniformities have not been extensively investigated using experimental or numerical approaches. The only relevant study of a non-uniform flow width that was found is a field study by Papanicolaou and Hilldale (2002) of a lateral channel expansion. Using ADV measurements at a single flood level and basing their analysis on the vorticity equation (Equation 1.11 in Chapter 1), they observed that turbulence intensities were anisotropic, meaning that the terms $\left(\overline{u_3'^2 - u_2'^2}\right)$ and $\left(\overline{u_2'u_3'}\right)$ are non-zero and contribute to the generation of turbulence and secondary flow of Prandtl's second type. Controlled physical and numerical experiments would help to further illuminate the key dynamics.

Cross-section shape affects the distribution of secondary flows and turbulence generation in meandering channels (Frothingham and Rhoads, 2003; Fong et al., 2009; Jamieson et al., 2010), and over alternate bars in a straight channel (Lisle et al., 1993; Lanzoni, 2000a, 2000b). However, the author is not aware of any studies that have looked at the development of secondary flow over straight channels with asymmetrical beds in isolation. This situation would require a condition in which the shape of the cross-section transitioned from a symmetrical or rectangular cross-section to an asymmetrical section without a change to the total cross-sectional area of flow. In this way the effect of the shape transition would not be contaminated by the effect of a bulk acceleration or deceleration.

### 2.3.4 Type V: Local Perturbation, Impulse

A subject that has received considerable attention is the design and construction of bridge abutments and spur dikes, also called groynes (groins in the United States), barbs or flow deflectors (Melville, 1992, 1997; Schmidt et al., 1993). The effect of these structures on scour has been well documented. A number of recent studies have combined experimental work with improved numerical simulations using RANS and LES modelling schemes to improve understanding of the effect on flow dynamics, including secondary flows, as a means of improving their design for river training and habitat restoration (Ettema and Muste, 2004; Nagata et al., 2005; Haltigin et al., 2007a; 2007b; Koken and Constantinescu, 2008a, 2008b; Kuhnle et al., 2008).

A common approach to understanding the effect of a single spur dike on flow dynamics has been to pair a

RANS numerical model with measurements from a physical model for validation. Ouillon and Dartus (1997) applied this approach in a study that was primarily concerned with thalweg flow alignment and the areal extent of the flow-separation region downstream of the dike. The simulations documented the development of 3-D flow at the toe of the dike where flows are strongly directed towards the centre of the channel. Nagata *et al.* (2005) also used the RANS equations with a $k$-$\varepsilon$ turbulence model, but removed the assumption of hydrostatic pressure to obtain detailed estimates of shear stress around the toe of the spur dike. Kuhnle *et al.* (2008) investigated the case of a spur dike with overtopping flow and found that the streamwise length of the separated zone was only about $1.6L$ (where $L$ is the distance that the dike protrudes into the channel), which is much shorter than the distances of $5L$ to $12L$ that have been found for unsubmerged dikes. It instead appears that submerged dikes are more similar to backwards facing steps, because the streamwise length of the separated zone was $4Y$ (where $Y$ is the height of step), which is within the typical range of $4Y$ to $6Y$ (Nelson *et al.*, 1995). The experimental work of Biron *et al.* (2005) was combined with a RANS model to investigate flow through paired deflectors set at different angles to the side wall (Haltigin *et al.*, 2007a, 2007b). Results showed that the zone of secondary flow was sensitive to the angle of the deflector, with relatively larger zones of significant secondary flow for deflectors angled upstream, and zones of deepest scour from the experimental work corresponding with zones of significant downwelling in the flat-bed numerical simulations.

Similar to what has been found for curved channels, there is some debate as to whether the steady and unsteady RANS models can accurately predict secondary flow around dikes and deflectors. An important experimental study for channels with a single spur dike is that of Ettema and Muste (2004). This study investigated how the length of the re-circulation zone and the distance required for the thalweg to re-align with the channel centreline was a function of channel size. The key result was that thalweg alignment with the channel centreline did not always correspond with the size of the recirculation zone. It was shown that the relatively strong vorticity and mixing within the shear zone in narrower channels lead to a contraction of the separation zone, while slowing the recovery of flow symmetry such that the lateral distribution of flow at the end of the separation region tended to remain skewed. This result demonstrates how the generation of turbulence (Prandtl's second kind of secondary flow) can modify secondary flow originally generated by the mean flow direction being skewed around the spur dike.

Koken and Constantinescu (2008a) applied an LES numerical model to the problem of a single spur dike in order to understand the role of coherent structures. This study detailed the vortical structures around the spur dike, including the main horseshoe vortex oriented on the horizontal plane near the bed of the channel and the vortex tubes oriented vertically that were shed periodically downstream from the spur dike. High bed shear stress values were associated with the region of strong acceleration near the tip of the spur dike and where vertical vortex tubes were shed and translated downstream in a detached shear layer. The reattachment point of the vertical vortex tubes was at $x/D \sim 13$. RANS models may be insufficient to understand separated flows that are dominated by such unsteady vortex shedding. The additional detail provided by LES modelling may help to resolve secondary flow and turbulence subject to sudden point disturbances such as spur dikes.

## 2.4 DISCUSSION

The studies discussed in this short review of turbulence and secondary flow in non-uniform channels adopt a reductionist approach in that they isolate one important type of complex geometry as a means of simplifying the results. In a complex system such as a gravel bed river, where feedback loops and non-linear processes are important considerations, this approach is obviously going to reach some scientific limits. The interaction between the flow and a mobile bed will produce a wide range of channel geometries with continuous variation of channel dimensions rather than a stepped series of discrete perturbations to the flow. As shown by Ettema and Muste (2004), the reductionist approach cannot always anticipate the flow phenomena that can emerge from the interaction of multiple boundary layers. These complex dynamics may be critical for understanding the genesis and maintenance of secondary flows in rivers. Nevertheless, the relative paucity of data in simple nonuniform types combined with some examples of clear explanations that have been developed (Koken and Constantinescu, 2008a; Blanckaert, 2009) suggest that the reductionist approach can be useful for teasing apart the complex interactions of flow that make it difficult to study in the field.

Most bedforms and non-uniform sections in rivers can be physically constructed using a combination of the five basic types outlined in the previous section. For example, a meandering channel with a pool in the bend will be characterized by a combination of a curved channel, non-uniform flow depth, as the flow depth increases into the pool and decreases out of the pool, non-uniform cross-sectional shape that is generally more symmetrical in the straight part of the meander and asymmetrical in the bend, and possibly some changes to the overall width of the channel. Even in a straight pool the increase in the depth of the channel as flow comes into the pool will lead to a deceleration of the bulk flow, but the asymmetrical shape of the channel may cause lateral concentration of flow and thereby induce acceleration in the thalweg of the channel. It is very difficult to study all of these effects simultaneously.

The results from simplified models can be used to interpret field measurements. For example, in riffle-pools, the velocity reversal hypothesis has been debated for many years (Keller, 1971; Caamano et al., 2009). By aligning themselves with experiments in simplified non-uniform flow environments, MacVicar and Roy (2007) were able to show that such a reversal can only be a partial explanation of pool maintenance because it cannot explain the mobility of particles in the upstream portion of the pool, where depth is increasing. Similarly, physical experiments in a simplified representation of a pool demonstrate that secondary flows will result in lateral flow convergence through the middle of a pool (MacVicar and Rennie, 2009). This result indicates that lateral flow convergence as observed in field cases (Booker et al., 2001; MacWilliams et al., 2006) is a product of the non-uniform water depth in the pool. Similar explanations of observed phenomena in other environments are likely to result from simplifying complex geometry as much as possible.

A further recommended approach is to consider the simplified flat-bed case as a baseline study to which more realistic representations of the bed can be added. Koken and Constantinescu (2008b), for example, followed their flat-bed study with a mobile-bed study to understand how the final bed configuration modifies the flow. Using a combination of measurements and LES simulations, they showed that the final bed configuration stabilizes the horseshoe vortex system in the flow past the spur dike and eliminates some of the minor vortices that were apparent in the flat-bed simulation. Patches of high vorticity were shown to move against the mean slope of the scour hole, and are thought to explain the convection of material out of the scour hole and the lateral growth of the hole. Recent closure schemes for the incorporation of sand- and gravel-sized roughness elements into numerical models should allow the effect of this additional layer of complexity to be reasonably understood (Hardy et al., 2010; Stoesser, 2010), although roughness modelling over large-scale channel non-uniformities has yet to be demonstrated, perhaps because the computational cost remains prohibitive.

A more general understanding of the effect of non-uniform flow on turbulence and secondary flow is likely to result from a consideration of disturbance and recovery. A common approach in the reviewed studies is to measure the distance required for the system to regain some sort of equilibrium, for example the length of the separation zone downstream of spur dikes (Ettema and Muste, 2004) or the length of the zone in which a transient value for Coles' wake parameter occurs within a zone of increasing flow depth (Onitsuka et al., 2009). The disturbances to turbulence and secondary flow are likely to be significant for sediment transport and bedform scaling, just as the size of the wake layer is important for the scaling of sand dunes (Best, 2005). Continued research into this developing area is likely to produce new insights into the dynamics of rivers.

## 2.5 REFERENCES

Abad, J.D. and Garcia, M.H. 2009a. Experiments in a high-amplitude Kinoshita meandering channel: 1. Implications of bend orientation on mean and turbulent flow structure. *Water Resources Research* **45**: W02401. doi:10.1029/2008 WR007016.

Abad, J.D. and Garcia, M.H. 2009b. Experiments in a high-amplitude Kinoshita meandering channel: 2. Implications of bend orientation on bed morphodynamics. *Water Resources Research* **45**: W02402. doi:10.1029/2008 WR007017.

Afzalimehr, H. 2010. Effect of non-uniformity of flow on velocity and turbulence intensities over a cobble-bed. *Hydrological Processes* **24**: 331–341.

Afzalimehr, H. and Rennie, C.D. 2009. Determination of bed shear stress in gravel-bed rivers using boundary-layer parameters. *Hydrological Sciences Journal* **54**: 147–159.

Best, J., 2005. The fluid dynamics of river dunes: A review and some future research directions. *Journal of Geophysical Research-Earth Surface* **110**: F04S02. doi: 10.1029/2004 JF000218.

Biron, P.M., Robson, C., Lapointe, M.F. and Gaskin, S.J. 2005. Three-dimensional flow dynamics around deflectors. *River Research and Applications* **21**: 961–975.

Blanckaert, K. 2009. Saturation of curvature-induced secondary flow, energy losses, and turbulence in sharp open-channel bends: Laboratory experiments, analysis, and modeling. *Journal of Geophysical Research – Earth Surface* **114**: F03015. doi:10.1029/2008 JF001134.

Blanckaert, K. and deVriend, H.J. 2004. Secondary flow in sharp open-channel bends. *Journal of Fluid Mechanics* **498**: 353–380.

Blanckaert, K. and DeVriend, H.J. 2005. Turbulence structure in sharp open-channel bends. *Journal of Fluid Mechanics* **536**: 27–48.

Booij, R. 2003. Measurements and large eddy simulations of the flows in some curved flumes. *Journal of Turbulence* **4**: N8. doi:10.1088/1468-5248/4/1/008.

Booker, D.J., Sear, D.A. and Payne, A.J. 2001. Modelling three-dimensional flow structures and patterns of boundary shear stress in a natural pool-riffle sequence. *Earth Surface Processes and Landforms* **26**: 553–576.

Caamano, D., Goodwin, P., Buffington, J.M., Liou, J.C.P. and Daley-Laursen, S. 2009. Unifying Criterion for the Velocity

Reversal Hypothesis in Gravel-Bed Rivers. *Journal of Hydraulic Engineering* **135**: 66–70.

Ettema, R. and Muste, M. 2004. Scale effects in flume experiments on flow around a spur dike in flatbed channel. *Journal of Hydraulic Engineering* **130**: 635–646.

Fong, D.A., Monismith, S.G., Stacey, M.T. and Burau, J.R. 2009. Turbulent Stresses and secondary currents in a tidal-forced channel with significant curvature and asymmetric bed forms. *Journal of Hydraulic Engineering* **135**: 198–208.

Frothingham, K.M. and Rhoads, B.L. 2003. Three-dimensional flow structure and channel change in an asymmetrical compound meander loop, Embarras River, Illinois. *Earth Surface Processes and Landforms* **28**: 625–644.

Haltigin, T.W., Biron, P.M. and Lapointe, M.E. 2007a. Three-dimensional numerical simulation of flow around stream deflectors: The effect of obstruction angle and length. *Journal of Hydraulic Research* **45**: 227–238.

Haltigin, T.W., Biron, P.M. and Lapointe, M.F. 2007b. Predicting equilibrium scour-hole geometry near angled stream deflectors using a three-dimensional numerical flow model. *Journal of Hydraulic Engineering* **133**: 983–988.

Hardy, R.J., Best, J.L., Lane, S.N. and Carbonneau, P.E. 2010. Coherent flow structures in a depth-limited flow over a gravel surface: The influence of surface roughness. *Journal of Geophysical Research-Earth Surface* **115**: F03006. doi:10.1029/2009 JF001416.

Jamieson, E.C., Post, G. and Rennie, C.D. 2010. Spatial variability of three-dimensional Reynolds stresses in a developing channel bend. *Earth Surface Processes and Landforms* **35**: 1029–1043.

Keller, E.A. 1971. Areal sorting of bed material: the hypothesis of velocity reversal. *Geological Society of America Bulletin* **82**: 753–756.

Kironoto, B.A. and Graf, W.H. 1995. Turbulence characteristics in rough non-uniform open-channel flow. *Proceedings of the Institution of Civil Engineers-Water Maritime and Energy* **112**: 336–348.

Koken, M. and Constantinescu, G. 2008a. An investigation of the flow and scour mechanisms around isolated spur dikes in a shallow open channel: 1. Conditions corresponding to the initiation of the erosion and deposition process. *Water Resources Research* **44**: W08406. doi:10. 1029/2007 WR006489.

Koken, M. and Constantinescu, G. 2008b. An investigation of the flow and scour mechanisms around isolated spur dikes in a shallow open channel: 2. Conditions corresponding to the final stages of the erosion and deposition process. *Water Resources Research* **44**: W08407, doi:10. 1029/2007 WR006491.

Kuhnle, R.A., Jia, Y.F. and Alonso, C.V. 2008. Measured and simulated flow near a submerged spur dike. *Journal of Hydraulic Engineering* **134**: 916–924.

Lanzoni, S. 2000a. Experiments on bar formation in a straight flume 1. Uniform sediment. *Water Resources Research* **36**: 3337–3349.

Lanzoni, S. 2000b. Experiments on bar formation in a straight flume 2. Graded sediment. *Water Resources Research* **36**: 3351–3363.

Lisle, T.E., Iseya, F. and Ikeda, H. 1993. Response of a channel with alternate bars to a decrease in supply of mixed-size bedload – a flume experiment. *Water Resources Research* **29**: 3623–3629.

MacVicar, B.J. and Rennie, C.D. 2009. Lateral distribution of turbulence and secondary currents in a non-uniform open channel flow. *Proceedings of the 33rd IAHR Congress,* *9–14 August, Vancouver, Canada* (CD-ROM: ISBN: 978-90-78046-08-0). International Association for Hydro-environmenal Engineering and Research (IAHR).

MacVicar, B.J. and Roy, A.G. 2007. Hydrodynamics of a forced riffle pool in a gravel bed river: 1. Mean velocity and turbulence intensity. *Water Resources Research* **43**: W12401. doi: 10.1029/2006 WR05272.

MacWilliams, M.L.J., Wheaton, J.M., Pasternack, G.B., Street, R.L. and Kitanidis, P.K. 2006. Flow convergence routing hypothesis for pool-riffle maintenance in alluvial rivers. *Water Resources Research* **42**: W10427. doi: 10.1029/2005 WR004391.

Melville, B.W. 1992. Local scour at bridge abutments. *Journal of Hydraulic Engineering* **118**: 615–631.

Melville, B.W. 1997. Pier and abutment scour: Integrated approach. *Journal of Hydraulic Engineering* **123**: 125–136.

Nagata, N., Hosoda, T., Nakato, T. and Muramoto, Y. 2005. Three-dimensional numerical model for flow and bed deformation around river hydraulic structures. *Journal of Hydraulic Engineering* **131**: 1074–1087.

Nelson, J.M., Shreve, R.L., McClean, S.R. and Drake, T.G. 1995. Role of near-bed turbulence structure in bed load transport and bed form mechanics. *Water Resources Research* **31**: 2071–2086.

Nezu, I. 2005. Open-channel flow turbulence and its research prospect in the 21st century. *Journal of Hydraulic Engineering* **131**: 229–246.

Nezu, I. and Nakagawa, H. 1993. *Turbulence in Open-channel Flows*. International Association for Hydraulic Research Monograph Series. Rotterdam, A.A. Balkema.

Onitsuka, K., Akiyama, J. and Matsuoka, S. 2009. Prediction of velocity profiles and Reynolds stress distributions in turbulent open-channel flows with adverse pressure gradient. *Journal of Hydraulic Research* **47**: 58–65.

Ouillon, S. and Dartus, D. 1997. Three-dimensional computation of flow around groyne. *Journal of Hydraulic Engineering* **123**: 962–970.

Papanicolaou, A.N. and Hilldale, R. 2002. Turbulence characteristics in gradual channel transition. *Journal of Engineering Mechanics* **128**: 948–960.

Schmidt, J.C., Rubin, D.M. and Ikeda, H. 1993. Flume simulation of recirculating flow and sedimentation. *Water Resources Research* **29**: 2925–2939.

Song, T. and Chiew, Y.M. 2001. Turbulence measurement in nonuniform open-channel flow using acoustic doppler velocimeter (ADV). *Journal of Engineering Mechanics* **127**: 219–231.

Stoesser, T. 2010. Physically realistic roughness closure scheme to simulate turbulent channel flow over rough beds within the framework of LES. *Journal of Hydraulic Engineering* **136**: 812–819.

Stoesser, T., Kara, S., MacVicar, B.J. and Best, J.L. 2010a. Turbulent flow over a mildly sloped pool-riffle sequence. *Proceedings of Riverflow – International Conference on Fluvial Hydraulics, Braunschweig, Germany, 8–10 September*, pp. 163–168.

Stoesser, T., Ruether, N. and Olsen, N.R.B. 2010b. Calculation of primary and secondary flow and boundary shear stresses in a meandering channel. *Advances in Water Resources* **33**: 158–170.

van Balen, W., Blanckaert, K. and Uijttewaal, W.S.J. 2010. Analysis of the role of turbulence in curved open-channel flow at different water depths by means of experiments, LES and RANS. *Journal of Turbulence* **11**: 1–34.

Van Balen, W., Uijttewaal, W.S.J. and Blanckaert, K. 2009. Large-eddy simulation of a mildly curved open-channel flow. *Journal of Fluid Mechanics* **630**: 413–442.

Yang, S.Q. and Chow, A.T. 2008. Turbulence structures in non-uniform flows. *Advances in Water Resources* **31**: 1344–1351.

Yang, S.Q. and Lim, S.Y. 1997. Mechanism of energy transportation and turbulent flow in a 3-D channel. *Journal of Hydraulic Engineering* **123**: 684–692.

Yang, S.Q., Xu, W.L. and Yu, G.L. 2006. Velocity distribution in a gradually accelerating free surface flow. *Advances in Water Resources* **29**: 1969–1980.

# 3

# Aspects of Secondary Flow in Open Channels: A Critical Literature Review

## Athanasios (Thanos) N. Papanicolaou

## 3.1 INTRODUCTION

Nikora and Roy (Chapter 1, this volume) should be complimented for tackling one of the most challenging problems in several disciplines (e.g., geomorphology, hydraulic engineering, physical geography, and stream ecology): the origin, mechanics, effects, and inter-relations of secondary flows with the primary mean flow and turbulence. In particular, the focus of their excellent thematic paper is on: (i) the theoretical frameworks for studying secondary flows, (ii) inter-relations between turbulence and secondary flows, and (iii) secondary flow effects on hydraulic resistance, sediment dynamics, and mixing in river channels.

Secondary flows are one of the main processes affecting stream flow characteristics (e.g., the dip of maximum velocity below the water surface) and fluvial processes (e.g., mixing, transport of sediment, bank erosion and meandering) (Leopold, 1994). Prandtl (1925) distinguished two fundamental mechanisms responsible for the generation of secondary flows: (i) skewing of the mean shear stress by either a transverse pressure gradient or body force (skew-induced secondary flows or secondary flows of Prandtl's first kind) and (ii) anisotropy of turbulent fluctuations (stress-induced secondary flows or secondary flows of Prandtl's second kind). The skew-induced secondary flows are primarily attributed to channel planform configurations (e.g., convex and concave reaches in meandering channels) and the stress-induced secondary flows are due to local cross-sectional irregularities and/or boundary roughness (e.g., bank expansion or constriction, and the presence of longitudinal bedforms).

Although secondary flows have been the subject of a considerable amount of research over the last decades for different hydrologic and geomorphic conditions (e.g., Gessner, 1973; Bradshaw, 1987; Nezu and Nakagawa,

1993; Colombini and Parker, 1995; McLelland et al., 1999; Papanicolaou and Hilldale, 2002, Wang, 2005), aspects of the way these flows originate and are maintained along a channel are not well understood (Tsinober, 2009). The following discussion elaborates on some aspects of secondary flow addressed in the keynote paper with emphasis on Prandtl's second kind of secondary flows and the inter-relation of channel bed geometry and secondary flows. It also points to the need for future research to examine the implications of secondary flows for suspended sediment transport.

## 3.2 SECONDARY FLOWS AND CHANNEL FORM

Within the first eight pages of their chapter (Sections 1.1 and 1.2, this volume) Nikora and Roy provide an exhaustive critical review of a number of theoretical frameworks available for describing secondary flows in rivers. They point out that most of the presented frameworks stem from the Navier–Stokes (momentum) equation for instantaneous velocities and pressure, representing its different forms and, thus, essentially containing the same information (Tennekes and Lumley, 1972). However, in each equation this information is presented differently, highlighting particular facets of the secondary flows or of the type of problem that is under investigation. The authors brilliantly use the description in the theoretical developments of secondary flows not only to outline the past and ongoing progress made in this area, but also to reveal the several shortcomings that hinder further understanding of the underlying mechanisms of secondary flows. Nikora and Roy mostly centred their attention on the fact that "most theoretical and experimental studies have been based on one or another equation, rarely involving joint consideration of two or more equations,

*Gravel-bed Rivers: Processes, Tools, Environments*, First Edition. Edited by Michael Church, Pascale M. Biron and André G. Roy.
© 2012 John Wiley & Sons, Ltd. Published 2012 by John Wiley & Sons, Ltd.

thus reflecting authors' preferences, specific research questions, and/or data availability". They add: "such a narrowly focused approach could be a reason for discrepancies in interpretation of physical mechanisms creating and maintaining secondary flows in straight and curved channels."

I fully concur with this statement and believe that secondary flow research across disciplines (e.g., geography, geomorphology, and mechanical/civil/biological systems engineering) is highly fragmented. For example, more traditional fluid mechanics studies treat secondary flows and geometric characteristics of channels as two disconnected processes. However, we have recently determined that channel constriction and expansion, and other channel bed anomalies have an effect on Prandtl's second kind of secondary flows (e.g., Papanicolaou and Hilldale, 2002). Based on detailed 3-D flow measurements collected via an acoustic doppler velocimeter (ADV) at a cross-section that is located downstream of a gradual channel expansion, Papanicolaou and Hilldale found that turbulent intensities increase toward the free surface, indicating the transfer of a higher momentum flux from the channel bed to the free surface, which contradicts common wisdom. Results for the normalized stress components in the streamwise and transverse direction show behaviour similar to that of the intensities. It was found that a channel expansion creates an unbalanced turbulent stress distribution along the cross-section plane, thus, affecting the distribution of the turbulent intensities and resulting in turbulence anisotropy (El-shewey and Joshi, 1996). To further examine the validity of the above assertion a comparison between the streamwise velocity and the secondary current velocity was provided. It was shown that the secondary velocity is less than 20–30% of the mainstream velocity, which suggested that the secondary current is due to turbulence anisotropy (Nezu and Nakagawa 1993).

Further, the relations between coherent turbulent flow structures, eddy cascade, and secondary currents, which are discussed in Section 1.3 of this volume, are still treated in the literature as de-coupled processes, whereas they are actually dynamically linked, as recent studies show (e.g., Abad and Garcia, 2009a, 2009b; Knight *et al.*, 2009; Sanjou and Nezu, 2009; Gyr, 2010; Sukhodolov and Kaschtschejewa, 2010). Many important problems, like ecosystem management in morphologically unstable areas of streams (e.g., streams with changes in the bed roughness or elevation in the transverse direction) where secondary flow and turbulent interactions are expected to be dominant, cut across disciplinary boundaries. This fragmented approach poses a significant challenge to the current and future developments in river theory and applications for scientists and engineers.

## 3.3  SECONDARY FLOWS AND CHANNEL ROUGHNESS

Another important aspect found in the secondary flows literature is the relation of secondary flows to the bed roughness differential and the aspect ratio. Along that line of thinking, the authors describe the work of Albayrak (2008), among others. The Albayrak (2008) study suggests that the number of cells at a particular aspect ratio may depend on the properties of bed roughness. I would also like to highlight the study by Wang (2005), which strongly confirms the findings of Albayrak (2008) and others that the intensity of cellular secondary flows is closely associated with the amplitude of the perturbations of the bed roughness or bed surface. All experiments were performed by Wang in a straight flume with a rectangular cross-section at the Hydraulics Laboratory of Nanyang Technological University. Six sets of artificial longitudinal bedforms were used for generating cellular secondary flows. These bedforms can be categorized into bed strips and bed ridges. The bed strips, being distinguished by lateral periodic variations in the bed roughness, were comprised of smooth and sediment-roughened plates, of which the surfaces were placed at the same level across the channel. In contrast, the bed ridges were characterized by lateral periodic variations in the bed elevation only. Figure 3.1a shows simplified secondary flow cells over rough and smooth strips of unequal width, whereas Figure 3.1b is a schematic of secondary flow cells over rectangular ridges (both experiments were performed with identical flow conditions and aspect ratio). The reader can clearly discern that there are two pairs of flow cells within the region covering one ridge and one trough (Figure 3.1a). In contrast there is only one pair of flow cells over the same lateral distance for roughness strips (Figure 3.1a). Briefly, there is a strong correspondence between channel bed geometry and secondary flows, and these observations may help to improve formulations for channel morphodynamics.

## 3.4  SECONDARY FLOWS AND RIVER MORPHODYNAMICS

Discussions in Sections 1.4–1.6 about the secondary flow effects on hydraulic resistance, sediment dynamics, and mixing in river channels reinstate the importance of available flow-sediment observations which describe these interactions. The few existing observations do not provide a systematic representation of the "connectivity" of different physical processes in understanding the secondary flow mechanics, or their inter-relations with other river processes such as sediment transport, mixing, and morphodynamics. Furthermore, our limited understanding of the interactions impedes further development

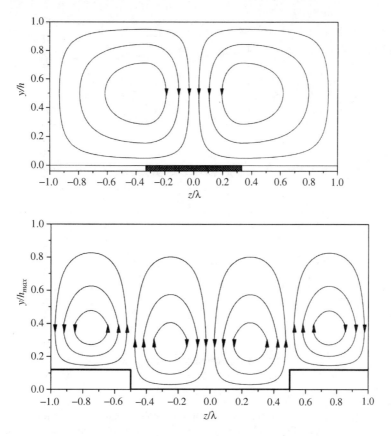

**Figure 3.1**   (a) Simplified secondary flow cells over rough and smooth strips with unequal width; $h$ = flow depth and $\lambda$ = width of the strip (after Wang 2005); (b) a schematic of secondary flow cells over rectangular ridges (after Wang 2005).

of physically based flow-morphodynamic models that closely simulate the intimate connection of secondary flows with the primary mean flow and turbulence processes.

Nikora and Roy discuss in Section 1.5 of their chapter the effects of secondary flows on sediment motion, however, the description of the effects of the secondary current on sediment is mostly qualitative. The discusser presumes that, due to limited space, the authors were not able to describe in detail the importance of secondary flow for sediment. Nonetheless, there are a handful of studies (e.g. Powell *et al.*, 1999) that provide insightful information in investigating the cross-stream variation in bedload transport. For instance, simultaneous measurements of bed-load discharge made at a number of locations across the widths of two coarse-grained ephemeral channels in Israel by Powell *et al.* (1999) reveal systematic cross stream variability in bedload rate. Their findings show that, on average, transport rates at the channel centre were about twice as much as those recorded at the channel margins. They have attributed these local varia-

tions to local differences in bed shear stress which, in turn, could be generated by sidewall drag in a symmetrical trapezoidal cross-section. The latter observation is consistent with laboratory evidence of lateral variations in shear stress due to the presence of secondary currents.

Finally, knowledge of secondary flow structures also provides implications for suspended sediment transport. One of the major influences of secondary flow on suspended sediment is that the secondary flow modifies the cross-flow trajectories of sediment particles or sediment path (Wang, 2005). Figures 3.2a and 3.2b show the travelling path of kaolin particles estimated by solution using analytical methods. These figures were constructed by considering the periodic and symmetrical characteristics of the secondary flow structure, whereby the stream function is expressed in the sine or cosine form. By assuming for low concentration conditions that the relative velocity between the sediment and flow is everywhere equal to the settling velocity, the sediment velocity, shown in Figure 3.2, is calculated as the summation of the fluid velocity and settling velocity.

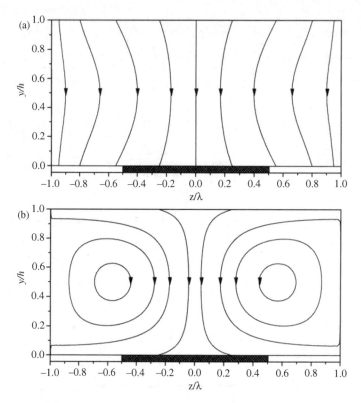

**Figure 3.2**  Traveling path of kaolin sediment particle computed using an analytical equation for the sediment velocity. (a) settling velocity > maximum upwelling fluid velocity; (b) settling velocity < maximum upwelling fluid velocity (after Wang 2005).

In Figure 3.2a the settling velocity is twice as large as the maximum upwelling fluid velocity. For this condition, the sediment concentration would vary only along, not across, the sediment paths, shown in Figure 3.2a, which may not be vertical, but remain uniform in the direction perpendicular to the sediment path. For the condition of cellular secondary flows (Figure 3.2b), the ratio of settling velocity with maximum upwelling fluid velocity is low and the trajectories of fine sediment particles are closed circles. In this case, the sediment tends to be trapped by the flow cells and the concentration tends to be homogenized within the two sets of concentric circles.

The chapter, however, offers a wide range of topics on secondary flows with the most interesting topics, to my thinking, being the inter-relations between turbulence and secondary flows, and secondary flow effects on hydraulic resistance, sediment dynamics, and mixing in river channels. In conclusion, this discussion intends to elaborate on some of the results presented by the authors with respect to secondary flows and to generate a discussion on the importance of performing 3-D turbulent flow measurements to precisely identify the effects of secondary flows on sediment motion.

## 3.5  CONCLUSIONS

Overall, the much needed review provided in Chapter 1 will be of substantial use to a broad readership. It offers useful results for an ongoing scientific area, but it has to be read with care in order to extract the gems. In this respect, the importance of the terms included in the different forms of the Navier–Stokes equations in relation to their contributions to secondary flow has not been fully presented (Xie, 1998).

## 3.6  REFERENCES

Abad, J.D. and Garcia, M.H. 2009a. Experiments in a high-amplitude Kinoshita meandering channel: 1. Implications of bend orientation on mean and turbulent flow structure. *Water Resources Research* **45**: W02401. doi: 10.1029/2008WR007016.

Abad, J.D. and Garcia, M.H. 2009b. Experiments in a high amplitude Kinoshita meandering channel: 2. Implications of bend orientation on bed morphodynamics. *Water Resources Research* **45**: W02402. doi: 10.1029/2008WR007017.

Albayrak, I. 2008. *An experimental study of coherent structures, secondary currents and surface boils and their interrelation in open-channel flow*. cole Polytechnique Fédérale de Lausanne, Thesis no. 4112. doi: 10.5075/epfl-thesis-4112.

Bradshaw, P. 1987. Turbulent secondary flows. *Annual Review of Fluid Mechanics* **19**: 53–74.

Colombini, M. and Parker, G. 1995. Longitudinal streaks. *Journal of Fluid Mechanics* **304**: 161–183.

El-shewey, M.I.A. and Joshi, S.G. 1996. A study of turbulence characteristics in open channel transitions as a function of Froude and Reynolds numbers using laser technique. In Advances in Fluid Mechanics (*Transactions of the Wessex Institute of Technology, Engineering Sciences*), pp. 363–372. doi: 10.2495/AFM960341.

Gessner, F. B. 1973. The origin of secondary flow in turbulent flow along a corner. *Journal of Fluid Mechanics* **58**, part 1: 1–25.

Gyr, A. 2010. The meander paradox – a topological view. *Applied Mechanics Reviews* **63**: Paper 020801. doi: 10.1115/1.4000725.

Knight, D.W., Aya, S., Ikeda, S., Nezu, I. and Shiono, K. 2009. Flow structure. Chapter 2 in Ikeda, S. and McEwan, I. K., editors. *Flow and Sediment Transport in Compound Channels: The Experience of Japanese and UK Research*. International Association for Hydraulic Research Monograph Series.

Leopold, L. B. 1994. *A View of the River*. Cambridge, MA, Harvard University Press.

McLelland, S.J., Ashworth, P., Best, J.L. and Livesey, J.R. 1999. Turbulence and secondary flow over sediment stripes in weakly bimodal bed material. *Journal of Hydraulic Engineering* **125**: 463–473.

Nezu, I. and Nakagawa, H. 1993. *Turbulence in Open-Channel Flows*. Rotterdam, A. A. Balkema.

Papanicolaou, A. N. and Hilldale, R. 2002. Turbulence characteristics in a gradual channel transition. *Journal of Engineering Mechanics* **128**: 948–960.

Powell, D.M., Reid I. and Laronne, J.B. 1999 Hydraulic interpretation of cross-stream variation in bedload transport rate in two straight alluvial channels. *Journal of Hydraulic Engineering* **125**: 1243–1252.

Prandtl, L. 1925. Bericht über Untersuchungen zur ausgebildete Turbulenz. *Zeitschrift für Angewandte Mthematik und Mechanik* **5**: 136–139.

Tennekes, H. and Lumley, J.L. 1972. *A First Course in Turbulence*. Cambridge, MA, MIT Press.

Tsinober, A. 2009. *An Informal Conceptual Introduction to Turbulence*. Berlin, Springer.

Sanjou, M. and Nezu, I. 2009. Turbulence structure and coherent motion in meandering compound open-channel flows. *Journal of Hydraulic Research* **47**: 598–610.

Sukhodolov, A. and Kaschtschejewa, E. 2010. Turbulent flow in a meander bend of a lowland river: Field measurements and preliminary results. *Proceedings of Riverflow, International Conference on Fluvial Hydraulics, Braunschweig, Germany, 8-10 September*, pp. 309–316.

Wang, Z. 2005. *Investigation of secondary flows in open channel with longitudinal bedforms*. Ph.D. thesis, School of Civil and Environmental Engineering, Nanyang Technological University.

Xie, Q. 1998. *Turbulent flows in non-uniform open channels: Experimental measurements and numerical modeling*. Ph.D. thesis, University of Queensland, Brisbane, Australia.

# Sediment Transport

# 4

# Gravel Transport in Granular Perspective

## Philippe Frey and Michael Church

## 4.1 INTRODUCTION

The overwhelming majority of fluvial sediment transport investigations have been focused on mass flux and its relation to the water flow. Yet after more than a century of work we have no satisfactory theory for bedload, an important component of the sediment load transported in contact with the stream bed. The extant transport formulae often overpredict the actual rate in gravel bed rivers by orders of magnitude (Bathurst, 2007). A large amount of research has been conducted on the influence of the fluid on grain entrainment and movement (Yalin, 1977; Graf, 1984; Julien, 1998; Parker, 2007). Yet aside from the pioneering work of Bagnold (1954), 1956), relatively little progress has been made in the study of grain–grain interactions in streams.

Progress has been made recently in the study of dry granular flows, but the knowledge gained has not, in general, diffused into the bedload science community. Research on granular flows is mainly published in the literature of physics, chemical engineering, and materials science, whereas bedload research has been published in the areas of river engineering, fluvial geomorphology, and geophysics. In this chapter, we seek to bring these fields closer together. The objective is to highlight ways in which understanding of bedload phenomena may be enhanced by adopting perspectives and results from the physics of granular flows.

Although transport of gravels and larger materials has been divided into three stages (Ashworth and Ferguson, 1989; Warburton, 1992), we consider here, for the sake of simplicity, two classes: mobility of local bed surface material with particles moving intermittently, most of the bed remaining static most of the time; and full mobility, when all grains move to a depth of several grain diameters. Our first class encompasses the first two recognized stages – transport over a static bed and partial transport of the surface layer. The granular phenomena in both stages are similar and transport is restricted to the bed surface. Grain–grain interactions over short time and length scales bear significantly on the predictability of both classes. But while sand bed channels characteristically experience full mobility transport, bedload in gravel bed channels typically is restricted to surface processes, except under exceptionally strong flows during major floods.

In this respect, what we call here a sand bed river (as opposed to a gravel bed river) has only partly to do with the grain size or texture. A sand bed channel can have a significant amount of textural gravel and, conversely, a gravel bed river usually includes a fair amount of textural sand. However, the range of grain sizes in gravel channels is usually higher than in sand channels. An important aspect that distinguishes sand and gravel rivers is that the ratio of the fluid shear stress to the incipient motion stress (which determines the transport stage) is usually much higher in sand bed channels than in gravel bed channels. In major floods, gravel bed rivers could be considered conceptually as sand bed channels in respect of the transport stage, except that the wider grain size range introduces additional complications into the physical processes and their modelling. However uncommon, full mobility does represent an important phenomenon in gravel transport and in natural hazard and risk management, especially in steep channels.

Granular physics has been developed mainly in the context of seeking to understand grain flows of industrial materials. An important difference between bedload transport and most experimental and industrial grain flows is that the latter usually entail relatively uniform material, whereas there commonly is a wide range of grain sizes present on the streambed. Hence, an important aspect of the bedload phenomenon concerns which grains move and how they become sorted.

In the next section we review some pertinent results from granular physics, especially in rheology, segregation, and discrete element modelling. In the following sections, we discuss how these results compare with

*Gravel-bed Rivers: Processes, Tools, Environments*, First Edition. Edited by Michael Church, Pascale M. Biron and André G. Roy.
© 2012 John Wiley & Sons, Ltd. Published 2012 by John Wiley & Sons, Ltd.

bedload phenomena, first for full mobility and second for surface processes. We then review some progress made on patch and bedload sheet dynamics, as their mechanisms of formation and migration could be better understood by closely considering grain–grain interactions. We close with a discussion of research directions that we hope will open new perspectives, both in fluvial geomorphology and in granular physics.

## 4.2    GRANULAR FLOWS

No single constitutive law reproduces the diversity of behaviours observed in cohesionless granular materials (Liu and Nagel, 1998; Forterre and Pouliquen, 2008). Fundamental characteristics of granular matter, such as inelastic (hence dissipative) interactions and a lack of separation between the microscopic grain scale and the macroscopic scale of the flow (Goldhirsch, 2003), condition this outcome. Granular flows are often classified into three different states (Jaeger *et al.*, 1996): a gas-like state in which the flow is very rapid and dilute, and the particles interact by collision (Goldhirsch, 2003); an intermediate state in which the material is dense, but flows like a liquid, the particles interacting both by collision and friction (MiDi, 2004); and a dense, quasi-static state in which the deformations are very slow and the particles interact by frictional contacts (Campbell, 2002). All three states (Figure 4.1) might be found in free surface flows and in both dry and liquid-mediated flows (Ottino and Khakhar, 2000).

In this paper, we make reference both to liquid-mediated grain flows, such as bedload transport in a stream, and to the "liquid" or dense state of granular flows, which may be dry or fluid-mediated. The "liquid state" refers to aggregate behaviour of the grain flow that resembles the behaviour of a true liquid.

From his experiments on grain–fluid mixtures in a Couette device – a pioneering contribution to both granular physics and knowledge of bedload – Bagnold (1954) recognized three different regimes of flow: "macro-viscous", transitional, and grain inertial. In the first, momentum imparted by the moving fluid to the particles is the most significant mobilizing process; in the last, most momentum transfer occurs between particles in the granular mixture. These regimes roughly correspond with gaseous- and liquid-state granular transport, as is now understood. Both states occur in bedload transport.

Dense granular flows have been studied (MiDi, 2004) in simple shear in both confined and free surface flows, especially with inclined chute and rotating drum configurations (Figure 4.2). Horizontal-axis, narrow rotating drums have been the most used, though they are not always representative of stationary shear flows (Ottino and Khakhar, 2000; Jain *et al.*, 2002; Hill *et al.*, 2003). Two main regimes have been identified, an avalanching regime and a rolling regime. While avalanching is important in rivers at the front of dunes and bars, we focus here on the "rolling" regime, which characterizes general gravel transport. Differences in size, density and other less important or less-studied properties lead to segregation, either by vibration or shearing (Duran, 1999). Important mechanisms relevant to bedload occur in the rolling regime, especially near the solid–liquid transition in granular behaviour. Probably the most important is size segregation by shearing in free surface granular flows.

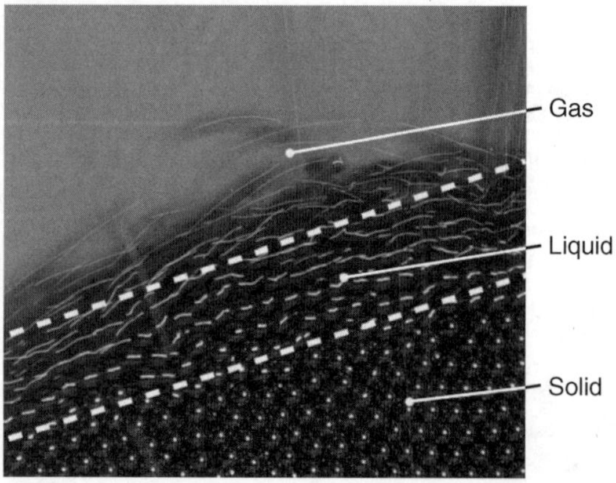

**Figure 4.1** Displacement regimes of a cohesionless granular flow in air (Forterre and Pouliquen, 2008). Reproduced by permission of Olivier Pouliquen.

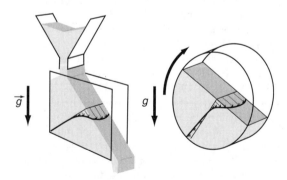

**Figure 4.2** The two typical devices used to study granular free surface flows over an erodible bed (inclined chute and horizontal-axis rotating drum). The solid black curves are the particle velocity profiles (Forterre and Pouliquen, 2008). Reproduced by permission of Olivier Pouliquen.

### 4.2.1 Size Segregation

Two distinct size segregation phenomena occur, both relevant to bedload flows. When the coarsest fractions are not moving, so-called spontaneous percolation occurs. Given a certain population of immobile grains (the bed), the conditions for smaller grains to percolate (fall by gravity) through the bed is a simple problem for a population of uniform spheres. When the ratio of the diameter of the larger to the smaller spheres is greater than 6.46, the smaller sphere passes through the smallest throat formed by three large spheres in tightly packed mutual contact, and can fall to the bottom of the sediment pile (Troadec and Dodds, 1993); when the ratio is equal to 4.45, the small sphere is just inscribed in the smallest cavities of the bed formed by four large spheres in open packed mutual contact (tetrahedron). Between these two values, the small spheres have a non-null probability of being blocked in a cavity and accumulated in the bed. When the distribution of sizes in the bed is not uniform or the shape is not spherical (Luchnikov *et al.*, 1999), the problem is more complicated. Even with a small quantity of fine particles the distribution of cavity sizes usually exhibits a larger range than for a monosized bed (Troadec and Dodds, 1993).

If the size ratio is close to unity, fine particles can percolate only through a moving bed, a phenomenon called "kinetic sieving" (Middleton, 1970, also called kinematic, dynamic, or random fluctuating sieving). Pioneering studies on kinetic sieving were performed by Bridgwater and co-workers (Drahun and Bridgwater, 1983). Segregation by size has been studied theoretically and experimentally in horizontal-axis rotating drums (Ottino and Khakhar, 2000; Thomas, 2000; Jain *et al.*, 2004), more rarely in inclined chute flow (Savage and Lun, 1988). Most experiments have been performed with small size ratios, rarely above 3. The usual net result is a downward flux of the smaller particles and an upward flux of larger particles, hence segregation (Figure 4.3). However, for ratios above 5, a reverse pattern occurs (Thomas, 2000; Felix and Thomas, 2004): the large grains are located at an intermediate level, evolving continuously from the surface to deeper levels, depending on the size ratio. This implies that effects other than the mere geometrical effect invoked in kinetic sieving play a role in size segregation.

### 4.2.2 Depth Profiles

Velocity and concentration profiles are another important feature because they can give access to the rheology of the granular flow if shear stress is known. Indeed, the apparent viscosity is the ratio of the shear stress to the shear rate (or velocity gradient in simple shear). Fluctuating velocity profiles are important too because

**Figure 4.3** Segregation of a tridisperse mixture in an inclined chute. Diameters of the glass beads: small white 150 μm, pink 350 μm, large dark 550 μm (image courtesy of N. Thomas and E. Martin, Université Aix-Marseille, France). (See the color version of this figure in color plate section.)

they permit computation of the "granular temperature" (a measure of energy intensity usually defined as the sum of the variances of the instantaneous velocity components). This variable is central in kinetic theory modelling of low-density granular flows (Goldhirsch, 2003). Moreover, number-density or concentration profiles are particularly useful for deriving the particle volume flux and the stress profile.

The mean granular velocity profile typically has an upward convex shape, with a linear profile in the upper part and an exponential decay toward zero in the lower part (Figure 4.4). Velocity profiles have been measured in a rotating drum both with dry beads and with beads

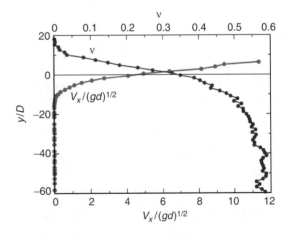

**Figure 4.4** Longitudinal velocity $V_x$ and concentration ν profiles over an erodible bed (grain diameter $D$). Inclined chute flow (slope 43°) between two vertical plates (width of 9 times the diameter). $y = 0$ corresponds to half the maximal concentration in the quasi-static zone. Data courtesy of P. Richard. Further details in (Richard *et al.*, 2008).

immersed in water and other liquids (Jain *et al.*, 2002, 2004). Whatever the bead sizes, fluid densities and viscosities, the velocity profile exhibits the same robust shape. The rheology of dense free surface granular flows has been investigated with measurements of mean and fluctuating velocity profiles (Orpe and Khakhar, 2007). In addition, the stress profile has been computed from the number-density profile using a force balance taking into account wall friction. The flow was found to comprise two layers: an upper low-viscosity layer and a lower layer of increasing viscosity.

Velocity and concentration profiles can also give a better insight into segregation. In an investigation of the kinetics of segregating mixtures of different sizes or densities (Hill and Zhang, 2008), it was found that the mean velocity profiles of the different components of the mixture are similar. In contrast, the fluctuating velocities of the different sizes are specific to a size class, implying that velocity fluctuations are a key element to understanding segregation.

### 4.2.3  Measurements and Modelling

A range of innovative and non-intrusive techniques has been used in granular flows to measure velocity and concentration profiles, including image processing (Jain *et al.*, 2004), diffusive wave-spectroscopy (Menon and Durian, 1997), magnetic resonance imaging (MRI) (Mueth *et al.*, 2000), and several radioactive tracer techniques (Doucet *et al.*, 2008). Although optical video techniques and particle image or tracking velocimetry have been used for bedload flow (Gotoh and Sakai, 1997; Böhm *et al.*, 2006), other techniques used in granular flows, such as the technique of matched refractive index (Mouilleron *et al.*, 2009), would be worth trying, especially to gain access to the entire 3-D layer.

Granular flows seem tailored for discrete descriptions ranging from idealized cellular automata to more sophisticated discrete element modelling (Meier *et al.*, 2007). In discrete element methods, the motion of each particle is solved using Newton's laws once the resultant of gravity and contact forces is known (Cundall and Strack, 1979). The method relies on the use of appropriate contact force models and parameters. The complexity of the macroscopic behaviour is achieved by modelling a large number of particles. Continuum description is at first sight not well suited to granular flows because the ratio of the system size to the particle size is much smaller than in typical fluid systems, leading to averaging problems. However, because of inelasticity, energy transport in granular materials does not extend more than a few particle diameters. A continuum description seems, then, as efficient as discrete descriptions, provided a relevant rheology is selected, which is

the crux of the problem (Goodman and Cowin, 1972; Forterre and Pouliquen, 2008). The merits of continuum models versus discrete models are widely discussed. A better understanding of granular flows may be achieved through complementary use of the two types of model (Meier *et al.*, 2007).

## 4.3  FULL MOBILITY TRANSPORT

Despite Bagnold's pioneering work, relatively little progress has been made toward understanding fluvial bedload transport as a granular phenomenon. It is interesting to ask to what extent the results in granular physics reviewed above may illuminate the phenomenon. Important differences between granular motion as usually studied, in both research and industrial contexts, and bedload transport in rivers include the very wide range of grain properties (size, shape, density,...) normally present in fluvial sediments, the highly irregular geometry of river channels (in alluvial channels, itself a consequence of the movement and deposition of bed material), and the highly variable forcing in rivers, both temporally and spatially (Haff, 1997).

In full mobility transport, there is a continuous bedload layer with several mobile grain layers beneath the surface. Several studies have investigated the trajectory of a single or a few saltating or rolling particles (Francis, 1973; Niño *et al.*, 1994; Ancey *et al.*, 2002, 2003), but only rare papers have addressed the particle velocity profile in a continuous bedload layer.

### 4.3.1  Velocity and Concentration Profiles

Velocities of the fluid/granular mixture have been measured inside the layer (typically, about 10 grain diameters thick) of an intense bedload flow (Sumer *et al.*, 1996). In the upper part and above the bedload layer, the velocity profiles followed the classical fluid logarithmic law. The lower part of the bedload layer followed a 3/4 power law. Concentrated bedload flows have also been studied under oscillatory conditions (Asano, 1995). Some particle velocity profiles showed an inflexion point with a tail that fit a 3/2 power law, resulting in the same qualitative shape as dry granular profiles. Some of these measurements were subsequently used for successful comparison with models addressing collisional grain flows based on kinetic theory (Jenkins and Hanes, 1998; Hsu *et al.*, 2004). Exponential particle velocity profiles have also been reported and compared with a discrete element model of three-size mixtures (Harada and Gotoh, 2008).

Free-surface flows of fluid/granular mixtures have been experimentally studied to model granular debris flows (Armanini *et al.*, 2005; Fraccarollo *et al.*, 2007; Larcher *et al.*, 2007). Some of the runs, called

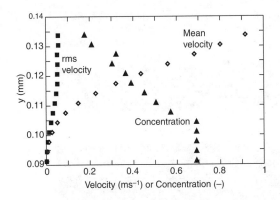

**Figure 4.5** Depth profiles of longitudinal mean velocity (diamonds), root-mean-squared fluctuation velocity (squares) and granular concentration (triangles). Data courtesy of L. Fraccarollo. Further details in (Larcher *et al.*, 2007).

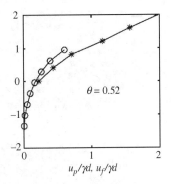

**Figure 4.6** Particle ($u_p$) and fluid ($u_f$) velocity profiles (*y*-axis is elevation scaled by the bead diameter) inside the moving layer of a sheared granular bed in a laminar Couette flow (o, particle; *, fluid; $\gamma$, shear rate; $d$, diameter; $\theta$, Shields number; at incipient motion, $\theta_c = 0.12$) (Mouilleron *et al.*, 2009). Reproduced by permission of Francois Charru.

oversaturated flows, are similar to intense bedload flows. Particle velocity profiles display the same upward convex shape as dry granular profiles with a linear part and an exponential decay (Figure 4.5). They have been modeled (Berzi and Jenkins, 2008) using a rheology developed in (MiDi, 2004).

All the foregoing results pertain to intense bedload flows, more typical of sand bed streams, with at least ten times the fluid shear stress necessary for grain incipient motion. We report further on less-intense bedload flows.

At the grain scale, a number of papers have recently been published investigating bedload dynamics driven by a laminar flow (Lobkovsky *et al.*, 2008; Mouilleron *et al.*, 2009; Ouriemi *et al.*, 2009). Although turbulent flows are ubiquitous in nature, bedload transport including saltation occurs whatever the flow regime, contrary to suspension, which necessitates a turbulent regime (Francis, 1973). Given the complexity of turbulence and its interaction with sediment transport (Campbell *et al.*, 2005; Sambrook Smith and Nicholas, 2005), it is tempting to study bedload under laminar conditions to remove the added complexity due to turbulence from a phenomenon already difficult to model *per se*. Mouilleron *et al.* (2009) used the technique of matched refractive index, permitting access to both the laminar fluid field and the motion of individual glass beads in an annular channel. They obtained both fluid and particle velocity profiles by particle image velocimetry and particle tracking, respectively. Particle velocity profiles have the same shape as in dry granular flows. Fluid and particle profiles inside the moving layer are the same for relatively low Shields numbers (up to about 4 times the incipient motion number), while a slip velocity is observed for higher flows (Figure 4.6).

Results have also been obtained on velocity and number-density profiles calculated from data pertaining to moderate bedload in turbulent flows with glass beads in a 2-D channel (Böhm *et al.*, 2004; Ancey *et al.*, 2008). The shear stress was only about twice that necessary to move the grains, and the grain motion extended to a depth of only 2–3 diameters, which is more typical of gravel beds. The velocity profile exhibits three segments (Figure 4.7a): an exponential tail at the transition between the stationary and the bedload layer; a linear domain; and a logarithmic region due mainly to saltating particles with velocities close to the fluid velocity. The lowest parts (exponential and linear) are similar to dry granular velocity profiles. The upper parts (linear and logarithmic) are similar to measurements on intense bedload flows (Asano, 1995; Sumer *et al.*, 1996). The number-density profiles are broken down into moving and quasi-immobile particles (less than 5% of the maximal particle velocity). The moving particle profile shows three peaks: the uppermost corresponding only to saltation and the two lower peaks essentially to rolling beads. Figure 4.7b shows for comparison a velocity profile calculated with particle image velocimetry in a monosized bedload experiment with natural gravel. This velocity profile has again the same shape as in dry granular flows. The exponential decay in bedload has recently been measured, perhaps for the first time, under unidirectional flow with natural material (Fraccarollo and Rosatti, 2009).

All these measurements further emphasize the value of considering natural bedload as a granular phenomenon. Indeed, velocity and number-density (or concentration) profiles can eventually help to establish a bedload rheology, using theoretical results obtained in granular flows.

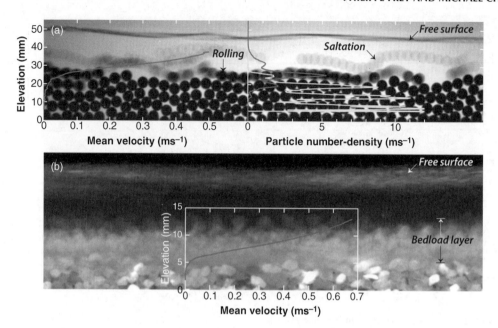

**Figure 4.7** (a) Mean streamwise particle velocity and number-density profiles (yellow immobile and red moving) calculated with data obtained by particle tracking velocimetry (Böhm *et al.*, 2006) on a temporal series of 8000 images (over 60.94s) in a 6.5 mm wide 2-D channel. The background image is the sum of 13 images (0.1 s). Slope of the channel: 10 %, diameter of the glass beads: 6 mm, water flux of $10.3 \times 10^{-3}$ m$^3$ s$^{-1}$ m$^{-1}$, solid flux of 20.6 beads s$^{-1}$ or $0.358 \times 10^{-3}$ m$^3$ s$^{-1}$ m$^{-1}$. (b) Mean streamwise particle velocity calculated by particle image velocimetry on a temporal series of 900 images (over 7.62 s) obtained with the experimental arrangement in (Recking *et al.*, 2008a). The background image is the sum of the entire series. Slope of the channel: 7%, width of 5 cm, mean diameter of the natural sediment: 2.3 mm, water flux of $10.0 \times 10^{-3}$ m$^3$ s$^{-1}$ m$^{-1}$, solid flux of $0.290 \times 10^{-3}$ m$^3$ s$^{-1}$ m$^{-1}$. Reproduced, with permission, from John Wiley & Sons, Ltd. (See the color version of this figure in color plate section.)

### 4.3.2 Size Segregation

Most studies in the bedload literature have concerned the spontaneous percolation of fine grains into immobile gravels (Beschta and Jackson, 1979; Frostick *et al.*, 1984; Lisle, 1989; Wooster *et al.*, 2008), although kinetic sieving has been qualitatively described (Einstein, 1968; Middleton, 1970; Parker and Klingeman, 1982). The motivations have been, variously, intrusion of fines into salmonid spawning beds, placer mineral concentration, and stratigraphical interpretation. Infiltration commonly is restricted to the top few centimeters or so beneath the surface due to pore clogging, creating sedimentary lamination. However it appears that lamination can also result from kinetic sieving within the moving layer, as evidenced by experiments performed on stratification of heterogeneous sand mixtures with different size and density ratios (Julien *et al.*, 1993).

In order to study kinetic sieving further, smaller beads were introduced upstream one by one into a bedload flow initially formed only of larger moving beads (as in Figure 4.7a). After a while a quasi-continuous layer of small particles developed beneath larger moving beads

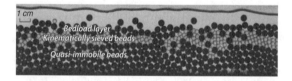

**Figure 4.8** Layers of smaller transparent beads under larger moving black beads as a result of kinetic sieving. Same channel as Figure 4.7a. Angle of the channel: 10%, diameter of the glass beads: 6 and 4 mm, water flux of $5.62 \times 10^{-3}$ m$^3$ s$^{-1}$ m$^{-1}$, solid flux of 6 mm beads: 9.1 beads s$^{-1}$ or $0.158 \times 10^{-3}$ m$^3$ s$^{-1}$ m$^{-1}$, solid flux of 4 mm beads: 0.5 beads s$^{-1}$ or $2.57 \times 10^{-6}$ m$^3$ s$^{-1}$ m$^{-1}$. This image was obtained 25 minutes after upstream introduction of the smaller beads. Reproduced, with permission, from John Wiley & Sons, Ltd.

and above quasi-immobile larger beads (Figure 4.8), as observed in granular flows (Hergault *et al.*, 2010).

### 4.3.3 Measurements

With the availability of a range of non-intrusive measurement techniques, the time is ripe for simultaneous measurement, in the laboratory at least, of fluid and particle velocity profiles, as well as concentration profiles, not only along a wall, but also at the channel centreline. This would lead to a bedload rheology that would, in turn, permit a more fundamental approach to modelling bedload phenomena. It would also yield better physical insight into the effect of bedload on the fluid (Recking et al., 2008b), including the shape of the fluid velocity profile, shear stress, and energy dissipation. To be successful, the measurements must be non-invasive. This has been a definitive problem in fluvial bedload research, but methods now available from granular physics investigations provide possible routes forward, at least for laboratory measurements. For example, Kleinhans et al. (2008) discuss potential applications and limitations of magnetic resonance imaging to coarse sediment visualization and sorting of fluvial sand–gravel mixtures. Finally a number of studies tend to show that some geomorphological mechanisms, such as meandering or braiding (Métivier and Meunier, 2003), or bar formation (Devauchelle et al., 2007), can be studied in microscale laminar flumes (Malverti et al., 2008).

### 4.3.4 Discrete Element Modelling

Discrete element modelling has rarely been applied to bedload transport. A 2-D system was modelled in a simple manner with molecular dynamics methods (Jiang and Haff, 1993). The injection of fine particles allowed qualitative investigation of the vertical mixing of particles. It was concluded that discrete element models are a developing paradigm not necessarily better than existing approaches, but representing a completely different framework. Discrete modelling has subsequently been used to study the transport of uniform particles under oscillatory flows (Gotoh and Sakai, 1997) and for particle entrainment (McEwan and Heald, 2001; McEwan et al., 2001). A bedload discrete model was proposed using a dynamic boundary condition for a mixed grain-size sediment bed with a refining of the near-bed turbulent velocity field (Schmeeckle and Nelson, 2003).

The use of discrete element modelling in environmental sciences has been outlined in a themed issue of the *Philosophical Transactions of the Royal Society of London* (Heald et al., 2004; Richards et al., 2004). Such modelling can reveal properties at the meso- and macroscales originating from microscale interactions, and can help to understand self-organizing behaviours. Indeed, discrete modelling of bi- or trimodal distributions of coarse sediments under waves has clearly shown segregation due to kinetic sieving (Calantoni and Thaxton, 2008; Harada and Gotoh, 2008). Discrete element modelling is not restricted to local or short-term processes.

It has also been applied to bedload, including grain-size sorting, for reach-scale long-term morphodynamic evolution (Hodge et al., 2007).

## 4.4 SURFACE PROCESSES

Processes restricted to the surface of the bed, where particles experience long periods of rest, have rarely been considered from a granular physics viewpoint. A phenomenological description of the transport in a stream has been given (Drake et al., 1988), as has the cumulative displacement of grains in streams over relatively long periods of time (Ferguson et al., 2002). Statistical analysis of surface displacements was initiated by Einstein (1936) and has been followed up in a considerable number of laboratory investigations (Nikora et al., 2002; Ancey et al., 2008). Field studies have been executed with marked tracer grains, (see review by Hassan and Ergenzinger (2003)). Near-field dispersion appears to follow an asymmetric distribution, such as a Gamma distribution (Hassan and Church, 1992), but further dispersion in streams is interrupted by zones of sediment congestion that are recognized as bars, with spacing in the range of 3–10 channel widths (Pyrce and Ashmore, 2003). Recent evidence (Hill et al., 2010) suggests that the net effect in mixed-size sediments may be for grains to exhibit a heavy-tailed distribution, with anomalously rapid dispersion of particle groups.

More interesting from a granular physics perspective are the interactions that occur amongst grains during transport. The propensity for grains of similar size to block each other leads to accumulations of similar sized grains in restricted areas of the channel bed. Two types of phenomena appear to be worthy of attention. Mobile materials tend to collect in patches of similar size in the streambed (see next section), a phenomenon that mediates the characteristic mobility and overall sediment flux (Paola and Seal, 1995; Nelson et al., 2009), while the largest stones in armoured streambeds – characteristically only marginally mobile – congregate into chains and cell-like arrangements (Figure 4.9a) that dramatically increase the overall stability of the bed (Laronne and Carson, 1976; Church et al., 1998).

The second case is particularly interesting from a granular perspective since the stone structures represent a natural case of granular "force chains" that have been studied in the laboratory for more than a decade (Cates et al., 1998; Liu and Nagel, 1998). In the extreme case of steep mountain channels with relatively large stones in them, stone lines become channel-spanning force chains that form a distinctive step-and-pool morphology and maintain a stable channel in situations when any unconstrained stone would be transported away (Church and Zimmermann, 2007).

**Figure 4.9** (a) Stone lines exposed at low flow on a gravel bed (River Tees, near Darlington, UK); (b) a bedform which may be identified as a bedload sheet. River Bléone, near Digne, France (Recking *et al.*, 2009). Reproduced, with permission, from American Geophysical Union.

In a pioneering contribution, the pairwise interaction of particles in saltation was modeled (Leeder, 1979). In the same spirit, a grain-based sediment transport model has been proposed (Hunt and Papanicolaou, 2003). The interaction of pairs of grains during transport on the bed surface has been modelled stochastically with the objective of reproducing stone structures (Tribe and Church, 1999; Malmaeus and Hassan, 2002; MacVicar *et al.*, 2006). Successful simulation required assumptions about the nature of grain–grain interactions, in particular about the way in which intercepted stones come to rest. Whilst this mode of investigation can suggest ideas, it does not solve the dynamical problem underlying the phenomenon.

## 4.5  BEDLOAD FLUCTUATIONS, SHEETS, AND PATCHES

This illustrative section is devoted to bedload fluctuations related to bedload sheets and patches, the understanding of which, as put forward by recent literature, could benefit from a better understanding of grain–grain interactions. Bedload fluctuations have been observed both in the field and in flume studies under quasi-steady water and sediment flux and in the absence of bedforms. Fluctuations were identified as early as the 1930s (Ehrenberger, 1931; Mühlofer, 1933; Einstein, 1937).

Field observations of fluctuations in bedload have increased since the 1980s (e.g., Jackson and Beschta, 1982; Reid *et al.*, 1985; Cudden and Hoey, 2003). Since conditions of constant water and sediment rate are rare in the field, bedload fluctuations could be simply viewed as the result of unsteady upstream flux. However, again in the 1980s, a number of detailed flume experiments definitively showed that fluctuations occur under a perfectly steady water flow and sediment influx (Hubbell, 1987; Iseya and Ikeda, 1987; Kuhnle and Southard, 1988). Fluctuations have been associated with bedload sheets (Kuhnle and Southard, 1988; Whiting *et al.*, 1988), themselves associated with migrating patches in the field (Dietrich *et al.*, 2005).

Bedload sheets are not well defined because they are complex features (Figure 4.9b). They develop as a result of interactions between coarse and fine fractions. The name "bedload sheet" was coined by Whiting *et al.* (1988), based on observations reported as follows: "Field observations in streams with beds of coarse sand and fine gravel have revealed that bedload moves primarily as thin, migrating accumulations of sediment, and coarse grains cluster at their leading edge. These accumulations are one or two coarse grains high and are much longer ... than their height. We propose the term 'bedload sheet' for these features, and we argue that they result from an instability inherent to bedload movement of moderately and poorly sorted sediment. In essence, coarse particles in the bedload slow or stop each other, trap finer particles in their interstices, and thus cause the coarse particles to become mobile again." (p. 105) Bedload sheet migration is associated with peak bedload discharges, resulting in large bedload flux variations of sometimes more than an order of magnitude (Gomez, 1983; Kuhnle and Willis, 1998).

In 2009, two articles shed a new light on bedload sheets. Nelson *et al.* (2009) focused on patchiness and its evolution when sediment supply is reduced. One type of patch, called a "free patch" because it migrates (in analogy with bar terminology), is acknowledged to actually be the same feature as a bedload sheet. The findings are based on two sets of experiments, one using a bimodal sand-gravel mixture (Iseya and Ikeda, 1987; Dietrich *et al.*, 1989) and the other, more recent, using a unimodal sand-free gravel mixture. One question discussed by Nelson *et al.* (2009) is whether bedload sheets can form in the absence of sand. Observation of free-patch (i.e., bedload-sheet) dynamics confirms the "catch and mobilize" process described by Whiting *et al.* (1988), even in the absence of sand. Their experiments suggest that the ratio of coarse to fine grain sizes is a key parameter, not the amount of sand *per se*. The passage of bedload sheets yielded a "tremendous short-term variability in sediment discharge" spanning nearly two orders of magnitude during the highest supply experiments (Nelson *et al.*, 2009). When bedload discharge peaks occurred, an increased flux of gravel with low sand content was observed (Figure 4.10). As sediment supply was reduced, bedload-sheet migration rates decreased and their spacing increased, completely disappearing with no sediment input.

Although the experiments were not set up to investigate the grain scale, Nelson *et al.* (2009) emphasized that the primary mechanism of formation and migration of these patches is grain–grain interaction. The time-averaged character of the process could be captured by a one-dimensional morphodynamical model, but of course not the "tremendous variability". It was suggested that the use of more complicated hydrodynamics (Seminara *et al.*, 1996) or particle-based modelling (Schmeeckle and Nelson, 2003; MacVicar *et al.*, 2006) is necessary to capture this variability. The passage of bedload sheets coincides with substantial increases in sediment flux, suggesting that the migration of free patches can be a primary cause of short-term fluctuations in sediment transport rate commonly observed in rivers and flumes. One conclusion by Nelson *et al.* (2009) is that bedload sheets are an inherent feature of gravel bed channels, so that understanding their dynamics is critical to improving bedload flux models.

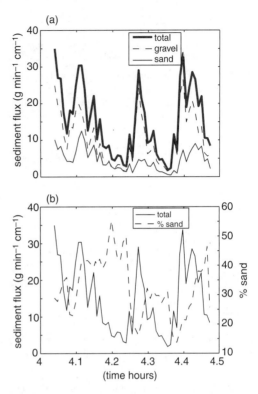

**Figure 4.10**  Sediment flux during a portion of the 17.4 g min$^{-1}$cm$^{-1}$ phase of the Tsukuba experiment. (a) The total rate of sediment transport along with the corresponding rates of sand and gravel transport. (b) The total sediment transport rate and the percentage of the load that was sand (Nelson *et al.*, 2009). Reproduced, with permission, from American Geophysical Union.

A second investigation by Recking *et al.* (2009) focused on the production and migration of bedload sheets. Experiments were carried out on steeper slopes, meaning shorter timescales and more easily distinguished phenomena. Fluctuations of mean and local slopes were systematically recorded. Although these experiments also were not designed to study the grain scale, some specific observations on segregation were made. In particular a very efficient vertical and longitudinal sorting process was evidenced with bed sample measurements (Figure 4.11). Upstream subsurface fining occurred that we can assume to result from a kinetic sieving process (see above). This resulted in aggradation and progressive surface coarsening until a maximum slope was attained. A sharp gravel flux increase then occurred resulting in local erosion and transport of finer gravel previously stored in the bed. This process was responsible for bedload sheet initiation. Bedload sheet migration resulted in alternating states similar to those described by Iseya and Ikeda (1987).

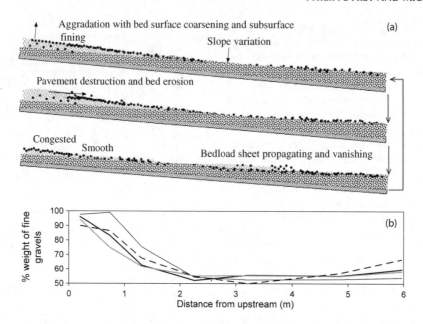

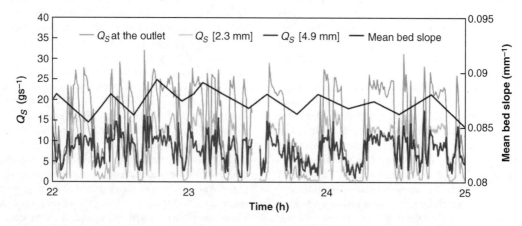

**Figure 4.11** (a) Aggradation-degradation cycles at the origin of bedload sheets. Reproduced, with permission, from Recking, 2006. (b) Four bed samplings indicating subsurface fining over a finite distance in the upstream section (their run 7) (Recking *et al.*, 2009). Reproduced, with permission, from American Geophysical Union.

In some runs, outgoing fractional solid discharges (Figure 4.12) were measured with a light table and high-frequency image analysis (Frey *et al.*, 2003). As in Nelson *et al.* (2009), peak bedload discharges associated with the leading edge of the bedload sheet were explained by the higher mobility of coarse gravels when transported with finer gravels. Finer gravel flux was severely reduced during bed coarsening to well below the expected value for uniform fine sediments, because

of segregation. The expected uniform value was attained only during the bedload sheet passage.

A difference between the experiments of Recking *et al.* (2009) and those of Nelson *et al.* (2009) pertains to the ratio between the coarser and the finer sizes. Based on their material grain size distributions and on recorded bedload sheet characteristics, Nelson *et al.* (2009) have suggested a minimum value of 4 because the coarse front of the sheet must trap the fines, which is only possible

**Figure 4.12** Continuous outlet solid discharge $Q_s$ (total and fractional) and mean bed slope over the entire length of the flume: see Figure 4.11a (Recking *et al.*, 2009). Reproduced, with permission, from American Geophysical Union. (See the color version of this figure in color plate section.)

above a certain ratio. This ratio is about 4 if the grain packing is idealized by tangent circles, as suggested by Nelson *et al.* (2009). This reasoning seems to be based on the idea that the coarser fraction is not moving. When the coarser substrate is not moving, infiltration (also called spontaneous percolation) can only occur for relatively high size ratios. In the experiments of Recking *et al.* (2009), bedload sheets appeared with a size ratio of only about two. The plausible explanation is that in these experiments coarser fractions of the bed surface were likely to move, which was also the case in experiments by Nelson *et al.* (2009). Therefore, the process is not spontaneous percolation anymore, but probably kinetic sieving, which can occur even with size ratios very close to unity. The basis for these inferences is clearly demonstrated in the work on granular flows.

Whereas much research has been conducted on spontaneous percolation in gravel bed rivers, we propose that further attention, informed by results obtained in granular physics, should be devoted to kinetic sieving and related segregation processes. Of course, in practice, for poorly sorted sediment under conditions where the coarsest fractions are not moving, both phenomena are likely to occur. We also believe that sedimentological and geomorphological interpretations would be enhanced by analysing spatial and temporal patterns of sediment observed in the field in light of these new results on bedload sheet dynamics. More generally, the seemingly very specific topic of bedload sheets shows how a better insight into grain–grain interactions could advance understanding of important phenomena in fluvial geomorphology.

## 4.6 PERSPECTIVES AND CONCLUSIONS

In this paper, we have leaned heavily on research performed outside the field of fluvial geomorphology. In doing so, we are not implying that the "fluid perspective" should be discarded. We are pointing out that grain–grain interactions may have been relatively neglected despite major advances in the field of granular physics. We believe that progress could easily be made by merging studies modelling, on the one hand, interactions between turbulent flows and bedload transport, and, on the other, grain–grain interactions, addressing the so-called fluid–grain coupling which is currently a very active research direction in the "powder and grain" community (Zhu *et al.*, 2008)

Of course bedload in gravel-bed rivers is more complex than the mere steady flux of uniform particles usually sufficient to model a large range of industrial flows. Indeed most results on granular flows and segregation pertain to the steady state, although time-dependent equations have been solved for the evolution

of the segregation, which operates very rapidly in dry granular flows (Gray and Chugunov, 2006). In bedload transport, the timescale of size sorting may well be longer, particularly in gravels. An important question, then, is how the timescale of the sedimentary process scales with the succession of floods of different duration and intensity in a stream. Answers to this question may be relevant or not, depending on the period of interest (instantaneous process, individual hydrological events, annual or centennial hydrology).

Most experiments in granular physics have been conducted with uniform or two-size distributions of spherical grains. There is a need, motivated by the success of bulk bedload transport prediction based on the two sizes of sand and gravel (Wilcock and Crowe, 2003), to investigate two-size mixtures with very different sizes. There is an urgent need to conduct experiments with natural materials of variable shape (and, eventually, density), and to conduct experiments with multisized distributions of materials. These effects will undoubtedly modulate some of the results obtained from granular experiments.

Altogether, it appears that a good basis exists in granular physics to improve our understanding of bedload transport at high rates, which are typically associated with sand bed channels and with extreme flows in relatively steep gravel bed channels. However, surface phenomena that would simulate moderate bedload transport – that is, transport of individual grains over a rough surface composed of similar grains – remain essentially uninvestigated in granular physics. While heuristic models have been constructed for the development of surface structures, the mechanisms that promote bed surface structures require additional experimental study before physically sound models may be developed. Stone lines and cells on the surface represent long-lived force chains; long-lived because, during most flows, their ultimate strength is not tested. This allows time for additional mechanisms to strengthen them beyond the state achieved in continuously deforming media. Hence, failure mechanisms are of particular interest (Church and Zimmermann, 2007).

Further research on bedload sheets and patches and, more generally, on fluctuations associated with grain sorting should focus on the grain scale. Both surface and full mobility processes may be acting. While imparting insight into the bedload problem, experiments on these phenomena would open a new perspective in the physics as well. We would like to share here our enthusiasm about this future research because it can encompass all scales from the grain to the river channel. Such research should benefit from an improved dialogue between the communities of granular media physicists and fluvial geomorphologists.

## 4.7 ACKNOWLEDGEMENTS

P. Frey acknowledges the support of Cemagref and the University of British Columbia, Department of Geography where this chapter was partly written while on sabbatical leave. This work is partly funded by the French "Institut National des Sciences de l'Univers" and "Agence Nationale de la Recherche" grant ANR GES-TRANS. M. Church is supported by the Natural Sciences and Engineering Research Council of Canada.

## 4.8 REFERENCES

Ancey, C., Bigillon, F., Frey, P. and Ducret, R. 2003. Rolling motion of a bead in a rapid water stream. *Physical Review E* 67: 011303.

Ancey, C., Bigillon, F., Frey, P., Lanier, J. and Ducret, R. 2002. Saltating motion of a bead in a rapid water stream. *Physical Review E* 66: 036306.

Ancey, C., Davison, A.C., Böhm, T., Jodeau, M. and Frey, P. 2008. Entrainment and motion of coarse particles in a shallow water stream down a steep slope. *Journal of Fluid Mechanics* 595: 83–114.

Armanini, A., Capart, H., Fraccarollo, L. and Larcher, M. 2005. Rheological stratification in experimental free-surface flows of granular-liquid mixtures. *Journal of Fluid Mechanics* 532: 269–319.

Asano, T. 1995. Sediment transport under sheet-flow conditions. *Journal of Waterway Port Coastal and Ocean Engineering* 121: 239–246.

Ashworth, P.J. and Ferguson, R.I. 1989. Size-selective entrainment of bed-load in gravel bed streams. *Water Resources Research* 25: 627–634.

Bagnold, R.A. 1954. Experiments on a gravity-free dispersion of large solid spheres in a Newtonian fluid under shear. *Proceedings of the Royal Society of London, A. Mathematical and Physical Sciences* 225: 49–63.

Bagnold, R.A. 1956. The flow of cohesionless grains in fluids. *Philosophical transaction of the Royal Society of London, A, Mathematical and Physical Science* 249(964): 235–297.

Bathurst, J.C. 2007. Effect of coarse surface layer on bed-load transport. *Journal of Hydraulic Engineering* 133: 1192–1205.

Berzi, D. and Jenkins, J.T. 2008. A theoretical analysis of free-surface flows of saturated granular-liquid mixtures. *Journal of Fluid Mechanics* 608: 393–410.

Beschta, R. L, and Jackson, W.L. 1979. Intrusion of fine sediments into a stable gravel bed. *Journal of the Fisheries Research Board of Canada* 36: 204–210.

Böhm, T., Ancey, C., Frey, P., Reboud, J.L. and Ducottet, C. 2004. Fluctuations of the solid discharge of gravity-driven particle flows in a turbulent stream. *Physical Review E* 69: 061307.

Böhm, T., Frey, P., Ducottet, C. *et al.* 2006. Two-dimensional motion of a set of particles in a free surface flow with image processing. *Experiments in Fluids* 41: 1–11.

Calantoni, J. and Thaxton, C.S. 2008. Simple power law for transport ratio with bimodal distributions of coarse sediments under waves. *Journal of Geophysical Research-Oceans* 113: C03003. doi: 10.1029/2007JC004237.

Campbell, C.S. 2002. Granular shear flows at the elastic limit. *Journal of Fluid Mechanics* 465: 261–291.

Campbell, L., McEwan, I., Nikora, V. *et al.* 2005. Bed-load effects on hydrodynamics of rough-bed open-channel flows. *Journal of Hydraulic Engineeringe* 131: 576–585.

Cates, M.E., Wittmer, J.P., Bouchaud, J.P. and Claudin, P. 1998. Jamming, force chains, and fragile matter. *Physical Review Letters* 81: 1841–1844.

Church, M. and Zimmermann, A. 2007. Form and stability of step-pool channels: Research progress. *Water Resources Research* 43: W03415. doi: 10.1029/2006WR005037.

Church, M., Hassan, M.A. and Wolcott, J.F. 1998. Stabilizing self-organized structures in gravel-bed stream channels: Field and experimental observations. *Water Resources Research* 34: 3169–3179.

Cudden, J.R. and Hoey, T.B. 2003. The causes of bedload pulses in a gravel channel: The implications of bedload grain-size distributions. *Earth Surface Processes and Landforms* 28: 1411–1428.

Cundall, P.A. and Strack, O.D.L. 1979. Discrete numerical-model for granular assemblies. *Geotechnique* 29: 47–65.

Devauchelle, O., Josserand, C., Lagree, P.Y. and Zaleski, S. 2007. Morphodynamic modeling of erodible laminar channels. *Physical Review E* 76. doi: 10.1103/PhysRev E.76.056318.

Dietrich, W.E., Kirchner, J.W., Ikeda, H. and Iseya, F. 1989. Sediment Supply and the Development of the Coarse Surface-Layer in Gravel-Bedded Rivers. *Nature* 340: 215–217.

Dietrich, W.E., Nelson, P.A., Yager, E. *et al.* 2005. Sediment patches, sediment supply and channel morphology. In Parker, G. and Garcia, M.H., editors. River, *Coastal and Esturarine Morphodynamics: RCEM 2005*. London, Taylor and Francis, 79–90.

Doucet, J., Bertrand, F. and Chaouki, J. 2008. Experimental characterization of the chaotic dynamics of cohesionless particles: application to a V-blender. *Granular Matter* 10: 133–138.

Drahun, J.A. and Bridgwater, J. 1983. The mechanisms of free-surface segregation. *Powder Technology* 36: 39–53.

Drake, T.G., Shreve, R.L., Dietrich, W.E., Whiting, P.J. and Leopold, L.B. 1988. bedload transport of fine gravel observed by motion-picture photography. *Journal of Fluid Mechanics* 192: 193–217.

Duran, J. 1999. *Sands, Powders And Grains: An Introduction to the Physics of Granular Materials (Partially Ordered Systems)* New York, Springer. [Translated from the French: *Introduction à la physique des matériaux granulaires*, 1997, Paris, Editions Eyrolles].

Ehrenberger, R. 1931. Direct bedload measurements on the Danube at Vienna and their results to date. *Die Wasserwirtschaft* 34: 1–9.

Einstein, H.A. 1936. *Der Geschiebetrieb als Wahrscheinlichkeitsproblem*. ETH Zürich, Doktor der technischen Wissenschaften. Zürich, Gebrüder Leemann & Co.

Einstein, H.A. 1937. The calibration of the bedload trap used in the Rhine. *Schweizerische Bauzeitung* 110: 29–32.

Einstein, H.A. 1968. Deposition of suspended particles in a gravel bed. *American Society of Civil Engineers. Journal of the Hydraulics Division* 94: 1197–1205.

Felix, G. and Thomas, N. 2004. Evidence of two effects in the size segregation process in dry granular media. *Physical Review E* 70: 051307 Part 1.

Ferguson, R.I., Bloomer, D.J., Hoey, T.B. and Werritty, A. 2002. Mobility of river tracer pebbles over different time-scales. *Water Resources Research* 38: 1045. doi: 10.1029/2001WR000254.

Forterre, Y. and Pouliquen, O. 2008. Flows of dense granular media. *Annual Review of Fluid Mechanics* 40: 1–24.

Fraccarollo, L. and Rosatti, G. 2009. Lateral bed load experiments in a flume with strong initial transversal slope, in sub- and supercritical conditions. *Water Resources Research* **45**: W01419. doi: 10.1029/2008WR007246.

Fraccarollo, L., Larcher, M. and Armanini, A. 2007. Depth-averaged relations for granular-liquid uniform flows over mobile bed in a wide range of slope values. *Granular Matter* **9**: 145–157.

Francis, J.R.D. 1973. Experiments on the motion of solitary grains along the bed of a water-stream. *Proceedings of the Royal Society of London. A. Mathematical and Physical Sciences* **332**: 443–471.

Frey, P., Ducottet, C. and Jay, J. 2003. Fluctuations of bed load solid discharge and grain size distribution on steep slopes with image analysis. *Experiments in Fluids* **35**: 589–597.

Frostick, L.E., Lucas, P.M. and Reid, I. 1984. The Infiltration of Fine Matrices into Coarse-Grained Alluvial Sediments and Its Implications for Stratigraphical Interpretation. *Journal of the Geological Society* **141**: 955–965.

Goldhirsch, I. 2003. Rapid granular flows. *Annual Review of Fluid Mechanics* **35**: 267–293.

Gomez, B. 1983. Temporal variations in bedload transport rates - the effect of progressive bed armouring. *Earth Surface Processes and Landforms* **8**: 41–54.

Goodman, M.A. and Cowin, S.C. 1972. A continuum theory for granular materials. *Archive for Rational Mechanics and Analysis* **44**: 249–266.

Gotoh, H. and Sakai, T. 1997. Numerical simulation of sheet-flow as granular material. *Journal of Waterway Port Coastal and Ocean Engineering* **123**: 329–336.

Graf, W.H. 1984. *Hydraulics* of sediment transport., 2nd edn, Water Resources Publications, Littleton, CO.

Gray, J. and Chugunov, V.A. 2006. Particle-size segregation and diffusive remixing in shallow granular avalanches. *Journal of Fluid Mechanics* **569**: 365–398.

Haff, P.K. 1997. Why prediction of grain behaviour is difficult in geological granular systems, *Proceedings of the 3rd International Conference on Powders and Grains, Durham, NC, 18–23 May*. Rotterdam, Balkema, pp. 61–64.

Harada, E. and Gotoh, H. 2008. Computational mechanics of vertical sorting of sediment in sheetflow regime by 3-D granular material model. *Coastal Engineering Journal* **50**: 19–45.

Hassan, M.A. and Church, M. 1992. The movement of individual grains on the streambed. In Billi, P., Hey, R.D., Thorne, C.R. and Tacconi, P.editors. *Dynamics of Gravel-bed Rivers*, Chichester, John Wiley & Sons, Ltd, 159–175.

Hassan, M.A. and Ergenzinger, P. 2003. Use of tracers in fluvial geomorphology. In Kondolf, G.M. and Piégay, H., editors. *Tools in Fluvial Geomorphology*. Chichester, John Wiley & Sons Ltd, 397–423.

Heald, J., McEwan, I. and Tait, S. 2004. Sediment transport over a flat bed in a unidirectional flow: simulations and validation. *Philosophical Transactions of the Royal Society of London, A. Mathematical, Physical and Engineering Sciences* **362**: 1973–1986.

Hergault, V., Frey, P., Métivier, F. *et al.* 2010. Image processing for the study of bedload transport of two-size spherical particles in a supercritical flow. *Experiments in Fluids* **49**: 1095–1107. doi: 10.1007/s00348-010-0856-6.

Hill, K.M. and Zhang, J. 2008. Kinematics of densely flowing granular mixtures. *Physical Review E* **77**: 061303.

Hill, K.M., DellAngelo, L. and Meerschaert, M.M. 2010. Heavy-tailed travel distance in gravel bed transport: An exploratory enquiry. *Journal of Geophysical Research* **115**: F00A14. doi: 10.1029/2009JF001276.

Hill, K.M., Gioia, G. and Tota, V.V. 2003. Structure and kinematics in dense free-surface granular flow. *Physical Review Letters* **91**: 064302.

Hodge, R., Richards, K. and Brasington, J. 2007. A physically-based bedload transport model developed for 3-D reach-scale cellular modelling. *Geomorphology* **90**: 244–262.

Hsu, T.J., Jenkins, J.T. and Liu, P.L.F. 2004. On two-phase sediment transport: sheet flow of massive particles. *Proceedings of the Royal Society of London Series A –Mathematical Physical and Engineering Sciences* **460**: 2223–2250.

Hubbell, D.W. 1987. Bedload sampling and analysis. In Thorne, C.R., Bathurst, J.C. and Hey, R.D., editors. *Sediment Transport in Gravel-Bed Rivers*. Chichester, John Wiley & Sons Ltd, 89–106.

Hunt, A.G. and Papanicolaou, A. 2003. Tests of predicted downstream transport of clasts in turbulent flow. *Advances in Water Resources* **26**: 1205–1211.

Iseya, F. and Ikeda, H. 1987. Pulsations in bedload transport rates induced by a longitudinal sediment sorting: a flume study using sand and gravel mixtures. *Geografiska Annaler, Series A* **69 A**: 15–27.

Jackson, W.L. and Beschta, R.L. 1982. A model of two-phase bedload transport in an oregon coast range stream. *Earth Surface Processes and Landforms* **7**: 517–527.

Jaeger, H.M., Nagel, S.R. and Behringer, R.P. 1996. Granular solids, liquids, and gases. *Reviews of Modern Physics* **68**: 1259–1273.

Jain, N., Ottino, J.M. and Lueptow, R.M. 2002. An experimental study of the flowing granular layer in a rotating tumbler. *Physics of Fluids* **14**: 572–582.

Jain, N., Ottino, J.M. and Lueptow, R.M. 2004. Effect of interstitial fluid on a granular flowing layer. *Journal of Fluid Mechanics* **508**: 23–44.

Jenkins, J.T. and Hanes, D.M. 1998. Collisional sheet flows of sediment driven by a turbulent fluid. *Journal of Fluid Mechanics* **370**: 29–52.

Jiang, Z, and Haff, P.K. 1993. Multiparticle simulation methods applied to the micromechanics of bed-load transport. *Water Resources Research* **29**: 399–412.

Julien, P.Y. 1998. Erosion and Sedimentation. Cambridge, Cambridge University Press.

Julien, P.Y., Lan, Y.Q. and Berthault, G. 1993. Experiments on Stratification of Heterogeneous Sand Mixtures. *Bulletin De La Sociéte Géologique De France* **164**: 649–660.

Kleinhans, M.G., Jeukens, C., Bakker, C.J.G. and Frings, R.M. 2008. Magnetic resonance imaging of coarse sediment. *Sedimentary Geology* **208**: 69–78.

Kuhnle, R.A. and Southard, J.B. 1988. Bed load fluctuations in a gravel bed laboratory channel. *Water Resources Research* **24**: 247–260.

Kuhnle, R.A. and Willis, J.C. 1998. Statistics of sediment transport in Goodwin Creek. *Journal of Hydraulic Engineering – ASCE* **124**: 1109–1114.

Larcher, M., Fraccarollo, L., Armanini, A. and Capart, H. 2007. Set of measurement data from flume experiments on steady uniform debris flows. *Journal of Hydraulic Research* **45**: 59–71.

Laronne, J.B. and Carson, M.A. 1976. Interrelationships between Bed Morphology and Bed-Material Transport for a Small, *Gravel-Bed Channel. Sedimentology* **23**: 67–85.

Leeder, M.R. 1979. Bedload dynamics – grain–grain interactions in water flows. *Earth Surface Processes and Landforms* **4**: 229–240.

Lisle, T.E. 1989. sediment transport and resulting deposition in spawning gravels, north coastal California. *Water Resources Research* **25**: 1303–1319.

Liu, A.J. and Nagel, S.R. 1998. Nonlinear dynamics – Jamming is not just cool any more. *Nature* **396**: 21–22.

Lobkovsky, A.E., Orpe, A.V., Molloy, R., Kudrolli, A. and Rothman, D.H. 2008. Erosion of a granular bed driven by laminar fluid flow. *Journal of Fluid Mechanics* **605**: 47–58.

Luchnikov, V.A., Medvedev, N.N., Oger, L. and Troadec, J.P. 1999. Voronoi-Delaunay analysis of voids in systems of nonspherical particles. *Physical Review E* **59**: 7205–7212.

MacVicar, B.J., Parrott, L. and Roy, A.G. 2006. A two-dimensional discrete particle model of gravel bed river systems. *Journal of Geophysical Research – Earth Surface* **111**: F03009. doi: 10.1029/2005JF000316.

Malmaeus, J.M. and Hassan, M.A. 2002. Simulation of individual particle movement in a gravel streambed. *Earth Surface Processes and Landforms* **27**: 81–97.

Malverti, L., Lajeunesse, E. and Metivier, F. 2008. Small is beautiful: Upscaling from microscale laminar to natural turbulent rivers. *Journal of Geophysical Research-Earth Surface* **113**: F04004. doi: 10.1029/2007JF000974.

McEwan, I.K. and Heald, J.G. 2001. Discrete particle modeling of entrainment from flat uniformly sized sediment beds. *Journal of Hydraulic Engineering* **127**: 588–597.

McEwan, I.K., Habersack, H.M. and Heald, J.G. 2001. Discrete particle modelling and active tracers: new techniques for studying sediment transport as a lagrangian phenomenon. In Mosley, M.P., editor. *Gravel-bed Rivers V*, Wellington, New Zealand, New Zealand Hydrological Society, 339–373.

Meier, S.W., Lueptow, R.M. and Ottino, J.M. 2007. A dynamical systems approach to mixing and segregation of granular materials in tumblers. *Advances in Physics* **56**: 757–827.

Menon, N. and Durian, D.J. 1997. Diffusing-wave spectroscopy of dynamics in a three-dimensional granular flow. *Science* **275**: 1920–1922.

Métivier, F. and Meunier, P. 2003. Input and output mass flux correlations in an experimental braided stream. Implications on the dynamics of bed load transport. *Journal of Hydrology* **271**: 22–38.

Middleton, G.V. 1970. Experimental studies related to problems of flysch sedimentation. In Lajoie, J.editor. *Flysch Sedimentology in North America*. St. John's, NL, Canada, Geological Association of Canada, 253–272.

MiDi G.D.R. 2004. On dense granular flows. *European Physical Journal E* **14**: 341–365.

Mouilleron, H., Charru, F. and Eiff, O. 2009. Inside the moving layer of a sheared granular bed. *Journal of Fluid Mechanics* **628**: 229–239.

Mueth, D.M., Debregeas, G.F., Karczmar, G.S. *et al.* 2000. Signatures of granular microstructure in dense shear flows. *Nature* **406**: 385–389.

Mühlofer. 1933. Investigations into suspended load and bedload of the river Inn, near Kirchbichl, Tirol. *Die Wasserwirtschaft*: 1–6.

Nelson, P.A., Venditti, J.G., Dietrich, W.E. *et al.* 2009. Response of bed surface patchiness to reductions in sediment supply. *Journal of Geophysical Research – Earth Surface* **114**: F02005. doi: 10.1029/2008JF001144.

Nikora, V., Habersack, H., Huber, T. and McEwan, I.K. 2002. On bed particle diffusion in gravel bed flows under weak bed load transport. *Water Resources Research* **38**: 1081. doi: 10.1029/2001WR000513.

Niño, Y., Garcia, M. and Ayala, L. 1994. Gravel saltation. 1. Experiments. *Water Resources Research* **30**: 1907–1914.

Orpe, A.V. and Khakhar, D.V. 2007. Rheology of surface granular flows. *Journal of Fluid Mechanics* **571**: 1–32.

Ottino, J.M. and Khakhar, D.V. 2000. Mixing and segregation of granular materials. *Annual Review of Fluid Mechanics* **32**: 55–91.

Ouriemi, M., Aussillous, P. and Guazzelli, E. 2009. Sediment dynamics. Part 1. Bed-load transport by laminar shearing flows. *Journal of Fluid Mechanics* **636**: 295–319.

Paola, C. and Seal, R. 1995. grain-size patchiness as a cause of selective deposition and downstream fining. *Water Resources Research* **31**: 1395–1407.

Parker, G. 2007. Transport of gravel and sediment mixtures. In Garcia, M.H., editor. *Sedimentation Engineering: Processes, Measurements, Modeling and Practice, Manual 110, Sedimentation Committee of the Environmental and Water Resources Institute*, American Society of Civil Engineers, 165–251.

Parker, G. and Klingeman, P.C. 1982. On why gravel bed streams are paved. *Water Resources Research* **18**: 1409–1423.

Pyrce, R.S. and Ashmore, P.E. 2003. The relation between particle path length distributions and channel morphology in gravel-bed streams: a synthesis. *Geomorphology* **56**: 167–187.

Recking, A. 2006. *An experimental study of grain sorting effects on bedload*, Ph.D. thesis, Insa Lyon.

Recking, A., Frey, P., Paquier, A. and Belleudy, P. 2009. An experimental investigation of mechanisms responsible for bedload sheet production and migration. *Journal of Geophysical Research – Earth Surface* **114**: F03010, doi: 10.1029/2008JF000990.

Recking, A., Frey, P., Paquier, A., Belleudy, P. and Champagne, J-Y. 2008a. Bed-load transport flume experiments on steep slopes. *Journal of Hydraulic Engineering* **134**: 1302–1310.

Recking, A., Frey, P., Paquier, A., Belleudy, P. and Champagne, J-Y. 2008b. Feedback between bed load transport and flow resistance in gravel and cobble bed rivers. *Water Resources Research* **44**: W05412. doi: 10.1029/2007WR006219. Correction. W08701. doi: 10.1029/WR007272.

Reid, I., Frostick, L.E. and Brayshaw, A.C. 1985. The incidence and nature of bedload transport during flood flows in coarse-grained alluvial channels. *Earth Surface Processes and Landforms* **10**: 33–44.

Richard, P., Valance, A., Metayer, J.F. *et al.* 2008. Rheology of confined granular flows: scale invariance, glass transition, and friction weakening. *Physical Review Letters* **101**: 248002.

Richards, K., Bithell, M., Dove, M. and Hodge, R. 2004. Discrete-element modelling: methods and applications in the environmental sciences. *Philosophical Transactions of the Royal Society of London, A. Mathematical, Physical and Engineering Sciences* **362**: 1797–1816.

Sambrook Smith, G.H. and Nicholas, A.P. 2005. Effect on flow structure of sand deposition on a gravel bed: Results from a two-dimensional flume experiment. *Water Resources Research* **41**: W10405. doi: 10.1029/WR003817.

Savage, S.B. and Lun, C.K.K. 1988. Particle-size segregation in inclined chute flow of dry cohesionless granular solids. *Journal of Fluid Mechanics* **189**: 311–335.

Schmeeckle, M.W. and Nelson, J.M. 2003. Direct numerical simulation of bedload transport using a local, dynamic boundary condition. *Sedimentology* **50**: 279–301.

Seminara, G., Colombini, M. and Parker, G. 1996. Nearly pure sorting waves and formation of bedload sheets. *Journal of Fluid Mechanics* **312**: 253–278.

Sumer, B.M., Kozakiewicz, A., Fredsoe, J. and Deigaard, R. 1996. Velocity and concentration profiles in sheet-flow layer of movable bed. *Journal of Hydraulic Engineering* **122**: 549–558.

Thomas, N. 2000. Reverse and intermediate segregation of large beads in dry granular media. *Physical Review E* **62**: 961–974.

Tribe, S. and Church, M. 1999. Simulations of cobble structure on a gravel streambed. *Water Resources Research* **35**: 311–318.

Troadec, J.P. and Dodds, J.A. 1993. Global geometrical description of homogeneous hard sphere. In Bideau, D. and Hansen, A., editors, *Disorder and Granular Media, Random Materials and Processes*. Amsterdam, Elsevier, 133–163.

Warburton, J. 1992. Observations of bed-load transport and channel bed changes in a proglacial mountain stream. *Arctic and Alpine Research* **24**: 195–203.

Whiting, P.J., Dietrich, W.E., Leopold, L.B., Drake, T.G., and Shreve, R.L. 1988. Bedload sheets in heterogeneous sediment. *Geology* **16**: 105–108.

Wilcock, P.R. and Crowe, J.C. 2003. Surface-based transport model for mixed-size sediment. *Journal of Hydraulic Engineering* **129**: 120–128.

Wooster, J.K., Dusterhoff, S.R., Cui, Y.T. *et al.* 2008. Sediment supply and relative size distribution effects on fine sediment infiltration into immobile gravels. *Water Resources Research* **44**: W03424. doi: 10.1029/2006WR005818.

Yalin, M. 1977. *Mechanics of Sediment Transport*, 2nd edn. Oxford, Pergamon Press.

Zhu, H.P., Zhou, Z.Y., Yangm R.Y. and Yu, A.B. 2008. Discrete particle simulation of particulate systems: A review of major applications and findings. *Chemical Engineering Science* **63**: 5728–5770.

## 4.9 DISCUSSION

### 4.9.1 Discussion by D. Rickenmann

In this chapter, Frey and Church summarize some key features of bedload sheets, such as the "catch and mobilize" process, an instability which has been associated with the bedload movement of moderately and poorly sorted sediment (Whiting *et al.*, 1988). In other studies, bedload sheets have been observed for a wide range of flow conditions, including channel gradients from 0.15% to 15%, and sheet migration has been associated with a peak solid discharge of the coarser gravel present in the sediment mixture (Recking *et al.*, 2009). Some of these elements may also be present during the formation of debris flows. For example, it can be observed that the formation of granular-type (coarse-grained or stony type) debris flows in steep channels may be associated with an intermittent stop-and-go process resulting from a temporary accumulation of solids and slurry upstream of a heap of coarse bedload sediment and a subsequent release of the accumulation once the driving forces have overcome the resisting forces. Visual observations of debris-flood conditions (sensu Hungr *et al.*, 2001) also indicate a pulsating behaviour of bedload movement, which has also been measured during intense fluvial bedload transport in steep streams for almost constant discharge conditions (Rickenmann, 1994; D'Agostino and Lenzi, 1999). I wonder whether the authors can comment on any possible analogy between the formation of bedload sheets and channel-type initiation of granular debris flows.

### 4.9.2 Discussion by G. Grant

Is there an implicit assumption of equilibrium bed level with respect to both segregation (as discussed by Frey) and exchange (as discussed by Haschenburger) processes? More broadly, how does aggradation or degradation affect these particle to particle exchanges and movement of particles within the bed? Clearly if the bed is aggrading, then the subsurface is being buried, so exchange must be from the surface to the subsurface. The opposite would be true for degrading systems. In either case, the overall bed elevation needs to be explicitly considered.

### 4.9.3 Discussion by P. Ashmore

One can imagine cases in which the height of mobile bars or depth of local scour exceeds $2D_{90}$ and in which the limit of active layer depth might, over time scales sufficient for bar and channel migration, approximate the amplitude of the bar/bed topography. Is it possible that a range of different burial depth distributions occur over the range of gravel river morpho-types with differing particle and bed mobility? For example, Figure 4.13 shows the amplitude of bed scour-fill in an active, proglacial braided river. Maximum amplitude of change during daily meltwater events is over 0.5 m, which presumably results in maximum burial depths of the same order. In this case $D_{90}$ is of the order of 0.1 m and active layer depth therefore exceeds $5D_{90}$.

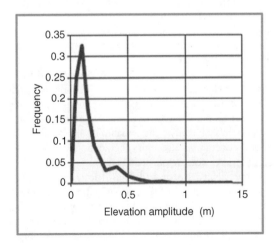

**Figure 4.13** Amplitude of bed scour and fill in an active, proglacial braided river.

### 4.9.4   Reply by P. Frey and M. Church

The discussants raise a number of interesting points about bedload sheets. A section was devoted to bedload sheets in the paper because bedload sheets are formed as a result of size segregation. A better knowledge of this ubiquitous feature may therefore benefit from investigations at the particle scale of granular interactions.

Rickenmann asks whether any possible analogy can be made between the formation of bedload sheets and channel-type initiation of granular debris flows. Indeed in both cases large instabilities develop resulting in fluctuations in bedload transport (e.g., Reid *et al.*, 1985; D'Agostino and Lenzi, 1999; Rickenmann, 1994) and in multiple surges in debris flows (see McCoy *et al.*, 2010 for *in situ* observations)

However, we would be cautious in making an analogy between the two phenomena. It is clear that size segregation (particularly kinetic sieving and mixing) plays a crucial role in both cases. In debris flows, the formation of a coarser front is obviously due to segregation as evidenced by experimental (Iverson *et al.*, 2010) and theoretical (Gray and Ancey, 2009) investigations. The mechanism for development of multiple surges is, however, unclear. Roll wave theory has been applied both for muddy and granular debris-flows (Trowbridge, 1987; Zanuttigh and Lamberti, 2007) and does not imply segregation processes, although the development of some roll waves has been shown to be linked with size segregation (Iverson *et al.* 2010). In bedload, bedload sheet propagation appears to be a combination of at least both size segregation and fractional two-phase transport dynamics (Recking *et al.*, 2009).

In short, although size segregation is an important process to be better investigated in both bedload and debris flows, other physical processes, different in each geophysical flow, are probably necessary to explain the observed instabilities.

Grant asks how does aggradation or degradation affect particle exchange with respect to segregation and bedload fluctuations. It is true that most experiments in the literature are performed at dynamical equilibrium. Some experiments investigate aggradational and/or degradational conditions although degradational conditions seem to have been less researched.

In the field, Rice *et al.* (2009) have described river bars built by the stacking of successive bedload sheets with size segregation such as would occur in kinetic sieving, while Madej *et al.* (2009) have conducted experiments in which bedload sheets and fluctuations of sediment output were present during aggradation. In contrast, they observed no bedload sheets and virtually no fluctuations during degradation.

Ashmore raises the question of the definition of the active layer, implying that the term has been applied both to the bed layer taking part in the active exchange with mobile sediment in the transport process, and to the total depth of bed sediment that may be disturbed over some arbitrary time period. The latter would include total scour and fill depths. Inasmuch as scour and fill occur progressively over time, the entire sediment column that is disturbed by such processes does not simultaneously take part in the active transport. The term "active layer" (an alternative would be "transport layer") originated with transport modelers (cf. Hirano, 1971; Parker, 1991; van Niekerk *et al.*, 1992; Hoey and Ferguson, 1994) who certainly intended the first interpretation given above. Experimental demonstration of an active layer of order $1–2D_{90}$ in thickness has been provided (Wilcock and McArdell, 1993; Wathen, 1995, quoted in Ferguson *et al.*, 1997). This is the interpretation intended in our paper and we believe it is the best interpretation.

## 4.10   DISCUSSION REFERENCES

D'Agostino V. and Lenzi, M.A. 1999. Bedload transport in the instrumented catchment of the Rio Cordon, Part II, Analysis of the bedload rate. *Catena* **36**: 191–204.

Ferguson, R.I., Hoey, T.B., Wathen, S.J. *et al.* 1997. Downstream fining of river gravels: integrated field, laboratory and modeling study. In Klingeman, P.C., Beschta, R. L, Komar, P.D. and Bradley, J.B., editors. *Gravel-bed Rivers in the Environment*. Highlands, Ranch, CO, Water Resources Publications, 85–114.

Gray, J. and Ancey, C. 2009. Segregation, recirculation and deposition of coarse particles near two-dimensional avalanche fronts. *Journal of Fluid Mechanics* **629**: 387–423.

Hirano, M. 1971. River bed degradation with armoring. *Proceedings of the Japan Society of Civil Engineers* **195**: 55–65 (in Japanese).

Hoey, T. B. and Ferguson, R. I. 1994. Numerical modeling of downstream fining by selective transport in gravel-bed rivers: model development and illustration. *Water Resources Research* **30**: 2251–2260.

Hungr, O., Evans, S., Bovis, M.J. and Hutchinson, J.N. 2001. A review of the classification of landslides of the flow type. *Environmental and Engineering Geoscience* **7**: 221–238.

Iverson, R.M., Logan, M., LaHusen, R.G. and Berti, M. 2010. The perfect debris flow? Aggregated results from 28 large-scale experiments. *Journal of Geophysical Research – Earth Surface* **115**: F03005. doi: 10.1029/2009JF001307.

Madej, M.A., Sutherland, D.G., Lisle, T.E. and Pryor, B. 2009. Channel responses to varying sediment input: A flume experiment modeled after Redwood Creek, *California. Geomorphology* **103**: 507–519.

McCoy, S.W., Kean, J.W., Coe, J.A. *et al.* 2010. Evolution of a natural debris flow: In situ measurements of flow dynamics, video imagery, and terrestrial laser scanning. *Geology* **38**: 735–738.

van Niekerk, A., Vogel, K.R., Slingerland, R.L. and Bridge, J.S. 1992. Routing of heterogeneous sediments over movable bed: model development. *Journal of Hydraulic Engineering* **118**: 246–261.

Parker, G. 1991. Selective sorting and abrasion of river gravel. I. Theory. *Journal of Hydraulic Engineering* **117**: 131–149.

Recking, A., Frey, P., Paquier, A. and Belleudy, P. 2009. An experimental investigation of mechanisms responsible for bedload sheet production and migration. *Journal of Geophysical Research – Earth Surface* **114**: F03010, doi: 10.1029/2008JF000990.

Reid. I., Frostick, L.E. and Layman, J.T. 1985. The incidence and nature of bedload transport during flood flows in coarse-grained alluvial channels. *Earth Surface Processes and Landforms* **10**: 33–44.

Rice, S.P., Church, M., Wooldridge, C.L. and Hickin, E.J. 2009. Morphology and evolution of bars in a wandering gravel-bed river; lower Fraser river, British Columbia, *Canada. Sedimentology* **56**: 709–736.

Rickenmann, D. 1994. Bedload transport and discharge in the Erlenbach Stream. In Ergenzinger, P. and Schmidt, K-H. editors. *Dynamics and Geomorphology of Mountain Rivers, Lecture Notes in Earth Sciences* **52**: 53–66.

Trowbridge, J.H. 1987. Instability of Concentrated Free-Surface Flows. *Journal of Geophysical Research-Oceans* **92**: 9523–9530.

Wathen, S. J. 1995. The effect of storage on sediment transfer processes in a small Scottish gravel bed river. Ph.D. thesis, St. Andrews University, Scotland.

Whiting, P.J., Dietrich, W.E., Leopold, L.B., Drake, T.G., and Shreve, R.L. 1988. Bedload sheets in heterogeneous sediment. *Geology* **16**: 105–108.

Wilcock, P. R. and McArdell, B. W. 1993. Surface-based fractional transport rates: mobilization thresholds and partial transport of a sand gravel sediment. *Water Resources Research* **29**: 1297–1312.

Zanuttigh, B. and Lamberti, A. 2007. Instability and surge development in debris flows. *Reviews of Geophysics* **45**: RG3006. doi: 10.1029/2005RG000175.

# 5

# On Gravel Exchange in Natural Channels

## Judith K. Haschenburger

## 5.1 INTRODUCTION

This paper extends the discussion of gravel transport presented by Frey and Church (Chapter 4, this volume) by focusing on the vertical exchange of gravel in natural channels with an emphasis on longer time scales. While grain exchange during bedload transport is well recognized, questions persist about the rates and depth of gravel exchange as part of the more general understanding of sediment dispersion. Most recent work on sediment exchange has emphasized the ingress of fine-grained sediment into gravel beds (e.g., Wooster et al., 2008) rather than the behaviour of coarse-grained sediment that controls bedload supply, builds surface structures, and dominates the grain–grain interactions described by Frey and Church.

Three specific topics are addressed: the role of grain size distributions in limiting exchange, the pathways and likelihood of exchange, and the depth of exchange. The latter two aspects are considered by grain size to reveal size-selective behaviour of the gravel fraction that contributes to size segregation. The reliance on field observations of tracer experiments (Table 5.1) and consideration of longer time scales provides a contrast to the gravel transport results derived from flume and numerical experimentation emphasized by Frey and Church (Chapter 4, this volume). While direct insights into the granular physics behind the exchanges cannot be explicitly articulated from these observations, the discussion provides insight for future experiments conducted in the field and flume, and through computer simulation.

## 5.2 GEOMETRIC LIMITS TO EXCHANGE SITES

The size distribution of surface sediment sets a general constraint on the vertical exchange of gravel, given the importance of the surface layer (Parker, 1990). When expressed in terms of grain area, the size distribution determines the number and size of exchange sites within a defined bed area. Surface cavities created by grain entrainment constitute possible exchange sites for kinematic sorting (also called kinetic sieving; Parker and Klingeman, 1982; Frey and Church, Chapter 4, this volume). Exchange should be partly geometrically controlled by the size of moving grains and dimensions of available surface cavities. Grain exchange that leads to size segregation has been shown to depend partially on the relative sizes of spheres in simple laboratory mixtures (e.g., Thomas, 2000).

Gravel beds differ in the range of sizes present and in two key characteristics, the modality of the distribution and the proportional relation between matrix and framework sediments, with a minimum of about 30% finer-sized sediment defining matrix-supported beds (see discussion in Church et al., 1987). The two key properties combine to give four characteristic mixtures: unimodal and bimodal matrix-supported sediment, and unimodal and bimodal framework-supported sediment. The strength of bimodality infuses additional variation. Modality and matrix-framework proportions are known to affect fractional entrainment and transport rates (Wilcock, 1992; Kuhnle, 1993; Wilcock et al., 2001).

How gravel bed characteristics might influence exchange can be initially explored by evaluating grain-to-cavity size ratios. Entrainment of a surface grain leaves, at a minimum, a cavity defined by the grain planimetric area, the combined long and intermediate axes, and depth, the short axis, based on typical grain orientation observed in the field. Deeper cavities may be achieved by the release of finer subsurface grains when surface grains are entrained, and movement of adjacent grains creates larger exchange areas. Nonetheless, this approximation provides a sufficiently realistic depiction of cavity size for an initial analysis, where exchange sites are quantified by the size distribution of cavities based on characteristic grain size distributions.

*Gravel-bed Rivers: Processes, Tools, Environments*, First Edition. Edited by Michael Church, Pascale M. Biron and André G. Roy.

**Table 5.1** Channel characteristics and tracer information for field studies[1]

| River[2] | Bed morphology | Width (m) | Slope (m/m) | Surface $D_{50}$ (mm) | Subsurface $D_{50}$ (mm) | Armour ratio | Surface $D_{90}$ (mm) | Multiple tracer generations or subreaches | Number of tracers[3] | Tracer size range (mm)[4] | Recovery rates (%) |
|---|---|---|---|---|---|---|---|---|---|---|---|
| Allt Dubhaig | Pool–riffle–bar with a downstream transition from medial, side, point, to submerged alternate bars | <10 to ~20 | 0.017 | 96 | 43 | 2.2 | 215 | Subreach T1 | 240 | 32–256 | 49–57 |
| | | | 0.013 | 101 | 49 | 2.1 | 118 | Subreach T2 | 320 | 16–180 | 50–54 |
| | | | 0.013 | 65 | 44 | 1.5 | 110 | Subreach T3 | 260 | 16–128 | 51–60 |
| | | | 0.006 | 32 | 28 | 1.1 | 109 | Subreach T4 | 240 | 16–128 | 58–69 |
| | | | 0.003 | 41 | 20 | 2.0 | 61 | Subreach T5 | 200 | 16–90 | 78–80 |
| | | | 0.003 | 23 | 13 | 1.8 | 36 | Subreach T6 | 200 | 16–90 | 85–88 |
| Carnation Creek | Pool–riffle–bar with mostly side bars | 9 to 27 | 0.009 | 30 to 47 | 19 to 32 | 1.6 | 63 to 118 | Yellow generation | 253 | 16–180 | 26–75[5] |
| | | | | | | | | Orange generation | 146 | 22–180 | 31–72[5] |
| | | | | | | | | Blue generation | 1164 | 16–256 | 40–96 |
| | | | | | | | | Green generation | 990 | 16–256 | 39–76 |
| Harris Creek | Pool–riffle–bar with side and medial bars | 10 to 20 | | 60 | 20 | 3.0 | 112 | 2 generations | 426, 700 | 16–520 | 25–35 |
| Lainbach River | Step-pool with side bars | 10 | 0.02 | See footnote[6] | | | | | 500–1000 | 30–170 | 23–100 |
| Nahal Hebron | Irregular low relief bars and pools | 3 to 5 | 0.016 | 70 | 35 | 2.0 | | | 282 | 45–180 | 80–93 |
| Nahal Og | Point and alternate bars with thalweg | 5 to 12 | 0.014 | 35 | 15 | 2.3 | | | 250 | 45–180 | 55–56 |
| Rio Cordon | Step-pool and riffle-pool[7] | | 0.14 | 90 | 38 | 2.4 | 330 | 2 generations | 860, 860 | 32–512 | 52–100 |

[1] Datasets are included in specific analyses when all needed information could be determined from published work or estimated with sufficient certainty

[2] Key references for each river are: Nahal Hebron – Hassan (1990); Nahal Og – Hassan (1990); Harris Creek – Hassan and Church (1994); Carnation Creek yellow and orange generations – Hassan and Church (1994); Carnation Creek blue and green generations – Haschenburger (1996, 2011); Lainbach River – Gintz *et al.* (1996); Rio Cordon – Lenzi (2004); Allt Dubhaig – Ferguson and Ashworth (1991), Ferguson and Wathen (1998), and Ferguson *et al.* (2002)

[3] All tracers deployed on the surface; sample sizes in order of generation where applicable

[4] Lower and upper limits

[5] Includes some recoveries where rates affected by the total length of channel searched; see Haschenburger (2011)

[6] Size range of sediment reported as 50–65 mm in pools and 290–800 mm in steps

[7] Tracers seeded in riffle reach, see Lenzi (2004)

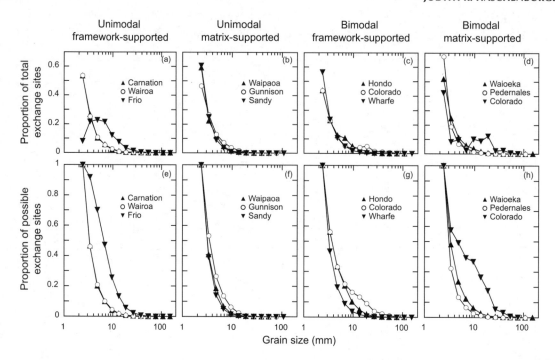

**Figure 5.1**　Total and possible exchange sites by grain size for characteristic gravel beds. Top diagrams illustrate the proportion of total exchange sites for a given grain size for sediment classified as: (a) unimodal framework-supported, (b) unimodal matrix-supported, (c) bimodal framework-supported, and (d) bimodal matrix-supported. Histograms shown as lines for visual clarity. Matrix-supported sediments contain 30% or more material <2 mm in size. Bottom diagrams show the proportion of exchanges sites that can accommodate a given grain size for sediment classified as: (e) unimodal framework-supported, (f) unimodal matrix-supported, (g) bimodal framework-supported, and (h) bimodal matrix-supported. The proportion of possible exchange sites was calculated assuming that the cavity is equal to or larger than the bedload grain, and therefore represents the proportion of all exchange sites that meets this criterion. Sources of grain size distributions are: Carnation (Haschenburger, 1996), Waipoa (Trafford, 1999), Colorado and Gunnison (J. Pitlick, pers. comm., 2010), Waioeka and Wairoa (Roest, 2005), Wharfe (Haschenburger *et al.*, 2007), and Frio, Hondo, Pedernales, and Sandy (Haschenburger, unpublished data).

For a collection of natural sediments the proportion of exchange sites generally decreases with grain size (Figures 5.1a–d). The largest proportion of sites is associated with the finest gravels except for the Frio River sediment, which contains less because it is an open framework gravel. Exchange sites derived from the largest gravels are very limited, which contributes to the propensity of these sizes to remain on the surface. While unimodal mixtures exhibit a systematic decline, some bimodal sediments show a temporary departure in the trend, which follows the bimodality gap and appears to reflect its strength.

Transformation to express the proportion of the exchange sites that can accommodate a given grain size reveals some differences among characteristic gravel beds (Figure 5.1e–h). The most pronounced difference lies in strongly bimodal mixtures, which create greater

potential for medium-sized gravel to be exchanged because more cavities of sufficient dimensions are available. Thus, a specific range of gravel sizes has a higher likelihood of utilizing surface cavities because of the increased availability of possible exchange sites.

The persistence of coarse surface layers during higher flows (Wilcock and DeTemple, 2005) suggests that geometric constraints operate not only during low intensity transport, but also at higher intensities. By extension, grain–grain interactions may be affected, regardless of the state of partial transport, because what happens to a particular bedload grain is influenced by the available exchange sites, the number and size of mobile grains, and the roughness of the bed (Nikora *et al.*, 2002).

Developing conditional probabilities that describe the kinematic sorting of mixed-size sediment must incorporate not only the geometric constraints on grain exchange that reflect bed sediment characteristics, but also the number and size of exchange sites that are active, which depends on the state of partial sediment transport. However, no relation exists to quantify how the state of partial transport changes the size distribution of active exchange sites for different characteristic bed sediments, although the probable role of grain size distributions has been acknowledged (Wilcock, 1997; Wilcock and McArdell, 1997). The experimental basis of partial transport concepts rests on a strongly bimodal sediment, a mixture that stands out from other characteristic sediments.

## 5.3  GRAVEL EXCHANGE

Conceptualizing the pathways of gravel exchange and their likelihood has typically entailed dividing the streambed into layers. While three-, four-, and ten-layer models have been employed (Hassan and Church, 1994; Ferguson and Hoey, 2002; Haschenburger, 2011), a two layer model (Schick et al., 1987) can maximize use of published results and is the least complicated model from which to generalize. Four exchange pathways are defined in this model: surface to surface, surface to subsurface, subsurface to surface, and subsurface to subsurface.

Exchanges may be accomplished through grain movement or adjustment to the depth of sediment overlying immobile grains through scour and fill.

Using the two-layer model, Schick et al. (1987) argued that gravel exchange exhibits an equilibrium which is recognized when the number of grains that are buried and re-exposed approaches limiting values. These values were envisioned to differ based on the degree of vertical mixing, which is driven by the extent of armour layer development. This criterion makes no distinction for grain size, and hence does not account for size-selective behaviour. Alternative criteria for attainment of equilibrium have been proposed (e.g., Hassan and Church, 1994) but are not pursued herein.

The first exchange of marked gravels deployed on the bed surface is either transfer into the subsurface or persistence on the surface. Field experiments using tagged gravels document that surface to subsurface exchanges generally increase with flood peak and can be significant (Figure 5.2), approaching 100% for a single flood or the dominant flood of a few events. Sensitivity of this exchange to flood size is highlighted by those rivers with multiple deployments (e.g., Carnation Creek and Lainbach River), in spite of any bias introduced by tracer deployment and recovery. Part of the scatter may reflect

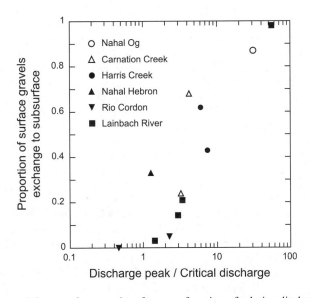

**Figure 5.2**  Exchange of gravel from surface to subsurface as a function of relative discharge. Observations represent first exchanges observed after deployment with proportions based on recovered tracers. Open symbols indicate surface median diameter ≤50 mm and closed symbols indicate median diameter >50 mm. Use of a discharge-based flow index permitted the largest compilation of published results. Critical discharge values were estimated from flood events with little or no tracer movement, depths of scour and fill and/or bedload transport rates when not explicitly reported. Published values taken from Hassan (1990), Hassan and Church (1994), Gintz et al. (1996), Lenzi (2004), and Haschenburger (2011).

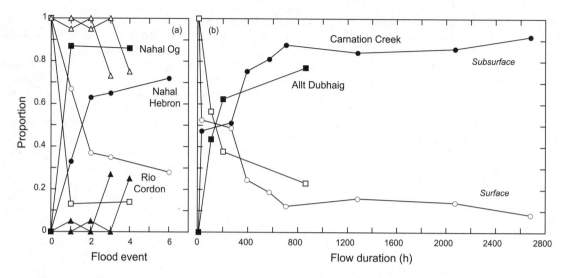

**Figure 5.3** Proportion of surface and subsurface gravels based on a two-layer model: (a) short-term studies and (b) longer-term studies. Open symbols indicate exposed tracers and closed symbols indicate buried tracers. Competent flow duration was estimated using published information about flow duration exceedence frequency in Allt Dubhaig and an individual hydrograph analysis in Carnation Creek. Published values taken from Hassan (1990), Haschenburger (2011), and Lenzi (2004), plus original observations for Allt Dubhaig (R. Ferguson, pers. comm., 2010).

differences in incipient motion definitions and the sizes of tracers relative to bed sediment.

Subsequent floods increase the net exchange of gravel into the subsurface (Figure 5.3a). The proportion of recovered tracers exposed on the surface declines to between 14% and 75% after no more than six floods. The attainment of limiting values and approach towards them are indicated in the trends of Nahal Og and Nahal Hebron, respectively. Over a longer flood sequence, most tracers are concentrated in the subsurface (Figure 5.3b). Proportions in Carnation Creek exhibit an apparent equilibrium after about 700 hours of competent flow, or 56 floods, which is largely maintained over subsequent events, while those in Allt Dubhaig suggest an approach toward equilibrium. The lack of an obvious limiting value in Allt Dubhaig may be because its achievement is a slower process than in Carnation Creek or because detection requires more frequent monitoring. For both rivers, proportions based on recovered tracers overestimate grain exposure because recovery rates tend to decline over time and unrecovered tracers are more likely to be buried. However, the bias appears to be only about 5% and 12% in Carnation Creek and Allt Dubhaig, respectively, when all unrecovered tracers are counted as buried.

The vertical evolution of marked surface grains into the subsurface involves more than surface to subsurface exchange, as documented by field tracing experiments that tracked buried grains. In one of the first such studies,

exchange probabilities for Nahal Hebron indicate that exchanges with surface grains become unlikely over several floods, as the dominance of subsurface residency is established. Exchange of surface grains declined to about 0.2, while the chance of re-exposure did not exceed 0.10 (Figures 5.4a and d).

Over the longer flood sequence in Allt Dubhaig and Carnation Creek, exchange shows weak re-exposure of grains to the surface and a strong tendency for buried grains to remain so (Figures 5.4b–c, e–f). Exchanges of surface grains are 20 to 40% more likely than in Nahal Hebron, with both rivers showing relatively consistent values over the latter part of the flood sequence. While exchange in Carnation Creek exhibits a fairly well-defined trend in all exchange probabilities after about 700 hours, exchanges originating from the subsurface in Allt Dubhaig show continued divergence (Figure 5.4e). If unrecovered tracers are assumed buried, exchange probabilities change by 10% or less based on Carnation Creek data.

This compilation of gravel exchange in a range of rivers reveals a general consistency in the dominance of particular exchange pathways that are sensitive to flood characteristics. Initial adjustment toward limiting values, which can be viewed as indicative of equilibrium exchange, is achieved relatively rapidly in most cases, as surface gravels are transferred to the subsurface. Time-scales for the approach toward or achievement of limiting values in natural rivers contrast sharply with the

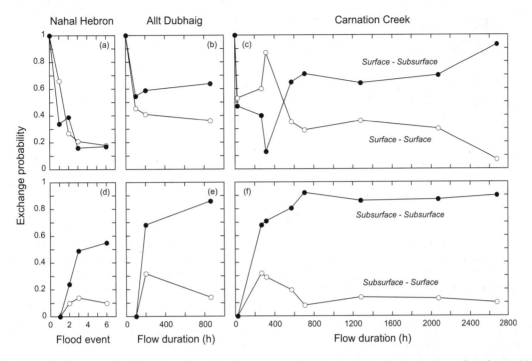

**Figure 5.4** Exchange probabilities based on a two-layer model. Exchange originating from the surface for: (a) Nahal Hebron, (b) Allt Dubhaig, and (c) blue generation in Carnation Creek, and from the subsurface for (d) Nahal Hebron, (e) Allt Dubhaig, and (f) blue generation in Carnation Creek. Open circles indicate exchange to surface and closed circles indicate exchange to subsurface. Nahal Hebron exchange probabilities from Hassan and Church (1992) and original observations for Allt Dubhaig (R. Ferguson, pers. comm., 2010) and Carnation Creek (Haschenburger, unpublished data).

typical length of flume and numerical experiments, spanning from four floods in one flood season in Nahal Og, to 56 floods over four flood seasons in Carnation Creek, to between 50 to 270 events in 3 to 15 flood seasons in Allt Dubhaig (the latter estimated from the equilibrium times reported by Ferguson and Hoey, 2002). Differences in exchange probabilities show some correspondence to the degree of armour layer development as quantified by the armour ratio (Figure 5.4; Table 5.1). The relative effectiveness of the floods captured in the field programmes may also play a role, but cannot be fully explored due to limitations in the available flow records. While definitive explanations for evident differences among rivers cannot be offered, it is worth noting that observations drawn from natural channels represent different states of partial transport, which are not generally documented or routinely reported. This limits interpretation and explanation.

## 5.4 EXCHANGE DEPTHS

Gravel exchange is constrained by the depth of bed activity, its absolute magnitude and distribution (Hassan and Church, 1994; Haschenburger, 1999; Wong

*et al.*, 2007). Flume and numerical experiments indicate that the depth of active sediment exchange is proportional to flow shear stress (Jiang, 1995; Sumer *et al.*, 1996; Wilcock and McArdell, 1997; Wong *et al.*, 2007). At high Shields numbers ($>0.5$) well-sorted sand-sized sediment can be activated to depths up to 60 grain diameters in a sheetflow regime (Sumer *et al.*, 1996), but at lower values more typical of conditions in gravel bed channels, depths are limited. Wilcock and McArdell (1997) deduced two grain diameters as an upper limit to the sediment exchange depth when the 90th percentile of the surface grain size distribution ($D_{90}$) quantified layer thickness. Field observations suggest that the depth of bed activity from scour and fill is typically a small proportion of the surface layer thickness (Carling, 1987; Hassan, 1990; Haschenburger, 1999) and that sediment exchange involves both the active exchange of mobile gravels and passive exchange of immobile gravels driven by imbalances in local bedload fluxes (Hassan, 1990; Haschenburger, 2011). Whether a universal upper limit exists has yet to be established, but limited field observations suggest values up to $2D_{90}$ for sediment exchange (e.g., Wilcock *et al.*, 1996; Haschenburger and Church, 1998; DeVries, 2002).

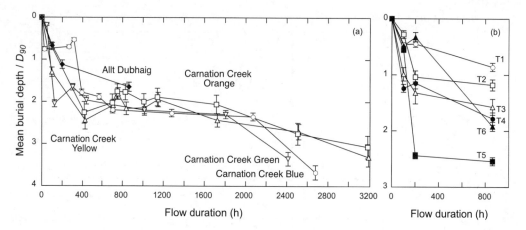

**Figure 5.5** Scaled burial depth as a function of competent flow duration: (a) Carnation Creek and Allt Dubhaig and (b) individual subreaches in Allt Dubhaig with modified ordinate scale. Tracer burial depths are scaled by the $D_{90}$, an estimate of the surface layer thickness. Burial depths in Allt Dubhaig were measured to the top of tracers. For this analysis, burial depths were adjusted by the tracer $c$-axis for consistency with Carnation Creek observations.

Over the long flood sequences in Allt Dubhaig and Carnation Creek, most adjustment in the scaled depth of gravel burial occurs relatively early in the sequence (Figure 5.5a). After 800 hours of competent flow, mean burial had reached about $2D_{90}$ in Carnation Creek, but only $1.6D_{90}$ in Allt Dubhaig, when considering both active and passive exchanges. Because recovery rates are less than 100% and it is more likely for unrecovered tracers to be buried, these depths are underestimated to some degree.

The deployment strategy in Allt Dubhaig reveals how gravel exchange can differ within a channel due to changes in local flow strength and bed material characteristics (Figure 5.5b). Scaled depths exhibit a fairly systematic downstream trend. Although mean burial depths are more variable across the subreaches, in part due to patterns in aggradation (Ferguson and Wathen, 1998; Ferguson et al., 2002), the large and systematic decline in the surface $D_{90}$ (Table 5.1) outweighs the variability in burial depths in the scaled values. The departure of subreach T6 from the downstream order may reflect the more subdued bed morphology and limited scour and fill (Table 5.1; R. Ferguson, pers. comm., 2010), an assertion supported by a mean burial depth that is only about half as deep as in the other subreaches.

An approach toward an upper limit of about $2D_{90}$ is suggested over a significant portion of the record in Carnation Creek, under conditions of relatively stable tracer recovery rates. The sharp increase in the blue and green tracers at the end of their record appears to reflect localized burial of grains near their deployment area and the bias introduced from higher recovery rates in this area. The increasing trend over the last two recoveries for the yellow and orange generations may be explained by mobility instead. Most recovered tracers were located in the finer-grained lower segment of the study reach, where scaled values are effectively increased because $D_{90}$ declines downstream.

Rates at which gravel exchange attains characteristic burial depths are initially relatively high (Figure 5.6), reflecting the dominance of surface to subsurface exchange. Subsequent rates decline to about 0.01 cm per hour of competent flow as mean burial depths stabilize. That the T6 subreach in Allt Dubhaig plots below the general trend suggests vertical dispersion is attained quickly when scour and fill is limited. Scatter may be introduced by errors associated with tracer recovery and the fact that flow duration fails to fully capture the control of flood size.

The trends in scaled burial depth reported herein integrate the history of gravel exchanges in the channels because they include both active and passive exchanges. As such these depths extend beyond those derived from the active grain exchanges typically considered in flume and numerical experiments. The depth to which gravel is exchanged shows some evidence of reaching a limiting value, which is equivalent to about two grain diameters or less, even when considering passive exchange. The release of bedload supply (and subsequent deposition) embedded in the concept of partial sediment transport provides a key mechanism for gravel exchange. In channels with mobile bedforms, such as channel bars, exchange depth may be set by the vertical dimension of the bedform. More generally, scour and fill, whether linked to local imbalances in

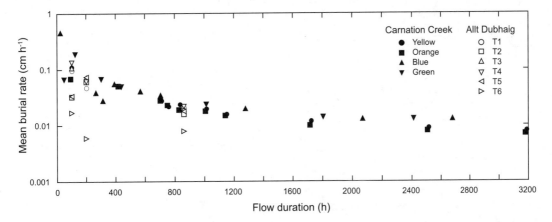

**Figure 5.6** Mean burial rates as a function of competent flow duration. Rates represent cumulative values and were calculated by dividing the mean burial depth at a given recovery by the total duration of competent flow up to that recovery. Burial depths for Allt Dubhaig adjusted as in Figure 5.5. Only long-term studies are shown.

bedload fluxes or change associated with moving bed-forms, defines the limits in which gravel exchange occurs in natural channels.

## 5.5  EXCHANGE AND SIZE SEGREGATION

Laboratory experiments and numerical models examining simple binary mixtures suggest that when a supply of relatively fine grains is introduced into a bed of coarser grains, the depth of their mixing is proportional to bed shear stress (Jiang and Haff, 1993) and that, at low feed rates, relatively fine grains form a nearly continuous layer toward the bottom of the sediment layers (Hergault et al., 2010). While the occurrence of granular processes that can sort grains has been documented for simple mixtures (e.g., Rosato et al., 1987; Félix and Thomas, 2004), it is unclear to what extent such processes operate in gravel bed rivers with their wide variability in grain size, shape, and packing. Previous field studies have discussed size-selective gravel exchange (e.g., Ferguson et al., 2002), but very few observations have been presented to fully quantify size effects.

How gravel exchange may contribute to size segregation is examined using observations from Carnation Creek. In terms of surface to subsurface exchange for mobile grains, finer gravels are mixed more extensively than coarser gravels (Figure 5.7). Further, an effect of flood size is evident in the systematically larger proportions for the larger flood. The extent of the exchange appears to be facilitated by the increased proportion of mobile grains and therefore reflects the state of partial transport, as might be expected.

Fractional exchange probabilities based on recovered tracers reveal that all four exchange pathways exhibit strong size-selective behaviour initially (Figure 5.8). Exchanges originating with surface grains show strong size effects over an extended period before merging to within 30%. In contrast, the strength of the size effect changes rapidly for gravels that originate from the sub-surface. Values merge to within 20% at around 700 hours,

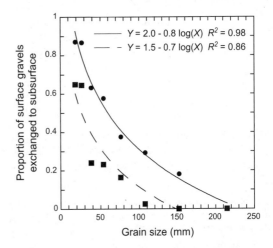

**Figure 5.7** Proportion of initial surface to subsurface exchange as a function of grain size in Carnation Creek. Circles indicate flood peak of $28.3 \, \text{m}^3 \, \text{s}^{-1}$ for blue generation and squares indicate maximum flood peak of $21.8 \, \text{m}^3 \, \text{s}^{-1}$ for green generation, which was followed by several smaller peaks less than half the magnitude. Only mobile tracers considered.

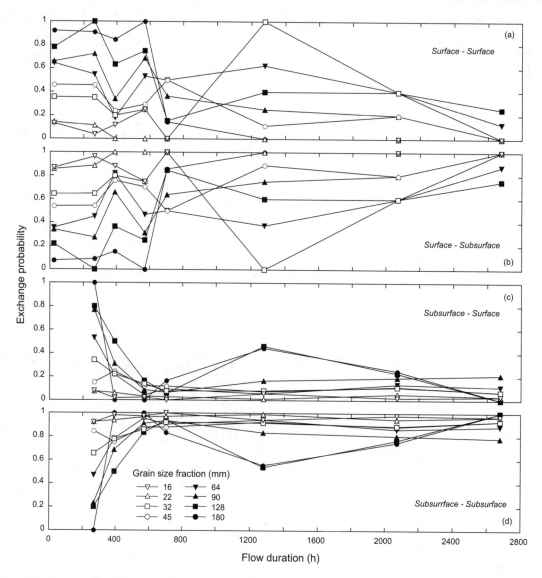

**Figure 5.8** Exchange probabilities for grain size fractions as a function of competent flow duration based on a two-layer model: (a) surface to surface, (b) surface to subsurface, (c) subsurface to surface, and (d) subsurface to subsurface. Half phi grain size fractions identified by lower limit. Observations based on recovered blue tracers in Carnation Creek.

except for the two largest fractions. Variability evident in the largest sizes reflects small sample sizes and localized aggradation that causes burial of most of the large tracers still residing near the deployment area.

Initial burial rates show a clear size effect; size fractions near or less than the median diameter of surface sediment are buried faster than coarser grains (Figure 5.9). However, the range of rates decreases significantly by the end of the first flood season (~270 hours of competent flow), indicating that the largest part of the vertical mixing process has been accomplished based on the flood

characteristics. Rates merge to within a small range after 700 hours and eventually decline to 0.01 cmh$^{-1}$, a rate that persists for the remaining floods.

These fractional results highlight a strong grain size effect for surface grains that are actively exchanged into the subsurface, with the extent depending on flood size. When both active and passive exchanges are considered over time, the strength of fractional size segregation declines substantially for a given population of surface grains, as expressed by exchange probabilities and rates of burial. Thus, understanding size segregation in natural

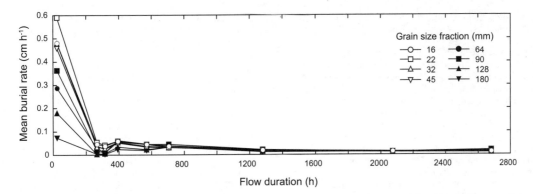

**Figure 5.9** Mean burial rates for individual grain size fractions as a function of competent flow duration. Half phi grain size fractions identified by lower limit. Values based on recovered blue tracers in Carnation Creek.

channels should account for both active and passive exchanges.

## 5.6 CONCLUSIONS

The results and discussion underscore the general tendency that bedload intensities typically observed in gravel bed rivers routinely involve the vertical exchange of gravels. Gravel transport is not a pure surface phenomenon, even at low transport intensities, and a comprehensive understanding must successfully couple surface and subsurface processes and take into account size-selective behaviour. While some tendencies in gravel exchange have been highlighted for natural channels, explanation for differences between rivers is partial at best. Further studies are needed that conduct critical tests of the relation between partial transport, characteristic bed sediments, and bed adjustment to establish a general view of gravel exchange in natural channels.

## 5.7 ACKNOWLEDGEMENTS

Field data were generously shared by Mike Church, Rob Ferguson, Marwan Hassan, John Pitlick, and Steve Rice. Research in Carnation Creek has been supported by grants from the Natural Sciences and Engineering Research Council of Canada (awarded to M. Church), Geological Society of America, University of Auckland Research Committee, and National Geographic Society (USA). The British Columbia Ministry of Forests operates the Carnation Creek field station.

## 5.8 REFERENCES

Carling, P.A. 1987. Bed stability in gravel streams, with reference to stream regulation and ecology. In Richards, K.S. editor. *River Channels: Environment and Process*. Oxford, Institute of British Geographers Special Publications Series no. 17, pp. 321–347.

Church, M.A., McLean, D.G., and Wolcott, J.F. 1987. River bed gravels: sampling and analysis. In Thorne, C.R., Bathurst, J.C.,and Hey, R, D., editors. *Sediment Transport in Gravel-bed Rivers*. Chichester, John Wiley & Sons Ltd., pp. 43–88.

DeVries, P. 2002. Bedload layer thickness and disturbance depth in gravel bed streams. *Journal of Hydraulic Engineering* **128**: 983–991.

Félix G. and Thomas, N. 2004. Evidence of two effects in the size segregation process in dry granular media. *Physical Review E* **70**: 051307.

Ferguson, R. and Ashworth, P. 1991. Slope-induced changes in channel character along a gravel-bed stream: the Allt Dubhaig, Scotland. *Earth Surface Processes and Landforms* **16**: 65–82.

Ferguson, R.I. and Wathen, S.J. 1998. Tracer-pebble movement along a concave river profile: virtual velocity in relation to grain size and shear stress. *Water Resources Research* **34**: 2031–2038.

Ferguson, R.I. and Hoey, T.B. 2002. Long-term slowdown of river tracer pebbles: generic models and implications for interpreting short-term tracer studies. *Water Resources Research* **38**, 1142. doi: 10.1029/2001WR000637.

Ferguson, R.I., Bloomer, D.J., Hoey, T.B., and Werritty, A. 2002. Mobility of river tracer pebbles over different time-scales. *Water Resources Research* **38**: 1045. doi: 10.1029/2001WR000254.

Gintz, D., Hassan, M.A., and Schmidt, K-H. 1996. Frequency and magnitude of bedload transport in a mountain river. *Earth Surface Processes and Landforms* **21**: 433–445.

Haschenburger, J.K. 1996. *Scour and fill in a gravel-bed channel: observations and stochastic models*. Ph.D. Thesis, University of British Columbia, Vancouver.

Haschenburger, J.K. 1999. A probability model of scour and fill depths in gravel-bed channels. *Water Resources Research* **35**: 2857–2869.

Haschenburger, J.K. 2011. Vertical mixing of gravel over a long flood series. *Earth Surface Processes and Landforms* **36**: 1044–4058.

Haschenburger, J.K. and Church, M. 1998. Bed material transport estimated from the virtual velocity of sediment. *Earth Surface Processes and Landforms* **23**: 791–808.

Haschenburger, J, K., Rice S.P., and Voyde, E. 2007. Evaluation of bulk sediment sampling criteria for gravel-bed rivers. *Journal of Sedimentary Research* **77**: 415–43.

Hassan, M.A. 1990. Scour, fill, and burial depth of coarse material in gravel bed streams. *Earth Surface Processes and Landforms* **15**: 341–356.

Hassan, M.A. and Church, M. 1992. The movement of individual grains on the streambed. In Billi, P., Hey, R.D., Thorne, C.R., and Tacconi, P. editors. *Dynamics of Gravel-bed Rivers*. Chichester, John Wiley & Sons Ltd, pp. 159–175.

Hassan, M.A. and Church, M. 1994. Vertical mixing of coarse particles in gravel bed rivers: a kinematic model. *Water Resources Research* **30**: 1173–1185.

Hergault, V., Frey, P., Métivier, F. *et al.* 2010. Image processing for the study of bedload transport of two-size spherical particles in a supercritical flow. *Experiments in Fluids* **49**. doi: 10.1007/s00248-010-0856-6.

Jiang, Z. 1995. The motion of sediment-water mixtures during intense bedload transport: computer simulation. *Sedimentology* **42**: 935–945.

Jiang, Z. and Haff, P.K. 1993. Multiparticle simulation methods applied to the micromechanics of bed load transport. *Water Resources Research* **29**: 399–412.

Kuhnle, R.A. 1993. Fluvial transport of sand and gravel mixtures with bimodal size distributions. *Sedimentary Geology* **85**: 17–24.

Lenzi, M.A. 2004. Displacement and transport of marked pebbles, cobbles and boulders during floods in a steep mountain stream. *Hydrological Processes* **18**: 1899–1914.

Nikora, V., Habersack, H., Huber, T. and McEwan, I. 2002. On bed particle diffusion in gravel bed flows under weak bed load transport. *Water Resources Research* **38**: 1081. doi: 10.1029/2001WR000513

Parker, G. 1990. Surface-based bedload transport relation for gravel rivers. *Journal of Hydraulic Research* **28**: 417–436.

Parker, G. and Klingeman, P.C. 1982. On why gravel bed streams are paved. *Water Resources Research* **18**: 1409–1423.

Roest, P. 2005. *Observations and predictions of porosity in gravel bed channels*. M.Sc. Thesis, University of Auckland, Auckland.

Rosato, A., Strandburg, K.J., Prinz, F. and Swendsen, R.H. 1987. Why the brazil nuts are on top: size segregation of particulate matter by shaking. *Physical Review Letters* **58**: 1038–1040.

Schick, A.P., Hassan, M.A., and Lekach, J. 1987. A vertical exchange model for coarse bedload movement: numerical considerations. *Catena* (supplement) **10**: 73–83.

Sumer, B.M., Kozakiewicz, A., Fredsoe, J. and Deigaard, R. 1996. Velocity and concentration profiles in sheet-flow layer of movable bed. *Journal of Hydraulic Engineering* **122**: 549–558.

Thomas, N. 2000. Reverse and intermediate segregation of large beads in dry granular media. *Physical Review E* **62**: 961–974.

Trafford, J. 1999. *Bedload transport at Kanakanaia, Waipaoa River, New Zealand*. M.Sc. Thesis, University of Auckland, Auckland.

Wilcock, P.R. 1992. Experimental investigation of the effect of mixture properties on transport dynamics. In Billi, P., Hey, R.D., Thorne, C.R.,and Tacconi, P. editors. *Dynamics of Gravel-Bed Rivers*. Chichester, John Wiley & Sons Ltd, pp. 109–130.

Wilcock, P.R. 1997. The components of fractional transport rate. *Water Resources Research* **33**: 247–258.

Wilcock, P.R. and McArdell, B.W. 1997. Partial transport of a sand/gravel sediment. *Water Resources Research* **33**: 235–245.

Wilcock, P.R. and DeTemple, B.T. 2005. Persistence of armor layers in gravel-bed streams. *Geophysical Research Letters* **32**: L08402. doi: 10.1029/2004GL021772.

Wilcock, P.R., Kenworthy, S.T. and Crowe J. C. 2001. Experimental study of the transport of mixed sand and gravel. *Water Resources Research* **37**: 3349–3358.

Wilcock, P.R., Barta, A.F., Shea, C.C., Kondolf, G.M., Matthews, W.V.G. and Pitlick, J. 1996. Observations of flow and sediment entrainment on a large gravel-bed river. *Water Resources Research* **32**: 2897–2909.

Wong, M., Parker, G., DeVries, P., Brown, T.M. and Burges, S.J. 2007. Experiments on dispersion of tracer stones under lower-regime plane-bed equilibrium bed load transport. *Water Resources Research* **43**: W03440. doi: 10.1029/2006WR005172.

Wooster, J.K., Dusterhoff, S.R., Cui, Y. *et al.* 2008. Sediment supply and relative size distribution effects on fine sediment infiltration into immobile gravels. *Water Resources Research* **44**: W03424. doi: 10.1029/2006WR005815.

## 5.9    DISCUSSION

### 5.9.1    Discussion by David Milan

Haschenburger in her discussion successfully applies Schick's conceptual model of clast exchange processes to explain the vertical evolution of tracer clasts in the bed at Carnation Creek, Canada, and Allt Dubhaig, Scotland. It is to be expected that the fate of individual clasts is strongly influenced by the depositional loci, with tracers deposited on bars being stored *in situ* for longer periods in comparison to those deposited in the submerged channel. The Allt Dubhaig study site shows strong downstream fining, and also marked changes in channel typology, with a pseudo-braided reach with mid-channel bars at the upstream end and a meandering reach with pool-riffle bedforms and point bars further downstream. The fate of clasts deposited on a mid-channel bar may differ somewhat from those deposited on a point bar. Clasts deposited on top of the point bar during high stage conditions may become inactive if subsequently buried and if the bar is aggrading outwards (away from the depositional loci of the tracer). The inner edge of the bar will become stabilized over time and vegetated, further reducing the possibility of remobilization of any buried clast. Conversely, clasts deposited on mid-channel bars are more likely to stay active, as long as the bars are in the active part of the channel width. It would be interesting to know whether any reach-to-reach differences in the nature of the vertical exchange mechanism had been detected in the Allt Dubhaig data.

### 5.9.2    Reply by Judy Haschenburger

The discussion raises an interesting point about the details of vertical exchange associated with channel-bar dynamics. Although distinguishing vertical exchange mechanisms by bar type in Allt Dubhaig cannot be established with the available dataset, some comments can be offered based on the 1999 recovery data where the depositional environment of tracers was noted. The downstream trend in channel morphology is well described (see Ferguson and Ashworth, 1991), but based on tracer observations, a mutually exclusive division of bar types between the subreaches does not exist. By 1999, tracers were distributed in medial bars from T1 through T5, except for T3, in side bars from T1 through T6, and in point bars from T2 through T6, with the number in medial bars the smallest. If only the subreaches where tracers were found in all three bar types are considered, which controls for grain mobility given downstream changes in flow shear stress and bed material, there is no significant difference in mean burial depths across bar types at a 0.05 significance level, but the result is marginal (one-way ANOVA, $p$-value $= 0.06$). Additionally, tracers stored in bars that were stationary between 1993 and 1999 show larger mean depths than those that had moved to a bar by the end of the period, although the depths for side and point bars, where sufficient replication exists, are identical ($20 \pm 1$ cm versus $21 \pm 1$ cm). Although these results hint at the possibility that type-specific bar dynamics affect patterns of vertical exchange, no causal link has been established between tracer position and residence time, and bar evolution. During the tracer field experiment, broad patterns of aggradation were documented by cross-sectional survey (see Ferguson and Wathen, 1998; Ferguson et al., 2002) but no detailed analysis of bar mobility was completed (R. Ferguson, pers. comm., 2011). Ferguson and Ashworth (1991) speculated that patterns in volumetric rates of channel change may reflect bedload transfers that differ based on channel bar mobility, but the temporal resolution of the results prevented a definitive conclusion on the matter. Collectively, these facts make it difficult to assign a specific mechanism for the vertical distribution of gravels in Allt Dubhaig; burial depths could be related to bars as sediment storage units, different dynamics of the bar types, or general patterns of channel aggradation. There is a need to more fully connect vertical exchange processes to streambed adjustment, which should include coupling tracer position and mobility to documented bar evolution. The experimental work on point bars by Pyrce and Ashmore (2005) could serve as an effective baseline from which to further investigate the problem.

## 5.10   DISCUSSION REFERENCES

Ferguson, R. and Ashworth, P. 1991. Slope-induced changes in channel character along a gravel-bed stream: the Allt Dubhaig, Scotland. *Earth Surface Processes and Landforms* **16**: 65–82.

Ferguson, R.I. and Wathen S.J. 1998. Tracer-pebble movement along a concave river profile: virtual velocity in relation to grain size and shear stress. *Water Resources Research* **34**: 2031–2038.

Ferguson, R.I., Bloomer, D.J., Hoey, T.B., and Werritty, A. 2002. Mobility of river tracer pebbles over different timescales. *Water Resources Research* **38**: 1045. doi: 10.1029/2001WR000254.

Pyrce, R.S. and Ashmore, P.E. 2005. Bedload path length and point bar development in gravel-bed river models. *Sedimentology* **52**: 839–857.

# Modelling Morphodynamics

# 6

# Morphodynamics of Bars in Gravel-bed Rivers: Bridging Analytical Models and Field Observations

## Guido Zolezzi, Walter Bertoldi, and Marco Tubino

## 6.1 INTRODUCTION

Understanding the morphodynamics of river bars is relevant for both scientific and practical reasons. Bars were early recognized as basic fundamental units of alluvial streams that repeat themselves along river corridors, albeit with varying degrees of regularity, across different fluvial morphologies. Bars therefore represent key observational features for understanding the dynamics of alluvial channel patterns. Practical interest in the study of bars has often related to the need to control their development and migration in river systems, with the aim of improving navigation and preventing structural damage or undesired channel shift. Only recently, emerging paradigms in river management increasingly recognize the relevance of bars for several physical and biogeochemical processes that are essential for sustaining a variety of river ecosystem functions (Gurnell *et al.*, 2001; Marzadri *et al.*, 2010).

Bars play an essential role in the morphodynamics of gravel bed rivers through bedform–planform interactions governed by mutual feedback processes. The present knowledge of bar morphodynamics results from a combination of field and laboratory observations, and mathematical models. A considerable number of theoretical and laboratory-scale models have been proposed in the last half century to understand bar dynamics in alluvial channels and to predict their main properties based on reach-averaged channel characteristics (e.g. Jaeggi, 1984; Colombini *et al.*, 1987; Tubino *et al.*, 1999; Lanzoni, 2000). Within the modelling literature, a major contribution to process understanding has been made by adopting a specific class of mathematical models that are named "analytical" because they provide closed-form approximate solutions of the complete system of differ-

ential governing equations for water and sediment flow. To this end they necessarily rely on a series of simplifying assumptions, whilst retaining the key physical effects. In past decades this facilitated process understanding through analytical solutions requiring negligible computational time. One of the major achievements in this sense has been detecting the fundamental instability governing bar development, analogous to that characterizing smaller-scale bedforms. Despite their simplifying assumptions, analytical models have effectively been used to predict typical spatial scales and to facilitate physical insight into basic processes governing channel pattern selection and bedform–planform interactions.

On the other hand, as argued by Church and Rice (2009), field studies on medium-term bar dynamics are relatively few, if compared to the vast modelling literature (but see Welford, 1994; Hooke, 2009). This is probably due to the long observational period required to include multiple channel-forming events in order to capture the features of bar dynamics at the proper timescale.

The aim of this chapter is to bridge theoretical and field observations on bars in gravel bed rivers by reviewing recent theoretical developments and applying existing analytical models to alluvial rivers with different planform morphologies. Strictly speaking, analytical models have been formulated with reference to single-thread streams with fully transporting cross-sections. Here we aim to explore the broader applicability of analytical models for river bars, which includes a wide spectrum of channel morphologies, from straight, to meandering and braiding. Together with a systematic effort to frame model predictions within field data from natural streams, this represents the main novel feature with respect to previous work.

*Gravel-bed Rivers: Processes, Tools, Environments*, First Edition. Edited by Michael Church, Pascale M. Biron and André G. Roy.
© 2012 John Wiley & Sons, Ltd. Published 2012 by John Wiley & Sons, Ltd.

The paper first reviews the key assumptions, structure, and solution approaches of an established class of analytical models of bar morphodynamics, also with the aim of introducing the typical terminology that is employed by these models (Section 6.2). Then, applications of analytical models to single-and multiple-thread rivers are used to illustrate to what extent these models can effectively predict bar dynamics in real streams and their interaction with the planform morphology (Sections 6.3 and 6.4). The concluding Section 6.5 finally discusses the key ingredients for effective model applications, along with the main open issues that need to be addressed in future research.

## 6.2 ANALYTICAL MODELS OF BARS IN GRAVEL BED RIVERS: FORMULATION, TERMINOLOGY, AND SOLUTION APPROACH

Mathematical modelling of bar morphodynamics in single-thread channels is commonly achieved through the approximate solution of the depth-averaged momentum equations and continuity equations for water and sediment flows, along with appropriate closure relations that relate sediment transport rate and friction to local flow properties. Such a depth-averaged approach, properly accounting for 3-D effects with vanishing depth-averages (secondary flows) through curvature-based parameterization, has been demonstrated, by a variety of studies, to be appropriate to investigate bar morphodynamics when effective sediment transport mostly occurs

as bedload (e.g. Colombini *et al.*, 1987; Schielen *et al.*, 1993; Garcia and Nino, 1993; Tubino *et al.*, 1999).

Bar models are commonly based on a series of simplifying assumptions with the aim of focusing on the fundamental morphodynamic processes, while keeping the mathematical problem amenable to analytical treatment. It is often assumed that the channel is fed by a representative constant value of discharge, the grain size is uniform, and the sediment transport mainly occurs as bedload at a rate that is in equilibrium with the stream transport capacity. The effects of flow unsteadiness (Tubino, 1991), grain size heterogeneity (Lanzoni and Tubino, 1999) and suspended load (Tubino *et al.*, 1999; Federici and Seminara, 2006) have also been investigated within the same class of analytical bar models, although they will not be discussed in detail within the present work.

The governing mathematical system, for the general case of a single-thread channel with spatially varying channel width and curvature (see Figure 6.1) can be cast in the following dimensionless form:

$$U^* \frac{\partial U^*}{\partial s^*} + V^* \frac{\partial U^*}{\partial n^*} + \frac{\partial H^*}{\partial s^*} + \beta \frac{\tau_s^*}{D^*} = v f_{10}^* + v^2 f_{20}^* + \delta f_{01}^* + v \delta f_{11}^*$$

(6.1)

$$U^* \frac{\partial V^*}{\partial s^*} + V^* \frac{\partial V^*}{\partial n^*} + \frac{\partial H^*}{\partial n^*} + \beta \frac{\tau_n^*}{D^*} = v g_{10}^* + v^2 g_{20}^* + \delta g_{01}^* + v \delta g_{11}^*$$

(6.2)

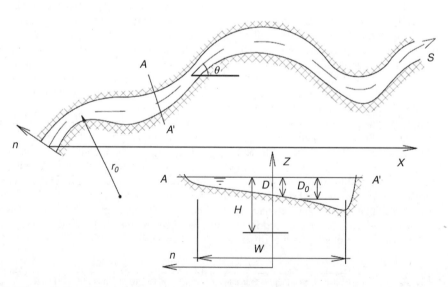

**Figure 6.1**  Mathematical notations.

$$\frac{\partial (D^* U^*)}{\partial s^*} + \frac{\partial (D^* V^*)}{\partial n^*} = v m_{10}^* + + \delta m_{01}^* \qquad (6.3)$$

$$(1-p)\frac{\partial \eta^*}{\partial t^*} + \left[\frac{\partial q_s^*}{\partial s^*} + \frac{\partial q_s^*}{\partial n^*}\right] = v n_{10}^* + \delta n_{01}^* \qquad (6.4)$$

Each dimensionless variable, which we denote by a star (*), is obtained from its dimensional correspondent by normalizing it with a representative value. These scaling quantities are typically reach-averaged parameters: the reach-averaged channel width $W_0$ for the streamwise and transverse coordinates $(s,n)$, the reach-averaged water depth $D_0$ for the local water depth and free surface elevation $(D,H)$ and the reach-averaged flow velocity $U_0$ for the depth-averaged velocity field $(U,V)$ (see also sketch in Figure 6.1). We note that the reach-averaged channel width is adopted as the normalizing factor for the planimetric coordinates because bar morphology actually displays relevant horizontal variations at this scale. When spatial width variations are accounted for, the local width $W$ (instead of its reach-averaged value) is used to stretch the spanwise coordinate $n$.

In Equations (6.1–6.4) $\eta^* = H^* - D^*$ is the local bed surface level and $p$ is sediment porosity. Furthermore

$$\beta = \frac{W_0}{D_0}, v = \frac{W_0}{r_0}, \delta = \frac{W_{\max} - W_0}{W_0} \qquad (6.5)$$

are the reach-averaged values of the width–depth ratio and the dimensionless amplitudes of the longitudinal variations of channel curvature and width, respectively, with $r_0$ representing a typical measure of bend curvature radius and $W_{\max}$ the maximum width. The above spatial variations of channel geometry are in general assumed to

be sufficiently regular and therefore amenable to Fourier representation.

Finally, $(\tau_s^*, \tau_n^*)$ is the bottom stress vector and $(q_s^*, q_n^*)$ is the bedload vector. The former is modelled as aligned with the near bed velocity vector and expressed in terms of a local friction coefficient $C_f$; the latter is assumed to be determined by local flow conditions together with gravity effects (Talmon et al., 1995) that deviate the sediment particle trajectory from the direction of the mean bottom stress (the standard Einstein scaling is adopted for sediment transport). The above closures introduce two further dimensionless parameters:

$$\tau_* = \frac{F_0^2 C_f}{\Delta d_s}|U^*|^2, d_s = \frac{d}{D_0} \qquad (6.6)$$

that represent the reach-averaged values of the Shields stress and of the relative roughness, respectively, with $\Delta$ denoting the relative submerged density, $d$ the mean sediment diameter, and $F_0$ the reach-averaged Froude number.

We note that time variability in Equations (6.1–6.4) is restricted to the bed level $\eta^*$, since time derivatives of flow quantities have been omitted, assuming that flow almost instantaneously adapts to bed variations. Therefore the time scaling is set by the Exner equation. Furthermore, typical boundary conditions for Equations (6.1–6.4) set the impermeability of lateral walls to both flow and sediments:

$$(U^*, V^*) \cdot \mathbf{n_b^*} = (q_s^*, q_n^*) \cdot \mathbf{n_b^*} = 0 \text{ at the banks} \qquad (6.7)$$

with the $\mathbf{n_b^*}$ unit vector normal to the bank lines. Implicit in the above procedure is the assumption that channel

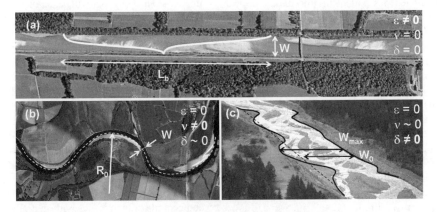

**Figure 6.2** Illustrative sketch of: (a) alternate bar geometry in a rectified river reach (the Rhine River in Liechtenstein, image from Google Earth); (b) nearly constant width meander geometry (Adda River, Italy, image from Google Earth); (c) straight channel with regular width oscillations (Dora di Veny, NW Italy, the authors). Each case is illustrative of a reference analytical problem where only one of the three perturbation parameters (respectively $\varepsilon$; $v$; $\delta$) is nonvanishing. Reproduced, with permission, from Google Corporation. (See the color version of this figure in color plate section.)

banks are fixed, at least when solving the morphodynamic model at the time scale that is relevant for bed processes, which implies that bank and bed evolution can be decoupled. It is worth noting that assuming the bed configuration to adapt instantaneously to changing river shape has been set as a basic hypothesis for most theoretical models proposed so far to investigate the planform development of single-thread channels (e.g. Howard, 1992; Seminara et al., 2001).

The resulting depth-averaged morphodynamic model cannot be solved analytically, i.e., in closed form, because of its mathematical complexity. Therefore, two options are commonly pursued: numerical solutions of the full governing system or approximate analytical solutions that can be obtained in nearly closed form when the physics of the process suggests reasonable simplifying assumptions that enable one to use perturbation techniques. However obtained, the solution of the above model allows us to compute the time-variable bed configuration and flow field in curvilinear channels with variable width, given reach-averaged values of the dimensionless parameters (Equations 6.5, 6.6). Details on the derivation of the system (6.1–6.4) as well as the complex algebraic expression of the functions ($f_{ij}$, $g_{ij}$, $m_{ij}$, $p_{ij}$) are reported in Luchi (2009).

River bars have been classified as *free* or *forced* (Seminara and Tubino, 1989), this terminology having a precise physical and mathematical meaning. *Free* bars are those forming spontaneously in almost straight reaches or laboratory flumes as a consequence of the inherent instability of the flow-cohesionless bed system. Bars are *forced* when they arise from some physical constraint that may be exerted by the river shape or by local effects. Mathematically free bars appear as solutions of the homogeneous part of the morphodynamic problem, expressed by the left-hand side of Equations (6.1–6.4), while the forcing effect of curvature and width variation is expressed by the right-hand side of the governing system.

As pointed out before, a broad class of analytical bar models is based on solutions obtained through perturbation methods, which allow us to seek approximate, asymptotic solutions of mathematical problems when the physics significantly depends on one or more key small parameter (e.g. Holmes, 1995). One of the advantages of analytical solutions is that they allow very easy distinction between the various types of bars, and therefore focus on the key physical effects controlling their dynamics. Figure 6.2 qualitatively illustrates the three small parameters relevant to bar morphodynamics.

The parameter $\varepsilon$ is the theoretically infinitesimal amplitude of *free* bars that can also develop in the absence of geometrical constraints (when $v = \delta = 0$).

Typical examples are the regular trains of alternate bars developing in reaches that have been artificially straightened, as in the Liechtenstein reach of the Rhine River (Figure 6.2a). The mathematical expression for the morphological structure of free bars, at the leading order of approximation in $\varepsilon$, is as follows:

$$\eta^* = \eta_0^* + \underbrace{\varepsilon \cdot \eta_1^*}_{\text{amplitude}} \times \underbrace{\exp[(\lambda s^* + \omega t^*)]}_{\text{long. and temporal structure}}$$

$$\times \underbrace{\sin\left(\frac{\pi}{2} m y^*\right)}_{\text{lateral structure}} + c.c., \tag{6.8}$$

where the exponential notation for cosine functions is employed, *c.c.* denoting the conjugate of a complex number and

$$\lambda = \lambda_{re} + i\lambda_{im}, \quad \omega = \omega_{re} + i\omega_{im} \tag{6.9}$$

are complex numbers representing key bar properties: (i) the longitudinal wavelength of bars $L_b = \frac{2\pi}{\lambda_{im}}$; (ii) the spatial damping of bars, $\lambda_{re}$; (iii) the temporal growth/decay rate of the bar amplitude, $\omega_{re}$, and (iv) bar migration speed, $\omega_{im}$. The transverse structure of bar morphology (alternate, central, multiple) is expressed by the number of bars $m$ laterally developing in the channel. Several stability analyses of the homogeneous system (Colombini et al., 1987) have demonstrated the existence of an inherent instability of the flow-cohesionless bed system which produces bar-like bed patterns, provided the width–depth ratio $\beta$ is larger than a threshold value falling in the range 10–20 that depends on the reach-averaged hydraulic conditions.

The other two small parameters ($v$ and $\delta$) define the magnitude of planform non-uniformities that force the altimetric and flow response at different orders of approximations. The $i$ $j$th order will be denoted by the notation $O$ ($v^i \delta^j$). The forcing terms are basically of two types. The forcing effect of curvature is due to both linear $O(v)$ and non-linear $O(v^2)$ terms that would also appear in meandering channels with constant width. Channel width variations force the system in the form of a first-order contribution $O(\delta)$ that coincides with that corresponding to a straight channel with variable width. Moreover the $O(v\delta)$ term represents mixed forcing due to width and curvature variations, an effect which therefore is only present in meandering channels with longitudinal width variations. The values of $v$ and $\delta$ are therefore associated with the amplitude of bars forced by geometrical constraints, like point bars in meander bends, forced by channel curvature, and central bars in reaches with spatial width variations. These bars are steady, because they remain fixed with respect to the channel planform itself ($\omega = 0$).

Free and forced bars interact with each other when channel curvature and/or width vary in space. Kinoshita and Miwa (1974) experimentally investigated the interplay between migrating bars and a weakly meandering planform. Above a threshold curvature, bars cannot migrate further and are turned into steady point bars, having the same wavelength as the meandering channel. Analytical modelling has subsequently reproduced quantitatively free-forced interactions in meanders with constant width (Tubino and Seminara, 1990), as well as in straight reaches with regular width oscillations, where they are eventually turned into steady central bars, possibly triggering channel bifurcation (Repetto and Tubino, 1999).

## 6.3 MORPHODYNAMICS OF STEADY BARS IN SINGLE-THREAD CHANNELS

*Steady point* bars in river meanders are probably the most popular type of forced bars that have been investigated theoretically in past decades (Seminara, 2006; Camporeale *et al.*, 2007). They present an alternate bar morphology and their amplitude is reasonably constant in space, provided the planform forcing is also spatially regular. Because steady bars do not move relative to the channel planform, they determine persistent scour and topographic steering of flow with respect to the banks, thus being much more effective than migrating bars in affecting the planform dynamics.

Theoretical developments have also embraced a broader class of steady bar morphologies, focusing on their effect on the planform evolution of single-thread channels. Spatially damped alternate bars, also occurring in straight reaches (Struiksma *et al.*, 1985; Mosselman *et al.*, 2006) have been interpreted as the topographic expression of the phenomenon of 2-D morphodynamic influence (Zolezzi and Seminara, 2001a). Moreover the occurrence of forced mid-channel (instead of point) bars in meander bends has been analytically modelled (Luchi *et al.*, 2010b) in the light of their dynamic role in connection with the spatial oscillations of channel width, a typical feature of transitional channel morphologies between meandering and braiding. The aim of the present section is therefore to review these recent theoretical developments and to relate them to data from natural gravel bed rivers. This exercise illustrates to what extent applications of analytical bar models can support process understanding and physical insight into the morphodynamics of single-thread gravel bed streams.

### 6.3.1 Alternate Bars and Morphodynamic Influence

Permanent forcing effects on bar morphodynamics can be of two major types: localized or distributed in space. Steady bars related to localized discontinuities in channel geometry are damped in the longitudinal direction, unlike, for instance, point bars in meanders that are associated with the continuous forcing role of curvature (in space). What has been recently called "2-D morphodynamic influence" (Zolezzi and Seminara, 2001a) is the phenomenon whereby a localized perturbation in river planform geometry makes itself felt several widths upstream or downstream through spatially damped bars. The geometric disturbance can be a discontinuity in channel curvature or localized channel narrowing. Because these bars are typically much longer than their migrating counterparts (up to 20 times bankfull width), morphodynamic influence can affect bank erosion and planform evolution at relatively great distances from the disturbance location. A typical example is the so called "overdeepening" or "overshoot" phenomenon associated with downstream (Struiksma *et al.*, 1985) and upstream (Zolezzi and Seminara, 2001b, Zolezzi *et al.*, 2005) damped steady bars.

The channel aspect ratio $\beta$ controls whether this phenomenon occurs predominantly upstream or downstream from the disturbance location. Upstream influence takes place only when $\beta$ falls above a threshold value (relatively shallow and wide channels), while downstream influence is dominant in deeper and narrower channels. The threshold aspect ratio is determined by reach-averaged conditions and it is termed resonant since it coincides with the value $\beta_R$ of Blondeaux and Seminara (1985) that defines the theoretical conditions at which the linear $O(\nu)$ solution exhibits a resonant behaviour. The value $\beta_R$ separates two distinct regimes of morphodynamic influence, which are therefore called super-resonant and sub-resonant, respectively. Geometrical disturbances, related to both anthropogenic and natural factors, may therefore affect planform evolution at very different locations along the stream depending on whether its regime is sub- or super-resonant. Such a picture has been theoretically and experimentally confirmed, but a close correspondence with field observations is still missing. Also of practical relevance is understanding which factors may control whether a single-thread stream is sub- or super-resonant, and to what extent these controls are autogenic or allogenic.

To this end Zolezzi *et al.* (2009b) explored the predictions of the analytical steady bar model of Zolezzi and Seminara (2001a) applied to a bankfull dataset consisting of more than 100 single-thread gravel bed river reaches (Parker *et al.*, 2007). Figure 6.3 shows the ratio $\beta/\beta_R$ between the actual bankfull aspect ratio and its resonant value computed with bankfull characteristics of every reach in the dataset. This ratio can be interpreted as a measure of the relative distance of the reach from resonant conditions. The apparently sparse cloud of points reveals a consistent trend with the bankfull value of the Shields stress $\tau_*$: black triangles represent the average $\beta/\beta_R$ value over all reaches with $\tau_*$ belonging to adjacent, equal intervals with spacing $\Delta\tau_* = 0.02$. A shift

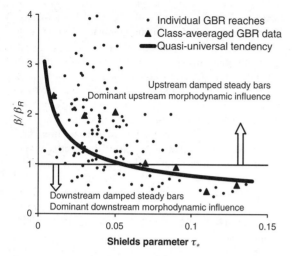

**Figure 6.3** Relative distance from resonant conditions for a large number of gravel bed single-thread river reaches (small dots); average values for reaches with bankfull Shields stress $\tau_*$ falling into equally spaced intervals ($\Delta\tau_* = 0.02$, black triangles); quasi-universal tendency of 2-D morphodynamic influence for single-thread alluvial gravel bed rivers (continuous line). Based on Zolezzi et al. (2009b).

from super- to sub-resonant conditions clearly appears when moving from reaches with lower bankfull values of $\tau_*$ to higher. This would imply that localized geometric disturbances in gravel bed rivers with bankfull Shields stress close to the critical value for bedload movement can also cause significant planform alteration in the upstream direction. The associated damped steady bars would instead develop only downstream of the disturbance location when the bankfull $\tau_*$ is closer to 0.1 or higher. Such a trend is consistent with the quasi-universal relation (continuous line) that can be derived for $\beta/\beta_R$ using the bankfull predictor proposed by Parker et al. (2007).

The above outcomes provide insight into which factors may control the regime of 2-D morphodynamic influence of a single-thread gravel-bed river reach. Inspection of the environmental characteristics of the reaches in the dataset indicates that the upstream influence (= super-resonant regime) is predicted for streams with relatively high sediment supply, poorly vegetated and low-cohesion channel banks, which are typically associated with relatively shallow and wide channels. Moreover, larger values of the relative roughness and lower values of the Shields stress tend to reduce the resonant value $\beta_R$, thus resulting in $\beta/\beta_R > 1$. To the extent that the above features can be considered intrinsic properties of gravel bed channels, this would imply an inherent, or autogenic

tendency of gravel bed streams to behave super-resonantly, which causes the morphodynamic effects of localized disturbances to be felt several channel widths upstream of their location.

### 6.3.2 Mid-Channel Bars and Channel Width Variations in Meanders

Mid-channel or central bars often appear as distinctive and significant elements of gravel bed meandering channels (Hooke, 1986; Knighton, 1972), although their dynamics have been much less studied in comparison with those associated with the point bar morphology. Contrary to point bars, they are associated with a symmetrical cross-sectional profile. Mid-channel bars may sometimes evolve into vegetated islands and are often associated with spatial oscillations of the channel width (Zolezzi et al., 2009a). Insight into the related physical processes can also contribute to a better understanding of the morphodynamics of transitional morphologies (wandering) between meandering and braiding.

Relatively few field observations are available, and a first mechanistic model for the development of mid-channel bars in single-thread, meandering rivers has been proposed only recently by Luchi et al. (2010b), on the basis of the theoretical framework presented in Section 6.2. Based on existing field and experimental observations, and on the recent field analysis by Luchi et al. (2010a), two different forcing mechanisms have been proposed to be responsible for central topographical patterns in meanders, respectively forced by the spatial oscillations of bankfull channel curvature and width. The width-forced mechanism had already been modelled by Repetto et al. (2002) in straight channels: at a linear level – $O(\delta)$ – it produces a laterally symmetrical bed shear stress pattern that promotes mid-channel bars close to the widest section. The curvature-forced mechanism can produce mid-channel bars also in equiwidth meandering streams, but a non-linear model – $O(v^2)$ – is required to reproduce the associated laterally symmetrical alterations of the sediment transport capacity.

Referring to natural river systems, however, it is not straightforward to understand which of the two mechanisms can be dominant in a given river reach. Here an attempt in this direction is proposed, with reference to Figure 6.4. The analytical model for mid-channel bars proposed by Luchi et al. (2010b) is applied to two meander bends (displayed in the left-hand side of the diagram) taken from the analyses of Hooke (1986) and Knighton (1972) on the rivers Dane and Dean, respectively. Hooke (1986) made a systematic study of the dynamics of mid-channel bars in several meander bends of the River Dane, observing that bar deposition mostly occurred in downstream parts of developing bends and in

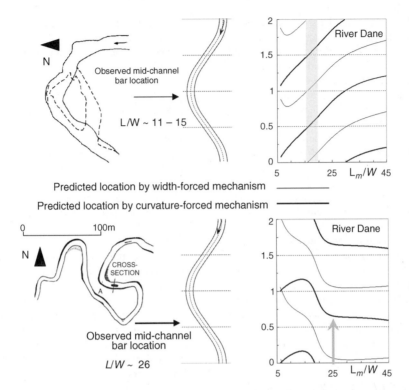

**Figure 6.4**  Predicted mid-channel bar locations in the reaches of the River Dane (upper panel) and of the River Dean (lower panel). Heavy lines refer to curvature-forced mid-channel bars, while light lines correspond to width-forced bars. In both cases the wavelength ranges and values corresponding to the field data have been graphically highlighted by a light grey band (upper panel) and arrow (lower panel) dashed lines. Adapted from Knighton (1972), Hooke (1986), and Luchi *et al.* (2010b).

association with channel width variations. A sample bend is reproduced in the upper panel of Figure 6.4. The curves in the two plots on the right-hand side of Figure 6.4 represent how the predicted location of forced mid-channel bars shifts along one full meander loop, depending on the value of the ratio $L_m/W_0$ between meander arclength and channel width. Thin lines indicate the position of mid-channel bars forced by width variations, and thick lines the position of those forced by curvature variations. These model predictions are based on reach averaged bankfull conditions reported in the above field studies and also in Hooke and Harvey (1983) and Hooke (2008).

The ratio $L_m/W_0$ in the examined bends of the River Dane showing characteristic cycles of mid-channel bar development ranges between 11 and 15. In such a range width variations force the development of mid-channel bars just downstream of bend apexes (dashed lines), in qualitative agreement with the observation that "bars are commonly in low-curvature downstream parts of developing bends" (Hooke 1986, p. 847). This, along with the fact that "(bank) erosion precedes (bed) deposition at

most of the sites" (*ibidem*, p. 848) might support the idea that mid-channel bars observed in the River Dane may be predominantly due to a width-forced mechanism.

Different considerations seem to apply to the longer, well-developed meander bend of the River Dean; it has a $L_m/W_0$ ratio of about 26, and the growth of a mid-channel bar has been observed by Knighton (1972) to occur close to meander inflection. The model indicates that for $L_m/W_0 = 26$ (see the grey arrow in the lower plot) meander inflection would be the chosen location of curvature-forced mid-channel bars, thus suggesting that the central bar observed by Knighton (1972) could be mainly related to non-linear effects. For the same hydraulic conditions, the width-forced mechanism would tend to operate very close to the bend apex where, however, neither significant widening nor mid-channel bar development have been observed.

Disentangling these two mechanisms can also indicate an approach to understanding whether spatial variations in channel width have a forcing or following function with respect to mid-channel bars, a still-debated issue. The steady, steering topographical effect associated with curvature-forced mid-channel bars causes persistent flow divergence, producing a laterally symmetrical near-bank excess longitudinal velocity close to the central bar. This can result in symmetrical bank erosion, thus producing a local widening tendency. Because the wavelength of these mid-channel bars is roughly half that of the meander loop, a central scour hole is expected further downstream (at a $L_m/4$ distance): analogously, this triggers flow convergence and a consequent peak of the main flow thread in the central portion of the channel a few widths downstream of the scour region itself. This would reduce the near-bank shear stress, thus promoting a local narrowing tendency. The steady character of the process can affect meander planform by forcing the development of spatial width oscillations, even from an originally equiwidth channel. In this case, the development of spatial width variations is forced by mid-channel bars. In other cases, the local unbalance between erosion and accretion processes at opposite banks (Lauer and Parker, 2008) can be the major factor responsible for the generation of channel width variations, independent of the previous existence of central bars which, in turn, may be forced by such developed width oscillations.

## 6.4   ANALYTICAL BAR MODELS AND MULTIPLE-THREAD CHANNEL MORPHODYNAMICS

Analytical bar models formulated and solved according to the approach presented in Section 6.2 rely on the hypothesis of a fully sediment-transporting cross-section. Furthermore, they assume that banks are much stronger than the bed, such that the characteristic time scales of the two processes are clearly distinct and therefore the morphodynamic problem greatly simplifies: banks are kept fixed when analysing bar features, while bank development is studied on a much longer time scale, assuming an equilibrium bed configuration. For these reasons their application to multiple-thread braided streams is still a challenging issue.

The presence of multiple branches, each one with its own different spatial and temporal scales, and the complexity and high dynamism of the network, determine a system that stays quite far from the configuration hypothesized in analytical models. In particular, the cross-section variability of flow parameters is much higher in a braided river, and sediment transport does not occur in the whole width, not even at bankfull conditions (Nicholas, 2000; Bertoldi et al., 2009a). Furthermore, bar and bank processes cannot be decoupled. In spite of these differences, many field and laboratory observations give support to the idea that the bar dynamics in both transitional (Church and Rice, 2009) and braided

river morphologies (Ashmore, 2001; Bertoldi and Tubino, 2005; Hundey and Ashmore, 2009) exhibit features that are similar to those observed in single-thread river channels. The observed analogies indicate that similar processes may occur in single-and multiple-thread river channels. The question arises, then, whether analytical bar models, developed for single-thread streams, may also be applied to a broader class of alluvial river morphologies.

The aim of the present section is to explore a suitable approach for such considerations and to discuss the role of bars in braided river morphodynamics and channel pattern selection. In particular, the role of migrating bars in setting the spatial and temporal scales of a gravel-bed braided network and their effect in controlling the morphodynamics of a bifurcation in a braided stream are discussed in this section, together with a recently proposed application of bar predictors to define alluvial river patterns (Crosato and Mosselman, 2009). The proposed examples indicate that analytical bar models can be reasonably employed for braided and transitional river morphologies, both for improving process understanding and for the prediction of typical spatial scales (longitudinal and lateral), as has been done for decades for single-thread rivers.

### 6.4.1   Alternate Bars and Longitudinal Scales in Braided Rivers

The existence of characteristic spatial scales in braided rivers is still debated. A classical claim is that networks show dynamic scaling and a self-affine pattern (e.g. Foufoula-Georgiou and Sapozhnikov, 2001), implying that no particular length scale can be assessed. Recently Hundey and Ashmore (2009) showed that laboratory and actual braided rivers show a clear scaling associated with the spacing between consecutive bifurcations and confluences. Developing an idea presented by Ashmore (2001), the authors showed that such "link-length" scales linearly with the mean width of the main channel. The average bifurcation–confluence distance is found to be 4 to 5 times the mean channel width. This braiding length scale was then related to the wavelength of alternate bars evolving in the initially straight channel from which the braided network was developed in the experiments. The alternate bars dynamically interact with the banks, causing a mutual feedback that results in a configuration with large width variations and steady, more central bars, eventually inducing the flow to bifurcate (Bertoldi and Tubino, 2005).

These observations suggest that the evolution of alternate bars in a non-fixed width context might be crucial to investigating braiding occurrence and evolution, which indicates the suitability of analytical bar models.

A key issue is then to devise an effective approach to apply bar predictors in these contexts.

The scaling relation found by Hundey and Ashmore (2009) involves the width of the main channel, i.e. the largest branch in the network that usually carries a large proportion of the total discharge. This is a new perspective in scaling braided rivers. Analytical models aimed at predicting the occurrence of a braided pattern (Parker, 1976; Fredsoe, 1978; Crosato and Mosselman, 2009) refer to the entire corridor width for the computation of reach-averaged hydraulic and geometrical conditions. However, braided river morphodynamics are not well represented by these averaged conditions since they are driven by local parameters, which exhibit a significant transverse variability (Nicholas, 2000; Bertoldi et al., 2009a).

Recently, laboratory and field observations undertaken by the group at the University of Western Ontario and the University of Trento have focused on the definition of the active part of a braided river as that subject to sediment transport, where morphological activity is expected. As reported by Egozi and Ashmore (2008) and Bertoldi et al. (2009a) a braided river under formative conditions shows a proportion of active width (or active number of branches) generally lower than half of the total wet. This quantifies the well-known characteristic of gravel bed braided rivers that exhibit only few active channels, together with a markedly uneven water distribution in the network (e.g. Mosley, 1982; Stojic et al., 1998). Braided river dynamics is often governed by only one or two active channels, or a limited active

part of a cross-section. An effective approach to the application of analytical bar models to multithread river morphologies must incorporate these observations and be based on the geometry and hydraulics of the "active" regions. Input model parameters such as the width–depth ratio and the dimensionless shear stress should therefore be computed referring to the portion of the cross-section that is morphologically active.

We now illustrate how the use of differently computed parameters affects the application of analytical bar models referring to two field examples: (i) the Fraser River, Canada (Church and Rice, 2009) and (ii) the Tagliamento River, Italy.

The gravel reach of the Lower Fraser River shows a mildly braided pattern, with the channels separated by relatively stable vegetated islands and less stable gravel bars. As reported by Church and Rice (2009) these bars show an average wavelength of about 5 km, with each bar 1.5 to 3 km long (see Table 6.1 for the measured and computed parameters). The reach is 1500 m wide, but the active part is restricted to the main channel, which is roughly 500 m wide. Mean flow depth also varies when considering the active part; it increases from 3.4 m to 6.6 m when considering the deepest part where sediment transport occurs (data extrapolated from Church and Rice, 2009). Reported data have been used to compute two sets of parameters, using the whole river area ("average" parameters) and the morphologically active proportion ("active" parameters). Considering the active instead of the average parameters reduces the width to depth ratio from 440 to 76. Table 6.1 reports the threshold

**Table 6.1** Measured and computed parameters for the Fraser River and two reaches of the Tagliamento River

| | Fraser | | | Tagliamento Cornino | | | Tagliamento Flagogna | | |
|---|---|---|---|---|---|---|---|---|---|
| $Q_2$ [m$^3$s$^{-1}$] | 9790 | | | 1400 | | | 1000 | | |
| $D_{50}$ [m] | 0.03 | | | 0.04 | | | 0.04 | | |
| s | 0.00045 | | | 0.0036 | | | 0.0028 | | |
| | Average | Main active | | Average | Main active | | Average | Main active | |
| W [m] | 1500 | 500 | | 840 | 300 | | 500 | 150 | |
| D [m] | 3.4 | 6.6 | | 1.1 | 1.7 | | 1.25 | 2.15 | |
| β | 441 | 76 | | 764 | 176 | | 400 | 70 | |
| θ | 0.031 | 0.060 | | 0.060 | 0.093 | | 0.053 | 0.091 | |
| ds | 0.009 | 0.005 | | 0.036 | 0.024 | | 0.032 | 0.019 | |
| | Analytical models | | Measured | Analytical models | | Measured | Analytical models | | Measured |
| β alternate | 21.6 | | | 19.2 | | | 18.4 | | |
| β central | 90.0 | | | 78.8 | | | 76.2 | | |
| β multiple | 161.8 | | | 141.0 | | | 134.1 | | |
| bar length [m] | 10959 | 3653 | 2640 | 3566 | 1274 | 500 | 3570 | 1071 | 500 |
| m | 12.2 | 2.2 | 2.0 | 76.0 | 15.5 | 11.0 | 37.5 | 5.8 | 7.0 |

values of the aspect ratio above which alternate, central or multiple bars are more likely to develop, based on mean annual flood ($Q_2$), measured longitudinal slope, and median bed material particle size (e.g. Church and Rice, 2009).

According to the theory of Colombini *et al.* (1987), a width-to-depth ratio larger than 90 is required to form central bars in the case of the Fraser River. Therefore, using the active parameters, analytical models predict that Fraser River is in the alternate bar regime rather than multiple bar regime, which is more consistent with the observed morphology (Church and Rice, 2009). Similarly, the observed lengths of these bars range between 2 and 3 km which corresponds to a wavelength of approximately 5 km. Analytical predictions suggest a dimensionless wave number approximately equal to 0.4. Using the active width this corresponds to a bar wavelength of 4 km, while using the total river width results in a length of nearly 11 km.

Data from the Tagliamento River provide two further examples from two different reaches. The Tagliamento is a large gravel bed braided river with an active corridor width up to 1500 m. Average and active parameters are reported in Table 6.1. Two automated digital cameras, taking pictures with a temporal interval of 1 hour, have been installed on cliffs above the Flagogna and Cornino reaches (Bertoldi *et al.*, 2010). The high temporal resolution provides great detail of morphological changes during floods, which can be quantified from the rectified images. Figure 6.5 shows an example in the Cornino reach; pictures cover an approximately 1 km long reach. Images are taken during a bankfull flood that occurred on 30 October, 2008. The left picture shows the configuration near peak conditions, whereas the right one illus-

trates the falling limb, about 4 days later. At peak stage the flow width is almost equal to the braidplain. However, the active part of the river is mainly concentrated within the channel on the right-hand side of the network (left side of image), where a series of large bars can be observed. The bar fronts are clearly recognizable in the picture and successive images show their downstream migration. The second image, at a much lower flow stage, shows that these bars moved several metres downstream and eventually emerged, splitting the flow into a series of small branches. For a bankfull flood like the one discussed here, the width-to-depth ratio of the entire wetted river is 764. However, using only the main active branch, the width-to-depth ratio decreases to 176, a value that falls slightly above the range of central bar instability (Table 6.1). This is more consistent with visual observations on the evolving bed topography at high flow stage.

On the other hand, bar wavelength is approximately 500 m, while the computed length for central bars is about 1.2 km, even using only the active channel. A possible explanation for this overestimate is that bars increase in length over time (Church and Rice, 2009) and may not have reached equilibrium length during the flood. During this formative event the downstream bar was indeed observed to migrate faster with respect to the upstream bar, resulting in a longer shape at the end of the flood. This indicates that equilibrium conditions were not achieved during the flood pulse.

A second explanation for this overprediction can be related to the decoupling between bed and bank processes that is assumed in the model, leading to the assumption that channel width is constant in time. Cohesionless systems, such as gravel bed braided rivers

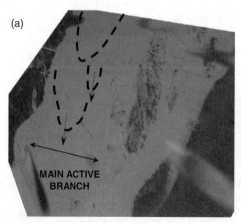
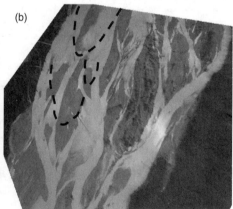

**Figure 6.5** Bar dynamics during a bankfull flood on the Tagliamento River at Cornino reach. (a) 30 October, 2008, 11.00, discharge approximately 1200 m³ s⁻¹; (b) 3 November, 2008, 9.00 (150 m³ s⁻¹). Flow is directed from top to bottom of images.

are characterized by similar temporal scales for bed and bank evolution, leading to a strong interaction, where width variations affect short-term bars dynamics, slowing their migration and shortening their length (see Bertoldi and Tubino, 2005).

### 6.4.2 Channel Pattern Prediction Through Analytical Bar Models

Analytical bar models developed in the 1970s (Parker, 1976; Fredsoe, 1978) have been used to predict the channel pattern of alluvial rivers, based on the most unstable lateral mode $m$ of free migrating bars in a given reach. Such a criterion, when $m = 1$, implies that meandering would evolve from a straight channel as a consequence of selective bank erosion associated with migrating bars, which has been lately recognized as physically meaningful, though still not relevant for meandering, only when bed and banks timescales are comparable.

Crosato and Mosselman (2009) recently revisited this approach based on the idea that steady bars should be more effective than migrating bars to condition the river planform style because of the time scale associated with their dynamics. The resulting river morphology has been defined by Crosato and Mosselman (2009) as meandering if $m < 1.5$, transitional for $1.5 < m < 2.5$ and braiding for $m > 2.5$. The most probable number of bars $m$ in a reach is obtained by Crosato and Mosselman (2009) as the ratio of the reach-averaged width-to-depth ratio to the resonant $\beta$ value of the first bar mode for the hydraulic conditions of the same reach. When computed with a second-order steady bar model like that of Struiksma et al. (1985), $m$ takes a relatively simple form (Crosato and Mosselman, 2009, Eq. 19):

$$m = \frac{\beta}{\beta_R^{(1^{st}\text{mode})}} = 0.17g \frac{(b-3)W^3 S}{\sqrt{\Delta d C Q}} \tag{6.10}$$

The integer part of $m$ represents the resonant lateral bar mode closest to the actual river conditions: it can therefore be taken as a good representation of the most probable number of bars in the reach, from which the channel pattern is readily predicted. Crosato and Mosselman (2009) indicate that the predictor tends to overestimate the observed value of $m$ for rivers with larger width-to-depth ratio, typically corresponding to braided morphologies. Nonlinear effects are suggested as one of the possible causes for such a discrepancy. Another explanation for the observed mismatch comes from the idea of using morphologically active values of channel width in Equation (6.10) instead of the wet ("average") values, which can result in very different predictions, particularly at large $\beta$.

We have tested the performance of the bar pattern predictor using both approaches in four different river reaches encompassing all the three different planform styles: meandering (River Bollin, UK, data from Luchi et al. 2010a), transitional (Fraser River, Canada, data from Church and Rice, 2009, and in Table 6.1) and braiding (Flagogna and Cornino reaches of the Tagliamento River, Italy, data in Table 6.1). Results are reported in Figure 6.6.

For the single-thread meandering River Bollin in the UK (Hooke, 2003), the predicted value of $m$ decreases from 2.4 to 1.0 when using active instead of wet parameters, against an observed value of 1. The predicted channel pattern correctly shifts from transitional to the observed meandering.

For the Fraser River reach examined by Church and Rice (2009) $m$ decreases from 12 to 2.4 when the active part is considered. The predicted pattern correctly changes from braided to transitional, which matches the actual morphology more closely. Indeed, Church and Rice (2009) highlight that the general pattern of this reach of the Fraser River can be schematized as a single-thread river with alternate bars (see their Figure 10).

For the two reaches of the Tagliamento both approaches predict a braided pattern, although use of the active parameters provides a better match between computed and observed number of bars.

Results reported in Figure 6.6 therefore point out that the application of analytical models using active values of the input parameters greatly enhances their effectiveness in replicating observed features. Indeed

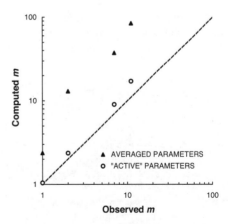

**Figure 6.6** Comparison between observed and computed most probable number of steady bars $m$ (Crosato and Mosselman, 2009) for the Tagliamento and Flagogna reaches of the Tagliamento River (Table 6.1), the Fraser River (Church and Rice, 2009), and the River Bollin (Hooke, 2003). Two different sets of parameters (wet and active) have been used (Table 6.1).

this approach is more consistent with the model assumption that the whole cross-section is transporting sediments. On the contrary, the use of averaged (wet) parameters is not always the best choice and can lead to large differences between predicted and observed behaviours. The distance between averaged and local conditions increases with cross-section complexity, and is more marked at low sediment mobility (but see also the approach proposed by Paola (1996) and Nicholas (2000) for higher morphological complexity. In single-thread streams such differences are less relevant.

Deviations from field observations can also be expected due to the linear character of Crosato and Mosselman's (2009) predictor, which refers to flat bed as the reference configuration. Luchi *et al.* (2010b) (see also Section 6.3.2) find that non-linearities can force mid-channel bars in single-thread, meandering streams, which therefore might locally display a transitional ($m = 2$) instead of a meandering ($m = 1$) morphology. Furthermore, non-linear competition among multiple transverse modes has been detected as responsible for reducing the transversal bar mode. Laboratory and numerical experiments on the evolution of a very wide, single-thread channel have shown that initially unstable multiple row bars are more likely to evolve towards a central or even an alternate bar pattern after non-linear mode competition occurs (e.g., Fujita, 1989; Enggrob and Tjerry, 1999).

### 6.4.3 Bar Controls on the Dynamics of Channel Bifurcations

Flow bifurcation is a key process leading to the development of a braided network. Bifurcations control water and sediment distribution in the branches, therefore determining their morphological evolution. In recent years knowledge of bifurcation has greatly improved, thanks to field and laboratory observations, as well as mathematical modelling (e.g., Bolla Pittaluga *et al.*, 2003; Federici and Paola, 2003; Zolezzi *et al.*, 2006; Miori *et al.*, 2006; Edmonds and Slingerland, 2008; Kleinhans *et al.*, 2008; Tubino and Bertoldi, 2008). These studies investigate bifurcation stability and show that a series of internal (width–depth ratio, shear stress of the upstream channel) and external (presence of vegetation, channel curvature) parameters are crucial in controlling the way discharge is diverted into the distributaries.

Bifurcation dynamics can be strongly controlled by interaction with alternate bars. The occurrence of sediment bars at the node and their migration is an element that can dramatically affect the water distribution in the network. Burge (2006) reports detailed data on five bifurcations on the anabranching cobble-gravel Renous River, Canada. Images show that in four cases a large bar occurred at the entrance of one of the distributaries, strongly limiting water flow into that branch. Similarly, a sequence of pictures taken on the Tagliamento River shows that evolution of a bifurcation can be dominated by the migration of alternate bars. Figure 6.7 shows the evolution of a fairly symmetric bifurcation formed after a bankfull flood at the end of October 2008. In the following 5 months, four flow pulses occurred that reworked the bifurcation, leading to a partial closure of the left branch.

Observed dynamics can be related to the migration of alternate bars in the upstream channel. After a December flood, a triangular bar moved at the inlet of the right distributary, inducing a more unbalanced water partition. Channel width increased in the left branch, whereas the right branch narrowed. After the subsequent

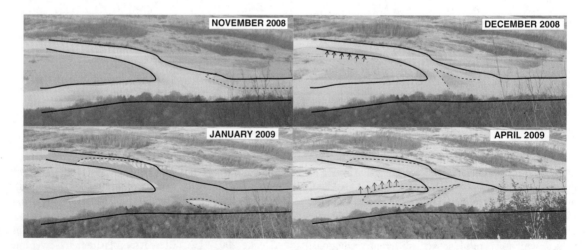

**Figure 6.7**   Bifurcation evolution in the Flagogna reach, Tagliamento River. Flow is from right to left.

flow pulse in January 2009, the bar fully entered the right branch, increasing the bed elevation in this branch. High flows in February and March further increased this difference in bed elevation between the two branches. In the April 2009 picture the right branch has shrunk to a few metres wide channel, and the previous bar is completely attached to the left bank. At the same time a second bar detectable in the upstream channel in January has moved into the left distributary. The increased width of the branch induced a large central deposit to form, deeply transforming the initially Y-shaped bifurcation.

Using the methodology of the previous section, it is possible to compute the characteristic morphological parameters in this bifurcation. The width-to-depth ratio is equal to about 400 when computed for the whole river width, but decreases to 70 when considering only the main active branch, which is 150 m wide. At the same time, the dimensionless shear stress increases from 0.053 (slightly above the threshold for sediment movement) to 0.09. This increase in shear stress explains the high sediment mobility observed in this reach, with the main branch changing morphology completely several times within a year (see also Li *et al.*, 2008; Bertoldi *et al.*, 2009c). According to the theory of Colombini *et al.* (1987), the threshold width-to-depth ratio for alternate bar formation is about 18, whereas central bars are more likely to develop for values larger than 76. The observed ratio in the main branch ($\beta \sim 70$) falls slightly below this threshold for central bars. This is consistent with the field observations that show mainly an alternate pattern, with detectable central bar structures only after widening of the main branch.

The interaction between bars and bifurcations has been tackled in recent work by Bertoldi *et al.* (2009b). The authors expanded the model developed by Bolla Pittaluga *et al.* (2003) and Miori *et al.* (2006), including the effect of alternate bar migration. The results of the theoretical analysis performed by Colombini *et al.* (1987) were used, combined with a simple 1-D model, with the bifurcation considered as a two-cell node in which transverse water and sediment exchanges are allowed. Bars are represented by a periodic sinusoidal forcing that increases the sediment yield in one of the bifurcations. Bar height and migration speed were computed as a function of the upstream channel hydraulics, according to the model of Colombini *et al.* (1987).

The model shows that a number of different interactions are possible, mainly depending on the width-to-depth ratio of the upstream flow. Bars can deeply affect the bifurcation when they are high and slow enough to completely close the inlet of one branch or force most of the water to switch from one branch to the other. This usually occurs when the width–depth ratio is large enough. On the other hand, when the width-to-depth ratio is lower than approximately 30, bars show a smaller amplitude and do not strongly affect the bifurcation evolution, causing only slight unbalance of the water distribution. Results are summarized in Figure 6.8 as a function of the width-to-depth ratio and of the Shields stress. Four possible behaviours can be identified, depending on how much the bifurcation is affected by the bar migration. A bifurcation can be perturbed by the bars, which can be either not able to divert the main flow from one branch to the other (case 2: bar – perturbed) or strong enough to switch the dominant branch (case 3: bar –

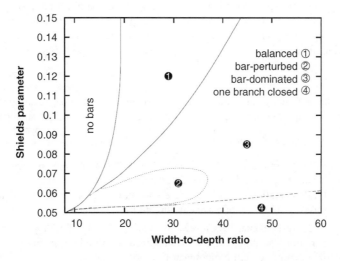

**Figure 6.8** The four possible behaviours of a bifurcation interacting with migrating bars. Modified from Bertoldi *et al.* (2009d).

dominated). In the latter case bar migration significantly changes the water distribution in the network, affecting the morphological evolution of the entire braided system. The other two possibilities are a balanced bifurcation, slightly affected by the bars (case 1) and the complete closure of one of the distributaries, when the bar completely obstructs its inlet (case 4).

The reported case on the Tagliamento River has a value of $\beta$ approximately equal to 35 and a dimensionless shear stress $\tau_*$ of 0.085. The analytical model correctly predicts the observed bar-dominated bifurcation morphodynamics, with a strongly unbalanced discharge distribution.

## 6.5  CONCLUSIONS AND RESEARCH PERSPECTIVES

Bars "essentially define the style and morphology of unconfined alluvial rivers" (Church and Rice, 2009) through mutual feedback processes between bedform and planform. Analytical models for bar morphodynamics have mostly referred to single-thread channels with regular planform geometries because they have been formulated referring to totally sediment-transporting cross-sections. These models solve the governing momentum and continuity equations for water and sediments through analytical techniques, which can be used, provided several simplifying assumptions are made. Their development and application in recent decades has allowed great insight into the basic features of bars in straight and meandering streams. As also embedded in analytical models, bars may be forced by spatial variations in river shape or develop as the result of a free instability mechanism, and may migrate or keep fixed relative to the channel planform. The predictions of analytical bar models have mainly been tested through controlled experiments in laboratory flumes, while systematic comparison with field observation on bar

dynamics in various types of river morphologies is still lacking.

This chapter reflects an attempt to progressively fill the gap between models and field observations through model applications to a number of field cases, including both meandering and braided gravel bed river reaches, in order to broaden the applicability of analytical bar models to increasingly complex river morphologies, like transitional and braided. The five selected field applications have focused on steady bars in meandering rivers and on migrating bars in transitional and braided streams. Another application relates to the model-based prediction of channel pattern based on the most probable number of steady bars in a reach. The examined types of bars in relationship with the planform morphology are summarized in Table 6.2.

The outcomes reveal that migrating free alternate bars can set characteristic spatial scales of complex braided networks and control the evolution of channel bifurcations. Braided rivers, despite their appearance as contemporary evolving multichannel systems, structure their morphological functioning according to spatial scales that may reflect the morphodynamics of a single-thread channel with the same active width as the braided stream for the given formative event. Observations resulting from published data (Church and Rice, 2009) and from high temporal resolution automated image acquisition (Bertoldi et al., 2010) confirm that bars in the wandering Fraser River and in the braided Tagliamento River migrate in the recognizable active corridor during formative events. The predicted bar pattern and wavelength agree fairly well with observed values in some cases, when morphologically active input parameters are used to compute bar properties. Finally, from model application to single-thread streams, possible physical explanations for the presence of steady mid-channel bars in meandering channels can be proposed and hypotheses can be formulated about the

**Table 6.2**  Synthesis of the morphological characteristics (alternate, central) of bars examined in the present paper in relation to channel pattern (meandering, braiding). The section number referring to each subtopic is reported in brackets

|  | Single-thread river reaches | Multiple-thread river reaches |
| --- | --- | --- |
| Alternate ($m=1$) | (3.1) Morphodynamic influence due to steady bars *forced* by local disturbances; (4.3) Migration of *free* alternate bars in upstream branches of channel bifurcations | (4.1) *Free* alternate bars migrating during flow and flood pulses setting characteristic length scales (link-length) in braided rivers |
| Mid-channel or central ($m=2$) | (3.2) Mid-channel bars *forced* by spatial variations of either channel width (linear process) or curvature (nonlinear process) | (4.1) Migrating free central bars during flow/flood pulses in braided streams |

environmental factors that are likely to control the regime of 2-D morphodynamic influence, which displays itself through spatially damped steady bars.

The exercise presented in this chapter reveals promising directions to improve insight into river morphodynamics through the use of analytical bar models thanks to their specific focus on process understanding. Their application to a broad range of river morphologies poses several challenges, and only a few of these can be considered settled issues. Namely, we have shown that in order to translate model input from reach-averaged to suitable channel-scale parameters, knowledge of the morphologically active part of the cross section is needed. The following major issues must be considered for future research into this perspective.

First, significant improvements can be expected if the strong decoupling is relaxed between bedform and planform processes, based on the assumption of a typical hierarchy of scales, whereby the river bed evolves much more slowly than the flow field and much faster than its planform. The presented applications already indicate (Table 6.2) that the type of bar most likely to affect channel planform depends on the relative timescales of bed and bank evolution. When these are comparable, as in braided systems, migrating bars can produce significant planform changes; when they are markedly different, as in single-thread rivers with cohesive banks, only steady bars can significantly affect the planform dynamics because the related pattern of near-bank shear stress affects the banks at more persistent locations.

Mathematically speaking, the presence of comparable timescales implies that the properties of the analytical solution can be significantly modified. The possibility of still achieving analytical solutions should be carefully verified. Also, the relation between the flow and bed timescales should be re-examined. When flood events are very rapid, as in the Tagliamento River, bars might not reach their equilibrium shape and length, while analytical models are often based on equilibrium assumptions with constant discharge. A starting point could be the analytical model of Tubino (1991), accounting for the relation between the morphological time scale of bar growth and that of the flow or flood pulses.

Second, in single-thread channels, the width-to-depth ratio decreases in the rising limb of flood events, bankfull conditions possibly falling below the threshold for bar formation. This implies that at lower (still formative) stages, conditions might be more favourable for bars to develop. This is particularly relevant in very dynamic systems, such as gravel bed braided rivers, where relatively small flow pulses may induce morphological changes, at least in the main active branch (e.g., Bertoldi et al., 2010).

Finally, limited-domain effects are typical of intertwined branches in braided streams: therefore the typical assumption of an indefinite longitudinal domain does not apply in this case and should be relaxed to achieve more consistency with natural situations.

## 6.6 ACKNOWLEDGEMENTS

This work has been developed within the research grants "Morphodynamical processes in river and riparian ecosystems - PRIN 2006" and "Hydrodynamic transport processes and biomorphodynamics of river corridors - PRIN 2009" funded by the Italian Government (MIUR) and the University of Trento, "RIMOF2", funded by the Fondazione CaRi Verona, Vicenza, Belluno e Ancona, "Linking geomorphological processes and vegetation dynamics in gravel-bed rivers", funded by the Fondazione Cassa di Risparmio di Padova e di Rovigo. Walter Bertoldi's research is presently funded by the Leverhulme Trust.

## 6.7 REFERENCES

Ashmore, P. 2001. Braiding phenomena: statics and kinetics. In Mosley, M.P., editor. *Gravel Bed Rivers V*. Wellington, New Zealand Hydrological Society, pp. 95–121.

Bertoldi, W. and Tubino, M. 2005. Bed and bank evolution of bifurcating channels. *Water Resources Research* **41**: W07001, doi: 10.1029/2004WR003333.

Bertoldi, W., Ashmore, P. and Tubino, M. 2009a. A method for estimating the mean bed load flux in braided rivers. *Geomorphology* **103**: 330–340.

Bertoldi, W., Zanoni, L., Miori, S., Repetto, R., and Tubino, M. 2009b. Interaction between migrating bars and bifurcations in gravel bed rivers. *Water Resources Research* **45**: W06418. doi: 10.1029/2008WR007086.

Bertoldi, W., Zanoni, L., and Tubino, M. 2009c. Planform dynamics of braided streams. *Earth Surface Processes and Landforms* **34**: 547–557.

Bertoldi, W., Zanoni, L., and Tubino, M. 2010. Assessment of morphological changes induced by flow and flood pulses in a gravel bed braided river: the Tagliamento River (Italy). *Geomorphology* **114**: 348–360.

Blondeaux, P. and Seminara, G. 1985. A unified bar-bend theory of river meanders. *Journal of Fluid Mechanics* **157**: 449–470. doi: 10.1017/S0022112085002440.

Bolla Pittaluga, M., Repetto, R., and Tubino, M. 2003. Channel bifurcation in braided rivers: equilibrium configurations and stability. *Water Resources Research* **39**: 1046. doi: 10.1029/2001WR001112.

Burge, L. 2006. Stability, morphology and surface grain size patterns of channel bifurcation in gravel-cobble bedded anabranching rivers. *Earth Surface Processes and Landforms* **31**: 1211–1226.

Camporeale, C., Perona, P., Porporato, A., and Ridolfi, L. 2007. Hierarchy of models for meandering rivers and related morphodynamic processes. *Reviews of Geophysics* **45**: RG1001, doi: 10.1029/2005RG000185.

Church, M. and Rice, S. 2009. Form and growth of bars in a wandering gravel-bed river. *Earth Surface Processes and Landforms* **34**: 1422–1432.

Colombini, M., Seminara, G. and Tubino, M. 1987. Finite-amplitude alternate bars. *Journal of Fluid Mechanics* **181**: 213–232.

Crosato, A. and Mosselman, E. 2009. Simple physics-based predictor for the number of river bars and the transition between meandering and braiding. *Water Resources Research* **44**: W03424. doi: 10.1029/2008WR007242.

Edmonds, D. and Slingerland, R. 2008. Stability of delta distributary networks and their bifurcations. *Water Resources Research* **44**: W09426. doi: 10.1029/2008WR006992.

Egozi, R. and Ashmore, P. 2008. Defining and measuring braiding intensity. *Earth Surface Processes and Landforms* **33**: 2121–2138.

Enggrob, H. and Tjerry, S. 1999. Simulation of morphological characteristics of a braided river. In *Proceedings of RCEM 1999 – Symposium on River, Coastal and Estuarine Morphodynamics, Genova, Italy, 6-10 September*, pp. 273–291.

Federici, P. and Paola, C. 2003. Dynamics of bifurcations in noncohesive sediments. *Water Resources Research* **39**: 1162. doi: 10.1029/2002WR001434.

Federici, B. and Seminara, G. 2006. Effect of suspended load on sandbar instability. *Water Resources Research* **42**: W07407. doi: 10.1029/2005WR004399.

Foufoula-Georgiou, E. and Sapozhnikov, V. 2001. Scale invariances in the morphology and evolution of braided rivers. *Mathematical Geology* **33**: 273–291.

Fredsoe, J. 1978. Meandering and braiding of rivers. *Journal of Fluid Mechanics* **84**: 607–624.

Fujita, Y. 1989. Bar and channel formation in braided streams. In Ikeda, S. and Parker, G., editors. *River Meandering*. American Geophysical Union, Water Resources Monograph **12**, pp. 417–462.

Garcia, M. and Nino, Y. 1993. Dynamics of sediment bars in straight and meandering channels: experiments on the resonance phenomenon. *Journal of Hydraulic Research* **31**: 739–761.

Gurnell, A., Petts, G., Hannah, D. *et al.* 2001. Riparian vegetation and island formation along the gravel-bed Fiume Tagliamento, Italy. *Earth Surface Processes and Landforms* **26**: 31–62.

Holmes, M. 1995. *Introduction to Perturbation Methods*, Texts in Applied Mathematics 20. New York, Springer-Verlag.

Hooke, J. 1986. The significance of mid-channel bars in an active meandering river. *Sedimentology* **33**: 839–850.

Hooke, J. 2003. River meander behaviour and instability: a framework for analysis. *Transactions Institute of British Geographers* **28**: 238–253.

Hooke, J. 2008. Temporal variations in fluvial processes on an active meandering river over a 20-year period. *Geomorphology* **100**: 3–13.

Hooke, J. 2009. Morphodynamics of bar formation in meandering rivers. *Eos, Transactions of the Ametrican Geophysical Union, Fall Meeting Supplement* **90**(52). Abstract H41B-0888.

Hooke, J. and Harvey, A. 1983. Meander changes in relation to bend morphology and secondary flows. In Collinson, J.D. and Lewin, J., editors. *Modern and Ancient Fluvial Systems*. International Association of Sedimentologists, Special Publication 6 pp. 121–132.

Howard, A. 1992. Modelling channel migration and floodplain sedimentation in meandering streams. In Carling, P.A. and Petts G.E., editors. *Lowland Floodplain Rivers: Geomorphological Perspectives*. Chichester, John Wiley & Sons, Ltd, pp. 1–41.

Hundey, E. and Ashmore, P. 2009. Length scale of braided river morphology. *Water Resources Research* **45**: W08409, doi: 10.1029/2008WR007521.

Jaeggi, M. N. R. 1984. Formation and effects of alternate bars. *Journal of Hydraulic Engineering* **110**: 142–156.

Kinoshita, R. and Miwa, H. 1974. River channel formation which prevents downstream translation of transverse bar. *Shinsabo* **94**: 12–17 [in Japanese].

Kleinhans, M., Jagers, H., Mosselman, E., and Sloff, C. 2008. Bifurcation dynamics and avulsion duration in meandering rivers by one-dimensional and three-dimensional models. *Water Resources Research* **44**: W08454. doi: 10.1029/2007WR005912.

Knighton, A. 1972. Changes in a braided reach. *Geological Society of America Bulletin* **83**: 3813–3822.

Lanzoni, S. 2000. Experiments on bar formation in a straight flume 1. Uniform sediment. *Water Resources Research* **36**: 3351–3363.

Lanzoni, S. and Tubino, M. 1999. Grain sorting and bar instability. *Journal of Fluid Mechanics* **393**: 149–174.

Lauer, J. and Parker, G. 2008. Net local removal of floodplain sediment by river meander migration. *Geomorphology* **96**: 123–149. doi: 10.1016/j.geomorph.2007.08.003.

Li, S., Millar, R., and Islam, S. 2008. Modelling gravel transport and morphology for the Fraser river gravel reach, *British Columbia*. *Geomorphology* **95**: 206–222.

Luchi, R. 2009. *The effect of width and curvature variations on river meander morphodynamics*. Ph.D. thesis, Doctoral School in Environmental Engineering, University of Trento, Italy.

Luchi, R., Hooke, J., Zolezzi, G., and Bertoldi, W. 2010a. Width variations and mid-channel bar inception in meanders: River Bollin (UK). *Geomorphology*: 1–8.

Luchi, R., Zolezzi, G., and Tubino, M. 2010b. Modelling mid-channel bars in meandering channels. *Earth Surface Processes and Landforms* **35**: 902-917. doi: 10.1002/esp.1947.

Marzadri, A., Tonina, D., Bellin, A., Vignoli, G., and Tubino, M. 2010. Semi-analytical analysis of hyporheic flow induced by alternate bars. *Water Resources Research* **46**: W07531. doi: 10.1029/2009WR008285.

Miori, S., Repetto, R., and Tubino, M. 2006. A one-dimensional model of bifurcations in gravel bed channels with erodible banks. *Water Resources Research* **42**: W11413. doi: 10.1029/2006WR004863.

Mosley, M. 1982. Analysis of the effect of changing discharge on channel morphology and instream uses in a braided river, Ohau river, New Zealand. *Water Resources Research* **18**: 800–812.

Mosselman, E., Zolezzi, G., and Tubino, M. 2006. The over-deepening theory in river morphodynamics: two decades of shifting interpretations. In Ferreira, R.M.L., Alves, E.C.T.L., Leal, J.G.A.B., and Cardoso, A.H., editors. *Proceedings of RiverFlow 2006, Lisbon, Portugal, 6-8 September*. London, Taylor & Francis Group, pp. 1175–1183.

Nicholas, A. 2000. Modelling bedload yield in braided gravel bed rivers. *Geomorphology* **36**: 89–106.

Paola, C. 1996. Incoherent structure: Turbulence as a metaphor for stream braiding. In Ashworth, P.J., Bennett, S.J., Best, J. L., and McLelland, S.J., editors. *Coherent Flow Structures in Open Channels*. Chichester, John Wiley & Sons, Ltd, pp. 705–723.

Parker, G. 1976. On the cause and characteristic scales of meandering and braiding in rivers. *Journal of Fluid Mechanics* **76**: 457–480.

Parker, G., Wilcock, P.R., Paola, C., Dietrich, W.E., and Pitlick, J. 2007. Physical basis for quasi-universal relations describing bankfull hydraulic geometry of single-thread gravel bed rivers. *Journal of Geophysical Research – Earth Surface* **112**: F04005, doi: 10.1029/2006JF000549.

Repetto, R. and Tubino, M. 1999. Transition from migrating alternate bars to steady central bars in channels with variable width. In *Proceedings of RCEM 1999 – Symposium on River, Coastal and Estuarine Morphodynamics, Genova, Italy, 6-10 September*, pp. 605–614.

Repetto, R., Tubino, M., and Paola. C. 2002. Planimetric instability of channels with variable width. *Journal of Fluid Mechanics* **457**: 79–109.

Schielen, R., Doelman, A., and De Swart, H. E. 1993. On the nonlinear dynamics of free bars in straight channels. *Journal of Fluid Mechanics* **252**: 325–356.

Seminara, G. 2006. Meanders. *Journal of Fluid Mechanics* **554**: 271–297.

Seminara, G. and Tubino, M. 1989. Alternate bars and meandering: Free, forced and mixed interactions. In Ikeda S. and Parker, G., editors, *River Meandering*. American Geophysical Union, Water Resources Monographs **12**, pp. 267–320.

Seminara, G., Zolezzi, G., Tubino, M., and Zardi, D. 2001. Downstream and upstream influence in river meandering. Part 2. Planimetric development. *Journal of Fluid Mechanics* **438**: 213–230.

Stojic, M., Chandler, J., Ashmore, P., and Luce, J. 1998. The assessment of sediment transport rates by automated digital photogrammetry. *Photogrammetric Engineering and Remote Sensing* **64**: 387–395.

Struiksma, N., Olesen, K., Flokstra, K., and deVriend, H. 1985. Bed deformation in curved alluvial channels. *Journal of Hydraulic Research* **23**: 57–79.

Talmon, A. M., Struiksma, N., and Van Mierlo, M. 1995. Laboratory measurements of the direction of sediment transport on transverse alluvial-bed slopes. *Journal of Hydraulic Research* **33**: 495–517.

Tubino, M. 1991. Growth of alternate bars in unsteady flows. *Water Resources Research* **27**: 37–52.

Tubino, M. and Bertoldi, W. 2008. Bifurcations in gravel-bed streams. In Habersack, H., Piegay, H., and Rinaldi, M., editors, *Gravel-Bed Rivers VI: From Process Understanding to River Restoration*. Amsterdam, Elsevier. Developments in Earth Surface Processes **11**, pp. 135–161.

Tubino, M. and Seminara, G. 1990. Free-forced interactions in developing meanders and suppression of free bars. *Journal of Fluid Mechanics* **214**: 131–159. doi: 10.1017/S0022112090000088.

Tubino, M., Repetto, R., and Zolezzi, G. 1999. Free bars in rivers. *Journal of Hydraulic Research* **37**: 759–775.

Welford, M. 1994. A field test of Tubino's (1991) model of alternate bar formation. *Earth Surface Processes and Landforms* **19**: 287–297.

Zolezzi, G. and Seminara, G. 2001a. Downstream and upstream influence in river meandering. Part 1. General theory and application of overdeepening. *Journal of Fluid Mechanics* **438**: 183–211.

Zolezzi, G. and Seminara, G. 2001b. Upstream influence in erodible beds. *Physics and Chemistry of the Earth. Part B – Hydrology, Oceans and Atmosphere* **26**(1), 65–70. doi: 10.1016/S1464-1909(01)85016-4.

Zolezzi, G., Bertoldi, W., and Tubino, M. 2006. Morphological analysis and prediction of channel bifurcations. In Sambrook Smith, G.H., Best, J.L., Bristow, C.S., and Petts, G.E., editors, *Braided Rivers: Process, Deposits, Ecology and Management*. Oxford, Blackwell. International Association of Sedimentologists, Special Publication **36**, pp.233–256.

Zolezzi, G., Guala, M., Termini, D., and Seminara, G. 2005. Experimental observation of upstream overdeepening. *Journal of Fluid Mechanics* **531**: 191–219.

Zolezzi, G., Luchi, R., and Tubino, M. 2009a. Coupling the dynamics of channel width and curvature in meandering rivers: a perspective on fluvial patterns. In *Proceedings of RCEM 2009 Conference, Santa Fe, Argentina, 4-7 October*. London: Taylor & Francis Group, pp. 120–140.

Zolezzi, G., Luchi, R., and Tubino, M. 2009b. Morphodynamic regime of gravel bed, single-thread meandering rivers. *Journal of Geophysical Research – Earth Surface* **114**: F01005. doi: 10.1029/2007JF000968.

## 6.8 DISCUSSION

### 6.8.1 Discussion by Ronel Barzilai

It is acceptable in the ecological literature to use shape statistics in order to compare the linearity, circularity, fractal dimension etc. of a patch. It seems like this might be a way to model the bar variation with time. However, one thing that should be taken into consideration in that is the variation in shape due to water stage variation.

### 6.8.2 Discussion by Rob Ferguson

The Shields stress is one of the parameters in your analytical results. Obviously it must affect rates of bar growth, whether forced by curvature or by variation in width. Does it also affect the predicted locations of bar growth within a reach? And if so, could floods of different magnitude cause bar growth in different places?

### 6.8.3 Discussion by David Gaeuman

Predictions of bar modes from an analytical bar model are compared with field examples. Model results represent idealized bar forms, whereas bar configurations in streams are much less ordered. Components of natural bars are formed under the influence of different discharges, and by multiple processes. Relatively large discharges may be responsible for creating gross bed topography that is later dissected to create the individual "bars" recognized by an observer. For example, erosion of riffles in meander crossings (bar mode 1) often produce emergent bars that could potentially be interpreted as a mode 2 configuration. It is therefore worthwhile to consider how the idealized forms predicted by the models might appear in real streams so that we can be sure to compare apples with apples.

### 6.8.4 Discussion by Jonathan Laronne

The morphodynamics of diffluences, studied less intensely and more recently than that of confluences, is yet to be studied in more detail. The varying bed texture between a major anabranch, which is expected to be deeper and more armoured, in comparison to a smaller, more elevated and less armoured channel may be very relevant to the morphodynamics of diffluences. Similarly, higher banks of major branches may be more stable, being more armoured due to bank collapse and accumulation of coarser clasts. How might these textural effects be studied analytically and by physical models?

### 6.8.5  Reply by the Authors

In our view the use of shape statistics in this case can be particularly useful with the aim of quantifying morphological parameters of recognized ecological relevance associated with the shape of river bars and with their variation with water stage. An example is the quantification of the shoreline length with varying flow stage; it is a measure of the interface between the aquatic and terrestrial habitats, and for this reason it is widely used to characterize the diversity of habitats in a river reach. On the other hand, these types of statistics do not appear to be very useful with respect to morphodynamic modelling of bars. Of more interest in the analysis of bar morphodynamics, particularly when comparing model outcomes with data from laboratory experiments or field surveys, can be the use of 2-D Fourier transform or of similar data-processing techniques (see also response to discussion by Gaeuman, below).

Ferguson's observation gives the opportunity for further comment on how analytical bar models can be applied to a practical situation. The model can predict the locations at which bars are expected to grow along a meander for given constant values of the aspect ratio $\beta$, defined in Equation (6.5), the Shields stress $\tau_*$ and the relative roughness $d_s$, both defined in Equation (6.6). Because the model assumes steady flow conditions, it can be suitable to reproduce the morphodynamic effect of unsteady flood events only when their duration is long enough compared to the typical morphological time scale of bed evolution expressed by the Exner Equation (6.4).

In single-thread meandering channels floods of increasing magnitudes reasonably result in: (i) reduced aspect ratios; (ii) increased Shields stress, and (iii) reduced relative roughness. According to model prediction, these types of variations all produce a coherent effect on the predicted mid-channel bar location along a meander. The main parameter controlling this effect seems to be the dimensionless meander wavelength $L/W$. Specifically, for relatively short meanders ($L/W$ <15–20), bar location shifts upstream when the Shields stress increases and when the aspect ratio and the relative roughness decrease. Therefore floods of larger magnitude can be expected to result in mid-channel bar growth at more upstream locations compared to smaller, still formative, flood events. The opposite behaviour is predicted for longer meander bends, i.e. when $L/W$ >15–20.

The response to Gaueman's question is not straightforward. It can be useful to first focus on the correspondence between processes incorporated in the model and those that actually determine the bed shape at a given time in a river. The controlling processes often mutually interact and give rise to irregular patterns. In addition, flow unsteadiness can shape different types of bedform within the same flood event. The examined formative event in the Cornino reach of the Tagliamento River has produced different types of bed patterns at high (Figure 6.5a) and low (Figure 6.5b) flow. High flow conditions are much closer to the model assumptions, and therefore the central bar pattern ($m = 2$), visually detected at high flow, has been chosen for the comparison between modelling outcomes and field data. Analytical bar models indeed cannot reproduce morphodynamics at below "barfull" stage; they assume that sediment transport occurs over the whole cross-section and refer to a steady constant discharge. A critical issue for practical applications is the availability of bed evolution data during the high stage of formative events. For the present work this has been solved, at least to a first approximation, thanks to the availability of high-frequency oblique photos of the considered river reach. The increasing availability of sophisticated river monitoring equipment will result in increased availability of this type of data in the near future.

Once the proper bed data are available, the methodology for suitable processing and comparison with analytical results is still not established at present. Such methods should be used to extract "ordered" topographical information from bed surveys, in order to produce "field apples" to be compared with "simulated apples". A starting point can be that often used to compare experimental data collected in mobile-bed laboratory flumes (e.g. Colombini et al., 1992; Zolezzi et al., 2005) with bar model prediction. It consists of the application of a 2-D Fourier transform to the bed elevation function. Extending this approach to field cases, however, must cope with additional difficulties related, for instance, to bankline detection.

Laronne is right in his statement that investigation of diffluence morphodynamics is less advanced than that of confluences. Despite recent studies that have shed some light on this process, many issues still need to be addressed. One of these is grain size distribution and armouring in the distributaries. There are a few field analyses (Frings and Kleinhans, 2005; Burge, 2006) that show differences in grain size at bifurcations. It is not clear whether there are general trends and whether the main branch is always coarser. When sedimentation is occurring in the smallest branch, finer sediments can be found, in this case reducing the difference in flow velocity and bed shear stress. A detailed study is needed in order to explain this point. In our view, both physical and numerical modelling could help. In particular, new remote sensing techniques (e.g., Dugdale *et al.*, 2010) could improve the accuracy and detail of field and laboratory investigations on bed textural properties.

## 6.9  DISCUSSION REFERENCES

Burge, L. 2006. Stability, morphology and surface grain size patterns of channel bifurcation in gravel-cobble bedded anabranching rivers. *Earth Surface Processes and Landforms* **31**: 1211–1226.

Colombini, M., Tubino, M., and Whiting, P. 1992. Topographic expression of bars in meandering channels. In editors. *Dynamics of Gravel Bed Rivers*. Chichester, John Wiley & Sons, Ltd, pp. 457–474.

Dugdale, S., Carbonneau, P., and Campbell, D. 2010. Aerial photosieving of exposed gravel bars for the rapid calibration of airborne grain size maps. *Earth Surface Processes and Landforms* **35**: 627–639.

Frings, R. and Kleinhans, M. 2005. Effects of river bifurcations on downstream fining. Poster presented at the Gravel-Bed Rivers 6 Conference, Austria, September 6–10.

Zolezzi, G., Guala, M., Termini, D., and Seminara, G. 2005. Experimental observation of upstream overdeepening. *Journal of Fluid Mechanics* **531**: 191–219.

# 7

# Field Observations of Gravel-bed River Morphodynamics: Perspectives and Critical Issues for Testing of Models

## Nicola Surian

## 7.1 INTRODUCTION

A major issue pointed out by Zolezzi et al. (Chapter 6, this volume) is that the analytical models of bar dynamics have rarely been tested with field observations. In the past, analytical models have commonly been tested with laboratory experiments (e.g., Lanzoni, 2000), but one can argue that physical models are simplified representations of rivers. If we want to know the real applicability of these models for understanding and predicting channel processes, more field observations are needed. Several tests of analytical models will offer the possibility to better define their potential and limitations. For instance, it would be worth further exploring their application to braided or transitional morphologies, and to understand better which processes and parameters can, or cannot, be predicted.

This discussion deals with field observations of bar dynamics and, in general, of river morphodynamics. If much work has been done in the past on this topic through physical, analytical and numerical modelling, the same cannot be said for field observations. Is it now more feasible to carry out field-based research? Are there specific aspects that should be taken into account, especially when field observations are used to test models? The discussion addresses this type of question and is specifically focused on the following three issues: (i) new technologies and their potentials in field studies; (ii) equilibrium and unstable conditions of river channels; and (iii) active channel width.

In the first section, after a brief review of field studies on bar dynamics, I discuss how new technologies, specifically remote-sensing techniques, are making it more feasible to carry out field studies in comparison with some years ago. The next section deals with the stability of river channels. The identification of stability conditions (i.e., equilibrium or disequilibrium) is crucial to compare field observations and models appropriately, specifically for those models, like analytical models, that assume equilibrium conditions. Finally, the last section concerns the measurement of active channel width. In their chapter, Zolezzi et al. show that active channel width is a crucial parameter for analytical models. Recent research on braided river morphodynamics also points out its relevance.

## 7.2 FIELD STUDIES ON BAR DYNAMICS: NEW PERSPECTIVES FROM REMOTE-SENSING TECHNIQUES?

In their chapter, Zolezzi et al. mention that there are not many field studies on bar dynamics. This may seem surprising considering the amount of research carried out on rivers over the last 50–60 years, but this is the case if we refer to studies that analysed bar morphology over short ($10^0$ yr) or medium ($10^1$ yr) time scales and not studies dealing with other properties of bars (e.g., sedimentology, stratigraphy). Studies considering bar dynamics over several years are very rare, good examples being the work of Hooke (2007, 2008) and Church and Rice (2009). In some other studies bar morphology was analysed over a few years (e.g., Bennett et al., 1998; Bartholdy and Billi, 2002). Aerial photographs, historical maps and topographic surveys were used in those studies for re-constructing and monitoring bar dynamics. The reason that field studies have been so rare up to now may be explained by the fact that: (i) long-term monitoring is often not easy in practice, as it requires funding projects on the same topic and (ii) availability of aerial

*Gravel-bed Rivers: Processes, Tools, Environments*, First Edition. Edited by Michael Church, Pascale M. Biron and André G. Roy.
© 2012 John Wiley & Sons, Ltd. Published 2012 by John Wiley & Sons, Ltd.

photographs and technology to analyse images effectively (e.g., GIS) was commonly more limited up to 15–20 years ago. Probably the first issue has not changed in recent years, and it is even more difficult now to continue research efforts in the same direction for several years. On the other hand, technologies for monitoring river channels have notably changed, opening new perspectives for field studies on bar dynamics.

The point I would like to discuss here is that available data and techniques make it more feasible to carry out field studies on bar dynamics in comparison with some years ago. Remarkable changes have occurred in remote sensing over the last ten years or so. Besides aerial photographs, which have been used for a long time, multispectral images and LiDAR are becoming fundamental tools in river studies (e.g., Heritage and Hetherington, 2007; Rumsby et al., 2008; Marcus and Fonstad, 2008). Multispectral images have been increasingly used because of: (i) availability of high resolution images (e.g., IKONOS, QuickBird; WorldView) and (ii) satellite images have become much more accessible in terms of cost. Availability of satellite images with high spatial resolution means that medium-sized streams can now be studied, not only using aerial photographs, but also with satellite images, therefore increasing temporal resolution of the analysis (Table 7.1). Satellite data are also more and more accessible (e.g., free access to Landsat archive), giving the opportunity to use such data, even in studies supported by low budgets. LiDAR data are becoming more accessible and technology is improving quickly (e.g., "green LiDAR"), giving the opportunity to analyse morphological changes in terms of erosion/deposition volumes using DEMs (e.g., Hicks et al., 2008), instead of cross-sections or longitudinal profiles.

In terms of tools for analysing and monitoring bar morphology and dynamics, two aspects are crucial:

spatial scale, dependent on river size, and temporal scale, dependent on degree of river dynamics. The first aspect, as mentioned above, is not a major problem anymore, since aerial and satellite images now offer a wide range of spatial resolutions. On the other hand, more attention should be paid to selecting measurement tools appropriate to capture of the dynamics of bars without missing relevant aspects. Aerial photographs or satellite images are fine for rivers that are not very dynamic, while continuous or very frequent monitoring is required for more dynamic systems. Aerial photographs, taken with a frequency of about five years, were effectively used on the lower Fraser River, a large wandering river, where bars have an existence of about 100 years (Church and Rice, 2009). Conversely, much more frequent data are needed where bars develop in a few years or shorter periods of time, such as in braided rivers. Hourly or daily frequency can be obtained with a fixed camera (Bertoldi et al., 2010) and terrestrial laser scanner (TLS) (Milan et al., 2007).

## 7.3 SELECTION OF TEST REACHES: EQUILIBRIUM AND UNSTABLE CONDITION OF RIVER CHANNELS

Although the examples presented in the chapter by Zolezzi et al. show good agreement between analytical models and field data, to understand to what extent analytical models, and models in general, are capable of describing river behaviour, several tests with field data should be carried out in the future. One of the criteria to be considered when a river, or a certain river reach, is selected to analyse bar dynamics, is river condition in terms of stability. A relevant issue is whether a river is in equilibrium condition or, conversely, in unstable

**Table 7.1**  Characteristics of some satellite-sensor systems with medium and high spatial resolution

| Satellite-Sensor | Spectral range ($\mu$m) | Spatial resolution (m) | Temporal resolution (days) | Image size (km) |
|---|---|---|---|---|
| Landsat 7–ETM+ | MS: 0.45–12.5 PAN: 0.52–0.9 | MS: 30 PAN: 15 | 16 | $183 \times 170$ |
| ASTER | MS: 0.52–11.65 | MS: 15, 30 or 90 | 4 to 16 | 60 (width) |
| SPOT 5 | MS: 0.50–1.75 PAN: 0.48–0.71 | MS: 10 or 20 PAN: 2.5 or 5 | 26 | $60 \times 60$ |
| IKONOS | MS: 0.45–0.85 PAN: 0.45–0.90 | MS: 4 PAN: 1 | 3 to 5 | 13 (width) |
| QuickBird | MS: 0.45–0.90 PAN: 0.45–0.90 | MS: 2.4 PAN: 0.6 | 2 to 3 | 16.5 (width) |
| WorldView-2 | MS: 0.40–1.04 PAN: 0.45–0.80 | MS: 1.8 PAN: 0.5 | 1 to 4 | 16.4 (width) |

Note: MS = multispectral bands; PAN = panchromatic band.

condition. For instance, since analytical models assume that bedload is in equilibrium with stream transport capacity, the reaches selected to test models should be in, or close to, an equilibrium condition. We may also be interested in studying bar dynamics of unstable channels (e.g., incising or aggrading channels), but in this case we should not expect analytical models to be able to predict channel behaviour correctly. The need for a better understanding of medium-term channel evolution and recognition of possible trends of channel adjustments will be illustrated through two examples.

The Brenta and the Tagliamento rivers are in northeastern Italy, drain from the Alps, and exhibit (or used to exhibit in the case of the Brenta) a braided morphology. These rivers, like many rivers in Italy, underwent notable channel adjustments over the past decades in response to a range of human activity (sediment mining, channelization, dams, slope afforestation, torrent control works) that substantially altered the sediment regime (Surian and Cisotto, 2007; Surian et al., 2009). In the Brenta River, channel width decreased dramatically from 1960 to 1981, while a widening phase has occurred since then (Figure 7.1a). Bed incision occurred with higher magnitude during the phase of narrowing (approximately 2 m in 20 years) and then continued with decreasing intensity (Figure 7.1a). It may be argued that, in this reach, the Brenta River was close to an equilibrium condition from 1930 to 1960, very unstable from 1960 to 1981 and then, up to 2003, still unstable, although less than in the previous period. Channel evolution in the Tagliamento River was similar to that in the Brenta River, but some differences may be pointed out. Channel narrowing and bed incision were very pronounced from 1970 to the late 1980s, while in the following period the channel seemed not far from a new condition of equilibrium (Figure 7.1b). Channel widening was less intense than in the Brenta River and bed incision is exhausted at present. In both cases, gravel mining had a key role in driving channel changes during the major phase of narrowing and incision (Surian et al., 2009). The fact that the Brenta River is still in an unstable condition may be due to an overall decrease of sediment supply from the catchment, which causes an imbalance between bedload and transport capacity in this reach.

How can we use these field data when the goal is modelling river morphodynamics? Analytical models could be appropriately applied to that reach of the Tagliamento over the last 20 years or so and, probably, the last ten years would represent the condition closer to equilibrium. On the other hand, the Brenta River does not offer an opportunity to test analytical models except, probably, for the period before 1960. Considering that unstable conditions (i.e., channel adjustments) have been

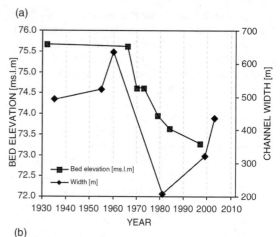

(a)

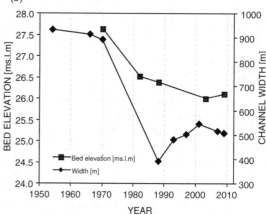

(b)

**Figure 7.1**   Channel width and bed-level changes in the Brenta River (a) and in the Tagliamento River (b).

identified in many rivers worldwide, re-construction of trends of channel adjustment is needed for reliable validation of analytical or numerical models.

## 7.4   ACTIVE CHANNEL WIDTH IN BRAIDED RIVERS

A key issue raised by Zolezzi et al. is that the use of active channel width, instead of wet width, significantly increases the performance of analytical models. Besides, recent research on braided rivers (Egozi and Ashmore, 2008, 2009; Bertoldi et al., 2009, 2010; Bertoldi and Ashmore, 2010) has shown that definition of the active channel width is crucial for understanding morphodynamics and sediment transport in braided rivers. Active channel width is defined as that part of the river active in terms of bedload transport and, therefore, morphologically active. The concept of active channel width is strictly connected to that of active braiding intensity

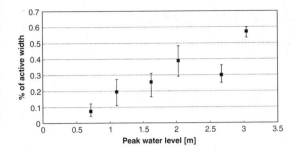

**Figure 7.2** Percentage of active channel width as a function of water level (Tagliamento River) (Bertoldi *et al.*, 2010). Reproduced, with permission, from Elsevier.

(Ashmore, 2001). Measurements of active width have been carried out mainly in flume experiments (e.g., Egozi and Ashmore, 2009; Bertoldi *et al.*, 2009), while there are few field data (e.g., Bertoldi *et al.*, 2010). In flume experiments, active width has commonly been between 0.3 and 0.6 of the wet width, while lower values (0.1–0.3) were measured in the field when moderate formative events were analysed (Figure 7.2). The first issue that I would like to discuss is: how can we measure active width in the field? Then, with the aim of linking field observations with modelling, which formative condition can be used for modelling (e.g., for analytical models)?

Estimation of active width requires measurement of channel morphology before and after a single flood. This is not an easy activity, especially in braided rivers with irregular flow regimes (i.e., not fed by glaciers). Existing field measurements of active channel width were obtained using fixed cameras and surveying a certain number of cross-sections (Bertoldi *et al.*, 2010; Bertoldi and Ashmore, 2010). Considering that fixed cameras cannot be installed in certain conditions (e.g., absence of a cliff close to the river corridor), TLS could be considered as another option to obtain frequent temporal surveys. Probably, TLS would not make the survey easier or faster, but it would offer the opportunity to analyse the whole channel topography (DEMs) rather than single sections. Topographic surveys could be integrated by the use of tracers (e.g., painted sediments, PIT tags) to analyse sediment mobility. For instance, using several painted areas along single cross-sections, Mao and Surian (2010) obtained good evidence of sediment mobility, and thus of channel activity, for different formative events (Figure 7.3). If sediment transport is used to define the active width, a question may arise about interpretation of different types of transport that can be observed. Specifically, it might not be obvious how to treat partial transport conditions. Would this condition always be an evidence of channel activity or would it be so only when significant partial transport occurs (i.e., several particles move and particle paths are of several metres)?

Egozi and Ashmore (2009) suggest that a universal function describing the trend in $BI_A/BI_T$ ratio ($BI_A$ and $BI_T$ are, respectively, active and total braiding intensity) over a range of dimensionless stream power may exist (Figure 7.4). Considering that a strict relationship may be expected between the $BI_A/BI_T$ ratio and active channel/wet channel ratio (Bertoldi *et al.*, 2009), it would be worth further exploring the relation between active width and dimensionless stream power through field observations. This will require observations of different formative events and, hopefully, in different rivers. On the other hand, definition of a representative formative discharge would be useful for modelling, and also for comparisons among rivers. I suggest that *barfull stage*, rather than bankfull stage, be used as the representative stage of formative conditions, the barfull stage being that condition when water overtops all bars, but not islands. Using the barfull stage observations in stable or unstable rivers (i.e., incising or aggrading) could be compared. However, if the bankfull stage is used, the comparison may be less reliable since this stage may represent different flow conditions, even along a single river (e.g., if magnitude of channel incision varies along the river).

## 7.5 FINAL REMARKS

- The chapter by Zolezzi *et al.* highlights the need for testing models using field observations, and it represents a very good example to think about the need to investigate river processes through a combination of different approaches. Models (physical, analytical, numerical) and field observations both have some limitations, therefore only a critical interplay between these approaches can lead to significant advances in river science (e.g., Ferguson, 2008; Kleinhans, 2010).

- Besides observations of single case studies and general theories (models), analysis at the regional scale, such as that of Piégay *et al.* (2009) on braided rivers in southeastern France, could offer useful insights into understanding and predicting river processes. This type of analysis may represent an intermediate step to move from understanding the behaviour of a specific river to general theories.

- Recent technological advances offer several opportunities for future field studies on river morphodynamics. However, it should be recognized that some difficulties remain, particularly in highly dynamic

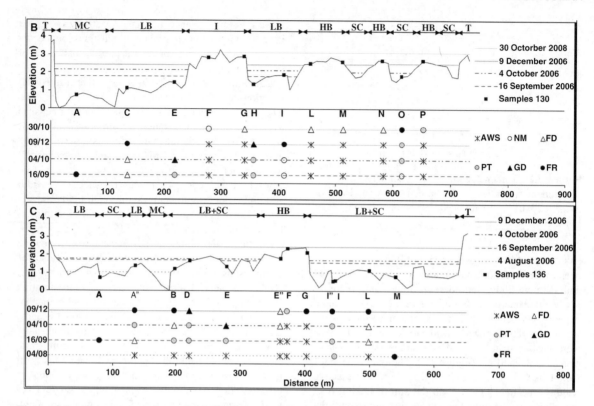

**Figure 7.3** Two cross-sections of the Tagliamento River where different formative events were monitored using painted sediments located in different morphological units (MC: main channel; SC: secondary channel; LB: low bar; HB: high bar; I: island; FD: floodplain; T: terrace). The lower graphs show the effects of floods over the painted areas (AWS: painted area above water stage; NM: no sediment motion; FD: deposition of fine sediments; PT: partial transport; GD: gravel deposition; FR: full removal of the painted sediments) (Mao and Surian, 2010). Reproduced, with permission, from Elsevier.

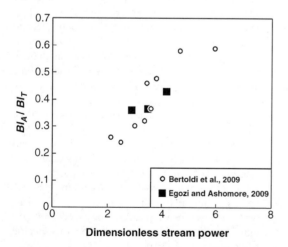

**Figure 7.4** $BI_A/BI_T$ versus dimensionless stream power from different flume experiments (Egozi and Ashmore, 2009). Reproduced, with permission, from American Geophysical Union.

systems characterized by frequent, unpredictable, formative events (e.g., Brasington *et al.*, 2010).

- Short-term observations should be put into a longer temporal framework to better understand channel condition in terms of equilibrium/disequilibrium. This is particularly true when short-term observations are used to validate models that assume an equilibrium condition (e.g., analytical models). On the other hand, historical re-constructions of channel evolution and instability often lack robust theories which could be better developed through modelling.

- Active channel width could be a key parameter in future research on large gravel-bed rivers. Some efforts should be made to define different strategies for its measurement in the field and to build larger datasets that could be used for testing general relationships, such as that between active width and dimensionless stream power.

## 7.6 ACKNOWLEDGEMENTS

I thank Ellen Wohl for helpful comments on the paper.

## 7.7 REFERENCES

Ashmore, P. 2001. Braiding phenomena: statics and kinetics. In Mosley, M.P. Editor. *Gravel-bed Rivers V.* Wellington, New Zealand Hydrological Society, pp. 95–114.

Bartholdy, J. and Billi, P. 2002. Morphodynamics of a pseudomeandering gravel bar reach. *Geomorphology* **42**: 293–310.

Bennett, S.J., Simon, A., and Kuhnle, R.A. 1998. Temporal variations in point bar morphology within two incised river meanders, Goodwin Creek, Mississippi. In Abt, S.R., Young-Pezeshk, J., and Watson, C.C., editors, *Proceedings of Water Resources Engineering '98.* Reston, American Society of Civil Engineers, pp. 1422–1427.

Bertoldi, W. and Ashmore, P. 2010. Active width of gravel-bed braided rivers. Poster presented at the Gravel-bed Rivers 7 Workshop, Tadoussac, Canada, 6–10 September.

Bertoldi, W., Zanoni, L., and Tubino, M. 2009. Planform dynamics of braided rivers. *Earth Surface Processes and Landforms* **34**: 547–557.

Bertoldi, W., Zanoni, L., and Tubino, M. 2010. Assessment of morphological changes induced by flow and flood pulses in a gravel bed braided river: the Tagliamento River. *Geomorphology* **114**: 348–360.

Brasington J., Williams R., Vericat D. *et al.* 2010. Hyperscale monitoring and modelling of the braided Rees River, New Zealand. Poster presented at the Gravel-bed Rivers 7 Workshop, Tadoussac, Canada, 6–10 September.

Church, M. and Rice, S.P. 2009. Form and growth of bars in a wandering gravel-bed river. *Earth Surface Processes and Landforms* **34**: 1422–1432.

Egozi, R. and Ashmore, P. 2008. Defining and measuring braiding intensity. *Earth Surface Processes and Landforms* **33**: 2121–2138.

Egozi, R. and Ashmore, P. 2009. Experimental analysis of braided channel pattern response to increased discharge. *Journal of Geophysical Research* **114**: F02012. doi: 10.1029/2008JF001099.

Ferguson R. 2008. Gravel-bed rivers at the reach scale. In Habersack, H., Piégay H., and Rinaldi, M. editors. *Gravel-bed Rivers VI: From Processes Understanding to River Restoration.* Amsterdam, Elsevier. Developments in Earth Surface Processes 11, pp. 33–53.

Heritage, G. and Hetherington, D. 2007. Towards a protocol for laser scanning in fluvial geomorphology. *Earth Surface Processes and Landforms* **32**: 66–74.

Hicks, D.M., Ducan, M.J., Lane, S.N., Tal, M., and Westway, R. 2008. Contemporary morphological change in braided gravel-bed rivers: new developments from field and laboratory studies, with particular reference to the influence of riparian vegetation. In Habersack H., Piégay H. and Rinaldi M. editors. *Gravel-Bed Rivers VI: From Process Understanding to River Restoration.* Amsterdam, Elsevier. Developments in Earth Surface Processes 11, pp. 557–584.

Hooke, J.M. 2007. Spatial variability, mechanisms and propagation of change in an active meandering river. *Geomorphology* **84**: 277–296.

Hooke, J.M. 2008. Temporal variations in fluvial processes on an active meandering river over a 20-year period. *Geomorphology* **100**: 3–13.

Kleinhans, M.G. 2010. Sorting out river channel patterns. *Progress in Physical Geography* **34**: 287–326.

Lanzoni, S. 2000. Experiments on bar formation in a straight flume 1. Uniform sediment. *Water Resources Research* **36**: 3351–3363.

Mao, L. and Surian, N. 2010. Observations on sediment mobility in a large gravel-bed river. *Geomorphology* **114**: 326–337.

Marcus, W.A. and Fonstad, M.A. 2008. Optical remote mapping of rivers at sub-meter resolutions and watershed extents. *Earth Surface Processes and Landforms* **33**: 4–24.

Milan, D.J., Heritage, G.L., and Hetherington, D. 2007. Application of 3D laser scanner in the assessment of erosion and deposition volumes and channel change in a proglacial river. *Earth Surface Processes and Landforms* **32**: 1657–1674.

Piégay, H., Alber, A., Slater, L., and Bourdin, L. 2009. Census and typology of braided rivers in the French Alps. *Aquatic Sciences* **71**: 371–388.

Rumsby, B.T., Brasington, J., Langham, J.A. *et al.* 2008. Monitoring and modelling particle and reach-scale morphological change in gravel-bed rivers: applications and challenges. *Geomorphology* **93**: 40–54.

Surian, N. and Cisotto, A. 2007. Channel adjustments, bedload transport and sediment sources in a gravel-bed river, Brenta River, Italy. *Earth Surface Processes and Landforms* **32**: 1641–1656.

Surian, N., Ziliani, L., Comiti, F., Lenzi, M.A., and Mao, L. 2009. Channel adjustments and alteration of sediment fluxes in gravel-bed rivers of Northeastern Italy: potentials and limitations for channel recovery. *River Research and Applications* **25**: 551–567.

# 8

# Morphodynamics of Bars in Gravel-bed Rivers: Coupling Hydraulic Geometry and Analytical Models

## Robert G. Millar

## 8.1 INTRODUCTION

Theoretical numerical models have been widely and successfully used in fluvial hydraulics to simulate physical processes and to gain insight into many aspects of bar morphodynamics, planform morphology, channel pattern, and meander dynamics. Analytical models are a subset of numerical models in which certain further simplifying assumptions are made, which can reduce often considerable mathematical complexity down to workable and practical solutions. Zolezzi *et al.* (Chapter 6, this volume) provide a comprehensive review.

The purpose of this discussion chapter is not to critique the analytical models *per se*, but rather to argue that these models alone are limited as they can provide only part of the solution. Specifically, channel parameters such as width, width–depth ratio, dimensionless shear stress, relative depth, channel slope, or Froude number must generally be specified as "inputs" to the analytical models in order to determine useable solutions. For example, it has been demonstrated (Zolezzi *et al.*, 2009) that deformation waves can propagate both upstream and downstream within single-thread meandering rivers (termed super- and subresonance), and that the direction of propagation is controlled by width–depth ratio. If width–depth ratio is known, then the propagation direction of deformation waves can be determined. The more fundamental question then is what controls the width–depth ratio, because this is ultimately what determines whether a meandering river will behave super- or subresonantly. Channel pattern and prediction of meandering and braided channels provides another instance in which analytical models have been successfully applied to natural rivers. This will be used to demonstrate how analytical model results can be extended by coupling with hydraulic geometry.

## 8.2 PREDICTION OF CHANNEL PATTERNS

The application of analytical linear-stability models to morphodynamic processes has a long and well-established history. Various models have been developed to simulate the initiation and growth of instabilities, which have described features ranging from sand ripples and dunes (1-D) to larger features including bars, and meander and braid wavelengths (2-D). With respect to the prediction of channel patterns, Parker (1976), Fredsoe (1978) and Crosato and Mosselman (2009) have made notable contributions.

The complexity of the models make them rather difficult and even intimidating for those lacking the strongest fluid mechanics and analytical backgrounds. Fortunately, rather simple general predictors can be derived. For transition from meandering to braiding, the following predictors have been proposed:

$$\text{Parker (1976): } W/D \approx F_R/S \tag{8.1}$$

$$\text{Fredsoe (1978): } W/D \approx 50 \tag{8.2}$$

$$\text{Crosato and Mosselman (2009): } 4 = 0.17g\frac{7}{\sqrt{(s-1)d_{50}}}\frac{W^3 S}{CQ} \tag{8.3}$$

*Gravel-bed Rivers: Processes, Tools, Environments*, First Edition. Edited by Michael Church, Pascale M. Biron and André G. Roy.
© 2012 John Wiley & Sons, Ltd. Published 2012 by John Wiley & Sons, Ltd.

amongst others. ($W$ = channel width, $D$ = channel depth, $F_R$ = Froude number, $S$ = channel slope, $g$ = gravitational acceleration, $d_{50}$ = median bed grain diameter, $s$ = sediment specific gravity, $Q$ = discharge, and $C$ = Chezy coefficient).

Of the three, the predictor proposed by Fredsoe (1978) is the simplest and states that the transition from meandering to braiding occurs at around a $W/D$ ratio of about 50. Narrower and deeper channels will tend to be single-thread or meandering, and wider and shallower channels will be braided. Wandering or anabranching rivers, which represent a transitional morphotype, should take a $W/D$ ratio of around 50.

For these gravel bed data, the simple predictor from Fredsoe (1978) of bankfull $W/D$ = 50 appears to discriminate very well between the different morphologies, with relatively little overlap between meandering and braided (Figure 8.1). Also, the channels described as wandering or anabranching lie within the space between the two main channel types, which is consistent with wandering representing a transitional morphology.

The empirical success of Fredsoe's theoretical predictor is certainly impressive. However, the practical application is limited because it requires the $W/D$ ratio to be specified. For a particular river, if one can measure the $W/D$ ratio, than there is no need to resort to Fredsoe's predictor to determine if the river is meandering or braiding, you can simply look for yourself! This illustrates the limitation of the various channel pattern predictors, as well as the theoretical analytical models in general. Values of key controlling parameters such as $W/D$ ratio, $W$, $S$, or dimensionless shear stress must generally be known *a priori* in order to apply the models.

### 8.2.1 Controls on W/D Ratio

Because the channel pattern appears so strongly controlled by $W/D$ ratio, it begs the question what are the independent variables that control the $W/D$ ratio, because, by inference, the same variables would also control the channel pattern.

Applying rational regime theory, Millar (2005) derived the following simplified expression for the bankfull $W/D$ ratio of gravel rivers as a function of dimensionless discharge $Q^*$, slope $S$, and the relative strength of the banks versus the channel bed $\mu'$:

$$W/D = 155 Q^{*0.53} S^{1.23} \mu'^{-1.74} \qquad (8.4)$$

wherein $Q^* = Q/d_{50}^2 \sqrt{gd_{50}(s-1)}$. Substituting Fredsoe's $W/D = 50$, and using a value of $\mu' = 1$ (corresponding to loose, non-cohesive gravel banks with no significant bank vegetation effects), the following dimensionless solution is obtained (Eaton et al., 2010):

$$S^* = 0.40 Q^{*-0.43} \qquad (8.5)$$

where $S^*$ is the transitional slope between meandering and braiding. Note that Equation (8.5) is purely theoretical, yet agrees very well in form with the well-known Leopold and Wolman (1957) dimensional empirical relation:

$$S^* = 0.0125 Q^{-0.44} \qquad (8.6)$$

Henderson (1963) revised the original Leopold and Wolman (1957) relation to include grain size, an obvious omission. Henderson's revised predictor can be reorganized into a dimensionless form (Eaton et al., 2010):

$$S^* = 0.28 Q^{*-0.44} \qquad (8.7)$$

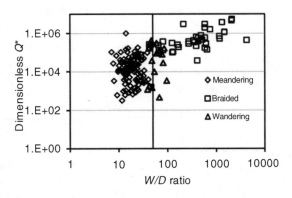

**Figure 8.1** Bankfull $W/D$ ratio of meandering, braided, and wandering/anabranching gravel-bed rivers. The $W/D$ ratio of 50 from Fredsoe (1978) is indicated for reference. Data are plotted using dimensionless discharge, $Q^* = \dfrac{Q}{d_{50}^2 \sqrt{gd_{50}(s-1)}}$ for convenience only.

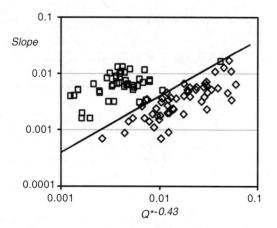

**Figure 8.2** Meandering and braided rivers described as having weak or no bank vegetation. The theoretical transition slope (Equation 8.5), which is based on bankfull $W/D = 50$ provides good separation of the two channel types.

Clearly, apart from a modest difference in the coefficient, Equations (8.5), which is purely theoretical, and (8.7), which is purely empirical, are very similar.

For gravel-bed rivers where bank vegetation is weak or absent. Assuming that a value of $\mu' \approx 1$ can be assumed. For these rivers, Equation (8.5) provides a clean separation between the meandering and braided streams (Figure 8.2). The transitional wandering/anabranching rivers show more scatter (Figure 8.3), although do plot mostly about the theoretical transition. By definition, wandering channels split and flow around vegetated islands, so it is possible that these channels are affected by bank vegetation, and therefore the assumed value of $\mu' = 1$ may not be valid.

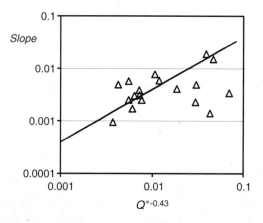

**Figure 8.3** Wandering/anabranching rivers. We expect these channels to plot near the theoretical transition slope (Equation 8.5). There is considerable scatter in the data.

In summary, the theoretical meandering–braiding transition Equation (8.5) from Eaton *et al.* (2010) can be viewed as an alternate expression of Fredsoe's (1978) predictor $W/D = 50$. It is very similar to the Leopold and Wolman (1957) relation, and provides good separation between meandering and braided gravel rivers where the banks are not strongly influenced by bank vegetation.

### 8.2.2  Most Probable Number of Bars, M

Eaton *et al.* (2010) also proposed a theoretical expression for the number of channel divisions, which is similar to Crosato and Mosselman's (2009) definition of *m*, the most probable number of steady bars:

$$m = \left(\frac{S}{S^*}\right)^{2.32} \tag{8.8}$$

Equation (8.8) is derived directly from (8.5), and is based on the idea that a wandering or braided river is composed of *m* single-thread anabranching channels, and $m = 2$ represents the transition between meandering and braided rivers. Equation (8.8) allows *m* to be computed using *Q*, *S*, and $d_{50}$, in contrast to Crosato and Mosselman's expression (Equation 8.3), which also requires the channel width, *W*, be known. The results are shown in Figure 8.4, and indicate good agreement with observation for the same data used by Zolezzi *et al.* (Chapter 6, this volume).

The relation between $W/D$ ratio, channel pattern, and *m* is shown in Figure 8.5. The average values of *m* calculated for the meandering, wandering, and braided channel types using Equation (8.8) are 0.65, 2.1, and 47, respectively.

## 8.3  SUMMARY AND CONCLUSIONS

Hydraulic geometry can provide key input parameters that must generally be specified in order to apply analytical morphodynamic models. In the example worked through here, $W/D$ ratio obtained from rational regime theory is coupled with Fredose's (1976) theoretical predictor to derive a meandering/braiding predictor (Eaton *et al.*, 2010) that is very similar in form to the classic Leopold and Wolman (1957) relation. The resultant theoretical predictor successfully discriminates between channel types, and demonstrates the more fundamental controls of discharge, grain size, slope, and bank strength on channel pattern. Furthermore, the Eaton *et al.* predictor can be further developed to yield a new theoretical relation for the number of channel divisions or mid-channel bars (Equation 8.8).

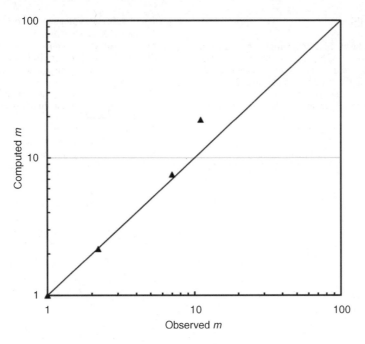

**Figure 8.4** Comparison between the observed number of probable steady bars, $m$, and the computed values using Equation (8.8) for the same data used by Zolezzi *et al.* (Chapter 6, this volume).

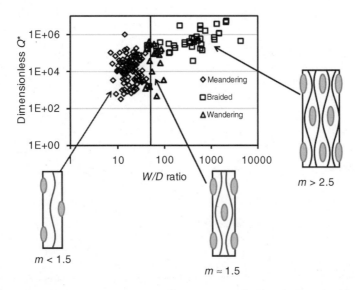

**Figure 8.5** *W/D* ratio, channel pattern, and the most probable number of steady bars (braiding index).

The same approach could be extended to other analytical models. Hydraulic geometry can provide width, *W/D* ratio, relative depth, $D/d_{50}$, dimensionless shear stress, or other input parameters for the analytical models. There is potential to then combine the two approaches and develop new relations that are based on the more fundamental controls such as discharge, grain size, and sediment load. Potentially, hydraulic geometry and analytical models can also benefit bridging with field observations.

## 8.4  REFERENCES

Crosato, A. and Mosselman, E. 2009. Simple physics-based predictor for the number of river bars and the transition between meandering and braiding. *Water Resources Research* **45**: W03424. doi: 10.1029/2008WR007242.

Eaton, B.E., Millar, R.G., and Davidson, S. 2010. Channel patterns: braided, anabranching, and single-thread. *Geomorphology* **120**: 353–364.

Fredsoe, J. 1978. Meandering and braiding of rivers. *Journal of Fluid Mechanics* **84**: 609–624.

Henderson, F.M. 1963. Stability of alluvial channels. *American Society of Civil Engineers Transactions* **128,** Part I: 657–654.

Leopold, L.B. and Wolman, M.G. 1957. *River channel patterns: braiding meandering and straight.* United States Geological Survey Professional Paper 262-B: 39–85.

Millar, R.G. 2005. Theoretical regime relations for mobile gravel-bed rivers with stable banks. *Geomorphology* **64**: 207–220.

Parker, G. 1976. On the cause and characteristic scales of meandering and braiding in rivers. *Journal of Fluid Mechanics* **76**: 457–478.

Zolezzi, G., Luchi, R., and Tubino, M. 2009. Morphodynamic regime of gravel bed, single-thread meandering rivers. *Journal of Geophysical Research* **114**: F01005. doi: 10.1029/2007JF000968.

# 9

# Modelling Sediment Transport and Morphodynamics of Gravel-bed Rivers

## Erik Mosselman

## 9.1 INTRODUCTION

Mathematical models of morphodynamics compute bed level changes and changes in bed sediment composition as a result of open channel hydraulics and sediment transport. They have found widespread application in river engineering and fluvial geomorphology. This chapter reviews some aspects of the present state of knowledge regarding morphodynamic models of gravel-bed rivers: non-uniform sediment (Section 9.2), analytical solutions (Section 9.3), bank erosion and accretion (Section 9.4), vegetation dynamics (Section 9.5), and validation (Section 9.6). For these aspects, the chapter also identifies trends and challenges ahead. The concluding section (Section 9.7) presents the challenges in the framework of Syvitski *et al.*, (2009), who identify up-scaling, process coupling, model coupling, data systems, high-performance computing, and model testing as the challenges for the morphodynamic modelling community in general.

The first and most obvious trend is the continuing development of knowledge and computer technology, leading to models of greater detail that, at the same time, can be run feasibly for longer river reaches and longer periods of time. The dimensionality of models increases, from 1-D to 2-D depth-averaged for reach-scale models and from 2-D width-averaged or depth-averaged to 3-D for models on a local scale. Morphodynamic models mostly compute the flow using a Reynolds-averaged momentum equation, but excursions into large-eddy simulation have been made. Direct numerical simulation has come within reach for the motion of sediment, but customary models remain based on empirical transport relations and a volumetric sediment balance or Exner equation. Sediment non-uniformity is an essential feature of gravel-bed rivers. Section 9.2 reviews the classical approach to modelling non-uniform sediment, and

indicates areas for improvement. Deeper insights into improvements have been obtained from analytical solutions that are reviewed in Section 9.3.

A second trend for gravel-bed rivers lies in the area of application. One's first image of a gravel-bed river might be a braided river with gravel bars, in a natural environment and preferably wadeable to carry out field work for research. However, the focus of research and modelling moves increasingly to larger gravel-bed rivers in more populated and urban areas, where every inch is optimized to meet demands for safety against flooding, navigation, hydropower, aggregate mining, water supply, and the like, often at the cost of ecological values. The management of these rivers is almost industrial, putting high demands on accuracy in design, implementation, and monitoring. The bed of the river Rhine, for instance, is routinely corrected by gravel nourishment (Figure 9.1) and is inspected by using a diving bell several metres under water, which can be conveniently reached by descending a staircase (Figure 9.2). Similar high demands are put on projects to counter the adverse effects on ecology in these rivers, even though river restoration is often limited here to cosmetic embellishment, gardening or, as Parker (2004) puts it, "disneylandification", rather than truly letting nature take its course. The high demands on accurately predicting the morphological effects of interventions also imply high demands on model reliability and, hence, model validation. Section 9.6 advocates setting international standards for model validation in fluvial morphodynamics.

A third trend is that morphodynamic models are becoming a standard element in decision-making for river projects where many stakeholders are involved. This makes the communication of model results a major issue, as most stakeholders will not have a background in fluvial morphodynamics. Moreover, stakeholders will

*Gravel-bed Rivers: Processes, Tools, Environments*, First Edition. Edited by Michael Church, Pascale M. Biron and André G. Roy.
© 2012 John Wiley & Sons, Ltd. Published 2012 by John Wiley & Sons, Ltd.

**Figure 9.1**  Gravel nourishment to correct the morphology of the river Rhine (courtesy Saskia van Vuren).

have differing attitudes to mathematical models, from awe to outright rejection. Proper communication requires good explanations of what models can do and what they cannot. Models represent certain aspects of reality, but they are not replicas of reality. Similarly, scale model buildings in miniature parks may accurately reproduce the shadows cast on the streets but, unlike their real counterparts, they will not have toilets inside you can flush. So, notwithstanding the increasing demands on accuracy, it is also increasingly important to acknowledge model uncertainty and to deal with this uncertainty explicitly. Van der Klis (2003) and Van Vuren (2005) develop a probabilistic approach to river morphodynamics by deriving 95% confidence intervals from Monte Carlo simulations. The trend towards becoming a standard tool also means that models are sold commercially and applied by users who had no role in developing them. This leads to subspecialization among modellers and the need to carry out modelling in a team to cover the different categories of knowledge. Here Van

**Figure 9.2**  (a) River bed inspection ship "Carl Straat" of the Wasser- und Schiffahrtsamt Duisburg-Rhein, Germany (source: www.wsa-duisburg-rhein.wsv.de); (b) staircase to the bed of the river Rhine (courtesy Gertjan Geerling); (c) standing on the gravel bed of the river Rhine, several metres under the water level (courtesy Gertjan Geerling). Reproduced from http://www.wsa-duisburg-rhein.wsv.de/wir_ueber_uns/Wasserfahrzeuge/Carl_Straat.html © Wasser- und Schifffahrtsamt Duisburg-Rhein, Germany.

Zuylen *et al.* (1994) distinguish: (i) domain knowledge based on common sense and expertise from experience with real rivers, (ii) knowledge about model concepts such as the underlying mathematical equations, (iii) knowledge about model constructs such as grids, time steps, and initial and boundary conditions, and (iv) knowledge about model artifacts such as user interfaces and file formats.

A fourth trend, finally, is that morphodynamic modelling moves from mere interactions between underwater bed topography and fluid dynamical processes to the evolution of earth-surface elevation as a result of interactions with fluid dynamics, ecodynamics, geodynamics, and human activities. Section 9.4 reviews the interactions with bank erosion and accretion, and Section 9.5 the interactions with vegetation dynamics. Accounting for the interactions between fluvial morphodynamics and vegetation dynamics is not just a matter of coupling processes or models. It involves interdisciplinary co-operation between ecologists and physics-based modellers who are trained with different paradigms and terminology. Interactions from the coupling of processes or models can produce complex phenomena in model results, for which it is not always clear whether they represent physical reality or a numerical artifact. Section 9.3 argues that analytical solutions can provide more clarity on this.

Large gravel-bed rivers, such as the river Rhine, have a large ratio of flow depth to sediment grain size. Most points in this chapter hold for both high and low values of this ratio. Rivers with low ratios of flow depth to grain size, however, pose additional problems to modelling because of their stronger spatial and temporal variations in width, the many factors that influence their hydraulic roughness, their spatial variations in flow regime, and the behaviour of pool-riffle sequences (Bradley *et al.*, 1998). These problems are beyond the scope of the present chapter.

## 9.2   EROSION, TRANSPORT, AND DEPOSITION OF NON-UNIFORM SEDIMENT

Morphologically active gravel-bed rivers display a wide range of grain sizes. Segregation of these grains during processes of erosion, transport, and deposition gives rise to spatial grain-sorting phenomena such as coarse bed surface layers, downstream fining, coarser-grained riffles in straight channels, and finer-grained point bars in meandering rivers. Grain sorting also affects the longitudinal river profile, as well as the patterns and dimensions of bars, riffles, and pools. The intimate relation between bed topography and bed sediment composition

makes sediment composition a central element in river morphology. It has become customary in the modelling of fluvial morphodynamics to use the term "graded sediment" as a synonym for "non-uniform sediment", although this is not fully correct, because non-uniform sediment includes, not only widely graded sediment, but also narrowly graded bimodal and trimodal sediment distributions. Most mathematical models treat all these distributions in the same way.

The classical approach to modelling river morphology with non-uniform sediment is based on: (i) division of the sediment mixture into separate fractions, (ii) transport formulae and mass conservation equations for each of the separate fractions, (iii) hiding-and-exposure corrections to the critical shear stress of each of the fractions (Egiazaroff, 1965; Ashida and Michiue, 1972, 1973), and (iv) an active layer or transport layer affected by erosion and sedimentation (Hirano, 1972). The hiding-and-exposure corrections account for the interactions between the different fractions. Hiding or shielding makes relatively fine grains in a mixture less mobile than they would be in uniform sediment, because they protrude less into the flow than surrounding coarser grains. Likewise, exposure makes relatively coarse grains in a mixture more easily entrained, because they protrude more.

The classical approach, however, has many shortcomings that have been explored to some extent, but remain areas of research and model development. Hiding and exposure act not only on the critical shear stress, but also on the effective bed shear stress (Einstein and Chien, 1953, referenced by Ribberink, 1987), which depends on the surface roughness of the bed. This roughness varies in a complex manner with bed sediment composition under conditions of partial mobility in which the coarsest fractions are immobile and the transport of the finest fractions is supply-limited. Sand may be transported in the interstices of a gravel layer if the amounts are low, thus hardly affecting bed roughness, but also as isolated sand dunes when the amounts are higher, with dimensions different from what would occur in the absence of the underlying gravel. Hiding and exposure are also likely to play a role in the effect of gravity pull along transverse bed slopes on moving grains. This role is still unknown. It is not clear, for instance, whether the proper mobility parameter to be used in the weighting function for gravity pull is the Shields parameter for each individual grain size fraction or an overall Shields parameter for an average grain size.

Another limitation of the classical approach is that the porosity is assumed constant. The models by Parker and Cui (1998) and Cui and Parker (1998) include a relation for an effective porosity under the assumption that the gravel interstices are fully filled by sand, but they note

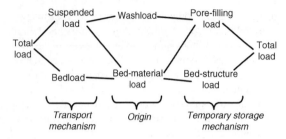

**Figure 9.3** Classification of sediment transport after Frings *et al.*, 2008.

that complete filling is unlikely to be realized due to partial bridging and clogging effects. Moreover, the filling and emptying of the pores of the coarser grains represents a temporary storage of sediment that does not cause any change in bed level. Frings *et al.* (2008) therefore propose an additional division of the total sediment load into bed-structure load and pore-filling load (Figure 9.3). Bed-structure load is defined as the coarse portion of the bed-material load that interacts with the bed structure and hence contributes to bed level changes. Pore-filling load is defined as the fine portion of the sediment load that infiltrates between the pores of the larger grains if the flow decelerates. By strict definition, this should be the fine portion of the bed-material load, but it could also include temporary storage of washload in ephemeral streams.

Morphological computations using the classical approach appear to depend much on the thickness of the active layer. This thickness is often equated to half the average height of the bed forms. However, a thicker active layer is needed to account for the statistical variability in dune dimensions, because sporadic deeper troughs between bed forms can exchange material at a larger depth under the bed surface. The active layer becomes even thicker when discharge variations cause variations in transverse bed slopes in river bends or generate sedimentation and erosion waves at locations where overbank flows leave and re-enter the main channel. Calibration of mathematical models generally confirms that the active layer must be considerably thicker than half the height of the bed forms. Mosselman and Sloff (2008) find that the bed topography computed using a 2-D depth-averaged model of the Rhine remains unrealistically constant if the active layer is chosen to be as thin as half the height of the bed forms. Section 9.3 explains this on the basis of an analytical solution of the mathematical model. Tuijnder (2010) observes that Struiksma's (1999) bedload reduction function for supply-limited transport over non-erodible layers matches his experimental findings if the active-layer thickness is taken equal to 1.5 times the average dune height. Sloff

and Ottevanger (2008) find in numerical computations for the river Rhine that a thick active layer is needed to stabilize the location of the gravel–sand transition. They find migration of the transition to slow down as the active layer is chosen to be thicker. This is also evident from Parker's (1991) equations for aggradational river profiles of permanent form. Nonetheless, for realistic active layers, the migration can only be stopped completely by fulfilling additional conditions, such as abrasion, basin subsidence, or base level rise (Parker and Cui, 1998).

The sensitivity of morphological computations to the oversimplified single active layer has led to more refined modelling approaches, such as the addition of an exchange layer in Ribberink's (1987) two-layer model and the introduction of a depth-continuous continuity model for vertical sediment exchange by Parker *et al.* (2000), Blom (2003) and Blom *et al.* (2003a, 2003b). Multiple-layer approaches are used for the book-keeping of sediment deposited and buried by natural sedimentation or artificial nourishment. They store information on deeper bed sediment composition for later erosion, a feature which also allows process-based geological modelling of alluvial stratigraphy.

The erosion, transport, and deposition of non-uniform sediment remain complex processes for which customary model formulations are often too simplistic. Improved formulations may be derived from detailed measurements in the laboratory or in the field, but also from detailed numerical modelling based on direct numerical simulation. Schmeeckle and Nelson (2003), for instance, compute the motion of individual spherical sediment particles, while keeping track of interparticle interactions. Such detailed models are not intended for direct application to real rivers, but once validated, they form a numerical research lab to collect data for the development of parameterized model formulations on longer spatial and temporal scales. This upscaling of detailed processes into more practical formulations forms a major challenge in modelling the erosion, transport, and deposition of non-uniform sediment.

## 9.3 ANALYTICAL SOLUTIONS

Mathematical modelling is often primarily understood as numerical solution of mathematical equations using a computer. However, the equations can also be solved analytically under special conditions. The solutions may be zero-order (referring to steady uniform states), linear (retaining only the linear parts of Taylor expansions of the equations), or non-linear. Analytical solutions are complementary to numerical solutions, as they offer additional insights into the fundamental behaviour of the corresponding physical system. Designing numerical models requires theoretical analyses to determine the appropriate numerical scheme, the time step, and the type and location of the boundary conditions to be imposed. Theoretical analyses also help the optimization of calibration strategies for numerical models, as they reveal which parameters are responsible for different aspects of the solution. They help the interpretation of results from numerical models as well, because numerical solutions may exhibit spurious wiggles, phase lags, or attenuation that in this way can be distinguished from real physical phenomena. Furthermore, analytical solutions provide exact solutions for certain idealized cases that may serve as validation cases for numerical models. Finally, they can be used as rapid assessment models or rules of thumb.

Notwithstanding these powerful qualities, analytical solutions remain just approximations of the real world, as they require a simplification of the mathematical equations or the assumption that variations with respect to a basic state have very small amplitudes. For good reason, linear and non-linear dynamics are sometimes likened to elephant and weakly non-elephant zoology. Linear analyses, for instance, can predict the essential features of alternate bars and meander point bars very well, but they appear incapable of predicting the bar patterns of highly braided rivers (Mosselman, 2006; Crosato and Mosselman, 2009). Fully non-linear analyses usually require the strongest simplifications. The non-linear stability analysis of river bifurcations by Wang *et al.* (1995), for instance, assumes uniform flow along with erosion and sedimentation spread uniformly over the full lengths of the river branches.

Ribberink (1987) and Lanzoni and Tubino (1999) pioneered the development of theoretical analyses of river morphodynamics with non-uniform sediment; Ribberink in one dimension and Lanzoni and Tubino in two dimensions. Ribberink's seminal analysis can be used to illustrate the wide range of insights and applications that can be obtained from such an analysis. He integrates mass conservation equations for individual sediment size fractions over the full sediment mixture and combines the resulting equation for sediment composition with quasi-steady flow equations and the sediment balance or Exner equation, assuming capacity-limited sediment transport as a function of depth-averaged flow velocity and bed sediment composition, without lag effects. He then carries out an analysis of characteristics of the set of equations, which reveals how information propagates in the mathematical system. The analysis leads to the following equation for the celerities, $c$, of perturbations in bed level and bed sediment composition:

$$(c-c_{bed})(c-c_{mix})-\xi c = 0 \qquad (9.1)$$

with

$$c_{bed} = \frac{bq_S}{(1-\varepsilon)(1-Fr^2)h} \qquad (9.2)$$

$$c_{mix} = \frac{D_{mT}}{D_m}\frac{q_S}{(1-\varepsilon)\delta} \qquad (9.3)$$

$$\xi = \frac{D_{mT}-D_m}{(1-\varepsilon)\delta}\frac{\partial q_S}{\partial D_m} \qquad (9.4)$$

Here, $b =$ the degree of non-linearity in the dependence of sediment transport rate on flow velocity, defined as $b = (u/q_S)(\partial q_S/\partial u)$. Its value is always above 3, equal to 5 for the Engelund–Hansen transport predictor, and even larger close to the sediment mobility threshold; $c =$ celerity of bed level and bed sediment composition perturbations; $c_{bed} =$ reference celerity of bed level perturbations; $c_{mix} =$ reference celerity of bed sediment composition perturbations; $D_m =$ median grain size of bed material; $D_{mT} =$ median grain size of sediment in transport; $Fr =$ Froude number, defined as $Fr = u/\sqrt{gh}$; $g =$ acceleration due to gravity; $h =$ flow depth; $q_s =$ volumetric sediment transport rate per unit width, excluding pores; $u =$ depth-averaged flow velocity; $\delta =$ thickness of active layer; $\varepsilon =$ porosity; $\xi =$ parameter representing the interactions between bed topography and bed sediment composition.

Equation (9.1) readily shows that the celerities, $c$, are equal to the reference celerities, $c_{bed}$ and $c_{mix}$, if $\xi = 0$, i.e., if $D_{mT} = D_m$. This means that bed level evolution and bed sediment composition evolution do not interact if the material in transport is equal to the material of the bed, which is generally true if the river experiences overall sedimentation. The positive values of the reference celerities evident from Equations (9.2) and (9.3) imply that bed topography information and bed sediment composition information travel from upstream to downstream. They hence require conditions at the upstream boundary. The wavelike behaviour of propagating features implies that the mathematical system has a hyperbolic character, according to a terminology based on the similarity between the characteristic equations of second-order partial differential equations and the discriminants of conic sections. The celerities also put an upper limit to the time step according to the Courant–Friedrichs–Lewy condition for numerical solution using explicit time-marching schemes.

Interactions between bed level evolution and bed sediment composition evolution occur if $\xi \neq 0$. Ribberink (1987) realized that the roots of Equation (9.1) can become complex if $\xi < 0$, with the remark that the latter is a necessary but not a sufficient condition for this. Complex roots hence occur in certain cases where the sediment in transport is coarser than the underlying material of the bed ($D_{mT} > D_m$), because sediment transport rates invariably decrease with increasing grain sizes ($\partial q_S / \partial D_m < 0$). The complex roots are problematic, because they change the hyperbolic character of the system into an elliptic character. This may not only render the chosen numerical solution procedure inappropriate, but also conflicts with fundamental principles in physics. An elliptic system requires conditions at both upper and lower boundaries of the independent variables. This is no problem if all independent variables are space coordinates, but does present a problem if one of the independent variables is time, as in the case of Ribberink's analysis, because the required condition at the upper time boundary implies the present to depend on the future. This insight into the limitations of the existing mathematical model formulations was another reason, in addition to the limitations of a single active layer explained in Section 9.2, why Ribberink (1987) developed a two-layer model and why Parker *et al.* (2000), Blom (2003) and Blom *et al.* (2003a, 2003b) developed a depth-continuous continuity model for vertical sediment exchange.

Mosselman and Sloff (2007) use the expressions for the reference celerities to assess the importance of the active-layer thickness, $\delta$. Equations (9.2) and (9.3) yield the following ratio of characteristic time scales:

$$\frac{T_{mix}}{T_{bed}} = \frac{c_{bed}}{c_{mix}} = \frac{b}{1-Fr^2} \frac{D_m}{D_{mT}} \frac{\delta}{h} \qquad (9.5)$$

wherein $T_{bed}$ denotes the characteristic time scale for bed level evolution and $T_{mix}$ is the characteristic time scale for bed sediment composition evolution. The ratio of time scales is hence proportional to the ratio of active-layer thickness to flow depth. If $\delta \ll h$, the sediment composition of the bed responds immediately to the initial bed topography in a way that eliminates gradients in sediment transport capacity, after which the bed topography remains unchanged. If $\delta \gg h$, the evolution of the bed topography is forced by the initial sediment composition pattern, while the bed sediment composition remains unchanged. A combined evolution of bed topography and bed sediment composition is only possible if approximately $5\delta$ and $h$ have the same order of magnitude. Application of a 2-D depth-averaged model to parts of the Rhine where bed topography changes are known to occur shows that the active-layer thickness must be larger than what might be inferred from dune dimensions during average flow conditions. One possible explanation is that floods with high dunes are an important factor for the morphological development of the river bed. Another explanation is that the active-layer thickness depends not only on river-bed variations due to migrating dunes, but also on river-bed variations due to variations in discharge.

Mosselman *et al.* (2008) use the analysis to improve the calibration of a 2-D morphological model. The large number of calibration parameters produces problems of equifinality in the sense that different combinations of calibration parameter values can produce the same bed topography. It is difficult to decide which combination is the right one. The model is therefore calibrated on as many different morphological phenomena as possible: the longitudinal bed profile, the pattern of bars and pools, the sediment transport rates, and the celerities of bed level perturbations. Often, however, these different phenomena are correlated and hence not independent. Equation (9.2), for instance, shows a strong correlation between sediment transport rate and celerity of bed level perturbations. This correlation becomes weaker if the transported sediment differs from the underlying material of the bed ($\xi \neq 0$). Identifying situations in which this occurs offers a possibility to use sediment transport rate and the celerity of bed level perturbations as independent phenomena for calibration.

The limitation that the analysis of characteristics represents variations with small amplitude can be illustrated by considering the propagation of a sedimentation front with a finite height, $\Delta z_b$. The expression for $c_{bed}$ in Equation (9.2) offers a rapid assessment method or rule of thumb for the propagation speed, $c_{front}$, but this equation is an exact solution for infinitely low fronts only. The true propagation speed is bounded by an upper limit because the forward accretion cannot exceed the amount of sediment arriving from upstream: $c_{front}\Delta z_b \leq q_S/(1-\varepsilon)$. The rule of thumb can be expected to yield reliable estimates, as long as $c_{bed}$ is well below the upper limit, which corresponds to the following condition for the height of the front:

$$\frac{\Delta z_b}{h} \ll \frac{(1-Fr^2)}{b} \qquad (9.6)$$

A major challenge for future theoretical analyses lies in the trend of coupling processes and models. Interactions between the different processes and models will increase model complexity and render proper model validation more difficult. Analytical solution methods are pre-eminent tools to come to grips with the complex phenomena that emerge from process interactions.

## 9.4 BANK EROSION AND BANK ACCRETION

Three modes can be discerned in the morphological response of rivers to natural changes or human interventions: bed level changes, planform changes, and changes in bed sediment composition. Planform changes are produced by bank retreat as a result of erosion and bank advance as a result of accretion. The erosion is determined by water flow, sediment transport, bank properties, water quality, and mechanical action. The water flow can be related to river discharge, return currents during ship passages, ship waves, wind waves, and groundwater seepage. The latter can be induced after flooding, and is hence related to river discharge, but can also be related to land use and precipitation (Fox et al., 2007). The relevant bank properties include bank material weight and texture, shear strength and cohesive strength, physico-chemical properties, bank height, and cross-sectional shape, groundwater level and permeability, stratigraphy, tension cracks, vegetation, ice and bank protection structures. The ASCE Task Committee on Hydraulics, Bank Mechanics, and Modeling of River Width Adjustment (1998) presents an overview of mechanisms. Banks erode by either entrainment of individual particles or mass failure under gravity with subsequent removal of slumped debris. The stability of a bank with respect to mass failure depends on the balance of forces on the most critical potential failure surface. Fluvial entrainment at the toe can trigger mass failure by increasing the bank height between top and toe, by oversteepening the bank and by undermining the bank. The failure can thus be a slide along a planar or rotational surface, but also a collapse of a cantilevered overhang. Tension cracks and high pore water pressures can trigger mass failure too. The most favourable conditions for high pore water pressures occur during rapid drawdown in the river following a flood. Vegetation can both increase and decrease the stability of river banks. Grasses and shrubs of low biomass usually improve the resistance to erosion. They reduce near-bank flow velocities, they cover the soil, and their roots and rhizomes reinforce the soil. Whether trees increase or decrease bank stability depends on a number of factors. Thorne and Osman (1988) describe how type, age, health, and density of trees influence bank stability.

Studies on bank erosion in soil mechanics are traditionally limited to determining whether or not a bank fails. What happens after failure, however, is important for river planform evolution. The slumped debris breaks up into smaller parts and is evacuated by fluvial entrainment. The new bank profile is subsequently subjected to toe erosion until a new failure occurs. Thorne and Osman (1988) apply this cycle of bank profile deformation, mass failure and subsequent fluvial removal of slumped debris to river widening. Darby and Thorne (1996) and Darby et al. (1996) combine fluvial entrainment and mass wasting algorithms with a model for steady uniform flow in straight channels to simulate width adjustment. Langendoen and Alonso (2008) and Langendoen and Simon (2008) combine such algorithms with unsteady, gradually varying 1-D flow equations. Thorne and Osman (1988) argue that the average bank retreat on longer time scales is governed by toe erosion, irrespective of the volumes and frequencies of intermediate mass failures. This justifies the use of simpler bank erosion models in which the rate of retreat is proportional to the excess shear stress or excess flow velocity above a certain critical value (Figure 9.4, left). Ikeda et al. (1981) use such a simple formulation for bank erosion in their meander model based on a 1-D linear near-bank flow perturbation equation and a 2-D planform evolution model. Later meander models adopt the same approach to bank erosion, sometimes adding a proportionality between bank retreat and excess bank height. Currently available meander models may have different degrees of sophistication, as reviewed by Camporeale et al. (2007) and Crosato (2007, 2008), but they all assume opposite bank advance to equal bank retreat, maintaining a constant width. Mosselman (1992, 1998) releases the constant-width limitation by adding the same simple bank erosion formulation to a 2-D model for flow and morphology. Darby et al. (2002) improve this model by adding their fluvial entrainment and mass wasting algorithms. Rinaldi et al. (2008) link a groundwater flow model to a 2-D hydrodynamic model with fluvial erosion and a bank stability model.

Bank accretion has received much less attention in research than bank erosion, and its mechanisms are hence known less well. Possible accretion mechanisms include:

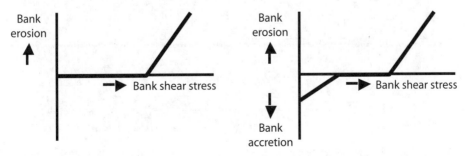

**Figure 9.4**   Simple models for bank erosion (left) and bank erosion and accretion (right).

(i) near-bank overloading of suspended sediment, (ii) development of a point bar during high discharges and subsequent emergence from the water level during low flow stage or channel incision, (iii) re-distribution of sediments by wind, and (iv) trapping of fine sediments by vegetation. The assumption in meander models that opposite bank advance equals bank retreat raises the question of what the simple formulation for bank erosion actually represents. Does it truly represent erosion or does it also reflect mechanisms of accretion? Nanson and Hickin (1983) observe on the Beatton River that bank retreat slows down when point-bar deposition and associated inner-bank advance cannot keep up with it. Bank advance and retreat are inter-related and, as a result, migrating river channels are wider than non-migrating ones under the same discharge and sediment conditions. Mosselman *et al.* (2000) reproduce this behaviour in an axisymmetric model for flow and morphology in a river bend, modelling bank erosion and accretion separately, as shown in Figure 9.4 (right). The range of bank shear stresses for which banks neither erode nor accrete implies that stable widths are essentially multivalued and depend on the history of previous conditions (Blench, 1969). Parker *et al.* (2011) develop a meander model with separate formulations for bank erosion and accretion.

More sophisticated submodels for bank accretion remain a major challenge. Another challenge is the numerical treatment of shifting bank-lines in 2-D and 3-D models of rivers with arbitrary geometries. Defining bank-lines along the nearest grid lines of a rectangular computational grid produces staircase lines that impede any reasonable determination of the hydraulic loads on the banks. Mosselman's (1992; 1998) adaptive curvilinear boundary-fitted grid seemed to solve that problem, but arbitrary bank erosion appears to deform such a grid prohibitively within a few bank-line update steps. A promising approach seems to be that shifting bank-lines are followed as separate moving objects on a fixed grid, solving flow and sediment transport in the vicinity of the bank-lines using local cut-cell techniques or locally unstructured grids. This is a current line of research at Deltares. Numerical inaccuracies, however, will remain even then. The thresholds for bank erosion and bank accretion imply that incorrect overmigration due to too large a time step is not necessarily restored in a next time step. Furthermore, Crosato (2007) shows the numerical treatment of evolving meander planforms to create inaccuracies that make it necessary to use bank erodibility coefficients as calibration parameters.

## 9.5 VEGETATION DYNAMICS AND ECOMORPHOLOGY

Vegetation dynamics are often as essential to river morphology as the dynamics of flowing water and sediment (Figure 9.5). Vegetation reduces flow velocities, deflects flows, protects banks, and stabilizes newly accreted parts of the river bed. Trees may also destabilize banks and become floating debris after the bank on which they stood collapses. The smaller a river, the more prominent is the influence of vegetation, but even accretion of islands in the mighty Brahmaputra is affected

**Figure 9.5** Vegetation affecting gravel-bed river morphology, Skykomish River, USA. (Taken during Gravel Bed Rivers IV, 1995).

by the planting of catkin reed (*Saccharum spontaneum*) by local residents. Pannekoek and van Straaten (1984) note that records of subsurface alluvial stratigraphy indicate that all rivers were braided before the Silurian period, in which the first plants with roots and rhizomes appeared, suggesting vegetation to be a pre-requisite for the occurrence of alluvial rivers with a single meandering channel. Experiments by Gran and Paola (2001), Tal *et al.* (2004), Tal and Paola (2007) and Braudrick *et al.* (2009) confirm the reduction of braiding intensity by vegetation. Parker (1998) explains the conditions for meandering from a self-reinforcing combination of fine sediments and vegetation that produces just the right floodplain erodibility to allow inner bank accretion to keep pace with opposite outer bank erosion. Here reduced bank erosion is only one side of the medal; vegetation also speeds up bank accretion. In turn, development of riparian vegetation is governed by conditions of flowing water and sediment. The mutual interactions make up a complex system for which mathematical models are still in their infancy.

Interactions between vegetation and morphodynamics are the realm of ecomorphology or biogeomorphology, a term coined by Viles (1988), whose book contains a contribution by Gregory and Gurnell (1988) on such interactions in fluvial environments. Tsujimoto (1999) represents vegetation in a 2-D morphological model as elements producing flow drag. He uses this model to simulate his laboratory experiments on the development of sand islands with and without vegetation, as well as his experiments on channel narrowing and degradation associated with vegetation encroachment and multiterrace formation. Jang and Shimizu (2007) numerically simulate laboratory experiments with and without floodplain vegetation using a 2-D model, including bank erosion, representing vegetation by its effect on both flow drag and the angle of repose of bank slopes. A braided channel developed in the absence of vegetation, a narrower meandering planform if vegetation was present. Perona *et al.* (2009) analyse a simplified morphological model of intermittent floods, bed erosion, sediment exposure on gravel bars, and vegetation settlement.

Baptist (2005) proposes a submodel for the effects of vegetation on flow and sediment transport in which the vegetation provides part of the flow resistance at elevations in the water column higher than the bed, thus modifying vertical flow velocity and sediment concentration profiles, and reducing bed shear stresses and bedload rates. The submodel has been verified against laboratory data and implemented in a 2-D numerical model of river morphodynamics. Baptist *et al.* (2007) present extensions of the original submodel. Samir Saleh and Crosato (2008) and Crosato and Samir Saleh (2011) add a submodel for vegetation settlement to this model.

Figure 9.6 shows some results. Again, the model qualitatively reproduces the formation of a multichannel braided river if vegetation development is absent and the formation of a single-thread meandering channel if vegetation develops simultaneously. Nonetheless, at least three areas need further research and development. First, the effects of vegetation on erosion are not reproduced well. This requires modelling of soil binding by roots, as well as subdivision of the substratum into layers. Second, Baptist's submodel can handle only one type of vegetation per location, whereas combinations of different types at the same location occur in reality, e.g., combinations of trees with shrubs or grasses underneath. Third, Crosato and Samir Saleh's representation of vegetation settlement and development could be improved by employing more realistic submodels for vegetation colonization and succession.

Coupling vegetation dynamics to sediment transport and morphodynamics is a clear challenge in biogeomorphology. The challenges, however, go well beyond the mere coding of different process descriptions into a single modelling framework. Combining vegetation dynamics with morphodynamics requires cooperation between ecologists and the physics-based modellers with backgrounds in hydraulic engineering and physical geography. They represent different worlds with different terminology and different mindsets. Scientific explanations in ecology usually have a teleological character because biological mechanisms operate in such a way that successive stages are better adapted to the environment, preserving and reproducing the corresponding genes. This is not a general principle in physics, where mechanisms do not produce evolution towards better states. Admittedly, there is an "ecological" line of thought in river morphology that assumes rivers to develop towards an optimum state of minimum energy dissipation or maximum sediment transport capacity, but that line does not stand the test of rigorous scrutiny. For instance, the principle that natural rivers develop towards a geometry of maximum sediment transport would imply that river narrowing by human intervention would invariably lead to sedimentation, contrary to common observation.

Differences in mindset appear also in terminology. For instance, ecologists speak of "ecosystem services" where engineers would use the word "functions". The term reflects that ecologists consider items such as navigability and hydropower as gifts of nature, meriting gratitude. Engineers do not use the term "ecosystem" for abiotic processes and take a more utilitarian standpoint. The word "function" suggests that rivers have the intrinsic purpose of providing navigation waterways and hydropower to society, requiring optimization by engineers if they do not fulfill this purpose well enough.

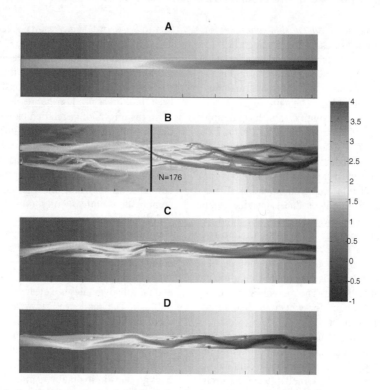

**Figure 9.6** Numerical simulation of morphological development from an initial configuration (A) to situations after 10 years in the cases of no floodplain vegetation (B), low-density floodplain vegetation (C), and high-density floodplain vegetation (D). Variable discharge, including overbank flows. Legend bar: bed level in metres above datum (Samir Saleh and Crosato, 2008). Reproduced, with permission, from Crosato, A., 2010, Numerical Study on the Effects of Floodplain Vegetation on River Planform Style in Earth Surface Processes and Landforms 6 v.36 © 2010 British Geomorphological Research Group.

The world knows many ecologists who are open to the paradigms of mechanistic river morphodynamics, and many engineers and physical geographers who are open to the paradigms of ecology. There are also many fruitful collaborations in river restoration projects. As yet, however, this has not resulted in a general unified framework for fluvial ecomorphology. Every collaboration somehow needs to re-invent the wheel. Developing a unified framework presents a challenge on its own.

## 9.6 VALIDATION

The quality of a model is evaluated by verification and validation, in a pragmatic sense, because absolute verification and validation are impossible (Oreskes *et al.*, 1994). Verification regards the quality of the calibration for a specific case. Validation addresses more generally the quality of the computer code, through consistency checks as well as verifications. The validation of morphodynamic models merits special attention. Comparisons between measured and computed cross-sections provide an incomplete picture, because the essential dynamics of the river bed manifest themselves

in the patterns of bars and pools. Figure 9.7 provides an example for Yen and Lee's (1995) laboratory experiment of bed deformation and grain sorting in a 180° bend. The experimental results show a deep outer bend and a shallow inner bend, superimposed by two bar-pool pairs. One pair has an outer-bend pool at 50° and an inner-bend bar at 80°. The other pair has an outer-bend pool beyond 180° and an inner-bend bar at 170°. Although Yen and Lee's grain sorting and variable discharges hamper an unequivocal analytical demonstration, this double bar–pool pair might be ascribed to overdeepening (Struiksma *et al.*, 1985; Parker and Johanneson, 1989), which is one of the most fundamental phenomena in 2-D depth-averaged and 3-D fluvial morphodynamics. The simulation shown in the figure does reproduce this phenomenon, but not at the same locations. A mere comparison of measured and computed cross-sections does not reveal this deficiency and is hence insufficient for proper validation. Validation might be placed on a better footing by defining clear acceptance criteria that are not limited to simple error bands around computed bed topographies. The criteria should also address the reproduction of characteristic features such as wavelengths, phase shifts, and adaptation times.

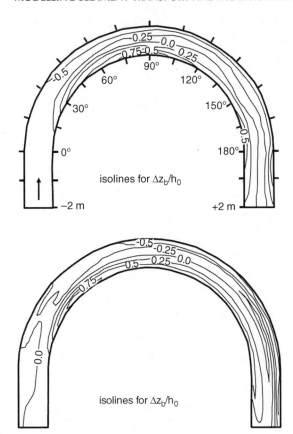

**Figure 9.7** Bed topography in curved-flume experiment by Yen and Lee (1995): measurements (upper) and debatable simulation (lower).

Ideally, the fluvial morphodynamics community would formulate an agreed set of elementary validation cases along with corresponding acceptance criteria. Three types of cases might be distinguished:

- *Hypothetical cases*: cases that have been designed in such a way that elementary properties, correctness and robustness of the model can be tested. These cases may test, for instance, that the results are invariant under grid mirroring or grid rotation. They may also be idealized cases for which analytical solutions are available. Hypothetical cases can be defined easily without the need of any database.
- *Laboratory cases*: well-documented and reproducible laboratory tests. A selection of cases might be based on a list of key functionalities for applications in river engineering and fluvial geomorphology, such as straight reaches versus bends, two-stage channels, steady versus unsteady flows, and uniform versus graded sediments.

- *Field cases*: well-documented field cases with good measured data.

The laboratory cases call for careful documentation of the experimental set-ups in particular, because it may be desirable to repeat certain benchmark experiments later when new measurements techniques have become available or when the testing of more advanced numerical models requires additional information.

Industrial validation of commercial software is usually more extensive and rigorous than the academic validations published in peer-reviewed scientific journals. Yet industrial validation has its caveats too. The validation of each new software version is often automated on the basis of numerous cases in a test bank, comparing new computational results with results from the previous version. Small departures from previous results might be accepted, but eventually add up to a large departure from the original measurements in the laboratory or in the field. The automated procedure must hence be verified regularly.

## 9.7 CONCLUSIONS

Trends in modelling sediment transport and morphodynamics of gravel-bed rivers include the continuing development of knowledge and computer technology, the shift of focus towards larger gravel-bed rivers in more populated and urban areas, the increasing use of morphodynamic models in projects where many stakeholders are involved, and the shift from mere interactions between underwater bed topography and fluid dynamical processes to the evolution of earth-surface elevation as a result of interactions with fluid dynamics, ecodynamics, geodynamics, and human activities.

The present state of knowledge has been reviewed for erosion, transport, and deposition of non-uniform sediment, analytical solutions, bank erosion and accretion, vegetation dynamics, and validation. The challenges identified for these aspects fit the more general list of morphodynamic modelling challenges of Syvitski *et al.* (2009): upscaling, process coupling, model coupling, data systems, high-performance computing, and model testing. For gravel-bed rivers, the main challenge of *upscaling* regards the translation of detailed process models into more practical formulations for the erosion, transport, and deposition of non-uniform sediment. Challenges of *process coupling* and *model coupling* arise from the inclusion of bank erosion, bank accretion, and vegetation dynamics. Bank accretion merits particular attention, as research on its mechanisms has been neglected compared to bank erosion. The numerical treatment of shifting bank lines merits attention too, because adaptive, structured, boundary-fitted grids do not offer a satisfactory solution. For the interaction with vegetation dynamics, the challenges go beyond the mere coupling of processes or models. They include the development of a unified framework for fluvial ecomorphology, with paradigms and terminology shared by both ecologists and the physics-based modellers with backgrounds in hydraulic engineering and physical geography. Furthermore, process coupling calls for theoretical analyses to deepen the understanding of the complex phenomena that emerge from interactions. Direct numerical simulation of discrete sediment particles is the main challenge of *high-performance computing*. Finally, the challenge of *model testing* lies in the development of a set of elementary validation cases, along with corresponding criteria for acceptance, that is agreed by the international fluvial morphodynamics community.

## 9.8    ACKNOWLEDGEMENTS

I thank Alessandra Crosato and Kees Sloff for fruitful discussions that were indispensable for the writing of this chapter. I thank Wes Lauer and Richard Hardy for their thoughtful comments and suggestions to improve the chapter.

## 9.9    REFERENCES

ASCE Task Committee on Hydraulics, Bank Mechanics, and Modeling of River Width Adjustment. 1998. River width adjustment. II: Modeling. *Journal of Hydraulic Engineering* **124**: 903–917.

Ashida, K. and Michiue, M. 1972. Study on hydraulic resistance and bedload transport rate in alluvial streams. *Japan Society of Civil Engineers Transactions* **206**: 59–69.

Ashida, K. and Michiue, M. 1973. Studies on bed-load transport in open channel flows. International Association for Hydraulic Research, *Proceedings of the International Symposium on River Mechanics, Bangkok, Thailand, January 9–12*, **A36**: Paper 407–418.

Baptist, M.J. 2005. *Modelling floodplain biogeomorphology*. Ph.D. thesis, Delft University of Technology. ISBN 90-407-2582-9.

Baptist, M.J., Babovic, V., Rodríguez Uthurburu, J. *et al.* 2007. On inducing equations for vegetation resistance. *Journal of Hydraulic Research* **45**: 435–450.

Blench, T. 1969. *Mobile-bed Fluviology*. Edmonton, University of Alberta Press.

Blom, A. 2003. *A vertical sorting model for rivers with non-uniform sediment and dunes*. Ph.D. thesis. University of Twente, University Press, Veenendaal, the Netherlands, ISBN 90-9016663-7.

Blom, A., Ribberink, J.S., and de Vriend, H. 2003a. Vertical sorting in bed forms. Flume experiments with a natural and a tri-modal sediment mixture. *Water Resources Research* **39**: 1025. doi:10.1029/2001WR001088.

Blom, A., Ribberink, J.S., and Parker, G. 2003b. Sediment continuity for rivers with non-uniform sediment, dunes, and bed load transport. In Gyr, A. and Kinzelbach, W., editors, *Sedimentation and Sediment Transport: At the Crossroad of Physics and Engineering*, Dordrecht, Kluwer Academic, pp. 179–182.

Bradley, J.B., Williams, D.T., and Walton, R. 1998. Applicability and limitations of sediment transport modeling in gravel-bed rivers. In Klingeman, P.C., Beschta, R.L., Komar, P.D., and Bradley, J.B., editors, Gravel-bed Rivers in the Environment. Highlands Ranch, CO, Water Resources Publications, pp. 543–578.

Braudrick, C.A., Dietrich, W.E., Lieverich, G.T., and Sklar, L.S. 2009. Experimental evidence for the conditions to sustain meandering in coarse-bedded rivers. *Proceedings of the National Academy of Sciences USA* **106**: 16936–16941.

Camporeale, C., Perona, P., Porporato, A., and Ridolfi, L. 2007. Hierarchy of models for meandering rivers and related morphodynamic processes. *Reviews of Geophysics* **45**: RG1001. doi:10.1029/2005RG000185.

Crosato, A. 2007. Effects of smoothing and regridding in numerical meander migration models, *Water Resources Research* **43**: W01401. doi:10.1029/2006WR005087.

Crosato, A. 2008. *Analysis and modelling of river meandering*. Ph.D. thesis, Delft University of Technology, IOS Press, ISBN 978-1-58603-915-8.

Crosato, A. and Mosselman, E. 2009. Simple physics-based predictor for the number of river bars and the transition between meandering and braiding, *Water Resources Research* **45**: W03424. doi: 10.1029/2008WR007242.

Crosato, A. and Samir Saleh, M. 2011. Numerical study on the effects of floodplain vegetation on river planform style. *Earth Surface Processes and Landforms* **36**: 711–720. doi: 10.1002/esp.2088.

Cui, Y. and Parker, G. 1998. The arrested gravel front: stable gravel-sand transitions in rivers; Part 2: General numerical solution. *Journal of Hydraulic Research* **36**: 159–182.

Darby, S.E. and Thorne, C.R. 1996. Numerical simulation of widening and bed deformation of straight sand-bed rivers. I: Model development. *Journal of Hydraulic Engineering* **122**: 184–193.

Darby, S.E., Alabyan, A., and van de Wiel, M.A. 2002. Numerical simulation of bank erosion and channel migration for meandering rivers. *Water Resources Research* **38**: 1163. doi: 10.1029/2001WR000602.

Darby, S.E., Thorne, C.R., and Simon, A. 1996. Numerical simulation of widening and bed deformation of straight sand-bed rivers. II: Model evaluation. *Journal of Hydraulic Engineering* **122**: 194–202.

Egiazaroff, I.V. 1965. Calculation of non-uniform sediment concentrations. *American Society of Civil Engineers, Journal of the Hydraulics Division* **91**: 225–247.

Einstein, H.A. and Chien, N. 1953. *Transport of Sediment Mixtures with Large Ranges of Grain Sizes*. United States Army Corps of Engineers, Mississippi River Division, Sediment Series No. 2.

Fox, G.A., Wilson, G.V. Simon, A. *et al.* 2007. Measuring streambank erosion due to groundwater seepage: correlation to bank pore water pressure, precipitation and stream stage. *Earth Surface Processes and Landforms* **32**: 1558-1573. doi: 10.1002/esp.1490.

Frings, R.M., Kleinhans, M.G., and Vollmer, S. 2008. Discriminating between pore-filling load and bed-structure load: a new porosity-based model, exemplified for the river Rhine. *Sedimentology* **55**: 1571–1593.

Gran, K. and Paola, C. 2001. Riparian vegetation controls on braided stream dynamics. *Water Resources Research* **37**: 3275–3283.

Gregory, K.J. and Gurnell, A.M. 1988. Vegetation and river form and processes. In Viles, H.A., editor, *Biogeomorphology*. Oxford, Blackwell, pp. 11–42.

Hirano, M. 1972. Studies on variation and equilibrium state of a river bed composed of nonuniform material. *Japanese Society of Civil Engineers Transactions* **4**: 128–129.

Ikeda, S., Parker, G., and Sawai, K. 1981. Bend theory of river meanders, Part 1, Linear development. *Journal of Fluid Mechanics* **112**: 363–377.

Jang, C.-L. and Shimizu, Y. 2007. Vegetation effects on the morphological behavior of alluvial channels. *Journal of Hydraulic Research* **45**: 763–772.

Langendoen, E.J. and Alonso, C.V. 2008. Modeling the evolution of incised streams: I. Model formulation and validation of flow and streambed evolution components. *Journal of Hydraulic Engineering* **134**: 749–762.

Langendoen, E.J. and Simon, A. 2008. Modeling the evolution of incised streams: II. Streambed erosion. *Journal of Hydraulic Engineering* **134**: 905–915.

Lanzoni, S. and Tubino, M. 1999. Grain sorting and bar instability. *Journal of Fluid Mechanics* **393**: 149–174.

Mosselman, E. 1992. *Mathematical Modelling of Morphological Processes in Rivers with Erodible Cohesive Banks.* Communications on Hydraulic and Geotechnical Engineering No.92-3, Delft University of Technology. ISSN 0169-6548.

Mosselman, E. 1998. Morphological modelling of rivers with erodible banks. *Hydrological Processes* **12**: 1357–1370.

Mosselman, E. 2006. Bank protection and river training along the braided Brahmaputra-Jamuna River, Bangladesh. In Sambrook Smith, G.H., Best, J., Bristow, C.S., and Petts, G.E., editors. Braided Rivers; Process, Deposits, Ecology and Management. Oxford, Blackwell. International Association of Sedimentologists Special Publication 36, pp. 277–287.

Mosselman, E. and Sloff, C.J. 2008. The importance of floods for bed topography and bed sediment composition: numerical modelling of Rhine bifurcation at Pannerden. In Habersack, H., Piégay, H., and Rinaldi, M., editors, Gravel Bed Rivers VI – From Process Understanding to River Restoration. Amsterdam, Elsevier. Developments in Earth Surface Processes 11, pp. 161–180.

Mosselman, E., Shishikura, T., and Klaassen, G.J. 2000. Effect of bank stabilization on bend scour in anabranches of braided rivers. *Physics and Chemistry of the Earth, Part B*, **25**: 699–704.

Mosselman, E., Sloff, K., and van Vuren, S. 2008. Different sediment mixtures at constant flow conditions can produce the same celerity of bed disturbances. In Altinakar, M., Kokpinar, A., Gogus, M. *et al.* editors. *River Flow 2008, Proceedings of the International Conference on Fluvial Hydraulics, Çeşme, Izmir, Turkey, 3–5 September, 2008.* Ankara, Kubaba, pp. 1373–1377.

Nanson, G.C. and Hickin, E.J. 1983. Channel migration and incision on the Beatton River. *Journal of Hydraulic Engineering* **109**: 327–337.

Oreskes, N., Shrader-Frechette, K., and Belitz, K. 1994. Verification, validation, and confirmation of numerical models in the earth sciences. *Science* **263**: 641–646.

Pannekoek, A.J. and van Straaten, L.M.J.U. 1984. *Algemene geologie*, 4th edn, Groningen, Wolters-Noordhoff [in Dutch].

Parker, G. 1991. Selective sorting and abrasion of river gravel. II: Applications. *Journal of Hydraulic Engineering* **117**: 150–171.

Parker, G. 1998. River meanders in a tray. *Nature* **395**: 111–112.

Parker, G. 2004. The uses of sediment transport and morphodynamic modeling in stream restoration. *Proceedings of the World Water and Environmental Resources 2004 Congress,* *Salt Lake City, June 2 –July 1*, American Society of Civil Engineers.

Parker, G. and Cui, Y. 1998. The arrested gravel front: stable gravel-sand transitions in rivers; Part 1: Simplified analytical solution. *Journal of Hydraulic Research* **36**: 75–100.

Parker, G. and Johanneson, H. 1989. Observations on several recent theories of resonance and overdeepening in meandering channels. In Ikeda, S. and Parker, G. editors. *River Meandering*. American Geophysical Union, Water Resources Monograph 12, pp. 379–415.

Parker, G., Paola, C. and Leclair, S. 2000. Probabilistic Exner sediment continuity equations for mixtures with no active layer. *Journal of Hydraulic Engineering* **126**: 818–826.

Parker, G., Shimizu, Y., Wilkerson, G.V. *et al.* 2011. A new framework for modeling the migration of meandering rivers. *Earth Surface Processes and Landforms* **36**: 70-86. doi: 10. 1002/esp.2113.

Perona, P., Camporeale, C., Perucca, E. *et al.* 2009. Modelling river and riparian vegetation interactions and related importance for sustainable ecosystem management. *Aquatic Sciences* **71**: 266–278.

Ribberink, J.S. 1987. *Mathematical Modelling of One-dimensional Morphological Changes in Rivers with Non-uniform Sediment*. Communications on Hydraulic and Geotechnical Engineering, No. 87-2, Delft University of Technology, ISSN 0169-6548.

Rinaldi, M., Mengoni, B., Luppi, L., Darby, S.E. and Mosselman, E. 2008. Numerical simulation of hydrodynamics and bank erosion in a river bend, *Water Resources Research* **44**: W09428. doi: 10.1029/2008WR007008.

Samir Saleh, M. and Crosato, A. 2008. Effects of riparian and floodplain vegetation on river patterns and flow dynamics. In Gumiero, G., Rinaldi, M., and Fokkens, B., editors, *Proceedings of the 4th ECRR International Conference on River Restoration, South Servolo Island, Venice, Italy, 16–21 June.* ECRR-CIRF Publication, printed by Industrie Grafiche Vicentine S.r.l, pp. 807–814.

Schmeeckle, M.W. and Nelson, J.M. 2003. Direct numerical simulation of bedload transport using a local, dynamic boundary condition. *Sedimentology* **50**: 279–301.

Sloff, C.J. and Ottevanger, W. 2008. Multiple-layer graded-sediment approach: Improvement and implications. In Altinakar, M., Kokpinar, M.A., Gogus, M. *et al.*, editors, *River Flow 2008, International Conference on Fluvial Hydraulics Proceedings, Çeşme, Izmir, Turkey, 3–5 September.* Ankara, Kubaba Publications, pp. 1447–1456.

Struiksma, N. 1999. Mathematical modelling of bedload transport over non-erodible layers. *IAHR Symposium on River, Coastal and Estuarine Morphodynamic Proceedings, Genova, Italy, 6–10 September*, Vol. I, pp. 89–98.

Struiksma, N., Olesen, K.W., Flokstra, C., and de Vriend, H. J. 1985. Bed deformation in curved alluvial channels. *Journal of Hydraulic Research* **23**: 57–79.

Syvitski, J.P.M., Slingerland, R.L., Burgess, P. *et al.* 2009. Morphodynamic models: An overview. In Vionnet, C.A., García, M. H., Latrubesse, E. M., and Perillo, G. M. E., editors, *River, Coastal and Estuarine Morphodynamics: RCEM 2009 Proceedings, Santa Fe, Argentina, 21–25 September*, pp. 3–20.

Tal, M., Gran, K., Murray, A.B., Paola, C., and Hicks, D.M. 2004. Riparian vegetation as a primary control on channel characteristics in multi-thread rivers. In Bennett, S.J. and Simon, A., editors, *Riparian Vegetation and Fluvial Geomorphology: Hydraulic, Hydrologic, and Geotechnical Interaction*. American Geophysical Union, Water Science and Applications 8, pp. 43–58.

Tal, M. and Paola, C. 2007. Dynamic single-thread channels maintained by the interaction of flow and vegetation. *Geology* 35: 347–350.

Thorne, C.R. and Osman, A.M. 1988. Riverbank stability analysis. II: Applications. *Journal of Hydraulic Engineering* 114: 151–172.

Tsujimoto, T. 1999. Fluvial processes in streams with vegetation. *Journal of Hydraulic Research* 37: 789–803.

Tuijnder, A.P. 2010. *Sand in short supply; Modelling of bedforms, roughness and sediment transport in rivers under supply-limited conditions*. Ph.D. thesis, University of Twente, ISBN 978-90-9025123-3.

Van der Klis, H. 2003. *Uncertainty analysis applied to numerical models of river bed morphology*. Ph.D. thesis, Delft University of Technology, Delft University Press, ISBN 90-407-2440-7.

Van Vuren, B.G. 2005. *Stochastic modelling of river morphodynamics*. Ph.D. thesis, Delft University of Technology, Delft University Press, ISBN 90-407-2604-3.

Van Zuylen, H.J. van Dee, D.P., Mynett, A. E. *et al.* 1994. Hydroinformatics at Delft Hydraulics. *Journal of Hydraulic Research* 32, (Extra Issue *Hydroinformatics*): 83–136.

Viles, H.A., editor. 1988. *Biogeomorphology*. Oxford, Blackwell.

Wang, Z.B., Fokkink, R.J., de Vries, M., and Langerak, A. 1995. Stability of river bifurcations in 1D morphodynamic models. *Journal of Hydraulic Research* 33: 739–750.

Yen, C.L. and Lee, K.T. 1995. Bed topography and sediment sorting in channel bend with unsteady flow. *Journal of Hydraulic Engineering* 121: 591–599.

## 9.10   DISCUSSION

### 9.10.1   Discussion by Chris Parker

As fluvial geomorphologists, we repeatedly claim that our attempts to model sediment transport and morphodynamics at intermediate to large spatial scales are inhibited by restricted data availability. In particular, modellers often indicate that data describing bed material size are not available at a sufficiently detailed resolution. Despite this, models of fluvial morphodynamics have been shown to fit observations "fairly well" when high-resolution bed material size data are not available (often they are interpolated from sparse measurements or automatically generated by running the model – "warming it up"). If high-resolution bed material size data were available would this improve the accuracy of modelling outputs or does the fact that bed material size is just one of several mutually adjusting interdependent variables mean that its accurate parameterization at a high spatial resolution is not strictly necessary? Essentially I am asking whether the self-organizing nature of the various degrees of adjustment within fluvial morphodynamics precludes the need to parameterize boundary conditions in a comprehensively reductionist manner?

### 9.10.2   Discussion by Helmut Habersack

This very interesting chapter gives an excellent overview on modelling sediment transport and morphodynamics.

The following comments are related to erosion, transport, and deposition of non-uniform sediment, and validation of numerical models. Classical models contain, for example, empirical sediment transport formulas which may under- or overpredict transport rates in the field (Habersack and Laronne, 2002; Habersack *et al.*, 2008). Furthermore, for example, the prediction of long-term bed level changes needs a previous simulation of the historically observed morphodynamics. Thus, before validation, a meaningful calibration of the numerical model is necessary, whereby direct field measurements of sediment transport and an accurate monitoring data set of morphodynamics over time are necessary (Habersack *et al.*, 2010). The calibration can also include the adjustment of empirical formulas and the optimization of the numerical model itself concerning non-uniformity, layer composition, hiding, and exposure etc. (Tritthart *et al.*, 2010). After a successful calibration the described validation with independent field data is absolutely necessary, including the call for elementary validation cases.

### 9.10.3   Discussion by Timothy Randle

The chapter mentions the interaction between vegetation growth and river hydraulics. Please also comment on the potential for modelling the evolution of riparian terrestrial habitat and aquatic habitat over time.

### 9.10.4   Reply by Erik Mosselman

I thank the discussants for raising the points of data requirements, calibration, and river habitats, and I thank Wes Lauer for further discussions on those points. Chris Parker wonders whether rivers might organize themselves into a unique morphological state for given overall flow and sediment conditions, irrespective of variations in the initial distribution of bed sediment composition. This would be analogous to a marble rolling in a bowl, which invariably ends up in the lowest point of the bowl, irrespective of its initial position. Such a development into a unique state may be true for the bed topography in a river with fixed banks and uniform sediment. However, it is not true for the combined development of bed topography and bed sediment composition, because a quasi-equilibrium morphology without gradients in sediment transport capacity can be attained by an infinite number of combinations of bed level gradients and bed sediment composition gradients. That model results often fit "fairly well" to observations can be ascribed, at least partly, to calibration. The large number of calibration parameters in complex 2-D morphodynamic models offers many degrees of freedom for obtaining a good fit, but it remains difficult to decide which combination of parameter settings is the right one. The strategy mentioned in the chapter to calibrate on as many different morphological phenomena as possible reduces this ambiguity only to a limited extent. Consequently, because high-resolution bed material size data allow for the development of more sophisticated submodels for elementary processes and for more precise calibration and verification, they certainly do represent a useful source for improving model performance.

Helmut Habersack underscores the importance of calibration too. Calibration precedes *verification* when applying a model to a specific situation, but it does not always need to precede *validation*. The chapter mentions three types of validation cases, i.e., hypothetical, laboratory, and field cases. The latter two types do require calibration as they represent model applications to specific situations, but no calibration is needed for the hypothetical cases. Thus the following order arises: (i) software validation, involving calibration only partly, (ii) model schematization for a specific situation, (iii) calibration, (iv) verification, and (v) application. Data on morphological change over time provide the firmest basis for calibration. Direct sediment transport data can be helpful, but are of secondary importance for a good calibration (Mosselman, 2005).

Timothy Randle draws attention to the potential for modelling the evolution of river habitats over time. Hydrodynamic and morphodynamic model outputs such as inundation frequency, water depth, flow velocity, bed surface composition, and substrate composition determine habitat suitability. A major question is how these model outputs can be translated into meaningful inputs for habitat suitability. Are average values relevant or, rather, extreme values, durations of occurrence or values in specific seasons? This remains an important area for collaborative research by ecologists and physics-based modellers.

## 9.11 DISCUSSION REFERENCES

Habersack, H. and Laronne, J.B. 2002. Evaluation and improvement of bedload discharge formulas based on Helley-Smith sampling in an alpine gravel bed river. *Journal of Hydraulic Engineering* **128**: 484–499.

Habersack, H., Seitz, H., and Laronne, J.B. 2008. Spatio-temporal variability of bedload transport rate: analysis and 2D modelling approach. *Geodinamica Acta* **21**: 67–79.

Habersack, H., Seitz, H., and Liedermann, M. 2010. Integrated automatic bedload transport monitoring. In Ray, J.R., Laronne, J.B. and Marr, J.D.G. editors. *Bedload-Surrogate Monitoring Technologies: US Geological Survey Scientific Investigations Report* 2010-5091 pp. 218–235. Available only online from http://pubs.usgs.gov/sir/2010/5091/papers/listofpapers.html.

Mosselman, E. 2005. Basic equations for sediment transport in CFD for fluvial morphodynamics. In Bates, P.D., Lane, S.N., and Ferguson, R.I. editors. *Computational Fluid Dynamics; Applications in Environmental Hydraulics*. Chichester, JohnWiley & Sons, Ltd, pp. 71–89.

Tritthart, M., Schober, B., Liedermann, M., and Habersack, H. 2010. Numerical modeling of sediment transport in the Danube River: uniform vs. non-uniform formulation. In Dittrich, A., Koll, Ka., Aberle, J., and Geisenhainer, P., editors. *River Flow 2010, Braunschweig, 8–10 September, Bundesanstalt für Wasserbau*, Vol. 2, pp. 977–984.

# 10

# The Potential of using High-resolution Process Models to Inform Parameterizations of Morphodynamic Models

## Richard J. Hardy

## 10.1 INTRODUCTION

This contribution covers several aspects of sediment transport and morphodynamics modelling in gravel-bed rivers and highlights several important current problems which merit resolution. In the conclusions of his paper, Mosselman (Chapter 9, this volume) develops the argument of Syvitski *et al.* (2009) that current trends in modelling sediment transport and morphodynamics of gravel-bed rivers are in general: (i) upscaling current models to study sediment transport at the reach length; (ii) process coupling to improve physical representation; (iii) the coupling of submodels to consider different processes operating in the fluvial environment over a range of spatial and temporal scales; (iv) the application of high-performance computing and data systems to increase both the spatial and temporal resolution at which these models can be applied; and (v) model testing, including benchmarking for validation. In particular, the argument is made that the main challenge in upscaling is in regard to the translation of detailed process models into more practical formulations for the erosion, transport, and deposition of non-uniform sediment for reach scale applications. It is the particular theme of upscaling that is considered here and it is suggested that an improvement in the empirical transport relations used in the morphodynamic modelling of gravel bed rivers can potentially be derived from a combined computational fluid dynamics approach linked with a discrete particle model.

## 10.2 PROCESS MODELLING OF GRAVEL BED RIVERS

The application and development of numerical models in fluvial geomorphology are now well documented; models are particularly useful in identifying emergent behaviour where there are combinations of processes acting over several scales that may exhibit strong process interaction and feedbacks. This is of particular importance when the behaviour of a whole system is of interest, possibly over either large spatial or temporal scales, which cannot readily be understood from the measurement of individual components in isolation because the system of interest behaves in a non-linear manner, in which the outputs are not proportional to the inputs across the entire range (Phillips, 1999). However, it is suggested herein that in many current morphodynamic models there is considerable process simplification and averaging which prevents both the complexity of the system and the feedbacks being accurately represented, and therefore models are highly dependent on arbitrary parameterization, for example the active depth used with the Exner equation.

Since the inception of modern process studies of sediment transport (e.g., DuBoys, 1879; Gilbert, 1914), the standard assumption of sediment transport equations has focused on a concept of a sediment mass flux and its correlation with the fluid flow. The fundamental equations of fluid motion have existed since the nineteenth century in the form of the Navier–Stokes equations

*Gravel-bed Rivers: Processes, Tools, Environments*, First Edition. Edited by Michael Church, Pascale M. Biron and André G. Roy.
© 2012 John Wiley & Sons, Ltd. Published 2012 by John Wiley & Sons, Ltd.

(Batchelor, 1967) and assume that a fluid is a continuum (Tritton, 1988) and fluid flow is governed by the basic principles of conservation of mass and momentum. For shallow flows, as typically found in gravel-bed rivers, where the ratio of mean depth to effective roughness height is often less than 10–20 in flood conditions and less than 5 during low-flow conditions (Charlton et al., 1978; Bathurst, 1978), the flow is largely unidirectional, turbulent, and the downstream and cross-stream dimensions greatly exceed the depth dimension (Jirka and Uijttewaal 2004). The numerical prediction of flow in gravel-bed rivers is therefore not straightforward, as the flow is strongly influenced by topographical forcing that changes over both space and time. The major challenges for numerical modelling are thus the representation of topography, and its derivative roughness, and modelling turbulence. However, in many current morphodynamic models of gravel bed rivers there is a simple representation of flow.

Although there are substantial challenges in flow modelling, they are by no means as complex as the challenges in developing a sediment transport model. Sediment material can be transported by: (i) suspension, an advanced stage of transport (Graf, 1998); (ii) saltation, the unsuspended transport of particles in the form of consecutive hops within the near-bed region which is generally considered the dominant mode of bedload transport (Niño and Garcia, 1994); and (iii) rolling and sliding, which occur to a lesser extent, mainly near the threshold of entrainment and in between individual saltation events (Bridge and Dominic, 1984). Due to the ratio of forces, gravel is rarely transported in suspension, but even if only transport mechanisms 2 and 3 are considered, three different stages of transport have been observed: (i) finer materials which have originated upstream passing over a locally static bed; (ii) partial transport of local bed material where there may be independent grain movement; and (iii) equal mobility of grains (Jackson and Beschta, 1982; Ashworth and Ferguson, 1989), all of which may involve the processes of either saltation, rolling, or sliding. Therefore, for a representative numerical model all processes acting over several scales should be considered. However, a numerical description of the hydraulics and sediment transport processes in current morphodynamic models is far from complete as they do not consider the complex interactions between river bed morphology, flow, and sediment transport.

The structure of near-bed turbulence determines the dynamics of sediment transport and the development of bed morphology through complex feedback relations (Clifford et al., 1992; Ashworth, 1996). However, an analytical description of turbulent flow and sediment entrainment, transport, and deposition is subject to significant errors due to the poor parameterization of physical processes (McEwan and Heald, 2001), for example that velocity profiles are frequently used to determine the mean boundary shear stress (McLean et al., 1999), which may be inadequate to describe the effect of bed roughness on flow characteristics (Papanicolaou et al., 2001). Figure 10.1 demonstrates an extracted velocity profile over a gravel bed collected using PIV. If Reynolds stresses are calculated at $0.2\,z/h$, an order of magnitude variation will be observed. Therefore, such averaging obscures the complex, non-linear interaction of wake decay, boundary-layer development, and topographically induced acceleration and deceleration; this leads to an inaccurate estimate of boundary stress, particularly skin friction, which is essential in sediment transport.

Although the importance of the hydraulics is apparent, they are not always specifically included in gravel transport models. Two classes of process-based sediment transport models have evolved, either a simple representation of hydraulics with the process representation concentrated on sediment transport dynamics and interactions (e.g., Sklar and Dietrich, 2004; Barry, 2004), or a coupled hydraulic-sediment scheme in which sediment dynamics are driven by high process hydraulics (e.g., Hardy, 2005). However, as demonstrated below, hydraulics can be predicted.

## 10.3 MODELLING FLOW IN A GRAVEL BED RIVER USING A COMPUTATIONAL FLUID DYNAMICS APPROACH

The merits of applying computational fluid dynamics (CFD) to understand flow processes in gravel-bed rivers are well documented (Hodskinson and Ferguson, 1998; Sinha et al., 1998; Gessler et al., 1999; Nicholas and Sambrook Smith, 1999; Bradbrook et al., 2000; Booker et al., 2001; Ferguson et al., 2003; Lane et al., 2003, 2004; Hardy et al., 2007; Carney et al., 2006) for both individual morphological units (e.g., meanders, confluences) and high-resolution millimeter-scale applications of flow around individual gravel particles (see Figure 10.2). In several of these applications it has been questioned whether the bed microtopography should be represented physically as part of the channel geometry or parametrically through an exaggerated value of the roughness height in a log law representation of flow in the cells adjacent to the bed (Hodskinson and Ferguson, 1998; Sinha et al., 1998; Gessler et al., 1999; Nicholas and Smith, 1999; Bradbrook et al., 2000; Booker et al., 2001; Ferguson et al., 2003). Different approaches have been developed, including additional computed drag terms associated with different grain sizes (Carney et al.,

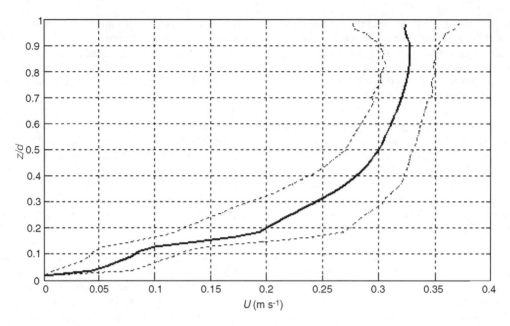

**Figure 10.1** An example of a velocity profile collected in a flume by particle imaging velocimetry over a gravel surface. The solid line marks the time-averaged profile, while the dotted line shows variability around the mean generated by turbulent structures demonstrated by $\pm$ one standard deviation of the $U$-component. The variability caused by turbulent structures cause an order of magnitude increase in the Reynolds Stress at 0.2 $z/d$ when the standard deviation component is considered.

(2006), or explicitly representing the bed through a mass flux scaling algorithm (MFSA) incorporated in the continuity equation (Lane *et al.*, 2004; Hardy *et al.*, 2005) to provide further insight into flow (Figure 10.2). Applying MFSA within a large-eddy simulation framework (e.g., Hardy *et al.*, 2007) has enabled classical turbulent structures such as arch vortices (Hunt *et al.*, 1978), as well as

regions of momentum exchange in the downstream wake of protruding clasts, which are similar to structures that have been previously measured in the field (Buffin-Bélanger and Roy, 1998), to be detected and visualized. This approach has demonstrated that there are two distinct scales of boundary influence: (i) a scale that is associated with clusters of particles which create undulations in the

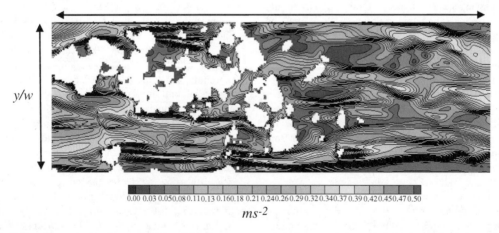

**Figure 10.2** An example of a prediction of flow over a gravel surface applying computational fluid dynamics. The image shows a plan view of the river bed with flow from left to right. White regions represent pebbles. (See the color version of this figure in color plate section.)

bed surface similar to kölks, which result in changes in the time and length scales and magnitudes of the associated turbulence; and (ii) large or isolated clasts which result in similar processes, but over a smaller length scale. This emphasizes that the measured flow variability at any one point in a natural river will contain both locally derived flow structures and structures inherited from upstream, according to the range of scales of topography. However, such hydraulics have rarely been applied to drive sediment transport schemes, even though velocity profiles can be extracted that demonstrate considerable variance around the mean (Figure 10.1).

## 10.4  IS DISCRETE PARTICLE MODELLING AN UNDERUSED METHOD IN GRAVEL-BED RIVERS?

The most frequently used approach to model sediment transport, as demonstrated in the Chapter 9, is a standard Eulerian approach, in which sediment is considered to be either eroded or deposited over space, and as long as mass is conserved, neither the origin of the eroded material nor the location of the deposited material is considered. Due to the spatial and temporal scale at which sediment transport is typically investigated, the equation base developed relies upon empirical coefficients that circumvent the need to consider process. However, as Frey and Church (Chapter 4, this volume) argue, discrete particle models are still underused in developing process understanding in gravel transport, although they have been demonstrated to be a beneficial methodological approach to study particle motion (see Richards et al., 2004; Cleary and Prakash, 2004; Heald et al., 2004). This approach follows a Lagrangian philosophy and equations governing particle motion have been used, especially in the prediction of the trajectories of saltating particles (e.g., Tsuchiya, 1969; Francis, 1973; Reizes, 1978; Hayashi and Ozaki, 1980; Murphy and Hooshiari, 1982; Wiberg and Smith, 1985; Lee and Hsu, 1994; Niño and García, 1994; Niño et al., 1994; Bauer et al., 1998). This approach has previously been applied to gain an understanding of both the kinematic and geometric characteristics of the particle saltation process, which in turn has been used to develop a model of bedload transport (Yalin, 1963).

Several of these models have predicted mean values of saltation characteristics (saltation length, height, and particle velocity) which agreed well with experimental results. This has led to the development and application of discrete particle models which are based on a standard momentum equation for an individual particle e.g.

$$m_p \frac{\partial U_p}{\partial t} = D_p(U - U_p) + m_p g - V_p \nabla_p \qquad (10.1)$$

where $m_p$ is the particle mass, $U_p$ is the particle velocity, $t$ is time, $D_p$ is the particle drag function, $U$ is the flow velocity, $g$ is the acceleration of gravity, $V_p$ is the particle volume, and $\nabla_p$ is the continuous-phase pressure gradient. This approach has been used to understand particle entrainment (McEwan and Heald, 2001; McEwan et al., 2001), bed load transport (Schmeeckle and Nelson, 2003) and grain-size sorting for reach-scale long-term morphodynamic evolution (Hodge et al., 2007). It can reveal properties at both the meso- and macro scales that have been characterized from microscale interactions, which enables an understanding of self-organizing behaviours. However, to date such models have poor hydraulic representations driving the particle motion.

## 10.5  SEDIMENT TRANSPORT PREDICTIONS WITH HIGH-RESOLUTION HYDRAULICS

There has recently been an increase in the use of models coupling computational fluid dynamics and discrete element modelling for multiphase flows (Zhu et al., 2008), although there has been limited application to gravel bed rivers. However, as demonstrated in Figure 10.3, particle dynamics can be observed in high-resolution applications. Here it can be seen that the particle is transported in a localized area of low flow and a region of possible deposition in front of a large pebble. However, the localized hydraulics in front of the particle, a possible suppressed saddle point vortex (Hunt et al., 1978), transport the particle within a confined area until a tertiary vortex (Hunt et al., 1978) entrains the particle into the shear flow over the particle and into a hydraulically induced hop. This demonstrates the spatial variability and the hydraulic processes operating in these environments. It is demonstrated that a spatial difference of millimetres can affect the forces acting on the particle and the possible transport mechanism. Once the particle has been transported over the large clast, the transport mechanism changes to saltation and the particle moves down slope.

## 10.6  HOW CAN THIS INFORMATION BE USED TO SCALE UP?

When considering bedload transport at the reach scale, there is no real physical equation, and mass conservation is often considered in terms of a continuity principle (Exner equation) for the bed morphology (elevation) and assumes that that there is no lateral sediment inflow:

$$\frac{\partial \eta}{\partial t} = -\frac{1}{\varepsilon_0} \nabla \cdot q_s \qquad (10.2)$$

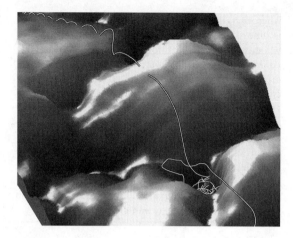

**Figure 10.3** The localized sediment dynamics of an individual particle.

where $\eta$ is the bed elevation, $t$ is time, $q_s$ is sediment transport rate, and $\varepsilon_o$ is the packing density. Mosselman (this volume) discusses the difficulty in parameterizing this equation and, in particular, the thickness of the active layer. He suggests that thickness is often equated to half the average height of the bed forms. However, a thicker active layer is needed to account for the statistical variability in bed forms as they can exchange material at a larger depth under the bed surface. The active layer becomes even thicker when discharge variations cause variations in transverse bed slopes in river bends, or generate sedimentation and erosion waves at locations where overbank flows leave and re-enter the main channel. Finally, this classical approach assumes that the packing density is constant, although several approaches have been developed to overcome this assumption (e.g., Parker and Cui, 1998; Cui and Parker, 1998).

It is suggested that this problem could potentially be resolved by the linkage of a computational fluid dynamics scheme with a discrete particle model. Scenario testing using different hydraulic conditions and turbulent conditions would provide a statistical range of outcomes for physically defined variables on particle size transport characteristics, enabling improved parameterizations of both the active layer of transport and the bed porosity post deposition.

## 10.7  DISCUSSION AND CONCLUSIONS

It is suggested here that a potential means to improve reach length morphodynamic models is by scenario testing gravel transport and deposition through the development and application of a combined CFD–discrete particle model. The process information derived from these types of models could then be used to improve the reach length scale model parameterizations, through a stochastic approach, for models of sediment transport. This in some ways may revert to Einstein's (1937, 1950) concept which recognized the appeal of stochastic models for bedload transport where particle motion was considered as a series of random length steps separated by rests of random duration. Instead of treating sediment transport as a random walk using a series of assumptions, all of the complexity, interaction, and variability in the factors that affect the erosion, transport, and deposition of sediment can be encapsulated in a probability distribution. The CFD–discrete particle model could be used to inform the probability distribution. This would lead to improved spatial and/or temporal parameterizations of reach length morphodynamic models.

## 10.8  REFERENCES

Ashworth, P.J. 1996. Mid-channel bar growth and its relationship to local flow strength and direction. *Earth Surface Processes and Landforms* **21**: 103–123.

Ashworth, P.J. and Ferguson, R.I. 1989. Size-selective entrainment of bed-load in gravel bed streams. *Water Resources Research* **25**: 627–634.

Barry, J.J., Buffington, J.M., and King, J.G. 2004. A general power equation for predicting bed load transport rates in gravel bed rivers. *Water Resources Research* **40**: W10401. doi: 10.1029/2004WR003190.

Batchelor, G.K. 1967. *An Introduction to Fluid Dynamics.* Cambridge, Cambridge University Press.

Bathurst, J.C. 1978. Flow resistance of large scale roughness, *Journal of Hydraulic Engineering* **104**: 1587–1603.

Bauer, B.O., Yi, J.C., Namikas, S.L., and Sherman, D.J. 1998. Event detection and conditional averaging in unsteady aeolian systems. *Journal of Arid Environments* **39**: 345–375.

Booker, D.J., Sear, D.A., and Payne, A.J. 2001. Modelling three-dimensional flow structures and patterns of boundary shear stress in a natural pool–riffle sequence. *Earth Surface Processes and Landforms* **26**: 553–576.

Bradbrook, K.F., Lane, S.N., and Richards, K.S. 2000. Numerical simulation of time-averaged flow structure at river channel confluences. *Water Resources Research* **36**: 2731–2746.

Bridge, J.S. and Dominic, D.F. 1984. Bed-load grain velocities and sediment transport rates, *Water Resources Research* **20**: 476–490.

Buffin-Bélanger, T. and Roy, A.G. 1998. Effects of a pebble cluster on the turbulent structure of a depth-limited flow in a gravel-bed river. *Geomorphology* **25**: 249–267.

Carney, S.K., Bledsoe, B.P., and Gessler, D. 2006. Representing the bed roughness of coarse-grained streams in computational fluid dynamics. *Earth Surfaces Processes and Landforms* **31**: 736–749.

Charlton, F.G., Brown, P.M. and Benson, R.W. 1978. *The hydraulic geometry of some gravel rivers in Britain.* Hydraulics Research Station, Wallingford, England. Report IT180.

Cleary, P.W. and Prakash, M. 2004. Discrete-element modelling and smoothed particle hydrodynamics: potential in the environmental sciences. *Philosophical Transactions of the Royal Society A* **362**: 2003–2030.

Clifford, N.J., Robert, A., and Richards, K.S. 1992. Estimation of flow resistance in gravel-bedded rivers: a physical explanation of the multiplier of roughness length. *Earth Surface Processes and Landform* **17**: 111–126.

Cui, Y. and Parker, G. 1998. The arrested gravel front: stable gravel-sand transitions in rivers. Part 2: General numerical solution. *Journal of Hydraulic Research* **36**: 159–182.

DuBoys, M. 1879. Le Rhône et les rivières à lit affouillable. *Annales des Ponts et Chaussées* Série 5, XVIII: 141–195.

Einstein, H.A. 1937. The calibration of the bedload trap used in the Rhine, *Schweizerische Bauzeitung* **110**: 29–32.

Einstein, H.A. 1950. *The Bed-load Function for Sediment Transportation in Open Channel Flows*. USDA Soil Conservation Service, Washington, D.C. Technical Bulletin 1026.

Ferguson, R.I., Parsons, D.R., Lane, S.N., and Hardy, R.J. 2003. Flow in meander bends with recirculation at the inner bank. *Water Resources Research*, **39**: 1322. doi: 10.1029/2003WR001965.

Francis, J.R.D. 1973. Experiments on the motion of solitary grains along the bed of a water-stream. *Proceedings of the Royal Society of London A*. **332**: 443–471.

Gessler, D., Hall, B., Spasojevic, M., Holly, F., Pourtaheri, H., and Raphelt, N. 1999. Application of 3D mobile bed, hydrodynamic model. *Journal of Hydraulic Engineering* **125**: 737–749.

Gilbert, G.K. 1914. *The Transportation of Debris by Running Water*. United States Geological Survey, Professional Paper 86.

Graf, W.H. 1998. *Fluvial Hydraulics: Flow and Transport Processes in Channels of Simple Geometry*. Chichester, John Wiley & Sons, Ltd.

Hardy, R.J. 2005. Modeling granular sediment transport within a CFD framework. *Earth Surface Processes and Landforms* **30**: 1069–1076.

Hardy, R.J., Lane, S.N., Ferguson, R.I., and Parsons, D.R. 2007. Emergence of coherent flow structures over a gravel surface: a numerical experiment, *Water Resources Research*, **43**: W03422. doi: 10.1029/2006WR004936.

Hardy, R.J., Lane, S.N., Lawless, M.R. *et al.* 2005. Development and testing of numerical code for treatment of complex river channel topography in three-dimensional CFD models with structured grids. *Journal of Hydraulic Research* **43**: 468–480.

Hayashi, T. and Ozaki, S. 1980. On the unit step length of saltation of sediment particles in the bed-load layer. *Proceedings of the Third Symposium on Stochastic Hydraulics, Tokyo, Japan, 26–28 July*. International Association for Hydraulic Research.

Heald, J., McEwan, I., and Tait, S. 2004. Sediment transport over a flat bed in a unidirectional flow: simulations and validation. *Philosophical Transactions of the Royal Society of London A*. **362**: 1973–1986.

Hodge, R., Richards, K., and Brasington, J. 2007. A physically-based bedload transport model developed for 3-D reach-scale cellular modelling. *Geomorphology* **90**: 244–262.

Hodskinson, A. and Ferguson, R.I. 1998. Modelling separation flow in meander bends. *Hydrological Processes* **12**: 1323–1338.

Hunt, J.C.R., Abell, C.J., Peterka, J.A., and Woo, H. 1978. Kinematic studies of the flow around free or surface mounted obstacles: applying topology to flow visualization. *Journal of Fluid Mechanics* **86**: 179–200.

Jackson, W.L. and Beschta, R.L. 1982. A model of two-phase bedload transport in an Oregon Coast Range stream. *Earth Surface Processes and Landforms* **7**: 517–527.

Jirka, G.H. and Uijttewaal, W.S.J. 2004. Shallow flows: a definition. In Jirka, G.H. and Uijttewaal, W.S.J., editors, Shallow Flows. London, Taylor and Francis Group, pp. 3–14.

Lane, S.N., Hardy, R.J., Elliot, L., and Ingham, D.B. 2003. High resolution numerical modelling of three dimensional flows over complex river bed topography. *Hydrological Processes* **16**: 2261–2272.

Lane, S.N., Hardy, R.J., Elliot, L., and Ingham, D.B. 2004. Numerical modelling of flow processes over gravelly-surfaces using structured grids and a numerical porosity treatment. *Water Resources Research* **40**: W01302. doi: 10.1029/2002WR001934.

Lee, H.Y. and Hsu, I.S. 1994. Investigation of saltating particle motions. *Journal of Hydraulic Engineering* **120**: 831–854.

McEwan, I. and Heald, J. 2001. Discrete particle modeling of entrainment from flat uniformly sized sediment beds. *Journal of Hydraulic Engineering* **127**: 588–597.

McEwan, I.K., Habersack, H.M., and Heald, J.G. 2001. Discrete particle modelling and active tracers: new techniques for studying sediment transport as a Lagrangian phenomenon. In Mosley, M.P.,editor, Gravel-bed Rivers V. Wellington, New Zealand Hydrological Society, pp. 339–373.

McLean, S.R., Wolfe, S.R., and Nelson, J.M. 1999. Predicting boundary shear stress and sediment transport over bed forms. *Journal of Hydraulic Engineering* **125**: 725–736.

Murphy, P.J. and Hooshiari, H. 1982. Saltation in water dynamics. *Journal of Hydraulic Engineering* **108**: 1251–1267.

Nicholas, A.P. and Sambrook Smith, G.H. 1999. Numerical simulation of three dimensional flow hydraulics in a braided channel. *Hydrological Processes* **13**: 913–929.

Niño, Y. and Garcia, M. 1994. Gravel saltation 2: modeling. *Water Resources Research* **30**: 1915–1924.

Niño, Y., Garcia, M., and Ayala, L. 1994. Gravel saltation. 1. Experiments. *Water Resources Research* **30**: 1907–1914.

Papanicolaou, A.N., Diplas, P., Dancey, C.L., and Balakrishnan, M. 2001. Surface roughness effects in near-bed turbulence: implications to sediment entrainment, *Journal of Engineering Mechanics* **127**: 211–218.

Parker, G. and Cui, Y. 1998. The arrested gravel front: stable gravel-sand transitions in rivers; Part 1: Simplified analytical solution. *Journal of Hydraulic Research* **36**: 75–100.

Phillips, J.D. 1999. *Earth Surface Systems: Complexity, Order and Scale*. Oxford, Blackwell.

Reizes, J.A. 1978. Numerical study of continuous saltation. *Journal of Hydraulic Engineering* **104**: 1303–1321.

Richards, K.S., Bithell, M., Dove, M., and Hodge, R. 2004. Discrete-element modelling: methods and applications in the environmental sciences. *Philosophical Transactions of the Royal Society of London A* **362**: 1797–1816.

Schmeeckle, M.W. and Nelson, J.M. 2003. Direct numerical simulation of bedload transport using a local, dynamic boundary condition. *Sedimentology* **50**: 279–301.

Sklar, L. and Dietrich, W.E. 2004. A mechanistic model for river incision into bedrock by saltating bedload. *Water Resources Research* **40**: W06301. doi: 10. 1029/2003 WR002496.

Sinha, S.K., Sotiropoulos, F., and Odgaard, A.J. 1998. Three-dimensional numerical model for flow through natural rivers, *Journal of Hydraulic Engineering* **124**: 13–24.

Syvitski, J.P.M., Slingerland, R.L., Burgess, P. *et al.* 2009. Morphodynamic models: An overview. In Vionnet, C.A., García, M.H., Latrubesse, E.M., and Perillo, G.M.E., editors, *Proceedings, River, Coastal and Estuarine Morphodynamics. RCEM 2009, Santa Fe, Argentina, 21–25 September*, pp. 3–20.

Tritton, D.J. 1988. Physical fluid dynamics, 2nd ed. Oxford, Oxford Science Publications.

Tsuchiya, Y. 1969. On the mechanics of saltation of a spherical sand particle in a turbulent stream. *Proceedings of the 13th International Association of Hydraulic Research Congress, Kyoto, Japan, 1-5 September*, vol. 2, pp. 191–198.

Wiberg, P.L. and Smith, J.D. 1985. A theoretical model for saltating grains in water. *Journal of Geophysical Research* **90**: 7341–7354.

Yalin, M.S. 1963. An expression for bed-load transportation. *Journal of the Hydraulics Division* **89**: 221–251.

Zhu, H.P., Zhou, Z.Y., Yang, R.Y., and Yu, A.B. 2008. Discrete particle simulation of particulate systems: A review of major applications and findings. *Chemical Engineering Science* **63**: 5728–5770.

# 11

# The Importance of Off-channel Sediment Storage in 1-D Morphodynamic Modelling

## J. Wesley Lauer

## 11.1 INTRODUCTION

Alluvial rivers adjust their boundaries in response to changes in sediment and water loads. Because forcing parameters such as climate are often characterized over decadal to millennial time scales, and because major changes in river systems can take significant time to exhibit themselves, it is important to develop and test models for morphodynamic change that are intended to run over similar time scales. Presently, numerous computer models are available for simulating short-term (decadal or shorter) evolution of bed profiles and grain-size distributions across a range of scales and modelling dimensions (see Papanicolaou *et al.*, 2008). However, while much as been accomplished in terms of detailed 2-D and 3-D sediment transport modelling (Cao and Carling, 2002; Mosselman, Chapter 9, this volume), it is still difficult for complex, multidimensional models to converge to appropriate conditions over decadal to millennial time scales and spatial scales of entire river reaches.

Perhaps the most successful long-term approaches involve the use of coupled channel/landscape evolution models (e.g., Coulthard and Macklin, 2003; Coulthard *et al.*, 2008; Tucker and Hancock, 2010). In these models, complex behaviour generally emerges as a function of thresholds in sediment transport and lags between sediment storage and re-mobilization. Because their spatial domain generally involves entire catchments, they allow for the simulation of detailed sediment production processes, as well as tracing of sediments from a particular source. However, the application of these models is labour intensive and potentially requires detailed topographic, lithologic, land-use, and climatic information, and, in some cases, a proxy record for historic climate (e.g.,

Coulthard *et al.*, 2008). Validation is problematic because much of the depositional record is lost as sediment is re-worked. Furthermore, the sometimes complex behaviour of these models, which in many cases is contingent upon a previous system state, may prevent them from providing more than a general representation of likely reach-specific response. Ensemble means for a series of many model runs with stochastically varying input may be the most that can be hoped for. Perhaps for these reasons, it is not yet common practice to use landscape evolution models to answer specific reach-scale questions.

Width-averaged, 1-D models for flow and morphodynamic evolution of bed and grain-size distribution represent an alternative (though traditional) approach for evaluating reach-scale responses to long-term changes in boundary conditions. The goal of the present contribution is twofold. First, recent developments in the application of 1-D models toward assessing long-term (multiple decades or longer) evolution of individual river reaches are briefly summarized. Second, because much of the recent work does not explicitly incorporate off-channel sediment storage, a procedure for such accounting in a 1-D framework is illustrated using a very simple numerical model. While the model intentionally neglects a range of processes that are obviously important, the storage and subsequent re-supply of bed sediment results in a surprisingly complex behaviour, even without multidimensional interaction between the flow field and the bed.

## 11.2 REVIEW OF 1-D PROFILE MODELLING APPROACHES

The few studies that have addressed site-specific river evolution at reach-scale and over time scales of at least

*Gravel-bed Rivers: Processes, Tools, Environments*, First Edition. Edited by Michael Church, Pascale M. Biron and André G. Roy.
© 2012 John Wiley & Sons, Ltd. Published 2012 by John Wiley & Sons, Ltd.

multiple decades have generally followed one of two approaches. The first and most common involves the use of a 1-D width-averaged representation of bed elevation and grain-size distribution evolution within an active layer of a channel. The number of models capable of this type of simulation is quite large (see Papanicolaou et al., 2008). Following this approach, Ferguson and Church (2009) used the 1-D width-averaged SEDROUT model to broadly represent the down-valley pattern of alluvial deposition over roughly 60 years within a rapidly aggrading reach of the Fraser River, British Columbia. Despite the absence of lateral deposition, the model reproduced observed sediment fluxes reasonably well, particularly when width was varied spatially according to the surveyed geometry. Over longer simulations, it is not clear how variability in width would best be handled, but Ronco et al. (2009) have presented an approach for spatial averaging along large rivers that partially addresses this problem. Verhaar et al. (2008, 2010) used SEDROUT to simulate the response of several tributaries of the Saint Lawrence River to projected climate change over a 100-year period. Results depended strongly on the setting of the rivers being modelled, particularly whether they are presently aggrading or degrading. Pizzuto et al. (2008) developed a model for the conservation of both gravel and mud within the confines of a bedrock-controlled alluvial channel and used this to illustrate the potential response of fine material fluxes in urbanizing systems to potential land-use and climate changes. Other decadal-scale applications of relatively traditional 1-D models include Wu et al., (2004), Cui and Parker (2005), and Martín-Vide et al. (2010).

A second but less common approach to 1-D bed profile modelling recognizes that over long time scales, valley evolution involves the transfer of both bed material and fine-grained suspendable load (i.e., bar material) to the floodplain. In many alluvial systems, and particularly in braided or wandering gravel bed rivers flowing through wide valleys, a large portion of the bed-material size sediment in the system may be stored in off-channel deposits. When time scales become long, it becomes important to allow this material to interact with the channel. One of the first studies to incorporate such storage into a 1-D modelling framework was that of Wright and Parker (2005) in their model for downstream fining along the sand-bed Fly River, Papua New Guinea. In their model, down-channel sediment flux was computed based on 1-D, width-averaged hydraulics. However, any divergence in flux was assumed to result in a change in elevation across a region wider than the channel bed (i.e., across the entire floodplain), using a modified form of the Exner equation. The net effect of such an approach is to greatly slow overall morphodynamic change.

While the above models assume temporally constant channel width, this assumption has been relaxed by some authors. Approaches include: (i) full coupling between bank retreat and bed stability (e.g., Langendoen et al., 2009), (ii) a partition between bed and bank change based on an extremal hypothesis, or (iii) an empirical width closure. However, width change may be less important than other model details. Chinnarasri et al. (2008) compared the GSTARS 2.1 model (Simões and Yang, 2008), which discriminates between bed and bank change in such a way that overall stream power is minimized, with the traditional constant width HEC-6 model over a 14-year period on the Pasak River, Thailand. The differences between the two models appear to be minimal, and probably have more to do with differences in the flow description than with temporal evolution (or lack thereof) in overall width. Approach (c), which often involves the use of a constant bankfull Shields stress (Dade and Friend, 1998; Parker et al., 2007) has been applied most frequently for valley-filling problems where the temporal and spatial domains are relatively large, and is thus often associated with approaches that distribute bed material across a region larger than the active channel bed. See Paola (2000) for an extensive theoretical background. It has been particularly useful in braided systems or alluvial fan-deltas (e. g., Parker et al., 1998), where it can help identify the relative proportion of the braid plain occupied by a channel, but it has also been applied to sand-bed rivers with very low Froude numbers, where the diffusive morphodynamic behaviour present under steady-uniform flow becomes more wave-like (Parker et al., 2008; Lauer et al., 2008). In these cases, the relative fraction of bed material in the off-channel deposit strongly influences the overall rates of valley profile evolution. This parameter probably varies in time as a function of overall aggradation rate, and, in most systems, has not been measured.

## 11.3   INFERENCES BASED ON PLANIMETRIC CENTRELINE EVOLUTION MODELS

Because lateral fluxes and the overall composition of the lateral storage reservoir can play an important role in moderating the overall evolution of a river valley (Aalto et al., 2008), it is worth briefly discussing what can be inferred from the large body of literature describing planform evolution of single-thread river channels. Such models are generally based on linearized solutions for coupled water and sediment flow through a channel (see Camporeale et al., 2008; Crosato, 2009; Parker et al., 2011). The initial development of these models allowed for their application to relatively long-term planform evolution of river floodplains (Howard 1992; Sun *et al*. 1996; Camporeale *et al*., 2008), sometimes as part of broader landscape evolution models (see Tucker and Hancock, 2010 and references therein). However, because it has not always been clear how to specify the lateral erodibility coefficient (although see Constantine *et al*., 2009) or how extensively this coefficient depends on numerical assumptions (Crosato, 2007), the actual time period represented by many long-term studies remains unclear. Nevertheless, these applications show that, although the details of migration at a given bend are still not perfectly predictable at local scale (and may never be, primarily because of the unpredictable nature of bend cutoff processes), over the long term, channel patterns along many meander belts are statistically similar and can involve relatively frequent re-occupation of a large part of the floodplain.

Traditional 1-D profile models (in fact, all models for mass movement through storage reservoirs) require assumptions regarding the statistical distribution of particle waiting times and step lengths. According to standard reservoir theory (Bolin and Rodhe, 1973), if a storage reservoir is well mixed, as in a traditional active layer for a stream bed, the distribution of waiting times for particles leaving the reservoir is the same as the age distribution, and both are exponentially distributed. In the context of meandering river systems, several authors have independently hypothesized that the distribution of floodplain age is exponential (Everitt, 1968; Nakamura and Kikuchi, 1996), providing some justification for treading floodplains as simple storage reservoirs in much the same way that an active layer is treated. However, note that recently, Skalak and Pizzuto (2010) observed age distributions for fine sediment in bedrock-controlled rivers that followed a power function form, and Phillips *et al*. (2007) found sediment significantly younger than would be implied by a purely exponential distribution along the rapidly aggrading Waipaoa River, New Zealand, partly because much of the older sediment was stored below the level of the channel bed.

Because the simpler 1-D planform models are not particularly difficult to implement, and because the randomness in these models is probably a result of channel cutoff (Camporeale *et al*., 2008), they offer a useful method for studying floodplain age distributions. Figure 11.1 presents the results of a simple numerical simulation using the IPS model (Ikeda *et al*., 1981) along the meandering (but sand-bed) Strickland River, Papua New Guinea. The model was developed as part of a larger study whose goal is to route geochemical tracers through the alluvial valley, and is conceptually similar to the model presented by Camporeale *et al*. (2008). Neck cutoff was included wherever the channel

approached within one channel width of another channel through the lateral migration process. In the IPS model, the average sinuosity or tortuosity (total channel length divided by valley length) that the model converges to over the long term depends on the friction coefficient. Since the object of the present work is not to include all appropriate physics, but is instead simply intended to provide some insight into typical age distributions for floodplains of actively meandering rivers, this was treated as a calibration parameter and was adjusted until the overall sinuosity matched the sinuosity observed from satellite images, given reasonable estimates of the other input parameters. The erodibility factor in the model was adjusted to give long-term average migration rates similar to those presented by Aalto *et al*. (2008).

Time since channel occupation (i.e., age) was stored on a 250 m by 250 m grid. While the overall age distribution is not particularly distinguishable from an exponential distribution (Figure 11.1), there are regions of the model domain that are perhaps somewhat older than would be expected from an exponential model. This could be due to local shielding of the floodplain from re-working, particularly near the upstream boundary, or simply because the channel occupies the centre of the floodplain slightly more often than the edges (see Camporeale *et al*., 2008). However, the model illustrates the surprisingly "random" re-working in a system dominated by frequent channel cutoff. In essence, channel cutoff, because of its unpredictable nature and strong influence on nearby migration rates, causes the portions of a floodplain that are reworked in a given centennial-scale period to be rather unpredictable and allows a roughly equal chance for any part of the floodplain to be re-worked during that period. It thus provides some justification for simply lumping the entire floodplain into the mass conservation domain of 1-D vertical profile evolution models, at least where the object of the modelling is not to identify stochastic variability across the floodplain, but is instead to simulate general, reach-scale trends over hundreds of years.

## 11.4 1-D PROFILE MODELLING WITH ACTIVE RESERVOIRS FOR CHANNEL AND LATERAL STORAGE

The tendency of channels (meandering or not) to re-work unpredictable portions of their valleys provides a simple mechanism for addressing long-term questions regarding valley-average sediment storage and discharge from such systems. Off-channel storage of bed material (gravel in gravel-bed rivers), bar material (usually gravel and/or sand), and upper floodplain material (usually sand

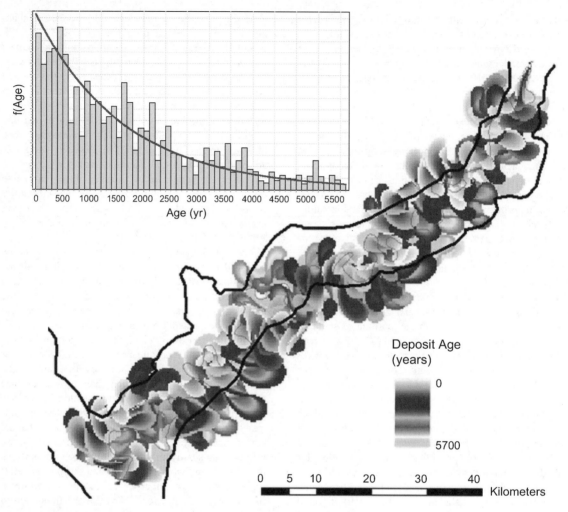

**Figure 11.1** Simulated ages for Strickland River floodplain, Papua New Guinea, after 5700 simulated years. The solid black lines represent the edge of the meander belt as observed from satellite imagery. The faint line illustrates the channel position in 1972. The histogram in the upper right shows the observed and best-fit exponential distribution of ages for the entire system. (See the color version of this figure in color plate section)

or mud) can be accounted for in a separate storage reservoir that evolves over time and influences sediment transport processes within the channel. This approach has been used by Lauer and Parker (2004) to represent coupled channel bed/floodplain surface evolution in a system conveying bed material (sand) and washload (mud). It was also used to represent the movement of sediment tracers in the mud fraction through the floodplain of the gravel-bed Clark Fork River, Montana (Lauer and Parker, 2008a and 2008b), as a function of an arbitrarily specified floodplain age distribution, and is presently being adapted for tracing both bed material and fine sediment through the Le Sueur River basin, Minnesota.

At its heart, a 1-D model with off-channel storage requires a mechanism for specifying lateral fluxes of bed material between the channel and the off-channel reservoir. Ideally, the model should incorporate a feedback between the geometry of these reservoirs, their history, and the sediment exchange rate between them. A key simplifying assumption is that lateral shifting by the channel can result in a net local supply of sediment at the eroding banks (Lauer and Parker, 2008c). The net supply can occur because: (i) the channel has incised, resulting in old eroding banks being somewhat higher than new point bars, or (ii) the old floodplain has accumulated overbank fines, in this case resulting in a net supply of fine material. (Note also that the tendency for eroding banks to be longer than corresponding point bar banks also results in a local net supply of bed sediment associated with channel elongation. However, this imbalance is probably balanced at reach scale by deposition in abandoned channel courses.)

Modelling lateral storage and resupply requires a mechanism for generating imbalances in lateral flux that can lead to net temporary storage. Perhaps the simplest approach is based on the hypothesis that rivers rapidly build bars to a relatively constant elevation (Braudrick, 2009), after which time sediment is simply added to the bars laterally up to this elevation. This is supported by the data of Church and Rice (2009) on the Fraser River, where, throughout the aggrading gravel reach, gravel bars tend to be built to a relatively constant height above the average level of the active bed. To the extent that the channel reworks this sediment, it represents a potential source of bed material should the main channel be starved of sediment by a reduction in the upstream load. Conversely, if the channel is aggrading, the average elevation of new bars would tend to be somewhat higher than the average floodplain elevation, resulting in net storage of sediment in the floodplain and a reduction in overall storage in the bed region from what would occur were the channel bed the only storage region in the model. The evolution of the channel-side deposit can thus represent a stabilizing mechanism for the evolution of the channel itself, although the extent of this effect probably depends on the grain-size distribution within the storage reservoir.

## 11.5   A SIMPLE 1-D MODEL WITH OFF-CHANNEL STORAGE

The rest of this contribution describes a very simple model for storage and re-supply of bed sediment in a bed-material-dominated system. The model is not intended to have fidelity in representing all important sediment transport processes and would be inappropriate for application to a real river in a management context. Instead, the goal is to study the potential importance of lateral storage using the simplest possible assumptions so that any interesting behaviour can be unequivocally attributed to storage effects. The model represents the channel and floodplain as a set of well-mixed sediment reservoirs, each containing the same single size class of sediment. While selective transport is certainly important in modelling gravel-bed rivers, grain-size effects can lead to complex morphodynamic behaviour. Since the object here is simply to study the potential effects of off-channel storage, assuming a single grain size helps clarify the interpretation of results. For additional simplicity, the entire cut bank is assumed to be composed of gravel, so that the potential effect of fine sediment

deposition on the overbanks or upward fining in point bars is also neglected.

Each storage reservoir corresponds with a channel segment of length $\Delta x_c$. The length of the corresponding valley segment is $\Delta x$, and the ratio $\Delta x_c/\Delta x$ is defined as the valley average sinuosity $\Omega$. The channel is assumed to migrate laterally through the valley at an absolute average rate $c$ that is constant for the duration of the model run, leaving behind a layer of point-bar gravel of characteristic height $H_{bar}$ above the bed (Figure 11.2). In other words, the lateral flux from channel to floodplain per unit channel length is fixed everywhere and for all time and equals $cH_{bar}$. The flux from the off-channel reservoir back to the channel, however, is assumed to vary as a function of the average storage in the off-channel reservoir (consistent with the floodplain having an exponential age distribution). Assuming a constant porosity $\lambda$ and constant channel and floodplain widths $B_c$ and $B_f$, respectively, the volume in this reservoir is proportional to its average thickness $H_f$ (i.e., to the difference in elevation between the bed and the average floodplain elevation). The return flux to the channel per unit channel length is thus $cH_f$. A further simplification involves decomposing $H_f$ into the sum of $H_{bar}$ and a thickness $T$ that represents the difference between new point-bar elevation and average floodplain elevation, so that the net rate of sediment transfer from channel to floodplain per unit channel length is $c(H_f - H_{bar}) = cT$. Note that if the channel is aggrading rapidly, $T$ may be negative, indicating that the crests of new bars are higher than the average floodplain surface.

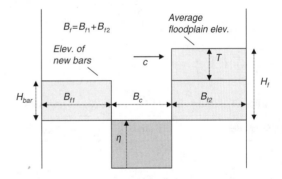

**Figure 11.2**   Geometric representation of the valley section. The darker region represents the channel bed (active layer plus all underlying sediment). The lighter region represents the off-channel reservoir (sediment stored adjacent to channel above the channel bed). $T$ represents the difference in elevation between new point bars and the average off-channel surface, so that $cT$ represents the net lateral return flux to the channel (or into storage, if $T < 0$).

Sediment conservation requires two separate mass conservation equations, one for the channel bed (sediment distributed across width $B_c$) and one for the off-channel reservoir (sediment distributed across the entire floodplain width $B_f = B_{f1} + B_{f2}$, the subscripts referring to left and right banks respectively). Note that an important source of sediment to the floodplain reservoir is through the bottom of the reservoir, which moves vertically at rate $d\eta/dt$ across the entire width of the valley. Also note that if multiple grain sizes were considered, a detailed accounting of valley stratigraphy would be required because of the moving boundary.

With $Q_s$ representing the sediment flux in the channel, and noting that $dT/dt = dH_f/dt$ since $H_{bar}$ is constant, mass conservation for the bed and floodplain, respectively, is stated as follows:

$$(1-\lambda)\frac{d\eta}{dt}\Delta t B_c \Delta x_c = \left[ Q_s|_{x_c} - Q_s|_{x_c+\Delta x_c} + Tc(1-\lambda)\Delta x_c \right]\Delta t \tag{11.1}$$

$$(1-\lambda)\frac{dT}{dt}\Delta t B_f \Delta x = -(1-\lambda)\frac{d\eta}{dt}\Delta t B_f \Delta x - (1-\lambda)cT\Delta t\Delta x_c \tag{11.2}$$

Because only a single grain size is considered, no active layer is required within the channel, greatly simplifying the problem (but admittedly at the expense of physical realism).

In differential form, the equations are:

$$\frac{\partial\eta}{\partial t} = -\frac{1}{1-\lambda}\frac{1}{B_c}\frac{\partial Q_s}{\partial x_c} + \frac{cT}{B_f} \tag{11.3}$$

$$\frac{\partial T}{\partial t} = -\frac{\partial\eta}{\partial t} - \frac{cT\Omega}{B_f} = \frac{1}{(1-\lambda)B_c}\frac{\partial Q_s}{\partial x_c} - cT\left(\frac{1}{B_c} + \frac{\Omega}{B_f}\right) \tag{11.4}$$

These are solved here using a simple Euler scheme, with the divergence in bed sediment flux computed using a width-averaged flow description and a modified Meyer-Peter–Müller sediment load equation (Wong and Parker, 2006). To ensure that the only complexity in the model results from sediment storage effects, flow is assumed steady and uniform, and is partitioned between channel and floodplain using a simplified Chézy equation to determine flow depth $H$, given discharge $Q$:

$$U_c = C_{z,c}\sqrt{gHS} \tag{11.5a}$$

$$U_f = \begin{cases} C_{zf}\sqrt{g(H-H_{bar}-T)S\Omega} & ; \quad H > H_{bar}+T \\ 0 & ; \quad H \leq H_{bar}+T \end{cases} \tag{11.5b}$$

$$Q = U_c H B_c + U_f(H-H_{bar}-T)B_f \tag{11.5c}$$

Sediment load is then computed by weighting with a flow duration curve. An upwinding method is used when estimating the divergence of sediment flux for the weighted load, with an upwinding coefficient $\alpha = 0.6$.

### 11.5.1  Model Application and Discussion

The model is applied with input parameters that crudely represent the Ain River, a medium-sized meandering gravel-bed river draining the Jura region of eastern France. A summary of key parameters is provided in Table 11.1. Four cases are considered, with each run starting from a graded condition wherein slope and sediment load are constant for the reach. Then the sediment feed is either cut in half (runs a and b), leading

**Table 11.1**  Summary of key model input parameters

| Parameter | Value | Units | Description |
|---|---|---|---|
| $H_{bar}$ | 3 | m | point bar thickness |
| $C$ | 1 | m yr$^{-1}$ | average migration rate |
| $\lambda$ | 0.2 | | porosity |
| $Q_s(0)$ | $4 \times 10^{-4}$ | m$^3$ s$^{-1}$ | annual average upstream load at equilibrium |
| $D$ | 0.0375 | m | median grain size |
| $R$ | 1.7 | | submerged specific gravity |
| $B_c$ | 100 | m | channel width |
| $B_f$ | 1000 | m | floodplain width |
| $C_{z,c}$ | 8.9 | | non-dimensional Chézy coefficient for channel |
| $C_{zf}$ | 1.2 | | non-dimensional Chézy coefficient for floodplain |
| $\Omega$ | 1.2 | | sinuosity |

to incision of the channel, or doubled (runs c and d), leading to aggradation. For each sediment supply rate (i.e., either double or half the graded load), the model is run with lateral exchange rates set at a relatively high value ($c = 1\,\mathrm{m\,a}^{-1}$, runs a and c) or a relatively low value ($c = 0.5\,\mathrm{m\,a}^{-1}$, runs b and d). Both are within the plausible range for long-term, reach-average migration rates. The differences between complementary sets of runs (runs a and b, or runs c and d, respectively) are thus due entirely to differences in lateral exchange.

Model results are illustrated in Figure 11.3, which presents temporal changes in bed elevation and thickness parameter $T$ for each run, and in Figure 11.4, which presents spatial variability in relative bed elevation and parameter $T$ at selected times. Note that in all cases, morphdynamic change is largest at the upstream end of the reach. This is an artefact of the fixed downstream boundary condition for bed elevation, which limits morphodynamic evolution near the downstream boundary of the system. For runs a and b, the reduction in sediment supply at the upper end of the reach causes the channel to incise rapidly (Figure 11.3a, b), and in both cases, the system ultimately converges to the same lower slope (Figure 11.4a, b). However, the approach toward the graded slope depends on the extent of lateral re-working. For the higher reworking rate, (run a, $c = 1$ m yr$^{-1}$), the average floodplain elevation tracks the bed elevation closely throughout the entire run, resulting in a parameter $T$ that remains relatively constant through time (Figure 11.3a). However, for a 50% reduction in the exchange rate, the channel degrades much more rapidly because of the absence of the moderating effect of lateral sediment supply (Figure 11.3b). $T$ becomes sufficiently large that even low-probability floods are contained within the channel, further increasing sediment transport rates and, in the case of run b, causing the bed to incise below the level necessary to achieve a "graded" slope. This is eventually corrected when the sediment supply associated with the large value of $T$ causes the entire channel to slowly aggrade back toward the graded condition (Figure 11.3b). In essence, when migration rates are sufficiently low, the channel temporarily creates a set of terraces that, while not resolved in detail, are: (i) initially able to focus flow energy into the channel zone, and (ii) eventually capable of supplying enough sediment to stabilize the system. However, the constant lateral re-working of the floodplain reservoir ultimately removes the terraces after the new grade associated with the final sediment feed is achieved, as illustrated in Figures 11.4a and b after roughly 1000 simulated years.

For runs c and d, wherein load is increased rather than decreased, the response is inverted, but the overall dependency on lateral re-working is still present. In these runs, the channel aggrades in response to the increase in load and approaches the graded condition smoothly where lateral exchange is sufficiently high (Figure 11.3c). However, when the migration rate is low (run d), the channel cannot distribute its sediment across the valley, so the bed aggrades sufficiently rapidly to create a large deficit in sediment storage in the floodplain (i.e., $T \ll 0$), particularly near the upstream end of the reach where aggradation is greatest (Figure 11.4d). This is associated with a reduction in the channel's ability to convey sediment, so the system aggrades further. As in run b, the channel overshoots the graded condition, only returning to this state several hundred years later once the channel has transferred a sufficient amount of sediment to the off-channel reservoir. In the case of run d, the bed oscillates around its graded position several times before eventually converging (Figure 11.3d), leading to the somewhat counterintuitive result that a stepwise increase in sediment load is at least temporarily (and many years later) associated with a channel that is somewhat incised into its floodplain (i.e., $T > 0$, as shown for the upper half of the reach at $t = 500$ years in Figure 11.4d). The key result from the simple modelling exercise is its illustration of potentially significant differences in channel behaviour associated with relatively small changes in lateral exchange, a parameter that is completely neglected in almost all 1-D morphodynamic models. Even in an extremely simple representation of an alluvial system, storage in the floodplain allows for complex, wave-like behaviour of a type that is not possible in simple 1-D bed-material conservation models (at least for 1-D models where grain size is fixed). Lags between storage and later re-supply are essential for this kind of wave-like behaviour to form. In other respects, the model is admittedly a dramatic oversimplification of real river processes, particularly those associated with selective transport and lateral exchange. However, selective transport of bed material could be incorporated into a similar 1-D model with an appropriate accounting of bed stratigraphy and bar grain size structure.

Fine sediment deposited through overbank processes would also probably significantly influence the results of the model runs presented here, particularly runs c and d, wherein aggradation of the bed causes the floodplain to flood frequently. An increase in flood frequency is likely to also increase overbank deposition rates, increasing $T$ in a way presently not accounted for and thus forcing some of the flow energy to remain within the channel. Furthermore, cohesive overbank sediment would probably cause lateral migration rates (and thus overall exchange) to decrease if the average fines content in overbank sediment stored within the floodplain reservoir increased sufficiently.

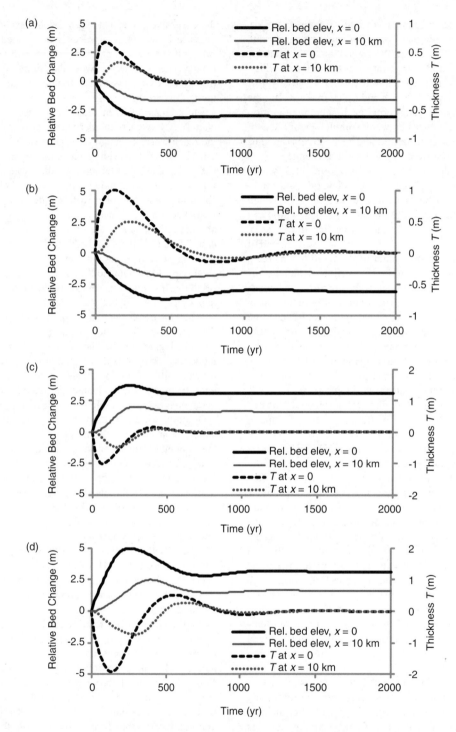

**Figure 11.3**  Temporal response of channel bed (relative to initial position) and thickness parameter $T$ to: (a) run a, a 50% reduction in upstream load at migration rate $c = 1\,\mathrm{m\,a^{-1}}$; (b) run b, a 50% reduction in upstream load at $c = 0.5\,\mathrm{m\,a^{-1}}$; (c) run c, a 50% increase in upstream load at $c = 1\,\mathrm{m\,a^{-1}}$; and (d) run d, a 50% increase in upstream load at $c = 0.5\,\mathrm{m\,a^{-1}}$. Note that for both the low exchange rate runs (runs b and d), the channel bed overshoots its final graded bed position and that the parameter $T$ switches sign several times over the course of the run.

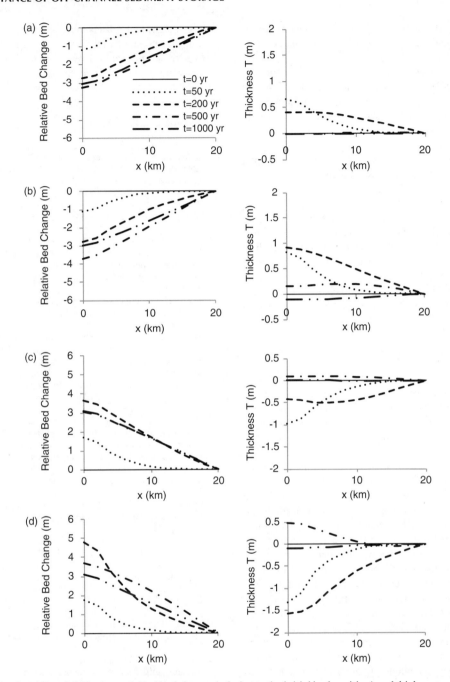

**Figure 11.4** Spatial variability in modelled bed change (relative to the initial bed position) and thickness parameter $T$, at various times for: (a) run a (reduced upstream load, high exchange); (b) run b (reduced upstream load, low exchange); (c) run c (increased upstream load, high exchange); and (d) run d (increased upstream load, low exchange). Note that for $T > 0$, lateral migration results in a net transfer of sediment from floodplain storage to the active channel, and for $T < 0$, lateral migration results in a net transfer from channel to floodplain. In all runs, $T$ eventually converges to zero, but in both low-exchange rate runs, $T$ is still far from zero, even after 500 simulated years. Also note that $T$ can shift sign in a single run, particularly if the lateral exchange rate is low.

A more realistic 1-D model that incorporates lateral exchange would thus require a full description of the role of fine-grained sediment.

The model clearly neglects several other important processes as well. These include the complex, 3-D nature of floodplain flow (particularly at the channel-floodplain interface), long-term changes in overall channel width, and the effects of individual flood hydrographs. However, these are often neglected in 1-D width-averaged models. The complexity remaining in the system despite the absence of these processes points towards several additional issues that should be addressed by centennial-scale modelling projects. These include the need for some way to constrain the overall fraction of mud in the valley fill (probably related to the relative frequency of laterally and vertically accreted sediments, which in turn should be related to the ratio between the lateral reworking rate and the vertical aggradation rate), and the overall control on reach-average exchange rates, which may change as the system evolves and boundary conditions change.

## 11.6   CONCLUSIONS

While detailed models for 2-D and 3-D flow and sediment transport continue to evolve, there is a continuing need for simplified 1-D models of channel evolution in order to assess the likely effects of changing climate and land-use patterns over centennial time scales. A significant deficiency in many existing 1-D models is the inability to account for off-channel sediment storage. In the context of gravel-bed systems, full accounting of off-channel storage will require either full landscape evolution codes (that at least resolve channel/floodplain patterns) or simplified approaches that spread sediment into off-channel reservoirs. If the age distribution of the off-channel reservoir is known, and particularly if it is exponentially distributed, there is theoretical justification for representing sediment movement through the system without detailed 3-D stratigraphic accounting. In the model presented here, a feedback develops between down-channel sediment flux and discharge that leads to long lags between storage and subsequent lateral re-supply of bed sediment. The results show that the reach-averaged magnitude of lateral exchange between the bed and the off-channel reservoir plays a primary role in controlling the long-term adjustment of the bed profile.

## 11.7   ACKNOWLEDGEMENTS

I am very gratedful to Ian Tromble, who performed most of the coding for the IPS-based migration-rate model. Hérve Piégay and Adrien Alber provided input data used for the development of the lateral storage model and also provided helpful feedback regarding the model structure. This work was supported through NSF grant OCE-0742476.

## 11.8   REFERENCES

Aalto, R., Lauer, J.W., and Dietrich, W.E. 2008. Spatial and temporal dynamics of sediment accumulation and exchange along Strickland River floodplains (PNG), over decadal-to-centennial time scales. *Journal of Geophysical Research* **113**: 01S04. doi: 10.1029/2006JF000627.

Bolin, B. and Rodhe, H. 1973. A note on the concepts of age distribution and transit time in natural reservoirs. *Tellus* **25**: 58–62.

Braudrick, C.A., Dietrich, W.E., Leverich, G.T., and Sklar, L.S. 2009. Experimental evidence for the conditions necessary to sustain meandering in coarse-bedded rivers. *National Academy of Sciences Proceedings* **106**: 16936–16941.

Camporeale, C., Perucca, E., and Ridolfi, L. 2008. Significance of cutoff in meandering river dynamics. *Journal of Geophysical Research, Earth Surface* **113**: F01001. DOI: 10.1029/2006JF000694.

Cao, Z and Carling, P.A. 2002. Mathematical modeling of alluvial rivers: reality and myth. Part I: General review. *Water and Maritime Engineering* **154**: 207–219.

Chinnarasri, C., Tingsanchali, T., and Banchuen, S. 2008. Field validation of two river morphological models on the Pasak River, Thailand. *Hydrological Sciences Journal* **53**: 818–833.

Church, M. and Rice, S.P., 2009. Form and growth of bars in a wandering gravel-bed river. *Earth Surface Processes and Landforms* **34**: 1422–1432.

Constantine, C.R., Dunne, T., and Hanson, G.J. 2009. Examining the physical meaning of the bank erosion coefficient used in meander migration modeling. *Geomorphology* **106**: 242–252.

Coulthard, T.J. and Macklin, M.G. 2003. Modeling long-term contamination in river systems from historical metal mining. *Geology* **31**: 451–454.

Coulthard, T.J., Lewin, J.L., and Macklin, M.G. 2008. Non-stationarity of basin scale sediment delivery in response to climate change. In Habersack, H., Piégay, H., and Rinaldi, M. editors. Gravel Bed Rivers VI: From Process Understanding to River Restoration. Amsterdam, Elsevier. Developments in Earth Surface Processes **11**, pp. 337–358.

Crosato, A. 2007. Effects of smoothing and regridding in meander migration models. *Water Resources Research* **43**: W01401. doi: 10.1029/2006WR005087.

Crosato, A. 2009. Physical explanations of variations in river meander migration rates from model comparison. *Earth Surface Processes and Landforms* **34**: 2078–2086.

Cui, Y. and Parker, G., 2005. Numerical model of sediment pulses and sediment-supply disturbances in mountain rivers. *Journal of Hydraulic Engineering* **131**: 646–656.

Dade, B. and Friend, P. 1998. Grain-size, sediment-transport regime, and channel slope in alluvial rivers. *Journal of Geology* **106**: 661–675.

Everitt, B.L. 1968. Use of the cottonwood in an investigation of the recent history of a flood plain. *American Journal of Science* **266**: 417–439.

Ferguson, R. and Church, M. 2009. A critical perspective on 1-D modeling of river processes: Gravel load and aggradation in lower Fraser River. *Water Resources Research* **45**: W11424. doi: 10.1029/2009WR007740.

Howard, A.D. 1992. Modelling channel migration and floodplain sedimentation in meandering streams. In Carling, P.A. and Petts, G.E. editors. *Lowland Floodplain Rivers: Geomorphological Perspectives*. Chichester, John Wiley & Sons Ltd, pp. 1–41.

Ikeda, S., Parker, G., and Sawai, K. 1981. Bend theory of river meanders: I. Linear development. *Journal of Fluid Mechanics* **112**: 363–377.

Langendoen, E.J., Wells, R.R., Thomas, R.E., Simon, A., and Bingner, R.L. 2009. Modeling the evolution of incised streams III: Model application. *Journal of Hydraulic Engineering* **135**: 476–486.

Lauer, J.W. and Parker, G., 2004. Modeling channel-floodplain co-evolution in sand-bed streams. In Sehlke, G., Hayes, D.F., and Stevens, D.K. editors. *Proceedings of the World Water and Environmental Resources Congress, Salt Lake City, June 27–July 1*. American Society of Civil Engineers.

Lauer, J.W. and Parker, G. 2008a. Modeling framework for sediment deposition, storage, and evacuation in the floodplain of a meandering river, part I: theory. *Water Resources Research* **44**: W04425. doi: 10.1029/2006WR005528.

Lauer, J.W. and Parker, G. 2008b. Modeling framework for sediment deposition, storage, and evacuation in the floodplain of a meandering river, part II: application to the Clark Fork River, Montana. *Water Resources Research* **44**: W08404. doi: 10.1029/2006WR005529.

Lauer, J.W. and Parker, G. 2008c. Net local removal of floodplain sediment by river meander migration. *Geomorphology* **96**: 123–149.

Lauer, J.W., Parker, G., and Dietrich, W.E., 2008. Response of the Strickland and Fly River confluence to postglacial sea level rise. *Journal of Geophysical Research* **113**, F01S06. doi: 10.1029/2006JF000626.

Martín-Vide, J.P., Ferrer-Boix, C., and Ollero, A. 2010. Incision due to gravel mining: Modeling a case study from the Gállego River, Spain. *Geomorphology* **117**: 261–271.

Nakamura, F. and Kikuchi, S. 1996. Some methodological developments in the analysis of sediment transport processes using age distribution of floodplain deposits. *Geomorphology* **16**: 139–145.

Paola, C. 2000. Quantitative models of sedimentary basin filling. *Sedimentology* **47**(Supplement 1): 121–178.

Papanicolaou, A. N., Elhakeem, M., Krallis, G., Prakash, S., and Edinger, J., 2008. Sediment transport modeling review—current and future developments. *Journal of Hydraulic Engineering* **134**: 1–14.

Parker, G., Muto, T., Akamatsu, Y., Dietrich, W.E. and Lauer, J.W., 2008. Unraveling the conundrum of river response to rising sea level from laboratory to field. Part II. The Fly-Strickland River System, Papua New Guinea. *Sedimentology* **55**: 1657–1686.

Parker, G., Paola, C., Whipple, K.X. *et al.* 1998, Alluvial fans formed by channelized fluvial and sheet flow, II, Application. *Journal of Hydraulic Engineering* **124**: 996–1004.

Parker, G., Shimizu, Y., Wilkerson, G.V. *et al.* 2011. A new framework for modeling the migration of meandering rivers. *Earth Surface Processes and Landforms* **36**: 70–86.

Parker, G., Wilcock, P.R., Paola, C., Dietrich, W.E., and Pitlick, J., 2007. Physical basis for quasi-universal relations describing bankfull hydraulic geometry of single-thread gravel bed rivers. *Journal of Geophysical Research, Earth Surface* **112**: F04005. doi: 10.1029/2006JF000549.

Phillips, J.D., Marden, M., and Gomez, B., 2007. Residence time of alluvium in an aggrading fluvial system. *Earth Surface Processes and Landforms* **32**: 307–316.

Pizzuto, J., Moglen, G., Palmer, M., and Nelson, K., 2008. Two model scenarios illustrating the effects of land use and climate change on gravel riverbeds of suburban Maryland, U.S.A. In Habersack, H., Piégay, H., and Rinaldi, M. editors. *Gravel Bed Rivers VI: From Process Understanding to River Restoration*. Amsterdam, Elsevier. Developments in Earth Surface Processes **11**, pp. 359–381.

Ronco, P., Fasolato, G., and Di Silvio, G. 2009, Modelling evolution of bed profile and grain size distribution in unsurveyed rivers. *International Journal of Sediment Research* **24**: 127–144.

Simões, J.M. and Yang, C.T., 2008. GSTARS computer models and their applications, Part II: Applications. *International Journal of Sediment Research* **23**: 299–315.

Skalak, K. and Pizzuto, J. 2010. The distribution and residence time of suspended sediment stored within the channel margins of a gravel-bed river. *Earth Surface Processes and Landforms* **35**: 435–446.

Sun, T., Meakin, P., Jøssang, T., and Schwarz, K. 1996. A simulation model for meandering rivers. *Water Resources Research* **32**: 2937–2954.

Tucker, G.E. and Hancock, G.R. 2010. Modelling landscape evolution. *Earth Surface Processes and Landforms* **35**: 28–50.

Verhaar, P.M., Biron, P.M., Ferguson, R.I., and Hoey, T.B. 2008. A modified morphodynamic model for investigating the response of rivers to short-term climate change. *Geomorphology* **101**: 674–682.

Verhaar, P.M., Biron, P.M., Ferguson, R.I., and Hoey, T.B. 2010. Numerical modelling of climate change impacts on Saint-Lawrence River tributaries. *Earth Surface Processes and Landforms* **35**: 1184–1198.

Wong, M. and Parker, G. 2006. Reanalysis and correction of bed-load relation of Meyer-Peter and Müller using their own database. *Journal of Hydraulic Engineering* **132**, 1159–1168. doi: 10.1061/(ASCE)0733-9429(2006)132:11(1159).

Wu, W., Vieira, D.A., and Wang, S.S.Y. 2004, One-dimensional numerical model for nonuniform sediment transport under unsteady flows in channel networks. *Journal of Hydraulic Engineering* **130**: 914–923.

Wright, S. and Parker, G. 2005. Modeling downstream fining in sand-bed rivers. I: Formulation. *Journal of Hydraulic Research* **43**: 612–619.

## 11.9 NOTATION

| | |
|---|---|
| $B_c$ | Channel width (m) |
| $B_f$ | Floodplain width (m) |
| $C_{z,c}$ | Dimensionless Chézy coefficient for channel |
| $C_{z,f}$ | Dimensionless Chézy coefficient for floodplain |
| $c$ | Reach-average lateral migration rate ($\mathrm{m\,s^{-1}}$) |
| $g$ | Gravitational constant ($\mathrm{m\,s^{-2}}$) |
| $H$ | Flow depth in channel (m) |
| $H_{bar}$ | Characteristic point bar thickness (m) |
| $H_f$ | Average floodplain thickness above channel bed (m) |
| $Q$ | Water discharge ($\mathrm{m^3\,s^{-1}}$) |
| $Q_s$ | Sediment discharge ($\mathrm{m^3\,s^{-1}}$) |
| $S$ | Channel Slope |

| | | | |
|---|---|---|---|
| $T$ | Difference between average floodplain elevation and elevation of new point bars (m) | $x_c$ | Down-channel coordinate (m) |
| | | $x$ | Down-valley coordinate (m) |
| $t$ | Time (year, cf Figures 3 and 4) | $\eta$ | Channel bed elevation (m) |
| $U_c$ | Flow velocity in channel (m s$^{-1}$) | $\lambda$ | Sediment deposit porosity |
| $U_f$ | Flow velocity in floodplain (m s$^{-1}$) | $\Omega$ | Average sinuosity |

# River Restoration and Regulation

# 12

# Stream Restoration in Gravel-bed Rivers

## Peter R. Wilcock

## 12.1  INTRODUCTION

Now widely practiced, stream restoration remains an industry whose growth has outpaced the science and engineering needed to support it. This review identifies challenges facing development of a robust, reliable, and cost-effective stream restoration methodology and practice. Considering both practice and research perspectives, this chapter defines elements of a successful restoration profession and presents some of the challenges to its implementation.

This review is based largely on the author's efforts to better understand the state of stream restoration practice as part of a programme to determine the most effective ways that science and engineering research can improve that practice. It is addressed primarily to those in the research community. There is a real need for a more active and productive relationship between research and practice, and this paper attempts to define some of the most pressing topics. The review is based primarily on experience with stream restoration as practiced in the United States, although most of the concepts and challenges are general. Because much of stream restoration practice in the United States is based on methods that are incompletely published and transmitted primarily through private short courses, it is difficult to write a conventional review citing the basis and reference for current methods. Indeed, it is difficult to find a complete foundational logic of current practice from available information and implemented projects. Nonetheless, it is possible to identify important assessment and design challenges that could be addressed in a more productive research–practice interaction.

An underlying goal of this review is to enumerate opportunities by which research might productively contribute to an improved practice. A further goal is to argue that a more effective research–practice collaboration requires a much better understanding on the part of researchers of the challenges faced by those in restoration practice. There is a pressing need for those in research to contribute more directly to restoration practice. Not every problem need be completely solved in order to provide useful methods and tools. A quantitative answer need only be good enough to provide clear guidance regarding assessment and design choices. Even a highly uncertain prediction of a stream's response to restoration actions can be effectively used in a decision context if the uncertainty is clearly and transparently communicated. For example, it may be sufficient to predict the sign of changes in sediment storage in a reach, rather than the specific sediment volume at any particular time. Or it may be sufficient to identify that the rate of sediment supply is well below a threshold above which channel performance is sensitive to sediment supply, in which case the simpler methods for designing a threshold channel may be used. Some difficult scientific problems may be finessed through clever specification of design goals and by taking advantage of local conditions. Without a good understanding of the problems faced in stream restoration practice, contributing research has a good chance of being irrelevant, inaccessible, and unused.

It is important to note at the beginning that essential elements of the stream restoration industry are about neither streams nor restoration. First, the term restoration has become a catch-all phrase for a wide range of manipulations of stream channels and their riparian corridor. Actions intended for enhancement, rehabilitation, mitigation, landscaping, or simple clean-up are grouped under the term restoration. The primary objectives of a stream project may focus on infrastructure protection or social amenities in an urban community, factors that have no immediate connection with returning the system to some earlier state. We preserve here this now-common misuse of the term restoration, following the argument that no objective is intrinsically wrong or dominant, and that all actions in streams should be considered within an integrated approach that includes ecosystem restoration as a persistent option. Second, stream restoration is not defined solely by actions directed toward the ecological

*Gravel-bed Rivers: Processes, Tools, Environments*, First Edition. Edited by Michael Church, Pascale M. Biron and André G. Roy.
© 2012 John Wiley & Sons, Ltd. Published 2012 by John Wiley & Sons, Ltd.

or geomorphic condition of a stream. Stream restoration is very much a social activity. Restoration actions are an intentional social choice, proposed in response to human impacts, risks, and opportunities. Restoration addresses societal goals, some of which (infrastructure protection, aesthetics, recreation, education, community building) are explicitly human in purpose. The social elements – particularly the social benefits – are real and may in some cases provide the strongest case for a worthwhile project.

Finally, a different kind of social interaction must be mastered in developing a successful stream restoration practice: the social interaction between practice and research. This has been incomplete and at times contentious. Friction between research and practice has sometimes skewed communication and inhibited development of a more mature and effective profession (Wilcock, 1997). A successful research–practice interaction is characteristic of a mature profession and essential for developing a more effective and professional practice. The most effective path forward is to focus on the elements of a superior approach, rather than the failings of existing methods.

## 12.2 RESTORATION PRACTICE AND THE RESEARCH PERSPECTIVE

Stream restoration has undergone rapid growth and is now a widespread activity in the United States. Practitioners have a diverse range of backgrounds (River Restoration Northwest, 2003). Professional training in engineering and natural science is becoming more common, driven in part by legal and regulatory requirements, and fostered by the emergence of large engineering firms as key players. The driving force behind the broad emergence of stream restoration in the United States has been one remarkable person, Dave Rosgen, and the methodology that he has developed, which has come to be known as Natural Channel Design (NCD).

Many of the concepts cited as providing the foundation of stream restoration have a rich history in geomorphological research of the mid-twentieth century, but appear to have no formal demonstration of their effectiveness or accuracy in the context of channel design. The conceptual basis for NCD is the equilibrium fluvial geomorphology represented by the hydraulic geometry (Leopold and Maddock, 1953; Leopold et al., 1964) and the association of bankfull channel dimensions with a flood frequency of 1–1.5 years return interval (Wolman and Miller, 1960; Leopold et al., 1964). With a focus on the equilibrium channel, the NCD approach to stream design seeks a template in a nearby or idealized channel that the designer judges to be suitable. Finding a suitable equi-

librium channel for a template is a difficult task, particularly in disturbed watersheds (where one would hope that restoration activities are focused). It is well documented that watershed and stream channel disturbances can take decades to centuries to work their way through a channel network. It can be argued that no streams are in equilibrium because the necessary stationarity of the driving conditions of water and sediment supply are uncommon, if not rare. The difficulty in finding an appropriate template channel is widely encountered in practice (e.g., Sortman, 2004) and designs following NCD instructions may identify a template or reference reach, but not use it in any substantial way in the design. More critically, no method has been developed for predicting the appropriate template in a way that links cause and effect in a logically complete and testable framework. At best, the design can be tested after the fact for its ability to transport the supplied sediment with the available flow.

In response to manifest problems with a template approach, and as an implicit response to the risk associated with uncertain and incomplete design methodologies, stream restoration practice has evolved away from a simple imprint of generic channel patterns toward more subtle manipulations in which the existing channel geometry, pattern, and slope are often preserved, but fixed in place by large rock placed in the bed and banks. Although still presented as NCD (often as a client or competitive requirement), this type of project shares as much with older approaches using armouring and rip-rap as it does with any meaningful restoration. Another emerging trend in stream restoration practice focuses on floodplain re-connection. In order to produce frequent overbank flow, channels are designed to be much smaller than those indicated by the typical flood frequency of the design flow used in NCD. These channels are also often anchored by instream and floodplain hard spots, thereby inhibiting a dynamic channel.

Many in academic and government research have watched the growing application of NCD methods with concern and a sometimes imperfect understanding of the efforts of those attempting to apply it resourcefully. Research–practice interactions have been at times unproductive, even bitter, fueled by reports of clients mandating NCD methods and accounts of job candidates with weeks of experience in short courses being hired in preference to those with advanced academic preparation in geomorphology, river engineering, or stream ecology.

A common theme in both research and practice is that a careful history of the channel and its watershed is needed such that the essential drivers of channel change – the supply of water and sediment – can be linked to observed channel behaviour. This is a traditional theme in geomorphology, but remains a tall order under the best of circumstances. The contingent and transient response of the channel to past events cannot be known exactly, the future water and sediment supply can only be estimated statistically, and our ability to predict across a wide range of time and space scales is limited. It might seem that designing a channel to meet specific design objectives is an impossible task, but many stream channels are being designed and rebuilt, often with claimed success. The challenge is to develop methods that are sufficiently robust that meaningful, testable predictions can be made to provide the basis for design. The amount of successful development and implementation of rigorous design methods is discouragingly limited. The application of current science can also appear limited in preference to the dominant equilibrium geomorphological paradigm of 50 years ago.

Part of the problem is that researchers have not provided methods that are accessible, relevant, and practical (Wilcock, 1997). This is not an easy task – it requires understanding the demands of stream channel design in a real-world context. Every aspect of stream dynamics need not (and cannot) be understood before management actions are designed and implemented. Clever planning and design decisions can in some cases finesse tough problems and still meet project objectives. For those technical problems that cannot be avoided, robust tools are needed to address design needs with demonstrable reliability. A successful evaluation of the desirable and the predictable requires a robust decision analysis system. Although no complete restoration methodology has emerged from the research perspective, many of the tools needed have been developed, or could be developed with current understanding. Advances in restoration practice will require close collaboration through which research results find their way into practice and challenges from practice are used to inform research priorities.

## 12.3 ELEMENTS OF A SUCCESSFUL STREAM RESTORATION PROFESSION

At the root of professional stream restoration practice is an explicit, rational connection between cause and effect, linking objective and action in a predictive, testable framework. This provides a basis for evaluating trade-offs, incorporating uncertainty, and learning from doing. Objectives must be specific, relevant, quantitative, and predictable. Although the outline of such a decision process can be found in many documents, it is yet to be implemented in a complete, rational, testable form using predictive methods.

Methods used to evaluate and finalize design options must be explicit and robust. Uncertainty must be explicitly incorporated into the design process. A practicable

method cannot depend in a sensitive way on accurate specification of details of water and sediment supply. Rather, designs must be robust, such that their response to future events will fall within acceptable bounds.

Because streams respond to changes in environmental drivers over a broad range of time and space scales, in most cases the success of a restoration design will depend directly on the level of understanding of the watershed and channel history. The tools needed to estimate sediment supply to the restoration site will need to include time scales of decades to millennia in order to reliably account for important drivers.

A key to developing a successful stream restoration profession is an essential and pervasive interaction among science, engineering, decision analysis, and practice. None of these perspectives is sufficient on its own, but must be explicitly combined in developing a framework that supports project assessment and design decisions. Better tools without context or direction produce numbers with unknown value. Superior decision methods without credible predictions cannot produce useful decisions. Uncertainty in predictions must be defined from the best science, but must also feed back into the decision process. Some design challenges may be addressed with existing or new predictive tools; others may be addressed by re-formulating the design objectives or by finding creative combinations of design elements. The most effective assessment and design options require a continuous two-way interaction between restoration science, engineering, practice, and decision analysis.

## 12.4 CHALLENGES

The underlying goal of this paper is to identify particular topics for which focused attention and predictive methods from the research community could benefit the science and practice of stream restoration. These focus primarily on physical components of the problem: the supply of water and sediment and the response of the stream channel. Some of the topics are rather general and some are specific to particular information needs of the practice community. The list is not meant to be exhaustive and, in fact, depends strongly on the author's particular experience and opinion. By enumerating these challenges, the hope is to encourage discussion, collaboration, and the development of new methods, and to promote wider awareness or more effective application of existing methods.

### 12.4.1 Improved Estimation of Sediment Supply

River channel dynamics depend on sediment supply, yet our ability to reliably estimate sediment supply remains poor. There is a pressing need for robust methods for estimating sediment supply and its uncertainty. Of the broad challenges in fluvial geomorphology, prediction of sediment supply is perhaps the most integrative and therefore intellectually challenging. The very wide range of watershed characteristics and contingencies, and the uncertain nature of future conditions of climate and land use, mean that perfect predictions of sediment supply are unobtainable. Fortunately, high accuracy is generally not needed in order to make effective decisions about stream performance. Continual progress has been made in developing better observations and explanation of sediment yield. New approaches offer rich opportunities for more accurate and practical prediction of sediment supply. The advent of high-resolution topography and spatial analysis tools allow for topographically sensitive scaling up of local observations of sediment production. The mere passage of time has made some classic approaches increasingly relevant. In many locations, 60–80 years of aerial photography are available, such that historical analysis of watershed and channel change can be routine. Many opportunities now exist to directly measure sediment yield over decadal time scales thanks to the mid-twentieth century dam-building era and the construction of many stormwater management facilities 25–40 years ago. Sediment yield estimates can now be tested against not only observed accumulation in ponds and reservoirs, but also against proportional source apportionment using sediment fingerprinting and estimates of watershed-scale denudation rates using cosmogenic radionuclides.

*Research challenge:* The geomorphic community is getting closer to making reliable estimates of sediment supply. Nonetheless, watershed models used in current practice too often rely on estimates of sediment supply that have little basis in actual mechanisms and rates, and do not include effective means for estimating sediment storage. A mix of classic and new methods can be marshalled to develop useful estimates of sediment supply to specific locations in a channel network. A range of methods is needed, requiring different levels of effort and supporting information, each with specified supply rate and grain size with described uncertainty. We have the prospect of routinely providing sediment yield estimates of useable reliability in the coming years.

### 12.4.2  Clarifying the Conceptual Basis for Stream Channel Design

Approaches to stream design can be divided into two categories – analogue and process-based. In the analogue approach, the size, shape, slope, and planform of the channel are based on a template developed from a combination of regional relations for bankfull geometry and a reference reach selected to represent desired conditions in the channel (Rosgen, 2007). Both are strongly conditioned by the expectation that the bankfull discharge should have a recurrence interval of order 1.2–1.5 years. In a process-based approach, the water and sediment supply are first specified, and the channel size and slope are determined to explicitly transport the supplied sediment with the available water (e.g., Copeland et al., 2001).

These two approaches have been presented as complementary, with either as a possible option (Shields et al., 2003). The relation between the two approaches is more intertwined. A template approach can provide useful information on channel geometry, but provides no direct basis for accommodating changing water and sediment supply. The absence of a cause–effect linkage eliminates any rational basis for learning or for correcting the method if a constructed channel performs poorly. Because the template approach contains no explicit connection between cause and effect, it cannot be a sufficient basis for channel design. This must be accomplished in subsequent steps that evaluate the flow competence and transport capacity of the template design (Rosgen, 2007).

A mechanistic approach, while explicitly linking water and sediment supply to channel design, does not specify a particular channel geometry (e.g., width) and recourse is often made to the same "typical" conditions upon which the template method is based. For example, one approach specifies the slope and depth needed to transport the supplied sediment with the available water for a range of channel widths (Figure 12.1a; Copeland et al., 2001). The width used in the design may be selected to match a value that falls within typical values for the given drainage area and valley conditions. The width may be selected using a calculated value of the effective discharge (the peak of the curve formed by multiplying the sediment rating curve with the discharge pdf, indicating the flow producing the most transport over time. Although the effective discharge approach incorporates sediment transport information, it suffers from the same liability as using the hydraulic geometry to pick a channel dimension: it is based on the strong assumption that a stable channel should be sized to the effective discharge, a condition broadly observed (with exceptions) for self-formed channels under stationary, equilibrium conditions.

The fundamental advantage of the process-based approach is that, having specified a channel width (for whatever reason), the remaining geometric properties of slope and depth are specifically determined for the specified design flow and its associated sediment load. The choice of channel width is flexible within bounds, but the slope and depth are determined by flow and transport relations.

If using a template approach for channel design, one must still verify that the channel can carry the supplied sediment with the available flow. If using a mechanistic analysis, one must still make a choice of channel dimension (e.g., width). In either case, one cannot ignore the requirements of transport capacity and flow competence. Clear thinking on these fundamental concepts is a requirement for a rigorous approach to stream channel design, particularly because it can help to clearly identify those steps in a design process in which strong assumptions are made. A successful, professional design approach replaces dependence on such assumptions, with specific drivers and mechanisms such that cause and effect are rationally linked, uncertainty can be assessed, and methods can be improved in light of observed performance.

*Research challenge:* An important role that can be played by research is to clearly and precisely articulate the essential drivers and mechanisms behind different restoration design options. Although the choices made regarding objectives and tradeoffs are the province of stakeholders, research can make those choices and tradeoffs clear, provide predictive links (with uncertainty) between management action and river response, and construct a rational and transparent framework within which decisions can be made. The connection between channel geometry, water and sediment supply, and stream channel design is widely accepted in the stream restoration community, but the rational linkages have yet to be completely specified in a complete, predictive, and accessible form that is useful to the practice community. A bright line must be drawn around the assumptions upon which the equilibrium template approach depends. An alternative, process-based approach must be developed completely and presented in an accessible and useful form.

### 12.4.3  Designing Channels for the Range of Water and Sediment Supply

Existing process-based tools for designing alluvial channels focus on conditions at the design (bankfull) stage. As discussed in the previous section, these relations provide a rational basis for selecting a combination of channel width, depth, and slope that will transport the supplied sediment at the design discharge. A more complete method would identify the combination of channel width, depth, and slope that would give a transport capacity that balances the sediment input over the range of flows that a channel will experience. In practice, various combinations of slope, width, and depth can be incorporated in a trial design and the (supply – capacity) sediment balance can be evaluated over the full flow duration curve. Although not complex, this type of calculation is rare in practice. Complications include uncertainty in the estimated sediment supply and transport capacity (Section 12.4.6) and evaluation of the configuration of sediment accumulated or evacuated from the reach.

*Research challenge:* Accessible channel design methods are needed that account for the range of water and sediment supply that the stream will experience.

### 12.4.4  Is There a Single Correct Design Discharge?

For many years, stream channels have been designed to a narrow range of bankfull discharge (typically the 1.1–1.5 years return interval on the annual flood series). Recently, stream restoration practice has expanded to include designs with a very small bankfull channel, thereby producing frequent overbank events and a moist, "re-connected" riparian corridor. This has sparked a debate in the practice community about the appropriate design discharge. Design "failures" (typically cases in which accumulation or evacuation of sediment produces rapid channel change) are often attributed to the selection of the "wrong" design discharge. Because channel dimension is not usually linked to the supply of water and sediment in any explicit fashion, this debate hinges on the untestable assumption of a single, stable equilibrium channel form adjusted to a "correct" bankfull discharge. Channels designed to a flow with a 1.1–1.5 years return interval rely on the broad correlation between equilibrium channel size and flood frequency that supports the classic hydraulic geometry derived from Leopold and Maddock (1953) *et seq.* But most channels requiring re-construction may be expected to have experienced changes in water and supply such that nature and duration of channel adjustment must be assessed and no equilibrium channel dimension may exist. A relevant question regarding the choice of a very small bankfull channel is whether such channels are sustainable, particularly in regimes with a non-negligible sediment supply.

*Research challenge:* A very practical question that should be intriguing to the gravel-bed river research community is whether there is a single correct design discharge for a channel. Can different flows be selected as the bankfull design discharge in order to meet various ecological and social objectives or is there a narrow range of bankfull flows that will produce acceptable river behaviour? The scatter in width-discharge plots of the downstream hydraulic geometry suggests that equilibrium channels can have a relatively wide range of widths for a particular discharge.

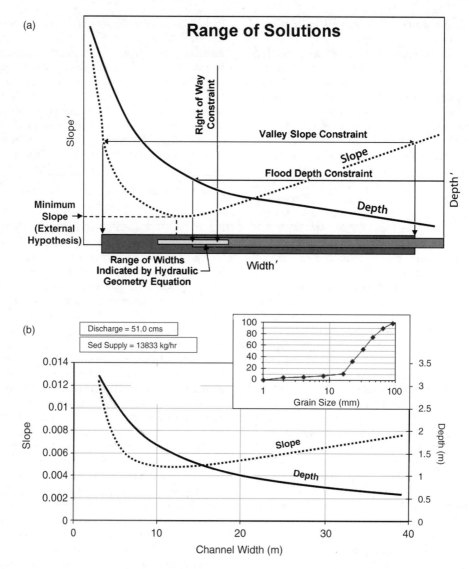

**Figure 12.1**  Two channel design charts, giving channel slope and depth required to transport a specified sediment load at a specified discharge. (a) Generic form of the Copeland method, implemented in *SAM* and *HEC-RAS*. Reproduced, with permission, from Copeland, R., McComas, D.N., Thorne, C.R., Soar, P.J., Jonas, M.M. and Fripp, J.B. 2001. Hydraulic Design of Stream Restoration Projects. U.S. Army Engineer Coastal and Hydraulics Laboratory, HL TR-01-28. Calculations are made using single-size transport formulas. (b) Design diagram using the Wilcock–Crowe transport model, as coded in the software *iSURF*. Water and sediment supply indicated on diagram.

But this broad correlation does not mean that an equivalent range of widths might produce desirable behaviour for particular stream channels (often judged as limited or negligible stream channel adjustments over periods of years to decades). The channel design methods illustrated in Figure 12.1 suggest that a range of widths may be chosen as long as the appropriate channel slope and depth are selected such that the supplied sediment will be transported with the avail-

able flow. Is any choice of width acceptable and, if not, what determines the limits that would produce acceptable behaviour of a designed channel?

### 12.4.5  Design Methods for Sediment Continuity

Improved predictions are needed to estimate sediment continuity with respect to alongstream variation in channel geometry. The design charts in Figure 12.1 provide a combination of width and slope that will transport the supplied sediment with the available water, but for a channel with a natural variation in geometry, to which segments of the channel should this slope/width combination be applied? Should it be applied to the slope of the entire reach, to individual riffle-to-riffle segments, or to a relatively straight and symmetrical cross-over section between bends? If straight reaches are designed to carry the supplied sediment with the available flow, can the balance of the reach geometry (particularly pools and bends) be designed relative to the straight reach? The information available to describe alongstream variation in channel size, shape, and slope is diverse and largely empirical (e.g., Soar and Thorne, 2001). A specific topic for which better guidance is needed is the pool and bend geometry needed to transport the sediment supply, particularly the coarsest fractions. Channel designers are concerned that a reach with a coarse sediment supply may have significant deposition in the approach to pools, producing an aggrading bar that can force the flow against the opposite bank, producing undesirable bank recession.

*Research challenge:* Current guidance for alongstream variation in channel geometry and slope is inadequate to support a predictive approach to stream design. Most channels are currently designed using generalized plots of dimensionless channel geometry that cannot be demonstrated to provide adequate performance. The gravel-bed river research community can provide useful methods using currently available tools. This topic would seem to be particularly well suited to numerical modelling of the interaction between channel geometry (channel width, depth, bend radius of curvature, bar morphology) and a range of discharge and sediment supply.

### 12.4.6 Methods for Handling Uncertainty

Uncertainty is rarely included in the planning and design of restoration projects. Efforts have been made to define a risk-based approach (e.g., Niezgoda and Johnson, 2007), but consideration of uncertainty and consequences is usually either informal or absent. This can lead to channel designs that are overly conservative, with increased costs and reduced opportunity for dynamic conditions. For example, many projects in the past decade have moved in a direction of overdesign and overuse of hard structures. For enlarged urban channels, an increasingly common approach is to minimally alter channel geometry and slope, thereby maintaining a large transport capacity (to prohibit inchannel deposition) while anchoring the bed and banks with rock structures in order to prevent bed incision and bank erosion. Some designs function more like a slurry pipe than a natural channel. This approach gives precedence to channel

stability – a static channel geometry – over other possible channel conditions. Although reducing uncertainty in channel performance, this intrusive approach is likely to be more expensive than alternatives and is not likely to provide the dynamic in-channel topography often judged to be important for ecological performance.

Addressing uncertainty in stream restoration planning involves two important steps, both of which can benefit from more direct involvement with the research community. First, uncertainty in predicted quantities must be assessed. In the case of sediment transport and associated morphodynamic change, the primary source of uncertainty is in the input to hydraulic and transport formulas. A simple approach to quantifying uncertainty is to specify uncertainty in the input and use a Monte Carlo analysis to estimate uncertainty in the calculated result (Wilcock, 2004; Wilcock *et al.*, 2009). This approach is conceptually simple and can be adopted by practitioners in ordinary design practice (Figure 12.2).

The second step in incorporating uncertainty in stream restoration is to develop methods that explicitly incorporate uncertainty in the design process. For a threshold channel, uncertainty in bed stability at the design flow can be combined with the probability of that flow to determine the annual probability of failure (defined as transport of bed material at the design flow). This probability can then be incorporated into an assessment of acceptable risk and the associated costs and benefits of different channel designs. For a mobile-bed channel, the potential for sediment accumulation or evacuation is based on estimates of sediment supply and transport capacity in the design reach, both of which are subject to uncertainty. A common approach is to calculate sediment transport rates in both the design reach and an upstream supply reach. Uncertainty is disregarded on the assumption that the errors made in both calculations may cancel, such that the balance between supply and capacity will be approximately correct. In general, this assumption is a poor one because of the strongly nonlinear relation between sediment transport rate and flow, and the difficulty in estimating the fraction of washload in different reaches. Independent assessment of uncertainty must be made for both supply and design reaches and then combined in an assessment of the possible sediment accumulation or evacuation in the design reach. Once the sediment balance and its uncertainty are estimated, the consequences of sediment imbalance can be evaluated in determining acceptable risk for a dynamic channel versus the cost and lost benefits associated with an overhardened, threshold channel with excess transport capacity, but little natural dynamics.

*Research challenge:* Along with improving methods for calculating transport rates and channel change, research should provide more realistic and accessible

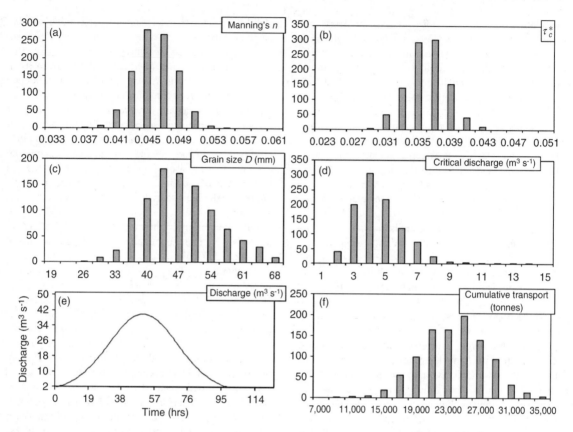

**Figure 12.2**  Example output from a Monte-Carlo estimate of uncertainty in the critical discharge for incipient motion (d) and the cumulative transport rate (f) over a specified hydrograph (e). Output uncertainty arises from user-specified uncertainty in Manning's $n$ (a), critical Shields number (b), and grain size (c). The 90% range in output is typically a factor of 2 to 3 for critical discharge. The range in cumulative transport is more variable, depending primarily on the overall magnitude of the transport and, hence, the amount by which the calculated shear exceeds the critical shear for incipient motion. This spreadsheet is used to demonstrate uncertainty in calculated transport to students of diverse background in one-week short courses.

methods for estimating uncertainty in those estimates. By becoming better informed regarding the constraints, choices, and options for stream channel design, those in research can provide more relevant methods that can be incorporated in a risk assessment of restoration options.

### 12.4.7  The Role of Higher Dimensional Models

In typical practice, sparse information on boundary conditions will limit the utility of 2-D and 3-D flow, transport, and morphodynamic models. Further, reliable application of such models requires capabilities in hydrodynamics and sediment transport that are beyond those commonly available in practice. The limitations of multidimensional models are often poorly understood by the practice community, who may mistakenly assume that more complex models produce more accurate answers. Higher-dimensional models find useful direct application in situations in which project objectives, such as the exclusion of fish and sediment at water diversion structures, require careful local attention. In such cases, the special expertise provided by firms with reliable modelling capability can be advantageous. Another, perhaps more important, application of multidimensional morphodynamic models remains underutilized. With suitable validation, such models can be used as numerical flumes to explore a wide range of conditions in order to develop design charts that can be used to evaluate channel response to various design choices. Among the topics for which this type of applied research can immediately contribute to stream restoration practice are: (i) design charts for alongstream variation in profile and channel geometry to give minimal alongstream variation in sediment storage (Section 12.4.5), (ii) bend adjustment to increases or decreases in sediment supply, and (iii) the tradeoff between width and depth for channels providing desired transport properties at a specified design discharge.

*Research challenge:* Numerical morphodynamic models have been available for 30 years. It is time to put them to work developing reliable and accessible design charts for those engaged in stream restoration practice. This is not a minor applied topic. These charts generalize our understanding of river dynamics in a most basic way, presenting important challenges in identifying the relevant controlling variables and developing an appropriate dimensionless space for general and robust description of channel geometry.

### 12.4.8 Combining Decision Analysis and Predictive Methods

Stream restoration projects often have multiple objectives. These objectives may conflict and tradeoffs among them must be evaluated. There is considerable uncertainty in predicting the outcomes of most restoration actions. Despite these challenges, methods exist for objective and transparent decision-making. A multiobjective decision analysis framework has been articulated for stream restoration (Reichert *et al.*, 2007; Corsair *et al.*, 2009). These methods can accommodate uncertainty and support the rational comparison of non-commensurate objectives such as ecological lift, infrastructure protection, and aesthetic benefits. The outstanding challenge for those in the research community is to more explicitly link prediction in the natural system with decision-making procedures in the social system. Much of the focus in multidisciplinary science has been on physical and biological linkages. Stream restoration is a social activity and a stronger integration between the natural and decision sciences is needed to advance the science and practice of stream restoration. It can sometimes surprise those in geomorphology and engineering that effective decisions may be made without detailed, accurate predictions of the system response to management actions. At the same time, the quality and acceptance of those decisions will be improved by physical predictions that are both relevant and accurate.

*Research challenge:* By collaborating on actual stream restoration cases with those in decision science, geomorphologists and engineers will be better able to identify and address problems that are relevant to stream restoration practice. In the author's experience, they are also likely to find their understanding of basic physical processes to be challenged, because relevant and useful answers to management problems often require knowledge at or beyond current understanding, particularly if the focus is on true prediction within the context of environmental management decision making.

## 12.5 CONCLUSIONS

There is a real opportunity for the research community to more directly improve the profession of stream restoration. This will require a closer understanding of the challenges facing the practice community. Not all questions must be answered, nor all processes predicted, in order to develop a successful stream design. At the same time, research that leads to better prediction of management-relevant factors will improve the assessment and implementation of restoration actions. The time is right for an improved connection between research and practice. A significant fraction of the research community has an interest in practical solutions. A growing proportion of the practice community has the necessary background, skills, and interest to take a more rigorous and predictive approach to stream restoration. Development of a professional stream restoration practice is possible in the coming years.

## 12.6 REFERENCES

Copeland, R., McComas, D.N., Thorne, C.R. *et al.* 2001. *Hydraulic Design of Stream Restoration Projects*. US Army Engineer Coastal and Hydraulics Laboratory, HL TR-01-28.

Corsair, H.J., Ruch, J.B., Zheng, P.Q., and Hobbs, B.F. 2009. Multicriteria decision analysis of stream restoration: potential and examples. *Group Decision and Negotiation*, **18**: 387–417. doi: 10.1007/s10726-008-9148-4.

Leopold, L.B. and Maddock T. Jr., 1953. *The Hydraulic Geometry of Stream Channels and Some Physiographic Implications*, United States Geological Survey Professional Paper 252.

Leopold, L.B., Wolman, M.G., and Miller, J.P. 1964. *Fluvial Processes in Geomorphology*. San Francisco, W.H. Freeman and Co.

Niezgoda, S.L. and Johnson, P.A. 2007. A case study in cost-based risk assessment for selecting a stream restoration design method for a channel relocation project. *Journal of Hydraulic Engineering*, **133**: 468–481.

Rosgen, D. 2007. Rosgen geomorphic channel design. In *Stream Restoration Design*, National Engineering Handbook, Part 654. Natural Resources Conservation Service, United States Department of Agriculture, Chapter 11.

Reichert, P., Borsuk, M., Hostmann, M. *et al.* 2007. Concepts of decision support for river rehabilitation. *Environmental Modeling & Software* **22**: 188–201.

River Restoration Northwest (RRNW), 2003. *Report on 2003 Survey of River Restoration Professionals*. www.rrnw.org.

Shields, F D, Copeland, R.R., Klingeman, P.C., Doyle, M.W., and Simon, A. 2003. Design for stream restoration. *Journal of Hydraulic Engineering* **129**: 8: 575–584.

Soar, P. and Thorne, C.R. 2001. *Channel Restoration Design for Meandering Rivers*, US Army Engineer Coastal and Hydraulics Laboratory, ERDC/CHL CR-01-1.

Sortman, V.L. 2004. Complications with urban stream restorations: Mine Bank Run, a case study. In Clar, M., Carpenter, J.,

Hayes, D.E., and Slate, L. *Protection and Restoration of Streams 2003*, Proceedings of Symposium held 23–26 June 2003 Philadelphia, PA. American Society of Civil Engineers, pp. 431–436.

Wilcock, P.R. 1997. Friction between science and practice: the case of river restoration. *Eos, Transactions of the American Geophysical Union* **78**(41): 454.

Wilcock, P.R. 2004. Sediment transport in the restoration of gravel-bed rivers. In Sehlke, G., Hayes, D.F., and Stevens, D. K., editors, *Proceedings of the ASCE Environmental and Water Resources Institute Annual Congress, Salt Lake City, 27 June–1 July*. American Society of Civil Engineers. ISBN 10-0784407371

Wilcock, P., Pitlick, J., and Cui, Y. 2009. *Sediment Transport Primer: Estimating Bed-Material Transport in Gravel-bed Rivers*. General Technical Report RMRS-GTR-226. Fort Collins, CO, US Department of Agriculture, Forest Service, Rocky Mountain Research Station. www.stream.fs.fed.us.

Wolman, M. G and Miller, J.P. 1960. Magnitude and frequency of forces in geomorphic processes. *Journal of Geology* **68**: 54–74.

## 12.7  DISCUSSION

### 12.7.1  *Discussion by George Heritage and David Milan*

Wilcock provides a usefully critical review of the state of restoration science in the United States. A similar review of practice in the United Kingdom would no doubt draw similar conclusions regarding current practice, with a reliance placed on regime theory and a concentration of restoration activity centred around a few approaches (re-meandering, riffle construction, backwater creation). We completely agree with Wilcock regarding the need for stronger science in the area of river restoration, and greater awareness and uptake amongst practitioners. The best practitioners should also be at the forefront of the research. Up to now the restoration paradigm has been to design for stasis, however, this is highly questionable. We would all argue that rivers are by their very nature dynamic and have been one of the principal agents of landscape change in temperate areas throughout the Holocene epoch.

As Wilcock points out on several occasions, river systems are responding to changes in the flow and sediment regime over a variety of spatial and temporal scales. As an example, we often view river floodplains as static features in restoration design, but they have evolved significantly throughout the Holocene, as long-term stores of glaciofluvial sediment have been re-worked. On a more practical restoration level, bank erosion issues are commonplace but are often highly localized, with the river reacting to individual flood events. This concentration of change and rapidity of response is important when considering the relatively small scales at which the majority of river restoration

schemes are attempted (individual geomorphic/habitat units through to a reach of a few kilometres). It is over these scales that the river is most sensitive and responsive, reacting both to the imposed change and to short-term stochastic variation in the flow and sediment supply. As such the imposition of a channel geometry defined either by regime theory or analogue sediment continuity approaches will not lead to stability over the time scales relevant to restoration.

It is also argued that designing for stasis is not consistent with river restoration ideals that aim to restore both form and function. As an example, a newly meandered channel that achieves stability through transport continuity will not naturally exhibit the differential pattern of coarse sediment deposition essential for point bar development and associated meander migration. Successional development of bar top vegetation communities will be restricted and short-term morphologic variability will be suppressed.

As a further discussion point we would also raise a concern that restoration practice often appears to have a pre-conceived view of restored river form, applying a few, well-used, approaches to create morphologies and habitats characteristic of a generic river type. The literature should be full of examples of subsequent failures, however, it is not. These failures have arisen from poor consideration of sediment transport and flow-related processes at the design stage and through a more fundamental misreading of the character and dynamics of the river locally, failing to recognize the direction the system wants to take towards a dynamic equilibrium. Instead the vast majority of publications linked to restoration remain positive, as the restoration industry is allowed to move on to the next project applying flawed science in an *ad hoc* way. We hope that Wilcock's progressive and insightful review will impact on restoration practice.

### 12.7.2  *Discussion by Joanna Curran*

Stream restorations have a tendency to fall into one of two spatial scales: either the reach scale or the catchment scale. The reach scale is too limited in its consideration of channel morphology, making the catchment scale preferred. However, it is not always possible to conduct a restoration project across an entire catchment, particularly in urban areas. Infrastructure changes the flow paths significantly in urban areas, often disconnecting the urban catchment from what would have been its natural area.

This comment proposes for consideration an infrastructure scale for urban restorations which encompasses the river reach, the immediate surrounding urban areas (including lawns and roads), and the source areas for any major pipes that discharge into the river reach. Changes to channel hydrology due to routing stormwater can dramatically alter channel hydrology and an infrastructure spatial scale is meant to emphasize the role of stormwater in creating the problems many restoration projects seek to correct. Many urban restorations continue to be conducted at the reach scale because the catchment scale is not practical. An infrastructure scale provides an intermediate spatial scale that can encourage those designing and performing restorations to include a reduction of stormwater impacts (for example, through rooftop disconnection) as part of their restoration plans. Adoption of this scale could reduce the need for heavy machinery in restoration and increase the likelihood of stabilizing channel morphology over the long term.

### 12.7.3 Discussion by Nicola Surian

I completely agree with Wilcock's statement that "...in most cases the success of a restoration design will depend directly on the level of understanding of the watershed and channel history" and I would like to put some emphasis on these aspects which are not discussed in detail in the paper. Analysis of channel changes, re-construction of channel evolutionary trajectories and understanding causes of changes (e.g., analysing human impact at basin and reach scales) are fundamental to address some key questions for stream restoration (e.g., Habersack and Piégay, 2008; Brierley et al., 2008). For instance questions such as: (i) what is the magnitude of channel change?, (ii) to what extent can the stream be restored?, (iii) which management strategy can be adopted (e.g., no action, interventions at reach scale, interventions at catchment scale)? Some recent works on gravel-bed rivers in Italy have tried to show how to use knowledge of channel evolution and sediment dynamics in river restoration (Rinaldi et al., 2009; Surian et al., 2009).

The potential of channel recovery was analysed in five gravel-bed rivers of north-eastern Italy (Surian et al., 2009). These rivers have undergone notable adjustments in the last 100 years, specifically narrowing by up to 76%, incision by up to 8.5 m, and changes in channel morphology (e.g., from braided to single-thread). Alteration of sediment fluxes, mainly due to in-channel mining, has been the main factor driving such channel adjustments. Evolutionary trends show that channel recovery is ongoing in several reaches, since widening and aggradation have occurred over the last 15–20 years. This channel recovery has been possible because sediment mining has significantly decreased or ceased along the study reaches. However, several constraints still exist on sediment fluxes (e.g.,

dams). To assess the potentials and limitations of channel recovery, the analysis proceeded in two steps: first, the identification of the trajectories of channel evolution over the last 100 years, and particularly in the last 15–20 years; second, the definition of three different scenarios of channel evolution over the next 40–50 years according to different management strategies (i.e., basin- and reach-scale interventions, reach scale only, and no interventions). Trajectories of channel evolution defined four categories of channel taking into account the evolution over the last 15–20 years: (A) high recovery, (B) moderate recovery, (C) slight recovery or no significant changes in channel morphology, and (D) no channel recovery.

Without any intervention, channel recovery would be possible in those reaches which have a relatively high degree of connectivity with upstream sediment sources or tributaries. However, further incision and narrowing could be expected in those reaches where connectivity is low or very low. Reach-scale interventions, such as the definition of an erodible corridor and removal of some bank protections, are the most feasible interventions to allow an increase in the supply of coarse sediment. This should help those reaches suffering from reduced upstream connectivity to reach an equilibrium condition (e.g., categories B and C), while it could lead to significant channel recovery in those reaches where bedload transport has been altered to a minor extent (e.g., category A). A more substantial channel recovery could be obtained through interventions at the basin scale (e.g., adoption of open check dams and sediment transfer downstream of dams). As for limitation for channel recovery, this study pointed out that, even though both reach- and basin-scale interventions may be carried out, it is likely that channels will not recover to the morphology they exhibited in the first half of the twentieth century, since sediment yield and connectivity will remain less than during the nineteenth century and the first half of the twentieth century. This issue is very relevant to define realistic goals in river restoration. Finally, it is worth noting that the conceptual model used in that study (Surian et al., 2009) relies on some simplified assumption (e.g., no dramatic changes in land use and human activities in the future), thus more complex evolutionary trajectories could be identified if effects of climate changes, large floods, or remarkable land-use changes were taken into account.

### 12.7.4 Reply by Peter Wilcock

Clifford (Chapter 13, this volume) provides a welcome extension of the discussion of stream restoration to include the UK experience. He also broadens the discussion regarding the appropriate definition of management actions from enhancement to rehabilitation to restoration. If we begin from the perspective that stream management is a social choice, using actions taken to address societal goals, then the appropriate starting point for any action is a clear and specific statement of objectives. These objectives might specifically arise from one's definition of restoration or they might be independently stated, and the degree to which the project falls on the rehabilitation to restoration continuum can be judged after the fact. Regardless of the extent to which the social objectives lead to restoration, or toward anything found in nature, for that matter, the imperative of precise, quantitative, and predictable objectives allows the scientist and engineer to use rational methods to assess design alternatives (including doing nothing) for achieving those objectives.

Clifford proposes that observations of the performance of existing stream projects, as well as existing watershed assessments, should be more commonly used to rigorously evaluate restoration practice and options. Although this is undoubtedly true, the diverse settings and actions taken and the poor documentation of many projects, currently make the prospect of learning from existing projects somewhat daunting. In addition to the need for better documentation of restoration projects and more consistent monitoring of their performance, any opportunity to learn from existing projects will also require a committed effort to archive and synthesize monitoring data. To date, the author is not aware of adequate investment being made to perform this essential service. There is also a deeper challenge to using existing projects to guide development of improved restoration science and practice: the absence of a rational assessment and design approach that links objective and action in a predictive, testable framework. It is difficult to use performance data to improve any design method based on untestable assumptions. Without an explicit and rational connection between cause and effect, there is little basis for altering the method in response to monitoring observations.

Heritage and Milan emphasize the dynamic nature of stream channels, which conflicts with the tendency in many restoration projects to build static channels. Certainly a static channel cannot provide the full range of geomorphic and ecologic function of a dynamic channel, and there are no doubt cases in which a fully dynamic channel would be appropriate. At the same time, there are many instances in which a channel with active bankline migration is deemed unacceptable in order to protect infrastructure. In these cases, innovative science is needed to determine the degree of natural function that is possible within a channel that is prohibited from migrating and to assess the lost function such that the tradeoff with infrastructure protection can be clearly evaluated.

Curran raises an important point regarding the need to consider larger scales in restoration assessment and design. In this case, she suggests using an infrastructure scale for urban streams in order to accommodate stormwater inputs from adjacent developed land and storm sewers. An effective way to incorporate these important elements of the urban hydrologic landscape into a stream restoration plan is to begin the planning process with very clear and specific objectives. Rather than designing a stream project according to a locally popular template and then listing a menu of benefits that might accrue, one could begin with specific objectives – such as contained floods, reduced pollutant discharge, or lowered water temperature – and then evaluate the stream project's ability to achieve those objectives. For many water quality objectives, it is likely that the most effective solution will be to address the problems at their source (within the infrastructure on which Curran focuses), rather than in the stream.

Surian emphasizes the link between the stream channel and the watershed at a larger scale, noting the connection between recovered sediment supply and the potential for channel recovery. These comments are particularly valuable because they point to the appropriate location for restoration action. If a restored channel requires an active sediment load, actions at the channel scale will not accomplish the desired restoration. Rather, the necessary management actions are required higher in the watershed. A narrow focus on an individual reach can lead to a restoration plan that does not link cause and effect or to the acceptance of degraded conditions of water and sediment supply, whereas a broader focus to the contributing watershed may identify the source of the problem and allow the local channel to recover on its own.

Snyder's (Chapter 14, this volume) example of stream restoration for salmon recovery in Maine provides an excellent illustration of the importance of shifting the focus to upstream sediment supply in order to provide the ingredients needed for a dynamic stream channel and acceptable habitat.

## 12.8   DISCUSSION REFERENCES

Brierley G.J., Fryirs K.A., Boulton A., and Cullum C. 2008. Working with change: the importance of evolutionary perspectives in framing the trajectory of river adjustment. In Brierley G.J. and Fryirs K.A. editors. *River Futures. An Integrative Scientific Approach to River Repair*, Washington, Island Press, 65–84.

Habersack H. and Piégay H. 2008. River restoration in the Alps and their surroundings: past experience and future challenges.

In Habersack H., Piégay H., and Rinaldi M. editors. *Gravel-bed Rivers VI - From Process Understanding to River Restoration*. Amsterdam, Elsevier. Developments in Earth Surface Processes 11, pp. 703–738.

Rinaldi M., Simoncini C., and Piégay H. 2009. Scientific strategy design for promoting a sustainable sediment management: the case of the Magra River (Central – Northern Italy). *River Research and Applications* **25**: 607–625.

Surian N., Ziliani L., Comiti F., Lenzi M.A., and Mao L. 2009. Channel adjustments and alteration of sediment fluxes in gravel-bed rivers of north-eastern Italy: potentials and limitations for channel recovery. *River Research and Applications* **25**: 551–567.

# 13

# River Restoration: Widening Perspectives

## Nicholas J. Clifford

## 13.1 INTRODUCTION

As Wilcock (Chapter 12, this volume) points out, stream restoration is an increasingly popular and widespread form of environmental management intervention, and one which is likely to gain in its public profile as much by its failures as by its successes. Wilcock emphasizes a key role for fluvial geomorphology in strengthening the scientific and conceptual base for stream restoration, thereby improving design criteria (exemplified best in relation to a critique of "Natural Channel Design" (NCD)). He also draws attention to the need for: more basic information on the sediment status of reaches and catchments, a more open and flexible approach to handling uncertainties, and a more sophisticated analysis of the social dimensions of stream restoration activity. Of the many points highlighted in his wide-ranging review and critique, there are some foundational issues to consider. These both connect and divide (fluvial) geomorphology as a science from stream restoration as a form of environmental practice. They also bear further scrutiny as possible means to effect change in future stream restoration activity. Defining unambiguously, and adopting, key terms; clarifying and broadening views of river form and river function; making better use of basic information; re-assessing the multiple roles geomorphologists might play in restoration efforts; and attempting a more subtle analysis of restoration as an example of the interplay between science, practitioners, and society are some of these points which are discussed below.

## 13.2 MATTERS OF DEFINITION

One of the fundamental issues in debating, teaching, or researching stream restoration is the unresolved matter of definition. This may be approached in at least two ways, neither of which has yet resulted in the kind of explanatory closure required to mount or sustain a scientific critique. First, there is a longstanding recognition that restoration intervention in streams occurs along a notional gradient of intervention and project goals. This gradient is partly parameterized with respect to the current form (structure) and function (ecosystem service) of the stream environment, both of which are assumed to be degraded from an initial, or natural, condition. Intervention is also guided by the desired trajectory of improvement and change. Full return to a pre-existing structural and functional state is restoration; partial return is rehabilitation; enhancement is improvement, but not along a trajectory toward some past natural condition (Cairns, 1991). Defined in this way, the terms have clear meaning and carry very different implications for practice, and scientific assessment and criticism – it is a pity, therefore, that the term "restoration" persists as a catch-all which masks such important differences.

A second approach to defining "stream restoration" involves a less formal match to the range of stream interventions and to the communities of practice associated with them. Stream restoration is thus variously an academic, professional, semi-organised, more-or-less institutionalised; partially regulated; or entirely *ad hoc* community-based knowledge set, with an ever-growing range of exemplars. Presented in this way, use of the term stream restoration begs questions of how, why, and if it will ever be possible to make scientific sense of such varied practice; to learn from past successes and failures; and whether stream restoration is "scientific" in important senses of the term. It also echoes Wilcock's critique insofar as a sociological (and sociology of science) examination of restoration activity is badly needed (see below). It should, as well, remind us of the tenor of early seminal reviews (most notably in Gore (1985)) which mark the beginning of river restoration as a definite subdiscipline of environmental science, partly because they identify just such a sociology.

*Gravel-bed Rivers: Processes, Tools, Environments*, First Edition. Edited by Michael Church, Pascale M. Biron and André G. Roy.
© 2012 John Wiley & Sons, Ltd. Published 2012 by John Wiley & Sons, Ltd.

## 13.3 TOWARDS INTELLIGENT DESIGN: SORTING FORM FROM FUNCTION AND ALTERNATIVES TO THE ALLUVIAL PARADIGM

It is perhaps not surprising that geomorphologists have, either consciously or unconsciously, emphasized adjustment of river form in their approaches to, and discussions of, stream restoration. This does, however, have at least two important consequences, one of which forms the focus of Wilcock's review. From the outset, it implies that the channel should (or must) be seen as a conveyor of water and sediments which are at least in some form of quasi-equilibrium condition over some meaningful design time and space scale. The search necessarily follows, therefore, to identify the alluvial condition, to reproduce this, and hence to attempt to find a fixed design for the channel. But in reality, the channel must adapt to continually varying conditions. Although this search is a traditional, and a rich source of geomorphological debate, it is hardly suited as an input to the practitioner community which is likely to be increasingly regulated and litigated, which needs certainty to raise capital, and clear measures of "success" to ensure its long-term viability. Moreover, it may, on closer inspection, prove illogical for a science which is essentially historical (Simpson, 1963) and which has made a virtue of coupling association with indeterminacy in process–form relations (Leopold and Langbein, 1963). It certainly provides nothing like an engineering prototype, nor should it, therefore, be assessed in the same way.

Recognition of this is at the heart of Wilcock's "relaxed" approach to stream design and the requisite geomorphological input, stressing trajectories of change, indicative criteria, and reduced uncertainty. Without such a relaxation, there is an inevitable reification of what might be termed a kind of "design parameterization by proxy", which necessarily resorts to generalized hydraulic geometries (just re-visit the early and withering critique by Mackin (1963), or Ferguson (1986) before advocating this), stream classification (whether NCD or River Styles (Brierley and Fryirs, 2005)) or the various "templates". Although general principles can be reconciled with certain time- and space-averaged conditions (see, for example, cross-sectional hydraulic geometry and the principle of least action for *straight alluvial* channels (Huang *et al.*, 2002)). All of these are context-specific substitutes for the detail of that nested hierarchy of spatially distributed form–process feedbacks within which almost all intervention inevitably takes place. It is a hierarchy that geomorphologists understand and can *explain* well (take for example, river metamorphosis and its derivations (following Schumm, 1969); and the long-standing explanatory schemes revisited by Lane and

Richards (1997)). However, explanation is not readily translated into prediction. One approach to effect prediction is to employ engineering-type and often empirical simplifications (Parker, 1979). Another is to deploy complex quasi-numerical representations rather than stable balance models. For early approaches exemplifying this, contrast the stable stream balance of Lane (1955) with Rubey's (1952) model of channel form (see Clifford (2008) for further comment). For recent perspectives, see Pizzuto (2003) and Church (2006).

Second, restoration practice is frequently not primarily concerned with form, but with function, and a function which is often driven by ecological requirements and processes. There are, then, several competing paradigms for stream restoration (Clifford, 2007). Geomorphological input is situated differently with respect to each of these, sometimes well down the list of specialisms to be consulted or included. Some rather sobering observations apply. A rather pessimistic review of restoration successes and failures (Ormerod, 2004), for example, starts from a restoration ecology perspective and proceeds to identify the concentration on physical habitat (i.e., geomorphological) design popularized by Brooks and Shields (1996) as one of the prime reasons for general failure.

Again, looking Figure 13.1 it becomes almost worryingly clear that function can fix form in a way with little or no geomorphological appeal: the channel has adequate conveyance, with unvegetated smooth boundaries; it has a sinuous planform and is more aesthetically appealing than a straight culvert; there is a vegetated flood plain (of sorts); and allowance is made for connectivity insofar as marginal drainage is promoted. But there is no geomorphology. The channel is totally engineered, low maintenance and, probably habitat-free, but *it works* in the context for which it is intended, and would be seen by many as a successful stream restoration.

Including hard rock or concrete to anchor or stabilize is not, of course, part of the alluvial, geomorphological paradigm, as Wilcock observes, but it provides the very closure of an otherwise indeterminate and unpredictable system, which is classic of engineering design. The alternative, of designing-in variability, or allowing for a degree of post-project dynamism is still a relatively novel concept, but should be tried more often if there is (literally) room for manoeuvre and if a natural sediment supply exists (see Gurnell *et al.*, 2006). Ecologists have suggested that this requires the setting of generous tolerances on design functional requirements to reflect the degree of ignorance and paucity of research (Bergen *et al.*, 2001) – another way of embracing uncertainty in the decision-support framework that Wilcock describes.

Another under-represented geomorphological response to reducing uncertainty in stream restoration may be to abandon the impossible alluvial ideal as

**Figure 13.1**   A "restored" stream in Nevada, USA.

approached from design of channel form, and explore instead greater control on water or sediment inputs either locally or at the catchment scale (Lane *et al.*, 2008), crucially also recognizing the co-determinant of channel form – vegetation (Corenblit *et al.*, 2007).

## 13.4   IMPROVING INVENTORY FROM THE STOCK OF ALTERED RIVER SYSTEMS

River restoration occurs when a degraded, disturbed, or altered channel state is perceived or identified. This implies notions of a pristine, pre-disturbance, or at the very least, a more desirable state to recover. It is also increasingly recognized that channel reaches should be set within the (sub)catchment context of a mosaic of altered, less altered and nearer-natural conditions which reflect simpler and more complex land-use and channel management histories. In current restoration practice, providing this contextual fit is the role of the reference reach, the template or the style, but this is approached on a case-by-case, operational, rather than strategic basis. Identifying what, where, how, when, and for how long stream intervention might or could take place, should, by contrast, now be a priority, and would again go some way to improving the science base, reducing uncertainty, and providing better-informed decision-support. It is possible to envisage how this might be promoted in a variety of ways.

As a basic science need, routinely deploying the range of inventory and reconnaissance techniques at a regional level (e.g., forms of catchment baseline survey and fluvial audit; Downs and Thorne, 1996) could yield GIS and models of restoration potential, and also be indicative of the kind/degree of intervention most suited at particular locations and for given purposes. To stitch together the various GIS layers presupposes some knowledge of how and why components should be combined for the multitude of restoration objectives, and it is here that geomorphology could play a central, and pivotal role, given basic knowledge of slope, width, discharge, and land use, and identification of thresholds and envelopes relating to key restoration variables.

Placing the growing number of restoration exemplars into a catchment context, cross-correlating with a range of morphological and process variables, motivating factors, and indications of success and failure, would be a start. Take Figures 13.2 and 13.3 for example – what geomorphological (and other) story would be told by overlaying the information they contain? Are there already patterns in the location of restoration with differing drivers we have yet to examine? Much of the commentary of restoration assumes that improvement will occur by more complete integration of process knowledge: that "science" must be applied. However, there is sufficient history and variety of restoration activity to use the restoration efforts

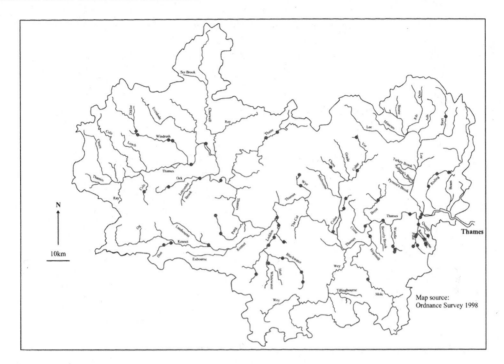

**Figure 13.2** Location of inventorized river restoration projects in the Thames Basin, United Kingdom, 1979–1999. Reproduced, with permission, from Robinson, D. 2003. Identification and characterisation of restored river reaches in urban areas. Unpublished Ph.D. thesis, University of London, United Kingdom.

themselves as part of the investigative science base. Gurnell *et al.* (2007), for example, examined existing restorations and other channel management sites in conjunction with an urban river survey methodology, to provide a process-based classification which might improve stream design choice for use at catchment and local scales (Figures 13.4 and 13.5).

Similar reasoning could be extended to national level. Greater use of surveys designed for compliance purposes definitely offers more with respect to identifying natural and modified environmental gradients relating to channel type and condition. These could be used to inform choice of restoration option and indicate likely viability. In the United Kingdom, for example, there is a national scale audit in the River Habitat Survey (RHS; Raven *et al.*, 1997). Figure 13.6, derived from the RHS, illustrates the characterization and assessment of habitat at the mesoscale of river systems.

This relates flow and sediment characteristics to the provision of habitats for aquatic communities based on the concepts of physical biotopes and functional habitats (Newson, 2002). Overlapping circles symbolize the overlap in physical characteristics between different biotope units, which form a spectrum rather than discrete units. Correlations at this broad level provide an appropriate simplification of the complex river environ-

ment for practical river management. Such features are readily identifiable in the field, and are, therefore, conducive to rapid reconnaissance methods for assessing habitat quality. Moreover, they also link concepts across science disciplines at a level that is practical for river management and conservation. This kind of "broad-scale, top-down" science goes some way to meeting the requirements of those advocating a "new" scientific approach to restoration (Clarke *et al.*, 2003; Wohl *et al.*, 2005) while avoiding some of the complications of interdisciplinary research encountered by bottom-up team-building (see, for example Harvey, 2006). It could also be one way of improving and refining approaches such as the River Styles Framework (Brierley and Fryirs, 2005) which couple geomorphological, hydrological, and ecological attributes across scales from the river patch and cross-section through river reaches to the wider catchment.

## 13.5 THE SOCIETAL AND SOCIAL DIMENSIONS

As Wilcock points out, there is a strong case for geomorphologists to become more informed as to the nature and significance of social dimensions of river restoration as a form of practice. There is definitely scope for an

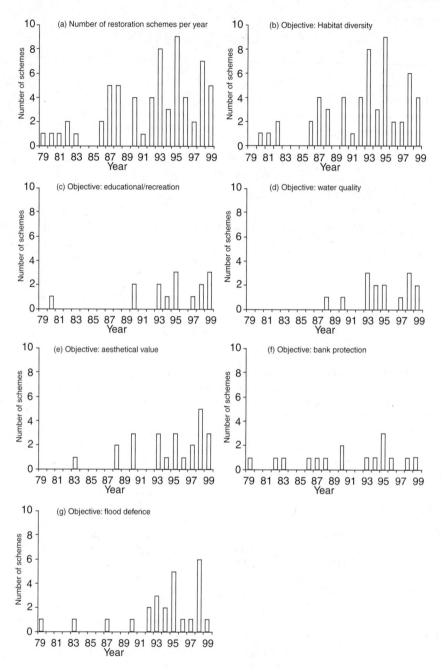

**Figure 13.3** Driving factors in river restoration in the Thames Basin, United Kingdom, 1979–1999. Reproduced, with permission, from Robinson, D. 2003. Identification and characterisation of restored river reaches in urban areas. Unpublished Ph.D. thesis, University of London, United Kingdom.

analysis of stream restoration using the sociology of scientific knowledge – of where knowledge resides, where it is produced, and who disseminates it. NCD is perhaps the clearest and starkest example of the consequences of interplay between a formalized elite with a particular knowledge base who control and disseminate this to practitioners for the assumed public good. Less obvious examples might be attempts at codification and organized communication – see for example the United Kingdom River Restoration Centre.

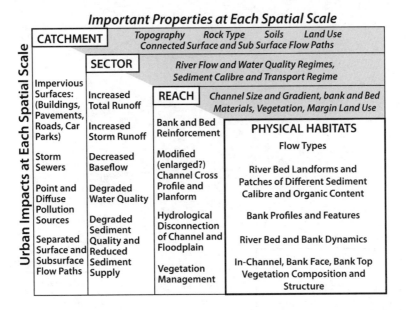

**Figure 13.4** Comparison of catchment properties and river characteristics in relation to typical urban modifications and impacts. Reproduced, with permission, from Figure 2 in Gurnell *et al.* (2007), © *Geography Compass*, Blackwell.

There are also other clear social dimensions. Much restoration is community based, and the activity requires funds from public or private bodies. Further, all scientific activity in the environment is now open to public, as well as legislative scrutiny. As early as 1998, Boon identified publicity and media representation as the necessary fifth dimension of river restoration. A more nuanced understanding of the role of science and the scientist is,

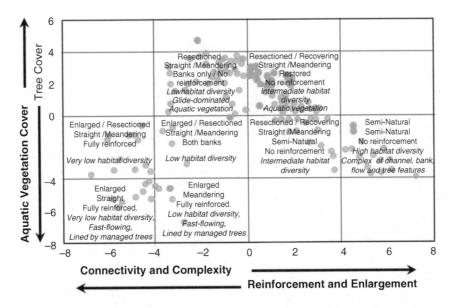

**Figure 13.5** Results of multivariate statistical analysis classifying urban rivers into various types based on multiple gradients reflecting engineering intervention, degree of hydrological complexity and function, corridor tree cover, and aquatic vegetation cover. Reproduced, with permission, from Figure 3 in Gurnell *et al.* (2007). © *Geography Compass*, Blackwell.

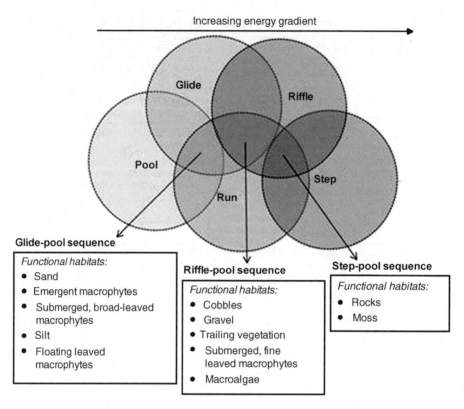

**Figure 13.6** Characterisation and assessment of habitat at the mesoscale of river systems. Adapted from Figures 4 and 5 in Harvey *et al.* (2008): © *Journal of Environmental Management,* Elsevier.

therefore, crucial. In a recent volume dedicated to the restoration of aquatic systems, Livingstone (2006) identifies a hierarchy of seven foundations which are ideally present. Scientific knowledge and input is the first, but only one of these. The others are, in order: regulation and enforcement; public education; economic and political considerations; legal actions; and the news media. The geomorphologist, as a professional expert, is directly linked to these through public education and possibly regulation: it is less clear how the role relates to the other considerations.

Without a nuanced view of science and societal dimensions, there is a danger that scientists/geomorphologists implicitly follow a linear and hierarchical model of knowledge generation, dissemination, and project activation, in which it is scientific information and input which first gains the attention of stakeholders and public, and which then shapes attitudes and actions. More or less participation on the part of the public and "stakeholders" might variously be seen as threatening, weakening, or in some way complicating the restoration process, with participation either excluded, or incorporated only in a token manner, in fear of outright citizen power.

A more nuanced view incorporates the science input as one (not necessarily privileged) component of action in a more holistic and non-hierarchical framework. Each viewpoint, knowledge exchange, and eventual management intervention is decided on a case-specific basis (see Clark, 2002). What may emerge from this are less obviously "scientific" solutions and outcomes in restoration efforts. Rather, the outcomes reflect social conceptions of the ideal or preferred river, going beyond or even replacing scientific designs. Stream "naturalization" is an example of such an emerging paradigm in river restoration (e.g., Eden *et al.*, 2000; Rhoads *et al.*, 2008) and depends on social visions of "naturalness" in specific contexts. The perspective is championed as particularly relevant for intensively managed landscapes, where the capacity to return a system to a "pre-disturbance" reference condition is highly limited. Ultimately the goals and objectives of such naturalization are social – so much so that some believe that the process of negotiating and implementing a restoration scheme is as, or more, important than the scientific success or failure which results from it (McDonald *et al.*, 2004).

## 13.6 CONCLUSIONS

Given the high, and growing, profile of stream restoration, and the claims made by advocates of its various techniques, it is timely to subject the activity to more intense academic scrutiny. There are, however, problems in developing an appropriate critique, which offers constructive points for the future, and which allows for an enhanced science input alongside some very non-scientific needs. Neither fluvial geomorphology nor stream restoration are exact sciences. Both deal with imprecise information which is highly time-space specific: herein lies the source of both strengths and weaknesses in better-combining the two. Questioning the viability of some foundational geomorphological concepts and approaches, identifying a wider range of geomorphological tools and inputs to restoration efforts, alongside a more reflexive consideration of science, environment, and society are some of those actions that might contribute to the active and productive collaboration between scientists and practitioners, and to the "professionalisation" of stream restoration that Wilcock foresees.

## 13.7 ACKNOWLEDGEMENTS

Research on river restoration in London and the Thames Basin was conducted by Daniel Robinson as part of a Ph.D. funded by University College London, under the joint supervision of N.J. Clifford and J.R. French. The author is grateful to Professor Mike Church for suggesting changes to the text to improve its clarity.

## 13.8 REFERENCES

Bergen, S.D., Bolton, S.M., and Fridley, J.L. 2001. Design principles for ecological engineering. *Ecological Engineering* **18**: 201–210.

Boon, P.J. 1998. River restoration in five dimensions. *Aquatic Conservation: Marine & Freshwater Ecosystems* **8**: 257–264.

Brierley, G.J. and Fryirs, K.A. 2005. *Geomorphology and River Management*. Oxford, Blackwell.

Brookes, A. and Shields, D.F., editors. 1996. *River Channel Restoration*. Chichester, John Wiley & Sons, Ltd.

Cairns, J. 1991. The status of the theoretical and applied science of restoration ecology. *The Environment Professional* **13**: 186–194.

Church, M. 2006. Bed material transport and the morphology of alluvial river channels. *Annual Review of Earth and Planetary Sciences* **34**: 325–354.

Clark, M.J. 2002. Dealing with uncertainty: adaptive approaches to sustainable river management. *Aquatic Conservation: Marine and Freshwater Ecosystems* **12**: 347–363.

Clarke, S.J., Bruce-Burgess, L., and Wharton, G. 2003. Linking form and function: towards an eco-hydromorphic approach to sustainable rive restoration. *Aquatic Conservation* **13**: 439–450.

Clifford, N.J. 2007. River restoration: paradigms, paradoxes and the urban dimension. *Water Science and Technology: Water Supply* **7**: 57–68.

Clifford, N.J. 2008. Channel form and process, *c*. 1890 – 1965. In Burt, T.P., Chorley, R.J., Brunsden, D., Cox, N.J. and Goudie, A.S., editors. *The History of the Study of Landforms*, Vol. 4 London, The Geological Society, pp. 217–324.

Corenblit, D., Tabacchi, E., Steiger, J., and Gurnell, A. 2007. Reciprocal interactions and adjustments between fluvial landforms and vegetation dynamics: a review of complementary approaches. *Earth Science Reviews* **84**: 56–86.

Downs P.W. and Thorne C.R. 1996. A geomorphological justification of river channel reconnaissance surveys. *Transactions of the Institute of British Geographers*, **21**: 455–468.

Eden, S., Tunstall, S., and Tapsell, S. 2000. Translating nature: river restoration as nature-culture. *Environment and Planning D: Society and Space* **18**: 257–273.

Ferguson, R. I. 1986. Hydraulics and hydraulic geometry. *Progress in Physical Geography* **10**: 1–31.

Gore, J. A., editor. 1985. *The Restoration of Rivers and Streams: Theories and Experience*. Ann Arbor, MI, Butterworth.

Gurnell, A.M., Lee, M., and Souch, C. 2007. Urban rivers: hydrology, geomorphology, ecology and opportunities for change. *Geography Compass* **1**: 1118–1137.

Gurnell, A.M., Morrissey, I.P., Boitsidis, A.J. *et al.* 2006. Initial adjustments within a new river channel: interactions between fluvial processes, colonising vegetation and bank profile development. *Environmental Management* **38**: 580–596.

Harvey, D.R. 2006. RELU special issue: editorial reflections. *Journal of Agricultural Economics* **57**: 329–336.

Harvey, G., Clifford, N.J., and Gurnell, A.M. 2008. Towards an ecologically meaningful classification of the flow biotope for river inventory, rehabilitation, design and appraisal purposes. *Journal of Environmental Management* **88**: 638–650.

Huang, H.Q., Nansen, G.C. and Fagan, S.D 2002. Hydraulic geometry of straight alluvial channels and the principle of least action. *Journal of Hydraulic Research* **40**: 153–160.

Lane, E.W. 1955. The importance of fluvial morphology in hydraulic engineering. *Proceedings of the American Society of Civil Engineers* **81**: 1–17.

Lane, S.N. and Richards, K.S. 1997. Linking river channel form and process; time, space and causality revisited. *Earth Surface Processes and Landforms* **22**: 249–260.

Lane, S.N., Reid, S.C., Tayefi, T., Yu, D., and Hardy, R.J. 2008. Reconceptualising coarse sediment delivery problems in rivers as catchment-scale and diffuse. *Geomorphology* **98**: 227–249.

Leopold, L.B. and Langbein, W.B. 1963 Association and indeterminacy in geomorphology. In Albritton, C.C., Jr., editor. *The Fabric of Geology*. Stanford, CA, Freeman, Cooper, pp. 184–92.

Livingstone, R.J. 2006. *Restoration of Aquatic Systems*. Boca Raton, FL, CRC Press.

Mackin, J.H. 1963: Rational and empirical methods of investigation in geology. In Albritton, C.C., Jr., editor. *The Fabric of Geology*. Stanford, CA, Freeman, Cooper, pp. 135–163.

McDonald, A., Lane, S.N., Haycock, N.E., and Chalk, E.A. 2004. Rivers of dreams: on the gulf between theoretical and practical aspects of an upland river restoration. *Transactions of the Institute of British Geographers* NS **29**: 257–281.

Newson, M.D. 2002. Geomorphological concepts and tools for sustainable river ecosystem management. *Aquatic Conservation: Marine and Freshwater Ecosystems* **12**: 365–379.

Ormerod, S.J. 2004. A golden age of river restoration science? *Aquatic Conservation: Marine and Freshwater Ecosystems* **14**: 543–549.

Parker, G. 1979. Hydraulic geometry of active gravel rivers. *American Society of Civil Engineers, Journal of the Hydraulics Division* **105**: 1185–1201.

Pizzuto, J.E. 2003. Numerical modeling of alluvial landforms. In Kondolf, G.M. and Piegay, H.editors. *Tools in Fluvial Geomorphology*. Chichester, John Wiley & Sons, Ltd, pp. 577–595.

Raven, P.J., Fox, P., Everard, M., Holmes, N.T.H., and Dawson, F.H. 1997. River habitat survey: a new system for classifying rivers according to their habitat quality. In Boon, P.J. and Howell, D.L.editors. *Freshwater Quality: Defining the Indefinable?* Edinburgh, The Stationery Office, pp. 215–234.

Rhoads, B.L., Garcia, M.H., Rodriguez, J. *et al.* 2008. Evaluating the geomorphological performance of naturalized rivers. In Darby, S. and Sear, D., editors. *River Restoration: Managing the Uncertainty in Restoring Physical Habitat.* Chichester, John Wiley & Sons, Ltd, pp. 209–228.

Robinson, D. 2003. *Identification and characterisation of restored river reaches in urban areas.* Unpublished Ph.D. thesis, University of London, United Kingdom.

Rubey, W.W. 1952. *Geology and mineral resources of the Hardin and Brussels quadrangles (in Illinois).* United States Geological Survey, Professional Paper 218.

Schumm, S.A., 1969. River metamorphosis. *American Society of Civil Engineers, Journal of the Hydraulics Division* **95**: 255–73.

Simpson, G.G. 1963. Historical science. In Albritton, C.C. Jr, editor. *The Fabric of Geology.* Stanford, CA, Freeman, Cooper, pp. 24–48.

Wohl, E., Angermeier, P.L, Bledsoe, B. *et al.* 2005. River restoration. *Water Resources Research* **41**: W10301. doi: 10.1029/2005WR003985.

## 13.9 DISCUSSION

### 13.9.1 Discussion by Bruce MacVicar

It is an interesting point that was made by Clifford about whether geomorphology can be used as a predictive rather than just a diagnostic tool. If we start from the assumption that geomorphology is not and cannot be a predictive science, and if we further specify that prediction is necessary for sufficient control of the system in restoration design, then we are limited to describing river systems that we can fully understand. This carries the risk that we then make the same errors that led us to the need for stream restoration in the first place, namely the oversimplification of rivers into channels and the ignorance of poorly understood processes occurring at the smaller (often biological) and larger (typically geological) scales. There must be a way of lowering risk and incorporating geomorphologic elements in stream restoration designs so that we can avoid repeating the mistakes of the past.

### 13.9.2 Reply by N.J. Clifford

The discussion raises an important distinction between natural, open systems, which are well understood, but which may necessarily be indeterminate, and those where a degree of control can render future change either determinate, or at least predictable with a given statistical

probability. Parker (1979) provides an early analysis of alluvial channel modelling which addresses this distinction. Various methodological and philosophical debates within geomorphology are summarized by Richards (1996) and Richards *et al.* (1997). There are numerous discussions in hydrology which address the asymmetry between improved explanation and lack of commensurate predictive success (e.g., Beven, 2001). These also examine the paradox that better prediction may be achieved with reduced-complexity models, rather than by further developing physically parameterized ones.

From a conceptual standpoint, uncertainty is inherent in fluvial systems. This may be a problem for intervention designs which attempt to fully re-create (or allow for) a complete range of natural channel dynamics with unconstrained water and sediment inputs. However, most designs are not like that: there will be some constraint on input and/or response. Provided the nature and degree of constraint is known, there should be determinate solutions. Essentially, this is what channel engineering has always relied upon. In raising the issue in this chapter, the intent was to direct attention away from the use of "geomorphological design" as a naturalistic paradigm for river restoration, and more towards its utility in improving contextualization of designs. In other words, geomorphological knowledge and methods can be used to identify the appropriate degree and kind of constraint involved, and ultimately, help to broaden the range of design options.

With respect to scale-integration across physical and biological systems, there has, in the United Kingdom at least, been an active research programme which addresses the "meso-scale" (Newson and Newson, 2000). The meso-scale encompasses interaction between physical habitat (biotopes composed of differing velocity, depth, and sediment combinations) and biological response (functional habitats composed of distinct species assemblages). Clifford *et al.* (2006) review the strengths and weaknesses of the approach to date. In addition, there has been progress in relating environmental gradients identified at larger spatial scales (regional and catchment) to local form–process interactions (reach and subreach). This employs a hybrid methodology based upon inventory/reconnaissance survey, statistical modelling and field measurement (Harvey *et al.*, 2008).

## 13.10 DISCUSSION REFERENCES

Beven, K. 2001. On explanatory depth and predictive power. *Hydrological Processes* **15**: 1099–1085.

Clifford, N.J., Harmar, O.P., Harvey, G., and Petts, G.E. 2006. Physical habitat, eco-hydraulics and river design: a review and re-evaluation of some popular concepts and methods.

*Aquatic Conservation, Marine and Freshwater Science* **16**: 389–408.

Harvey, G.L., Clifford, N.J., and Gurnell, A.M. 2008. Towards an ecologically meaningful classification of the flow biotope for river inventory, rehabilitation, design and appraisal purposes. *Journal of Environmental Management* **88**: 638–650.

Newson, M.D. and Newson, C.L. 2000. Geomorphology, ecology and river channel habitat; mesoscale approaches to basin-scale challenges. *Progress in Physical Geography* **24**: 195–217.

Parker, G. 1979. Hydraulic geometry of active gravel rivers. *American Society of Civil Engineers, Journal of the Hydraulics Division* **105**: 1185–1201.

Richards, K.S. 1996. Samples and cases: generalization and explanation in geomorphology. In Rhoads, B.L. and Thorn, C.E., editors. *The Scientific Nature of Geomorphology*. Chichester, John Wiley & Sons, Ltd, pp. 171–190.

Richards, K.S., Brooks, S., Clifford, N.J., Harris, T., and Lane, S.N. 1997. Real geomorphology: theory, observation and testing. In Stoddart, D.R., editor. *Process and Form in Geomorphology*. London, Routledge, pp. 265–292.

# 14

# Restoring Geomorphic Resilience in Streams

## Noah P. Snyder

## 14.1 INTRODUCTION

My purpose in this chapter is to broaden the discussion of river restoration to consider projects beyond direct modification of channel geometry. This contribution is a discussion of Wilcock's (Chapter 12, this volume) review of stream restoration in gravel-bed rivers. While channel re-construction is a high-profile and popular restoration technique, it also has the potential for ineffectiveness, failure and great expense. The toolbox of river restoration also includes projects from culvert replacement to large woody debris placements to dam removal. Particularly in nonurban areas, habitat restoration goals may be best served by these types of projects because they may enhance the river's ability to restore itself. My essential point is simple: ideally, restoration projects should enhance morphodynamic feedbacks in channels so that rivers are resilient to future changes in hydrology and sediment supply in their watersheds (e.g., Palmer *et al.*, 2005; Newson and Large, 2006). I suggest that understanding trajectories of channel evolution in response to land-use and climate change is an important area of further fluvial geomorphic research in support of restoration objectives. I begin my discussion by underscoring several of Wilcock's main points.

## 14.2 REACTIONS TO THE WILCOCK REVIEW

Wilcock's review is an excellent assessment of the state of the profession of stream restoration and the role of fluvial geomorphic research in improving restoration practice. The emphasis is on Natural Channel Design (NCD), which is wise because, while this view of stream restoration is dominant in practice in the United States, it was developed on a relatively narrow scientific basis focused on the equilibrium channel paradigm. Wilcock summarizes the limitations and potential problems with this approach.

I agree that understanding watershed context and history, and particularly sediment supply, are pre-requisites for designing channel restoration projects. Techniques for rapid evaluation of sediment supply are sorely needed and vital for all types of riparian restoration. Particularly in areas of low sediment supply rate, knowing this may greatly simplify the channel design process.

I also agree with Wilcock's view of the importance of acknowledging the social aspects of stream restoration, and working toward a healthy and robust research–practice interaction. In my experiences in northern New England, USA (described in more detail below), I have been pleased to find a strong spirit of collaboration among academic researchers, government land managers, consultants, and environmental organizations. The common view is that the synergy between research and practice can only enhance both. Several annual meetings (e.g., the Maine Water Conference, http://www.umaine.edu/WaterResearch/mwc/index.htm) and a National Science Foundation Research Coordination Network (http://www.umaine.edu/searunfish/) serve as ongoing venues for enhancing research–agency–practitioner interactions in the region. I suspect that similar venues for interaction exist in many regions where stream restoration is practiced.

Wilcock's review focuses on stream restoration projects that involve direct alteration of channel geometry, as opposed to the wider suite of projects that might be included in the category of riparian restoration. This is a reasonable scope, particularly because of the focus of NCD on equilibrium channels, but restoration practice is broader, and the practitioner community needs to know about (and be encouraged to use) a wider variety of restoration approaches. In my discussion below, I focus on projects that seek to restore stream processes more

*Gravel-bed Rivers: Processes, Tools, Environments*, First Edition. Edited by Michael Church, Pascale M. Biron and André G. Roy.
© 2012 John Wiley & Sons, Ltd. Published 2012 by John Wiley & Sons, Ltd.

generally, and particularly morphodynamic feedbacks in the channel. This view builds on Wilcock's skepticism with the equilibrium basis for NCD. I acknowledge that direct modification of channel geometry is probably the most high-profile (and controversial) type of stream restoration, especially in settings with infrastructure near the channel. In my experience citizens (e.g., watershed-based non-profit organizations) interested in implementing stream restoration projects can be drawn to the channel alterations, because of the prominence of the NCD approach, and the obvious and visible nature of the projects, when other types of projects may be far more effective in achieving ecological goals and have less opportunity for spectacular failure.

## 14.3 RESTORATION OF STREAM GEOMORPHIC RESILIENCE

### 14.3.1 Geomorphic Resilience

Rivers are dynamic systems. Channel morphology evolves in response to water and sediment discharge, among many other factors. Both factors have changed, are changing, and will continue to change due to shifting land use and climate. Restoration to a pre-disturbance reference condition is a difficult (if not impossible) goal, as has been noted by others (e.g., Palmer *et al.*, 2005 and references therein). For example, Walter and Merritts (2008) found that Colonial-era mill-dam deposits are pervasive in the US Mid-Atlantic Piedmont region, forming what appear to be floodplains, but are actually fill terraces, in many valley bottoms. They show that the pre-Colonial riparian morphology was quite different than that seen today, including anabranching channels interspersed in a wide wetland complex. A restoration practice suggested by this finding is manual excavation of millpond sediment and creation of wide, low valley bottoms that flood frequently (Wilcock, 2008; Palmer, 2009). Walter and Merritts (2008) do not specifically advocate this approach in their paper. Such a practice probably is not practical over large areas (i.e., along the length of whole river networks), and potentially not useful. The conditions that existed in pre-Colonial North America do not exist today (due to land-use change, urbanization, and subsequent changes in runoff patterns and volumes; reduction in beaver populations; climate change; Wilcock, 2008; Burchsted *et al.*, 2010). In my view, restoration practice should focus on allowing rivers to be resilient to ongoing and future environmental changes in their watersheds (Palmer *et al.*, 2005).

Resilience is the ability of an ecosystem to tolerate disturbance without shifting to a different state controlled by different processes. Resilience is a well-established concept in ecology (Holling, 1973). Classic

examples include eutrophication in lakes, where the entire ecologic community can flip and lock into a new state as a result of water quality degradation. Resilience is clearly a relevant concept to fluvial geomorphology. Disturbances can cause fundamental and quasi-permanent shifts in process regimes. A primary example is dam construction, which can result in fundamental changes in hydrology (e.g., Magilligan *et al.*, 2003) and channel form (e.g., Rubin *et al.*, 2002; Grant *et al.*, 2003; Walter and Merritts, 2008). Given that watershed conditions are changing, and that rivers have an inherent ability to respond to changes through erosion and sediment deposition in their channels, we should focus restoration on practices that enhance the geomorphic resilience of rivers (Palmer *et al.*, 2005). Further, restoration of the conditions that facilitate morphodynamic feedback processes means that the river does much of the restoration work. Depending on local context, this view can yield restoration projects, including dam removal, bridge and culvert improvements, careful land-use planning in valley bottoms (e.g., Montgomery, 2004), large woody debris (LWD) placements, and re-construction of channel geometry.

### 14.3.2 Example from Maine, USA

The dramatic decline of Atlantic salmon and other anadromous fish populations from rivers in the northern New England region of the United States (National Research Council, 2004; Limburg and Waldman, 2009) has motivated considerable interest in stream restoration. While numerous factors (e.g., overfishing and changing ocean conditions) contributed to the decline, habitat loss and degradation by dam construction and in-channel timber transport in the nineteenth and twentieth centuries are clearly important (National Research Council, 2004). In particular, the poor survival of Atlantic salmon fry, parr, and smolts bred in hatcheries and stocked in Maine rivers is thought to be related to a decline of physical habitat quality. The relative accessibility of stream (compared to ocean) habitat, combined with strong grassroots (most Maine watersheds have associated citizen-based environmental organizations) and agency interest, has motivated many stream restoration projects as a means to increase fish populations. Around the time of publication of the National Research Council (2004) report, the focus of many of these efforts was on decreasing inputs of fine sediment (sand and mud) to river systems, because of the belief (likely coming from studies in high-gradient rivers of the North American Pacific Coast) that high suspended load and associated fine sedimentation was a culprit for poor fish survival (e.g., Arter, 2003).

Since that time, several studies have demonstrated that low large woody debris (LWD) loading (Magilligan *et al.*, 2008) and low bedload sediment supply (Snyder *et al.*, 2008) are potential causes of habitat degradation in this landscape. A feedback process driven by interaction among the research, agency, consultant, and non-profit communities has shifted the focus of restoration activities to projects such as LWD additions, dam removals, and replacement of undersized culverts. In 2008 Project SHARE (http://www.salmonhabitat.org/), a non-profit organization focused on salmon habitat restoration in Downeast Maine, received federal funds to replace 53 culverts on logging roads in watersheds that contain important salmon habitat.

The salmon rivers of coastal Maine clearly demonstrate the importance of geologic context in designing restoration projects (Snyder *et al.*, 2008; Wilkins and Snyder, 2011). In this low-gradient, post-glacial landscape, sediment is supplied to rivers largely via erosion of glacial deposits, rather than weathering and mass wasting on hillslopes. This means that sediment is sourced locally and stochastically, particularly when and where rivers and tributaries impinge on eskers and outwash deposits. Furthermore, the presence of numerous mainstem lakes and low-gradient wetlands (the results of glacial erosion and/or beaver dams) means that bedload transport is discontinuous along the rivers (Burchsted *et al.*, 2010). Dam construction for mills and log drives in the seventeenth to twentieth centuries served to enhance these discontinuities. Preliminary analysis (Strouse and Snyder, 2010) of bank stratigraphy indicates that legacy sediment exists upstream of some breached dams in these rivers, although likely not on the scale observed by Walter and Merritts (2008). Removal of roughness elements (LWD, boulders, mid-channel islands) to facilitate inchannel timber transport during the nineteenth and twentieth centuries resulted in channels that today are probably straighter, smoother, and less complex than those in the pre-disturbance state. Evidence of this situation is seen in straight channels with little obvious (e.g., gravel bars) or direct (marked particle studies; Snyder *et al.*, 2008) evidence of bedload transport.

For the rivers to return to a presumed more dynamic and resilient state that includes channel migration, bar formation, and bank construction, which are thought to be conducive to high-quality habitat, the rivers need to transport sediment. In this context, stabilization of eroding banks where they exist (typically glacial, not fluvial, deposits) may be a counterproductive use of restoration funds; the trouble is not too much fine sediment, but too little. Sediment inputs are vital to the re-construction of channel complexity via morphodynamic feedback processes: sand and mud make overbank deposits and raise new vegetated banks; and gravel builds mobile bars. In places in Maine with higher sediment load (i.e., those downstream of large, actively eroding glacial deposits),

the signs of a channel still resilient to changes are clear: bar construction and migration, in-channel sediment sorting, storage of fine sediment on overbank deposits, even in places clearly impacted by log drives, splash dams and associated legacy sedimentation. Such reaches can include much of the quality salmon spawning habitat mapped in the watersheds (Snyder *et al.*, 2008). This view of river processes in Maine points to a focus on restoration of sediment transport continuity: replacing undersized culverts, removal of small dams and remnant dams, and LWD additions to increase scour. It is important to note that such an approach may be unfeasible in more developed regions because re-establishing bank erosion may result in channel migration and damage to infrastructure in riparian corridors.

### 14.3.3  Trajectories of Channel Change

My addition to Wilcock's list of challenges to the fluvial geomorphic research community is to improve our understanding of the trajectories of channel change. Rivers with altered channel form due to land-use changes are presumably in the process of responding to the present-day water and sediment regime in their watersheds. For example, using historical photographs, Walter and Merritts (2008) observed that rivers first incise and then widen after mill dam breaching. Such findings motivate additional questions. What is the timescale of this response? When after dam breaching or removal does chronic bank erosion slow and different morphodynamic processes (e.g., bar formation, development of multithread channels, riparian vegetation growth) begin to dominate? What restoration strategies can accelerate this process?

The rates and processes of channel response provide a means of prioritizing restoration. If, after a major land-use change such as dam removal, a river erodes and evolves toward a different (and ecologically desirable) morphodynamic state rapidly, then in-channel modifications may not be necessary. Such an approach may not be acceptable in watersheds where the delivery of large quantities of sediment to estuaries downstream is a separate motivation for restoration. Other systems (such as some of the Maine rivers described above) may be on a slow trajectory of channel change (indicated by little bank erosion or bar formation) which may motivate other types of restoration activities that seek to accelerate the creation of morphologic diversity in the channel. In general, we should seek restoration solutions that work with the existing trajectories of channel change we observe in altered rivers.

Historical images are a simple and powerful tool for understanding past conditions and the trajectory of landscape change (Bierman *et al.*, 2005). Time series of aerial photographs are particularly useful for fluvial studies (e.g., Gaeuman et al., 2003; O'Connor et al., 2003; Snyder and Kammer, 2008; Walter and Merritts, 2008; Burchsted et al., 2010), because they can be integrated quantitatively into a GIS-based analysis, with a pixel size (~1 m) less than channel width. Studies of river morphologic evolution after planned dam removals (e.g., Doyle et al., 2005; Major et al., 2008; Pearson et al., 2011) provide another powerful means to understand time scales of channel change, particularly after we have a decade or more of monitoring of such experiments.

## 14.4 SUMMARY AND CONCLUSIONS

My essential points support and extend those of Wilcock (Chapter 12, this volume): (i) watershed geologic history and context are critical to designing restoration strategies; (ii) restoration should focus not on equilibrium channel conditions, but on restoring resilience; (iii) whenever possible, projects should focus on enabling morphodynamic feedbacks so that rivers can restore themselves; and (iv) understanding trajectories of channel change in systems responding to land-use changes is an important avenue of restoration research. In the ideal case, restoring resilience results is a win-win-win situation in which the rivers provide ecosystem services (better water quality, fish production), economic benefits (flood control via in-channel storage, lack of erosion of infrastructure, less need for ongoing restoration projects), and recreational opportunities. Of course, in practice, social and economic factors, particularly the construction of infrastructure (buildings, roads, bridges) in riparian corridors, strongly limits the range of available restoration options. Downstream factors may also be important. For instance, fine sediment delivery from rivers to estuaries is an issue in many watersheds. Such factors may push practitioners toward different restoration projects in different landscapes, depending on local geologic, climatic, and land-use conditions.

## 14.5 ACKNOWLEDGEMENTS

The ideas in this contribution stem from research funded by the National Fish and Wildlife Foundation Maine Atlantic Salmon Conservation Fund (award 2005-0009-020) and the National Science Foundation (award #0645343).

## 14.6 REFERENCES

Arter, B. 2003. *Narraguagus River Watershed Nonpoint Source Pollution Management Plan*. Cherryfield, Maine, USA, Narraguagus River Watershed Council and Project SHARE. http://www.salmonhabitat.org/outreach/nrwmp.html.

Bierman, P.R., Howe, J., Stanley-Mann, E. et al. 2005. Old images record landscape change through time. *GSA Today* 15(4): 4–10. doi: 10.1130.1052-5173(2005)015<4:OIRLCT>2.0.CO;2.

Burchsted, D., Daniels, M., Thorson, R., and Vokoun, J. 2010. The river discontinuum: applying beaver modifications to baseline conditions for restoration of forested headwaters. *BioScience* 60: 908–922. doi: 10.1525/bio.2010.60.11.7.

Doyle, M.W., Stanley, E.H., and Harbor, J.M. 2003. Channel adjustments following two dam removals in Wisconsin. *Water Resources Research* 39: 1011. doi: 10.1029/2002WR001714.

Gaeuman, D.A., Schmidt, J.C., and Wilcock, P.R. 2003. Evaluation of in-channel gravel storage with morphology-based gravel budgets developed from planimetric data. *Journal of Geophysical Research* 108: doi: 6001. 10.1029/2002JF000002.

Grant, G.E., Schmidt, J.C., and Lewis, S.L. 2003. A geological framework for interpreting downstream effects of dams on rivers. In O'Connor, J.E. and Grant, G.E., editors. *A Peculiar River: Geology, Geomorphology, and Hydrology of the Deschutes River, Oregon*. American Geophysical Union, Water Science and Applications Series 7 pp. 209–225.

Holling, C.S. 1973. Resilience and stability of ecological systems. *Annual Review of Ecology and Systematics* 4: 1–23. http://www.jstor.org/stable/2096802.

Limburg, K.E. and Waldman, J.R. 2009. Dramatic declines in North Atlantic diadromous fishes. *BioScience* 59: 955–965. doi: 10.1525/bio.2009.59.11.7.

Magilligan, F.J., Nislow, K.H., and Graber, B.E. 2003. Scale-independent assessment of discharge reduction and riparian disconnectivity following flow regulation by dams. *Geology* 31: 569–572.

Magilligan, F.J., Nislow, K.H., Fisher, G.B. et al. 2008. The geomorphic function and characteristics of large woody debris in low gradient rivers, coastal Maine, USA. *Geomorphology* 97: 467–482. doi: 10.1016/j.geomorph.2007.08.016.

Major, J.J., O'Connor, J.E., Grant, G.E. et al. 2008. Initial fluvial response to removal of Oregon's Marmot Dam, *Eos, Transactions of the American Geophyical Union* 89: 241–242.

Montgomery, D.R. 2004. Geology, Geomorphology, and the restoration ecology of salmon. *GSA Today* 14(11): 4–12. doi: 10.1130/1502-5173(2004)014<4:GGATRE>2.0.CO;2.

National Research Council (NRC) 2004. *Atlantic salmon in Maine*. National Academies Press. http://www.nap.edu/catalog/10892.html.

Newson, M.D. and Large, A.R.G. 2006. "Natural" rivers, "hydromorphological quality" and river restoration: a challenging new agenda for applied fluvial geomorphology. *Earth Surface Processes and Landforms* 31: 1606–1624, doi: 10.1002/esp.1430.

O'Connor, J.E., Jones, M.A., and Haluska, T.L. 2003. Flood plain and channel dynamics of the Quinault and Queets Rivers, Washington, USA. *Geomorphology* 51: 31–59.

Palmer, M.A., Bernhardt, E.S., Allan, J.D. et al. 2005. Standards for ecologically successful river restoration. *Journal of Applied Ecology* 42: 208–217. doi: 10.1111/j.1365-2664.2005.01004.x.

Palmer, M.A. 2009. Reforming watershed restoration: science in need of application and applications in need of science. *Estuaries and Coasts* 32: 1–17, doi: 10.1007/s12237-008-9129-5.

Pearson, A.J., Snyder, N.P., and Collins, M.J. 2011. Rates and processes of channel response to dam removal with a sand-filled impoundment, *Water Resources Research* 47: 1–15, doi: 10.1029/2010WR009733.

Rubin, D.M., Topping, D.J., Schmidt, J.C. *et al*. T.S. 2002. Recent sediment studies refute Glen Canyon Dam hypothesis. *Eos, Transactions of the American Geoophysical Union* **83**: 273, 277–278.

Snyder, N.P., Castele, M.R., and Wright, J.R. 2008. Bedload entrainment in low-gradient paraglacial coastal rivers of Maine, U.S.A.: Implications for habitat restoration. *Geomorphology* **103**: 430–446. doi: 10.1016/j.geomorph. 2008.07.013.

Snyder, N.P. and Kammer, L.L. 2008. Dynamic adjustments in channel width in response to a forced diversion: Gower Gulch, Death Valley National Park, *California. Geology* **25**: 187–190. doi: 10.1130/G24217A.1.

Strouse, S.R. and Snyder, N.P. 2010. Do post-glacial river valleys in northern New England store mill-dam legacy sediments? *American Geophysical Union, Fall Meeting 2010, San Francisco, 13–17 December*. Abstract PA31E-1589.

Walter, R.C. and Merritts, D.J. 2008. Natural streams and the legacy of water-powered mills. *Science* **319**: 299–304. doi: 10.1126/science.1151716.

Wilcock, P. 2008. What to do about those dammed streams. *Science* **321**: 910–911.

Wilkins, B.C. and Snyder, N.P. 2011. Geomorphic comparison of two Atlantic coastal rivers: toward an understanding of physical controls on Atlantic salmon habitat. *River Research and Applications* **27**: 135–156. doi: 10.1002/rra.1343.

# 15

# The Geomorphic Response of Gravel-bed Rivers to Dams: Perspectives and Prospects

## Gordon E. Grant

## 15.1  INTRODUCTION

Dams and reservoirs represent the single most profound human alteration of the fluvial system. In almost all cases, dams interrupt and modify the downstream flux of sediment through watersheds; they typically also affect the flow regime. Because they directly influence the two overarching controls of channel form – sediment and water – dams have the potential to alter the entire hierarchy of channel variables (*sensu* Schumm and Lichty, 1965).

The geomorphic literature is replete with case studies of river response to dam regulation, with review papers and monographs providing useful reference (e.g., Petts 1980, 1984; Williams and Wolman, 1984; Brandt, 2000; Grant *et al.*, 2003; Petts and Gurnell, 2005; Schmidt and Wilcock, 2008.) Beyond case studies, however, there is a growing need to develop predictive tools and models that can be used to forecast likely channel response to dam construction and operation. Motivating the need for such tools is the recognition that dams and their flow regimes are likely to be a focal point for energy, ecology, and economy in the future. There is increasing interest in changing or modifying flow regimes at existing dams to meet various objectives (more natural or normative flow regimes, controlled floods, or ecological or geomorphic restoration) (e.g., Poff *et al.*, 2007). Many rivers are likely to experience altered flow regimes due to climate changes, and modifying dam operations may be one approach to mitigate or accommodate such alterations (Payne *et al.*, 2004). At the same time, hydropower is widely seen as a relatively clean and low-emission source of energy, although there is some debate on this point (Fearnside, 1997). Both economic development and environmental pressures are already resulting in major

dam construction in the developing world, and these pressures are likely to grow in the future (Oud, 2002). These converging trends underscore the need for improved predictive capacity to help guide management decisions with respect to dam construction and operation around the world.

Developing such predictive models represents a significant challenge for fluvial geomorphology. Predicting the effects of dams on rivers can be viewed as an acid test for the discipline as a whole. A dam represents a discrete, geographically localized, and measurable perturbation of the fluvial system. The effect of a dam on the distribution and magnitude of flows is known or can be reasonably specified, and the trap efficiency of the reservoir, and hence magnitude of change to sediment flux, is equally predictable. The ability of geomorphologists to rigorously forecast changes to the downstream river's planform, hydraulic geometry, grain-size distribution, and slope from changes in the controlling variables of discharge and sediment supply represents a real-world application and test of the most fundamental principles of the science. Because the boundary conditions are generally known, predicting geomorphic response of rivers to dams is an ideal experiment and learning opportunity.

The questions posed by this paper are: Where do we stand with respect to this type of quantitative prediction? Is our ability to predict downstream response improved by focusing on the effects of dams on a specific type of channel, those with beds primarily composed of gravel? Motivating the second question is the observation that despite decades of geomorphic research demonstrating that rivers occupy distinct process domains as a function of where they sit in the landscape (e.g., Schumm, 1977; Montgomery, 1999), and a wide range of approaches to

*Gravel-bed Rivers: Processes, Tools, Environments*, First Edition. Edited by Michael Church, Pascale M. Biron and André G. Roy.
© 2012 John Wiley & Sons, Ltd. Published 2012 by John Wiley & Sons, Ltd.

river classification (see Kondolf *et al.*, 2003 for review), there has been very little emphasis on looking at the effects of dams through the lens of specific river morphologies. One exception is the work of Gaeuman *et al.* (2005), who examined the difference between gravel-bed and sand-bed reaches along the same river to changes in flow (due in part to upstream regulation) and sediment supply. This approach has not been widely followed, however.

The object here is to consider whether there are distinctive aspects of gravel-bed rivers that might constrain the wider range of potential responses to impoundment and thus improve prediction. Beginning with some considerations about the number and location of dams on gravel-bed rivers, I follow with a brief discussion of the history of predicting geomorphic responses to dams on rivers in general. Both analytical approaches and field studies are then examined to determine whether there is a characteristic style of channel adjustment below dams on gravel-bed rivers. Finally, I consider future research directions and implications for management. The focus is specifically on dams that are large enough to have the capacity to measurably affect the flux of water, sediment, or both, thereby excluding the effects of weirs and small check dams. Diversion dams are included insofar as they affect water and sediment transport, but the specific effects of diversions are not considered, since the issue of de-watering and re-watering channels adds another

dimension to the problem (see Ryan, 1997; Baker *et al.*, 2010 for recent reviews).

## 15.2   A GLOBAL PAUCITY OF DATA

No one knows how many dams are located on gravel-bed rivers, or any other type of river for that matter. Our inability to conduct a quantitative census points to data gaps that limit our understanding of the scale and dimension of dam issues globally. The problem is twofold: first, we don't know where all the gravel-bed rivers are, and second, virtually all local or national databases treat dams and their associated reservoirs as points in space; attributes that are associated with these points focus on the dimensions and characteristics of the dam (length, height, construction materials) or reservoir (volume, surface area), without any reference to the channel on which the dam is located. For example, the Dams, Lakes and Reservoirs Database for the World Water Development Report is a global databank of 633 large impoundments from a series of world dam registers published by the International Commission on Large Dams (ICOLD) and International Water Power and Dam Construction (IWPDC) (available at: http://wwdrii.sr.unh. edu) (Figure. 15.1). "Large" dams are defined as over 75 m in height or producing $1 \times 10^6 \, m^3$ of storage. Only latitude and longitude for each dam are given, and with 30-minute resolution for both, this would make it

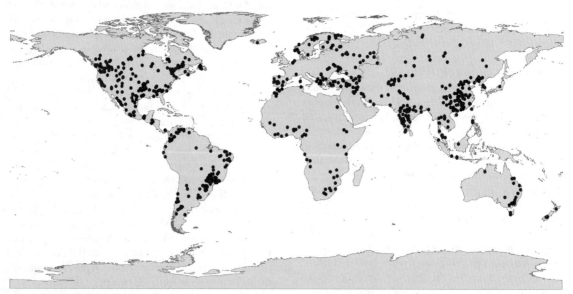

• Large reservoir site

**Figure 15.1**   Location of large dams contained in the global databank of 668 large impoundments from a series of world dam registers published by ICOLD and IWPDC (ICOLD, 1984, 1984; IWPDC, 1989; 1994); data available at: wwdrii.sr.unh.edu.

impossible to map the dams onto an accurate channel network. The US Army Corps of Engineers maintains the United States National Inventory of Dams (NID; available at: https://nid.usace.army.mil). The database includes over 79 000 dams that equal or exceed 7.6 m in height and exceed $1.8 \times 10^4 \, m^3$ of storage, or that equal or exceed $6.2 \times 10^5 \, m^3$ storage and exceed 1.8 m in height, or that pose a significant or high risk to life or property if they were to fail. The dataset that accompanies these dams and reservoirs is more extensive than the ICOLD dataset, and includes drainage area of the dam as one of its attributes. There are no data on the channel itself, however. A potentially more useful, although spatially limited, data set is one maintained by local reservoir management agencies in Japan, termed here the Japanese Reservoir Database (JRD). Detailed information on channel characteristics associated with 131 dams, including stream gradient, along with annual surveys of sediment and woody debris has permitted spatial analysis of controls on woody debris export (Seo *et al.*, 2008; Fremier *et al.*, 2009; Seo and Nakamura, 2009).

The lack of grain-size data for channels where dams are located reflects a general paucity of such data for most rivers – even those where long-term USGS stream gauging sites are located. In the absence of such data, even a reach-averaged channel slope along with discharge could be used to predict grain size, following a recast Strickler equation (e.g., Henderson, 1966, pp. 453–454). But with the exception of the JRD, slope data are lacking for all major dam datasets. For the JRD, channel slopes range from 0.02–0.26, clearly placing most if not all channels within the domain of gravel-bed

streams (Seo *et al.*, 2008). Drainage area alone provides a very indirect estimate of discharge (since runoff per unit area varies widely) or the character of the channel, but in conjunction with slope data permits the channel to be geomorphically classified, at least to a first approximation (Montgomery and Buffington, 1998). On-going (but *ad hoc*) efforts to digitize the location of dams and reservoirs using platforms such as Google Earth (see: http://www.kcl.ac.uk/schools/sspp/geography/research/emm/geodata/geowikis.html) could improve the georeferencing of dams in such a manner as to permit more detailed analyses in the future.

## 15.3 CHARACTERIZING THE GEOMORPHIC RESPONSE OF RIVERS TO IMPOUNDMENT

The chronology of scientific investigations on the geomorphic response of rivers to dams reflects a sometimes wandering trajectory from field studies of dams on individual rivers to comparative empirical analyses of dams on multiple rivers, through conceptual models of channel response, and, most recently, analytical and predictive models (Figure 15.2). The science of predicting geomorphic response to dams began over 50 years ago with field studies of the effects of dams on individual rivers, such as the Colorado (e.g., Borland and Miller, 1960) and Rio Grande, (e.g., Lawson, 1925), as well as efforts to understand the causes and rates of bed degradation below dams (Komura and Simons, 1967; Pemberton, 1976). Early papers on hydraulic geometry

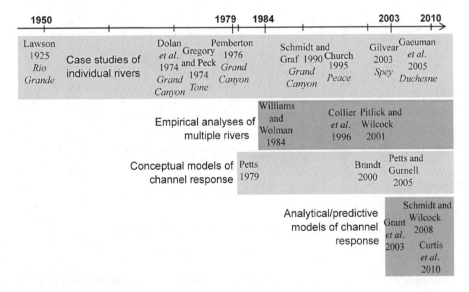

**Figure 15.2** Chronology of primary approaches for examining geomorphic response of rivers to dam removal highlighting keystone or representative papers.

adjustments below dams expanded the range of potential impacts (Gregory and Park, 1974; Park, 1977). Petts (1979) offered one of the first examples of a conceptual model for depicting geomorphic response through space and time. (Figure 15.3). But it was not until the publication of the classic paper by Williams and Wolman (1984) that these studies were synthesized into a set of empirical relations. The conclusions of that paper were generalized trends supported by data, rather than analytical and predictive models (Figure 15.4). Wolman (pers. comm., 1982) commented about the difficulty of extracting general relations from the data, particularly with regard to predicting the depth and downstream extent of bed incision below dams.

In the 25 years since publication of Williams and Wolman's report, the scientific literature on understanding and predicting effects of dams on rivers has followed three distinct themes: (i) case studies of geomorphic effects of individual dams or dam complexes on specific rivers; (ii) conceptual models based on geomorphic first principles that broadly predict the direction and magnitude of channel changes; and most recently (iii) analytical models based on coupled flow and sediment transport relations that provide more rigorous predictions of potential channel changes (Table 15.1). Although not directly making this distinction, a recent review paper on the subject of geomorphic response to dams by Petts and Gurnell (2005) provides a useful summary of much of this work, emphasizing both the conceptual approaches and the importance of folding considerations of riparian vegetation dynamics into geomorphic response models. While some of the more recent analytical approaches are not included in their state-of-the science assessment, it serves as a good and reasonably comprehensive assessment of the field, and will not be duplicated here. Beginning with an early analytical approach (Figure 15.5), I emphasize progress in quantitative prediction that these new methods allow.

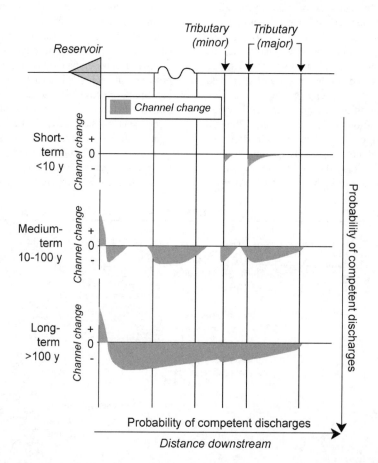

**Figure 15.3**  Conceptual model of longitudinal and temporal trends in channel width below a dam. Negative values correspond to channel narrowing while positive values correspond to channel widening. Reproduced, with permission, from Petts, G.E. 1979. Complex response of river channel morphology subsequent to reservoir construction. *Progress in Physical Geography*, **3**: 329–362.

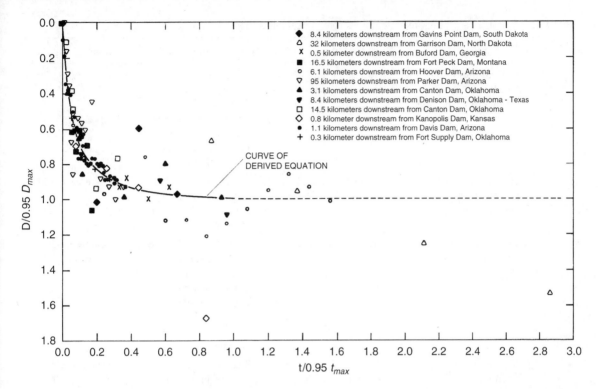

**Figure 15.4** Normalized depth of degradation (*D*) as a function of normalized time (*t*) for 12 rivers after dam closure. Reproduced, with permission, from Williams, G.P. and Wolman, M.G. 1984. Downstream effects of dams on alluvial rivers. United States Geological Survey, Professional Paper 1286.

Emerging from this entire body of work to date is the wide range of downstream geomorphic responses that follow dam construction and river regulation. Petts (1984) provides a useful and simple framework for categorizing downstream response, distinguishing three broad styles of adjustment:

- *Passive response*, where flows are reduced below the river's competence threshold and channel dimensions are reduced accordingly but without significant change in bed elevations;
- *Degradation,* where bed elevations and lateral deposits are scoured as the channel moves toward a new equilibrium with the reduced sediment supply; and
- *Aggradation*, where reductions in discharges and competence due to dam operation are of sufficient magnitude to limit the channel's ability to entrain and transport sediment delivered by tributary or other inputs downstream of the dam, resulting in an increase in bed elevation.

Generally, both field studies and analytic models of river response focus on assigning one or more of these response styles to specific reaches and periods of time.

The complexity of predicting downstream response is due to several factors. While a dam represents a point perturbation to the fluvial system, a diverse suite of influences, inputs, and driving forces operating below the dam immediately come into play, making interpretation of the dam's effects more difficult. Downstream of the dam, water may be supplied from tributaries; sediment may be supplied from tributaries or available in the channel bed, banks, and floodplains; the channel boundaries may be constrained by bedrock or entirely alluvial and unconstrained. Typically, the flux of sediment from tributaries or channel storage is not well known. These extrinsic controls can also vary spatially. The response of the downstream channel can therefore be viewed as a trajectory of potential changes that are not entirely predictable from first principles (Grant *et al.*, 2003) – a classic example of deterministic uncertainty (*sensu* Phillips, 1994).

### 15.3.1 Recent Analytical Approaches

As previously indicated, a great deal of work has been done to describe both theoretical and documented examples of channel response to dams on rivers. Although

**Table 15.1** Variables useful in prediction of morphological adjustment

| Metric | Description | Application | Data required | Source |
|--------|-------------|-------------|---------------|--------|
| $T^*$ | Ratio of pre- to post-dam frequency of sediment-transporting flows | Change in sediment transport capacity | Measured or modelled Critical threshold of flow required to transport sediment of particular grain size Pre- and post-dam flow regime | Grant *et al.*, 2003 |
| $S_G^*$ | Ratio of below to above-dam sediment supply | Change in sediment supply with distance downstream | Measured or modelled sediment supply for both main channel and tributaries | Grant *et al.*, 2003 |
| $S_S^*$ | Ratio of pre- to post-dam slope | Predicts sediment surplus of deficit | Measured or modelled sediment supply and sediment transport rate, for grain size of interest, pre- and post-dam flow regime and grain-size distribution | Schmidt and Wilcock, 2008 |
| $\tau^*$ | Bed incision index based on Shield's number | Potential for bed incision based on competence of post-dam flows | Stage discharge relationship; pre-dam gradient; grain-size distribution | Schmidt and Wilcock, 2008 |
| $A_*$ | Proxy for degree of dam influence down-stream of dam | Prediction of channel width for channels at or below tributary junctions | Drainage area at dam and points of interest downstream | Curtis *et al.*, 2010 |

much of the theoretical work prior to 2000 was fairly abstract, predicting general tendencies and trends as a function of the relation between the magnitude and direction of flow alteration and sediment supply, within the past 10 years a growing body of work has sought to develop a more rigorous predictive framework. Beginning with Brandt (2000), who used general formulations derived from Lane's (1955) balance between available stream power, sediment supply, and calibre, there have been several efforts to place predicting downstream effects of dams on a more solid technical foundation. Several of these recent approaches, developed to estimate trend or magnitude of probable response of rivers to impoundment, are considered here. These approaches introduce new predictive variables for evaluating predictive response and are summarized in Table 15.1. Following a brief description, each approach is examined from the standpoint of whether it provides evidence for a characteristic style of fluvial response of gravel-bed rivers to impoundment.

### 15.3.1.1 Semi-quantitative Estimation of Trend

Grant *et al.* (2003) developed a semi-analytical approach by proposing that geomorphic "response space" to dams could be defined in relation to two overarching controls: the change in the fraction of time that the river experiences flows capable of transporting sediment, and the upstream to downstream change in sediment supply. In a sense, these two axes capture the arms of Lane's balance. The first axis represents the change in the energy available for sediment transport due to the dam, and is defined by the fraction of time $T$ that flow $Q$ is greater than critical flow for sediment transport ($Q_{cr}$) downstream of the dam or:

$$T = \frac{\sum t_{(Q \geq Q_{cr})}}{\sum t_{(Q)}} \qquad (15.1)$$

where $t_{(Q)}$ refers to time at flow $Q$. The effect of the dam on the fractional time of sediment transport can be expressed as the dimensionless ratio $T^*$ between the

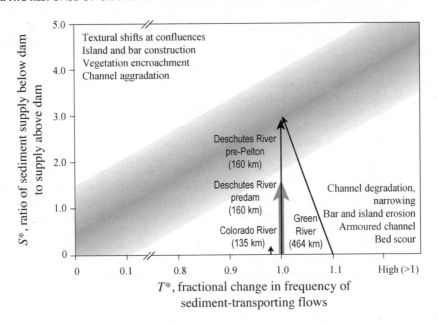

**Figure 15.5**  Predicted morphologic response to river impoundment as a function of two dimensionless variables, $T^*$ and $S_G^*$, as defined in text. Shown are trajectories of change for rivers selected to show a diversity of responses. Reproduced, with permission, from Grant, G.E., Schmidt, J.C. and Lewis, S.L. 2003. A geological framework for interpreting downstream effects of dams on rivers. In O'Connor, J.E. and Grant, G.E., editors. *A Peculiar River. American Geophysical Union, Water Science and Applications* **7**: 203–219.

pre-dam ($T_{pre}$) and post-dam ($T_{post}$) frequency of sediment-transporting flows:

$$T^* = \frac{T_{post}}{T_{pre}} \qquad (15.2)$$

Grant *et al.* (2003) note that this definition of $T$ and $T^*$ is grain-size dependent, since the magnitude, and hence frequency, of competent flows varies by grain size. In practice, transport thresholds are usually indexed to a particular grain size, $D_{50}$. $T^*$ may also vary over time in response to textural adjustments downstream. As the channel bed armours, $T_{post}$ may actually decrease, even with no change in the dam-imposed flow regime. Here lies one key aspect of the response of gravel-bed rivers to dams: *the presence of a mixed grainsize, which is typical of gravel-bed streams, creates the opportunity for textural adjustments that would not be present if the grain-size distribution were more homogeneous, as in sand-bed channels.*

A related complication is that both $T$ and $T^*$ can change over time as channel geometry adjusts to the changed flow and sediment regimes due to the dam. As previously noted, this implies that downstream change is best viewed as a trajectory of response (in both space and time) rather than a singular and deterministic value.

The other axis represents the rate of sediment resupply below the dam ($S_B$) relative to the sediment flux above

the dam ($S_A$); this is defined by another dimensionless ratio, $S_G^*$ as:

$$S_G^* = \frac{S_B}{S_A} \qquad (15.3)$$

The $G$ in the subscript is used to distinguish this variable from the $S^*$ defined by Schmidt and Wilcock (2008, below), which is denoted here as $S_S^*$. As Grant *et al.* (2003) note, large dams that capture virtually all bedload will have $S_B$, hence $S_G^* = 0$. Downstream of the dam, $S_G^*$ will increase as a function of input from hillslopes and tributaries, defining a longitudinal trajectory of change. Tributary flux is not typically known, but can be estimated from regional sediment yield relations or sediment transport models. Channel adjustment will also vary accordingly, as discussed below. Although $S_G^*$ is defined in terms of total mass flux above and below the dam, it is likely that the dam will impose changes in the type and calibre of sediment supply as well. Such changes are partially captured by the change in $T^*$, but a further (and unexplored) refinement may be to consider a size-dependent $S_G^*$ – to consider defining $S_G^*$ separately for the coarse and fine fractions.

Grant *et al.* (2003) propose that these two dimensionless variables, $T^*$ and $S_G^*$ (Table 15.1), can be thought of as defining a morphologic response space (Figure 15.5); the corresponding plot has been used to broadly predict or explain morphologic response of rivers in different geographic settings (Wampler, 2004; Kummu and Varis, 2007; Ambers, 2007).

What does this approach tell us about the response of gravel-bed rivers to dams? From first principles, $T$ (either pre- or post-dam) for gravel-bed rivers is likely to be relatively small; that is, the frequency of sediment-transporting flows tends to be much less for gravel- than for sand-bed rivers. Entrainment frequencies for gravel are typically given as slightly less than bankfull flow ($Q_{bf}$) (Andrews, 1984; Whiting et al., 1999; Torizzo and Pitlick, 2004), whereas sand transport on many rivers occurs at much more frequent flows. For example, detailed sediment sampling in the Grand Canyon reveals sand transport occurring from 40 to 97% of the time, depending on season (Topping, 2000a, 2000b). Wilcock (1998) and Wilcock and Kenworthy (2002) shows a three- to fourfold increase in critical dimensionless shear stress for gravel versus sand entrainment. Gravel-bed rivers are fundamentally more stable than sand-bed rivers, and the presence of a dam does not alter that fact. Therefore, $T_{pre}$ (and $T_{post}$) in gravel-bed streams is usually small and, for dams that reduce peak flows (flood control dams), $T^*$ will be less and sometimes much less than 1, depending on the degree to which peak flows are reduced. Trapping efficiency for coarse sediment in reservoirs is usually very high, approaching 100% (Brune, 1953). So the response of most gravel-bed rivers, at least immediately downstream of flood control dams, will generally lie in the lower right-hand quadrant of the plot, where channel degradation and bed armouring are the dominant adjustment mechanisms (Figure 15.5). Although plotted together, degradation and armouring are somewhat antagonistic processes, in the sense that armouring may limit degradation.

Sand-bed streams, on the other hand, are likely to have $T^*$ much closer to 1, since reduction in peak flows is usually offset by an increase in base flows, and $Q_{cr}$ is generally exceeded for virtually all flows. This brings up a second key difference between the response of gravel- versus sand-bed channels below dams: *gravel-bed streams are active a small fraction of the time, whereas bed material is in transport at some small rate at virtually all flows in sand-bed streams. Hence channel changes and adjustments in gravel-bed streams will inevitably be slower and take longer to be reflected in channel morphology.*

One situation where other responses are possible is where low-storage dams are operated to reduce peak flows, but are also periodically flushed of their accumulated sediments. In this case, bed aggradation can occur below the dam (upper left-hand quadrant), as described by Salant et al. (2006). The other, more common, case

where bed aggradation can occur below dams in gravel-bed rivers is where sediment is introduced from tributaries or other sources. As discussed below, the nature of the channel response can vary depending on the grain size and amount of introduced sediment.

Although Figure 15.5 can be used to predict the general direction and magnitude of channel response, there are a number of limitations to this approach. First, it is only semi-quantitative in the sense that the axis values are poorly constrained, as is the general shape of the response surface. The central portion of the graph, which indicates how local factors, including bedrock geology and channel geometry, can control or override hydraulic and sedimentalogic factors, is similarly poorly constrained. Moreover, the data used to derive $T^*$ and $S_G^*$ can be difficult to obtain, requiring measurements of sediment transport and estimates of sediment flux that are not readily available. Finally, as previously indicated, $T^*$ is both grain-size dependent and can change over time in response to morphodynamic adjustments, such as armouring and changes in channel geometry, and $S_G^*$ changes over space in response to downstream inputs. As discussed by Grant et al. (2003), the response surface in Figure 15.5 is best viewed as a general trajectory of change rather than a rigorous prediction.

### 15.3.1.2 Quantitative Prediction of Trend and Magnitude

A more quantitative approach to predicting downstream effects of dams was developed by Schmidt and Wilcock (2008), who used three dimensionless metrics characterizing the sediment mass balance, bed incision potential, and magnitude of flood reduction to predict downstream response. This last metric, $Q^*$, had little explanatory power and is not considered here. In particular, they defined the sediment mass balance using a reformulation of Lane's (1955) balance, in terms of the ratio of pre-dam to post-dam slope needed to transport the rate and calibre of the sediment supply at the imposed discharge, which they defined as $S_S^*$ (again the subscript is introduced here to distinguish from $S^*$ as previously defined by Grant et al. (2003)):

$$S_S^* = \frac{S_{post}}{S_{pre}} = \sqrt{\frac{qs_{post}}{qs_{pre}}} \left( \frac{q_{pre}}{q_{post}} \right) \left( \frac{D_{post}}{D_{pre}} \right)^{0.75} \quad (15.4)$$

where $S$ is the slope necessary to transport the sediment supply of rate $qs$ and calibre $D$ at flow rate $q$; the subscripts refer to pre- and post-dam. $S_S^* > 1$ implies that for the change in flow produced by the dam, there must be an increase in post-dam slope in order to transport the post-dam sediment supply; this corresponds to a post-dam sediment surplus. Conversely, a post-dam sediment deficit exists when $S_S^* < 1$. Although such a sediment surplus or deficit could be interpreted as indicating whether the downstream bed will aggrade or incise, Schmidt and Wilcock (2008) argue that an additional criterion that must be met is that the post-dam flows are competent to transport sediment and actually incise the bed. They define a bed incision index in terms of a Shield's number $\tau^*$:

$$\tau^* \propto \frac{h_{post} S_{pre}}{D_B} \qquad (15.5)$$

where $h_{post}$ is defined as the mean depth of post-dam floods, $S_{pre}$ is the pre-dam gradient, and $D_B$ is a characteristic grain size. The Shields number is the ratio of downstream shear stress to submerged particle weight or:

$$\tau^* = \frac{hS}{(G-1)D_B} \qquad (15.6)$$

where $G$ is the specific gravity of sediment particles. Empirical results from application of this and the previous metric suggest that bed incision will occur where $S_s^* > 1$ and $\tau^* > 0.1$. Similar to $S_G^*$, sediment mass balance as defined by $S_s^*$ varies with distance downstream from the dam as sediment is re-supplied from tributaries, and may also vary with time.

The metrics (see Table 15.1) developed by Schmidt and Wilcock (2008) show real promise in terms of placing prediction of downstream response of rivers to dams on a more rigorous foundation. Despite the many assumptions that underlie this approach, they show that combining a metric for sediment mass balance (essentially sediment transport capacity) and flow competence is reasonably successful in identifying where channels have aggraded or incised. Moreover, the data suggest that there may be discernible thresholds in both $S_s^*$ and $\tau^*$. If so, this approach provides an *a priori* basis for predicting channel response.

This approach also provides insight into the adjustment of gravel-bed rivers below dams. Of the 14 river reaches used to test the metrics, only four (upper Colorado, Trinity, upper Snake, and Deschutes Rivers) were gravel-bed reaches. Of these, the upper Colorado and Snake were in sediment surplus ($S_s^*$ ranging from 1.18 to 1.61), the Deschutes showed the greatest sediment deficit ($S_s^*$ ranging from 0.08 immediately below the dam to 0.76 approximately 160 km downstream), and the Trinity had reaches showing both deficit ($S_s^* = 0.35$, immediately downstream from the dam) and surplus ($S_s^* = 1.40$ more than 13 km downstream). All gravel-bed streams had very low bed incision indices (ranging from

0.01–0.05), reflecting their greater stability. What is most significant is that despite the large range of sediment mass balance, the range of observed changes in channel bed elevation was very small, less than 0.5 m of either incision or aggradation, with most responses very close to zero (Figure 7a in Schmidt and Wilcock, 2008). Compare this with their reported range of bed elevation changes for rivers with finer (sand and fine gravel) beds, from 2.5 m of aggradation (Rio Grande below Elephant Butte) to 4 m of incision (Colorado River below Parker and Hoover Dams).

These data are broadly consistent with other published accounts of downstream response of rivers to dams. Williams and Wolman (1984) did not provide comprehensive grain-size data for the population of dams that they studied. Of the rivers for which they did report grain-size data from pebble counts, only two – the Smoky Hill River below Kanopolis Dam in Kansas, and the Red River below Denison Dam in Oklahoma – appear to be gravel-bed; measured grain size was approximately 20 mm on the Smoky Hill River below the dam, and 50–60 mm on the Red River. Incision rates are on order of 1 m for the Smoky Hill River and 2.5 m for the Red River immediately below the dam; both incision rates decrease with distance downstream (Figure 14 in Williams and Wolman, 1984). Grain sizes were measured 13 to 16 years after closure, however, so the pre-dam grain-size distribution is difficult to establish. Much less incision, approximately 0.2 m, is reported by Salant *et al.* (2006) for the Black River, a gravel-bed ($D_{50} = 130$ mm) stream in eastern Vermont. Wampler (2004) reported an average of 0.3 up to 1.0 m of incision below River Mill Dam on the Clackamas River in Oregon; $D_{50}$ ranged from 5–10 cm. The Peace River, a classic gravel-bed channel in British Columbia, Canada, has degraded no more than 0.5 m below Bennett Dam (M. Church, pers. comm., 2010). Kellerhals (1982) similarly notes lack of degradation on at least three other gravel-bed Canadian rivers. Gaeuman *et al.* (2005) compare the complex response of gravel-bed to sand-bed reaches subject to the same flow and sediment alteration due to dams and flow diversions on the Duchesne River in Utah. The gravel-bed reaches narrowed, then aggraded and widened in response to varying flow regimes, while the sand-bed channels aggraded and avulsed, then incised.

### 15.3.1.3 Importance and Prediction of Armouring

The key conclusion to extract from this admittedly incomplete census of the literature is that the magnitude of bed elevation change due to dam closure alone in gravel-bed rivers is generally relatively small, on order of 1 m or less of degradation. A primary reason for this is the natural armouring process that results from the mixed grain size. Armouring limits the magnitude of degradation by increasing bed $D_{50}$, thereby requiring flows of increasing competence in order to entrain the bed. This armouring can result from both the decreased magnitude of peak flows and the decreased sediment supply from upstream. The conclusion that channel beds tend to armour below dams is hardly novel; dam construction engineers anticipated it in the design of Glen Canyon Dam (Pemberton, 1976), and Williams and Wolman (1984, p. 29) describe the process succinctly:

> Few if any natural channels are underlain by perfectly uniform sediments. Because magnitude and frequency of high flows are significantly decreased by dams, and because released flows may not be able to transport sizes previously moved by higher flows, successive flows can winnow finer materials from the bed. Progressive winnowing concentrates the coarser fraction. As degradation proceeds, the average particle size on the bed increases, possibly resulting in a surface or armor of coarse particles alone. This idealized theory has long been accepted in engineering planning.

Agreement on the mechanism of armouring remains more elusive than suggested in the paragraph above (see Wohl, 2000, pp. 95–97). But the key point here, and what has perhaps been underappreciated, is that because the range of grain sizes in gravel-bed rivers is fundamentally greater than finer bed rivers, gravel-bed rivers will tend to armour much more readily; as a consequence the downstream effects of dams on channel incision will be less pronounced.

Predicting the intensity, longitudinal extent, or time scales of armouring remains a challenge, though theoretically possible. Empirically, the coarsening of channel beds below dams occurs relatively rapidly, typically within the first 5 to 10 years following dam closure (see Williams and Wolman, 1984, Figure 13), while the downstream extent of coarsening appears to be on order of 10–20 km, diminishing downstream (see Williams and Wolman, 1984, Figure 14). Longer distances (up to 70 km) were noted for some rivers, such as the Colorado below Hoover Dam. Wampler (2004) noted surface coarsening on the Clackamas River on the order of two to three times $D_{50}$ that extended 3 km downstream of the dam and resulted in skeletal boulder bars with little residual gravel (Figure 15.6).

In theory, we can predict intensity or time scale of armouring from first principles, but in practice there has been little work to rigorously develop and test predictions. Such predictions would be useful for constraining both the magnitude and time scales of bed degradation below dams. They would also be valuable for predicting depth of scour of fish redds in rivers (May *et al.*, 2009). Recent advances in remote monitoring of changes in the size distribution of bed material using digital photogrammetry (e.g., Graham *et al.*, 2005; Carbonneau *et al.*, 2004, 2005, 2006) may improve the situation here, but widespread application of these techniques is still a distance off (Marcus and Fonstad, 2008).

In general, we can better predict the degree of armouring than the time scale over which armour will develop. For example, Parker and Sutherland (1990) showed that the surface composition of both the static armour that

**Figure 15.6**   Coarse gravel bar devoid of fines, located approximately 1.5 km below River Mill Dam on the Clackamas River, OR, USA. Photo by Peter Wampler.

results from selective transport (as described by Williams and Wolman, above), and the mobile armour which forms during bedload transport of non-uniform sediment, could be numerically predicted from a known set of flow conditions and a bedload transport rate. Given that armour development below dams is most likely in response to clear water releases, a focus on static armour development seems warranted; the grain-size distributions of both the static and mobile armour were similar to each other in any case (Parker and Sutherland, 1990). As demonstrated by Parker (2004), and Parker et al. (2007), the armour layer that develops in response to time-varying hydrographs results in an equilibrium grain-size distribution that is somewhat independent of the immediate flow history.

Predicting the time scale over which armour develops, on the other hand, is more problematic. A critical issue is the time scale to reach equilibrium; this sets the adjustment time for the channel as a whole downstream of the dam and is a function of the thickness of the active layer, which exchanges with the surface layer under conditions of bedload transport. This thickness is not well constrained, however, but typically defined as some multiple of the maximum grain size, $nD_{90}$. For example, data from DeVries (2002) suggests $1.5\,D_{90}$, while Haschenberger and Church (1998) report a range from 0.4 to $2.0\,D_{90}$; the latter is close to the value proposed by Wilcock and McArdell (1997). The point is that the thicker the active layer, the more exchange and overturning occurs, hence longer time required to reach equilibrium (G. Parker, 2010, pers. comm.). Recent flume studies show that the active layer scales with both grain size and flow strength (Wong et al., 2007). A simple one-layer model based on kinematic wave theory that assumes an active layer thickness equal to $D_{100}$ has been proposed, but gives highly idealized results (Bettess and Frangipane, 2003).

In the absence of more analytical methods, perhaps the simplest approach to estimating time required to reach a bed pavement in equilibrium with the flows below a dam would be to calculate the size of sediment that is likely to be stable under the post-dam flow regime, and consider the fraction of the bed material that is finer than this grain size. Re-casting Equation (15.5) as:

$$D_B \propto \frac{h_{post}S_{post}}{\tau^*} \qquad (15.7)$$

where $S_{post}$ refers to the post-dam slope, one can solve for the grain size $D_B$ that is likely to be stable for the predicted range of post-dam flows and depths. Assuming that grain size $D_B$ represents the nth percentile of the surface grain-size distribution, then the time $T_a$ for an equilibrium pavement may be estimated as the time required for flows to transport that volume of sediment made up of size fractions $D_B$, obtainable from the flow

release schedule coupled to an appropriate sediment transport relation.

In sum, new analytical approaches advance our ability to predict downstream geomorphic response to dams as general trends in the direction and magnitude of adjustments. Textural coarsening of the surface layer and bed incision are the predominant responses, with the former limiting the latter to only a few metres or less; in some cases little or no incision occurs. Predicting the time scale over which armouring develops, the resulting grain size of the bed, and the longitudinal extent of armouring below the dam are less certain, although empirical evidence suggests that textural adjustments occur rapidly – within 5–10 years following dam closure.

Armouring is not the only mechanism limiting degradation below dams, however. Local controls, such as presence of bedrock in the channel can also limit incision, as in the case of Hoover Dam on the Colorado River (Williams and Wolman, 1984), the Glenbawn Dam in New South Wales, Australia (Erskine, 1985), and other rivers.

### 15.3.1.4 Longitudinal Trends and the Role of Tributaries

The focus thus far has been on evaluating where we stand with respect to predicting downstream effects of dams on gravel-bed rivers using basic principles of channel adjustments in response to changing sediment and flow regimes. As previously noted, however, such alluvial controls are not fixed, but change with distance downstream, primarily in response to inputs of water and sediment from tributaries. Until recently, there has been little effort to rigorously characterize how these tributary inputs change the style of adjustment. Such inputs can result in the nature of the response transforming from degradational to aggradational domains (Grant et al., 2003), or from sediment deficit to sediment surplus (Schmidt and Wilcock, 2008). A key factor appears to be the grain size of the sediment contributed relative to the mainstem channel competency and capacity. Here I examine new approaches to evaluating the response of gravel-bed rivers to influx of both coarse (sediment whose calibre is equal or greater than the mainstem bed material) and fine (sediment whose caliber is less than the mainstem bed material) sediment into regulated reaches downstream of dams. Again, the intent is to explore where we stand with respect to making rigorous predictions of dam-related impacts.

*Coarse Sediment Influx:* There is abundant literature documenting how tributary input of coarse material can aggrade the channel bed below dams, resulting in coarse-grained deposits and rapids that form distinct slope breaks or steps in the longitudinal profile at tributary junctions (Graf, 1980; Kieffer, 1985; Petts and Thoms, 1987; Magirl et al., 2005). This arises if dam operations reduce peak flows, and thereby flow competence and the channel's capacity to excavate material delivered down tributaries. Such a scenario resulted in a stepped longitudinal profile on the mainstem Peace River following river regulation (Church, 1995). An interesting ancillary effect of flow regulation on the Peace was that the tributaries tended to degrade near their confluences with the mainstem due to lower peak flows – hence flood stages – on the mainstem, and asynchrony in flood discharges between the tributaries and the mainstem (M. Church, pers. comm., 2010).

A detailed analysis of channel changes at tributary junctions below two dams in New England where peak flow has been reduced revealed both bar growth and bed coarsening at and downstream of tributary junctions with concomitant narrowing of channel width (Curtis et al., 2010); they also note fining of the bed upstream of confluences. The mainstem channel bed immediately downstream of the confluence appears to reflect the grain size of the tributary more than the grain size of the upstream mainstem, as has been noted by others (Graf, 1980; Petts and Thoms, 1987). Following the general approach of Schmidt and Wilcock (2008), Curtis et al. (2010) have developed a quantitative analysis that generally predicts the magnitude of adjustment of both channel slope and width in response to the changed flow regime. This analysis rests on the assumption that the Shield's parameter of the formative flows (both pre- and post-dam) is near the critical value required for the mobilization of the average size sediment on the bed; that is $\tau^* \approx \tau^*_{cr}$. This assumption, in turn, is supported by the work of Dade and Friend (1998), along with hydraulic modelling. The concept is that under both the pre- and post-dam flow regime, the channel geometry, slope, and grain size adjust to maintain this near equality. From this, they show how the ratio of pre- to post-dam slope ($S*$) at tributary junctions varies as a function of $A*$ (Table 15.1), which they define as the drainage area A at some point below a dam (for example at a tributary junction) normalized by the drainage area at the dam, $A_{dam}$, or:

$$A* = \frac{A - A_{dam}}{A} \qquad (15.8)$$

$A*$ therefore approaches 1 as drainage area increases below a dam and the proportion of dam-influenced drainage area diminishes. They also demonstrate that the same analysis can be used to predict channel width adjustment below dams, and argue that the time scale of adjustment for channel width might be on the order of a century or more for the channel geometry to reach equilibrium with the new flow regime. As with the work previously cited, these analyses provide a much firmer foundation for predicting dam effects that includes the role of downstream tributaries that deliver coarse sediment.

*Fine Sediment Influx:* A different situation applies where fine sediment is delivered from tributaries to the mainstem of a gravel-bed channel that has been regulated by a dam. Whereas the response of the channel to coarse bedload input is limited by the competence of the channel to transport the material, the response to fine-grained input is limited by the sediment transport capacity of the channel, since the available shear stress is almost always greater than that necessary to mobilize sediment (Dade and Friend, 1998). That is not to say that all fine sediment input to a gravel-bed river will necessarily be transported downstream, however. If post-dam flows, hence transport capacity, are sufficiently reduced, the effect will be aggradation of fine sediment at and downstream of tributary junctions, fining of the bed surface layer, and intrusion of fine sediment into interstices in the gravel. Classic examples of this include the Trinity River downstream of Lewiston Dam (Wilcock et al., 1996a; Trush et al., 2000), the Green River below Flaming Gorge Dam (Andrews, 1986; Allred and Schmidt, 1999), and the upper Colorado River (Van Steeter and Pitlick, 1998). Gaeuman et al. (2005) note that fine sediment from gully erosion entered but did not aggrade the Duchesne River following water diversions and reservoir construction, but aggradation did occur when coarser gravel with the same calibre as the bed material was eroded from bank deposits. Both the geomorphic and ecological consequences of these impacts may be severe, including loss of invertebrate or aquatic habitats, stabilization of bars by vegetation, and changes in the frequency of bedload transport (for review, see Pitlick and Wilcock, 2001).

The nature of this problem lends itself to the idea of flushing or sediment maintenance flows – deliberate releases of flows that are capable of entraining the fine material stored in the surface and subsurface of the bed. Identifying the flows required to flush fines from the bed without entraining the gravel layer, which is often limited below sediment trapping dams, and viewed as a resource, is a delicate problem, however, since some dilation of the bed is required in order to entrain fines stored in gravel interstices.

Recent progress in specifying such flows has been made by using rating curves for sand and gravel transport, together with estimates of the efficiency of pool sediment trapping and upward flux of sand from the subsurface of the bed, and coupling these with sand and gravel routing algorithms (Wilcock et al., 1996b). These

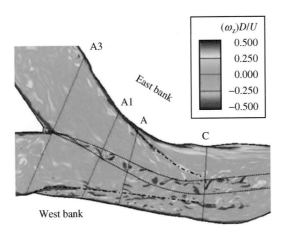

**Plate 1 (Figure 1.5)**  Instantaneous vorticity at the confluence visualized with the contours on the water surface (Miyawaki *et al.*, 2009).

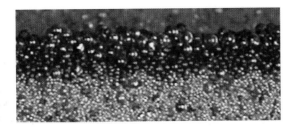

**Plate 1 (Figure 4.3)**  Segregation of a tridisperse mixture in an inclined chute. Diameters of the glass beads: small white $150\,\mu m$, pink $350\,\mu m$, large dark $550\,\mu m$ (image courtesy of N. Thomas and E. Martin, Université Aix-Marseille, France).

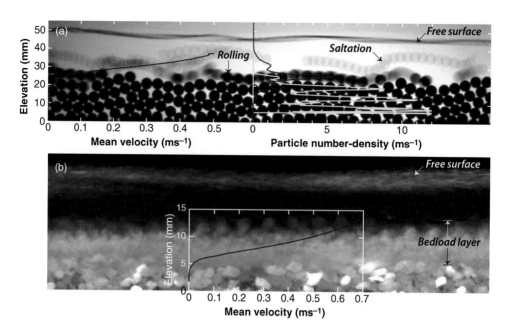

**Plate 2 (Figure 4.7)** (a) Mean streamwise particle velocity and number-density profiles (yellow immobile and red moving) calculated with data obtained by particle tracking velocimetry (Böhm *et al.*, 2006) on a temporal series of 8000 images (over 60.94s) in a 6.5 mm wide 2-D channel. The background image is the sum of 13 images (0.1 s). Slope of the channel: 10 %, diameter of the glass beads: 6 mm, water flux of $10.3 \times 10^{-3} \, m^3 \, s^{-1} \, m^{-1}$, solid flux of 20.6 beads $s^{-1}$ or $0.358 \times 10^{-3} \, m^3 \, s^{-1} \, m^{-1}$. (b) Mean streamwise particle velocity calculated by particle image velocimetry on a temporal series of 900 images (over 7.62 s) obtained with the experimental arrangement in (Recking *et al.*, 2008a). The background image is the sum of the entire series. Slope of the channel: 7%, width of 5 cm, mean diameter of the natural sediment: 2.3 mm, water flux of $10.0 \times 10^{-3} \, m^3 \, s^{-1} \, m^{-1}$, solid flux of $0.290 \times 10^{-3} \, m^3 \, s^{-1} \, m^{-1}$. Reproduced, with permission, from John Wiley & Sons, Ltd.

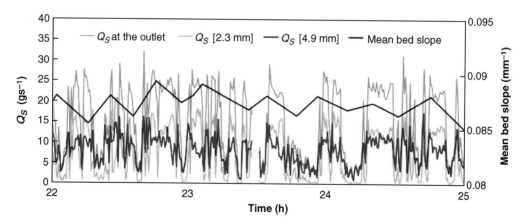

**Plate 2 (Figure 4.12)** Continuous outlet solid discharge $Q_s$ (total and fractional) and mean bed slope over the entire length of the flume: see Figure 4.11a (Recking *et al.*, 2009). Reproduced, with permission, from American Geophysical Union.

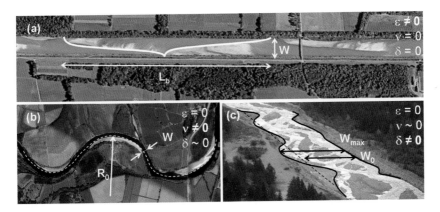

**Plate 3 (Figure 6.2)**  Illustrative sketch of: (a) alternate bar geometry in a rectified river reach (the Rhine River in Liechtenstein, image from Google Earth); (b) nearly constant width meander geometry (Adda River, Italy, image from Google Earth); (c) straight channel with regular width oscillations (Dora di Veny, NW Italy, the authors). Each case is illustrative of a reference analytical problem where only one of the three perturbation parameters (respectively $\varepsilon$; $\nu$; $\delta$) is nonvanishing. Reproduced, with permission, from Google Corporation.

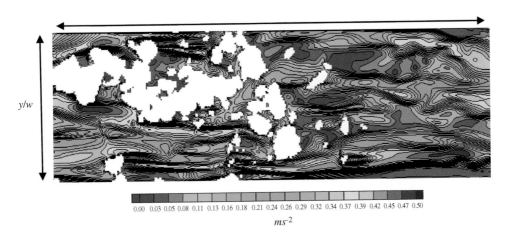

0.00 0.03 0.05 0.08 0.11 0.13 0.16 0.18 0.21 0.24 0.26 0.29 0.32 0.34 0.37 0.39 0.42 0.45 0.47 0.50

$ms^{-2}$

**Plate 3 (Figure 10.2)**  An example of a prediction of flow over a gravel surface applying computational fluid dynamics. The image shows a plan view of the river bed with flow from left to right. White regions represent pebbles.

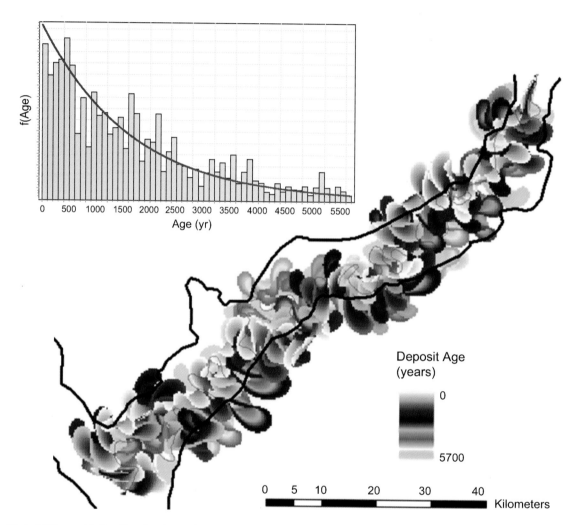

**Plate 4 (Figure 11.1)** Simulated ages for Strickland River floodplain, Papua New Guinea, after 5700 simulated years. The solid black lines represent the edge of the meander belt as observed from satellite imagery. The faint pink line illustrates the channel position in 1972. The histogram in the upper right shows the observed and best-fit exponential distribution of ages for the entire system.

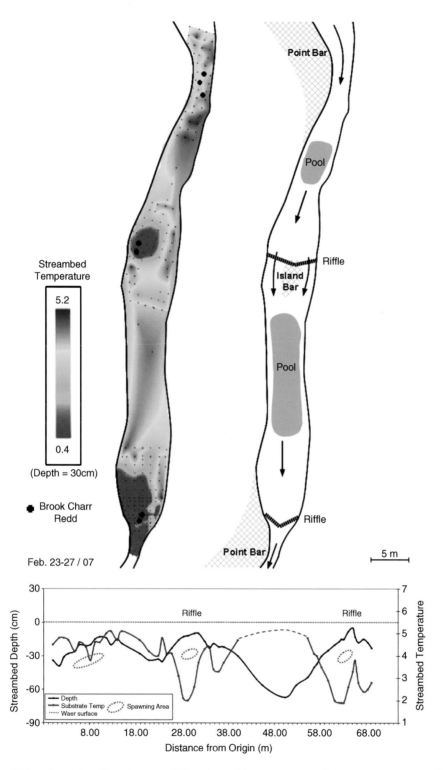

**Plate 5 (Figure 17.3)** Examples of brook trout redd locations with respect to gravel temperatures measured in the middle of embryo incubation season (February). Stream bed temperatures, measured at 15 cm depth in the substrate, are an indication of the warmer groundwater's contribution to local hyporheic water. Surface water is 0.5 °C during surveys. Egg pockets are located in riffle zones with large surface water contributions in reaches with appreciable groundwater upwelling in pools. (From Jan Franssen, unpublished doctoral research.)

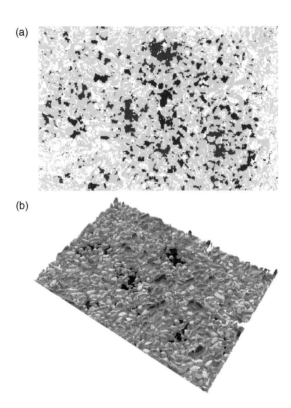

**Plate 6 (Figure 19.1)**   (a) DEM of Difference showing elevation changes before and after 6 hours of crayfish activity. Red areas indicate positive changes in elevation that exceed $D_{50}$ and blue areas indicate negative changes that exceed $D_{50}$ (pit and mound construction). Areas of orange show changes between $\pm D_{50}$ (grain re-arrangement) and areas of white indicate no change according to the minimal discernable difference of $\pm 1$ mm. (b) DEM of the disturbed surface showing pit and mound structures. Blue is low elevation, brown is high elevation. Flow was from left to right in both cases and the area shown is 0.6 by 0.4 m.

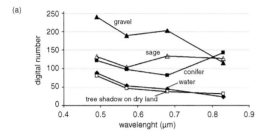

(a)

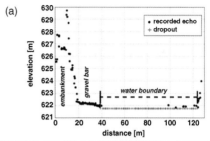

(a)

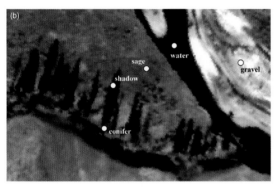

(b)

(b)

**Plate 7 (Figure 21.1)** (a) Spectral reflectance plots of water, gravel, sage, conifers in sunlight, and conifer shadow on dry land. The approximate locations of the locations where the spectra were collected are shown in (b), which is a 1 m resolution, pan-sharpened IKONOS image of Soda Butte Creek, Wyoming, USA. The similarity of spectral reflectance over open water and shadow confuses automated image-based classifications. The distinctive shapes associated with the shadows suggest that shape-based feature-detection algorithms may provide a means to separate shadows from water in the future.

**Plate 7 (Figure 21.2)** LiDAR returns from water surfaces. (a) Many of the terrestrial LiDAR signals along a 2 m cross-sectional swath are absorbed over water, leading to "dropouts" that have to be modelled to map the water surface. Reproduced, with permission, from Höfle, B., Vetter, M., Pfeifer, N., Mandlburger, G. and Stötter, J. 2009. Water surface mapping from airborne laser scanning using signal intensity and elevation data. *Earth Surface Processes and Landforms* **34**: 1635–1649 (b) The density of LiDAR returns increases over rough water surfaces. Reproduced, with permission, from English, J. 2009. Effectiveness of extracting water surface slopes from LiDAR data within the active channel: Sandy River, Oregon, USA. M.S. Thesis, Department of Geography, University of Oregon, Eugene.

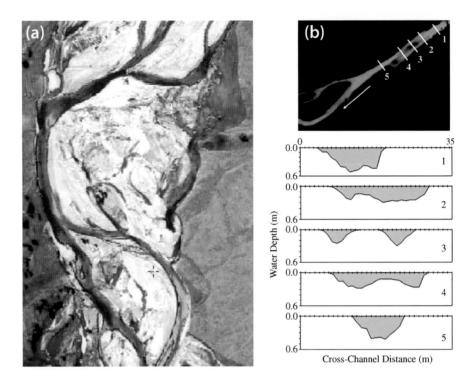

**Plate 8 (Figure 21.5)** Optical measurements of water depth without ground-based measurements using the HAB technique (Fonstad and Marcus, 2005). (a) A bathymetric map of the Lamar River, Wyoming, USA, based on airborne imagery. Deeper water is indicated by darker blue. Flow is from top to bottom. Deep areas are correctly shown in areas of flow convergence and on the outside of bends. (b) Cross-sections derived from satellite data for Soda Butte Creek, Wyoming USA. The satellite-based measurements correctly capture the emergence and disappearance of a mid-channel bar. Figures are modified from Fonstad and Marcus (2005), Figures 11 and 15, respectively. Reproduced, with permission, from Fonstad, M.A. and Marcus, W.A. 2005. Remote sensing of stream depths with hydraulically assisted bathymetry (HAB) models. *Geomorphology* **72**: 107–120.

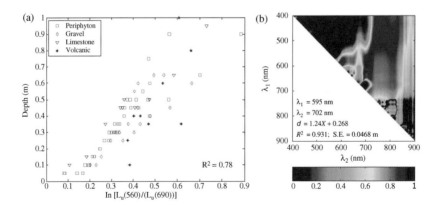

**Plate 8 (Figure 21.6)** The use of natural logarithms of band ratios for depth estimates with optical imagery. (a) The ratios normalize for variations in reflectance over different substrates. Reproduced, with permission, from Legleiter, C.J., Roberts, D.A., Marcus, W.A. and Fonstad, M.A. 2004. Passive remote sensing of river channel morphology and in-stream habitat: physical basis and feasibility. *Remote Sensing of Environment* **93**: 493–510. (b) The range of modeled $r^2$ values for measured versus estimated depths, Lamar River, Wyoming, USA, 19 August, 2006. Reproduced, with permission, from Legleiter, C.J., Roberts, D.A. and Lawrence, R.L. 2009. Spectrally based remote sensing of river bathymetry. *Earth Surface Processes and Landforms* **34**: 1039–1059. Red colours indicate higher $r^2$ values. The best predictor of depths occurs using a ratio of the natural logarithms of the 702 nm and 595 nm bands.

can provide useful estimates of the flow discharges needed, and also highlight the importance of pool dredging as an adjunct to flushing flows.

### 15.3.2  Width Adjustments and the Role of Vegetation

Although this paper has tended to emphasize vertical adjustments to the channel, changes in channel width are also important. Both channel narrowing and widening have been reported, although narrowing appears to be more common. Gaeuman *et al.* (2005) describe both processes for a regulated gravel-bed reach of the Duchesne River; they attribute narrowing to fine sediment accumulation along channel margins and backwaters, and widening to feedback between bed aggradation and infrequent transport events concentrating erosion along lateral channel margins, leading to introduction of more coarse sediment.

Vegetation plays a key role in mediating channel narrowing. As noted by Petts and Gurnell (2005), vegetation acts to stabilize bars and other channel surfaces that have either been formed or stranded by the dam-induced changes in flow regime. Typically this results in dramatic channel narrowing, as documented in the Trinity, Green, and Colorado River examples already cited. Gilvear (2003) documented channel narrowing accompanying vegetation encroachment along benches over a 60-year timeframe on the River Spey in Scotland. Rates of vegetation encroachment and channel narrowing on both the Duchesne and Spey are strongly influenced by the flow regime itself, particularly the presence or absence of large flows.

In all of these cases, the primary mechanism leading to narrowing was deposition of fine sediment (primarily sand) along channel margins that was subsequently colonized by vegetation, even though the channel beds were composed of gravel. An interesting though unanswered question is the relative importance of vegetation as a stabilizing influence in gravel- versus sand-bed channels. One is tempted to claim that vegetation exerts a greater role in sand-bed channels, since the cohesion afforded by its root systems would seem to impart stability to otherwise unstable substrates and surfaces. On the other hand though, if many gravel-bed rivers are poised close to the critical threshold for transport under formative flows, as suggested earlier, then the increased flow resistance coupled with root cohesion might easily tip the balance in favour of stability for vegetated bars. Recent efforts to physically model the role of vegetation in the laboratory in coarse-grained channels certainly suggest that vegetation plays a dominant role in influencing channel form and pattern (Gran and Paola, 2001; Tal and Paola, 2007; Braudrick *et al.*, 2009).

We are still some distance from being able to predict width adjustments below dams, however. In general, predicting width adjustments in channels in response to changing flow regime remains one of the more difficult challenges, since deterministic models of bank erosion and deposition are still rudimentary. Moreover, the importance of vegetation, both as a promoter of deposition and a component of hydraulic roughness introduces a suite of biological processes (colonization, propagation, reproduction, mortality) that do not lend themselves to process-based modelling, and may not be directly coupled to the flow regime. Empirical studies remain the best approach to constraining the magnitude and direction of planform changes.

## 15.4  SOME PERSPECTIVES AND CONCLUSIONS

The number of dams that regulate the flux of water and sediment on gravel-bed rivers worldwide is unknown. Perhaps as global databases coupled with remote sensing improve, a more coherent picture will emerge, not only of where dams sit, but of what types of rivers they affect. Building spatial databases that characterize the fundamental descriptors of river channels – slope, grain size, channel dimensions, and bed morphology – represents an ambitious, though tractable task that would dramatically improve our ability to predict geomorphic response of rivers, not just to impoundment, but to other anthropogenic and natural drivers of channel change.

Over 50 years of field observations from around the world reveal that the geomorphic response of rivers downstream of dams has to be viewed as a trajectory of potential changes that are not entirely predictable from first principles. The new analytical approaches and data presented here, however, suggest that knowing the grain size of the channel below a dam can provide, at least to a first approximation, much-needed information about the likely direction and magnitude of dam-induced changes to river geomorphology. This conclusion echoes the one put forth by Gaeuman *et al.* (2005; p.205): "…the uncertainty inherent in predicting the direction of channel adjustment could be reduced by distinguishing between gravel-bed and sand-bed channels and by considering the size of the imposed sediment load relative to the bed material size". The evidence indicates that bed incision on most gravel-bed rivers below dams is typically modest – on the order of a metre or two or less. The mixed grain-size ranging from sand to large gravel that is typical of many gravel-bed streams creates the opportunity, through selective entrainment, winnowing, and scour, for textural adjustments that would not be present if the grain-size distribution were more homogeneous, as

**Table 15.2**  Current level of confidence with respect to quantitative prediction of geomorphic response of rivers to dams: high (++), moderate (+) or low (?)

| Response | Vertical Adjustments | Textural Adjustments | Lateral Adjustments (with tribs) | Lateral Adjustments (no tribs) |
|---|---|---|---|---|
| Direction | ++ | ++ | ++ | + |
| Magnitude | + | + | + | + |
| Timing | + | ? | + | + |
| Longitudinal Extent | + | ? | + | ? |
| Persistence | ? | ? | ? | ? |

in sand-bed channels. The ensuing bed coarsening and armouring limits bed incision to values much smaller than found in finer-grained channels.

New generations of analytical tools and metrics offer real prospects for predicting downstream changes due to impoundment (Table 15.1). We now have the capacity to generally predict the direction, magnitude, and timing of bed incision and armour development, as well as to anticipate the kinds of changes that are likely to occur at tributary junctions (Table 15.2). Less well developed are the tools to predict changes in channel width, the longitudinal extent of adjustments, or the persistence of dam-related impacts. These tools provide a strong foundation for moving forecasts of fluvial response out of the realm of simple conceptual approaches and towards more technically defensible predictive models.

What are some of the management implications of this trend? Will increased capacity for more rigorous predictions of the consequence of damming rivers result in improved management decisions? The jury is of course still out, but some observations may have bearing. First, more quantitative prediction is not likely to result in fundamental changes to management, in that the general direction of dam-induced changes in channel morphology has been known for decades. It is, however, likely to better constrain the magnitude and timing of response, and this may result in more efficient strategies for anticipating and mitigating change. For example, a more rigorous prediction of the extent and magnitude of incision below a dam may obviate the need for expensive countermeasures such as erosion control structures and check dams. Perhaps more importantly, the types of metrics presented here have utility for answering key questions that invariably come up when contemplating dam construction or re-licensing. For example, a critical question faced by dam managers is whether and how much gravel to introduce below a dam to offset the effects of sediment trapping on aquatic habitat and other river resources. A more quantitative prediction of channel scour and incision, and armour development can

provide a first-order estimate of the volumes of gravel needed and some idea as to what grain sizes may be appropriate. Alternatively, current efforts to re-think operating schedules and flow regimes for existing dams, such as The Nature Conservancy's "Sustainable Rivers Project" (see: http://www.nature.org/initiatives/ freshwater/partnership/) employ limited tools to evaluate the effects of proposed flow regimes on channel morphology; the approaches outlined here would expand that toolbox. Prediction of downstream effects becomes even more critical when rivers cross international boundaries, and upstream decisions with respect to dam construction and operation affect downstream river populations, managers, and ecosystems. The approaches described here can provide a common technical foundation for negotiation and mitigation (Kummu and Varis, 2007).

That being said, we should not consider the problem of predicting downstream adjustments to dams a closed problem. Significant challenges await, which will keep the next generations of geomorphologists and river managers happily occupied or frustrated, depending on your point of view. It is one thing to be able to speak to the likely effects of a particular dam and flow regime on a channel; it is quite another to design a flow regime to provide a range of physical and ecological benefits. Yet that is the challenge, as the operation and even existence of many dams is being re-considered in light of changing environmental and societal concerns. Optimizing a flow regime involves a very complex calculus that includes ecological, geomorphic, and economic considerations, and no one has designed a template for this type of analysis. The tools and approaches described here can help resolve predictions of physical changes to channels, but few tools exist to provide robust models of ecological responses.

Moreover, dams are not the only impact on rivers, and do not function alone in changing flow and sediment regimes. Characterizing geomorphic response to multiple drivers and stressors in a basin is a much more daunting challenge, because the responses are not unique or linear, and responses to multiple drivers can be synergistic or antagonistic. There have been relatively few studies that place dam impacts within a broader context of watershed changes, and those that do exist tend to rely more on historical analyses and measurements than analytical tools to weave a compelling narrative (e.g., Wallick *et al.*, 2008).

Taking the long view, then, interpreting the response of gravel-bed rivers to dams must be viewed within a broader framework that includes the full range of anthropogenic and natural drivers of system change: climatic variation, channelization, urbanization, and even efforts to restore rivers. All of these represent interventions in the fluvial system that must be accounted for if we are to understand how our rivers are changing. Analytical approaches will continue to provide useful foundations for this effort, but must be complemented by comprehensive case studies and histories drawing on diverse types of data. Every river is different, every dam is unique, and understanding the impact of the latter on the former will always have an element of art to complement the science.

## 15.5 ACKNOWLEDGEMENTS

The author would like to thank Mike Church, Gary Parker, Jack Schmidt, and Peter Wilcock for helpful discussions and data, and Sarah Lewis and Kathryn Ronnenberg for editorial and review suggestions. Reviews by David Gaeuman, David Gilvear, and Colin Rennie greatly improved the manuscript.

## 15.6 REFERENCES

Allred, T.M. and Schmidt, J.C. 1999. Narrowing by vertical accretion along the Green River near Green River, Utah. *Geological Society of America Bulletin* **111**: 1757–1772.

Ambers, R.K.R. 2007. Effects of a small, century-old dam on a second-order stream in the Virginia Piedmont. *Southeastern Geographer* **47**: 181–201.

Andrews, E.D. 1984. Bed-material entrainment and hydraulic geometry of gravel-bed rivers in Colorado. *Geological Society of America Bulletin* **95**: 371–378.

Andrews, E.D. 1986. Downstream effects of Flaming Gorge Reservoir on the Green River, Colorado and Utah. *Geological Society of America Bulletin* **97**: 1012–1023.

Baker, D.W., Bledsoe, B.P., Albano, C.M., and Poff, N.L. 2010. Downstream effects of diversion dams on sediment and hydraulic conditions of Rocky Mountain streams. *River Research and Applications* doi: 10.1002/rra.1376.

Bettess, R. and Frangipane, A. 2003. A one-layer model to predict the time development of static armour. *Journal of Hydraulic Research* **41**: 179–194.

Borland, W.M. and Miller, C.R. 1960. Sediment problems of the lower Colorado River. American Society of Civil Engineers, *Journal of the Hydraulic Division* **86**: 61–87.

Brandt, S.A. 2000. Classification of geomorphological effects downstream of dams. *Catena* **40**: 375–401.

Braudrick, C.A., Dietrich, W. E, Leverich, G.T., and Sklar, L.S. 2009. Experimental evidence for the conditions necessary to sustain meandering in coarse-bedded rivers. *Proceedings of the National Academy of Sciences, USA* **106**: 16936–16941.

Brune, G. M. 1953. Trap efficiency of reservoirs. *Transactions of the American Geophysical Union* **34**: 407–418.

Carbonneau, P.E., Lane, S.N., and Bergeron, N.E. 2004. Catchment-scale mapping of surface grain size in gravel bed rivers using airborne digital imagery. *Water Resources Research* **40**: W07202. doi: 10.1029/2003WR002759.

Carbonneau, P.E., Bergeron, N.E., and Lane, S.N. (2005) Texture-based image segmentation applied to the quantification of superficial sand in salmonid river gravels. *Earth Surface Processes and Landforms*, **30**: 121–127.

Carbonneau, P.E., Lane, S.N., and Bergeron, N.E. 2006. Feature based image processing methods applied to bathymetric measurements from airborne remote sensing in fluvial environments. *Earth Surface Processes and Landforms* **31**: 1413–1423.

Church, M. 1995. Geomorphic response to river flow regulation: case studies and time-scales. *Regulated Rivers* **11**: 3–22.

Curtis, K.E., Renshaw, C.E., Magilligan, F.J., and Dade, W.B. 2010. Temporal and spatial scales of geomorphic adjustments to reduced competency following flow regulation in bedload-dominated systems. *Geomorphology* **118**: 105–117. doi: 10.1016/j.geomorph.2009.12.012.

Dade, W.B. and Friend, P.F. 1998. Grain-size, sediment-transport regime, and channel slope in alluvial rivers. *Journal of Geology* **106**: 661–675.

DeVries, P. 2002. Bedload layer thickness and disturbance depth in streams. *Journal of Hydraulic Engineering* **128**: 983–991.

Erskine, W.D. 1985. Downstream geomorphic impacts of large dams: The case of Glenbawn Dam, NSW. *Applied Geography* **5**: 195–210.

Fearnside, P. 1997. Greenhouse-gas emissions from Amazonian hydroelectric reservoirs: the example of Brazil's Tucuruí Dam as compared to fossil fuel alternatives. *Environmental Conservation* **24**: 64–75.

Fremier, A.K., Seo, J.I., and Nakamura, F. 2009. Watershed controls on the export of large wood from stream corridors. *Geomorphology* **117**: 33–43. doi: 10.1016/j.geomorph. 2009.11.003.

Gaeuman, D., Schmidt, J.C., and Wilcock, P.R. 2005. Complex channel responses to changes in stream flow and sediment supply on the lower Duchesne River, Utah. *Geomorphology* **64**: 185–206.

Gilvear, D.J. 2003. Patterns of channel adjustment to impoundment of the upper River Spey, Scotland (1942–2000). *River Research and Applications* **19**: 1–15, doi: 10.1002/rra.741.

Graf, W. 1980. The effect of dam closure on downstream rapids. *Water Resources Research* **16**: 129–136. doi: 10.1029/WR016i001p00129.

Graham, D.J., Rice, S.P., and Reid, I. 2005. A transferable method for the automated grain sizing of river gravels. *Water Resources Research* **41**: W07020.

Gran, K. and Paola, C. 2001. Riparian Vegetation Controls on Braided Stream Dynamics. *Water Resources Research* **37**: 3275–3283. doi: 10.1029/2000WR000203.

Grant, G.E., Schmidt, J.C., and Lewis, S.L. 2003. A geological framework for interpreting downstream effects of dams on rivers. In O'Connor, J.E. and Grant, G.E., editors. *A Peculiar River*. American Geophysical Union, Water Science and Applications 7, pp. 203–219.

Gregory, K. and Park, C.C. 1974. Adjustment of river channel capacity downstream from a reservoir. *Water Resources Research* **10**: 870–873.

Haschenberger, J.K. and Church, M. 1998. Bed material transport estimated from the virtual velocity of sediment. *Earth Surface Processes and Landforms* **23**: 791–808.

Henderson, F.M. 1966. *Open Channel Flow*. New York, Macmillan.

ICOLD 1984 (1988). *World Register of Dams*. 1984 full edition (1988 update) Paris. International Commission on Large Dams.

IWPDC. International Water Power and Dam Construction. 1989. *The World's Major Dams and Hydro Plants*. Global map. Sutton, Surrey, UK, Reed Business Publishing.

IWPDC. 1994. *Handbook*. Sutton, Surrey, UK, Reed Business Publishing.

Kellerhals, R. 1982. Effect of river regulation on channel stability. In Hey, R.D., Bathurst, J.C., and Thorne, C.R., editors. *Gravel-Bed Rivers*. Chichester, John Wiley & Sons, Ltd, 685–705.

Kieffer, S.W. 1985. The 1983 hydraulic jump in Crystal Rapid: Implications for river-running and geomorphic evolution in the Grand Canyon. *Journal of Geology* **93**: 385–406.

Komura, S. and Simons, D.B. 1967. River bed degradation below dams. American Society of Civil Engineers, *Journal of the Hydraulics Division* **93**: 1–14.

Kondolf, G.M., Montgomery, D.R., Piegay, H., and Schmitt, L. 2003. Geomorphic classification of rivers and streams. In Kondolf, G.M. and Piegay, H., editors. *Tools in Fluvial Geomorphology*. Chichester, John Wiley & Sons, Ltd, pp. 171–204.

Kummu, M. and Varis, O. 2007. Sediment-related impacts due to upstream reservoir trapping, the Lower Mekong River. *Geomorphology* **85**: 275–293.

Lane, E.W. 1955. The importance of fluvial morphology in hydraulic engineering. *Proceedings of the American Society of Civil Engineers* **81**: Paper 745, 1–17.

Lawson, J.M. 1925. Effect of Rio Grande storage on river erosion and deposition. *Engineering News Record* **95**: 327–334.

Magirl, C.S., Webb, R.H., and Griffiths, P.G. 2005. Changes in the water surface profile of the Colorado River in Grand Canyon, Arizona, between 1923 and 2000. *Water Resources Research* **41**: W050201. doi: 10.1029/2003WR002519.

Marcus, W.A. and Fonstad, M.A. 2008. Optical remote mapping of rivers at sub-meter resolutions and watershed extents. *Earth Surface Processes and Landforms* **33**: 4–24. doi: 10.1002/esp

May, C.L., Pryor, B., Lisle, T.E., and Lang, M. 2009. Coupling hydrodynamic modeling and empirical measures of bed mobility to predict the risk of scour and fill of salmon redds in a large regulated river. *Water Resources Research* **45**: W05402. doi: 10.1029/2007WR006498.

Montgomery, D.R. 1999. Process domains and the river continuum. *Journal of the American Water Resources Association* **35**: 397–410.

Montgomery, D.R. and Buffington, J.M. 1998. Channel process, classification and response. In Naiman, R. and Bilby, R., editors. *River Ecology and Management*. New York, Springer Verlag, pp. 13–24.

Oud, E. 2002. The evolving context for hydropower development. *Energy Policy* **30**: 1215–1223.

Park, C.C. 1977. Man-induced changes in stream channel capacity. In Gregory, K.J., editor. *River Channel Changes*. Chichester, John Wiley & Sons, Ltd, pp. 121–144.

Parker, G. 2004. Response of the gravel bed of a mountain river to a hydrograph. *Proceedings of the International Conference on Slopeland Disaster Mitigation, Taipei, Taiwan, 5–6 October* (available at http://vtchl.uiuc.edu/people/parkerg/_private/ConferenceProceedings/Taiwan04Parker.pdf)

Parker, G. and Sutherland, A.J. 1990. Fluvial armor. *Journal of Hydraulic Research* **28**: 529–544.

Parker, G., Hassan, M., and Wilcock, P. 2007. Adjustment of the bed surface size distribution of gravel-bed rivers in response to cycled hydrographs. In Habersack, H., Piegay, H. and., Rinaldi, M., editors. *Gravel-bed Rivers VI: From Process Understanding To River Restoration*. Amsterdam, Elsevier, Developments in Earth Surface Processes 11, pp. 241–289.

Payne, J.T., Wood, A.W., Hamlet, A.F., Palmer, R.N., and Lettenmaier, D.P. 2004. Mitigating the effects of climate change on the water resources of the Columbia River Basin. *Climatic Change* **62**: 233–256.

Pemberton, E.L. 1976. Channel changes in the Colorado River below Glen Canyon Dam. In *Proceedings of the Third Federal Inter-Agency Sedimentation Conference, Denver, CO*, pp. 5-61–5-73.

Petts, G.E. 1979. Complex response of river channel morphology subsequent to reservoir construction. *Progress in Physical Geography* **3**: 329–362.

Petts, G.E. 1980. Long-term consequences of upstream impoundment. *Environmental Conservation* **I7**: 325–332.

Petts, G.E. 1984. *Impounded Rivers*. Chichester, John Wiley & Sons, Ltd.

Petts, G.E. and Gurnell, A.M. 2005. Dams and geomorphology: research progress and future directions. *Geomorphology* **71**: 27–47.

Petts, G.E. and Thoms, M.C. 1987. Morphology and sedimentology of a tributary confluence bar in a regulated river – North Tyne, UK. *Earth Surface Processes and Landforms* **12**: 433–440.

Phillips, J.D. 1994. Deterministic uncertainty in landscapes. *Earth Surface Processes and Landforms* **19**: 389–401.

Pitlick, J. and Wilcock, P.R. 2001. Flow, sediment transport, and aquatic habitat in large rivers. In Dorava, J., Fitzpatrick, F., Montgomery, D., and Palcsak, B., editors. *Geomorphic Processes and Riverine Habitat*. American Geophysical Union, Water Science and Application 4, pp. 185–198.

Poff, N. L, Olden, J.D., Merritt, D.M., and Pepin, D.M. 2007. Homogenization of regional river dynamics by dams and global biodiversity implications. *Proceedings of the National Academy of Sciences, USA* **104**: 5732–5737.

Ryan, S. 1997. Morphologic response of subalpine streams to transbasin flow diversion. *Journal of the American Water Resources Association* **33**: 839–854.

Salant, N.L., Renshaw, C.E., and Magilligan, F.J. 2006. Short and long-term changes to bed mobility and bed composition under altered sediment regimes. *Geomorphology* **76**: 43–5. doi: 10.1016/j.geomorph.2005.09.003

Schmidt, J.C. and Wilcock P. R. 2008. Metrics for assessing the downstream impacts of dams. *Water Resources Research* **44**: W04404. doi: 10.1029/2006WR005092.

Schumm, S.A. 1977. *The Fluvial System*. New York, Wiley-Interscience.

Schumm, S.A. and Lichty, R.W. 1965. Time, space, and causality in geomorphology. *American Journal of Science* **263**: 110–119.

Seo, J.I. and Nakamura, F. 2009. Scale-dependent controls upon the fluvial export of large wood from river catchments. *Earth Surface Processes and Landforms* **34**: 786–800. doi: 10.1002/esp.1765.

Seo, J.I., Nakamura, F., Nakano, D., Ichiyanagi, H., and Chun, K.W. 2008. Factors controlling the fluvial export of large woody debris, and its contribution to organic carbon budgets at watershed scales. *Water Resources Research* **44**: W04428. doi: 10.1029/2007WR006453.

Tal, M. and Paola, C. 2007. Dynamic single-thread channels maintained by the interaction of flow and vegetation. *Geology* **35**: 347–350.

Topping, D.J., Rubin, D.M., and Vierra, L.E., Jr 2000a. Colorado River sediment transport. 1. Natural sediment supply limitation and the influence of Glen Canyon Dam. *Water Resources Research* **36**: 515–542.

Topping, D.J., Rubin, D.M., Nelson, J.M., Kinzel, P.J., III, and Corson, I.C. 2000b. Colorado River sediment transport. 2. Systematic bedelevation and grain-size effects of sand supply limitation. *Water Resources Research* **36**: 543–570.

Torizzo, M. and Pitlick, J. 2004. Magnitude-frequency of bed load transport in mountain streams in Colorado. *Journal of Hydrology* **290**: 137–151.

Trush, W.J., McBain, S.M., and Leopold, L.B. 2000. Attributes of an alluvial river and their relation to water policy and management. *Proceedings of the National Academy of Sciences, USA* **97**: 11858–11863.

Van Steeter, M.M. and Pitlick, J. 1998. Geomorphology and endangered fish habitats of the upper Colorado River 1. Historic changes in streamflow, sediment load and channel morphology. *Water Resources Research* **34**: 287–302.

Wallick, J.R., Grant, G.E, Lancaster, S.T., Bolte J.P., and Denlinger, R.P. 2008. Patterns and controls on historical channel change in the Willamette River, Oregon USA. In Gupta, A.V., editor. *Large Rivers: Geomorphology and Management*. Chichester, John Wiley & Sons, Ltd, pp. 491–516.

Wampler, P. 2004. *Contrasting geomorphic responses to climatic, anthropogenic, and fluvial change across modern to millennial time scales, Clackamas River, Oregon*. Ph.D. thesis, Department of Geosciences, Oregon State University.

Whiting, P.J., Stamm, J.F., Moog, D.B., and Orndorff, R.L. 1999. Sediment-transporting flows in headwater streams. *Geological Society of America Bulletin* **111**: 450–466.

Wilcock, P.R. 1998. Two-fraction model of initial sediment motion in gravel-bed rivers. *Science*, **280**: 410–412.

Wilcock, P.R. and Kenworthy, S.T. 2002. A two-fraction model for the transport of sand–gravel mixtures. *Water Resources Research* **38**: 1194. doi: 10.1029/2001WR000684.

Wilcock, P.R. and McArdell, B.W. 1997. Partial transport of a sand-gravel mixture. *Water Resources Research* **33**: 235–245.

Wilcock, P.R., Barta, A.F., Shea, C.C. *et al.* 1996a. Observations of flow and sediment entrainment on a large gravel-bed river. *Water Resources Research* **32**: 2897–2909.

Wilcock, P.R., Kondolf, G.M., Matthews, W.V.G., and Barta A.F. 1996b. Specification of sediment maintenance flows for a large gravel-bed river. *Water Resources Research* **32**: 2911–2921.

Williams, G.P. and Wolman, M.G. 1984. *Downstream Effects of Dams on Alluvial Rivers*. United States Geological Survey, Professional Paper 1286.

Wohl, E. 2000. *Mountain Rivers*. American Geophysical Union, Water Resources Monograph 14.

Wong, M., Parker, G., DeVries, P., Brown, T.M., and Burges, S.J. 2007. Experiments on dispersion of tracer stones under lower-regime plane-bed equilibrium bed load transport. *Water Resources Research* **43**: W03440. doi: 10.1029/2006WR005172

## 15.7   DISCUSSION

### 15.7.1   Discussion by Bruce MacVicar

One interesting point from the chapter was that new construction of large dams has shifted to the developing world, with large projects in sub-Saharan Africa, India, and China. It is worth noting that the developed world is also experiencing an explosion of new dam construction, with many thousands of mini-dams being constructed specifically for stormwater management. These dams collect water from what would have been small headwater swales and streams and then control outflow to address various goals, including water quality, quantity, and sediment criteria. They are interesting cases of dams because they have no power or irrigation utility. There is considerable debate as to how best to utilize these dams to mitigate problems such as urban river degradation. It may be useful to use the available research on stream response to dams as a means of improving the design of stormwater management facilities.

### 15.7.2   Reply by Gordon E. Grant

MacVicar makes an interesting point that the locus of dam construction in developed countries has shifted towards small ("mini") dams that are being built for various purposes, including in places not normally associated with dam construction (i.e., urban environments). Although not mentioned, another arena where dam construction may be increasing is for low head or microhydropower dams. In principle, the analytical approaches discussed here should help engineers and planners predict the downstream consequences of these new developments, and design dams accordingly. It is likely that the relatively small storage volumes associated with these low head projects will have only a modest effect on an individual basis. More significant channel changes could be anticipated if large numbers of these structures are built throughout a basin, in which case the cumulative effect could be more pronounced.

# 16

# Mitigating Downstream Effects of Dams

## David Gaeuman

## 16.1 INTRODUCTION

Gordon Grant's contribution to this volume provides a wide-ranging review of the main uncertainties surrounding geomorphic responses downstream from dams, and some of the approaches to reducing those uncertainties. In particular, that discussion highlights some recent physically based models for predicting the style and probable magnitude of channel adjustments that are likely under various regulation scenarios (e.g., Brandt, 2000; Grant et al., 2003; Schmidt and Wilcock, 2008). These response models are important tools for communicating to policy-makers the linkages between changing boundary conditions, pre-regulation channel characteristics, and subsequent channel adjustments. Such communication is urgently needed if future environmental management decisions are to be better informed than those of the past. The fact that dam-induced morphological adjustments often seem to take society by surprise may be as much a function of ineffective communication as of insufficient scientific understanding. Dam building is a political and economic activity more than a scientific one. As a result, the political forces behind these projects have sometimes neglected consideration of important questions, or failed to engage the appropriate expertise for addressing them. For example, it appears that the potential for geomorphic adjustment was entirely ignored when trans-basin flow diversions exporting 90% of the inflow to California's Trinity Reservoir to the Sacramento basin were implemented in the 1960s. That flow schedule, which reduced annual daily peak flows in the Trinity River at Lewiston, California, from a pre-dam average of $526\,\mathrm{m}^3\,\mathrm{s}^{-1}$ to about $4.7\,\mathrm{m}^3\,\mathrm{s}^{-1}$ in the first few decades after dam closure, was based entirely on supplying the volume of water necessary to inundate salmonid redds on existing spawning riffles (Moffett and Smith, 1950).

Numerous instances in which dam construction and subsequent dam operations have compromised the ecological integrity of downstream reaches are documented in the geomorphic and ecological literature (e.g., Petts, 1980; Power et al., 1996; Wilcock et al., 1996; Van Steeter and Pitlick, 1998; Milhous, 1998; Erskine et al., 1999; McHenry and Pess, 2008). In such instances, resource managers are often faced with the daunting task of mitigating for the effects of flow and sediment regulation in an effort to rehabilitate downstream habitats. Although the physical principles are the same for either case, predicting the geomorphic consequences of a given dam operation scenario and mitigating for those consequences differ in some important respects. The former involves identifying the type and perhaps the magnitude of geomorphic change that will occur as a result of changes in the boundary conditions imposed at the reservoir gates. It is likely that those boundary conditions will change in known ways or be constrained to a relatively narrow range of possibilities determined by dam operating plans, e.g., peak flows will be reduced, baseflow discharge may increase, the supply of bed material from upstream will be eliminated. Mitigating for the consequences of these changes, by contrast, involves choosing specific management actions from a large number of possibilities, and specifying the magnitudes of those actions. Successful rehabilitation demands the manipulation of a complex system with many degrees of freedom to achieve and maintain a desired state. In practice, the desired state incorporates an array of physical, social, and ecological objectives, some of which may be mutually exclusive or otherwise contradictory (Schmidt et al., 1998). The overwhelming complexity inherent in balancing the full gamut of these objectives is beyond the scope of the present discussion, which is restricted to a few simple physical objectives that are relevant to gravel-bed rivers.

It is well known that dams often alter downstream physical conditions by reducing sediment transport capacity via reductions in peak flow magnitudes or, in the case of trans-basin diversions, total discharge volumes,

*Gravel-bed Rivers: Processes, Tools, Environments*, First Edition. Edited by Michael Church, Pascale M. Biron and André G. Roy.
© 2012 John Wiley & Sons, Ltd. Published 2012 by John Wiley & Sons, Ltd.

and by cutting off the supply of bed-material sediments from upstream. In gravel-bed streams, the loss of flood peak flows competent to mobilize the bed surface can cause the channel substrate and planform to become static, or frozen in place (Church, 1995). If flows are occasionally competent to transport the more mobile gravel sizes on the bed, these sizes will be exported downstream, leading to progressive bed coarsening and a decrease in bed mobility over time (Williams and Wolman, 1984). In these situations, physical rehabilitation objectives may include increasing gravel mobility and gravel supplies by implementing high flow releases and gravel augmentation. Abundant literature exists concerning the specification of flow releases intended to entrain gravel (e.g., Andrews and Nankervis, 1995; Kondolf and Wilcock, 1996; Nelson, 1996; Wilcock et al., 1996; Milhous, 1998), and no attempt to delve further into that topic will be made here. Instead, I wish to discuss some of the scientific challenges associated with managing gravel augmentations downstream from dams. I will also illustrate a few approaches to addressing those challenges with some analyses and results from the Trinity River.

## 16.2 GRAVEL AUGMENTATION DOWNSTREAM FROM DAMS

Gravel augmentation is an increasingly common practice, particularly on the west coast of the United States, beginning with supplementation of spawning riffles in the Trinity River below Lewiston Dam in the 1970s (Kondolf and Minear, 2004). In the years since, gravel augmentation programmes of one sort or another have been implemented in the Sacramento River in California and a number of tributaries to the Sacramento–San Joaquin river system, including Clear Creek and the American, Merced, Mokelumne, Tuolumne, Stanislaus, and Yuba Rivers, as well as in several streams outside of California, such as the Campbell River in British Columbia, and the Green and Cowlitz Rivers in Washington (Bunte, 2004). Early gravel additions, such as those in the Trinity River in the 1970s and 1980s took the form of artificial spawning riffles constructed upstream from grade control structures intended to keep the spawning gravel in place (Krause et al., 2010). However, modern gravel augmentations in the Trinity River and elsewhere are increasingly being implemented for geomorphic purposes. The intent of a geomorphic gravel augmentation is to supply gravel at a rate and with a particle size distribution that will support the geomorphic processes that maintain channel complexity, substrate quality, and physical habitat integrity.

Neglecting economic, logistical, and regulatory issues, the key uncertainties regarding geomorphic gravel augmentation include:

- What is the optimal range of particle sizes for gravel augmentation in a given river?
- How much gravel is needed to support geomorphic and habitat objectives over the long term?
- How will gravel added at a given location propagate downstream, and how long will it take?

### 16.2.1 Augmentation Particle Size Distribution

The first problem listed above, that of specifying the particle size distribution for augmentation gravel, is usually constrained to a relatively narrow range defined by ecological considerations, such as the spawning needs of the fish that inhabit the stream. Beyond that, particle sizes in a geomorphic augmentation must also be fine enough that the material can be entrained under the regulated flow regime. Although this second requirement can be assessed relatively easily using standard geomorphic analyses, choosing an optimum particle size distribution for a gravel augmentation is complicated by the fact that particle size is intertwined with the quantity of augmentation material that will be required. Therefore, the problem of narrowing the range of ecologically appropriate particle sizes to an optimum prescription for a given stream is best considered part of the problem of defining augmentation quantity.

### 16.2.2 Augmentation Quantity

The level of complexity involved in determining the quantity of gravel needed for an augmentation project depends on the project objectives. Quantities needed to construct a spawning riffle are relatively easy to specify by calculating the volume of the riffle, and perhaps accounting for settling of the material following placement. A review of the available documentation regarding gravel augmentation plans and designs, which, as Bunte (2004) pointed out, is rather fragmentary, suggests that the volumes of constructed riffles have determined augmentation quantities in the majority of gravel additions performed to date. This appears to have been the primary design method for augmentations on, for example, the American (USBR, 2008), Mokelumne (Pasternack et al., 2003), and Merced Rivers (Stillwater Sciences, 2006) in California and the Campbell River (DFO, 2002) in British Columbia. Augmentation volumes for the Campbell River, and perhaps the Merced River, were derived simply as the product of the spawning habitat area to be restored and the gravel depth required for spawning. In the case of the American and Mokelumne Rivers, 2D hydraulic modelling was used to ensure that designed riffles would create hydraulic conditions favourable for salmonid habitat. This approach was later applied to a gravel addition in the Trinity River in 2007 and 2008 (Brown and Pasternack, 2008).

Specifying augmentation quantities is considerably more difficult when the placed material is intended to support long-term geomorphic objectives, such as building bars and promoting alluvial dynamics in downstream reaches. On one hand, it is tempting to take the view that more geomorphic activity is always better than less, and that the best quantity for a geomorphic augmentation is the largest that is logistically and economically feasible. However, there is some evidence that bed topography, and presumably physical habitat diversity, is reduced when bed-material sediment supplies are unusually large (Lisle, 1982; Yarnell, 2006). Adding very large quantities of gravel to a stream can also interfere with recreation and navigation, and may threaten property and infrastructure through bank erosion or increased flood stages due to bed aggradation. In the interest of being ecologically, economically, and socially responsible, it is necessary to estimate a gravel augmentation rate that approximates the rate at which the receiving reach can transport it without undergoing unacceptable changes in channel geometry (the definition of "unacceptable change" obviously depends on project-specific circumstances). The task can be approached using either computational or empirical methods. Either way, monitoring, and adaptive management during project implementation are necessary to refine initial estimates.

Generally speaking, a computational approach involves calculating the gravel transport capacity for the reach under the present or anticipated regulated flow regime. For example, gravel augmentation quantities for the Green River in Washington were compared with gravel transport capacity determined by applying the Meyer-Peter and Müller sediment transport relation to the regulated hydrology downstream from Howard Hanson Dam (USACE, 2003). A major difficulty with this approach is that bedload transport rates are extremely difficult to compute accurately. Large errors can occur even for the relatively simple problem of computing total bedload transport rates (Wilcock, 2001; Barry, 2004). Accurately computing fractional transport rate, as would be needed to determine transport capacities of the specific gravel size fractions in a gravel augmentation, is even more difficult (Gaeuman et al., 2009). A somewhat more subtle difficulty with the direct application of sediment transport equations is that the relation between fractional bedload transport rates, and the quantity and size distribution of the bed-material supply is indirect. Bed-material supply characteristics and flow hydraulics control the grain-size distribution of the bed surface, which in turn mediates the transport rates that can be generated under the prevailing hydraulic conditions (Parker and Klingeman, 1982). The interdependence among bedload supply, bed surface, and transport characteristics implies that there is no straightforward solution to the computational problem – similar hydraulic conditions can produce different transport rates that correspond to different sediment supply and bed surface characteristics. This complication can be accommodated to some extent through the use of a morphodynamic model that incorporates bed surface and substrate evolution. Studies using 1D morphodynamic models have been used to evaluate gravel augmentation needs on the Sacramento and Trinity Rivers in California, although in the case of the Sacramento River, the modelling was apparently intended to evaluate the potential longevity of a gravel addition rather than to specify the augmentation quantity (Stillwater Sciences, 2007).

Two different modelling approaches have been used to develop current recommendations regarding the quantity and size distribution for long-term gravel augmentations in the Trinity River downstream from Lewiston Dam. The first of these exploited the linkage between bed surface characteristics and gravel transport/supply rates to evaluate the effectiveness of various gravel augmentation feed rates and size distributions for reducing reach-averaged bed surface particle sizes to a range that is suitable for salmonid spawning. For that analysis, the Wilcock–Crowe bedload equations (Wilcock and Crowe, 2003) were inverted (Curran and Wilcock, 2005) to compute equilibrium bed surface textures that would be expected to develop under various quantities and size distributions of bedload supply (Gaeuman, 2008). Results suggest that the long-term addition of approximately 9000 metric tons of coarse sediment between 10 and 125 mm in diameter results in a significant reduction in bed surface particle sizes with a relatively modest volume of coarse sediment added (Figure 16.1). Subsequent analysis of gravel augmentation scenarios for the Trinity River using a 1D morphodynamic model developed at the University of Illinois gave similar results (Viparelli et al., 2011).

Empirical approaches to quantifying long-term gravel needs downstream from dams involve scaling the augmentations according to gravel transport rates in unregulated streams that are similar in size and character. Although an empirical approach has the potential to side-step the numerous uncertainties and approximations that abound in computational methods, gravel transport information that is directly applicable to the reach being rehabilitated is seldom available. Reliable reports documenting long-term bedload yields in gravel-bed rivers are scarce, and few still separate the gravel load from the total bedload. That separation is critical, since the total bedload may actually be composed chiefly of sand and relatively fine gravel (Lisle, 1995; Whiting et al., 1999; Andrews, 2000). Where long-term gravel yield estimates are available, they are often derived from morphology-based sediment budgets (Martin and Church, 1995;

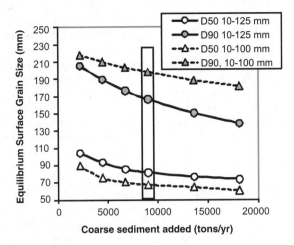

**Figure 16.1** Variation in modelled equilibrium median and 90th percentile surface grains sizes for different coarse sediment augmentation quantities and size limits in the Trinity River below Lewiston Dam. The vertical rectangle indicates the recommended augmentation volume suggested for the Trinity River by Gaeuman (2008).

McLean and Church, 1999; Ham and Church, 2000; Gaeuman *et al.*, 2003). Morphology-based methods are particularly well suited to quantifying gravel fluxes, because the volume of clast-support gravel deposits is relatively insensitive to the presence of sand in the voids or in the transported bedload.

For the Trinity River, some information regarding potential gravel transport rates under the regulated flow regime can be gleaned from bedload samples collected over the course of annual spring high flow releases at multiple locations downstream from Lewiston Dam since 2004 (Gaeuman *et al.*, 2009). These bedload samples are sieved and used to compute annual sediment loads for both sand and gravel. The most downstream sampling location is near Douglas City, California, 29 km downstream from Lewiston Dam. Four significant sediment-producing tributaries enter the river between the dam and that location. The Douglas City reach is therefore thought to be relatively unaffected by the loss of the gravel supply from the upper basin (USFW and HVT, 1999). The average annual peak flow over the 6 years from 2004 through 2009 is 190 m³ s⁻¹, a discharge magnitude with an expected return frequency of about 1.9 years under current dam operating plans (USDI, 2000). The average annual gravel flux computed for the Douglas City sampling location for the same time period is 4335 metric tons, or about half the current recommended annual rate for augmentations downstream from Lewiston Dam. The annual gravel flux at Douglas City is considerably larger than those measured upstream (e.g., the average annual flux for the same time period for a sampling location 3 km below Lewiston Dam is 1826

metric tons). Nonetheless, it is uncertain whether the gravel flux measured at Douglas City represents unencumbered gravel transport that can serve as a reference for upstream augmentation activities, as opposed to a reduced transport rate in a sediment-starved system.

In the absence of reliable data on gravel yields in appropriate reference streams, general tendencies of gravel-bed streams as expressed in regime equations may be worth considering. A set of semi-empirical hydraulic geometry relations proposed by Parker *et al.* (2007) includes the following equations useful for computing the dimensionless gravel yield at bankfull flow:

$$Q_b^* = 0.0033 Q^{*0.551} \tag{16.1}$$

$$Q = \frac{Q}{\sqrt{gD_{s50}}\, D_{s50}^2} \tag{16.2}$$

$$Q_b^* = \frac{Q_b}{\sqrt{GD_{s50}}\, D_{s50}^2} \tag{16.3}$$

where $Q^*$ is the dimensionless bankfull water discharge, $D_{s50}$ is the median gravel size on the bed surface, and $Q$ and $Q_b$ are the volumetric bankfull water discharge and bankfull gravel yield, respectively.

In this set of equations, gravel particle size ($D_{s50}$) is inextricably tied to the global scaling of the remaining variables. For constant $Q$, increasing $D_{s50}$ decreases $Q^*$, which corresponds to an increase in channel slope ($S$) according to:

$$S = 0.11 Q^{*-0.344} \tag{16.4}$$

The net result is that increasing $D_{s50}$ produces an increase in $Q_b$. This behaviour is the reverse of what would occur if grain sizes were suddenly increased in an individual real-world stream, but is appropriate for representing the fundamental scaling properties of gravel-bed streams. For present purposes, its significance is simply that particle size cannot be gamed as a free variable to explore different potential gravel yields for a given stream. Appropriate scaling must instead be derived from the geometric parameters of the stream to be analysed. An example application from the Trinity River is presented below.

Under current dam operating plans, the dominant channel-forming discharge in the Trinity River below Lewiston Dam is estimated to be between 170 and 225 $m^3 s^{-1}$ (Gaeuman, 2008). The average channel slope through the stream segments that receive gravel augmentations is about 0.0024. Using $Q = 200\,m^3\,s^{-1}$ and an average slope of 0.0024 through the stream segments that receive gravel augmentations, Equations (16.2) and (16.4) indicate that $D_{s50} = 68$ mm is consistent with the scaling of the regulated Trinity River. This is generally similar to the values of $D_{s50}$ corresponding to augmentation volumes of 9000 metric tons per year or more shown in Figure 16.1. Applying Equation (16.1) and using $D_{s50} = 68$ mm in Equation 16.3) produces an estimated bankfull gravel flux of 1143 metric tons per day. According to current dam operating plans, discharges exceeding $160\,m^3\,s^{-1}$ (0.8$Q$) will occur an average of 8.2 days per year, suggesting that the regulated Trinity River is scaled to accommodate a long-term gravel yield in the neighbourhood of 9380 metric tons per year. This result is in remarkably good agreement with the recommendation illustrated in Figure 16.1 and with those of Viparelli et al. (2011).

## 16.3 DOWNSTREAM PROPAGATION AND RESPONSE TIME

Questions concerning how and when gravel augmentations are likely to influence fluvial processes and channel morphology in downstream reaches are perhaps the most difficult of all to answer. These are essentially questions about how gravel slugs, i.e., localized large inputs of coarse sediments, evolve as the material is transported downstream. At the core of the issue is whether local concentrations of coarse sediment tend to disperse in place, or whether they tend to translate downstream as coherent waves. The implications of this uncertainty for managing gravel augmentations are profound.

Where the downstream propagation of introduced gravel is dominated by translation, managers could potentially add large quantities of gravel at a few long-term augmentation sites with the expectation that the benefits of the augmentation will eventually propagate to downstream reaches. The remaining questions would then be focused on the rate of downstream propagation and whether steps should be taken to speed up the process. If slug evolution turned out to be dominated by dispersion, on the other hand, gravel additions may yield significant benefits only in the immediate vicinity of the augmentation. Gravel particles that "peel off" the leading edge of the slug could become too widely dispersed to materially alter downstream channel morphology or the availability of habitat features such as spawning riffles. In that case, a large number of local augmentation sites or extremely large augmentation quantities may be needed to adequately cover the stream segment targeted for rehabilitation.

A number of recent studies conducted in laboratory flumes (Lisle et al., 1997; Cui et al., 2003a; Sklar et al., 2009) or by numerical simulation of transport in prismatic channels (Lisle et al., 2001; Cui et al., 2003b; Cui and Parker, 2005; Greimann et al., 2006) suggest that the evolution of gravel slugs is dominated by dispersion. However, these studies do not consider the possibility that geomorphic structures found in natural streams may cause dispersed slugs to be re-constituted at downstream storage areas. For example, dispersed gravel may re-constitute into a coherent slug where channel curvature or obstructions produce fixed bar forms, or in so-called "response reaches", where incoming sediment interacts with the existing channel morphology (Wathen and Hoey, 1998). As yet unpublished studies in the Trinity River and in Grass Valley Creek, a tributary to the Trinity River, suggest that morphological factors, as well as differences in the bed surface texture within versus downstream from a gravel slug, substantially influence slug behaviour.

### 16.3.1 Gravel Augmentation Monitoring Results

Much as with the documentation regarding gravel augmentation designs noted above, published reports detailing the performance of gravel augmentation activities are relatively scarce. Bunte (2004, p.10) wrote "final project reports are available from only a very few projects. Interim reports have either not been published yet or are rarely available. . ." This is still largely true. It may be of interest to note that, of the documents that are available via the internet or other sources, monitoring plans are considerably more common than monitoring results. Moreover, the majority of the geomorphic monitoring reports that do appear are implementation reports documenting as-built conditions. Subsequent reports describing project evolution appear infrequently on an irregular basis, or never.

The few available reports that describe the geomorphic performance of gravel augmentations tend to offer broad-brush conclusions regarding the mobility of the placed gravel. Perhaps the most informative of the currently available geomorphic monitoring reports details the results of gravel augmentations in the Green River through 2005 (USACE, 2006). According to that report, 95% of the gravel placed as berms along the active channel margin was mobilized, resulting in the creation or improvement of nearly 5 ha of new spawning habitat over a downstream distance of about 3 km. The latest available report on augmentation activities on the Tuolumne River indicates that gravel placement has improved salmonid spawning habitat, but that the placed gravel was found to be too coarse to be entrained by flows as intended (DWR, 2004). A report discussing the outcome of gravel augmentations on the Campbell River concluded only that spawning habitat in the river had increased and that methods used to place the gravel were effective (Oceans and Community Stewardship, 2002). A recent report discussing the results of gravel augmentations at seven locations along the Trinity River since 2008 shows varied results (TRRP, 2011). As of the summer of 2010, the gravel placed at most of these sites remained within several channel widths of where it was introduced, with local effects ranging from the development of greater bed and bar relief to pool filling. However, the dynamics at a few sites was characterized by almost complete mobilization and downstream dispersion of the placed material.

## 16.4 SUMMARY

The scientific challenges related to identifying and quantifying the downstream effects of dams extend to the rehabilitation of the affected stream reaches, as well as predicting the consequences of dam construction and operation. Rehabilitation efforts span a wide range of physical, ecological, and social objectives, including the restoration of fisheries resources and aquatic habitats. Gravel augmentation is increasingly being used to support geomorphic processes in stream reaches where natural gravel supplies have been cut off by dams. The aim of geomorphic gravel augmentations is to supply gravel at a rate and with a particle size distribution that will support the alluvial processes that maintain channel complexity and substrate quality, without creating new ecological or social problems.

Quantifying the rate at which a given stream can or should transport gravel of a particular size distribution is an inexact science. Gravel transport capacities can be readily calculated via a variety of methods, but computational results are potentially subject to large errors and their accuracy can be difficult to assess. Empirical data quantifying long-term gravel loads in streams is exceed-

ingly scarce in the geomorphic literature. Reports of bedload yields are somewhat more common, but are of limited use for defining typical gravel loads because bedload typically includes a large component of sand and very fine gravel. Our collective ability to define appropriate gravel augmentation rates stands to benefit greatly from targeted studies designed to quantify long-term gravel fluxes in naturally functioning streams, especially streams that might serve as references for re-habilitation. Morphology-based methods are particularly well-suited to the task.

Additional questions related to the manner and rate at which sediment slugs propagate downstream also remain to be answered. The degree to which a gravel slug translates downstream as a coherent wave has major implications for augmentation management. Most investigations into the behaviour of gravel slugs to date have been conducted in laboratory flumes or via numerical models based on simple channel geometry. Additional research examining the propagation properties of gravel concentrations in natural rivers with variable morphology and bed surface characteristics is needed.

## 16.5 REFERENCES

Andrews, E.D. 2000. Bed material transport in the Virgin River, Utah. *Water Resources Research* **36**: 585–596.

Andrews, E.D. and Nankervis, J.M. 1995. Effective discharge and the design of channel maintenance flows for gravel-bed rivers. In Costa, J.E., Miller, A.J., Potter, K.W., and Wilcock, P.R., editors, *Natural and Anthropogenic Influences in Fluvial Geomorphology*. American Geophysical Union, Geophysical Monograph **89**: 151–164.

Barry, J.J., Buffington, J.M., and King, J.G. 2004. A general power equation for predicting bed load transport in gravel bed rivers, *Water Resources Research* **40**: W10401. doi: 10.1029/2004WR003190.

Brandt, S.A. 2000. Classification of geomorphological effects downstream of dams. *Catena* **40**: 375–401.

Brown, R.A. and Pasternack, G.B. 2008. Engineered channel controls limiting spawning habitat rehabilitation success on regulated gravel-bed rivers. *Geomorphology* **97**: 631–654. doi: 10.1016/j.geomorph.2007.09.012.

Bunte, K. 2004. *Gravel mitigation and augmentation below hydroelectric dams: A geomorphological perspective*. Report to the Stream Systems Technology Center, USDA Forest Service, Rocky Mountain Research Station, Fort Collins, CO.

Church, M. 1995. Geomorphic response to river flow regulation: Case studies and time-scales. *Regulated Rivers: Research and Management* **11**: 3–22.

Cui, Y., and Parker, G. 2005. Numerical model of sediment pulses and supply disturbances in mountain rivers. *Journal of Hydraulic Engineering* **131**: 646–656.

Cui, Y., Parker, G., Lisle, T.E. *et al.* 2003a. Sediment pulses in mountain rivers: 1. Experiments. *Water Resources Research* **39**: 1239. doi: 10.1029/2002WR001803.

Cui, Y., Parker, G., Pizzuto, J., and Lisle, T.E. 2003b. Sediment pulses in mountain rivers: 2. Comparison between experiments and numerical predictions. *Water Resources Research* **39**: 1240. doi: 10.1029/2002WR001805.

Curran, J.C. and Wilcock, P.R. 2005. Effect of sand supply on transport rates in a gravel-bed channel. *Journal of Hydraulic Engineering* **131**: 961–967.

DFO (Fisheries and Oceans Canada). 2002. *Investigation into the stability of gravel placed in the Campbell River during 1997 and 1998*. Report to British Columbia Hydro and Power Authority, Burnaby, British Columbia.

DWR (California Department of Water, Resources). 2004. *Tuolumne River La Grange gravel addition project Phase II geomorphic monitoring report*. California Department of Water Resources, San Joaquin District, Fresno, CA.

Erskine, W.D., Terrazzolo, N., and Warner, R.F. 1999. River rehabilitation from the hydrogeomorphic impacts of a large hydro-electric power project: Snowy River, Australia. *Regulated Rivers: Research and Management* **15**: 3–24.

Gaeuman, D. 2008. *Recommended Quantities and Gradations for Long-term Coarse Sediment Augmentation Downstream from Lewiston Dam*. Trinity River Restoration Program, Technical Monograph TM-TRRP-2008-2, Weaverville, CA.

Gaeuman, D., Andrews, E.D., Krause, A., and Smith, W. 2009. Predicting fractional bedload transport rates: application of the Wilcock–Crowe equations to a regulated gravel-bed river. *Water Resources Research* **45**: W06409. doi: 10.1029/2008WR007320.

Gaeuman, D., Schmidt, J.C., and Wilcock, P.R. 2003. Evaluation of in-channel gravel storage with morphology-based gravel budgets developed from planimetric data. *Journal of Geophysical Research* **108**: 6001. doi: 10.1029/2002JF000002.

Grant, G.E., Schmidt, J.C., and Lewis, S.L. 2003. A geological framework for interpreting downstream effects of dams on rivers. In O'Connor, J.E., and Grant, G.E., editors. *A Peculiar River*. American Geophysical Union, Water Science and Application 7, pp. 203–219.

Greimann, B., Randle, T., and Huang, J. 2006. Movement of finite amplitude sediment accumulations. *Journal of Hydraulic Engineering* **132**: 731–736, doi: 10.1061/(ASCE)0733-9429(2006)132:7.(731)

Ham, D.G. and Church, M. 2000. Bed-material transport estimated from channel morphodynamics: Chilliwack River, British Columbia. *Earth Surface Processes and Landforms* **25**: 1123–1142.

Kondolf, G.M. and Minear, J.T. 2004. *Coarse Sediment Augmentation on the Trinity River below Lewiston Dam: Geomorphic Perspectives and Review of Past Projects*. Report to the Trinity River Restoration Program, Weaverville, CA.

Kondolf, G.M. and Wilcock, P.R. 1996. The flushing flow problem: Defining and evaluating objectives. *Water Resources Research* **32**: 2589–2599.

Krause, A., Wilcock, P.R., and Gaeuman, D. 2010. One hundred and fifty years of sediment manipulation on the Trinity River, CA. *Proceedings of the 9th Federal Interagency Sedimentation Conference, 27 June–1 July, 2010, Las Vegas, NV* (CD/ROM).

Lisle, T.E. 1982. Effects of aggradation and degradation on riffle-pool morphology in natural gravel channels, Northwestern California. *Water Resources Research* **18**: 1643–1651.

Lisle, T.E. 1995. Particle size variation between bed load and bed material in natural gravel bed channels. *Water Resources Research* **31**: 1107–1118.

Lisle, T.E., Cui, Y., Parker, G., Pizzuto, J.E., and Dodd, A.M. 2001. The dominance of dispersion in the evolution of bed material waves in gravel-bed rivers. *Earth Surface Processes and Landforms* **26**: 1409–1420.

Lisle, T.E., Pizzuto, J.E., Ikeda, H., *et al.* 1997. Evolution of a sediment wave in an experimental channel. *Water Resources Research* **33**: 1971–1981.

Martin, Y. and Church, M. 1995. Bed-material transport estimated from channel surveys: Vedder River, British Columbia. *Earth Surface Processes and Landforms* **20**: 347–361.

McHenry, M.L. and Pess, G.R. 2008. An overview of monitoring options for assessing the response of salmonids and their aquatic ecosystems in the Elwha River following dam removal. *Northwest Science* **82**: 29–47.

McLean, D.G. and Church, M. 1999. Sediment transport along the lower Fraser River: 2. Estimates based on the long-term gravel budget. *Water Resources Research* **35**: 2549–2559.

Milhous RT. 1998. Modelling of instream flow needs: The link between sediment and aquatic habitat. *Regulated Rivers: Research and Management* **14**: 79–94.

Moffett, J.W. and Smith, S.E. 1950. *Biological Investigations of the Fishery Resources of Trinity River, California*. United States Fish and Wildlife Service, Special Scientific Report: Fisheries 12, Washington DC.

Nelson, J.M. 1996. Predictive techniques for river channel evolution and maintenance. *Water Air and Soil Pollution* **90**: 321–333.

Oceans and Community Stewardship. 2002. *Campbell River 2001 Spawning Gravel Placement*. Final Report.

Pasternack, G.B., Wang, C.L., and Merz, J. 2003. Application of a 2D hydrodynamic model to design of reach-scale spawning gravel replenishment on the Mokelumne River, *California*. *River Research and Applications* **20**: 205–225. doi: 10.1002/rra.748.

Parker, G. and Klingeman, P.C. 1982. On why gravel bed streams are paved. *Water Resources Research* **18**: 1409–1423.

Parker, G., Wilcock, P.R., Paola, C., Dietrich, W.E., and Pitlick, J. 2007. Physical basis for quasi-universal relations describing bankfull hydraulic geometry of single-thread gravel bed rivers. *Journal of Geophysical Research* **112**: F04005. doi: 10.1029/2006JF000549.

Petts, G.E. 1980. Long-term consequences of upstream impoundment. *Environmental Conservation* **7**: 325–332.

Power, M.E., Dietrich, W.E., and Finlay, J.C. 1996. Dams and downstream aquatic biodiversity: potential food web consequences of hydrologic and geomorphic change. *Environmental Management* **20**: 887–895.

Schmidt, J.C. and Wilcock, P.R. 2008. Metrics for assessing the downstream effects of dams. *Water Resources Research* **44**: W04404. doi: 10.1029/2006WR005092.

Schmidt, J.C., Webb, R.H., Valdez, R.A., Marzolf, G. R., and Stevens, L.E. 1998. Science and values in river restoration in the Grand Canyon. *BioScience* **48**: 735–747.

Sklar, L.S., Fadde, J., Venditti, J.G. *et al.* 2009. Translation and dispersion of sediment pulses in flume experiments simulating gravel augmentation below dams. *Water Resources Research* **45**: W08439. doi: 10.1029/2008WR007346.

Stillwater Sciences. 2006. *Merced River Ranch channel-floodplain restoration: Design rationale*. Report to CALFED Ecosystem Restoration Program, Sacramento, California. Technical Memorandum 8.

Stillwater Sciences. 2007. *Sacramento River ecological flows study: The unified gravel and sand model (TUGS) simulation of the Sacramento River between Keswick Dam and Clear Creek*. Final Report to The Nature Conservancy and the CALFED Ecosystem Restoration Program, Sacramento, CA.

TRRP (Trinity River Restoration, Program). 2011. *WY2010 Implementation Monitoring Report*. TRRP Technical Report, Weaverville, CA. Contact the author or the TRRP office (http://www.trrp.net) for a copy of the report.

USACE (United States Army Corps of, Engineers). 2003. *Green River fish habitat restoration pilot project – Zone 1*. Final Design Report, USACE Seattle District.

USACE (United States Army Corps of, Engineers). 2006. *Howard Hanson Dam additional water storage project. Zone 1 fish habitat restoration project, Green River, Washington*. Water Year 2005 Monitoring Report, USACE Seattle District.

USBR (United States Bureau of, Reclamation). 2008. *Lower American River salmonid spawning gravel augmentation and side-channel habitat establishment program*. Final Environmental Assessment, USBR Mid-Pacific Region, Sacramento, California.

USDI (United States Department of, Interior). 2000. *Record of Decision: Trinity River Mainstem Fishery Restoration Final EIS/EIR*. Washington DC.

USFW and HVT (United States Fish and Wildlife Service and Hoopa Valley, Tribe). 1999. *Trinity River Flow Evaluation Study Final Report*. Report to the US Department of Interior, Washington, DC.

Van Steeter, M.M. and Pitlick, J.P. 1998. Geomorphology and endangered fish habitat of the upper Colorado River 1. Historic changes in streamflow, sediment load, and channel morphology. *Water Resources Research* **34**: 287–302.

Viparelli, E., Gaeuman, D., Wilcock, P.R., and Parker, G. 2011. A model to predict the evolution of a gravel bed river under an imposed cyclic hydrograph and its application to the Trinity River. *Water Resources Research* **47**: W02533. doi: 10.1029/2010WR009164.

Wathen, S.J. and Hoey, T.B. 1998. Morphological controls on the downstream passage of a sediment wave in a gravel-bed stream. *Earth Surface Processes and Landforms* **23**: 715–730.

Whiting, P.J., Stamm, J.F., Moog, D.B., and Orndorff, R.L. 1999. Sediment-transporting flows in headwater streams. *Geological Society of America Bulletin* **111**: 450–466.

Williams, G.P. and Wolman, M.G. 1984. *Downstream Effects of Dams on Alluvial Rivers*. United States Geological Survey, Professional Paper 1286.

Wilcock, P.R. 2001. Toward a practical method for estimating sediment-transport rates in gravel-bed rivers, *Earth Surface Processes and Landforms* **26**: 1395–1408.

Wilcock, P.R. and Crowe, J.C. 2003. Surface-based transport model for mixed-size sediment. *Journal of Hydraulic Engineering* **129**: 120–128.

Wilcock, P.R., Kondolf, G.M., Matthews, W.V.G., and Barta, A.F. 1996. Specification of sediment maintenance flows for a large gravel-bed river. *Water Resources Research* **32**: 2911–2921.

Yarnell, S.M., Mount, J.F., and Larsen, E.W. 2006. The influence of relative sediment supply on riverine habitat heterogeneity. *Geomorphology* **80**: 310–324. doi: 10.1016/j.geomorph.2006.03.005.

# Ecological Aspects of Gravel-bed Rivers

# 17

# River Geomorphology and Salmonid Habitat: Some Examples Illustrating their Complex Association, from Redd to Riverscape Scales

Michel Lapointe

## 17.1 INTRODUCTION

Given the wealth of research in recent decades on fish habitats in running waters, a review of this vast field (let alone of salmonid habitat science) would be so superficial as to be practically useless. What follows has a different and more limited ambition. This opinion piece argues for the need for geomorphologists interested in river ecosystems to develop an awareness of some of the complexities implicit in "riverine habitat", as a scientific concept. I also hope to highlight the unique contributions that river geomorphologists can make to understanding fish habitats. This will be done by illustrating typical methodological challenges incurred in research on salmonid habitats, in particular spawning habitat, using examples ranging from micro to larger "riverscape" scales. This chapter presents less a review of what we know and more a discussion of what we would like to know about salmonid habitat, along with the author's views on some of the emerging challenges in advancing on this front.

Like many other physical scientists who become interested in river ecosystem science, my original approach to habitat questions was quite direct and limited: I would ask an ecologist colleague what type of instream or riparian habitat patch was used by a given organism. I would then volunteer back some geomorphic insights into where else such patches could be found, how they were formed and what would happen to them under given anthropogenic or hydro-climatic disturbances. Indeed, such casual exchanges often constitute a natural starting point to rich interdisciplinary collaborations.

However, in interdisciplinary research, an overly superficial engagement with collaborators' disciplinary models does constrain collaboration. The budding "habitat geomorphologist" may discover that the (to her or him) exciting insights supplied on that particular habitat patch, although welcome, may be of limited immediate interest to an ecologist collaborator, who has many possible factors to ponder in understanding a fish population's current state. The ecologist may be less concerned about this particular habitat's availability than with some specific biotic interaction with another organism. Or he or she may be focusing attention on a more limiting habitat type used by a different life stage of this same fish. And lack of interdisciplinary engagement generally works both ways: the geomorphologist's richer textured understanding of the organization and physical dynamics of riverine habitats may lead her/him to formulate hypotheses related to a river's "landscape ecology" or to ecological disturbance pathways that may not be easily appreciated or seem salient to the collaborating ecologist, possibly less versed in landscape structure and process.

This paper argues that a geomorphologist should acquire a relatively rich view of the diversity of riverine habitats. Familiarity with ecological principles is necessary for effective fundamental work on river ecosystem science or, more simply, for applied, collaborative work on impact mitigation or habitat restoration (see also Rice *et al.*, 2010a, 2010b). In what follows, I will illustrate these points with selected examples of how various geomorphic processes play key roles in fashioning salmonid habitat quality and distribution and I will refer

*Gravel-bed Rivers: Processes, Tools, Environments*, First Edition. Edited by Michael Church, Pascale M. Biron and André G. Roy.
© 2012 John Wiley & Sons, Ltd. Published 2012 by John Wiley & Sons, Ltd.

readers to some recent literature on these topics. Examples given do not aim to review the breadth of current knowledge; rather, they are used to illustrate the complex scientific questions and methodological problems underlying fundamental work at this interface. The author assumes full responsibility for a considerable amount of speculation in this chapter and for leaving uncited, regrettably, much interesting and recent work on river salmonid habitat, broadly defined.

### 17.1.1   Habitat Preferences are Complex and Contextual

Habitat science is the study of relations among species and their environments. In some applications, the river engineer or geomorphologist may be well justified in limiting the biological focus to estimating mathematical "fish production equivalents", in the form of "weighted habitat units" (WUA) for any fish species and life stage of interest. However, when preferences are poorly defined for a particular fish–ecosystem pair, and when deeper collaboration with local ecologists is possible, it may be useful to consider what can be inferred from observed fish data gathered from a complex river environment. This is the approach illustrated in this chapter.

The geomorphologist or river engineer engaged along this path may very rapidly detect a lack of enthusiasm on the part of research ecologists for habitat suitability and preference models, such as those used in the classic Instream Flow Incremental Methodology (IFIM; Bovee et al., 1998). There are many reasons for this which cannot be summarized here. Some key ones are discussed in Anderson et al. (2006). Among them is the complexity of the habitat preference concept itself. Although an organism's environmental "tolerances" can be tested in the laboratory, habitat preferences are not in general fixed and directly exportable across ecosystems. Habitat "preferences" are in general highly contextual: antecedent disturbances, current environmental conditions, and status of predators, competitors, and local food sources can all modify detailed habitat preferences (Southwood, 1977; Warren and Liss, 1980; Frissell et al., 1986). Preferences can only be observed in specific, natural contexts while, hopefully, some general lessons are learned despite their observed plasticity. This is particularly true for salmonids, a group in which many species are extremely "adaptable", across populations and individuals, in their habitat choices, life histories, and overall phenotype (which is any observable trait or characteristic under the control of an organism's genotype interacting with its environment) (Taylor, 1991). For example, individual fish in the same population can differ in their choice of anadromy or stream resident life cycle (see Zimmerman and Reeves, 2000; 2002) and

various "runs" of a given species in the same river may use different seasonal cues for spawning, etc.

Biologists know that habitat preferences are not really fixed in time; neither over ecological time (simply put, the time scale of population cycles, as environment, resources, competition, and predation pressures vary) nor, even less, over evolutionary time scales, as species evolve by natural selection. Clearly, tolerances and preferences are aspects of an organism's phenotype that can evolve over time. In the case of small, relatively isolated populations of salmonids, significant changes in phenotype have been observed over just a few decades (for an example, see Koskinen et al., 2002). *For such reasons, Habitat preferences have been described as self-organizing properties of biological systems and thus are inherently difficult to predict* (Anderson et al., 2006). In effect, the habitat used by a given organism (A) depends on how other biota (B, C) are using the shared environment, both now and over recent evolutionary time. Moreover, with regard to the latter organisms (B, C), the converse is also true (their habitat use adjusts in response to A).

In summary, habitat is a complex interaction between an organism and its biotic and abiotic environments, at one point in evolution, and the habitat use in any given system may be difficult to predict in detail from observations in other systems. Although applied work must rely on some *a priori* insights on habitat use and value, the habitat geomorphologist should have an open mind and seek local insight from fish ecologists (and wildlife technicians) into such details as changes in the local fish population's habitat use with population pressures and species invasions, as well as with atypical hydrological or climatic contexts.

Recent and impassioned debates on the various issues complicating the hydraulic modelling of stream habitat quality can be found in Lancaster and Downes (2010a), with successive replies in Lamouroux et al. (2010) and Lancaster and Downes (2010b). These are continuing debates concerning the extent to which observations of the very local conditions (patch characteristics) in which animals are found under given "fair weather" conditions can be trusted to yield solid predictions of an animal's ability to grow and reproduce in various habitats. While hydraulic science is ultimately based on fundamental, physically based governing equations, some may argue that ecohydraulics modellers unjustifiably treat habitat preference curves as if they were analogous to "ecological governing equations", with similar predictive power to mass or momentum conservation laws.

In the next section 17.2, some of the complexities in defining habitat preferences will be illustrated, using current research on salmonid spawning habitat, a topic close to the heart of fluvial geomorphologists naturally interested in gravel substrate, erosion, sediment transport, and barforms. The object of Section 17.2 is not to fully review this topic (see, for example, Kondolf, 2000; Moir *et al.*, 2004), but to illustrate some of the complex, multiscale inferential issues and questions increasingly raised in investigating salmonid spawning habitat. To end the chapter, in Section 17.3 I will broaden discussion to a landscape ecology perspective, where fish production depends not only on spawning habitat, but also on the proximity of other important salmonid habitats, such as rearing and refuge habitats. A common thread, which I hope is amply demonstrated in both Sections 17.2 and 17.3, is the need to look beyond patch scale conditions to understand fish habitats. Hotspots of spawning activity or of fish abundances need to be understood in their broader "riverscape" context (Ward, 1997): the hotspot may depend as much on attributes of the river reach, valley segment, or tributary proximity as on local substrate, depth, and velocity at patch scale.

## 17.2  SALMONID SPAWNING HABITAT

Spawning habitat was chosen as the focus of this first section (rather than salmonid rearing or refuge habitats, briefly discussed in Section 17.3) because of the geomorphologist's natural interest in processes controlling reach-scale morphological and sedimentary patterns, factors directly implicated in spawning site selection. This will allow me, I hope, to illustrate in more detail the multiscale aspects of the geomorphic controls on redd site selection. However, one has to be cautious about any generalization on salmonid habitats. There are many distinct salmonid species and most of these include geographically widespread populations which use as spawning habitats combinations of lakes, running waters, and coastal environments. No one pattern may apply everywhere, as will also be illustrated in this section.

Various human disturbances (damming, forestry, urban expansion, etc.) can degrade salmonid reproductive habitat in rivers. To prioritize protection of the most important reproductive habitats, one first has to locate them. As will be seen, spawning activity in some populations is clustered, leaving unused many bars with spawning substrate and flow conditions that seem otherwise suitable. What factors explain such clustering? More broadly, how do we determine where the highest-quality spawning habitats are located for a given population? As will be shown below, the answers to this simple question are obscured by various methodological and conceptual issues.

In theory, the quality of spawning habitat at a patch in a given salmonid ecosystem could be measured by "*in situ*" observations of embryo incubation success up to emergence from the gravel. However, such data are rarely available. Custom-designed, artificial incubating cells rarely fully replicate natural conditions (in terms of susceptibility to fines ingress or to scour disturbance, factors which depend on cell design). Critically, instream data on "egg to emergence" survival are rare and generally of poor reliability. Even where female egg deposition estimates can be made at individual redds, *in situ* capture of live fry in flowing water and during week-long emergence periods is a major challenge. By default, the basis for our core knowledge of salmonid spawning habitat thus lies in observed trends in both precise location and substrate conditions at selected redd sites, complemented by a general understanding of embryo incubation tolerances gained from limited laboratory experiments.

Because of the general absence of good, *in-situ*, "survival to emergence" data, we must presume when analysing such spawning site data that sites selected by fish are most often of good reproductive quality. This is a reasonable presumption from a biological standpoint, for a few reasons. As salmonids display homing to natal streams and some degree of spawning site fidelity (Quinn *et al.*, 2006), adults that choose poor reproductive habitat see their progeny preferentially eliminated, decreasing the pool of adults returning to the poor quality spawning reach. Moreover, in addition to imprinting of location, inherited site-selection preferences based on local environmental cues must play a role. Thus, the subset of a cohort of embryos surviving as adult spawners is, by implication, more likely to have retained from their parents a genotype and phenotype which favours instinctive spawning in conditions suitable for reproductive success. In some systems, however, competition for relatively scarce spawning habitat (or environmental disturbances, such as new obstructions to migration) are known to lead spawners to lay eggs in settings that are atypical or clearly marginal in quality. Such limits must be borne in mind when considering unusual redd locations.

### 17.2.1  Some Inherent Challenges in Understanding Spawning Habitat Selection

Spawning habitat preferences are defined in terms of environmental characteristics (which must be inferred from our main "observable", the locations of selected spawning sites). As we will see, inferring the former (preferences) from the latter (observed redd locations) requires complex hypothesis formulation and testing. This involves testing a variety of possible controls on progeny survival that act at the patch, reach, and segment scales, controls which I will describe in the following subsections.

Any given redd and surrounding reach has, associated with it, multiple layers of biotic and abiotic characteristics and related cues that the fish may detect and seek out, singly or in combination. The requirements, long documented in the literature (Kondolf and Wolman, 1993), for substrate pavement sizes that are not too coarse (so as to inhibit redd excavation by the female) and of fine sediment contents that are not so high as to "entomb" embryos, may represent physically based tolerances and, as will be seen, leave room for the existence of narrower preferences. Are observed spawning sites selected mostly for surface or subsurface substrate composition; for particular depth and velocity of flow over the redd; for the strength, chemistry and temperature of shallow, subsurface (hyporheic) flow around the redd; or because of location with respect to other habitat features useful to the emergent fry? Spawning sites are likely selected based on some weighting of all of these factors and the weightings may well change with species and ecosystem. Note also that given the multiscale processes at work here (ranging from patch-scale substrate composition, to reach-scale controls on pool-riffle morphology, hyporheic flow, and fine sediment transport patterns, etc.) testing relevant hypotheses requires habitat characterizations that are both high resolution and large in spatial extent (cf. the challenge of data acquisition at "intermediate spatial scales" described by Fausch et al. (2002)).

The following sections describe in some detail various questions raised in understanding spawning-site preferences at the patch and reach scales. Section 17.3 of this chapter will then broaden to a discussion of the challenges of understanding habitat complementation and salmonid landscape ecology at watershed scales.

### 17.2.1.1 When and how does Fish Embryo Mortality Occur?

The incubation period for salmonid embryos is generally many months long (particularly for late fall, low temperature spawners) and key incubating habitat characteristics that influence embryo development (such as fine sediment content, oxygen levels, and temperature near egg pockets) can change over this extended incubation period. This poses real challenges for understanding the effective controls on development and mortality rates, ultimate controls of habitat selection. Thus, little is known concerning the phase of embryo incubation ("pre-eyed, eyed, hatched, re-sorbed yolk sac stages") at which limiting conditions may be reached in some of the variables listed above. Nor do we have the ability yet to observe, in situ, such thresholds in developmental processes and mortality events.

Of particular interest to geomorphologists, in this regard, is the relevant time frame to study sedimentary composition around egg pockets. Grain size conditions at freshly created redds and the sedimentology of the

ambient, undisturbed bar can both be documented through redd surveys immediately after spawning. But, in general, both these may differ from conditions affecting embryo development during the incubation and fry emergence seasons, over post-spawning weeks or months. Strong surface currents at spawning sites generally flush away substantial fines (especially the finest fractions) from redds freshly created by the spawning female (Kondolf et al., 1993). Barring subsequent fines infiltration, conditions in fresh redds are often compatible with high survival to emergence (Tonina and Buffington, 2009a; Zimmermann and Lapointe, 2005). The implication is that what really matters with regard to clogging of egg pocket flow or entombment of embryos are fines infiltration events that occur post-spawning, due to freshets over the incubation months separating egg pocket creation from fry emergence.

To summarize, we rarely have access to redd-specific data on overall survival to emergence or, even less, to data on changing biotic and abiotic conditions in egg pockets over the entire incubation period. In this context, the problem of determining what are the effective local conditions controlling reproductive success, the driver of site preference, is, to say the least, non-trivial. *In effect, we must attempt to infer, purely from site-selection data, an animal's weightings for various habitat characteristics or "cues", detectable at patch and reach scales, cues that themselves correlate with probabilities of reproductive success over the months separating spawning from emergence.* This reflects a broader challenge in habitat science: in many cases, we can only directly observe an animal's site selection and activity at the time of sighting, whereas processes at the site controlling growth and survival over longer periods are much harder to study.

### 17.2.1.2 Is Spawning Habitat Quality Mainly Defined by Substrate Texture?

In applied, habitat conservation work, geomorphologists tend to define good spawning habitat mainly in terms of sediment texture and location with respect to bar forms (e.g. "spawners seek clean gravels of the right size located at the pool 'tailout', approaching the following riffle crest"). In part, this focus on grain sizes and fines content is a natural response to the fines overload driving spawning habitat deterioration (often due to forestry, flow regulation, or road work impacts on which the geomorphologist is consulted; Waters, 1995; Greig et al., 2005). However, the focus put on sediment texture appears to be too narrow. This issue matters considerably, because the most intensely used and productive spawning habitats (those providing, in aggregate, the most population support) may fail to be protected if too broad a definition of what constitutes good habitat is used (for example, one focusing just on bar texture). Overestimates of spawning habitat availability may, in practice, lead to less efficient habitat conservation.

A notable theme in the recent literature on spawning habitat has been the recognition that, for some salmonid populations, other, more complex factors, beyond patch-scale substrate composition (and depth and velocity of overlying flow) appear to play important roles in spawning habitat selection (Geist and Dauble, 1998; Knapp and Preisler, 1999). Based on an analysis of redd data of fall spawning, chinook salmon (*Onchorhynchus tshawytscha*) along the Columbia River, Geist *et al.* (2000) show that spawning habitat use is often highly clustered in a distinct subset of areas within the range of potential habitat with suitable substrate, depth, and velocity conditions conventionally used to define quality spawning sites. Such a clustering effect is supported by similar findings elsewhere (Chapman, 1943; Vronskiy, 1972).

In a related vein, after analyzing the statistical performance of various redd site predictors on a large set of Chinook redd data from central Idaho streams, Isaak *et al.* (2007) concluded that the best predictors of selected sites were not the traditional metrics of habitat quality (preferred substrate, depth, and velocity), but rather what they termed "spatial characteristics" of the habitat, specifically size of spawning area and "interconnectivity" across spawning bars. The authors inferred from this the possible existence of "biogenic" clustering of redd sites,

presumably based on the extent of spawning habitat available for large congregations of spawners.

For Atlantic salmon (*Salmo salar*), there is also evidence from redd data along Quebec rivers that spawning habitat preferences may not be restricted only by substrate size characteristics (although these do impose broad limits, akin to tolerances). Instead, one often observes that redd numbers and egg deposition can be concentrated in a subset of bars and reaches within the "good substrate" window (Figure 17.1). Redd densities can attain extreme values in such favoured reaches for reasons that appear to be unexplained by substrate or local depth and velocity conditions. The next sections explore what might be some of the non-textural determinants of spawning site selection in a few studied salmonid populations.

### 17.2.1.3 Factors that Impact Reproductive Success, beyond Substrate Patch Characteristics

"Neighborhood effects" are invoked in landscape ecology when the use of a specific location may be related more to the use of nearby habitats than to the characteristics of the habitat itself (Isaak *et al.*, 2007; Mull and Wilzbach, 2007). An increasingly recognized challenge in ecology is matching the spatial scales of habitat measurements to the scales at which organisms perceive and respond to the environment (Keitt and Urban, 2005). Part of the poor predictive power of conventional, patch-scale spawning habitat preferences just mentioned may

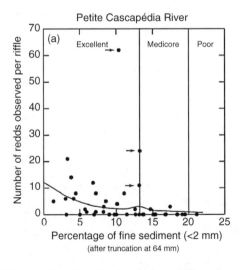 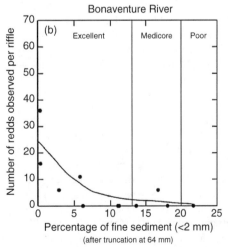

**Figure 17.1** Number of redds observed per riffle over two years plotted against the percentage of fine material in the substrate of the Petite Cascapedia (a) and Bonaventure (b) rivers. *Sites marked with arrows correspond to anomalous riffles situated at the head of alluvial islands.* Quality categories are based on the Fredle Index (Lotspeich and Everest, 1981) for spawning substrate. Samples were truncated at 64 mm. Redd locations were surveyed in 1998–1999 in the Petite Cascapedia River and 1999–2000 in the Bonaventure River. Lowess trend lines are fitted to the data.

be due to a scale mismatch concerning broader characteristics that control local reproductive success.

Beyond texture, depth and velocity at the spawning patch itself, other reach and segment-scale characteristics may theoretically affect reproductive success at a redd. An egg pocket in a given cobble patch is embedded in a complex, multiscale environment that has a number of more or less independent abiotic characteristics, all of which can play some role in enhancing progeny survival, and hence the spawner's "fitness" through natural selection. Importantly, many of these characteristics are not captured by local, redd-site data. These may include the amount of sand in pools upstream (which can affect fines loads over and thus ingress into the redd, during incubation season freshets) and the overall reach-scale bed morphology, particularly the vertical and lateral extent of the spawning bar complex. In pool-riffle type reaches, anomalous bar volume and morphology in channel inflection zones affect local surface water slopes between the successive pools that frame the bar complex. This water slope controls depth/velocity conditions of surface flow over redds, often located upstream of riffle crests; these hydraulic conditions then affect turbulence and the fines infiltration regime into the egg pocket.

Most importantly, this local, pool-to-pool slope also affects hydraulic head gradients that drive hyporheic water through gravel interstices within the bar and control flow rates around any egg pocket in the bar (Zimmermann and Lapointe, 2005; Buffington and Tonina, 2009; Tonina and Buffington, 2009b). Hyporheic flow below the bar surface in this context involves a mixture of surface water that penetrates the bed at bar heads with variable proportions of groundwater seeping upward into the bed. The hyporheic flow percolating around egg pockets can have variable speed, temperature, and chemistry, depending on the local subsurface gradients and the mix of surface and groundwater at play, factors which can also depend on stratigraphic and topographic factors at valley and reach scales. Notably, the surface water to groundwater proportions of the hyporheic mix around the egg pocket at a particular site affects the oxygen fluxes to embryos (recent, surface water may be better oxygenated) as well as the incubation temperature regime (groundwater is warmer than surface water in winter, cooler in summer). An illustration of this variability will be provided in Section 17.2.1.5. Dissolved oxygen and temperature levels in hyporheic water, in turn, directly affect the embryo development rate, and thus the date and condition at hatching and emergence (Acornley, 1999; Youngson et al., 2004; Grieg 2007).

There are compelling reasons why the physico-chemical characteristics of hyporheic water at redd sites should matter to site selection. It is clear from salmonid biology that fry mortality is very high in the first weeks after emergence, while fry condition and timing of emergence are crucial to access to food resources in early summer (Milner et al., 2003). Thus site factors determining incubation conditions should exert strong selective pressures (and thus may be reflected in spawning site preferences). In short, "reproductive success" depends not only on factors affecting the percentage of eggs surviving to emergence, but also, in principle, on factors such as hyporheic temperature that affect the timing of emergence.

### 17.2.1.4   A "New Frontier": Hyporheic Flow Patterns as Controls on Spawning Site Selection

Recent literature discussed in Section 17.2.1.3 suggests that factors beyond patch-scale substrate texture and overlying depth and velocity affect redd site selection. As the temperature, oxygen content, and velocity of interstitial flow through the egg pocket control the egg incubation processes, increasing attention is being given to the link between redd site selection and local hyporheic flow characteristics just below the bar surface.

Based on piezometer and morphological data collected near observed chinook redd sites in the Hanford reach of the Columbia River, Geist and Dauble (1998) (Table 17.1) argue that overall bar morphology as well as location with respect to bar form are important determinants of redd site choice. These factors are said to affect both the strength and direction (upward or downward) of hydraulic gradients below the gravel–water interface, in turn influencing hyporheic flow rates, dissolved oxygen content, and incubation temperature regimes around eggs at potential redd sites.

Geist et al. (2000) noted that chinook redds in the Columbia River are often clustered in areas of distinct channel complexity. In such areas, alluvial islands and split channels typically translate into higher hydraulic resistance and higher, reach-scale water slope. This, in turn, implies greater downstream hydraulic gradients below channel beds and bars, driving stronger hyporheic flows (Buffington and Tonina, 2009; Tonina and Buffington, 2009b). Similarly, for Atlantic salmon, there is also field evidence (Coulombe-Pontbriand and Lapointe, 2004a and Figure 17.1) that redds are more abundant near anomalously voluminous mid-channel bars or on the upstream sides of islands, where local hyporheic gradients are steeper and where one might expect strong hyporheic flow (assuming constant permeability).

Not much is known, however, about the differential effects on reproductive success of upwelling, downwelling, or streamwise interstitial flow of similar strength (or of the effects of the precise mix of groundwater and surface water within the local hyporheic water). Similarly, little is known about whether these effects

**Table 17.1** List of typical physical habitat parameters used in previous studies to describe fall chinook salmon (*Oncorhynchus tshawytscha*) spawning habitat (empirically derived) and additional characteristics whose inclusion were suggested by Geist and Dauble (1998)[a]

| Traditional characteristics | Additional characteristics |
| --- | --- |
| Water depth | Longitudinal and transverse slope |
| Water velocity | Channel morphology (channel pattern, channel islands, bedforms, and lateral activity) |
| Substrate size | Hyporheic temperature, dissolved oxygen, pH, and electrical conductivity |
| | Near-bed velocity gradient |
| | Vertical hydraulic gradient (upwelling and downwelling) |
| | Substrate depth, stability, permeability, and porosity |
| | Hydraulic conductivity and transmissivity |
| | Presence or absence of natural bedforms (e.g., dunes and/or ripples) and their type, shape, amplitude, frequency, etc. |
| | Rate of bedform migration |
| | Presence of groundwater springs |

[a] Traditional characteristics are usually measured at the microhabitat scale (100 m) in large rivers. Additional characteristics could be measured at various spatial scales. Reproduced, with permission, from Geist, D.R. and Dauble, D.D. 1998. Redd site selection and spawning habitat use by fall chinook salmon: the importance of geomorphic features in large rivers. *Environmental Management* **22**: 655–669. doi: 10.1007/s002679900137.

vary in importance across salmonid species, populations, and river contexts. As will be seen, this is an aspect of spawning preferences much in need of clarification.

Upwelling zones, for example, are said to play a role, both in brook trout (*Salvelinus fontinalis*) and bull trout (*Salvelinus confluentus*) spawning-site selection, among other species. Some brook trout are known to spawn in groundwater upwelling zones located in lake bottoms (Snucins *et al.*, 1992; Curry and Noakes, 1995; Blanchfield and Ridgway, 1997). This preference for upwelling at redds is unsurprising for any lake-spawning salmonid. In a lake (or any impounded stream, upstream of beaver dams, etc.) where there is little or no slope to the water surface, horizontal head gradients just below the substrate must be minimal or nil: at such sites, the interstitial flow required for incubation success can only be driven by vertical head gradients, directed either upward or downward. However, in the temperate climates where Brook trout are found, downward "outflow seepage" (aquifer re-charge from lake waters) is unlikely and thus cannot in general supply the needed vertical gradients. Logically, therefore, only groundwater upwelling (inflow seepage zones) can provide sites for salmonids spawning on lake bottoms. Notably, some salmonid species also spawn in coarse, littoral rubble along lake shores, where wave effects can also drive sufficient interstitial flow to maintain embryo development.

It has long been remarked that some strains of brook trout also spawn near groundwater upwellings in streams (Webster and Eiriksdottir, 1976; Witzel and MacCrimmon, 1983; Essington *et al.*, 1998; Petty *et al.*, 2005; Curry and MacNeill, 2004), where they have occasionally been observed to spawn, even in coarse sand-rich substrates (Curry and MacNeill, 2004). However, scale mismatch in the data concerning upwelling conditions at exact redd locations affect many such observations and still cloud our understanding of hyporheic or upwelling preferences for stream-spawning trout. It often remains unclear in this literature whether upwelling (either observed or just inferred) occurred at trout redds or merely nearby, within the immediate spawning reach. Groundwater upwellings on the bed of small, headwater brook trout streams can occur quite sporadically, in some cases through discrete, metre-scale "upwelling chimneys" that occur where high, sub-bed, vertical gradients coincide with more permeable underlying strata (Schmidt *et al.*, 2007).

In headwater trout streams, which are narrow, with short wavelength bar forms and side terraces flanking the channel bed intermittently, vertical gradients in substrate can vary over short distances. Thus detection of upwelling patterns at known redd sites requires high spatial resolution data sets on vertical hydraulic gradients collected precisely at redds, not metres away. These should be combined with gravel temperature, conductivity and, ideally, oxygen records collected at the depth of egg pockets (as the local hyporheic temperature regime can be used as an indicator of vertical groundwater influx rate, (Conant, 2004; Anderson, 2005)).

Furthermore, the precise adaptive function of upwelling preferences for stream spawners remains unclear.

Are the posited benefits of upwellings to egg development associated with higher interstitial flow rate, or are
they related to warmer incubation temperatures brought
on by more groundwater input to the egg pocket?
(Recall that, for fall-spawning populations such as
brook trout, egg pockets located in upwellings experience higher gravel temperatures over winter, and thus
faster and more stable incubation rates.) Further complicating this picture, local upwelling around the egg
pocket might also, in theory, have the benefit of limiting
fines ingress during the incubation season; although,
again, this process is poorly quantified. Weighing
against such possible benefits, groundwater upwellings
can be detrimental in some hydrogeological contexts;
for example, "older" groundwater may lower the oxygen content of incubating environments, possibly inducing embryo mortality.

Some of these complex questions are beginning to be
explored for bull trout, a member of the same genus
(*Salvelinus*) as brook trout. Based on work conducted
in northwestern Montana (Baxter and Hauer, 2000)
and northeastern British Columbia (Baxter and
McPhail, 1999), it has been speculated that upwelling
groundwater flow may be important for redd site selection at the reach scale to temper winter stream water
temperatures. However, upwellings present in the reach
may not be selected at the spatial scale of the redd patch
itself, possibly to ensure stronger dissolved oxygen
levels around the developing eggs (see Figure 17.2 for
an illustration of reach-scale and patch-scale hyporheic
exchanges within a valley segment). Indeed, Vronskiy
and Leman (1991) observed that chinook salmon
spawned in the Kamchatka River, Russia, at downwelling sites. Based on such observations, Gaust and Dauble
(1998) argue that the strength of the hyporheic flow itself,
whether it is upwelling, downwelling, or parallel to the
bed surface, may be what matters more generally to
salmonid redd location. Clearly this aspect of spawning
preferences requires further research.

### 17.2.1.5  Potential for Inter-Regional Variability in a Species' Spawning Preferences

Hyporheic flow is by definition a mix of surface and
groundwater contributions. We have seen that the
groundwater contribution to winter-time hyporheic flow
around the egg pocket exerts a strong effect on incubation
season temperatures and thus on fry emergence dates for
fall spawners. Since fry mortality in the weeks following
emergence is very high, any factor affecting this mortality, such as the timing of fry emergence, should have
strong adaptive significance. It would follow that
groundwater upwelling preferences might vary geographically, across regions and populations, as they may

depend on the regional timing of surface water warming
and the start of benthic production in streams, the food
base for emergent fry.

In watersheds located above 500 m elevation in the
Réserve Faunique des Laurentides, (north of Quebec
City, 49°N), which support abundant populations of
fall-spawning, resident brook trout, winter temperatures are cold (January mean of −16 °C) and stream ice
breakup is delayed to mid-May. Yet, the great thickness of the winter snowpack on this high precipitation
plateau substantially insulates forest soils from the
winter cold (mean annual snowfall is 6.4 m while mean
1 March standing snow depth is 0.9 m). Groundwater
temperatures remain above 5 °C in these Boreal watersheds, despite much colder mean annual air temperatures (0.3 °C). If trout egg pockets were located over
groundwater-rich upwelling sites in these streams,
with egg incubation at a, near steady, 5 °C, eggs
spawned in early fall would emerge in February, at
a time when the streams are still ice-covered and fry
are unlikely to feed.

In a pattern reminiscent of the Baxter and
Hauer (2000) model of bull trout spawning site selection, preliminary data (J. Franssen, pers. comm. and
manuscript in preparation, February 2011) suggest that
in these systems, trout often spawn in reaches with
observed groundwater seepage (possibly preventing
stream water freezing to the bed over riffles, despite
cold winter temperatures). However, most trout redds
themselves, within these reaches, are not located preferentially at upwelling zones (where shallow gravel
remains over winter at 5 °C); rather, redds are mainly
located near riffle patches, where colder (1–2 °C)
winter surface waters entering the bar dominates interstitial flow around egg pockets, effectively ensuring
that fry do not emerge before mid-May breakup
(Figure 17.3).

Preferences for upwelling versus downwelling conditions may well be geographically variable. In contrast
to the Boreal ecosystem discussed above, one could
speculate that in lower latitude regions with relatively
low winter snowpack and earlier spring thaw, for example in interior mountain drainages in the USA, brook
trout spawners might select different hyporheic settings
from those noted above. At more temperate latitudes,
spawners might select egg pocket locations on warmer
groundwater upwellings to favour earlier fry emergence, coincident with earlier snowmelt recession, thus
ensuring earlier access to territory and food. It thus
seems theoretically possible that the role of groundwater
inputs at redds may vary geographically, as well as with
salmonid species and spawning habitat preferences
(e.g., lakes versus instream preferences). Such potential
variability across species and ecosystems should always

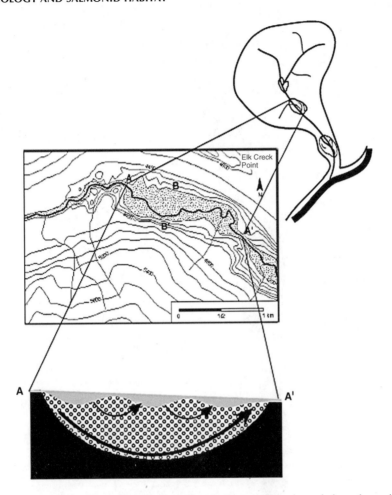

**Figure 17.2**  Illustration of the top-down view of intermediate-scale controls on hyporheic exchange in a drainage basin. A–A' and B–B' denote the length and the maximum valley bottom width of the bounded alluvial valley segment, respectively. The cross-sectional diagram (A–A') illustrates how reach-scale (large arrow) and bedform-scale (small arrows) hyporheic exchange typically occurs within a bounded alluvial valley segment. The stippling denotes the alluvial valley fill. (Figure taken from Baxter and Hauer, 2000.)

be borne in mind before generalizing from local observations.

### 17.2.2  Testing Hypotheses Concerning Spawning Preferences

The previous sections gave examples of key issues emerging in recent investigations of spawning preferences of various salmonid populations. Is there a systematic way of studying such complex questions? *A priori*, one can imagine three types of enquiries that might triangulate us towards solid conclusions:

(1)  Do good quality redd location data, with measurements of all hypothesized control variables at both selected and surrounding non-selected sites at various scales, support the given habitat preference hypothesis?

(2)  Do lab (or *in situ*) experiments confirm that the particular suite of suspected environmental preferences (whether involving fine sediments, interstitial water velocity, dissolved oxygen, temperature regime, etc.) indeed affect reproductive success as hypothesized? Through which physiological and physical processes is this control exerted (for example, are infiltrating fines affecting embryo development mostly through lower flow rates, through mechanical abrasion of the membrane, or through fry entombment)?

A final question can also be relevant.

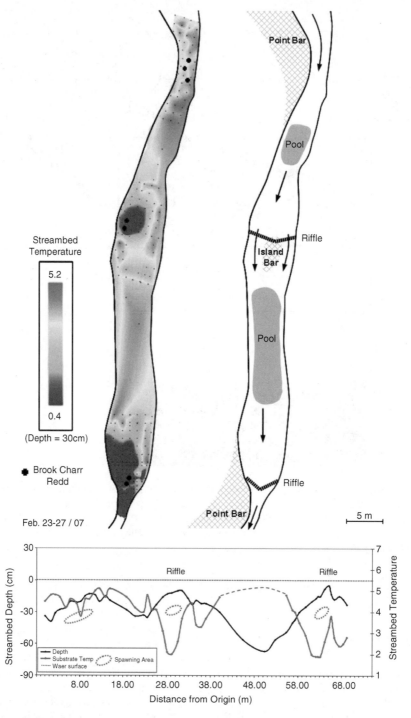

**Figure 17.3** Examples of brook trout redd locations with respect to gravel temperatures measured in the middle of embryo incubation season (February). Stream bed temperatures, measured at 15 cm depth in the substrate, are an indication of the warmer groundwater's contribution to local hyporheic water. Surface water is 0.5 °C during surveys. Egg pockets are located in riffle zones with large surface water contributions in reaches with appreciable groundwater upwelling in pools. (From Jan Franssen, unpublished doctoral research.) (See the color version of this figure in color plate section)

(3) Can spawners detect (and respond to) environmental cues associated with the habitat characteristics of interest so that they can in effect become, through selection pressures, preferred habitat characteristics?

Potentially favourable (or unfavourable) local conditions that spawners cannot detect through environmental cues can neither be "sought" nor avoided. For example, local groundwater inflow of a synthetic chemical, toxic to embryos, cannot be part of an avoidance response if the spawner's olfaction cannot detect it. Contaminated groundwater might thus create an "ecological trap" for spawner populations cued to seek upwellings, for example.

Clearly, determining which combinations of spawning habitat characteristics are detectable (and sought) by spawners in any given ecosystem and subpopulation is not a trivial scientific problem. In most cases, preferences are simply inferred through systematic analysis of habitat selection data combined with limited laboratory or *in situ* incubation experiments. Although painstaking field and lab manipulations could be imagined to test possible cues used by spawners (Question 3 above), few such studies have been conducted (however, see Smith (2003) for a brief review of trout sensory and cognitive processes).

### 17.2.2.1   Possible Cues for Degree of Substrate Mobility and Potential Egg Pocket Scour

The question of possible cues used by spawning fish can be illustrated with respect to avoidance of mortality through flood scour of redds. Some salmonids appear to avoid river bars, reaches, and segments where the substrate mobility regime may lead to egg pocket scour, even if those locations have substrate within preference ranges and are accessible to spawners. Moir *et al.* (2009) show that salmonid spawning sites in the Pacific Northwest occur most frequently in reach- and segment-scale morphological units that, at formative flows, have low mobility of spawning substrates, as determined through estimates of excess shear stress at reach scales. But what are the relevant environmental cues that could explain this preference pattern (cf. Question 3 above)? Clearly, fish do not have access to estimates of mean annual flood, excess shear stresses, or to scour chain data. However, through natural selection, fish can "evolve" instinctual preferences to avoid any set of environmental cues strongly correlated with reproductive failure through scour, explaining how spawning in "unstable gravel reaches" may be avoided. For example, spawners could have evolved an instinctual avoidance of shallow and sporadic cobble patches overlying bedrock in canyon

reaches. They may instinctively avoid spawning in reaches with high sand content in the gravel cobble surface layer, substrate characteristics that may be indicative of recent, upstream avulsions, landslide inputs, or other types of high sediment loadings producing enhanced substrate and macroform instability. However, such hypotheses concerning the exact avoidance cues remain untested.

DeVries (1997) and Montgomery *et al.* (1999) document preferences for depths of egg pocket emplacement that may be related to substrate mobility. Here the instinctual cue for spawners simply relates to the depth of egg burial, which for many salmonids seems to be a depth that is slightly greater than two times the $D_{90}$ of the bed surface, which over flat bar surfaces indeed approximates the maximum thickness mobilized by the mean annual flood (Wilcock *et al.*, 1996). It is plausible that spawners straying from this depth cue produce fewer surviving progeny, gradually eliminating this behaviour from the population.

In summary, one can hypothesize that a number of such local- and reach-scale characteristics having an impact on reproductive success can be detected by the spawners, and thus become, through differential selection, environmental cues defining preferred habitat. The proportion of groundwater inputs might be detectable by the female during redd excavation through temperature or geochemical cues. The strength of horizontal, hyporheic flow below the gravel surface is correlated (through local water slope) with depth–velocity conditions in the overlying water column; substrate permeability is correlated with substrate fines content; all site factors that the spawners presumably can sense and respond to.

### 17.2.3   Towards Some General Hypotheses Concerning Salmonid Spawning Preferences

To conclude this section, I will synthesize these various arguments into some broad, testable hypotheses concerning salmonid spawning preferences. I have argued above (Section 17.2.1.5) that site selection for various degrees of groundwater inputs affects embryo incubation temperatures and hence fry emergence dates. One might first hypothesize that, across populations within the broad climatic range of salmonid occurrence, redd site selection for relative groundwater contributions may vary with the seasonal climate conditions in the particular ecosystem to ensure proper synchronization of fry emergence with prey availability in any stream.

A second and more general hypothesis would state that salmonid reproductive success strongly depends on the female selecting a site offering a suite of habitat conditions that will minimize what are arguably the most direct causes of egg mortality throughout the incubation season: egg pocket scour or dessication, as well as embryo asphyxiation (oxygen deficiency) or entombment, both strongly associated with overly high fines content around egg pockets.

As discussed above, minimizing egg scour during freshets, the first of these threats, appears to depend on the female avoiding reaches with visible cues of unusually high bed material load (as well as instinctively laying egg pockets below the active gravel layer thickness, scaled by local $D_{90}$; Wilcock et al., 1996; De Vries, 1997). For Atlantic salmon in Boreal watersheds where winter flows are at a minimum, winter-time embryo desiccation and freezing appears to be avoided by the female's preference for spawning away from channel margins, in deeper water near the thalweg, where water flows all winter over the redd, beneath the ice cover.

A more complex question is how and to what extent spawners can detect and actively avoid the third threat, sites where high fines loads may infiltrate the substrate over the incubation months, killing embryos through asphyxiation and entombment? Alternatively, to what extent might salmonids partly "hedge" this risk of fines intrusion by choosing sites with stronger intergravel flow gradients, thus counteracting the lower conductivity of egg pockets that are initially relatively richer in fines or that acquire fines after spawning?

The theoretical possibility of such hedging in patch selection follows from basic principles of interstitial hydraulics. High fines content is detrimental to egg survival as it lowers hydraulic conductivity and thus interstitial flow velocities, inhibiting the transport of oxygen to, and metabolic wastes from, the developing embryo. Yet, according to Darcy's law, the detrimental effects of a 50% lower conductivity can be mitigated if hydraulic gradients twice as strong are present to drive interstitial flow. In theory, this tradeoff might to some extent favour spawning sites with higher hyporheic gradients. Indeed, for some salmonid populations there is evidence, discussed earlier (Section 17.2.1.4), that redds may be preferentially located in zones with greater interstitial flow, with highest redd densities in reaches with large, emergent bar complexes or alluvial islands, anomalously high reach slopes and thus stronger hyporheic gradients through bars (Tonina and Buffington, 2009b).

However, other embryo mortality processes can limit this hedging effect. Excess fines intrusion also abrades membranes and entombs embryos and it is unlikely that these mechanical effects can be fully compensated by stronger interstitial velocities. If these detrimental mechanical effects are strong, irrespective of hydraulic gradients and flow rates, spawners should actively avoid sites with higher potential for fines intrusion (assuming environmental cues are available for fish to identify such sites).

### 17.2.3.1 Experiments on the Interactive Effects of Variations in Fines Content and Hydraulic Gradient Strength on Salmon and Trout Embryo Incubation Success

Along with my collaborator Normand Bergeron, I conducted a number of laboratory incubation experiments to test aspects of the tradeoffs just discussed. We specifically investigated the extent to which the lower permeability of fines-rich substrate can be compensated by strong hydraulic gradients across the egg pocket. Some of these results are presented here, in part to illustrate the contribution of experimentation in such research (as per point 2, Section 17.2.2).

Two separate sets of laboratory incubation experiments were run, with salmon and trout eggs, respectively, using a wide range of hydraulic gradients and sediment mixtures typical of spawning substrates observed in the field. The earlier results on Atlantic salmon incubation have been published (Lapointe et al., 2004). Both sets of experiments demonstrate that there is indeed a positive but non-linear effect of gradient strength on embryo survival to emergence, strongest for relatively clean substrates. Interestingly, for fines-rich (lower permeability) substrate this mitigation effect (measured by reduced mortality to emergence) tends to weaken markedly or disappear. For fines-rich substrates, substantial mortality was observed even in cases where large imposed hydraulic gradients maintained high interstitial flow velocities (Figure 17.4).

Notably, both sets of experiments invalidate any a priori expectation that to ensure reproductive success, it is sufficient to maintain a specific minimum, or threshold, flow velocity and thus oxygen flux around the eggs. No such velocity threshold was found for either species, whether the threshold is expressed as a bulk (Darcy) velocity (water flux per cross-sectional area) or as a mean interstitial flow velocity (mean flow rate through pore spaces). High mortality invariably occurred even at moderate to high flow rates, when fines content (particularly for fine sand and silt fractions) exceeds thresholds. The observed effect of high fines content on embryo mortality, non-mitigable by higher gradients and interstitial flow rates, appear to be partly associated with mechanical effects (in particular embryo entombment after hatching: Franssen et al., in press).

### 17.2.4 Are there Optimal Reaches that Combine Low Potential for Fines Ingress with Stronger Hyporheic Flows at Spawning Sites?

Based on the above considerations, one can hypothesize that to maximize embryo survival, salmonids may

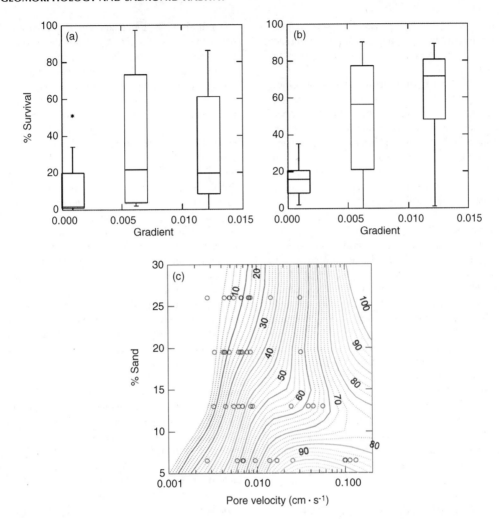

**Figure 17.4** Box plots showing effects of increasing the imposed hydraulic gradient on egg-to-emergence survival of Atlantic salmon embryo for (a) silt-rich (> 1.5%) and (b) silt-poor (< 1.5%) sediment mixtures. Variability in survival at any gradient reflects the large range of sand and silt contents tested. For a given interstitial velocity (c), the percentage survival (represented by the isolines) to emergence of fry decreases with increasing sand content in the substrate. (Figures taken from Lapointe *et al.*, 2004)

preferentially select redd patches which are located in steep, complex bar reaches, as these redd sites enhance interstitial flow regime. However, to minimize excessive fines intrusion into egg pockets during the incubation months, spawners may simultaneously avoid reaches with widespread sand veneers in pools (or sand pockets at channel margins or in lee of bed clusters), thus limiting the supply of bed surface fines for entrainment to redd patches during freshets.

Various other processes may limit potential fines intrusion into redds located in such complex bar reaches: when redds are located at the tailout of large pools impounded upstream of more massive riffles, flows overpassing the

redds are accelerating rapidly, as the riffle crest is approached. Because of the unusual steepness of the riffle face located just downstream in such cases, these flows have relatively high flow velocities for the water depths as they approach the crest (high Froude number). In such a setting, these high velocities maintain relatively high shear stresses and turbulent intensities over the redd patch, theoretically limiting the potential for settling into egg pockets of any of the small load of fine sands making it out of the large pool (itself, an effective fines trap under most incubation season flows). Such reach-scale geomorphic settings (relatively low sand evacuation from large pools and tailouts approaching large bar complexes with steep riffles) may thus ensure low potential for fines ingress, while the unusually strong hyporheic flows can mitigate the effects of any fines ingress occurring during the incubation period.

This hypothesis could be tested (as per point 1, Section 17.2.2) against data on redd densities across a large set of riffle-pool reaches with variable riffle face (or pool to pool) slopes (higher slopes should be preferred) and variable sand contents in pools and channel margins (higher sand content reaches should be avoided). Fines ingress cans set at pool tailouts over a range of riffle amplitudes could test the hypothesis that the ingress regime is more benign in the preferred morphological settings.

In this section I discussed the interactions among a large number of detailed physical processes that are known to affect salmonid egg survival to emergence. The complexity of many of the individual processes and their interactions was presented as illustrative of the challenges of really understanding this type of habitat. Some of these processes with emerging visibility in the literature have been poorly studied so far (in particular too little is known about the temperature, dissolved oxygen, and velocity regimes of intersticial flow at preferred redd sites, factors that directly affect incubation outcomes). More fundamentally, I hope this long discussion illustrated how patch-scale, reach-scale, and even segment-scale characteristics, in combination, control key reproductive processes. These processes and these scales need to be considered in spawning-habitat preference modelling, in addition to patch-scale grain size composition.

## 17.3 A "RIVERSCAPE" PERSPECTIVE INTO SALMONID HABITAT SCIENCE

The previous section mainly discussed how various environmental characteristics at the reach and patch scale can affect the incubating embryo and emergent fry. However, spawning beds that are located too far from suitable rearing habitat for older juveniles should also be avoided because of increased mortality of progeny. In this section, I will broaden the view of links between geomorphology and salmonid habitat to discuss how larger scale characteristics of a riverscape can hinder or support a salmonid fry's subsequent growth, either to instream reproductive maturity (in the case of a resident salmonid) or to smolt stage and migration to sea (for an anadromous fish). This will entail a brief discussion of the landscape ecology of salmonid fishes.

Such a broader spatial focus reflects a maturing and integration of the principles of river ecology with those of landscape sciences over recent decades. In much cited conceptual papers, Poff (1997) and Ward (1997) argued

for a multiscale understanding of the complex links between fluvial landscape structures and river ecosystem structure and functions. Poff (1997) claimed that understanding patterns of distribution and abundance of lotic species (plants and animals) requires that we test theoretical predictions about functional relationships between species and their environments across a range of spatial and temporal scales. Fausch et al. (2002, p. 483) compellingly argue that ". . .a continuous view of rivers is essential for effective research and conservation of their fishes and other aquatic biota – a view not just of disjunct reaches but of the entire spatially heterogeneous scene of the river...". As pointed out by the latter authors, the requirements surrounding the spatial grain (the finest resolution studied) and the extent (the size of the entire studied area) of data gathering implied in a landscape ecology perspective are considerable and require continued developments in remote sensing of riverine habitats.

A major conceptual development here has been to largely supersede earlier views of fairly simple downstream trends in biotic structure and function along river networks (for example, in the River Continuum Concept (RCC) of Vannote et al., 1980). The RCC focused mainly on the lower rungs of the food web and arguably had limited predictive power, in any case, for highly mobile organisms like salmonid fish. The "predictable continuum" paradigm has now been replaced by a fuller appreciation of the diversity in structural organization of habitat across neighbouring watersheds located in the same region, in the "uniqueness" of individual "riverscapes". Ward (1997), indeed, argued that lotic productivity and biodiversity patterns reflect the structure of a given "riverscape", with its unique succession of valley segment types, "sedimentary links" (Rice et al., 2001; Davey and Lapointe, 2007), tributary-related discontinuities in water chemistries and biota, etc. Such perspectives are just beginning to be applied to understanding how a "riverscape's" unique structure may control both size and resilience of its salmonid populations, topics briefly discussed below.

### 17.3.1 Top-Down Watershed Level Controls on Habitat Characteristics at Reach and Patch Scales

To simplify, I will divide here into two main components the abundant recent literature uncovered through keyword searches using "landscape" or "riverscape" along with "fish habitats" and "fish population ecology". The first component, with the most diverse and developed contributions, deals with how large-scale riverscape features, such as watershed area, stream order, lithotype, and valley segment characteristics, determine or constrain habitat characteristics at a patch or reach scale (Montgomery, 1999; Montgomery et al., 1999;

Thompson and Lee, 2000; Pess *et al.*, 2002). The important principle at work here is that in any hierarchical system, such as a watershed, smaller-scale features (e.g., patch- and reach-scale habitat characteristics, such as substrate, temperature, velocities and depths, wetted areas) are by definition constrained by characteristics of the larger-scale units in which they are embedded (thus hierarchy) and that these constraints must be well understood to model system structure (Frissell *et al.*, 1986; Poole, 2002).

Highly relevant illustrations of landscape-scale controls on the character of local salmonid habitat have been provided by Montgomery, Buffington, and others, who have made major contributions to our understanding of watershed and valley segment-scale determinants of salmonid habitat availability in the western USA (Montgomery *et al.*, 1999; Buffington *et al.*, 2004; May and Lee, 2004; Burnett *et al.*, 2007). In particular, the work on variable substrate mobility regimes as determinants of spawning habitat distribution at watershed scales was mentioned in a previous section (17.2.2.1). In a similar vein, Davey and Lapointe (2007) showed how in one Boreal river in the Canadian Shield, the spotty distribution of Atlantic salmon spawning reaches is determined by the large-scale, sedimentary link segmentation of the river, as a consequence of the strong constraint imposed on the possibility of spawning activity by repeated, link-scale, downstream fining sequences. Investigating such "top-down" controls is part of a long tradition of enquiry in watershed science. Although such top-down controls on salmonid habitat have clear management implications, I assume here that the general idea of such watershed-scale controls on reach characteristics, expressed, for example, in hydraulic geometry laws, are very familiar to geomorphologists and do not warrant review here.

In the limited space of this chapter, I propose to highlight a second, newer, and conceptually distinct aspect of processes linking landscape-scale structure with salmonid habitats. This emerging literature focuses on how detailed landscape organization imposes constraints on salmonid habitat "complementation", across contrasting but interconnected reaches along the river. How do geomorphic processes in riverscapes structure the 'landscape ecology' of salmonids and other fishes?

### 17.3.2 Focus on Salmonid "Landscape Ecology", Habitat Heterogeneity, and Complementation

A characteristic of riverscapes as ecosystems is that their animal communities are structured by relatively strong, long-distance connectivity (via water) across highly heterogeneous habitats and by a complex temporal regime of disturbances on which the ecosystem structure depends (particularly with regard to bed morphology, sedimentology, and riparian vegetation). These characteristics allow the existence of fish life-history strategies involving displacements across relatively distant habitats and a complex metapopulation structure that enhances species persistence despite local environmental disturbances. In this section, the focus is on the population-level support provided by the unique spatial organization of reach, valley, and tributary types across watersheds, that forms the signature of each riverscape.

Stream ecologists are increasingly aware of the importance of watershed-scale spatial organization to the "landscape ecology" of stream organisms. Barriers to dispersal that hamper along-stream movement, such as dams, natural falls, high-gradient reaches, or reaches with unusual temperature regimes, are particularly important in relatively more-linear habitats like streams, because all fish moving across segments encounter them. Le Pinchon *et al.* (2009) argue that, because stream fishes use different patches of vital habitats during daily movements and seasonal migrations, "complementation" relationships across habitats (defined as the spatial proximity of non-substitutable resources) are important to maintain viable populations (see Dunning *et al.*, 1992). Frissell *et al.* (1986), Schlosser (1991, 1995), Poole (2002) and Fausch *et al.* (2002), have similarly emphasized the need to take into account the heterogeneity and connectivity of river habitat types, with a focus on the spatial organization of complementary habitats for given organisms in daily, seasonal, and life-cycle displacements.

### 17.3.2.1 Salmonid Habitat Complementation

How does the unique structure of a riverscape affect salmonid community composition, population size, and stability? This is an exciting research area in which geomorphology and river remote sensing, allied with fish ecology and improved tracking technologies, can contribute much in coming decades. The freshwater part of the life history of salmonids depends on a number of distinct habitat types (Groot and Margolis, 1991). The coarsest such classification would distinguish spawning habitats used for egg incubation and different rearing habitats for juvenile fish as they grow in age and size, as well as habitats facilitating migration of adults and their pre-spawning residence in rivers (Kocik and Ferreri, 1998; White and Rahel, 2008). In some cases, a particular river location may also have unusual habitat value for organisms for reasons that may not be obvious during benign environmental conditions, as in the localized thermal refugia habitats (Torgersen *et al.*, 1999; Ebersole *et al.*, 2003) or ephemeral streams (Wigington *et al.*, 2006).

Although not much is known about valley segment-scale habitat complementation patterns for salmonids, there is evidence that the abundance of older salmonid juveniles or adults is not necessarily limited by the availability of only one type of habitat, such as spawning habitat. White and Rahel (2008) demonstrate through a study of age-class abundances of cutthroat trout in various stream systems in Wyoming that widespread spawning and fry habitat in a system may not lead to high abundances of older juveniles and smolts unless sufficient complementary summer pool habitats (here associated with beaver dams and large organic debris) are also present in the system to shelter these larger individuals. They argue that in Wyoming streams, "...habitat complementation is important for the co-existence of multiple age-classes of fish and that the adjacency of spawning habitat and refugia is crucial for the persistence of fish, particularly in the face of environmental stress associated with drought" (White and Rahel, 2008, p. 881).

The importance of drought conditions in the "spatial patterning" of complementary salmonid habitats in some ecosystems is further illustrated by the recent work of Boughton *et al.* (2009) in the California Chaparral. This work focuses on rainbow trout (*Oncorhynchus mykiss*), a fish that spawns in spring, the end of the high runoff season in these watersheds. The authors document movement patterns between spawning and juvenile habitats that are dependent on elevation, flow intermittency, and temperature regime. They observed that reaches with suitably sized spawning gravels tend to occur both in intermittent tributaries and in the perennial mainstem (although the latter segment was too warm for over-summering). However, they noted that in early summer, juvenile rainbows occurred at similar densities in the intermittent and perennial tributaries, but larger fish (over 10 cm in length) had greater densities in perennial tributaries with deeper pool habitats.

### 17.3.2.2 Riverscape Scale Determinants of Salmonid Production

Section 17.2 of this chapter focused mostly on hydrogeomorphic processes acting at reach scale that appear to underlie spawning habitat quality. In practice, of course, an exclusive focus on conservation of spawning habitat assumes that this habitat type is the one limiting population-carrying capacity in an ecosystem. However, as seen in Section 17.3.2, the fluvial geomorphologist should be aware that in many river ecosystems, other complementary river habitats (for rearing of older juvenile year classes or for thermal refuge) may also be limiting and act as bottlenecks to population size.

When this is the case, a "riverscape ecology" perspective is required to determine in which sections of river

valley an optimal spatial organization of complementary habitats allows higher fish biomass and production rates. The general notion of fish productivity hotspots related to local habitat complementation is not new. With respect to rivers, this was implicit, for example, in Poole's (2002) Hierarchical Patch Dynamics (HPD) model that argues that each river network is a unique, patchy discontinuum from headwaters to mouth, with a longitudinal series of alternating stream segments with different geomorphological structures. The HPD was meant to provide a framework for studying and understanding the ecological importance (to biomass or to production rates) of each stream's individual pattern of habitat transitions.

Such a "landscape productivity hotspot" perspective (one that inherently meshes the large with the smaller spatial scales, *sensu* Fausch *et al.*, 2002) is beginning to be applied to salmonids. In a mostly conceptual paper, Kocik and Ferreri (1998) argued that the complementary habitats for Atlantic salmon spawning and juvenile rearing along a river are naturally organized into segments they called functional habitat units (FHU), each with distinct and contrasting productive capacity, which they identified as the basic units of salmonid production. They demonstrated through theoretical simulations that the size and spatial organization of FHUs along a system can influence both salmon production levels and population resilience to environmental disturbances.

In this spirit, my lab has begun to test simple "landscape ecology" models of Atlantic salmon production for southern Quebec rivers. In these systems, various lines of evidence suggest that spawning habitat itself is often not limiting; rather, that salmon production may be limited by proximity of complementary rearing and refuge habitats. In Quebec watersheds, anadromous Atlantic salmon runs are much smaller than Pacific salmonid runs in comparably sized watersheds flowing to the west coast of North America. Superimposed redds are not common in Quebec salmon rivers and typically many sections of "good spawning beds" are unused by adults in any given year. Mortality during Quebec's severe winter conditions of course plays a role in limiting population sizes. Boulder and large-cobble-rich reaches seem to provide key winter refuges for large parr in the form of abundant, large-diameter, interstitial hiding and resting spaces near the bed surface (Cunjak *et al.*, 1998; Huusko *et al.*, 2007).

Coulombe-Pontbriand and Lapointe (2004*a*, 2004*b*) presented indirect evidence suggesting that in the Petite Cascapédia River (Gaspé Peninsula, Québec), rearing and refuge habitat for larger salmon juveniles (parr) are limiting fish production. Spawning habitat availability and fry densities along the Petite Cascapedia are comparable to those in neighbouring watersheds with similar hydroclimate, such as the Bonaventure River. However, overall parr densities and returning salmon runs are much smaller in the Petite Cascapedia River, consistent with the fact that boulder-rich rearing habitat for older juveniles is more limited (relative to spawning habitat) in that river system.

Landscape ecology type predictions concerning fish production "hotspots" along river segments may be tested using electrofishing data on abundances of older juvenile fish, as in the study just described. However, predictions of total anadromous salmonid production are ideally tested, where such data exist, through the size of smolt runs, these being the export from a watershed to the sea of freshwater-produced, anadromous salmon. Alternatively, in the absence of data on smolt runs for many systems, variability in watershed production across a limited region can also be indexed by the size of the return spawning run, which is made up of that fraction of smolts that survived mortality at sea and are returning to reproduce in their natal streams.

Overall, Atlantic salmon rivers in the Gaspé Peninsula of Quebec present a 20 to 1 variability in the average numbers of returning adult salmon per $km^2$ of watershed area (the median "specific run size" in Gaspé rivers is approximately one returning adult per $km^2$ of watershed) with a similar variability across watersheds in adults per total km of river length. Kim and Lapointe (2011) hypothesized that, at any given watershed area or total stream length, the relative spatial organization of different essential, complementary habitats is an important factor controlling the production of smolts and, by extension, can be used as a predictor of the interannual average number of adults returning each year to spawn. To test this, we developed a very simple riverine landscape ecology model that uses easily accessible topographic map and airphoto sources to identify optimally productive river segments based on large-scale river and valley features and top-down predictions of the associated availability of key, complementary salmon habitats (here: spawning beds, quality rearing habitats for older 1+ and 2+ parr and large "holding pools" where adults congregate over summer as they wait for the fall spawning season). The components of this landscape ecology model are consistent with theory and with available data on redd sites and parr abundance patterns in these systems (Kim, 2009).

Based on such evidence, Kim and Lapointe (2011) hypothesize that "optimally productive" river segments (Figure 17.5) require a combination of deep, low-velocity "holding pools" (mostly found in bedrock canyons in these particular Gaspé riverscapes), as well as abundant rearing and spawning habitats (found in confined and unconfined valley meander segments), all available within a maximum of approximately 15 river km. Although these "optimal" segments are distinct from Kocik and Ferreri's (1998) Functional Habitat Units (FHUs),

the approach is conceptually akin. The ability of the resultant landscape ecology model to predict salmon run sizes (25-year average salmon runs for each watershed) was tested across 14 rivers in the Gaspé Peninsula, Quebec. The aggregate length of "optimally productive habitat", as defined in our model, was a strong predictor of the average size of the annual salmon runs for these watersheds ($R^2 = 0.913$, $p < 0.0005$; Figure 17.6a). Furthermore, "specific" salmon run sizes were quite accurately predicted through this approach after the effects of scale (watershed area or total stream length) were removed ($R^2 = 0.771$, $p < 0.0005$; Figure 17.6b).

The importance of accounting for the connectivity of the different types of habitat is demonstrated in Figure 17.6c; if a maximum distance requirement (15 km, as stated above) is ignored, the predictive strength of the model decreases radically ($R^2 = 0.098$, $p = 0.276$). As shown in Figures 17.6a and 17.6b, our river segment-scale production model also much more accurately predicted specific run size than did a higher resolution scale Atlantic salmon habitat assessment method currently used by local wildlife agencies (Figure 17.6d); the latter approach notably ignores the spatial organization of complementary habitats.

Of course, here as ever, strong correlation (Figures 17.6a, b) neither demonstrates causation nor confirms the exact nature of underlying mechanisms. To test directly the key ecological assumptions underlying such simple landscape models, one could in theory conduct genetic "parental assignation" of juveniles found in various segments (using "microsatellite genetic markers") identifying them as progeny of individual adults, sampled in various holding pools. One could also conduct mark-recapture estimates of survival rates to smoltification of tagged emergent fry collected and tagged at various distances from holding pools along the system.

### 17.3.3 Conclusion: Riverscape Science will Strengthen the Integration of Geomorphology and River Ecology

I have tried in this chapter to demonstrate through very selected examples that the prospects for fruitful collaboration between salmonid ecologists and geomorphologists over the next decades are exciting. In Section 17.2.1, I have argued that it is not a trivial scientific task to unravel which of the multidimensional characteristics of the reach containing redd sites spawners were actually selecting for. This basic problem is compounded when one takes into account longer-distance river interconnections between spatially distinct, but complementary habitat types used over the fish's life cycle, including adult refuge and juvenile rearing. Examples have been given in Section 17.3 showing how the challenge of

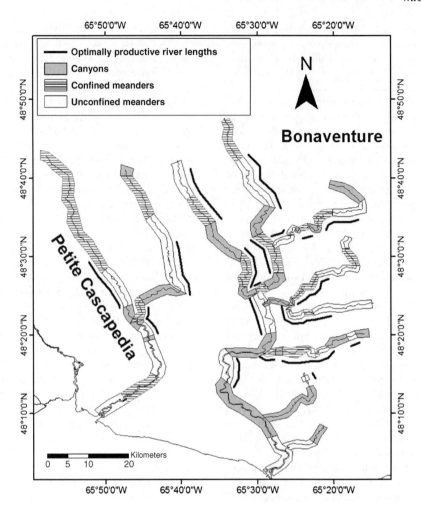

**Figure 17.5** The Petite Cascapedia and Bonaventure Rivers (Gaspé Peninsula, Canada), along with their major tributaries, were partitioned into three types of geomorphic segments (see legend) and "optimally productive" river segments were identified (bold lines) based on riverscape ecology principles reflecting necessary complementarity and proximity of spawner holding pools, spawning beds, and rearing habitat for parr (see discussion in text). Illustrating a consistent trend across 14 Gaspé rivers (cf. Figure 17.6a) the Bonaventure has a much larger specific run size than the Petite Cascapedia (1.10 versus 0.33 adult salmon per unit watershed area) that appears to be explained by its greater availability of optimally productive habitat (44% versus 28% of total accessible salmon stream kilometre in optimally productive habitat). (See also Kim and Lapointe, 2011.)

understanding the intensity of use of any given single "habitat" depends on interpreting the complex web of local-, reach-, and segment-scale geomorphic conditions that give this location value for biota. Of course, this broader "riverscape" perspective on fish habitat does entail data-gathering challenges, such as the need for combining fine grain, large extent spatial analysis of both biotic and abiotic data (Fausch *et al.*, 2002).

There is little doubt that the next decades will witness an explosion in the use of high-resolution remote-sensing techniques applied to river networks. Ongoing advances in lower cost, high-resolution and multispectral image

acquisition (both satellite and aircraft based) and habitat modelling at valley segment scales are encouraging in this regard (Torgersen *et al.*, 1999, 2001; Carbonneau *et al.*, 2004, 2005, 2006; Chapters 21–24, this volume). These developments, in synergy with further refinements and miniaturization of fish tagging and tracking technologies, will allow the next generation of river ecosystem scientists to better unravel the ecology of complementary habitat use and production hotspots.

Ongoing refinements in performance and lowering of costs of genotyping techniques will also allow us to better understand the micro-evolutionary underpinnings of sal-

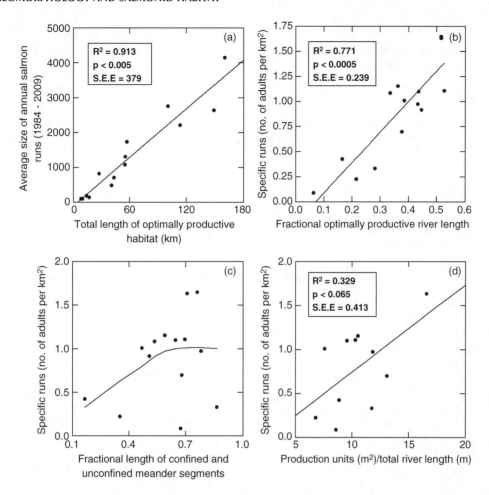

**Figure 17.6** For watersheds in the Gaspé Peninsula of Canada, the aggregate length of optimally productive habitat in a given watershed is a strong predictor of the average size of the annual salmon run (a), even when the effects of scale are removed (b). If the spatial organization of the different types of habitat is ignored (in this case by considering bedrock canyons as unproductive despite their value in providing oversummer holding pools for adults) when identifying optimally productive habitat, the predictive power of the model decreases substantially (c). A reach-scale habitat assessment model employed by local wildlife agencies and which does not account for habitat complementarity, proved to be a weaker predictor of the specific salmon runs (d). "S.E.E." denotes the standard error of the estimate. (See also Kim and Lapointe, 2011.)

monid adaptation to local conditions across watersheds and regions. Geomorphologists might also note emerging developments in a research area called "landscape genetics" (Heggenes and Røed, 2006; Holderegger and Wagner, 2006) that will allow us to better understand the importance of river ecosystem structure for biodiversity conservation.

In the current context of growing, climate-change-driven concern for water resources and biodiversity, we are witnessing rapidly increasing capabilities in remote sensing and field data acquisition as well as develop-

ments in numerical modelling and a growing awareness among fish ecologists of the "uniqueness" and complexity of individual riverscapes. This context provides very interesting possibilities for decisive collaborations between ecologists and geomorphologists (who have the expertise and detailed understanding of the physical structure and temporal dynamics of river habitat). The prospects for future scientific advances in understanding of riverine habitats are clear if biological and physical river scientists are willing to invest the time and effort needed for true interdisciplinarity.

## 17.4   ACKNOWLEDGEMENTS

This chapter profited greatly from the detailed comments of Christian Torgersen and Stephen Rice.

## 17.5   REFERENCES

Acornley, R.M. 1999. Water temperatures within spawning beds in two chalk streams and implications for salmonid egg development. *Hydrological Processes* **13**: 439–446. doi: 10.1002/(SICI)1099-1085(19990228)13:3<439::AID-HYP748>3.0.CO;2-E.

Anderson, M.P. 2005. Heat as a ground water tracer. *Ground Water* **43**: 951–968. doi: 10.1111/j.1745-6584.2005.00052.x.

Anderson, K.E., Paul, A.J., McCauley, E. *et al.* 2006. Instream flow needs in streams and rivers: The importance of understanding ecological dynamics. *Frontiers in Ecology and the Environment* **4**: 309–318. doi: 10.1890/1540-9295(2006)4 [309:IFNISA]2.0.CO; 2.

Baxter, C.V. and Hauer, F.R. 2000. Geomorphology, hyporheic exchange, and selection of spawning habitat by bull trout (*Salvelinus confluentus*). *Canadian Journal of Fisheries and Aquatic Sciences* **57**: 1470–1481. doi: 10.1139/cjfas-57-7-1470.

Baxter, J.S. and McPhail, J.D. 1999. The influence of redd site selection, groundwater upwelling, and over-winter incubation temperature on survival of bull trout (*Salvelinus confluentus*) from egg to alevin. *Canadian Journal of Zoology* **77**: 1233–1239. doi: 10.1139/cjz-77-8-1233.

Blanchfield, P.J. and Ridgway, M.S. 1997. Reproductive timing and use of redd sites by lake-spawning brook trout (*Salvelinus fontinalis*). *Canadian Journal of Fisheries and Aquatic Sciences* **54**: 747–756. doi: 10.1139/cjfas-54-4-747.

Boughton, D.A., Fish, H., Pope, J., and Holt, G. 2009. Spatial patterning of habitat for Oncorhynchus mykiss in a system of intermittent and perennial streams. *Ecology of Freshwater Fish* **18**: 92–105. doi: 10.1111/j.1600-0633.2008. 00328.x.

Bovee, K.D., Lamb, B.L., Bartholow, J.M. *et al.* 1998. *Stream Habitat Analysis Using the Instream Flow Incremental Methodology.* United States Geological Survey, Biological Resources Division. Information and Technology Report USGS/BRD-1998-0004.

Buffington, J.M. and Tonina, D. 2009. Hyporheic exchange in mountain rivers II: Effects of channel morphology on mechanics, scales, and rates of exchange. *Geography Compass* **3**: 1038–1062. doi: 10.1111/j.1749-8198.2009.00225.x.

Buffington, J.M., Montgomery, D.R., and Greenberg, H.M. 2004. Basin-scale availability of salmonid spawning gravel as influenced by channel type and hydraulic roughness in mountain catchments. *Canadian Journal of Fisheries and Aquatic Sciences* **61**: 2085–2096. doi: 10.1139/f04-141.

Burnett, K.M., Reeves, G.H., Miller, D.J. *et al.* 2007. Distribution of salmon-habitat potential relative to landscape characteristics and implications for conservation. *Ecological Applications* **17**: 66–80. doi: 10.1890/1051-0761(2007)017 [0066:DOSPRT]2.0.CO; 2.

Carbonneau, P.E., Bergeron, N.E., and Lane, S.N. 2005. Automated grain size measurements from airborne remote sensing for long profile measurements of fluvial grain sizes. *Water Resources Research* **41**: W11426. doi: 10.1029/ 2005WR003994.

Carbonneau, P.E., Lane, S.N., and Bergeron, N.E. 2004. Catchment-scale mapping of surface grain size in gravel bed rivers using airborne digital imagery. *Water Resources Research* **40**: W0720211. doi: 10.1029/2003WR002759.

Carbonneau, P.E., Lane, S.N., and Bergeron, N.E. 2006. Feature based image processing methods applied to bathymetric measurements from airborne remote sensing in fluvial environments. *Earth Surface Processes and Landforms* **31**: 1413–1423. doi: 10.1002/esp.1341.

Chapman, W.M. 1943. The spawning of chinook salmon in the main Columbia River. *Copeia* **3**: 168–170.

Conant, B., Jr 2004. Delineating and quantifying ground water discharge zones using streambed temperatures. *Ground Water* **42**: 243–257. doi: 10.1111/j.1745-6584.2004.tb02671.x.

Coulombe-Pontbriand, M. and Lapointe, M. 2004a. Geomorphic controls, riffle substrate quality, and spawning site selection in two semi-alluvial salmon rivers in the Gaspé Peninsula, *Canada. River Research and Applications* **20**: 577–590. doi: 10.1002/rra.768.

Coulombe-Pontbriand M. and Lapointe, M. 2004b. Landscape controls on boulder-rich, winter habitat availability and their effects on Atlantic salmon (*Salmo salar*) parr abundance in two fifth-order mountain streams. *Canadian Journal of Fisheries and Aquatic Sciences* **61**: 648–658. doi: 10.1139/ F04-023.

Cunjak, R.A., Prowse, T.D., and Parrish, D.L. 1998. Atlantic salmon (*Salmo salar*) in winter: "the season of parr discontent?" *Canadian Journal of Fisheries and Aquatic Sciences* **55** (Supplement 1): 161–180. doi: 10.1139/cjfas-55-S1-161.

Curry, R.A. and MacNeill, W.S. 2004. Population-level responses to sediment during early life in brook trout. *Journal of the North American Benthological Society* **23**: 140–150. doi: 10.1899/0887-3593(2004)023<0140:PRTSDE>2.0.CO;2.

Curry, R.A. and Noakes, D.L.G. 1995. Groundwater and the selection of spawning sites by brook trout (*Salvelinus fontinalis*). *Canadian Journal of Fisheries and Aquatic Sciences* **52**: 1733–1740. doi: 10.1139/f95-765.

Davey, C. and Lapointe, M. 2007. Sedimentary links and the spatial organization of Atlantic salmon (*Salmo salar*) spawning habitat in a Canadian Shield river. *Geomorphology* **83**: 82–96. doi: 10.1016/j.geomorph.2006.06.011.

DeVries, P. 1997. Riverine salmonid egg burial depths: review of published data and implications for scour studies. *Canadian Journal of Fisheries and Aquatic Sciences* **54**: 1685–1698. doi: 10.1139/cjfas-54-8-1685.

Dunning, J.B., Danielson, B.J., and Pulliam, H.R. 1992. Ecological processes that affect populations in complex landscapes. *Oikos* **65**: 169–175.

Ebersole, J.L., Liss, W.J., and Frissell, C.A. 2003. Thermal heterogeneity, stream channel morphology, and salmonid abundance in northeastern Oregon streams. *Canadian Journal of Fisheries and Aquatic Sciences* **60**: 1266–1280. doi: 10.1139/f03-107.

Essington, T.E., Sorensen, P.W., and Paron, D.G. 1998. High rate of redd superimposition by brook trout (*Salvelinus fontinalis*) and brown trout (*Salmo trutta*) in a Minnesota stream cannot be explained by habitat availability alone. *Canadian Journal of Fisheries and Aquatic Sciences* **55**: 2310–2316. doi: 10.1139/cjfas-55-10-2310.

Fausch, K.D., Torgersen, C.E., Baxter, C.V., and Li, H.W. 2002. Landscapes to riverscapes: bridging the gap between research and conservation of stream fishes. *BioScience* **52**: 483–498. doi: 10.1641/0006-3568(2002)052[0483: LTRBTG]2.0.CO; 2.

Franssen, J., Blais, C., Lapointe, F., *et al.* in press. Asphyxiation and entombment mechanisms in fines rich spawning substrates: experimental evidence with brook trout embryos. *Canadian Journal of Fisheries and Aquatic Sciences.*

Frissell, C.A., Liss, W.J., Warren, C.E., and Hurley M. *D.* 1986. A hierarchical framework for stream habitat classification: viewing streams in a watershed context. *Environmental Management* 10: 199–214. doi: 10.1007/BF01867358.

Geist, D.R. and Dauble, D.D. 1998. Redd site selection and spawning habitat use by fall chinook salmon: the importance of geomorphic features in large rivers. *Environmental Management* 22: 655–669. doi: 10.1007/s002679900137.

Geist, D.R., Jones, J., Murray, C.J., and Dauble, D.D. 2000. Suitability criteria analyzed at the spatial scale of redd clusters improved estimates of fall Chinook salmon (*Oncorhynchus tshawytscha*) spawning habitat use in the Hanford Reach, *Columbia River. Canadian Journal of Fisheries and Aquatic Sciences* 57: 1636–1646. doi: 10.1139/cjfas-57-8-1636.

Greig, S.M., Sear, D.A., and Carling, P.A. 2005. The impact of fine sediment accumulation on the survival of incubating salmon progeny: Implications for sediment management. *Science of the Total Environment* 344: 241–258. doi: 10.1016/j.scitotenv.2005.02.010.

Greig, S.M., Sear, D.A., and Carling, P.A. 2007. A review of factors influencing the availability of dissolved oxygen to incubating salmonid embryos. *Hydrological Processes* 21(3): 323–334.

Groot, C. and Margolis, L. 1991. *Pacific Salmon Life Histories.* Vancouver, British Columbia, UBC Press.

Heggenes, J. and Red, K.H. 2006. Do dams increase genetic diversity in brown trout (*Salmo trutta*)? Microgeographic differentiation in a fragmented river. *Ecology of Freshwater Fish* 15: 366–375. doi: 10.1111/j.1600-0633.2006.00146.x.

Holderegger, R. and Wagner, H.H. 2006. A brief guide to Landscape Genetics. *Landscape Ecology* 21: 793–796. doi: 10.1007/s10980-005-6058-6.

Huusko, A., Greenberg, L. Stickler, M. *et al.* 2007. Life in the ice lane: the winter ecology of stream salmonids. *River Research and Applications* 23: 469–491.

Isaak, D.J., Thurow, R.F. Rieman, B.E., and Dunham, J.B. 2007. Chinook salmon use of spawning patches: Relative roles of habitat quality, size, and connectivity. *Ecological Applications* 17: 352–364. doi: 10.1890/05-1949.

Keitt, T.H. and Urban, D.L. 2005. Scale-specific inference using wavelets. *Ecology* 86: 2497–2504. doi: 10.1890/04-1016.

Kim, M.S. 2009. *The controls of sedimentary links on the spatial distribution of Atlantic salmon* (Salmo salar) *juveniles and spawning activity along rivers in the Gaspé Peninsula, Canada.* M.Sc. thesis, Department of Geography, McGill University, Montreal, Quebec.

Kim, M.S. and Lapointe, M. 2011. Regional variability in Atlantic salmon (*Salmo salar*) riverscapes: a simple landscape ecology model explaining the large variability in size of salmon runs across Gaspé watersheds, Canada. *Ecology of Freshwater Fishes* 20: 144–156.

Knapp, R.A. and Preisler, H.K. 1999. Is it possible to predict habitat use by spawning salmonids? A test using California golden trout *(Oncorhynchus mykiss aguabonita). Canadian Journal of Fisheries and Aquatic Sciences* 56: 1576–1584. doi: 10.1139/cjfas-56-9-1576.

Kocik, J.F. and Ferreri, C.P. 1998. Juvenile production variation in salmonids: population dynamics, habitat, and the role of spatial relationships. *Canadian Journal of Fisheries and Aquatic Sciences* 44(Suppl. 1): 191–200. doi: 10.1139/cjfas-55-S1-191.

Kondolf, G.M. 2000. Assessing salmonid spawning gravel quality. *Transactions of the American Fisheries Society* 129: 262–281. doi: 10.1577/1548-8659(2000)129<0262: ASSGQ>2.0.CO; 2.

Kondolf, G.M. and Wolman, M.G. 1993. The size of salmonid spawning gravels. *Water Resources Research* 29: 2275–2285. doi: 10.1029/93WR00402.

Kondolf, G.M., Sale, M.J., and Wolman, M.G. 1993. Modification of fluvial gravel size by spawning salmonids. *Water Resources Research* 29: 2265–2274. doi: 10.1029/93WR00401.

Koskinen, M.T., Haugen, T.O., and Primmer, C.R. 2002. Contemporary fisherian life-history evolution in small salmonid populations. *Nature* 419: 826–830. doi: 10.1038/nature01029.

Lamouroux, N., Mérigoux, S., Capra, H., *et al.* 2010. The generality of abundance-environment relationships in microhabitats: A comment on Lancaster and Downes (2009). *River Research and Applications* 26: 915–920. doi: 10.1002/rra.1366.

Lancaster, J. and Downes, B.J. 2010a. Linking the hydraulic world of individual organisms to ecological processes: putting ecology into ecohydraulics. *River Research and Applications* 26: 385–403. doi: 10.1002/rra.1274.

Lancaster, J. and Downes, B.J. 2010b. Ecohydraulics needs to embrace ecology and sound science, and to avoid mathematical artifacts. *River Research and Applications* 26: 921–929. doi: 10.1002/rra.1425.

Lapointe, M., Eaton, B., Driscoll, S., and Latulippe, C. 2000. Modelling the probability of salmonid egg pocket scour due to floods. *Canadian Journal of Fisheries and Aquatic Sciences* 57: 1120–1130. doi: 10.1139/cjfas-57-6-1120.

Lapointe, M.F., Bergeron, N.E., Bérubé, F., Pouliot, M.-A., and Johnston, P. 2004. Interactive effects of substrate sand and silt contents, redd-scale hydraulic gradients, and interstitial velocities on egg-to-emergence survival of Atlantic salmon (*Salmo salar*). *Canadian Journal of Fisheries and Aquatic Sciences* 61: 2271–2277. doi: 10.1139/f04-236.

Le Pichon, C., Gorges, G., Baudry, J., Goreaud, F., and Boët, P. 2009. Spatial metrics and methods for riverscapes: quantifying variability in riverine fish habitat patterns. *Environmetrics* 20: 512–526. doi: 10.1002/env.948.

Lotspeich, F.B. and Everest, F.H. 1981. A new method for reporting and interpreting textural composition of spawning gravel. United States Department of Agriculture, Pacific Northwest Forest and Range Experiment Station, *Research Note* PNW-RN-369: 11p.

May, C.L. and Lee, D.C. 2004. The relationships among in-channel sediment storage, pool depth, and summer survival of juvenile salmonids in Oregon Coast Range streams. *North American Journal of Fisheries Management* 24: 761–774. doi: 10.1577/M03-073.1.

Milner, N.J. Elliott, J.M., Armstrong, J.D. *et al.* 2003. The natural control of salmon and trout populations in streams. *Fisheries Research* 62: 111–125. doi: 10.1016/S0165-7836 (02)00157-1.

Moir, H.J. Gibbins, C.N., Soulsby, C., and Webb, J. 2004. Linking channel geomorphic characteristics to spatial patterns of spawning activity and discharge use by Atlantic salmon (*Salmo salar* L.). *Geomorphology* 60: 21–35. doi: 10.1016/j.geomorph. 2003.07.014.

Moir, H.J., Gibbins, C.N., Buffington, J.M. *et al.* 2009. A new method to identify the fluvial regimes used by spawning salmonids. *Canadian Journal of Fisheries and Aquatic Sciences* 66: 1404–1408. doi: 10.1139/F09-136.

Montgomery, D.R. 1999. Process domains and the River Continuum. *Journal of the American Water Resources Association* 35: 397–410. doi: 10.1111/j.1752-1688.1999.tb03598.x.

Montgomery, D.R., Beamer, E.M., Pess, G.R., and Quinn, T.P. 1999. Channel type and salmonid spawning distribution and abundance. *Canadian Journal of Fisheries and Aquatic Sciences* 56: 377–387. doi: 10.1139/cjfas-56-3-377.

Mull, K.E. and Wilzbach, M.A. 2007. Selection of spawning sites by Coho salmon in a northern California stream. *North American Journal of Fisheries Management* 27: 1343–1354. doi: 10.1577/M06-054.1.

Pess, G.R., Montgomery, D.R., Steel, E.A. *et al.* 2002. Landscape characteristics, land use, and coho salmon (*Oncorhynchus kisutch*) abundance, Snohomish River, Wash., U.S.A. *Canadian Journal of Fisheries and Aquatic Sciences* 59: 613–623. doi: 10.1139/f02-035.

Petty, J.T., Lamothe, P.J., and Mazik, P.M. 2005. Spatial and seasonal dynamics of brook trout populations inhabiting a central Appalachian watershed. *Transactions of the American Fisheries Society* 134: 572–587. doi: 10.1577/T03-229.1.

Poff, N.L. 1997. Landscape filters and species traits: Towards mechanistic understanding and prediction in stream ecology. *Journal of the North American Benthological Society* 16: 391–409. doi: 10.2307/1468026.

Poole, G.C. 2002. Fluvial landscape ecology: addressing uniqueness within the river discontinuum. *Freshwater Biology* 47: 641–660. doi: 10.1046/j.1365-2427.2002.00922.x.

Quinn, T.P., Stewart, I.J., and Boatright, C.P. 2006. Experimental evidence of homing to site of incubation by mature sockeye salmon, *Oncorhynchus nerka. Animal Behaviour* 72: 941–949. doi: 10.1016/j.anbehav.2006.03.003.

Rice, S.P., Greenwood, M.T., and Joyce, C.B. 2001. Tributaries, sediment sources, and the longitudinal organisation of macroinvertebrate fauna along river systems. *Canadian Journal of Fisheries and Aquatic Sciences* 58: 824–840. doi: 10.1139/cjfas-58-4-824.

Rice, S.P., Lancaster, J., and Kemp, P. 2010a. Experimentation at the interface of fluvial geomorphology, stream ecology and hydraulic engineering and the development of an effective, interdisciplinary river science. *Earth Surface Processes and Landforms* 35: 64–77. doi: 10.1002/esp.1838.

Rice, S.P., Little, S., Wood, P.J., Moir, H.J., and Vericat, D. 2010b. The relative contributions of ecology and hydraulics to ecohydraulics. *River Research and Applications* 26: 363–366. doi: 10.1002/rra.1369.

Schlosser, I.J. 1991. Stream Fish Ecology: A Landscape Perspective. *BioScience* 41: 704–712.

Schlosser, I.J. 1995. Critical landscape attributes that influence fish population dynamics in headwater streams. *Hydrobiologia* 303: 71–81. doi: 10.1007/BF00034045.

Schmidt, C., Conant, B., Jr, Bayer-Raich, M., and Schirmer, M. 2007. Evaluation and field-scale application of an analytical method to quantify groundwater discharge using mapped streambed temperatures. *Journal of Hydrology* 347: 292–307. doi: 10.1016/j.jhydrol.2007.08.022.

Smith, R. 2003. *The Mind of the Trout: A Cognitive Ecology for Biologists and Anglers*. Madison, WI, University of Wisconsin Press.

Snucins, E.J., Curry, R.A., and Gunn, J.M. 1992. Brook trout (*Salvelinus fontinalis*) embryo habitat and timing of alevin emergence in a lake and a stream. *Canadian Journal of Zoology* 70: 423–427. doi: 10.1139/z92-064.

Southwood, T.R.E. 1977. Habitat, the templet for ecological strategies? *The Journal of Animal Ecology* 46: 336–365.

Taylor, E.B. 1991. A review of local adaptation in Salmonidae, with particular reference to Pacific and Atlantic salmon.

*Aquaculture* 98: 185–207. doi: 10.1016/0044-8486(91)90383-I.

Thompson, W.L. and Lee, D.C. 2000. Modeling relationships between landscape-level attributes and snorkel counts of chinook salmon and steelhead parr in Idaho. *Canadian Journal of Fisheries and Aquatic Sciences* 57: 1834–1842. doi: 10.1139/cjfas-57-9-1834.

Tonina, D. and Buffington, J.M. 2009a. A three-dimensional model for analyzing the effects of salmon redds on hyporheic exchange and egg pocket habitat. *Canadian Journal of Fisheries and Aquatic Sciences* 66: 2157–2173. doi: 10.1139/F09-146.

Tonina, D. and Buffington, J.M. 2009b. Hyporheic exchange in mountain rivers I: Mechanics and environmental effects. *Geography Compass* 3: 1063–1086. doi: 10.1111/j.1749-8198.2009.00226.x.

Torgersen, C.E., Faux, R.N., McIntosh, B.A., Poage, N.J., and Norton, D.J. 2001. Airborne thermal remote sensing for water temperature assessment in rivers and streams. *Remote Sensing of the Environment* 76: 386–398. doi: 10.1016/S0034-4257(01)00186-9.

Torgersen, C.E., Price, D.M., Li, H.W., and McIntosh, B.A. 1999. Multiscale thermal refugia and stream habitat associations of chinook salmon in northeastern Oregon. *Ecological Applications* 9: 301–319. doi: 10.1890/1051-0761(1999)009[0301:MTRASH]2.0.CO; 2.

Vannote, R.L., Minshall, G.W., Cummins, K.W., Sedell, J.R., and Cushing, C.E. 1980. The river continuum concept. *Canadian Journal of Fisheries and Aquatic Sciences* 37: 130–137. doi: 10.1139/f80-017.

Vronskiy, B.B. 1972. Reproductive biology of the Kamchatka River chinook salmon [*Oncorhynchus tshawytscha* (Walbaum)]. *Journal of Ichthyology* 12: 259–273.

Vronskiy, B.B. and Leman, V.N. 1991. Spawning stations, hydrological regime, and survival of progeny in nests of chinook salmon, *Oncorhynchus tshawytscha,* in the Kamchatka River Basin. *Voprosy Ikhtiologii* 31: 282–291.

Ward, J.V. 1997. An expansive perspective of riverine landscapes: pattern and process across scales. *Gaia* 6: 52–60.

Warren, C.E. and Liss, W.J. 1980. *Adaptation to aquatic environments*. In Lackey, R.T. and Nielsen, L.editors. *Fisheries management*. Oxford, Blackwell Scientific Publications pp. 15–40.

Waters, T.F. 1995. *Sediment in Streams: Sources, Biological Effects and Control.* Bethesda, MD, American Fisheries Society.

Webster, D.A. and Eiriksdottir, G. 1976. Upwelling water as a factor influencing choice of spawning sites by brook trout (*Salvelinus fontinalis*). *Transactions of the American Fisheries Society* 105: 416–421. doi: 10.1577/1548-8659(1976)105<416:UWAAFI>2.0.CO; 2.

White, S.M. and Rahel, F.J. 2008. Complementation of habitats for Bonneville cutthroat trout in watersheds influenced by beavers, livestock, and drought. *Transactions of the American Fisheries Society* 137: 881–894. doi: 10.1577/T06-207.1.

Wigington, Jr., P.J., Ebersole, J.L., Colvin, M.E. *et al.* 2006. Coho salmon dependence on intermittent streams. *Frontiers in Ecology and the Environment* 4: 513–518. doi: 10.1890/1540-9295(2006)4[513:CSDOIS]2.0.CO; 2.

Wilcock, P.R., Barta, A.F., Shea, C.C. *et al.* 1996. Observations of flow and sediment entrainment on a large gravel-bed river. *Water Resources Research* 32: 2897–2909. doi: 10.1029/96WR01628.

Witzel, L.D. and MacCrimmon, H.R. 1983. Redd-site selection by brook trout and brown trout in southwestern Ontario streams. *Transactions of the American Fisheries Society* 112: 760–771. doi: 10.1577/1548-8659(1983)112<760:RSBBTA>2.0.CO; 2.

Youngson, A.F., Malcolm, I.A., Thorley, J.L., Bacon, P.J., and Soulsby, C. 2004. Long-residence groundwater effects on incubating salmonid eggs: low hyporheic oxygen impairs embryo development. *Canadian Journal of Fisheries and Aquatic Sciences* **61**: 2278–2287. doi: 10.1139/f04-217.

Zimmerman, C.E. and Reeves, G.H. 2000. Population structure of sympatric anadromous and non-anadromous *Onchorhynchus mykiss*: evidence from spawning surveys and otolith microchemistry. *Canadian Journal of Fisheries and Aquatic Sciences* **57**: 2152–2162. doi: 10.1139/cjfas-57-10-2152.

Zimmerman, C.E. and Reeves, G.H. 2002. Identification of steelhead and resident rainbow trout progeny in the Deschutes River, Oregon, revealed with otolith microchemistry. *Transactions of the American Fisheries Society* **131**: 986–993. doi: 10.1577/1548-8659(2002) 131 <0986:IOSARR>2.0.CO; 2.

Zimmermann, A.E. and Lapointe, M. 2005. Intergranular flow velocity through salmonid redds: sensitivity to fines infiltration from low intensity sediment transport events. *River Research and Applications* **21**: 865–881. doi: 10.1002/rra.856.

# 18

# Incorporating Spatial Context into the Analysis of Salmonid–Habitat Relations

Christian E. Torgersen, Colden V. Baxter, Joseph L. Ebersole, and Robert E. Gresswell

## 18.1 INTRODUCTION

Habitat use and availability studies have long been used to understand fish–habitat relations and develop predictive models in fisheries management. Lapointe (Chapter 17, this volume) addresses many of the strengths of this approach, specifically for quantifying linkages between geomorphology and fish habitat. Despite the well-documented limitations of correlative models that relate the population density of organisms to habitat characteristics (Railsback et al., 2003; Lancaster and Downes, 2010), this approach still has much to offer aquatic ecology in terms of setting the broader context within which ecological processes (i.e., growth, reproduction, and behaviour) interact and influence the distribution and abundance of organisms (Thomson et al., 1996). This applies particularly to gravel-bed rivers, which (i) are dynamic spatially and temporally, (ii) range in size from several to tens of metres in width, and (iii) are characterized by flows that make experimentation and manipulation difficult at scales that are relevant to the diverse life histories of lotic fishes (Fausch et al., 2002). Thus, it is expected that statistical models that assess habitat associations and seek to predict the distribution and abundance of fish in relation to physical factors (e.g., channel form, flow, and water quality) will continue playing a role – albeit in conjunction with process-based investigations of movement, growth, and behaviour – in studying and conserving lotic fishes. It is along these lines, and specifically regarding salmonid fishes, that this chapter responds to the review and synthesis provided by Lapointe (Chapter 17, this volume).

Habitat preferences are highly "complex and contextual" (see Section 17.2). In spite of centuries of work and the availability of sophisticated computer modelling tools, there is much room for improvement in describing and quantifying fish–habitat relations (Walton and Cotton, 1676; Bjornn and Reiser, 1991; Smith, 1994; Guisan et al., 2002; Railsback and Harvey, 2002; Rosenfeld, 2003). The challenge lies not just in having the appropriate statistical tools, but in obtaining more complete information on where the fish are located and what is available to them in both space and time. Lapointe acknowledges that there are many potential explanations for this problem and suggests that "Part of the poor predictive power of conventional, patch-scale spawning habitat preferences just mentioned may be due to a scale mismatch concerning broader characteristics that control local reproductive success." The specific issue of a scale mismatch as one such explanation for the poor fit of fish–habitat models is a propos and has been described for stream fishes at scales ranging from metres to hundreds of kilometres (Dunham and Vinyard, 1997; Peterson and Dunham, 2010). However, this raises the general question: Why is the predictive power of fish–habitat models so poor? This general question is particularly germane to the aim of the chapter by Lapointe, which is to provide some background for geomorphologists who may be interested in relating physical patterns in fluvial geomorphology to biological responses to address the needs of natural resource managers.

In the following discussion, we address the question raised by Lapointe of why it is so difficult to predict salmonid–habitat relations. We acknowledge that this cannot be an exhaustive treatment of the subject and therefore identify what we believe are several key issues that demonstrate the importance of explicitly incorporating spatial context into the analysis of fish–habitat data. Specifically, our goals are to (i) describe uncertainty in fish–habitat relations as is reflected in correlative models, (ii) elucidate the potential problems with using density (i.e., abundance normalized by area or length) as a response variable in statistical models, (iii) illustrate how uncertainty in correlative models can

*Gravel-bed Rivers: Processes, Tools, Environments*, First Edition. Edited by Michael Church, Pascale M. Biron and André G. Roy.
© 2012 John Wiley & Sons, Ltd. Published 2012 by John Wiley & Sons, Ltd.

be alleviated by using spatially explicit data to predict the locations of areas with locally high abundance, and (iv) demonstrate how increasing the scale of the area, or length, over which population density is calculated can lead to improved predictive power. Our emphasis is on spatial context (i.e., scale and location), but it is important to note that the same principles may be applied with some modification to temporal context which, although very important, is beyond the scope of this chapter.

## 18.2  UNCERTAINTY IN FISH–HABITAT RELATIONS

Bivariate scatterplots and least-squares regression are common techniques used for assessing fish–habitat relations. Although much more sophisticated statistical methods are increasingly being applied in salmonid ecology, demonstrating correlation with scatterplots is one of the most powerful ways to present scientific data. Moreover, bivariate scatterplots provide a visual method for assessing uncertainty in the relation between response and explanatory variables. Peterson and Dunham (2010) describe three different types of uncertainty in fisheries management: environmental uncertainty, statistical uncertainty, and structural uncertainty. In this chapter, we focus on structural uncertainty in species–habitat relations specifically in relation to the influence of spatial scale. Structural uncertainty derives from "the inability to determine accurately the processes or models that best represent system dynamics (e.g., the relation between geomorphology, streamflow, habitat availability, and fish population demographics)" (Peterson and Dunham, 2010, p.101).

For the purposes of illustration, we used data from three streams to examine the relation between salmonid abundance and pool area. The three study streams fit the characterization of "gravel-bed" rivers and streams described in this volume. To eliminate the potentially confounding influence of broad-scale upstream–downstream gradients in species distribution, we selected fish species that were present throughout the extent of each of their respective streams. Data on juvenile Chinook salmon (*Oncorhynchus tshawytscha*) and rainbow trout (*O. mykiss*) were collected in the Wenaha River, a medium-sized (width: 5–38 m) tributary to the Grande Ronde River located in northeastern Oregon (USA); field work was conducted in July, 1999 during an extensive snorkeling survey of all pools in 35 km of the main stem (see descriptions of the study area and methods in Baxter, 2001; Torgersen *et al.*, 2006) (Figures 18.1a and b). Coastal cutthroat trout (*O. clarkii clarkii*) data were collected in August, 2001 using single-pass electrofishing in all pools throughout the entire fish-bearing portion of the stream network (11 km in total) of Camp

Creek, a small (width: 0.5–13 m) tributary to the Umpqua River in western Oregon (see Torgersen *et al.*, 2004; Gresswell *et al.*, 2006) (Figure 18.1c). Juvenile coho salmon (*O. kisutch*) data were collected in July–August, 2004 during snorkeling surveys of all pools in 30 non-contiguous ~400 m reaches distributed throughout the West Fork Smith River basin, a small- to medium-sized (width: 1–19 m) tributary to the Umpqua River in western Oregon (Ebersole *et al.*, 2009). Pools were defined as a geomorphically distinct channel unit based on scour and associated bedform topography (Bisson *et al.*, 1982; Hawkins *et al.*, 1993). Pool area was calculated by multiplying channel unit length by the width. The methods for identifying pools and enumerating salmonids in pools were consistent among the separate studies for which the data were collected. Riffles were not included in the analysis because the methods with which they were sampled varied among the different studies.

Bivariate scatterplots of salmonid abundance and pool area were typical of salmonid–habitat relations (Figure 18.1). The fit of the data to simple linear models was generally poor ($r^2 \leq 0.54$) and was highly variable among species and streams. What was striking about these data – as will be discussed in the following section on density as a measure of abundance – was that area was expected to be a very good predictor of fish abundance for the simple reason that more fish can occupy larger pools. In Figure 18.1, it is important to note: (i) the small number of data points with both high abundance and large area, and (ii) the large number of points clustered near the origin. Data points at either ends of the fitted relation have a large effect on the perceived relation, even though there is considerable scatter between these two extremes (e.g., low area with low abundance versus high area with high abundance). Interestingly, if fewer samples had been collected, the relations may have appeared tighter, assuming that the extreme values at either end of the fitted relation had still been captured. Spatially continuous data (Figures 18.1a, b, and c) thus have both the advantage of capturing variation in the data and the disadvantage of making it more difficult to discern consistent patterns (Torgersen *et al.*, 2008).

The relatively high degree of scatter illustrates variability in the relation between salmonid abundance and pool area (Figure 18.1). Moreover, the relatively low number of data points with both high fish abundance and large area complicates the interpretation of these relations. Many investigators are reticent to remove these data points from analysis because (i) every data point represents significant work in the field, and (ii) these points have a lot of leverage on the fit ($r^2$) and statistical significance of the relation. This is by no means a criticism; it is merely a consequence of the complexity of fish–habitat relations. Some of the most instructive

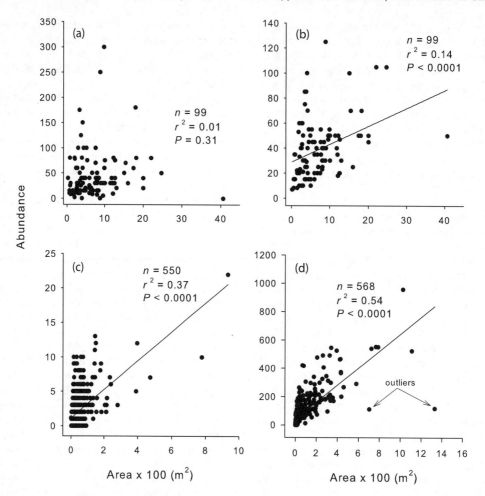

**Figure 18.1** Relations between pool area and abundance for four species of salmonids in three gravel-bed streams: juvenile Chinook salmon (a) and rainbow trout (b) (Wenaha River, summer 1999); coastal cutthroat trout (c) (Camp Creek, summer 2001); and juvenile coho salmon (d) (West Fork Smith River, summer 2004). Fitted lines for significant relations ($P < 0.05$) and $r^2$ values are from simple linear regression of pool area versus abundance.

and influential examples of salmonid–habitat relations show similar "noisy" patterns (Inoue *et al.*, 1997; Connolly and Hall, 1999; Isaak and Hubert, 2004; Wissmar *et al.*, 2010). These challenges are not unique to salmonid ecology and have been addressed by multiple authors in ecology (Thomson *et al.*, 1996; Cade *et al.*, 1999; Dunham *et al.*, 2002; Lancaster and Belyea, 2006). These papers provide excellent explanations of the difficulty of modelling species-abundance–environment relations and suggest alternative statistical methods (e.g., quantile regression) for interpreting and analyzing correlations in data when the ecological response (i.e., abundance) shows a "factor-ceiling" or "wedge-shaped" pattern, indicating that the habitat variable may be acting as a limiting factor rather than a single dominant "controlling" factor (Thomson *et al.*,

1996; Cade *et al.*, 1999). This "wedge-shaped" pattern is apparent in Figure 18.1a (for other examples see Dunham *et al.*, 2002; Zoellick and Cade, 2006), in which both high and low abundances occur where pool area is low, but high abundances generally do not occur where pool area is high. These "wedge-shaped" relations may be due to a number of factors, including (i) other important explanatory variables that were excluded from the model, (ii) undefined "error" associated with sampling methods, and (iii) spatial context (Thomson *et al.*, 1996).

## 18.3  PROBLEMS WITH DENSITY AS A MEASURE OF ABUNDANCE

The decision to normalize counts or estimates of the abundance of organisms based on the sampled length, area, or volume is an essential step in the process of analyzing scientific data. As with any data transformation, there are assumptions that must be made in the interpretation of the results, particularly when density is used in habitat preference models. For example, it is widely acknowledged that the density of organisms can be a misleading indicator of habitat quality (Van Horne, 1983; Science Citation Index (SCI): cited 960 times). However, it is poorly recognized in salmonid ecology that there can be problems with using density as a measure of abundance (Grant *et al.*, 1998; SCI: cited 71 times). These potential problems are numerous, and it is beyond the scope of this chapter to address them exhaustively. Therefore, we focus on aspects of the problem that are specifically related to the spatial context of density measurements. For example, error that arises from incorrectly using density as a measure of abundance can contribute to uncertainty – as described in the previous section – and illustrates the importance of explicitly considering spatial context in quantifying in fish–habitat relations. We believe that these problems may be particularly pronounced in gravel-bed rivers and streams due to the effects of scale, territory size, and variations in the bedform topography of pools (*sensu* Grant *et al.*, 1998). For example, in headwater streams, coastal cutthroat trout in small pools in higher-gradient reaches tend to be distributed more uniformly within channel units than trout in pools located in larger, lower-gradient reaches (Torgersen and Gresswell, unpublished data). Thus, two different pools may have similar abundances of trout (and area useable by trout), but after normalizing by area, the larger pool will have a lower density. The same concept applies when scaling up to evaluate numbers of trout in relation to pool area and number of pools in a given reach or stream: two streams may have the same pool area, but have different numbers of pools for a given stretch of stream. Due to territory size, cover, and the usable area by trout, number of pools may be a better predictor of trout abundance than pool area.

The assumption in normalizing by length, area, or volume is that there is a predictable relation between numbers of fish and the spatial dimensions of the sampled unit. The convention in salmonid ecology of demarcating sampling units according to geomorphic channel units (e.g., pools, riffles, and glides) and normalizing fish counts by the area of the sampled unit is based on well-founded theory and empirical data (Frissell *et al.*, 1986; Hankin and Reeves, 1988). However, when comparing among species, across watersheds, and among reaches along the longitudinal stream profile, we found that the relation between salmonid abundance and pool area was inconsistent (Figure 18.1). Further investigation is needed to evaluate the relation

between sampled area and salmonid abundance in riffle habitats and at larger spatial scales in which pool and riffle habitats are combined. We were not able to examine the relation between salmonid abundance and area in riffle habitats because riffles were sampled differently in the separate studies from which the data in Figure 18.1 were derived. However, we expect that there may be a better fit between area and salmonid abundance in riffles than in pools, particularly as unit length increases and the effects behavioural interactions related to cover and territory size are reduced (*sensu* Grant *et al.*, 1998).

Relations between salmonid abundance and pool area were difficult to discern for juvenile Chinook salmon and rainbow trout in the Wenaha River (Figure 18.1a, b). Although the trend of increasing abundance with area appears to be positive and is statistically significant for rainbow trout ($P < 0.01$) (but not for juvenile Chinook), the scatterplots suggest a high degree of variability in these relations. There are many potential explanations for the poor fit between salmonid abundance and area in the Wenaha River (e.g., other limiting habitat variables, the presence of other fish species or predators, food availability), and these other factors could be addressed by including other explanatory variables in the statistical model. However, the important lesson learned from these data is that abundance (not normalized abundance, i.e., density) may be the more appropriate response variable. In fact, depending on the research question, it may be helpful to include the spatial dimensions of the sampled unit (area or length) as separate variables in the statistical model on equal footing with other explanatory variables. An effective alternative would be to collect data in uniformly sized units. This approach was employed with excellent results by Deschenes and Rodriguez (2007), who used a hierarchical model to predict the abundance of brook trout (*Salvelinus fontinalis*) based on stream habitat features in $600 \times 75$ m reaches in tributaries throughout the Cascapedia River basin in Quebec (Canada).

Even when salmonid abundance appears to be relatively highly correlated with area (Figures 18.1c, d), normalizing by area could still make it difficult to interpret habitat relations. An unexpected consequence of a high correlation between abundance and area (e.g., Figure 18.1d) is that finding additional statistically significant explanatory variables after the data have been normalized by area may be difficult because so much of the relation may have been already explained by area. In some cases, area itself is the explanatory variable that is most ecologically relevant and should be evaluated explicitly. For example, removing two outliers beneath the diagonal in Figure 18.1d increases the $r^2$ value to 67%, a considerably high value for a fish–habitat model. This high $r^2$ value suggests that space at the habitat-unit level may be the dominant factor limiting the abundance of juvenile coho salmon in portions of the West Fork Smith River (Ebersole *et al.*, 2009).

## 18.4    PREDICTING THE LOCATIONS OF AREAS WITH LOCALLY HIGH ABUNDANCE

In many instances, the relation between salmonid abundance and habitat features may be noisy, even when the relations are evaluated with sophisticated regression techniques and after addressing potential problems with density (e.g., Cade *et al.*, 1999; Dunham *et al.*, 2002). Situations such as these indicate that spatial context (location) and scale (which will be addressed in the following section) may be making salmonid–habitat relations difficult to interpret. One approach to this problem is to use spatial regression techniques that include spatial autocorrelation in the model (Guisan *et al.*, 2002), but even these tools may not adequately address the influences of location (i.e., juxtaposition and proximity) on salmonid behaviour. Moreover, if location is of interest, as it often is in ecological settings, it may be desirable to elucidate its role explicitly (an issue highlighted by Lapointe). Various approaches have been used to solve this problem and, unfortunately for the practitioner, they all require specific adaptation for the unique ecological setting and species involved (Knapp and Preisler, 1999; Fukushima, 2001; Moir *et al.*, 2004; Isaak *et al.*, 2007; Murray, 2009). We applied a simple approach to illustrate graphically how logistic regression can be used to predict the locations – as opposed to the actual densities – of areas with locally high abundance (Torgersen *et al.*, 1999; Torgersen and Close, 2004).

To demonstrate the effectiveness of logistic regression for predicting the locations of areas with locally high salmonid abundance, we re-analysed data from the distribution of adult Chinook salmon and stream habitat in the Middle Fork John Day River, Oregon, (for details on the study area and methods see Torgersen *et al.*, 1999) (Figure 18.2). Visual inspection of longitudinal patterns in the distribution of salmon abundance, pool numbers, and water temperature indicated that peaks in salmon abundance corresponded with troughs in temperature and peaks in pool density (Figure 18.2). However, multiple linear regression using these two explanatory variables showed a very poor fit (adjusted $r^2 = 0.28$) of the observed and predicted values (Figure 18.3). Although the wedge-shaped pattern in the scatterplot of predicted versus observed values suggested that there may be associations between these variables and salmon abundance (*sensu* Dunham *et al.*, 2002), the results of the regression were not convincing. In contrast, when logistic regression was used to statistically compare the locations of peaks and troughs (binary response variable: peak = 1, trough = 0) in salmon numbers with spatial patterns of pool density and water temperature, the model correctly predicted 78% of the observations based on a classification table with a cut-off level of 0.5 ($P = 0.5$) for the predicted values (Torgersen *et al.*, 1999). This analysis confirmed the patterns of spatial association that were visually apparent in Figure 18.2 but could not be detected using standard multiple linear regression.

Understanding the role of spatial context, and specifically local discontinuities or patchiness, in fish–habitat relations constitutes a new frontier in stream fish ecology. Influences of biotic factors, such as inter- and intraspecific interactions, on local discontinuities in fish distribution are poorly understood and deserve greater attention (Angermeier *et al.*, 2002). Although the importance of discontinuities in the longitudinal progression of biotic and abiotic patterns has been emphasized in riverine ecology, most notably by Poole (2002), the role of discontinuities in salmonid ecology has been poorly described. This may be because spatially continuous data collection, which is labour intensive and relatively uncommon, is required to identify such patterns. Lapointe succinctly summarizes this issue in paraphrasing Isaak *et al.* (2007): "the best predictors of selected sites [for spawning] were not the traditional metrics of habitat quality (preferred substrate, depth and velocity) but rather...'spatial characteristics' of the habitat...[and] the existence of a 'biogenic' clustering of redd sites based mainly on 'geometric' characteristics of spawning habitat." There is much to be learned about these aspects of habitat selection, particularly at the interface between fluvial geomorphology and salmonid ecology. For example, the link discontinuity concept proposed by Rice *et al.* (2001) has not been tested as a factor in determining the longitudinal distribution of salmonids. Preliminary evidence suggests, however, that areas with locally high abundance of Atlantic salmon (*Salmo salar*) parr may be associated with locations of sedimentary links (M. Lapointe, McGill University, and N. Bergeron, INRS, Quebec, Canada, pers. comm.) even though their actual density is not (Bouchard and Boisclair, 2008).

## 18.5    SCALING UP FOR GREATER PREDICTIVE POWER

Typical investigations of salmonid–habitat relations are conducted at either fine, or very coarse scales. However, scales intermediate to these may be the most important for understanding stream fish populations because these are the scales where stream fishes complete their life history (Fausch *et al.*, 2002). Thus, the difficulty in

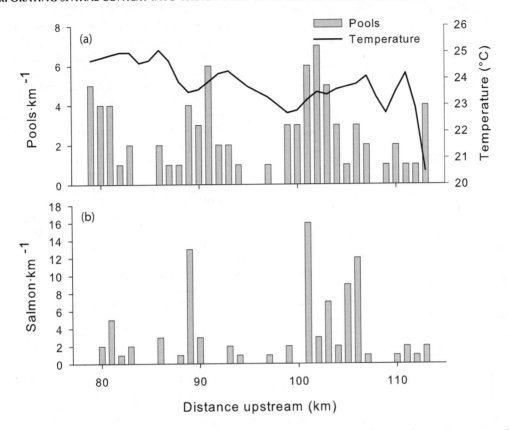

**Figure 18.2** Longitudinal patterns of the number of deep pools and mean remotely sensed water temperature (a) and adult Chinook salmon abundance (b) in summer 1994, Middle Fork John Day River (MFJD), Oregon (USA). Data from spatially continuous surveys are summarized as the mean (water temperature) or density (number·km$^{-1}$) in 1 km bins. Distance upstream from the confluence of the MFJD with the North Fork John Day River is indicated on the $x$-axis (see Torgersen *et al.*, 1999)

modelling salmonid–habitat relations stems from the overarching problem of scale (Wiens, 1989). The crux of the problem as applied to salmonid–habitat relations is that where fine-scale characteristics may be suitable, coarser-scale and perhaps less understood factors come into play, giving the appearance that fish are occupying suboptimal habitat and not fully utilizing the best habitats. Lapointe emphasizes this problem and stresses the importance of investigating habitat relations at multiple scales. We also advocate this view, but add the caveat that the nature of salmonid–habitat relations may change from that of a limiting factor at fine scales to a single dominant "controlling" factor at coarser scales and vice versa (*sensu* Dunham *et al.*, 2002; Lancaster and Belyea, 2006). This makes it very difficult to simultaneously evaluate habitat associations at multiple scales because the type of analysis required may change from logistic regression or quantile regression for limiting factors to linear regression for controlling factors, depending upon the question and scale(s) of interest. The

standard practice of predicting salmonid abundance at a fine scale (e.g., a channel unit or even a series of channel units) based on a suite of progressively larger-scaled explanatory variables can be very effective at solving this problem (Peterson and Dunham, 2010), but still addresses only local abundance responses which may not be as relevant to the life history of the species of interest (*sensu* Fausch *et al.*, 2002).

We propose that in order to gain more predictive power and address salmonid response at ecologically important intermediate scales, it may be helpful to coarsen, or "scale up", the spatial grain (i.e., length or area) of both the response and explanatory variables. Coarsening the scale of the response and explanatory variables helps to obtain tighter correlative relations (i.e., less uncertainty and higher $r^2$ values) because at coarser scales the nature of the relation is more likely to be a single dominant "controlling" factor, as opposed to a limiting factor. For example, the association between the abundance of Chinook salmon and water temperature at "intermediate"

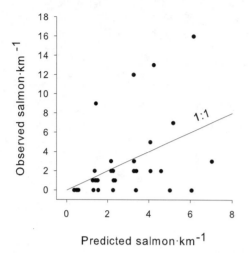

**Figure 18.3** Predicted versus observed values from multiple linear regression of salmon·km$^{-1}$, pools·km$^{-1}$, and water temperature. The diagonal line indicates a 1:1 relation.

scales shown in Figures 18.2 and 18.3 is indicative of a limiting factor and could only be detected with logistic regression because the range in temperature is within the thermal tolerances of the species. At broader scales throughout entire basins and over latitudinal gradients, the relation between water temperature and Chinook salmon abundance is indicative of a single dominant "controlling" factor due to the greater range in temperatures from lethal to optimal. Unfortunately, scaling up the response variable does come at a cost because it means that more length or area must be surveyed in order to obtain an accurate estimate of total abundance in the sampled unit. The mean abundance derived from a statistical sample of channel units selected randomly from a reach is not likely to be a precise estimate of total reach abundance unless fish are distributed uniformly, which for the reasons discussed in previous sections, is highly unlikely in natural river systems.

Lapointe (Figure 17.6) provides an excellent example of how scaling up the response and explanatory variables leads to better predictive power. By relating the abundance of returning adult Atlantic salmon (i.e., the run size) to the total length of optimally productive valley segments in a watershed, Kim and Lapointe (2010) were able to explain an unusually high degree of variation ($r^2 = 0.8$–$0.9$) in salmon run size. Note that the response and explanatory variables were not mean values obtained from a sample of channel units or reaches in each watershed. Rather, they were derived from (i) census data of returning adults per watershed (over multiple years), and (ii) the total amount of optimal habitat derived from interpretation of aerial photos for entire watersheds. A similar approach, in terms of using coarser "intermediate-scale" response and explanatory variables was used by Baxter and Hauer (2000) to predict with a high degree of precision ($r^2 > 0.8$) the number of bull trout (*Salvelinus confluentus*) redds in watersheds, valley segments, and reaches, based the proportion of bounded alluvial valley segments and the magnitude of ground-water input. In this study, upwelling at watershed, valley-segment, and reach scales was important for mediating winter temperatures and preventing the build-up of ice which could directly affect egg-to-fry survival. Thus, upwelling exhibited a controlling relation with redd density and could be effectively modelled with direct correlation analysis, whereas at finer scales, the relationship between redd abundance and the magnitude and direction of hyporheic exchange was less predictable and indicative of a limiting relation. Other work of this type has shown strong relations between valley segment configuration and salmonid distribution (Boxall *et al.*, 2008). Observations by Lapointe (Chapter 17, this volume) corroborate these findings and yet illustrate that more work is needed to understand interactions among biological and physical processes that influence redd site selection by salmonids at multiple scales.

In this discussion, we have highlighted several areas of inquiry that not only provide opportunities for collaboration between fluvial geomorphologists and salmonid ecologists, but also represent important theoretical topics in riverine ecology. There is much to be gained through mutual exchange of ideas between aquatic ecologists and fluvial geomorphologists, but in order for this collaboration to flow smoothly across disciplines, it is important to explicitly identify differences in "knowledge structure" (Benda *et al.*, 2002). These differences are pronounced in physical versus ecological sciences and usually involve contrasting perceptions of scale and uncertainty (*sensu* Peterson and Dunham, 2010), and this is where we have focused our discussion. The intersection of different domains of understanding can be the source of conflict, but also the fertile ground of discovery. It is our aim to advance the latter by identifying areas in salmonid ecology that pose real challenges in the discipline and pertain particularly to the structure and function of gravel-bed rivers and streams.

## 18.6   ACKNOWLEDGEMENTS

Many of the ideas presented in this manuscript arose out of discussions with J. A. Jones in the Department of Geosciences at Oregon State University. Constructive reviews were provided by P. Connolly, J. Dunham, M. Lapointe, and an anonymous reviewer. The authors also wish to thank N. Bergeron and the organizers and participants of the 7th Gravel-bed Rivers Conference

2010 for the inspiring discussions that helped bring these ideas to fruition. Example data sets were collected with funding from the Bonneville Power Administration (Project No. 88-108), the Environmental Protection Agency (EPA), the EPA/National Science Foundation Joint Watershed Research Program (Grant R82-4774-010), and the Cooperative Forest Ecosystem Research Program, a consortium of the US Geological Survey Forest and Rangeland Ecosystem Science Center, the US Bureau of Land Management, Oregon State University, and the Oregon Department of Forestry. Any use of trade, product, or firm names is for descriptive purposes only and does not imply endorsement by the US Government.

## 18.7 REFERENCES

Angermeier P.L., Krueger, K.L., and Dolloff, C.A. 2002. Discontinuity in stream-fish distributions: Implications for assessing and predicting species occurrence. In Scott, J.M., Heglund, P.J., Morrison, M.L. *et al.*. editors. *Predicting Species Occurrences: Issues of Accuracy and Scale.* Washington, D.C., Island Press, pp. 519–527.

Baxter, C.V. 2001. *Fish movement and assemblage dynamics in a Pacific Northwest riverscape.* Ph. D. dissertation. Oregon State University, Corvallis.

Baxter, C.V. and Hauer, F.R. 2000. Geomorphology, hyporheic exchange, and selection of spawning habitat by bull trout (*Salvelinus confluentus*). *Canadian Journal of Fisheries and Aquatic Sciences* **57**: 1470–1481.

Benda, L.E., Poff, N.L., Tague, C. *et al.* 2002. How to avoid train wrecks when using science in environmental problem solving. *Bioscience* **52**: 1127–1136.

Bisson, P.A., Nielsen, J.L., Palmason, R.A., and Grove, L.E. 1982. A system of naming habitat types in small streams, with examples of habitat utilization by salmonids during low streamflow. In Armantrout, N.B., editor. *Acquisition and Utilization of Aquatic Habitat Inventory Information.* Bethesda, MD, American Fisheries Society, Western Division, pp. 62–73.

Bjornn, T.C. and Reiser, D.W. 1991. Habitat requirements of salmonids in streams. In Meehan, W.R., editor. *Influences of Forest and Rangeland Management of Salmonid Fishes and their Habitats.* Bethesda, MD, American Fisheries Society, pp. 83–138.

Bouchard, J. and Boisclair, D. 2008. The relative importance of local, lateral, and longitudinal variables on the development of habitat quality models for a river. *Canadian Journal of Fisheries and Aquatic Sciences* **65**: 61–73.

Boxall, G.D., Giannico, G.R., and Li, H.W. 2008. Landscape topography and the distribution of Lahontan cutthroat trout (*Oncorhynchus clarki henshawi*) in a high desert stream. *Environmental Biology of Fishes* **82**: 71–84.

Cade, B.S., Terrell, J.W., and Schroeder, R.L. 1999. Estimating effects of limiting factors with regression quantiles. *Ecology* **80**: 311–323.

Connolly, P.J. and Hall, J.D. 1999. Biomass of coastal cutthroat trout in unlogged and previously clear-cut basins in the central Coast Range of Oregon. *Transactions of the American Fisheries Society* **128**: 890–899.

Deschenes, J. and Rodriguez, M.A. 2007. Hierarchical analysis of relationships between brook trout (*Salvelinus fontinalis*) density and stream habitat features. *Canadian Journal of Fisheries and Aquatic Sciences* **64**: 777–785.

Dunham, J.B. and Vinyard, G, L. 1997. Incorporating stream level variability into analyses of site level fish habitat relationships: Some cautionary examples. *Transactions of the American Fisheries Society* **126**: 323–329.

Dunham, J.B., Cade, B.S., and Terrell, J, W. 2002. Influences of spatial and temporal variation on fish–habitat relationships defined by regression quantiles. *Transactions of the American Fisheries Society* **131**: 86–98.

Ebersole, J.L., Colvin, M.E., Wigington, P.J. *et al.* 2009. Hierarchical modeling of late-summer weight and summer abundance of juvenile coho salmon across a stream network. *Transactions of the American Fisheries Society* **138**: 1138–1156.

Fausch, K.D., Torgersen, C.E., Baxter, C.V., and Li, H.W. 2002. Landscapes to riverscapes: Bridging the gap between research and conservation of stream fishes. *Bioscience* **52**: 483–498.

Frissell, C.A., Liss, W.J., Warren, C.E., and Hurley, M.D. 1986. A hierarchical framework for stream habitat classification: Viewing streams in a watershed context. *Environmental Management* **10**: 199–214.

Fukushima, M. 2001. Salmonid habitat-geomorphology relationships in low-gradient streams. *Ecology* **82**: 1238–1246.

Grant, J.W.A., Steingrimsson, S.O., Keeley, E.R., and Cunjak, R.A. 1998. Implications of territory size for the measurement and prediction of salmonid abundance in streams. *Canadian Journal of Fisheries and Aquatic Sciences* **55** (Supplement 1): 181–190.

Gresswell, R.E., Torgersen, C.E., Bateman, D.S. *et al.* 2006. A spatially explicit approach for evaluating relationships among coastal cutthroat trout, habitat, and disturbance in small Oregon streams. In Hughes, R.M., Wang, L.,and Seelbach, P.W.editors. *Landscape Influences on Stream Habitats and Biological Assemblages.* Bethesda, MD, American Fisheries Society, pp. 457–471.

Guisan, A., Edwards, T.C., and Hastie, T. 2002. Generalized linear and generalized additive models in studies of species distributions: Setting the scene. *Ecological Modelling* **157**: 89–100.

Hankin, D.G. and Reeves, G.H. 1988. Estimating total fish abundance and total habitat area in small streams based on visual estimation methods. *Canadian Journal of Fisheries and Aquatic Sciences* **45**: 834–844.

Hawkins, C.P., Kershner, J.L., Bisson, P.A. *et al.* 1993. A hierarchical approach to classifying stream habitat features. *Fisheries* **18**: 3–12.

Inoue, M., Nakano, S., and Nakamura, F. 1997. Juvenile masu salmon (*Oncorhynchus masou*) abundance and stream habitat relationships in northern Japan. *Canadian Journal of Fisheries and Aquatic Sciences* **54**: 1331–1341.

Isaak, D.J. and Hubert, W, A. 2004. Nonlinear response of trout abundance to summer stream temperatures across a thermally diverse montane landscape. *Transactions of the American Fisheries Society* **133**: 1254–1259.

Isaak, D.J., Thurow, R.F., Rieman, B.E., and Dunham, J, B. 2007. Chinook salmon use of spawning patches: Relative roles of habitat quality, size, and connectivity. *Ecological Applications* **17**: 352–364.

Kim, M. and Lapointe, M. 2010. Regional variability in Atlantic salmon (*Salmo salar*) riverscapes: A simple landscape ecology model explaining the large variability in size of salmon runs across Gaspé watersheds, *Canada. Ecology of Freshwater Fish* **20**: 144–156.

Knapp, R.A. and Preisler, H.K. 1999. Is it possible to predict habitat use by spawning salmonids? *A test using California golden trout (Oncorhynchus mykiss aguabonita). Canadian Journal of Fisheries and Aquatic Sciences* **56**: 1576–1584.

Lancaster, J. and Belyea, L.R. 2006. Defining the limits to local density: alternative views of abundance–environment relationships. *Freshwater Biology* **51**: 783–796.

Lancaster, J. and Downes, B.J. 2010. Linking the hydraulic world of individual organisms to ecological processes: putting ecology into ecohydraulics. *River Research and Applications* **26**: 385–403.

Moir, H.J., Gibbins, C.N., Soulsby, C., and Webb, J. 2004. Linking channel geomorphic characteristics to spatial patterns of spawning activity and discharge use by Atlantic salmon *(Salmo salar* L.). *Geomorphology* **60**: 21–35.

Murray, K. 2009. *Spatial and temporal analysis of Chinook salmon redds from historical and current aerial surveys on the Cowlitz River, Washington*. M.S. thesis. University of Washington, Seattle.

Peterson, J.T. and Dunham, J.B. 2010. Scale and fisheries management. In Hubert, W. and Quist, M.editors. *Inland Fisheries Management*. Bethesda, MD, American Fisheries Society, pp. 81–105.

Poole, G.C. 2002. Fluvial landscape ecology: Addressing uniqueness within the river discontinuum. *Freshwater Biology* **47**: 641–660.

Railsback, S.F. and Harvey, B.C. 2002. Analysis of habitat selection rules using an individual-based model. *Ecology* **83**: 1817–1830.

Railsback, S.F., Stauffer, H.B., and Harvey, B, C. 2003. What can habitat preference models tell us? Tests using a virtual trout population. *Ecological Applications* **13**: 1580–1594.

Rice, S.P., Greenwood, M.T., and Joyce, C.B. 2001. Tributaries, sediment sources, and the longitudinal organisation of macroinvertebrate fauna along river systems. *Canadian Journal of Fisheries and Aquatic Sciences* **58**: 824–840.

Rosenfeld, J. 2003. Assessing the habitat requirements of stream fishes: An overview and evaluation of different approaches. *Transactions of the American Fisheries Society* **132**: 953–968.

Smith, C.L. 1994. *Fish Watching: An Outdoor Guide to Freshwater Fishes*. Ithaca, NY, Cornell University Press.

Thomson, J.D., Weiblen, G., Thomson, B.A., Alfaro, S., and Legendre, P. 1996. Untangling multiple factors in spatial distributions: Lilies, gophers, and rocks. *Ecology* **77**: 1698–1715.

Torgersen, C.E. and Close, D.A. 2004. Influence of habitat heterogeneity on the distribution of larval Pacific lamprey (*Lampetra tridentata*) at two spatial scales. *Freshwater Biology* **49**: 614–630.

Torgersen, C.E., Baxter, C.V., Li, H.W., and McIntosh, B.A. 2006. Landscape influences on longitudinal patterns of river fishes: Spatially continuous analysis of fish-habitat relationships. In Hughes, R.M., Wang, L.,and Seelbach, P.W.editors. *Landscape Influences on Stream Habitats and Biological Assemblages*. Bethesda, MD, American Fisheries Society, pp. 473–492.

Torgersen, C.E., Gresswell, R.E., and Bateman, D.S. 2004. Pattern detection in stream networks: Quantifying spatial variability in fish distribution. In Nishida, T., Kailola, P.J., and Hollingworth, C.E.editors. *GIS/Spatial Analyses in Fishery and Aquatic Sciences*, Vol. **2**, Saitama, Japan, Fishery-Aquatic GIS Research Group, pp. 405–420.

Torgersen, C.E., Gresswell, R.E., Bateman, D.S., and Burnett, K.M. 2008. Spatial identification of tributary impacts in river networks In Rice, S.P., Roy, A.G.,and Rhoads, B.L., editors. *River Confluences, Tributaries and the Fluvial Network*. Chichester, John Wiley & Sons Ltd, pp. 159–181.

Torgersen, C.E., Price, D.M., Li, H.W., and McIntosh, B.A. 1999. Multiscale thermal refugia and stream habitat associations of chinook salmon in northeastern Oregon. *Ecological Applications* **9**: 301–319.

Van Horne, B. 1983. Density as a misleading indicator of habitat quality. *Journal of Wildlife Management* **47**: 893–901.

Walton, I. and Cotton, C. 1676. *The Compleat Angler: Or, The Contemplative Man's Recreation*. London.

Wiens, J.A. 1989. Spatial scaling in ecology. *Functional Ecology* **3**: 385–397.

Wissmar, R.C., Timm, R.K., and Bryant, M. 2010. Radar-derived digital elevation models and field-surveyed variables to predict distributions of juvenile coho salmon and Dolly Varden in remote streams of Alaska. *Transactions of the American Fisheries Society* **139**: 288–302.

Zoellick, B.W. and Cade, B.S. 2006. Evaluating redband trout habitat in sagebrush desert basins in southwestern Idaho. *North American Journal of Fisheries Management* **26**: 268–281.

# 19

# Animals and the Geomorphology of Gravel-bed Rivers

Stephen P. Rice, Matthew F. Johnson and Ian Reid

## 19.1 INTRODUCTION

Lapointe (Chapter 17, this volume) argues for a fuller and more critical consideration of the nature of the relation between the physical environment and stream organisms, specifically salmonid fish, at local and catchment scales. His fundamental argument is that geomorphologists can offer more to an integrated river science than mapping and defining physical habitat patches; an excellent point of departure. Fluvial geomorphology does have much more to offer, but as Lapointe suggests, this depends on geomorphologists engaging more deeply with ecological theory and, of course, reciprocal engagement by ecologists with the geomorphologists' understanding of river morphodynamics. In this sense, Lapointe's chapter contributes to a growing body of work that calls for better interdisciplinary efforts between fluvial geomorphologists and lotic ecologists, and seeks to identify pathways to achieving that goal (Palmer and Bernhardt, 2006; Dollar et al., 2007; Vaughan et al., 2009; Rice et al., 2010).

Following discussion of Lapointe's general themes, we explore an understudied aspect of the interaction between biota and the physical environment of streams and rivers: the role of animals as geomorphological agents. By emphasizing the two-way interaction between biotic and abiotic elements in gravel-bed rivers, this topic exemplifies the need to develop our view of "habitat". In particular, a growing body of work has demonstrated how biotic components of the river system exert strong influences on channel geomorphology and hydrology, and it is therefore increasingly apparent that the relation between the physical environment and biota is not one way and top-down, in which the physical environment defines a habitat template, but is one of feedbacks and self-regulation (Naiman et al., 2000; Reinhardt et al., 2010) where plants, animals, flow, and sediments interact to define the ecosystem. Following a necessarily brief review of available work, we report on experiments to investigate the impact of the signal crayfish (*Pacifastacus leniusculus*) on bedload sediment transport in gravel-bed rivers. In several parts of the world, this is a highly successful invasive species and therefore represents a special case: the animal has been released from the suite of factors that would limit its vigour and abundance in its native environment (Wolff, 2002) and encounters environments unadjusted to its presence. There is therefore the potential for enhanced sedimentological and morphological impacts, compared to native species (Harvey et al., 2011).

## 19.2 IT IS NOT ONLY "HABITAT" THAT MATTERS

Lapointe's paper emphasizes the complexity and spatio-temporal contextuality of "habitat" and therefore the difficulty of finding widely applicable or definitive rules that link animal presence, density or diversity to physical conditions. This issue is increasingly recognized, especially in the ecological literature, where it has been argued that empirical associations between environmental variables, like water velocity or depth, and biotic variables, like species density, community composition, or population biomass, do not constitute a robust understanding of the controls on organism, population, community, or ecosystem ecology (e.g., Anderson et al., 2006; Rypel and Bayne, 2009). In turn, some have argued that because a "habitat-centric" approach is deeply engrained in the lexicon of river managers there is a broad and dangerous knowledge gap between the understanding of physical–biological interactions and the tools deployed by practitioners charged with maintaining healthy aquatic ecosystems (e.g., Lancaster and Downes, 2010a).

*Gravel-bed Rivers: Processes, Tools, Environments*, First Edition. Edited by Michael Church, Pascale M. Biron and André G. Roy.
© 2012 John Wiley & Sons, Ltd. Published 2012 by John Wiley & Sons, Ltd.

In river restoration practice, for example, the habitat-centric view aligns with the misplaced belief that the introduction or manipulation of physical structures will *necessarily* yield ecological "improvements" – the so-called "Field of Dreams" hypothesis: *If we build it (the habitat), they (the animals) will come* (Palmer *et al.*, 1997). In reality, population density and the potential for population density to increase are affected by many factors other than manipulation of local flows and morphology, including animal dispersal, barriers to dispersal, large-scale or long-term disturbance, and species interactions. This is why some placement practices have been effective, while others show no benefits or fail entirely (Thompson and Stull, 2002; Roni *et al.*, 2008). In addition, local increases in the density of a target species at a rehabilitation site may simply reflect local immigration from neighbouring habitats that does not represent a meaningful improvement in biotic status. Without broad evaluation of populations in contiguous reaches, which is rare, it is not possible to claim any net increase in population.

Similarly in ecohydraulics, instream flow needs are routinely evaluated using abundance–environment relations (or habitat suitability curves) and associated habitat-based association models (e.g., PHABSIM; Bovee, 1982 *et seq.*) that aim to predict the amount of available habitat that is of value to a particular target species under a given flow condition or flow regime. Although these approaches are widely used (Tharme, 2003) and have stoutly been defended as useful, general, and theoretically robust (e.g., Lamouroux *et al.*, 2010), critics suggest that reliance on these habitat-centric models rather than other types of modelling tool, which they argue are informed by deeper ecological understanding (e.g., population demographic or individually based bioenergetic models), is problematic. Amongst other criticisms, they point out that the population density or biomass of a species is ultimately caused by vital rates (births, deaths, and migration) not environmental factors *per se*, that statistical descriptions of abundance-environment relations are often weak and lack clear mechanistic understanding, and that freshwater fauna have complex, spatially extensive life cycles that can involve terrestrial, marine, or lentic phases, so that local physical conditions cannot predict population characteristics (Hudson *et al.* 2003; Anderson *et al.*, 2006; Lancaster and Downes, 2010a, 2010b). This debate is important because models like PHABSIM are used to make important management decisions about environmental flows. Proponents highlight the development of innovative, holistic approaches that aim to accommodate a broad range of physical and biological processes in the design of environmental flows (Tharme, 2003; Richter, 2003), while detractors claim there has been inadequate

testing of whether habitat changes caused by flow manipulation produce anticipated changes in population characteristics (Souchon *et al.*, 2008) and suggest that the approach remains limited by an over-emphasis on the role of physical habitat.

Despite these debates about the role of "habitat" and the value of "habitat-centric" approaches, few would disagree with the main message in Lapointe's paper – that there is still much to learn about the mechanistic interaction of physical and biological factors in river systems. For example, Petts *et al.* (2006) argue for "*new science/knowledge to address the emerging issue of variability within fluvial ecosystems and the integration of physical and biological processes from first principles*" (Petts *et al.*, 2006, p. 281). Here, we focus on one relatively understudied aspect of this interaction: the impact of animals on the geomorphological processes and forms in gravel-bed rivers. This is one arena, of many in river science, where there is substantial potential for fruitful interdisciplinary progress at the interface of geomorphology, ecology, and hydrology (Naiman, *et al.*, 2000; Rice *et al.*, 2010).

## 19.3 GEOMORPHOLOGICAL IMPACTS OF ANIMALS IN GRAVEL-BED RIVERS

### 19.3.1 Overview and Scope

Despite a long history of interest in the interactions between fauna and geomorphological processes, both in terrestrial (e.g., Darwin, 1881) and riverine settings (e.g. Reudemann and Schoonmaker, 1938), mainstream geomorphology has, in general, failed to consider the importance of animals as geomorphic agents (Butler, 1995). This omission is increasingly challenged by broader developments that emphasize the importance for geomorphology of understanding biotic–abiotic interactions (Corenblit *et al.*, 2007; Reinhardt *et al.*, 2010), for example, within the frameworks of earth system science and integrated earth surface dynamics (Paola *et al.*, 2006; Rice and Mackin, 2008). There is greater awareness of the fundamental link between life and Earth surface processes across landscapes (Dietrich and Perron, 2006), through geological time (Corenblit and Steiger, 2009) and, relevant here, within fluvial geomorphology (Tal and Paola, 2007; Hassan *et al.*, 2008; Osterkamp and Hupp, 2010; Westbrook *et al.*, 2011) and alluvial sedimentology (Ward *et al.*, 2000; Davies and Gibling, 2010).

To varying degrees, these efforts are supported by conceptual frameworks, including biogeomorphology (Viles, 1988), which recognises the role of all organisms, zoogeomorphology (Butler, 1995), which exclusively deals with the geomorphic effects of animals, excluding humans, and ecosystem engineering (Jones et al., 1994; Wright and Jones, 2006), which explicitly recognizes that modification of physical environments by organisms, including habitat maintenance or creation, affects aspects of resource availability and thence ecology. Moore (2006) provides a useful review of ecosystem engineering in rivers, suggesting that the impact of organisms on their environment and the wider ecosystem depends on three key biological attributes (behaviour, body size, and population density) mediated by one key abiotic factor – the hydrological regime. As the following review of animal impacts on river geomorphology makes clear, geomorphological factors (topography, morphology, sediment characteristics, and sediment regime) also control the impact that organisms can have on their physical environment.

Consistent with our own work in this area, this review largely is restricted to the role of fish and invertebrates in directly affecting coarse-grained river channel substrates and bedload sediment transport. There is insufficient space to review broader zoogeomorphic impacts on river and floodplain geomorphology. Thus, we do not reiterate the well-documented impacts of North American and, to a lesser extent, European beavers (Castor canadensis and Castor fiber) on river channel and valley geomorphology – by far the most studied zoogeomorphic agent in rivers (Naiman et al. 1988; Butler 1995, 2006; Gurnell, 1998). It is sufficient to point out that the impacts of these animals are considerable. Butler and Malanson (2005) estimated that total sediment storage in beaver ponds across North America was between 3 and $125 \times 10^9$ m$^3$ prior to European settlement and that now, despite major reductions in beaver numbers due to hunting and land-use changes, the equivalent figures are 0.75 to $3.85 \times 10^9$ m$^3$. Entrapment of these very large volumes of sediment, now and in the past, has profound landscape-scale implications for the hydrology and geomorphology of upland gravel-bed rivers, as well as for sediment supply to downstream reaches (Westbrook et al., 2011). We also sidestep a large body of work concerning the impacts of domestic livestock, particularly cattle, on stream bank stability and sediment production (see reviews in Kauffman and Krueger, 1984; Trimble and Mendel, 1995; and Agouridis, 2005). Therein, there is a general consensus that unmanaged grazing leads predominantly to increased bank erosion, channel widening, and sediment production (e.g., Trimble 1994; Magilligan and McDowell, 1997; Laubel et al., 2003) as livestock damage river banks by direct trampling, by grazing protective vegetation and by adding a mass surcharge that can promote bank slumping (Trimble and Mendel, 1995).

Similarly, we do not consider how animal populations across landscapes affect drainage basin sediment loads and hydrology and thereby have a strong indirect influence on river channel functions and morphology. However, see Butler (2006) for a broad introduction to these interactions, Trimble and Mendel (1995) for an overview of the role of domesticated cattle in the United States, Hall and Lamont (2003) for a useful conceptualization of the issue in Alpine environments and Sidle and Zeigler (2010) for an example of the impact that the largest living land animal in Asia, the Asiatic elephant (Elephas maximus) can have on runoff and sediment yield. Finally, we do not review a large body of work on how the synergies and ecological functioning of riparian hydrology, vegetation, and animal communities affect fluvial geomorphology (Naiman et al., 2000); for example, the impact on gravel-bed river geomorphology of intensified riparian herbivory following removal of top carnivores (wolves, Canis lupus, and cougar, Puma concolor) in the United States (Beschta and Ripple, 2006; 2008; Ripple and Beschta, 2006).

### 19.3.2 Impact of Fish in Gravel-Bed Rivers

Salmonids directly re-work fluvial substrates during nest building in shallow gravel beds. Moore et al. (2004) observed that the swimming action of sockeye salmon (Oncorhynchus nerka) resulted in mobilization of fine sediment, but it is bed disturbance during redd construction that has been most widely documented. As the female fish excavates her redd, lateral flexions clean interstitial fines from the substrate, increasing permeability and porosity, and coarsening the surface (Field-Dodgson, 1987; Kondolf et al., 1993; Peterson and Foote, 2000). Moore et al. (2004) measured a fivefold increase in fine sediment accumulation in areas of Alaskan rivers where salmon were excluded. Montgomery et al. (1996) found that spawning activity caused a 33–39% increase in median surface grain size in Kennedy Creek, Washington and a 56–57% increase in Montana Creek, Alaska, USA. These modifications allow a flow of surface water through the egg pocket that ensures temperature regulation, oxygenation, and removal of metabolites (Chapman, 1988; Grieg et al., 2006; Tonina and Buffington, 2009). The size and density of redds is dependent on the salmonid species (Burner, 1951) so that the impact of redd-building varies between species. For example, Sockeye salmon in the Alaskan streams studied by Moore et al. (2004) built nests of between 2.1 and 4.1 m$^2$ that were, on average, 0.2 m deep. Sockeye can attain densities in Alaskan streams of at least $1500$ km$^{-2}$ (Peterson and Foote, 2000), from which Moore (2006) estimated that salmon have consistently disturbed more than 5000 m$^2$ of the bed surface every summer over the last 50 years; roughly 30% of the available area.

Using particle tracer data at sites in the Stuart-Takla system, British Columbia, Gottesfeld *et al.* (2004) found that spawning Sockeye caused vertical mixing of bed materials on the same order of magnitude as flood events. For the same streams, Hassan *et al.* (2008) reported relatively low armour ratios, typically between 1 and 1.4, indicating that re-working disrupts the formation of stabilizing bed surface structures. Montgomery *et al.* (1996) also noted that redd gravels were more loosely packed and lacked imbrication relative to un-spawned patches. This reduction in surface structure should reduce critical entrainment stresses for redd gravels and thereby promote bedload transport. However, bed coarsening and improved bed material sorting are expected to counteract this effect, and the topography created by spawning increases form drag, dissipating shear stress, and reducing the basal shear available to drive bedload transport. The impact of spawning on bed sediment entrainment depends on these opposing effects and empirical evidence is equivocal. Montgomery *et al.* (1996) concluded that the effect of spawning was reduced substrate mobility in one of their study streams, but Hassan *et al.* (2008) found that spawning activity, including direct movement, accounted for between one third and one half of the annual bedload flux in four small streams in the Stuart–Takla system, leading them to suggest that mass spawning can be a major influence on bedload yield in mountain gravel-bed rivers. For the same streams, bedload trap data reveal that bedload accumulations were greater, for similar hydraulic conditions, during spawning periods than during non-spawning periods and that the density of spawning fish was a useful predictor of bedload yield (Macdonald *et al.* 2010). On Kanaka Creek, British Columbia, Rennie and Millar (2000) observed greater scour depths in the tailspills of chum salmon (*Oncorhynchus keta*) redds than in the adjacent bed or in the redds themselves, suggesting that impacts on bedload transport are highly localized.

In addition to the pervasive impact on gravel-bed sediment structure and bedload transport, redd-building produces a distinctive, hummocky bed topography (Montgomery *et al.*, 1996; Hassan *et al.*, 2008) of depressions and tailspills. Concentration of redds in approximately transverse parallel lines produces bed forms that are akin to gravel dunes (see Figure 1 in Field-Dodgson, 1987 for a striking illustration). In Forfar Creek, one of their small study streams in the Stuart–Takla system, Gottesfeld *et al.* (2008) observed the creation then eradication of these features by prolonged redd building at a popular spawning site. Further spawning trimmed bar edges and filled pools to produce a relatively uniform morphology of bioturbated gravels.

Individual redds and small bed forms are likely to be transient, washed out by subsequent high flows. However, in larger rivers in British Columbia, Gottesfeld *et al.* (2008) have recorded well-organised gravel dune fields extending for hundreds to thousands of metres that survive from year to year. The dunes have amplitudes up to 1.5 m and wavelengths of 10–20 m. These are thought to be the product of Chinook salmon (*Oncorhynchus tshawytscha*) that are sufficiently large and powerful to build features that withstand winter high flows. Such dune fields are most common down-stream of lake outlets that buffer catchment storm flows and trap sediment.

Most of the research on bed disturbance by salmonids is based on Pacific salmon species that are larger and spawn in higher densities than their Atlantic counter-parts, such as brown trout *(Salmo trutta)* and Atlantic salmon *(Salmo salar)*. The cumulative effects of these species may, nevertheless, be important, as could the activity of non-salmonid fish. Many non-salmonid fish construct nests by moving gravels, including species of bream (Pierce *et al.,*1987; Thorp, 1988), chub (Lachner, 1952), lamprey (Stone, 2006), bass (Winemiller and Taylor, 1982) and stickleback (Rushbrook and Barber, 2008). The foraging activity of many fish species also results in disturbance of the bed (Pringle and Hamazaki, 1998). A number of species of detrivorous, tropical fish have been found to significantly reduce fine sediment accrual at foraging sites (Flecker, 1996, 1997; Flecker and Taylor, 2004). Power (1990) demonstrated that armoured catfish (*Loricariidae*) could clear sediment from bedrock in the Rio Frijoles, Panama. Statzner *et al.* (2003b) found in experimental channels that barbel (*Barbus barbus*) and gudgeon (*Gobio gobio*) could decrease the accumulation of fine sediment on gravel substrates, as well as modify the bed elevation, which they interpreted as indicating a change in substrate structure and topography. Carp (*Cyprinus carpio)* have also been found to re-suspend sediments when foraging (Breukelaar *et al.* 1994; Parkos *et al.* 2003; Chumchal *et al.*, 2005; Miller and Crowl, 2006; Roozen *et al.* 2007; Matsuzaki *et al.* 2009), as have bream (*Abramis brama*), tench (*Tinca tinca*), and ruffe (*Gymnocephalus cernus*) (Persson and Svensson 2006a, 2006b).

### 19.3.3 Impact of Invertebrates in Gravel-Bed Rivers

Despite their relatively small size, freshwater invertebrates (for example, insect larvae) can occur in densities of thousands per square metre with potentially significant cumulative impacts on grain stability and sediment fluxes. For example, Hydropsychid caddisfly larvae stabilize gravelly materials by binding grains together with silk that is spun to construct filter nets and retreats (Statzner *et al.*, 1999; Cardinale *et al.*, 2004). Johnson *et al.* (2009) compared the critical shear stresses required to entrain graded fine gravels from three test substrates: those colonized in a river bed to natural densities (1200–4700 m$^{-2}$) by *Hydropsyche angustipennis*, *H. contubernalis* and *H. pellucidula* over a period of 30 days; substrates conditioned by the same river flows, but from which the hydropsychids were excluded; and unstructured substrates unconditioned by river flows. For 4–6 mm gravels, the average critical entrainment stress for the colonized substrates, where silk nets and retreats were prolific, was 35% greater than for the river conditioned substrates and 38% greater than for the unstructured substrates. The equivalent percentages for 6–8 mm gravels were 23% and 31% respectively. These results not only reveal the important impact of these animals on fine gravel mobility, but also suggest that the magnitude of their effect can be at least as important as other low-flow conditioning, for example by biofilm development, ingress of fines, and structural development which, together, did not significantly increase the critical shear stress of conditioned trays in these experiments.

Bearing in mind that sand and fine gravel fractions are present in patches on the surface of many gravel-bed rivers, including in pools (Lisle and Hilton, 1999), that these surface fines contribute to the bedload before armour break-up (Lisle, 1995) and that sand availability is a key determinant of gravel transport (Wilcock *et al.*, 2001), it is then intriguing to consider the large-scale implications of fine-gravel stabilization by Hydropsychid larvae for sand and gravel transport in gravel-bed rivers. These impacts are difficult to assess and it is likely that their effect is spatially patchy and temporally intermittent as a function of variability in larvae distributions, the grain size characteristics of surface sediment patches and the magnitude of entraining flows. Nevertheless, the cumulative impact could be significant because hydropsychids are one of the most widespread and abundant families of freshwater invertebrates worldwide (Wallace and Merritt, 1980) and, in the United Kingdom, for example, larvae of Hydropsychidae are present all year round (Boon, 1979; Edington and Hildrew, 1995).

There are numerous other examples in the literature of how invertebrate larvae and freshwater shrimps can modify the distribution of fine, matrix sediment, acting like "tiny bulldozers" (Boulton, 2000, p. 56) and winnowing sand grains from interstitial spaces when foraging (Pringle and Blake, 1994; March *et al.*, 2002; Visoni and Moulton, 2003; Moulton *et al.*, 2004; De Souza and Moulton, 2005) with hunger levels significantly increasing the disturbance (Statzner *et al.*, 1996: Zanetell and Peckarsky, 1996). In the absence of explicit experiments and measurements we can only speculate that these modifications could affect local sand availability and gravel–sand ratios, with implications for gravel transport

rates at patch scales (Ikeda and Iseya, 1988; Jackson and Beschta, 1984; Wilcock *et al.*, 2001; Curran and Wilcock, 2005).

Crayfish provide an excellent example of how large freshwater crustaceans can affect fluvial morphology and processes. Some species of crayfish burrow extensively into bank and bed material (Holdich, 2002; Barbaresi *et al.*, 2004) which can destabilize river banks (Guan, 1994). Some crayfish species live in terrestrial floodplains and burrow to the water-table, creating complex burrow systems with surface "chimneys" (Hobbs, 1981).

A widely reported impact of crayfish on bed sediment composition is the winnowing, from the substrate, of fine sediment (Parkyn *et al.*, 1997; Creed and Reed, 2004; Usio and Townsend, 2004; Helms and Creed, 2005; Matsuzaki *et al.*, 2009). Statzner *et al.* (2000; 2003a), working in small artificial channels (0.2 m wide, 1.25 m$^2$ total area), found that more sediment was eroded from an unstructured gravelly substrate with sand covering when the crayfish *Orconectes limosus* was present, than from control substrates without crayfish. The critical shear stress for sand-sized particles was reduced by 50–75% in the presence of the animals. In the North River, North Carolina, USA, Fortino (2006) noted that crayfish-related reductions in fine bed sediments were not observed in winter due to a decline of crayfish activity in cold temperatures. Mobilization of fine sediment is associated with the movement of legs and contact between the substrate and abdomens of walking crayfish (Usio and Townsend, 2004). Statzner *et al.* (2003a) reported that the presence of the crayfish (*O. limnosus*) altered the topography of the gravel–sand substrates in their experimental channels. A measured increase in mean bed elevation was interpreted as indicating that gravel consolidation was reduced by crayfish (Statzner and Peltret, 2006). In addition to these impacts on bed materials, crayfish also appear to affect the availability and mobilization of suspended sediments and increase turbidity (Angeler *et al.*, 2001). Preliminary research conducted on a low energy United Kingdom river dominated by fine substrates suggests that nocturnal increases in crayfish activity are associated with a greater frequency of sediment suspension events, with potential implications for suspended sediment fluxes at catchment scales (Harvey *et al.*, 2011).

## 19.4 UNDERSTANDING THE MECHANISMS OF ANIMAL IMPACTS: LABORATORY AND FIELD EXPERIMENTS WITH SIGNAL CRAYFISH

While previous work has revealed the potential for crayfish to affect fine sediment transport, there is little knowledge of how crayfish impact coarse bed-sediment structures, especially water-worked gravels, and thereby influence gravel stability. We undertook a programme of work designed to illuminate and quantify the disturbance of gravel substrates by crayfish and directly link this to bed mobility. In this section we review some of that work and, unlike the preceding review, include methodological detail to illustrate the need for careful experimentation, in both the laboratory and field, when seeking to understand the mechanisms by which animals affect river geomorphology.

Signal crayfish (*Pacifastacus leniusculus*) are a highly successful invasive species throughout Europe and parts of Asia. They occur at densities exceeding $10 \, m^{-2}$ and are now widely distributed throughout United Kingdom freshwaters (Holdich, 2002). They are large benthic animals (adults are typically 10 to 14 cm in length) and are reportedly more aggressive and active (Bubb *et al.*, 2002; Dunn *et al.*, 2009) than the native United Kingdom species, white-clawed crayfish (*Austropotamobius pallipes*). Moore's three criteria for organism impact of behaviour, body size and population density are therefore satisfied and the potential for large-scale disruption of river bed materials is clear.

We first conducted a series of still-water and flume experiments designed to tackle several key questions (What size of particles can crayfish move? Do crayfish affect surface structures? How are particle movements accomplished?) and measure the impacts of substrate alterations on gravel entrainment. We then undertook a programme of field observations designed to establish whether crayfish spend time on substrate patches characterized by the grain-size fractions used in our experiments. If they do not, then our laboratory findings are of little consequence. Details of this work can be found in Johnson *et al.* (2010, 2011) and Johnson (2011) and here we provide only a brief summary. Third, we have instigated additional laboratory experiments, reported here in full, that investigate whether interactions between crayfish are important. We were interested in whether density-dependent changes in behaviour have implications for bed sediment structures and sediment mobility.

### 19.4.1 Summary of Still-Water and Flume Experiments with Individual Crayfish

Still-water experiments were conducted in opaque aquaria ($0.6 \times 0.4 \times 0.4$ m) using narrowly graded gravel substrates composed of half-phi fractions. DEMs of difference (DoDs) derived from consecutive laser scans were used to measure volumetric changes in gravel surfaces following exposure to crayfish. Animals had a substantial impact on most substrates within 6 hours and could move material up to 38 mm in diameter, with a submerged weight

approximately six times that of the individuals used in the experiments. For grain-size fractions between 8 and 38 mm individual signal crayfish moved, on average, $450 \, cm^{3}$ of material in a $2400 \, cm^{2}$ area over a 24 hour period, equating to a displacement of $1.7 \, kg \, m^{-2} \, d^{-1}$ after accounting for porosity. They altered significantly the topography of the surfaces by constructing shallow pits, within which they sheltered, and piling excavated material into mounds (Figure 19.1) (Johnson *et al.*, 2010).

To investigate the influence of these effects on bed structures and gravel entrainment we used a 0.6 m wide flume to water-work 11–16 mm fluvial gravel, then released individual crayfish into the flume for a period of 6 hours. A fine-wire cage, with a footprint of $0.24 \, m^{2}$, open to the bed, was used to contain the crayfish so that areal animal density was $4.16 \, m^{-2}$. While crayfish were in the flume the laboratory was darkened, because they are nocturnal, and a water cooling system maintained flume water temperature at approximately 15 °C. Laser

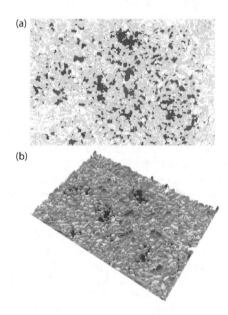

(a)

(b)

**Figure 19.1** (a) DEM of Difference showing elevation changes before and after 6 hours of crayfish activity. Red areas indicate positive changes in elevation that exceed $D_{50}$ and blue areas indicate negative changes that exceed $D_{50}$ (pit and mound construction). Areas of orange show changes between $\pm D_{50}$ (grain re-arrangement) and areas of white indicate no change according to the minimal discernable difference of $\pm 1$ mm. (b) DEM of the disturbed surface showing pit and mound structures. Blue is low elevation, brown is high elevation. Flow was from left to right in both cases and the area shown is 0.6 by 0.4 m. (See the color version of this figure in color plate section)

scans of the gravel surfaces before and after water-working, as well as before and after crayfish activity, were used to generate DEMs that allowed comparison of topography and structural character. To quantify these changes we used Smart's inclination index ($I_l$) which describes the difference between the number of positive and negative inclinations across a surface (Smart et al., 2004; Millane et al., 2006). Imbricate structure is reflected in an asymmetric distribution of inclinations in a streamwise direction, with more positive inclinations and increasingly positive values of $I_l$. Crayfish behaviours were recorded using underwater video cameras (Figure 19.2a).

The re-arrangement of surface grains associated with 6 hours of individual crayfish activity was found to have a significant impact on the structure of water-worked gravels, partially undoing the imbrication of surface grains (Johnson et al., 2011). For example, 6 hours of crayfish activity on 11–16 mm water-worked surfaces visibly and measurably reduced imbrication with an average reduction in $I_l$ of 37%.

After the 6 hour period of crayfish activity, test section gravels were entrained by a relatively high flow that ran for 2 hours. Movement of grains was recorded with digital video cameras. A grain was defined as being mobile if it was displaced a distance greater than a single grain diameter from its original location. Error analysis found that the maximum error in counting grains was not greater than 5% of the total. During these entrainment tests, nearly twice as many grains were mobilized from substrates disturbed by crayfish than from control surfaces that were not exposed to crayfish (Johnson, 2011). We attribute this increased mobility to the disturbance of stabilizing surface structures, and particularly the partial destruction of imbrication, accomplished by walking, foraging, and digging (Figure 19.2b). Topographic alterations (pits and mounds) may also contribute to the observed increase in mobility because loosened grains in the mound are overexposed, but it is also possible that the modified topography augments form drag and thereby reduces available bed shear, which would counteract this effect to some degree. Resolution of this issue requires detailed hydraulic measurements of disturbed and undisturbed surfaces, which we have not yet made.

### 19.4.2 Linking Laboratory Findings to Field Impacts

Signal crayfish were tracked in a 3 m wide, 20 m long meandering reach of the River Bain, Lincolnshire, UK, with passive integrated transponder (PIT) tags. The aim was to quantify the lengths of time crayfish were present on substrate units with grain-size characteristics similar to those used in our laboratory experiments. A series of 16 antennae were buried beneath discrete facies and

**Figure 19.2** (a) Flume arrangement showing test section, crayfish containment structure, video cameras, and laser scanner; (b) Photograph of a signal crayfish moving grains during pit-digging activity. The grain in the centre of the image is approximately 16 mm across and is being pulled toward and beneath the body by the chelae.

connected to a multipoint decoder which also acted as a data-logger, continuously recording the time, date, tag number, and antenna number, for every occasion when a tagged crayfish was present over an antenna. A total of 65 signal crayfish (approximately five at any one time) were tracked over a 150 day period.

Crayfish showed some preference for the bed beneath marginal macrophyte stands and areas of low flows, particularly on a small point bar. Although crayfish sheltered in these areas, on average spending 40% of their monitored time there, they regularly made excursions into other, more exposed, areas of the bed characterized by a variety of substrate types. Substrate was not a good determinate of crayfish presence as crayfish spent extended periods on all facies within the reach (Johnson, 2011). Crayfish were regularly active on patches of open framework gravels similar in size to those used in flume experiments, on average spending 20% of their monitored time there. Considering that crayfish have been shown to have a significant impact on these gravel sizes in only 6 hours, this supports the hypothesis that signal crayfish could have significant geomorphic impacts on gravel mobility at channel width or larger scales.

### 19.4.3 Conspecific Interaction: Behavioural Effects with Two Crayfish

#### 19.4.3.1 Methods

Experimental procedures were as for the single crayfish experiments except that in each of six replications, two adult crayfish of the same sex and approximately the same size were simultaneously introduced to the test area so that areal density of animals was 8.33 m$^{-2}$. Crayfish activity was summarized by counting the total number of seconds that each crayfish was engaged in different recognizable behaviours during their deployment. Five categories of behaviour were used: walking, foraging, digging, stationary, and aggressive interaction (fighting, posturing). We subsampled 120 minutes of the 360 minutes of recording, classifying behaviours for minutes 0 to 10 and 30 to 40 in each hour. A sixth category of behaviour – climbing on the cage walls – was excluded from the analysis. On average, crayfish spent up to 20% of their time climbing on the cage walls, presumably because the cage confined their movement and because it offered a means of escape from aggressive interactions. Without confinement crayfish behaviours are likely to be different, but we did not evaluate that quantitatively here. The behaviours, bed disturbance, and entrainment rates measured with two crayfish were compared with equivalent results from a random selection of six single-crayfish experiments and, for entrainment, six control runs without any crayfish.

#### 19.4.3.2 Behaviour

When two crayfish were present they spent approximately 17% of the time interacting – usually fighting. In each experimental run one individual became dominant, often after an early period of confrontation. Figure 19.3a shows that the dominant individuals spent a significantly lower proportion of their time stationary (t-test, $df = 10$, $p < 0.01$) and walking (t-test, $df = 10$, $p = 0.02$) than did single crayfish, but spent a greater

proportion of time foraging (t-test, $df = 6$, $p = 0.06$). There were no significant differences in the proportion of time spent digging. The subordinate animals also spent less time walking, but similar amounts of time stationary, foraging, and digging compared with single crayfish. When two crayfish were present there were, therefore, significant behavioural differences, albeit in one of the two individuals. The dominant animal may have foraged more and spent less time inactive than its single counterpart because it was in a competitive situation and had established its superiority.

From our observations, it is possible to group different activities according to their impact on bed materials: when crayfish are stationary, no changes take place; digging causes topographic change; and grain rearrangement is caused by a combination of walking, foraging, and, in the case of two crayfish, their interaction. Figure 19.3b shows that the combined effect of two crayfish is a much greater total time engaged in activities that affect grain rearrangement (t-test, $df = 10$, $p < 0.01$) and slightly more total time engaged in activities that affect topography (t-test, $df = 7$, $p = 0.08$).

#### 19.4.3.3 Bed Disturbance and Gravel Entrainment

Despite these behavioural differences, DoDs reveal that volumetric changes in surface topography caused by the presence of crayfish are not different between cases when one or two individuals are present (t-tests, $df = 10$; Table 19.1). This indicates that the behavioural differences have no impact on net surface change. Figure 19.4 compares inclination indices for loose, water-worked, and crayfish-impacted substrates, and clearly shows the significant impact of crayfish on water-worked gravels (as described above). For a single animal the mean $I_l$ value drops from 0.070 for the water-worked beds to 0.044 after crayfish deployment, and for two crayfish the respective values are 0.070 and 0.032. The lower mean value after deployment of two crayfish is consistent with the reasonable possibility that two crayfish can accomplish greater disorganization of a water-worked bed compared with a single animal; for example, because of the greater total number of minutes that the bed is subject to grain-rearranging activities and the changed nature of those activities, particularly the increase in foraging behaviour on the part of the dominant animal. However, the difference in post-deployment mean values is not significant ($\alpha = 0.10$).

While the presence of crayfish has a clear and significant impact on entrainment rate, there is only a small increase in the mean entrainment rate from beds exposed to two crayfish rather than one crayfish (Figure 19.5). This is consistent with the possibility that slight

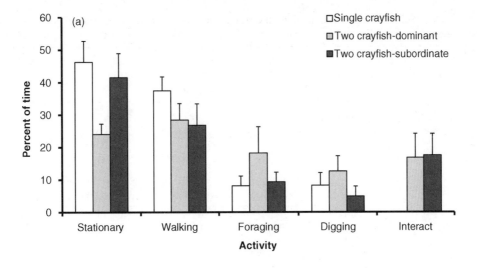

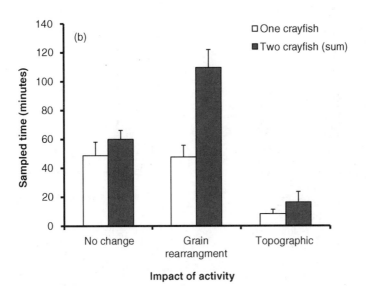

**Figure 19.3** (a) Comparison of the behaviour of single crayfish ($n = 6$) and pairs of crayfish ($n = 6$) during 6 hour flume deployments. Bars are mean percentage of time engaged in observed activities and error bars are two times the standard error. Classification was undertaken for a subsample of 120 minutes. Time spent climbing on the cage was excluded. (b) Differences between single ($n = 6$) and paired ($n = 6$) deployments in the total amount of time engaged in activities likely to alter bed topography and rearrange grains. Bars are means and error bars are two times the standard error.

reductions in $I_I$ resulted in reduced bed stability, but the difference is not significant (t-test, $\alpha = 0.10$).

In sum, these results demonstrate that conspecific interaction affects the behaviour of individual animals, with the potential for significant impacts on bed materials. However, despite the slightly larger reduction of imbrication and slightly higher entrainment rates for beds exposed to two crayfish, it is not possible to conclude that changed behaviour caused significant changes in either bed structure or bed mobility. These

results are likely to be sensitive to the confinement space we used and are restricted to consideration of only one or two crayfish, rather than larger numbers. Further work is necessary to explore the role of these factors.

### 19.4.4 Summary: Crayfish, Bed Disturbance, Grain Mobility, and Ecosystem Engineering

Whilst previous studies have shown that crayfish can have an impact on gross transport, particularly of sand

**Table 19.1**   Substrate disturbance measured as volumetric change (cm$^3$) after exposure to crayfish within the flume test area. Normalized values are expressed as the volumetric change per unit area of exposed bed surface (m$^3$ m$^{-2}$)

| | Volume change (cm$^3$) | | Normalized (m$^3$ m$^{-2}$) | |
| --- | --- | --- | --- | --- |
| | Mean | 2 SE | Mean | 2 SE |
| *Grain rearrangement* | | | | |
| **1 crayfish** | 120.1 | 27.1 | 0.00050 | 0.00011 |
| **2 crayfish** | 114.6 | 25.1 | 0.00048 | 0.00010 |
| *Pit and mound construction* | | | | |
| **1 crayfish** | 43.1 | 15.2 | 0.00018 | 0.00006 |
| **2 crayfish** | 58.7 | 19.5 | 0.00025 | 0.00008 |

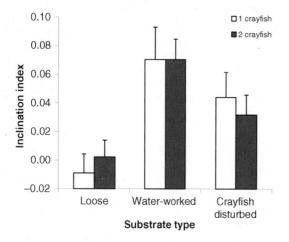

**Figure 19.4**   Alterations of surface structure measured using the inclination index of Smart *et al.* (2004) for 11–16 mm gravel substrates. Means ($\pm$ 2 standard errors, $n = 6$) for initial, unstructured surfaces, for the same surfaces after water-working and for the same surfaces after deployment of one or two crayfish. Higher values of the index indicate greater imbrication.

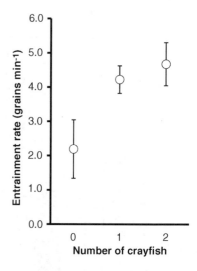

**Figure 19.5**   Particle entrainment from water-worked beds of 11–16 mm gravel exposed to zero, one, or two crayfish. Mean ($\pm$ 2 standard errors, $n = 6$) number of grains mobilized per minute for a subsample of 24 minutes during a 2 hour run (see text for details).

fractions, our experiments show that crayfish can alter the structure and topography of gravel beds composed of particles up to 38 mm in diameter. Behavioural analysis confirms that crayfish rearrange surface bed materials both by digging, which accomplishes topographic change, and by dislodging and re-arranging water-worked grains during walking and foraging. We have established a direct link between these bed modifications and increases in the entrainment of gravel particles. Crayfish are therefore capable of causing changes in surface grain arrangements that counteract the natural gains in stability which develop as gravelly beds become structured during periods when excess shear remains relatively low (Reid and Frostick, 1984; Church *et al.*, 1998; Oldmeadow and Church, 2006; Haynes

and Pender, 2007; Lamarre and Roy, 2008). Moreover, for a typical lowland river in the United Kingdom, we have shown that signal crayfish spend a considerable amount of time on gravelly substrates and therefore have the opportunity to affect these changes. Notwithstanding the need to investigate further the interactions between topographic change, near-bed hydraulics, and changes in entrainment stresses caused by grain rearrangement, this work supports the hypothesis that signal crayfish have a significant effect on bed material mobility in streams and rivers, which raises the possibility that they may also affect bedload transport rates.

In rivers, animals share space with other individuals of the same species (conspecific interaction) and with other species (interspecific interaction), competing for mates and resources. A fundamental question when scaling up laboratory studies to river-scale impacts is to understand how these interactions affect animal behaviour and whether any behavioural changes affect the zoogeomorphic impact. Moore (2006) highlights the importance of animal density, suggesting that higher densities of ecosystem engineers will have larger impacts up to some saturation point. The nature of this relation between density and impact in part depends on the relation between behavioural changes and increased density. Our initial examination of this relation for signal crayfish suggests that crayfish behaviours relevant to sediment reworking are affected by conspecific interaction, but that for the experimental arrangement here, at least, slight reductions in bed structuring and increased grain mobility were not significantly different from those caused by individual crayfish. These results add to limited and unresolved work on interspecific effects by Statzner and Sagnes (2008). They found that the presence of fish (gudgeon, *Gobio gobio*) which have been shown to rework substrates, and crayfish did not have an additive effect on substrate disturbance when present together, indicating the potentially complex effects of communities of organisms on sediment reworking.

The impact of fluvial substrate reworking by signal crayfish on other biota remains unquantified, but is likely to be significant where crayfish destabilize the river bed and so deny insect larvae, for example, stable substrate refugia during floods. By increasing involuntary drift, bed destabilization may be detrimental to insect larvae, but, because crayfish have been found to shelter during flood events, it seems unlikely that bed destabilization would be detrimental to crayfish themselves. Ecosystem engineering provides a conceptual framework within which to examine the feedbacks between zoogeomorphic effects and the wider biotic community, and is one area where future efforts should be focused.

## 19.5  CONCLUSIONS

"Habitat", as conventionally considered by most geomorphologists and engineers, refers to the physical environment that provides a template upon which biological processes are played out and ecological patterns are developed. Lapointe (Chapter 17, this volume) highlights the need to develop a richer view of habitat in which geomorphology and ecohydrology do more than map and model habitat patches. We wholeheartedly agree that, by recognizing local context and the importance of biological as well as physical processes for ecological patterns, interdisciplinary river science can gain the better mechanistic understanding of the

links amongst flora, fauna, hydraulics, and sediments that are necessary to underpin sustainable river management.

There is rapidly growing interest in the truly interactive nature of biotic and abiotic elements across geomorphology and this is particularly apparent in fluvial science. We reviewed one aspect of this interaction – the role of freshwater fishes and benthic invertebrates in affecting sediments and transport processes in gravel-bed rivers – and used our work with signal crayfish to illustrate how small-scale laboratory and field experiments can inform understanding of the processes involved. Culled from this literature and our own experiments with crayfish, Figure 19.6 is a simplified conceptual model that summarizes the links between animal activities and sediment fluxes in gravel-bed rivers. This view of the problem emphasizes the need to consider impacts both on bed stability and on channel hydraulics because the potentially contrasting effects of animals on these processes remain largely unknown (Montgomery *et al.*, 1996; Hassan *et al.* 2008). Importantly, this model sits within a larger framework that is not shown, in which changes in bed condition, changes in bed topography and changes in sediment fluxes all feed back to animal behaviour and ecosystem functioning in largely unknown ways. The diagram is also limited to consideration of direct animal impacts and omits indirect "food web" or trophic effects; for example, caused by animals grazing on algae or macrophyte stands that damage stabilizing biofilms or change vegetation-induced flow resistance. As Naiman *et al.* (2000) point out for the wider context of river corridor functioning, these interactions are important.

Fish and benthic invertebrates, with the exception of the largest salmonids (see Gottesfeld, 2008), do not leave explicit landform signatures like beaver or cattle and it is therefore difficult to demonstrate their importance for fluvial morphodynamics. Their effects remain hidden and they might be regarded as forgotten, "Cinderella", geomorphological agents. Flume experiments, like those reported here for crayfish, and small-scale field experiments can be used to build a better mechanistic understanding of their impacts, but a substantial challenge is to design observation programmes and large-scale field experiments that can quantify their impacts at river scales. We have begun to do this in our crayfish work. For those species that affect gravelly bed sediments, their global ubiquity, high densities and activity levels nevertheless suggest that extremely large quantities of energy are collectively expended in modifying river bed sediments and near-bed hydraulics. It therefore seems reasonable to assume that fish and invertebrates are important actors in gravel-bed rivers with as yet undiscovered and

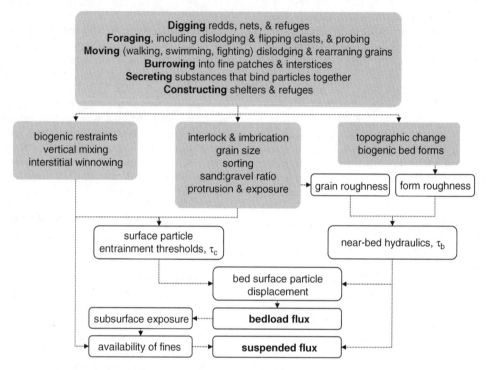

**Figure 19.6** Fish and invertebrate impacts on gravel-bed sediments and processes. $\tau_b$ is bed shear stress and $\tau_c$ is critical bed shear stress required for entrainment.

unquantified impacts on channel morphology and sediment fluxes.

## 19.6   REFERENCES

Agouridis, C.T., Workman, S.R., Warner, R.C., and Jennings, G.D. 2005. Livestock grazing management impacts on stream water quality: a review. *Journal of the American Water Resources Association* **41**: 591–606.

Anderson, K.E., Paul, A.J., McCauley, E. *et al.* 2006. Instream flow needs in streams and rivers: the importance of understanding ecological dynamics. *Frontiers in Ecology and Environment* **4**: 309–318.

Angeler, D.G., Sánchez-Carillo, S., García, G., and Alvarez-Cobelas, M. 2001. The influence of *Procambarus clarkia* (Cambaridae, Decapoda) on water quality and sediment characteristics in a Spanish floodplain wetland. *Hydrobiologia* **464**: 89–98.

Barbaresi, S., Tricarico, E., and Gherardi, F. 2004. Factors inducing the intense burrowing activity of the red-swamp crayfish, *Procambarus clarkia,* an invasive species. *Naturwissenschaften* **91**: 342–345.

Beschta, R.L. and Ripple, W.J. 2006. River channel dynamics following extirpation of wolves in northwestern Yellowstone National Park,USA. *Earth Surface Processes and Landforms* **13**: 1525–1539.

Beschta, R.L. and Ripple, W.J. 2008. Wolves, trophic cascades, and rivers in Olympic National Park,USA. *Ecohydrology* **1**: 118–130.

Boon, P.J. 1979. Studies on the spatial and temporal distribution of larval Hydropsychidae in the North Tyne river system (Northern England). *Archiv fur Hydrobiologie* **85**: 336–359.

Boulton, A.J. 2000. The functional role of the hyporheos. *Vehandlungen der Internationalen fur theoretische und angewandte Limnologie* **27**: 51–63.

Bovee, K.D. 1982. *A Guide to Stream Habitat Analysis Using the Instream Flow Incremental Methodology.* Instream Flow Information Paper 12.FWS/OBS-82/26. United States Department of the Interior, Fish and Wildlife Service, Office of Biology Services, Washington, DC.

Breukelaar, A.W., Lammens, E., Breteler, J., and Tatrai, I. 1994. Effects of benthivorous bream (*Abramis brama*) and carp (*Cyprinus carpio*) on sediment resuspension and concentrations of nutrients and chlorophyll-a. *Freshwater Biology* **32**: 113–121.

Bubb, D.H., Thom, T.J., and Lucas, M.C. 2006. Movement dispersal and refuge use of co-occurring introduced and native crayfish. *Freshwater Biology* **51**: 1359–1368.

Burner, C.J. 1951. Characteristics of spawning nests of Columbia River salmon. *U.S. Fish and Wildlife Service Fisheries Bulletin,* **61**: 97–110.

Butler, D.R. 1995. *Zoogeomorphology: Animals as Geomorphic Agents.* Cambridge, Cambridge University Press.

Butler, D.R. 2006. Human-induced changes in animal populations and distributions, and the subsequent effects on fluvial systems. *Geomorphology* **79**: 448–459.

Butler, D.R. and Malanson, G.P. 2005. The geomorphic influences of beaver dams and failures of beaver dams. *Geomorphology* **71**: 48–60.

Cardinale, B.J., Gelmann, E.R., and Parker, M.A. 2004. Net spinning caddisflies as stream ecosystem engineers: the influence of *Hydropsyche* on benthic substrate stability. *Functional Ecology* **18**: 381–387.

Chapman, D.W. 1988. Critical review of variables used to define effects of fines in redds of large salmonids. *Transactions of the American Fisheries Society* **117**: 1–21.

Chumchall, M.M., Nowlin, W.H., and Drenner, R.W. 2005. Biomass-dependent effects of common carp on water quality in shallow ponds. *Hydrobiologia* **545**: 271–177.

Church, M., Hassan, M.A., and Wolcott, J.F. 1998. Stabilizing self-organized structures in gravel-bed stream channels: field and experimental observations. *Water Resources Research* **34**: 3169–3179.

Corenblit, D. and Steiger, J. 2009. Vegetation as a major conductor of geomorphic changes on the Earth surface: toward evolutionary geomorphology. *Earth Surface Processes and Landforms* **34**: 91–96.

Corenblit, D., Steiger, J., Gurnell, A., and Tabacchi, E. 2007. Darwinian origin of landforms. *Earth Surface Processes and Landforms* **32**: 2070–2073.

Creed, R.P., Jr. and Reed, J.M. 2004. Ecosystem engineering by crayfish in a headwater stream community. *Journal of the North American Benthological Society* **23**: 244–236.

Curran, J.C. and Wilcock, P.R. 2005. Effect of sand supply on transport rates in a gravel-bed channel. *Journal of Hydraulic Engineering* **131**: 961–967.

Darwin, C.R. 1881. *The Formation of Vegetable Mould, Through the Action of Worms, with Observations on their Habitat*. London, John Murray.

Davies, N.S. and Gibling, M.R. 2010. Cambrian to Devonian evolution of alluvial systems: The sedimentological impact of the earliest plants. *Earth Science Reviews* **98**: 171–200.

De Souza, M.L. and Moulton, T.P. 2005. The effects of shrimps on benthic material in a Brazilian island stream. *Freshwater Biology* **50**: 592–602.

Dietrich, W.E. and Perron, J.T. 2006. The search for a topographic signature of life. *Nature* **439**: 411–418.

Dollar, E.S.J., James, C.S., Rogers, K.H., and Thoms, M.C. 2007. A framework for interdisciplinary understanding of rivers as ecosystems. *Geomorphology* **89**: 147–162.

Dunn, J.C., McClymont, H.E., Christmas, M., and Dunn, A.M. 2009. Competition and parasitism in the native White Clawed Crayfish *Austropotamobius pallipes* and the invasive Signal Crayfish *Pacifastacus leniusculus* in the UK. *Biological Invasions* **11**: 315–324.

Edington, J.M. and Hildrew, A., G. 1995. *Caseless Caddis Larvae of the British Isles: A Key with Ecological Notes*. Cumbria, Freshwater Biological Association, Scientific Publication No. 53.

Field-Dodgson, M.S. 1987. The effect of salmon redd excavation on stream substrate and benthic community of two salmon spawning streams in Canterbury, New Zealand. *Hydrobiologia* **154**: 3–11.

Flecker, A.S. 1996. Ecosystem engineering by a dominant detrivore in a diverse tropical stream. *Ecology* **77**: 1845–1854.

Flecker, A.S. 1997. Habitat modification by tropical fishes: environmental heterogeneity and the variability of interaction strength. *Journal of the North American Benthological Society* **16**: 286–295.

Flecker, A.S. and Taylor, B.W. 2004. Tropical fishes as biological bulldozers: density effects on resource heterogeneity and species diversity. *Ecology* **85**: 2267–2278.

Fortino, K. 2006. Effect of season on the impact of ecosystem engineers in the New River, NC. *Hydrobiologia* **559**: 463–466.

Gottesfeld, A.S., Hassan, M.A., and Tunnicliffe, J.F. 2008. Salmon bioturbation and stream process. *American Fisheries Society Symposium* **65**: 175–193.

Gottesfeld, A.S., Hassan, M.A., Tunnicliffe, J.F., and Poirier, R.W. 2004. Sediment dispersion in salmon spawning streams: the influence of floods and salmon redd construction. *Journal of the American Water Resources Association* **40**: 1071–1086.

Grieg, S.M., Sear, D.A., and Carling, P.A. 2006. A review of factors influencing the availability of dissolved oxygen to incubating salmonid embryos. *Hydrological Processes* **21**: 323–334.

Guan, R.-Z. 1994. Burrowing behaviour of signal crayfish, *Pacifastacus leniusculus* (Dana), in the River Great Ouse, England. *Freshwater Forum* **4**: 155–168.

Gurnell, A.M. 1998. The hydrogeomorphological effects of beaver dam-building activity. *Progress in Physical Geography* **22**: 167–189.

Hall, K. and Lamont, N. 2003. Zoogeomorphology in the Alpine: some observations on abiotic-biotic interactions. *Geomorphology* **55**: 219–234.

Harvey, G.L., Moorhouse, T.P., Clifford, N.J. *et al.* 2011. Evaluating the role of invasive aquatic species as drivers of fine sediment-related river management problems: the case of the signal crayfish (*Pacifastacus leniusculus*), *Progress in Physical Geography* **35**: 517–533.

Hassan, M.A., Gottesfeld, A.S., Montgomery, D.R. *et al.* 2008. Salmon-driven bedload transport and bed morphology in mountain streams. *Geophysical Research Letters* **35**: L0440. doi: 10.1029/2007GL032997.

Haynes, H. and Pender, G. 2007. Stress history effects on graded bed stability. *Journal of Hydraulic Engineering* **133**: 343–349.

Helms, B.S. and Creed, R.P. 2005. The effects of 2 coexisting crayfish on an Appalachian river community. *Journal of the North American Benthological Society* **24**: 113–122.

Hobbs, H.H., Jr., 1981. The crayfishes of Georgia. *Smithsonian Contributions to Zoology* **318**: 1–549.

Holdich, D.M. 2002. Background and functional morphology. In: Holdich, D.M., editor, *Biology of Freshwater Crayfish*. Oxford, Blackwell Science Ltd.

Hudson, H.R., Byrom, A.E., and Chadderton, W.L. 2003. *A Critique of IFIM – Instream Habitat Simulation in the New Zealand Context*. Science for Conservation 231. Wellington, New Zealand Department of Conservation.

Ikeda, H. and Iseya, F. 1988. *Experimental Study of Heterogeneous Sediment Transport*. Tsukuba, Japan, University of Tsukuba, Environmental Research Centre, Report 12.

Jackson, W.L. and Beschta, R.L. 1984. Influences of increased sand delivery on the morphology of sand and gravel channels. *Journal of the American Water Resources Association* **20**: 527–533.

Johnson, M.F. 2011. *The disturbance of fluvial gravel substrates by signal crayfish (Pacifastacus leniusculus) and the implications for coarse sediment transport in gravel-bed rivers*. Unpublished Ph.D. thesis, Loughborough University, UK.

Johnson, M.F., Reid, I., Rice, S.P., and Wood, P.J. 2009. Stabilization of fine gravels by net-spinning caddisfly larvae. *Earth Surface Processes and Landforms* **34**: 413–423.

Johnson, M.F., Rice, S.P., and Reid, I. 2010. Topographic disturbance of subaqueous gravels by signal crayfish (*Pacifastacus leniusculus*). *Geomorphology* **123**: 269–278.

Johnson, M.F., Rice, S.P., and Reid, I. 2011. Increase in coarse sediment transport associated with disturbance of gravel river beds by signal crayfish (*Pacifastacus leniusculus*), *Earth Surface Processes and Landforms*, doi: 10.1002/esp.2192.

Jones, C.G., Lawton, J.H., and Shachak, M. 1994. Organisms as ecosystem engineers. *Oikos* **69**: 373–386.

Kauffman, J.B. and Krueger, W.C. 1984. Livestock impacts on riparian ecosystems and streamside management implications: A review. *Journal of Range Management* **37**: 430–438.

Kondolf, G.M., Sale, M.J., and Wolman, M.G. 1993. Modification of fluvial gravel size by spawning salmonids. *Water Resources Research* **20**: 2265–2274.

Lachner, E.A. 1952. Studies of the biology of the cyprinid fishes of the chub genus Nocomis of Northwestern United States. *American Midland Naturalist* **48**: 433–466.

Lamarre, H. and Roy, A.G. 2008. A field experiment on the development of sedimentary structures in a gravel-bed river. *Earth Surface Processes and Landforms* **33**: 1064–1081.

Lamouroux, N., Mérigoux, S., Capra, H. *et al.* 2010. The generality of abundance-environment relationships in microhabitats: a comment on Lancaster and Downes (2009). *River Research and Applications* **26**: 915–920. doi: 10.1002/rra.1366.

Lancaster, J. and Downes, B.J. 2010a. Linking the hydraulic world of individual organisms to ecological processes: putting ecology into ecohydraulics. *River Research and Applications* **26**: 385–403.

Lancaster, J. and Downes, B.J. 2010b. Ecohydraulics needs to embrace ecology and sound science, and to avoid mathematical artefacts. *River Research and Applications* **26**: 921–929. doi: 10.1002/rra.1425

Laubel, A., Kronvang, B., Hald, A.B., and Jensen, C. 2003. Hydromorphological and biological factors influencing sediment and phosphorous loss via bank erosion in small lowland rural streams in Denmark. *Hydrological Processes* **17**: 3443–3463.

Lisle, T.E. 1995. Particle size variations between bed load and bed material in natural gravel bed channels. *Water Resources Research* **31**: 1107–1118.

Lisle, T.E. and Hilton, S. 1999. Fine bed material in pools of natural gravel bed channels. *Water Resources Research* **35**: 1291–1304.

Macdonald, J.S., King, C.A., and Herunter, H. 2010. Sediment and salmon: The role of spawning sockeye salmon in annual bed load transport characteristics in small, interior streams of British Columbia. *Transactions of the American Fisheries Society* **139**: 758–767.

Magilligan, F.J. and McDowell, P.F. 1997. Stream channel adjustments following elimination of cattle grazing. *Journal of the American Water Resources Association* **33**: 867–878.

March, J.G., Pringle, C.M., Townsend, M.J., and Wilson, A.I. 2002. Effects of freshwater shrimp assemblages on benthic communities along an altitudinal gradient of a tropical island stream. *Freshwater Streams* **47**: 377–390.

Matsuzaki, S.S., Usio, N., Takamura, N., and Washitani, I. 2009. Contrasting impacts of invasive engineers on freshwater ecosystems: an experiment and meta-analysis. *Oecologia* **158**: 673–686.

Millane, R.P., Weir, M.I., and Smart, G.M. 2006. Automated analysis of imbrication and flow direction in alluvial sediments using laser-scan data. *Journal of Sedimentary Research* **76**: 1049–1055.

Miller, S.A. and Crowl, T.A. 2006. Effects of common carp (*Cyprinus carpio* L.) on macrophytes and invertebrate communities in a shallow lake. *Freshwater Biology* **51**: 85–94.

Montgomery, D.R., Buffington, J.M., Peterson, N.P., Schuett-Hames, D., and Quinn, T.P. 1996. Stream-bed scour, egg burial depths, and the influence of salmonid spawning on bed surface mobility and embryo survival. *Canadian Journal of Aquatics and Fisheries Science* **53**: 1061–1070.

Moore, J.W. 2006. Animal ecosystem engineers in streams. *Bioscience* **56**: 237–246.

Moore, J.W., Schindler, D.E., and Scheuerell, M.D. 2004. Disturbance of freshwater habitats by andromous salmon in Alaska. *Oecologia* **139**: 298–308.

Moulton, T.P., De Souza, M.L., Silveira, R.M.L., and Krsulovic, F.A.M. 2004. Effects of ephemeropterans and shrimps on periphyton and sediments in a coastal stream (Atlantic forest, Rio de Janeiro Brazil). *Journal of the North American Benthological Society* **23**: 868–881.

Naiman, R.J., Elliott, S.R., Helfield, J.M., and O'Keefe, T.C. 2000. Biophysical interactions and the structure and dynamics of riverine ecosystems: the importance of biotic feedbacks. *Hydrobiologia* **410**: 79–86.

Naiman, R.J., Johnston, C.A., and Kelly, J.C. 1988. Alteration of North American streams by beaver. *Bioscience* **38**: 753–762.

Oldmeadow, D.F. and Church, M. 2006. A field experiment on streambed stabilization by gravel structures. *Geomorphology* **78**: 335–350.

Osterkamp, W.R. and Hupp, C.R. 2010. Fluvial processes and vegetation – Glimpses of the past, the present, and perhaps the future. *Geomorphology* **116**: 274–285.

Palmer, M.A. and Bernhardt, E.S. 2006. Hydroecology and river restoration: Ripe for research and synthesis. *Water Resources Research* **42**: W03S07. doi: 10.1029/2005WR004354.

Palmer, M.A., Ambrose, R.F., and Poff, N.L. 1997. Ecological theory and community restoration ecology. *Restoration Ecology* **5**: 291–300.

Paola, C., Foufoula-Georgiou, E., Dietrich, W.E. *et al.* 2006. Toward a unified science for the Earth's surface: opportunities for synthesis among hydrology, geomorphology, geochemistry, and ecology. *Water Resources Research* **42**: W03S10. doi: 10.1029/2005WR004336.

Parkos, J.J., Santucci, V.J., and Wahl, D.H. 2003. Effects of adult common carp (Cyprinus carpio) on multiple trophic levels in shallow mesocosms. *Canadian Journal of Fisheries and Aquatic Science* **60**: 182–192.

Parkyn, S.M., Rabeni, C.F., and Collier, K.J. 1997. Effects of crayfish (*Paranephrops planifrons*: Parastacidae) on instream processes and benthic faunas: a density manipulation experiment. *New Zealand Journal of Marine and Freshwater Research* **31**: 685–692.

Persson, A. and Svensson, J.M. 2006a. Effects of benthivorous fish on biogeochemical processes in lake sediments. *Freshwater Biology* **51**: 1298–1309.

Persson, A. and Svensson, J.M. 2006b. Vertical distribution of benthic community responses to fish predators, and effects on algae and suspended material. *Aquatic Ecology* **40**: 85–95.

Peterson, D.P. and Foote, C.J. 2000. Disturbance of small-stream habitat by spawning sockeye salmon in Alaska. *Transactions of the American Fisheries Society* **129**: 924–934.

Petts, G.E., Nestler, J., and Kennedy, R. 2006. Advancing science for water resources management. *Hydrobiologia* **565**: 277–288.

Pierce, C.L., Musgrove, K.A., Ritterpusch, J. and Carl, N.E. 1987. Littoral invertebrate abundance in bluegill spawning colonies and undisturbed areas of a small pond. *Canadian Journal of Zoology* **65**: 2066–2071.

Power, M.E. 1990. Resource enhancement by indirect effects of grazers: armored catfish, algae, and sediment. *Ecology* **71**: 897–904.

Pringle, C.M. and Blake, G.A. 1994. Quantitative effects of atyid shrimp (Decapoda: Atyidae) on the depositional environment in a tropical stream: use of electricity for experimental exclusion. *Canadian Journal of Fisheries and Aquatic Science* **51**: 1443–1450.

Pringle, C.M. and Hamazaki, T. 1998. The role of omnivory in a neotropical stream: separating diurnal and nocturnal effects. *Ecology* **79**: 269–280.

Reid, I. and Frostick, L.E. 1984. Particle interaction and its effects on thresholds of initial and final bedload motion in coarse alluvial channels. In Koster, E.H. and Steel, R.J., editors. *Sedimentology of Gravels and Conglomerates*: Calgary, Canadian Society of Petroleum Geologists, Memoir 10, pp. 61–69.

Reinhardt, L., Jerolmack, D., Cardinale, B.J., Vanacker, V., and Wright, J. 2010. Dynamic interactions of life and its landscape: feedbacks at the interface of geomorphology and ecology. *Earth Surface Processes and Landforms* **35**: 78–101.

Rennie, C.D. and Millar, R.B. 2000. Spatial variability of streambed scour and fill: a comparison of scour depth in Chum Salmon (*Oncorhynchus keta*) redds and adjacent bed. *Canadian Journal of Fisheries and Aquatic Science* **57**: 928–938.

Reudemann, R. and Schoonmaker, W.J. 1938. Beaver-dams as geologic agents. *Science* **88**: 523–525.

Rice, S.P. and Macklin, M.G. 2008. Geomorphology and earth system science: A reflection. *Earth Surface Processes and Landforms* **33**: 2118–2120.

Rice, S.P., Lancaster, J.L., and Kemp, P.S. 2010. Experimentation at the interface of fluvial geomorphology, stream ecology and hydraulic engineering and the development of an effective, interdisciplinary river science. *Earth Surface Processes and Landforms* **35**: 64–77.

Richter, B.D., Mathews, R., Harrison, D.L., and Wigington, R. 2003. Ecologically sustainable water management: managing river flows for ecological integrity. *Ecological Applications* **13**: 206–224.

Ripple, W.J. and Beschta, R.L. 2006. Linking a cougar decline, trophic cascade, and catastrophic regime shift in Zion National Park. *Biological Conservation* **133**: 397–408.

Roni, P., Hanson, K., and Beechie, T. 2008. Global review of the physical and biological effectiveness of stream habitat rehabilitation techniques. *North American Journal of Fisheries Management* **28**: 856–890.

Roozen, F., Lurling, M., Vlek, H. *et al.* 2007. Resuspension of algal cells by benthivorous fish boosts phytoplankton biomass and alters community structure in shallow lakes. *Freshwater Biology* **52**: 977–987.

Rushbrook, B.J. and Barber, I. 2008. A comparison of nest building by three-spined sticklebacks *Gasterosteus aculeatus* from still and flowing waters. *Journal of Fish Biology* **73**: 746–752.

Rypel, A.L. and Bayne, D.R. 2009. Hydrologic habitat preferences of select southeastern USA fishes resilient to river ecosystem fragmentation. *Ecohydrology* **2**: 419–427.

Sidle, R.C. and Zeigler, A.D. 2010. Elephant trail runoff and sediment dynamics in Northern Thailand. *Journal of Environmental Quality* **39**: 871–881.

Smart, G.M., Aberle, J., Duncan, M., and Walsh, J. 2004. Measurement and analysis of alluvial bed roughness. *Journal of Hydraulic Research* **42**: 227–237.

Souchon, Y., Sabaton, C., Deibel, R. *et al.* 2008. Detecting biological responses to flow management: missed opportunities; future directions. *River Research and Applications* **24**: 506–518.

Statzner, B. and Peltret, O. 2006. Assessing potential abiotic and biotic complications of crayfish-induced gravel transport in experimental streams. *Geomorphology* **74**: 245–256.

Statzner, B. and Sagnes, P. 2008. Crayfish and fish as bioturbators of streambed sediments: assessing the joint effects of species with different mechanistic abilities. *Geomorphology* **93**: 267–287.

Statzner, B., Arens, M.F., Champagne, J-Y., Morel, R., and Herouin, E. 1999. Silk producing stream insects and gravel erosion: significant biological effects on critical shear stress. *Water Resources Research* **35**: 3495–3506.

Statzner, B., Fievet, E., Champagne, J-Y., Morel, R., and Herouin, E. 2000. Crayfish as geomorphic agents and ecosystem engineers: biological behaviour affects sand and gravel erosion in experimental streams. *Limnology & Oceanography* **45**: 1030–1040.

Statzner, B., Fuchs, U., and Higler, L.W.G. 1996. Sand erosion by mobile predaceous stream insects: implications for ecology and hydrology. *Water Resources Research* **32**: 2279–2287.

Statzner, B., Peltret, O. and Tomanova, S. 2003a. Crayfish as geomorphic agents and ecosystem engineers: effect of a biomass gradient on baseflow and flood-induced transport of gravel and sand in experimental streams. *Freshwater Biology* **48**: 147–163.

Statzner, B., Sagnes, P., Champagne, J-Y., and Viboud, S. 2003b. Contribution of benthic fish to the patch dynamics of gravel and sand transport in streams. *Water Resources Research* **39**: 1309. doi: 10.1029/2003WR002270.

Stone J. 2006. Observations on nest characteristics, spawning habitat, and spawning behaviour of pacific and western brook lamprey in a Washington stream. *Northwestern Naturalist* **87**: 225–232.

Tal, M. and Paola, C. 2007. Dynamic single-thread channels maintained by the interaction of flow and vegetation. *Geology* **35**: 347–350.

Tharme, R.E. 2003. A global perspective on environmental flow assessment: emerging trends in the development and application of environmental flow methodologies for rivers. *River Research and Applications* **19**: 397–441.

Thompson, D.M. and Stull, G.N. 2002. The development and historic use of habitat structures in channel restoration in the United States: The grand experiment in fisheries management. *Geographie Physique et Quaternaire* **56**: 45–60.

Thorp, J.H. 1988. Patches and the responses of lake benthos to sunfish nest-building. *Oecologia* **76**: 168–174.

Tonina, D. and Buffington, J.M. 2009. A three-dimensional model for analyzing the effects of salmon redds on hyporheic exchange and egg-pocket habitat. *Canadian Journal of Fisheries and Aquatic Sciences* **66**: 2157–2173.

Trimble, S.W. 1994. Erosional effects of cattle on streambanks in Tennessee, U.S.A. *Earth Surface Processes and Landforms* **19**: 451–464.

Trimble, S.W. and Mendel, A.C. 1995. The cow as a geomorphic agent – a critical review. *Geomorphology* **13**: 233–253.

Usio, N. and Townsend, C.R. 2004. Roles of crayfish: consequences of predation and bioturbation for stream invertebrates. *Ecology* **85**: 807–822.

Vaughan, I.P., Diamond, M., Gurnell, A.M. *et al.* 2009. Integrating ecology with hydromorphology: a priority for river science and management. *Aquatic Conservation: Marine and Freshwater Ecosystems* **19**: 113–125.

Viles, H.A., editor. 1988 *Biogeomorphology*. Oxford, Blackwell.

Visoni, S.B.C. and Moulton, T.P. 2003. Effects of shrimp on periphyton and sediments in Atlantic forest streams: an exclusion experiment. *Acta Limnologica Brasil* **15**: 19–26.

Wallace, J.B. and Merritt, R.W. 1980. Filter-feeding ecology of aquatic insects. *Annual Review of Entomology* **25**: 103–132.

Ward, P.D., Montgomery, D.R., and Smith, R. 2000. Altered river morphology in South Africa related to the Permian-Triassic extinction. *Science* **289**: 1740–1744.

Westbrook, C.J., Cooper, D.J., and Baker, B.W. 2011. Beaver assisted river valley formation. *River Research & Applications* **27**: 247–256. doi: 10.1002/rra.1359

Wilcock, P.R., Kenworthy, S.T., and Crowe, J.C. 2001. Experimental study of the transport of mixed sand and gravel, *Water Resources Research* **37**: 3349–3358.

Winemiller, K.O. and Taylor, D.H. 1982. Smallmouth bass nesting behaviour in a small Ohio stream. *Ohio Journal of Science* **82**: 266–273.

Wolff, L.M. 2002. Why alien invaders succeed: support for the escape-from-enemy hypothesis. *The American Naturalist* **160**: 705–711.

Wright, J.P. and Jones, C.G. 2006. The concept of organisms as ecosystem engineers ten years on: progress, limitations, and challenges. *Bioscience* **56**: 203–209.

Zanetell, B.A. and Peckarsky, B.L. 1996. Stoneflies as ecological engineers – hungry predators reduce fine sediments in stream beds. *Freshwater Biology* **36**: 569–577.

## 19.7 DISCUSSION

### 19.7.1 Discussion by Joanna Curran

You have documented the ability of fish to move individual gravel clasts on the bed surface. Through their actions, the fish can change the surface structure of a gravel bed, disrupt an armour layer, reduce imbrication, and alter microcluster population and structure. From the video, it did not appear that the fish then created a new bed structure, unlike the large salmon redds documented elsewhere, that would re-create bed surface stability. The fish are necessarily impacting the mobility of the bed surface, most likely reducing the critical shear stress necessary for entrainment. Can you comment on how much you believe the fish contribute to a reduction in bed surface structure and an increase in bed mobility?

### 19.7.2 Discussion by Gordon Grant

A comment followed by a question. It is interesting to note the contrast between the discussions framed by Torgerson and Rice. Torgerson points to something we all expect to be important, i.e., the correspondence between hydraulic patterns, geomorphic forms, and fish habitat, and shows why the linkage may be weak. Rice, on the other hand, points to something we might tend to view as unimportant, i.e., the role of very small biotic organisms in channel morphology, and suggests that it might play a heretofore under-appreciated role in channel dynamics and evolution. My question is how we distinguish whether such biotic interactions are, in fact, important. Just noting that organisms can, for example, secrete substances that bind bed particles together is not enough; we have to know if such biotic "glue" makes a difference for entrainment, roughness, etc.

### 19.7.3 Reply by Stephen P. Rice

These questions go to the heart of two key issues. First, we do not know the extent to which fish behaviours, like nest building and grain re-arrangements during foraging, affect bed structure and grain mobility. There is certainly evidence that spawning sockeye salmon (*Oncorhynchus nerka*) can affect bed material mobility and bedload fluxes (Hassan *et al.*, 2008) but the mechanisms involved are unclear. Spawning salmon cause a direct downstream transfer of sediment, but also affect the distribution of available grain sizes, the fabrics and structures of bed sediments, and the topography of the bed surface, each of which may have implications for sediment availability. Montgomery *et al.* (1996) make the important point that changes to bed surface topography during redd building are likely to also affect bed shear stress distributions, potentially reducing drag and thence particle mobility. Similar effects may occur as a result of particle re-arrangement and the destruction of water-worked fabrics or microforms. Disentangling the effects of increased particle availability and reduced near-bed stresses is one area that requires careful consideration.

While we know that many fish species engage in behaviours that affect parameters of importance for bedload transport in gravel-bed rivers (Figure 19.6), empirical investigations are extremely rare. To our knowledge, the handful of papers referenced here represent all of the published work that focuses on the geomorphic impacts rather than ecological consequences of bed disturbance by fish. This paucity of empirical information means that we cannot construct an evidence-based understanding of: (i) the extent and degree to which fish and other animals influence the bed and flow parameters of interest nor (ii) the extent and degree to which these effects feed through to measurable or important differences in bedload flux.

This second point relates directly to Grant's question. We agree wholeheartedly that it is not enough to merely demonstrate that instream fauna *can* influence the entrainment, near-bed hydraulics or transport rates of bed materials via the pathways laid out in Figure 19.6. Experimental control in laboratory or outdoor flumes is required to tease apart and identify the important mechanisms and their relative roles, but this work is largely redundant without then relating experimental results to field situations to investigate whether biotic effects make a difference in the environment (Johnson, 2009; Johnson *et al.*, 2010; Rice *et al.*, 2010). Making this connection may be easier for large animals that have a clear and visible impact; for example, production of spawning dunes (salmon), construction of dams (beaver) or poaching of the land surface (cattle). Identifying the reach or catchment scale impact of much smaller "Cinderella" species, that are not readily visible and do not cause obvious physical modifications, may require greater effort. It is possible to think of grand schemes that might be used to investigate the impact of such animals at field scales (for example, large-scale exclusion studies using paired reaches with pre- and post-treatment monitoring). Alternatively, it may be possible to develop incremental programmes of work that build a picture of the likelihood that a particular animal has an impact in the field (as we illustrate for our crayfish work by establishing that crayfish do spend time on the substrates that flume experiments show they can affect). In either case, there are a number of basic considerations that might guide attempts to understand better the implications of small-scale experimental observations of animal impacts for fluvial geomorphology in the field:

(1) What are the potential impacts of experimental arrangements on the key behaviours and activities that affect hydraulic or geomorphological processes? How might those behaviours be different in the field (where there are biotic interactions, more space, physical patchiness, and uncontrolled physical factors to consider) and what are the consequences for the impacts on physical processes that were observed in the artificial environment?

(2) What are the spatial and temporal distributions of the animals and their behaviours in the field? What are the spatial and temporal distributions of the physical conditions (substrates, flows) under which animals are understood to have an effect? What is the coincidence of these two sets of factors in space and time?

(3) What is the magnitude of any demonstrable net field impact relative to those other factors that are known to control sediment transport rates?

Notwithstanding the considerable empirical challenge that these issues present, the work that has been done to date by Statzner, ourselves, and others indicates that small animals may have a profound effect on bed stability and coarse-grained transport and we hope that the conceptualization of the problem presented in Figure 19.6 provides a framework for future work in this area.

# 20

# Geomorphology and Gravel-bed River Ecosystem Services: Workshop Outcomes

**Normand Bergeron and Joanna Eyquem**

## 20.1 INTRODUCTION

It is widely recognized that rivers provide valuable services to humans; for example, provision of water for agriculture, industry and human consumption, transportation of goods, recreational opportunities, and habitat for aquatic organisms. However, human activities also exert significant pressure on river ecosystems, resulting in changes to the physical and biological processes that are required to produce the very services from which we currently benefit. Because river ecosystem services are not commonly valued in monetary terms, it is difficult to demonstrate the economic benefits resulting from the preservation and/or restoration of rivers. As pointed out by Loomis *et al.* (2000), failure to quantify ecosystem values often results in an implicit value of zero being placed on ecosystem services. Fluvial forms and processes are evidently key components of the production of river ecosystem services and fluvial geomorphologists therefore have a key role to play in their identification and evaluation. To date, however, fulfilment of this role has been limited. Thus, although appropriate methods of valuing ecosystem services are still a matter of debate, we suggest that it is vital for fluvial geomorphologists to become more actively involved in this relatively new, yet rapidly expanding and increasingly important, area of applied research.

In view of the limited knowledge within the gravel-bed river research community concerning river ecosystem services, the GBR7 scientific committee selected this topic as the subject of the conference workshop. The workshop was intended to provide an informative and interactive introduction to ecosystem services in the context of gravel-bed rivers. More specifically, the objectives of the workshop were to:

- provide all participants with a common background to the concept of river ecosystem services;

- bring the perspective of the gravel-bed river research community into this evolving area of applied research;
- demonstrate how ecosystem services and their evaluation can be potentially used to benefit river management and restoration;
- stimulate the gravel-bed river research community to undertake research into this new area of study.

This chapter presents the salient points and outcomes of the workshop, which was held on 8 September 2010 in Tadoussac (Québec, Canada) and attended by an international group of over 80 delegates.

## 20.2 WORKSHOP STRUCTURE

The workshop comprised presentations and break-out group work sessions (a copy of the program is contained in Appendix A). In advance of the workshop, delegates were provided with a summary of the program and asked to read two papers (Costanza *et al.*, 1997; Boyd and Banzhaf, 2007) as useful background information.

### 20.2.1 Presentations

The first part of the workshop consisted of a series of presentations to provide delegates with a common understanding of the definition of ecosystems services and established evaluation methods. Dr Karin Limburg provided a personal perspective of the evolution of the concept of ecosystem services, particularly describing her role in assessing the value of marine-related ecosystem services leading up to the publication of the Costanza *et al.* (1997) paper. Ms Joanna Eyquem subsequently provided an overview of different environmental evaluation methods and practical applications, together with a brief discussion of some of the key challenges.

*Gravel-bed Rivers: Processes, Tools, Environments*, First Edition. Edited by Michael Church, Pascale M. Biron and André G. Roy.
© 2012 John Wiley & Sons, Ltd. Published 2012 by John Wiley & Sons, Ltd.

Following a short break, Dr Normand Bergeron presented the work that had previously been undertaken as part of the "Workshop on Indicators of Final Ecosystem Services for Streams" in July 2009 (Ringold *et al.*, 2009a). The next two sections present in greater detail the content of the presentations by Joanna Eyquem and Normand Bergeron, respectively.

### 20.2.1.1 How much is it Worth? – An Overview of Evaluation Methods

In order for delegates to take part in the practical elements of the workshop, an introduction to environmental evaluation methods was provided. This introduction considered different types of ecosystem values together with a range of methods for their evaluation. Practical examples were used to illustrate how values may be monetized, including cost-benefit methods that have already been introduced as a tool to decision-making.

Various different types of ecosystem value may contribute to the total economic value of an ecosystem service, as illustrated in Figure 20.1. The challenge is that some of these values are not associated with defined quantities and no market price is established through direct trade. Environmental evaluation methods therefore commonly seek to establish the "willingness to pay" of consumers using alternative methods. Willingness to pay for some ecosystem services may be revealed through the market prices of related goods that are bought or sold to enjoy the service. In other cases, values may be imputed by estimating what people are willing to pay, or the cost of actions they are willing to take, to avoid the adverse effects that would occur if these services were lost, or to replace the lost services. Where neither of these

alternatives is feasible, it may be possible to ask people to state their willingness to pay using surveys based on hypothetical situations. An overview of common evaluation methods and examples discussed during the workshop is provided in Table 20.1.

The selection of an appropriate and practicable approach to evaluation of ecosystem services depends on several aspects, including the type of value of interest, data requirements, inherent limitations of evaluation methods, the degree of detail required, and the time and resources available. Frequently, a lack of available resources limits the effort that can be applied to evaluation of ecosystem services and prohibits the use of more data-intensive methods.

However, in recent years, pragmatic approaches to environmental evaluation have been adopted so that environmental benefits or costs can be taken into account as part of the decision-making process. Examples include multicriteria analysis, scoring and weighting approaches, and staged ranking methods. A key example is the recently updated United Kingdom Flood and Coastal Erosion Risk Management Appraisal Guidance, which describes a scoring and weighting methodology whereby indicative economic values can be assigned to non-monetized benefits of habitat creation or costs of habitat loss when evaluating alternative flood or coastal erosion risk management options (UK Environment Agency, 2010).

### 20.2.1.2 Outcomes of the Workshop on "Indicators of Final Ecosystem Services for Streams"

The workshop, held in July 2009 in Denver (Colorado, USA), was sponsored by the Western Ecology Division

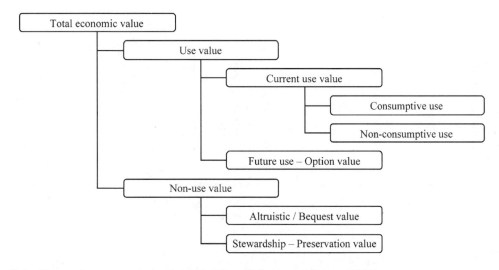

**Figure 20.1** Types of ecosystem value (modified from Huppert and Kantor, 1998).

**Table 20.1** Methods of economic evaluation (based on King and Markowitz, 2000)

| Willingness to Pay | Method | Description | Example |
|---|---|---|---|
| Revealed | Market Price Method | Estimates the economic value of ecosystem products or services that are bought and sold in commercial markets | Market price of fish or wood resources |
|  | Productivity Method | Estimates the economic value of ecosystem products or services that contribute to the production of commercially marketed goods | Improved water quality may result in decreased chlorination costs to produce drinking water |
|  | Hedonic Pricing Method | Estimates economic values for ecosystem services that directly affect market prices of some other good | Increase in house prices as a result of increased proximity to local green space |
|  | Travel Cost Method | Estimates economic values associated with sites that are used for recreation. Assumes that the value of a site is reflected in how much people are willing to pay to travel to visit the site | Transport and time related costs of travelling to a site for recreational fishing |
| Imputed | Damage Cost Avoided, Replacement Cost, and Substitute Cost Methods | Estimates economic values based on costs of avoided damages resulting from lost ecosystem services, costs of replacing ecosystem services, or costs of providing substitute services | Valuing flood protection benefits of wetlands by measuring:<br>• the cost of flood damages avoided<br>• the cost of constructing substitute flood protection, such as flood walls |
| Stated | Contingent Valuation Method | Estimates both use and non-use, or "passive use" values. Asks people to directly state their willingness to pay for specific environmental services, based on a hypothetical scenario | Asking households whether they would support removal of dams to triple salmon populations at a set annual cost that varies between households |
|  | Choice Experiments | Similar to CVM but asks people to make a sequence of choices between hypothetical scenarios associated with a specific cost. Values are inferred by the trade offs that are made | Asking households to choose between restoration of different stream attributes associated with different costs |
| Other | Benefit Transfer Method | Used to estimate economic values for ecosystem services by transferring available information from studies already completed in another location and/or context | Values for recreational fishing in a particular region may be estimated by applying measures of recreational fishing values from a study conducted in another region |

and the Ecosystems Services Research Program of the United States Environmental Protection Agency. It gathered 25 participants from various institutions (academia, government, agencies, private sector, non-government organizations) and with different areas of expertise (ecology, social sciences, physical habitat, biology, sampling methods, etc.). This workshop is particularly important to the field of river ecosystem services because it was the first step in specifically focusing on the relations between streams and human wellbeing. The main objective of the workshop was to produce a list of indicators of final ecosystem services directly valued by society and usable in nationwide stream-monitoring programs.

The workshop relied heavily on the concept of "final ecosystem services" and the related concepts of "intermediate ecosystem services" and "production functions" as defined in Boyd and Banzhaf (2007). In their paper, these authors argued that ecology and economics had so far failed to standardize the definition and measurement of ecosystem services and that there was a need to consistently define the units of account to be used for measuring the contributions of nature to welfare. For this reason, they advocated the need to clearly distinguish between "final" and "intermediate" ecosystem services. In their approach, final ecosystem services are viewed as the components of nature that are directly enjoyed, consumed, or used to yield human wellbeing. They are thus the "end product of nature" and are the "units" upon which the valuation of ecosystem should be based. Final services are to be distinguished from intermediate ecosystem services that are not directly consumed by humans, but that are necessary to produce final services. Taking the example of recreational trout angling, a list of possible indicators of final services could include the "abundance of the trout population", the "length of fishable stream" and the "aesthetics of the surroundings". However, "good substrate" and "clean water" would constitute indicators of intermediate services because they are not directly consumed by trout anglers, but are linked by ecological production functions to the "abundance of the trout population".

Another important reason to distinguish between final and intermediate services is to avoid double-counting the value of intermediate goods (Boyd and Banzhaf 2007). For example, valuing both "good substrate" and "abundance of the trout population" would double-count the service of good substrate because its effect is already embodied in the "abundance of the trout population". Boyd and Banzhaf (2007) also stressed that a given component of an ecosystem could be a final service in one context, but an intermediate service in another. For example, although the indicator "clean water" was an intermediate service in the trout angling example, it would be considered as a final service for providing drinking water to a municipality. Although this may seem odd, they argued that the same property is present in conventional welfare accounting where, in the case of harvested apples for example, apples are counted if they are sold as apples in stores, but they are not counted if they are used to make apple sauce because their value is embodied in the value of apple sauce. Finally, Boyd and Banzhaf (2007) underlined that final services are ecological "things" or components of nature, not functions or process. For example, according to their definition, water purification is not a final service because it is not directly consumed by humans. It rather is a function that helps produce the clean water that constitutes the final service used by humans. Thus ecosystem processes and functions are not end-products of nature, although they have an immense value in the provision of final ecosystem services. There is therefore an urgent need to understand and model them thoroughly in order to predict how damage to ecosystems will depreciate the value of final services or to predict how restoration programs may help improve their value.

The main outcome of the Colorado workshop was a conceptual matrix listing different beneficiary groups that may "use" the services provided by streams, together with indicators of the final ecosystem services that may be provided. The work undertaken in drafting the Indicator Working Hypothesis matrix (Ringold et al., 2009b) was presented at the GBR7 conference workshop, although the actual draft matrix was not provided to delegates. This was in order to avoid influencing the ideas of the delegates present during the interactive portion of the workshop.

### 20.2.2 Break-out Group Session

From the outset of the organization process, the intent was to use the workshop as an opportunity to produce tangible outputs that would help further develop the concept of ecosystem services in relation to rivers. Following the presentations, a structured break-out group session was organized for this purpose. This session aimed to draw on the expertise of those present at the GBR7 conference to advance the work of Ringold et al., (2009b), in particular in terms of geomorphology-related ecosystems services.

Delegates were asked to work in 10 groups of up to 10 people, with each group representing one of the following river beneficiaries: (i) farmer irrigating commercial cereal crops; (ii) electricity company producing hydro-electricty using a large-scale dam; (iii) gravel and sand extraction company; (iv) commercial sturgeon fishing company; (v) municipality providing drinking water for a large city; (vi) riverside residential property owner;

**Table 20.2** Final Ecosystem Services Identified as "Consumed" by Different Beneficiary Groups by Workshop Participants

| Beneficiary Group | Amount (water) | Timing (water)[3] | Temperature (water) | Conductivity (water) | Stream bed (substrate) | Clarity (water) | Dissolved oxygen | Chemicals | Odour | Pathogens | Ecosystem health/biointegrity | Fish | Wildlife | Plants | Genetic diversity | Aesthetics | Total number of final services identified as "consumed" (of 16) | Other final services identified |
|---|---|---|---|---|---|---|---|---|---|---|---|---|---|---|---|---|---|---|
| (1) Farmer irrigating commercial cereal crops | ✓ *(1)* | ✓ *(1)* | | ✓ *(5)* | | | | ✓ *(2)* | | | | | | | | | 4 | Suspended sediment load *(2)* Channel morphology *(3)* *Stable bed and banks* |
| (2) Electricity company producing hydro-electricity using a large-scale dam | ✓ *(2)* | ✓ *(1)* | | | | | | | | | | | | | | | 2 | Sediment load *(2)* |
| (3) Gravel and sand extraction | | | | | ✓ *(1,2)* | | | ✓ | | | | | | | | | 2 | Amount (sediment) |
| (4) Commercial sturgeon fishing company | | | | | | | | | | | | ✓ *(1,2,6)* | | | | | 1 | - |
| (5) Municipality providing drinking water for a large city | ✓ *(1,3)* | ✓ *(1)* | ✓ | ✓ | | ✓ *(2)* | | ✓ | ✓ | ✓ | | | | | | | 8 | Timing (sediment) *(1)* Channel morphology (accessibility) *(1)* |
| (6) Riverside residential property owner | ✓ | ✓ | ✓ | | | ✓ | | | | | ✓ | ✓ | ✓ | ✓ | | ✓ | 9 | *Bank stability* *(1,2,7)* |

| Beneficiary group | Flow velocity, turbulence | Channel morphology (bedforms) *(4)* | Channel morphology (accessibility) | Channel morphology (diversity) *(1,2,6)* | Channel morphology (dimensions) *(2,3,4)* | Stable bed and banks *(1,2)* | |
|---|---|---|---|---|---|---|---|
| (7) Whitewater rafting enthusiast | ✓ *(6)* | ✓ *(2)* | | ✓ | | | *3* |
| (8) Recreational salmonid fly-fisherman | ✓ | | ✓ *(1,2)* | | | | *4* *(1)* |
| (9) River landscape photographer | | ✓ | | ✓ | | | *4* *(1)* |
| (10) Commercial transportation company (goods) | ✓ *(1)* | ✓ *(1)* | | | | | *2* |
| **Number of beneficiary groups identified as "consuming" final service (out of 10)** | 7 | 8 | 2 | 2 | 3 | 3 | 0 3 1 1 1 3 1 1 0 3 **39** |

Key to geomorphological intermediate services identified from matrix wall chart
*(1)* Channel & floodplain morphology, *(2)* Sediment transport regime (amount, timing, sizing), *(3)* Stable channel, *(4)* Gradient, *(5)* Weathering, *(6)* Flow velocity & turbulence, *(7)* Bank Material

(vii) whitewater rafting enthusiast; (viii) recreational salmonid fly-fisherman; (ix) river landscape photographer; (x) commercial transportation company (goods). Each group was provided with a set of detailed written instructions for completing two group tasks, together with a response booklet for recording the outcomes of group discussion.

For the first task, delegates were asked to respond to the following questions in the context of their river beneficiary:

(1) Which final ecosystem services (of a list provided – see Appendix B) are important to your beneficiary?
(2) Are there any other final services that you think are relevant?
(3) Is geomorphology relevant in providing the final services to your beneficiary? (A draft list of geomorphological intermediate services was provided as a starting point – see Appendix C.)
(4) What geomorphological intermediate services are most important?

Responses to questions (1) to (3) were recorded in the response booklet, whilst responses to the final question (4) were recorded using post-it notes which delegates affixed to a matrix wall chart based on the draft Indicator Working Hypothesis matrix (Ringold *et al.*, 2009b).

For the second task, delegates were asked to select the final ecosystem service "consumed" by their beneficiary group that was most related to geomorphology – i.e., a geomorphological final service or one strongly dependant on geomorphological intermediate services. Considering this final service, groups were asked to respond to the following questions:

(1) What is important about this final service to your beneficiary and how can we measure it?
(2) Do we understand the relation between any supporting geomorphological intermediates services you have identified and the final service?
(3) Considering your responses to (1) and (2) what information is currently lacking?
(4) How could the value of the final ecosystem service be measured (i.e., in $)? (A table of potential evaluation methods and their advantages and disadvantages, extracted from Abaza and Rietbetgen-McCracken (1998), was provided for reference.)

Each of the tasks was allocated a period of 30 minutes, however additional time was allowed to enable groups to complete the tasks and conclude their discussions. Throughout the break-out session the workshop organizers circulated among the groups to facilitate discussion and provide clarification as required.

### 20.2.3  Plenary Discussion

Following completion of the tasks, an open, unstructured plenary discussion was held to gather the views of delegates having undertaken the tasks, focusing on their impressions of the approach, potential uses, limitations, and next steps. At the end of the session the response booklets were collected and the information on the matrix wall chart documented to enable the organisers to analyse the outcomes of the workshop.

## 20.3  WORKSHOP OUTCOMES

### 20.3.1  Findings of the Break-out Group Session

The outcomes of the workshop are presented by task in this section. It should be stressed that these results are presented at face value as outcomes of the workshop to provide a basis for further analysis rather than as definitive or exhaustive findings.

*20.3.1.1  Task 1: How does Geomorphology Contribute to Final Ecosystem Services for Your Beneficiary Group?*

*(a) Which final ecosystem services are important to your beneficiary?*
The final ecosystem services identified as being "consumed" directly by the beneficiaries being considered are identified in Table 20.2. The results clearly illustrate how different final ecosystem services are important to different beneficiaries. Each of the final ecosystem services was identified as being "consumed" by at least one of the beneficiary groups under consideration, with the exception of dissolved oxygen and genetic diversity. The final services that were identified for most beneficiary groups were the amount and timing of water in the river. It is also notable that while some beneficiaries were identified as requiring only one or two final services, others were indicated to "consume" a range of up to nine final services.

*(b) Are there any other final services that you think are relevant?*
The additional final services identified by workshop delegates as being "consumed" directly by the beneficiary groups under consideration are also identified in Table 20.2. These final services have been integrated as appropriate into the working list of final ecosystem services contained in Appendix B.

*(c) Is geomorphology relevant in providing the final services to your beneficiary?*
Many different geomorphological intermediate services were identified as necessary to the production of final ecosystem services "consumed" by the beneficiaries

considered. A summary of the intermediate services identified in relation to each of the final services, incorporating all group responses, is provided in Table 20.3. The phrasing of the responses has been standardized in order to identify common intermediate services.

The findings presented in Table 20.3 indicate that channel and floodplain morphology, channel stability, sediment transport regime (amount, timing, and size), and flow velocity and turbulence were identified as geomorphological intermediate services supporting several of the final ecosystem services.

*(d) What geomorphological intermediate services are most important?*

The geomorphological intermediate services that were perceived as most important were annotated using post-it notes on the matrix wall chart. The findings from the wall chart are summarised within Table 20.2 using numbered annotations. The findings illustrate that channel and floodplain morphology (including lateral and longitudinal connectivity) and sediment transport regime (incorporating amount, timing and size) are key geomorphological intermediate services necessary to support many of the final ecosystem services identified as "consumed" by the beneficiary groups.

### 20.3.1.2 Task 2: How can Geomorphology Contribute to Evaluation of Ecosystem Services?

The workshop group responses to the questions posed as part of the second task are summarized in Table 20.4. A recurring theme within these responses is the need for further investigation and quantification of sediment supply, transport, and deposition of both coarse and fine sediment, in order to understand catchment function. The potential increased use of modelling techniques or remote-sensing methods for simulating sediment processes, measuring channel bed elevation or monitoring channel planform change, is highlighted.

### 20.3.2 Plenary Discussion

The workshop was organized on the assumption that few participants would be very familiar with economic evaluation methods and the concept of ecosystem services. A visual survey of participants prior to the break-out groups confirmed that the majority of participants in the workshop were geomorphological specialists, together with a limited number of ecologists. Few participants had prior experience of applying the concept of ecosystem services or undertaking environmental economic evaluation. The ideas expressed within the plenary discussion consequently concerned the fundamental use of ecosystem services and environmental valuation rather than detailed methodological discussions. The main discussion points

can be divided into those concerning definition of ecosystem services, balancing of potential conflicts of interest and use of economic evaluation.

Due to the interrelated nature of geomorphological processes, many participants found it difficult to define separate final and intermediate ecosystem services. There was also some confusion regarding the concept that the same service may be classified as a final service or an intermediate service depending on the beneficiary user being considered. The expression of geomorphic diversity as a specific service was highlighted as a particular difficulty. In addition, it was felt that the need to take into account "disservices" (e.g., flooding for residential landowners) was also a challenge in defining services.

The fact that different final services are required by some beneficiary groups, while they are actually disservices to other groups formed another point of discussion regarding conflicts of interest. This raised several questions, including which group's preference was more important and who was in a position to choose between different groups. It may be possible to consider the balance, for example by expressing the net economic value of each service, but it was considered that, on a catchment-basin scale, there are too many users to realistically consider in this way.

There was an appreciation that evaluation of the services associated with a river ecosystem in monetary terms may help to express the true cost of environmental impacts or benefits of river restoration. However, there were also concerns that apportionment of a monetary value may suggest that a river could be bought or traded by commercial means, whereas it was felt that any monetary value could not realistically reflect the true worth of a river as part of a wider, balanced ecosystem. The potential use of ecosystem services to promote "doing nothing" (and avoid environmental costs) was also discussed alongside the notion that compensation for non-exploitation of resources may be economically viable (the example was cited of set-aside payments made to farmers not to cultivate re-created wetland areas). Consideration of the implications of this latter concept on an international scale was more controversial.

### 20.3.3 Post-workshop Feedback

Following the workshop, the organizers received significant feedback from participants throughout the rest of the GBR7 conference and in written correspondence after the event. Most expressed their support for bringing this area of application research into a forum for discussion with a mainly academic audience, most of whom had limited prior knowledge of ecosystem services or environmental evaluation methods. Key concerns among those who remain sceptical of the appropriateness of the

**Table 20.3** Geomorphological intermediate ecosystem services identified by workshop participants

| Final ecosystem service | Geomorphological intermediate services necessary to production of final ecosystem service | Example of influence/pathway of effect |
| --- | --- | --- |
| Amount (water) | Channel & floodplain morphology (including lateral and longitudinal connectivity) | Influence of floodplain storage in reducing downstream discharge |
| | Stable channel | Influence of channel stability on the efficiency of drinking water abstraction |
| | Flow velocity and turbulence | Influence of velocity and turbulence on the area of water suitable for white-water rafting |
| Timing (water) | Channel & floodplain morphology (including lateral and longitudinal connectivity) | Influence of floodplain storage in attenuating flows |
| Temperature (water) | Channel morphology | Influence of channel depth on water temperature |
| Conductivity | Sediment transport regime | Influence of suspended fine sediment on conductivity |
| | Weathering | Influence of weathering on supply of fine sediment load |
| Stream bed (substrate) | Sediment transport regime (including sizing) | Influence of sediment transport on the size of bed substrate |
| Clarity | Sediment transport regime | Influence of fine sediment supply and transportation on turbidity |
| Chemicals | Sediment transport regime | Influence of sediment in distribution and storage of adsorbed chemicals |
| Fish | Channel & floodplain morphology (including lateral and longitudinal connectivity) | Influence of pool-riffle morphology on availability of diverse physical habitat conditions (e.g., depths) |
| | Flow velocity and turbulence | Influence of flushing flows on availability of clean gravel suitable for spawning |
| | Sediment transport regime (amount, timing, sizing) | Influence of sediment supply on the availability of clean gravel suitable for spawning |
| | Stream bed substrate | Influence of substrate on availability of clean gravel suitable for spawning |
| Wildlife | Channel morphology | Influence of pool-riffle morphology on availability of diverse physical habitat conditions (e.g. depths) |
| | Sediment transport regime | Influence of sediment supply on the distribution of sediment |
| Aesthetics | Channel morphology | Influence of channel form in providing aesthetically pleasing landscapes (e.g.. meanders) |
| Suspended sediment load | Sediment transport regime | Influence of fine sediment supply on suspended sediment load |

| Channel morphology (includes stable form & diversity) | Bank material | Influence of bank material on bank erosion rates and channel dimensions |
| | Channel stability | Influence of bank instability on bank erosion rates and channel dimensions |
| | Flow velocity and turbulence | Influence of velocity on development of pool-riffle morphology |
| | Gradient | Influence of gradient on channel planform |
| | Sediment transport regime | Influence of sediment deposition in reducing channel dimensions |

**Table 20.4** Methods of measurement, geomorphological linkages, further data/research requirements and potential evaluation methods identified by workshop delegates

| Final ecosystem service | Important criteria | Indicators/metrics | Already measured? | Understanding of linkages between geomorphological intermediate services and final service | Further data/research requirements | Potential methods for estimating value ($) of service |
|---|---|---|---|---|---|---|
| Amount (water) | Discharge – maintenance of volume of water behind dam | Precipitation, seasonality, basin volume | Precipitation, inflows and loss of storage are monitored | Geomorphological concern relating to sediment inputs that reduce storage volume capacity over time | Suspended sediment quantification of sources and fluxes/ turbidity measurements. Understanding of downstream impacts and mitigation due to sediment transport disturbance | • Economic models relating storage volume/discharge to value of electricity produced |
| Stream bed (substrate) | Rate of sediment supply (replenishment) post extraction | Sediment sources, rate of sediment supply, seasonal variations | Typically insufficient data to enable quantification | Difficult to measure amounts and timing of sediment supply and link this with timing of water supply | Methods of estimating catchment-scale sediment supply, potentially using modelling techniques | None identified |
| Clarity | Low turbidity and colour | Turbidity Colorimeter | Techniques are available and applied | Bank stability relates to fine sediment generation and therefore turbidity. Riparian buffers//vegetation increase stability and also filter overland flow. Catchment land use has a strong influence | Location and quantification of sediment sources, understanding of efficacy relating to dimensions of buffer zones | • Costs incurred by municipal drinking water authority to improve clarity (e.g., filtration) |

| | | | | | | |
|---|---|---|---|---|---|---|
| Fish | Distribution, population demographics, biomass, fish health | Many parameters, e.g. catch weight per area, species, number, size, age, health | Some parameters measured, though data may be privately held by fishing companies. Other parameters not routinely measured but techniques are available | Broad understanding of how flow, sediment delivery and ecosystem structure influence fish. However, much uncertainty with regard to quantification or prediction of impacts. An active area of research | Quantification of complex linkages in geomorphic systems and how these are reflected in: Long-term monitoring Studies of fish behaviour/response to cues Improved understanding of interannual salmonid run dynamics or variation Adaptation to changing temperature and flow regimes | • Market price of saleable adults that are harvested sustainably • Market price of caviar that are harvested sustainably • Economic benefits from salmonid fishing tourist industry (e.g. licenses) • Surveys/choice experiments to establish "willingness to pay" of fishermen |
| Aesthetics | Ecosystem health, wildlife, plants | Bird/wildlife/plant populations | To varying extents dependant on species or communities of concern | Linkages to geomorphology are largely indirect and not completely understood | None identified | • Difference in property values (sale or professional valuation) between similar properties with/without river view |
| Channel morphology (includes stable form & diversity) | Bank stability | Bank retreat rates | Measured from historic aerial photographs, widely available | Link between bank stability and bank retreat clear. Importance of meandering, riparian vegetation and sediment supply less well understood | Regular aerial photography Improved/automated methods for tracking river position Underlying causes of instability require research | • Estimate cost of loss of land (e.g. lost production/revenue) • Cost of replacing irrigation infrastructure • Cost of bank stabilization measures |
| | Bed stability | Aggradation/ degradation rates | Can be quantified where specific data available | Link between bank stability and bank retreat is clear Importance of meandering and sediment supply is less well understood | Data relating to vertical change (e.g. using remote sensing methods) Underlying causes of instability require research | • Cost of replacing irrigation infrastructure • Damages caused by flooding due to aggradation |

*(Continued)*

**Table 20.4** (*Continued*)

| Final ecosystem service | Important criteria | Indicators/metrics | Already measured? | Understanding of linkages between geomorphological intermediate services and final service | Further data/research requirements | Potential methods for estimating value ($) of service |
|---|---|---|---|---|---|---|
| | Flow velocity/turbulence | Whitewater classification/grading | Gradings based on expert judgement | Sediment transport needed to maintain bedforms and local gradient changes | None identified | • Survey of rafters based on travel-cost method<br>• Revenue of commercial rafting companies<br>• Costs of building artificial rafting facilities |
| | Channel dimensions | Width and depth of channel | Yes techniques readily available | Influence of sediment supply, transport and influence on changes in channel dimensions not as readily understood | None identified | • Costs of intervention to enable navigation<br>• Increase in value of cargo shipped as a result of channel modification (e.g. additional cargo weight) |

concept include the subjectivity involved in evaluation methods and the view that it is not possible to express the true intrinsic value of river ecosystems in monetary terms.

## 20.4  FUTURE RESEARCH AND CHALLENGES

The enthusiastic response of participants, both during and after the event, suggests that the workshop achieved its primary goal of raising awareness and interest in the concept of river ecosystem services among the gravel-bed river research community. It is hoped that this enthusiasm will translate into increased involvement of fluvial geomorphologists in the identification and evaluation of river ecosystem services in support of river management, preservation, and restoration initiatives.

It is recognized that there are many challenges within this rapidly evolving area of research, in particular due to the need to incorporate subjective values. Currently, however, option appraisal and cost–benefit analyses are being undertaken largely without incorporating any measure of the value of river ecosystem services, which may lead to inappropriate decisions or inaction due to a lack of perceived net benefit. There is therefore significant scope for development of innovative approaches that could potentially be widely applied to more fully recognize the value of rivers in our decision-making processes. There are a number of steps that could be readily taken to improve the dataset available for research. For example, it is rare that river management projects fully report the realized economic costs associated with implementing river-management changes and even fewer projects include post-project analysis to assess the environmental benefits and/or costs realized. Documentation and provision of access to design, planning, installation, maintenance, and monitoring costs could potentially assist in valuing river ecosystem services in the future, but would require greater co-operation between researchers and practitioners in the private and public sectors.

Indeed, the interdisciplinary and applied nature of this field of research makes communication and integration of work undertaken by researchers from different communities and backgrounds of prime importance. This includes those from disciplines with whom fluvial geomorphologists have not traditionally worked (for example economists). Rather than being a challenge, this represents a significant and stimulating opportunity to share knowledge and expertise. As a first step, it is hoped that the outcomes from this workshop will help those already involved in evaluation of river ecosystem services to take greater account of the role of fluvial geomorphology in the production of river ecosystem services. This may in turn result in a larger number of joint, multidisciplinary research opportunities for those

interested in taking this emerging field of applied geomorphological research forward.

## 20.5  ACKNOWLEDGEMENTS

The workshop organisers would like to thank Dr Karen Limburg for providing us with the benefit of her extensive experience within this area of research, in particular her presentation and assistance in facilitating the workshop. We would also like to thank Paul Ringold and Dixon Landers for their valuable help and comments during the planning stages of the workshop, Michel Lapointe for assistance in organization of the workshop on the day, the organizing committee of the GBR7 conference for their encouragement and support, and all participants, whose expertise and enthusiasm made this introductory workshop a stimulating experience for all involved.

## 20.6  REFERENCES

Abaza, H. and Rietbetgen-McCracken, J. 1998. *Environmental Valuation: A Worldwide Compendium of Case Studies.* United Nations Environment Programme, Environmental Economics Series 26.

Boyd, J. and Banzhaf, S. 2007. What are ecosystem services? The need for standardized environmental accounting units. *Ecological Economics* **63**: 26–28.

Costanza, R., d'Arge, R., de Groot, R. *et al.* 1997. The value of the world's ecosystem services and natural capital. *Nature* **387**: 253–260.

Huppert, D.D. and Kantor, S. 1998. Economic perspectives on the ecology and management of rivers. In Naiman, R. and Bilby, R.E., editors. *Ecology and Management of Streams and Rivers in the Pacific Northwest Coastal Ecoregion.* New York, Springer-Verlag, Chapter 23.

King, D.M and Markowitz, K.J 2000. *Ecosystem Valuation.* United States Department of Agriculture, Natural Resources Conservation Services and National Oceanographic and Atmospheric Administration. url: http://www.ecosystemvaluation.org/index.html [Accessed: April 12, 2011].

Loomis, J.L., Kent, P., Strange, L., Fausch, K., and Covich, A. 2000. Measuring the total economic value of restoring ecosystem services in an impaired basin: results from a contingent valuation survey. *Ecological Economics* **33**: 103–117.

Ringold, P.L., Boyd, J., Landers, D., and Weber, M. 2009a. Report from the Workshop on Indicators of Final Ecosystem Services for Streams. Meeting held in Denver, Colorado, July 13-16 Ecosystems Services Research Program, United States Environmental Protection Agency. Report EPA/600/R-09/137: 56 pp. url: http://www.epa.gov/nheerl/arm/streameco/index.html [Accessed: April 12, 2011].

Ringold, P.L., Boyd, J., Landers, D., and Weber, M. 2009b. Indicator working Hypothesis. United States Environmental Protection Agency. URL: http://www.epa.gov/nheerl/arm/streameco/index.html [Accessed: April 12, 2011].

UK Environment Agency. 2010. *Flood and coastal erosion risk management appraisal guidance.* London, March 2010. url: http://www.environment-agency.gov.uk/research/planning/116705.aspx [Accessed: April 12, 2011].

## 20.7 APPENDIX A: PROGRAM OF THE GBR7 WORKSHOP ON GRAVEL-BED RIVER ECOSYSTEM SERVICES HELD 8 SEPTEMBER, 2010 IN TADOUSSAC, QUÉBEC (CANADA)

**How much is a gravel bed river worth? A workshop on Gravel Bed River Ecosystem Services**
**Organizers:** Normand Bergeron, Joanna Eyquem, and Michel Lapointe

How much is our favourite object of study worth? What are the services gravel-bed rivers render to aquatic ecosystems, and what are their values?

Answering these questions may provide river managers with more robust arguments to support protection and restoration of gravel-bed rivers. This workshop aims to provide an introduction to this new, yet rapidly expanding and increasingly essential, area of applied research. More specifically, the objectives of the workshop are to:

- provide all participants with a common background to the concept of river ecosystem services;
- bring the perspective of the gravel bed river research community into this not yet stabilized area of applied research;
- demonstrate how ecosystem services and their evaluation can be potentially used to benefit river management and restoration;
- stimulate the gravel bed river research community to undertake research into this new area of study.

The workshop will begin with two keynote presentations providing basic background information on the topic of ecosystem services. First, Dr Karin Limburg (State Uiversity of New York at Syracuse) will present a general introduction to the concept of ecosystem services as it applies to aquatic ecosystems. Subsequently, Joanna Eyquem (Parish Geomorphic) will provide an overview of economic methods of valuing ecosystem goods and services, including practical case studies demonstrating economic valuation of river-related ecosystem services.

We will then present the main outcomes of the workshop on "Indicators of Final Ecosystem Services for Streams" that was organized in July 2009 by the Ecosystem Services Research Program of the United States Environmental Protection Agency. The results of this workshop will form the basis of break-out group discussions, which will be designed to help map out how we can best contribute to and more fully utilize the concept of ecosystem services in gravel-bed rivers research. The break-out groups will comprise 7–8 delegates and a group leader.

The following plenary session will provide an occasion to compile the work of our break-out groups and to discuss some key questions relating to the future direction of gravel-bed river ecosystems services, priority areas for monitoring/research and how we can best present and use the outputs from the workshop.

**Workshop program**
**14h00–14h10 Welcoming remarks. Objectives and structure of the workshop.**
N. Bergeron, INRS-ETE, J. Eyquem, Parish Geomorphic

**14h10–14h50 Aquatic ecosystem services**
Keynote speaker: **Karin Limburg, SUNY Syracuse** (Talk 30 min, Q&A 10 min)

**14h50–15h30 How much is it worth?**
Keynote speaker: **Joanna Eyquem, Parish Geomorphic** (Talk 20 min, Q&A 10 min)
*15h30–16h00 Break and Refreshments*

**16h00–16h15 Outcomes of workshop on "Indicators of Final Ecosystem Services for Streams"**
N. Bergeron, INRS-ETE

**16h15–16h30 Presentation of break-out group discussion format and tasks**
J. Eyquem, Parish Geomorphic

**16h30–17h30 Break-out group work**
**17h30–18h15 Plenary session**

## 20.8 APPENDIX B: WORKING LIST OF FINAL ECOSYSTEM SERVICES ASSOCIATED WITH RIVERS

**Quantity**
- Amount (water)
- Timing (water)
- ***Amount (sediment)***
- ***Timing (sediment)***

**Quality – Physical**
- Temperature (water)
- Conductivity (water)
- Clarity (water)
- ***Flow velocity/turbulence***
- Bed substrate
- ***Suspended sediment load***
- ***Channel morphology***
- ***Stable bed***
- ***Stable bank***

**Quality – Chemical**
- Dissolved oxygen
- Chemicals
- Odor

**Quality – Biological**
- Pathogens
- Ecosystem health/biotic integrity

- Fish
- Wildlife
- Plants
- Genetic diversity

**Quality – Landscapes**

- Aesthetics

Elements in ***bold italics*** are those added to the original list presented by Ringold *et al*. (2009) and incorporate the outcomes from this workshop.

## 20.9 APPENDIX C: WORKING LIST OF GEOMORPHOLOGICAL INTERMEDIATE ECOSYSTEM SERVICES ASSOCIATED WITH RIVERS

**Water**

- Quantity
- Timing
- Velocity
- Turbulence
- Quality
- Ice

**Sediment**

- Sediment transport size
- Sediment transport amount
- Sediment transport timing
- Sediment transport quality
- Bed material size
- Bed material amount
- Bed material quality
- Bank material

**Morphology**

- Channel gradient
- Channel dimensions
- Channel form
- Channel pattern
- Bank gradient
- Bars
- Bedforms

# Tools for Study

# 21

# Remote Sensing of the Hydraulic Environment in Gravel-bed Rivers

## W. Andrew Marcus

## 21.1  INTRODUCTION

River scientists have a rich history of using film-based aerial photographs to map rivers and channel changes (Gilvear and Bryant, 2003). Since the mid-1990s, however, the nature of remote sensing of rivers has radically changed with the advent of new types of imagery (e.g., LiDAR), platforms ranging from hand-held poles to satellites, finer spatial resolution multispectral digital imagery, a new generation of investigators trained in GIScience, and advances in software and computers. These advances have enabled river scientists to develop techniques for measuring variables ranging from bed sediment size at centimetre resolutions to water discharge over basin areas of $100\,000\,\mathrm{km}^2$ and more. Much of this research has focused on the relatively clear water settings of gravel- and cobble-bed streams, because most sensors require clear water to observe the stream bottom.

This chapter reviews techniques for remote sensing of variables that can be used to characterize and model active channel hydraulics, highlighting techniques that have achieved the highest accuracies using aerial or satellite-based imagery from optical and active sensors. The majority of the chapter focuses on techniques for mapping:

(1)  the river planform, including the extent of the water surface and lateral channel change over time;
(2)  the vertical environment, including water surface and stream bed elevations, slopes, water depth, and erosion and deposition of the channel bed; and
(3)  sediment size.

These sections do not report on research using near-ground platforms and associated techniques, nor do they cover variables not used in most hydraulic models.

A brief section therefore directs readers to recent literature on these topics. The chapter closes with a discussion of future developments, needs, and applications for remote sensing of river hydraulics.

The chapter assumes that the reader has a basic knowledge of remote-sensing concepts. In particular, the following discussion assumes an understanding of different types of resolution (spatial, temporal, spectral, radiometric), the basic characteristics of optical and active sensors, and the general nature of airborne and satellite platforms. These topics are covered in every introductory remote sensing text. Gilvear and Bryant (2003) also provide an excellent overview of many of these topics in the context of fluvial geomorphology.

The emphasis on optical and active imagery reflects the wide use of these sensors to map parameters relevant to river hydraulics. Optical imagery captures reflected sunlight in visible and shortwave infrared bands. Colour air photos and Landsat imagery (not including the thermal band) are examples of optical images. In contrast, active imaging devices send out a signal that bounces off the surface(s), then record the time of the signal's return to determine distance. In some cases the nature of the signal (e.g., strength of return or polarization) is used to determine surface characteristics, such as whether a river surface is smooth or perturbed. LiDAR and radar are active imaging devices. Readers should be aware that the focus on active or optical sensors omits thermal sensors, even though there have been significant recent advances in thermal monitoring of streams (Handcock et al., 2006).

The large number of techniques reviewed in this article prevents the listing of algorithms for each method. Readers should turn to the cited articles to investigate the underlying equations.

*Gravel-bed Rivers: Processes, Tools, Environments*, First Edition. Edited by Michael Church, Pascale M. Biron and André G. Roy.
© 2012 John Wiley & Sons, Ltd. Published 2012 by John Wiley & Sons, Ltd.

## 21.2   THE PLAN VIEW OF THE RIVER

### 21.2.1   Identifying the Wetted Channel

A surprisingly confounding task in remote sensing of rivers is figuring out where the wetted channel area is, a task that is crucial for discharge estimates, flood modelling, habitat classification, and validation of hydraulic models. How can it be so difficult to automate the identification and classification of something that can be seen so easily with the naked eye on black and white or colour imagery? The answer is that we often forget the complex operations we conduct with the human eye–brain combination. Defining the wetted channel requires a mix of processes ranging from identifying variations in colour and brightness to detecting surface textures to approximating channel boundaries where they extend beneath

canopy. All of these can be mimicked with various algorithms, but no one package yet incorporates them all.

Water strongly absorbs light in the red and especially in the shortwave infrared wavelengths. Algorithms for mapping water extent in clear-water streams using optical imagery therefore classify the water portions of the image by identifying areas of very low reflectance (in contrast, turbid streams can have relatively high reflectance values). Unfortunately, areas of shadow, especially in dense forest canopy, have equally low reflectance values, leading to confusion of shadow and water (Figure 21.1a). Even when shadows and water are correctly identified, shadows make it difficult to extract features like depth from the river, because shadows make the water appear darker and therefore deeper than surrounding sunlit areas.

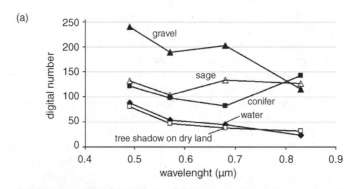

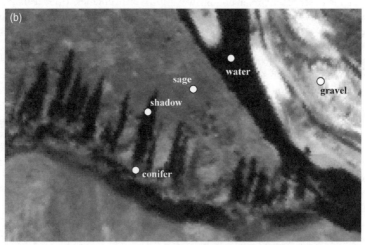

**Figure 21.1**   (a) Spectral reflectance plots of water, gravel, sage, conifers in sunlight, and conifer shadow on dry land. The approximate locations of the locations where the spectra were collected are shown in (b), which is a 1 m resolution, pan-sharpened IKONOS image of Soda Butte Creek, Wyoming, USA. The similarity of spectral reflectance over open water and shadow confuses automated image-based classifications. The distinctive shapes associated with the shadows suggest that shape-based feature-detection algorithms may provide a means to separate shadows from water in the future. (See the color version of this figure in color plate section)

Many authors have addressed issues of shadow removal from terrestrial observations (for a range of different approaches, see Rossi *et al.*, 1994; Li *et al.*, 2005; Richter and Muller, 2005). Ongoing efforts to remove shadow from river images suggest that shape-detection algorithms may provide a solution, because shadows have such distinct boundaries (Figure 21.1b). No studies have yet been published, however, on shadow removal over aqueous surfaces. The issue of shadow removal therefore remains one of the fundamental challenges to remotely mapping the extent of the wetted channel with optical imagery (Marcus and Fonstad, 2008).

Shadows, however, pose less of a problem at the coarser spatial resolutions and larger spatial extents typically observed from satellites in large rivers (>100 m in width). It is thus possible to map water extents in larger rivers using the shortwave infrared signal from satellite-based sensors such the Landsat Thematic Mapper (Kishi *et al.*, 2001), AVHRR (Sheng *et al.*, 2001), and the EO-1 hyperspectral sensor (Ip *et al.*, 2006). In turn, discharge can be estimated from the river extent if: (i) there are nearby gauges that enable correlations of river surface area and discharge (Brakenridge *et al.*, 2005) or (ii) if there are digital elevation models (DEMs) that make it possible to calculate the valley volume filled by water, which can then be coupled with hydrological models to estimate discharge (Smith, 1997).

Unfortunately, clouds severely limit the use of both airborne and satellite-based optical imagery. During times of flooding, when water surface mapping is often the most critical, it therefore is often impossible to acquire optical imagery of the river.

In contrast, radar is an active sensor that penetrates cloud cover and, depending on wavelength and canopy density, vegetation. Researchers are therefore increasingly turning to automated image classification routines using satellite-based radar to map water extent and discharge, especially in remote or ungauged river systems (e.g., Horritt *et al.*, 2001; Alsdorf *et al.*, 2007; Schumann *et al.*, 2007). Space-based radar data also cover the same location frequently, which is excellent for flow monitoring during the rising or falling limbs of large multiday floods. However, the spatial resolution of most radar is relatively poor compared to optical sensors or LiDAR, limiting water surface mapping to larger rivers. Some 1 m resolution radar is now available (the TerraSAR-X in SpotLight mode), but these shorter wavelengths are strongly back-scattered by vegetation so that canopy near the stream's edge can obscure the channel.

LiDAR has the fine-scale resolution needed to map water surface area at metre accuracies, but only a few studies have examined the potential for LiDAR to classify water surface areas of rivers. A relatively brief, but useful review of LiDAR physics over river surfaces is provided in the mapping work of Höfle *et al.* (2009). The 1064 nm infrared signal used by most airborne terrestrial LiDAR systems is largely absorbed by water, leading to a generally lower number and lower intensity of signal returns over rivers (Figure 21.2a) (in contrast to the blue-green wavelength of bathymetric LiDAR that penetrates the water column and can be used for depth detection, as is discussed later). Classification algorithms with infrared LiDAR can therefore use intensity-of-return thresholds to identify water surfaces (Brennan and Webster, 2006). Moreover, more turbulent surfaces generate a greater density of LiDAR returns (English, 2009), suggesting that terrestrial LiDAR could potentially be used to map variables related to surface roughness (Figure 21.2b).

However, variations in vegetation cover, specular surfaces, or surfaces like roads with poor returns can be misclassified when only density-of-return criteria are used. To overcome this, Hicks *et al.* (2006) used the variance in LiDAR intensity and altimetry differences from first and last returns to classify riparian ground cover and wetted areas. Antonarakis *et al.* (2008) coupled a surface roughness parameter with signal intensity to classify water surfaces, thus taking advantage of the relatively flat surfaces of water to achieve classification accuracies ranging from 95 to 99%. Höfle *et al.* (2009) took this work several steps further, noting that LiDAR signals from water vary with look angle and atmospherics. By adjusting for these factors, Höfle *et al.* were even able to model areas with laser dropouts (i.e., no returns) and achieve water surface classification accuracies over 98%.

Despite these high accuracies, identifying the wetted channel remains a problem in many settings. At present, automated procedures for identifying the wetted channel area with standard remote-sensing software are available only for space-borne radar imagery. LiDAR techniques require special algorithms that are not included with standard remote-sensing software, while shadows from trees, hills, or other local features continue to pose a major obstacle to identifying water with optical imagery. In most instances, investigators thus must manually edit or program procedures for classifying the wetted river channel on a case-by-case basis, substantially slowing the process of studying features within rivers. Developing programs that accurately classify the wetted channel *and* incorporating these programs into existing software packages would be a significant contribution to remote sensing of rivers.

### 21.2.2 Mapping River Planform and Planform Change

The use of remote-sensing imagery to map the planform evolution of rivers has a long tradition in geomorphology

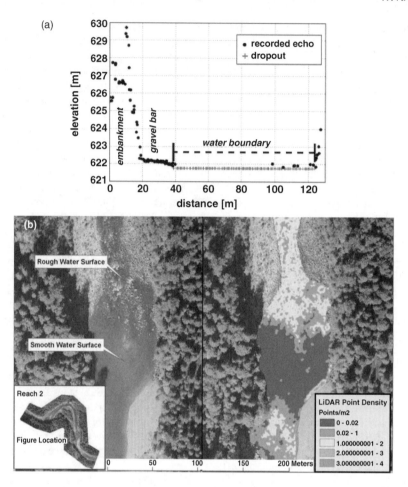

**Figure 21.2** LiDAR returns from water surfaces. (a) Many of the terrestrial LiDAR signals along a 2 m cross-sectional swath are absorbed over water, leading to "dropouts" that have to be modelled to map the water surface. Reproduced, with permission, from Höfle, B., Vetter, M., Pfeifer, N., Mandlburger, G. and Stötter, J. 2009. Water surface mapping from airborne laser scanning using signal intensity and elevation data. *Earth Surface Processes and Landforms* **34**: 1635–1649 (b) The density of LiDAR returns increases over rough water surfaces. Reproduced, with permission, from English, J. 2009. Effectiveness of extracting water surface slopes from LiDAR data within the active channel: Sandy River, Oregon, USA. M.S. Thesis, Department of Geography, University of Oregon, Eugene. (See the color version of this figure in color plate section.)

dating back to the earliest aerial photos. The process is conceptually simple; changes in the position of some feature (e.g., the bank) are measured on photos from different dates to determine variations over time. Researchers and river managers have used manual classification with remote-sensing imagery to map channel change for decades. The methods are well established and widely reviewed (e.g., Trimble, 1991; Lawler, 1993; Alsdorf and Lettenmaier, 2003; Gilvear and Bryant, 2003).

Despite all this work, however, planform mapping and change detection remain problematic for river scientists attempting to apply these techniques at watershed extents, especially when using multiple high-resolution

images acquired from aircraft. Change detection at large area extents using aerial imagery requires: (i) assigning geographic co-ordinates to each image so it can be co-registered with other images; (ii) adjusting brightness between photos so that features retain the same reflectance value and are classified the same way on different images (this assumes the user is applying an automated classification across multiple images); (iii) detecting key features (e.g., the bank) so that key variables (e.g., wetted channel width) or differences between dates can be calculated, and (iv) incorporating error analyses across multiple images to assess which change is "real." All of these tasks can be accomplished relatively easily using existing techniques on a photo-by-photo basis, but become prohibitively time consuming with the hundreds to thousands of high-resolution aerial images needed to characterize variations over tens to hundreds of kilometres.

Unfortunately, relatively little effort has been expended on how to automate and batch process large numbers of airborne images for purposes of river analysis. For example, georectifying images is essential to measuring changes in position over time, yet almost all researchers still accomplish this manually on a photo-by-photo basis. To the degree that automated approaches exist, they typically require significant programming expertise, as in the case of Höfle *et al.*'s (2009) technique for using LiDAR to identify bank location. Some researchers are developing methods to automatically co-register and map key features across thousands of images (Dugdale and Carbonneau, 2009), but at present the programs are proprietary and not widely available. However, changes are occurring in this regard. Pavelsky and Smith (2008), for example, developed a freeware program for extracting the channel centreline and channel widths along entire river courses. Although not yet a reality, ever more researchers are discussing ways to create more open source programs.

Error analysis also remains a major stumbling block to change detection. Too frequently, error is ignored in planform change detection, with any measured change assumed to be real (Hughes *et al.*, 2006). Particularly with older photos, it may not be possible to georectify the imagery to better than a few metres of positional accuracy, which reduces the degree of change that can be detected over time. Orthorectification with digital elevation models can improve these results, but at a significant cost in terms of processing time. Regardless of the technique and its accuracy, developing techniques for incorporating error analysis into large, multi-image data sets is essential to supporting good science and management decisions.

## 21.3 THE VERTICAL DIMENSION

### 21.3.1 Water Surface Elevations and Slopes

River scientists have long been frustrated by the need to use valley or channel bed slopes as a substitute for energy slope in hydraulic modelling. Water surface slopes are a better estimator of the energy slope because they integrate the effects of varying topography, turbulence structures, and flow momentum. However, measuring water surface elevations and deriving water surface slopes over long reaches of stream can be problematic with ground-based measurements. Remote sensing provides a potential mechanism for providing detailed, broad-extent, synoptic measurements of river surface elevations and slopes.

One approach to remotely measuring water elevations and slopes is to measure the elevation of the water at the channel's edge using classical photogrammetric approaches. This is not an ideal solution because the water elevation may vary across the channel due to super elevation effects. Aerial photo approaches rely on applying classical photogrammetric techniques to determine the elevation of dry surfaces immediately adjacent to the wetted channel. These elevations can then be interpolated across the channel to develop water surface elevation maps (Westaway *et al.,* 2000, 2001).

Several issues, however, potentially limit the applicability of the photogrammetric approach. First, there must be stereo pairs where the same side-channel elevation points can be identified on both photos (homologous point pairs); something that can be difficult in vegetated streams especially. Moreover, to capture local reach-scale variations in elevation, the flights must be fairly low in order to generate the necessary parallax between images. This means that image scale generally needs to be approximately 1:5000 or finer, which requires special flights, further adding to the cost and logistical burden. If historical imagery exists, however, photogrammetric techniques provide the potential to examine changes in elevation and slope over time.

Active sensors that directly record returns from the water's surface or dry land at the channel edge provide an alternative for measuring elevations and slopes (Magirl *et al.*, 2005; Snyder, 2009). As noted above, a major obstacle to using active imagery is determining which signals come from the water's surface and the channel; the "Where is the river?" question discussed previously. Locating the channel can be done using some of the signal classification algorithms previously discussed. Alternatively, existing flow path models that are a standard component of GIS software can be coupled with LiDAR or radar-generated DEMs to identify channel locations. However, this approach can break down in low gradient sinuous streams, at which point channel paths can be identified from aerial photos or topographic maps (Snyder, 2009).

The precision of radar or LiDAR measurements varies with the resolution of the sensor and spatial extent over which the measurements are taken. Radar, with its wavelengths on the order of centimetres to metres, works best in larger river systems (Figure 21.3a). Radar cannot, however, resolve elevations to the same accuracy and spatial resolution as LiDAR, which has wavelengths on the order of a micrometre ($10^{-6}$ m). Personal experiences of the author indicate that shorter wavelength X-band radar can provide reasonable water surface elevations over distances of several hundred metres or more,

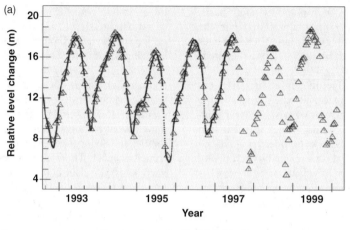

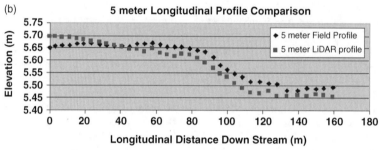

**Figure 21.3** Active sensor measurements of water surface elevations. (a) Space-borne TOPEX/POSEIDON radar (triangles) can measure fluctuations at the scale of metres that agree closely with gauge observations (solid line) Reproduced, with permission, from Birkett, C.M., Mertes, L.A.K., Dunne, T., Costa, M.H. and Jasinski, M.J. 2002. Surface water dynamics in the Amazon Basin: Application of satellite radar altimetry. *Journal of Geophysical Research,* **107**: 8059. doi: 10.1029/ 2001JD000609; (b) high-quality terrestrial LiDAR can capture variations in water surface elevations at cm resolution over horizontal distances as short as a few metres. Reproduced, with permission, from English, J. 2009. Effectiveness of extracting water surface slopes from LiDAR data within the active channel: Sandy River, Oregon, USA. M.S. Thesis, Department of Geography, University of Oregon, Eugene. The LiDAR data represent an average for the entire channel width, while the field data are for points along the channel edge.

although significant effort must be put into screening anomalous measurements. Previous works shows that LiDAR provides accurate measurements of elevation and longitudinal profiles over distances of a kilometre or more (Magirl *et al.*, 2005; Snyder, 2009). Very high quality LiDAR even can accurately measure water surface elevations and slopes over distances as short as 5 m (English, 2009) (Figure 21.3b).

Airborne LiDAR profiles avoid the spurious steps created by DEMs and topographic contour maps (Snyder, 2009). English (2009) compared water surface elevations measured with a total station and airborne terrestrial LiDAR for a reach in the Sandy River, Oregon (Figure 21.3b). The standard deviation of differences (field data – LiDAR) was only 1.3 cm, and no elevation was off by more than 4.7 cm. A regression of field versus LiDAR elevations yielded an $r^2$ of 0.94. The correlation decreased to 0.37 when field-based slopes were com-

pared to LiDAR slopes averaged over a 5 m distance because of the multiplicative error in the rise-over-run calculation. However, the $r^2$ value increased to 0.79 when slopes were calculated over a 20 m interval. These results indicate that LiDAR can provide accurate measurements of water surface slope over distances as short as a single riffle-pool sequence.

It is important to have an accurate and properly calibrated geoidal model when using LiDAR and radar systems that rely on GPS positioning. Otherwise, spurious results may result and, in low gradient rivers, even show the water to be flowing uphill.

### 21.3.2 Water Depth and Channel Bed Elevation

Remote sensing of subsurface channel topography and water depths has received tremendous attention since the 1990s. This emphasis represents a shift from viewing the channel as a series of connected cross-sections to viewing the channel as having continuous topography best characterized by digital elevation models (DEMs) (Lane, 2000) and continuous variations in water depth best characterized by remote-sensing imagery (Fonstad and Marcus, 2005). Remote sensing provides an ideal medium for creating DEMs or mapping bathymetry at reach to watershed extents because the imagery provides continuous coverage (Marcus and Fonstad, 2008).

DEMs of channel topography can be generated using *photogrammetric approaches* with high-resolution stereo pairs typically collected from low flying aircraft. Photogrammetric approaches measure the elevation of the channel bottom and water surface at the channel edge, which in turn enables estimates of water depth. Lane *et al.* (2010) provide a succinct overview of the history of photogrammetric methods for measuring elevations and depths of subaqueous river beds.

*Optical techniques* use multiband aerial or satellite imagery coupled with either ground-based depth measurements or equations for light absorption in water to estimate water depths. Optical methods map only the water depth without any associated elevations. Fonstad and Marcus (2005) and Marcus and Fonstad (2008) summarize optical methods for measuring river depths, while Legleiter *et al.* (2004, 2009) and Legleiter and Roberts (2005) systematically develop the theory for optical remote sensing of depths in rivers.

*Blue-green LiDAR* maps the elevation of the channel bottom and, depending on the water depth and the algorithm used, the elevation of the water surface. Often the water surface cannot be clearly delineated, in which case the blue-green LiDAR can be coupled with near infrared LiDAR or the Raman backscatter signal to determine water depths above the channel bottom. Allouis *et al.* (2010) provide a good summary of the general concepts behind use of blue-green LiDAR, Raman, and near infrared signals to measure depths.

Major limitations to all these approaches include the need to have an unobstructed line of sight to the river (e.g., no overhanging trees) and the need for relatively clear water. The photogrammetric approach works only in clear water rivers where the bottom can be seen. LiDAR and optical approaches work best when the bottom can be seen, but can generate some useful depth data where the bottom is obscured, so long as turbidities remain relatively low.

### 21.3.2.1 Photogrammetry

Photogrammetric depth measurements in marine environments date to at least the 1940s (Lundahl, 1948), but it is only since the mid-1990s that these techniques have been modified for rivers, which pose particular challenges to photogrammetry. As noted earlier, the low relief of river beds necessitates low flight elevations to differentiate the small variations in bed elevations and water depths, which are often on the order of several metres or less. Accurately locating matching point pairs on stereo photos of rivers also is problematic for a variety of reasons. Vegetation can mask near-shore features, making it impossible to find equivalent points on more than one photo. Moreover, the similarity of texture within many features (e.g., sand bars) can make it difficult to locate matching points on separate photos. Finally, photogrammetric solutions to mapping elevations along rivers are two-media problems, requiring separate elevation solutions for the dry and submerged surfaces. This has been a significant challenge because it requires measurement of water surface elevations in order to calculate the refraction effects on subaqueous elevation measurements (Lane *et al.*, 2010).

Westaway *et al.* (2000, 2001) developed a purely photogrammetric solution to the two-media problem (combined photogrammetric-optical solutions are described later). In their approach, they determined matching points on stereo pairs by searching for pixels of similar brightness and contrast based on correlations at increasing resolutions (Lane *et al.*, 2000). After finding matching points, the procedure used standard photogrammetric techniques to calculate the elevation of dry surfaces. Water surface elevations were determined using kriging to interpolate between dry elevations adjacent to the wetted channel. Within the wetted channel, refraction either caused bed elevations to seem higher than they were (i.e., the water seemed more shallow) or created situations where the camera did not "see" the bed in shallow water, leading to poor point matches on stereo pairs. After screening out these false point matches, the procedure corrected for refraction using methods developed from earlier studies (Fryer, 1983) to calculate bed elevations in the wetted channel. The wetted and dry bed data were then merged using a Delauney triangulation to generate a full surface DEM (Figure 21.4a).

Elevation errors derived from this approach were randomly distributed and similar in magnitude on exposed surfaces and in shallow waters, but errors in deeper water scaled with water depth (Figure 21.4b). The degree to which these errors were "real" or a function of different measuring techniques is an open question. Ground-based stream surveys were used to validate photogrammetric methods. The field measurements identify depths between cobbles and gravels, while image-based techniques typically "see" the tops of the substrate. Similar issues have surfaced in remote sensing of other variables. Apparent errors in remote-sensing measurements or classification may be more indicative of differences in measurement approach than of poor

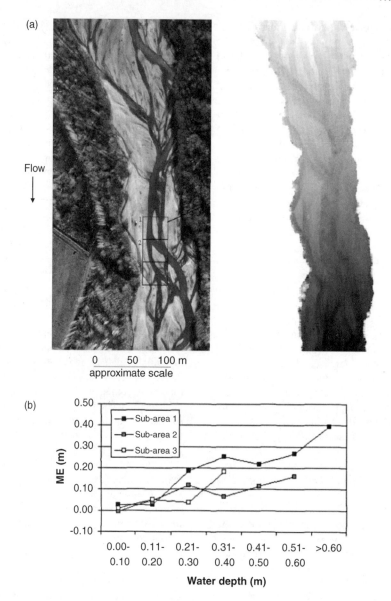

**Figure 21.4** Photogrammetric measurements of channels bed elevations. (a) A DEM produced for the channel bed of the North Ashburton River, New Zealand. Reproduced, with permission, from Westaway, R.M., Lane, S.N. and Hicks, D.M. 2000. Development of an automated correction procedure for digital photogrammetry for the study of wide, shallow gravel-bed rivers. *Earth Surface Processes and Landforms* **25**: 209–226. (b) Increases in mean error of channel bed elevation measurements with increases in depth. Reproduced, with permission, from Westaway, R.M., Lane, S.N. and Hicks, D.M. 2001. Airborne remote sensing of clear water, shallow, gravel-bed rivers using digital photogrammetry and image analysis. *Photogrammetric Engineering and Remote Sensing* **67**: 1271–1281.

measurement by the sensing devices and algorithms (see Marcus, 2002 and Legleiter *et al.*, 2002 in the context of biotypes; Marcus *et al.*, 2003 in the context of fluvial wood).

The photogrammetric method developed by Westaway *et al.* (2000, 2001) generated a standard deviation of error

in depth measurements that varied between 9 and 15 cm in different segments of the stream, with no significant difference between a relatively simple refraction correction and a more complex one. These magnitudes of the standard deviation of error are similar to those associated with optical methods for estimating *depths* only, which typically are on the order of 15 cm (Fonstad and Marcus, 2005; Lejot *et al.*, 2007) to 30 cm (Westaway *et al.*, 2003; Lane *et al.*, 2010). In a different experiment assessing bed *elevation* errors, Westaway *et al.* (2003) documented a mean error of 17 to 18 cm and a standard deviation of the error of 23 to 26 cm for elevations of exposed surfaces. The mean error on wet surfaces was 36 cm, with a standard deviation of 33 cm.

### 21.3.2.2    Optical Approaches to Measuring Water Depth

Optical approaches to measuring water depth are simple in concept, taking advantage of the fact that deeper water is darker. Or, to be more precise, deeper water is darker up to the point where backscatter creates a relatively constant reflectance, regardless of increasing depth, and assuming other factors such as substrate colour, turbidity, and aquatic vegetation do not also generate variations in darkness (Legleiter *et al.*, 2004, 2009). The "deeper is darker" observation can be translated into quantitative measurements by correlating ground measurements of depth to water brightness, or by using optical equations that describe light attenuation in water.

The correlation approach is the simplest of all remote-sensing depth measurement techniques and the most widely applied to date. To implement the optical correlation approach, one must have: (i) imagery at a fine enough spatial resolution to capture depth variations throughout the stream (e.g., 5 m pixel resolution is a poor choice for a stream that is only 5 m wide) and (ii) ground-based depth measurements when the discharge and stream bed topography are similar to when the imagery is acquired. This latter constraint means the ground measurements generally should coincide with the time-of-flight, which is a significant logistical constraint and prevents ready use of the correlation approach with historical imagery.

To derive depths from the imagery using the correlation approach, the ground measurements are regressed against the spectral values at those same locations. The regression equation developed from the correlation is then applied to the spectral values throughout the remainder of the imagery to estimate depths at each pixel. The $r^2$ values for correlations of measured versus estimated depths using this approach are typically on the order of 0.80 or higher (see Table 1 in Marcus and Fonstad, 2008).

Marcus *et al.* (2003) found that subsetting the stream by biotypes enabled better characterization of depths and associated errors, with $r^2$ values for depths ranging from 0.67 in high gradient riffles where white water prevents the sensor from "seeing" the water column to 0.99 in low turbulence glides. Likewise, Lejot *et al.* (2007) noted that subsetting the image by substrate type improved depth

estimates, with $r^2$ values ranging from 0.81 in alluvial substrates to 0.90 in areas with subaquatic vegetation (SAV).

The correlation approach has the advantage of being simple and generally accurate. Correlations, however, require ground-based measurements at time-of-flight and are not grounded in theory that can be used to evaluate and modify measurements under varying conditions. Researchers thus have recently turned to physically based models to map stream depths.

Lyzenga (1978, 1981) developed the baseline for characterizing light movement through water in the absence of ground calibration data. The complexity of river systems, however, has prevented transference of fully parameterized physical models to fluvial settings. Fonstad and Marcus (2005) dealt with this issue by adopting a much simplified version of light transmittance, coupling the Beer–Lambert law of light absorption with the Manning equation and conservation of discharge to estimate depths. Their approach requires ground-based data on discharge at the time of flight and slope, but does not require any depth measurements. It therefore is appropriate for locations where there is a nearby discharge monitoring station or where regional curves can be used to estimate discharge. The goodness-of-fit for regressions ranged from as low as 0.22 in the turbulent gravel and cobble-bed Lamar River of Wyoming to 0.77 in the less turbulent Brazos River of Texas. Regardless of the $r^2$ values, general channel bathymetry and channel cross-sections using this approach were consistent with geomorphological expectations of deep water in areas of flow convergence and outer bends (Figure 21.5). This general accuracy is typical of most remote-sensing investigations; estimates of depth at any one point may be in error, but overall global accuracies are good (Marcus and Fonstad, 2008).

Alternatively, Legleiter *et al.* (2004, 2009) and Legleiter and Roberts (2005) adapted the Hydrolight radiative transfer model (Mobley, 1994) to more fully characterize the physics of light movement through complex river environments. Regressions of their modelled versus measured water depths generated $r^2$ values ranging from 0.70 to 0.98, depending on which combination of bottom reflectances, turbidity, surface roughness, and spectral and spatial resolutions they examined (Legleiter *et al.*, 2009). Legleiter and Roberts (2005) concluded that optical physics can tell us a great deal about the river environment, but that the accuracy and precision of depth estimates vary spatially with channel morphology and thus cannot be defined based solely on optical physics.

Physically based models that do not require ground calibration data offer the potential for being used with historical data. Unfortunately, most historical,

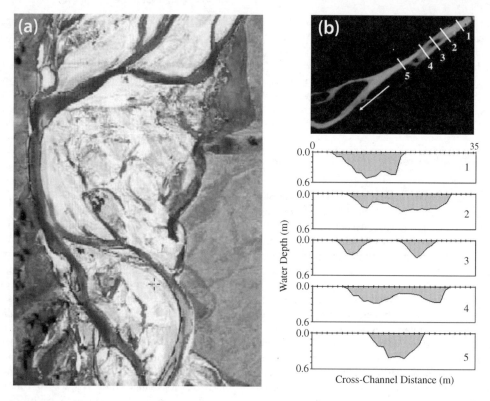

**Figure 21.5** Optical measurements of water depth without ground-based measurements using the HAB technique (Fonstad and Marcus, 2005). (a) A bathymetric map of the Lamar River, Wyoming, USA, based on airborne imagery. Deeper water is indicated by darker blue. Flow is from top to bottom. Deep areas are correctly shown in areas of flow convergence and on the outside of bends. (b) Cross-sections derived from satellite data for Soda Butte Creek, Wyoming USA. The satellite-based measurements correctly capture the emergence and disappearance of a mid-channel bar. Figures are modified from Fonstad and Marcus (2005), Figures 11 and 15, respectively. Reproduced, with permission, from Fonstad, M.A. and Marcus, W.A. 2005. Remote sensing of stream depths with hydraulically assisted bathymetry (HAB) models. *Geomorphology* **72**: 107–120. (See the color version of this figure in color plate section.)

film-based air photos were exposed to maximize contrast of terrestrial features, which minimized contrast within the darker river channel. Coupled with low optical quality and coarse spatial resolution, this makes it impossible to generate quality depth measurements from most historical black and white air photos. Users should also be aware that in the process of converting film to digital imagery, scanners often automatically adjust colour and contrast to "enhance" the image, which in turn introduces significant error into optically based depth measurements (Walther *et al.*, 2011). Moreover, the coarse spatial resolution of most satellite and airborne imagery prior to the 1990s makes it difficult at best to apply these techniques to measure depths prior to these dates. However, as higher-resolution satellite and airborne digital data became available in the 1990s, depth measurements using these data have become possible.

Regardless of whether the correlation approach or a physical model is used, the quality of results varies with the spectral bands used for the regressions. If only a single spectral band is used, many researchers use the red band because it generally generates the highest $r^2$ values, although green can generate reasonable results. The blue band is largely avoided because it is subject to scattering in both the atmosphere and the water. High-quality black and white imagery can also be used with the correlation approach (Lane *et al.*, 2010). When multiple bands are available, multiple regressions of the spectral values versus measured depth often generate better depth estimates then a one-variable regression (Marcus *et al.*, 2003; Gilvear *et al.*, 2007; Lejot *et al.*, 2007). Alternatively, Legleiter *et al.* (2004, 2005, 2009) showed via field-based measurements and theoretical arguments that using the natural logarithm of band ratios normalizes for factors such as substrate colour and aquatic vegetation

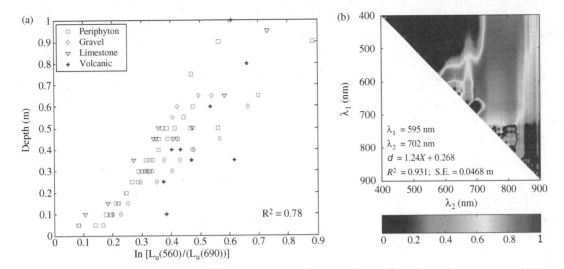

**Figure 21.6** The use of natural logarithms of band ratios for depth estimates with optical imagery. (a) The ratios normalize for variations in reflectance over different substrates. Reproduced, with permission, from Legleiter, C.J., Roberts, D.A., Marcus, W.A. and Fonstad, M.A. 2004. Passive remote sensing of river channel morphology and in-stream habitat: physical basis and feasibility. *Remote Sensing of Environment* **93**: 493–510. (b) The range of modeled $r^2$ values for measured versus estimated depths, Lamar River, Wyoming, USA, 19 August, 2006. Reproduced, with permission, from Legleiter, C.J., Roberts, D.A. and Lawrence, R.L. 2009. Spectrally based remote sensing of river bathymetry. *Earth Surface Processes and Landforms* **34**: 1039–1059. Red colours indicate higher $r^2$ values. The best predictor of depths occurs using a ratio of the natural logarithms of the 702 nm and 595 nm bands. (See the color version of this figure in color plate section.)

that cause brightness to vary independent of depth (Figure 21.6a). If multispectral or hyperspectral images are available, the work of Legleiter *et al.* (2009) can be used to select the optimal bands to use in the ratio (Figure 21.6b).

Another issue that arises in all optical techniques is that illumination varies within and between images, so that variations in darkness are not necessarily indicative of variations in depth. The ratio approach is one approach to correct for this effect. Ratios, however, do not work in the context of black and white imagery or scanned film-based imagery where digital values may not represent true reflectance values. In these situations, one can re-scale the brightness values of images to calibration targets. Carbonneau *et al.* (2005) developed an auto-mated procedure for this purpose that improved the $r^2$ values for correlation-based depths using the red band from 0.20 before rescaling to 0.58 afterward.

### 21.3.2.3 Combined Photogrammetric-Optical Approaches

Optical approaches generate maps that show depth var-iations, but not absolute elevation changes (Figure 21.5). They therefore fail to provide the elevation change and slope information needed for hydraulic modelling. In contrast, photogrammetric approaches generate digital elevation models (Figure 21.4), but require stereo pair coverage and identification of matching points on the stream bottom. Merging photogrammetric and optical techniques creates the potential to avoid some of the weaknesses of each method.

Westaway *et al.* (2003) coupled optical correlation with photogrammetry to develop a DEM for wetted and dry portions of a channel. To accomplish this, they first used maximum likelihood classification, a standard tech-nique in optical remote sensing, to separate wet, dry, and vegetated areas using true colour imagery. In the river portion of the channel they converted the red-green-blue (RGB) spectral values to natural logarithms, which created a linear relation between depth and spectral values. Depths measured in the field at the time-of-flight and spectral values at those same locations were used to generate a regression equation for estimating depths throughout the remainder of the stream. Elevations of the dry channel bed and water surface were measured using the photogrammetric approaches discussed above (Westaway *et al.*, 2000, 2001). They then developed a DEM of the wetted channel by subtracting the river depth values from the water surface elevations. The require-ment of ground measurements at the time-of-flight, however, means the technique cannot be used with historical imagery.

Lane *et al.* (2010) overcame this limitation by developing a technique in which historical ground-based depth data are not needed so long as there is stereo coverage of the wetted channel. In simple terms, Lane *et al.* used variants of the photogrammetric approaches already discussed to generate dry channel DEMs and to derive water depths in the limited number of locations where matching points could be identified on the channel bottom. They then used these depths to calibrate a simple physical model relating image brightness to depth. In turn, this equation was used to derive depths throughout the channel, including areas that were deeper than could be measured using standard photogrammetry or contemporary LiDAR techniques. This technique generated depth estimates with mean errors varying from 2.5 to 18 cm (depending on setting and photos), and standard deviations of error ranging from 18 to 31 cm.

In real terms, however, application of the Lane *et al.* (2010) approach is far more complex, requiring methodologies for transferring precision ground control data to historical imagery, for error corrections, and for depth-brightness modelling. Despite this complexity, the potential of the technique is exciting, enabling use of black-and-white historic imagery to develop DEMs and characterize channel change. Use of the technique is limited, however, to areas where: (i) high-quality ground control points can be identified on historical imagery that can also be surveyed in the present; (ii) fine-resolution imagery is available (generally on the order of approximately <1:6000); and (iii) image brightness correlates to water depth, which can be a problem with lower-quality historic images.

### 21.3.2.4 Bathymetric LiDAR

LiDAR determines surface elevations by measuring the time it takes a pulse of light to reach a ground target and return to the sensor. Bathymetric LiDAR sends out a light pulse in the blue-green portion of the spectrum. Portions of this signal return to the sensor via reflection from the water surface, backscattering from the water column, or reflection from the stream bottom. In an ideal case, one can easily delineate the portions of the return signal reflecting off the water surface and stream bottom, making it possible to calculate surface and bottom elevations and water depths (Figure 21.7a). As a general rule of thumb, bathymetric LiDAR surveys can measure depths ranging up three times the Secchi depth in relatively clear water to two times the Secchi depth in more turbid conditions (Guenther *et al.*, 2000), where a Secchi depth is the maximum depth at which a black and white Secchi disk can be seen from above with the naked eye.

Bathymetric LiDAR avoids many obstacles encountered with image-based techniques (Hilldale and Raff, 2008). Shadowing, surface textures of the water, sun angle and glint pose problems for photogrammetric or optical approaches, but generally do not disturb LiDAR measurements. LiDAR can be acquired in cloudy conditions, although aircraft must fly below or near the cloud base. Ground data are not required to calibrate LiDAR measurements, although field surveys are useful (as with any technique) for assessing measurement error.

LiDAR approaches, however, face significant limitations in rivers. From a logistical perspective, bathymetric LiDAR instruments are relatively rare, so flights are hard to schedule and costly. From a signal-processing perspective, the strength and shape of the return signal are strongly affected by refraction at the water surface, bubbles in the water column, turbidity, and to some degree by bottom reflectance, complicating signal interpretation. In water less than approximately 2 m deep, the surface and bottom returns merge with the backscatter signal from the water column, resulting in a single peak return that obscures the simple interpretation suggested by Figure 21.7 (Allouis *et al.*, 2010). LiDAR signals are also subject to specular reflection that can overload the receiver and "blind it" to relatively weak signals from the stream bottom that arrive only a few billionths of a second later in shallow streams (Kinzel *et al.*, 2007). Moreover, not all bathymetric LiDAR sensors are created equal. The SHOALS (Scanning Hydrographic Operational Airborne LiDAR Survey) or similar instruments, for example, have large footprints where the signal captures an area up to several metres in diameter. This works well in marine settings, but can be problematic in streams where major depth variations or mixed terrain (e.g., exposed bar and water) can occur over these distances. It is for this reason that researchers have begun to examine narrow footprint bathymetric LiDAR like the Experimental Advanced Airborne Research LiDAR (EAARL) system, which typically has a footprint of 15 to 20 cm (McKean *et al.* 2009a, 2009b).

LiDAR research in streams has tended to focus on ways to separate the water surface and stream bottom portions of the return signal. One set of approaches is to mathematically de-convolve (i.e., split apart) the single blue-green wave form into its surface and bottom return components. Kinzel *et al.* (2007), for example, found single peak returns at all depths less than 1 m in the Platte River. Used a standard terrestrial LiDAR equation and the assumption that the single peak represented the stream bed elevation, they created a stream bed DEM with a root mean square error (RMSE) of 0.35 m, but with a bias towards estimates that were lower than ground truth elevations. The applications of a single value to correct the bias in both submerged and dry areas, however, led to overestimating the streambed elevation, especially at depths greater than 0.4 m. This was because

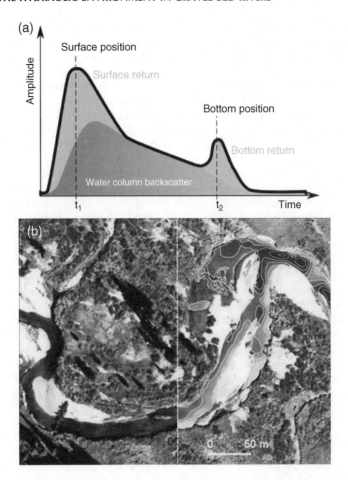

**Figure 21.7** LiDAR measurement of depths. (a) Blue-green LiDAR returns in deep water generate a double peak that indicates the location of the water surface and stream bottom. At more shallow depths (approximately <2 m), the return signal often displays only one peak, complicating the analysis. Reproduced, with permission, from Allouis, T., Bailly, J.-S., Pastol, Y. and Le Roux, C. 2010. Comparison of LiDAR waveform processing methods for very shallow water bathymetry using Raman, near-infrared, and green signals. *Earth Surface Processes and Landforms* **35**: 640–650; (b) Colour-infrared photography with LiDAR-generated bathymetry overlaid on the right-hand portion of the stream. The contour interval is 30 cm, but McKean *et al.* report the data support a 20 cm interval. Reproduced, with permission, from McKean, J., Issak, D. and Wright, W. 2009a. Improving stream studies with a small–footprint green lidar. *EOS: Transactions of the American Geophysical Union* **90**: 341–342. The River Bathymetry Toolkit (RBT) is available online at http://www.fs.fed.us/rm/boise/AWAE/projects/river_bathymetry_toolkit.shtml. (See the color version of this figure in color plate section.)

the adjustment failed to account for the differential speed of light in air ($0.15\,\mathrm{m\,ns^{-1}}$) and water ($0.11\,\mathrm{m\,ns^{-1}}$), the exponential decay of the laser pulse in water, and water column backscatter, all of which alter the form and magnitude of the waveform. A bathymetric model that incorporated these factors to identify the portions of the wave associated with surface and bottom returns reduced the RMSE to 0.24 m and removed the bias.

Using multiple instruments provides an alternative method for deconvolving the water surface and bottom reflectance portions of the return signal. Blue-green LiDAR (typically with a wavelength of 520 or 532 nm) provides a return from throughout the water column, while infrared LiDAR (1064 nm) has a weak return from the water surface, but no return below the surface. One thus can align the blue-green and infrared LiDAR returns, then subtract the infrared return to remove the surface component of the blue-green signal. This identifies the stream bottom elevation, although the processing is significantly more complex than is suggested by the term "subtract." Allouis *et al.* (2010) used this approach to generate water depth data with a mean error of only 4.2 cm and a standard deviation of the error of 25 cm. Their techniques decreased the minimum detectable depth from 1.8 m, which was the minimum depth detected using just the blue-green signal on its own, to 1.0 m.

Some LiDAR systems include a sensor to detect the red Raman signal (647 nm) that is generated when water partially scatters and changes the wavelength of the blue-green signal (Guenther et al., 1994). The shapes of the Raman return signal can be classed into different categories that correspond to different depth classes (Pe'eri and Philpot, 2007). Allouis et al. (2010) conducted a variant of this method to derive depths with a mean error of 3.1 cm and standard deviations of the error of 40.3 cm. The minimum detectable depth was 0.5 m.

To date, there are still substantial variations in findings regarding minimum detectable depths and depth resolutions. McKean et al. (2009a), using the EAARL, were able to map water depths as shallow as 10 to 20 cm. They noted that the greatest discrepancies between bathymetric LiDAR results and ground truth data occurred in areas of sharp topographic curvature and steep slopes. In general, they found that measured stream widths, maximum depths, and slopes fell within 5% of ground-based measurements. Hilldale and Raff (2008) also noted the effects of local topography. In the relatively low-gradient Yakima River, they documented a standard deviation of the depth error of only 0.2 m. The error increased to 0.29 to 0.53 m on the Trinity River of California, probably due to the steep drops along the river, where local gradients are as high as 100%. These high gradients made it difficult to define the water surface with LiDAR. Hilldale and Raff (2008) suggest that increasing the point density of the LiDAR coverage would probably improve the overall accuracy, because there would be less interpolation between points. Likewise, a smaller pulse footprint size and tighter pulse density will enhance the capacity to resolve changes in topography in areas with rapidly changing configurations, such as along banks.

### 21.3.2.5 Radar and Gravity Measurements

Direct measurements of river depths and velocities can be acquired with ground-penetrating radar suspended above stream beds on bridges or cableways (Spicer et al., 1997; Costa et al., 2000). These approaches have not yet seen widespread application and testing, but they hold great promise for at-a-site monitoring over time.

At a much broader spatial extent and with spatial resolutions on the order of $10^1$ to $10^2$ m, space-based radar provides a means for indirect measurements of water surface elevations and floodplain depths during inundation (Smith, 1997). The concept is a simple one; the radar is used to create a DEM of the water surface that is accurate to within several centimetres of vertical resolution (Alsdorf and Lettenmaier, 2003). Inundation depths are calculated by generating a DEM of the floodplain during low flow periods. Water depths are calculated by: (i) using the DEM to measure the height reached by the waters at their furthest extent, then extending this surface across the inundated area to calculate depths above the floodplain DEM, or (ii) calculating the differences between the water surface elevation measured from radar and the DEM. Coupling these data with hydrologic models provides estimates of discharge (e.g., Bjerklie et al., 2003). These techniques are seeing increasing use, especially in large, ungauged rivers or in areas where political boundaries and remoteness make direct gauging difficult or impossible (Brakenridge et al., 2005).

At spatial extents of 100 000s km², space-based measurements of the earth's gravitation flux are sufficiently sensitive to document variations in surface water mass. Researchers have used monthly Gravity Recovery and Climate Experiment (GRACE) satellite data to document changes in seasonal water storage in the river basins of the Amazon (Tapley et al. 2004) and the Congo (Crowley et al., 2006). Syed et al. (2005) combined gravity measurement with an atmospheric water budget model to estimate discharges in the Mississippi and Amazon. Although not yet applied to gravel bed rivers per se, the work to date suggests that gravity monitoring could be a useful tool for tracking changes in water storage in large basins of mountainous or deglaciated regions typical of gravel-bed rivers. These applications, however, would have to normalize for other factors (e.g., snow) that also affect the mass balance and gravitational field.

### 21.3.3 Vertical Change Detection and Error

Contemporary approaches for measuring bed elevation changes and erosion/deposition still rely primarily on ground-based measurements using total stations, drop lines, sonar, or similar instruments. These techniques provide local measurements, but do not measure change at segment or catchment extents. The capacity of remote-sensing techniques to measure depths and elevations throughout watersheds means that it should now be possible to map erosion/deposition throughout basins. If those measurements are to be meaningful, however, it is critical that the error in change detection be quantified.

Lane et al. (2003) developed a probabilistic approach for understanding the propagation of error in determining differences between remote-sensing-based DEMs and, more specifically, in determining volumes of erosion and deposition. They applied these concepts to DEM data derived from photogrammetric and laser altimetry for exposed parts of a braided river, and to DEM data derived from coupling optically derived depths with the LiDAR/ photogrammetric elevations for dry areas (Westaway *et al.*, 2003). Several key findings derived from their analysis. First, error propagates rapidly when combining DEMs. One therefore should *not* assume that the accuracy associated with an individual DEM is the precision associated with the difference between two DEMs. Second, the accuracy depends on the technique (e.g., optical, photogrammetric, or altimetry) used to create the DEM and the nature of the surface being mapped. For example, the standard deviation of the error in difference calculation between DEMs ranged from 0.16 to 0.37 m over surfaces that were dry at the times of flight, but were 0.30 to 0.41 m for surfaces that were inundated at the time of both flights (see Table IV in Lane *et al.*, 2003). Third, and in line with the first two issues, errors are almost universally higher than the precision one would assume from first principles and manufacturer's documents. Project design therefore should be based on the nature of the surfaces being investigated, the associated measurement techniques, acceptable levels of random error, and the acceptable levels of information loss associated with setting different thresholds of detectable change (Figure 21.8a).

Lane *et al.* (2003) used a threshold of 0.40 m to determine whether differences between DEMs would be accepted as "real" and not just a function of error. Although this threshold eliminated some sites of erosion or deposition, it still highlighted clear patterns of change in the Waimakariri River, New Zealand (Figure 21.8a). Brasington *et al.* (2003), however, used a more rigorous 95% confidence interval in the River Feshie, Scotland, which generated minimum thresholds of detection of 0.41 m, 0.64 m, and 0.80 m for dry–dry, wet–dry, and wet–wet comparisons, respectively. This more stringent threshold meant the remote-sensing survey missed over 60% of channel deposition and 40% of erosion relative to a higher-precision ground survey. Wheaton *et al.* (2009) developed a fuzzy inference analysis that allowed them to retain more of the erosion/deposition information at the Feshie site. Their system incorporated anecdotal information on where differences were real, as well as data documenting the spatial coherence of erosion/ deposition patterns and the distinctive elevation change signatures of geomorphic change. Regardless of the technique, vertical change detection with remote sensing requires the user to balance the tremendous increase in spatial coverage against the loss of local accuracy relative to ground-based surveys.

## 21.4  BED SEDIMENT SIZE

Many hydraulic models and all sediment transport models include a parameter for bed sediment size. Despite the importance of this factor, however, there is relatively little research on remote sensing of bed sediment size because of the limitations of spatial resolution. Existing methods for estimating size (e.g., $D_{50}$ or $D_{84}$) using standard colour imagery cannot detect variations among sediments that are smaller than the pixel resolution (Carbonneau, 2005). Spatial resolutions on the order of 3 cm or smaller therefore are needed to distinguish variations within a significant portion of the gravel fraction because gravel spans the range of 0.2 cm to 6.4 cm. Although easily obtainable with ground-based photo sieving (Carbonneau *et al.*, 2003), resolution at this level requires exceptionally high quality, close-range aerial imagery with specifications that exceed those typically used with aerial imagery. Rainey *et al.* (2003) demonstrated that 1.75 m, 11-band imagery could be coupled with linear unmixing approaches to extract clay, silt, and sand percentages in fine-grained estuarine sediments. The technique was not tested in gravel-bed systems, however, and only rarely is multispectral imagery available at this fine a spatial resolution.

Despite these obstacles, investigators have shown that sediment size can be mapped from airborne platforms at catchment extents. To date, all the techniques for measuring bed sediments use image texture to estimate sediment size. The concept is a simple one; as sediments become larger they cast larger shadows, which in turn create more contrast in the image. Larger bed sediments are therefore more varied in their textural appearance.

To capture this phenomenon mathematically, Carbonneau *et al.* (2004, 2005) first reduced their 3 cm resolution, red-green-blue imagery to an 8-bit gray scale, which emphasized brightness differences between pixels and highlighted size-driven textural variations. They quantified the texture on the gray images by measuring the 2-D semi-variance within a $33 \times 33$ pixel moving window. A linear regression demonstrated a strong correlation between local semi-variance and $D_{50}$ within the window ($r^2 = 0.80$ over dry sediment, 0.85 over submerged sediment). They used different equations over submerged and exposed sediments because the water dampened the semi-variance, limiting use of the equations to depths between 0 and 1500 mm. Using these regressions, Carbonneau *et al.* (2005) were able to map $D_{50}$ for 86% of the active channel along 80 km of the St Marguerite River, Quebec (Figure 21.9). Only the portions of the river deeper than 1.5 m could not be mapped. The precision of the sediment size estimates was $\pm 11$ mm over dry surfaces, $\pm 13$ mm for sediments at depths between 0 and 0.5 m, and $\pm 15$ mm at depths between 0.5 and 1.5 m.

Carbonneau *et al.* (2005) noted that the error of estimate increased up to a $D_{50}$ of about 90 mm of particle size, at which point the error stabilized. This may result

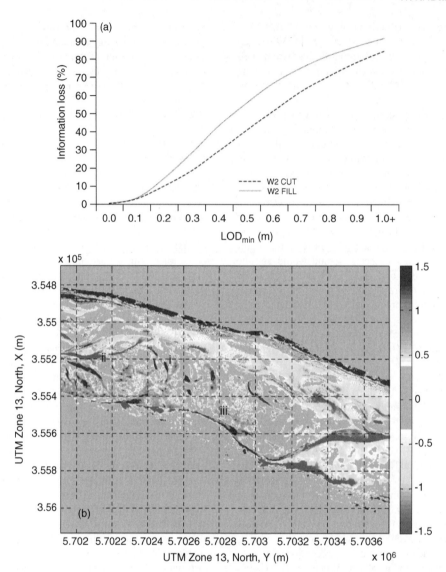

**Figure 21.8**  Implications of error for mapping erosion and deposition. (a) The tradeoff between the acceptable limit of detection (LOD) and the amount of erosion or deposition that is detected by subtracting DEMs for the Waimakariri River, New Zealand. Reproduced, with permission, from Lane, S.N., Westaway, R.M. and Hicks, D.M. 2003. Estimation of erosion and deposition volumes in a large, gravel-bed, braided river using synoptic remote sensing. *Earth Surface Processes and Landforms* **28**: 249–271. (b) Erosion and deposition in the South Saskatchewan River, Canada, derived from comparison of DEMs with the minimum detectable limit of erosion set at 0.40 m. Reproduced, with permission, from Lane, S.N., Widdison, P.E., Thomas, R.E., Ashworth, P.J., Best, J.L., Lunt, I.A., Sambrook Smith, G.H. and Simpson, C.J. 2010. Quantification of braided river channel change using archival digital image analysis. *Earth Surface Processes and Landforms* **35**: 971–985. (See the color version of this figure in color plate section.)

from the fact that fewer large particles are included in a $33 \times 33$ moving window, thus reducing the sample size, although colour variations may also drive the difference. In addition, glare off the water can result in spurious measurements that need to be manually deleted or avoided by using a polarizing lens on the camera. Verdú

*et al.* (2005) evaluated a multiple regression linking different semi-variance components to size fractions on exposed sediments and found correlations ranging from 0.66 for $D_{10}$ to 0.86 for $D_{50}$.

One of the major limitations to the textural techniques has been the need to collect ground data to calibrate the

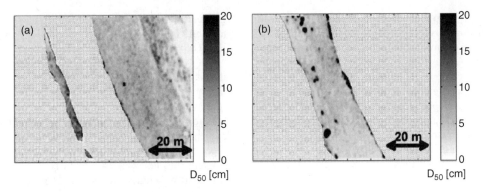

**Figure 21.9** Mapping of $D_{50}$ in the St, Marguerite River, Quebec over dry surfaces (a) and submerged surfaces (b). Reproduced, with permission, from Carbonneau, P.E., Bergeron, N. and Lane, S.N. 2005. Automated grain size measurements from airborne remote sensing for long profile measurements grain sizes. *Water Resources Research* **41**: W11426. doi: 10.1029/2005WR003994.

semi-variance model. Dugdale *et al.* (2010) therefore developed an aerial photosieving technique for measuring clast sizes directly from high spatial resolution imagery. They found that ground-based and aerial size measurements generated identical slopes for the regressions used to set up calibration equations, although the aerial photosieving had a systematic bias to overestimate sediment size by $0.45\varphi$ (i.e. a factor of 1.36). The results indicate that aerial photos with spatial resolutions on the order of 3 cm can now be used to map gravel-bed rivers, even in the absence of field data.

## 21.5 OTHER VARIABLES AND PLATFORMS

The focus of this chapter has been on techniques for documenting variables widely used in stream hydraulic models, which means that there are many river variables *not* addressed, but for which there is a substantial body of remote-sensing literature. These variables include: turbidity and suspended sediment (Mertes *et al.*, 2002), fluvial wood (Marcus *et al.,*2003; Smikrud and Prakash, 2006; MacVicar *et al.*, 2009), submerged aquatic vegetation (Silva *et al.*, 2008), biotypes (Marcus, 2002; Hilldale and Raff, 2008), and stream temperatures (Handcock *et al.*, 2006). Likewise, the focus on the active, scoured channel means that a vast literature on optical remote sensing of floodplain vegetation is not reviewed (see any remote sensing text book, e.g., Jensen, 2007), nor is the rapidly evolving research on LiDAR characterization of floodplain vegetation (Straatsma, 2008), floodplain hydraulics (Mason *et al.*, 2003; Casas *et al.*, 2006; Straatsma and Baptist, 2008), and floodplain geomorphology (Jones *et al.*, 2007). Readers should turn to the cited references to start investigating these topics.

The focus of this review has been on aerial and satellite imagery, which can document variations at submetre resolution across entire catchments. However, there are also ground- and water-based remote-sensing devices and methods for mapping river systems at local extents. These techniques include using: sonar to measure water depths (Ferrari and Collins, 2006), laser-scanning from boats to map microtopography (Alho *et al.*, 2009), laser scanning from the ground to map biotypes and surface texture (Milan *et al.*, 2010), ground-based radar to measure water depths and velocity (Costa *et al.*, 2000), photo sieving to document sediment size (Carbonneau *et al.*, 2003), and ground-based photogrammetry to characterize water depth and channel change (Butler *et al.*, 2002). In addition, the same airborne or space-based techniques reviewed in this article can be replicated at very fine spatial resolutions and frequent return intervals using near-ground aerial platforms such as hand-held poles (Bird *et al.,*2010), kites (Smith *et al.*, 2009), tethered blimps and balloons (Vericat *et al.*, 2008), remote control drones (Lejot *et al.*, 2007) and sensors placed on nearby canyon walls (Chandler *et al.*, 2002). Readers should turn to the cited references for additional literature on these topics.

Finally, the article's focus on the highest-accuracy techniques led to an emphasis on recent literature. Broader historical treatments of the field are contained in reviews by Mertes (2002), Gilvear and Bryant (2003), Feurer *et al.* (2008), Marcus and Fonstad (2008), and Gao (2009).

## 21.6 FUTURE NEEDS AND DIRECTIONS

Remote sensing of rivers is coming of age. In the 1990s the appearance of widely available, high spatial resolution, digital, colour, and multispectral imagery coupled with the advent of LiDAR spawned a remarkable proliferation of remote-sensing techniques for mapping and monitoring rivers. Despite the large number of sensors and techniques now available, however, there remain major opportunities for improving remote sensing of the hydraulic environment. Major areas where investigators are already focusing their work include: (i) improvements to existing techniques, (ii) development of new applications, (iii) improved access to data and algorithms, and (iv) theory development and application to fundamental questions regarding rivers. To this list should be added the need to develop ethical guidelines regarding appropriate use of high spatial resolution river data.

The opportunity for improving existing techniques is large in a field as young as remote sensing of rivers. Almost every article cited in this review outlines potential ways that techniques could be improved by better data, improved algorithms, and/or testing across a wider range of conditions. In addition, it would be helpful to know where different techniques are potentially applicable. For example, there are no maps at regional or continental scales that display the locations of gravel- or cobble-bed streams where: (i) the channel is visible from the air, and/or (ii) the water is sufficiently clear to enable views of the stream bottom. Such a map would provide

guidance on where passive sensors might (or might not) be useful for mapping channel morphology and hydraulics. The survey could be conducted manually simply by "flying" GoogleEarth. The need to improve existing techniques and test them in a wider variety of settings means that the opportunity for master's thesis levels of study is remarkable.

Likewise, there remains ample opportunity for development of new techniques. Fundamental issues such as separating shadow from water remain a major obstacle (Marcus and Fonstad, 2008), yet solutions may be as simple as transferring techniques from other subfields. For example, object-based mapping holds great promise for identifying and removing shadows, yet has not been formally investigated (Carbonneau, pers. comm., 2009). There is also tremendous room for fusion of data and models to derive hydraulic variables such as velocity, Froude numbers, and stream power (e.g., Jordan and Fonstad, 2008).

Perhaps the single greatest obstacle to widespread adoption of river remote-sensing techniques is the perceived (and sometime actual) complexity of the methods.

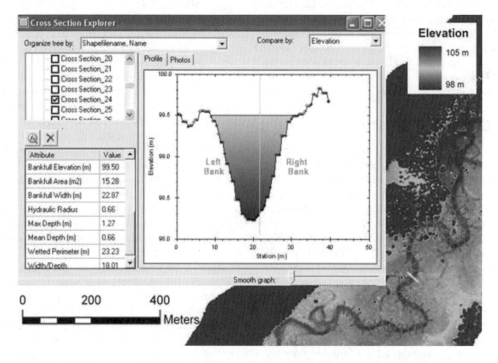

**Figure 21.10** The McKean *et al.* (2009a) ArcGIS-based River Bathymetry Toolkit graphical user interface for extracting cross sections and other hydraulic variables from high-resolution aquatic-terrestrial DEMs. The data and cross-section in the inset are from the cross-section identified by light line on the channel. Other lines show additional cross section to be collected. From figure S2 of McKean *et al.*, 2009a (http://www.agu.org/pubs/eos-news/supplements/2009/mckean_90_39.shtml). Reproduced, with permission, from McKean, J., Issak, D. and Wright, W. 2009a. Improving stream studies with a small–footprint green lidar. *EOS: Transactions of the American Geophysical Union* **90**: 341–342. (See the color version of this figure in color plate section.)

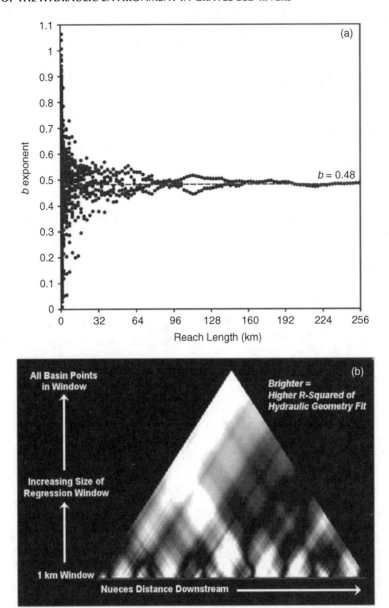

**Figure 21.11** Implications of high-resolution, basin-extent remote sensing data for theory testing. (a) The hydraulic geometry width exponent, $b$, varies dramatically with width and location along 700 km of the Lena River, only stabilizing when river lengths of 60 to 90 km are obtained. Reproduced, with permission, from Smith, L.C. and Pavelsky, T.M. 2008. Estimation of river discharge, propagation speed, and hydraulic geometry from space: Lena River, Siberia. *Water Resources Research* **44**: W03427. doi:10.1029/2007WR006133, 2008; (b) likewise, the $b$ exponent varies with location and scale throughout the Nueces River, Texas. Reproduced, with permission, from Fonstad, M.A. and Marcus, W.A. 2010. High resolution, basin extent observations and implications for understanding river form and process. *Earth Surface Processes and Landforms* **35**: 680–698. The inability of hydraulic geometry to capture morphologic variations has implications for applications of this theory at local scales and sets the stage for development of new theories to explain river structure and behaviour.

In recent years, authors have tried to overcome this issue by making software solutions available. For example, there are now Matlab programs available for fuzzy definition of error between DEMs (Wheaton *et al.* 2009) and for correcting variable illumination between images (which generates errors in depth mapping) (Carbonneau *et al.*, 2006). Pavelsky and Smith (2008) posted an IDL script for defining channel centrelines and widths, while Fonstad and Marcus (2005) coded their depth estimation procedures into an Excel spreadsheet. Substantial obstacles to the non-specialist remain, however, because so many programs are specific to just one application and many require programming knowledge. Some of the most promising lines of research therefore are occurring where authors are scripting a variety of remote-sensing applications into commonly used software. McKean *et al.* (2009a), for example, have developed an ArcGIS River Bathymetry Toolkit that will automatically extract common geomorphic and ecologic channel measures from high-resolution data from any source (Figure 21.10). Likewise, Dugdale and Carbonneau (2009) are developing a Matlab-based Fluvial Information System (FIS) that works with multiple high-resolution images to automate a wide range of otherwise very time consuming and potentially complex tasks.

The implications of basin-extent, high-resolution data for understanding river systems are only just beginning to be explored. Smith and Pavelsky (2008), for example, measured widths at 0.25 spacing along 700 km of the Lena River, Siberia, in order to develop remote-sensing-based rating curves linking width to discharge. They found that the width exponent ($b$) in hydraulic geometry equations only stabilized at length scales of 60 to 90 km (two to three times the valley width) (Figure 21.11a). In a similar fashion, but in the much smaller Nueces River of Texas, Fonstad and Marcus (2010) found that the $b$ exponent varied dramatically with both location and length scales (Figure 21.11b). Such findings have significant implications for predicting river morphology and hydrology in other settings. This work also highlights the fundamental problem of determining how to visualize submetre resolution data over tens to hundreds of kilometres.

There are many (as of yet) unrealized opportunities to apply the new techniques to mapping, modelling, and understanding gravel-bed rivers. Continuous and detailed maps of bed topography and water surfaces generated from remote sensing can, for example, provide superior input parameters and validation data for 2-D and 3-D models. Likewise, the metre resolution maps of variations in bed sediment size provide a remarkable opportunity for mapping and understanding sedimentary facies.

As a final note, almost none of the articles on remote sensing of rivers discusses the ethics of mapping sub-metre habitat at basin extents. Given the importance of gravel-bed rivers to water supply and to many species, some of them endangered, it is important that the river community begin to assess issues related to the access and use of basin-extent, high-resolution river data. As with human subject surveys, the river-science community needs to develop protocols for mapping, monitoring, and reporting on detailed habitat data. Otherwise, the very techniques we have worked so hard to develop may be used to over-exploit and destroy the rivers that most of us doing the research wish to protect and preserve.

## 21.7 ACKNOWLEDGMENTS

My understanding of remote sensing of rivers and the content of this paper have benefited tremendously from conversations, correspondence, or collaboration with Normand Bergeron, Joe Boardman, Patrice Carbonneau, Mark Fonstad, David Gilvear, D. Murray Hicks, Stuart Lane, Carl Legleiter, Jim McKean, and Suzanne Walther. Much of the material presented here was developed with sabbatical support from the Department of Geography, University of Oregon and a Distinguished International Fellowship at the Department of Geography, University of Durham.

## 21.8 REFERENCES

Alho, P., Kukko, A., Hyyppä, H. *et al.* 2009. Application of boat-based laser scanning for river survey. *Earth Surface Processes and Landforms* **34**: 1831–1838.

Allouis, T., Bailly, J-S., Pastol, Y., and Le Roux, C. 2010. Comparison of LiDAR waveform processing methods for very shallow water bathymetry using Raman, near-infrared, and green signals. *Earth Surface Processes and Landforms* **35**: 640–650.

Alsdorf, D.E. and Lettenmaier, D.P. 2003. Tracking fresh water from space. *Science* **301**: 1491–1494.

Alsdorf, D., Bates, P.D., Melack, J., Wilson, M., and Dunne, T. 2007. Spatial and temporal complexity of the Amazon flood measured from space. *Geophysical Research Letters* **34**: L08402. doi: 10.1029/2007GL029447.

Antonarakis, A.S., Richards, K.S., and Brasington, J. 2008. Objects-based land cover classification using airborne LiDAR. *Remote Sensing of Environment* **112**: 2988–2998. doi: 10.1016/j.rse.2008.02.004

Bird, S., Hogan, D., and Schwab, J. 2010. Photogrammetric monitoring of small streams under a riparian forest canopy. *Earth Surface Processes and Landforms* **35**: 952–970.

Birkett, C.M., Mertes, L.A.K., Dunne, T., Costa, M.H., and Jasinski, M.J. 2002. Surface water dynamics in the Amazon Basin: Application of satellite radar altimetry. *Journal of Geophysical Research*, **107**: 8059. doi: 10.1029/2001JD000609.

Bjerklie, D.M., Dingman, D.L., Vörösmarty, C.J., Bolster, C.H., and Congalton, R.G. 2003. Evaluating the potential for measuring river discharge from space. *Journal of Hydrology* **278**: 17–38.

Brakenridge, G.R., Nghiem, S.V., Anderson, E., and Chien, S. 2005. Space-based measurement of river runoff. *EOS: Transactions of the American Geophysical Union* 86: 185–192.

Brasington, J., Langham, J., and Rumbsy, B. 2003. Methodological sensitivity of morphometric estimates of coarse fluvial sediment transport. *Geomorphology* 53: 299–316.

Brennan, R. and Webster, T.L. 2006. Object-oriented land cover classification of lidar-derived surfaces. *Canadian Journal of Remote Sensing*, 32: 162–172.

Butler, J.B., Lane, S.N., Chandler, J.H., and Porfiri, E. 2002. Through-water close range digital photogrammetry in flume and field environments. *Photogrammetric Record* 17: 419–439.

Carbonneau, P.E. 2005. The threshold effect of image resolution on image-based automated grain size mapping in fluvial environments. *Earth Surface Processes and Landforms* 30: 1687–1693.

Carbonneau, P.E., Bergeron, N., and Lane, S.N. 2005. Automated grain size measurements from airborne remote sensing for long profile measurements grain sizes. *Water Resources Research* 41: W11426. doi: 10.1029/2005WR003994.

Carbonneau, P.E., Lane, S.N., and Bergeron, N.E. 2003. Cost-effective non-metric close-range digital photogrammetry and its application to a study of coarse gravel river beds. *International Journal of Remote Sensing*, 24: 2837–2854.

Carbonneau, P.E., Lane, S.N., and Bergeron, N.E. 2004. Catchment-scale mapping of surface grain size in gravel bed rivers using airborne digital imagery. *Water Resources Research* 40: W07202. doi: 10.1029/2003WR002759.

Carbonneau, P.E., Lane, S.N., and Bergeron, N. 2006. Feature based image processing methods applied to bathymetric measurements from airborne remote sensing in fluvial environments. *Earth Surface Processes and Landforms* 31: 1413–1423.

Casas, A., Benito, G., Thorndycraft, V.R., and Rico, M. 2006. The topographic data source of digital terrain models as a key element in the accuracy of hydraulic flood modeling. *Earth Surface Processes and Landforms* 31: 444–456.

Chandler, J.H., Ashmore, P., Paola, C., Gooch, M.J., and Varkaris, F. 2002. Monitoring river channel change using terrestrial oblique digital imagery and automated digital photogrammetry. *Annals of the Association of American Geographers* 92: 631–644.

Costa, J.E., Spicer, K.R., Cheng, R.T. *et al.* 2000. Measuring stream discharge by non-contact methods: A proof of concept experiment. *Geophysical Research Letters* 27: 553–556.

Crowley, J.W., Mitrovica, J.X., Bailey, R.C., Tamisiea, M.E., and Davis, J.L. 2006. Land water storage within the Congo Basin inferred from GRACE satellite gravity data. *Geophysical Research Letters* 33: L19402. doi: 10.1029/2006GL027070.

Dugdale, S.J. and Carbonneau, P. 2009. *The Fluvial Information System User Manual*. Revision 1.1. APEM Ltd and Durham University.

Dugdale, S.J., Carbonneau, P.E., and Campbell, D. 2010. Aerial photosieving of exposed gravel bars for the rapid calibration of airborne grain size maps. *Earth Surface Processes and Landforms* 35: 627–639.

English, J. 2009. *Effectiveness of extracting water surface slopes from LiDAR data within the active channel: Sandy River, Oregon, USA*. M.S. Thesis, Department of Geography, University of Oregon, Eugene.

Ferrari, R.L. and Collins, K.L. 2006. Reservoir survey and data analysis. In Yang, C.T., editor. *Erosion and Sedimentation Manual*, United States Department of the Interior, Bureau of Reclamation, Technical Service Center, Denver, Colorado, Chapter 9. Available online at http://www.usbr.gov/pmts/sediment/projects/index.html.

Feurer, D., Bailly, J-S., Puech, C., LeCoarer, Y., and Viau, A. 2008. Very high resolution mapping of river immersed topography by remote sensing. *Progress in Physical Geography* 32: 1–17.

Fonstad, M.A. and Marcus, W.A. 2005. Remote sensing of stream depths with hydraulically assisted bathymetry (HAB) models. *Geomorphology* 72: 107–120.

Fonstad, M.A. and Marcus, W.A. 2010. High resolution, basin extent observations and implications for understanding river form and process. *Earth Surface Processes and Landforms* 35: 680–698.

Fryer, J.G. 1983. A simple system for photogrammetric mapping in shallow-water. *Photogrammetric Record* 11: 203–208.

Gao, J. 2009. Bathymetric mapping by means of remote sensing: Methods, accuracy and limitations. *Progress in Physical Geography* 33: 103–116.

Gilvear, D.J. and Bryant, R. 2003. Analysis of aerial photography and other remotely sensed data. In Kondolf, G.M. and Piegay, H. editors. *Tools in Fluvial Geomorphology*. Chichester, John Wiley & Sons, Ltd, pp. 133–168.

Gilvear, D.J., Hunter, P., and Higgins, T. 2007. An experimental approach to the measurement of the effects of water depth and substrate on optical and near infra-red reflectance: a field-based assessment of the feasibility of mapping submerged instream habitat. *International Journal of Remote Sensing* 28: 2241–2256.

Guenther, G.C., Cunningham, A.G., LaRocque, P.E., and Ried, D.J. 2000. Meeting the accuracy challenge in airborne LiDAR bathymetry. *Proceedings of EARSeL-SIG Workshop LiDAR No. 1, Dresden, Germany, June 16–17*, pp. 1–27.

Guenther, G., LaRocque, P.E., and Lillycrop, W. 1994. Multiple surface channels in SHOALS airborne lidar. *SPIE: Ocean Optics XII* 2258: 422–430.

Handcock, R.N., Gillespie, A.R., Cherkauer, K.A. *et al.* 2006. Accuracy and uncertainty of thermal-infrared remote sensing of stream temperatures at multiple spatial scales. *Remote Sensing of Environment* 100: 427–440.

Hicks, D.M., Shankar, U., Duncan, M.J., Rebuffe, M., and Aberle, J. 2006. Use of remote-sensing technology to assess impacts of hydro-operations on a large, braided, gravel-bed river: Waitaki River, New Zealand. In Sambrook Smith, G. H., Best, J.L., Bristow, C.S., and Petts, G.E. editors. *Braided Rivers – Process, Deposits, Ecology and Management*. Interntional Association of Sedimentologists Special Publication 36 Oxford, Blackwell, pp. 311–326.

Hilldale, R.C. and Raff, D. 2008. Assessing the ability of airborne LiDAR to map river bathymetry. *Earth Surface Processes and Landforms* 33: 773–783.

Höfle, B., Vetter, M., Pfeifer, N., Mandlburger, G., and Stötter, J. 2009. Water surface mapping from airborne laser scanning using signal intensity and elevation data. *Earth Surface Processes and Landforms* 34: 1635–1649.

Horritt, M.S., Mason, D.C., and Luckman, A.J. 2001. Flood boundary delineation from synthetic aperture radar imagery using a statistical active contour model. *International Journal of Remote Sensing* 22: 2489–2507.

Hughes, M.L., McDowell, P.F., and Marcus, W.A. 2006. Accuracy assessment of georectified aerial photographs: Implications for measuring lateral channel movement in a GIS. *Geomorphology* 74: 1–16.

Ip, F., Dohm, J.M., Baker, V.R. *et al.* 2006. Flood detection and monitoring with the Autonomous Sciencecraft Experiment onboard EO-1. *Remote Sensing of Environment* 101: 463–481.

Jensen, J.R. 2007. *Remote Sensing of the Environment: An Earth Resource Perspective*. London, Pearson Prentice Hall.

Jones, A.F., Brewer, P.A., Johnstone, E., and Macklin, M.G. 2007. High-resolution interpretative geomorphological mapping of river valley environments using airborne LiDAR data. *Earth Surface Processes and. Landforms* **32**: 1574–1592.

Jordan, D.C. and Fonstad, M.A. 2005. Two-dimensional mapping of river bathymetry and power using aerial photography and GIS on the Brazos River, Texas. *Geocarto* **20**: 1–8.

Kishi, S., Song, X., and Li, J. 2001. Flood detection in Changjiang 1998 from Landsat-TM data. *Space Technology* **20**: 99–105.

Kinzel, P.J., Wright, C.W., Nelson, J.M., and Burman, A.R. 2007. Evaluation of an experimental LiDAR for surveying a shallow, braided, sand-bedded river. *Journal of Hydraulic Engineering* **133**: 838–842.

Lane, S.N. 2000. The measurement of river channel morphology using digital photogrammetry. *Photogrammetric Record* **16**: 937–957.

Lane, S.N., James, T.D., and Crowell, M.D. 2000. The application of digital photogrammetry to complex topography for geomorphological research. *Photogrammetric Record* **16**: 793–821.

Lane, S.N., Westaway, R.M., and Hicks, D.M. 2003. Estimation of erosion and deposition volumes in a large, gravel-bed, braided river using synoptic remote sensing. *Earth Surface Processes and Landforms* **28**: 249–271.

Lane, S.N., Widdison, P.E., Thomas, R.E. *et al.* 2010. Quantification of braided river channel change using archival digital image analysis. *Earth Surface Processes and Landforms* **35**: 971–985.

Lawler, D.M. 1993. The measurement of river bank and lateral channel change: a review. *Earth Surface Processes and Landforms* **18**: 777–821.

Legleiter, C.J. and Roberts, D.A. 2005. Effects of channel morphology and sensor spatial resolution on image-derived depth estimates. *Remote Sensing of Environment* **95**: 231–247.

Legleiter, C.J., Marcus, W.A., and Lawrence, R. 2002. Effects of sensor resolution on mapping in-stream habitats. *Photogrammetric Engineering and Remote Sensing* **68**: 801–807.

Legleiter, C.J., Roberts, D.A., and Lawrence, R.L. 2009. Spectrally based remote sensing of river bathymetry. *Earth Surface Processes and Landforms* **34**: 1039–1059.

Legleiter, C.J., Roberts, D.A., Marcus, W.A., and Fonstad, M.A. 2004. Passive remote sensing of river channel morphology and in-stream habitat: physical basis and feasibility. *Remote Sensing of Environment* **93**: 493–510.

Lejot, J., Delacourt, C., Piegay, H. *et al.* 2007. Very high spatial resolution imagery for channel bathymetry and topography from an unmanned mapping controlled platform. *Earth Surface Processes and Landforms* **32**: 1705–1725.

Li, T., Gong, P., and Sasagawa T. 2005. Integrated shadow removal based on photogrammetry and image analysis. *International Journal of Remote Sensing* **26**: 3911–3929.

Lundahl, A.C. 1948. Underwater depth determination by aerial photography. *Photogrammetric Engineering* **14**: 454–462.

Lyzenga, D.R. 1978. Passive remote-sensing techniques for mapping water depth and bottom features. *Applied Optics* **17**: 379–383.

Lyzenga, D.R. 1981. Remote sensing of bottom reflectance and water attenuation parameters in shallow water using aircraft and Landsat data. *International Journal of Remote Sensing* **2**: 71–82.

MacVicar, B.J., Piégay, H., Henderson, A. *et al.* 2009. Quantifying the temporal dynamics of wood in large rivers: field trials of wood surveying, dating, tracking, and monitoring techniques. *Earth Surface Processes and Landforms* **34**: 2031–2046.

Magirl, C.S., Webb, R.H., and Griffiths, P.G. 2005. Changes in water surface profile of the Colorado River in Grand Canyon, Arizona, between 1923 and 2000. *Water Resources Research*, **41**: W05021. doi: 10.1029/2003WR002519.

Marcus, W.A. 2002. Mapping of stream microhabitats with high spatial resolution hyperspectral imagery. *Journal of Geographical Systems* **4**: 113–126.

Marcus, W.A. and Fonstad, M.A. 2008. Optical remote mapping of rivers at sub-meter resolutions and watershed extents. *Earth Surface Processes and Landforms* **33**: 4–24.

Marcus, W.A., Legleiter, C.J., Aspinall, R.J., Boardman, J.W., and Crabtree, R.L. 2003. High spatial resolution, hyperspectral (HSRH) mapping of in-stream habitats, depths, and woody debris in mountain streams. *Geomorphology* **55**: 363–380.

Mason, D.C., Cobby, D.M., Horritt, M.S., and Bates, P.D. 2003. Floodplain friction parameterization in two-dimensional river flood models using vegetation heights derived from airborne scanning laser altimetry. *Hydrological Processes* **17**: 1711–1732.

McKean, J., Issak, D., and Wright, W. 2009a. Improving stream studies with a small–footprint green lidar. *EOS: Transactions of the American Geophysical Union* **90**: 341–342.

McKean, J., Nagel, D., Tonina, D., *et al.* 2009b. Remote sensing of channels and riparian zones with a narrow-beam aquatic-terrestrial LIDAR. *Remote Sensing* **9**: 1065–1096. doi: 10.3390/rs1041065.

Mertes, L.A.K. 2002. Remote sensing of riverine landscapes. *Freshwater Biology* **47**: 799–816.

Mertes, L.A.K., Dekker, A., Brakenridge, G.R., Birkett, C., and Létourneau G. 2002. Rivers and lakes. In Ustin, S.L. editor. *Natural Resources and Environment, Manual of Remote Sensing*. New York, John Wiley & Sons, Inc.

Milan, D.J., Heritage, G.L., Large, A.R.G., and Entwistle, N.S. 2010. Mapping hydraulic biotopes using terrestrial laser scan data of water surface properties. *Earth Surface Processes and Landforms* **35:** 918–931.

Mobley, C.D. 1994. *Light and Water: Radiative Transfer in Natural Waters*. San Diego, Academic Press.

Pe'eri, S. and Philpot, W. 2007. Increasing the existence of very shallow-water LIDAR measurements using the red-channel waveforms. *IEEE Transactions on Geoscience and Remote Sensing* **45**: 1217–1223.

Pavelsky, T.M. and Smith, L.C. 2008. RivWidth: A software tool for the calculation of river widths from remotely sensed imagery. *IEEE Geoscience and remote Sensing Letters* **5**: 70–73.

Rainey, M.P., Tyler, A.N., Gilvear, D.J., Bryant, R.G., and McDonald, P. 2003. Mapping intertidal estuarine sediment grain size distributions through airborne remote sensing. *Remote Sensing of Environment*, **86**: 480–490.

Richter, R. and Muller, A. 2005. De-shadowing of satellite/airborne imagery. *International Journal of Remote Sensing* **26**: 3137–3148.

Rossi, R.E., Dungan, J.L., and Beck, L.R. 1994. Kriging in the shadows: geostatistical interpolation for remote sensing. *Remote Sensing of the Environment* **49**: 32–40.

Schumann, G., Hostache, R., Puech, C. *et al.* 2007. High-resolution 3-D flood information from radar imagery for flood hazard management. *IEEE Transactions on Geoscience and Remote Sensing*, **45**: 1715–1725.

Sheng, Y., Gong, P., and Xiao, Q. 2001. Quantitative dynamic flood monitoring with NOAA AVRR. *International Journal of Remote Sensing* **22**: 1709–1724.

Silva, T.S.F., Costa, M.P.F., Melack, J.M., and Novo, E.M.L. 2008. Remote sensing of aquatic vegetation: theory and applications. *Environmental Monitoring and Assessment* **140**: 131–145.

Smikrud, K.M. and Prakesh, A. 2006. Monitoring large woody debris dynamics in the Unuk River, Alaska using digital aerial photography. *GIScience and Remote Sensing* **43**: 142–154.

Smith, L.C. 1997. Satellite remote sensing of river inundation area, stage, and discharge: A review. *Hydrologic Processes* **11**: 1427–1439.

Smith, L.C. and Pavelsky, T.M. 2008. Estimation of river discharge, propagation speed, and hydraulic geometry from space: Lena River, Siberia. *Water Resources Research* **44**: W03427. doi: 10.1029/2007WR006133, 2008.

Smith, M.J., Chandler, J., and Rose, J. 2009. High spatial resolution data acquisition for the geosciences: kite aerial photography. *Earth Surface Processes and Landforms* **34**: 155–161.

Snyder, N.P. 2009. Studying stream morphology with airborne laser elevation data. *EOS, Transactions of the American Geophysical Union* **90**: 45–46.

Spicer, K.R., Costa, J.E., and Placzek, G. 1997. Measuring flood discharge in unstable stream channels using ground penetrating radar. *Geology* **25**: 423–426.

Straatsma, M.W. 2008. Quantitative mapping of hydrodynamic vegetation floodplain forests under leaf-off conditions using airborne laser scanning. *Photogrammetric Engineering and Remote Sensing* **74**: 987–998.

Straatsma, M.W. and Baptist, M.J. 2008. Floodplain roughness parameterization using airborne laser scanning and spectral remote sensing. *Remote Sensing of Environment* **112**: 1062–1080.

Syed, T.H., Famiglietti, J.S., Chen, J. *et al.* 2005. Total basin discharge for the Amazon and Mississippi River basins from GRACE and a land-atmosphere water balance. *Geophysical Research Letters* **32**: L24404. doi: 10.1029/2005GL024851.

Tapley, B.D., Bettadpur, S., Ries, J.C., Thompson, P.F., and Watkins, M.M. 2004. GRACE measurements of mass variability in the Earth system. *Science* **305**: 503–505.

Trimble S. 1991. Historical sources of information for geomorphological research in the United States. *Professional Geographer* **43**: 212–228.

Vericat, D., Brasington, J., Wheaton, J., and Cowie, M. 2008. Accuracy assessment of aerial photographs acquired using lighter-than-air blimps: Low-cost tools for mapping river corridors. *River Research and Applications* **25**: 985–1000. doi: 10.1002/rra1198.

Verdú, J.M., Batalla, R.J., and Martínez-Casasnova, J.A. 2005. High-resolution grain-size characterisation of gravel bars using imagery and geo-statistics. *Geomorphology* **72**: 73–93.

Walther, S.C., Marcus, W.A., and Fonstad, M.A. 2011. Evaluation of high resolution, true colour, aerial imagery for mapping bathymetry in clear water rivers without ground-based depth measurements. *International Journal of Remote Sensing* **32**: 4343–4363.

Westaway, R.M., Lane, S.N., and Hicks, D.M. 2000. Development of an automated correction procedure for digital photogrammetry for the study of wide, shallow gravel-bed rivers. *Earth Surface Processes and Landforms* **25**: 209–226.

Westaway, R.M., Lane, S.N., and Hicks, D.M. 2001. Airborne remote sensing of clear water, shallow, gravel-bed rivers using digital photogrammetry and image analysis. *Photogrammetric Engineering and Remote Sensing* **67**: 1271–1281.

Westaway, R.M., Lane, S.N., and Hicks, D.M. 2003. Remote survey of large-scale braided rivers using digital photogrammetry and image analysis. *International Journal of Remote Sensing* **24**: 795–816.

Wheaton, J.M., Brasington, J., Darby, S.E., and Sear, D.A. 2009. Accounting for uncertainty in DEMs from repeat topographic surveys: improved sediment budgets. *Earth Surface Processes and Landforms* **35**: 136–156. doi: 10.1002/esp.1886.

## 21.9 DISCUSSION

### 21.9.1 Discussion by Peter Ashmore

We have exciting new technologies for high-resolution mapping of gravel river morphology. I wonder if this very high resolution is always necessary for resolving morphodynamics of rivers and this brings to mind two points for discussion: (i) Whether any thought has been given to what resolution, precision, and density of data are needed for particular problems and therefore the appropriate technology and data to use; (ii) whether these higher-resolution data have been used to assess the minimum requirements for reaching equivalent (statistical?) information of, for example, bed elevation change, and whether this might also be applied retrospectively to older, low-resolution data sets to assess their overall reliability.

### 21.9.2 Discussion by Stephen Rice

Despite substantial advances in using these technologies to extract useful information about fluvial environments, the author has pointed out that there are limitations and challenges to be overcome. Some of these pertain to the availability and user-friendliness of the tools themselves, but others are technical issues. Technical limitations must reflect, in part at least, the fact that many of the technologies we are using were not designed for fluvial geomorphologists, but for a different market – perhaps the US military, for example. What are the prospects for our community to become engaged with manufacturers in the design and/or modification of instruments that are more tuned to our specific requirements? What is the experience of the author in developing relationships with relevant companies and what advice does he have for engaging with providers as a means of overcoming technical limitations?

### 21.9.3 Discussion by Noah P. Snyder

Airborne LiDAR is spectacular when compared to traditional digital elevations models (DEMs). With traditional DEMs (generated from topographic maps) you could measure channel slopes only over elevation changes on the order of the contour interval of the original map source (~3 m in the best cases). With airborne LiDAR, you can resolve water surface elevations within half a metre, so you can measure slopes over much shorter lengths. This opens up exciting opportunities in tectonic fluvial geomorphology and habitat mapping at the reach scale (hundreds of metres length or less). See Snyder (2009) for a longer discussion of this topic, including limitations of LiDAR for gravel-bed rivers.

### 21.9.4  Reply by W. Andrew Marcus

The three comments identify intertwined issues that are central to future river studies that use remote sensing. Rice asks the question: can sensors and remote data acquisition for river applications be improved through more direct collaboration with data providers? Ashmore's query targets the kind of information that might be provided to data providers, asking what information on resolution, precision, and data density should be specified to optimize data collection for specific river applications? Snyder's statement provides a partial answer to Ashmore's question in the context of LiDAR. Finally, Ashmore asks whether high-resolution, remotely sensed data can be used to evaluate the accuracy of older, lower-resolution data sets for characterizing fluvial parametres.

The fact that sensors and platforms have almost universally been designed and operated for applications *outside* rivers has long been an obstacle to river applications. As early as the first black and white photographs, most film was exposed to heighten contrast among terrestrial features. Accomplishing this requires intermediate exposures to avoid over-saturating bright areas, which leads to the relatively dark features of rivers being chronically under-exposed. The litany of similar problems for river scientists continues to this day: spatial resolutions are typically overly coarse for river applications in smaller streams (Marcus et al.,2003), coordinate information is too imprecise to co-register images where small errors can lead to placement of terrestrial features on top of aqueous features (Wright et al.,2000), and the exposures and radiometric resolutions of river images are often inadequate to map key features (Legleiter et al., 2002).

Working with sensor developers and data providers seems an obvious solution to this issue, but is more easily said than done. The most significant obstacle is that groups studying rivers typically have small budgets compared to the military, commercial interests, or government entities. Because sensor and platform design flows to money, this leaves river scientists without much influence when talking to design engineers and operators.

In response to this obstacle, river scientists and managers have developed several approaches to gaining more control over sensor specifications and platform operations. One option is to develop large user groups who collaborate on developing research initiatives and government funding around a particular application. The Surface Water and Ocean Topography (SWOT) satellite mission is an example of this approach (e.g., Jung et al., 2010). In the context of aerial imagery and at more moderate cost, river scientists are re-tooling the EAARL bathymetric LiDAR and software system to get better reflection from dark substrates, increase data density, and improve separation of surface and bed reflections, all of which will enhance river applications (McKean, 2009; pers. comm., 2010). Alternatively, at the lower cost end, researchers are adapting existing technologies by coupling digital recording devices to tethered balloons or poles (e.g., Bird et al.,2010) or drones (e.g., Lejot et al., 2007). Unfortunately, after almost 20 years of mostly bad experiences working directly with data providers, it is this author's view that collaborating with operators on a good faith basis does little to change operations; actual control of the instrument and platform is required to achieve good results in rivers for specialized applications. The incentive of changing operations simply to enable good science offers little incentive to companies who are on incredibly tight deadlines with multimillion dollar clients.

This is not to say, however, that all existing imagery is poor for river applications. Snyder (2009, and his comment above) makes this point in the context of near infrared LiDAR imagery. Likewise, the many successful applications noted in the chapter above point to the potential to use existing sensors and platforms for successful river mapping. Before purchasing imagery or arranging for special image acquisition, however, the key point is that the success of the application will vary widely with the spatial, spectral, radiometric, and temporal resolutions of the instruments – a note that leads to Ashmore's query regarding optimal specifications for river applications.

Unfortunately there is no one answer for what constitutes optimal image specifications, other than to note that the requirements will vary with the application at hand. For example, present techniques for measuring subaqueous sediment size require optical imagery with a spatial resolution approximating that of the sediment size (Carbonneau, 2005). Mapping sediment size in gravel-bed rivers therefore requires imagery with spatial resolutions on the order of several centimetres. In contrast, depth measurements with optical imagery can actually improve with coarser spatial resolution, which "blends' the many micro-variations that can result from turbulence, substrate, glint, and so forth (Walther et al., 2011).

Absent any simple rule for all occasions, the user must turn to existing literature regarding specifications.

Articles that explicitly investigate sensor and image requirements for different applications are: biotypes (Legleiter *et al.*, 2002; Marcus, 2002; Marcus *et al.*, 2003); depth measurements from optical imagery using physical modeling approaches (Legleiter and Roberts, 2005; Legleiter *et al.*, 2009); optical depth measurements using photogrammetric approaches (Lane *et al.*, 2003); depth change detection using photogrammetry (Lane *et al.*, 2003, 2010); depth measurement with blue-green LiDAR (McKean *et al.*, 2009a); substrate size (Carbonneau, 2005); and large wood (Marcus *et al.*, 2003). In addition, Hicks (Chapter 23, this volume) provides an excellent overview of accuracies of depth measurements and depth-change-over-time calculations associated with different remote-sensing approaches and instruments. Finally, a fundamental issue facing all river scientists is how to define accuracy for the purposes of specific applications, which in turn constrains which approaches and sensors to use. For example, in building a true "riverscape" with billions of data points that map the stream continuously in three dimensions, one must sacrifice precision and local accuracy (Carbonneau *et al.*, in press). Whether this is acceptable depends on the application at hand.

Ashmore's final query is whether high-resolution, remotely sensed data can be used to evaluate the reliability of older, lower resolution data sets? In theory, the answer is: "Yes." However, while the use of modern high-resolution, remote-sensing measurements to validate, calibrate or correct other, lower-resolution measurements makes sense conceptually, there is little (if any) research on the topic. In practice, one of the biggest obstacles is adequate co-registration of old measurements to new, image-based data in a dynamic, changing system. In rivers, for example, differences in location of just a metre can be the difference between a dry bank and a pool. If this difference shows up over two different dates, it may be impossible to know if it represents real change, an error in the original measurement, or a slight mismatch in coordinate location. It thus seems likely that revisiting historic, low-resolution data with new, image-based measurements will work best for larger extent areal or volumetric measurements, where slight differences in location of one measurement are less likely to skew the entire outcome.

## 21.10   DISCUSSION REFERENCES

Bird, S., Hogan, D., and Schwab, J. 2010. Photogrammetric monitoring of small streams under a riparian forest canopy. *Earth Surface Processes and Landforms* **35**: 952–970.

Carbonneau, P.E. 2005. The threshold effect of image resolution on image-based automated grain size mapping in fluvial environments. *Earth Surface Processes and Landforms* **30**: 1687–1693.

Carbonneau, P., Fonstad, M.A., Marcus, W.A., and Dugdale, S. In press. Making riverscapes real. *Geomorphology*.

Jung, H.C., Hamski, J., Durand, M. *et al.* 2010. Characterization of complex fluvial systems using remote sensing of spatial and temporal water level variations in the Amazon, Congo, and Brahmaputra Rivers. *Earth Surface Processes and Landforms* **35**: 294–302.

Lane, S.N., Westaway, R.M., and Hicks, D.M. 2003. Estimation of erosion and deposition volumes in a large, gravel-bed, braided river using synoptic remote sensing. *Earth Surface Processes and Landforms* **28**: 249–271.

Lane, S.N., Widdison, P.E., Thomas, R.E. *et al.* 2010. Quantification of braided river channel change using archival digital image analysis. *Earth Surface Processes and Landforms* **35**: 971–985.

Legleiter, C.J. and Roberts, D.A. 2005. Effects of channel morphology and sensor spatial resolution on image-derived depth estimates. *Remote Sensing of Environment* **95**: 231–247.

Legleiter, C.J., Marcus, W.A., and Lawrence, R. 2002. Effects of sensor resolution on mapping in-stream habitats. *Photogrammetric Engineering and Remote Sensing* **68**: 801–807.

Legleiter, C.J., Roberts, D.A., and Lawrence, R.L. 2009. Spectrally based remote sensing of river bathymetry. *Earth Surface Processes and Landforms* **34**: 1039–1059.

Lejot, J., Delacourt, C., Piegay, H. *et al.* 2007. Very high spatial resolution imagery for channel bathymetry and topography from an unmanned mapping controlled platform. *Earth Surface Processes and Landforms* **32**: 1705–1725.

Marcus, W.A. 2002. Mapping of stream microhabitats with high spatial resolution hyperspectral imagery. *Journal of Geographical Systems* **4**: 113–126.

Marcus, W.A., Legleiter, C.J., Aspinall, R.J., Boardman, J.W., and Crabtree, R.L. 2003. High spatial resolution, hyperspectral (HSRH) mapping of in-stream habitats, depths, and woody debris in mountain streams. *Geomorphology* **55**: 363–380.

Marcus, W.A., Legleiter, C.J., Aspinall, R.J., Boardman, J.W., and Crabtree, R.L. 2003. High spatial resolution, hyperspectral (HSRH) mapping of in-stream habitats, depths, and woody debris in mountain streams. *Geomorphology* **55**: 363–380.

McKean, J., Issak, D., and Wright, W. 2009a. Improving stream studies with a small–footprint green lidar. *EOS: Transactions of the American Geophysical Union* **90**: 341–342.

McKean, J., Nagel, D., Tonina, D., *et al.* 2009b. Remote sensing of channels and riparian zones with a narrow-beam aquatic-terrestrial LIDAR. *Remote Sensing* **9**: 1065–1096. doi: 10.3390/rs1041065.

Snyder, N.P. 2009. Studying stream morphology with airborne laser elevation data. *EOS, Transactions of the American Geophysical Union* **90**: 45–46.

Walther, S.C., Marcus, W.A., and Fonstad, M.A. 2011. Evaluation of high resolution, true colour, aerial imagery for mapping bathymetry in clear water rivers without ground-based depth measurements. *International Journal of Remote Sensing* **32**: 4343–4363.

Wright, A., Marcus, W.A., and Aspinall, R.J. 2000. Evaluation of multispectral, fine scale digital imagery as a tool for mapping stream morphology: *Geomorphology* **33**: 107–120.

# LiDAR and ADCP Use in Gravel-bed Rivers: Advances Since GBR6

## David J. Milan and George L. Heritage

## 22.1 INTRODUCTION

Marcus (Chapter 21, this volume) presents a comprehensive review of the applications and advances of aerial and satellite remote-sensing approaches to fluvial systems. Aerial light detection and ranging (LiDAR) is highlighted by Marcus as a key technique for remotely sensing rivers for a variety of hydrological and morphological applications. Although LiDAR data acquired from aerial platforms provide a means of gathering information over large areas (e.g., catchment scale), finer-scale information such as bed elevation, water depth, and grain size are often subject to root mean square errors (RMSE) that are larger than the changes being measured. There is often a high cost associated with data obtained from aerial platforms, and the temporal frequency of survey acquisition may be restricted due to both cost and poor atmospheric conditions (e.g., cloud). Instruments deployed from terrestrial- and aquatic-based platforms overcome these issues; they retrieve higher-resolution data, are cheaper to deploy and sites may potentially be sampled more frequently. This discussion focuses upon the recent advances using terrestrial- and aquatic-based platforms, in addition to providing more focus on the advances made in LiDAR in relation to river studies. A key data gap with LiDAR studies is the difficulty in obtaining data from the submerged bed in shallow rivers (<0.3 m), characteristic of gravel-bed river environments. The role of acoustic Doppler current profiling (ADCP), as a possible means of obtaining the data from this environment is explored.

## 22.2 LiDAR

The application of LiDAR to fluvial systems has seen a rapid increase since 2000, partly due to wider availability of hardware and the introduction of terrestrial LiDAR.

LiDAR systems have evolved from being research tools to widely available commercial tools. The number of river studies published utilizing LiDAR has taken a sharp increase since 2005; from an average of one publication a year between 2000 and 2005, to seven a year between 2005 and 2010 (Table 22.1).

### 22.2.1 Aerial Infrared LiDAR

Aerial LiDAR is mounted either on a small aircraft or a helicopter, which is usually flown anywhere between 300 and 2000 m altitude (Table 22.2), where it measures distances to the earth's surface based on the time of return flight of the laser pulse. Pulsed laser scanners use a high frequency (typically 25 000 to 150 000 laser pulses per second), eye-safe infrared laser source (1064 nm wavelength) emitted in precisely defined angular directions controlled by a spinning mirror arrangement. Distances are initially referenced to the position of the aircraft. The trajectory of the aircraft itself is determined through an on-board dGPS that receives data that are post-processed and then corrected, based upon the position of a base station located over a known benchmark. The attitude (pitch, yaw, and roll) of the aircraft during the survey is recorded by an inertial measurement unit (IMU) consisting of high-precision orthogonal gyroscopes and accelerometers. Distance, position, and IMU data are used in conjunction with a geoid model to determine longitude, latitude, and elevation for survey points on the ground (see Heritage and Large, 2009 for a more detailed review of instrument types). Point measurement density depends on laser frequency, aircraft speed, altitude, ground terrain, and vegetation. Research published to date indicates that point densities at best are of the order of 5 points $m^{-2}$ (Cavalli *et al.*, 2008), but more commonly in the order of 1–3 points $m^{-2}$ (Höfle *et al.*, 2009). However, current instruments used by the United Kingdom

*Gravel-bed Rivers: Processes, Tools, Environments*, First Edition. Edited by Michael Church, Pascale M. Biron and André G. Roy.
© 2012 John Wiley & Sons, Ltd. Published 2012 by John Wiley & Sons, Ltd.

**Table 22.1** Terrestrial, aerial, and bathymetric LiDAR studies in river environments

| Scale | Study | River | Details |
|---|---|---|---|
| *Terrestrial* | | | |
| Clast–patch | Hodge et al. (2009a and 2009b) | Feshie and Bury Green Brook, UK | High-resolution survey (35–54 pts cm$^{-1}$) data for 1 m$^2$ patches of bar surfaces. DEMs produced. Grain size and structure information collected |
| | Heritage and Milan (2009) | South Tyne, UK | Gravel patch information extracted from bar surface scans. Grain roughness data extracted through filtering data using standard deviation moving window over point cloud |
| | Milan (2009) | Kingsdale Beck, UK | TLS data are used as the boundary for 3-D hydraulic modelling over gravel patches |
| Bar scale | Entwistle and Fuller (2009) | Kingsdale Beck, UK | Surface grain size and facies determination |
| | Heritage and Milan (2009) | South Tyne, UK | Grain roughness maps of whole bar surfaces demonstrated |
| | Heritage et al. (2009) | Nent, UK | Survey strategies and interpolation methods for DEM construction assessed using TLS dataset of gravel bar as control |
| | Alho et al. (2009) | Pulmankijoki River, Finland | Bar surfaces scanned to an accuracy of 2 cm in $x,y$ and 4 cm in $z$. Data linked into larger survey at reach scale involving BoMMS |
| | Milan et al. (2009) | Rede, UK | Grain roughness and morphological changes over a sequence of floods is demonstrated |
| Reach scale | Heritage and Hetherington (2007) | Wharfe, UK | Protocols for use of TLS in river morphological survey presented for single thread 150 m channel |
| | Milan et al. (2007) | Ferpecle, Swiss Alps | Daily repeat survey and sediment budgeting exercise conducted on a 5881 m$^2$ area of proglacial river |
| | Straatsma et al. (2008) | Rhine (Ijssel and Waal tributaries) Netherlands | River floodplains and vegetation surveyed (1000 m$^2$) |
| | Wasklewicz and Hattanji (2009) | Ashio mountains, Japan | Hillslope–headwater stream coupling. Morphological analysis of headwater streams (100 m length). Cross-section data extracted from point cloud |
| | Pizzuto et al. (2010) | Brandywine Creek, South River, US | Bank erosion assessment |
| | Morche et al. (2008) | Reintal valley, Germany | Erosion scar assessment, slope-channel coupling sediment budgeting |
| | Jaboyedoff et al. (2009) | Saint-Barnabe-Nord, Canada; Sorge river, Switzerland | Slope-channel coupling (<250 m reach) |
| | Milan et al. (2010) | Rede, UK | Water surface roughness mapping related to instream habitat (<200 m reach) |
| | Antonarakis et al. (2009; 2010) | Garonne and Allier, France | Riparian leaf and tree scanning for resistance estimation in flood modelling |

*(Continued)*

**Table 22.1** (Continued)

| Scale | Study | River | Details |
|---|---|---|---|
| *Aerial*<br>Reach scale | Jones *et al.* (2007) | Dee and Teifi UK | Morphological mapping of river floodplains ($<3$ km reaches) |
| | Bowen and Waltermire (2002) | Green River, US | River corridor survey (1.5 km reach) |
| | Alho *et al.* (2009) | Pulmankijoki River, Finland | BoMMS TLS surveying of river channel from a boat, linked in with bar-scale TLS. 0.7 km$^2$ covered in 85 mins |
| | Cavalli *et al.* (2008) | Rio Cordon, Italy | Differentiation of channel morphology based upon surface roughness. 2725 m reach analysed |
| | Charlton *et al.* (2003) | Coquet, UK | Appraisal of accuracy of aerial LiDAR for gravel-bed river re-survey (2 km reach) |
| | Gilvear *et al.* (2004) | Forth, UK | River hydromorphology of estuaries (1 km reaches) |
| | French (2003) | Blyth, UK | Use of LiDAR data for hydraulic modelling of estuary (10 km reach) |
| | Marks and Bates (2000) and Bates *et al.* (2003) | Stour, UK | Floodplain flow modelling (12 km reach) |
| | Cobby *et al.* (2001) | Severn, UK | Flood modelling. 144 km$^2$ area surveyed |
| | Matgen *et al.* (2007) | Alzette, Luxembourg | Flood modelling ($<10$ km reach) |
| | Chust *et al.* (2008) | Bidasoa, France/Spain border | Estuarine habitat mapping |
| | Aggett and Wilson (2009) | Naches river, US | Hydraulic modelling ($<400$ m reaches) |
| | Höfle *et al.* (2009) | Inn and Hintereisferner, Austria | Water surface mapping (20 km and 3 km reaches) |
| | Overton *et al.* (2009) | Murray, Australia | Floodplain vegetation mapping and flood modelling |
| | Notebaert *et al.* (2009) | Dijle and Ambleve | Geomorphological mapping, short-term morphological change, sediment budgeting. Reaches $<3$ km in length |
| Catchment scale | Pirotti and Tarolli (2010) | Rio Cordon, Italy | Channel network extraction. Catchment area 0.7 km$^2$ |
| | Murphy *et al.* (2008) | Swan Hills, Canada | Stream network modelling 193 ha catchment |
| | James *et al.* (2007) | South Carolina piedmont, US | Gully and headwater stream mapping in forested areas (800 and 1600 km$^2$ areas) |
| | Hopkinson *et al.* (2009) | Lake O'Hara, US | Watershed characterization (14 km$^2$ catchment) |
| *Bathymetric*<br>Reach scale | Kinzel *et al.* (2006; 2007) | Platte, US | Bathymetric LiDAR, EAARL system |
| | Hilldale and Raff (2007) | Yakima and Trinity, US | Bathymetric LiDAR using SHOALS-1000T system ($<220$ km) |
| | Hilldale (2007) | | Bathymetric LiDAR used in 2-D hydraulic modelling of aquatic habitat |
| | Bailly *et al.* (2010) | Gardon, France | Bathymetric LiDAR using Hawkeye II system (1.5 km reach) |

**Table 22.2** LiDAR instrumentation used in fluvial and hydrologic studies[1]

| Instrument | Wave-length | Range/Altitude (m) | Accuracy | Point density/spacing | Footprint size | Speed of data capture | Scan angle | Studies |
|---|---|---|---|---|---|---|---|---|
| **Terrestrial infrared LiDAR** | | | | | | | | |
| Riegl LMS Z-210 | 0·9 µm | <100 m | 5 mm | | | | 8000–12000 pts s$^{-1}$ | 0·036° in the vertical and 0·018° in the horizontal step-width angle (0·072°) | Heritage and Hetherington (2007); Milan et al. (2007); Milan et al. (2010) |
| Leica Scan station HDS3000 | | <100 m | 1.3 mm (mean of 3 scans), Position 6 mm at 50 m | 35–54 pts cm$^{-1}$ prior to filtering, 17–30 pts m$^{-2}$ post filtering | 6 mm at 50 m | 3000–4000 pts s$^{-1}$ | 360°×270° FoV | Straatsma et al. (2008); Hodge et al (2009a and b); Wasklewicz and Hattanji (2009) |
| Optech ILRIS-3D | 1500 nm | Range 3–1500 m | Range 7 mm @ 100 m, position 8 mm @ 100 m | | | 2500 pts s$^{-1}$ | | Morche et al. (2008); Jaboyedoff et al. (2009) |
| Leica HDS6000 | | | 2 cm in $x,y$ and 4 cm in $z$ | Point spacing of 6 mm at 10 m | | | | Alho et al. (2009) |
| FARO LS 880HE80 | | | | 15.7 mm at 20 m | | 8000 pts over one rev scanning mirror | 360° angular resolution of 0.045° | Alho et al. (2009) |
| Trimble GS2000 | | | 1.3 mm at 100m | | | | | Pizzuto et al. (2010) |
| **Aerial infrared LiDAR** | | | | | | | | |
| Optech 2033 | | Altitude 800 m | | | | | | Marks and Bates (2000); Bates et al. (2003); Jones et al. (2007) |
| Optech ALTM1020 | 1047 nm | Altitude 800 m | RMSE of ±0.10 m to ±0.15 m | 1 point per 7 m$^2$ | | | scan angle ±19°, scan rate 13 Hz, pulse rate 5 kHz | Cobby et al. (2001); Charlton et al. (2003); French (2003); Gilvear et al. (2004) |
| Not reported | | | 0.43 m RMSE for $z$ | | | | | Bowen and Waltermire (2002) |
| Mace system | | | | 0.13 points m$^2$, point spacing 2.8 m | | | | James et al. (2007) |
| Comp 32 system | | | | 0.1 points m$^2$, point spacing 3.24 m | | | | James et al. (2007) |
| OPTECH ALTM 3100 | 1064 nm | 1000 m 500–2000 m | 0.13–0.14 m (RMSE) | 5 points m$^2$, 1–4 m | 0.3 m at 1000 m 0.6 m at 2000 m | | | Cavalli et al. (2008); Hopkinson et al. (2009); Holfe et al. (2009); Pirotti and Tarolli (2010) *(Continued)* |

**Table 22.2** (*Continued*)

| Instrument | Wave-length | Range/Altitude (m) | Accuracy | Point density/spacing | Footprint size | Speed of data capture | Scan angle | Studies |
|---|---|---|---|---|---|---|---|---|
| Optech ALTM 3025 | 1064 nm | | 0.15 m (RMSE) | | | | | Chust *et al.* (2008) |
| Optech ALTM 2050 | 1064 nm | | | | | | ± 20 degrees | Holfe *et al.* (2009) |
| AeroScan laser scanner | | | Horizontal ±40 cm, vertical ±20 cm | 1.4–3.2 points m$^2$ Point spacing of 3.77 m | | | | Aggett and Wilson (2009) |
| **Aerial bathymetric/bathymetric-infrared combined LiDAR** | | | | | | | | |
| Optech SHOALS-1000T | 1064 nm and 532 nm | 300 m | ±0.25 m | | | | | Hilldale and Raff (2007) |
| Hawkeye II system | 1064 nm and 532 nm | | 0.2–0.32 m | Submerged channel was 0.9 pts m$^{-2}$ | | | | Bailly *et al.* (2010) |
| EAARL | 532 nm | 300 m at 50 ms$^{-1}$ | RMSE for z for exposed areas of 0.11 m and for submerged areas 0.18 m | 2 pts per 2.5 m in the centre and 2 pts per 4 m along edges of 240 m swath | 0.15 m | 21 scans s$^{-1}$ | | Kinzel *et al.* (2007) |

[1]Terrestrial and aerial near-infrared and aerial bathymetric LiDAR are differentiated. Entries are organized based on the date of the earliest published study utilizing the instrument. Blank entries represent instances in which data were not reported or were not applicable.

Environment Agency can achieve point densities of up to 16 points $m^{-2}$.

Whilst this resolution is suitable for surveying small river catchments (e.g., Pirotti and Tarolli, 2010) and mesoscale channel morphology (e.g., Charlton et al., 2003) it is not suitable for finer-scale morphological characterization or for capturing grain-scale roughness. Most river studies have concentrated on long reaches 2–200 km in length (Table 22.1). Vertical accuracy at best on flat surfaces is of the order of ±0.15 m (RMSE). Bowen and Waltermire (2002) suggest that whilst this vertical accuracy may be obtained for uniform flat surfaces, undulating and varied terrain is likely to give poorer vertical accuracy, and quote a value of 0.43 m RMSE for the elevation value ($z$). Good data returns may be obtained from solid ground surfaces and vegetation, with fewer from water surfaces. Infrared LiDAR has been used to detect water surfaces using both aerial (Höfle et al., 2009) and terrestrially-based platforms (Milan et al., 2010). Retrieval of data from the submerged part of the river channel is, however, problematic, and is perhaps the major challenge in river studies where data on depth and submerged roughness/grain size are crucial to developing the hydraulic modelling and habitat quantification aspects of the technique. Infrared LiDAR is attenuated by water, such that no returns are obtained from the river bed. As a consequence LiDAR data have been combined with passive techniques applied in the submerged areas of the channel to produce full river topographic maps (e.g., Hicks et al., 2001; Lane et al., 2003).

### 22.2.2 Terrestrial LiDAR

Terrestrial LiDAR hardware is very similar to that used on aerial platforms, however most of the instruments are designed for surveying objects at closer range (typically < 100 m). Furthermore, a broader range of manufacturers produce terrestrial LiDAR systems in comparison to aerial LiDAR (Table 22.2). Although terrestrial LiDAR cannot survey areas as large as aerial LiDAR, the instruments can provide greater vertical accuracy (± 5 mm) and higher point densities. This has been shown to produce high quality DEMs of river beds (Heritage et al., 2009) which, in turn, has led to improved sediment budgeting (Milan et al., 2007), and more detailed insights into processes of channel response. A further significant advantage of terrestrial LiDAR is the ability to obtain data on surface roughness (Heritage and Milan, 2009; Hodge et al., 2009a). This information is of critical importance for numerical hydraulic modelling studies, and sediment transport equations. Without the restrictions of having to rely on aircraft, re-surveys of areas may be conducted more frequently. Terrestrial

LiDAR may be deployed during cloudy conditions, however atmospheric conditions such as fog or drizzle can hamper surveys.

Terrestrial LiDARs are set up on a tripod and the feature of interest is scanned obliquely. To make sure no areas of shadow exist in the scan, multiple scans are taken around the feature of interest, which also increases point resolution and accuracy. A series of reflectors placed in the scanning environment act as fixed points enabling the sequence of scans to be merged into one larger point cloud, with the aid of post-processing computer software (Heritage and Hetherington, 2007).

### 22.2.3 Bathymetric LiDAR

Bathymetric LiDAR is a more recent technological advance that uses laser light in the blue-green wavelength (532 nm) to overcome attenuation through the water column. Bathymetric LiDAR is advantageous over other remote-sensing methods that are used to retrieve depth information (e.g., aerial black and white imagery, multispectral imagery, and hyperspectral imagery) in that data can be obtained concurrently from dry areas of the bed and from the floodplain, providing a full dataset for areas of submergence and potential submergence. The development of this instrumentation has been slow due to eye-safety issues linked to the wavelengths being used. Most blue-green LiDAR systems overcome this by spreading the laser spot intensity over a much larger area (Kinzel et al., 2007). Initial use of bathymetric LiDAR has concentrated upon coastal environments, and it has only recently been applied to rivers (Hilldale and Raff, 2006; Kinzel et al., 2007; Bailly et al., 2010). Hilldale and Raff (2007) suggest it is not yet possible to use bathymetric LiDAR at the microscale (equivalent to the size of a cobble) for numerical modelling or geomorphological analysis because mean errors and standard deviations are too large. Bathymetric LiDAR appears best suited to survey at the mesoscale, e.g., pool, glide, and riffle (Hilldale and Raff, 2007; Bailly et al., 2010). Hilldale (2007) has further demonstrated that bathymetric data are of sufficient quality to simulate river habitat using a 2-D hydraulic model. However, the lower limit of depth detection for bathymetric LiDAR is also an issue, as this is around 0.5 m (Pe'eri and Philpot, 2007). Gravel-bed river science commonly deals with depths less than this. Kinzel et al. (2007), using the experimental NASA EAARL system, have obtained more encouraging results working on a braided sand-bed river, where they obtained RMSE for $z$ for exposed areas of 0.11 m and for submerged areas 0.18 m. More recently Bailly et al. (2010) using the Hawkeye II system found the minimum detectable depth to be 0.32 m (weighted error standard deviation using block kriging).

## 22.3 APPLICATION OF ADCP FOR COMBINED DEPTH AND VELOCITY SURVEY

In addition to direct measurement of depth using bathymetric LiDAR, Marcus (Chapter 21, this volume) identifies aerial photogrammetry and aerial/satellite-based optical approaches (using multiband sensors) as important remote approaches capable of surveying flow depth at large scales. ADCP technology, primarily used to measure and map velocity profiles, provides a further remote means of measuring flow depth at the reach-scale. The advantage of this approach over other remote-sensing methods is the ability to capture data underneath trees and overhanging banks. Modern ADCPs can be used in shallow water, characteristic of gravel-bed rivers, and thus have an advantage over current bathymetric LiDAR technology. Instrument manufacturers quote an accuracy for depth measurement equivalent to 1% of the flow depth, this compares with typical values of 15–30 cm found for photogrammetric and optical approaches (Westaway et al., 2003; Fonstad and Marcus, 2005; Lejot et al., 2007; Lane et al., 2010), and a RMSE of 0.18 m at best for bathymetric LiDAR (Kinzel et al., 2007). Although satellite-based platforms supporting the TerraSAR-X along-track interferometric synthetic aperture radar have recently been demonstrated to provide surface velocity data in river environments (Romeiser et al., 2009), ADCP provides a low cost alternative that is suited to reach-scale surveys obtaining relatively low-density data compared to LiDAR, but generally at a scale sufficient to define ecologically relevant scales in river systems.

### 22.3.1 ADCP Principles and Operating Limits

ADCPs utilize the principle that the frequency of an emitted sound wave from a moving object is affected by the motion of the object, becoming compressed (higher frequency) as the object approaches and extended (reduced frequency) as the object recedes. A constant-frequency sound wave emitted into moving water will be reflected off suspended particles. The frequency of the reflected sound wave changes due to the velocity of the suspended particles in the water column. The change in frequency, recorded back at the point of emission, may be used to determine the speed of the water moving the particle along. If a series of sound waves from known sources is directed into the water column, the 3-D velocity field may be determined from the returned set of pulses, providing information on current trajectory as well as speed. Modern ADCPs are able to emit a rapid series of sound pulses through the water column, recording the modified return frequencies and defining current

speed and direction in segments of the flow throughout the water column. The time taken for the sound waves to return to the ADCP defines the flow depth. These instruments require immersion to work, and are typically used with boat- or shore-based platforms.

Fixed position ADCP devices emitting multiple beams at different angles can thus be used to define the channel boundary and cross-section velocity field, and these data can be used to determine instantaneous discharge. The use of ADCP devices from a moving platform is also developing with RTK or dGPS positioning equipment integrated onboard to define the position of the ADCP across the water surface (e.g., Sime et al., 2007). Pitch, roll, and yaw sensors detect rotation about the downstream, cross-stream, and vertical, and the combined positional, rotational, and Doppler data generate a 3-D dataset of the velocity field.

ADCP use is restricted by the operational frequency of the instrument. Water acts as an efficient absorber of high-frequency energy. Lower frequency sound waves may extend several tens of metres through a water column, but suffer the disadvantage of travelling much more slowly than light. The slow speed of the sound pulse restricts the speed of the moving platform before return signals are missed. Furthermore the footprint of the soundwave impacting on a surface increases with decreasing frequency, resulting in increased areal averaging and loss of local topographic detail. Lower-frequency sound waves emitted from sub-bottom sonar profilers can also penetrate soft bed sediment and reflect off horizons with different density, and may potentially be used to characterize bed sedimentology. Higher-frequency sound pulses allow greater measurement precision and faster data collection, but cannot be used in deep water (>5 m). It is the development of these higher-frequency units that is opening up new opportunities to measure flow and morphology in rivers where shallow water is common.

The intensity of return received back at an ADCP instrument is also directly related to the number of particles encountered in the water column. Hence suspended sediment load and transport rates may also be calculated from the data. Current ADCP instruments are suitable for use in shallow water environments. They also cover a wide velocity range ($0$–$20\,\mathrm{m\,s^{-1}}$) measuring down to $0.001\,\mathrm{m\,s^{-1}}$ to a precision within 0.25% of the measured velocity value. Sample volumes may be as small as $0.02\,\mathrm{m^3}$. ADCP has also been used to measure bedload transport rates (see Rennie, Chapter 25, this volume).

### 22.3.2 Review of the Use of ADCP Technology

Early work on remotely measuring flow patterns utilized low-frequency Doppler devices for large-scale oceanographic, near-shore, and estuary studies (e.g., Simpson and Oltmann, 1993; Stacey *et al.*, 1999). Their use in measuring discharge in riverine environments has expanded since the turn of the century (see Muste *et al.*, 2004). Dinehart and Burau (2005a) have used ADCP data to identify well defined flow regions and secondary flow paths within a reach, confirming previous observational evidence. They were able to capture detailed bathymetry over a series of profile runs and link this to changes in suspended sediment concentration as defined using ADCP intensity data (Dinehart and Burau, 2005b). Sime *et al.* (2007), using a transect-based approach, have demonstrated the application of ADCPs for retrieving shear stress data from gravel-bed rivers. ADCPs have been used to survey channel morphology of large rivers, including the Brahmaputra (Richardson and Thorne 2001), helping to elucidate morphometric thresholds for channel bifurcation. Detailed 3-D hydraulic data have also been retrieved from smaller gravel-bed channels. For example, Wilcox and Wohl (2007) report on the 3-D hydraulics for a short (30 m) reach of a step-pool channel, demonstrating the extreme stage-dependent hydraulic variation characteristic of this channel type. Channel morphology derived from ADCP instrument data have also been used to define initial model boundary data for flow and sediment transport modelling. For example, Tiron *et al.* (2009) used a 1-D model to investigate processes operating through a cutoff meander on the River Danube, whilst Li *et al.* (2008) have used ADCP data for 2-D modelling of morphologic change and gravel transport along a complex wandering channel.

## 22.4 EXAMPLE STUDIES

### 22.4.1 Roughness Studies

Marcus (Chapter 21, this volume) highlights the use of aerial imagery for grain-size detection, which has the potential to be applied at the catchment scale (e.g., Carbonneau *et al.*, 2004). There have also been developments in the use of digital imagery and automated processing techniques that provide accurate representations of grain size, but are limited to small areas (e.g., Butler *et al.*, 2001; Sime and Ferguson, 2003; Rubin, 2004; Graham *et al.*, 2005; Buscombe, 2008). Following a simple filtering procedure, terrestrial LiDAR point clouds provide a means of mapping grain roughness and grain size at intermediate (reach) scales.

#### 22.4.1.1 Grain Roughness and Grain Size

Through filtering the point cloud derived from terrestrial LiDAR, it is possible to extract information on surface roughness. Grain roughness of gravel beds is an important parameter in hydraulic models, whilst grain-size character is important for instream benthos and the success of fish spawning (Kondolf *et al.*, 2008). Grain roughness and size are usually derived from a Wolman count (see Wolman, 1954) taken from a geomorphic unit. This procedure requires the sampler to randomly measure the intermediate axis of 100 clasts taken from the bed surface for each unit. Cumulative grain-size curves may be produced from the data, and often the $D_{84}$ is related to the surface roughness (e.g., Hey, 1979). The drawback with this conventional approach is that no information is retrieved concerning spatial variability in surface texture across the bed at the geomorphic unit scale. Furthermore, the method is intrusive, requiring the bed fabric to be disturbed during the process of sampling. Heritage and Milan (2009) and Hodge *et al.* (2009a) have both used data-filtering approaches to extract roughness information from terrestrial LiDAR point clouds through treating the point cloud as a random elevation field. Working on exposed bars at Lambley on the South Tyne and the River Rede, in northern England, Heritage and Milan (2009) extracted the standard deviation ($\sigma$) of all the $z$ values in a moving-window equivalent to the size of the largest visible clast, over the point cloud. Standard deviation values, used to represent grain roughness, were then attributed to a 1 cm regular grid. Grain roughness maps are then produced from the grid (Figure 22.1). This procedure allows grain roughness to be assessed remotely, and provides fine spatial detail not retrieved from conventional Wolman counts. Changes in surface texture may be monitored through re-survey and grain roughness change maps may be produced (Figure 22.1b).

Terrestrial LiDAR is able to survey only the extent to which grains protrude, i.e., the grain roughness, and cannot provide any information on buried or hidden parts of the clast. Despite this, terrestrial LiDAR-derived grain roughness does show a strong relation with grain size. Heritage and Milan (2009) found very strong linear relations between patch roughness ($2\sigma$) and Wolman counts (Figure 22.2), although the character of the relation appeared to vary between patches, possibly relating to variations in grain exposure (degree of burial) and imbrication (Hodge *et al.*, 2009a). Further research is needed to investigate the potential of terrestrial LiDAR to usefully characterize grain roughness and grain size.

#### 22.4.1.2 Biotope Mapping

The term "biotope" is used to describe instream "physical" or "hydraulic" habitat. Biotopes are distinguished by the hydraulics (water surface flow type; Figure 22.3a) associated with a particular morphology, bed slope, and local bed roughness, over a range of flows

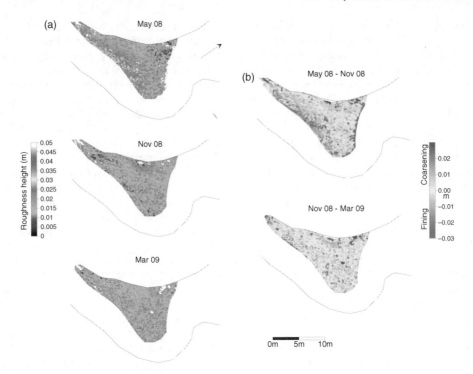

**Figure 22.1** (a) Grain roughness maps, and (b) grain roughness change maps for the River Rede. Grain roughness, measure of clast protrusion, is derived from taking the standard deviations ($\sigma_z$) of elevations in a moving window over the point cloud, usually equivalent to the size of the largest clast. $\sigma_z$ values are then attributed to a 1 cm regular grid. (See the color version of this figure in color plate section.)

(Padmore *et al.*, 1998). Links between biotopes and instream biota have recently been demonstrated for macroinvertebrate communities (Reid and Thoms, 2008). Since the introduction of the European Union Water Framework Directive, biotope mapping in Europe is becoming increasingly integrated into river corridor survey as a means of logging instream river health (Dodkins *et al.*, 2005). Biotope mapping is based on visual differentiation of surface flow type by trained observers. Despite this, the procedure remains a subjective exercise and is open to identification errors. Milan *et al.* (2010) have used terrestrial LiDAR to quantitatively map water surface flow type by measuring water surface roughness taken from first return scans (Heritage and Large, 2009). Different surface flow types exhibit different surface roughness (Figure 22.3a). The point cloud is filtered using a moving window, this time equivalent to the size of the smallest biotope present (e.g., 0.5 m diameter), and by taking the standard deviation of elevations in the moving window and assigning these to a 0.1 m regular grid. Water surface roughness maps are then produced, which can be related to characteristic water surface roughness delimiters for certain biotopes (Figure 22.3b).

### 22.4.2 Morphological Change

Milan *et al.* (2007) highlighted the advantages of terrestrial LiDAR in a daily re-survey of an active proglacial channel in the Swiss Alps, demonstrating that large reaches (5881 m²) can be surveyed on a daily basis. These workers fitted surfaces (DEMs) to merged point clouds (five scans), and produced DEMs of difference to identify spatial patterns of scour and fill over a 10 day period at the start of the meltwater season in June, 2004. Differences in error between wet and dry areas need to be considered during DEM differencing, and an appropriate level of change detection (LoD) needs to be applied to the respective areas of each DEM in the subtraction. Some laser returns were obtained from the submerged part of the channel, partly due to its shallow nature (generally <0.1 m); vertical errors in the wet part of the channel were found to be greater ($\sigma = 0.047$ m) compared to the dry part ($\sigma = 0.020$ m). Differentiating wet and dry areas accurately on the DEM is problematic and was done manually by Milan *et al.* (2007). A more robust basis for separating wet and dry areas is to use the laser intensity data retrieved from the incident surface. Analysis of laser intensity returns reveals distinct differences

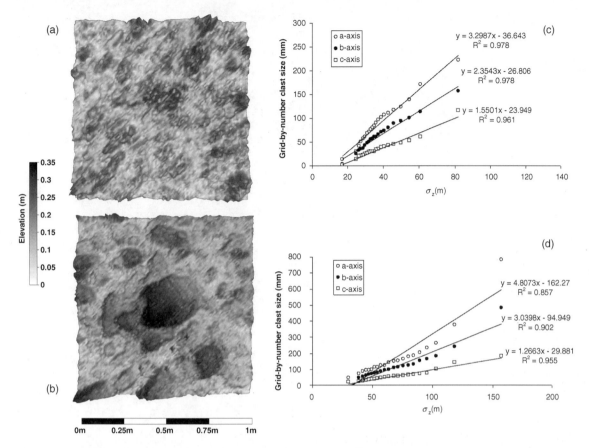

**Figure 22.2** Grain-scale terrestrial LiDAR: (a) and (b) DEMs of 1 m² gravel patches taken from a bar at Lambley, demonstrating differences in surface roughness, (c) and (d) relation between conventionally measured grain size (*a*, *b* and *c* axes) taken from the gravel patches in (a) and (b), and the terrestrial LiDAR-derived grain roughness. Reproduced, with permission, from Heritage, G.L. and Milan, D.J. 2009. Terrestrial laser scanning of grain roughness in a gravel-bed river. *Geomorphology* **113**: 4–11.

in intensity readings from wet and dry areas (Figure 22.4a). Wet and dry areas of the DEM may be separated by using a threshold return intensity and the appropriate error may then be accounted for in the respective parts of the DEM (Figure 22.4b).

### 22.4.3 ADCP Utilization to Characterize the Flow Character Around a Mid-Channel Bar

It is generally recognized that the identification and mapping of instream ecological units is largely a subjective exercise due to the lack of appropriate field survey instruments that can capture detail at the relevant spatial and temporal scales (Marcus, 2002; Legleiter and Goodchild, 2005; Clifford *et al.*, 2006; Heritage *et al.*, 2009). Instruments such as ADCPs may be used to address this issue as it captures the data relevant to determination of Froude number, which is used to define hydraulic habitat

through biotope characterization. An ADCP survey was conducted during December 2009 on a wandering gravel-bed reach on the River Wharfe between Buckden and Starbotton, Yorkshire, UK. The reach was surveyed at low and intermediate flows, both of which bifurcated around a large mid-channel bar.

A SonTek™ M5 ADCP and dGPS unit mounted on a floating hydroboard were used to collect data on water velocity and depth from up to 20 equally sized cells (bins) in the water column (minimum bin size is 2 cm). The stated accuracy for velocity measurements from the ADCP is $\pm 0.001$ m s$^{-1}$ with a profiling range of 0.06 to 5 m (distance) and $\pm 20$ m s$^{-1}$ (velocity). Depths of between 0.1 and 2 m were encountered during the survey, well within the range of the instrument.

Velocity and depth data obtained from the ADCP were used to calculate Froude number (*Fr*) and these data were interpolated to generate the spatial pattern of hydraulic

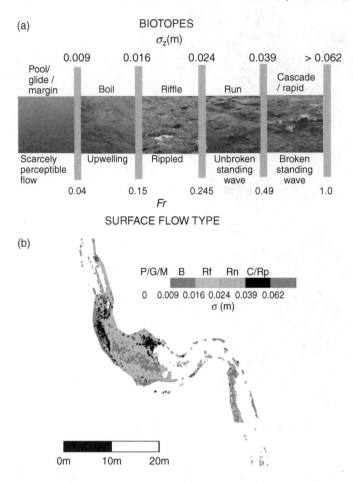

**Figure 22.3** Application of terrestrial LiDAR for water surface roughness mapping for biotope assessment; (a) conceptual model linking water surface roughness (Milan *et al.*, 2010) and Froude number (Newson *et al.*, 1998) delimiters (the boundary between each biotope is fuzzy in nature, and should be considered transitional rather than rigid). Reproduced, with permission, from Entwistle, N., Milan, D.J., and Heritage, G.L. 2010. Biotope mapping using combined LiDAR and acoustic Doppler profiler survey. BHS 3rd International Symposium, Managing Consequences of a Changing Global Environment. Newcastle University, 21–23 July. Proceedings: http://www.ceg.ncl.ac.uk/ bhs2010/ (b) water surface roughness map highlighting distribution of biotopes for the River Rede. P: pool; G: glide; M: marginal deadwater; B: boil; Rf: riffle; Rn: run; C: cascade; Rp: rapid. Reproduced, with permission, from Milan, D.J., Heritage, G.L., Large, A.R.G. and Entwistle, N. 2010. Identification of hydraulic biotopes using terrestrial laser scan data of water surface properties. *Earth Surface Processes & Landforms* **35**: 918–931. Their figure 9. (See the color version of this figure in color plate section.)

variation for the reach (Figure 22.5). Pool-riffle morphology is clearly picked out by variations in flow depth, where a maximum flow depth of just over 2 m was recorded in a pool towards the upstream end of the reach. A backwater pool is also evident on the right bank towards the tail end of the reach. Variations in mean column velocity may also be seen, with greatest velocities occurring over riffles with peaks in the order of

$1.5\,\mathrm{ms}^{-1}$, and the lowest velocities occurring either in pools or in the backwater area where velocities below $0.1\,\mathrm{ms}^{-1}$ were found, supporting the expected pattern at low flow (see Milan *et al.*, 2001). Variations in *Fr* (Figure 22.5c) show lowest values in pools. Small areas of critical and supercritical flow, as displayed by unbroken and broken standing waves on the water surface respectively, are found on the riffles.

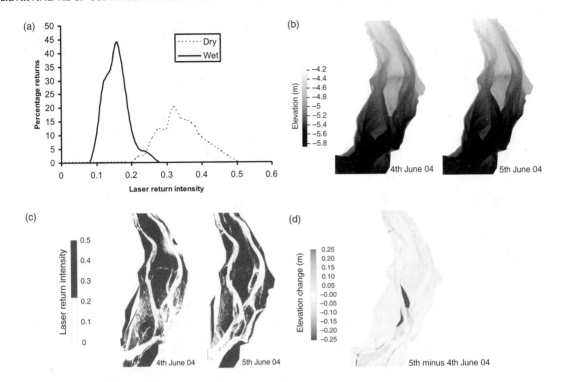

**Figure 22.4**    Terrestrial LiDAR resurvey of a proglacial braided river in the Swiss Alps June 2004: (a) population of laser intensity returns from dry and wet areas of the study reach on 5 June; (b) DEMs of study reach for 4 and 5 June; (c) laser return intensity maps for study reach; blue areas indicate all those where returns were below 0.22 (threshold value taken from Figure 22.4a above), which appear to represent dry bar surfaces, the white areas are those areas where returns are in excess of 0.22, and appear to match up with he locations of submerged parts of the channel; (d) DoD for 5 June minus 4 June surface showing areas of scour and fill. Reproduced, with permission, from Milan, D.J., Hetherington, D. and Heritage, G.L. 2007. Application of a 3D laser scanner in the assessment of erosion and deposition volumes in a proglacial river. *Earth Surface Processes & Landforms* **32**: 1657–1674. Their figures 6 and 7. (See the color version of this figure in color plate section.)

### 22.4.4   Submerged Bed-integrated LiDAR and ADCP

A Riegl™ LMSZ210 scanner was used at the site on the River Wharfe and integrated with the ADCP depth data to generate a DEM for use in the River2D flow modelling package. River2D is a 2-D, depth-averaged finite-element hydrodynamic model. It has been used successfully for modelling natural streams and rivers displaying both supercritical and subcritical flow and variable wetted area. The model is optimized for rapid convergence to steady-state conditions. The digital elevation model of the study reach was degraded to a uniform 1 m data grid and input into the River2D software to generate a 1 m resolution surface mesh using a uniform triangulation algorithm. Surface roughness was defined using the local bed level variation derived from the original survey data. The ADCP used in the study (see Section 22.4.3) has five sensors which provide local flow depth variation linked

to change in the bed topography. The variation amongst individual depths was used to determine local bed roughness, assuming a horizontal water surface datum. Inflow and outflow discharge and flow stage boundaries were set during hydraulic model runs based on low flow survey data and high flow 1-D backwater model estimates. These were refined within the program during model runs to satisfy the conservation of mass and momentum equations. Six discharges were modelled, ranging from low flow up to bankfull stage (0.36, 1, 3, 5, 10, and $20\,\mathrm{m}^3\,\mathrm{s}^{-1}$) and local flow depth and velocity data extracted for each 1 m wetted area node in the model. These data were then transformed to Froude number.

Hydraulic patterns for each modelled flow are shown in Figure 22.6 as biotope areas (see Wadeson and Rowntree, 1998; Newson *et al.*, 1998; Figure 22.3a) based on the Froude number distribution through the reach. It is

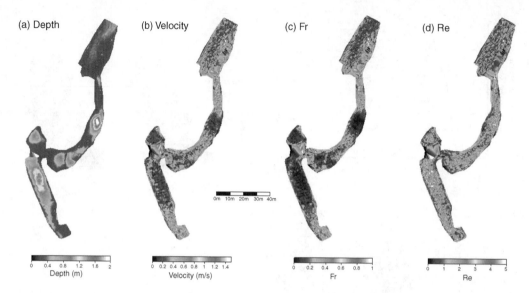

**Figure 22.5**   Hydraulic data obtained using the ADCP for River Wharfe site; (a) water depth; (b) mean column velocity; (c) *Fr*; and (d) $Re \times 10^{-6}$. Data were interpolated using TINs and maps were produced from a 0.1 m grid. Flow direction is from the top of the page downwards. Reproduced, with permission, from Entwistle, N., Milan, D.J., and Heritage, G.L. 2010. Biotope mapping using combined LiDAR and acoustic Doppler profiler survey. *BHS 3rd International Symposium, Managing Consequences of a Changing Global Environment.* Newcastle University, 21–23 July. British Hydrological Society, Proceedings, Their figure 5. (See the color version of this figure in the color plate section.)

clear from the changing colours of the biotope maps that there is a gradual move from lower energy to higher energy biotopes as discharge increases. At flows below $1 \, \text{m}^3 \, \text{s}^{-1}$ (summer levels) pool biotopes are dominant behind the riffle sites and higher-energy biotope units are restricted to shallower flow areas. As flow increases to general winter levels ($3–5 \, \text{m}^3 \, \text{s}^{-1}$) higher energy biotopes extend across the pool areas with rippled flow and unbroken standing waves gaining dominance. The large transverse bar extending downstream off of the central bar surface becomes very energetic and displays a wide variety of biotope types as its wetted area is increased at higher discharges. Although the low flow pool biotopes maintain a degree of uniformity, transforming to higher-energy rippled areas, the activation of the right bank subchannel and the increasing influence of the downstream transverse bar serve to further increase biotope diversity during flood flows (10 and $20 \, \text{m}^3 \, \text{s}^{-1}$).

The pattern of biotope dominance is clear, with pools declining in areal extent as flow increases, largely being replaced by unbroken standing waves. The changing energy regime is reflected in a change in the skew of the biotope distribution from lower-energy units to higher-energy units. The increased wetted area across the downstream transverse bar feature ensures that overall biotope diversity does not decline at higher discharges.

The patterns of biotope distribution and dominance are both interesting and unique. Modelling discharges across the whole flow regime at the site offers insights into hydraulic habitat patterns that have rarely, if ever, been measured in nature. The results confirm a general increase in higher-energy biotopes as discharge increases and a loss of pools in favour of unbroken standing waves. It also shows that in morphologically diverse areas, the expected increase in biotope uniformity with discharge does not occur. This is due to submergence of different morphologies (e.g., mid-channel bar) that increase biotope diversity, particularly along marginal areas.

## 22.5   FUTURE DEVELOPMENTS TOWARDS GBR8

Considerable progress has been made with regard to the application of infrared LiDAR to fluvial systems since GBR6. The use of LiDAR is likely to continue to grow as aerial LiDAR datasets become more widespread and terrestrial LiDAR systems become increasingly adaptable and available. Aerial LiDAR has proven particularly useful for flood modelling purposes and for coarse-scale morphological analysis. Grain-scale resolution LiDAR is now retrievable using terrestrial LiDAR at the reach-scale, although limited to dry areas of river bed.

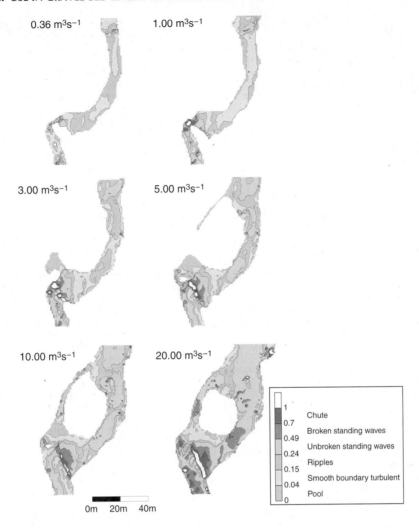

**Figure 22.6** Changing biotope distribution with increasing flow for the River Wharfe study site using the River2D hydraulic model. (See the color version of this figure in color plate section.)

Grain-scale high-resolution topographic models of river reaches that integrate exposed and submerged areas of the river bed will improve hydraulic modelling. However, care must be exercised with regard to error when utilizing LiDAR systems at the limit of their capability. Although bathymetric LiDAR has been shown to successfully map meso-scale morphological features (e.g., pools, and riffles), retrieval of data at the precision required for CFD modelling is still not possible. The use of ADCPs in conjunction with terrestrial LiDAR appears to offer a very successful way forward to retrieve high-quality survey data for both dry and wet areas of the bed, and has the advantage of providing high-resolution hydraulic data. Developments in bathymetric LiDAR are needed to improve data gathered from shallow rivers over long channel reaches and whole catchments.

## 22.6    REFERENCES

Aggett, G.R. and Wilson, J.P. 2009. Creating and coupling a high-resolution DTM with a 1-D hydraulic model in a GS for scenario-based assessment of avulsion hazard in a gravel-bed river. *Geomorphology* **113**: 21–34.

Alho, P., Kukko, A., Hyyppä, H. *et al.* 2009. Application of boat-based laser scanning for river survey. *Earth Surface Processes and Landforms* **34**: 1831–1838.

Antonarakis, A.S., Richards, K.S., Brasington, J., and Bithell, M. 2009. Leafless roughness of complex tree morphology using terrestrial laser scanning. *Water Resources Research* **45**: W10401. doi: 10.1029/2008WR007666.

Antonarakis, A.S., Richards, K.S., Brasington, J., and Muller, E. 2010. Determining leaf area index and leafy tree roughness using terrestrial laser scanning. *Water Resources Research* **46**: W06510. doi: 10.1029/2009WE008318.

Bailly, J., Le Coarer, Y., Languille, P., Stigermark, C., and Allouis, T. 2010. Geostatistical estimations of bathymetric

LiDAR errors on rivers. *Earth Surface Processes and Landforms* **35**: 1199–1210.

Bates, P.D., Marks, K.J., and Horritt, M.S. 2003. Optimal use of high-resolution topographic data in flood inundation models. *Hydrological Processes* **17**: 537–557.

Bowen, Z. and Waltermire, R.G. 2002. Evaluation of light detection and ranging (LiDAR) for measuring river corridor topography. *Journal of the American Water Resources Association* **38**: 33–41.

Buscombe, D. 2008. Estimation of grain-size distributions and associated parameters from digital images of sediment. *Sedimentary Geology* **210**: 1–10.

Butler, J.B., Lane, S.N., and Chandler, J.H. 2001. Automated extraction of grain-size data from gravel surfaces using digital image processing. *Journal of Hydraulic Research* **39**: 519–529.

Carbonneau P.E., Lane, S.N., and Bergeron, N.E. 2004. Catchment-scale mapping of surface grain size in gravel bed rivers using airborne digital imagery. *Water Resources Research* **40**: W07202. doi: 10.1029/2003WR002759.

Cavalli, M., Tarolli, P., Marchi, L. and Fontanna, G.D. 2008. The effectiveness of airborne LiDAR data in the recognition of channel-bed morphology. *Catena* **73**: 249–260.

Charlton, M.E., Large, A.R.G., and Fuller, I.C. 2003. Application of airborne LiDAR in river environments: the river Coquet, Northumberland, UK. *Earth Surface Processes and Landforms* **28**: 299–306.

Chust, G., Galparsoro, I., Borja, Á., Franco, J., and Uriarte, A. 2008. Coastal and estuarine habitat mapping, using LiDAR height and intensity and multispectral imagery. *Estuarine, Coastal and Shelf Science* **78**: 633–643.

Clifford, N.J., Harmar, O.P., Harvey, G., and Petts, G.E. 2006. Physical habitat, eco-hydraulics and river design: a review and re-evaluation of some popular concepts and methods. *Aquatic Conservation, Marine and Freshwater Science* **16**: 389–408.

Cobby, D.M., Mason, D.C., and Davenport, I.J. 2001. Image processing of airborne scanning laser altimetry data for improved river flood modeling. *Journal of Photogrammetry and Remote Sensing* **56**: 121–138.

Dinehart R.L. and Burau J.R. 2005a. Averaged indicators of secondary flow in repeated acoustic Doppler current profiler crossings of bends. *Water Resources Research* **41**: W09405. doi: 10.1029/2005WR004050.

Dinehart R.L. and Burau J.R. 2005b. Repeated surveys by acoustic Doppler current profiler for flow and sediment dynamics in a tidal river. *Journal of Hydrology* **314**: 1–21.

Dodkins I., Rippey B., Harrington, T.J. *et al.* 2005. Developing an optimal river typology for biological elements within the Water Framework Directive. *Water Research* **39**: 3479–3486.

Entwistle, N.S. and Fuller, I.C. 2009. Terrestrial laser scanning to derive the surface grain size character of gravel bars. In Heritage, G.L. and Large, A.R.G., editors. *Laser Scanning for the Environment Sciences*. Oxford, Wiley-Blackwell, pp. 102–114.

Fonstad, M.A. and Marcus, W.A. 2005. Remote sensing of stream depths with hydraulically assisted bathymetry (HAB) models. *Geomorphology* **72**: 107–120.

French, J.R. 2003. Airborne LiDAR in support of geomorphological and hydraulic modeling. *Earth Surface Processes and Landforms* **28**: 321–335.

Gilvear, D., Tyler, A., and Davids, C. 2004. Detection of estuarine and tidal river hydromorphology using hyperspectral and LiDAR data: Forth estuary, Scotland. *Estuarine, Coastal and Shelf Science* **61**: 379–392.

Graham, D.J., Rice, S.P., and Reid, I. 2005. A transferable method for the automated grain sizing of river gravels. *Water Resources Research* **41**: W07020. doi: 10.1029/2004 WR003868.

Heritage, G.L. and Large, A.R.G. 2009. Principles of 3D laser scanning. In Heritage, G.L. and Large, A.R.G., editors. *Laser Scanning for the Environment Sciences*. Oxford, Wiley-Blackwell, pp. 21–34.

Heritage, G. and Hetherington, D. 2007. Towards a protocol for laser scanning in fluvial geomorphology. *Earth Surface Processes and Landforms* **32**: 66–74.

Heritage, G. L. and Milan, D.J. 2009. Terrestrial laser scanning of grain roughness in a gravel-bed river. *Geomorphology* **113**: 4–11.

Heritage, G.L., Milan, D.J., Large, A.R.G., Fuller, I., and Hetherington, D. 2009. Influence of survey strategy and interpolation model upon DEM quality. *Geomorphology* **112**: 334–344.

Hey, R.D. 1979. Flow resistance in gravel-bed rivers, American Society of Civil Engineers, *Journal of the Hydraulics Division* **91**: 365–379.

Hicks, D. M., Duncan, M. J., Walsh, J. M., Westaway. R. M., and Lane. S. N. 2001. New views of the morphodynamics of large braided rivers from high-resolution topographic surveys and time-lapse video. In Dyer., F.J., Thoms, M.C., and Olley, J.M., editors. *The Structure, Function and Management Implications of Fluvial Sedimentary Systems*. International Association for Hydrological Sciences, Publication 276, pp. 373–380.

Hilldale, R.C. 2007. Using bathymetric LiDAR and a 2-D hydraulic model to quantify aquatic habitat. *Proceedings of the World Environmental and Water Resources Congress, Tampa, FL, 15–19 May*. American Society of Civil Engineers, CD-ROM.

Hilldale, R.C. and Raff, D. 2007. Assessing the ability of airborne LiDAR to map river bathymetry. *Earth Surface Processes and Landforms* **33**: 773–783.

Hodge, R., Brasington, J., and Richards, K. 2009a. *In situ* characterization of grain-scale fluvial morphology using terrestrial laser scanning. *Earth Surface Processes and Landforms* **34**: 954–968.

Hodge, R., Brasington, J., and Richards, K. 2009b. Analysing laser-scanned digital terrain models of gravel bed surfaces: linking morphology to sediment transport processes and hydraulics. *Sedimentology* **56**: 2024–2043.

Höfle, B., Vetter, M., Pfeifer, N., Mandlburger, G., and Stötter, J. 2009. Water surface mapping from airborne laser scanning using signal intensity and elevation data. *Earth Surface Processes and Landforms* **34**: 1635–1649.

Hopkinson, C., Hayashi, M., and Peddle, D. 2009. Comparing alpine watershed attributes from LiDAR, photogrammetric, and contour-based digital elevation models. *Hydrological Processes* **23**: 451–463.

Jaboyedoff, M., Demers, D., Locat, J. *et al.* 2009. Use of terrestrial laser scanning for the characterization of retrogressive landslides in sensitive clay and rotational landslides in river banks. *Canadian Geotechnical Journal* **46**: 1379–1390.

James, L.A., Watson, D.G., and Hansen, W.F. 2007. Using LiDAR data to map gullies and headwater streams under forest canopy: South Carolina, *USA. Catena*, **71**: 132–144.

Jones, A, F., Brewer, P.A., Johnstone, E., and Macklin, M.G. 2007. High-resolution interpretive geomorphological mapping of river valley environments using airborne LiDAR data. *Earth Surface Processes and Landforms* **32**: 1574–1592.

Kinzel, P.J., Wright, C.W., and Nelson, J.M., 2006. Application of an experimental scanner for surveying a braided river channel. In *Proceedings of the 8th Interagency Sedimentation Conference, 2–6 April, 2006, Reno, Nevada*, Sub Committee on Sedimentation, CD-ROM.

Kinzel, P.J., Wright, C.W., Nelson, J.M., and Burman, A.R. 2007. Evaluation of an experimental LiDAR for surveying a shallow, braided, sand-bedded river. *Journal of Hydraulic Engineering* 133: 838–842.

Kondolf, G.M., Williams, J.G., Horner, T.C., and Milan, D.J. 2008. Quantifying physical degradation of spawning habitat. In Sear, D., DeVries, P., and Greig, S., editors. *Salmon Spawning Habitat in Rivers: Physical Controls, Biological Responses and Approaches to Remediation*. American Fisheries Society Symposium, 65: 249–274.

Lane, S.N., Widdison, P.E., Thomas, R.E. *et al*. 2010. Quantification of braided river channel change using archival digital image analysis. *Earth Surface Processes and Landforms* 35: 971–985.

Lane, S.N., Westaway, R.M., and Hicks, D.M. 2003. Estimation of erosion and deposition volumes in a large, gravel-bed, braided river, using synoptic remote sensing. *Earth Surface Processes and Landforms* 28: 249–271.

Legleiter, C. and Goodchild, M. 2005. Alternative representations of in-stream habitat: classification using remote sensing, hydraulic modeling, and fuzzy logic. *International Journal of Geographical Information Science* 19: 29–50.

Lejot, J., Delacourt, C., Piegay, H. *et al*. 2007. Very high spatial resolution imagery for channel bathymetry and topography from an unmanned mapping controlled platform. *Earth Surface Processes and Landforms* 32: 1705–1725.

Li, S.S., Millar, R.G., and Islam, S. 2008. Modelling gravel transport and morphology for the Lower Fraser River, British Columbia. *Geomorphology* 95: 206–222.

Marcus, W.A. 2002. Mapping of stream microhabitats with high spatial resolution hyperspectral imagery. *Journal of Geographical Systems* 4: 113–126.

Marks, K. and Bates, P. 2000. Integration of high-resolution topographic data with floodplain flow models. *Hydrological Processes* 14: 2109–2122.

Matgen, P., Schumann, G., Henry, J.B., Hoffman, L., and Pfister, L. 2007. Integration of SAR-derived river inundation areas, high-precision topographic data and a river flow model toward near real-time flood management. *International Journal of Applied Earth Observation and Geoinformation* 9: 247–263.

Milan, D.J. 2009. Terrestrial laser scan-derived topographic and roughness data for hydraulic modelling of gravel-bed rivers. In Heritage, G.L. and Large, A. R. G. *Laser Scanning for the Environment Sciences*. Oxford, Wiley-Blackwell, pp. 133–146.

Milan, D.J., Heritage, G.L., and Entwistle, N. 2009. Detecting grain roughness change and sorting patterns in a gravel-bed river using terrestrial laser scanning. *Proceedings of the 33rd Congress of the International Association for Hydraulic Engineering and Research (IAHR), Vancouver, Canada, 10–14 August, 2009*. CD-ROM, IAHR. ISBN: 978-90-78046-08-0.

Milan, D.J., Heritage, G.L., Large, A.R.G., and Charlton, M.E. 2001. Stage-dependent variability in shear stress distribution through a riffle-pool sequences. *Catena* 44: 85–109.

Milan, D.J., Heritage, G.L., Large, A.R.G., and Entwistle, N. 2010. Identification of hydraulic biotopes using terrestrial laser scan data of water surface properties. *Earth Surface Processes & Landforms* 35: 918–931.

Milan, D.J., Hetherington, D., and Heritage, G.L. 2007. Application of a 3D laser scanner in the assessment of erosion and deposition volumes in a proglacial river. *Earth Surface Processes & Landforms* 32: 1657–1674.

Morche, D., Schmidt, K-H., Sahling, I., Herkommer, M., and Kutschera, J. 2008. Volume changes of alpine sediment stores in a state of post-event disequilibrium and the implications for downstream hydrology and bed load transport. *Norsk Geografisk Tidsskrift* 62: 89–101.

Murphy, P.N., Ogilvie, J., Meng, F., and Arp, P. 2008. Stream network modeling using LiDAR and photogrammetric digital elevation models: a comparison and field verification. *Hydrological Processes* 22: 1747–1754.

Muste, M., Yu, K., Pratt, T., and Abraham, D. 2004. Practical Aspects of ADCP Data Use for Quantification of Mean River Flow Characteristics: Part II: Fixed-Vessel Measurements. *Flow Measurement and Instrumentation* 15: 17–28.

Newson, M.D., Harper, D.M., Padmore C.L., Kemp J.L., and Vogel, B. 1998. A cost-effective approach for linking habitats, flow types and species requirements. *Aquatic Conservation: Marine and Freshwater Ecosystems* 8: 431–446.

Notebaert, B., Verstraeten, G., Govers, G., and Poesen, J. 2009. Qualitative and qualitative applications of LiDAR imagery in fluvial geomorphology. *Earth Surface Processes and Landforms* 34: 217–231.

Overton, I.C., Siggins, A., Gallant, J.C., Penton, D., and Byrne, G. 2009. Flood modeling and vegetation mapping in large river systems. In Heritage, G.L. and Large, A. R. G. *Laser Scanning for the Environment Sciences*. Oxford, Wiley-Blackwell, pp. 220–244.

Padmore, C.L., Newson, M.D., and Charlton, M.E. 1998. In-stream habitat in gravel-bed rivers: identification and characterization of biotopes. In Klingeman, P.C., Beschta, R.L., Komar, P.D., and Bradley, J.B., editors. *Gravel-bed Rivers in the Environment*. Highlands Ranch, CO, Water Resources Publications, pp. 345–364.

Pe'eri, S. and Philpot, W. 2007. Increasing the existence of very shallow-water LiDAR measurements using the red-channel waveforms. *IEEE transactions on Geoscience and Remote Sensing* 45: 1217–1223.

Pirotti, F. and Tarolli, P. 2010. Suitability of LiDAR point density and derived landform curvature maps for channel network extraction. *Hydrological Processes* 24: 1187–1197.

Pizzuto, J., O'Neil, M., and Stotts, S. 2010. On the retreat of forested, cohesive riverbanks. *Geomorphology* 116: 341–352.

Reid, M.A. and Thoms, M.C. 2008. Surface flow types, near-bed hydraulics and the distribution of stream macroinvertebrates. *Biogeosciences* 5: 1043–1055.

Richardson, W.R. and Thorne, C.R. 2001. Multiple Stream Flow and Channel Bifurcation in a Braided River. *Geomorphology* 38: 185–196.

Romeiser, R., Suchandt, S., Runge, H., Steinbrecher, U., and Grunler, S. 2009. First analysis of TerraSAR-X along-track InSAR-derived current fields. *Geoscience and Remote Sensing* 48: 820–829.

Rubin, D.M. 2004. A simple autocorrelation algorithm for determining grain size from digital images of sediment. *Journal of Sedimentary Research* 74: 160–165.

Sime, L.C. and Ferguson, R.I. 2003. Information on grain sizes in gravel-bed rivers by automated image analysis. *Journal of Sedimentary Research* 73: 630–636.

Sime, L.C., Ferguson, R.I., and Church, M. 2007. Estimating shear stress from moving boat acoustic Doppler velocity measurements in a large gravel-bed river. *Water Resources Research* 43: W03418. doi: 10.1029/2006WR005069.

Simpson, M.R. and Oltmann, R.N. 1993. *Discharge Measuring System using an Acoustic Doppler Profiler with Applications to Large Rivers and Estuaries*. United States Geological Survey Water-Supply Paper 2395.

Stacey, M.T., Monismith, S.G., and Burau, J.R. 1999. Measurements of Reynolds stress profiles in tidal flows. *Journal of Geophysical Research* **104**: 10933–10949.

Straatsma, M.W., Warmink, J.J., and Middelkopp, H. 2008. Two novel methods for field measurements of hydrodynamic density of floodplain vegetation using terrestrial laser scanning and digital parallel phography. *International Journal of Remote Sensing*, **29**: 1595–1617.

Tiron, L., Le Coz, J., Provansal, M. *et al.* 2009. Flow and sediment processes in a cutoff meander of the Danube Delta during episodic flooding. *Geomorphology* **106**: 186–197.

Wadeson, R.A. and Rowntree, K.M. 1998. Application of the hydraulic biotope concept to the classification of instream habitats. *Aquatic Ecosystem Health and Management* **1**: 143–157.

Wasklewicz, T. and Hattanji, T. 2009. High-resolution analysis of debris flow-induced channel changes in a headwater stream, Ashio Mountains, Japan. *The Professional Geographer* **61**: 231–249.

Westaway, R.M., Lane, S.N., and Hicks, D.M. 2003. Remote survey of large-scale braided rivers using digital photogrammetry and image analysis. *International Journal of Remote Sensing* **24**: 795–816.

Wilcox, A. C. and Wohl, E. E. 2007. Field measurements of three-dimensional hydraulics in a step-pool channel. *Geomorphology* **83**: 215–231.

Wolman, M.G. 1954. A method of sampling coarse river-bed material: *American Geophysical Union Transactions* **35**: 951–956.

## 22.7   DISCUSSION

### 22.7.1   Discussion by R. Hodge

Milan and Heritage highlight the use of terrestrial laser scanning (TLS) for collecting high-resolution topographic data from fluvial gravel surfaces, and demonstrate how these data can be used both to monitor topographic change and to measure surface roughness. New techniques to quantify sediment properties and morphology are particularly timely, given the increasing appreciation of the role that sediment structure plays in controlling sediment entrainment.

We have used TLS data to create digital elevation models (DEM) of fluvial gravel surfaces; these DEMs capture the surface topography at the scale of individual grains. The errors inherent in TLS data can be significant compared to the grain size, therefore a methodology for data collection, filtering, and processing was developed in order to minimize errors (Hodge *et al.*, 2009a). Quantifying errors in the DEM is difficult because of the practicalities of measuring high-resolution surface topography using alternative techniques; however,

simulated TLS does provide a method of error quantification (Hodge, 2010).

Analysis of these high-resolution DEMs has demonstrated that grain-scale properties, including grain imbrication, orientation, and exposed area can be measured from them (Hodge *et al.*, 2009b). Through combination with field-based pivoting angle measurements, grain-size specific distributions of entrainment shear stress can also be calculated, directly linking sediment structure to grain entrainment.

### 22.7.2   Reply by D. Milan and G.L. Heritage

The authors very much agree with the statements made by Hodge based on her and her co-authors research. It is essential that an appropriate error assessment be conducted on TLS data and that grossly erroneous data generated by the laser scanner be removed. Errors linked to the scanning system and survey technique are inevitable, although often these are relatively small compared with the gross variation of the surfaces scanned. There is an obvious danger here though that the overall accuracy achieved by TLS combined with the extremely large volume of collected data encourages the immediate use of the data without considering error. This is particularly true of the macro-scale use of TLS which has dominated the early research in this area (Hodge *et al.*, 2009a). Hodge (2010) notes this when discussing the results of scanning coarse grained surfaces. Across finer surfaces, however, she clearly demonstrates the influence of laser-induced error on surface representation, although the large number of points contained in the overall dataset still reproduced the properties of the original surface.

## 22.8   DISCUSSION REFERENCES

Hodge, R.A. 2010. Using Simulated Terrestrial Laser Scanning to analyse errors in high-resolution scan data of irregular surfaces. *ISPRS Journal of Photogrammetry and Remote Sensing* **65**: 227–240.

Hodge, R.A., Brasington, J., and Richards, K. 2009a. In-situ characterisation of grain-scale fluvial morphology using Terrestrial Laser Scanning. *Earth Surface Processes and Landforms* **34**: 954–968.

Hodge, R.A., Brasington, J., and Richards, K. 2009b. Analysing laser-scanned Digital Terrain Models of gravel bed surfaces: linking morphology to sediment transport processes and hydraulics. *Sedimentology* **56**: 2024–2043.

# 23

# Remotely Sensed Topographic Change in Gravel Riverbeds with Flowing Channels

## D. Murray Hicks

## 23.1 INTRODUCTION

The aim of this chapter is to stimulate discussion on the application of remote sensing to quantifying, with confidence, the "vertical dimension" and changes thereof in gravel-bed river channels – in other words, remote surveying of river channel topographic and morphologic change.

Marcus (Chapter 21, this volume) concludes his review of this topic with the statement: "Regardless of the technique, vertical change detection with remote sensing requires the user to balance the tremendous increase in spatial coverage against the loss of local accuracy relative to ground-based surveys". He precedes this statement with some figures that suggest that a lot of actual riverbed topographic change lies below the threshold of detection by remote sensing. Is this really so, or does it depend on the application?

Typical needs for riverbed topographic change information cover a range of applications. For example, river engineers require repeat surveys for riverbed gravel management, bed level trend detection, bedload transport estimation via the "morphological" method, and morphological model validation; ecologists are interested in bed disturbance and physical habitat and its modification by floods; while geomorphologists can use patterns of morphologic change to interpret processes.

For all of these needs, what we would ideally like is a widely available, affordable, one-pass remote-surveying system that delivers, at reach scale at least, synoptic, high-spatial density point elevations over both dry and wet areas of riverbed at accuracies commensurate with ground surveys ($\sim$ cm). At present, with airborne systems we fall short of this ideal mainly because of limitations of accuracy, and the difficulty and degraded accuracy of dealing with wetted channels. While terrestrial laser scanning may resolve the precision constraint and improves on spatial density, this is at the expense of survey speed and is still constrained to dry areas of riverbed.

This paper expands on these issues, first reviewing the "wetted channel problem" then addressing what can be reliably extracted from remotely sensed difference surveys. I begin with wetted channel surveying because: (i) it is the weak link and (ii) appreciating the source and nature of its errors is useful when interpreting meaningful change from the results of repeat riverbed topographic surveys.

## 23.2 THE WETTED CHANNEL PROBLEM

The wetted channel problem occurs because for dry areas of riverbed there are affordable, readily available ground or aerial techniques that can deliver high-resolution topographic data, but for underwater topography the vast majority of us have to use other technologies that are often difficult to apply and invariably deliver inferior accuracy. Even for the lucky few able to access/afford bathymetric LiDAR systems that deliver seamless dry–wet datasets, degraded accuracy through water remains an issue. For example, while McKean et al. (2009) report point bed level RMS accuracies of 0.1–0.25 m for the EAARL system (of which there are only two sets in operation, J. Buffington, pers. comm., 2010), Hilldale and Raff (2008) report mean errors of 0.1–0.22 m and standard errors of 0.14–0.53 m for the commercially available SHOALS-1000T™ system; these being of the same order as the errors for other remote-sensing options over wetted channels (e.g., Westaway et al., 2003; Brasington et al., 2003; Hicks et al., 2006).

*Gravel-bed Rivers: Processes, Tools, Environments*, First Edition. Edited by Michael Church, Pascale M. Biron and André G. Roy.
© 2012 John Wiley & Sons, Ltd. Published 2012 by John Wiley & Sons, Ltd.

Five years ago, there was some expectation that by now we would all have readily accessible bathymetric LiDAR sets and alternative approaches would be discarded. For various reasons (mainly availability and cost) this has not eventuated, and so we need to retrieve the other methods from the bin and for the foreseeable future make serious use of them.

Setting laser-bathymetry aside then, there are three broad techniques available for surveying wetted channel topography: remote sensing, ground surveys, and inverse modelling. These are discussed below, generally within the context of a concurrent non-bathymetric LiDAR survey.

### 23.2.1 Remote Sensing

As detailed by Marcus (Chapter 21, this volume), the remote-sensing options (excluding bathymetric LiDAR) amount to some type of image-based (or optical) depth mapping, with wet-bed elevations generated by subtracting water depth from a water surface elevation model.

The water surface elevation model can be derived from laser returns from the water surface. These returns need to be extracted from the raw laser dataset by first masking the dry-bed returns, and this is usually done with a wet–dry classification procedure. One simple classification approach is using laser return intensity (since the pulse intensity returned from water tends to be low), but this on its own creates confusion when wet–dry boundaries are based only on intensity contours. An expedient fix is through manual editing. A more powerful way to classify wet–dry boundaries is through classification of optical imagery. This should be available anyway if that is the method chosen for depth mapping, and its advantages are that it: (i) has more "channels" available (e.g., RGB, compared with the monochrome of laser intensity), (ii) usually has better spatial (i.e., pixel) density at the water's edge, and (iii) provides a more informative underlay image to assist manual editing of the wet–dry boundary line. Once the wetted area has been masked, it is TINed and gridded, and it is also usual to numerically smooth the water surface model to remove random error. If point density is sufficiently high, only a small smoothing window is needed, thus minimizing local bias in areas of high water surface curvature.

A water surface elevation model can also be derived using digital photogrammetry. Since elevation fixes by this method from the water surface itself are typically poor or confused, the usual approach is to fit a TIN across the water surface, linking dry points along the water edges. This is error-prone, however, due to the "water's edge" points not being exactly at the water level and where significant water surface curvature exists, such as at pool-riffle transitions and diffluences. The latter is of particular concern if the project objective is to derive a 2-D hydrodynamic model of a braided river, where the distribution of water at diffluences is critically dependent on the bed elevation of the control sections. For these reasons, at least in the author's experience, a laser-scanned water surface model is preferable.

Image-based depth mapping relates depth to the spectral characteristics of sunlight reflected/scattered from water bodies. As detailed by Marcus, quantitative relations can be established by empirical calibration of image spectral characteristics to depths sampled concurrently with the image acquisition (the correlation approach) or they can be theoretically (i.e., physically) based with no or less of a need for field data.

With either approach, confusions develop due to spatial variations in ambient light (e.g., due to hill, cloud, and vegetation shadows), water surface reflectance, bottom reflectance and, sometimes, water turbidity. To some degree, these can be minimized by relating depth to relative intensity, for example, by using ratios of intensity by spectral band rather than absolute values. Also, pre-classification by substrate type, aquatic vegetation cover, and/or hydraulic setting – and developing calibrations for each class – improves accuracy. Slight water turbidity (due to light back-scattering by fine sediment suspended within the water column) can help mask confusions created by varying substrate, but if the water is too turbid the light scattering "saturates" only a short distance below the water surface and the image characteristics become independent of depth. Even with clear water, there is a limiting depth of light penetration. These effects mean that the characteristics of the uncertainty (accuracy and precision) can change with depth, the ambient environment, and the sensing platform. For example, Hicks et al. (2006), using multispectral imagery, found the optically sensed depth "saturating" at ∼ 2.0 m (Figure 23.1), while RGB-based depth mapping by Brasington et al. (2003) saturated at less than 1.0 m.

While not dependent on depth measurements, most physically based approaches require some environmental information (e.g., substrate characteristics, water turbidity – Marcus, Chapter 21, this volume). Moreover, to avoid blunders they should strictly be verified with an independent set of depth measurements.

Also, for the depth map to overlay the dry-bed and water surface DEM, the imagery must be orthorectified to the same projection and datum as the concurrent LiDAR project. This process can be streamlined without ground control by matching features between the real imagery and the imagery generated from the LiDAR intensity, and by using the LiDAR-based DEM. Alternatively, modern airborne imaging platforms can now use on-plane navigation systems (as used with LiDAR) to

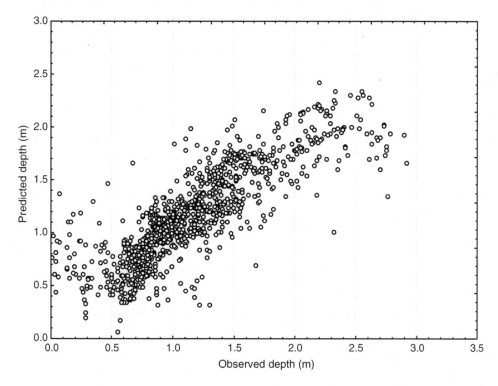

**Figure 23.1** Comparison of sounded (observed) depths and depths predicted from multispectral imagery, Lower Waitaki River, New Zealand (from Hicks *et al.*, 2006). Predicted depth "saturates" at ~2.0 m. When compared against GPS+sounding bed level data, the riverbed DEM generated by subtracting the MS-mapped depths from a LiDAR-derived water surface DEM had ME = 0.08 m and SDE = 0.23 m. Reproduced, with permission, from Hicks, D.M., Shankar, U., Duncan, M.J., Rebuffe, M. and Aberle, J. 2006. Use of remote-sensing technology to assess impacts of hydro-operations on a large, braided, gravel-bed river: Waitaki River, New Zealand. In Sambrook Smith, G.H., Best J.L., Bristow, C.S. and Petts, G.E., editors. Braided rivers - process, deposits, ecology and management. International Association of Sedimentologists, Special Publication 36, Oxford, Blackwell: 311–326.

position and orient the image frame (on the fly, literally) without the need for ground control.

So, where we are currently is: (i) there are established methods available to map water depth from imagery; (ii) at least a modicum of field data are still required, if only for validation checks and to characterize the uncertainty; (iii) existing professional acquisition systems can now supply geosynchronized laser-scanned topography and imagery, relieving the "end-user" of this chore; (iv) often substantial manual editing is required to correct confusions; and (v) the error associated with the derived bed elevation stems from both the water surface modelling step and the water depth mapping step, and each step is wont to produce patches of locally systematic error. Unfortunately, unless recognized and managed, the latter can dominate overall survey error statistics, leading to possible misinterpretations and/or good data being discarded with bad.

### 23.2.2  Ground-based Options

Ground-based options to rapidly survey wetted channel topography over large extents include RTK-GPS surveys, either wading or using a boat with an acoustic sounding system. Acoustic depth sensors include single-beam "altimeters", multibeam/swath systems, and multipurpose acoustic systems that map the velocity field as well as the depth. Boat options include small, unmanned craft tethered to the banks, paddle-craft such as kayaks, remote-control mini-boats, jet-boats, and hovercraft. Since gravel-bed rivers tend to be relatively steep, shallow, and fast, and because it is usually better to survey them at low flow when the area of wetted bed is minimized, navigation with any single method can be difficult, so flexibility is required. For example, boat access into shallow water zones that provide hydraulic controls (e.g., riffle-heads and diffluences) is often constrained by the cruising speeds required for echo-sounding or the skills of the operator. Safe navigation can also be thwarted by riparian vegetation.

While most ground-based methods deliver bed elevations to centimetre-scale accuracy, the challenge is to provide an adequate density and placement of survey lines that in the time and budget available delivers an acceptable interpolation error. This is being advanced in two ways. First, multibeam echo-sounders (MBES) improve on single-beam systems, with of the order of several hundred beams scanning at 20–30 Hz. They typically have beam angles of ∼150°, so they cover swaths of width 10–12 × depth (e.g., 10–12 m in 1 m water depth). Constraints are that MBESs are limited to depths > 0.5 m and have a sizeable "deck unit" that would be a tight squeeze in a kayak. Acoustic Doppler current profilers (ADCPs), with typically four acoustic heads, also provide multibeam capability. Some ADCPs are now small enough to be operated from un-manned or paddled craft and have blanking depths as small as 0.15 m, but systems to extract multibeam bed topography from them are not yet widely available. Second, "smart" bathymetric survey systems are being developed that analyse the quality of the bed topography being acquired "on the fly" so that the survey can be steered to areas with poor coverage and interpolation error (A Blake, USGS, pers. comm., 2011). However, a smart tracking algorithm to optimize interpolation for gravel-bed channels has yet to emerge.

Thus, the key limitations with commonly available ground-based technologies are navigation/access, trackline placement, point-density and interpolation, and the time commitment.

### 23.2.3 Inverse Modelling

Inverse modelling involves using hydraulic principles to estimate the submerged bed level, beginning with a water surface digital elevation model (DEM) and knowing the water discharge and bed roughness. Smart et al. (2009), for example, describe an iterative procedure which follows after preliminary masking of the wetted channels and creation of a water surface DEM from LiDAR returns. An initial, uniform estimate of depth is subtracted from the water surface DEM to provide a starting bed DEM, which is then used with a 2-D hydrodynamic model to produce a refined depth model. This is repeated until the modelled water surface DEM converges on the observed DEM (Figure 23.2). Comparison of the modelled bed DEM with bed elevations surveyed with RTK-GPS showed an over-reach mean error (ME) of 0.136 m and standard deviation of error (SDE) of 0.319 m. Degraded performance occurred at Froude number

settings < 0.3 (e.g., in pools, particularly deep ones); excluding these areas the ME reduced to 0.073 m and the SDE to 0.212 m. The approach was considered adequate to predict flood levels from subsequent model runs, but the accuracy statistics show that it has limitations for detecting morphologic change (at least at its current stage of development). It nonetheless provides a way to check for blunders generated with optical bathymetric mapping techniques.

### 23.2.4 Mixed Approaches

From the above, there appears to be no obvious single approach to the wetted channel problem, at least if maximum accuracy over 2-D domains is required. The way forward appears to be to use a combination of ground and remote-sensing methods, relying principally on the remote sensing, but using ground methods to collect calibration data, validation data sufficient to map the error characteristics of the remote-sensing products, and supplementary data in patches where a reconnaissance inspection of the project area shows that the remote-sensing product will be biased or inadequate (such as pools deeper than the optical saturation depth or channels masked by trees).

## 23.3 EXTRACTING MEANINGFUL CHANGE IN BED LEVEL AND VOLUME FROM REMOTELY SENSED SURVEYS

When considering the reality of erosion and deposition mapped from repeat riverbed surveys, Marcus (this volume) quotes figures from Brasington et al. (2003) from a 0.024 km$^2$ subreach of the braided River Feshie. These indicated 95% confidence interval thresholds of change detection (ToD) between remote-sensed surveys of 0.41–0.8 m. These are sobering uncertainties when one considers that they are typical of the relative relief of braided gravel-bed channels. This concern is heightened when Brasington et al. show that when compared against highly accurate ground survey data that captured the riverbed change over a year-long epoch, their remote sensing would only have been able to reliably detect 32% of the actual volume of channel deposition, 60% of the channel erosion, and ∼17% of the net volume change. Do these apparently poor results tell us to abandon remote sensing for riverbed surveying, or should we persevere and if so how? It is instructive to begin with a short review.

### 23.3.1 DEMs, DoDs, and LoDs

The essential problem is to define and manage uncertainty in riverbed DEMs of difference (DoDs), which are created by subtracting DEMs from component surveys. The first

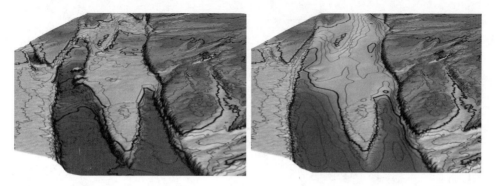

**Figure 23.2**  Top: DEM from Waiau River, New Zealand. Green-brown areas are dry riverbed surveyed by LiDAR. Blue areas are wetted channels derived after six iterations of inverse application of 2-D hydrodynamic model. Contours at 0.2 m intervals; bold line maps water's edge; flow is top to bottom. Bottom: DEM of same reach with wetted areas mapped with RTK-GPS. For inverse method over wetted areas, ME = 0.136 m, SDE = 0.319 m relative to GPS. Reproduced, with permission, from Smart, G.M., Bind, J. and Duncan, M. 2009. River bathymetry from conventional LiDAR using water surface returns. In Anderson, R.S., Braddock, R.D. and Newham, L.T.H. (eds) 18th World IMACS Congress and MODSIM09 International Congress on Modelling and Simulation. Modelling and Simulation Society of Australia and New Zealand and international Association for Mathematics and Computers in Simulation: 2521–2527. ISBN: 978-0-9758400-7-8. (See the color version of this figure in color plate section.)

thing is to define the uncertainty in elevation for each point in the individual DEMs, and that begins with identifying the error sources. These include errors with raw measured points (instrument precision, calibration errors, such as in relating image brightness to water depth and associated confusions, operator blunders) and errors relating to interpolation onto a fixed grid (raw point density, topographic complexity, interpolation model). Typically, these are bundled together and quantified by comparison with a set of high-quality ground survey data in terms of the mean error (ME) and standard deviation of error (SDE). The former identifies any bias, while the latter indicates the precision of the point elevation. When surveying methods are mixed, such as using different approaches for dry and wet parts of the riverbed (Brasington *et al.*, 2000; Westaway *et al.*, 2003), different precisions are adopted.

When a DoD is created, the elevation change on the DoD is considered to be reliable (that is, due to process-induced deposition or erosion, rather than error-induced noise) if it exceeds a minimum level of detection (LoD). The LoD may simply be defined as the root-sum-squares (RSS) of the errors on the matching points of the two DEMs, but the preferred approach (e.g., Brasington *et al.*, 2000; Lane *et al.*, 2003) is to regard the error (when normalized by the RSS) as having a Student's t-distribution, thus allowing a probability to be assigned to a given LoD (or alternatively, each elevation change can be assigned a probability of being real). The higher the confidence level assigned, the higher the elevation change must be before being accepted as real. By this process, the

DoD can either be filtered of change beneath the LoD or it can be qualified in terms of the likelihood that the mapped change is real (Figure 23.3). Lane *et al.* (2003, 2004) went on to show that if the points on a DoD were spatially independent, then the error in the spatial mean elevation change, and hence the error in volume change over an area, could be propagated by an RSS approach.

Wheaton *et al.* (2010) pointed out a number of deficiencies in this general procedure. They centre on observations that there is typically spatial variability in the error surface over DEMs that is coherent and often predictable. The upshot is that global or simply stratified (e.g., wet–dry) SDE values can produce LoDs that reject relatively low-relief changes (such as gravel-sheet deposits) while retaining spurious high-relief changes (such as apparent bank erosion due to poorly mapped bank slopes on either or both DEMs). Moreover, should changes be rejected if they are below the LoD but persistent over patch or bar scales?

It is useful to return briefly to the River Feshie work reported by Brasington *et al.* (2003, 2004) to illustrate these issues within the context of a remotely sensed survey typical of many over the past decade. They surveyed their 300 × 80 m study reach both with densely spaced RTK-GPS (providing a "ground truth") and by remote sensing with a combination of digital photogrammetry for dry parts of the river bed, a calibrated optical approach to map water depth, and water's-edge TINing to model the water surface. Both the ground-based and remotely sensed surveys were interpolated to a common grid, enabling a grid of errors to be developed. Analysis

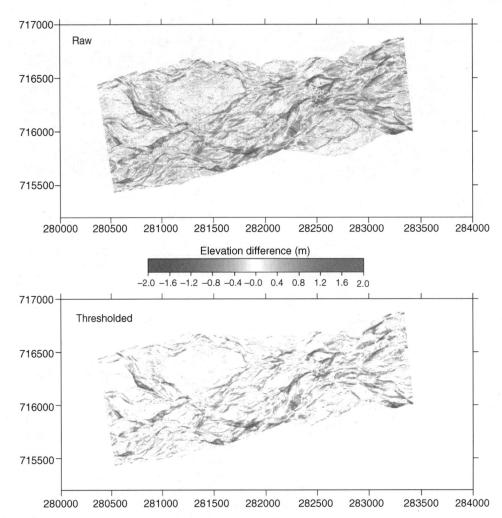

**Figure 23.3**  DEMs of difference for 3.5 km reach of Waimakariri River, New Zealand, between February 1999 and February 2000. Surveyed with digital photogrammetry for dry-bed areas, empirical optical approach for wet areas. Top: raw DoD. Bottom: DoD thresholded using 68% confidence level LoDs (±0.292 m for dry–dry comparison, ±0.344 m for wet–dry, ±0.386 m for wet–wet). Flow is left to right. Map units in metres. Reproduced, with permission, from Lane, S. N., Westaway, R.M. and Hicks, D.M. 2003. Estimation of erosion and deposition volumes in a large, gravel-bed, braided river using synoptic remote sensing. *Earth Surface Processes and Landforms* **28**: 249–271. (See the color version of this figure in color plate section.)

of this error surface showed greater imprecision over wet areas (SDE = 0.29 m) compared with dry areas (SDE = 0.148 m), and (using the RSS approach for combining errors in differences) provided the basis for the 95% confidence interval thresholds-of-change detection that have been mentioned above – i.e. 0.41 m for dry–dry bed comparisons, 0.64 m for wet–dry, and 0.80 m for wet–wet comparisons.

In fact, Brasington *et al.* (2003) showed that a lot of the overall SDE in the wetted channel areas of their final remotely sensed DEM was generated by patches of sys-

tematic error induced by shortcomings in the remote-sensing methodology. For example, in Figure 23.4 (which maps the error in their final photogrammetric DEM relative to their ground-surveyed DEM) the (blue) patch of over-estimated elevation at the top of the reach is in a ~2.4 m deep pool that was deeper than the light penetration depth (~1 m), while (red) patches of under-estimated bed elevation relate to inaccuracies in modelling the water surface (due to the points selected to define the water's edge and the algorithm used to smooth the water surface, which performed poorly in areas of high water surface

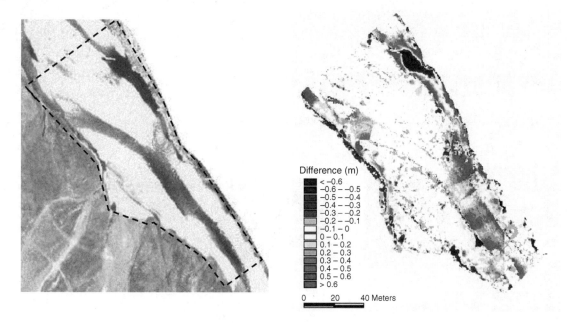

**Figure 23.4** Left: surveyed reach of River Feshie, Scotland; river flows bottom to top. Right: map of residual error between corrected photogrammetric DEM and DEM from high-resolution ground-based survey. Blue pixels where remotely sensed DEM over-estimates bed level, red where it under-estimates. Overall ME $= 0.08$ m, SDE $= 0.22$ m. Blue patch at top is a 2.4 m deep pool; red patches mark areas of inaccurate water-surface modelling. Reproduced, with permission, from Brasington, J., Langham, J. and Rumsby, B. 2003. Methodological sensitivity of morphometric estimates of coarse fluvial sediment transport. *Geomorphology* **53**: 299–316. (See the color version of this figure in color plate section.)

curvature). The upshot is that over parts of the wetted channels their remotely sensed DEM was more precise than indicated by the overall SDE, and there was more information lost from their DoD than was necessary. The problem in application is knowing where such error patches occur. The obvious lesson from the Feshie experience is to collect more ground-based data, collecting enough not only to calibrate the optical model, but to map the error surface, and, if necessary, identifying where remote-sensing data need to be substituted with ground data.

### 23.3.2 Recent Developments

Wheaton *et al.* (2010) used more recent surveys of the River Feshie to illustrate two linked approaches that explicitly manage spatial variability and coherence in DEM error surfaces. The first approach uses fuzzy set theory to map the spatial variability of the uncertainty over a DEM. The fuzzy inference system (FIS) approach used is based on the premise that there exists at least some vague appreciation of what factors (termed "inputs") contribute to the uncertainty in DEM-point elevation,

and even though these may not be directly quantified or quantifiable, at least they can be rated on a linguistic scale (e.g., low, medium, high). Moreover, a set of rules can be defined that rate the uncertainty level of all combinations of the contributing factors (termed "outputs"). Simple functions representing the input factors are calibrated using field data and enable a quantified estimate of the uncertainty for each output class. Every DEM point is classified in terms of the error-contributing factors and is assigned a weighted uncertainty value. In the Feshie case, Wheaton *et al.* provided input knowledge on survey point density, slope, and GPS point quality. While sounding complicated, the FIS approach is really little more than a formal and generalized treatment of what has been done intuitively to date. For example, the adoption of different errors for wet and dry areas (e.g., Westaway *et al.*, 2003; Brasington *et al.*, 2003) may be viewed as a FIS with one input type (i.e., survey method) that requires rules for wet and dry survey methods.

Wheaton *et al.*'s second innovation was to index each point in a DEM in terms of the degree to which it lies within a spatially contiguous window of erosion or

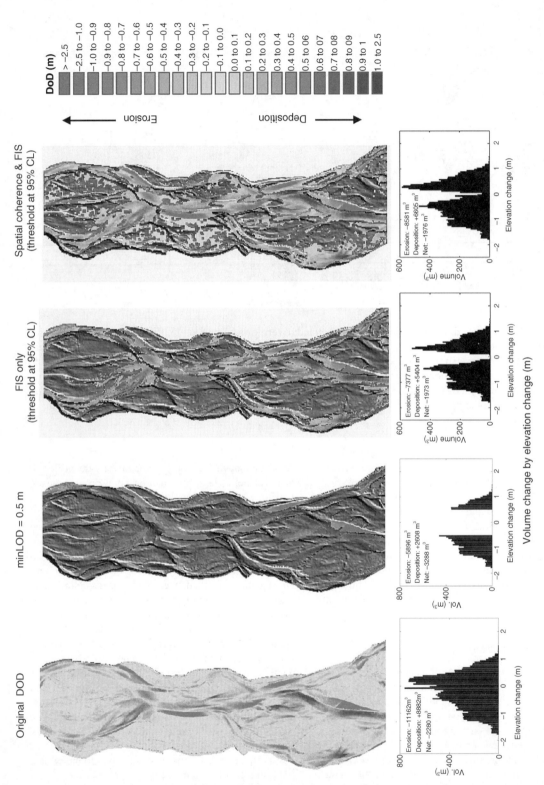

**Figure 23.5** DEMs of difference between River Feshie surveys in 2006 and 2007 (top row) and volumes of erosion and deposition distributed by elevation change above level of detection (bottom row). From left to right: original DoD with no thresholding; thresholding at 0.5 m elevation change; thresholding at 95% confidence level using FIS to refine LoD; applying FIS and Bayesian updating using spatial contiguity index. Reproduced, with permission, from Wheaton, J.M., Brasington, J., Darby, S.E. and Sear, D.A. 2010. Accounting for uncertainty in DEMs from repeat topographic surveys: improved sediment budgets. *Earth Surface Processes and Landforms* **35**: 136–156. (See the color version of this figure in color plate section.)

deposition. The derived spatial continuity indices are then transformed into conditional probabilities that each cell is erosional or depositional. This means, for example, that where a point showing erosion less than the LoD would normally be discarded, when it is surrounded by like points it is highly likely that the erosion is actually real and so it should be kept. They employ Bayes' theorem to use this conditional probability to update the original *a priori* probability of significant change determined through the FIS approach. Thus, the two approaches together enable the reliability of a DoD to be refined by taking account of: (i) spatial variation in the factors contributing to measurement error in the component DEMs and (ii) spatial coherence in the erosion and deposition patterns. In the Feshie example, application of these approaches recovered greater volumes of significant erosion and deposition, and provided richer detail on the bar-scale transfers of gravel (Figure 23.5).

While the Bayesian-updating FIS approach was applied to ground survey data in this example, it is equally suited to dealing with mixed-method remotely sensed datasets, such as in the earlier Feshie example discussed above and the Waimakariri dataset of Westaway *et al.* (2003). It would appear particularly relevant to bathymetric surveys, where the factors influencing spatial variability in DEM quality are becoming increasingly appreciated (i.e., depth saturation, substrate confusions, water surface modelling deficiencies, point density, and so on).

### 23.3.3 Volume Change Uncertainty and Patchy Systematic Error

One issue requiring improvement is the spatial integration of volume change (whether erosion, deposition, or net) from DoDs. This is particularly important when using volume change with the morphological method for estimating bedload transport, both at the reach scale and for discrete erosion/deposition units. As discussed above, remotely sensed gravel riverbed DoDs usually contain patches of systematic error due to local inadequacies in at least one component of the survey approach (e.g., deep pools). In such cases, application of the Lane *et al.* (2003) approach, which assumes that the errors at individual DoD nodes are independent of those at adjacent nodes, will underestimate the spatially propagated error in volume change or mean bed level.

Returning again to the Feshie example, the ground-based data of Brasington *et al.* (2003) showed that their final version remotely sensed DEM had a mean bed level error of 0.02 m (i.e., when node errors are averaged over all grid points, wet and dry). While fundamental differences between ground and photogrammetric-

based methods (e.g., point versus pixel-cluster matching) may have influenced some of this bias, it must be due, in part at least, to the patches of systematic error which, while positive in some places and negative in others (Figure 23.4), did not fully cancel over the surveyed reach. This mean elevation error indicates that the error in volume above some datum over the $24\,000\,\mathrm{m}^2$ reach area is $480\,\mathrm{m}^3$, thus (by the RSS approach) the error in the net volume difference between two surveys by the same methodology should be $679\,\mathrm{m}^3$, and only net change greater than this should be considered real. Conversely, applying the approach of Lane *et al.* (2003), with a grid spacing of 1 m and assuming conservatively a global SDE of 0.29 m (using the wet result of Brasington *et al.* for both wet and dry grid nodes), the standard error on net volume change is only $63.5\,\mathrm{m}^3$ (or $124\,\mathrm{m}^3$ if the DEM elevation uncertainty is set at $1.96 \times$ SDE).

What is required is for the uncertainty in local volume change to be propagated on a patch basis rather than node by node. This requires knowledge of spatial variability in the local mean error, as well as the variability in the precision, and an appreciation of the cause of this error.

In principle, the FIS–Bayesian method could also be applied to this problem. Thus, the way forward – particularly with wetted channel remote-sensing – is to collect enough data not only to calibrate the optical methods, but to map, or at least sample in adequate detail, the local mean and variance of the bed elevation error surface (see Figure 23.4). Indeed, when the local mean error surface is well enough understood and quantified, it is perhaps better to simply remove it by adjusting the DEM. For example, Westaway *et al.* (2003) and Lane *et al.* (2004) found "banding" in DoDs produced by subtracting DEM mosaics derived from digital photogrammetry of a $\sim 3.5 \times 1\,\mathrm{km}$ reach of the braided, gravel-bed Waimakariri River. This banding was traced to the bundle adjustment process, which led to the propagation of random error in camera positions and orientations into locally systematic error in the DEM. This understanding led to the development of solutions that removed much of the locally systematic error over dry-bed areas at the post-processing stage.

So, to return to the question posed in the introduction to this section: no, we need not abandon remote sensing for surveying erosion and deposition volumes, as there has been progress developing more effective methods to sort signal from noise. However, this does come at the cost of collecting more check data in the field – to the extent of needing a well-planned strategy that is reactive to the conditions encountered and, as a last resort, being prepared to use ground-data to patch in topography where remote sensing simply can't deliver.

## 23.4 BALANCING SPATIAL DETAIL AGAINST VERTICAL ACCURACY

Despite the accuracy issues, the key advantage of remotely sensed riverbed topography datasets is their spatial detail. In some applications, this may be just as important as vertical accuracy in tipping the balance towards adopting remote sensing. An example is the use of cross-section networks to monitor reach-averaged bed levels and gravel volumes to manage gravel resources, monitor aggradation/degradation trends, or monitor flood conveyance capacity. While section lines may be accurately surveyed, the reach-averaged change is sensitive to interpolation errors between sections (e.g., Fuller *et al.*, 2003).

In New Zealand, where many rivers once braided freely and avulsed over Holocene alluvial fans, confinement has led to concentrated aggradation that has required regular gravel extraction (e.g., Griffiths, 1979). This has traditionally been managed with the aid of quasi-regular surveys of cross-section networks using conventional ground-based methods (Basher, 2006). Section spacing appears to have been generally set on an intuitive basis rather than designed with errors in mind; typically, it is of the order of 1 km, but is some-

times reduced along reaches of greater concern (and vice versa). Sometimes, sections are surveyed at the rate of a few per year in a cyclic process, so a truly synoptic reach-scale survey is never captured. Currently, however, some river managers are considering whether to abandon the cross-section networks in favour of synoptic LiDAR surveys, thus embracing the second dimension. Should they be? Or is the reduction in spatial interpolation error offset by reduced absolute accuracy?

This question was addressed by Lane *et al.* (2003), who generated 1 m grid DEMs from four repeat, remotely sensed surveys of their Waimakariri River study reach (using digital aerial photogrammetry or airborne LiDAR for the dry-bed topography and image-based depth mapping for wet areas). By assuming no error in these DEMs, they computed "most accurate" values for the changes in reach-averaged bed level between surveys. Cross-sections were then extracted from each DEM at a given spacing and used to calculate the reach-averaged bed level for that cross-section spacing, for comparison against the "most accurate" value. Repeating the procedure multiple times for each section spacing enabled the mean and standard deviation of the relative error to be quantified. The results (e.g., Figure 23.6) showed relative mean and sampling errors increasing rapidly as section

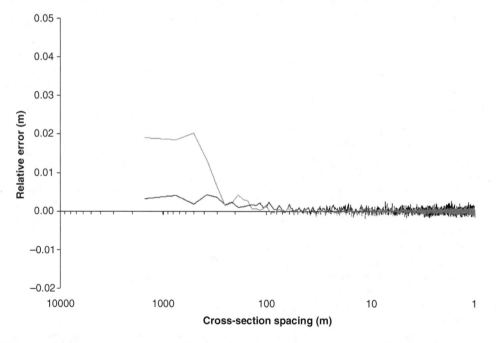

**Figure 23.6** Mean (black) and standard deviation (grey) of the relative error in mean bed level estimated against cross-section spacing for a 3.5 km reach of the braided Waimakariri River, New Zealand. Both are relative to the mean bed level change calculated by differencing 1 m grid DEMs surveyed in February 2000 and May 2000. Reproduced, with permission, from Lane, S.N., Westaway, R.M. and Hicks, D.M. 2003. Estimation of erosion and deposition volumes in a large, gravel-bed, braided river using synoptic remote sensing. *Earth Surface Processes and Landforms* **28**: 249–271.

spacing increased beyond 100–200 m (which corresponds to about $^1/_4$–$^1/_2$ a morphological unit scale). The relative mean error associated with section spacing passed the absolute uncertainty in reach-averaged bed level change associated with a LiDAR survey (based on comparison with ground-surveyed check data) when the section spacing exceeded $\sim 500$ m. Coincidently, the typical cross-section spacing for the Waimakariri River is 500–800 m (Griffiths, 1979). Thus in that location, simply in terms of accuracy of reach-averaged bed level change, the case for LiDAR may be marginal; however, LiDAR would also deliver richer information on within-reach gravel build-up, showing where gravel extraction should be focused.

A similar local accuracy versus spatial interpolation tradeoff applies in the choice between 1-D (cross-section based) and 2-D (DEM based) hydrodynamic modelling approaches for quantifying reach-averaged instream habitat (Jowett et al., 2008). In that case the focus is on channels wetted at low flow, thus the method for surveying these is critical. In braided channels particularly, accurate mapping of shallow water ($< 0.2$–$0.3$ m) is required to assess bird-wading habitat and fish passage, while local patches of systematic error at hydraulic controls and diffluences can significantly influence the flow distribution amongst braids and the boundaries of habitat units. In this context, the performance of existing remote-sensing technologies, even bathymetric LiDAR, remains marginal.

## 23.5 CONCLUSIONS

With bathymetric LiDAR hard to access because of cost or availability issues, optical methods remain the pragmatic remote-sensing option for surveying wetted channel topography in gravel-bed rivers. These, however, may involve significant error due to both the water surface modelling step and the water depth mapping step, with each prone to producing patches of locally systematic error. The way forward is to collect enough ground-based check data to characterize the spatial variability not only in bed-level precision but also in local mean bed level, and, if necessary, to patch gaps.

The main issues with ground-based technologies are navigation/access to channels, track-line placement, point-density and interpolation, and the time commitment. With data on water surface elevation, roughness, and discharge, inverse hydrodynamic modelling provides an alternative to optical remote sensing, or at least a way to improve water surface DEM definition along waters edges and areas of high curvature.

A key challenge with mapping and quantifying volumes of erosion and deposition from DoDs is determining the reliability of the observed elevation changes (i.e., separating signal from noise). The thresholding, or LoD, approach has been recently improved by new techniques that enable the reliability of a DoD to be refined by (i) taking account of spatial variation in the factors contributing to measurement error in the component DEMs and (ii) taking account of spatial coherence in erosion and deposition patterns.

Further improvement is required in the way that error is propagated when reach- and bar-scale erosion and deposition volumes are totalled, taking account of spatial variability in the local mean error as well as the precision.

While the spatial detail delivered by remote-sensing surveys means that they can deliver greater precision in reach-scale mean bed level or volume changes than do traditionally spaced cross-sections, this advantage can be offset by residual mean errors associated with the remote sensing. Similarly, 2-D hydrodynamic models based on remotely sensed DEMs can reduce spatial interpolation errors within instream habitat assessments, but this may be offset by degraded bed level accuracy over hydraulic controls and along shallow channel margins.

## 23.6 ACKNOWLEDGMENTS

The content of this paper has benefitted greatly from my association with and/or the work of my NIWA colleagues Maurice Duncan, Ude Shankar, Graeme Smart, and Jo Bind, and my antipodean colleagues Stuart Lane, Richard Westaway, and James Brasington. Support from the (New Zealand) Foundation for Research, Science, and Technology under Contract C01X0308 is gratefully acknowledged.

## 23.7 REFERENCES

Basher, L. 2006. Monitoring of Riverbed Stability and Morphology by Regional Councils in New Zealand: Application to Gravel Extraction Management. Landcare Research Contract Report 0506/138. Nelson, Landcare Research Ltd.

Brasington, J., Langham, J., and Rumsby, B. 2003. Methodological sensitivity of morphometric estimates of coarse fluvial sediment transport. Geomorphology 53: 299–316.

Brasington, J., Rumsby, B.T., and McVey, R.A. 2000. Monitoring and modelling morphological change in a braided gravel-bed river using high resolution GPS-based survey. Earth Surface Processes and Landforms 25: 973–990.

Fuller, I.C., Large, A.R.G., Charlton, M.E., Heritage, G.L., and Milan, D.J. 2003. Reach-scale sediment transfers: an evaluation of two morphological budgeting approaches. Earth Surface Processes and Landforms 28: 889–903.

Griffiths, G.A. 1979. Recent sedimentation history of the Waimakariri River, New Zealand. Journal of Hydrology (New Zealand) 18: 6–28.

Hicks, D.M., Shankar, U., Duncan, M.J., Rebuffe, M., and Aberle, J. 2006. Use of remote-sensing technology to assess impacts of hydro-operations on a large, braided, gravel-bed river: Waitaki River, New Zealand. In Sambrook Smith, G.H., Best, J.L., Bristow, C.S., and Petts, G.E., editors. *Braided Rivers – Process, Deposits, Ecology and Management.* International Association of Sedimentologists, Special Publication 36. Oxford, Blackwell, pp. 311–326.

Hilldale, R.C. and Raff, D. 2008. Assessing the ability of airborne LiDAR to map river bathymetry. *Earth Surface Processes and Landforms* **33**: 773–783.

Jowett, I.G., Hayes, J.W., and Duncan, M.J. 2008. *A Guide to Instream Habitat Survey Methods and Analysis.* NIWA Science and Technology Series 54.

Lane, S.N., Westaway, R.M., and Hicks, D.M. 2003. Estimation of erosion and deposition volumes in a large, gravel-bed, braided river using synoptic remote sensing. *Earth Surface Processes and Landforms* **28**: 249–271.

Lane, S.N., Reid, S.C., Westaway, R.M., and Hicks, D.M. 2004. Remotely sensed topographic data for river channel research: the identification, explanation and management of error. In Kelly, R., Drake, N., and Barr, S. editors. *Spatial Modelling of the Terrestrial Environment.* Chichester, John Wiley & Sons, Ltd, pp. 113–136.

McKean, J., Nagel, D., Tonina, D. *et al.* 2009. Remote sensing of channels and riparian zones with a narrow-beam aquatic-terrestrial lidar. *Remote Sensing* **1**: 1065–1096.

Smart, G.M., Bind, J., and Duncan, M. 2009. River bathymetry from conventional LiDAR using water surface returns. In Anderson, R.S., Braddock, R.D., and Newham, L.T.H., editors, *Proceedings of the 18th World IMACS Congress and MODSIM09 International Congress on Modelling and Simulation.* Modelling and Simulation Society of Australia and New Zealand and International Association for Mathematics and Computers in Simulation, pp. 2571–2527.

Westaway, R.M., Lane, S.N., and Hicks, D.M. 2003. Remote survey of large braided, gravel-bed rivers using digital photogrammetry and image analysis. *International Journal of Remote Sensing* **24**: 795–815.

Wheaton, J.M., Brasington, J., Darby, S.E., and Sear, D.A. 2010. Accounting for uncertainty in DEMs from repeat topographic surveys: improved sediment budgets. *Earth Surface Processes and Landforms* **35**: 136–156.

# 24

# Modern Digital Instruments and Techniques for Hydrodynamic and Morphologic Characterization of River Channels

## Marian Muste, Dongsu Kim, and Venkatesh Merwade

## 24.1  INTRODUCTION

New stresses and demands on surface water resources from increasing world population and rising global living standards are requiring a better fundamental understanding and management of our rivers. Observation, theory, and analysis form the pillars of scientific and observational studies of river systems. While river analysis has been greatly improved by the advent of the digital revolution and the advancement of numerical simulations, the way we observe river characteristics has changed only in the past decade or so. Until recently, flow hydrodynamics was still measured using mechanical velocity meters that used the force of water to rotate a propeller, a method that has been used since the beginning of the previous century. During the past 20 years, the availability of inexpensive computing power, electronics, and sensing technology has led to the development of digital velocity instruments for measuring and mapping river hydrodynamics. The new and emerging developments in flow instrumentation are significantly improving our capabilities to measure velocity, discharge, and flow dynamics in rivers.

Consequently, velocity meters based on acoustics, electromagnetic waves, and imaging river are replacing traditional mechanical meters in most measurement locations in the United States. For example, 33% of all gauging stations managed by the United States Geological Survey (USGS) use acoustic instruments to estimate discharge (Muste *et al.*, 2008). Approximately 57% of all USGS discharge measurements that could be made from a boat, cableway, or bridge were made with an acoustic doppler current profiler (ADCP); whereas 27% of all wading measurements were made with an acoustic doppler velocimeter (ADV). This new generation of instruments offers superior measurement efficiency, performance, and safety when operated in normal and extreme flow environments (e.g., low and high flows in shallow and deep rivers). Moreover, digital instrumentation can measure velocities faster over larger areas, at higher spatial resolutions and at a more reasonable cost than previous mechanical instruments. The new generation of instruments is capable of measuring spatially distributed 2-D and 3-D kinematic features that can be related to important morphologic (e.g., Kostachuck *et al.*, 1989; Carling *et al.*, 2000; Wilbers and Ten Brinke, 2003) and hydrodynamic (e.g., Lane *et al.*, 2000; Parsons *et al.*, 2005, 2007) aspects of natural rivers.

In addition to river hydrodynamics, river morphology plays a major role in understanding and modelling of instream hydraulic, ecological, and biochemical processes (e.g., Julien *et al.*, 2002; Kostaschuk *et al.*, 2004). Conventional techniques used for measuring morphologic attributes such as cross-sectional area and width–depth ratio are based on an assumption of 1-D flow. In a 1-D domain, river morphology is described by extracting information from cross-sectional surveys. Although the techniques used for measuring 1-D river morphology are well established and have been used for several engineering and scientific investigations, their applicability is limited in truly capturing the 3-D nature of river systems. Because of growing concerns regarding

---

the effect of human impacts on overall stream health and ecology, the desire to acquire rapidly 2-D and 3-D river morphologic data is also growing.

While not presented herein, it should be mentioned that recent instrument development also targets the investigation of the micro-characteristics of the sand- and gravel-bed rivers: turbulence (Roy et al., 2004; Lacey and Roy, 2007), bed characteristics (Graham et al., 2010; Cohen et al., 2010) and dynamics (Dinehart, 1992; Carling et al., 2000). Many of these studies are conducting comparisons among various techniques in order to assess their capabilities, limitations, and implementation suitability for various practical applications (MacVicar et al., 2007; Fox and Belcher, 2009). Overall, it can be concluded that given the enhanced availability, efficiency, and performance of the new generation of instruments, there is an obvious trend to shift the investigation of detailed aspects of flow mechanics from the laboratory to the natural environment.

This paper reviews contemporary instrumentation and associated methodologies for characterizing river hydrodynamics and morphology using minimally intrusive or remote-sensing techniques. The minimally intrusive techniques described in the review are acoustic-based instruments, whereas remote-sensing digital techniques include RAdio Detection And Ranging (RADAR), LIght Detection And Ranging (LiDAR), and image-based instruments that do not need to be in contact with the water body during measurements. The paper starts by describing the measurement principles, instrument configuration and the measurement output (i.e., river bathymetry, velocity, and discharge). Next, a description of how these highly proficient measurement methods go beyond providing conventional data by providing new insights into 3-D river systems, including new research opportunities, is presented.

## 24.2 ACOUSTIC RIVER INSTRUMENTATION

Most contemporary instruments for rivers are based on acoustic principles, in which the instrument transmits short pulses in the water column and subsequently listens to the returned signal. One subcategory of these instruments uses the "time of travel" principle to determine either velocity or depth. These acoustic velocimeters determine the bulk flow velocity in the water column based on the travel time of an acoustic pulse between two targets located in a direction oblique to the flow (Ruhl and Simpson, 2005). From the same subcategory are acoustic instruments for depth measurement (sonars) that use the time it takes for the echo return to determine the distance between probe and the target (de Moustier, 1988). Most of the acoustic instruments for measurement

of velocity, however, use the Doppler principle to measure velocities at a point or along a line of sight (RDI, 1996). They are minimally intrusive – the instrument transducer is in contact with the water body – and the signals are sent away from the sensor.

Acoustic instruments can be operated from moving boats, by wading, or by fixing them on channel banks or structures for long-term measurements. They have fewer mechanical parts than conventional instruments, offer relatively high spatial and temporal sampling resolution, and require few calibrations. Moreover, they allow measurements in field settings where conventional measurements are very difficult or costly to obtain. Acoustic techniques have profoundly changed the way morphologic and hydrodynamic data are collected by researchers, engineers, and technicians. Besides using acoustic instruments for routine operations on water delivery projects, in water treatment plants, at stream gauging stations, and in many other water-resources-related projects, these instruments are increasingly being used for in situ scientific studies (Shields et al., 2003; Kostaschuk et al., 2004; Shugar et al., 2010).

### 24.2.1 Velocity Measurements Using Acoustic Methods

Most instruments used for velocity measurements are based on the Doppler effect (Figure 24.1a.), in which an acoustic pulse (ping) of a known frequency ($F$) is sent out by a transducer into the water column along the acoustic beam. A fraction of that acoustic pulse is reflected by small particles in the water and returns to the transducer at a frequency ($F'$) that has been shifted due to the Doppler effect (RDI, 1966). The water velocity along the acoustic beam is determined using the Doppler shifts of sound waves reflected from the particles moving with the water velocity ($V$). The change in signal amplitude or frequency (the frequency shift is actually determined from the slope at zero shift of the covariance function; Miller and Rochwarger, 1972) in conjunction with the travel time is used to estimate the location of the measurement and the velocities along the beam path.

Acoustic velocimeters are built in a wide variety of configurations, depending on the number of transducers and beams, and their deployment in the field. A mono-static velocimeter sends and receives acoustic signals through one transducer; whereas a bistatic velocimeter sends and receives acoustic signals through separate transducers. Only the velocity component along the beam path is measured. A velocimeter can use one or more acoustic beams and, based on the beam geometry, can provide 1-D, 2-D, or 3-D velocity components. They can be operated from fixed positions or in motion. Short descriptions of the most commonly used acoustic instruments used for velocity measurements are presented below.

### 24.2.1.1 Acoustic Doppler Velocimeters (ADV)

These instruments measure flow velocities using the Doppler shift principle (Kraus *et al.*, 1994). The instrument consists of a sound emitter, three sound receivers, and a signal-conditioning electronic module bundled in a light portable casing that can be easily attached to a wading rod. An ADV can measure 2-D or 3-D water velocity components within a small sampling volume (of the order 1 cm$^3$) at short distances (between 5 and 18 cm) from the instrument head (see Figure 24.1b), with sampling frequencies up to 200 Hz. Using additional measurements for the flow depth and distance between vertical profiles obtained from repeated measurements at various depths, the stream discharge can be estimated. ADVs are well suited to characterize mean flow and turbulence characteristics in natural streams, including gravel beds (Nikora and Goring, 2000; Fox and

Belcher, 2009), but quite limited for measurements in large rivers.

### 24.2.1.2 Horizontal Acoustic Doppler Current Profilers (HADCPs)

These specialized instruments utilize monostatic transducers that are fixed on special side-facing mounts (see Figure 24.1c). Acoustic pulses are sent into the water body along two horizontal diverging beams. Signal-processing software is used to analyse the returning beams to calculate multiple velocities from numerous range-gated sample volumes (bins) along the beam path. Both the size and number of these bins can be controlled from the HADCP firmware, with the bins spaced evenly along the main beam axis. The HADCP output is a time series of two-component horizontal water velocity profiles along a line across the channel cross-section. Using an index-velocity method (Rantz, 1982), the simultaneous HADCP velocities are converted to depth-averaged velocities across the section (Le Coz, 2008).

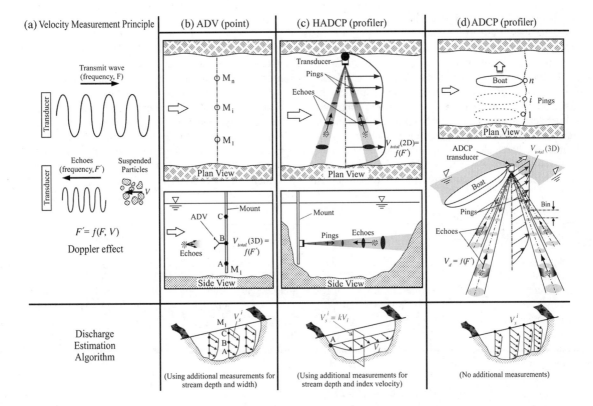

**Figure 24.1** Acoustic Doppler velocity instruments: (a) illustration of the Doppler effect; (b) acoustic Doppler velocimeter for point measurements; (c) horizontal acoustic Doppler current profiler for instantaneous horizontal velocity profiles; (d) acoustic Doppler current profilers for instantaneous measurement of vertical velocity profiles.

Empirical fits are needed to determine the index velocity and for filling in the missing velocities in areas unmeasured by the instrument (Le Coz, 2008). With bathymetry and depth externally measured, HADCP profiles can be used for estimating stream discharge, which is currently their main application in hydrometry.

### 24.2.1.3  Acoustic Doppler Current Profilers (ADCPs)

These instruments have been continuously developed since their inception in the early 1980s (Christensen and Herrick, 1982; Simpson, 1986, 2001; Gordon 1989). There is a vast literature describing the ADCPs underlying principles, configuration, and operational aspects (e.g., Gordon, 1989; Simpson and Oltmann, 1993; RDI, 1996; SonTek, 2000). ADCPs transmit sound pulses (pings) pointing in several directions (typically three or four) in the water column, and subsequently listen to the returning echoes from particles moving in the acoustic beam (Figure 24.1d). The echo received from a pulse traveling through the water column is range-gated to produce successive segments, called depth cells or bins (see Figure 24.1d). The relative velocity between ADCP and particles in each depth cell is determined by comparing transmitted and echoed acoustic signals characteristics. Velocity is inferred using single pulse (narrow-band systems) or two or morel pulses sent in short series (broad-band systems).

The pulses sent in different directions sense velocity components along the beam directions. Under the assumption that water currents are uniform (homogeneous) across layers of constant depth, a trigonometric transformation is used to convert the velocity along the beams into three velocity components associated with a Cartesian coordinate system attached to the instrument. At least three acoustic beams are required to characterize fully the 3-D velocity vector. The multibeam arrangement of ADCPs has a major drawback due to the fact that velocity components at a given depth are measured at different locations. Consequently, the size of the measurement volume for an ADCP operated at a fixed position has a constant height for all depths and a cross-section that increases with depth, as illustrated in Figure 24.1d. Most of the ADCP measurements in rivers have been, and still are, conducted from moving boats to obtain discharges. However, ADCPs measure with relative ease multicomponent instantaneous velocities along a profile in the column of water, over the cross-section, and within a river reach (Dinehart and Burau, 2005a; Szupiany et al., 2007). More details about the frequently used ADCPs are provided in Table 24.1.

Constraints of the ADCP architecture and operating principles make them unfeasible for measurements near solid boundaries or free surface. Measurements near free surfaces are affected by sensor submergence and operation (Muste et al., 2006), whereas water velocities measured near the river bottom are affected by acoustic beam side-lobe interference. Generally velocities in the top and bottom regions are discarded and replaced by assumed velocities. Water velocities measured by ADCP attached to a boat are relative to the boat to which the ADCP is attached. Therefore, if the boat moves, its velocity relative to the channel bed needs to be measured to calculate the actual velocity in the water column. The most popular procedure for measuring boat translation velocity is bottom-track (BT), which assumes a fixed channel bed, and determines the relative velocity between boat and river bed using long acoustic pulses. However, if the bed is in motion, the sediment concentration near the bed is high, or the river bottom is outside the ADCP's BT range, the calculation of actual boat velocity, and hence the water velocity is incorrect. To

**Table 24.1**  Specifications for commonly-used ADCPs

| Frequency (KHz) | 250 | 600 | 600 | 1000 | 1200 | 1200 | 1500 | 3000 |
|---|---|---|---|---|---|---|---|---|
| Velocity Mode | N/A | 1,12 | 5,8,11 | N/A | 1,12 | 5,8,11 | N/A | N/A |
| Operation | NB | BB | PC | NB | BB | PC | PC | NB |
| Instrument | SonTek ADP | RDI Rio Grande | RDI Rio Grande | SonTek M9 | RDI Rio Grande | RDI Rio Grande | SonTek PC-ADP | SonTek M9/S5 |
| Beam Angle (deg) | 25 | 20 | 20 | 25 | 20 | 20 | 15 | 25 |
| Max range (m) | 180 | 45 | 7 | 30 | 12 | 3.5 | 5 | 5 |
| Sample volume (m) | 1.0–10 | 0.5–4 | 0.1–0.5 | 0.02–0.5 | 0.25–2 | 0.05–0.25 | 0.02 | 0.02–4 |
| Velocity range (ms$^{-1}$) | 10 | 10 | 0.5–1 | 20 | 10 | 0.5–1 | 2.5 | 20 |
| Accuracy (cm s$^{-1}$) | 1% velocity | 0.25 | 0.25 | 0.25 | 0.2 | 0.25 | 0.1 | 0.002 |
| Resolution (cm s$^{-1}$) | 0.1 | 0.1 | 0.1 | 0.1 | 0.1 | 0.1 | 0.01 | 0.1 |

Acronyms in the table represent: NB – Narrow-band; BB – Broad-band; PC – Pulse-coherent. Remarks: Sampling volume is characterized by the height of the cell (bin).

handle such situations, a differential geographical positioning system (DGPS) can alternatively be used.

Instrument manufacturers (e.g., RDI, 1996) state 0.25% accuracy for the full measurement range. Manufacturer specifications, however, may vary depending on measurement environment, operating conditions, instrument settings, and operator experience (Shih *et al.*, 2000; Oberg *et al.*, 2005; Gonzalez-Castro and Muste, 2007).

Several investigations have explored the potential of ADV and ADCP to provide turbulence characteristics that play an important role in sediment transport, bed scour, and habitat restoration (Lohrmann *et al.*, 1990; Voulgaris and Trowbridge, 1998, Stacey *et al.*, 1999; Nystrom, 2001; Muste *et al.*, 2010). While this assessment is still in progress, there are indications that the instruments in the present configurations have limited capabilities to measure the finer structure of the turbulent flow. Among the causes of these limitations are: the large size of the measurement volumes (from centimetres to metres – inherently spatially averaging the flow within the sensor's probe) and the relatively low sampling frequency. Some researchers (e.g. Stacey *et al.* 1999) have attempted to circumvent this problem by utilizing the variance of individual beam velocities to estimate Reynolds stresses. However, this approach requires that measured variance is the actual true variance. Moreover, ADCP measurements include a substantial amount of noise (Rennie and Millar, 2007), which renders this technique difficult. These findings call for more research in order to substantiate specific improvements that instrument manufacturers should focus on in the future.

While both ADV and ADCP have profoundly changed the way hydraulic data are collected, ADCPs are increasingly popular in riverine environments, both for estimation of discharges (Simpson, 2001) and for capturing flow features which previously could only be documented in the laboratory (Dinehart and Burau, 2005b).

Among the new innovative applications of ADCPs in support of riverine research are: (i) characterization of mean flow characteristics (e.g., González-Castro *et al.*, 1996; Muste *et al.*, 2004); (ii) estimation of turbulence quantities (e.g., Stacey *et al.*, 1999, Lu and Lueck, 1999a, 1999b; Schemper and Admiraal, 2002; Nystrom *et al.*, 2002; Howarth, 2002; Kawanisi, 2004; Lane *et al.*, 2008); (iii) characterization of the spatial distribution of velocities in riverine habitats and bed survey (Shields *et al.*, 2003, Gaeuman and Jacobson, 2006); (iv) estimation of the longitudinal dispersion coefficient for river flow (Carr *et al.*, 2006, 2007; Kim *et al.*, 2007a); (v) estimation of bedload transport in gravel rivers (Rennie *et al.*, 2002; Rennie and Millar, 2007), and (vi) suspended sediment concentration (Wall *et al.*, 2006, Topping *et al.*, 2007, Gray and Gartner, 2009).

### 24.2.2 Bathymetry Measurements Using Acoustic Methods

Relatively new, but quite intensively used acoustic instruments for measuring river bathymetry are the depth sounders (see Figure 24.2). Depth sounders (also known as echosounders) can provide 3-D representation of river morphology by conducting mobile surveys with sounders attached to boats. Echosounders have been used in the oceanographic community since the advent of sonar in the 1940s (e.g., de Moustier, 1988; Kostachuck *et al.*, 1989; Pratson and Edwards, 1996; Parsons *et al.*, 2005; Mayer, 2006), but their use for mapping river bathymetry is fairly recent. The most common echosounder that is used to measure river bathymetry is based on single beam operation that creates one bathymetry point per emitted signal (pulse) (Kostaschuk and Villard, 1996; Carling *et al.*, 2000; Julien *et al.*, 2002; White and Hodges, 2005; Merwade *et al.*, 2006). The set-up for mapping river bathymetry

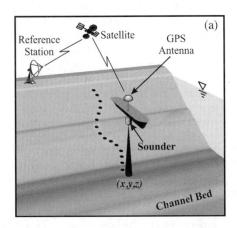

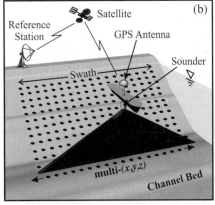

**Figure 24.2**   Depth echosounder using: (a) single beam and (b) multibeam.

involves using a boat-mounted echosounder coupled to a GPS as shown in Figure 24.2a. The GPS unit is equipped with an antenna that is capable of receiving differential GPS (DGPS) corrections. The echosounder or transducer emits a sound pulse (ping) in the water, and the pulse gets reflected back to its source as an echo after hitting the channel bottom. The time interval between the initiation of the sound pulse and the echo returned from the channel bed is used to determine the depth of the channel bed from the source. The boat is moved throughout the river reach to collect bathymetry along a track. A single beam echosounder emits one signal or pulse, thus producing one $(x, y, z)$ bathymetry point per ping (LCSI, 2000).

Bathymetry mapping with the single-beam echosounder is expensive in terms of time and effort. In the water resources community, 2-D and 3-D hydrodynamic models, which are becoming common in modelling flows, turbulence, and other processes, need higher-resolution bathymetry as input to be able to perform accurate simulation and deliver better results compared to 1-D models. As a result, even the bathymetry produced by a single beam echosounder is sometimes inadequate to prepare accurate high-resolution models. Consequently, single beam echosounders are now being replaced by multibeam echosounders (MBES; Julien *et al.*, 2002; Wilbers and Ten Brinke, 2003; Parsons *et al.*, 2005; Eilertsen and Hansen, 2007; Nittrouer, 2008) which produce a swath of river bathymetry by emitting multiple signals at the same time (Denbigh, 1989). With MBES, a transducer emits an acoustic beam that is narrow along the boat track and wide across the boat track, thus creating a swath of bathymetry measurements, as illustrated in Figure 24.2b. As the boat moves, these swaths overlap, and produce a high-resolution river bathymetry surface. Some of the main characteristics of MBES are acoustic frequency, maximum angular aperture, number of beams, and beam spacing (Orange *et al.*, 1999). Frequency affects the spatial resolution, wave attenuation, and sub-bottom penetration. Spatial resolution and wave attenuation increase with frequency, whereas sub-bottom depth penetration (e.g., wave penetrating into soft sediments) decreases with higher frequency. Therefore, high-frequency transducers are desired for river studies to get accurate higher-resolution bathymetry. For example, a 455 kHz SeaBat™ 8125 system from Reson (www.reson.com) can be used in water bodies varying in water depth from 0.5 to 500 m, with a reported vertical resolution of 6 mm. The maximum angular aperture determines the swath width, with typical values ranging from 90° to 150°.

Using a sound pulse to record river bathymetry is only one of the two functions a MBES can perform. MBES can also function as a sidescan sonar to create an image of a river bed. Instead of only measuring the depth to the river bed using travel time, a sidescan sonar reveals information about the river bed composition by taking advantage of different sound-absorbing and -reflecting properties of different bed materials using the amplitude or strength of returned signals. The same signal that records water depth through travel time is analysed for amplitude (power) information. Objects that protrude from the bed, such as metals (strong reflectors), reflect stronger signals compared to clay or sand. Thus, strength of return signals is continuously recorded to create a picture of the river bed, which can be examined for its composition (LCSI, 2000). River bathymetry in conjunction with sidescan images becomes a powerful dataset to explore a river bed in greater detail. While the main objective of echosounding surveys is to collect high-resolution bathymetry, the resulting data have wide applications in many areas connected to river channels, such as hydrodynamic modelling (Andréfouëta *et al.*, 2006), sediment transport (Abraham and Pratt, 2002), fish habitat modelling (Hilldale, 2007), and characterization of the bedform morphology (Best, 2005; Kostaschuk and Best, 2005; Parsons *et al.*, 2005; Hanrahan, 2006). General specifications of both single and multibeam echosounders are presented in Table 24.2.

## 24.3  CLOSE-RANGE REMOTE-SENSING RIVER INSTRUMENTATION

The emerging techniques for characterizing river morphology and hydrodynamics are inspired by ground and aerial close-range remote-sensing technology developed for the geophysical and coastal engineering areas in recent decades. The main advantage of this new generation of riverine measurement instruments over the acoustic techniques presented in the previous sections is that they do not require direct contact with the water body to be measured. Consequently, there is no need for boat deployments for most of these techniques. Velocity measurements are taken from the river banks or a structure located along or across the river. Bathymetric surveys can be made either close to the free surface using suspended cableways, or remotely with the instruments carried by planes flying at low altitudes. Linking the terrestrial and riverine survey techniques allow integration of geomorphology, hydrology, ecology, and tectonics for studying complex stream processes in rivers, their floodplains and watersheds at unprecedented spatial and temporal resolutions (Quadros, 2008).

Mapping the velocity distribution at the free surface can be obtained by short segments of recordings of images or radio waves returned from the free surface. Velocity measurements can only be attained if the free surface contains "patterns" that can be recognized in the recorded images or retuned waves. The patterns can

**Table 24.2** Specifications of acoustic methods for bathymetry measurements

| Method | Depth Range | Accuracy | Strengths | Limitations | Applicability |
|--------|-------------|----------|-----------|-------------|---------------|
| Single Beam | 0–1200 m | Up to 1 cm[a] | Relatively inexpensive and easy to use | Limited spatial coverage[b] | Small narrow river reaches with relatively homogenous river bed |
| Multibeam | 0.5–3000 m | Up to 1 cm[a] | Spatial coverage in the form of a swath is better than single beam; can also provide sidescan imagery | Expensive[b] | Wider river reaches with non-shallow depth |

[a] accuracy is affected by frequency.
[b] data quality is affected by vessel noise, water quality and sediment reflectivity.

occur naturally at the free surface (e.g., free-surface waviness, kolks, or boils produced by large-scale channel turbulence) or can be added in order to support the measurement process. Non-contact bathymetry mapping instruments are the most recent developmental efforts in this area, and are currently undergoing fast evolution and continuous evaluation. Therefore, only operating principles of these instruments are covered in this chapter. The most extensively tested technology in this category is the ground-penetrating radar (GPR), which can provide bathymetry profiles in river cross-sections and sediment stratigraphy in the river bed (Leclerc and Hickin, 1997; Lin et al., 2009). Parallel efforts are carried out to develop non-contact river bathymetry instruments based on LiDAR techniques (Snyder, 2009). Both bathymetric measurement systems range-gate the transmitted wave returns, and associate the characteristics of the return signal with changes in the media (water versus solids) or stratification of the subsurface. The processed signals lead to bathymetric surveys in a river cross-section or over whole river reaches.

### 24.3.1 Velocity Mapping Using Remote Sensors

#### 24.3.1.1 Large-Scale Particle Image Velocimetry (LSPIV)

Developments over the last three decades in optics, acoustics, electronics, and computer hardware and software have triggered a rapid implementation of image- and radar-based techniques for measuring river surface currents (Costa et al., 2000; Muste et al., 2008). The first image-based velocity measurements in rivers were made in Japan in the mid 1990s (Fujita and Komura, 1994; Aya et al., 1995). As most of the measurements were taken over surfaces much larger than those in traditional Particle Image Velocimetry (PIV), the technique was dubbed large-scale PIV (LSPIV). A thorough review of LSPIV from its inception to date is provided in Muste et al. (2008).

A schematic of the LSPIV procedural steps from image acquisition to measurement output is presented in Figure 24.3a. In essence, LSPIV entails several steps: flow visualization, illumination, image recording, and image processing. Given that LSPIV images cover large areas usually recorded from an oblique angle to the flow surface, an additional step of image ortho-rectification is customarily involved.

The most critical aspect of the LSPIV usage in field conditions is the visualization of the free surface. Visualization can be accomplished with a variety of tracers. A favourable measurement situation is when naturally occurring seeding or patterns are floating at the free surface. They can consist of foam, light debris, or small free-surface deformations created by turbulent eddies intersecting the free surface. An alternative seeding surrogate is the specular reflection formed by incident light interacting with the free-surface deformations (Creutin et al., 2002). Free-surface waviness is generated by large-scale turbulent structures intersecting the free surface or wind acting on the free surface. In the absence of "natural seeding", addition of a material contrasting with the background waterbody colour, light enough to trace the flow accurately, large enough to be detected at the individual particle level or in particle clumps, and uniformly dispersed onto the free surface within the measured area can give good LSPIV measurements. Convenient seeding alternatives include use of dry tree leaves, wood debris, or other ecologically harmless materials, such as biodegradable eco-foam peanuts (an off-the-shelf granular packaging material containing 99% corn syrup).

Raw LSPIV data are instantaneous water surface velocity fields spanning flow areas up to thousands of square metres. Image visualization, illumination, and image recording are strongly inter-related, and, therefore, selection of one approach for a given step imposes the types of devices or approaches available for the remaining steps. The selection of the approaches and their integrated operation in conventional PIV is

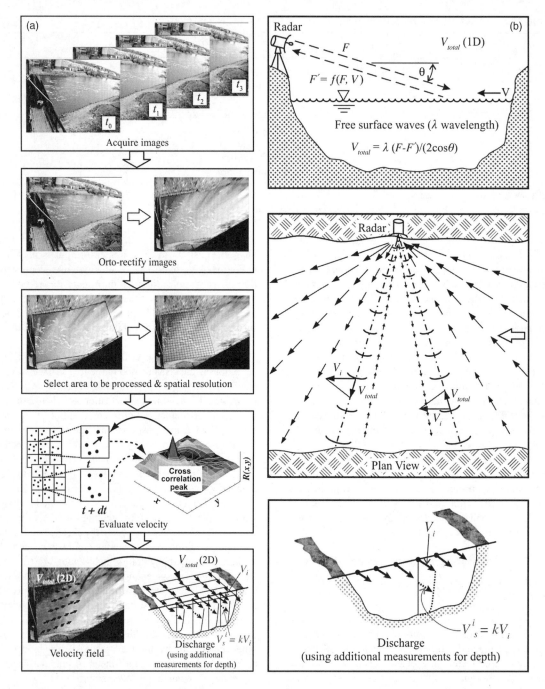

**Figure 24.3** Principles of operation and procedures associated with the velocity mapping techniques. (a) large-scale particle image velocimetry, (b) surface-velocity radar.

driven by well-established rules of thumb regarding the concentration of the visualization patterns, their size with respect to the image-processing parameters, and the desirable particle displacement in a series of images (Adrian, 1991). In order to extract accurate flow data

from distorted images, they have to be rectified by an appropriate image transformation scheme (Mikhail and Ackermann, 1976).

LSPIV algorithms for estimating velocities are the core of the measurement technique. In essence, a pattern-matching technique is applied to the image intensity distribution in a series of images, as illustrated in Figure 24.3a. The similarity index for patterns enclosed in a small interrogation area fixed in the first image is calculated for the same-sized window within a larger search area selected in the second image using an image velocimetry algorithm (e.g., Fujita *et al.*, 1998). The window pair with the maximum value for the similarity index is assumed to be the pattern's most probable displacement between two consecutive images. Once the distance between the centres of the respective small windows is obtained, velocity can be calculated by dividing it by the time difference between consecutive images. This local searching process is applied successively over the entire image, resulting in 2-D vector fields.

The key advantage of image velocimetry is that it measures instantaneous velocities in a flow plane (see Figure 24.3a). Using images instead of transducer output makes image velocimetry more user-friendly. The technique does not require calibration and allows reprocessing of the raw information with variable spatial and temporal resolutions to obtain flow details. The mean vector field, turbulence characteristics, flow patterns (streamlines, pathlines), vorticity, and discharges can all be readily obtained from the raw image-based measured velocities. The grid-attached nature of the measurements efficiently complements the requirements for the calibration and validation of numerical simulations. LSPIV surface velocity in conjunction with bathymetry can provide flow rates in streams. The method used for estimation of the discharge is the velocity-area method (VAM), as illustrated in Figure 24.3a. The channel bathymetry can be obtained from direct surveys using specialized instruments (e.g., sonars or acoustic doppler current profilers). The channel bathymetry can be surveyed at the time of the LSPIV measurements, or prior to them, under the assumption that bathymetry is not changing in the time interval between the bed and free-surface measurements. Surface velocities at several points along the surveyed cross-section ($V_i$ in Figure 24.3a) are computed by linear interpolation from neighbouring grid points of the PIV-estimated surface velocity vector field. Assuming that the shape of vertical velocity profile is the same at each point $i$, the depth-averaged velocity at each $i$ vertical, $V_s^i$, is related to the free-surface velocity by a velocity index, $k$. The discharge for each river subsection ($i, i + 1$) is computed following the classical VAM procedure (Rantz, 1982).

### 24.3.1.2 *Surface-Velocity Radar*

Microwave radars have been extensively used in remote sensing of the ocean surface since the mid 1990s (McGregor *et al.*, 1997). With direct support of the USGS's Hydro 21 Committee, radar-based techniques have been extended to riverine environments (Costa *et al.*, 2000). Several configurations and constructive details have been tested over a relatively short time interval (Plant and Keller, 1990; Melcher *et al.*, 1999). While the technique continues to evolve, the monostatic geometry (that allows setting the instrument components close to each other) is described here for illustration purposes (Teague *et al.*, 2003). Figure 24.3b illustrates the deployment of an ultra-high frequency (UHF, i.e., microwave at 350 MHz) radar system for a river measurement situation. Surface currents can be determined by measuring the Doppler shift in the signal scattered back to the radar antenna from a rough water surface. UHF uses predominantly Bragg-type scattering (Plant and Keller, 1990), whereby the approaching and receding wave energy can be separated and processed independently. The instrument detects only velocity along its line of sight, and therefore, the radial currents perceived by the radar look like those shown in Figure 24.3b.

Most often the free surface roughness needed for acquiring the measurements is produced by winds or by internally generated free surface waves of 2 to 4 cm wavelengths (Melcher *et al.*, 1999). Under low wind and flow conditions, sufficient surface roughness may not be present to produce backscatter above system noise levels, and thus, under such conditions, the techniques presented in this paper may not yield a measurement. The microwave techniques presented here are expected to work well at moderate to high flows and may prove especially valuable during floods.

Use of surface velocity radars requires some general knowledge of the dominant flow velocity because raw free surface velocities can only be measured if the flow is not perpendicular to the wave direction propagation. The actual direction of the flow is determined using the raw measurements obtained as described above in conjunction with assumed models for the flow to be measured. The simplest direction-finding algorithm is the one assuming that the flow is parallel to banks with only a small cross-river component. Cross-channel velocity profiles can subsequently be calculated for several streamwise locations. Similar to LSPIV, an index velocity relates the measured surface velocity to depth-averaged velocity. Stream discharge can be subsequently obtained using conventional VAM procedures (Rantz, 1982).

### 24.3.2 *Bathymetry Mapping Using Remote Sensors*

#### 24.3.2.1 *Airborne LiDAR Bathymetry (ALB)*

These systems emerged from the coastal engineering area (Irish and White, 1998; Lillycop *et al.*, 2001), but recently have been tested for river bathymetry surveys (McKean *et al.*, 2009). Development of ALB for bathymetry mapping is driven by the growing need to efficiently and accurately represent high-resolution river channel geometry to study fluvial environments for flow hydraulics, flood routing, sediment transport, aquatic habitat, and monitoring of geomorphic changes (Hilldale and Raff, 2007).

Bathymetric LiDAR systems operate in a manner that is similar to their airborne LiDAR mapping (ALM) counterpart for terrestrial surveys, with one notable exception. Bathymetric systems transmit two light waves, one in the infrared and one in the green spectrum, and are capable of detecting two returns that delineate the water surface and the river or seabed (see Figure 24.4a). The infrared band is quickly absorbed, and is therefore used to detect the water surface, while the green band is used as the optimum colour to achieve maximum penetration in shallow water. Because of the increased energy required to penetrate the denser medium of water, ALB systems operate at a much slower scan rate than terrestrial systems. To avoid scattering of short laser pulses in the water column, ALB systems use much longer pulses for bathymetry mapping. An ALB pulse is generated as a digital waveform, making it easier to detect the smallest variances in the returns, including perturbations in the water column.

Bathymetry mapping is a stand-alone LiDAR data product. Despite the high cost of acquiring an ALB system, the methodology offers significant savings in operational cost and increased productivity compared to conventional survey methods. ALB systems are generally flown from small aircraft, and mapping can be conducted in clear water that is up to 50 m deep. Penetration of ALB signals, however, depends on water

clarity, and it decreases with increased water turbidity. Integration of the terrestrial LiDAR with bathymetric LiDAR is a powerful methodology to seamlessly and efficiently map rivers, their floodplains, and their watersheds at unprecedentedly high spatial resolutions (Quadros, 2008).

Hilldale and Raff (2007) used ALB to collect bathymetry on gravel-bed reaches in two river basins (Yakima in Washington and Trinity in California) in the western US to assess the quality of the data for numerical modelling and geomorphic assessment. They found that the ALB data was suitable for micro-scale modeling, but some meso-scale features such as pools, riffles, and glides are relatively better defined compared to large boulders and rootwads. The overall accuracy of the ALB data was comparable to the terrestrial LiDAR and bathymetry obtained through photogrammetry. Although, ALB has found wide applications in coastal systems, in gravel-bed rivers – which also have shallow water depths (less than 1 m) – data from ALB should be used with caution and in conjunction with other field data to gain confidence in the data quality. For example, Bailly *et al.* (2008) used ALB data for the Gardon, gravel-bed river in southern France, and found that ALB data were unable to produce accurate water depths. However, a prior calibration of LiDAR with turbidity was able to produce better estimates of water depth and bed forms.

### 24.3.2.2   Ground-Penetrating Radar (GPR)

This technology operates in a fashion similar to sonar, except that GPRs emit electromagnetic energy pulses instead of acoustic energy pulses. GPR systems have been commercially available for geomorphologic and

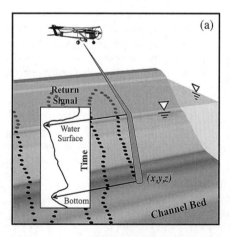
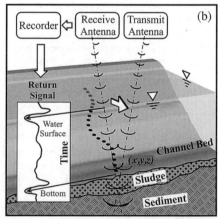

**Figure 24.4**   Non-contact bathymetry surveying instruments using: (a) airborne LiDAR bathymetry; and (b) ground-penetrating radar.

geotechnical applications since the 1970s (Moorman and Michel, 1997). These non-contact bathymetry instruments were originally developed to identify natural features such as sediment stratigraphy and interfaces, as well as natural and man-made objects including cables, pipes, boats, outboards, logs, and other artifacts buried deeply in sediments. They have been gradually tested and customized for implementation in riverine environments, including gravel-bed rivers (Costa *et al.*, 2000; Pelpola and Hickin, 2004; Wooldridge and Hickin, 2006). GPR can be suspended from a bank-operated cableway and transported across the channel 2 to 4 feet above the water surface, or can be operated from boats or helicopters (Melcher *et al.*, 1999). The continuous and slow motion across the channel produces a radar image of the water and soil column, and GPRs can be used for both open- and ice-covered water bodies (Moorman and Michel, 1997).

GPRs can use either separate transmitting and receiving antennas or only one antenna containing both functions (see Figure 24.4b). The radar system emits an electromagnetic (ELM) wave which propagates away from the transmitter antenna until it finds a reflector that sends the ELM wave to the receiver antenna. ELM waves travel at high speeds (0.3 m ns$^{-1}$ in air and 0.033 m ns$^{-1}$ in water). The electromagnetic properties of a material are related to soil composition and water content, both of which control the speed and attenuation of ELM waves (Mellett, 1995). ELM wave reflections are a result of contrasts in the dielectric permittivity between adjacent materials. Greater contrasts in dielectric permittivities produce stronger reflections, and therefore, ELM waves will reflect off soil interfaces having different electromagnetic properties. When the wave hits a buried object or a boundary with different dielectric constants, the receiving antenna records variations in the reflected return signal, as illustrated in Figure 24.4b. The accuracy of GPR measurements is adversely affected by high conductivity of the medium through which they propagate.

### 24.3.3 Passive Methods for Bathymetry

The above methods can be considered active methods in which the illumination is provided by a device. The other category, in which the illumination is provided by the sun, includes passive methods such as photogrammetric and spectral methods. In photogrammetric methods the image geometry is used to extract information (Westaway *et al.*, 2001, 2003; Feurer *et al.*, 2007), whereas in spectral methods, water depth is related to image reflectance to derive bathymetry (e.g., Winterbottom and Gilvear, 1997; Westaway *et al.*, 2003; Carbonneau *et al.*, 2003; Lyzenga *et al.*, 2006). Lane (2000, 2001)

provides a history and review of photogrammetry in river applications. Recent articles by Gao (2009) and Feurer *et al.* (2008) also provides a review of both active and passive methods with regard to their potential and issues in producing high-resolution river bathymetry, including providing an overview of general characteristics (e.g., resolution, accuracy, and applicability) of different methods (see Table 24.3).

In addition to the review of existing approaches, Feurer *et al.* used an unmanned aerial vehicle (UAV) to compare the photogrammetric approach with the spectral approach. Results showed that spectral approach was able to produce reasonable results at coarser resolutions (1 m and higher), but the photogrammetric approach required very high-resolution ground data and bottom texture. Legleiter *et al.* (2009) developed an optimal band ratio analysis (OBRA) algorithm to retrieve river bathymetry from images when the remotely sensed signal is dominated by bottom-reflected radiance. Application of OBRA to three gravel-bed reaches in Yellowstone National Park, USA produced reasonable bathymetric maps. In another study, Legleiter and Roberts (2009) took a bottom-up (streambed to remote sensing) approach to evaluate the requirements of remote-sensing images to describe the streambed of interest. Such an approach may be useful to develop remote-sensing methods to meet the specific needs of different river bathymetries across a range of fluvial systems and scales.

## 24.4 DEMONSTRATION OF INSTRUMENT CAPABILITIES

This section illustrates the capabilities of modern velocity- and depth-measuring instruments to provide with ease, accuracy, and convenience an impressive volume of digital data that further enables unprecedented characterization of river morphology and hydrodynamics. Out of the plethora of the instruments and techniques described earlier, description of one instrument for velocity measurements and one instrument for bathymetry mapping is provided for illustrative purposes.

To demonstrate the capabilities for measuring hydrodynamic variables, ADCP data collected along two study reaches are used, specifically, a Kissimmee River reach in Florida (Muste *et al.*, 2007) and Pool 16 of the Mississippi River (Young, 2006). Hydrodynamic data were collected with a 1200 kHz four beam ADCPs from Teledyne RDI.

For Kissimmee River, 14 repeated moving boat profiles and 12 fixed location measurements were collected at the site. The average channel width at this location is 40 m, maximum depth is 4 m, mean flow velocity is 0.78 m s$^{-1}$, and stream discharge is 13.6 m$^3$ s$^{-1}$. Single-ping ADCP data were acquired from a boat tethered at tag lines anchored on the river banks. The approximate travel

**Table 24.3** Specifications of remote sensing methods for bathymetry measurements (reproduced from Gao (2009))

| Method | System | Depth Range | Accuracy | Affecting Factors | Strengths | Limitations | Best Use |
|---|---|---|---|---|---|---|---|
| Non-imaging | LIDAR | Up to 70 m | Up to 15 cm | Water clarity, bottom material, surface state, background light | Wide depth range; Concurrent measurement not essential | Expensive Limited swath width | Diverse environments of a narrow range (e.g., several km wide) |
| Imaging | Microwave | Shallow to deep | Low | Image resolution slicks, fronts, waves | Over large areas Not subject to cloud cover | Not so accurate | Open oceanic waters |
| Imaging | Optical-analytical | Up to 30 m | High | Water quality, atmospheric conditions | Based on physical process, Accurate | Complex as several input parameters are required; Concurrent sea truth essential | Turbid and shallow inland waters, estuaries and river channels |
| Imaging | Optical-empirical | Up to 30 m | variable | Atmospheric calibration, water turbidity, bottom reflectance | Simple to implement Accurate at certain depth; | Limited depth Accuracy lower at a larger depth;- Concurrent sea truth essential | Near shore and coastal waters; open waters |
| Imaging | Video | Tidal height | High | Image resolution | Able to reveal minor bathymetric change | Restrictive area Bathymetry along profiles | Intertidal zone and estuaries |

time of the boat along the transect was 5 minutes, which produced a spacing of 5 cm between consecutive pings that were emitted every 0.4 seconds. With an exclusion of 0.65 m from the free surface and 0.36 m from the bottom, the vertical profiles were sampled every 25 cm, which defined the extent of depth cells (bins). The 12 fixed boat profiles were sampled with a spacing of approximately 3 m along the transect. For each fixed location, the boat was anchored for 2.5 minutes time duration to capture adequately local mean flow characteristics. The vertical spacing of the ADCP data for fixed-point measurements was identical to moving boat measurements at respective locations.

While the Kissimmee River measurements were acquired at one cross section, the Pool 16 Mississippi River data were collected with multiple transects to describe a portion of the river. Mississippi data were collected for assessment of mussel colony habitat (Young, 2006). Twenty moving boat transects were surveyed along Pool 16 reach with an approximate spacing of 60 m between adjacent transects. The average channel width of Pool 16 reach is 280 m, maximum depth is 5.5 m, mean flow velocity was 0.3 m s$^{-1}$, and stream discharge was 317.4 m$^3$ s$^{-1}$. The approximate travel time of the boat along Pool 16 transects was 17 minutes, which produced a spacing of 0.5 m between consecutive pings that were emitted every 0.9 seconds. The vertical profiles were sampled every 10 cm, which defined the bin size for these data.

Demonstration of morphologic measurements is done using MBES data collected for a 5 km reach along the Brazos River in Texas. These data can be used to extract information that is produced by conventional methods (cross-sectional surveys), as well as new information that is available as a result of high-resolution bathymetry.

The MBES data for Brazos River were collected by Texas Water Development Board (TWDB) using 240 kHz SeaBat™ 8101 with titanium sonar head from Reson Inc. and Trible Pro-XRS GPS. The signals returned to the system were processed by Reson 6042 data collection software to produce a 0.5 m digital terrain model (DTM) of the river bed. The final data from Reson 6042, $(x, y, z)$ points, were then exported to a shapefile in ArcGIS to extract river features. In addition to MBES bathymetry, sidescan images were also collected by TWDB for the same reach. Rapid acquisition of high-resolution bathymetry from MBES enables extraction of different river features which otherwise would require separate survey campaigns with conventional methods. In addition, the spatial resolution associated with data collected with conventional methods is inadequate for extracting micro-scale features such as dunes, pools, and riffles. Features that can be extracted from ADCP and MBES data are categorized into three types: linear, areal, and surfaces. Each category is discussed in more detail in the next section.

### 24.4.1 River Hydrodynamics

#### 24.4.1.1 1-D Characterization of Stream Cross-Section

Individual ADCP pings practically provide 3-D instantaneous velocities along verticals in the water column and depth measurement at the measurement location. When operated from a moving boat the resulting data are voluminous. For example, the operational settings used for the Kissimmee River transects produced about 800 pings and 8000 bins in each transect (Figure 24.5). Areas with missing data are usually filled through extrapolation algorithms such as power and log laws. The data can be

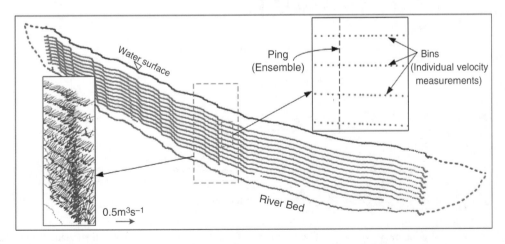

**Figure 24.5** Instantaneous velocities acquired by ADCP operated from moving boat across the stream cross-section. (See the color version of this figure in color plate section.)

used to determine the dominant velocity direction along a cross-section, which in most cases defines the river direction. Average cross-sectional velocities and depth can be used to estimate other flow parameters such as Froude number and aspect ratio. Discharge can be estimated by using either custom algorithms specifically developed for ADCP measurements collected from moving boats (Christensen and Herrick, 1982) or conventional algorithms such as the velocity-area method (Boiten, 2000) for fixed measurements across a cross-section.

### 24.4.1.2 2-D Characterization of Stream Cross-Section

ADCP operations at fixed points can provide accurate description of mean flow and selected turbulence aspects (Muste *et al.*, 2010). The extensive data collected by ADCP in each bin can provide vertical profiles of mean velocity and turbulence characteristics under various flow conditions (Nystrom *et al.*, 2002; Muste and Kim, 2007). Time-averaged velocity profiles obtained from ADCP data collected at fixed points in the Kissimmee River are illustrated in Figure 24.6. The total velocity vectors (using all three velocity components provided by ADCP) shown in Figure 24.5 can be

averaged for each bin along a vertical to produce profiles of mean velocity in the water column, as illustrated in Figure 24.6a. Average mean velocity in all bins at a fixed point can be averaged to produce depth-averaged velocity for each point, as shown in Figure 24.6b, which characterizes the stream through a vector field in the horizontal plane. Finally, the velocity measurements in each bin can be used to produce a traverse velocity distribution across the stream cross-section, as shown in Figure 24.6c, which characterizes the stream through a vector field in the vertical plane.

### 24.4.1.3 3-D Characterization at Reach Scale

Reach-scale flow-field analyses are needed for various hydrodynamic modelling studies, including quantification of aquatic habitat zones across a range of scales (Shields, 2003). In principle, the 1-D and 2-D quantities and representations discussed earlier can be extrapolated at reach scale through spatial averaging. The spatial averaging in this context refers to averaging of velocities collected from moving boats. The data are averaged over small travel distances over areas where the flow is uniform (away from edges, obstacles in the flow, depth changes). Spatial averaging of ADCP data enables to obtain 2-D and

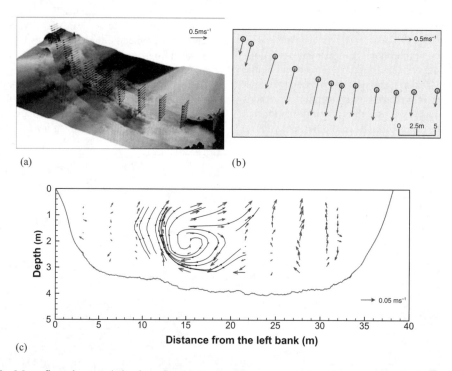

(a)                                    (b)

(c)

**Figure 24.6** Mean flow characteristics from fixed point ADCP measurements: (a) mean vertical velocity distributions; (b) depth-averaged profile; (c) mapping of the velocity distribution in the stream cross-section. (See the color version of this figure in color plate section.)

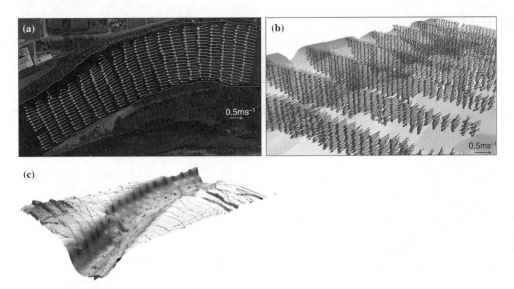

**Figure 24.7** River morphology and mean hydrodynamic characteristics obtained from ADCP measurements acquired in Pool 16 in Mississippi River; (a) 2-D reach scale river representation of spatially double-averaged (spanwise and vertical averaging) velocity field; (b) 3-D velocity field obtained by spatially averaged ADCP transect measurements within the reach; (c) spatially interpolated river morphology based on individual beam ADCP data. (See the color version of this figure in color plate section.)

3-D velocity fields at reach scale. Reach-scale ADCP data include multiple cross-sections that are spatially distributed to cover a targeted reach. Reach-scale river representation is illustrated using data for Pool 16 in the Mississippi River (see Figure 24.7). 2-D depth-averaged velocity vectors are shown in Figure 24.7a, while 3-D vertical velocity distributions are shown in Figure 24.7b by spatially averaging over 3 m span across each transect.

An ADCP can also provide depth information similar to a single beam echosounder. When the ADCP is moved across a transect, a river cross-section is created in addition to the acquired velocity measurements. These cross-sections can be interpolated to create a surface, as shown in Figure 24.7c. This bed surface is obtained from the 20 cross-sections using the four ADCP beams corrected for pitch and roll. The ADCP computes water depth by using pulses that are distinct from those used to estimate velocities in the water column. Usually, the depths recorded by the inclined ADCP beams (typically 20–30°) are averaged to provide a depth surrogate associated with the instrument axis. The divergent beam configuration, criticized for playing a negative role in the measurement of velocity with ADCP, becomes an advantage for the depth measurements as the ADCP acts similarly to a multibeam sonar. While it is expected that ADCPs are capable of measuring accurately the depth along individual beams, there is not a final verdict on the accuracy of the ADCP to measure bathymetry.

### 24.4.2 River Morphology

#### 24.4.2.1 Linear Features

Linear (sometimes also referred as 1-D) features that can be extracted from MBES data include channel cross-sections and the thalweg. The channel centreline and bank lines are also linear features, but they generally do not contain elevation information, and can be extracted from other data sources such as aerial photographs. Cross-sections and the thalweg are used in all hydraulic, ecological, and aquatic models that use the 1-D flow assumption to compute cross-section averaged variables. Because of the continuous bathymetry available from MBES, data can be extracted at various resolutions, thus enabling efficient data retrieval to fit the objectives of different modelling and research studies. In addition, because the channel bed is invisible in the presence of water, it is difficult to determine *a priori* the best cross-section to capture the required details. With MBES data, several cross-sections in the same vicinity can be visualized to choose the right cross-section. A slight change in survey location can yield cross-sections with different shapes and morphologic properties, as demonstrated by five different locations and survey configurations in Figure 24.8a. At another location along a meandering bend, however, the cross-sectional shape and properties are relatively similar for different survey locations (Figure 24.8b). Similarly, a thalweg profile can be

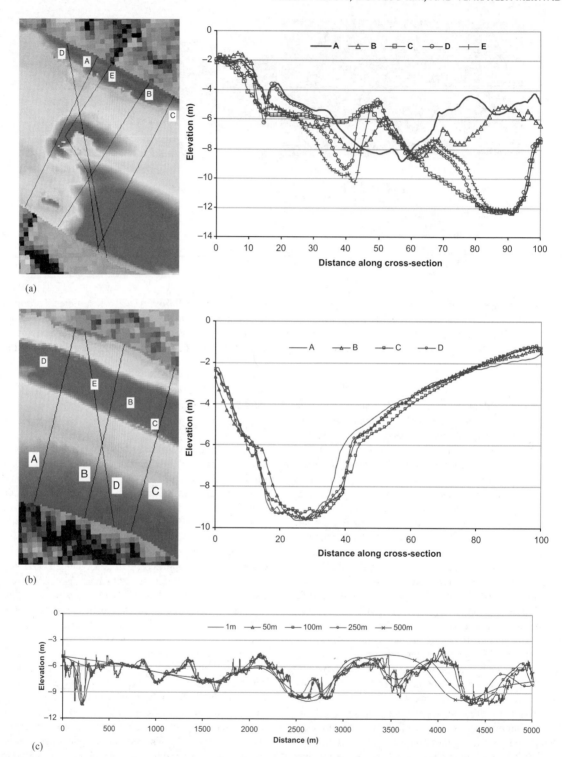

**Figure 24.8** Linear features extraction from Brazos River MBES data: (a) cross-section locations at a bridge and corresponding ground profiles; (b) cross-section locations at a meandering bend and corresponding ground profiles; (c) thalweg profiles for different sampling intervals. (See the color version of this figure in color plate section.)

different depending on the spacing of surveyed points using conventional methods (Figure 24.8c). A MBES surface can be used to create thalweg profiles of different resolutions to pick an appropriate profile. A thalweg profile can also give an idea of critical locations for extracting cross-sections.

### 24.4.2.2 Areal Features

MBES data can be used to extract areal features such as pools, riffles, and islands that are useful in hydraulic modelling, geomorphology, and habitat mapping. A traditional technique used for mapping pools and riffles is "habitat typing", in which an observer walks along the channel with a tape and measures lengths of pools and riffles (Madej, 1999). Habitat typing is a subjective method which is affected by discharge and operator variability. With MBES data, simple GIS-based queries of depths can yield a map of pools and riffles (Figure 24.9). Besides simple depth-based queries, advanced exploratory analysis using slope, curvature, and aspect can also be used to characterize river morphologic features (Song and Shan, 2008).

In addition to areal extent, attributes such as average depth and volume, which are not possible to estimate from conventional techniques, can be easily estimated from MBES data using standard GIS tools. Areal extent of river features such as pools and riffles is inadequate to understand river processes and aquatic conditions because pools with similar areas and even depths may have different topography. Therefore, the ability to compute additional variables such as depth and volume is extremely useful in tracking the changes occurring in river systems.

### 24.4.2.3 Surfaces

Although linear and areal features extracted from MBES data tend to be more accurate and of higher resolution compared to data extracted from conventional methods, the greatest benefit of having MBES data is the ability to visualize, interpret, and use river bathymetry as a 3-D surface. A bathymetry surface from MBES in conjunction with sidescan sonar can reveal details that are not easily captured with conventional techniques. A MBES surface can provide details on extent, depth, and volume of a river feature, while a sidescan image can show the exact nature of the feature. For example, in a MBES surface it is possible to see a bridge pier, extent of erosion or deposition, and depth variations around a bridge pier, but a sidescan image can show details such as woody debris around the pier (Figure 24.10a).

Similarly other non-natural details (human interventions) which may appear ambiguous from MBES bathymetry can be confirmed by looking at the corresponding sidescan image to reduce the uncertainty in MBES data, and incorporate these details into engineering and scientific investigations. For example, the MBES surface for the Brazos shows some rectangular, unrecognizable irregularities in the bathymetry data at one location (Figure 24.10b), but when these data are interpreted in conjunction with sidescan sonar, it is evident (confirmed by visual inspection during the survey) that the river bank at this location is protected by rectangular frames. In addition to these macro-details, other minute details that are important in hydrodynamic and sediment modeling, such as sand dunes, which cannot be captured with conventional techniques, are easily visible with MBES data (Figure 24.10a).

## 24.5  DISCUSSION AND CONCLUSIONS

This paper provides an overview of the capabilities of selected state-of-the-art techniques for river measurements and specific applications of two acoustic instruments, ADCP and MBES, for providing information on various aspects of river hydrodynamics and morphology. Besides enabling extraction of information that is generally available through laborious conventional methods, ADCP and MBES can provide a wealth of additional information that is critical for understanding and modelling river processes. Spatial and temporal averaging of ADCP-measured velocities can provide a 3-D view of river hydrodynamics that is rarely available in previous hydraulic and hydrologic studies. Similarly, the 3-D view of river bathymetry obtained with MBES data is critical for characterization of both macro- and micro-scale features that are not possible to capture with traditional methods.

Although individual MBES and ADCP data provide a wealth of critical information regarding river hydrodynamics and processes and create plenty of research opportunities, it is the coupling of these two techniques that opens doors to opportunities that were unthinkable in the recent past. High-resolution bathymetry from MBES enables modelling of hydrodynamic processes at much finer scale. These finer-scale models require extensive calibration and validation data that now can be obtained from ADCP. For example, the reliable prediction of flow resistance and sediment transport in alluvial channels is a classical problem in hydraulics, fluvial geomorphology, and sedimentology that has challenged researchers over the last century. The dominant role of bed forms such as dunes in controlling resistance and transport is recognized as probably the source of the greatest difficulty (Lyn et al., 2002) due to the highly non-linear interaction between the erodible alluvial bed and the flow. Coupling of MBES data with velocity measurements from ADCP may enable solution of this and other practical problems

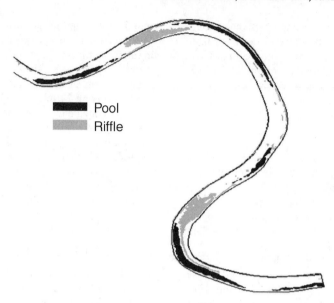

**Figure 24.9**   Areal extent of pool and riffle areas derived from MBES data for the Brazos reach.

that until now could have been addressed only through laboratory investigations.

Besides smaller-scale high-quality research, MBES data have potential to contribute to regional efforts such as the United States Federal Emergency Management Agency (FEMA) Digital Flood Insurance Rate Maps (DFIRM) programme. Currently, efforts have been initiated to collect LiDAR for the whole United States to prepare more accurate flood maps (NAS, 2007). MBES data can be collected and integrated with LiDAR to create high-resolution digital terrain models for rivers and floodplains to address flood mapping and other related issues at different scales.

The United States Geological Survey (USGS) operates over 7000 streamflow gauging stations in the United States. These stations provide near real-time streamflow data at all stations over the internet (http://waterdata. usgs.gov/nwis). Most streamflow records are based on a stage-discharge rating curve, which relates water depth or stage to streamflow at each location. Thus, streamflow is estimated from stage records using the stage-discharge rating curve. Because stream bed and banks change over time, the stage-discharge rating curves need to be updated through regular measurements of river depth, width, and velocity at gauging locations. Over the past several years, the USGS has replaced conventional techniques for velocity and discharge measurements, including cross-sectional surveys, with ADCP in recognition of its abilities with regard to speed, accuracy, 3-D view of the flow field, and ease of use during high floods. As a result, a large amount of fine-scale velocity data is being

assembled at a national level. While the USGS uses ADCP data mainly for updating stage discharge curves at each station, these data in conjunction with bathymetry, sediment, and other observations can be used to look at many research issues at different locations and scales. In addition, these ADCP observations can be combined with topographic data to develop regional river models to provide streamflow at any point along a river.

Although new opportunities are emerging from MBES and ADCP data, these data also bring new challenges. This mainly includes storage of the massive datasets available from these methods. For example, 20 velocity measurements along a cross-section are replaced by thousands or more velocity measurements in multiple directions. Similarly, simple cross-sectional surveys are replaced by millions of bathymetry points (a 5 km reach of Brazos River has 1.7 million bathymetry points). As a result of the massive volume of data produced by these contemporary instruments, the hydrologic community is currently focused on the design and development of information systems for storing, assembling, processing, and querying available data for the myriad needs of scientists, engineers, and practitioners. These efforts include the development of Arc Hydro (Maidment, 2002), Arc Marine (Wright *et al.*, 2007) and CUAHSI HIS observation data models (Horsburgh *et al.*, 2008), among others. These models developed to cater to specific needs in individual areas, are however not sufficient to accommodate the 3-D hydrodynamic or bathymetric information available through MBES and ADCP. As a result, a new data model labelled Arc River

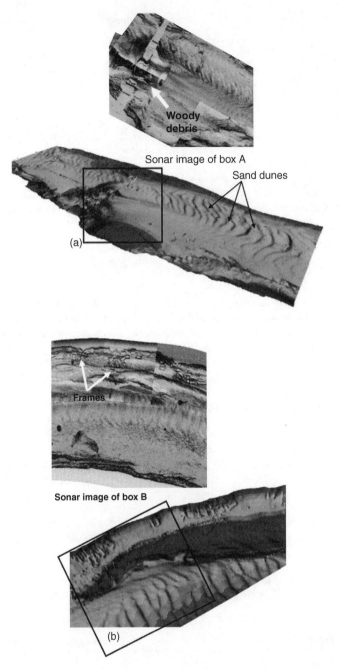

**Figure 24.10** MBES bathymetry surface and corresponding sidescan image showing: (a) the location of bridge piling and woody debris; (b) details of frames installed for bank protection. (See the color version of this figure in color plate section.)

is being developed at IIHR-Hydroscience & Engineering (Kim *et al.*, 2007b). Arc River is a customized data repository that extends Arc Hydro's 1-D river network model to accommodate the 3-D hydrodynamic and bathymetric information for river systems.

The considerations above discuss the advances brought by the reviewed techniques for the hydrologic and hydraulic communities by enabling them to uniquely and efficiently characterize river channels and networks from a macro- (or global) perspective. These considerations are

**Table 24.4** Capabilities and limitations of the reviewed techniques to acquire measurements in gravel-bed environments

| Instrument | Advantages | Disadvantages |
|---|---|---|
| **ACOUSTIC Point (ADV)** | Quasi -non-intrusive (requires deployment)<br>Robust for field work<br>Good spatial and temporal resolution | Difficult to deploy in shallow, fast, rough-bed rivers |
| **Profilers (HADCP, ADCP)** | Quasi- nonintrusive (requires deployment)<br>Fast deployment, setting, operation, and data acquisition and control<br>Potential for acquiring micro-scale measurements (bed-load, sediment concentration, turbulence aspects) | Difficult to deploy in shallow, fast, rough-bed rivers<br>Large measurement volume due to the multi-beam probe configuration<br>Quasi low sampling frequency<br>Up to 6% unmeasured areas near boundaries |
| **Sounders (multibeam)** | Fully characterization of river geometry<br>Distinguishes bed-surface roughness<br>Potential to measure in-situ bed load transport (using acoustic images) | Difficult to deploy in shallow, fast, rough-bed rivers |
| **IMAGE**<br>**LSPIV** | Non-intrusive technique: can be efficiently used in shallow, fast and rough-bed rivers<br>Use of free-surface texture to visualize the flow movement (also indicator of the bed roughness and river status)<br>Instantaneous 2-D velocity field<br>Continuous development – relies on conventional video imaging | When not naturally available, seeding is required for free-surface visualization<br>Sensitive to adverse measurements conditions such as wind, rain, snow<br>Requires illumination (natural or artificial) |
| **RADAR**<br>**Free-surface Velocity** | Non-intrusive technique: can be efficiently used in shallow, fast and rough-bed rivers<br>Can measure continuously over the diurnal cycle | Measures at a point, one-velocity component<br>Sensitive to adverse measurement conditions (wind, rain, snow)<br>Well defined and uniform free-surface waviness |
| **Ground-penetrating** | Non-intrusive: can be efficiently used in shallow, fast and rough-bed rivers | Expensive<br>Still under development |
| **LIDAR**<br>**Airborne** | Non-intrusive technique: can be efficiently used in shallow, fast and rough-bed rivers | Expensive<br>Low scanning speed |
| **Terrestrial** | High productivity | Still under development |

valid for both sand-bed and gravel-bed rivers. Table 24.4 highlights the capabilities and limitations of these instruments when operated in gravel-bed river environments.

In conclusion, acoustic, image, and radar-based methods are changing the field of river science and engineering by enabling rapid acquisition of high-resolution, accurate data related to river morphology and hydrodynamics in digital formats. Besides providing data that were available through conventional methods, these new methods are providing fine-scale datasets to investigate research issues that were only possible through laboratory experiments in the past. In addition, these high-resolution data can be used in conjunction with other regional datasets such as USGS streamflow and national hydrography datasets, and LiDAR, to address river-related regional issues. As the technology continues to develop, higher-resolution data covering large areas and multiple scales will be available enabling improved understanding of the dynamics of the river processes through in-situ observations acquired at the scales at which the processes occur.

## 24.6  ACKNOWLEDGEMENTS

We are thankful to the Texas Water Development Board for supplying MBES data for the Brazos River reach in Texas, IIHR-Hydroscience and Engineering for the data from the Mississippi River, and South-Florida Management District for the ADCP data for Kissimmee River. The first author gratefully acknowledges the partial support provided by the National Science Foundation grant EAR 0843798 (R. Keltz, Program Manager). We are also thankful to André Roy, Colin Rennie, and Dan Parsons for their substantial comments and suggestions during the critical review of the paper.

## 24.7  REFERENCES

Abraham, D. and Pratt, T. 2002. *Quantification of Bed-load Transport using Multibeam Survey Data and Traditional Methods*. United States Army Engineer Research and Development Center, Vicksburg, MS. *ERDC/CHL CHETN-VII-4*. http://chl.wes.army.mil/library/publications/chetn-vii-4.pdf

Adrian, R.J. 1991. Particle-Imaging Techniques for Experimental Fluid Mechanics. *Annual Review of Fluid Mechanics* **23**: 261–304.

Andréfouëta, S., Ouillon, S., Brinkman, R. *et al.* 2006. Review of solutions for 3D hydrodynamic modeling applied to aquaculture in South Pacific atoll lagoons. *Marine Pollution Bulletin* **52**: 1138–1155.

Aya, S., Fujita, I., and Yagyu, M. 1995. Field observation of flood in a river by video image analysis. Japan Society of Civil Engineers *Proceedings of Hydraulic Engineering* **39**: 447–452.

Bailly, J.-S., LeCoarer, Y., Allouis, T. *et al.* 2008. Bathymetry with LiDAR on gravel-bed rivers: quality and limits. *Annual General Assembly, Vienna, 14–18 April*. European Geosciences Union, Abstract EGU 2008-A-04967.

Best, J. 2005. The Fluid dynamics of river dunes: a review and some future research directions. *Journal of Geophysical Research* **110**: F04S02. doi:10.1029/2004JF000218

Boiten, W. 2000. *Hydrometry*. Rotterdam, the Netherlands, IHE Delft Lecture Note Series.

Carbonneau, P.E., Lane, S.N., and Bergeron, N.E. 2003. Cost-effective non-metric close-range digital photogrammetry and its application to a study of coarse gravel river beds. *International Journal of Remote Sensing* **24**: 2837–2854.

Carling, P.A., Golz, E., Orr, H.G., and Radecki-Pawlik, A. 2000. The morphodynamics of fluvial sand dunes in the River Rhine near Mainz, Germany: I. Sedimentology and morphology *Sedimentology* **47**: 227–252.

Carr, M.L. and Rehmann, C.R. 2007. Measuring the dispersion coefficient with an acoustic Doppler current profiler. *Journal of Hydraulic Engineering* **133**: 977–982.

Carr, M.L., Rehmann, C.R., and Gonzalez, J.A. 2006. Comparison between dispersion coefficients estimated from a tracer study and ADCP measurements. Examining the confluence of environmental and water concerns. *Proceedings of the World Environmental and Water Resources Congress 2006*. ASCE Conference Proceedings doi: 10.1061/40856 (200)170. CD-Rom.

Cohen, E.A., Dudley, R.D., Liao, Q., Variano, E.A., and Liu, P. L.-F. 2010. An *in situ* quantitative imaging profiler for the measurement of high concentration sediment velocity. *Experiment in Fluids* **49** 77–88 doi: 10.007/s00348-009-0801-8

Costa, J.E., Spicer, K.R., Cheng, R.T. *et al.* 2000. Measuring stream discharge by non-contact Methods: a proof-of-concept experiment. *Geophysical Research Letters* **27**: 553–556.

Christensen, J.L. and Herrick, L.E. 1982. *Mississippi River Test 1*. El Cajon, CA, United States Geological Survey.

Creutin, J.D., Muste, M., and Li, Z. 2002. Traceless quantitative alternatives for measurements in natural streams, *Proceedings of the ASCE-IAHR Joint Conference, Hydraulic Measurements and Experimental Methods, Estes Park, CO, 28 July–1 August*, CD-ROM

de Moustier, C. 1988. State of the art in swath bathymetric survey systems. *International Hydrographic Review* **65**: 25–54.

Denbigh, P.N. 1989. Swath bathymetry: Principles of operation and an analysis of errors, *IEEE Journal of Ocean Engineering* **14**: 289–298.

Dinehart, R.L. 1992. Evolution of coarse gravel bed forms: field measurements at flood stage. *Water Resources Research* **28**: 2667–2689.

Dinehart, R.L. and Burau, J.R. 2005a. Averaged indicators of secondary flow in repeated acoustic Doppler current profiler crossings of bends. *Water Resources Research* **41**: W09405. doi: 10.1029/2005WR004050

Dinehart, R.L. and Burau, J.R. 2005b. Repeated surveys by acoustic Doppler current profiler for flow and sediment dynamics in a tidal river. *Journal of Hydrology* **314**: 1–21.

Eilertsen, R.S. and Hansen, L. 2007. Morphology of river bed scours on a delta plain revealed by interferometric sonar. *Geomorphology* **94**: 58–68.

Feurer, D.J., Bailly, S., Coarer, Y.L., Puech, C., and Viau, A.A. 2007. On the use of very high resolution optical images to map river bathymetry: upscaling from aerial to satellite imagery. *Second Space for Hydrology Workshop, 12–14 November, Geneva. Surface Water Storage and Runoff: Modeling, In-situ Data and Remote Sensing*, CD-ROM

Feurer, D.J., Bailly, S., Puech, C., Coarer, Y.L., and Viau, A.A. 2008. Very high resolution mapping of river-immersed topography by remote sensing. *Progress in Physical Geography*, **32**: 403–419.

Fox, J.F. and Belcher, B.J. 2009. Comparison of LSPIV, ADV, and PIV data that is decomposed to measure structure of turbulence over a gravel-ded. *Proceedings of the 33rd Congress, Vancouver, BC, Canada, 9-14 August*. International Association for Hydraulic Research, CD-ROM

Fujita, I. and Komura, S. 1994. Application of video image analysis for measurements of river-surface flows. Japan Society of Civil Engineers *Annual Journal of Hydraulic Engineering* **38**: 733–738 [in Japanese].

Fujita, I., Muste, M. and Kruger, A., 1998. Large-scale particle image velocimetry for flow analysis in hydraulic applications. *Journal of Hydraulic Research* **36**: 397–414.

Gaeuman, D. and Jacobson, R.B. 2006. Acoustic bed velocity and bed load dynamics in a large sand bed river. *Journal of Geophysical Research* **111**: F02005. doi: 10.1029/2005JF000411

Gao, J. 2009. Bathymetric mapping by means of remote sensing: methods, accuracy and limitations. *Progress in Physical Geography* **33**: 103–116.

González, J.A., Melching, C.S., and Oberg, K.A. 1996. Analysis of open-channel velocity measurements collected with an Acoustic Doppler Current Profiler. *Proceedings of RiverTech 96, Chicago, IL, Vol. 2.* International Water Resources Association pp. 838–845.

Gonzalez-Castro, J. and Muste, M. 2007. Framework for estimating uncertainty of ADCP measurements from a moving boat using standardized uncertainty snalysis. *Journal of Hydraulic Engineering* **133**: 1390–1411.

Gordon, R.L. 1989. Acoustic measurement of river discharge. *Journal of Hydraulic Engineering* **133**: 1390–1411.

Graham, D.J., Rollet, A-J., Piegay, H., and Rice, S.P. 2010. Maximizing the accuracy of image-based surface sediment sampling techniques. *Water Resources Research* **46**: W02508. doi: 10.1029/2008WR006940

Gray, J.R. and Gartner, J.W. 2009. Technological advances in suspended-sediment surrogate monitoring. *Water Resources Research* **45**: W00D29. doi: 10.1029/2008WR007063

Hanrahan, T.P. 2006. Bedform morphology of salmon spawning areas in a large gravel-bed river. *Geomorphology* **86**: 529–536.

Hilldale, R.C. 2007. Using bathymetric LiDAR and a 2-D hydraulic model to quantify aquatic habitat. *Proceedings of the World Environmental and Water Resources Congress, Tampa, FL, 15-19 May.* American Society of Civil Engineers, CD-ROM

Hilldale, R.C. and Raff, D. 2008. Assessing the ability of airborne LiDAR to map river bathymetry. *Earth Surface Processes and Landforms* **33**: 773–783.

Horsburgh, J.S., Tarboton, D.G., Maidment, D.R., and Zaslavsky, I. 2008. A relational model for environmental and water resources data. *Water Resources Research* **44**: W05406. doi: 10.1029/2007WR006392

Howarth, M.J. 2002. Estimates of Reynolds and bottom stress from fast sample ADCPs deployed in continental shelf seas. *Proceedings of the ASCE-IAHR Joint Conference, Estes Park, CO, 28 July–1 August, Hydraulic Measurements and Experimental Methods,* CD-ROM

Irish, J.L. and White, T.E. 1998. Coastal engineering applkications of high-resolution lidar bathymetry. *Coastal Engineering* **35**: 47–71.

Julien, P.Y., Klaassen, G.J., Ten Brinke, W.B.M., and Wilbers, A.W.E. 2002. Case study: bed resistance of Rhine River during 1998 folod. *Journal of Hydraulic Engineering* **128**: 1042–1050.

Kawanisi, K., 2004. Structure of turbulent flow in a shallow tidal estuary. *Journal of Hydraulic Engineering* **130**: 360–370.

Kim, D., Muste, M., and Weber, L. 2007a. Software for assessment of longitudinal dispersion coefficient using acoustic-Doppler current profiler measurements. *Proceedings of the 32nd Congress, Venice, Italy, 1-6 July.* International Association for Hydraulic Research, CD-ROM.

Kim, D., Muste, M., and Weber, L. 2007b. Arc River: multi-dimensional relational geodatabase for representation of river characteristics. *Proceedings of the ASCE-IAHR, Joint Conference, Lake Placid, NY, 10–12 September. Hydraulic Measurements and Experimental Methods* p. 445.

Kostaschuk, R. and Best, J. 2005. Response of sand dunes to variations in tidal flow: Fraser Estuary, Canada. *Journal of Geophysical Research* **110**: F04S04. doi: 10.1029/2004JF000176.

Kostaschuk, R.A. and Villard, P.V. 1996. Flow and sediment transport over large subaqueous dunes: Fraser River, Canada. *Sedimentology* **43**: 849–863.

Kostachuck, R.A., Church, M.A., and Luternauer, J.L. 1989. Bedforms, bed material, and bedload transport in a salt-wedge estuary: Fraser River, British Columbia. *Canadian Journal of Earth Sciences* **26**: 1440–1432.

Kostaschuk, R., Villard, P., and Best, J. 2004. Measuring velocity and shear stress over dunes with acoustic Doppler profiler. *Journal of Hydraulic Engineering* **130**: 932–936.

Kraus, N.C., Lohrmann, A., and Cabrera, R. 1994. New acoustic meter for measuring 3D laboratory flows. *Journal of Hydraulic Engineering* **120**: 406–412.

Lacey, R.W.J. and Roy, A.G. 2007. A comparative study of the turbulent flow field with and without a pebble cluster in a gravel bed river. *Water Resources Research* **43**: W05502. doi: 10.1029/2006WR005027

Lane, S.N., Bradbrook, K.F., Richards, K.E., Biron, P.M., and Roy, A.G. 2000. Secondary circulation cells in river channel confluence: measurement artefacts or coherent flow structures? *Hydrologic Processes* **14**: 2047–2071.

Lane, S.N. 2001. The measurement of gravel-bed river morphology. In Mosley, M.P. (Ed.), *Gravel Bed Rivers V.* Wellington, New Zealand Hydrological Society, pp. 291–320.

Lane, S.N., Parsons, D.R., Best, J.L. *et al.* 2008. Causes of rapid mixing at a junction of two large rivers: Rio Parana and Rio Paraguay, Argentina, *Journal of Geophysical Research* **113**: F02024. doi: 10.1029/2006JF000745.

LCSI (L-3 Communications SeaBeam Instruments) 2000. *Multibeam Sonar Theory of Operation,* http://www.mbari.org/data/mbsystem/formatdoc/ (accessed 6 July 2011)

Le Coz, J., Pierrefeu, G., and Paquier, A. 2008. Evaluation of river discharges monitored by a fixed side-looking Doppler profiler. *Water Resources Research* **44**: W00D09. doi: 10.1029/2008WR006967.

Leclerc, R. and Hickin, E.J. 1997. Ground penetrating radar stratigraphy of a meandering river floodplain, South Thompson River, British Columbia: *Geomorphology* **21**: 17–38.

Legleiter, C.J. and Roberts, D.A. 2009. A forward image model for passive optical remote sensing of river bathymetry. *Remote Sensing of Environment* **113**: 1025–1045.

Legleiter, C.J., Roberts, D.A., and Lawrence, R.L. 2009. Spectrally based remote sensing of river bathymetry. *Earth Surface Processes and Landforms* **34**: 1039–1059.

Lillycop, W.J., Johnson, P., Lejdebrink, U., and Pope, R.W. 2001. Airborne lidar hydrography: requirements for tomorrow. *Proceedings of Oceanology International. Meeting at Miami, FL, 3–5 April.* Paper 5-7, CD

Lin, Y.T., Schuettpelz, C.C., Wu, C.H., and Fratta, D. 2009. A combined acoustic and electromagnetic wave-based techniques for bathymetry and subbottom profiling in shallow waters. *Journal of Applied Geophysics* **68**: 203–218.

Lohrmann, A., Hackett, B., and Roed, L.P. 1990. High resolution measurements of turbulence, velocity and stress using pulse-to-pulse coherent sonar. *Journal of Atmospheric and Oceanic Technology* **7**: 19–37.

Lu, Y. and Lueck, R.G. 1999a. Using broadband ADCP in a tidal channel. Part I: Mean flow and shear. *Journal of Atmospheric and Oceanic Technology* **16**: 1556–1567.

Lu, Y. and Lueck, R.G. 1999b. Using broadband ADCP in a tidal channel. Part II: Turbulence. *Journal of Atmospheric and Oceanic Technology* **16**: 1568–1579.

Lyn, D.A., McLean, S.R., Bennett, *et al.* 2002. Flow and transport over dunes. *Journal of Hydraulic Engineering* **128**: 726–728.

Lyzenga, D.R., Malinas, N.P., and Tanis, F.J. 2006. Multispectral bathymetry using a simple physically based algorithm. *IEEE Transactions on Geoscience and Remote Sensing* **44**: 2251–2259.

MacVicar, B.J., Beaulieu, E., Champagne, V., and Roy, A.G. 2007. Measuring water velocity in highly turbulent flows: field tests of an electromagnetic current meter and acoustic Doppler velocimeter. *Earth Surface Processes and Landforms* **32**: 1412–1432.

Madej, M.A. 1999. What can thalweg profiles tell us? A case study from Redwood Creek, California. *Watershed Management Council Networker* **8**: http://watershed.org/news/sum_99/11_thalweg_profiles.htm

Maidment, D.R. (Ed.), 2002. *Arc Hydro – GIS for Water Resources*. Redlands, CA, ESRI Press.

Mayer, L.A. 2006. Frontiers in seafloor mapping and visualization. *Marine Geophysical Researches* **27**: 7–17.

McGregor, J.A., Poulter, E.M., and Smith, M.J. 1997. Ocean surface currents obtained from microwave sea-echo Doppler spectra. *Journal of Geophysical Research* **102**: 25227–25236.

McKean, J., Isaak, D., and Wright, W. 2009. Improving stream studies with a small-footprint green Lidar. *Eos, Transactions of the American Geophysical Union* **90**: 341–342.

Melcher, N.B., Cheng, R.T., and Haeni, F.P. 1999. Investigating technologies to monitor open-channel discharge by direct measurement of cross-sectional area and velocity flow. Hydrological Engineering for Sustainable Water Resource Management at the Turn of the Millennium, *28th Congress, Graz, Austria, 22–27 August*. International Association for Hydraulic Research Paper,188. CD-ROM.

Mellett, J.S. 1995. Ground penetrating radar applications in engineering, environmental management, and geology. *Journal of Applied Geophysics* **33**: 157–166.

Merwade, V.M., Maidment, D.R., and Goff, J.A. 2006. Anisotropic considerations while interpolating river channel bathymetry. *Journal of Hydrology* **331**: 731–741.

Mikhail, E.M. and Ackermann, F. 1976. *Observation and Least Square*. New York, IEP – A Dun-Donnelley Publisher.

Miller, K.S. and Rochwarger, M.M. 1972. A covariance approach to spectral moment estimation. *IEEE Transactions on Information Theory* **18**: 588–596.

Moorman, B.J. and Michel, F.A. 1997. Bathymetric mapping and sub-bottom profiling through lake ice with ground-penetrating radar. *Journal of Paleolimnology* **18**: 61–73.

Muste, M. and Kim, D. 2007. AdcpXP: Software for Processing and Visualization of ADCP Measurements. Invited Speaker Presentation, ADCPs in Action 2007, San Diego, CA

Muste, M., Kim, W., and Fulford, J. 2008. Mapping river hydrodynamics with non-intrusive measurements. World Meteorological Organization, Geneva. *WMO Bulletin* **57**: 163–169.

Muste, M., González-Castro, J.A., Yu, K., and Kim, D. 2006. *Accuracy of ADCP Discharge Measurements for Rating of Flow-control Structures*. Iowa Institute of Hydraulic Research Report. Iowa City, IA, IIHR-Hydroscience & Engineering, The University of Iowa.

Muste, M., Kim, D., and Gonzalez-Castro, J.A. 2010. Near-transducer errors in ADCP measurements: experimental findings, *Journal of Hydraulic Engineering* **136**: 275–289.

Muste, M., Vermeyen, T., Hotchkiss, R., and Oberg, K. 2007. Acoustic velocimetry for riverine environments. *Journal of Hydraulic Engineering* **133**: 1297–1299.

Muste, M., Yu, K., Pratt, T., and Abraham, D. 2004. Practical aspects of ADCP data use for quantification of mean river flow characteristics: part II: Fixed-vessel measurements. *Journal of Flow Measurement and Instrumentation* **15**: 17–28.

NAS (National Academy of Sciences) Committee on Floodplain Mapping Technologies. 2007. *Elevation Data for Floodplain Mapping*. Washington, DC, National Academy Press.

Nikora, V. and Goring, D.G. 2000. Flow turbulence over fixed and weakly mobile gravel beds. *Journal of Hydraulic Engineering* **126**: 679–690.

Nittrouer, J.A., Allison, M.A., and Campanella, R. 2008. Bedform transport rates for the lowermost Mississippi River, *Journal of Geophysical Research* **113**: F03004. doi: 10.1029/2007JF000795.

Nystrom, E.A. 2001. *Applicability of acoustic Doppler profilers to measurements of mean velocity and turbulence parameters*. M.S. Thesis, University of Illinois at Urbana-Champaign, IL

Nystrom, E.A., Oberg, K.A., and Rehmann, C.R. 2002. Measurement of turbulence with acoustic Doppler current profilers - sources of error and laboratory results. *Proceedings of the ASCE-IAHR Joint Conference, Estes Park, CO, 28 July–1 August. Hydraulic Measurements and Experimental Methods 2002*, CD-ROM.

Oberg, K.A., Morlock, S.E., and Caldwell, W.S. 2005. *Quality-assurance Plan for Discharge Measurements using Acoustic Doppler Current Profilers*. United States Geological Survey, Scientific Investigations Report 2005-5183

Orange, D.L., Angell, M., and Lapp, D. 1999. Applications of multibeam mapping to exploration and production; detecting seeps, mapping geohazards, and managing data overload with GIS. *The Leading Edge* **18**: 495–501.

Parsons, D.R., Best, J.L., Lane, S.N. *et al.* 2007. Form roughness and the absence of secondary flow in a large confluence-diffluence, Rio Paraná, Argentina *Earth Surface Processes Landforms* **32**: 155–162.

Parsons, D.R., Best, J.L., Orfeo, O. *et al.* 2005. Morphology and flow fields of a three-dimensional dunes, Rio Paraná, Argentina: results from simultaneous multibeam echo sounding and acoustic Doppler current profiling, *Journal of Geophysical Research* **110**: F04S03. doi: 10.1029/2004JF000231.

Pelpola, C. and Hickin, E.J. 2004. Long-term bed-load transport rate based on air photo and ground-penetrating radar surveys of fan-delta growth, Coast Mountains, British Columbia, *Geomorphology* **57**: 169–181.

Plant, W.J. and Keller, W.C. 1990. Evidence of Bragg scattering in Microwave Doppler spectra of sea return. *Journal of Geophysical Research* **95**: 16299–16310.

Pratson, L.F. and Edwards, M. 1996. An introduction to advances in seafloor mapping using side-scan sonar and multibeam bathymetry. *Marine Geophysical Researches* **18**: 601–605.

Quadros, N.D., Collier, P.A., and Fraser, C.S. 2008. Integration of bathymetric and topographic Lidar: a preliminary investigation. *Remote Sensing and Spatial Information Sciences* **37**: 1299–1304.

Rantz, S.E. and others. 1982. *Measurement and Computation of Streamflow, Vol. 2: Computation of Discharge*. United States Geological Survey, Water Supply Paper 2175.

RDI (1996) *Acoustic Doppler Current Profilers – Principle of operation, A Practical Primer*. San Diego, CA, RD Instruments.

Rennie, C.D. and Millar, R.G. 2007. A deconvolution technique to separate signal from noise in gravel bedload velocity data. *Journal of Hydraulic Engineering* **133**: 845–856.

Rennie, C.D., Millar, R.G., and Church, M.A. 2002. Measurement of bedload velocity using an acoustic Doppler current profiler. *Journal of Hydraulic Engineering* **128**: 473–483.

Roy, A.G., Buffin-Belanger, T., Lamarre, H., and Kirkbride, A.D. 2004. Size, shape and dynamics of large-scale turbulent flow structures in a gravel-bed river, *Journal of Fluid Mechanics* **500**: 1–27.

Ruhl, C.A. and Simpson, M.R. 2005. *Computation of Discharge using the Index-velocity Method in Tidally Affected Areas*. United States Geological Survey, Scientific Investigations Report 2005–5004.

Schemper, T.J. and Admiraal, D.M. 2002. An examination of the application of acoustic Doppler current profiler measurements in a wide channel of uniform depth for turbulence calculations. *Proceedings of the ASCE-IAHR Joint Conference, Estes Park, CO, 28 July-1 August, Hydraulic Measurements and Experimental Methods 2002*, CD-ROM

Shields, F.D., Knight, S.S., Testa, S., and Cooper, C.M. 2003. Use of acoustic Doppler current profilers to describe velocity distributions at the reach scale. *Journal of the American Water Resources Association* **39**: 1397–1408.

Shih, H.H., Payton, C., Sprenke, J., and Mero, T. 2000. Towing basin speed calibration of acoustic Doppler current profiling instruments. *Proceedings of the ASCE-IAHR Joint Conference, Minneapolis, MN, 30 July–2 August, Water Resources Engineering and Water Resources Planning and Management 2000*, CD-ROM

Shugar, D.H., Kostaschuk, R., Best, J.L. *et al.* 2010. On the relationship between flow and suspended sediment transport over the crest of a sand dune, Rio Parana, Argentina *Sedimentology* **57**: 252–272.

Simpson, M.R. 1986. Evaluation of a vessel-mounted acoustic Doppler current profiler for use in rivers and estuaries. *Proceedings of the Third Working Conference on Current Measurement, Washington, DC*. IEEE pp. 106–121.

Simpson, M.R. 2001. *Discharge Measurements using a Broadband Acoustic Doppler Current Profiler*. Unites States Geological Survey, Open-File Report 01-1.

Simpson, M.R. and Oltmann, R.N. 1993. *Discharge-measurement System using an Acoustic Doppler Current Profiler with Applications to Large Rivers and Estuaries*. United States Geological Survey, Water-Supply Paper 2395.

Snyder, N.P. 2009. Studying stream morphology with airborne laser elevation data. *EOS, Transactions American Geophysical Union* **90**: 45–46.

Song, Y.K. and Shan, J. 2008. An adaptive approach to topographic feature extraction from digital terrain models. *Photogrammetric Engineering and Remote Sensing* **75**: 281–290.

SonTek. 2000. Doppler velocity log for ROV/AUV applications. *SonTek Newsletter*, **6**(1) San Diego, CA, SonTek.

Stacey, M.T., Monismith, S.G., and Burau, J.R. 1999. Observations of turbulence in partially stratified estuary. *Journal of Physical Oceanography* **29**: 1950–1970.

Szupiany, R.N., Amsler, M.L., Best, J.L., and Parsons, D.R. 2007. Comparison of fixed- and moving-vessel flow mea-

surements with an aDp in a large river, *Journal of Hydraulic Engineering* **133**: 1299–1309.

Teague, C.C., Barrick, D.E., Lilleboe, P.M., and Cheng, R.T. 2003. Initial River Test of a Monostatic Riversonde Streamflow Measurement System. In: Rizoli, J.A., editor, *Proceedings of the IEEE/OES Working Conference on Current Measurement Technology, New York, NY* pp. 46–50.

Topping, D.J., Wright, S.A., Melis, T.S., and Rubin, D.M. 2007. High-resolution measurements of suspended-sediment concentration and grain size in the Colorado River in Grand Canyon using a multi-frequency acoustic system, *Proceedings of the 10th International Symposium on River Sedimentation, 1-4 Aug, Moscow, Russia, Vol. III* pp. 330–339.

Voulgaris, G. and Trowbridge, J.H. 1998. Evaluation of the acoustic Doppler velocimenter for turbulence measurements, *Journal of Atmospheric and Oceanic Technology* **15**: 272–289.

Wall, G., Nystrom, E., and Simon, L. 2006. *Use of an ADCP to Compute Suspended Sediment Discharge in the Tidal Hudson River, New York*. United States Geological Survey, Scientific Investigation Report 2006–5055.

Westaway, R., Lane, S., and Hicks, D. 2001. Remote sensing of clear-water, gravel-bed rivers using digital photogrammetry, *Photogrammetric Engineering and Remote Sensing* **67**: 1271–1281.

Westaway, R., Lane, S., and Hicks, D. 2003. Remote survey of large-scale braided, gravelbed rivers assessing digital photogrammetry and image analysis, *International Journal of Remote Sensing* **24**: 795–815.

Wilbers, A.W.E. and Ten Brinke, W. B. M. 2003. The response of subaqueous dunes to floods in sand and gravel bed reaches of the Dutch Rhine. *Sedimentology* **50**: 1013–1034.

Winterbottom, S.J. and Gilvear, D.J. 1997. Quantification of channel bed morphology in gravel-bed rivers using airborne multispectral imagery and aerial photography. *River Research and Applications* **13**: 489–499.

White, L. and Hodges, B. 2005. Filtering the signature of submerged large woody debris from bathymetry data. *Journal of Hydrology* **309**: 53–65.

Wooldridge, C.L. and Hickin, E.J. 2005. Radar architecture of channel bars in wandering gravel-bed rivers. *Journal of Sedimentary Research* **75**: 884–860.

Wright, D.J., Blongewicz, M.J., Halpin, P.N., and Breman, J. 2007. *Arc Marine: GIS for a Blue Planet*. Redlands, CA, ESRI Press.

Young, N.C. 2006. *Physical Characterization of Freshwater Mussel Habitats in Upper Mississippi River Pool 16*. Doctoral Dissertation, The University of Iowa, Iowa City, IA.

## 24.8    DISCUSSION

### 24.8.1    *Discussion by Jonathan B. Laronne*

In addition to the methods mentioned in this presentation, two other novel methods are relevant to gravel-bed rivers:

(1)    The use of 3-D ADVs is problematic when suspended sediment concentration is very high. In such instances use may be made of electromagentic current meters, some of which can currently monitor 3-D velocities at frequencies as high as 75 Hz.

(2)    The determination of water discharge during rising flood level is difficult in most gravel-bed rivers due to the rapidity of water rise. A novel

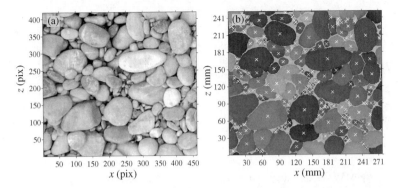

**Figure 24.11** Example of an application of image-processing techniques for object detection: (a) raw image of a typical gravel bed in top view; (b) result of a refined version of Graham *et al.*'s (2005) image-processing algorithm. Here, each area interpreted as a single grain is colour-coded in a different grayscale and the midpoint of the non-boundary element is marked by a white cross.

technique is based on the Doppler shift in the transmission of radar signals by a Radar Velocity Gun. Such hand-held instruments are easy to use, inexpensive, and may provide the means to determine water surface velocity throughout an entire river section or its variation across a wide river during fast hydrograph rises.

### 24.8.2 Discussion by Martin Detert

Both the keynote authors and the discussants should be complimented for their comprehensive overview of acoustic velocity instruments, complemented by techniques based on RADAR, LiDAR, and photo-optical approaches. However, with regard to the heading of the chapter, the focus should be brought to two supplemental techniques that have come into use more and more in recent times or that bear at least a high potential to gain innovative insights into the secrets of gravel bed rivers: pressure sensors using the piezo-effect, and image-based object detection techniques.

(1) The hydrodynamics of flow over gravel beds is determined by the intricate interaction between turbulent velocity fields and pressure fields. However, most past studies concerning gravel beds underlying open-channel flow focused on velocity measurements alone, although the bed pressure regime gives more direct information on the flow forces that act on the bed. Piezo-based pressure sensors have been used both in laboratory (e.g., Hofland *et al.*, 2005) and field studies (Smart and Habersack, 2007). On a point scale, these pressure sensors can be used to obtain information on time series statistics like turbulence intensity profiles, histograms, and spectral analysis (Detert

*et al.*, 2010a). On a multidimensional scale, the detailed analysis of an array of pressure sensors can even be used to re-construct the instantaneous structure of bed pressure fields (Detert *et al.*, 2010b).

(2) Object recognition techniques are widely used in several industrial, medical, and biological applications (e.g., Neumann *et al.*, 2006), where the object properties like, for example, boundaries, textures, or colours are well pronounced. These techniques are very promising for studying several aspects in gravel-bed rivers as well, although their application remains, as yet, only partially exploited. Graham *et al.* (2005) were one of the first groups that combined the purposes of the object-oriented programming of Matlab and recent developments in digital image acquisition to measure the surface grain-size distribution of gravel. In principle, their algorithm uses the information of the grayscale shading supplemented by a watershed procedure. Figure 24.11 gives a snapshot of a typical result of an algorithm based on Graham *et al.*'s (2005) image-processing algorithm, mainly refined by edge-detection methods. However, image-processing techniques like this can be used for a much wider area of fluvial interests, e.g., development of banks or other significant geomorphic breaklines, analysing (cray-)fish movement or low-cost measurement of several aspects of the environment of gravel-bed rivers.

### 24.8.3 Discussion by Jay Lacey

Research interest in the *in situ* characterization of turbulent flow in rivers and estuaries has grown substantially in recent years. High-frequency velocity measurements are obtained, for the most part, using electromagnetic current meters (ECMs) and acoustic Doppler velocimeters (ADVs). ADVs are more commonly used and measure three component (3C) velocities at frequencies as high as 200 Hz at a single point. The sampling volume is approximately 1 cm³ in size and is located at a distance of 5 or 10 cm from the transmitter (depending on probe geometry). Since averaging takes place within the sampling volume the smallest turbulent length scales measurable by ADVs are on the order of the sampling volume size (0.01 m).

The main drawback of ADVs is that they can obtain only a single point measurement at a given time. For multiple measurements, (required to characterize the vertical velocity profile or velocity field) the instrument needs to be displaced in a step-by-step process or multiple ADVs need to be deployed. An attractive alternative to ADVs for measuring time-averaged velocity profiles is the acoustic Doppler current profiler (ADCP). As outlined in the keynote chapter, this instrument has the capabilities of collecting multiple velocity samples throughout the water depth simultaneously and therefore can measure a velocity profile with a single deployment.

A critical distinction between ADVs and ADCPs is that, while ADVs estimate velocities from a very small sampling volume, ADCPs, due to their beam geometry, obtain samples over a much larger area. The extent of the area is based on the angle of the individual beams with the vertical axes (i.e., angles of $\theta = 15°$ to $25°$ depending on ADCP type). For a four beam, $\theta = 25°$, ADCP, the 3C velocity samples at a specific depth (bin) is determined from the four beams which are separated by a horizontal distance $L\text{Horiz} = 2z \tan \theta = 0.93z$ where $z$ is the vertical distance from the transducer face. This shows that not only are the velocities derived and averaged over a horizontal distance comparable with the depth of the bin, but that the horizontal averaging distance increases with depth. As the 3C velocities are derived from beams with a large separation, it is crucial that flow is homogeneous over this extent. If not, velocities will be biased and the resulting velocity profiles may be invalid.

The distinction between ADVs and ADCPs should be made clear to research scientists wishing to use ADCPs as an attractive alternative to ADVs. ADCPs have very limited capabilities for measuring turbulence and the output statistics will be biased due the physical nature of the instrument. For turbulence intensity (estimated by standard deviations of the instantaneous velocity components), it must be recognized that turbulent scales smaller than the sampling volume over which averaging occurs cannot be resolved. Secondly, due to the geometry of the beams, bins closer to the ADCP have smaller sampling volumes. Therefore velocity time series collected closer to the ADCP will contain more variance

associated with the finer-scale turbulent fluctuations than will velocities recorded at greater $z$. The inconsistent sampling volume may result in a bias towards elevated turbulence levels with proximity to the ADCP. Some studies have estimated Reynolds ($Re$) shear stresses using ADCP data through a statistical variance method (Stacey et al.,1999; Nystrom et al.,2007). In theory $Re$ shear stresses are defined as the time-averaged momentum flux for a differential fluid element. Therefore, by definition, $Re$ stresses are derived for an infinitesimally small fluid volume. Estimating $Re$ stresses from velocity components separated by large distances is highly questionable and should be avoided.

### 24.8.4 Response by M. Muste, D. Kim, and V. Merwade

Thank you to the discussants for the comments and the additional information provided. Given the vast number of instruments that are used for documenting rivers in general, including gravel-bed, the authors chose to present non-intrusive instruments that are capable to characterize rivers up to the reach scale. The instruments used for local characterization of the streams (cross-sections, verticals) are also numerous and they might constitute themselves a subject for a stand-alone chapter.

(1) Indeed the use of electromagnetic current meters (www.decaturradar.com) is a good solution for high sediment flows given the saturation of the return signals produced by the suspended sediment. For fairly clear water conditions however, the ADV should be chosen over the current meter as the latter is an intrusive instrument that actually reports the impact velocity as the flow is approaching the sensor body.

(2) The radar-based velocimeter is a point measurement instrument that provides one component of velocity as described above. The measurement protocol for this instrument is based on several constraints and assumptions briefly presented next. One of the constraints is that the instrument measures velocity only along its "line of sight". Signals received from locations at the free surface perpendicular to the instrument line of sight do not carry the information needed to estimate velocities. Consequently, the instrument has to be positioned strategically, typically opposite to the flow direction. Alternatively, the angle between the instrument line of sight and the flow direction must be specified in order to obtain a correct reading of the local velocity. The prerequisite assumption for this instrument is that the free surface has sufficient "roughness patterns" for the gun to detect the Bragg

scattering. The patterns (usually produced by wind acting at the free surface and by the breakup of the turbulence structure protruding at the free surface) are assumed to move with the same velocity as that of the channel flow at the surface. Strong winds acting on the free surface can, however, violate this assumption so the reported velocity should be considered with caution.

The instruments brought to our attention by Detert pertain to the family of techniques used to characterize the stream micro-scales, so they were intentionally omitted from our review paper. Short comments are added below to address the comments in the order in which they were made.

(1)  The investigation of the flow hydrodynamics in gravel beds is well complemented by the pressure field measurements even if at this time this quantity can be only observed at a point and over time as the discussant has illustrated in his comments.

(2)  Colour detection for identification of the texture and consequently inference of the substrate nature and additional characteristics (size distribution, spatial clustering, etc.) is a substantial contribution for many hydrodynamic-morphodynamic studies, especially in gravel-bed experimental work focused on micro-scale investigations. For macro-scale investigations, an extensive illustration of the current measurement technique capabilities is provided by Marcus (Chapter 21, this volume), one of the keynote lectures in GBR7.

Lacey's comments are useful for warning the users about the accuracy (or lack of) and practical value of the quantities (especially turbulence) reported by ADVs and ADCPs. There is a need to trace the accuracy of these instruments to primary standards (laser-Doppler velocimetry or comparable) in order to interpret the measurements conducted with ADCP and ADV. Such studies have been conducted for ADV (e.g., Voulgaris and Trowbridge, 1998), but much work is needed for the same purpose with respect to ADCP. The discussion provides a good basis for suggesting to the manufacturers of these instruments the next lines of research and development for the above-mentioned instruments.

## 24.9  DISCUSSION REFERENCES

Detert, M., Nikora, V., and Jirka, G.H. 2010a. Synoptic velocity and pressure fields at the water-sediment interface of streambeds. *Journal of Fluid Mechanics* **660**: 55–86.

Detert, M., Weitbrecht, V., and Jirka, G.H. 2010b. Laboratory measurements on turbulent pressure fluctuations in and above gravel beds. *Journal of Hydraulic Engineering* **136**: 779–789.

Graham, D.J., Rice, S.P., and Reid, I. 2005. A transferable method for the automated grain sizing of river gravels. *Water Resources Research* **41**: W07020. doi: 10.1029/2004WR003868.

Hofland, B., Booij, R., and Battjes, J.A. 2005. Measurement of fluctuating pressures on coarse bed material. *Journal of Hydraulic Engineering* **131**: 770–781.

Neumann, B., Held, M., Liebel, U. *et al.* 2006. High-throughput RNAi screening by time-lapse imaging of live human cells. *Nature Methods* **3**: 385–390.

Nystrom, E.A., Rehmann, C.R., and Oberg, K.A. 2007. Evaluation of Mean Velocity and Turbulence Measurements with ADCPs. *Journal of Hydraulic Engineering* **133**: 1310–1318.

Smart, G.M. and Habersack, H.M. 2007. Pressure fluctuations and gravel entrainment in rivers. *Journal of Hydraulic Research* **45**: 661–673.

Stacey, M.T., Monismith, S.G., and Burau, J.R. 1999. Measurements of Reynolds stress profiles in unstratified tidal flow. *Journal of Geophysical Research* **104**: 10933–10949.

Voulgaris, G. and Trowbridge, J.H. 1998. Evaluation of the acoustic Doppler velocimeter for turbulence measurements. *Journal of Atmospheric and Oceanic Technology* **15**: 272–289.

# Mapping Water and Sediment Flux Distributions in Gravel-bed Rivers Using ADCPs

## Colin D. Rennie

## 25.1 INTRODUCTION

Muste *et al.* (Chapter 24, this volume) have presented a comprehensive overview of recent advances in experimental methods and instrumentation available for field studies in rivers. In their primary examples they have demonstrated the utility of acoustic methods such as acoustic Doppler current profilers (ADCPs) for measurement of 3-D flow fields and combined use of multibeam echosounders and sidescan sonars for high-resolution measurement and visualization of bathymetry. Their examples, however, are from large sand-bed rivers. The purpose of this discussion is to demonstrate that similar results can be obtained in gravel-bed rivers using an ADCP. This chapter has two principal objectives. First, ADCP measurements in gravel-bed versus sand-bed rivers are compared, with particular emphasis on the influence of flow turbulence upon the reliability of velocity measurements in each river type. The intent is to assess whether measurement protocols for spatial surveys should differ between gravel-bed and sand-bed rivers. Second, ADCP surveys are used to map spatial distributions of flow depth, velocity, and apparent bedload velocity. Two gravel-bed case studies are presented: the relatively deep wandering Fraser River, Canada and the relatively shallow braided Rees River, New Zealand. The case studies demonstrate the unprecedented spatial coverage achievable with ADCP spatial surveys, such that it is possible to identify bedload transport pathways within a reach. In both case studies it is observed that locations of bedload transport are more related to local sediment supply than local flow competence.

## 25.2 GRAVEL-BED VERSUS SAND-BED ADCP MEASUREMENTS

First, consider the differences between gravel-bed and sand-bed rivers that are relevant for measuring 3-D flow and sediment transport fields with an ADCP. This discussion will centre on the two elements that contribute to uncertainty of ADCP measurements: real temporal turbulent fluctuations and measurement errors. As a result of real fluctuations and measurement errors, an instantaneous measurement may be a poor realization of the local mean velocity (Muste *et al.*, 2004a, 2004b; Rennie and Church, 2010), and some degree of spatial or temporal averaging is required to obtain useful velocity distributions.

By definition, gravel-bed rivers have a coarser substrate and thus greater grain friction than sand-bed rivers. However, total friction tends to be greater in sand-bed rivers due to the bed form roughness of ripples and dunes. For rivers of comparable depth, the water velocity, friction slope, and shear velocity are greater in a gravel-bed river than a sand-bed river (Table 25.1). In Table 25.1, reach-averaged data are presented from the Fraser River and the Missouri River at similar flow stage (61–65% of the mean annual flood). Data are available from both a gravel-bed reach and a sand-bed reach of the Fraser River, and the channel dimensions of the Fraser gravel-bed reach and the Missouri sand-bed reach are similar. For uniform flow, Kironoto and Graf (1994) demonstrated that turbulence (root mean square of velocity fluctuations) is proportional to the shear velocity ($u^*$), and exponentially decays towards the free surface. Given that shear velocity is greater in gravel-bed rivers than

*Gravel-bed Rivers: Processes, Tools, Environments*, First Edition. Edited by Michael Church, Pascale M. Biron and André G. Roy.
© 2012 John Wiley & Sons, Ltd. Published 2012 by John Wiley & Sons, Ltd.

**Table 25.1** Comparison of sand-bed and gravel-bed rivers: Fraser and Missouri Rivers at similar flow stage (61–65% of the mean annual flood)

| | Reach-averaged conditions | | | | | | | | Local stationary ADCP profile | | | | | |
| --- | --- | --- | --- | --- | --- | --- | --- | --- | --- | --- | --- | --- | --- | --- |
| | $Q$, m$^3$ s$^{-1}$; ($Q$, %MAF) | $W$, m | $\langle H \rangle$, m | $\langle U \rangle$, m s$^{-1}$ | $D_{90}$, m | Water surface $S$ | $\tau$, N/m$^2$; ($u_*$, m s$^{-1}$) | Man. $n$ | $H$, m ($H_{max}$, m) | $u_*$, m s$^{-1}$ | $\overline{U}$, m s$^{-1}$ | $\overline{\sigma}_u$, m s$^{-1}$ | $\overline{\sigma}_\varepsilon$, m s$^{-1}$ | $\overline{\sigma}_s$, m s$^{-1}$ | $\frac{\overline{\sigma}}{\overline{U}}$ |
| **Gravel bed** | | | | | | | | | | | | | | |
| Fraser R. off Minto Island | 6000 (61) | 500 | 6 | 2.00 | ~0.08 | 0.00035 | 20.6 (0.144) | 0.031 | 7.03 (7.19) | 0.151 | 2.293 | 0.335 | 0.225 | 0.246 | 0.109 |
| Fraser R. off Queen's Bar | 6000 (61) | 500 | 6 | 2.00 | ~0.08 | 0.00035 | 20.6 (0.144) | 0.031 | 3.94 (4.41) | 0.145 | 1.860 | 0.362 | 0.221 | 0.286 | 0.159 |
| **Sand bed** | | | | | | | | | | | | | | |
| Missouri R. @Plowboy; thalweg large dunes | 3030 (65) | 500 | 6 | 1.01 | 0.0022[a] | 0.00016[a] | 9.4 (0.097) | 0.041 | 7.95 (8.12) | 0.128 | 2.368 | 0.312 | 0.237 | 0.259 | 0.111 |
| Missouri R. @Plowboy; no dunes | 3030 (65) | 500 | 6 | 1.01 | 0.0022[a] | 0.00016[a] | 9.4 (0.097) | 0.041 | 5.51 (5.73) | 0.105 | 1.309 | 0.316 | 0.226 | 0.221 | 0.172 |
| Fraser R. @Mission; small dunes | 6200 (63) | 530 | 11.3 | 1.04 | 0.002 | 0.000069 | 7.7 (0.088) | 0.041 | 11.27 (11.54) | 0.098 | 1.423 | 0.252 | 0.185 | 0.171 | 0.121 |

[a] from Gaeuman and Jacobson (2006), for Missouri River reach 33 km from the Plowboy reach.

$Q$ = discharge, MAF = mean annual flood, $W$ = width, $\langle U \rangle$ = reach averaged depth, $\langle U \rangle$ = reach averaged velocity, $D_{90}$ = 90$^{th}$ percentile particle size, $S$ = slope, $\tau$ = bed shear stress, $u_*$ = shear velocity, Man. $n$ = Manning's n roughness, H = average local depth, $H_{max}$ = maximum depth recorded in time series, $\overline{U}$ = depth averaged velocity, $U$ = average bin velocity, $\overline{\sigma}_u$ = depth averaged observed standard deviation of primary water velocity, $\overline{\sigma}_\varepsilon$ = depth averaged ADCP error velocity, $\overline{\sigma}_s$ = depth averaged estimated turbulence standard deviation, $\frac{\overline{\sigma}}{\overline{U}}$ = depth averaged turbulence intensity.

comparable sand-bed rivers, one would expect greater turbulence in a gravel-bed river. However, the presence of dunes and associated vortices due to flow separation at dune crests will also increase turbulence in a sand-bed river (Lapointe, 1992; Venditti and Bauer, 2005). Vortices in dune fields typically form kolk boils, which advect momentum and suspend sediment from the bed to the water surface. It is thus necessary to consider the relative importance of large coherent structures generated at the bed in the presence of dunes versus turbulence associated with depth-limited coherent structures which appear to be ubiquitous, even in gravel-bed rivers (Roy et al., 2004).

For stationary ADCP vertical profile data, Rennie and Church (2010) employed a pooled variance model to estimate the actual turbulence ($\sigma_s$), where $\sigma_s$ is the standard deviation of velocity fluctuations. Specifically, for each bin in the vertical profile, the average ADCP error velocity ($\sigma_\varepsilon$) was removed from the observed standard deviation of water velocity ($\sigma_u$):

$$\sigma_s = \sqrt{\sigma_u^2 - \sigma_\varepsilon^2} \qquad (25.1)$$

The ADCP error velocity is based on the difference between two redundant measurements of vertical velocity in a depth bin, and accounts for both Doppler noise and heterogeneity of actual velocities between beams. Based on the beam geometry, the error velocity for an RD Instruments Rio Grande ADCP is scaled such that it represents the error in horizontal velocity. In the gravel-bed Fraser River reach, Rennie and Church (2010) observed $\sigma_\varepsilon$ was greatest near the bed, particularly in deep locations, due to beam divergence and consequent increase in velocity heterogeneity between beams at greater depths. Velocity heterogeneity may also be greater near the bed in gravel-bed rivers due to local wakes generated off individual clasts or particle clusters, but the ADCP side-lobe error typically requires blanking of velocities nearest the bed. For rivers of similar conveyance capacity, sand-bed rivers are deeper than gravel-bed rivers (Church, 1992). Given that the assumption of velocity homogeneity between beams becomes more tenuous with increasing depth, one would expect greater violation of the homogeneity assumption in sand-bed rivers. Furthermore, the spatial heterogeneity of velocity in a dune field will exacerbate the homogeneity violation, particularly if individual beams insonify different dune elements such as the stoss and trough.

It should be acknowledged that Equation (25.1) requires the assumption that $\sigma_s$ and $\sigma_\varepsilon$ are mutually independent, which may not hold if increased turbulence increases the error velocity. Lastly, note that $\sigma_s$ repre-

sents only large-scale fluctuations encompassed by the divergent ADCP acoustic beams.

For the present analysis, Equation (25.1) is used with profiles collected in the Fraser River and Missouri River study reaches to estimate the magnitude of velocity fluctuation in each environment. Each stationary profile was based on at least 10 minutes of data collection, with boat translation limited to a few metres. All profiles were collected with an RD Instruments 1200 kHz Rio Grande ADCP using Water Mode 1 with 25 cm bins, with a sampling frequency of 1–2 Hz, depending on depth. Two gravel-bed profiles with differing depths and average velocities were collected in the Fraser River near Chilliwack, British Columbia on 23 June, 2006 (see Rennie and Church, 2010 for details of this survey). This portion of the Fraser River is characterized as a wandering gravel-bed river, with sufficient sediment load to induce the formation of mid-channel bars and vegetated islands. Two Missouri River profiles were collected on 28 May, 2008 in the Plowboy reach at River Mile 173 (see Jamieson et al., 2011 and in press for details of this survey). One profile was collected in the thalweg navigation channel where large dunes were present (average dune height and length of 2.5 m and 39 m, respectively), and the other was collected toward the left side of the channel, upstream of a series of large spur dikes, where no dunes were present. Flow was concentrated in the thalweg navigation channel due to the spur dikes. Dune celerity was not measured, but previous measurements of dune celerity in the Lower Missouri River range from 1 to 5 m h$^{-1}$ (Gaeuman and Jacobson, 2007), thus it can be assumed that the dune field was stationary during the ADCP measurements. Finally, the Fraser River sand-bed profile was collected on 8 June, 2010 in the centre of the straight single-thread reach immediately upstream of the Mission gauge (Water Survey Canada 08MH024) where small dunes were present (average dune height and length of 0.4 m and 10 m, respectively) (Rennie et al., unpublished data).

For each profile, Equation (25.1) was used to estimate $\sigma_s$ in each environment. The profiles of mean streamwise velocity ($U$), $\sigma_u$, $\sigma_\varepsilon$, and $\sigma_s$ are provided in Figure 25.1, and depth-averaged values are summarized in Table 25.1. As expected, both the error velocity and the observed variance tend to increase toward the bed. The results are reasonably consistent between river types, particularly when comparing the gravel-bed Fraser River and the Missouri River profiles. The average error velocities are similar between profiles (0.22 m s$^{-1}$ for the gravel-bed Fraser River, 0.23 to 0.24 m s$^{-1}$ for the Missouri River, and 0.19 m s$^{-1}$ for sand-bed Fraser River). It is noteworthy that error velocity was lowest in the sand-bed Fraser River, despite the greatest depth and thus greatest beam divergence for this profile. This suggests that the velocity

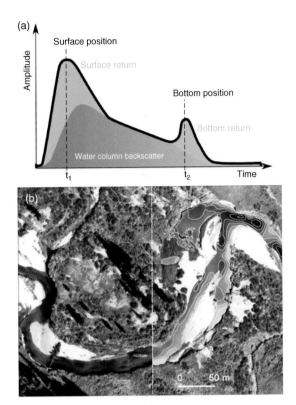

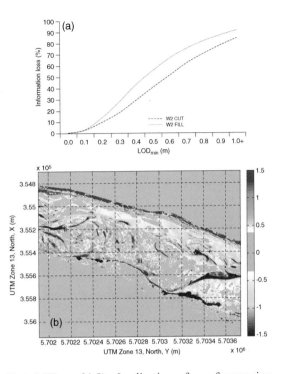

**Plate 9 (Figure 21.7)** LiDAR measurement of depths. (a) Blue-green LiDAR returns in deep water generate a double peak that indicates the location of the water surface and stream bottom. At more shallow depths (approximately <2 m), the return signal often displays only one peak, complicating the analysis. Reproduced, with permission, from Allouis, T., Bailly, J.-S., Pastol, Y. and Le Roux, C. 2010. Comparison of LiDAR waveform processing methods for very shallow water bathymetry using Raman, near-infrared, and green signals. *Earth Surface Processes and Landforms* **35**: 640–650; (b) Colour-infrared photography with LiDAR-generated bathymetry overlaid on the right-hand portion of the stream. The contour interval is 30 cm, but McKean *et al.* report the data support a 20 cm interval. Reproduced, with permission, from McKean, J., Issak, D. and Wright, W. 2009a. Improving stream studies with a small–footprint green lidar. *EOS: Transactions of the American Geophysical Union* **90**: 341–342. The River Bathymetry Toolkit (RBT) is available online at http://www.fs.fed.us/rm/boise/AWAE/projects/river_bathymetry_toolkit.shtml.

**Plate 9 (Figure 21.8)** Implications of error for mapping erosion and deposition. (a) The tradeoff between the acceptable limit of detection (LOD) and the amount of erosion or deposition that is detected by subtracting DEMs for the Waimakariri River, New Zealand. Reproduced, with permission, from Lane, S.N., Westaway, R.M. and Hicks, D.M. 2003. Estimation of erosion and deposition volumes in a large, gravel-bed, braided river using synoptic remote sensing. *Earth Surface Processes and Landforms* **28**: 249–271. (b) Erosion and deposition in the South Saskatchewan River, Canada, derived from comparison of DEMs with the minimum detectable limit of erosion set at 0.40 m. Reproduced, with permission, from Lane, S.N., Widdison, P.E., Thomas, R.E., Ashworth, P.J., Best, J.L., Lunt, I.A., Sambrook Smith, G.H. and Simpson, C.J. 2010. Quantification of braided river channel change using archival digital image analysis. *Earth Surface Processes and Landforms* **35**: 971–985.

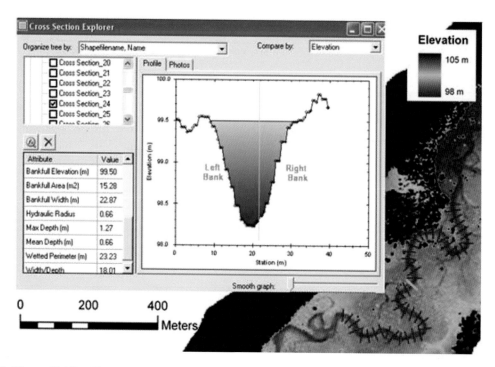

**Plate 10 (Figure 21.10)** The McKean *et al.* (2009a) ArcGIS-based River Bathymetry Toolkit graphical user interface for extracting cross sections and other hydraulic variables from high-resolution aquatic-terrestrial DEMs. (*See text for full caption.*)

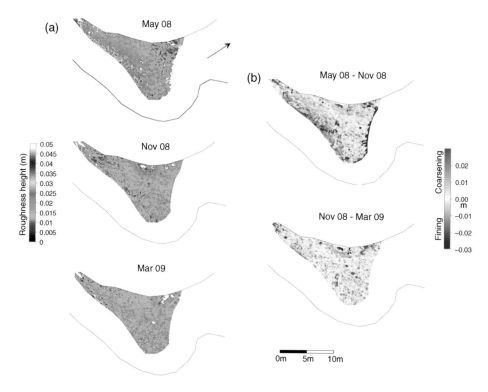

**Plate 10 (Figure 22.1)** (a) Grain roughness maps, and (b) grain roughness change maps for the River Rede. (*See text for full caption.*)

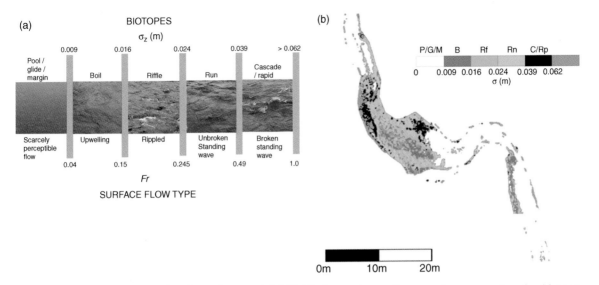

**Plate 11 (Figure 22.3)** Application of terrestrial LiDAR for water surface roughness mapping for biotope assessment; (a) conceptual model linking water surface roughness (Milan *et al.*, 2010) and Froude number (Newson *et al.*, 1998) delimiters (the boundary between each biotope is fuzzy in nature, and should be considered transitional rather than rigid). (*See text for full caption.*)

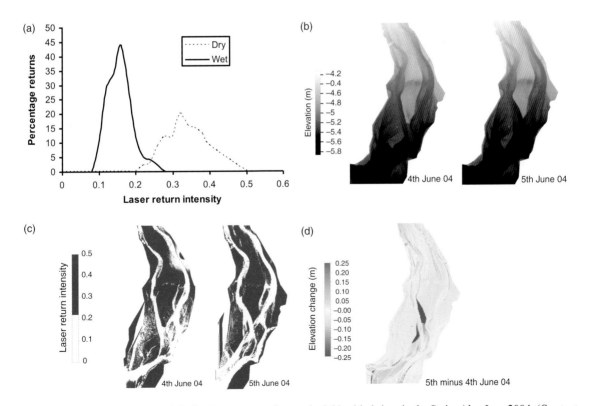

**Plate 11 (Figure 22.4)** Terrestrial LiDAR resurvey of a proglacial braided river in the Swiss Alps June 2004. (*See text for full caption.*)

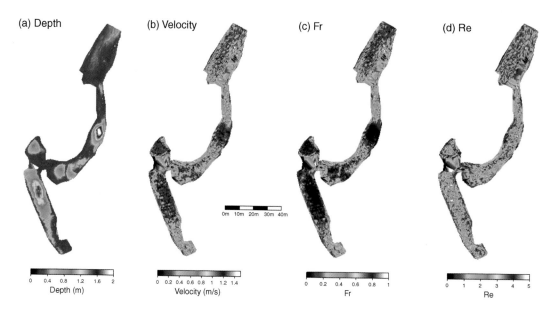

**Plate 12 (Figure 22.5)** Hydraulic data obtained using the ADCP for River Wharfe site; (a) water depth; (b) mean column velocity; (c) *Fr*; and (d) *Re* $\times 10^{-6}$. (*See text for full caption.*)

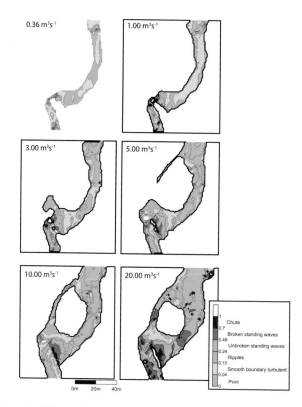

**Plate 12 (Figure 22.6)** Changing biotope distribution with increasing flow for the River Wharfe study site using the River2D hydraulic model.

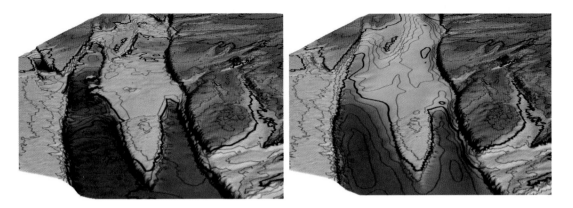

**Plate 13 (Figure 23.2)** Top: DEM from Waiau River, New Zealand. Green-brown areas are dry riverbed surveyed by LiDAR. (*See text for full caption.*)

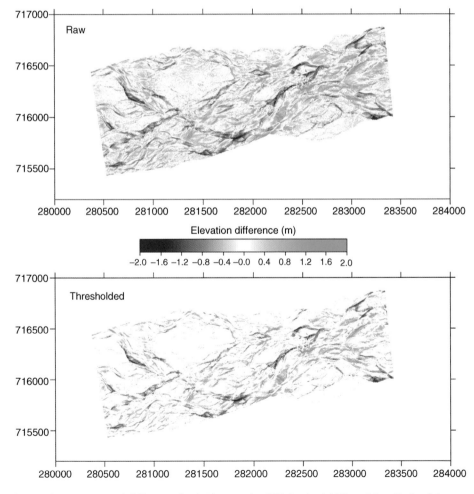

**Plate 13 (Figure 23.3)** DEMs of difference for 3.5 km reach of Waimakariri River, New Zealand, between February 1999 and February 2000. (*See text for full caption.*)

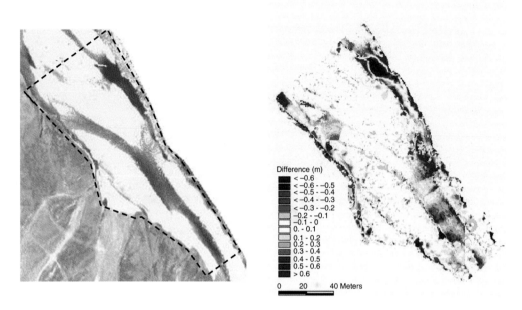

**Plate 14 (Figure 23.4)** Left: surveyed reach of River Feshie, Scotland; river flows bottom to top. (*See text for full caption.*)

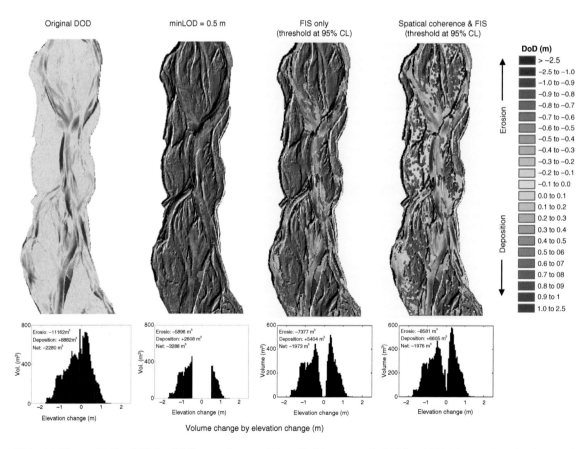

**Plate 14 (Figure 23.5)** DEMs of difference between River Feshie surveys in 2006 and 2007 (top row) and volumes of erosion and deposition distributed by elevation change above level of detection (bottom row). (*See text for full caption.*)

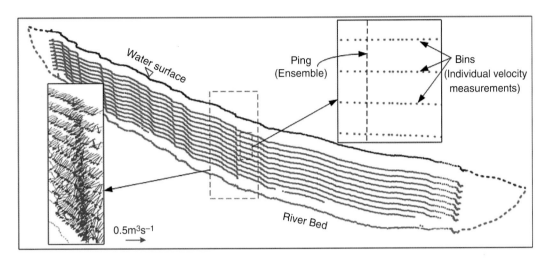

**Plate 15 (Figure 24.5)** Instantaneous velocities acquired by ADCP operated from moving boat across the stream cross-section.

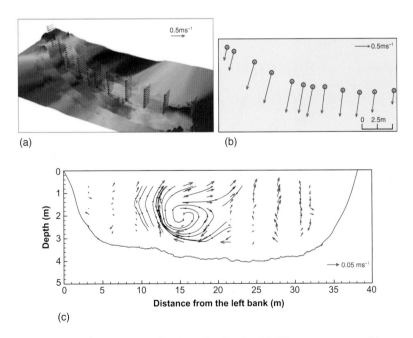

(a)

(b)

(c)

**Plate 15 (Figure 24.6)** Mean flow characteristics from fixed point ADCP measurements: (a) mean vertical velocity distributions; (b) depth-averaged profile; (c) mapping of the velocity distribution in the stream cross-section.

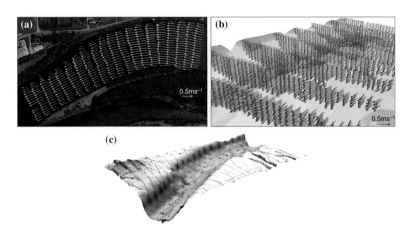

**Plate 16 (Figure 24.7)** River morphology and mean hydrodynamic characteristics obtained from ADCP measurements acquired in Pool 16 in Mississippi River. (*See text for full caption.*)

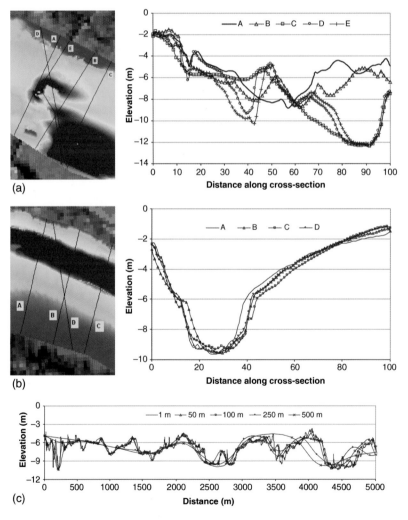

**Plate 16 (Figure 24.8)** Linear features extraction from Brazos River MBES data: (a) cross-section locations at a bridge and corresponding ground profiles; (b) cross-section locations at a meandering bend and corresponding ground profiles; (c) thalweg profiles for different sampling intervals.

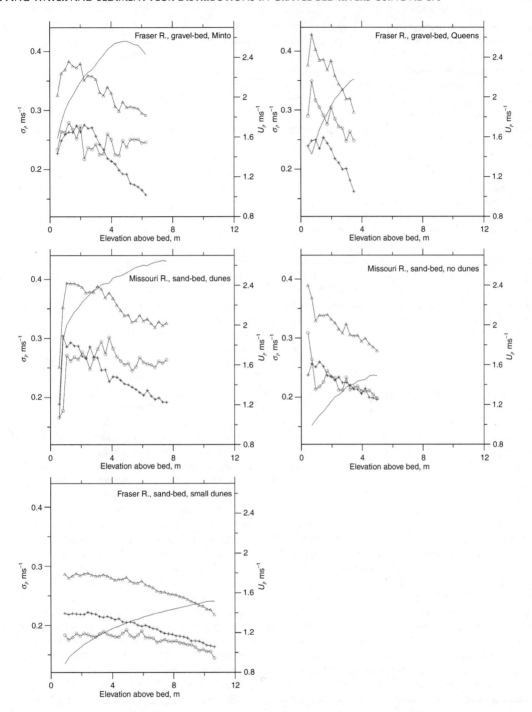

**Figure 25.1**   Profiles of mean streamwise velocity ($U$, no symbols), observed standard deviation of streamwise velocity ($\sigma_u$, $\Delta$ symbol), average error velocity ($\sigma_\varepsilon$, $+$ symbol), and calculated turbulence intensity using Equation (25.1) ($\sigma_s$, $\bigcirc$ symbol).

field was more spatially homogenous in the sand-bed Fraser River where only small dunes were present. The estimated depth-averaged turbulence standard deviations ($\overline{\sigma_s}$) tended to be greater in the gravel-bed profiles than the sand-bed profiles, except when large dunes were present. If large dunes are present, it appears that turbulence standard deviation in sand-bed rivers is comparable to that of gravel-bed rivers, presumably due to the generation of large-scale turbulent structures. Lastly, the turbulence intensities ($\frac{\overline{\sigma_x}}{U}$) were similar at all sites, with the largest value observed at the Missouri River without dunes.

Overall, error velocities and real turbulent fluctuations appear to be similar in gravel-bed and sand-bed rivers; thus similar ADCP survey intensity and interpolation procedures should be employed for mapping water velocity distributions in each river type. To confirm this analysis, it would be worthwhile to evaluate a large number of profiles from a range of gravel-bed and sand-bed rivers. To complete the analysis it would also be useful to consider double averaging procedures (e.g., McLean and Nikora 2006), which would account for spatial variability of turbulence characteristics within a river.

## 25.3   GRAVEL-BED SPATIAL DISTRIBUTIONS

In the following, spatial ADCP surveys are presented from two gravel-bed rivers: the wandering Fraser River in Canada, and the braided Rees River in New Zealand.

### 25.3.1   Fraser River

The Fraser River drains $250\,000\,\text{km}^2$ of southern British Columbia, Canada. At the town of Hope, 151 river km upstream of the river mouth, the river enters the alluvial Fraser Valley, where it proceeds to deposit its load of gravel. Spatially intensive ADCP surveys were performed over a 5.5 km study reach in the gravel-bed portion of the Fraser River near Chilliwack, British Columbia, during the falling limb of both the 2006 and 2007 freshets. A 1200 kHz RD Instruments Rio Grande ADCP was utilized, with 25 cm velocity bins and sampling frequency of 1–2 Hz. The study reach extended from just downstream of the confluence with the Harrison River to the downstream end of Queen's Island (see Rennie and Church, 2010, their Figure 1). As noted above, the study reach is a wandering gravel-bed river, with mid-channel bars and vegetated islands. Bedrock outcrops partially control the right bank of the river in this reach. Zones of erosion and deposition are related strongly to areas of flow convergence and divergence around the mid-channel islands. The main channel is

approximately 500 m wide, and the bed material ranges from cobble to sand, with bar surface $D_{50}$ ($D_{84}$) of about 22 mm to 35 mm (40 mm to 75 mm) (Sime et al., 2007; Rice and Church, 2010). At Mission, 25 km downstream from the lower limit of the study reach (Water Survey of Canada gauge 08MH024), the mean annual discharge is $3400\,\text{m}^3\,\text{s}^{-1}$, mean annual flood is $9800\,\text{m}^3\,\text{s}^{-1}$, and maximum freshet-driven flows exceed $13\,000\,\text{m}^3\,\text{s}^{-1}$ (McLean et al., 1999).

Using the data from these surveys, Rennie and Church (2010) presented the first maps of spatially distributed depth ($H$), depth-averaged water velocity ($U$), shear velocity ($u^*$), and apparent bed-load velocity ($v_a$) measured by ADCP in a large gravel-bed river reach (Figure 25.2). Apparent bed-load velocity is the bias in bottom tracking (Doppler sonar) due to near-bed particle motion, and serves as a metric of relative bedload transport (Rennie et al., 2002). Rennie and Church (2010) also assessed the uncertainty of these maps based on measured ADCP error velocities and modelled turbulent fluctuations of both water velocity and spatially averaged bedload. Flow during the 2006 survey was near the threshold for particle motion, whereas flow in 2007 was above bankfull, when full mobility of the bed material was expected. Only the 2006 maps are reproduced herein. The ADCP survey was based on single diagonal transects spaced an average of 110 m apart, which was less than a quarter of a channel width. The survey extent was sufficient to capture a full meander wavelength, with the thalweg crossing back and forth across the channel (Figure 25.2a). The deepest pools occurred in bends where the thalweg met channel banks, particularly when accompanied by bedrock control.

The maps shown in Figure 25.2 are remarkably coherent, with maximum $U$, $u^*$, and $v_a$ following the thalweg. The largest values occurred in channel bends at zones of flow convergence where the thalweg flow accelerated toward the bank. This was observed in both the 2006 moderate-flow and 2007 high-flow surveys. The uncertainty analysis demonstrated greater uncertainty of $U$ in shallower locations due to reduced depth averaging. Nevertheless, the uncertainty was much less than the observed signal, and the spatial distribution of $U$ was significant at the 95% confidence level. With respect to $u^*$, greater uncertainty was also observed for shallower profiles due to smaller number of velocity points in the profile, but uncertainty of $u^*$ was $<0.02\,\text{m s}^{-1}$ for all depths, if $u^*$ was calculated from velocity profiles based on averages of 11 ADCP single-ping profiles. Thus, most of the $u^*$ spatial distribution was also statistically significant. Lastly, the uncertainty of $v_a$ was comparable to the observed mean signal, but large values of $v_a$ were found to be statistically significant, and the locations of significant transport were mapped.

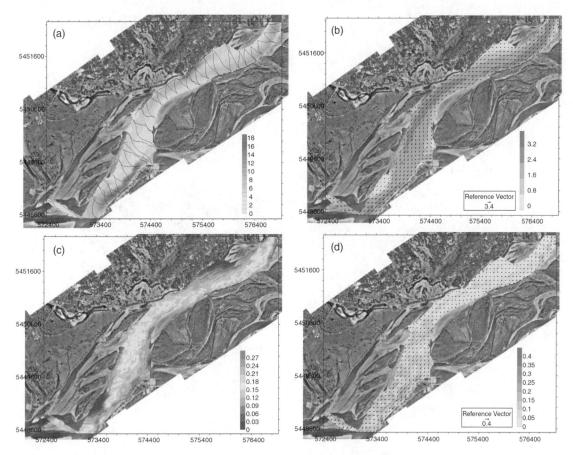

**Figure 25.2** Fraser River gravel-bed ADCP spatial survey, 24–25 June, 2006. All distributions interpolated using kriging with 25 m grid spacing. Map units are UTM coordinates in m: (a) water depth (m), overlain by boat track showing positions of ADCP measurements; (b) depth averaged water velocity (m s$^{-1}$), every third vector in Easting and Northing shown; (c) shear velocity (m s$^{-1}$); (d) apparent bedload velocity (m s$^{-1}$), every third vector in Easting and Northing shown. Reproduced, with permission, from Rennie, C.D., and M. Church (2010), Mapping spatial distributions and uncertainty of water and sediment flux in a arge gravel bed river reach using an acoustic Doppler current profiler. J. *Geophys. Res.* **115**, F03035, doi:10.1029/2009JF001556. (See the color version of this figure in color plate section.)

High values of $v_a$ should be indicative of bed material transport and, particularly in the high-flow year, it is likely that all grain sizes were in motion in the channel thalweg. However, in the lower-flow year the highest $v_a$ was observed outside the thalweg in a deep pool with a rapidly eroding cutbank (Figure 25.2d, at 574200 m E, 5449450 m N). This pool was scoured by the confluence flow of the main channel and a large side channel. A highly resolved survey of the confluence area was performed during the falling limb of the 2008 freshet (Gaskin *et al.*, 2010; Gaskin, 2010). Low shear velocities were calculated in this pool using the log law, even if only the lowest 20% of the velocity profile was utilized, but high positive vertical velocities were observed at the

eroding cut-bank. It appears that the cut-bank erosion was caused by highly turbulent, strongly 3-D flow generated by both the confluence shear layer (see, Boyer *et al.*, 2006) and flow separation from the channel bank. In this case, it is possible that transport along the river bed of relatively fine material from the channel bank dominated the $v_a$ signal.

### 25.3.2   Rees River

The Rees River drains a 405 km$^2$ basin in Central Otago, New Zealand. The ReesScan project was conducted over the summer 2009/2010 flood season in a 2.5 km long × 0.7 km wide slowly aggrading braided reach (Brasington, 2010).

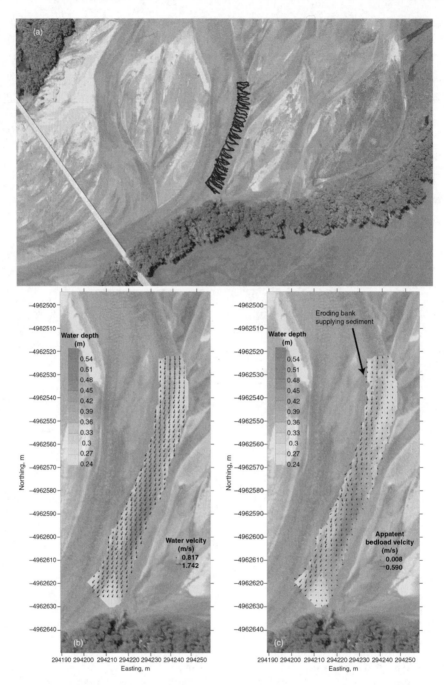

**Figure 25.3** Rees River gravel-bed ADCP spatial survey, 13 January, 2010. All distributions interpolated using kriging with 1.1 m grid spacing. Map units are arbitrary coordinates in m: (a) boat track showing positions of ADCP measurements within the braid plain; (b) depth-averaged water velocity (m s$^{-1}$), every second vector in Easting and Northing shown, overlain on water depth (m); (c) apparent bedload velocity (m s$^{-1}$), every second vector in Easting and Northing shown, overlain on water depth (m). Modified from Vericat *et al.* (2010). (See the color version of this figure in color plate section.)

Measurements included terrestrial laser-scanning surveys of bed morphology following each flood event (Brasington *et al.*, 2010), discharge and sediment monitoring, and ADCP stationary and spatial surveys of flow and apparent bedload velocity (Vericat *et al.*, 2010). Mean surface $D_{50}$ in the study reach ranged from 18 to 45 mm.

An ADCP spatial survey was conducted on 10 January, 2010 in the primary braid anabranch on the receding limb of a moderate flood (Figure 25.3). A 3 MHz Sontek S5 ADCP was deployed using a tethered boat. Velocity data were collected in 10 cm bins in the vertical at a sampling frequency of 1 Hz. Due to shallow depths (Figure 25.3b) insufficient bins were available to estimate shear velocity from velocity profiles. The study reach was 100 m long and about 13 m wide, ADCP transects were spaced an average of 1.4 m apart, and maximum transect spacing was less than 4 m (Figure 25.3a). Maps of spatially distributed $U$ (Figure 25.3b) and $v_a$ (Figure 25.3c) are provided herein.

The deepest part of the reach was observed in a scour pool at a confluence with a minor anabranch (at 294225 Easting, $-4962958$ Northing). The highest water velocity at the entrance to the reach was on the channel right, as flow converged on the upstream edge of a mid-channel bar. The core of high-water velocity transferred from the right bank to the left bank as flow converged in the confluence scour pool. On the other hand, the highest apparent bedload velocity hugged the right bank along the mid-channel bar. It is clear from Figure 25.3b that a bedload transport pathway occurred along the mid-channel bar margin. During the survey a cutbank on the mid-channel bar at the upstream end of the study reach was observed to be actively eroding due to flow convergence, effectively supplying sediment to the study reach (Figure 25.3c). The eroded sediment was observed to translate along the bar margin, thus providing visual corroboration of the transport pathway seen in Figure 25.3c. This visual observation was possible due to relatively clear water and shallow depths. Interestingly, this transport pathway did not follow the deepest part of the anabranch where water velocity was highest.

## 25.4 DISCUSSION AND CONCLUSIONS

The case studies from gravel-bed reaches of Fraser River and Rees River demonstrate that ADCP surveys can provide spatially distributed data for water velocity, shear velocity, and sediment transport. These results complement the sand-bed case studies presented by Muste *et al.* Furthemore, the analysis of ADCP errors and turbulent fluctuations in gravel-bed versus sand-bed rivers suggests that similar survey intensity and data smoothing/interpolation procedures are required for spatial surveys in each river type.

It is generally understood that bed material transport occurs where excess shear stress is available to mobilize local bed sediments (Mülhofer, 1933; Dietrich and Whiting, 1989). Sediment transport pathways observed by Mülhofer and by Dietrich and Whiting did not necessarily correspond to locations with the highest bed shear stress in the reach, because locations with high bed shear stress can be more heavily armoured. Regardless, high shear stress is generally considered to be required for bed material transport, and most bedload formulae calculate bedload as a function of bed shear. Morphodynamic numerical models of rivers generally employ such formulae to calculate sediment transport in the reach. Morphodynamic models are used to predict changes in channel morphology, which is critical for managing and protecting infrastructure and habitat.

In both of the field case studies presented above, highest apparent bedload velocity was observed immediately downstream of a source of sediment supply, in a location where shear velocity (Fraser River) or water velocity (Rees River) was observed to be relatively low. These results demonstrate the importance of sediment supply sources for determining bed material transport pathways in gravel-bed rivers with complex topography. These transport pathways determine the transfer of sediment through the reach, and thus determine the time evolution of channel morphology. Spatially distributed measurements of bed material transport are essential for determining these pathways, and the results presented above demonstrate that ADCP spatial surveys of $v_a$ can achieve this; morphodynamic models that assume high bedload as a function of only high bed shear cannot. A challenge for river researchers will be to develop morphodynamic models that can quantify local sediment supply by locating and quantifying zones of erosion and deposition. This will require coupling of advanced 3-D turbulent flow models, bank erosion algorithms, and sediment transport routines.

## 25.5 REFERENCES

Boyer C., Roy A.G., and Best J.L. 2006. Dynamics of a river channel confluence with discordant beds: Flow turbulence, bed load sediment transport, and bed morphology. *Journal of Geophysical Research* **111**: F04007. doi: 10.1029/2005JF000458.

Brasington, J. 2010. From grain to floodplain: hyperscale models of braided rivers. *Hydrolink* **4**: 52–53.

Brasington, J., Vericat, D., Hicks, M. *et al.* 2010. Hyperscale monitoring and modelling of the braided Rees River, New Zealand. *7th International Gravel-bed Rivers Workshop, Tadoussac, Québec, 6–10 September, Abstracts*, p. 23.

Church, M. 1992. Channel morphology and typology. In Calow, P. and Petts, G.E., editors. *The Rivers Handbook*. Oxford, Blackwell Science: 126–143.

Dietrich, W. E. and Whiting, P. 1989. Boundary shear stress and sediment transport in river meanders of sand and gravel. In Ikeda, S. and Parker, G., editors. *River Meandering*. American Geophysical Union, *Water Resources Mongraph* **12**: 1–50.

Gaeuman, D. and Jacobson, R.B. 2006. Acoustic bed velocity and bedload dynamics in a large sand bed river. *Journal of Geophysical Research* **111**: F02005. doi: 10.1029/2005JF0004111.

Gaeuman, D. and Jacobson R. B. (2007). Field assessment of alternative bed-load transport estimators. *Journal of Hydraulic Engineering*, **133**(12): 1319–1328.

Gaskin, J. 2010. *Intensive ADCP survey of a gravel-bed river confluence*. M.A.Sc thesis, University of Ottawa, Department of Civil Engineering.

Gaskin, J., Rennie, C.D., and Church, M.A. 2010. Intensive ADCP survey of a gravel-bed river confluence. Poster Presented at the 7th International Gravel-bed Rivers Workshop, Tadoussac, Québec, 6–10 September.

Jamieson, E.C., Rennie, C.D., Jacobson, R.B., and Townsend, R.D. In press. Evaluation of ADCP bed velocity in a large sand bed river: Moving versus stationary boat conditions. *Journal of Hydraulic Engineering*.

Jamieson, E.C., Rennie, C.D., Jacobson, R.B., and Townsend, R.D. In press. 3-D flow and scour near a submerged wing dike: ADCP measurements on the Missouri River. *Water Resources Research* **47**: W07544. doi:10.1029/2010WR010043.

Kironoto, B.A. and Graf, W. 1994. Turbulence characteristics in rough uniform open-channel flow. *Proceedings of the Institution of Civil Engineers, Water, Maritime and Energy* **106** (December): 333–344.

Lapointe, M. 1992. Burst-like sediment suspension events in a sand-bed river. *Earth Surface Processes and Landforms* **17**: 253–270.

McLean, S. and Nikora, V. 2006. Characteristics of turbulent unidirectional flow over rough-beds: Double-averaging perspective with particular focus on sand dunes and gravel beds. *Water Resources Research* **42**: W10409. doi: 10.1029/2005WR004708.

McLean, D. G., Church, M., and Tassone, B. 1999. Sediment transport along lower Fraser River: 1. Measurements and hydraulic computations. *Water Resources Research* **35**: 2533–2548.

Mülhofer L. 1933. Untersuchungen uber der Schwebstoff und Geschiebefurung des Inn nachst Kirchbichl, Tirol [Investigations into suspended load and bedload of the River Inn, near Kirchbichl, Tirol]. *Wasserwirtschaft* Heft 1–6.

Muste, M., Yu, K., Pratt, T., and Abraham, D. 2004a. Practical aspects of ADCP data use for quantification of mean river flow characteristics; Part II: fixed-vessel measurements. *Flow Measurement and Instrumentation* **15**: 17–28.

Muste, M., Yu, K., and Spasojevic, M. 2004b. Practical aspects of ADCP data use for quantification of mean river flow characteristics; Part 1: moving-vessel measurements. *Flow Measurement and Instrumentation* **15**: 1–16.

Rennie, C.D. and Church, M. 2010. Mapping spatial distributions and uncertainty of water and sediment flux in a large gravel-bed river reach using an aDcp. *Journal of Geophysical Research* **115**: F03035. doi: 10.1029/2009JF001556.

Rennie, C.D., Millar, R.G., and Church, M.A. 2002. Measurement of bed load velocity using an acoustic Doppler current profiler. *Journal of Hydraulic Engineering* **128**: 473–483.

Rice, S. P. and Church, M. 2010. Grain-size sorting within river bars in relation to downstream fining along a wandering channel. *Sedimentology* **57**: 232–251.

Roy, A.G., Buffin-Belanger, T., Lamarre, H., and Kirkbride, A.D. 2004. Size, shape and dynamics of large-scale turbulent flow structures in a gravel-bed river. *Journal of Fluid Mechanics* **500**: 1–27.

Sime, L.C., Ferguson, R.I., and Church, M. 2007. Estimating shear stress from moving boat acoustic Doppler velocity measurements in a large gravel-bed river. *Water Resources Research* **43**: W03418. doi: 10.1029/2006WR005069.

Venditti, J.G. and Bauer, B.O. 2005. Turbulent flow over a dune: Green River, Colorado, *Earth Surface Processes and Landforms* **30**: 289–304.

Vericat, D., Rennie, C., Brasington, J. *et al.* 2010. Bedload monitoring with acoustic bottom tracking: braided Rees River, New Zealand. Poster presented at the 7th International Gravel-bed Rivers Workshop, Tadoussac, Québec, 6–10 September.

# Steep Channels

# 26

# Recent Advances in the Dynamics of Steep Channels

## Francesco Comiti and Luca Mao

## 26.1 DEFINITION OF STEEP CHANNELS

Headwater catchments and their channels represent the majority of the world channel network (Benda *et al.*, 2005). Most of these river reaches are characterized by higher longitudinal gradients compared to lowland reaches. But, what is "steep" and what is "mild"? In this paper we will use the term "steep" to indicate those channels whose bed morphology, hydrodynamics, and sediment transport regime differ substantially from gravel-bed reaches at a lower slope, as will be illustrated below. Such a transition generally occurs for longitudinal slopes $S > 4$–5%, and is associated with the diffuse presence of cobbles, boulders, or bedrock outcrops of large dimension relative to the channel width. Therefore, steep channels (SCs) are a subset of mountain rivers defined by Montgomery and Buffington (1997) and Wohl (2000) as having $S > 0.2$%, and are most commonly "small channels" according to Church (1992), i.e., the channel width/surface-grain-size ratio is $<10$.

Indeed, steep streams should not be referred to as "gravel-bed rivers", but as cobble/boulder-bed channels because the sediment sizes most relevant for their dynamics are usually $>256$ mm (up to the order of metres). Gravel (as well as sand) can be present, but does not determine the structure of the bed. Also, SCs are very infrequently truly alluvial systems because they drain steep mountain basins whose hillslopes – and related processes, such as landslides, debris flows and avalanches – greatly affect channel boundaries (i.e., bed and banks). More commonly they are semi-alluvial (*sensu* Halwas and Church, 2002), i.e., only a portion of the bed sediment has been fluvially transported from upstream as bedload. The stream bed can be only partly adjustable by even high-magnitude floods because of the presence of very large, immobile boulders derived from colluvial or moraine deposits, and due to bedrock outcrops.

It is important to point out that specific processes relevant for bedrock rivers and mass transport processes (i.e., debris flows) will not be addressed here; the reader is directed to dedicated publications (for bedrock rivers, e.g., Tinkler and Wohl, 1998; Carling, 2006; for debris flows, e.g., Jakob and Hungr, 2005; Takahashi, 2007). However, even though bedload transport dominates channels with $S < 18$% (D'Agostino, 2010), hyperconcentrated and debris flow processes can be very important in the long-term dynamics of steep channels. Indeed, many SCs feature the occurrence of the entire range of such transport processes, depending on the recurrence interval of the flood event and on the active sediment supply sources (Mao *et al.*, 2009; Figure 26.1).

We will restrict our presentation to SCs of humid-temperate environments, i.e., channels in arid environments will not be addressed. The most relevant differences, determined by the contrasting flood and sediment supply regimes, lie in the lack of bed armouring in the channels of arid regions, which contrast with the armoured bed surface of SCs in humid environments (Laronne and Reid, 1993; Laronne *et al.*, 1994; Reid and Laronne, 1995; Hassan *et al.* 2006).

The purpose of the present paper is to provide an updated state of our understanding of the main physical processes in SCs (i.e., channel with $S > 5$%; alluvial and semi-alluvial). Although the number of publications on the topic has soared during the last two decades, only a few dedicated monographs are available (e.g., see Wohl, 2000; Lenzi *et al.*, 2000). The paper will first address the morphological configuration of SCs (Section 26.2), then move to their hydraulics (Section 26.3) and sediment transport processes (Section 26.4). For the sake of conciseness, the review will concentrate on the most recent works, i.e., the last 10 years, but in some cases older investigations will be discussed. To maintain the

*Gravel-bed Rivers: Processes, Tools, Environments*, First Edition. Edited by Michael Church, Pascale M. Biron and André G. Roy.
© 2012 John Wiley & Sons, Ltd. Published 2012 by John Wiley & Sons, Ltd.

**Figure 26.1** Alluvial and semi-alluvial steep channels may be dominated by fluvial transport processes for long periods, but the occurrence of debris floods, hyperconcentrated or even debris flows of infrequent recurrence may determine sudden dramatic channel adjustments. The photos illustrate Strimm creek (Italian Alps) before (a) and after (b) such an event. A bed incision of about 1–1.5 m took place.

focus of our review, we will not discuss the dynamics of large wood (see e.g., Haga *et al.*, 2002; Comiti *et al.*, 2006; Wohl and Goode, 2008; Wohl and Jaeger, 2009) or the "restoration" of steep channels by artificial step-pool sequences (see e.g., Lenzi, 2002; Weichert, 2005; Comiti *et al.* 2009b; Wang *et al.* 2009; Yu *et al.*, 2010).

## 26.2 CHANNEL MORPHOLOGY

A general characteristic of SCs is a stepped bed morphology (Figure 26.2), i.e., the longitudinal profile does not slope gently, but shows alternation of near-vertical drops (steps), scour holes (pools), and relatively regular, mild-sloping treads. Indeed, such an irregular profile has long being recognized as the fundamental element of distinction between SCs and lower-gradient rivers because it creates – at least for low to medium flow rates – a tumbling flow regime (Peterson and Mohanty, 1960; Judd, 1963) which will be analysed in detail in Section 26.3.

However, as pointed out by Zimmermann (2009), until recently most researchers appear to have overlooked the common – and in some cases extended – presence of morphological units other than steps and pools (i.e., those comprising the treads, Figure 26.2). Actually, "step pool channel" has become a sort of

synonym of steep channel, such that the morphology of high-gradient streams has been often characterized and analysed in terms of dimensions and spacing of steps and pools only. For a summary of morphological relations in step-pool channels, see, e.g., Chin and Wohl (2005) and Church and Zimmermann (2007).

Recently, investigators have focused on the complexity of bedforms present in SCs, which include step-pool sequences, but are not restricted to them (see below). So the question arising is: how many step-pool sequences should be present to define a certain reach as a step-pool reach (following, e.g., Montgomery and Buffington, 1997; Wohl, 2000)? Furthermore, a precise and widely recognized definition of step is still lacking, and this generates a great deal of inconsistency among investigations on step-pool channels (see below). Indeed, such issues can be tackled only by making clear the reference spatial scale at which a SC is to be analysed from a geomorphological perspective.

After a period (1980s and 1990s) when spatial regularity in channel features was widely seen and also expected in steep channels (e.g., Whittaker and Jaeggi, 1982; Chin, 1989; Abrahams *et al.* 1995), the current dominant perspective seems to have been reversed; investigators are increasingly recognizing the variability in step spacing and height (starting from Zimmermann

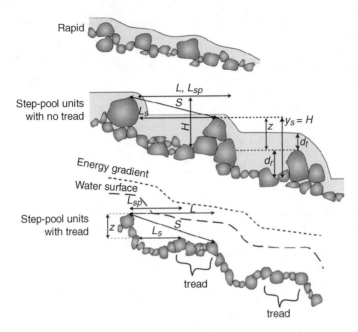

**Figure 26.2** Sketch of longitudinal profiles of rapid and step-pool sequences without and with treads. The morphology, extent, and relevance of treads have been so far overlooked by fluvial geomorphologists. Reproduced, with permission, from Church and Zimmermann (2007).

and Church, 2001, see below), thus defying the application of simplified predictive models. Associated with an inherently variable bed geometry, the existence of several mechanisms for step formation has become widely accepted after the innovative ideas proposed in Crowe (2002), Curran and Wilcock (2005) and Curran (2007). In addition, the relevance of a stochastic perspective in bed stability (from particle entrainment to step failure) and in step formation, driven by spatially random events, has almost completely taken over the deterministic, purely hydraulic models used so far (Church and Zimmermann, 2007; Zimmermann *et al.*, 2010).

Therefore, we believe that the "hottest" topics in the recent SC morphological studies can be identified as: (i) scaling and reach/unit nomenclature; (ii) step definition and its automated extraction from longitudinal bed profiles; (iii) mechanisms for step formation and their stability. Each of these topics will be treated separately below.

### 26.2.1 Scaling: What to?

The relevance of scaling issues in fluvial processes was effectively discussed by Church (2008) in the preceding GBR conference. Church (2008) addressed gravel-bed rivers in general, but briefly highlighted the peculiarity of shallow channels where flow depth is of the same order of magnitude as sediment size, for which distinctive scaling relations are envisioned. As mentioned before, such is the case for steep channels.

Indeed, a considerable degree of ambiguity still characterizes morphological terminology in mountain streams, mostly due to the scaling involved in the definition of reaches and units: How long is a channel reach? What are channel units? What is the rationale behind their definition? Should step pool morphology be seen at the reach or unit scale?

Channel width, $W$, has long been used as the fundamental metric for defining spatial scales in the channel network, mostly because $W$ correlates well with formative discharge $Q$ (Leopold and Maddock, 1953), and thus width is commonly used to define spatial scales in rivers (i.e., reaches, unit, subunits). Grant *et al.* (1990) defined the *reach* scale as having a channel length $L \sim 10^2$–$10^3$ $W$, the channel *unit* at a scale of $L \sim 10^0$–$10^1$ $W$, the channel *subunits* at a scale of $L \sim 10^{-1}$–$10^0$ $W$, and finally the particle scale (e.g., individual grains, boulders, or cobble clusters) as spanning the spatial range $L \sim 10^{-2}$–$10^0$ $W$.

On the other hand, the well-known classification scheme developed by Montgomery and Buffington

(1997) for mountain rivers refers to the *reach* scale, as defined by $L > 10–20 W$ (therefore very close to the unit scale identified by Grant *et al*. 1990), wherein "step-pools" and "cascades" are distinct morphological categories that include "steps" and "pools", which are identified as "units". Halwas and Church (2002), in their paper dedicated to the morphological units of very steep streams (>10%), defined a channel unit as "a morphologically distinct portion of channel, commonly one to a few channel widths in length".

More recently, Weichert (2005) proposed a division of scales paralleling that of Grant *et al*. It is relevant to highlight that: (i) Weichert (2005) states that riffles and steps belong to different scales (i.e., macro- and meso-scales, respectively) and therefore any attempt to establish analogies between their origin and geometry is not possible; and (ii) morphological patterns are related to channel width, but the micro-scale (i.e., sediment structure) to flow depth. This latter point is crucial in the definition of what are steps and what are not, and will be discussed later. Hassan *et al*. (2008) proposed instead a classification of bedforms for gravel-bed rivers in which step-pool *units* are placed at a mesoform level, along with riffles and pools. Recently, Zimmermann (2009) advocated the unit-scale status for a step pool *sequence*, on the evidence that truly "step pool" reaches, i.e., where all steps and pools span the entire channel width, as in the Montgomery and Buffington (1997) definition, are quite unusual, or at least are rather short (relative to $W$) in many mountain streams. Therefore, Zimmermann (2009) believes that the reach scale featuring either step pool or cascade *units* (*sensu* Halwas and Church, 2002) should be labelled as a "cascade" (as in Grant *et al*., 1990).

A striking conclusion emerges from the above presentation; a common definition and extent of channel reaches and units is still lacking (as also pointed out by Ferguson, 2008). We believe that the most sound way of tackling this issue is first to agree on the rationale (morphological and/or hydraulic) lying behind the definition of units and reaches. In our understanding, channel units are the elementary components of river beds, which are characterized by different hydraulic and sediment transport dynamics, and originate through different processes, e.g., local erosion and deposition. These differences are analysed at the flow depth scale associated with effective/formative discharges (see Section 26.2.2), which is on the order of the bankfull stage (Figure 26.3) with a recurrence interval of about 2–5 a (Lenzi *et al*. 2006a). Because steps and pools feature very distinct and contrasting hydrodynamics and sediment transport processes, we believe steps and pools should be two different units. Consequently, the spatial scale of channel units in steep channels can be envisaged to be of the order $L \sim 10^{-1}–10^{0} W$, with "short" (but

hydraulically relevant, see Section 26.2.2) steps defining the lower bound, which may eventually collapse to the sediment grain scale (i.e., surface $D_{84}$ or $D_{90}$), and "long" rapids the upper limit. Essentially, we propose to call units what Grant *et al*. (1990) named subunits.

As to the channel reach scale, this should be viewed (see also Ferguson, 2008) as the scale at which the varying hydrodynamic and transport patterns associated with the different channel units can be balanced out to provide spatially significant characteristics responsible for the large-scale morphological dynamics of streams. Of course, such characteristics must be linked to sediment transport processes and thus to sediment grain size and shear stress or stream power, in turn entailing representative average values of energy grade, flow velocity, and hydraulic radius. The relevance of the channel reach scale is clear, as it is the most appropriate to analyse river changes which may interfere with the human scale (Ferguson, 2008).

To this end, the reach scale proposed by Grant *et al*. (1990) and by Weichert (2005) seems to be too long (i.e., in channel width terms), especially for steep channels which are extremely variable (in terms of slope, width, and roughness) in the longitudinal direction due to external forcings such as landslides, debris fans, and rock outcrops (as pointed out in Section 26.1). As suggested by many geomorphologists, including Montgomery and Buffington (1997), Wohl and Merritt (2005, 2008), Ferguson (2008), and Hassan *et al*. (2008), the reach scale can be as small as $10 W$.

Even though we agree with Zimmermann (2009) on the fact that long stretches of well-defined steps and pools are not common, and that most steep channels feature a longitudinal alternation of steps, pools, and cascade units, we also believe that the distinction between the two end points of a natural continuum, that is, an "ordered" staircase-like system (step pool *reach*) versus a spatially "chaotic" ensemble of boulders and pocket (i.e., non-channel spanning) pools (cascade *reach*), still holds some value, especially when the range of slope in a given channel network is large. The assignment to one category or the other will depend on the relative proportion of step pool versus cascade *units*. However, for some applied purposes (see e.g., Rinaldi *et al*., 2011a, 2011b) the use of just one "all-inclusive" reach-scale category may be sufficient (indeed, differences in flow resistance between step pool and cascade reaches seem to be not significant, see Montgomery and Buffington, 1997; Mao *et al*., 2006; Comiti *et al*., 2007; Zasso and D'Agostino, 2007; David *et al*., 2010), but we think that naming it "cascade" may contribute to further misunderstanding. Hence, we tentatively propose to label the ensemble of step pool and cascade at the reach scale a "stepped bed" morphology. Channel units other than steps, pools, and cascades – e.g., riffles, rapids,

**Figure 26.3**    Three stretches of a steep channel (Rio Cordon, Italy) at low and high (RI ~ 2 a) flows. The two shown above (a–b, c–d) could be labelled as step pool reaches based on low flows, but note that steps in the foreground in (a–b) are relatively small and thus at "bankfull" stage are almost drowned out (rapid unit, see Figure 26.2). The wider reach below (e–f) features instead a cascade morphology.

chutes (Halwas and Church, 2002) – can be present in such a stepped bed reach in response to local changes in slope and width, but the hydrodynamic and sediment transport processes averaged along the entire reach should be dominated by a tumbling flow regime.

### 26.2.2  Step Definition and Reconnaissance

How large should a drop in the longitudinal profile be to be called a step? Again, scaling issues become crucial. A transverse rib or a small step (and the associated small pool downstream) can be very important for habitat diversity at low flows, whereas they may represent a negligible source of roughness during high, formative flows that submerge them. Indeed, when talking about steps, biologists and geomorphologists (Zimmermann et al., 2008) may well be referring to different units. This is reflected in different classifications in terms of morphological units of a given longitudinal profile, depending on the investigator, and on water stage. Such a problem arises because a widely accepted dimensional definition of step is still lacking.

The first researchers to explore objective methods to define steps from longitudinal profiles were Wooldridge and Hickin (2002). They used zero-crossing, bed elevation difference, and power spectral analysis, but concluded that visual identification was able to determine the geometry and classify bedform type better than the other methods.

Subsequently, Milzow et al. (2006) proposed an algorithm based on the concept that steps feature a higher local slope than adjacent units (i.e., pools, runs). Therefore, a step is identified as such if the slope between two points is greater than a critical slope of 0.45. If more adjacent points are all greater than the critical slope, then they are part of the same step.

The idea of Milzow et al. was developed further by Zimmermann et al. (2008), who found it to perform rather well when topographic data are collected at the "correct" spatial density, but quite poorly if dense survey data were used. The algorithm put forward by Zimmermann et al. (2008) applies a series of scale-free geometric rules that include minimum step length, minimum pool length, minimum residual depth, minimum drop height, and minimum step slope. Such rules performed as well as the mean response of several step pool researchers who were asked to classify long profiles, and also correspond with the channel morphologies as identified in the field. Importantly, Zimmermann et al. (2008) observed that their algorithm is most sensitive to the choice of minimum pool length and minimum drop height. It is relevant to point out that an adequately high spatial resolution (i.e., allowing one to clearly discern bedforms edges) is needed to apply the above-mentioned algorithms.

Despite the clear advantages of identifying steps in an objective way through the use of similar algorithms (see also Nickolotsky and Pavlowsky, 2006), there still is a problem in defining the most appropriate density and procedure to be adopted in the topographic survey of long profiles. Zimmermann et al. (2008) found that a single long profile with a fixed sampling interval poorly characterizes steps and pools and thus recommend a procedure for field surveys in which points correspond to breaks in slope. This requirement stresses how the identification of bed morphology in steep channels is time-consuming and subject to all field-related issues (weather, wadebility, accessibility). Therefore, alternative methods relying on remote sensing would be highly desirable. The first of such investigations in steep channels we are aware of is by Cavalli et al. (2008), who analysed the reach-scale morphology by means of morphological roughness based on a LiDAR-derived DTM (cell size 0.5 m). More recently, the same authors developed further the approach towards a 2-D geostatistical method (Trevisani et al., 2009). The tested indices included directional slope, directional curvature, and directional variograms. The final selection of geomorphometric indices was carried out to balance complexity and informative content.

Trevisani et al. (2009) found that the slope index is most useful for a general characterization of the channel profile and should be preliminary to the geostatistical indices. The integrated use of these indices seems effective to identify single morphological units, but still relies on manual processing (no automated or semi-automated recognition was achieved). This research field – the use of the long profile from a LiDAR-derived DTM in steep channels – appears very promising (see also Vianello et al., 2009), as high-resolution LiDAR data (either airborne or terrestrial) may likely represent the standard topographic technique in the near future. A terrestrial laser scanner was in fact recently used – in association with a total station – by David et al. (2010) to derive the DTM of a steep channel in the Colorado Rocky Mountains. Limitations due to LiDAR elevation errors and lack of water penetration may still hamper the general applicability of this method, especially with respect to deep channels with small steps.

A cheaper method for obtaining high resolution DTMs of channel beds is to overlap stereo imagery captured by digital non-metric cameras. Bird et al. (2010) recently presented a novel technique for the capture and analysis of close-range photos acquired from a non-metric camera suspended 10 m above the channel bed on a unipod. Operating under the forest canopy, the camera can frame the channel bed without obstructions. Bird et al. (2010) obtained DTMs of river beds with 0.03 m nominal ground resolution and vertical precision ranging from

± 0.01 to 0.1 m, depending on the quality of triangulation and the characteristics of the bed surface.

All these terrific research efforts have left an unanswered question though: how should we define a step? Wooldridge and Hickin (2002) defined it in terms of absolute elevation drop, Milzow *et al.* (2006) in terms of slope, and Zimmermann *et al.* (2008) relative to bankfull width. Algorithms can be optimized to match our field observations, but we still need to agree upon the *functional* concept of a step.

We believe that a functional geomorphological definition should be based on the effect of channel units on long-term bedload transport (i.e., the driver of morphological adjustments), which in steep channels was shown to be effective for normal floods (RI = 2–5 a, Lenzi *et al.*, 2006a). Only drops (bedrock, log, alluvial, or semi-alluvial) significantly affecting bedload transport (i.e., by augmenting flow resistance) at such flows should be named steps, or alternatively "major steps", following the classification proposed by Hayward (1980). Therefore, we propose to call step units those profile drops (the dimension $z$ in Figure 26.2) spanning the entire channel width and larger than the average bankfull flow depth measured just upstream of step crests, i.e., larger than critical flow depth ($Fr \sim 1$) at bankfull stage. This would be in accordance with preliminary evidence (see Section 26.3) showing that hydraulic jumps become submerged and lose a great deal of their effect on energy dissipation after such a threshold is passed.

### 26.2.3 Mechanisms for Step Formation

Step formation in step pool reaches is a very intriguing matter, and the debate over the "right" formative model is somehow analogous to the even longer discussion over the dynamics of meander generation in lowland rivers. In this chapter we do not aim to discuss in detail the different theories on step formation, which has been the subject of recent review papers (see Chin and Wohl, 2005; Church and Zimmermann, 2007). Indeed, step-pool morphology has received much more attention compared to cascade reaches, where steps may also be present but which do not present the – sometimes only apparent – spatial regularity exhibited in step-pool reaches. Even though steps imposed by fallen large wood elements (log steps) can heavily influence the channel morphology and hydraulics of SCs, especially in temperate old-growth forested basins (e.g., Marston, 1982; Curran and Wohl, 2003; Faustini and Jones, 2003; Gomi *et al.*, 2003; Mao *et al.*, 2008a), here we will focus on the formation of alluvial and semi-alluvial steps only.

Among the conceptual models for the formation of steps in high-gradient channels, there are those which emphasize the role of hydraulic processes, of random particle interactions, and those focusing on a variational approach, i.e., bed evolution maximizes/minimizes a certain target variable. Within the "hydraulic models", there are theories based on the presence of antidune trains over a fully mobile bed (Whittaker and Jaeggi, 1982; Ashida *et al.*, 1984; Grant and Mizuyama, 1991; Grant, 1997; Chin, 1999; Chartrand and Whiting, 2000; Lenzi, 2001), and others invoking local hydraulic processes (hydraulic jumps or standing waves) originated by stable steps or obstacles during flows which are not capable of fully mobilizing the bed (Judd, 1963; McDonald and Day, 1978; Allen, 1983; Ergenzinger, 1992; Comiti *et al.*, 2005; Comiti and Lenzi, 2006; Milzow *et al.* 2006).

In contrast, other investigators have focused on how variable step-pool geometry is in nature, and stressed the stochastic role of immobile keystone boulders in promoting step formation by particle interaction processes (Wohl and Grodek, 1994; Lee, 1998; Zimmermann and Church, 2001; Church and Zimmermann, 2007; Zimmermann *et al.* 2010). In these conceptual models, hydraulics (i.e., shear stress) still play a crucial role in determining the likelihood of step formation, but it is nevertheless constrained by random factors related to local immobile boundary conditions. These models, in particular the jammed state model (Church and Zimmermann, 2007; Zimmermann *et al.*, 2010), have the great merit to have included channel width $W$ as a fundamental variable for the morphological processes in steep channels, by introducing the jamming ratio ($W/D_{84steps}$). Also, the jammed state model adopts a probabilistic conceptual framework which is – in our opinion – crucial when analysing the dynamics of steep channels (Figure 26.4).

Starting from a different perspective, a variational approach (i.e., in which the maximization or minimization of some variable is the attractor of the system over time) has also been used to explain the formation of step and pool units, as well as riffles and pools (Yang, 1971). In particular, an evolutionary process of step-pool geometry leading towards maximum flow resistance and thus maximum stability was proposed (Abrahams *et al.*, 1995; Lenzi, 2001; Weichert, 2005; Chin and Phillips, 2006; Weichert *et al.* 2008; Wang *et al.*, 2009). This approach focuses on the overall functionality achieved by the bed configuration rather than on small-scale processes responsible for step formation. Therefore, this line of research must be viewed as complementary to hydraulic/stochastic formative models rather than as an alternative (similar to thermodynamics principles related to the non-linear dynamics of open systems).

However, the contest between deterministic (hydraulic) and stochastic (particle interaction) models has been shown to be irrelevant by the laboratory investigation of Crowe (2002) and Curran (2007), which demonstrated

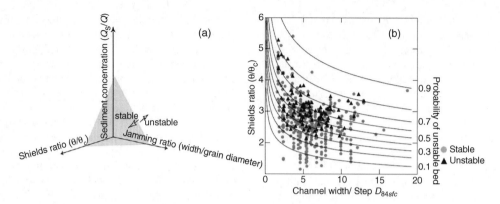

**Figure 26.4** (a) The jammed state concept for step stability initially put forward by Church and Zimmermann (2007). Reproduced, with permission, from Zimmermann (2009). (b) Flume data to test the probabilistic jammed state model presented in Zimmermann *et al.* (2010). Reproduced, with permission, from Zimmermann, A., Church, M. and Hassan, M.A. 2010. Step-pool stability: testing the jammed state hypothesis. *Journal of Geophysical Research* **115**: F02008.

how several processes of step formation, both hydraulic and stochastic, may be at play in a single channel during a formative flow. As further support, recent laboratory investigations (Weichert, 2005; Comiti *et al.*, 2009a; Zimmermann, 2009; Zimmermann *et al.*, 2010) have shown that antidune wavetrains are not formed on mobile beds where sediment mixture and slope are similar to real step pool channels, even though step spacing fits the Kennedy's diagram for antidune stability (Weichert, 2005; Weichert *et al.*, 2008).

Therefore, after almost three decades since its original formulation, there is now a large body of evidence that the antidunes theory should be abandoned. Nevertheless, standing waves and roller jumps originated by stable steps were observed to trigger the formation of some steps by deposition (Curran, 2007; Comiti *et al* 2009a). There is also evidence (Koll *et al.*, 2000, Curran, 2007) that step-forming mechanisms differ on relatively moderate gradients (<6–8%, where hydraulic processes are likely more relevant) when compared to steeper channels, where particle congestion and sediment transport intensity may become dominant (Zimmermann, 2009). Unfortunately, our knowledge of step formation in very steep channels (>9–10%) relies on relatively few studies (Whittaker and Jaeggi, 1982; Rosport, 1994, 1997; Tatsuzawa *et al.*, 1999; Koll, 2002; Weichert *et al.*, 2008; Comiti *et al.*, 2009a; Zimmermann *et al.*, 2010).

Finally, it must pointed out that increasing attention is being focused on the other side of the problem of step formation, step failure and subsequent bed erosion. Surely, the two aspects are tightly linked, but our knowledge is even scarcer for step stability than for step formation. For such a topic, the reader is referred to the works of Whittaker and Davies (1982), Whittaker

(1987), Rosport and Dittrich (1995); Chin (1998), Koll and Dittrich (2001), Crowe (2002), Comiti (2003), Comiti *et al.* (2005), Curran and Wilcock (2005), Weichert (2005), Church and Zimmerman (2007), Weichert *et al.* (2008, 2009), Zimmermann (2009) and Zimmermann *et al.* (2010). It is worth mentioning here that both Zimmermann (2009) and Comiti *et al.* (2009a) observed in the flume that the collapse of just one step – when apparently the bed had already attained equilibrium – triggered bed failure and upstream migrating headcuts moving up to steps that were stable enough to withstand toe erosion.

These events led to high sediment transport rates and a total re-working of upstream bed morphology, and such dynamics are actually the same as observed in previous flume experiments with boulder check dams mimicking step-pool sequences (Giacometti, 2000). This represents the reason why larger, deeply founded grade-control structures are built at the downstream end of check-dam sequences in steep channels (Comiti *et al.*, 2010b). However, it must be pointed out that in SCs the most dramatic and profound bed re-arrangements may take place during debris floods/hyperconcentrated flows (Lenzi, 2001; Mao *et al.*, 2009; Rickenmann and Koschni, 2010) and debris flows events, as already mentioned in the introduction and illustrated in Figure 26.1.

## 26.3 HYDRODYNAMICS AND FLOW RESISTANCE IN STEEP CHANNELS

### 26.3.1 General Characteristics

The hydraulics of steep channels is tremendously complex and very distinct from that of gravel-bed streams.

Such complexity can be ascribed to several topographical, hydrological, and morphological factors that are tied together – high average gradient, relatively low water discharge, and very poorly sorted bed sediments with the presence of large boulders (Bathurst, 1993). The direct consequence is that SCs are characterized by very low relative submergence (i.e., ratio $h/D$, $h$ being flow depth, and $D$ characteristic grain size) even during normal flood events, and macro-roughness conditions (Bathurst, 1978) are almost always present in these streams. The effects of macro-roughness on the basic hydrodynamics and flow resistance equations have been investigated for decades (see e.g., Bathurst, 1978; Wiberg and Smith, 1991; Smart et al., 2002), but only a few studies were carried out in SCs. These relatively few exceptions will be discussed later in this section.

### 26.3.2  The Tumbling Flow Regime

SCs differ considerably from low-gradient channels in terms of mechanisms of energy dissipation, as they feature a peculiar flow regime, named "tumbling flow" by Peterson and Mohanty (1960), which is characterized by a close alternation between super- and subcritical flow (i.e., $Fr >$ and $< 1$) along the channel. Such a regime is due to the presence of steps along the profile that are high enough, relative to flow depth, to cause the acceleration of the flow beyond critical conditions (i.e., $Fr = 1$). The supercritical jet thus issued from the step crest dissipates its high erosive power scouring a pool downstream, where flow decelerates and becomes subcritical with the formation of a hydraulic jump within the pool.

Virtually every pool (both channel-spanning as in step pool or narrower than the channel width as in cascade systems, Montgomery and Buffington, 1997) along a SC hosts a hydraulic jump which, summed up along a reach, likely represent a relevant component, in the form of spill resistance, of the overall flow resistance along the channel. Indeed, the presence of pools with roller jumps is recognized to be the main reason why alluvial SCs feature so large a flow resistance that the flow regime has been found, on a reach-averaged spatial scale, to be in subcritical regime ($Fr < 1$), both in the lab (Curran and Wilcock, 2005; Comiti et al., 2009a; Zimmermann, 2009; Zimmermann et al., 2010) and up to the level of frequently occuring flood events in the field (Comiti et al., 2007; Wilcox and Wohl, 2007).

Grant (1997) was the first to hypothesize that the critical regime ($Fr = 1$) was a severe constraint in step-pool streams, even at flood flows. Such recent evidence strikes against the common belief that high-gradient channels feature supercritical flows, which is erroneously supported by applying resistance formula developed for gravel-bed rivers to steep streams, and thereby underestimating resistance to flow.

However, a very relevant question is up to what flow rate spill resistance persists, i.e., when do the rollers of the hydraulic jumps disappear with step submergence (Figures 26.3 and 26.5). In fact, paralleling observations in stepped spillways, Chanson (1996) hypothesized the onset of the skimming flow regime – after the nappe (tumbling) flow regime – at flows high enough to mobilize the very coarse clasts that form steps. The skimming regime is characterized by supercritical conditions, high air concentration, and re-circulation eddies attached to the main flow stream at step corners. Many researchers (Ashida et al., 1984, Whittaker, 1987, Bathurst, 1993, Comiti and Lenzi, 2006, Church and Zimmermann, 2007) have long hypothesized that a marked change in flow resistance would occur when steps became submerged, which should correspond to the transition between nappe and skimming regimes. However, experimental tests by Lee and Ferguson (2002) did not give the expected results.

Recently, Comiti et al. (2009a) observed, for step-pool morphologies at 8–14% slope in a series of flume experiments, a sharp decrease in flow resistance (and $Fr$ increase up to slightly supercritical values) after a certain flow threshold was exceeded (Figure 26.5). Specifically, their results indicate that a shift from nappe to transitional or even skimming flow regime (see comment by Richardson, 2010, and reply by Comiti et al., 2010a) occurs when the $h_c/z$ ratio ($h_c$ being critical flow depth and $z$ step drop) attains values between 1.2 and 1.7. It was also noted that such a flow regime could persist only within a narrow flow range around step-forming discharges, because higher flow velocities lead to bed instability. However, the threshold range appeared wider and on average higher than anticipated from previous studies on stepped spillways. There is a need to verify these results further, especially regarding how different step-pool geometries may affect the threshold. Of course, the required field evidence is extremely hard to obtain, given the high flood magnitude (presumably RI $> 10$–20 a) which would make flow velocity measurement in prototype channels challenging at best, and surely very rare.

Even though it is widely accepted that the hydrodynamics in steep streams greatly differs from gravel-bed rivers, few investigations of the actual flow pattern have been carried out in the field, even at low flows (i.e., under a nappe flow). Wohl and Thompson (2000) measured velocity profiles and their fluctuations over steps and pools with a 1-D ECM. They observed that pools had wake turbulence from mid-profile shear layers generated by jet diffusion, whereas at step crests and on step treads bed-generated turbulence prevailed. They concluded that wake-generated turbulence is responsible for the higher energy dissipation occurring along step-pool reaches relative to smoother channels.

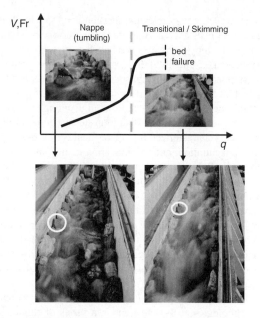

**Figure 26.5** Sketch representing longitudinally averaged flow velocity $V$ (and Froude number $Fr$) versus unit discharge $q$ as observed in the laboratory tests by Comiti *et al.* (2009a). Step destruction and consequent bed failure occurred at flow rates slightly higher than the threshold at which a rapid increase of velocity was measured. Images from nappe (left) and transitional/skimming (right) are shown for the same bed morphology. Circles highlight the same rock on the bank (pictures were taken from different positions).

Wilcox and Wohl (2007) collected 3-D measurements of time-averaged and turbulent velocity components using a 3-D acoustic Doppler velocimeter (ADV) in a step pool channel ($S = 11\%$) of the Colorado Rockies for various flows (up to 80% of the mean annual flow). They observed that the flow pattern is definitely more 3-D than in lower-gradient streams. Streamwise velocity is the largest contributor to overall velocity vector magnitudes, whereas cross-stream and vertical components contribute on average 20 and 15%, respectively. The largest contributions to turbulent kinetic energy derive from the vertical velocity component, especially in the pools (location of the hydraulic jumps). They also found that streamwise velocity is strongly affected by discharge variations and by the position along the bed profile (upstream versus downstream of steps). However, the performance of the ADV instrument was found to be severely limited by air bubbles, especially at the base of steps (Wilcox and Wohl, 2007). The application of this device in rougher, more irregular bed morphologies – causing widespread higher-flow aeration such as in cascade units – appears

quite problematic, but its potential to explore the hydraulics of step pool sequences has recently been confirmed (Wilcox *et al.*, 2011). Indeed, SCs typically feature high aeration; nonetheless this flow characteristic has been overlooked by geomorphologists, whereas engineers have long been studying – mostly in the flume – flow aeration and its effects in chute and stepped channels (see e.g., Chanson, 1993; Boes and Hager, 2003).

Valuable insights on aeration and hydrodynamics characteristics of hydraulic jumps occurring at large bedrock step-pools have been provided by Valle and Pasternack (2002; 2006a, 2006b, 2006c) who developed an innovative portable "crane" (the "River Truss") to carry out bed topography and flow velocity measurements. Subsequently, Wyrick and Pasternack (2008) developed a semi-analytical numerical model of step hydraulics to quantify energy dissipation and predict hydraulic jump regimes, accounting for discharge, jump submergence, and non-uniform channel geometry.

### 26.3.3  *Flow Resistance Partitioning*

The studies described in the previous section indicate that hydraulic jumps in SCs generate a great deal of energy dissipation and thus contribute substantially to the total flow resistance. Indeed, we believe that the key control exerted by hydraulic jumps in SCs should be explicitly addressed when attempting to establish a partitioning of flow resistance. For this reason, there is a need to expand the classical linear approach – whereby the different sources of resistance (grain, form, spill, bedload, large wood) are additive – developed for low-gradient rivers and gravel-bed rivers (see e.g., Meyer-Peter and Muller, 1948; Einstein and Barbarossa, 1952; Millar, 1999), which is at the moment the only available conceptual framework within which flow resistance partitioning is analyzed.

All the field investigations on flow resistance carried out so far on steep stepped channels (Curran and Wohl, 2003; MacFarlane and Wohl, 2003; Reid and Hickin, 2008; Comiti *et al.* 2007) have found that the grain component of total friction is rather small ($<10$–15%), and that friction terms other than grain (form, spill, large wood) dominate. However, Wilcox *et al.* (2006) and Wilcox and Wohl (2006) demonstrated through flume experiments that partitioning estimates for stepped channels are highly sensitive to the order in which components are calculated, and that linearly additive approaches inflate the values of components that are calculated by subtraction from measured (or estimated) components. Furthermore, Wilcox *et al.* (2006) showed that discharge (and thus flow depth) is the most important factor controlling the interaction among the different flow resistance components.

Recently, Comiti et al. (2009a) confirmed the key role of discharge in flow resistance partitioning, but estimated that grain resistance accounts for <10% of total resistance only within a tumbling (nappe) flow regime, where spill resistance was evaluated to make up at least 30%, the remaining part being form resistance induced by the macro-roughness characteristics of the bed. In a skimming regime, spill resistance drops because roller jumps are drowned out and the relative importance of grain resistance may increase up to 45% (Comiti et al., 2009a). Similar high values were determined by Canovaro et al. (2007) in flume tests with fixed transverse roughness elements.

However, a considerable challenge to the established knowledge on flow resistance partitioning has recently come from the flume experiments of Zimmermann (2009; see also Zimmermann, 2010, and Zimmermann et al., 2010). He did not observe any substantial variation in the friction factor during the development of a step-pool morphology starting from a plane bed, a morphology where step-pool-induced friction (i.e., the spill resistance component) is not present. In fact, one would expect to measure higher flow resistance on well-structured stepped morphologies compared to plane bed, as preliminarily observed by Montgomery and Buffington (1997) and recently clearly demonstrated by David et al. (2010). But also in the flume work by Comiti et al. (2009a, unpublished data) it was not possible to infer any significant difference in the friction factor between the initial and final phase of the bed evolution tests, and actually initial flow resistance values were on average slightly higher than at equilibrium.

Zimmermann (2009) suggests that most of the resistance in a step-pool reach is due to grain resistance, in evident contrast to the previously cited results, where grain resistance was not measured, but calculated using a resistance equation developed for a planar bed (i.e., no influence of step-pools) with a roughness height which should not represent form resistance (e.g., $D_{50}$ in the Keulegan formula; Millar and Quick, 1994). Putting together Zimmermann (2009) and Comiti et al.'s unpublished results, one may hypothesize that during the first minutes of the experiments (when the bed was still a plane), a relevant portion of the overall resistance was due to the intense bedload transport, which would "mask" the effects of a smoother bed morphology. Indeed, Recking et al. (2008) found an increase in flow resistance due to bedload transport in steep flume runs (e.g., Carbonneau and Bergeron, 2000; Campbell et al., 2005), and quantified its contribution, distinguishing three flow domains. However, it must be mentioned that such an increase in flow resistance due to bedload transport was not very evident in the steep flume experiments of either Rickenmann (1990, 1991) or Zimmermann (2009), and

therefore further research is needed to clarify the actual contribution of bedload transport on flow resistance in SCs.

Another reason why resistance might not generally increase whilst step pools are forming could be due to the fact that form resistance is higher on the initial plane bed because the flow is shallower (bed slope remains uniformly large) and thus rougher, whereas, when step-pools are formed, the flow becomes on average deeper (actual bed slope decreases at step treads) and thus less rough between successive steps. Furthermore, the contribution to energy dissipation by steps and pool units at near step-forming discharges could be relatively small because only form, not spill roughness, takes place when jumps are drowned out (Comiti et al., 2009a). The overall result is that a similar friction factor is measured before and after the bed adjustments. However, it must be emphasized that Zimmermann (2009, 2010) did not observe any clear distinction between nappe and skimming flow in his tests, whereas field measurements of flow resistance by David et al. (2010) in two creeks of the Rocky Mountains (USA) seem to confirm the existence of different flow regimes – which require different predictive models – depending on flow stage.

### 26.3.4 Modelling Flow Resistance

Compared to flow resistance partitioning, more investigations have attempted to model total flow resistance (and thus predict flow velocity) in steep alluvial channels, through either laboratory experiments (Bathurst, 1985; El Kashab, 1986; Rickenmann, 1990; 1991; Egashira and Ashida, 1991; Rosport, 1997; Maxwell and Papanicolau, 2001; Aberle and Smart, 2003, Weichert, 2005; Recking et al., 2008; Comiti et al., 2009a; Zimmermann, 2009), field measurements (Jarrett, 1984; Ruf, 1988; Marcus et al., 1992; Rickenmann, 1994; Palt, 2001; Comiti et al., 2007; Zasso and D'Agostino, 2007; Reid and Hickin, 2008), or both (Lee, 1998; Lee and Ferguson, 2002; Ferguson, 2007).

Several flow resistance equations have been proposed by each investigator. The emerging conclusion (see in particular Ferguson, 2007, and Zimmermann, 2010), is that adopting "classical" hydraulic approaches for the prediction of channel roughness (including Chezy, Manning and Darcy–Weisbach coefficients, using either power or log laws) is not the best solution for steep channels, where even the definition of the average hydraulic depth/radius can be problematic and the flow field (velocity profile) departs substantially from that featured in lower-gradient gravel-bed rivers. This latter evidence is tightly associated with the larger total flow resistance measured in SCs compared to its estimation based on extrapolating traditional approaches.

The most robust and reliable approach – yet more empirical and less physically based – appears to be a dimensionless hydraulic geometry, which entails the direct prediction of mean flow velocity ($V$) from unit discharge ($q$) and channel slope ($S$), where both $V$ and $q$ are made dimensionless by a measure of channel roughness (characteristic sediment size $D$ or bed standard deviation $\sigma$). First introduced by Rickenmann (1990, 1991), this approach was subsequently re-emphasized by Rickenmann (1994, 1996), re-proposed by Aberle and Smart (2003), and recently advocated by Comiti et al. (2007, 2009a) and David et al. (2010). However, the actual statistical superiority of such an approach was demonstrated only with the thorough cross-comparison carried out by Ferguson (2007) and Zimmermann (2009, 2010).

As to the best way to characterize bed roughness, the discussion is still open. In fact, despite the convincing results and arguments provided by Aberle and Smart (2003) and Weichert (2005) in favor of the standard deviation of bed elevation, many laboratory and field results (Comiti et al., 2007; 2009a; Reid and Hickin, 2008; Zimmermann, 2009; David et al. 2010) do not support it. In contrast, better results in terms of equations' predictive capabilities have been obtained using the step $D_{84}$ (Lee and Ferguson, 2002), the $D_{84}$ of the bed surface layer (Comiti et al., 2007; Zimmermann, 2009), and a sorting coefficient of sediment distribution ($D_{84}/D_{50}$, Reid and Hickin, 2008).

## 26.4  SEDIMENT TRANSPORT

The quantification of sediment transport is notoriously a difficult task in gravel-bed rivers, but even more in SCs. Overall, the prediction of sediment transport in high-gradient streams is hampered by their by their complex hydrodynamics and morphological and sedimentological dynamics. The present section will deal with bedload transport only (i.e., non-Newtonian flows and suspended transport will not be addressed) because it is directly related to channel morphology and flow resistance.

### 26.4.1  Incipient Motion

The most difficult parameter to specify for a reasonable evaluation of bedload transport in steep streams is incipient condition. Critical flow conditions for sediment entrainment have been expressed in several ways: in terms of critical unit discharge (e.g., Ferguson, 1994, Lenzi et al., 2006b), critical densimetric Froude number (e.g., Aguirre-Pe et al., 2003), and critical stream power (see later). However, the most common approach is the one based on the critical dimensionless shear stress (or Shields stress, $\tau_c^*$), defined as:

$$\tau_c^* = \tau_c/(\rho_s - \rho)gD \qquad (26.1)$$

in which $\tau_c$ is the critical shear stress at the incipient motion condition for the grain size $D$, and $\tau_c = \rho ghS$, wherein $h$ is the water depth, $S$ is the water surface slope, $g$ is the gravitational acceleration, and $\rho$ and $\rho_s$ are the fluid and sediment densities, respectively. Because most sediment transport events occur at flows that exceed the shear stress by less than 20% of its critical value (Ryan et al., 2002; Mueller et al., 2005; Lenzi et al., 2006a; Parker et al., 2007), bedload prediction can be severely biased by a small misevaluation of $\tau_c^*$. Buffington and Montgomery (1997) demonstrated that the range of $\tau_c^*$ can be threefold around 0.045 even in low-gradient gravel-bed rivers, due to the influence of measurement methods, channel morphology, bed roughness, and bed slope. Flume and field evidence reveal that critical Shields stress tends to increase with channel slope (Figure 26.6; Shvidchenko and Pender, 2000; Mueller et al., 2005; Lenzi et al., 2006b; Lamb et al., 2008).

The fact that a clast of a certain size tends to be more stable at a higher slope is somehow counterintuitive because of the theoretical increased component of gravity in the downstream direction. Lamb et al. (2008) recently analysed the potential causes of the reduction of sediment mobility at higher slope using a force-balance model and concluded that the main causes are the reductions in near-bed mean velocity and turbulent fluctuations at higher slopes due to the increase in relative roughness (Carollo et al., 2005). This conclusion is supported by recent experimental findings (Shvidchenko and Pender, 2000; Mueller et al., 2005; Armanini and Gregoretti, 2005; Vollmer and Kleinhans, 2007). Recking (2009) fit a velocity profile incorporating the roughness layer (based on the equations of Aguirre-Pe and Fuentes, 1990) to a force-balance model. The model satisfactorily estimated Shields stresses obtained from flume experiments and field measurements over a wide range of slopes, Reynolds numbers, and relative depths. Further investigations into the nature of velocity profiles within the roughness layer and its dependence on slope should increase the applicability of such models, especially when combined with incipient motion observations.

However, field data from the Rio Cordon in Italy (slope $S = 13.6\%$) and from the Tres Arroyos in Chile ($S = 7.6\%$; Mao et al., 2008b) indicate that the critical Shields stress for the $D_{50}$ of the sediment bed is actually much higher (Figure 26.6) than predicted by the model of Lamb et al. (see also later in this section).

The analysis of poorly sorted grain-size distributions would shed further light on the physical processes con-

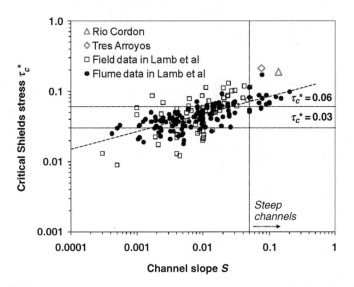

**Figure 26.6** Compilation of literature flume and field data showing the slope dependency of the critical Shields stress . Reproduced, with permission, from Lamb, M.P., Dietrich, W.E. and Venditti, J.G. (2008). Only a few data are available for steep channels (SCs), especially from the field. Data from step-pool streams with $S > 7\%$ (Rio Cordon and Tres Arroyos, Mao *et al.* 2008b) feature $\tau_c^*$ of about 0.2, plotting much higher than the regression equation proposed in Lamb *et al.* (2008, dashed line).

trolling the incipient motion of individual size fractions within a mixture. In fact, SCs exhibit very heterogeneous bed mixtures, and this introduces relative particle size complications in incipient motion assessment. A coarse clast is more easily entrained when surrounded by finer grains than when surrounded by other coarse grains because it is relatively more exposed to entraining forces. The contrary happens for fine clasts, which are hidden by coarse fractions and are thus more difficult to move. A further complication is due to a mobility reversal (coarser grains more mobile than finer), observed as downstream grain-size coarsening on aggrading deposits when the bed slope is higher than 2% (Solari and Parker, 2000).

Some flume and field measurements in gravel-bed rivers (Parker and Klingeman, 1982; Andrews, 1983; Kuhnle, 1992; Wilcock, 1993) suggest that the hiding/protrusion effect is compensated by the differences in particle weight, and thus sediments are entrained at the same shear stress irrespective of their size. This condition (called equal mobility) causes the exponent $b$ in Equation (26.2)

$$\tau_{ci}/\tau_{c50} = a(D_i/D_{50})^b \qquad (26.2)$$

to be equal to $-1$. The coefficient $a$ in Equation (26.2) corresponds to the Shields stress for the reference grain size $D_{50}$. However, other studies have reported values of $0 < b < -1$, thus implying a condition of size-selective entrainment with increasing shear stress.

Analysing bedload transport rate and distribution, and particle tracer displacement distance during five near-bankfull flood events in a step pool stream ($S = 8.8\%$), Marion and Weirich (2003) concluded that equal mobility of bedload is more evident than size selectivity, reporting a value of $b$ of $-0.73$. A value of $-0.63$ has been recently derived by Turowski *et al.* (2009) from the analysis of sediment transport in a monitored high-gradient Swiss torrent (Erlenbach), but a further particle tracing study on the same stream revealed a higher value ($b = -0.89$, Rickenmann, pers. comm., 2010). Similarly, Mao *et al.* (2008b), analysing bedload samples and particle displacement distances collected both after relatively low flows and after floods well above bankfull stage in two small, high-gradient streams (Rio Cordon and Tres Arroyos), found a value $b = -0.78$. In these streams, the finer sediment fractions (i.e., $D_i/D_{50}$ about 0.1) featured $\tau_c^*$ up to 1 (Mao and Lenzi, 2007; Mao *et al.*, 2008b).

By means of a series of sediment tracer analysis, Yager (2006) verified in the Erlenbach stream that during moderate events (up to 70% of bankfull) very coarse elements remained stable, and finer sediments on mobile patches underwent partial and size-selective transport. Analysing transport data collected at the Rio Cordon experimental monitoring station, Mao and Lenzi (2007) also concluded that equal mobility likely occurs only for very high-magnitude flows (RI > 50 a), whereas size-selective transport appears to dominate during ordinary events. In contrast, investigating the displacements of individual clasts in a Canadian step-pool stream through passive integrated transponder (PIT) tags, Lamarre and Roy (2008) observed equal mobility transport occurring during less than bankfull events.

As to the $\tau^*_{c50}$ (i.e., the coefficient $a$ in Equation 26.2), Mao et al. (2008b) reported a value of about 0.21, which is very high if compared with values obtained in low-gradient rivers (i.e., $\tau^*_{c50}$ in the range 0.04–0.09; Andrews, 1983; Carling, 1983; Ashworth and Ferguson, 1989; Lamb et al., 2008; see Figure 26.6). This was mostly attributed to the additional morphological drag due to the presence of step pools (see also Lenzi et al., 2006b). However, the apparent increase of critical Shields stress due to additional morphological sources of flow resistance may be difficult to assess correctly in steep streams.

Recently, use of the stream power approach to define the critical threshold for sediment entrainment has received more attention because it would be unaffected by additional sources of flow resistance. Compared to shear stress, the stream power is easier to determine and to calculate after a flood event, being a simple function of slope, discharge, and channel width. Bedload transport initiates above a critical value of stream power ($\omega_c$) that in Bagnold's (1980) formula was expressed as a function of water depth and size of the mobilized particles.

Re-considering the critical stream power from a theoretical point of view, Ferguson (2005) proposed a more general form of Bagnold's (1980) equation in which a distinction between transported ($D_i$) and bed roughness grain size ($D_{50}$) is provided. The new formulation also eliminates the need for critical flow depth and incorporates hiding/protrusion effects. Two general equations for critical stream power were proposed (based on logarithmic and power resistance laws), and Ferguson (2005) demonstrated that critical stream power is, in fact, unaffected by additional resistance due to bedforms because the increase in critical shear stress ($\tau_c$) is balanced by a reduction in critical mean velocity ($V_c$), thus leaving $\omega_c$ ($= \tau_c V_c$) invariant. The tendency identified by Petit et al. (2005) for small headwater channels to require a higher critical stream power to mobilize a given grain size has thus been explained by Ferguson (2005) in terms of differences in bed grain size and channel slope.

Mao et al. (2008b) compared Ferguson's predicted values and the critical stream power derived from field measurements in two steep streams and confirmed its good performance. Back-calculating the Shields critical parameter using Ferguson's formula and the field-derived critical stream power, they also confirmed that $\tau^*_{c50}$ was three times lower than the value derived in the field and affected by additional sources of resistance (i.e., form and spill). Recently, Gob et al. (2010) estimated, using a lichenometric approach, the specific critical stream power of flood events over the last 50 years in steep French boulder bed streams. Because differences in critical stream power are unaffected by additional sources of flow resistance, as described above, they explained the range of obtained values in terms of differences in sediment size and channel slope, as suggested by Ferguson (2005). Another way of expressing the incipient conditions for sediment entrainment that is free from field estimation of hydraulic radius/flow depth is the unit critical discharge approach (Bathurst et al., 1987; Ferguson, 1994) which has been successfully applied to a steep boulder-bed channel (Rio Cordon) by Lenzi et al. (2006b).

As to the flow frequency associated with bedload motion, Thompson and Croke (2008) analysed bedload transport data in southeast Australian streams of different morphology (from pool-riffle to cascade) in order to determine critical Shields stresses. They observed that the channels investigated are not competent to transport the $D_{50}$ grain of the surface layer at bankfull flows, in contrast to what is usually assumed (see Wohl and Wilcox, 2005) and also observed in the field in the Rio Cordon by Lenzi et al. (2006a).

### 26.4.2 Bedload Transport Rates

Bedload formulas (e.g., Meyer-Peter and Müller, 1948; Smart and Jaeggi, 1983; Rickenmann, 1997) often overestimate sediment transport rates by one or more orders of magnitude, and sediment rates are accurately predicted only under unlimited sediment availability and supply conditions (D'Agostino and Lenzi, 1999; Rickenmann, 2001; Gomez, 2006; Rickenmann and Koschni, 2010). SCs have high ratios of transport capacity to sediment supply (Montgomery and Buffington, 1997) and are characterized by a lack of significant inchannel sediment storage, and by seasonal or stochastic sediment inputs. D'Agostino and Lenzi (1999) reported a reasonable bedload prediction only for an unlimited-supply high-magnitude event in the Rio Cordon basin. Rickenmann (2001) and Rickenmann and Koschni (2010) corroborated this finding, verifying the poor prediction efficiency of bedload formulas in high-gradient streams (> 5% gradient), and attributed it to the low values of relative flow depth (< 4–6), additional form resistance and sediment supply limitation.

Taking advantage of a large collection of bedload field data from 24 gravel-bed rivers in Idaho (a third of which with slope > 2%), Barry et al. (2004) confirmed that formulas tend to overestimate sediment transported during ordinary events. Furthermore, they demonstrated the good performance of a simplified transport equation which is a function of only channel armouring (as a measure of the excess of transport capacity over the sediment supply) and drainage area (as a proxy for the absolute sediment supply). Bathurst (2007) pointed out that bedload formulas over-estimate sediment transport in mountain streams because they do not account for the effect of the armour layer limiting sediment supply during the first phase of sediment transport (fine sediments transported over an unbroken armour layer). Bathurst (2007) also quantified the critical conditions for the onset of the second phase of sediment transport (disruption of the armor layer) as a function of bed material size and channel slope.

A recent attempt to reduce the over-estimation of sediment transport in steep channels during ordinary flood events was carried out by Yager et al. (2007). They modified a shear stress-based bedload equation (Fernandez Luque and Van Beek, 1976) to account for the stress borne by coarse clasts considered immobile and for the limited availability of mobile sediment fractions. Bedload transport is a function of the portion of shear stress acting on the mobile sediments, and the stress partitioning takes into account the variable submergence of immobile grains and the area of the bed covered by mobile sediments. The bedload formula of Yager et al. (2007) relies on the $D_{50}$ of the mobile bed portion rather than the $D_{50}$ of the entire bed. The sediment transport prediction proved to be within an order of magnitude of values measured in a steep flume. Accepting that immobile grain protrusion and bed coverage by mobile sediment represent a proxy of the sediment supply, this approach has a strong potential to be successfully applied in the field upon incorporation of step spacing geometry and spill resistance. Yager (2006) also developed a model accounting for size-selective transport of the mobile bed sediments during near-bankfull flood events that do not destabilize the coarse and immobile clasts. The model was tested using a long data series provided by the monitoring station on the Erlenbach stream (Swiss Alps, Rickenmann, 1997; Rickenmann and McArdell, 2007) and predicted bedload transport to within an order of magnitude of the measured values.

A complete flow routing, sediment transport, and bed evolution model specific for SCs was developed by Papanicolaou et al. (2004). It combines, in a 1-D numerical model, hydrodynamic and sediment transport modules that accounts for multifractional bedload transport, and its predictive ability was tested with success through both laboratory and field data. A further attempt to model bedload routing in steep channels is the SETRAC model

(Rickenmann et al., 2006; Chiari, 2008; Chiari et al., 2010). SETRAC combines a modified Smart and Jaeggi (1983) flow resistance approach and Rickenmann's (1991) bedload formula. Form roughness losses are accounted for by an empirical adjustment acting on the energy slope calculation.

Overall, for a transport model to be valid over a wide range of flood magnitudes, a better understanding of the mobility conditions of isolated and step-forming boulders and the consequences of their movements – in terms of finer sediment availability – is required. It has been shown that step pool structures may be destabilized during very large events and that they re-arrange to form a new stable sequence over time (Lenzi, 2001; Lamarre and Roy, 2008). Lenzi et al. (2004) showed that sediment transport during flows following a high-magnitude flood (likely featuring hyper-concentrated conditions, Mao et al., 2009) is relatively higher than before the event, and mostly related to the increased sediment availability and to the lower channel roughness caused by breakage of step-pool sequences and of the armour layer (Figure 26.7). Very similar dynamics were described also for the Erlenbach (Turowski et al., 2009). In Japan, Imaizumi et al. (2009) conducted field monitoring of the bedload transport rates associated with an artificial sediment release at near-bankfull flows. They observed that the step pool sequences were not destroyed and that the sediment supplied enriched the bed of fine patches and reduced the exposure of boulders.

Experimental monitoring stations (for example the Erlenbach in Switzerland and the Rio Cordon in Italy) have provided invaluable insight into the long-term coupled dynamics of morphological features and sediment transport. Furthermore, they can represent an ideal resource to link bed morphology adjustment, sediment transport, flow resistance, immobile grain organization and protrusion, and fine-patch dynamics with the availability of sediment supplied by the basin, which remains the major source of uncertainties for a reliable estimation of sediment transport. Along with the magnitude and timing of sediment supply from sources at the basin scale (bank erosion, debris flows, landslides), the other process which needs to be better explored is the sediment storage and transfer within the channel network, from the smaller tributaries to the higher-order mountain streams.

Relatively cheap surrogate techniques for bedload monitoring (such as hydrophones) installed along the channel network could represent a valuable way of assessing sediment storage and transfer processes (e.g., Reid et al., 2007; Mizuyama et al., 2008), once calibrated against a bedload trap or other direct devices. Finally, a recent attempt to use optically stimulated luminescence to determine residence times of fine sediments within mountain streams (Thompson et al., 2007)

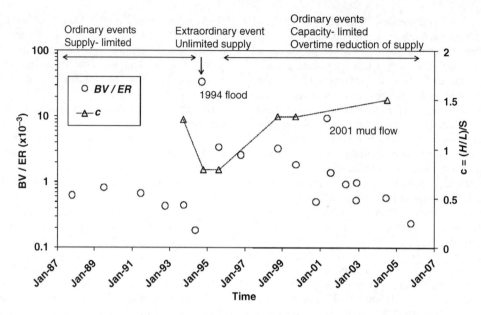

**Figure 26.7**   The dynamics of sediment supply condition and transport capacity in the Rio Cordon over the period 1987–2007, expressed in terms of the ratio between bedload volume (BV, m$^3$) and effective runoff (ER, $10^3$ m$^3$) for each flood. The destruction of step-pools and their re-shaping after the intense 1994 flood (RI > 50–70 a) is evident from the trend of the steepness factor derived from the longitudinal profile; $c = (H/L)/S$, with $S$ slope, $H$ step height and $L$ step wavelength. In 2001 a mud flow from a tributary caused a sudden increase in sediment supply to the main channel (modified from Lenzi, 2001 and Lenzi *et al.*, 2004). The value of $c$ for 2004 derives from Comiti *et al.* (2007). Reproduced, with permission, from Lenzi, M.A., Mao, L. and Comiti, F. (2004).

proved to be successful, which further enriches the set of indirect techniques for sediment dynamic study at the channel network scale.

## 26.5   CONCLUSIONS

The review provided above clearly indicates how little we still know about the processes which control the dynamics of flow, sediment transport, and the morphological evolution of steep channels. Indeed, boulder-bed channels are such complex systems that attempts to develop deterministic predictive models are likely to fail; thus probabilistic approaches are likely to be more suitable to describe their dynamics. Great headway has certainly been made compared to one decade ago, but there are still fundamental unknowns, especially regarding the flow and sediment fluxes during major flood events that are often responsible for dramatic changes in channel morphology and sediment availability at the river network and basin scales. To this end, experimental monitoring stations are crucial for the acquisition of hydrodynamics and sediment transport insights that otherwise need to be based on laboratory experiments only. These latter are undoubtedly very valuable for advancing

our knowledge of steep channels, provided that they are carefully designed to simulate properly the complex and stochastic flow–bed–bank interactions typical of steep channels. Also, in flume experiments, more attention should be given to the role of channel width and of bank roughness as they affect bed stability, as well as to conducting replicate tests.

Finally, we believe that the scientific community (geomorphologists, engineers, physicists) should endeavour to develop innovative technologies to monitor water and sediment fluxes over a range of flow stages, and these technologies should be implemented in long-term projects. Long-duration monitoring projects are vital to overcome the inherently great stability of steep channels at the shorter time scale. A more refined ability to estimate bed erosion/aggradation, flow velocity, and bedload transport volumes is of extreme relevance to address flood hazards as well as ecological management issues.

## 26.6   ACKNOWLEDGEMENTS

The authors are grateful to Joanna Curran and Dieter Rickenmann for their very helpful comments, which decidedly improved the manuscript. We thank Michael Lamb for providing his large database on sediment incipient motion, and Pascale Biron for her assistance and final editing. Finally, we are grateful to the GBR7 Organizing Committee for inviting us to present this overview at the conference.

## 26.7 REFERENCES

Aberle, J. and Smart, G.M. 2003. The influence of roughness structure on flow resistance on steep slopes. *Journal of Hydraulic Research* **41**: 259–269.

Abrahams, A.D., Li, G., and Atkinson, J.F. 1995. Step-pool streams: adjustment to maximum flow resistance. *Water Resources Research* **31**: 2593–2602.

Aguirre-Pe, J. and Fuentes, R. 1990. Resistance to flow in steep rough streams. *Journal of Hydraulic Engineering* **116**: 1374–1387.

Aguirre-Pe, J., Olivero, M.L., and Moncada, A.T. 2003. Particle densimetric Froude number for estimating sediment transport. *Journal of Hydraulic Engineering* **129**: 428–437.

Allen, J.R.L. 1983. A simplified cascade model for transverse stone-ribs in gravelly streams. *Proceedings of the Royal Society of London* A385: 253–266.

Andrews, E.D. 1983. Entrainment of gravel from naturally sorted riverbed material. *Geological Society of America Bulletin*. **94**: 1225–1231.

Armanini, A. and Gregoretti, C. 2005. Incipient sediment motion at high slopes in uniform flow conditions. *Water Resources Research* **41**: W12431. doi: 10.1029/2005WR004001.

Ashida, K., Egashira, S., and Ando, N. 1984. Generation and geometric features of step-pool bed forms. *Disaster Prevention Research Institute, Kyoto University, Annals* **27**: 341–353.

Ashworth, P.J. and Ferguson, R.I. 1989. Size-selective entrainment of bed load in gravel bed streams. *Water Resources Research* **25**: 627–634.

Bagnold, R.A. 1980. An empirical correlation of bedload transport rates in flumes and natural rivers. *Proceedings of the Royal Society of London* A 372: 453–473.

Barry, J.J., Buffington, J.M., and King, J.G. 2004. A general power equation for predicting bedload transport rates in gravel bed rivers. *Water Resources Research* **40**: W104001. doi: 10.1029/2004WR003190.

Bathurst, J.C. 1978. Flow resistance of large-scale roughness. American Society of Civil Engineers, *Journal of the Hydraulics Division* **104**: 1587–1603.

Bathurst, J.C. 1985. Flow resistance estimation in mountain rivers. *Journal of Hydraulic Engineering* **111**: 625–643.

Bathurst, J.C. 1993. Flow resistance through the channel network. In Beven, K. and Kirkby, M.J.editors. *Channel Network Hydrology*. Chichester, John Wiley & Sons, Ltd, pp. 69–98.

Bathurst, J.C. 2007. Effect of coarse surface layer on bed-load transport. *Journal of Hydraulic Engineering* **133**: 1192–1205.

Bathurst, J.C., Graf, W.H., and Cao, H.H. 1987. Bed load discharge equations for steep mountain rivers. In Thorne, C.R., Bathurst, J.C.,and Hey, R.D.editors. *Sediment Transport in Gravel-Bed Rivers*. Chichester, John Wiley & Sons, Ltd, pp. 453–491.

Benda, L., Hassan, M.A., Church, M., and May, C.L. 2005. Geomorphology of steepland headwaters: the transition from hillslopes to channels. *Journal of the American Water Resources Association* **41**: 835–851.

Bird, S., Hogan, D., and Schwab, J. 2010. Photogrammetric monitoring of small streams under a riparian forest canopy. *Earth Surface Processes and Landforms* **35**: 952–970.

Boes, R.M. and Hager, W.H. 2003. Two-phase flow characteristics of stepped spillways, *Journal of Hydraulic Engineering* **129**: 661–670.

Buffington, J.M. and Montgomery, D.R. 1997. A systematic analysis of eight decades of incipient motion studies, with special reference to gravel-bedded rivers. *Water Resources Research* **33**: 1993–2029.

Campbell, L., McEwan, I., Nikora, V.I. *et al.* 2005. Bed-load effects on hydrodynamics of rough-bed open-channel flows. *Journal of Hydraulic Engineering* **131**: 576–585.

Canovaro, F., Paris, E., and Solari, L. 2007. Effects of macro-scale bed roughness geometry on flow resistance. *Water Resources Research* **43**: W10414. doi: 10.1029/2006WR005727.

Carbonneau, P. and Bergeron, N.E. 2000. The effect of bedload transport on mean and turbulent flow properties. *Geomorphology* **35**: 267–278.

Carling, P.A. 1983. Threshold of coarse sediment transport in broad and narrow natural streams. *Earth Surface Processes and Landforms* **8**: 135–138.

Carling, P.A. 2006. The hydrology and geomorphology of bedrock rivers. *Geomorphology* **82**: 1–3.

Carollo, F.G., Ferro, V., and Termini, D. 2005. Analyzing turbulence intensity in gravel bed channels. *Journal of Hydraulic Engineering* **131**: 1050–1061.

Cavalli, M., Tarolli, P., Marchi, L., and Dalla Fontana, G. 2008. The effectiveness of airborne LiDAR data in the recognition of channel-bed morphology. *Catena* **73**: 249–260.

Chanson, H. 1993. Self-Aerated flows on chutes and spillways. *Journal of Hydraulic Engineering* **119**: 220–243.

Chanson, H. 1996. Comment on Step-pool streams: adjustment to maximum flow resistance by Abrahams, L.D., Gang, L. and Atkinson, J. K. *Water Resources Research* **32**: 3401.

Chartrand, S.M. and Whiting, P.J. 2000. Alluvial architecture in headwater streams with special emphasis on step-pool topography. *Earth Surface Processes and Landforms* **25**: 583–600.

Chiari, M. 2008. *Numerical modelling of bedload transport in torrents and mountain streams*. Ph.D. dissertation. University of Natural Resources and Applied Life Sciences, Vienna, Austria (available from www.bedload.at).

Chiari, M., Friedl, K., and Rickenmann, D. 2010. A one dimensional bedload transport model for steep slopes. *Journal of Hydraulic Research* **48**: 152–160.

Chin, A. 1989. Step-pools in stream channels. *Progress in Physical Geography* **13**: 391–408.

Chin, A. 1998. On the stability of step-pool mountain streams. *Journal of Geology* **106**: 59–69.

Chin, A. 1999. On the origin of step-pool sequences in mountain streams. *Geophysical Research Letters* **26**: 231–234.

Chin, A. and Phillips, J.D. 2006. The self-organization of step-pools in mountain streams. *Geomorphology* **83**: 346–358.

Chin, A. and Wohl, E. 2005. Toward a theory for step-pools in stream channels, *Progress in Physical Geography* **29**: 275–296.

Church, M. 1992. Channel morphology and typology. In Callow, P. and Petts, G.E.editors. The Rivers Handbook, Oxford, Blackwell, pp. 126–143.

Church, M. 2008. Multiple scales in rivers. In Habersack, H., Piégay, H. and Rinaldi, M.editors. *Gravel Bed Rivers VI: From Process Understanding to River Restoration*.

Amsterdam, Elsevier, Developments in Earth Surface Processes 11, pp. 3–32.

Church, M. and Zimmermann, A. 2007. Form and stability of step-pool channels: Research progress. *Water Resources Research* **43**: W03415. doi: 10.1029/2006wr005037.

Comiti, F. 2003. *Local scouring in natural and artificial step-pool systems.* Ph.D. thesis, Dipartimento Territorio e Sistemi Agro-Forestali, Università degli studi di Padova.

Comiti, F. and Lenzi, M.A. 2006. Dimensions of standing waves at steps in mountain rivers. *Water Resources Research* **42**: W03411. doi: 10.1029/2004WR003898

Comiti, F., Andreoli, A., and Lenzi, M.A. 2005. Morphological effects of local scouring in step-pool streams. *Earth Surface Processes and Landforms* **30**: 1567–1581.

Comiti, F., Andreoli, A., Lenzi, M.A., and Mao, L. 2006. Spatial density and characteristics of woody debris in five mountain rivers of the Dolomites (Italian Alps). *Geomorphology* **78**: 44–63.

Comiti, F., Cadol, D., and Wohl, E.E. 2009a. Flow regimes, bed morphology, and flow resistance in self-formed step-pool channels. *Water Resources Research* **45**: W04424. doi: 10.1029/2008WR007259.

Comiti, F., Cadol, D., and Wohl, E.E. 2010a. Reply to "Comment on Flow regimes, bed morphology, and flow resistance in self-formed step-pool channels" by K. *Richardson. Water Resources Research* **46**. W12804. doi: 10.1029/2010WR009699.

Comiti, F., Lenzi, M.A., and Mao, L. 2010b. Local scouring at check dams in mountain rivers. In Conesa-Garcia, M. and Lenzi, M.A.,editors, *Check Dams, Morphological Adjustments and Erosion in Torrential Streams*. New York, Nova Science Publishers, pp. 263–282.

Comiti, F., Mao, L., Lenzi, M.A., and Siligardi, M. 2009b. Artificial steps to stabilize mountain rivers: A post-project ecological assessment. *River Research and Applications* **25**: 639–659.

Comiti, F., Mao, L., Wilcox, A., Wohl, E., and Lenzi, M.A. 2007. Field-derived relationships for flow velocity and resistance in high-gradient streams. *Journal of Hydrology* **340**: 48–62.

Crowe, J. 2002. *An experimental study of the step-pool bed form.* Ph.D. thesis, John Hopkins University, Baltimore, Maryland.

Curran, J.C. 2007. Step-pool formation models and associated step spacing. *Earth Surface Processes and Landforms* **32**: 1611–1627.

Curran, J.C. and Wilcock, P.R. 2005. Characteristic dimensions of the step-pool configuration: an experimental study. *Water Resources Research* **41**: W0203. doi: 10.1029/2004WR003568.

Curran, J.H. and Wohl, E.E. 2003. Large woody debris and flow resistance in step-pool channels, Cascade Range, Washington. *Geomorphology* **51**: 141–157.

D'Agostino, V. 2010. Filtering-retention check dam design in mountain torrents. In Conesa-Garcia M., Lenzi M.A.,editors, *Check Dams, Morphological Adjustments and Erosion in Torrential Streams*. New York, Nova Science Publishers, pp. 185–210.

D'Agostino, V. and Lenzi, M.A. 1999. Bedload transport in the instrumented catchment of the Rio Cordon: Part II. Analysis of the bedload rate. *Catena* **36**: 191–204.

David, G.C., Wohl, E., Yochum, S.E., and Bledsoe, B.P. 2010. Controls on spatial variations in flow resistance along steep mountain streams. *Water Resource Research* **46**: W03513. doi: 10.1029/2009WR008134.

Egashira, S. and Ashida, K. 1991. Flow resistance and sediment transportation in streams with step-pool bed morphology. In

Armanini, A. and Di Silvio, G.,editors. *Fluvial Hydraulics of Mountain Regions, Lecture Notes in Earth Sciences*. Berlin, Springer-Verlag, pp. 45–58.

Einstein, H.A. and Barbarossa, N.L. 1952. River Channel Roughness. *American Society of Civil Engineers Transactions* **117**: 1121–1132.

El Khashab, A.M. 1986. Form drag resistance of two-dimensional stepped steep open channels. *Canadian Journal of Civil Engineering* **13**: 523–527.

Ergenzinger, P. 1992. Riverbed adjustments in a step-pool system: Lainbach, Upper Bavaria. In Billi, P., Hey, R.D., Thorne, C.R.,and Tacconi, P., editors. *Dynamics of Gravel-bed Rivers*. Chichester, John Wiley & Sons, Ltd, pp. 415–430.

Faustini, J.M. and Jones, J.A. 2003. Influence of large woody debris on channel morphology and dynamics in steep, boulder-rich mountain streams, western Cascades, Oregon. *Geomorphology* **51**: 187–205.

Ferguson, R.I. 1994. Critical discharge for entrainment of poorly sorted gravel. *Earth Surface Processes and Landforms* **19**: 179–186.

Ferguson, R.I. 2005. Estimating critical stream power for bed-load transport calculations in gravel-bed rivers. *Geomorphology* **70**: 33–41.

Ferguson, R.I. 2007. Flow resistance equations for gravel- and boulder-bed streams. *Water Resource Research* **43**: W05427.

Ferguson, R.I. 2008. Gravel-bed rivers at the reach scale. In Habersack, H., Piégay, H.,and Rinaldi, M., editors. *Gravel Bed Rivers VI: From Process Understanding to River Restoration.* Amsterdam, Elsevier, pp. 33–60.

Fernandez Luque, R.F. and Van Beek, R. 1976. Erosion and transport of bedload sediment. *Journal of Hydraulic Research* **14**: 127–144.

Giacometti, G. 2000. *Indagine sperimentale sullo scavo a valle di opere trasversali in alvei a media ed alta pendenza.* Ph.D. thesis, University of Padova, Padova, Italy [in Italian].

Gob, F., Bravard, J-P., and Petit, F. 2010. The influence of sediment size, relative grain size and channel slope on initiation of sediment motion in boulder bed rivers. A lichenometric study. *Earth Surface Processes and Landforms* **35**: 1535–1547. doi: 10.1002/esp.1994.

Gomez, B. 2006. The potential rate of bed-load transport. *Proceedings of the National Academy of Sciences USA* **103**: 17170–17173.

Gomi, T., Sidle, R.C., Woodsmith, R.D., and Bryant, M.D. 2003. Characterstics of channel steps and reach morphology in headwater streams, southeast Alaska. *Geomorphology* **51**: 225–242.

Grant, G.E. 1997. Critical flow constrains flow hydraulics in mobile-bed streams: A new hypothesis. *Water Resources Research* **33**: 349–358.

Grant, G.E. and Mizuyama, T. 1991. Origin of step-pool sequences in high gradient streams: a flume experiment. In *Japan-USA Workshop on Snow Avalanche, Landslide and Debris Flow Prediction and Control,* Tsukuba, Japan Science and Technology Agency, National Research Institute for Earth Science and Disaster Prevention, Japan, pp. 523–532.

Grant, G.E., Swanson, F.J., and Wolman, M.G. 1990. Pattern and origin of stepped-bed morphology in high gradient streams, western Cascades, Oregon, *Geological Society of America Bulletin* **102**: 340–352.

Haga, H., Kumagai, T., Otsuki, K., and Ogawsa, S. 2002. Transport and retention of coarse woody debris in mountain streams: An in situ field experiment of log transport and a field survey of coarse woody debris distribution. *Water Resources Research* **38**: 1126.

Halwas, K.L. and Church, M. 2002. Channel units in small, high gradient streams on Vancouver Island, British Columbia. *Geomorphology* 43: 243–256.

Hassan, M.A., Egozi, R., and Parker, G. 2006. Experiments on the effect of hydrograph characteristics on vertical grain sorting in gravel bed rivers. *Water Resources Research* 42: W09408. doi: 10.1029/2005WR004707.

Hassan, M.A., Smith, B.J., Hogan, D.L. *et al.* 2008. Sediment storage and transport in coarse bed streams: scale considerations. In Habersack, H., Piégay, H.,and Rinaldi, M., editors. *Gravel Bed Rivers VI: From Process Understanding to River Restoration*. Amsterdam, Elsevier, pp. 473–496.

Hayward, J.A. 1980. *Hydrology and Stream Sediments from Torlesse Stream Catchment*. Tussock Grasslands and Mountain Lands Institute, Lincoln College, New Zealand, Special Publication 17.

Imaizumi, F., Gomi, T., Kobayashi, S., and Negishi, J.N. 2009. Changes in bedload transport rate associated with episodic sediment supply in a Japanese headwater channel. *Catena* 77: 207–215.

Jakob, M. and Hungr, O.editors. 2005. *Debris Flow Hazards and Related Phenomena*. Berlin, Springer.

Jarrett, R.D. 1984. Hydraulics of high-gradient streams. *Journal of Hydraulic Engineering* 110: 1519–1539.

Judd, H.E. 1963. *A study of bed characteristics in relation to flow in rough, high-gradient natural channels*. Ph.D. thesis, Utah State University, Logan, Utah.

Koll, K. 2002. *Feststofftransport und Geschwindigkeitsverteilung in Raugerinnen*. Ph.D. thesis, Universität Fridericiana zu Karlsruhe, Germany.

Koll, K. and Dittrich, A. 2001. Influence of sediment transport on armoured surfaces. *International Journal of Sediment Research* 16: 201–206.

Koll, K.J., Aberle, J., and Dittrich, A. 2000. *Bed instability in steep mountain streams*. EROSLOPE II, Universität Fridericiana zu Karlsruhe: Institut für Wasserwirtschaft und Kulturtechnik, Karlsruhe, Germany.

Kuhnle, R.A. 1992. Fractional transport rates of bedload on Goodwin Creek. In Billi, P, Hey, R.D., Thorne, C.R. and Tacconi, P., editors. *Dynamics of Gravel-Bed Rivers*. Chichester, John Wiley & Sons, Ltd, pp. 141–155.

Lamarre, H. and Roy, A.G. 2008. The role of morphology on the displacement of particles in a step-pool river system. *Geomorphology* 99: 270–279.

Lamb, M.P., Dietrich, W.E., and Venditti, J.G. 2008. Is the critical Shields stress for incipient sediment motion dependent on channel-bed slope? *Journal of Geophysical Research* 113: F02008. doi: 10.1029/2007JF000831.

Laronne, J.B. and Reid, I. 1993. Very high bedload sediment transport in desert ephemeral rivers. *Nature* 366: 148–150.

Laronne, J.B., Reid, I., Yitshak, Y., and Frostick, L.E. 1994. The non-layering of gravel streambeds under ephemeral flow regimes. *Journal of Hydrology* 159: 353–363.

Lee, A.J. 1998. *The hydraulics of steep streams*. Ph.D. thesis, University of Sheffield, United Kingdom.

Lee, A.J. and Ferguson, R.I. 2002. Velocity and flow resistance in step-pool streams. *Geomorphology* 46: 59–71.

Lenzi, M.A., D'Agostino, V., and Sonda, D. 2000. *Ricostruzione morfologica e recupero ambientale dei torrenti. Criteri metodologici ed esecutivi*. Cosenza, Italy, Editoriale Bios [in Italian].

Lenzi, M.A. 2001. Step-pool evolution in the Rio Cordon, Northeastern Italy. *Earth Surface Processes and Landforms* 26: 991–1008.

Lenzi, M.A. 2002. Stream bed stabilization using boulder check dams that mimic step-pool morphology features in Northeastern Italy. *Geomorphology* 45: 243–260.

Lenzi, M.A., Mao, L., and Comiti, F. 2004. Magnitude-frequency analysis of bed load data in an Alpine boulder bed stream. *Water Resources Research* 40: W0720. doi: 10.1029/2003WR002961.

Lenzi, M.A., Mao, L., and Comiti, F. 2006a. Effective discharge for sediment transport in a mountain river: computational approaches and geomorphic effectiveness. *Journal of Hydrology* 326: 257–276.

Lenzi, M.A., Mao, L. and Comiti, F. 2006b. When does bedload transport begin in steep boulder-bed streams? *Hydrological Processes* 20: 3517–3533.

Leopold, L.B. and Maddock, T., Jr 1953. *The Hydraulic Geometry of Stream Channels and some Physiographic Implications*. United States Geological Survey, Professional Paper 252.

MacFarlane, W.A. and Wohl, E.E. 2003. Influence of step composition on step geometry and flow resistance in step-pool streams of the Washington Cascades. *Water Resources Research* 39: 1037.

Mao, L. and Lenzi, M.A. 2007. Sediment mobility and bedload transport conditions in an alpine stream. *Hydrological Processes* 21: 1882–1891.

Mao, L., Andreoli, A., Comiti, F., and Lenzi, M.A. 2008a. Geomorphic effects of large wood jams on a sub-antarctic mountain stream. *River Research and Applications* 24: 249–266.

Mao, L., Cavalli, M., Comiti, F. *et al.* 2009. Sediment transfer processes in two Alpine catchments of contrasting morphological settings. *Journal of Hydrology* 364: 88–98.

Mao, L., Comiti, F., and Lenzi, M.A. 2006. La resistenza al flusso in un torrente montano ad elevata pendenza con morfologia a step-pool. *Rivista di Ingegneria Agraria* 3: 29–38.

Mao, L., Uyttendaele, G.P., Iroume, A., and Lenzi, M.A. 2008b. Field based analysis of sediment entrainment in two high gradient streams located in Alpine and Andine environments. *Geomorphology* 93: 368–383.

Marcus, W.A., Roberts, K., Harvey, L., and Tackman, G. 1992. An evaluation of methods for estimating Mannings' n in small mountain streams. *Mountain Research and Development* 12: 227–239.

Marion, D.A. and Weirich, F. 2003. Equal-mobility bed load transport in a small, step-pool channel in the Ouachita Mountains. *Geomorphology* 55: 139–154.

Marston, R.A. 1982. The geomorphic significance of log steps in forest streams. *Association of American Geographers Annals* 72: 99–108.

Maxwell, A.R. and Papanicolaou, A.N. 2001. Hydraulic resistance of step-pool streams. In Phelps, D. and Sehlke, G., editors, *Bridging the Gap: Meeting the World's Water and Environmental Resources Challenges. Proceedings of World Water and Environmental Resources Congress 2001 Orlando, FL, 20–24 May*. American Society of Civil Engineers. doi: 10.1061/40569 (2001) 133. CD-ROM.

McDonald, T.J. and Day, B.C. 1978. *An Experimental Flume Study on the Formation of Transverse Ribs: Current Research, part A*. Geological Survey of Canada, Paper 78-1A, pp. 441–451.

Meyer-Peter, E. and Müller, R. 1948. Formulas for bed-load transport. *Proceedings of the 3rd Meeting, Stockholm, Sweden*. International Association for Hydraulic Structures Research, Appendix 2: 1-26.

Millar, R.G. 1999. Grain and form resistance in gravel-bed rivers. *Journal of Hydraulic Research* **17**: 303–311.

Millar, R.G. and Quick, M.C. 1994. Flow resistance of high-gradient gravel channels. In Cotroneo, V. and Rumer, R.R., editors, Hydraulic Engineering '94, New York, American Society of Civil Engineers, pp. 717–721.

Milzow, C., Molnar, P., McArdell, B.W., and Burlando, P. 2006. Spatial organization in the step-pool structure of a steep mountain stream (Vogelbach, Switzerland). *Water Resources Research* **42**: W04418. doi: 10.1029/2004WR003870.

Mizuyama, T., Yoshifumi, S., Laronne, J., Nonaka, M., and Matsuoka, M. 2008. Monitoring sediment transport in mountain torrents. *Interpraevent* **2008 1**: 425–431.

Montgomery, D.R. and Buffington, J.M. 1997. Channel-reach morphology in mountain drainage basins. *Geological Society of America Bulletin* **109**: 591–611.

Mueller, E.R., Pitlick, J., and Nelson, J. 2005. Variation in the reference Shields stress for bed load transport in gravel-bed streams and rivers. *Water Resource Research* **41**: W04006. doi: 10.1029/2004WR003692.

Nickolotsky, A. and Pavlowsky, R.T. 2006. Morphology of step-pools in a wilderness headwater stream: the importance of standardizing geomorphic measurements. *Geomorphology*, **83**: 294–306.

Palt, S. 2001. *Sedimenttransportprozesse im Himalaya-Karakorum und ihre Bedeutung für Wasserkraftanlagen.* Institut für Wasserwirtschaft und Kulturtechnik, Universität Karlsruhe.

Papanicolaou, A.N., Bdour, A., and Wicklein, E. 2004. One-dimensional hydrodynamic/sediment transport model applicable to steep mountain streams. *Journal of Hydraulic Research* **42**: 357–375.

Parker, G. and Klingeman, P.C. 1982. On why gravel bed streams are paved. *Water Resources Research* **18**: 1409–1423.

Parker, G., Wilcock, P.R., Paola, C., Dietrich, W.E., and Pitlick, J. 2007. Physical basis for quasi-universal relations describing bankfull hydraulic geometry of single-thread gravel bed rivers. *Journal of Geophysical Research* **112**: F04005, doi: 10.1029/2006JF000549.

Peterson, D.F. and Mohanty, P.K. 1960. Flume studies of flow in steep, rough channels. *American Society of Civil Engineers, Journal of the Hydraulic Division* **86**: 55–76.

Petit, F., Gob, F., Houbrechts, G., and Assani, A.A. 2005. Critical specific stream power in gravel-bed rivers. *Geomorphology*, **69**: 92–101.

Recking, A. 2009. Theoretical development on the effects of changing flow hydraulics on incipient bed load motion. *Water Resource Research* **45**: W04401, doi: 10.1029/2008WR006826.

Recking, A., Frey, P., Paquier, A., Belleudy, P., and Champagne, J.Y. 2008. Feedback between bed load and flow resistance in gravel and cobble bed rivers. *Water Resources Research* **44**: W05412, doi: 10.1029/2007WR006219.

Reid, D.E. and Hickin, E.J. 2008. Flow resistance in steep mountain streams. *Earth Surface Processes and Landforms* **33**: 2211–2240.

Reid, I. and Laronne, J.B. 1995. Bedload sediment transport in an ephemeral stream and a comparison with seasonal and perennial counterparts. *Water Resources Research* **31**: 773–781.

Reid, S.C., Lane, S.N., Berney, J.M., and Holden, J. 2007. The timing and magnitude of coarse sediment transport events within an upland, temperate gravel-bed river. *Geomorphology* **83**: 152–182.

Richardson, K. 2010. Comment on "Flow regimes, bed morphology, and flow resistance in self-formed step-pool channels" by Comiti, F., Cadol, D., Wohl, E. *Water Resources Research* **46**: W12803. doi: 10.1029/2010WR009550.

Rickenmann, D. 1990. *Bedload Transport Capacity of Slurry Flows at Steep Slopes.* Versuchsanstalt für Wasserbau, Hydrologie und Glaziologie, Eidgenossischen Technischen Hochschule, Zürich, Mitteilungen 103.

Rickenmann, D. 1991. Hyperconcentrated flow and sediment transport at steep slopes. *Journal of Hydraulic Engineering* **117**: 1419–1439.

Rickenmann, D. 1994. An alternative equation for the mean velocity in gravel-bed rivers and mountain torrents. In Cotroneo, V. and Rumer, R.R., editors, *Proceedings of Hydraulic Engineering '94, Vol. 1* American Society of Civil Engineers, New York, pp. 672–676.

Rickenmann, D. 1996. Fliessgeschwindigkeit in Wildbächen und Gebirgsflüssen. *Wasser, Energie, Luft* **88**: 298–303.

Rickenmann, D. 1997. Sediment transport in Swiss torrents. *Earth Surface Processes and Landforms* **22**: 937–951.

Rickenmann, D. 2001. Comparison of bed load transport in torrents and gravel bed streams. *Water Resources Research* **37**: 3295–3305.

Rickenmann, D. and Koschni, A. 2010. Sediment loads due to fluvial transport and debris flows during the 2005 flood events in Switzerland. *Hydrological Processes* **24**: 993–1007.

Rickenmann, D. and McArdell, B.W. 2007. Continuous measurement of sediment transport in the Erlenbach stream using piezoelectric bedload impact sensors. *Earth Surface Processes and Landforms* **32**: 1362–1378.

Rickenmann, D., Chiari, M., and Friedl, K. 2006. SETRAC – A sediment routing model for steep torrent channels. In Ferreira, R., Alves, E., Leal, J. and Cardoso, A., editors. River Flow 2006. London, Taylor & Francis, pp. 843–852.

Rinaldi, M., Surian, N., Comiti, F., and Bussettini, M. 2011a. *Guidebook for the Evaluation of Stream Morphological Conditions by the Morphological Quality Index (MQI).* Version 1. Rome, Istituto Superiore per la Protezione e la Ricerca Ambientale. ISBN: 978-88-448-0487-9. url: http://www.isprambiente.gov.it/site/en-GB/Publictions/Handbooks_and_Guidelines/Documents/manuale_66_2011.html.

Rinaldi, M., Surian, N., Comiti, F., and Bussettini, M. 2011b. The morphological quality index (IQM) for stream evaluation and classification. *Italian Journal of Engineering Geology and Environment* **11**(1): 17–36.

Rosport, M. 1994. Stability of torrent beds characterized by step-pool textures. *International Journal of Sediment Research* **9**: 124–132.

Rosport, M. 1997. Hydraulics of steep mountain streams. *International Journal of Sediment Research* **12**: 99–108.

Rosport, M. and Dittrich, A. 1995. Step-pool formation and stability – a flume study. In *Proceedings of the 6th International Symposium on River Sedimentation, New Delhi, India*, pp. 525–532.

Ruf, G. 1988. Neue Ergebnisse über die Fließgeschwindigkeit in sehr rauen Gerinnen (Wildbächen). *Interpraevent* **4**: 165–176.

Ryan, S.E. Porth, L.S., and Troendle, C.A. 2002. Defining phases of bedload transport using piecewise regression. *Earth Surface Processes and Landforms* **27**: 971–990.

Shvidchenko, A. and Pender, G. 2000. Flume study of the effect of relative depth on the incipient motion of coarse uniform sediments. *Water Resource Research* **36**: 619–628.

Smart, G.M. and Jaeggi, M.N.R. 1983. *Sediment Transport on Steep Slopes*. Versuchsanstalt für Wasserbau, Hydrologie und Glaziologie, Eidgenossischen Technischen Hochschule, Zurich, Mitteilungen 64.

Smart, G.M., Duncan, M.J., and Walsh, J.M. 2002. Relatively rough flow resistance equations. *Journal of Hydraulic Engineering* 128: 568–578.

Solari, L. and Parker, G. 2000. The curious case of mobility reversal in sediment mixtures. *Journal of Hydraulic Engineering* 12: 198–208.

Takahashi, T. 2007. *Debris Flow - Mechanics, Prediction and Countermeasures*. London, Taylor and Francis.

Tatsuzawa, H., Hayashi, H., and Hasegawa, K. 1999. Role of heterogeneous property of bed materials in the formation of step-pool systems in mountain streams. *Journal of Hydroscience and Hydraulic Engineering* 17: 37–45.

Thompson, C. and Croke, J. 2008. Channel flow competence and sediment transport in upland streams in southeast Australia. *Earth Surface Processes and Landforms* 33: 329–352.

Thompson, C., Rhodes, E., and Croke, J. 2007. The storage of bed material in mountain stream channels as assessed using Optically Stimulated Luminescence dating. *Geomorphology* 83: 307–321.

Tinkler, K.J. and Wohl, E.E.,editors. 1998. *Rivers Over Rock: Fluvial Processes in Bedrock Channels*. American Geophysical Union, Geophysical Monograph 107.

Trevisani, S., Cavalli, M., and Marchi, L. 2009. Reading the bed morphology of a mountain stream: a geomorphometric study on high-resolution topographic data. *Hydrology and Earth System Sciences Discussion* 6: 7287–7319.

Turowski, J.M., Yager, E.M., Badoux, A., Rickenmann, D., and Molnar, P. 2009. The impact of exceptional events on erosion, bedload transport and channel stability in a step-pool channel. *Earth Surface Processes and Landforms* 34: 1661–1673.

Valle, B. and Pasternak, G.B. 2002. TDR measurements of hydraulic jump aeration in the South Fork of the American River, California. *Geomorphology* 42: 153–165.

Valle, B. and Pasternack, G.B. 2006a. Submerged and unsubmerged natural hydraulic jumps in a bedrock step-pool mountain channel. *Geomorphology* 82: 146–159.

Valle, B. and Pasternack, G.B. 2006b. Field mapping and digital elevation modelling of submerged and unsubmerged hydraulic jump regions in a bedrock step-pool channel. *Earth Surface Processes and Landforms* 31: 646–664.

Valle, B. and Pasternack, G.B. 2006c. Air concentrations of submerged and unsubmerged hydraulic jumps in a bedrock step-pool channel. *Journal of Geophysical Research* 111: F03016. doi: 10.1029/2004JF000140.

Vianello, A., Cavalli, M., and Tarolli, P. 2009. LiDAR-derived slopes for headwater channel network analysis. *Catena* 76: 97–106.

Vollmer, S. and Kleinhans, M.G. 2007. Predicting incipient motion, including the effect of turbulent pressure fluctuations in the bed. *Water Resource Research* 43: W05410. doi: 10.1029/2006WR004919.

Wang, Z., Melching, C.S., Duan, X.H., and Yu, G.A. 2009. Ecological and hydraulic studies of step-pool system. *Journal of Hydraulic Engineering* 135: 705–717.

Weichert, R. 2005. Bed morphology and stability of steep open channels. Ph.D. thesis, Eidgenossischen Technischen Hochschule, Zurich, Switzerland.

Weichert, R.B., Bezzola, G.R., and Minor, H.E. 2008. Bed morphology and generation of step-pool channels. *Earth Surface Processes and Landforms* 33: 1678–1692.

Weichert, R.B., Bezzola, G.R., and Minor, H.E. 2009. Bed erosion in steep open channels. *Journal of Hydraulic Research* 47: 360–371.

Whittaker, J.G. 1987. Sediment transport in step-pool streams. In Thorne, C.R., Bathurst, J.C.,and Hey, R.D., editors. *Sediment Transport in Gravel-bed Rivers*. Chichester, John Wiley and Sons, Ltd, pp. 545–579.

Whittaker, J.G. and Davies, T.R.H. 1982. Erosion and sediment transport processes in step-pool torrents. In Walling, D.E., editor. *Recent developments in the Explanation and Prediction of Erosion and Sediment Yield*. International Association for Hydrological Sciences, Publication 137, pp. 99–104.

Whittaker, J.G. and Jaeggi, M.N.R. 1982. Origin of step-pool systems in mountain streams. American Society of Civil Engineers, *Journal of the Hydraulics Division* 108: 758–773.

Wiberg, P.L. and Smith, J.D. 1991. Velocity distribution and bed roughness in high-gradient streams. *Water Resources Research* 23: 1471–1480.

Wilcock, P.R. 1993. Critical shear stress of natural sediments. *Journal of Hydraulic Engineering* 119: 491–505.

step-poolWilcox, A.C. and Wohl, E.E. 2006. Flow resistance dynamics in step-pool channels: 1. Large woody debris and controls on total resistance. *Water Resources Research* 42: W05418. doi: 10.1029/2005WR004277.

Wilcox, A.C. and Wohl, E.E. 2007. Field measurements of three dimensional hydraulics in a step-pool channel. *Geomorphology* 83: 215–231.

Wilcox, A.C., Nelson, J.M., and Wohl, E.E. 2006. Flow resistance dynamics in step-pool channels: 2. Partitioning between grain, spill, and woody debris resistance. *Water Resources Research* 42: W05419. doi: 10.1029/2005 WR004278.

Wilcox, A.C., Wohl, E.E., Comiti, F., and Mao, L. 2011. Hydraulics, morphology and energy dissipation in an alpine step-pool channel. *Water Resources Research* 47 doi: 10.1029/2010WR010192.

Wohl, E.E. 2000. *Mountain Rivers*. American Geophysical Union, Water Resources Monograph 14.

Wohl, E.E. and Goode, J.R. 2008. Wood dynamics in headwater streams of the Colorado Rocky Mountains. *Water Resources Research* 44: W09429. doi: 10.1029/2007WR006522.

Wohl, E.E. and Grodek, T. 1994. Channel bed-steps along the Nahal Yael, Negev desert, Israel. *Geomorphology* 9: 117–226.

Wohl, E.E. and Jaeger, K. 2009. A conceptual model for the longitudinal distribution of wood in mountain streams. *Earth Surface Process and Landforms* 34: 329–344.

Wohl, E.E. and Merritt, D. 2005. Prediction of mountain stream morphology. *Water Resources Research* 41: W08419. doi: 10.1029/2004WR003779.

Wohl, E.E. and Merritt, D.M. 2008. Reach-scale channel geometry of mountain streams. *Geomorphology* 93: 168–185.

Wohl, E.E. and Thompson, D.M. 2000. Velocity characteristics along a small step-pool channel. *Earth Surface Process and Landforms* 25: 353–367.

Wohl, E.E. and Wilcox, A.C. 2005. Channel geometry of mountain streams in New Zealand. *Journal of Hydrology* 300: 252–266.

Wooldridge, C.L. and Hickin, E.J. 2002. Step-pool and cascade morphology, Mosquito Creek, British Columbia: a test of four analytical techniques. *Canadian Journal of Earth Sciences* 39: 493–503.

Wyrick, J.R. and Pasternack, G.B. 2008. Modeling energy dissipation and hydraulic jump regime responses to channel nonuniformity at river steps. *Journal of Geophysical Research* **113**: F03003. doi: 10.1029/2007JF000873.

Yager, E.M. 2006. *Prediction of sediment transport in steep, rough streams.* Ph.D. thesis, University of California, Berkeley.

Yager, E., Kirchner, J.W. and Dietrich, W.E. 2007. Calculating bedload transport in steep, boulder-bed channels. *Water Resources Research* **43**: W07418. doi: 10.1029/2006WR005432.

Yang, C.T. 1971. Formation of riffles and pools. *Water Resources Research* **7**: 1567–1574.

Yu, G., Wang, Z., Zhang, K., Duan, X., and Chang, T. 2010. Restoration of an incised mountain stream using artificial step-pool system. *Journal of Hydraulic Research* **48**: 178–187.

Zasso, V. and D'Agostino, V. 2007. Field analysis on the hydraulic roughness in an alpine stream: colluvial, cascade and step-pool reaches. *Quaderni di Idronomia Montana* **27**: 503–518 [in Italian].

Zimmermann, A. 2009. *Experimental investigations of step-pool channel formation and stability.* Ph.D. thesis, The University of British Columbia, Vancouver, Canada. https://circle.ubc.ca//handle/2429/7016.

Zimmermann, A. 2010. Flow resistance in steep streams: An experimental study. *Water Resoures Research* **46**: W09536. doi: 10.1029/2009WR007913.

Zimmermann, A. and Church, M. 2001. Channel morphology, gradient profiles and bed stresses during flood in a step-pool channel. *Geomorphology* **40**: 311–327.

Zimmermann, A., Church, M., and Hassan, M.A. 2008. Identification of steps and pools from stream longitudinal profile data. *Geomorphology* **102**: 395–406.

Zimmermann, A., Church, M., and Hassan, M.A. 2010. Step-pool stability: testing the jammed state hypothesis. *Journal of Geophysical Research* **115**: F02008. doi: 10.1029/2009JF001365.

## 26.8 DISCUSSION

### 26.8.1 *Discussion by Kristin Bunte*

In your excellent presentation of issues in steep channels, you have a diagram by Lamb *et al.* (2008) (slightly modified) that shows an increase in critical shear stress $\tau_c^*$ with channel slope ($S$) suggesting that values of $\tau_c^*$ fall mainly within 0.05 to 0.12 for steep channels. Data from your study streams superimposed on Lamb's figure indicate values of $\tau_c^*$ even higher. I would like to confirm your observation and show field data that demonstrate an even stronger increase of $\tau_c^*$ with $S$ in steep mountain streams with low sediment supply and high structural bed stability.

We have measured gravel bedload at 12 sites in coarse gravel- and cobble-bed Rocky Mountain streams with channel gradients of 1.2% to 9.3% (see Bunte *et al.* (2010) for site characteristics) over snowmelt high-flow seasons. Bedload traps were used for sampling. With their $0.2 \times 0.3$ m openings, a large 4 mm mesh width net to accommodate sample volumes of 10–20 l, and sampling times of up to one hour, bedload

traps were especially designed for representative collection of large, infrequently moving particles in streams with generally low sediment supply (Bunte *et al.*, 2004, 2007, 2008). These design criteria allowed us to be quite confident that the largest bedload particles sizes mobile at bankfull flow ($D_{max,bf}$) were sampled representatively. Based on fitted flow competence curves ($D_{max} = c\ Q^d$), the particle size typically mobile at bankfull flow (where $Q_{bf}$ is approximately equivalent to $Q_{1.5}$) was computed as

$$D_{max} = F \cdot c \cdot Q_{bf}^d \qquad (26.3)$$

wherein $F$ is the bias correction factor needed to account for the inherent underprediction of $y$-values from $x$ in a power function (Ferguson 1986, 1987), $c$ is a coefficient and $d$ an exponent. Knowing $D_{max\ bf}$, $S$, and the bankfull hydraulic radius ($R_{bf}$), the critical shear stress at bankfull flow ($\tau_{cbf}^*$) can be back-calculated (Bunte *et al.*, 2010). For study sites with $S$ of 3.8%–9.3% (steep channels), $\tau_{cbf}^*$ reached values of 0.17–0.67 (Figure 26.8), which are much higher than shown for the field data compiled by Lamb *et al.* (2008).

The study sites within the wide category of plane-bed streams moved particle sizes at bankfull flow that were up to twice the bed surface $D_{50}$ size at the most mobile sites and as small as half the bed surface $D_{50}$ at the less mobile sites. In contrast, the largest bankfull mobile particle sizes in steep channels were only 0.2–0.5 times the bed surface $D_{50}$, indicating that the bed $D_{50}$ particles can be mobilized only by extremely high flood events. Consequently, the critical shear stress required to move the bed surface $D_{50}$ ($\tau_{c50}^*$) would be higher (probably much higher) than values plotted for bankfull flow in Figure 26.8.

One could argue that roughness corrections of $R_{bf}$ to account for energy dissipation due to grain, form, and spill resistance on rough beds, in turn, would lower values for $\tau_{cbf}^*$ and $\tau_{c50}^*$. However, roughness correction values suitable for steep streams with their varied channel morphologies, particle-size distributions, and sediment supplies are neither easily available nor consistently applied. It thus appears that incipient motion predictions in steep channels would be better served by referring to high, back-calculated values of $\tau_{cbf}^*$ and $\tau_{c50}^*$ that are based on careful bedload measurements rather than to roughness-corrected values of $R_{bf}$ when computing mobile particle sizes for a specified flow or the critical flow for a specified particle size from a Shields-type approach.

### 26.8.2 *Discussion by Gordon Grant*

Here is a way to test whether the regular spacing between step pools results from hydraulic patterns established by

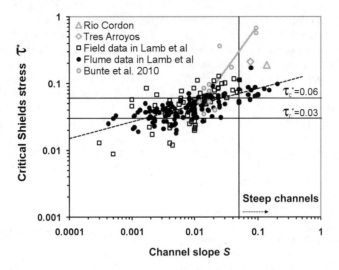

**Figure 26.8** Increase of critical Shield stress with increasing channel gradient. Base figure with black circles and open squares from Lamb *et al.* (2008) with modifications. Data plotted as gray-filled bullets refer to the studies by Bunte *et al.* 2010 (i.e., incipient motion conditions for the particle size mobilized at bankfull flows).

standing wave trains. The length scale for standing waves (*L*) or Kennedy wave number is given by:

$$L = \frac{2\pi v^2}{g} \tag{28.4}$$

If we assume (based on Grant, 1997) that at the step-forming discharge flow is near critical, then

$$Fr \approx 1 \approx \frac{v}{\sqrt{gy}} \tag{28.5}$$

Then

$$L = \frac{2\pi(gy)}{g} = 2\pi y \tag{28.6}$$

In other words, step spacing should be approximately equal to $2\pi$ times the critical or formative depth. This provides a first-order test of the standing wave train hypothesis. What do the data say?

### 26.8.3 Discussion by Jens Turowski

There is a need to differentiate between different types of hydrologic conditions in steep channels, and possibly in the formation of step pool sequences. In some streams, flood events capable of re-arranging the step pool morphology are driven by convective thunderstorms, which trigger a flashy response. For example, in the largest observed flood event on 20 June, 2007 in the Erlenbach, a small stream in the Swiss pre-Alps, which completely

re-arranged the step pool sequence, discharge increased from $5\,\mathrm{l\,s^{-1}}$ to $15000\,\mathrm{l\,s^{-1}}$ (a factor of 3000) within about half an hour (Turowski *et al.*, 2009). It is clear that in such an event no single discharge can be made uniquely responsible for the destruction of the old or the formation of the new step pool sequence. Other step pool channels may be driven by glacial meltwater. In such streams, discharge is typically slowly varying and an effective discharge approach may be suitable.

### 26.8.4 Reply by Francesco Comiti and Luca Mao

We are very glad that Kristine Bunte contributed to the discussion on incipient motion in high-gradient channels. The data she has added to the Lamb *et al.* (2008) graph are of great value as they are among the few field data available for steep channels. However, they represent critical Shields parameters for the grain sizes mobilized at bankfull stage which, as Bunte points out, were finer than $D_{50}$ in the steeper channels. Therefore, the actual value of the critical Shields parameter for the $D_{50}$ of the bed surface will strongly depend on the degree of size selectivity on the specific streams (exponent $b$ in Equation 26.2; see Mao *et al.*, 2008). Nonetheless, we agree with Bunte that the modelling of incipient sediment motion conditions in steep channels is sounder and more reliable when based on bedload transport measured in real streams. Also, it is quite clear that flume experiments carried out so far have not properly represented prototype conditions (both about hydrodynamics and sediment interactions) for steep channels.

As to the point raised by Gordon Grant on step spacing and standing waves, we agree that the assumption of critical conditions at the step-formation stage is absolutely reasonable, and potentially would enable us to look for a relation between step spacing and (critical) flow depth through the dimensions of standing waves ($L/h \sim 2\pi$, i.e., about 6), as was proposed by Comiti and Lenzi (2006). However, the problem is that the roller length in plunging flows also scales with the (subcritical sequent) flow depth with a similar coefficient (i.e., 5.7 for fully aerated flows, following Yasuda and Ohtsu, 2008; see also Valle and Pasternack 2006 for the distinction between submerged and unsubmerged jumps). Therefore, the mere existence of such a linear relation between step spacing and flow depth cannot be taken as an indication that steps also were formed by standing waves because the same relation would be consistent with formative models interpreting steps as depositional berms associated with roller jumps (e.g., Allen, 1983; Comiti et al., 2005; Comiti and Lenzi, 2006) or invoking exclusion zones where steps cannot form below stable steps due the turbulent stresses of hydraulic jumps (Curran and Wilcock, 2005). Indeed, we think that the widely observed inverse relation between channel slope and step spacing (Judd, 1963; Whittaker, 1987; Chin and Wohl, 2005) may at least partially be attributed to the fact that steeper channels present shallower flows (for similar discharges and channel width) and thus shorter standing waves/hydraulic jumps. However, steeper streams are also characterized by lower jamming ratios (i.e., channel width/grain diameter), which provides more chances for steps to be stable thanks to the denser presence of obstructions and bank-anchoring sites (Church and Zimmermann, 2007); that is, increasing the probability of shorter step spacing.

Finally, we agree with Jens Turowski on the relevance of the hydrologic regime to the morphological (and sediment) dynamics of steep channels. In streams featuring rapidly varying flow rates (flash flooding regime) the same step-pool geometry is likely to become destabilized at lower discharges (and thus more frequently, but always with a decadal time scale) than in snowmelt-dominated channels, where flood hydrographs are much flatter and thus the bed is subject to steadier flow variations possibly imparting higher stability to its structure. In fact, flume experiments have demonstrated that the history of antecedent flow conditions – including flows featuring stresses below the motion threshold – can strongly influence bed stability due to local particle rearrangement (Paphitis and Collins, 2005; Haynes and Pender, 2007). Still, the discharge associated with the instant when the step-pool sequence collapses can be considered the threshold for bed stability in either cases. However, as Turowski remarks, the discharge responsi-ble for shaping the new step-pool geometry cannot be regarded as a single value, but rather as a range, probably in both end-member flow regimes, because as the flood recedes steps keep on forming and collapsing until the bed is no longer movable by the flow. There is certainly a lack of knowledge on this topic, which should be explored in the field through long-term monitoring of step-pool reaches under different hydrological conditions. Also, further insights could be provided by step-pool formation/destruction flume experiments conducted under unsteady flow conditions, simulating hydrographs of different duration and magnitude.

## 26.9  DISCUSSION REFERENCES

Allen, J.R.L. 1983. A simplified cascade model for transverse stone-ribs in gravelly streams. Proceedings of the Royal Society of London **A385**: 253–266.

Bunte, K., Abt, S.R., Potyondy, J.P., and Ryan, S.E. 2004. Measurement of coarse gravel and cobble transport using a portable bedload trap. *Journal of Hydraulic Engineering* **130**: 879–893.

Bunte, K., Abt, S.R., Potyondy, J.P., and Swingle, K.W. 2008. A comparison of coarse bedload transport measured with bedload traps and Helley-Smith samplers. *Geodinamica Acta* **21**: 53–66.

Bunte, K., Abt, S.R., Swingle, K.W., and Potyondy, J.P. 2010. Bankfull mobile particle size and its predictions from a Shields-type approach. *Proceedings of the 4th Federal Interagency Hydrologic Modeling Conference and the 9th Federal Interagency Sedimentation Conference, Las Vegas, NV, 27 June–1 July, 2010. Session: sediment transport.* CD-ROM ISBN 978-0-9779007-3-2.

Bunte, K., Swingle, K., and Abt, S.R. 2007. *Guidelines for Using Bedload Traps in Coarse-bedded Mountain Streams: Construction, Installation, Operation and Sample Processing.* Fort Collins, CO, United States Department of Agriculture, Forest Service, Rocky Mountain Research Station, General Technical Report RMRS-GTR-191. http://www.agu.org/meetings/fm07/waisfm07.html.

Chin, A. and Wohl, E. 2005. Toward a theory for step-pools in stream channels. *Progress in Physical Geography* **29**: 275–296.

Church, M. and Zimmermann, A. 2007. Form and stability of step-pool channels: Research progress. *Water Resources Research* **43**: W03415. doi: 10.1029/2006wr005037.

Comiti, F. and Lenzi, M.A. 2006. Dimensions of standing waves at steps in mountain rivers. *Water Resources Research* **42**: W03411. doi: 10.1029/2004WR003898.

Comiti, F., Andreoli, A., and Lenzi, M.A. 2005. Morphological effects of local scouring in step-pool streams. *Earth Surface Processes and Landforms* **30**: 1567–1581.

Curran, J.C. and Wilcock, P.R. 2005. Characteristic dimensions of the step-pool configuration: an experimental study. *Water Resources Research* **41**: W02030. doi: 10.1029/2004WR003568.

Ferguson, R.I. 1986. River loads underestimated by rating curves. *Water Resources Research* **22**: 74–76.

Ferguson, R.I. 1987. Accuracy and precision of methods for estimating river loads. *Earth Surface Processes and Landforms* **12**: 95–104.

Grant, G.E. 1997. Critical flow constrains flow hydraulics in mobile-bed streams: A new hypothesis. *Water Resources Research* **33**: 349–358.

xHaynes, H. and Pender, G. 2007. Stress history effects on graded bed stability. *Journal of Hydraulic Engineering* **133**: 343–349.

Judd, H.E. 1963. *A study of bed characteristics in relation to flow in rough, high-gradient natural channels.* Ph.D. thesis, Utah State University, Logan, Utah.

Lamb, M.P., Dietrich, W.E., and Venditti, J.G. 2008. Is the critical Shields stress for incipient sediment motion dependent on channel-bed slope? *Journal of Geophysical Research* **113**: F02008. doi: 10.1029/2007JF000831.

Mao, L., Uyttendaele, G.P., Iroume, A., and Lenzi, M.A. 2008. Field based analysis of sediment entrainment in two high gradient streams located in Alpine and Andine environments. *Geomorphology* **93**: 368–383.

Paphitis, D. and Collins, M.B. 2005. Sand grain threshold, in relation to bed stress history: an experimental study. *Sedimentology* **52**: 827–838.

Turowski, J.M., Yager, E.M., Badoux, A., Rickenmann, D., and Molnar, P. 2009. The impact of exceptional events on erosion, bedload transport and channel stability in a step-pool channel. *Earth Surface Processes and Landforms* **34**: 1661–1673.

Valle, B. and Pasternack, G.B. 2006. Submerged and unsubmerged natural hydraulic jumps in a bedrock step-pool mountain channel. *Geomorphology* **82**: 146–159.

Whittaker, J.G. 1987. Sediment transport in step-pool streams. In Thorne, C.R., Bathurst, J.C.,and Hey, R.D., editors. *Sediment transport in gravel-bed rivers*. Chichester, John Wiley & Sons, Ltd, pp. 545–579.

Yasuda, Y. and Ohtsu, I. 2008. Flow characteristics of plunging flows in steep sloping channels with a horizontal channel portion. *Acta Mechanica* **201**: 95–104.

# 27

# Examining Individual Step Stability within Step-pool Sequences

### Joanna Crowe Curran

## 27.1 INTRODUCTION

Individual and step sequence stability lie at the nexus of a number of research topics in steep channels, including issues related to channel boundary roughness. While all steps in a step-pool sequence contribute to channel roughness, only stable steps can contribute in a predictable manner. If the number and spacing of steps frequently vary due to step instability, reliable estimates of total flow resistance and sediment transport rates through the channel during high flows will be difficult to develop. Information on step stability also has the potential to inform about the probability of step formation and destruction processes. For example, if the step destruction process under a known set of flow and sediment transport rates becomes predictable, the probability of step destruction for a given flow may become predictable. Because sediment transport rates have been shown to increase in the years immediately following a step destabilizing flow (Lenzi *et al.*, 2004; Turowski *et al.*, 2009), this type of predictability would prove useful. Pool development and scour depth are also related to step stability because a pool can form only while a step is stable. However, excessive scouring can also lead to step failure. The current research into pool formation and pool hydrodynamics is well summarized by Comiti and Mao (Chapter 26, this volume).

An exploration of step stability necessarily involves an examination of step formation and failure processes, and the role of step spacing. Step stability is hypothesized to be a function of these parameters as well as flow and sediment transport rates, and the ability of steps to adjust their location. This chapter summarizes the current state of research, and presents a new analysis of experimental data with the intention of furthering an understanding of individual and sequence step stability.

## 27.2 CURRENT RESEARCH

### 27.2.1 Steps

Full descriptions of the step-forming mechanisms are provided in Curran (2007) and well summarized by Comiti and Mao (Chapter 26, this volume). Step formation occurs by a limited number of processes. Most common is the rough-bed process, when the step-forming grain is arrested in its downstream transport by a rough patch on the bed surface. Also common is step exhumation, where the sediment around a step-forming grain is eroded and a formerly buried step becomes prominent in the channel profile. Approximately one-quarter of steps form at a berm (often referred to as a dune, due to its appearance) that develops downstream of an existing step and is in phase with a standing wave on the water surface.

An element essential to step formation and stability is a heterogeneous grain-size distribution which includes a large grain that can act as a step-forming grain (Tatsuzawa *et al.*, 1999; Comiti *et al.*, 2005; Curran and Wilcock, 2005; Weichert *et al.*, 2008; Zimmermann, 2009a). The size of the step-forming grain must be large enough such that a small number can span the channel width to form a step. This has been verified by both flume and field experiments, and is formulated as the jammed state hypothesis (Church and Zimmermann, 2007). In alluvial channels the step-forming grains are typically the largest clasts in the bed sediment. They are mobilized during large floods, causing step formation where they are able to create a jam across the channel width (Zimmermann, 2009b; Zimmermann *et al.*, 2010).

Hypothesized to be necessary for individual step stability is step sequence spacing that maximizes overall channel stability. This hypothesis has its roots in experiments by Abrahams *et al.* (1995), who developed a

*Gravel-bed Rivers: Processes, Tools, Environments*, First Edition. Edited by Michael Church, Pascale M. Biron and André G. Roy.
© 2012 John Wiley & Sons, Ltd. Published 2012 by John Wiley & Sons, Ltd.

relation between the ratio of step height to step spacing and channel bed slope, postulating that for maximum flow resistance a step sequence has a step height to step spacing ratio that is 1–2 times the channel slope, $S \leq H/L \leq 2S$. Step-pool sequences fit this relation when the distance between steps includes little to no tread, and is instead composed primarily of the pool (Church and Zimmermann, 2007; Weichert *et al.*, 2008). Flume experiments measuring the hydraulics of individual step-pool units found turbulence intensity and flow energy dissipation were at a maximum in the pool area immediately downstream of a step (Gimenez-Curto and Corniero, 2006; Pasternack *et al.*, 2006). The turbulent stresses generated by flows entering and exiting a pool establish a lower bound for the distance between sequential steps. The minimum measured step spacing, described as an exclusion zone, is often larger than the distance needed to maximize flow resistance over a step pool sequence (Gimenez-Curto and Corniero, 2003; Curran and Wilcock, 2005). A number of studies of steps in natural streams have recorded step spacing that is larger than the exclusion zone length, and thus does not fit the Abrahams relation despite the wide parameter range possible. These data have led many to question the validity of the Abrahams *et al.* relation (i.e., Chartrand and Whiting, 2000), and research continues to explore the parameters responsible for individual step stability, including the role and function of the pool (Zimmermann and Church, 2001; Comiti *et al.*, 2005).

### 27.2.2  Pools

Comiti *et al.* (2005) found that pools scour and develop so long as the upstream step remains stable. In the field, pool scour was extensive during floods lower in magnitude than those needed to mobilize the step-forming grain and subsequent to the step-forming flow (Lenzi *et al.*, 1999; Lenzi, 2001). As the pool scoured into the bed, step height increased. When unconstrained, pool scour continued until the step became over-steep and collapsed, with the step-forming grain toppling into the downstream pool (Rosport and Dittrich, 1995; Crowe, 2002). If steps were spaced closely together, the flow patterns between consecutive pools interfere to constrain the scour depth at the downstream step-pool pair (Lenzi *et al.*, 2003; Marion *et al.*, 2004; Comiti *et al.*, 2005). Pool interference increased the stability of the step toe on the upstream step and reduced the probability of step destruction through toppling. Under these conditions a step sequence develops with minimum spacing equal to the exclusion zone length and that fit the relation developed by Abrahams *et al.* (1995).

A stable step sequence formation process emerged from these observations. An initial step sequence is established during a large flood. Pools scour and any unstable steps are destroyed during smaller flood flows following the large flood. The resultant step sequence has lower step spacing and a hydraulic pattern that maximizes resistance in the channel, thus creating a stable step-pool sequence.

### 27.2.3  Step Failure

In flume studies, steps have been observed breaking and re-forming along the length of a channel so long as there is flow sufficient to mobilize the bed (Curran, 2007; Weichert *et al.*, 2008). Field studies have documented situations in which extreme floods caused destruction of entire step-pool sequences and in which smaller floods affected only a portion of steps, essentially re-arranging the step sequence and altering initial step spacing (Lenzi *et al.*, 1999; Lenzi, 2004; Turowski *et al.*, 2009). Turowski *et al.* (2009) report step-mobilizing floods in the Erlenbach for which over 90% of the steps were broken and re-arranged in two floods, while in the third, which had a lower discharge, only 30% of the steps were re-arranged. They were able to document the movement of individual boulders, including one boulder that was transported over a number of stable steps before depositing. This field evidence indicates that individual steps within a sequence can have different degrees of stability, allowing some steps to re-arrange while other steps remain stable.

## 27.3  NEW ANALYSES

A series of 17 feed flume experiments testing four discharge rates against five sediment transport rates provided an opportunity to document step formation and destruction processes, changes in step spacing, and step stability for over 300 steps. Previously, these data were examined to test hypotheses related to step spacing, and the experimental techniques are fully described elsewhere (Crowe, 2002; Curran and Wilcock, 2005; Curran, 2007). The data are now analysed for connections between step stability, step formation, and step failure. Step-forming grains were able to form jams across the channel width, but because the flume width was constant, the jammed state hypothesis (Zimmermann, 2009b) was not directly included in the analysis.

### 27.3.1  Step Failure

Four distinct methods of step destruction were observed during the flume experiments. They are divided into hydraulic and sediment categories, based on the interactions leading to step loss. Hydraulic processes are dominant in topple and burial loss mechanisms.

The topple mechanism occurs when a step becomes too steep due to extensive pool scour at its base. As a result, the step-forming grains at the step crest fall into the downstream pool and the remainder of the step form is eroded. Step burial occurs when sediment fills the pool and buries the step form. The hydraulics in the pool weaken, allowing deposition and the loss of the step. Burial is considered a step loss because the step is no longer apparent in the bed profile and does not contribute to channel resistance or step sequence spacing. Sediment interactions leading to step loss include slumping and impact mechanisms. During a step slump, the base of the step shifts forward into the pool and the step collapses. Step loss occurs as a result of processes internal to the step form and not related to the local hydraulics. Step destruction by impact occurs when a grain in transport impacts and dislodges the step-forming grain. The impact destabilizes the step bedform, causing it to collapse. Because the loss is dependent on the bedload transport, this is considered a loss mechanism dependent on sediment and not hydraulics. All the processes of step failure are illustrated in Figure 27.1.

Comiti and Mao (Chapter 26, this volume) identify upstream migrating headcuts that form following

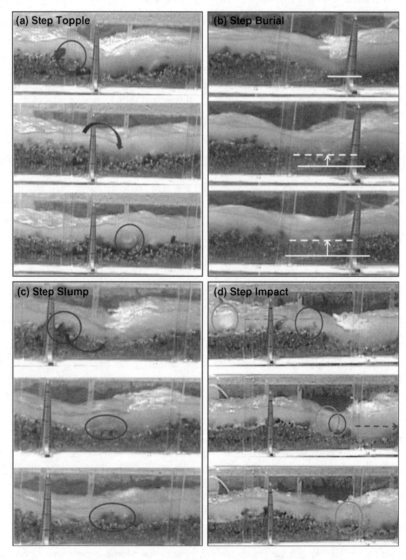

**Figure 27.1** Schematics of the step failure processes: (a) step over-steepens and topples into the pool; (b) step form is buried by sediment; (c) step form slumps into the pool; (d) step-forming grain is dislodged when impacted by sediment in transport.

downstream step failure as the most common step failure mechanism. Headcuts similar to those described were commonly observed during the experiments. When a headcut occurred, it was following a downstream step failure. As the headcut traveled upstream, it either instigated toppling of steps, where the headcut eroded into the base of the step, or ceased migration upon exhuming a buried step.

### 27.3.2 Step Stability

Step stability was measured as the length of time a step exists, and the longest lasting step from each run was considered to be the most stable step for that combination of flow and sediment transport rate (Table 27.1). When the discharge increased and sediment transport rate remained constant, decreasing the sediment concentration ratio $Q_s/Q$, average step stability decreased from 60 to 40% of run time. However, this trend was apparent only in the averaged data over the range of sediment transport rates at each flow and was not evident when comparing individual runs. Comparison between the individual experiments show that in all cases a single step existed for over 20% of the equilibrium run time and in one case, the stable step existed for 88% of the run time.

The process by which a step formed influenced the stability of that step, regardless of the sediment concentration ratio during step formation. The most stable steps in all the runs were formed by the rough-bed mechanism, while the least stable steps formed by the berm mechanism. The least stable steps in each run were those lasting less than three minutes, which corresponds to 1.2% of the median step existence time for steps from all the runs. These results indicate that interaction between sediment in transport and channel bed surface is an important factor for creating a stable step.

The experimental results also indicate that the probability of particular step failure processes is related to the sediment concentration ratio in the channel. In general, the failure of a step due to hydraulic forces was twice as frequent as failure due to sediment-related mechanisms. However, this was true only when all the steps formed

during the runs were used in the analysis. If steps existing for less than three minutes were removed from the data set, a different relation was observed, and sediment interaction mechanisms became more important at higher sediment concentration ratios. At the lowest sediment transport rate, which was also the lowest sediment concentration ratio, most steps were lost by toppling, a hydraulic loss process. With an increase in sediment transport rate and concentration ratio, steps were destroyed first through a combination of toppling and impact, then by a combination of burial and slumps. As sediment transport rates and concentrations reached a maximum, slumping became the dominant loss mechanism. Thus, the step destruction shifted from dependence on hydraulic forces to sediment interaction as the sediment concentration ratio increased.

Step burial and pool filling during flows under high sediment supply rates have been observed in field studies (Church and Zimmermann, 2007). The step-pool sequence re-developed as pools eroded and steps were excavated during flows subsequent to the extreme flood that buried the step-pool sequence. The importance of burial as a step loss mechanism under high sediment rates verifies the importance of pool scour in defining a step sequence in the channel profile.

### 27.3.3 Step Stability and Spacing

Whether the spacing between adjacent steps was equal to or greater than the exclusion zone may be a factor in the stability of the upstream and downstream steps. To evaluate the role that step spacing has on stability, the spacing of the most stable step relative to steps immediately upstream and downstream was examined for each run. The distance from the stable step to the closest upstream step was compared to the average step spacing for each run. In all but two cases, the spacing for the most stable step was shorter than the run average. When compared to the average spacing to the closest downstream step, 10 of the 17 runs had downstream step spacing shorter than the average. At first glance, it appeared that step stability was enhanced when the step

**Table 27.1**  Existence of the most stable step as a percentage of run time

| Discharge $Q_s$ | $0.0046 \, \mathrm{m^3 \, s^{-1}}$ | $0.0050 \, \mathrm{m^3 \, s^{-1}}$ | $0.0055 \, \mathrm{m^3 \, s^{-1}}$ | $0.0065 \, \mathrm{m^3 \, s^{-1}}$ | Average for $Q_s \, [\mathrm{gm^{-1} \, s^{-1}}]$ |
|---|---|---|---|---|---|
| $110 \, \mathrm{gm^{-1} \, s^{-1}}$ | 44.6 | 87.7 | | 23.3 | 51.9 |
| $475 \, \mathrm{gm^{-1} \, s^{-1}}$ | | 53.6 | 23.3 | | 38.5 |
| $750 \, \mathrm{gm^{-1} \, s^{-1}}$ | 63.2 | 46.2 | 74.3 | 65.2 | 55.1 |
| $1000 \, \mathrm{gm^{-1} \, s^{-1}}$ | 73.6 | 52.4 | 38.8 | 32.9 | 49.1 |
| $1250 \, \mathrm{gm^{-1} \, s^{-1}}$ | | 30.6 | 43.8 | | 37.2 |
| Average for Q $[\mathrm{m^3 \, s^{-1}}]$ | 60.5 | 49.3 | 45.1 | 40.5 | |

was consistently part of a step sequence. However, the evidence for this is complicated by the lack of an upstream or downstream step neighbouring the stable step for much of the run duration. An upstream step existed for more than half the run time for only six of the 17 experiments and a downstream step was present for over half the run time in seven of the 17 runs. On average, there was only one step neighbouring the stable step for 53% of total run time in the experiments. It was when there was a neighboring upstream step that the difference between the stable step spacing was less than the average step spacing during that run.

Across all experiments the most stable step was a step not static in its location. The centre of the step form was able to adjust or shift its location within its immediate area, both in the upstream and downstream directions. Adjustments were within the 30 cm exclusion zone defined for these experiments, and typically limited to a range between 10 and 30 cm. Where the step-forming grains were stable, but not positioned at the step face, the pool eroded to move the location of the step upstream. Erosion did not mobilize the step-forming grains, but instead shifted the mass of the step upstream by removing less-stable sediment from the step face. When the step shifts in the downstream direction, it was the result of one of two possible scenarios. Deposition at the face of the

step shifted the step location downstream by increasing the upstream step tread. More commonly, the step-forming grains rotated downstream, causing the step position to shift through a small slumping motion. The step-forming grains remained, but shifted into a more stable configuration. Figure 27.2 illustrates the existence of each step during 80 minutes of a flume run and provides an example of how individual steps can remain stationary or alter their position and spacing over time. The most stable step observed during this run is marked by the highlighted path.

Limited step mobility was evaluated for its importance to overall step stability by comparing the rate of step adjustment of stable and unstable steps. The number of adjustments by a stable step was scaled by the existence time of that step and compared to the average number of adjustments by all the steps scaled by the existence time for all steps (Table 27.2). Under each combination of flow and sediment transport rate, the number of location adjustments by the most stable step was greater than the average number per step. A total of 38% of all steps were immobile in their position, and these were the shortest lived steps during every run, regardless of step formation or failure mechanism. The rate of step adjustment was recalculated after removing from the dataset those steps with no position adjustments. The results were the same,

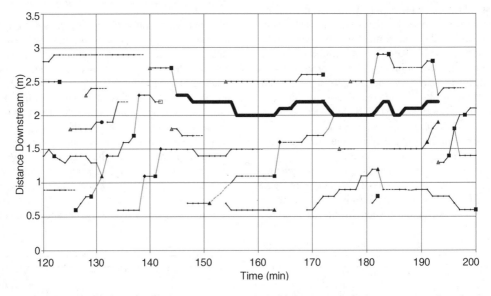

**Figure 27.2** Example of the temporal and spatial distribution of steps, step-formation processes, and step failure processes during 80 minutes of a flume run where $Q = 0.005 \, \mathrm{m}^3 \, \mathrm{s}^{-1}$ and $Q_s = 1000 \, \mathrm{gm}^{-1} \, \mathrm{s}^{-1}$. The longest lasting or most stable step is shown as a thick solid line. Step-formation processes: ◆ black diamond for rough bed; △ gray triangle for berm; dashed line when a step is excavated. Step break-up processes: ■ black square for slump; ▲ black triangle for topple; dashed line when a step is buried. Interactions between steps: dashed line represents the burial and excavation process; solid black line when a step migrates; gray line when the break-up of a step causes a step-forming grain to travel downstream or a knick-point to travel upstream.

**Table 27.2** Comparison of the average time span of mobile and immobile steps as a percent of total run time

| $Q[\mathrm{m}^3\,\mathrm{s}^{-1}]$ | $Q_s[\mathrm{gm}^{-1}\,\mathrm{s}^{-1}]$ | $Q_s/Q$ | $\tilde{\tau}/\tau_c$ | % immobile steps | Time span of immobile steps [%] | Time span of mobile steps [%] | Ratio of time spans of immobile to mobile steps |
|---|---|---|---|---|---|---|---|
| 0.0046 | 110 | 1.35 | 1.15 | 20 | 9.2 | 16.8 | 1.8 |
| 0.0050 | 110 | 1.25 | 1.23 | 39 | 4.3 | 22.0 | 5.1 |
| 0.0065 | 110 | 0.96 | 0.72 | 16 | 9.2 | 12.9 | 1.4 |
| 0.0050 | 475 | 5.38 | 0.80 | 29 | 5.9 | 10.8 | 1.4 |
| 0.0055 | 475 | 4.89 | 1.07 | 46 | 4.9 | 6.7 | 1.8 |
| 0.0046 | 750 | 9.23 | 1.10 | 29 | 12.8 | 17.4 | 1.4 |
| 0.0050 | 750 | 8.49 | 1.09 | 42 | 4.2 | 8.9 | 2.1 |
| 0.0050 | 750 | 8.49 | 1.23 | 28 | 3.2 | 7.7 | 2.4 |
| 0.0055 | 750 | 7.72 | 1.02 | 47 | 26.0 | 13.4 | 1.9 |
| 0.0065 | 750 | 6.53 | 0.95 | 48 | 13.0 | 23.5 | 1.8 |
| 0.0046 | 1000 | 12.31 | 1.07 | 50 | 13.7 | 30.2 | 2.2 |
| 0.0050 | 1000 | 11.32 | 1.10 | 50 | 15.1 | 28.6 | 1.9 |
| 0.0050 | 1000 | 11.32 | 1.06 | 28 | 5.2 | 11.6 | 2.2 |
| 0.0055 | 1000 | 10.29 | 1.08 | 50 | 5.1 | 11.6 | 2.3 |
| 0.0065 | 1000 | 8.71 | 1.23 | 32 | 10.7 | 16.3 | 1.5 |
| 0.0050 | 1250 | 14.15 | 1.10 | 52 | 4.4 | 9.1 | 2.1 |
| 0.0055 | 1250 | 12.86 | 0.80 | 52 | 4.6 | 8.8 | 1.9 |

All values are scaled by the existence time for step(s) in the run. Sediment concentration ratio $Q_s/Q$ and transport stage $\tilde{\tau}/\tau_c$ are also provided.

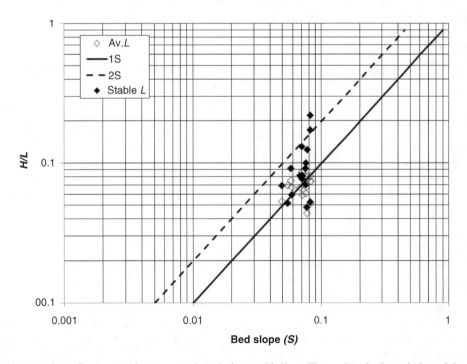

**Figure 27.3** Data from flume experiments are plotted along with lines illustrating the boundaries of the Abrahams relation, $S \leq H/L \leq 2S$. Hollow diamonds are calculated using average step height and average step spacing for each run. Solid diamonds are calculated using average step height and the spacing of the most stable step.

showing that the most stable steps were distinguished by a greater number of position shifts than the average of all step adjustments during each run. Immobile steps typically existed for between one and five minutes, or 4–15% of the run time. In contrast, mobile steps were stable for 9–30% of the run time. The data showed an increase of 50–100% in the stability of steps that were able to adjust their location during a run.

These experimental data were fit to the Abrahams *et al.* (1995) geometric relation, which has been hypothesized to be a definition of the step sequence geometry needed to maximize flow resistance in a steep channel. Using run-averaged step spacing and step heights, the experimental data clustered around and below the line for $H/L = S$ (Figure 27.3). When the spacing of the most stable step was used in place of the run-averaged spacing, the data plot across the stability range defined by Abrahams *et al.* (1995), with a majority of the data between $S$ and $2S$. Because the average step height for each run was used rather than the step height associated with the most stable step, it is possible that the data could provide a stronger fit to the Abrahams relation than the one shown. Regardless, these data indicated that the stability of the longest-lasting steps may be related to flow resistance generated by local step sequence geometry.

The ability of the step to shift its position appears to be a necessary characteristic for step stability. This observation aligns with field observations from the Italian Alps and the Swiss Prealps. In the Erlenbach, a flood was documented during which only a portion of the steps in the channel were removed, essentially re-setting the step spacing (Turowski *et al.*, 2009). Step geometry immediately following a step-mobilizing flood on the Rio Cordon in 1994 plotted outside the area of maximum flow resistance defined by the Abrahams relation. Individual steps were re-worked and their locations altered during lower flows following the large flood and the resulting step geometry better fit the Abrahams relation (Lenzi *et al.*, 1999; Lenzi, 2001).

## 27.4  SUMMARY

Step-pool sequences have been shown to re-arrange selectively during flows that mobilize only a portion of the steps, but the factors causing some steps to be lost or to change position while other steps remain stable are not well known. This paper explores the parameters important to the stability of individual steps within a step sequence.

Processes of step formation and destruction related to step stability, but did not appear to be the only controlling influence. Both field and flume studies documented a progression in step formation and failure mechanisms as sediment concentration increased. Step formation was predominantly through the rough bed process, although the berm process became more common at high sediment concentrations. When sediment transport rates were low, step loss was through toppling, a process related to local hydraulics and pool scour. As sediment concentrations increased, loss processes associated with sediment mechanisms were more prevalent.

Step stability showed a strong dependence on the ability of the step to adjust its immediate location. These adjustments did not mobilize the step-forming grains, but instead shifted the bulk of the step form within an area defined by the size of the exclusion zone. Those steps able to adjust their position existed 50–100% longer than steps that were immobile. The longest lasting, and therefore most stable, steps observed during the flume experiments all shifted in position, illustrating the connection between step stability and mobility. Immobile steps were quickly destroyed. Spacing between stable steps was smaller than the average step spacing for each flume experiment and, when applied to the Abrahams relation, a majority of the data plot within the area theorized to be the step geometry providing maximum flow resistance. In a natural river subject to floods of varying magnitudes, immobile steps may form during a step setting flood and then be removed under subsequent lower-magnitude floods that also enable mobile steps to adjust location. Final step sequence spacing is related most strongly to the spacing of the mobile steps, making these steps of greater importance for understanding steep channel processes.

## 27.5  ACKNOWLEDGEMENTS

The original experimental work was supported by a United States Environmental Protection Agency STAR Graduate Fellowship. The flume work was made possible with the help of Anna Johnson, Brendan DeTemple, Keith Ritchie, and Sean Smith. The author is very grateful to Peter Wilcock, Andre Zimmermann and Francesco Comiti for continuing discussions about the nature of step-pool systems and their comments on this work in particular.

## 27.6  REFERENCES

Abrahams, A.D., Li, G., and Atkinson, J.F. 1995. Step-pool streams: adjustment to maximum flow resistance. *Water Resources Research* **31**: 2593–2602.

Chartrand, S.M. and Whiting, P.J. 2000. Alluvial architecture in headwater streams with special emphasis on step-pool topography. *Earth Surface Processes and Landforms* **25**: 583–600.

Church, M. and Zimmermann, A. 2007. Form and stability of step-pool channels: research progress. *Water Resources Research* **43**: W03415. doi: 10.1029/2006WR005037.

Comiti, F., Andreoli, A., and Lenzi, M.A. 2005. Morphological effects of local scouring in step-pool streams. *Earth Surface Processes and Landforms* **30**: 1567–1581.

Crowe, J.C. 2002. *An experimental study of the step-pool bed form*. Ph.D. thesis. The Johns Hopkins University, Baltimore, MD.

Curran, J.C. 2007. Step-pool formation models and associated step spacing. *Earth Surface Processes and Landforms* **32**: 1611–1627.

Curran, J.C. and Wilcock, P.R. 2005. Characteristic dimensions of the step-pool bed configuration: an experimental study. *Water Resources Research* **42**: W02030. doi: 10.1029/2004WR003568.

Gimenez-Curto, L.A. and Corniero, M.A. 2003. Highest natural bed forms. *Journal of Geophysical Research* **108**: 3046. doi: 10.1029/2002JC001474.

Gimenez-Curto, L.A. and Corniero, M.A. 2006. Comment on "Characteristic dimensions of the step-pool bed configuration: An experimental study" by Joanna C. Curran and Peter R. Wilcock. *Water Resources Research* **42**: W03601. doi: 10.1029/2005WR004296.

Lenzi, M.A. 2001. Step-pool evolution in the Rio Cordon, Northeastern Italy. *Earth Surface Processes and Landforms* **26**: 991–1008.

Lenzi, M.A. 2004. Displacement and transport of marked pebbles, cobbles, and boulders during floods in a steep mountain stream. *Hydrological Processes* **18**: 1899–1914.

Lenzi, M.A., D'Agostino, V., and Billi, P. 1999. Bedload transport in the instrumented catchment of the Rio Cordon, Part I: Analysis of bedload records, conditions and threshold of bedload entrainment. *Catena* **36**: 171–190.

Lenzi, M.A., Mao, L., and Comiti, F. 2004. Magnitude-frequency analysis of bed load data in an Alpine boulder bed stream. *Water Resources Research* **40**: W07201. doi: 10.1029/2003WR002961.

Lenzi, M.A., Marion, A., and Comiti, F. 2003. Interference processes on scouring at bed sills. *Earth Surface Processes and Landforms* **28**: 99–110.

Marion, A., Lenzi, M.A. and Comiti, F. 2004. Effect of sediment size grading and sill spacing on scouring at grade-control structures. *Earth Surface Processes and Landforms* **29**: 983–993.

Pasternack, G.B., Ellis, C.R., Leier, K.A., Valle, B.L., and Marr, J.D. 2006. Convergent hydraulics at horseshoe steps in bedrock rivers. *Geomorphology* **82**: 126–145.

Rosport, M. and Dittrich, A. 1995. Step-pool formation and stability - a flume study.In Varma, C.V.J. and Rao, A.R.G., editors. *Sixth International Symposium on River Sedimentation, New Delhi, India, 7–11 November*. International Research and Training Centre on Erosion and Sedimentation, pp. 525–532.

Tatsuzawa, H., Hayashi, H., and Hasegawa, K. 1999. Role of heterogeneous property of bed materials in the formation of step-pool systems in mountain streams. *Journal of Hydroscience and Hydraulic Engineering* **17**: 37–45.

Turowski, J.M., Yager, E.M., Badoux, A., Rickenmann, D., and Molnar, P. 2009. The impact of exceptional events on erosion, bedload transport and channel stability in a step-pool channel. *Earth Surface Processes and Landforms* **34**: 1661–1673.

Weichert, R.B., Bezzola, G.R., and Minor, H.E. 2008. Bed morphology and generation of step-pool channels. *Earth Surface Processes and Landforms* **33**: 1678–1692.

Zimmermann, A.E. 2009a. *Experimental investigations of step-pool channel formation and stability. Ph.D. thesis*. The University of British Columbia, Vancouver, BC.

Zimmermann, A.E. 2009b. Step-pool formation and stability experiments. *33rd IAHR Congress: Water engineering for a sustainable environment*: International Association of Hydraulic Engineering and Research (IAHR) pp. 3431–3438.

Zimmermann, A. and Church, M. 2001. Channel morphology, gradient profiles and bed stresses during flood in a step-pool channel. *Geomorphology* **40**: 311–327.

Zimmermann, A., Church, M., and Hassan, M.A. 2010. Step-pool stability: testing the jammed state hypothesis. *Journal of Geophysical Research* **115**: F02008. doi: 10.1029/2009JF001365.

# 28

# Alluvial Steep Channels: Flow Resistance, Bedload Transport Prediction, and Transition to Debris Flows

## Dieter Rickenmann

## 28.1 INTRODUCTION

Studies on flow resistance in steep streams and shallow flows have received increasing attention in recent decades. However, for mountain rivers, characterized by coarse bed materials and steep slopes, traditional flow resistance relations generally provide poor predictions, with typical errors of $\pm 30\%$ (Bathurst, 2002). Several studies have shown that the traditional semi-logarithmic equation used to estimate flow resistance in deeper flows in more gently sloped channels may no longer be valid for shallow flows. Instead a power-law type flow resistance relation may be more appropriate for steeper and rougher channels:

$$\sqrt{\frac{8}{f}} = a\left(\frac{d}{D_x}\right)^b \tag{28.1}$$

wherein $f$ = Darcy–Weisbach flow resistance coefficient, $d$ = flow depth, $D_x$ = grain size of the bed material for which $x\%$ is finer, $a$ = empirical coefficient, and $b$ = empirical exponent. The exponent $b$ tends to increase from about 0 or 1/6 (Chezy equation or Manning–Strickler equation) up to about 1 for steep channels, i.e. it tends to increase with increasing bed slope and decreasing relative flow depth (Ferguson, 2007; Rickenmann and Recking, 2011); the exponent may possibly also decrease with increasing uniformity of the bed material distribution (Bathurst, 2002). Power-law type flow resistance relations can be transformed into dimensionless hydraulic geometry equations (Ferguson, 2007), which have been increasingly proposed for steep channels based both on flume and field observations (Aberle and Smart, 2003; Ferguson, 2007; Comiti et al., 2007,

2009; Zimmermann, 2010; Comiti and Mao, Chapter 26, this volume). Rickenmann (1991, 1994) introduced similar approaches, and Rickenmann and Recking (2011) have confirmed the suitability of such an approach based on more than 3000 field measurements, including rough and steep streams.

Flume experiments on bedload transport in steep channels basically show that traditional bedload transport equations can be extrapolated to steeper channels (Mizuyama, 1978; Smart and Jäggi, 1983; Rickenmann, 1991; Recking et al., 2008). However, in all these experiments macro-roughness bed structures have been largely absent, grain-size distributions of the bed material were rather uniform, and all grain sizes in the bed were typically in motion during the bedload transport measurements. However, several studies have demonstrated that observed bedload transport in natural steep streams can be several orders of magnitude smaller than those predicted by the laboratory-based transport equations (D'Agostino and Lenzi, 1999; Rickenmann, 2001; Barry et al., 2004; Rickenmann and Koschni, 2010). Likely reasons for this discrepancy are increased flow resistance (Rickenmann, 2001; Zimmermann, 2010) or a strong armour layer development, including imbrication, clustering, and particle wedging, all of which increase the structural stability of the bed and limit the sediment availability (Barry et al., 2004; Hassan et al., 2005; Bathurst, 2007). Although it may be difficult to discern which factors are most responsible for the under-prediction of transport rates in steep channels, approaches to account for the reduced energy available for transport (as compared to flows with larger relative flow depths) have shown some success in improving bedload transport predictions in steep streams (Govers and Rauws, 1986;

*Gravel-bed Rivers: Processes, Tools, Environments*, First Edition. Edited by Michael Church, Pascale M. Biron and André G. Roy.
© 2012 John Wiley & Sons, Ltd. Published 2012 by John Wiley & Sons, Ltd.

Palt, 2001; Rickenmann, 2005; Rickenmann et al., 2006; Yager et al., 2007; Badoux and Rickenmann, 2008; Chiari et al., 2010; Chiari and Rickenmann, 2010).

Direct observations of flow and sediment transporting characteristics in steep streams with bed slopes $S$ steeper than about 0.1 are limited, and understanding of the processes governing the transition from fluvial bedload transport to debris flows is poor. For $S > 0.20$ to 0.25, a streambed saturated with water is close to the limit for a soil mechanical instability which may lead to debris-flow initiation (Takahashi, 1991). Some support for this theoretical limit is provided by the observations of Smart and Jäggi (1983) in their flume experiments on bedload transport, in which the mobile bed became unstable, resulting in a debris-flow-like transport behaviour at $S = 0.25$. In addition, in steep headwater catchments a process type intermediate between fluvial sediment transport and debris flow may occur during rainstorm events, namely "debris floods" (Hungr et al., 2001) or "hyperconcentrated flow" (Costa, 1984). While the former term is more typically used in steep channels with relatively coarse material, the latter refers to flows with high fine-sediment concentrations. Some authors have proposed a rough distinction amongst floods, hyperconcentrated flows (or debris floods), and debris or mud flows based on sediment concentration, however Pierson and Costa (1987) and Hungr et al. (2001) point out that the limiting sediment concentration may be highly variable and may depend, for example, on sediment composition and mean flow velocity. Debris flows typically travel in surges, the frontal part commonly having higher sediment concentrations and carrying more coarse particles than the rear part of the surge, and the flow behaviour may change to debris flood and flood flow conditions towards the tail of a surge.

The objective of this paper is to discuss the importance of including proper estimates of flow resistance in bedload transport calculations and to examine some aspects related to the transition to debris flows. Both issues are addressed from a partly quantitative perspective, and thus expand the discussion presented in Comiti and Mao (Chapter 26, this volume). The first part deals with the increase in flow resistance in steep and rough streams, and presents an approach to partition between a "base-level" and a "macro-roughness" flow resistance. In the second part the flow resistance partitioning approach is applied to a data set of bedload transport in steep channels, and it is shown that the flow resistance partitioning approach improves bedload transport prediction in steep and rough streams. The third part illustrates that bedload transport rates and event sediment yields tend to increase in a continuous way without "jumps" in relations between the sediment transport and flow during the transition from fluvial bedload transport to debris flows.

A comparison of mean flow velocities in clear water flows and debris flows further suggests that there may be a continuous transition between the two processes.

## 28.2 FLOW RESISTANCE AND BEDLOAD TRANSPORT

### 28.2.1 Flow Resistance and Flow Resistance Partitioning in Steep Channels

Total flow resistance in gravel-bed streams has been divided into "grain" and "form" resistance, the latter term often including other sources of resistance such as spill drag, variation in cross-section geometry and flow width, and woody debris (Meyer-Peter and Müller, 1948; Parker and Peterson, 1980; Carson and Griffiths, 1987; Carson, 1987; Gomez and Church, 1989; Millar and Quick, 1994; Millar 1999). According to these studies, only the "grain" resistance part should be taken into account for bedload transport calculations, since a part of the flow energy is "lost" to form resistance. The concept of flow-resistance partitioning was also proposed for application in large lowland rivers with large relative flow depths (Einstein and Barbarossa, 1952). The topic of flow resistance partitioning is also addressed by Comiti and Mao (Chapter 26, this volume), and they particularly refer to the study of Zimmermann (2010) on flow resistance in steep channels with flume experiments including a wide range of flow conditions. Zimmermann (2010) did not observe any substantial variation in the friction factor during the development of a step pool morphology starting from a plane bed, assumed to represent grain resistance only. He concluded that the traditional concept of separating grain and form resistance does not make sense for shallow flows in steep streams. Indeed, in steep and rough streams it appears to be difficult to distinguish between grain and form resistance, since larger particles are also part of the bed, of macro-roughness elements and of the "bank", and may contribute to different types of resistance.

However, the importance to account for additional energy "losses" (or increased total flow resistance) in steep streams in the context of bedload transport calculations has been pointed out in several studies (Govers and Rauws, 1986; Palt, 2001; Rickenmann, 2001, 2005; Yager et al., 2007; Rickenmann and Koschni, 2010; Chiari et al., 2010; Zimmermann, 2010). In some of these studies, concepts similar to the grain/form resistance partitioning in lowland rivers were also applied in steep streams with some success. One of the major challenges in using this concept in steep streams is to quantify the additional flow resistance which reduces the flow energy available for bedload transport. Bedload transport equations for steep channels were typically developed and calibrated with flume experiments, where grain flow resistance was prevalent and macro-roughness bed elements were absent. Therefore traditional sediment transport formulas overestimate sediment transport rates in steep streams where most of the flow energy is lost to form and spill drag (Zimmermann, 2010). Both mean flow velocity and turbulence intensity near the bed were found to decrease with decreasing relative flow depth $d/D_x$ (Bayazit, 1976; Carollo et al., 2005; Lamb, et al., 2008), which may be important for bedload transport in steep and rough streams. According to the above discussion, some of the previous approaches to correct for over-estimation of bedload transport in steeper streams (e.g. Palt, 2001; Rickenmann, 2005; Chiari et al., 2010) can be considered as an attempt to separate between a base-level resistance and macro-roughness (sum of additional) flow resistance (Rickenmann and Recking, 2011), the latter type normally not being accounted for with traditional bedload transport formulas. The terminology of grain/form resistance partitioning as it was used in these reports appears incorrect, although the selected approach may still be valid.

As pointed out by Comiti and Mao (Chapter 26, this volume) steep channels are characterized by very low relative flow depth, with macro-roughness conditions possibly prevailing also during normal flood events. For example, in tumbling flow, flow conditions alternate between super- and subcritical along the channel. Associated hydraulic jumps lead to spill resistance and to a substantial increase in total flow resistance as compared to deeper flows in channels with milder bed slopes. Comiti et al. (2009) performed flume experiments replicating natural steep channel conditions, for which they also observed a transition to skimming flow conditions (with slightly supercritical Froude numbers). In these experiments, a sharp decrease in flow resistance at the transition from tumbling to skimming flow was documented. Comiti and Mao (Chapter 26, this volume) report a number of other studies which hypothesized that a decrease in flow resistance could occur when steps become submerged. However, they also mention experimental tests by Lee and Ferguson (2002) which did not support this assumption. Lee and Ferguson speculated that as smaller clasts are submerged, and wake-interference flow gives way to skimming flow, the reduction in total resistance is presumably more important than any increase in spill resistance in large hydraulic jumps over steps at high flows.

Ferguson (2007) presented a detailed discussion of the application of dimensionless hydraulic geometry equations in steep channel flows with small relative flow depths. Application of such an approach in steep and rough streams is also recommended by Comiti et al. (2007, 2009), Zimmermann (2010), and Comiti and Mao (Chapter 26, this volume). Ferguson (2007) used the dimensionless variables $U^* = U/(gD_{84})^{0.5}$ and $q^* = q/(gD_{84}{}^3)^{0.5}$ and proposed a flow resistance equation of the form:

$$U^* = kq^{*m}S^{(1-m)/2} \tag{28.2}$$

wherein $U =$ mean flow velocity, $g =$ gravitational acceleration, $D_{84} =$ grain size of the bed material for which 84% is finer, $q =$ discharge per unit channel width, $S =$ bed slope, $k =$ dimensionless coefficient, and $m =$ exponent. He also pointed to the equivalence between Equations (28.1) and (28.2) through the continuity equation, implying the following relations: $k = a^{(1-m)}$, $m = (2b+1)/(2b+3)$, and $b = (3m-1)/(2-2m)$. Ferguson showed that in Equation (28.2) $m$ varies from a value close to 0.33 (Chezy equation: $m = 0.33$; Manning–Strickler equation: $m = 0.4$) to a value close to 0.6 (steep channels), with a likely smooth transition from one domain to another. Rickenmann and Recking (2011) rearranged Equation (28.2) and defined two slightly modified dimensionless variables $U^{**} = U/(gSD_{84})^{0.5}$ and $q^{**} = q/(gSD_{84}{}^3)^{0.5}$, resulting in:

$$U^{**} = kq^{**m} \tag{28.3}$$

and

$$\frac{d}{D_{84}} = k^{-1}q^{**(1-m)} \tag{28.4}$$

They used a data set consisting of 2890 field measurements covering a wide range of flow conditions, with $0.01 < q^{**} < 8.1 \times 10^7$ and with $0.09 < (d/D_{84}) < 23000$. They found a reasonable similarity collapse when plotting both $U^{**}$ versus $q^{**}$ and $(d/D_{84})$ versus $q^{**}$, with a smooth transition from flows with larger to lower relative flow depths. A major advantage of the $U^{**}$ versus $q^{**}$ representation is to show that and how the exponent $m$ changes with decreasing values of $(d/D_{84})$ or $q^{**}$. The similarity collapse of the data using $U^{**}$ and $q^{**}$ supports the distinction of different roughness scales and facilitates comparison of between-site and at-a-site flow resistance. These aspects and the potential problem of spurious correlation between the new dimensionless variables are discussed in Rickenmann and Recking (2011).

Rickenmann and Recking (2011) evaluated several flow resistance equations, for cases of both a given flow depth and a given flow discharge, and concluded that the variable power equation (VPE) of Ferguson (2007) gave the best overall performance:

$$\sqrt{\frac{8}{f}} = \frac{a_1 a_2 (d/D_{84})}{\sqrt{a_1^2 + a_2^2 (d/D_{84})^{5/3}}} \tag{28.5}$$

wherein the coefficients $a_1 = 6.5$ and $a_2 = 2.5$ were used. Equation (28.5) represents a combination of Equation (28.1) with $b_1 = 1/6$ for small-scale roughness, and with $b_2 = 1$ for large-scale roughness, *sensu* Bathurst *et al.* (1981). Using the new dimensionless variables $U^{**}$ and $q^{**}$, the corresponding equations are given by Equation (28.3) with $k_1 = 3.074$ and $m_1 = 0.4$ for small-scale roughness, and with $k_2 = 1.443$ and $m_2 = 0.6$ for large-scale roughness, respectively. The advantage of transforming Equation (28.5) into the domain of Equation (28.3) is that this allows one to obtain an explicit version of the VPE for the case of given discharge $q$. To do so, the logarithmic matching technique, as proposed by Guo (2002) was used. The power law equations given by Equation (28.3) form the end members of a composite functional relation $U^{**} = \varphi(q^{**})$, and Equation (28.5) is used to determine the value of the ordinate at the intersection point of the two straight lines in the log-log plot. The resulting logarithmic matching equation is:

$$U^{**} = \frac{U_{tot}}{\sqrt{gSD_{84}}} = 1.443\, q^{**0.60} \left[ 1 + \left( \frac{q^{**}}{43.78} \right)^{0.8214} \right]^{-0.2435}$$

(28.6)

The exponent $m_1 = 0.4$ for small-scale roughness is largely constant for $q^{**} > 100$. The limiting value $q^{**} \approx 100$ corresponds approximately to the range $7 > (d/D_{84}) \geq 4$ in terms of Equation (28.4). In other words, for $q^{**} < 100$ the flow conditions are associated with intermediate- and large-scale roughness, according to Bathurst *et al.* (1981). Rickenmann and Recking (2011) assume that a base-level resistance is defined by the flow conditions with small-scale roughness, i.e., by Equation (28.3) with the values of $k_1$ and $m_1$:

$$U^{**} = \frac{U_o}{\sqrt{gSD_{84}}} = 3.074\, q^{**0.4}$$

(28.7)

In terms of Equation (28.1), base-level resistance is defined accordingly by a Manning–Strickler-type approach with the values of $a_1$ and $b_1$:

$$\sqrt{\frac{8}{f}} = 6.5 \left( \frac{d}{D_{84}} \right)^{1/6}$$

(28.8)

This assumption is analogous to estimates of "grain" or "base-level" resistance using the equation $(1/n_o) = p/D_{90}^{1/6}$ with a coefficient $p = 20$ to $22$ (Jäggi, 1984) and $p = 23.2$ (Wong and Parker, 2006), where $n_o$ = Manning's roughness coefficient related to "grain" resistance, and $D_{90}$ = grain size of the bed material for which 90% is finer. By extrapolating the power-law flow resistance Equation (28.7) for the domain $q^{**} > 100$ with small-scale roughness to the domain $q^{**} < 100$ with

intermediate- and large-scale roughness, Rickenmann and Recking (2011) proposed the following flow resistance partitioning in terms of $(f_o/f_{tot})^{0.5}$, where $f_o$ is associated with the "base-level" resistance, $(1 - f_{tot})$ is associated with the "macro-roughness" resistance, and $f_{tot}$ represents the total flow resistance:

$$\sqrt{\frac{8}{f_o}} = \frac{U_o(q)^{1.5}}{(gqS)^{0.5}}$$

(28.9)

where $U_o$ is calculated with Equation (28.7). Total flow resistance is calculated with the predicted velocity $U$ using the logarithmic matching Equation (28.6):

$$\sqrt{\frac{8}{f_{tot}}} = \frac{U_{tot}(q)^{1.5}}{(gqS)^{0.5}}$$

(28.10)

wherein $f_{tot}$ is the corresponding friction factor representing total flow resistance. Partitioning between base-level ($f_o$) and total resistance ($f_{tot}$) is then simply expressed as:

$$\sqrt{\frac{f_o}{f_{tot}}} = \left( \frac{U_{tot}(q)}{U_o(q)} \right)^{1.5}$$

(28.11)

Application of Equation (28.11) to the data set compiled by Rickenmann and Recking (2011) shows that macro-roughness resistance is a function of relative flow depth, starts to become important for $(d/D_{84})$ smaller than about 7–10, and increases with decreasing $(d/D_{84})$ in a roughly semi-logarithmic manner.

Bedload transport rates in steep channels are highly affected by a reduction in energy slope $S_o$ due to flow resistance. The reduced energy slope $S_o$ can be expressed by relating stream gradient to either Manning's roughness coefficient $n$ or the Darcy–Weisbach friction coefficient $f$ in the form:

$$\frac{S_o}{S} = \left( \frac{n_o}{n_{tot}} \right)^e = \left( \sqrt{\frac{f_o}{f_{tot}}} \right)^e$$

(28.12)

where the exponent $e$ is in the range 1.33–2 according to Meyer-Peter and Müller (1948), who determined a best fit exponent of $e = 1.5$ for their flume bedload transport data. In earlier studies (Rickenmann, 2005; Rickenmann *et al.*, 2006; Badoux and Rickenmann, 2008; Chiari *et al.*, 2010; Chiari and Rickenmann, 2010) a similar concept of flow-resistance partitioning as discussed above was applied to bedload transport calculations in steep streams. Although a misleading terminology for grain/form resistance partitioning was used in these reports, the estimation of the macro-roughness resistance component is thought to be correct, and it resulted in a slightly stronger reduction of the energy slope (for the same exponent $e$) than application of Equations (28.9) to (28.11). This earlier flow resistance partitioning was based on 373 field measurements of flow resistance, including shallow flows in steep streams (Rickenmann 1994, 1996), in contrast to the 2890 field measurements used by Rickenmann and Recking (2011). Back-estimation of $e$ from bedload data for the Austrian and Swiss flood events in 2005 resulted in a best fit exponent $e$ in the range of about 1.2–1.5 (Chiari and Rickenmann, 2010).

### 28.2.2 Bedload Transport Estimation in Steep Streams and Comparison With Field Data

Based on experiments of bedload transport in gravel-bed flumes at ETH in Zurich for bed slopes of $0.0004 \leq S \leq 0.20$ (Meyer-Peter and Müller, 1948; Smart and Jäggi, 1983; Rickenmann, 1990), a dimensionless bedload transport equation was developed (Rickenmann, 1991), which is given here in a slightly simplified form (Rickenmann, 2001):

$$\Phi_b = 2.5\theta^{0.5} \, (\theta - \theta_c) F_r \qquad (28.13)$$

wherein the dimensionless bedload transport rate $\Phi_b = q_b/[(s-1)gD_m^3]^{0.5}$, $q_b =$ bedload transport rate per unit channel width, $s = \rho_s/\rho$ is the ratio of solid to fluid density, $D_m =$ mean grain size, $\theta = dS/[(s-1)D_m]$ is the dimensionless shear stress, $\theta_c =$ dimensionless critical shear stress at initiation of bedload transport, $Fr = U/(gd)^{0.5}$ is the Froude number, and $s = 2.68$ is assumed for quartz grains in water. Using the definitions of $\Phi_b$ and $\theta$, and the continuity equation $q = dU$, (Equation 28.13) can be transformed into:

$$q_b = A(q - q_c)S^{1.5} \qquad (28.14)$$

wherein $q_c =$ critical discharge at initiation of bedload transport, and $A = 1.5$ according to the ETH Zürich flume experiments. An exact mathematical transformation would require multiplication of the term $q_c$ by $U/U_c$ (where $U_c$ is the critical velocity corresponding to the discharge for $\theta_c$); this factor is neglected here because $q_c$ is typically defined with an empirical function based on field and flume observations. It is also noted that Equation (28.14) is not strictly valid for the conditions of the steep flume experiments for which bedload concentrations were non-negligible (e.g. bedload-induced increase of mixture flow depth above about 10%); in this case the transformation of mixture flow depth used in Equation (28.13) into water discharge is more complex, and Equation (28.14) is not equivalent to Equation (28.13). Equation (28.14) is very similar to a bedload transport

equation proposed by Schoklitsch (1962), for which the coefficient $A$ is 0.93.

Arguments could also be made for an increase of the energy slope in steep streams. If only the ETH Zurich flume experiments with $S \geq 0.03$ are used, a regression analysis results in a bedload transport equation similar in form to Equation (28.14), but with a bed slope exponent of 2.0 instead of 1.5 (Rickenmann, 1991, 2001). In steep channels the bed-slope-parallel weight component of the particles favours bedload transport, and Abrahams (2003) and Abrahams and Gao (2006) proposed – following Schoklitsch (1914) – a correction by using an increased bed slope (or energy slope) $S_k$ as follows:

$$S_k = S[\sin\varphi_r/\sin(\varphi_r - \beta)] = Sa_k \qquad (28.15)$$

wherein $\varphi_r =$ friction angle of the submerged solid particles, and $\beta =$ angle of the bed inclination. Rickenmann (2005) applied Equation (28.15) in combination with Equation (28.14) to the ETH flume experiments and to experimental data on bedload transport at steep channel slopes from Aziz and Scott (1989). The calculations show a good agreement with the experimental observations and suggest that Equation (28.14) together with Equation (28.15) may be applied in a very large bed slope range $0.0004 \leq S \leq 0.20$, including steep slopes.

Using Equation (28.14), the bedload transport rate over the entire channel width $Q_b$ can be given in terms of total discharge $Q$ and critical discharge $Q_c$ as:

$$Q_b = A \, (Q - Q_c)S^{1.5} \qquad (28.16)$$

Only total bedload volumes over several flood events (typically over about a one year period) are known for some field data on bedload transport in Swiss torrents (Rickenmann, 2001). Integrating Equation (28.16) over the time of bedload transport results in:

$$G_E = AV_{re}S^{1.5} \qquad (28.17)$$

wherein $G_E =$ total bedload volume (excluding pore space), and $V_{re} =$ effective runoff volume.

The field data on bedload transport presented in Rickenmann (2001) include measurements from mountain rivers, gravel-bed streams, and torrents with bed slopes up to $S = 0.17$. These data are compared here with calculated bedload transport for the two cases: (i) using Equations (28.14) or (28.16) in combination with Equation (28.15) in Figure 28.1; and (ii) using in addition a correction to account for macro-roughness resistance (additional energy "losses") by using a reduced energy slope according to Equation (28.12) in Figure 28.2. For this comparison, the coefficient $A$ in Equations (28.14, 28.16), and (28.17) is back-calculated from the field data and shown in Figure 28.1 and

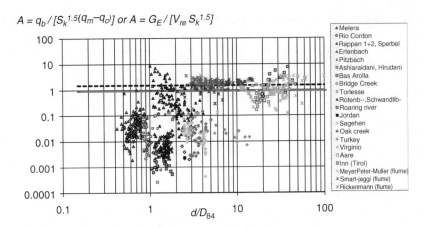

**Figure 28.1** The variable $A$ (coefficient) in the bedload transport Equations (28.14) or (28.17) in combination with Equation (28.15) has been back-calculated from field data given in Rickenmann (2001), and is compared with the flume-based coefficient of Equation (28.14), represented as thick dashed horizontal line, and the coefficient of the Schoklitsch (1962) equation, represented as thick gray horizontal line. The coefficient $A$ is shown versus the relative flow depth ($d/D_{84}$). (See the color version of this figure in color plate section.)

Figure 28.2 as a function of the (mean) relative flow depth $d/D_{84}$. For the field sites without flow depth information, $d$ is estimated using Equation (28.6) and the continuity equation. In contrast to the data and analysis presented in Rickenmann (2001, 2005) for the Erlenbach stream, a representative bed slope of $S = 0.105$ in a 50 m reach upstream of the measuring site is used in the analysis presented here. In addition, field data from the Roaring River in Colorado, USA (Bathurst *et al.*,

1986; Bathurst, 1987) and from the Ashiaraidani and Hirudani streams in Japan (Sawada *et al.*, 1985) are included here as well.

If a reduced energy slope accounting for macro-roughness resistance is considered, the back-calculated coefficients $A$ in Figure 28.2 plot closer to the value of $A = 1.5$ indicated from flume data (Rickenmann, 2001) or of $A = 0.93$ as inferred from field data (Schoklitsch, 1962), than without correction, as shown in Figure 28.1. The

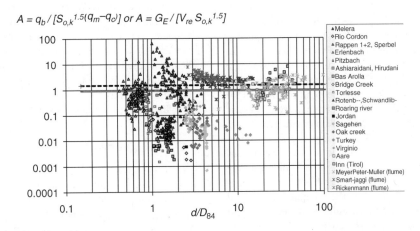

**Figure 28.2** The variable $A$ (coefficient) in the bedload transport Equations (28.14) or (28.17) in combination with Equation (28.15) has been back-calculated from field data given in Rickenmann (2001), and is compared with the flume-based coefficient of Equation (28.14), represented as thick dashed horizontal line, and the coefficient of the Schoklitsch (1962) equation, represented as thick gray horizontal line. In contrast to Figure 28.1, a reduced energy slope $S_o$ has been taken into account additionally, using Equations (28.11) and (28.12). The coefficient $A$ is shown versus the relative flow depth ($d/D_{84}$). (See the color version of this figure in color plate section.)

presented analysis thus indicates improved bedload transport predictions for the considered natural streams when applying a flow-resistance partitioning correction. However, it should be pointed out that the proposed correction is a very rough one which can provide only an order of magnitude improvement of bedload transport estimates. The new approach over-predicts bedload transport rates by up to two orders of magnitude in streams like the Sperbel and Rappengraben (Figure 28.2) where high sediment supply from the conglomerate basin lithology provides ample rounded particles but few cobbles and boulders necessary to form larger roughness elements on the bed and to cause a substantial energy reduction. Caution is also necessary when applying the proposed partitioning of flow resistance (Equation 28.11) to flume conditions with very high bedload concentrations, but lacking macro-roughness elements. Such conditions were present in the experiments by Smart and Jäggi (1983) and by Rickenmann (1991), with all particles in the mobile bed being in motion. According to Figures 28.1 and 28.2, this results in a non-plausible reduction of calculated bedload transport rates and an over-estimation of the coefficient $A$. This effect is partly also due to unrealistic (too small) flow depths being calculated with a $q$-based approach using $d = q/U$, while in reality measured mixture flow depths were considerably larger due to very high sediment concentrations (in excess of 20% increase in depth).

Abrahams *et al.* (2001) applied a slightly modified version of Equation (28.13) to rill flows at steep slopes with large roughness elements. For some of their experimental runs, they introduced a correction procedure to reduce predicted sediment transport rates, because for the flows including roughness elements, observed sediment transport rates were clearly smaller than those from the flume conditions that were the basis for their sediment transport equation. Further support for the necessity to correct bedload predictions for flows with intermediate- and large-scale roughness is provided by Yager *et al.* (2007) who developed a more complex method for bedload transport calculation in steep streams with large immobile boulders by considering form drag by rarely mobile grains and accounting for the limited availability of mobile sediment. Yager (2006) applied this approach to the Erlenbach stream and obtained a similar prediction accuracy with an agreement between predicted and observed bedload volumes to within about one order of magnitude. In comparison, the procedure outlined above to include a flow resistance partitioning for the Erlenbach data results also in an agreement between predicted and observed bedload volumes to within about one order of magnitude (Figure 28.2).

## 28.3   TRANSITION FROM BEDLOAD TRANSPORT TO DEBRIS FLOODS AND DEBRIS FLOWS

In the following part several equations to estimate bedload or sediment concentration at steep slopes are compared with field data from prototype experiments on debris flows in Kazakhstan (Rickenmann *et al.*, 2003). In these experiments artificial flood waves were triggered from a dammed ancient glacial lake, leading to rapid vertical and lateral erosion in a 700 m long channel reach incised in loosely compacted morainic material, with an average bed slope of the reach of $S \approx 0.30$. Here the data from four experiments performed from 1972 to 1976 are used, for which repeated cross-sectional surveys along the reach allow calculation of the average solid concentration of the flow having passed each subreach during each experiment. For a given experiment, the peak water discharge varied from 5 to 28 m$^3$ s$^{-1}$, the typical duration of the water release was about one hour, and the total entrained volume of solids (without pore space) varied from 12 000 to 84 000 m$^3$ (Rickenmann *et al.*, 2003).

Based on the steep flume experiments on bedload transport of Smart and Jäggi (1983) and Rickenmann (1991), and neglecting the critical conditions at initiation of motion, the following regression equation for the range $0.03 \leq S \leq 0.20$ was proposed (Rickenmann, 1990):

$$Q_b = 6.8QS^{2.1} \qquad (28.18)$$

This equation has a larger exponent for the bed slope factor than Equations (28.8) or (28.10) partly because no correction (see Equation 28.15) for the slope-parallel bedload weight was considered. Integrating Equation (28.18) over the time of an experiment and defining the mean volumetric sediment concentration as $C_s = V_b/(V_b + V_w)$, with $V_b$ = total eroded sediment load (excluding pore space) and $V_w$ = total water volume, and with $C^*$ = maximum packing density of the bed material, results in:

$$C_s/C^* = 6.8\,S^{2.1}/[C^*\,(6.8\,S^{2.1} + 1)] \qquad (28.19)$$

Tognacca (1999) performed steep flume experiments on debris flows for bed slopes within the range $0.25 \leq S \leq 0.70$. Analysing his experiments together with the data of Smart and Jäggi (1983) for the bed slope range $0.03 \leq S \leq 0.20$, he proposed the following regression equation:

$$C_s/C^* = [\tanh(9.0\,S_e^{0.85} - 2.4)/2.3] + 0.43 \qquad (28.20)$$

wherein $S_e$ is the energy line slope which is set here equal to the channel bed slope. Based on soil mechanical considerations and flume experiments, Takahashi (1991) proposed to express the so-called equilibrium sediment concentration of debris flows as (including here a normalization by $C^*$).

$$C_s/C^* = \tan\phi/[C^*(s-1)(\tan\phi-\tan\phi)] \qquad (28.21)$$

where $\phi =$ friction angle of the bed material, and Equation (28.21) is valid only in the range $C_s \leq 0.9\,C^*$.

The reach-length and time-integrated mean sediment concentrations for the Kazakhstan debris-flow experiments are compared with Equations (28.19) to (28.21) in Figure 28.3. For the calculations it was assumed that $S=S_e=\tan\beta$, $C^*=0.82$, and $\phi=36°$ in Equation (28.21). The observed sediment concentration $C_s$ represents a mean value over the time of each experiment and includes all sediment and water that entered a given reach with a mean reach slope $\beta$. The field data show a large scatter of $C_s$ for a given channel reach slope $S$, and the data may not be representative for equilibrium flow conditions which are assumed for the predictive equations. Particularly along the upper reaches of the channel and during the later part of the experiments (with lower discharges and probably less sediment entrainment) the flow conditions may have represented debris flood or even fluvial transport conditions (photos and film material taken during the experiments indicate high sediment concentrations at the front of the wave). It is also noted

that Equation (28.19) is extrapolated in Figure 28.3 far beyond the maximum channel slope of the flume experiments that form its basis. However, the three equations predict largely similar sediment concentrations and trends with increasing $S$ values. The lower limit of the field data refers primarily to the first phase of the debris-flow formation, and these data define a roughly similar trend for the increase of $C_s$ with $S$, which might indicate a smooth transition from fluvial bedload transport to debris flood to debris flow in terms of changing sediment concentrations. The cluster of data points which plot essentially above the lines defined by Equations (28.19) to (28.21) represent the more downstream reaches where more mature debris flow conditions could have been present.

Severe floods in August 2005 in Switzerland were associated with many debris flows in the headwater catchments and fluvial bedload transport along the mountain rivers. Rickenmann and Koschni (2010) analysed the observed bedload volumes transported by both types of processes (32 with fluvial bedload transport, 23 with debris flows) in terms of Equation (28.17) (Figure 28.4). They found that for channel gradients steeper than about 0.05 the observed sediment volumes transported by fluvial processes at relatively large flow intensities are clearly over-predicted (also when using other bedload transport equations), which likely results

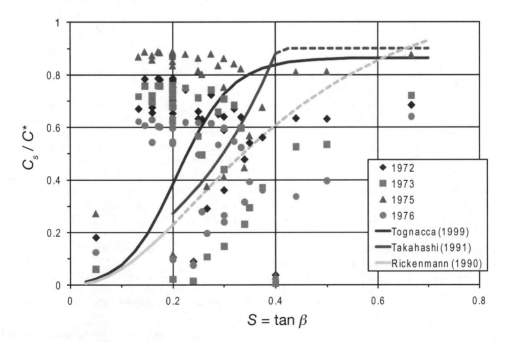

**Figure 28.3** Normalized volumetric sediment concentration $C_s/C^*$ versus channel slope $S$. Observational data from four prototype debris-flow experiments in Kazakhstan (1972–1976) are compared with (partly extrapolated) equations for bedload transport at steep slopes and for debris flows.

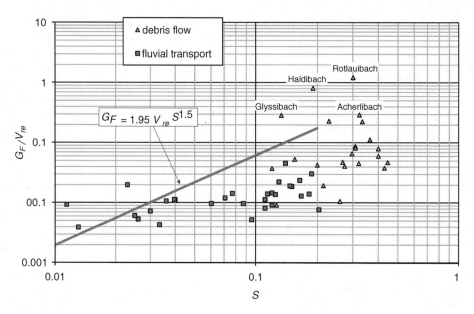

**Figure 28.4**  Fluvial bedload transport and debris flow events during the floods of August 2005 in Switzerland. Event volumes ($G_F$) normalized by effective runoff volumes ($V_{re}$) are shown versus the bed slope ($S$). Reproduced, with permission, from Rickenmann, D. and Koschni, A. 2010. Sediment loads due to fluvial transport and debris flows during the 2005 flood events in Switzerland. *Hydrological Processes* **24**: 993–1007. The blue line indicates the bedload transport Equation (28.11), accounting for 30% pore volume.

from non-accounted energy losses and supply limitation. This is in agreement with the findings in Section 28.2 relating to bedload transport observations associated primarily with low- and medium-intensity flows. For those events in August 2005 with debris flows as the dominant sediment transfer mechanism, sediment volumes show a large variability for given flood runoff volume and channel gradient. However, the majority of the debris-flow data are in line with the trend defined by the fluvial transport events (or by Equation 28.17 with a coefficient $A$ of roughly 0.15 instead of 1.5), indicating a continuous transition to debris-flood and debris-flow conditions. The debris-flow events with the largest magnitudes (sediment volumes) were associated with large sediment inputs by landslides. Marchi and D'Agostino (2004) used a data set with 125 debris-flow events from the Eastern Italian Alps, after having excluded two events triggered by landslide mobilization, and proposed the following empirical relation to estimate the debris-flow event magnitude $G_F$ (in m³), which refers to solid material including pore space and possibly organic material:

$$G_F = C_a A_c^{1.35} S^{1.7} \qquad (28.22)$$

wherein $A_c$ = catchment area (in km²) above the fan apex, and $C_a$ = empirical coefficient. Their best-fit coefficient is $C_a = 65000$, while for the August 2005 events in

Switzerland it is about $C_a = 16400$ (Rickenmann and Koschni, 2010). The data on debris-flow event magnitude in these two studies may have included flows with debris flood conditions, and it is recognized that many other factors, such as lithology and sediment availability in the catchment, probably are important with regard to event magnitude. Nevertheless, considering catchment area as a proxy for water discharge during a torrential flow event, there is some similarity between Equations (28.22) and (28.17) that may also support the hypothesis of a smooth transition from fluvial bedload transport to debris flood to debris flow in terms of changing sediment concentrations. Marchi and D'Agostino (2004) also made a rough estimate of the total runoff volume $V_r$ [in m³] which may have triggered the 125 debris-flow events, and found from regression analysis:

$$G_F = 2.9\, V_r\, S^{2.0} \qquad (28.23)$$

Equation (28.23) is quite similar to a time-integrated version of Equation (28.18) derived from steep flume experiments, although the coefficients differ by a factor of about two.

Recking *et al.* (2008) observed an increase of flow resistance due to bedload transport in steep flume experiments that is also confirmed by other studies (Carbonneau and Bergeron, 2000; Campbell *et al.*, 2005). However, Comiti and Mao (Chapter 26, this volume) note that such an increase in flow resistance due to bedload transport is not very evident in some of the steep flume experiments of Zimmermann (2010). A similar observation of small differences between fixed-bed conditions without transport and bedload transporting flows in steep flume experiments was made by Rickenmann (1991). At the other end of increasing flow strength and sediment concentrations, mean flow velocities of debris flows can be considered. Rickenmann (1999) analysed field data including 124 debris flows from different sites worldwide. He applied the following empirical equation to this debris-flow data:

$$U_{DF} = 2.1 \, Q_p^{0.33} \, S^{0.33} \qquad (28.24)$$

wherein $U_{DF}$ = front velocity of debris flow, and $Q_p$ = peak discharge of debris-flow front. Interestingly, Equation (28.24) was first developed as an empirical equation to predict water flow velocities in torrents and gravel-bed rivers (Rickenmann, 1994, 1996, 1998). For these conditions it was found to give predictions similar to those of another dimensionally consistent equation proposed by Rickenmann (1994, 1996); the original form of (28.24) is $U = C_b \, (g \, Q \, S/D_{90})^{1/3}$ where the non-dimensional coefficient $C_b$ was found to be fairly constant for $S \leq 0.1$. Equation (28.24) with a constant coefficient gave a reasonable and similarly good agreement ($r^2 = 0.70$) for the field observations both of the 124 debris flows and of 373 clear water flows (Rickenmann, 1999). This empirical evidence suggests that there may be some kind of smooth transition from fluvial bedload transport to debris flood to debris flow also in terms of mean flow velocities for given discharge and bed slope conditions. However, this very rough trend may not exclude that more subtle variations in flow resistance exist in steep channels for changing sediment concentrations in the flow.

## 28.4 CONCLUSIONS

Flow resistance in steep and rough streams is clearly increased as compared to deeper flows in more gently sloped gravel-bed streams, which are characterized by larger relative flow depth. The traditional concept of partitioning between "grain" and "form" resistance is difficult to apply in steep streams. For bedload transport calculations it appears to be more appropriate to distinguish between a base-level resistance and macro-roughness resistance, the latter type representing the sum of all additional resistance as compared to flow conditions with large relative flow depths representing base-level resistance. These additional energy "losses" were taken into account for bedload transport calcula-

tions for a number of gravel-bed streams including steep channels. The results show a generally better agreement with the bedload transport observations, as compared to the case of applying traditional bedload transport equations without taking into account flow-resistance partitioning.

With increasing bed slope, debris flows are more likely to occur in natural channels. Three approaches to estimate mean sediment concentration of flows at steep slopes were compared with field data of prototype experiments on debris flow formation. The first approach is theoretical and based on considerations for debris flow equilibrium conditions, while the second and third are empirical and based on flume experiments, both on fluvial bedload transport and on debris flows. All approaches show similar trends for increasing bed slopes. Sediment volumes of fluvial bedload transport and debris flow events, together with a trend defined by a bedload transport equation, suggest that on average there may be a more or less continuous increase in sediment loads when process type changes from fluvial to debris-flood to debris-flow conditions.

## 28.5 ACKNOWLEDGEMENTS

Thanks are due to Kristin Bunte and Francesco Comiti, whose constructive review comments helped to improve the manuscript.

## 28.6 REFERENCES

Aberle, J. and Smart, G.M. 2003. The influence of roughness structure on flow resistance on steep slopes. *Journal of Hydraulic Research* **41**: 259–269.

Abrahams, A.D. 2003. Bedload transport equation for sheet flow. *Journal of Hydraulic Engineering* **129**: 159–163.

Abrahams, A.D. and Gao, P. 2006. A bed-load transport model for rough turbulent open-channel flows on plane beds. *Earth Surface Processes and Landforms* **31**: 910–928.

Abrahams, A.D., Li, G., Krishnan, C., and Atkinson, J.F. 2001. A sediment transport equation for interrill overland flow on rough surfaces. *Earth Surface Processes and Landforms* **26**: 1443–1459.

Aziz, N.M. and Scott, D.E. 1989. Experiments on sediment transport in shallow flows in high gradient channels. *Hydrological Sciences Journal* **34**: 465–478.

Badoux, A. and Rickenmann, D. 2008. Berechnungen zum Geschiebetransport während der Hochwasser 1993 und 2000 im Wallis. *Wasser, Energie, Luft* **100**: 217–226 [in German].

Barry J.J., Buffington, J.M., and King, J.G. 2004. A general power equation for predicting bedload transport rates in gravel bed rivers. *Water Resources Research* **40**: W10401. doi: 10.1029/2004WR003190.

Bathurst, J.C. 1987. Critical conditions for bed material movement in steep, boulder-bed streams. In Beschta R.L., Blinn, T., Grant, G.E., Ice, G.G.,and Swanson, F.J.editors. *Erosion and Sedimentation in the Pacific Rim*. International

Association of Hydrological Sciences Publication 165, pp. 309–318.

Bathurst, J.C. 2002. At-a-site variation and minimum flow resistance for mountain rivers. *Journal of Hydrology* 269: 11–26.

Bathurst, J.C. 2007. Effect of coarse surface layer on bed-load transport. *Journal of Hydraulic Engineering* 133: 1192–1205.

Bathurst, J.C., Leeks, G.J.L., and Newson, M.D. 1986. Relationship between sediment supply and sediment transport for the Roaring River, Colorado, USA. In Hadley, R.F., editor, *Drainage Basin Sediment Delivery*, International Association of Hydrological Sciences Publication 159, pp. 105–117.

Bathurst, J.C., Li, R-M., and Simons, D.B. 1981. Resistance equation for large-scale roughness. American Society of Civil Engineers, *Journal of the Hydraulics Division* 107: 1593–1613.

Bayazit, M. 1976. Free surface flow in a channel of large relative roughness. *Journal of Hydraulic Research* 14: 115–126.

Campbell, L., McEwan, I., Nikora, V.I. *et al.* 2005. Bed-load effects on hydrodynamics of rough open-channel flows. *Journal of Hydraulic Engineering* 131: 576–585.

Carbonneau, P. and Bergeron, N.E. 2000. The effect of bedload transport on mean and turbulent flow properties. *Geomorphology* 35: 267–278.

Carollo, F.G., Fero, V. and Termini, D. 2005. Analyzing turbulence intensity in gravel bed channels. *Journal of Hydraulic Engineering* 131: 1050–1061.

Carson, M.A. 1987. Measures of flow intensity as predictors of bed load. *Journal of Hydraulic Engineering* 113: 1402–1421.

Carson, M.A. and Griffiths, G.A. 1987. Bedload transport in gravel channels. *Journal of Hydrology* (New Zealand) 26(1) (Special issue).

Chiari, M. and Rickenmann, D. 2010. Back-calculation of bedload transport in steep channels with a numerical model. *Earth Surface Processes and Landforms* 36: 805–815. doi: 10.1002/esp.2108.

Chiari, M., Friedl, K., and Rickenmann, D. 2010. A one dimensional bedload transport model for steep slopes. *Journal of Hydraulic Research* 48: 152–160.

Comiti, F., Cadol, D., and Wohl, E.E. 2009. Flow regimes, bed morphology, and flow resistance in self-formed step-pool channels. *Water Resources Research* 45: W04424. doi: 10.1029/2008WR007259.

Comiti, F., Mao, L., Wilcox, A., Wohl, E., and Lenzi, M.A. 2007. Field-derived relationships for flow velocity and resistance in high-gradient streams. *Journal of Hydrology* 340: 48–62.

Costa, J.E. 1984. Physical geomorphology of debris flows. In Costa, J.E. and Fleisher, P.J., editors. *Developments and Applications of Geomorphology*. Berlin, Springer, pp. 268–317.

D'Agostino, V. and Lenzi, M.A. 1999. Bedload transport in the instrumented catchment of the Rio Cordon. Part II. Analysis of the bedload rate. *Catena* 36: 191–204.

Einstein, H.A. and Barbarossa, N.L. 1952. River channel roughness. *American Society of Civil Engineers Transactions* 117: 1121–1146.

Ferguson, R. 2007. Flow resistance equations for gravel- and boulder-bed streams. *Water Resources Research* 43: W05427. doi: 10.1029/2006WR005422.

Gomez, B. and Church, M. 1989. An assessment of bedload sediment transport formulae for gravel bed rivers. *Water Resources Research* 25: 1161–1186.

Govers, G. and Rauws, G. 1986. Transporting capacity of overland flow on plane and on irregular beds. *Earth Surface Processes and Landforms* 11: 515–524.

Guo, J. 2002. Logarthmic matching and its application in computational hydraulics and sediment transport. *Journal of Hydraulic Research* 40: 555–565.

Hassan, M.A., Church, M., and Lisle, T.E. 2005. Sediment transport and channel morphology of small, forested streams. *Journal of the American Water Resources Association* 41: 853–876.

Hungr, O., Evans, S.G., Bovis, M.J., and Hutchinson, J.N. 2001. A review of the classification of landslides of the flow type. *Environmental and Engineering Geoscience* 7: 221–238.

Jäggi, M. 1984. Abflussberechnung in kiesführenden Flüssen. *Wasserwirtschaft* 74: 263–267 [in German].

Lamb, M.P., Dietrich, W.E., and Venditti, J.-G. 2008. Is the critical Shields stress for incipient sediment motion dependent on channel-bed slope? *Journal of Geophysical Research* 113: F02008. doi: 10.1029/2007JF000831.

Lee, A.J. and Ferguson, R.I. 2002. Velocity and flow resistance in step-pool streams. *Geomorphology* 46: 59–71.

Marchi, L. and d'Agostino, V. 2004. Estimation of debris-flow magnitude in the Eastern Italian Alps. *Earth Surface Processes and Landforms* 29: 207–220.

Meyer-Peter, E. and Müller, R. 1948. Formulas for bed-load transport. *Proceedings of the 2nd Meeting, Stockholm*. International Association for Hydraulic Structures Research, Appendix 2, pp. 39–64.

Millar, R.G. 1999. Grain and form resistance in gravel-bed rivers. *Journal of Hydraulic Research* 17: 303–311.

Millar, R.G. and Quick, M.C. 1994. Flow resistance of high-gradient gravel channels. In Cotroneo, V. and Rumer, R.R., editors. *Hydraulic Engineering '94*, American Society of Civil Engineers, New York, *Proceedings* 2: 717–721.

Mizuyama, T. 1977. *Bedload transport in steep channels*. Ph.D. dissertation, Kyoto University, Kyoto, Japan.

Palt, S.M. 2001. *Sedimenttransportprozesse im Himalaya-Karakorum und ihre Bedeutung für Wasserkraftanlagen*. Institut für Wasserwirtschaft und Kulturtechnik, Universität Karlsruhe (TH), Mitteilungen 209[in German].

Parker, G. And Peterson, A.W. 1980. Bar resistance of gravel-bed streams. *American Society of Civil Engineers, Journal of the Hydraulics Division* 106: 1559–1575.

Pierson, T.C. and Costa, J.E. 1987. A rheologic classification of subaerial sediment–water flows. Geological Society of America, *Reviews in Engineering Geology* 7: 1–12.

Recking, A., Frey, P., Paquier, A., Belleudy, P., and Champagne, J.Y. 2008. Feedback between bed load and flow resistance in gravel and cobble bed rivers. *Water Resources Research* 44: W05412. doi: 10.1029/2007WR006219.

Rickenmann, D. 1990. *Bedload Transport Capacity of Slurry Flows at Steep Slopes*. Versuchsanstalt für Wasserbau, Hydrologie und Glaziologie, Eidenossische Technischen Hochschule, Zürich, Mitteilungen 103.

Rickenmann, D. 1991. Hyperconcentrated flow and sediment transport at steep slopes. *Journal of Hydraulic Engineering* 117: 1419–1439.

Rickenmann, D. 1994. An alternative equation for the mean velocity in gravel-bed rivers and mountain torrents. In Cotroneo, V. and Rumer, R.R., editors. *Proceedings of Hydraulic Engineering '94, Vol. 1*, American Society of Civil Engineers, New York, pp. 672–676.

Rickenmann, D. 1996. Fliessgeschwindigkeit in Wildbächen und Gebirgsflüssen. *Wasser, Energie, Luft* 88: 298–303 [in German].

Rickenmann, D. 1998. Antwort zum Diskussionsbeitrag von W.H. Hager zu "Fliessgeschwindigkeit in Wildbächen und Gebirgsflüssen". *Wasser, Energie, Luft* **90**: 133–134 [in German].

Rickenmann, D. 2001. Comparison of bed load transport in torrents and gravel bed streams. *Water Resources Research* **37**: 3295–3305.

Rickenmann, D. 2005. *Geschiebetransport bei steilen Gefällen [Bedload transport at steep slopes].* Versuchsanstalt für Wasserbau, Hydrologie und Glaziologie, Eidgenossische Technischen Hochschule, Zürich, Mitteilungen **190**, pp. 107–119 [in German].

Rickenmann, D. and Koschni, A. 2010. Sediment loads due to fluvial transport and debris flows during the 2005 flood events in Switzerland. *Hydrological Processes* **24**: 993–1007.

Rickenmann, D. and Recking, A. 2011. Evaluation of flow resistance in gravel-bed rivers through a large field dataset. *Water Resources Research* **47**, W07538. doi: 10.1029/2010WR009793.

Rickenmann, D., Weber, D., and Stepanov, B. 2003. Erosion by debris flows in field and laboratory experiments. In Rickenmann, D. and Chen, C.L., edirors. *Debris-Flow Hazards Mitigation: Mechanics, Prediction, and Assessment.* Rotterdam, Millpress, pp. 883–894.

Rickenmann, D., Chiari, M., and Friedl, K. 2006. SETRAC - A sediment routing model for steep torrent channels. In Ferreira, R., Alves, E., Leal, J.,and Cardoso, A., editors. *River Flow 2006.* London, Taylor & Françis, pp. 843–852.

Schoklitsch, A. 1914. *Über Schleppkraft und Geschiebebewegung.* Leipzig und Berlin, Engelmann.

Schoklitsch, A. 1962. *Handbuch des Wasserbaus*, 3rd edition. Vienna, Springer.

Sawada, T., Ashida, K., and Takahashi, T. 1985. Sediment transport in mountain basins. In Takei, A., editor, *Proceedings of the International Symposium on Erosion, Debris Flow and Disaster Prevention, Tsukuba, Japan, 3–5 September.* Erosion Control Engineering Society, pp. 139–144.

Smart, G.M. and Jäggi, M.N.R. 1983. *Sediment Transport on Steep Slopes.* Versuchsanstalt für Wasserbau, Hydrologie und Glaziologie, Eidgenossische Technischen Hochschule, Zürich, Mitteilungen **64**, pp. 89–191.

Takahashi, T. 1991. *Debris flow.* International Association for Hydraulic Research Monograph Series, Balkema, The Netherlands.

Tognacca, C. 1999. *Beitrag zur Untersuchung der Entstehungsmechanismen von Murgängen.* Versuchsanstalt für Wasserbau, Hydrologie und Glaziologie, Eidenossische Technischen Hochschule, Zürich, Mitteilungen **164**.

Wong, M., and Parker, G. 2006. Reanalysis and correction of bed-load relation of Meyer-Peter and Müller using their own database. *Journal of Hydraulic Engineering* **132**: 1159–1168.

Yager, E.M. 2006. *Prediction of sediment transport in steep, rough streams.* Ph. D. thesis, University of California, Berkeley.

Yager, E.M., Kirchner, J.W., and Dietrich, W.E. 2007. Calculating bedload transport in steep, boulder-bed channels. *Water Resources Research* **43**: W07418. doi: 10.1029/2006WR005432.

Zimmermann, A. 2010. Flow resistance in steep streams: an experimental study. *Water Resources Research* **46**: W09536. doi: 10.1029/2009WR007913.

# Semi-alluvial Channels

# 29

# Semi-alluvial Channels and Sediment-Flux-Driven Bedrock Erosion

## Jens M. Turowski

## 29.1 INTRODUCTION

In the last decade research on bedrock channels and fluvial erosion has seen a remarkable increase in interest. It was recognized that these channels play a key role in the evolution of the whole landscape. They set the base-level for hillslope response, control the relief of a region, and are important agents of sediment transport (Whipple, 2004). The idea of a dynamic coupling between climate-driven erosion and tectonics received wide interest in the 1990s (Molnar and England, 1990; Willett, 1999), and triggered intensive research into bedrock channels and fluvial erosion. Fluvial geomorphologists have recognized that bedrock channels behave quite differently from alluvial channels, which river research had focused on for many decades (Tinkler and Wohl, 1998; Wohl and Merritt, 2001; Richardson and Carling, 2006).

The boundary of semi-alluvial channels is partly composed of alluvium and partly of bare rock. Bedrock channels have been defined to have a bare rock bed (e.g., Howard and Kerby, 1983; Montgomery et al., 1996; Montgomery and Buffington, 1997; Whipple, 2004). Streams flowing over thin alluvial cover on a bedrock surface have been variously called "alluvial" (e.g., Howard and Kerby, 1983), "bedrock" (e.g., Tinkler and Wohl, 1998) and "mixed-bedrock alluvial" (e.g., Whipple, 2004). Because individual floods can bring large amounts of sediment into a channel reach, which can reside there for some time afterwards, a classification based on the depth and extent of bed cover will yield different results, depending on when the stream is observed. Turowski et al. (2008b) suggested the definition "A bedrock channel cannot substantially widen, lower or shift its bed without eroding bedrock", thus emphasizing channel dynamics rather than bed morphology. As I will argue here, the dynamics of bedrock channel morphology are intimately connected to sediment transport in the stream. Most bedrock channels are in fact semi-alluvial, with a sand or gravel bed.

Wohl (1998) described the interaction of erosional processes and channel morphology in bedrock channels and identified driving and resisting forces for bedrock incision. Wohl (1998) and Wohl and Merritt (2001) proposed five classes of single flow path bedrock channels according to reach morphology (Figure 29.1). Similar to alluvial channels (Montgomery and Buffington, 1997), plane bed, pool-riffle, and step-pool channels have been observed in bedrock (Wohl and Grodek, 1994; Duckson and Duckson, 1995; Wohl, 1998, 1999; Wohl and Merritt, 2001; Wohl and Legleiter, 2002). In addition, one can identify channels with undulating walls and with inner channels as separate morphologies (Wohl et al., 1999: Wohl and Merritt, 2001). In the channel planform, straight, meandering, and anastomosing channels have been described (e.g., Moore, 1926; Wohl, 1998; Kale, 2005; Barbour, 2008). Thus, the forms observed in bedrock channels are as diverse as in alluvial channels, and various morphologies can be found within a single catchment (Figure 29.2). Often, partly or wholly alluviated reaches alternate with bare rock, and drainage area, local slope, bed topography, and the abundance of coarse woody debris all exert a strong control on whether a particular reach has a sediment cover (Montgomery et al., 1996, 2003; Massong and Montgomery, 2000; Keen-Zebert and Curran, 2009).

A wide range of fluvially sculpted surfaces and erosional bedforms can be observed in bedrock channels, controlled by substrate type, flow regime, and dominant erosion process (e.g., Allen, 1971; Tinkler, 1997; Springer and Wohl, 2002; Richardson and Carling, 2005). In turn, these bedforms influence flow hydraulics and with it the local distribution of erosion. For example, potholes can coalesce and connect to drive downward incision or form inner channels. In addition, bedforms provide resistance

*Gravel-bed Rivers: Processes, Tools, Environments*, First Edition. Edited by Michael Church, Pascale M. Biron and André G. Roy.
© 2012 John Wiley & Sons, Ltd. Published 2012 by John Wiley & Sons, Ltd.

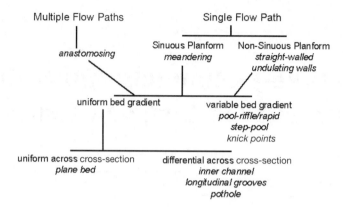

**Figure 29.1**  Typology of meso-scale bedrock channel morphologies. Reproduced, with permission, from Wohl, E.E. 1998. Bedrock channel morphology in relation to erosional processes. In Tinkler, K. and Wohl, E.E., editors, Rivers over Rock. Washington, DC. American Geophysical Union. 133–151.

**Figure 29.2**  Channel types and variability in the Liwu catchment, Taiwan. (a) Step pool morphology in the headwater regions. Canyon is ∼2 m wide. (b) Alluvial channel meanders in a narrow bedrock valley. The wetted channel is approximately 8 m wide. (c) Taroko Gorge with steep marble walls. Note the vegetation strip line approximately 30 m above the channel. (d) Braiding pattern in a valley with steep bedrock walls. Abundant sediment in all pictures was delivered in typhoon Long-Wang six months earlier.

to the flow and may contribute substantially to the total roughness of the bed (e.g., Wohl and Ikeda, 1997: Finnegan et al., 2007; Johnson and Whipple, 2007).

In this chapter I summarize the current state of knowledge on the morphology and dynamics of bedrock channels, with a focus on the effects of sediment on fluvial incision and channel morphology. Even though debris-flow erosion is dominant in many headwater catchments, it is not discussed here and I will concentrate on fluvial processes. I first give a definition of steady state in bedrock channels and outline the controls on steady-state channel morphology. This is followed by a description of the erosion processes thought to be most important, and mathematical models to describe them, with a particular emphasis on the stream power model. Then, I describe the role of sediment in determining morphology and dynamics of the channels. The article concludes with an outlook and some important current research questions.

## 29.2 CONTROLS ON CHANNEL MORPHOLOGY AND STEADY STATE

Local channel morphology is controlled by many different factors (Figure 29.3). In general, one can discriminate between steady-state and transient conditions. In a steady state, bedrock erosion equals base level lowering or rock uplift. This implies constant channel parameters (slope, width, etc.) through time if the boundary conditions are constant, e.g., in experiments, or a variation without long-term trend in natural conditions. To maintain steady state

the channel must fulfil three needs: (i) to transport the water supplied from upstream; (ii) to transport the sediment supplied from upstream (otherwise it aggrades); (iii) to erode at a rate matching tectonic uplift (otherwise the bed slope changes or a knickpoint is initiated). Boundary conditions that determine steady-state channel morphology can be classed into four categories (Turowski et al., 2009).

### 29.2.1 Climate and Discharge, Including Representative Discharge and Discharge Variability

The effective discharge is the discharge that does the same geomorphic work as the complete flood cycle, and is most often used as representative discharge. It is most frequently taken as bankfull flow, which is often identified to be equal to the magnitude of a flood with a return period of around two years. However, many bedrock channels lack a well-defined bank, making the recognition of bankfull flow difficult, and the mean discharge (e.g., Lague et al., 2005; Turowski et al., 2008b), or a certain percentile (e.g., Lavé and Avouac, 2001) have been used as representative values. Tinkler (1971) and Baker and Kale (1998) argued that the effective discharge in bedrock channels may well have return times of several decades.

As for alluvial channels (e.g., Leopold and Maddock, 1953), channel slope, width, depth, and mean flow velocity are often expressed as power functions of discharge along the channel, known as downstream hydraulic geometry (Hack, 1957; Montgomery and Gran, 2001;

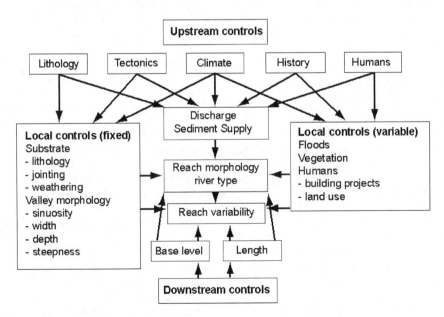

**Figure 29.3** Controls on channel morphology. Adapted from a concept by Schumm (2005).

Duvall *et al.*, 2004; Craddock *et al.*, 2007; Wohl and David, 2008).

$$S = k_S Q^{-\theta} \qquad (29.1)$$

$$W = k_W Q^w \qquad (29.2)$$

Here $S$ is the channel bed slope, $Q$ is the representative discharge, $W$ the channel width, and $k_S$ and $k_W$ are dimensional constants. Both exponents $\theta$ (the "concavity index") and $w$ vary between about 0.3 and 0.8 (Whipple, 2004). Similar equations have been used to describe the at-a-station hydraulic geometry, which is the variance of width, depth, and mean flow velocity with discharge at a given cross-section (Turowski *et al.*, 2008b). Equations (29.1) and (29.2) are thought to apply in steady-state conditions (see Whittaker *et al.*, 2007a, 2007b). Wohl (2004) argued that Equations (29.1) and (29.2) fail if the streams have insufficient power to move the coarse sediment in the channel.

The importance of discharge variability on channel morphology has been argued mainly from theoretical grounds (Tucker and Bras, 2000; Molnar, 2001; Snyder *et al.*, 2003b; Lague *et al.*, 2005; Huang and Niemann, 2006; Molnar *et al.*, 2006; Barbour *et al.*, 2009). However, there is direct field evidence for its effect on erosion rate (Hartshorn *et al.*, 2002; Dadson *et al.*, 2003; Kale and Hire, 2007) and planform channel geometry (Barbour *et al.*, 2009; Stark *et al.*, 2010).

Local climate has indirect effects on channel morphology. For example, temperature and precipitation affect weathering (changing substrate properties – see (ii) and mass wasting rates, and the type, density, and distribution of vegetation.

### 29.2.2   Substrate Properties, Including Rock Mass Strength, Jointing, and Weathering

Substrate has regularly been identified to exert a dominant control on channel and valley morphology (Bretz, 1924; Moore, 1926; Miller, 1991a; Lifton *et al.*, 2009). Substrate type and properties are known to determine the dominant process of erosion (Bretz, 1924; Hancock *et al.*, 1998; Whipple *et al.*, 2000a), and the types of erosional bedforms in the channel (Allen, 1971; Richardson and Carling, 2005). Sklar and Dietrich (2001) showed that experimental erosion rates are strongly controlled by substrate type and argued that the tensile strength is the relevant parameter determining the erodibility of massive rock. There are few systematic field studies investigating substrate control on channel morphology, but there is clear evidence for its importance (e.g., Wohl, 1999, 2008; Ehlen and Wohl, 2002; Wohl

and Achyuthan, 2002; Montgomery, 2004; Stock *et al.*, 2005; Jansen, 2006; Pelletier *et al.*, 2009). In general, a channel is expected to be narrower and steeper in more resistant lithology.

### 29.2.3   River Sediment Supply, Including Sediment Input, Grain Size Distribution and Grain Lithology

Sediment supply can enhance or inhibit erosion (Gilbert, 1877; Foley, 1980; Sklar and Dietrich, 1998), and erosion rate is both directly dependent on grain size (Sklar and Dietrich, 2001) and the mode of transport (e.g., bedload or suspension) (Brewer *et al.*, 1992; Lamb *et al.*, 2008). Thus, the grain-size distribution may strongly influence channel morphology (see Whipple and Tucker, 2002; Sklar and Dietrich, 2006, 2008; Attal and Lavé, 2009). No systematic field studies of these effects have yet been presented.

### 29.2.4   Tectonics and Base-Level Changes, Including the Uplift Pattern, the Location of Fracture Zones, and the Magnitude-Frequency Distribution of Earthquakes

The influence of tectonics is expected from theoretical work (e.g., Howard, 1994; Whipple and Tucker, 1999, 2002; Turowski *et al.*, 2009), and has been demonstrated in the laboratory (Turowski *et al.*, 2006) and in the field (e.g., Dolan *et al.*, 1978; Lavé and Avouac, 2001; Snyder *et al.*, 2003a; Duvall *et al.*, 2004; Whittaker *et al.*, 2007a). Turowski *et al.* (2009) have presented a theoretical analysis of tectonic forcing and summarized available field data (see also Yanites and Tucker, 2010). In general, higher uplift rates force the channel to be narrower and steeper. Base level changes can trigger knickpoints, which migrate up the channel. Knickpoints are often considered as indicators for transient states and may be a local focus of erosion in the channel (e.g., Seidl and Dietrich, 1992).

For steady-state channel cross-sections, the parameters in these four groups comprise the independent parameters of the system. The parameters of the channel cross-sectional morphology, such as flow width, depth and cross-sectional area, channel bed slope, and bed roughness comprise the dependent parameters and adjust to the boundary conditions.

## 29.3   PROCESSES OF BEDROCK EROSION

The bedrock boundary of a channel is shaped by erosion, and a thorough understanding of fluvial erosion processes is necessary to interpret and predict channel morphology. Here, I describe the physical processes leading to bedrock erosion.

### 29.3.1 Solution

Solution occurs when the rock is disintegrated by the solvent water in a chemical process. Solution can be the dominant erosion process in limestone and evaporites (Allen, 1971; Smith *et al.*, 1995; Richardson and Carling, 2005), but may also be active in other rock types such as marble. Some common bedrock bedforms such as scallops are shaped by solution processes. However, in many channels solution is probably less important than physical erosion processes.

### 29.3.2 Cavitation

In very high-velocity flows the fluid pressure may drop below the vapour pressure of water. Then bubbles can form, which become unstable if driven into areas with lower flow velocities. As the bubbles collapse, powerful water jets are ejected, which can damage nearby rock surfaces (Barnes, 1956; Hancock *et al.*, 1998; Whipple *et al.*, 2000a). Damage due to cavitation is well known in engineering applications, but it has been argued that the required flow velocities occur too rarely in natural streams for it to play a significant role in bedrock erosion (Hancock *et al.*, 1998). No conclusive field evidence has been presented so far.

### 29.3.3 Shear Detachment or Fluid Stressing

Flowing water exerts a shear force upon the bed it overflows, and particles can be entrained due to this force. It is well known that sediment transport rates and sediment entrainment are driven by excess shear stress over a threshold value, and a similar mechanism can be envisioned for bedrock erosion. It is widely thought that the process is important only in weakly consolidated rocks and clays (e.g., Howard, 1998).

### 29.3.4 Impact Erosion or Abrasion

Moving sediment particles in the flow may impact the bed and remove small splinters of the impacted rock material. This process is known as erosion in the wear literature and as abrasion in the geomorphological community. The impact of particles also drives crack propagation and weakens the substrate (and thus prepares for plucking) (e.g., Bitter, 1963; Wilson, 2009). Impact erosion is thought to be important in many natural environments.

### 29.3.5 Quarrying or Plucking

Quarrying or plucking is the removal of loose blocks from the rock and involves the combination of several processes. Existing cracks, joints, and planes of weakness in the material are enlarged by the impact of particles until individual blocks are loosened. The preparation of blocks has been termed macro-abrasion (Chatanantavet and Parker, 2009). Loose blocks can be entrained and removed by shear detachment. Although quarrying is thought to be important in jointed rock and should thus be common (Bretz, 1926; Hartshorn *et al.*, 2002), the process has been little studied and only preliminary laboratory work has been described (Dubinski and Wohl, 2005).

### 29.3.6 Knickpoint Migration

Knickpoints are over-steepened sections of the river long profile. Their migration is not an erosion process as such, but an interplay of several processes modulated by a channel-spanning bedform. Knickpoints can be triggered by changes in climate or local tectonics (Crosby and Whipple, 2006), by base-level drops (Whipple and Tucker, 1999), blocking of the channel by landslide material (Korup, 2006), and by lithologic contrasts (Miller, 1991b), or they can arise autogenically (Chatanantavet and Parker, 2009). Erosion may focus in a knick point due to high slope, causing it to migrate upstream. Knickpoints contribute to total channel lowering and transmit information on base level through the channel network, and thus play an important role in channel dynamics (Whipple and Tucker, 1999, 2002).

## 29.4 EROSION MODELS

There have been many attempts to cast descriptions of erosion processes into mathematical form. Following, I give a short overview over the most important formulations.

### 29.4.1 The Shear Stress/Stream Power Family of Erosion Models (Detachment-Limited Erosion)

Howard and Kerby (1983) proposed that bedrock erosion rate $E$ is proportional to a power function of bed shear stress of the dominant discharge:

$$E = \begin{cases} k_e(\tau-\tau_c)^a & \text{for} \quad \tau > \tau_c \\ 0 & \text{otherwise} \end{cases} \quad (29.3)$$

Here $k_e$ and $a$ are constants and $\tau$ is the shear stress at the bed. The erosion threshold $\tau_c$ is frequently neglected. Whipple *et al.* (2000a) developed versions of Equation (29.3) for several important erosion processes, including abrasion, cavitation, and plucking, with the exponent $a$ ranging from 1 to 5/2. Alternatively, Seidl *et al.* (1994) hypothesized that erosion rate is proportional to a power function of stream power.

$$E = \begin{cases} k_{sp}(SQ)^b & \text{for} \quad Q > 0 \\ 0 & \text{otherwise} \end{cases} \qquad (29.4)$$

Here $k_{sp}$ and $b$ are constants. $Q$ could be either a representative or an instantaneous value. With simple assumptions on hydraulics and hydrology, Equations (29.3) and (29.4) can be rewritten to yield (Howard, 1994; Whipple and Tucker, 1999; Snyder et al., 2000):

$$E = \begin{cases} KA^m S^n - \psi_e & \text{for} \quad KA^m S^n > \psi_e \\ 0 & \text{otherwise} \end{cases}, \qquad (29.5)$$

wherein $m$, $n$ and $K$ are constants, $A$ is the drainage area, and $\psi_e$ is a threshold term. Equation (29.5) is widely used to model bedrock erosion. It is often called the "detachment-limited erosion model" because it is thought to apply in situations in which the sediment transport capacity of the stream greatly exceeds sediment supply, and sediment evacuation from the catchment is limited by mass removal from the substrate rather than by the stream's ability to transport. In the following, it is referred to as the stream power model. The threshold $\psi_e$ is frequently neglected because in geomorphically effective floods it is much smaller than the active term (e.g., Howard and Kerby, 1983; Whipple et al., 2000a). Subsequently, it has been shown from field and laboratory data, and from theoretical arguments that the threshold cannot be neglected, especially when a realistic flood cycle is taken into account (Tucker and Bras, 2000; Molnar, 2001; Lague et al., 2003, 2005; Snyder et al., 2003b; Tucker, 2004). Other controls, such as sediment-flux effects, are sometimes incorporated into the prefactor $K$ (e.g., Whipple and Tucker, 2002).

### 29.4.2  Transport-Limited Erosion Models

In a transport-limited channel, the rate of sediment flux is equal to the transport capacity $Q_t$ of the stream, which is usually given by the equation (e.g., Smith and Bretherton, 1972; Whipple and Tucker, 2002):

$$Q_t = \begin{cases} k_t A^m S^n - \psi_t & \text{for} \quad k_t A^m S^n > \psi_t \\ 0 & \text{otherwise} \end{cases} \qquad (29.6)$$

Here, $k_t$ is a constant and $\psi_t$ is a threshold term. Note the similarity of Equations (29.5) and (29.6). The constants $m$ and $n$ do not necessarily have the same value as in Equation (29.5). Realizing that incision in a transport-limited system is determined by the downstream divergence of sediment flux, the erosion rate can be written as:

$$E = \frac{1}{(1-p)} \frac{d}{dx} \left( \frac{Q_t}{W} \right) \qquad (29.7)$$

wherein $p$ is the porosity of the deposited sediment and $x$ is the distance along the stream.

### 29.4.3  Hybrid Models: the $\xi$-$q$ Model

In landscape evolution models often both detachment-limited and transport-limited erosion models are implemented. A formulation combining both model types is the $\xi$-$q$ model (Davy and Crave, 2000; Davy and Lague, 2009). It reduces to a detachment-limited formulation when a free parameter, the transport length, becomes large, and to a transport-limited formulation when the transport length becomes small. For intermediate values, the model shows mixed behaviour. The transport length can be identified with the average distance an individual particle travels before being deposited.

### 29.4.4  Sediment Flux-Dependent Models

There are two conflicting effects of sediment transport on impact-driven erosion rates (Gilbert, 1877). More transported sediment leads to a higher number of impacts, increasing erosion rates (tools effect). On the other hand, more sediment in the channel shields the bed from impacts; decreasing erosion rates (cover effect). The cover effect can be due both to stationary and to moving sediment (Turowski et al., 2007); in the latter case moving particles interact more frequently as more sediment is available. These are the most important of various effects sediment flux can have on erosion rate, and several erosion laws have been proposed that include one or both of them (Sklar and Dietrich, 2006). I shall describe here only the two most commonly cited models, the undercapacity model (Beaumont et al., 1992) and the saltation-abrasion model (Sklar and Dietrich, 2004), and their derivatives.

#### 29.4.4.1  The Undercapacity Model

In the undercapacity model (Beaumont et al., 1992) the stream has a certain amount of energy available, which it uses to transport the delivered sediment load. Any excess energy is spent on bedrock erosion. This results in a linear decline of erosion rate with increasing sediment supply at otherwise constant conditions. Therefore, variants of the model are often termed "linear-decline models" (Whipple and Tucker, 2002). The decrease in erosion rate with increasing sediment supply resembles the cover effect; however, the idea leading to this decline is not based on the shielding effect of sediment.

#### 29.4.4.2  The Saltation-Abrasion Model and Variants

Assuming that erosion is driven by the impact of saltating bedload particles, the erosion rate can be written as the product of three terms (Sklar and Dietrich, 1998):

$$E = V_i I_r R_a \qquad (29.8)$$

wherein $V_i$ is the average volume of rock removed upon each individual impact, $I_r$ is the impact frequency, and $R_a$ describes the cover effect. Sklar and Dietrich (2004) quantified Equation (29.8) to yield:

$$E = KS_{eff}q_sR_a \qquad (29.9)$$

with

$$K = \frac{0.08\Delta\rho gY}{k_v\rho_w\sigma_t^2}\left[\frac{\tau^*}{\tau_c^*}-1\right]^{1/2} \qquad (29.10)$$

and

$$S_{eff} = \left[1-\left(\frac{u^*}{w_f}\right)^2\right]^{3/2} \qquad (29.11)$$

Here $Y$ is Young's modulus of the substrate, $k_v$ a dimensionless rock resistance coefficient, $\sigma_t$ the rock tensile strength, $\Delta\rho = \rho_s - \rho_w$ where $\rho_w$ and $\rho_s$ are the densities of water and sediment respectively, $\tau^* = \tau/\Delta\rho gd$ the Shields stress, and $\tau_c^*$ the critical Shields stress for the onset of motion of sediment, where $d$ the sediment grain diameter. $w_f$ is the particle fall velocity in still water, $u^* = (\tau/\rho_w)^{1/2}$ the shear velocity, and $q_s$ is the sediment flux per unit width in the river. $K$ describes substrate erodibility and sediment motion dynamics. The suspension-effect term $S_{eff}$ accounts for the increasing proportion of mobile sediment carried in suspension with rising shear stress. The linear dependence of $E$ on $q_s$ in Equation (29.9) models the tools effect. The cover term $R_a$ is discussed in more detail in Section 29.6.4. Whipple and Tucker (2002) simplified the model to study the long-profile evolution of bedrock channels and to develop testable criteria for model selection. Their version is generally known as the parabolic model, because a linear cover term leads to an overall parabolic dependence of erosion rate on sediment flux. Lamb et al. (2008) generalized the model to include abrasion by suspended load. Chatanantavet and Parker (2009) combined the saltation-abrasion model with a description of plucking to study the relative effect of the two processes and their influence on long-profile evolution.

## 29.5 BEDROCK CHANNELS IN THE STREAM POWER MODEL FRAMEWORK

### 29.5.1 Use of the Model

The stream power model has been widely used to make inferences about bedrock channel morphology and dynamics. The model can be readily identified with shear detachment (see Section 29.3.3), but is used as a general model encompassing all fluvial erosion processes.

A correlation between incision rates and stream power has been reported for several streams (Wohl, 1992, 1993; Wohl et al., 1994; Wohl and Ikeda, 1998; Kale and Hire, 2007; Yanites et al., 2010). The constants in Equation (29.5) can in principle be calibrated on field data, and this has been attempted with varying success (e.g., Seidl and Dietrich, 1992; Stock and Montgomery, 1999; Whipple et al., 2000b; Lavé and Avouac, 2001; Snyder et al., 2003a).

The stream power model has been extensively used in theoretical studies on channel long-profiles and in landscape evolution models (e.g., Howard, 1994; Lague et al., 2005; Tucker and Whipple, 2002; Whipple and Tucker, 1999), and to interpret field data on river incision and morphology (e.g., Kirby and Whipple, 2001; Montgomery and Gran, 2001; Korup and Schlunegger, 2007). Long profiles can easily be extracted from digital elevation models, making the analysis of a large number of streams possible. Neglecting the threshold term in Equation (29.5), channel bed slope can be written as a function of drainage area and erosion rate:

$$S = \left(\frac{E}{k_e}\right)^{1/n}A^{-\theta} \qquad (29.12)$$

The concavity index $\theta$ is equal to $m/n$ and independent of the erosion exponent $a$ (Equation 29.3) (Whipple and Tucker, 1999). A power-law dependence of slope on area is observed in many streams (compare with Equation 29.1), and these observations comprise the most important field evidence for the stream power model. A similar dependence can be obtained from the transport-limited formulation. The concavity index is thus not sufficient to discriminate the two models in the field and the transient behaviour of the channel needs to be considered (Whipple and Tucker, 2002). Channels respond to changes in the boundary conditions by the creation of a knickpoint, which then migrates upstream. In the stream power model, knickpoints retreat along the channel without changing shape, while in the transport-limited model, the knickpoint spreads and diffuses until it vanishes. Therefore, knickpoint behaviour can in principle be used to test different erosion models in the field.

The insensitivity of $\theta$ on $a$ suggests that local channel slope is independent of the dominant erosion process. Therefore, the channel long profile can be used to extract the spatial variation of erosion rate and thus, for steady-state channels, rock uplift rate (e.g., Seeber and Gornitz, 1983; Kirby and Whipple, 2001; Bishop, 2007).

Stark (2006) developed the first model where both slope and width can adjust freely to boundary conditions. He assumed a trapezoidal cross-sectional shape and used empirical relations to partition the available shear stress onto channel bed and walls. Wobus et al. (2006b, 2008) and Turowski *et al.* (2009) described models with freely evolving cross-sections. All these models predict a unique channel shape at steady state, such that channel width and slope are independent of initial conditions.

### 29.5.2 Problems With the Stream power Model

Despite the success of the stream power formulation, evidence is mounting that the model is insufficient to account for all aspects of fluvial bedrock erosion. Existing field data are scarce and often incomplete, and it is debated how to close the equations for a complete model of channel morphology. Tomkin *et al.* (2003) tested several erosion models, including the stream power model, the transport-limited model and a variant of the saltation-abrasion model, on detailed data from the steady-state channel of the Clearwater River, Washington State, USA. They concluded that none of the tested models adequately described the data, and some (including the stream power model with and without threshold) even gave physically implausible results. In a similar study, van der Beek and Bishop (2003) reported that for all of the tested models, suitable parameter values could be found that reproduced the observed channel morphology after simulating incision from known palaeo-channel profiles. Sklar and Dietrich (1998) argued that the environment in which the stream power model is applicable is limited to channels with intermediate slopes; it fails at low slopes because the bed alluviates, and at high slopes because debris flows become the dominant agents of erosion. They also showed that the apparently simple form of the model hides an underlying complexity. This makes it difficult to find unique parameter values that apply to the whole length of a stream (see Stock and Montgomery, 1999). Howard (1998) argued that even if the stream power model gives a correct process description of erosion, other processes, such as weathering, mass wasting, and the cover effect may dominantly control long-term erosion rates. Therefore, it may not be possible to successfully upscale the stream power model to reach- or catchment-wide erosion. In flume experiments, Johnson and Whipple (2010) observed that erosion rate is independent of shear stress if sediment supply and bed cover are held constant.

One of the assumptions leading to Equation (29.5) is the empirical scaling of channel width with discharge (Equation 29.2). Although similar scaling as for alluvial streams has been reported for bedrock channels (Equations 29.1 and 29.2), it has recently become clear that channel width is dependent on the magnitude and distribution of tectonic forcing (e.g., Lavé and Avouac, 2001; Snyder *et al.*, 2003a; Duvall *et al.*, 2004), and that the scaling breaks down for transient channels (Whittaker *et al.*, 2007a). Turowski *et al.* (2009)

reviewed data on tectonic forcing of channel width and concluded that a numerical model driving cross-sectional evolution with shear-stress-dependent erosion could not account for the downstream trends in channel width observed in most well-documented bedrock rivers.

## 29.6 THE ROLE OF SEDIMENT

In this section my aim is twofold. First, I want to argue that in most natural environments the effect of the sediment flux on bedrock erosion cannot be ignored. Second, I want to outline the current understanding of how sediment affects channel dynamics and morphology.

### 29.6.1 Process Scale

There are few direct observations of the relation between erosion rate and sediment flux. Sklar and Dietrich (2001) showed the influence of bedload transport on erosion in laboratory experiments (Figure 29.4). For given hydraulic conditions, the erosion rate rises to a maximum at small transport rates and falls to zero at high transport rates. The two regions to the left and the right of the maximum are known as tools-dominated and cover-dominated domains, respectively. No direct observation of either domain has been reported from field measurements. Turowski and Rickenmann (2009) showed that both tools and cover effects are active in the interaction of bedload particles with the channel bed in a mountain stream in Austria. However, the connection to erosion can only be made under the assumption that particle impacts drive incision.

Additional evidence comes from observations of engineering structures. In hydro-power plant water intakes, sediment is separated out in settling basins, providing clean water for power production. These basins are regularly flushed out. Despite high flow velocities and shear stress in the clear water flow behind the settling basin at the water intake at Bas Arolla in Switzerland, which has been in operation for more than 50 years, the structures show no evidence of scouring or other fluvial erosion. However, heavy scour is observed in the flushing channel for sediment removal and the concrete structures have to be replaced regularly.

### 29.6.2 Cross-Section and Reach scale

It is commonly observed that large sediment input to a channel can divert or delay channel incision (e.g., Korup, 2006; Ouimet *et al.*, 2008). On the cross-section and reach scale, evidence for the effect of sediment comes from the distribution of erosion across the channel. Lateral incision not only determines channel form, it also drives meandering. Strath terraces form when the

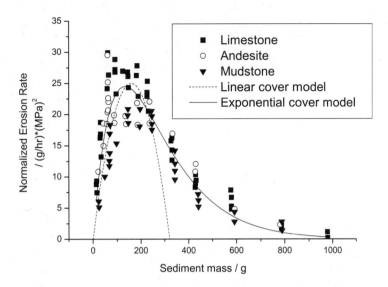

**Figure 29.4** Experimental erosion rates normalised for rock strength for three different types of rock (Sklar and Dietrich, 2001). Both tools and cover effects are active. The exponential model (Equation 29.14) for the cover effect gives a better description of the data than the linear model (Equation 29.13). Reproduced, with permission, from Turowkski, J., Lague, D., Hovius, N. 2007. Cover effect in bedrock abrasion: a new derivation and its implications for the modelling of bedrock channel morphology. *Journal of Geophysical Research* **112**, F04006, doi:10.1029/2006JF000697.

channel changes from a phase of lateral planation to vertical incision (Suzuki, 1982: Hancock and Anderson, 2002). Whether incised meanders evolve dynamically in bedrock channels, or whether the planform is inherited from a previous alluvial stage of the river has been debated for more than a century (Davis, 1893; Winslow, 1893; Shepherd, 1972; Barbour, 2008). Moore (1926) described extensive field observations and proposed that the amount of sediment in the channel determines whether it meanders actively or cuts vertically. If there is a lot of sediment available, the bed is protected from incision and erosion focuses on the channel walls. Lateral incision is dominant. Otherwise, erosion focuses in the thalweg, where most tools are available, fostering vertical incision. This hypothesis was confirmed in experimental channels cutting into artificial bedrock (Shepherd, 1972; Shepherd and Schumm, 1974). Bull (1979) proposed that if the ratio of available stream power to that necessary to transport the imposed sediment load is greater than one, the river incises V-shaped valleys vertically into bedrock; otherwise it cuts mainly laterally. Using similar ideas, Hancock and Anderson (2002) developed a numerical simulation to study terrace formation. Hartshorn *et al.* (2002) observed that in the Liwu River, Taiwan, erosion of the channel walls occurs during large floods, while small and medium discharges are responsible for thalweg lowering. Turowski *et al.* (2008a) showed that the distribution of shear stress across the Liwu channel at different flood stages cannot

account for this erosion pattern and suggested that large floods supply large sediment loads that shield the channel bed. The maximum erosion rate is expected near the top of the sediment cover, in the narrow region where a sufficient amount of tools is available for incision, but the shielding effect of the sediment is not important. In the Liwu River, the location of maximum sediment cover during typhoon Long-Wang coincided with the maximum erosion rate during the storm, supporting this hypothesis (Turowski *et al.*, 2008a). A similar relation between the distribution of erosion and the flood magnitude was observed for snow-melt floods in a bedrock channel in the Henry Mountains, USA (Johnson *et al.*, 2010). In addition, the relation is consistent with recent laboratory experiments (Johnson and Whipple, 2010), and with the observation that lower sediment flux in Taiwanese bedrock channels is associated with steeper channel walls (Turowski *et al.*, 2008b).

### 29.6.3  Catchment-Scale and Long-Term Landscape Evolution

Few studies have evaluated the effect of sediment flux on long-term basin development and channel long profiles. Johnson *et al.* (2009) observed that channels with abundant sediment in the Henry Mountains, USA, have steeper bed slopes and are less incised than their sediment-poor tributaries, even though the latter have smaller drainage areas. Thus, sediment cover can inhibit erosion and

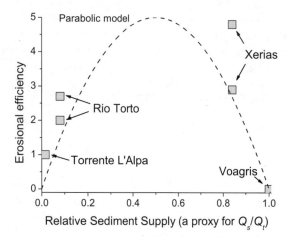

**Figure 29.5** Erosional efficiency of the Rio Torto and Torrente L'Alpa in Italy, and the Xerias and Voagris in Greece plotted as a function of relative sediment supply. See Cowie *et al.* (2008) for details of the measurements and calculations. Although many approximations and assumptions affect data quality, the results are clearly at odds with an erosion rate independent of sediment supply. The parabolic model, widely used to describe tools and cover effect in erosion, has been included to guide the eye.

control channel concavity. Cowie *et al.* (2008) estimated the long-term ratio of sediment supply and transport capacity for streams in Italy and Greece and showed that both tools and cover effects play an important role in determining erosion rates (Figure 29.5).

Many tributaries join the main channel not at the level of the valley, but over a waterfall. The abundance of hanging valleys in many mountain landscapes is predicted by sediment-flux-dependent erosion models and has been cited as evidence for the importance of sediment effects (Wobus *et al.*, 2006a). A later study cautioned against this conclusion (Crosby *et al.*, 2007); however, sediment-flux-dependent incision is still the most likely explanation.

### 29.6.4 Sediment Cover and Channel Dynamics

In a channel where the bed configuration has adjusted to sediment supply, we can identify two end-member states. If sediment supply exceeds local transport capacity ($Q_s > Q_t$), the bed will aggrade, and the cover term $R_a$ should equal zero. If no sediment is supplied ($Q_s = 0$), any locally stored material will be evacuated and the cover term should equal one. The simplest function connecting these two points is a linear equation (Sklar and Dietrich, 1998):

$$R_a = \begin{cases} 1 - \dfrac{Q_s}{Q_t} & Q_s < Q_t \\ 0 & Q_s \geq Q_t \end{cases} \qquad (29.13)$$

Equation (29.13) is widely used to model the cover effect. Turowski *et al.* (2007) gave a heuristic derivation of an exponential function for alluvial cover based on a simple stochastic argument:

$$R_a = \begin{cases} \exp\left\{ -\varphi \dfrac{Q_s}{Q_t} \right\} & Q_s < Q_t \\ 0 & Q_s \geq Q_t \end{cases} \qquad (29.14)$$

Equation (29.14) arises when assuming that homogeneous sediment is randomly distributed on a plane bed (Turowski, 2009). The cover factor $\varphi$ is a free parameter, which is one for a plane bed, and greater than one for existing field data. Equation (29.14) gives a better fit to the erosion data of Sklar and Dietrich (2001) (Figure 29.4). Available data from flume experiments do not currently allow us to discriminate effectively between the two models (Figure 29.6) (Chatanantavet and Parker, 2008; Turowski, 2009; Johnson and Whipple, 2010). Probably neither of these models correctly describes bed cover on the process scale, but they provide a starting point for further investigation.

In Equations (29.13) and (29.14) the ratio of sediment supply to transport capacity determines the importance of the cover effect. Common sediment transport formulas can be transformed to yield a linear relation between $Q_t$ and $Q$ (Rickenmann, 2001):

$$Q_t = \begin{cases} C(Q - Q_c) & Q > Q_c \\ 0 & Q \leq Q_c \end{cases} \qquad (29.15)$$

Bedload supply $Q_s$ can be written as a power function of discharge (Barry *et al.*, 2004):

$$Q_s = cQ^\lambda \qquad (29.16)$$

We can distinguish two cases: (i) the exponent $\lambda$ is larger than one, or (ii) $\lambda$ is smaller than one (Figure 29.7). In case (i) large floods supply more sediment than they can evacuate (Figure 29.7a). Then, intermittent sediment cover may hinder thalweg erosion for some time, until all deposits are evacuated by medium sized floods (Howard, 1998; Heritage *et al.*, 2004; Turowski *et al.*, 2008a; Johnson and Whipple, 2010; Lague, 2010). In case (ii) the channel aggrades during low and medium flows until it behaves like an alluvial river (Figure 29.7b). Large floods evacuate this sediment and cause bedrock erosion (Heritage *et al.*, 2004). This second type of behaviour seems to be common; many actively incising channels feature thick alluvial cover during low flow. Both types of behaviour can occur in different reaches of the same river (Heritage *et al.*, 2004). The coupling between sediment supply and transport capacity implies

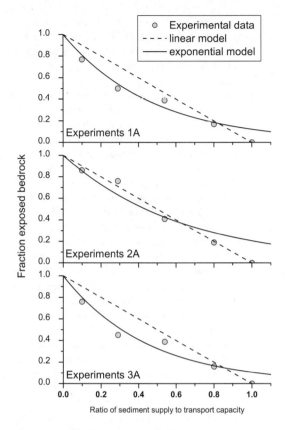

**Figure 29.6** Experimental observations on the cover effect in experiments 1A, 2A, and 3A reported by Chatanantavet and Parker (2008). Both linear (Equation 29.13) and exponential cover models (Equation 29.14) give similarly good fits. Reproduced, with permission, from Turowski, J.M. 2009. Stochastic modeling of the cover effect and bedrock erosion. *Water Resources Research* **45**: W03422. doi:10.1029/2008WR007262.

that the long-term cover effect may take a different form than those of either Equations (29.13) or (29.14). Lague (2010) showed that the precise short-term formulation does not have a strong influence on the form of the long-term cover function, which instead is dependent on the magnitude-frequency distribution of floods and the way sediment supply is coupled to discharge.

## 29.7 CONCLUSIONS AND RESEARCH NEEDS

Bedrock channels have come into the focus of geomorphic research in the recent decades. The stream power model was the first widely used formulation of fluvial bedrock erosion. However, recent evidence shows that the stream power model insufficiently describes erosion

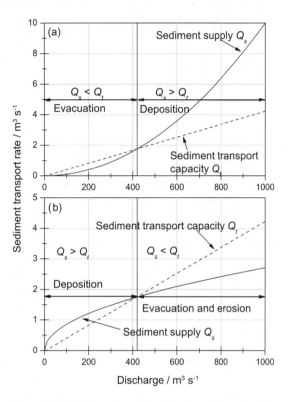

**Figure 29.7** Illustration of the simple model outlined in Equations (29.15) and (29.16). (a) Case (i): during large floods (here $>420 \, m^3 \, s^{-1}$) sediment supply exceeds transport capacity and sediment is deposited in the reach. Then, the thalweg is protected from erosion and incision occurs mainly on the channel walls. During subsequent small floods, the excess sediment is evacuated. Thalweg lowering occurs when sediment is scarce and the tools effect dominates. Then, incision focuses in the channel centre, where sediment transport is concentrated and most tools are available. (b) Case (ii): Excess sediment is supplied during small and medium floods, and the channel bed aggrades until the river behaves alluvial. The resident sediment is evacuated during large floods and bedrock erosion can occur.

processes. In particular, it has been demonstrated in field and laboratory studies that sediment effects such as the tools and cover effects play an important role and cannot be neglected. Bedrock channels are in general semi-alluvial. Despite new insights, many research questions remain open and some of the most important of these are listed below. The list is of course subjective and not exhaustive.

(i) Empirical data on short time-scale erosion is lacking in comparison to hydraulics, sediment transport and substrate properties to calibrate fluvial bedrock erosion laws. Even well-developed process laws like the saltation-abrasion law are largely based on engineering studies of non-natural materials (e.g., Bitter, 1963). Recent laboratory experiments are starting to rectify the situation (Sklar and Dietrich, 2001; Wilson, 2009), but detailed field data are lacking.

(ii) When and where is the stream power model applicable? Because of its apparently simple form, the stream power model is widely used in modelling studies. However, it is debatable in which environments it is actually applicable (Howard, 1998; Sklar and Dietrich, 1998).

(iii) Is it possible to define an effective discharge in a bedrock channel and how can it be measured in the field (Lague et al., 2005: Huang and Niemann, 2006)? Which channel width should correctly be used in models and how can it be measured in the field (Turowski et al., 2009)?

(iv) More high-quality field data on bedrock channels and the controls on channel morphology are needed (see Wohl and David, 2008). When used in landscape evolution models, different formulations of erosion laws often predict similar steady-state topographies, and it has been argued that the transient behaviour needs to be observed to discriminate between models (Whipple and Tucker, 1999; Whipple, 2004; Gasparini et al., 2007). Monitoring the temporal evolution of a stream in the field remains a major challenge.

(v) A new generation of models accounting for sediment effects on erosion on the reach and cross-section scales is needed. First efforts have been presented by Stark et al. (2009) and Lague (2010), but the generality of these models is limited.

(vi) Although there is field evidence for the importance of discharge variability on erosion rates (e.g., Hartshorn et al., 2002; Dadson et al., 2003), no field studies have yet been presented that investigate its control on channel morphology.

(vii) What is the feedback between sediment supply, erosion, channel morphology, and bed roughness? Bed roughness is commonly treated as an independent parameter in models of channel morphology (e.g., Finnegan et al., 2005; Wobus et al., 2006b; Turowski et al., 2009). However, in laboratory experiments roughness actively adjusts through the development of bedforms (Wohl and Ikeda, 1997; Finnegan et al., 2007; Johnson and Whipple, 2007, 2010). How exactly do bedforms develop (see Richardson and Carling, 2005; Wilson, 2009)? How can their

formation be incorporated into models? Also, the roughness of bare rock, of stationary, and of moving sediment differ, and this needs to be quantified (Chatanantavet and Parker, 2008; Recking et al., 2008).

(viii) Dated terraces are often used to infer the incision history of a stream. However, their formation needs to be re-investigated in light of the new insights on channel dynamics. The controls on the relation between channel and valley width are closely connected to terrace formation, and also provide open problems (see Suzuki, 1982; Hancock and Anderson, 2002; Brocard and van der Beek, 2006; Turowski et al., 2009).

(ix) How can process laws be scaled up to geological timescales? What is the functional form for erosion to be used in channel and landscape evolution? What is the role of cover versus tools effects on long time scales (see Cowie et al., 2008)? Turowski and Rickenmann (2009) showed that both tools and cover effect can be dominant at the same time at different locations in a channel cross-section, or at the same location at different times. Due to the non-linearity of the erosion models this makes upscaling of process laws even to the cross-section very difficult. Lague (2010) showed that upscaling of the cover effect to long time periods is largely independent of the precise formulation of the process law, which opens the question of how far the process laws need to be known for accurate modelling.

## 29.8   ACKNOWLEDGEMENTS

Many people have contributed to my understanding of bedrock channels in discussions, by commenting on my manuscripts, and by their own work. Foremost, I want to thank my teachers and colleagues N. Hovius, D. Lague, C. Stark, and J. Barbour, as they have deeply affected my thinking. Lague, Barbour, and A. Badoux gave helpful comments on previous versions of this manuscript. P. Carling, T. Lisle, and T. Buffin-Bélanger provided thoughtful criticisms, which helped to improve this chapter. I thank the attendees of GBR7 for comments and discussion.

## 29.9   REFERENCES

Allen, J.R.L. 1971. Transverse erosional marks of mud and rock: their physical basis and geological significance. *Sedimentary Geology* **5**: 167–385.
Attal, M. and Lavé, J. 2009. Pebble abrasion during fluvial transport: experimental results and implications for the

evolution of the sediment load along rivers. *Journal of Geophysical Research* **114**: F04023. doi: 10.1029/2009JF001328.

Baker, V.R. and Kale, V.S. 1998. The role of extreme floods in shaping bedrock channels. In Tinkler, K.J. and Wohl, E.E., editors. *Rivers over Rock: Fluvial Processes in Bedrock Channels.* American Geophysical Union, Geophysical Monograph 107, pp. 133–151.

Barbour, J.R. 2008. *The origin and significance of sinuosity along incising bedrock rivers.* Ph.D. thesis, Columbia University, New York.

Barbour, J.R., Stark, C.P., Lin, C. *et al.* 2009. Magnitude-frequency distributions of boundary shear stress along a rapidly eroding bedrock river. *Geophysical Research Letters* **36**: L04401. doi: 10.1029/2008GL035786.

Barnes, H.L. 1956. Cavitation as a geological agent. *American Journal of Science* **254**: 493–505.

Barry, J.J., Buffington, J.M., and King, J.G. 2004. A general power equation for predicting bed load transport rates in gravel bed rivers. *Water Resources Research* **40**: W10401. doi: 10.1029/2004WR003190.

Beaumont, C., Fullsack, P., and Hamilton, J. 1992. Erosional control of active compressional orogens. In McClay, K.R. editor. *Thrust Tectonics.* New York, Chapman and Hall, pp. 1–18.

Bishop, P. 2007. Long-term landscape evolution: linking tectonics and surface processes. *Earth Surface Processes and Landforms* **32**: 329–365.

Bitter, J.G.A. 1963. A study of erosion phenomena Part I. *Wear* **6**: 5–21.

Bretz, J.H. 1924. The Dalles type of river channel. *Journal of Geology* **24**: 139–149.

Brewer, P.A., Leeks, G.J.L., and Lewin, J. 1992. Direct measurement of in-channel abrasion processes. *Erosion and Sediment Transport Monitoring Programmes in River Basins (Proceedings of the Oslo Symposium, August 1992)* International Association for Hydrological Sciences Publication 210, pp. 21–29.

Brocard, G.Y. and van der Beek, P.A. 2006. Influence of incision rate, rock strength, and bedload supply on bedrock river gradients and valley-flat widths: Field-based evidence and calibrations from western Alpine rivers (southeast France). In Willet, S.D., Hovius, N., Brandon, M.T., and Fisher, D.M. editors. *Tectonics, Climate, and Landscape Evolution,* Geological Society of America, Special Paper 398, pp. 127–141.

Bull, W.B. 1979. Threshold of critical power in streams. *Geological Society of America Bulletin* **90**: 453–464.

Chatanantavet, P. and Parker, G. 2008. Experimental study of bedrock channel alluviation under varied sediment supply and hydraulic conditions. *Water Resources Research* **44**: W12446. doi: 10.1029/2007WR006581.

Chatanantavet, P. and Parker, G. 2009. Physically-based modeling of bedrock incision by abrasion, plucking, and macroabrasion. *Journal of Geophysical Research* **114**: F94918. doi: 10.1029/2008JF001044.

Cowie, P.A., Whittaker, A.C., Attal, M. *et al.* 2008. New constraints on sediment-flux-dependent river incision: Implications for extracting tectonic signals from river profiles. *Geology* **36**: 535–538.

Craddock, W.H., Burbank, D.W., Bookhagen, B., and Gabet, E.J. 2007. Bedrock channel geometry along an orographic rainfall gradient in the upper Marsyandi River valley in central Nepal. *Journal of Geophysical Research* **112**: F03007. doi: 10.1029/2006JF000589.

Crosby, B.T. and Whipple, K.X. 2006. Knickpoint initiation and distribution within fluvial networks: 236 waterfalls in the Waipaoa River, North Island, New Zealand. *Geomorphology* **82**: 16–38.

Crosby, B.T., Whipple, K.X., Gasparini, N.M., and Wobus, C.W. 2007. Formation of fluvial hanging valleys: Theory and Simulation. *Journal of Geophysical Research* **112**: F03S10. doi: 10.1029/2006JF000566.

Dadson, S.J., Hovius, N., Chen, H. *et al.* 2003. Links between erosion, runoff variability and seismicity in the Taiwan orogen. *Nature* **426**: 648–651.

Davis, W.M. 1893. The Osage River and the Ozark Uplift. *Science* **22**: 276–279.

Davy, P. and Crave, A. 2000. Upscaling local-scale transport processes in large-scale relief dynamics. *Physics and Chemistry of the Earth A* **25**: 533–541.

Davy, P. and Lague, D. 2009. The fluvial erosion/transport equation of landscape evolution models revisited. *Journal of Geophysical Research* **114**: F03007. doi: 10.1029/2008JF001146.

Dolan, R., Howard, A. and Trimble, D. 1978. Structural control of the rapids and pools of the Colorado River in the Grand Canyon. *Science* **2002**: 629–631.

Dubinski, I.M. and Wohl, E.E. 2005. Physical model of river erosion into jointed bedrock through quarrying. *EOS: Transactions of the American Geophysical Union,* Fall Meeting Supplement, Abstract H53D-0516.

Duckson, D.W. and Duckson, L. 1995. Morphology of bedrock step pool systems. *Water Resources Bulletin* **31**: 43–51.

Duvall, A., Kirby, E., and Burbank, D. 2004. Tectonic and lithologic controls on bedrock channel profiles and processes in coastal California. *Journal of Geophysical Research* **109**: F03002. doi: 10.1029/2003JF000086.

Ehlen, J. and Wohl, E.E. 2002. Joints and landform evolution in bedrock canyons. *Transactions, Japanese Geomorphological Union* **23**: 237–255.

Finnegan, N.J., Roe, G., Montgomery, D.R., and Hallet, B. 2005. Controls on the channel width of rivers: Implications for modelling fluvial incision into bedrock. *Geology* **33**: 229–232.

Finnegan, N.J., Sklar, L.S. and Fuller, T.K. 2007. Interplay of sediment supply, river incision, and channel morphology revealed by the transient evolution of an experimental bedrock channel. *Journal of Geophysical Research* **112**: F03S11. doi: 10.1029/2006JF000569.

Foley, M.G. 1980. Bed-rock incision by streams. *Geological Society of America Bulletin* **91**: 577–578.

Gasparini, N.M., Whipple, K.X., and Bras, R.L. 2007. Predictions of steady state and transient landscape morphology using sediment-flux-dependent river incision models. *Journal of Geophysical Research* **112**: F03S09. doi: 10.1029/2006JF000567.

Gilbert, G.K. 1877. Land sculpture. In *The Geology of the Henry Mountains.* United States Department of the Interior, Chapter V, pp. 99–150.

Hack, J.T. 1957. *Studies of Longitudinal Stream Profiles in Virginia and Maryland.* United States Geological Survey Professional Paper 294-B.

Hancock, G.S. and Anderson, R.S. 2002. Numerical modeling of fluvial strath terrace formation in response to oscillating climate. *Geological Society of America Bulletin* **114**: 1131–1142.

Hancock, G.S., Anderson, R.S., and Whipple, K.X. 1998. Beyond power: Bedrock river incision processes and form. In Tinkler, K.J. and Wohl, E.E., editors. *Rivers over rock: Fluvial processes in bedrock channels,* American Geophysical Union, *Geophysical Monograph* **107**: 237–260.

Hartshorn, K., Hovius, N., Dade, W.B., and Slingerland, R.L. 2002. Climate-driven bedrock incision in an active mountain belt. *Science* **297**: 2036–2038.

Heritage, G.L., Large, A.R.G., Moon, B.P., and Jewitt, G. 2004. Channel hydraulics and geomorphic effects of an extreme flood event on the Sabie River, South Africa. *Catena* **58**: 151–181.

Howard, A.D. 1994. A detachment-limited model of drainage basin evolution. *Water Resources Research* **30**: 2261–2285.

Howard, A.D. 1998. Long-profile development of bedrock channels: Interaction of weathering, mass wasting, bed erosion, and sediment transport. In Tinkler, K.J. and Wohl, E.E. editors. *Rivers over Rock: Fluvial Processes in Bedrock Channels*, American Geophysical Union, Geophysical Monograph 107, pp. 237–260.

Howard, A.D. and Kerby, G. 1983. Channel changes in badlands. *Geological Society of America Bulletin* **94**: 739–752.

Huang, X. and Niemann, J.D. 2006. An evaluation of the geomorphically effective event for fluvial processes over long periods. *Journal of Geophysical Research* **111**: F03015. doi: 10.1029/2006JF000477.

Jansen, J.D. 2006. Flood magnitude-frequency and lithologic control on bedrock river incision in post-orogenic terrain. *Geomorphology* **82**: 39–57.

Johnson, J.P. and Whipple, K.X. 2007. Feedbacks between erosion and sediment transport in experimental bedrock channels. *Earth Surface Processes and Landforms* **32**: 1048–1062.

Johnson, J.P. and Whipple, K.X. 2010. Evaluating the controls of shear stress, sediment supply, alluvial cover, and channel morphology on experimental bedrock incision rate. *Journal of Geophysical Research* **115**: F02018. doi: 10.1029/2009JF001335.

Johnson, J.P., Whipple, K.X., and Sklar, L.S. 2010. Contrasting bedrock incision rates from snowmelt and flash floods in the Henry Mountains, Utah. *Geological Society of America Bulletin* **122**: 1600–1615.

Johnson, J.P., Whipple, K.X., Sklar, L.S., and Hanks, T.C. 2009. Transport slopes, sediment cover, and bedrock channel incision in the Henry Mountains, Utah. *Journal of Geophysical Research* **114**: F02014. doi: 10.1029/2007JF000862.

Kale, V.S. 2005. The sinuous bedrock channel of the Tapi River, central India: Its form and processes. *Geomorphology* **70**: 296–310.

Kale, V.S. and Hire, P.S. 2007. Temporal variations in the specific stream power and total energy expenditure of a monsoonal river: The Tapi River, India. *Geomorphology* **92**: 134–146.

Keen-Zebert, A. and Curran, J.C. 2009. Regional and local controls on the spatial distribution of bedrock reaches in the Upper Guadelupe River, Texas. *Geomorphology* **112**: 295–305.

Kirby, E. and Whipple, K.X. 2001. Quantifying differential rock-uplift rates via stream profile analysis. *Geology* **29**: 415–418.

Korup, O. 2006. Rock-slope failure and the river long profile. *Geology* **34**: 45–48.

Korup, O. and Schlunegger, F. 2007. Bedrock landsliding, river incision, and transience of geomorphic hillslope-channel coupling: Evidence from inner gorges in the Swiss Alps. *Journal of Geophysical Research* **112**: F03027. doi: 10.1029/2006JF000710.

Lague, D. 2010. Reduction of long-term bedrock incision efficiency by short-term alluvial cover intermittency. *Journal of Geophysical Research* **115**: F02011. doi: 10.1029/2008JF001210.

Lague, D., Crave, A., and Davy, P. 2003. Laboratory experiments simulating the geomorphic response to tectonic uplift. *Journal of Geophysical Research* **108**: 2008. doi: 10.1029/2002JB001785.

Lague, D., Hovius, N., and Davy, P. 2005. Discharge, discharge variability and the bedrock channel profile. *Journal of Geophysical Research* **110**: F04006. doi: 10.1029/2004JF000259.

Lamb, M.P., Dietrich, W.E., and Sklar, L.S. 2008. A model for fluvial bedrock incision by impacting suspended and bed load sediment. *Journal of Geophysical Research* **113**: F03025. doi: 10.1029/2007JF000915.

Lavé, J. and Avouac, J.P. 2001. Fluvial incision and tectonic uplift across the Himalayas of central Nepal. *Journal of Geophysical Research* **106**: 26 561–26 591.

Leopold, L.B. and Maddock, T.J., Jr. 1953. *The Hydraulic Geometry of Stream Channels and some Physiographic Implications.* United States Geological Survey, Professional Paper 252.

Lifton, Z.M., Thackray, G.D., Kirk, R.V., and Glenn, N.F. 2009. Influence of rock strength on the valley morphometry of Big Creek, central Idaho, USA. *Geomorphology* **111**: 173–181.

Massong, T.M. and Montgomery, D.R. 2000. Influence of sediment supply, lithology and wood debris on the distribution of bedrock and alluvial Channels. *Geological Society of America Bulletin* **112**: 591–599.

Miller, J.R. 1991a. Controls on channel form along bedrock-influenced alluvial streams in south-central Indiana. *Physical Geography* **12**: 167–186.

Miller, J.R. 1991b. The influence of bedrock geology on knickpoint development and channel-bed degradation along downcutting streams in south-central Indiana. *Journal of Geology* **99**: 591–605.

Molnar, P. 2001. Climate change, flooding in arid environments, and erosion rates. *Geology* **29**: 1071–1074.

Molnar, P. and England, P. 1990. Late Cenozoic uplift of mountain ranges and global climate change: Chicken or egg? *Nature* **346**: 29–34.

Molnar, P., Anderson, R.S., Kier, G., and Rose, J. 2006. Relationships among probability distributions of stream discharges in floods, climate, bed load transport, and river incision. *Journal of Geophysical Research* **111**: F02001. doi: 10.1029/2005JF000310.

Montgomery, D.R. 2004. Observations on the role of lithology in strath terrace formation and bedrock channel width. *American Journal of Science* **304**: 454–476.

Montgomery, D.R. and Buffington, J.M. 1997. Channel-reach morphology in mountain drainage basins. *Geological Society of America Bulletin* **109**: 596–611.

Montgomery, D.R. and Gran, K.B. 2001. Downstream variations in the width of bedrock channels. *Water Resources Research* **37**: 1841–1846.

Montgomery, D.R., Abbe, T.B., Buffington, J.M. *et al.* 1996. Distribution of bedrock and alluvial channels in forested mountain drainage basins. *Nature* **381**: 587–589.

Montgomery, D.R., Massong, T.M., and Hawley, S.C. 2003. Influence of debris flows and log jams on the location of pools and alluvial channel reaches, Oregon Coast Range. *Geological Society of America Bulletin* **115**: 78–88.

Moore, R.C. 1926. Origin of inclosed meanders on streams of the Colorado Plateau. *Journal of Geology* **34**: 29–57.

Ouimet, W.B., Whipple, K.X., Crosby, B.T., Johnson, J.P., and Schildgen, T.F. 2008. Epigenetic gorges in fluvial landscapes. *Earth Surface Processes and Landforms* **33**: 1993–2009.

Pelletier, J.D., Engelder, T., Comeau, D. *et al.* 2009. Tectonic and structural control of fluvial channel morphology in metamorphic core complexes: The example of the Catalina-Rincon core complex, Arizona. *Geosphere* **5**: 363–384.

Recking, A., Frey, P., Paquier, A., Belleudy, P., and Champagne, J.Y. 2008. Feedback between bed load transport and flow resistance in gravel and cobble bed rivers. *Water Resources Research* **44**: W05412. doi: 10.1029/2007WR006219.

Richardson, K. and Carling, P.A. 2005. *A Typology of Sculpted Forms in Open Bedrock Channels*. Geological Society of America, Special Paper 392.

Richardson, K. and Carling, P.A. 2006. The hydraulics of a straight bedrock channel: Insights from solute dispersion studies. *Geomorphology* **82**: 98–125.

Rickenmann, D. 2001. Comparison of bed load transport in torrents and gravel bed streams. *Water Resources Research* **37**: 3295–3305.

Schumm, S.A. 2005. River Variability and Complexity. Cambridge, Cambridge University Press.

Seeber, L. and Gornitz, V. 1983. River profiles along the Himalayan arc as indicators of active tectonics. *Tectonophysics* **92**: 335–367.

Seidl, M.A. and Dietrich, W.E. 1992. The problem of channel erosion into bedrock. *Catena Supplement* **23**: 101–124.

Seidl, M.A., Dietrich, W.E. and Kirchner, J.W. 1994. Longitudinal profile development into bedrock: An analysis of Hawaiian channels. *Journal of Geology* **102**: 457–474.

Shepherd, R.G. 1972. Incised river meanders: Evolution in simulated bedrock. *Science* **178**: 409–411.

Shepherd, R.G. and Schumm, S.A. 1974. Experimental study of river incision. *Geological Society of America Bulletin* **85**: 257–268.

Sklar, L.S. and Dietrich, W.E. 1998. River longitudinal profiles and bedrock incision models: Stream power and the influence of sediment supply. In Tinkler, K.J. and Wohl, E.E. editors. *Rivers over Rock: Fluvial Processes in Bedrock Channels*, American Geophysical Union, Geophysical Monograph 107, pp. 237–260.

Sklar, L.S. and Dietrich, W.E. 2001. Sediment and rock strength controls on river incision into bedrock. *Geology* **29**: 1087–1090.

Sklar, L.S. and Dietrich, W.E. 2004. A mechanistic model for river incision into bedrock by saltating bed load. *Water Resources Research* **40**: W06301. doi: 10.1029/2003WR002496.

Sklar, L.S. and Dietrich, W.E. 2006. The role of sediment in controlling steady-state bedrock channel slope: Implications of the saltation-abrasion incision model. *Geomorphology* **82**: 58–83.

Sklar, L.S. and Dietrich, W.E. 2008. Implications of the saltation-abrasion bedrock incision model for steady-state river longitudinal profile relief and concavity. *Earth Surface Processes and Landforms* **33**: 1129–1151.

Smith, T.R. and Bretherton, F.P. 1972. Stability and the conservation of mass in drainage basin evolution. *Water Resources Research* **8**: 1506–1529.

Smith, D.I., Greenaway, M.A., Moses, C., and Spate, A.P. 1995. Limestone weathering in eastern Australia. Part 1: Erosion rates. *Earth Surface Processes and Landforms* **20**: 541–463.

Snyder, N.P., Whipple, K.X., Tucker, G.E., and Merritts, D.J. 2000. Landscape response to tectonic forcing: Digital elevation model analysis of stream profiles in the Mendocino triple junction region, northern California. *Geological Society of America Bulletin* **112**: 1250–1263.

Snyder, N.P., Whipple, K.X., Tucker, G.E., and Merritts, D.J. 2003a. Channel response to tectonic forcing: Field analysis of stream morphology and hydrology in the Mendocino triple junction region, northern California. *Geomorphology* **53**: 97–127.

Snyder, N.P., Whipple, K.X., Tucker, G.E., and Merritts, D.J. 2003b. Importance of a stochastic distribution of floods and erosion thresholds in the bedrock river incision problem. *Journal of Geophysical Research* **108**: 2117. doi: 10.1029/2001JB001655.

Springer, G.S. and Wohl, E.E. 2002. Empirical and theoretical investigations of sculpted forms in Buckeye Creek Cave, West Virginia. *Journal of Geology* **110**: 469–481.

Stark, C.P. 2006. A self-regulating model of bedrock river channel geometry. *Geophysical Research Letters* **33**: L04402. doi: 10.1029/2005GL023193.

Stark, C.P., Barbour, J.R., Hayakawa, Y.S. *et al.* 2010. The climatic signature of incised river meanders. *Science* **327**: 1497–1501.

Stark, C.P., Foufoula-Georgiou, E., and Ganti, V. 2009. A nonlocal theory of sediment buffering and bedrock channel evolution. *Journal of Geophysical Research* **114**: F01029. doi: 10.1029/2008JF000981.

Stock, J.D. and Montgomery, D.R. 1999. Geologic constraints on bedrock river incision using the stream power law. *Journal of Geophysical Research* **104**: 4983–4993.

Stock, J.D., Montgomery, D.R., Collins, B.D., Dietrich, W.E., and Sklar, L. 2005. Field measurements of incision rates following bedrock exposure: Implications for process controls on the long profile of valleys cut by rivers and debris flows. *Geological Society of America Bulletin* **117**: 174–194.

Suzuki, T. 1982. Rate of lateral planation by Iwaki River, Japan. *Transactions, Japanese Geomorphological Union* **3**: 1–24.

Tinkler, K.J. 1971. Active valley meanders in south-central Texas and their wider implications. *Geological Society of America Bulletin* **82**: 1783–1800.

Tinkler, K.J. 1997. Rockbed wear at a flow convergence zone in Fifteen Mile Creek, Niagara Peninsula, Ontario. *Journal of Geology* **105**: 263–274.

Tinkler, K.J. and Wohl, E.E. 1998. A primer on bedrock channels. In Tinkler, K.J. and Wohl, E.E. editors. *Rivers over Rock: Fluvial Processes in Bedrock Channels*. American Geophysical Union, Geophysical Monograph 107, pp. 1–18.

Tomkin, J.H., Brandon, M.T., Pazzaglia, F.J., Barbour, J.R., and Willett, S.D. 2003. Quantitative testing of bedrock incision models for the Clearwater River, NW, Washington State. *Journal of Geophysical Research* **108**: 2308. doi: 10.1029/2001JB000862.

Tucker, G.E. 2004. Drainage basin sensitivity to tectonic and climatic forcing: Implications of a stochastic model for the role of entrainment and erosion thresholds. *Earth Surface Processes and Landforms* **29**: 185–205.

Tucker, G.E. and Bras, R.L. 2000. A stochastic approach to modeling the role of rainfall variability in drainage basin evolution. *Water Resources Research* **36**: 1953–1964.

Tucker, G.E. and Whipple, K.X. 2002. Topographic outcomes predicted by stream erosion models: Sensitivity analysis and intermodel comparison. *Journal of Geophysical Research* **107**: 2179–2194.

Turowski, J.M. 2009. Stochastic modeling of the cover effect and bedrock erosion. *Water Resources Research* **45**: W03422. doi: 10.1029/2008WR007262.

Turowski, J.M. and Rickenmann, D. 2009. Tools and cover effects in bedload transport observations in the Pitzbach, Austria. *Earth Surface Processes and Landforms* **34**: 26–37.

Turowski, J.M., Lague, D., Crave, A., and Hovius, N. 2006. Experimental channel response to tectonic uplift. *Journal of Geophysical Research* **111**: F03008. doi: 10.1029/2005 JF000306.

Turowski, J.M., Lague, D., and Hovius, N. 2007. Cover effect in bedrock abrasion: A new derivation and its implication for the modeling of bedrock channel morphology. *Journal of Geophysical Research* **112**: F04006. doi: 10.1029/2006 JF000697.

Turowski, J.M., Hovius, N., Hsieh, M., Lague, D., and Chen, M. 2008a. Distribution of erosion across bedrock channels. *Earth Surface Processes and Landforms* **33**: 353–363.

Turowski, J.M., Hovius, N., Wilson, A., and Horng, M. 2008b. Hydraulic geometry, river sediment and the definition of bedrock channels. *Geomorphology* **99**: 26–38.

Turowski, J.M., Lague, D., and Hovius, N. 2009. Bedrock channel width response to tectonic forcing: Insights from a numerical model, theoretical considerations and comparison with field data. *Journal of Geophysical Research* **114**: F03016. doi: 10.1029/2008JF001133.

van der Beek, P. and Bishop, P. 2003. Cenozoic river profile development in the upper Lachlan Catchment (SE Australia) as a test of quantitative fluvial Incision models. *Journal of Geophysical Research* **108**: 2309. doi: 10.1029/2002 JB002125.

Whipple, K.X. 2004. Bedrock rivers and the geomorphology of active orogens. *Annual Reviews in Earth and Planetary Science* **32**: 151–185.

Whipple, K.X. and Tucker, G.E. 1999. Dynamics of the stream-power river incision model: Implications for height limits of mountain ranges, landscape response timescales, and research needs. *Journal of Geophysical Research* **104**: 17 661–17 674.

Whipple, K.X. and Tucker, G.E. 2002. Implications of sediment-flux-dependent river incision models for landscape evolution. *Journal of Geophysical Research* **107**: 2039. doi: 10.1029/2000JB000044.

Whipple, K.X., Hancock, G.S., and Anderson, R.S. 2000a. River incision into bedrock: Mechanics and relative efficacy of plucking, abrasion, and cavitation. *Geological Society of America Bulletin* **112**: 490–503.

Whipple, K.X., Snyder, N.P., and Dollenmayer, K. 2000b. Rates and processes of bedrock incision by the Upper Ukak River since the 1912 Novarupta Ash Flow in the Valley of Ten Thousand Smokes, Alaska. *Geology* **28**: 835–838.

Whittaker, A.C., Cowie, P.A., Attal, M., Tucker, G.E., and Roberts, G.P. 2007a. Bedrock channel adjustment to tectonic forcing: Implications for predicting river incision rates. *Geology* **35**: 103–106.

Whittaker, A.C., Cowie, P.A., Attal, M., Tucker, G.E., and Roberts, G.P. 2007b. Contrasting transient and steady-state rivers crossing active normal faults: new field observations from the central Apennines, Italy. *Basin Research* **19**: 529–556.

Willett, S.D. 1999. Orogeny and orography: The effects of erosion on the structure of mountain belts. *Journal of Geophysical Research* **104**: 28957–28981.

Wilson, A. 2009. *Fluvial bedrock abrasion by bedload: process and form.* Ph.D.thesis, Cambridge University.

Winslow, A. 1893. The Osage River and its meanders. *Science* **22**: 31–32.

Wobus, C.W., Crosby, B.T., and Whipple, K.X. 2006a. Hanging valleys in fluvial systems: Controls on occurrence and implications for landscape evolution. *Journal of Geophysical Research* **111**: F02017. doi: 10.1029/2005JF000406.

Wobus, C.W., Kean, J.W., Tucker, G.E., and Anderson, R.S. 2008. Modeling the evolution of channel shape: Balancing computational efficiency with hydraulic fidelity. *Journal of Geophysical Research* **113**: F02004. doi: 10.1029/ 2007JF000914.

Wobus, C.W., Tucker, G.E. and Anderson, R.S. 2006b. Self-formed bedrock channels. *Geophysical Research Letters* **33**: L18408. doi: 10.1029/2006GL027182.

Wohl, E.E. 1992. Bedrock benches and boulder bars: Floods in the Burdekin Gorge, Australia. *Geological Society of America Bulletin* **104**: 770–778.

Wohl, E.E. 1993. Bedrock channel incision along Piccaninny Creek, Australia. *Journal of Geology* **101**: 749–761.

Wohl, E.E. 1998. Bedrock channel morphology in relation to erosional processes. In Tinkler, K.J. and Wohl, E.E. editors. Rivers over Rock: Fluvial Processes in Bedrock Channels. American Geophysical Union, Geophysical Monograph 107, pp. 133–151.

Wohl, E.E. 1999. Substrate influences on step-pool sequences in the Christopher Creek drainage, Arizona. *Journal of Geology* **108**: 121–129.

Wohl, E.E. 2004. Limits of downstream hydraulic geometry. *Geology* **32**: 897–900.

Wohl, E.E. 2008. The effect of bedrock jointing on the formation of straths in the Cache la Poudre River drainage, Colorado Front Range. *Journal of Geophysical Research* **113**: F01007. doi: 10.1029/2007JF000817.

Wohl, E.E. and Achyuthan, H. 2002. Substrate influences on incised-channel morphology. *Journal of Geology* **110**: 115–120.

Wohl, E.E. and David, G.C.L. 2008. Consistency of scaling relations among bedrock and alluvial channels. *Journal of Geophysical Research* **113**: F04013. doi: 10.1029/ 2008JF000989.

Wohl, E.E. and Grodek, T. 1994. Channel bed-steps along Nahal Yael, Negev desert, Israel. *Geomorphology* **9**: 117–126.

Wohl, E.E. and Legleiter, C.J. 2002. Controls on pool characteristics along a resistant-boundary channel. *Journal of Geology* **111**: 103–114.

Wohl, E.E. and Ikeda, H. 1997. Experimental simulation of channel incision into a cohesive substrate at varying gradients. *Geology* **25**: 295–298.

Wohl, E.E. and Ikeda, H. 1998. Patterns of bedrock channel erosion on the Boso Peninsula, Japan. *Journal of Geology* **106**: 331–345.

Wohl, E.E. and Merritt, D.M. 2001. Bedrock channel morphology. *Geological Society of America Bulletin* **113**: 1205–1212.

Wohl, E.E., Greenbaum, N., Schick, A., and Baker, V. 1994. Controls on bedrock channel incision along Nahal Paran, Israel. *Earth Surface Processes and Landforms* **19**: 1–13.

Wohl, E.E., Thompson, D.M., and Miller, A.J. 1999. Canyons with undulating walls. *Geological Society of America Bulletin* **111**: 949–959.

Yanites, B.J. and Tucker, G.E. 2010. Controls and limits on bedrock channel geometry. *Journal of Geophysical Research* **115**: F04019. doi: 10.1029/2009JF001601.

Yanites, B.J., Tucker, G.E., Mueller, K.J. *et al.* 2010. Incision and channel morphology across active structures along the Peikang River, central Taiwan: Implications for the importance of channel width. *Geological Society of America Bulletin* **122**: 1192–1208.

# 29.10   DISCUSSION

## 29.10.1   Discussion by Kristin Bunte

The term "semi-alluvial" streams has been used mostly for bedrock channels that transport some gravel (J. Turowski, this chapter) or for gravel-bed streams in which gravel and cobble transport is affected by the presence of bedrock (e.g., Lamarre *et al.*, 2010). It would be quite helpful to add steep, coarse gravel- and cobble-bed channels with low sediment supply (typical of many high elevation Rocky Mountain streams) to this group. Such Rocky Mountain streams fit at least two of the "semi-alluvial" criteria put forth by Turowski: (i) bedrock limits the dynamics of streambed development and (ii) bedload moves in a thin layer over a poorly mobile or immobile bed. In low-sediment supply, steep Rocky Mountain streams, the bed experiences a great deal of structural stability due to particles wedging and interlocking with neighbouring particles, as well as by being firmly stuck in near-vertical, vegetated banks. The structural stability makes much of the bed functionally equivalent to bedrock for almost all high flow events except for perhaps very infrequent, extreme ones. Typically, some fine- and medium-size gravel, and even an occasional cobble, moves over those coarse beds without forcing the wedged particles out of their locked position. Wedging is also not limited to the coarsest particles (cobbles and boulders), but may include some of the coarse and medium gravel particles as well. Algae and moss growing on the bed surface attest to bed particle immobility during commonly occurring high-flow events. Similarly, in my experience of those streams, many coarse gravel and cobble surface particles can only be pried loose from the bed (e.g., during a pebble count) with the help of a trowel or a crowbar.

The advantage of formally categorizing steep mountain streams with low sediment supply and high bed stability as semi-alluvial would be improved predictions of bedload transport rates and critical flows. In practical terms this means flagging these streams as not having the properties and dynamics of alluvial streams (where even low flows move almost all bed material sizes) or threshold channels (where bankfull flows moves the bed surface $D_{50}$ size). Uncritical transfer of principles valid in alluvial and threshold channels to semi-alluvial streams leads to erroneous results in estimating incipient motion conditions and bedload transport rates.

## 29.10.2   Discussion by Rob Ferguson

You suggest that in many rivers large floods supply more sediment than they can evacuate, so that there is a protective alluvial cover until medium-sized floods evacuate it. Like Lague (2010) you model this by assuming that sediment supply is a simple power function of discharge (Equation 29.16), whereas transport capacity follows a threshold-excess function (Equation 29.15).

Is this an appropriate model for all kinds of bedrock reach? The supply has different sources depending on the tectonic setting. In young mountain ranges much of the supply is from failure of steep, close-coupled hillslopes, and the supply rate need not vary over time in the same way as does the river's transport capacity. But bedrock gorges also occur in old landscapes where rivers have incised into much flatter terrain because of post-glacial rebound. In this case the supply is predominantly from the alluvial river bed immediately upstream, and surely should follow the same kind of threshold-excess rating curve as the transport capacity within the gorge. Any fluctuation over time in sediment cover must then be due to a difference in the threshold for transport in the alluvial and bedrock reaches, a difference in channel width, or a combination of these. At one site in northern England that a colleague of mine has been monitoring for several years, there is some evidence that major floods sweep the gorge clear of sediment and lesser floods gradually replenish the cover. This variety of behaviour suggests that some detailed process studies of sediment transfers through semi-alluvial reaches would be instructive.

## 29.10.3   Discussion by Rebecca Hodge

As Turowski has outlined, sediment is a key component of bedrock river incision. The incision rate depends on the sediment size and mode of transport, and hence the sediment grain-size distribution may strongly influence the channel morphology. It is therefore desirable to be able to predict how sediment grain size will vary along a semi-alluvial channel; this means that it is necessary to be able to quantify grain-size-specific transport rates under semi-alluvial conditions. At present, alluvial sediment relations are commonly applied to semi-alluvial settings, however, whether this application is valid has not yet been rigorously tested.

Initial results from magnetic sediment tracing experiments indicate that semi-alluvial rivers can display different sediment dynamics to fully alluvial rivers, and it is suggested that the sediment dynamics are a function of a river's location along the bedrock–alluvial continuum. Magnetic tracer data were collected from two semi-alluvial rivers with 10 and 80% sediment cover. (The latter data were collected by L. Sklar.) In the river with 80% cover, sediment behaves as in an alluvial system, with size-selective transport and a gamma distribution of travel distances. In the river with 10% cover, transport is size-independent and travel distances do not fit a gamma distribution. Further research is necessary to identify the causes of these differences, but it is hypothesized that they result from differences in sediment depth, sediment packing and the distribution of sediment patches.

### 29.10.4    Reply by Jens M. Turowski

I agree that there may be some parallels between steep boulder-bed channels and bedrock channels in terms of sediment dynamics and that the term "semi-alluvial" may be used to make clear these parallels. Similar ideas were discussed by Meshkova et al. (Chapter 31, this volume), who suggested to use the term semi-alluvial, for example, for channels influenced by stationary wood and dense root networks.

Ferguson makes an excellent point. Of course, only in a certain subclass of bedrock channels do large floods supply most of the sediment, while small and medium floods evacuate. In fact, in my experience, most semi-alluvial channels have a more or less continuous sediment cover at low flow. As I have outlined, this behaviour can easily be incorporated into the simple model by choosing a supply exponent smaller than the transport capacity exponent. There may also be semi-alluvial channels in which supply matches capacity at all discharges; however, I expect these to be rare. The study by Heritage et al. (2004) is instructive, as they show that reaches with above-capacity supply at high discharge alternate with reaches with above-capacity supply at low discharge.

I agree that detailed process studies of sediment transfer through semi-alluvial reaches are necessary, and there is much we have to learn. In this respect, the simple model I have described highlights three points: (i) a single representative discharge, as often used for sand- or gravel-bed channels is not sufficient to capture the behaviour of semi-alluvial reaches, (ii) observations over a variety of flood stages are necessary to understand the sediment transport behaviour of the channel, and (iii) it is crucial to understand the sediment transport behaviour of the channel to understand its long-term development.

The point made by Hodge is similar to ones before: we need detailed studies of the sediment dynamics in semi-alluvial channels. The grain-size distribution is certainly an important aspect of this. I am very much looking forward to the final results of the mentioned study.

## 29.11    DISCUSSION REFERENCES

Heritage, G.L., Large, A.R.G., Moon, B.P., and Jewitt, G. 2004. Channel hydraulics and geomorphic effects of an extreme flood event on the Sabie River, South Africa. *Catena* **58**: 151–181.

Lague, D. 2010. Reduction of long-term bedrock incision efficiency by short-term alluvial cover intermittency. *Journal of Geophysical Research* **115**: F02011. doi: 10.1029/2008JF001210.

Lamarre, H., Marquis, G., Sicotte, K., Roy, M., and Roy, A.G. 2010. Dynamics of semi-alluvial systems. Poster presented at *Gravel-bed Rivers 7*. International Workshop held at Tadoussac, Quebec, 6–10 September.

# 30

# Transport Capacity, Bedrock Exposure, and Process Domains

## Thomas E. Lisle

## 30.1 INTRODUCTION

Turowski (Chapter 29, this volume) provides a comprehensive review of the rapidly developing field of bedrock erosion of semi-alluvial channels. He has distilled a large and dense literature, logically organized the subject matter, and identified the salient issues. Providing a guide to the literature with an exhaustive reference list is a service to those who want to understand this problem. The main challenges have been to understand a spectrum of processes and conditions governing bedrock erosion that are difficult to observe, so that models that are consistent with process can be formulated. It has become evident that a dominant control on bedrock erosion is exposure to the tool effects of particles in transport, since rates of wear of bedrock by impacting particles commonly exceed greatly rates of uplift (Sklar and Dietrich, 2001). Thus the attention to semi-alluvial channels is justified for increasing our understanding of drainage network evolution.

If the problem essentially reduces to the role of alluvial cover and tools, then a fundamental approach is to quantify spatial and temporal variations in transport capacity and sediment supply. This is especially relevant to the fluvial domain downstream of headwater channels, where the log-linearity of slope–area relations is consistent with log-linear relations between drainage area (the contributing area of sediment as well as discharge) and factors influencing transport capacity, including water discharge, hydraulic variables, and particle size (Stock *et al.*, 2005).

In this discussion, I raise the need to quantify relations between transport capacity and bedrock erosion to sediment supply within the fluvial domain. Upstream of the fluvial domain, I discuss processes that episodically expose and erode bedrock, including debris flows and gully headcut migration.

## 30.2 TRANSPORT CAPACITY IN THE FLUVIAL ZONE

### 30.2.1 Transport Capacity and Sediment Stage

Transport capacity mediates relations between sediment supply, alluvial cover, and bedrock exposure, which can be examined conceptually by attempting to plot transport capacity versus a measure of sediment supply, e.g., "sediment stage" or the depth of alluvial cover (Figure 30.1). It is well known that factors that influence transport rates (e.g., armouring, channel geometry, and roughness) commonly change as the channel aggrades or degrades in response to shifts in the balance between supply and transport (Lisle and Church, 2002; Demeter *et al.*, 2005; Chatanantavet and Parker, 2008; Johnson *et al.*, 2009). For example, armouring may increase and roughness increase in a sediment-starved channel with a decreasing sediment stage, thereby lowering transport capacity. Conversely, fine-grained sediment pulses can increase the mobility of large particles (Jackson and Beschta, 1984; Iseya and Ikeda, 1987; Wilcock and Kenworthy, 2002; Venditti *et al.*, 2010), thereby boosting transport capacity and possibly causing armoured channels to erode. However, the dynamics of transport capacity, which may be important to modelling drainage evolution, are poorly understood. Over what time scale and range of sediment stage should transport capacity be considered as dynamic or constant? Is there a dynamic equilibrium between transport capacity and sediment stage, which would define a common relation as a channel aggrades and degrades (scenario 1, Figure 30.1), or does transient disequilibrium created by changes in the rate of sediment supply cause channel response and transport capacity to vary as sediment stage is perturbed (scenario 2)? In reference to Turowski (Chapter 29, this volume), scenario 1 represents dynamic equilibrium with sediment

*Gravel-bed Rivers: Processes, Tools, Environments*, First Edition. Edited by Michael Church, Pascale M. Biron and André G. Roy.

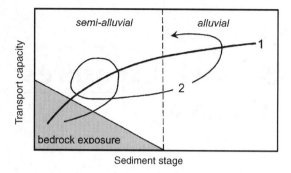

**Figure 30.1** Conceptual relations between bedrock exposure in a semi-alluvial channel, transport capacity, and sediment stage. Lines represent scenarios 1 and 2 in the text. In scenario 2, depressed transport capacity in an overall positive relation between transport capacity and sediment stage promotes increases in sediment stage during aggradation; enhanced transport capacity promotes decreases in sediment stage during degradation.

supply as a boundary condition governing average channel condition (manifested as transport capacity); scenario 2 represents transient conditions caused by short-term variations in supply.

Evidence for these behaviours is sparse. Lisle and Church (2002) found generally positive relations between sediment transport and storage in degrading, gravel-bed channels, which can be attributed primarily to increased armouring with declining sediment supply. Pryor et al. (in press) used a flume experiment to model response of a natural channel undergoing episodes of aggradation and degradation and finds departures from a common transport-sediment stage relation for different phases of aggradation-degradation episodes. Variations within a generally positive relation between sediment output and sediment storage were created by changes in channel morphology that lagged variations in rates of sediment supply. For example, as the channel incised and deepened, greater transport rates were achieved than during filling at the same sediment stage. This effect was greater in experimental runs with more disequilibrium at the height of aggradation before the sediment supply rate was reduced. These results indicate the dynamics described by scenario 2, and the similarity of observations of channel morphology and texture in the physical model and prototype supports this interpretation. Furthermore, cross-section surveys in the prototype channel (Cuneo Creek, northern California) show large differences in rates of loss in sediment storage between two degradational phases at the same values of stored sediment volume (Smith, 2004).

Madej et al. (2009) performed a similar experiment modelling aggradation-degradation episodes in Redwood Creek, which could represent a more distal channel in a drainage network. The range in particle size was not as wide as that in the experiment modelling Cuneo Creek and hysteresis in transport-storage relations was not as strong. Nevertheless, wandering of the plotted points in transport-storage space indicates the dynamics of scenario 2.

In conclusion, transport rates show a tendency to be high at high sediment stages, but transport capacity at a given sediment stage in a reach of channel is contingent on conditions resulting from its geomorphic history that may include periods of relative stability punctuated by large floods and sediment-input events. Variations in transport-storage relations are evident in the complex response of gravel-bed rivers to variations in sediment supply due to lags in sediment routing (Schumm, 1973) and transient increases in stored sediment associated with large floods (Kelsey, 1980; Hartshorn et al. 2002; Turowski et al., 2008). This suggests that the threshold of exposure and erosion of bedrock in channels is not associated with a consistent rate of sediment supply. Background conditions governing steady-state conditions, such as uplift rate (Turowski, Chapter 29, this volume) may pre-dispose a channel to effect bedrock erosion, but the critical balance between sediment supply and transport that leads to bedrock exposure is subject to transient conditions manifested in changing relations between transport capacity and sediment storage.

### 30.2.2 Feedbacks with Bedrock Exposure

A critical threshold in sediment stage is reached when bedrock becomes exposed on the channel bed and sloping banks (disregarding bedrock walls for this discussion). At this stage and lower, bedrock can be locally eroded by particle impact and drainage network evolution can proceed. For this reason, transport capacity has been defined specifically for the bedrock incision problem as the transport regime that maintains a complete alluvial cover (Sklar and Dietrich, 1998). Exposed bedrock commonly creates large-scale form roughness and locally alters skin friction, which influence transport capacity by altering hydraulic friction, transport surfaces, and the distribution of tractive forces (Demeter et al., 2005; Finnegan et al., 2007; Chatanantavet and Parker, 2008; Johnson et al., 2009).

An interesting dynamic between bedrock exposure, bedrock erosion, and sediment stage is apparent in semi-alluvial channels that are prone to form bar-pool sequences. In such channels, bedrock is commonly exposed locally as large obstructions that force scour and deposition in concert with the formation of bar-pool sequences (Figure 30.2). The patterns of flow and

**Figure 30.2** Bedrock obstruction in Jacoby Creek, northern California. The pool scoured around the right-bank obstruction terminates the upstream bar and is the origin of the next bar downstream. This pattern has remained fixed since the author's first visit here in 1978.

sediment transport they create are similar to those documented at bridge piers and abutments (Raudkivi and Ettema, 1983) and, if large enough, they can create flow structures that intersect sediment transport from the upstream bar, scour a pool, and set up hydraulic and sedimentological patterns that form the downstream bar (Lisle, 1986). Insofar as the bedrock forms are quasi-stable in the time scale in which bar-pool sequences are formed, a series of bedrock obstructions and bends can stabilize channels in forms that expose bedrock deeply and route particles in high-velocity flow paths along the bedrock. Whether bedrock is abraded chiefly by impacts of saltating particles along lanes of bedload transport or more generally by suspended sediment (Richardson and Carling, 2005), the deep exposure of bedrock in the energetic environment of pools at high flow would seem to promote abrasion. At the same time, bedrock obstructions tend to increase flow resistance, induce backwaters and eddies, and thereby promote deposition and alluvial coverage around the scoured area (Lisle, 1986). Thus, even at a relatively high sediment stage (broad alluvial cover and bar surfaces much higher than exposed bedrock), the bedrock may create a self-inflicting dynamic between channel topography, flow, and bedload transport.

## 30.3 UPSTREAM OF THE FLUVIAL ZONE

### 30.3.1 The Debris-Flow Domain

The transition from log-linear to curvilinear relations between drainage area and channel gradient marks a change in processes governing bedrock erosion from the fluvial domain downstream to a domain upstream where debris flows, weathering, and other processes not associated with threshold gravel-bed channels dominate erosion and transport of bed material (Stock and Dietrich, 2003). Although low-order tributaries commonly have drainage areas of $10^0$ km$^2$ or less, they comprise a large fraction of the total length of channels in a drainage network and are closely tied to hillslope processes that supply much of the sediment to the channel network. They are also sensitive to environmental stressors such as human impacts and climate change.

Broadly speaking, the convexity in the slope–area relation upstream of the fluvial domain can be interpreted as a zone of greater erosional efficiency: upstream of the threshold it takes less of a slope for a given drainage area to maintain an equilibrium profile than indicated by an extrapolation upstream of the fluvial relation. In the limit of slopes increasing to an angle of repose of alluvium or colluvium, such a loss of dependency of slope on area must be expected (Stock and Dietrich, 2003), but how do processes expose and erode bedrock in the intervening reaches? A modelling framework for debris-flow influences on profile development by Stock and Dietrich (in press) predicts curvilinear relations between slope and drainage area. One contributing factor is that sediment transport is more episodic than in fluvial reaches but, when they occur, transport events commonly evacuate the sediment cover to bedrock, allowing removal of weathered bedrock and providing a period of abrasion by saltating particles before the alluvial or colluvial cover is restored. Thus the problem is not one of balancing transport capacity and sediment supply, but one of the frequency and threshold of episodes that scour the alluvial/colluvial cover and expose bedrock to erosion.

Debris flows tend to be dominant in tectonically active terrains with hard bedrock that maintain steep slopes, have low rates of mechanical weathering, and produce large rocks that powerfully impact exposed bedrock. In contrast, softer rocks such as poorly indurated sediments tend to have higher rates of weathering and produce smaller rocks that are rapidly reduced by abrasion during transport. Here, I present a field example of a process governing profile development in headwater channels that is common in terrains with soft bedrock – gullying and headcut retreat.

### 30.3.2 The Gully Domain: Caspar Creek

The drainage of Caspar Creek in northern California (drainage area 10 km$^2$) is deeply incised into a flight of uplifted marine terraces formed over more than 300 000 years on Franciscan sandstone and shale (Merritts et al., 1991). Valley side slopes are steep, but mainstem channels and many tributary segments are bordered by narrow valley flats. Tributaries between 1.9 and 80 ha show signs of active gullying that has been accelerated by logging of the forest of coastal redwood (*Sequoia sempervirens*) and Douglas fir (*Pseudotsuga menziesii*) since the late nineteenth century (Reid *et al.*, 2010). Channel erosion of weathered alluvium, saprolite, and bedrock occurs in plunge pools of active headcuts, which are spaced at an average of 12 m. An alluvial cover is prevalent everywhere but in the plunge pools. Sediment transport in tributaries is affected by mass movement (e.g., debris flows and deep-seated landslides), but active gullies are nearly continuous in all tributaries. In the fluvial zone, lower gradients and the accumulation of a deeper cover of non-cohesive alluvium apparently suppresses headcut development, and channels are characteristic of threshold, gravel-bed channels with armour layers, wood-formed step-pools, bars, and riffle-pool sequences.

Similar to relations observed by Stock and Dietrich (2003), the relation between drainage area and channel slope shows a broad log-curvilinear relation in upstream reaches (Figure 30.3). The transition downstream to log-linearity is unclear, but could be construed to occur at approximately 1 km$^2$, which corresponds to the transition from gullied channels to threshold channels. The scatter of points also increases upstream of this point. This can be expected because the local slope at a headcut influences plunge-pool scour only weakly. The flow goes critical at the brink of the headcut regardless of flow conditions upstream, which are always in the subcritical range. Thus local slope is freer to vary than in the fluvial domain, although gradient limits the frequency of headcuts. Slopes above the transition to gullied channels are greater than about 0.04, which does not appear to be significantly

different than the lower limit of debris-flow influence in other basins (Stock and Dietrich, 2003; Stock *et al.*, 2005). However, drainage areas at the transition appear to be lower in the gully case (~1 km$^2$) than in the debris-flow case (~10$^1$ km$^2$). In both cases, a trend toward increased efficiency of channel incision can be linked to a transition in process that exposes bedrock at the time scale of an event and leaves it vulnerable to scour.

## 30.4 REFERENCES

Chatanantavet, P. and Parker, G. 2008. Experimental study of bedrock channel alluviation under varied sediment supply and hydraulic conditions. *Water Resources Research* **44**: W12446. doi: 10.1029/2007WR006581.

Demeter, G.I. and Sklar, L.S. 2005. The influence of variable sediment supply and bed roughness on the spatial distribution of incision in a laboratory bedrock channel. *American Geophysical Union, Fall Meeting, San Francisco CA, 5–9 December.* Abstract 53D-0519.

Finnegan, N.J., Sklar, L.S., and Fuller, T.K. 2007. Interplay of sediment supply, river incision, and channel morphology revealed by the transient evolution of an experimental bedrock channel. *Journal of Geophysical Research* **112**: F03S11. doi: 10.1029/2006JF000569.

Hartshorn, K., Hovius, N., Dade, W.B., and Slingerland, R.L. 2002. Climate-driven bedrock incision in an active mountain belt. *Science* **297**: 2036–2038.

Iseya, F. and Ikeda, H. 1987. Pulsations in bedload transport rates induced by a longitudinal sediment sorting: A flume study using sand and gravel mixtures. *Geografiska Annaler* **69A**: 15–27.

Jackson, W.L. and Beschta, R.L. 1984. Influences of increased sand delivery on the morphology of sand and gravel channels. *Water Resources Bulletin* **20**: 527–533.

Johnson, J.P., Whipple, K.X., Sklar, L.S., and Hanks, T.C. 2009. Transport slopes, sediment cover, and bedrock channel incision in the Henry Mountains, *Utah. Journal of Geophysical Research* **114**: F02014. doi: 10.1029/2007JF000862.

Kelsey, H.M. 1980. A sediment budget and an analysis of geomorphic process in the Van Duzen River Basin, North Coastal California, 1941-1975. *Geological Society of American Bulletin* **91**: 1119–1126.

Lisle, T.E. 1986. Stabilization of a gravel channel by large streamside obstructions and bedrock bends, Jacoby Creek, northwestern California. *Geological Society of America Bulletin* **97**: 999–1011.

Lisle, T.E. and Church, M. 2002. Sediment transport-storage relations for degrading gravel-bed channels. *Water Resources Research* **38**: 1219. doi: 1210.1029/2001WR001086.

Madej, M.A., Sutherland, D.G., Lisle, T.E., and Smith, B.S. 2009. Channel responses to varying sediment input: A flume experiment modeled after Redwood Creek, California. *Geomorphology* **103**: 507–519.

Merritts, D.J., Chadwick, O.A., and Hendricks, D.M. 1991. Rates and processes of soil evolution on uplifted marine terraces, northern California. *Geoderma* **51**: 241–275.

Pryor, B.S., Lisle, T.E., Montoya, D.S., and Hilton, S. in press. Transport and storage of bed material in a gravel-bed channel during episodes of aggradation and degradation: A field and flume study. *Earth Surface Processes and Landforms.*

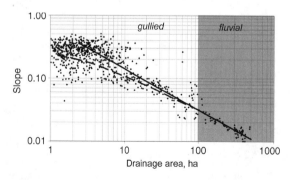

**Figure 30.3** Relation between drainage area and channel slope in Caspar Creek, northern California. Data were obtained by laser altimetry. Solid line represents log-linear relation for the fluvial domain; dashed line represents curvilinear relation for gullied domain.

Raudkivi, A.J. and Ettema, R. 1983. Clear-water scour at cylindrical piers. *Journal of Hydraulic Engineering* **109**: 338–351.

Reid, L.M., Dewey, N.J., Lisle, T.E., and Hilton, S. 2010. The incidence and role of gullies after logging in a coastal redwood forest. *Geomorphology* **117**: 155–169.

Richardson, K. and Carling, P.A. 2005. *A Typology of Sculpted Forms in Open Bedrock Channels*. Geological Society of America, Special Paper 392.

Schumm, S.A. 1973. Geomorphic thresholds and complex reponse of drainage systems. In Morisawa, M., editor. *Fluvial Geomorphology*. Binghamton, State University of New York, pp. 299–310.

Sklar, L.S. and Dietrich, W.E. 2001. Sediment and rock strength controls on river incision into bedrock. *Geology* **29**: 1087–1090.

Sklar, L.S. and Dietrich, W.E. 1998. River longitudinal profiles and bedrock incision models: stream power and the influence of sediment supply. In Tinkler, K.J. and Wohl, E., editors. *Rivers over Rock: Fluvial Processes In Bedrock Channels*.

American Geophysical Union, Washington DC. Geophysical Monograph 107: 237–260.

Stock, J. and Dietrich, W.E. 2003. Erosion of steepland valleys by debris flows: evidence of a topographic signature. *Water Resources Research* **39**: 1089. doi: 10.1029/2001WR001057.

Stock, J., Montgomery, D., Collins, B.D., Dietrich, W.E., and Sklar, L. 2005. Field measurements of incision rates following bedrock exposure: Implications for process controls on the long profi les of valleys cut by rivers and debris flows. *Geological Society of America Bulletin* **117**: 174–194.

Turowski, J.M., Hovius, N., Hsieh, M., Lague, D., and Chen, M. 2008. Distribution of erosion across bedrock channels. *Earth Surface Processes and Landforms* **33**: 353–363.

Venditti, J.G., Dietrich, W.E., Nelson, P.A. *et al.* 2010. Mobilization of coarse surface layers in gravel-bedded rivers by finer gravel bed load. *Water Resources Research* **46**: W07506. doi: 10.1029/2009WR008329.

Wilcock, P.R. and Kenworthy, S.T. 2002. A two-fraction model for the transport of sand/gravel mixtures. *Water Resources Research* **38**: 1194. doi: 1110.1029/2001WR000684.

# 31

# Nomenclature, Complexity, Semi-alluvial Channels and Sediment-flux-driven Bedrock Erosion

**Lyubov V. Meshkova, Paul A. Carling, and Thomas Buffin-Bélanger**

## 31.1   INTRODUCTION

The purpose of this discussion is not to provide a critique of the chapter by Turowksi, but to amplify issues that we think are important and to which Turowski's written contribution draws attention.

## 31.2   DEFINITION OF CHANNEL TYPES

For consistency of nomenclature it is worth noting that the term "rock-bed" river should be preferred as this is consistent with the accepted terms: "gravel-bed" river and "sand-bed" river. Turowski *et al.* (2008) commented on nomenclature but used both "rock-bed" and "bedrock" in their terminology; applying the former adjective to channel-shaping processes and the latter to a description of a channel at a given location in time. Both adjectives are used commonly in the literature and it is likely that attempts to introduce such a finessed differentiation and standardization will be resisted. In addition, often "bedrock" grammatically is a more convenient adjective than "rock-bed" and so both terms are used herein interchangeably.

Turowski *et al.* (2008, p.28) provided the following definition of a bedrock channel: "A bedrock channel cannot substantially widen, lower or shift its bed without eroding bedrock". Given that a lateral shift in a bedrock channel cannot be accomplished without erosion of the lateral margin we can simplify the definition of Turowski *et al.* (2008) to include only two, rather than three, adjustments in geometry through the statement: "A bedrock channel cannot adjust laterally, nor incise without eroding bedrock".

Turowski *et al.* (2008) also introduced a useful definition cartoon (Figure 31.1, parts a, b and c) that prompts

additional comment. Channel type A exists where there is negligible sediment accumulation on the bed and a negligible transported sediment load and as such this type of channel approaches an end-member classification of clear-water flow. Such channels are unusual in nature although some bedrock step-pool systems approach this condition (Carling *et al.*, 2005). Physical wear due to sparse sediment tool effects allows limited opportunity to adjust width or depth. Rather, at the extreme, corrosion and chemical weathering will be the primary mechanisms for inducing changes in channel geometry where the rock-type permits, and subaerial weathering will pertain in the case of all rock types. In principle, adding a substantial suspended load (but no bedload) would induce channel adjustments (Turowski *et al.*, 2008), for case A, through abrasion of both the side walls and the bed. However, it is difficult to envisage a natural system wherein suspended load was not associated with a bedload. This end-member channel type we refer to as a "rock-bed" or "bedrock" channel. We also include in Figure 31.1 the alluvial end-member for completeness.

Most natural bedrock channels studied to date would be classified as channel type B, as these systems contain a mobile bedload and usually a deposited sediment filament that covers at least a substantial part of the rock bed, although the side walls are bare bedrock. As soon as there is a significant alluvial content, the channel cannot be considered a bedrock channel; rather it is a "mixed bedrock-alluvial system". General reference to bedrock "constrained" and "confined" channels has been made previously (e.g., Montgomery and Buffington, 1997; Schumm, 2005), but below we provide more precise definitions.

Where the channel is laterally confined by competent bedrock, but there is a live bedload layer or an alluvial bed, there is less opportunity for lateral erosion, in

*Gravel-bed Rivers: Processes, Tools, Environments*, First Edition. Edited by Michael Church, Pascale M. Biron and André G. Roy.

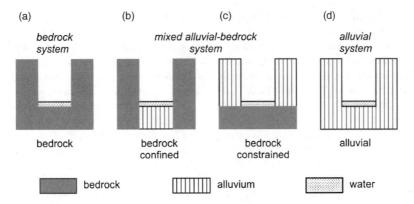

**Figure 31.1**    The end members in the continuum of channel types from bedrock to alluvial character.

contrast to a greater opportunity either to accrete the sediment fill or to erode the rock bed; the assumptions being that loose sediment is more erodible than the confining bedrock walls and the rock bed is more subject to abrasion by bedload than the side walls. This class of channel we refer to as "bedrock confined" and the channels are usually rather narrow with a sediment fillet at the base (Figure 31.1b). The third type of channel has a rock bed, but alluvial sidewalls. In this latter case, vertical incision is less readily accomplished in comparison with lateral erosion of the alluvium (Figure 31.1c) and to differentiate from class B, we term this channel type "bedrock constrained". We return to this class later, but it is class B which has been subject to the majority of research to date.

## 31.3    STEADY-STATE, DYNAMIC EQUILIBRIUM AND THE ROLE OF SEDIMENT

Turowski (Chapter 29, this volume) considers channels in steady state where bedrock erosion equals uplift. Here we do not challenge the conceptual model advanced by Turowski, but seek to clarify some issues which highlight the significance of any sediment fill to the equilibrium of a rock-bed channel. Steady state might be defined as "a stable condition that does not change over time or in which change in one direction is continually balanced by change in another". The alternative to steady state is defined by Turowski as "transient conditions". Transience implies impermanence to any adjustment and consequently this latter system state is a form of dynamic equilibrium. Dynamic equilibrium might be defined as "a lack of change in a system as inputs and outputs remain in balance because if changes do occur, then feedbacks will allow for correction". More usually the state of such a

system is such that the output continually changes, but remains within fairly narrow bounds. The output is characterized by a mean value and a bounded range around that mean value.

It is important to consider the implications of these two system states for the evolution of the geometry of a bedrock channel. Where uplift equals incision, the channel slot will deepen over time such that the side walls of the slot become higher. It is important to note that reference is made here to the depth of the slot and not the wetted depth. This is a simple example of a steady-state system, but note that an increasing slot depth has implications for the distribution of erosional forces on the channel boundary if discharge were to increase above a discharge reference value associated with a given wetted depth. Thus, although uplift supplies additional bedrock for erosion, the width–depth ratio of the slot changes through time with channel width changing less as the slot deepens. Although discharge variability through time may be important for adjustments in bedrock channel geometry, it is important to note that given a sufficiently low base level, a competent steady discharge can still lead to changes in the slot geometry through abrasion and solution, including width adjustments (Turowski *et al.*, 2008) if incision is halted. Even if channel geometry refers to a constant value of, say, width–depth ratio, the actual channel dimensions in principle could change; i.e., both width and depth increase whilst *W/d* remains static.

If we define the physical boundary of the channel as consisting of bedrock (i.e., width and depth, for example, are defined by the bedrock surfaces rather than any sediment fillet sitting on the bedrock), then a bedrock channel can only be in dynamic equilibrium (as defined above) if the overall size of the channel increases through time, as bedrock erosion is a one-way process. As noted above, *W/d* might remain constant, but overall slot size cannot remain constant. Either *W/d* has to change, in which case there is no dynamic equilibrium, or the channel size has to change. If *W/d* changes, as is likely, then a bedrock channel can only maintain dynamic equilibrium if there is sediment deposition on the bed to counter any bedrock erosion. Therefore the spatial disposition of sediment within mixed bedrock-alluvial streams is an important systems response to maintain dynamic equilibrium. Thus, in this context, the balance between a tools-dominated domain and a cover-dominated domain becomes of greater significance than determining the local vertical erosion rate alone; rather, the variation in the loci of sediment covers in space and time will influence the shape of the bedrock long profile, as well as any propensity for the river to move laterally.

Class C, the bedrock constrained system, is the least well-investigated type of river. The best published examples of such a system are reaches within the Orange River, South Africa (Tooth and McCarthy, 2004). The Orange River has a tendency to be anastomosed with locally two or more bedrock-floored channels with alluvial banks. Although the Orange River is a large system (individual channels up to $\sim$3000 m$^3$ s$^{-1}$), there are numerous examples of small, single-channel bedrock constrained channels in nature which seem to have been over-looked. The Mekong River in northern Cambodia near Kratie is a further example of a large, constrained system (Meshkova and Carling, in press) incised some 20 m into ancient alluvium (Figure 31.2) with a bedrock floor and with evidence of lateral stability since the mid-Quaternary. The Mekong is of particular interest because it is anastomosed, with a low Quaternary rate of vertical incision (possibly 40 to 100 m in 600 000 years; Carbonnel, 1972). Low incision rates in this case are not conditioned by an extensive sediment cover, but rather by a relatively low channel gradient (0.00027) close to the base level and by tectonic stability. The mean peak annual discharge for the last 90 years at Kratie is in excess of 50 000 m$^3$ s$^{-1}$ (MRC, 2009) and is contained within the channel boundary. However, although total peak power is high, around 132 300 W, this is distributed across an anastomosed channel network in places up to 5 km wide, giving an average unit stream power as low as 26 W m$^{-1}$, such that incision is slight and highly localized across the sections. Nevertheless, the annual power is sufficient to transport an annual suspended fine sand load of 160 megatonnes with an unknown sandy bedload component, there being negligible gravel. Despite the competence to transport sand, the river exhibits persistent zones of sedimentation and zones of bare bedrock (Figure 31.3). Quantitative study of air photographs has shown that the loci and size of sand bars have remained constant over the last 50 years or so. At the regional scale, and as might be expected, it is evident that bare rock reaches correspond to the steepest reaches of the river, with the intervening lower slope bedrock reaches having variable degrees of alluviation. However, it is the local controls on sedimentation in this complex anastomosed network that provide the reach-scale complexity in the sedimentation pattern and these controls are more difficult to ascertain.

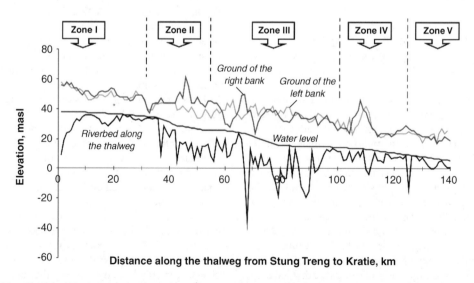

**Figure 31.2** The elevation of the riverbed, dry season water level and the ground elevation of the western and eastern banks of the Mekong in northern Cambodia. Modified after Meshkova and Carling, in press. Zones correspond to those explained in Figure 31.3.

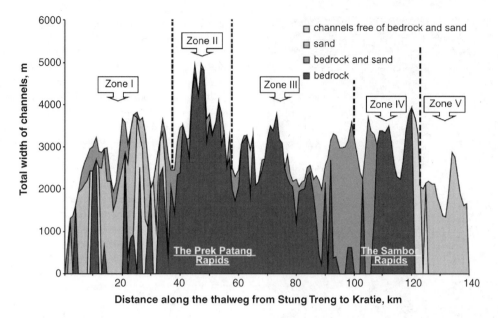

**Figure 31.3** Zonation of the channel of the Mekong shown in Figure 31.2 is based in part on the proportion of the channel width occupied by sand fillet over bedrock as shown here. The detail of sand distribution in Zones II and III in particular is complex and is highly simplified here. Modified after Meshkova and Carling, in press. Lightest sections are deep-water with indeterminate bed type. (See the color version of this figure in color plate section)

Yet these local controls may be important, inducing avulsion of individual Mekong subchannels (Meshkova and Carling, in press). These effects of alluviation in bedrock systems on backwater effects and channel shifting are only recently being explored (Humphrey and Konrad, 2000; Capart *et al.*, 2007). The Mekong in northern Cambodia remains a topic of investigation by the authors, with several luminescence dates imminent to define the incision history more precisely.

## 31.4   NEW CONCEPTS

### 31.4.1   *"Alluvial Overprint"*

To the north of Cambodia in southern Laos, the Mekong is also a bedrock constrained anastomosed system that is incised into ancient alluvium, flowing across bedrock. However, there has been considerable lateral movement during the Quaternary such that it is often bounded laterally by its own alluvium. Satellite images show that a regional-scale meandering pattern is super-imposed onto local bedrock control (Figure 31.4). The meandering pattern has not been investigated, but seemingly "sweeps" across the bedrock surface such that the meander planforms have the characteristics of an alluvial system. This style of alluviation we here term an "alluvial overprint" and the interaction of alluvial channel processes, including bank cutting and bank accretion with a

bedrock constraining floor, introduces further intriguing complexity to the future understanding of rock-bedded rivers and re-inforces the need to document these specific river styles (Heritage *et al.*, 2001).

### 31.4.2   *"Bedrock Footprint"*

The presence of moving sediments plays a key role in the evolution and nature of the bedrock sections in semi-alluvial channels. Similarly, several authors have highlighted that the presence of rock outcrops plays a crucial role in the morphodynamics of semi-alluvial channels. This issue is addressed here briefly using three recent examples from the literature.

Nicol and Hickin (2010) studied the planform geometry and the migration behaviour of confined meandering rivers. These are rivers in valleys that are laterally constrained and in which planform geometry of free meanders cannot develop fully. Figure 31.5 presents a LiDAR image from the Matane River, Eastern Québec, illustrating the planform geometry of such a confined meandering river. Although relations between planform geometry variables extracted from 23 locations along confined meandering rivers are generally not inconsistent with those for freely meandering rivers, Nicol and Hickin (2010) observed significant differences in the ratio of channel length/channel width and the bend curvature. For the migrating behaviour, they observed

**Figure 31.4** Anastomosed bedrock-constrained fluvial network of the Mekong River, Siphandone, southern Laos. Landsat-7, horizontal field of view approximately 40 km. Virgin and degraded forest (dark shades) on ancient alluvium flank the river system, whereas the recent river corridor is now largely denuded of natural vegetation (light shades). Although "linear" reaches of the river reflect structural control (e.g. black arrows), it is also evident that curvilinear alluvial-controlled reaches occur (e.g., white arrows) (see text for detail). Reproduced, with permission, from Carling, P.A. 2009. Geomorphology and Sedimentology of the Lower Mekong River. In Campbell, I.C., editor. *The Mekong: Biophysical Environment of an International River Basin*. New York, Academic Press: 77–111.

that these confined meandering rivers rarely develop cutoffs and that the dominating migrating pattern is the downstream translation of meander bends as a coherent waveform. These observations suggest specific morphodynamics and planform geometries that pertain for confined meanders.

Lamarre *et al.* (2010) compared a large number of alluvial and semi-alluvial river sections in order to identify the dominant control variables of the morphological features found in these two types of channels in several rivers of the Gaspé peninsula, Québec. Semialluvial river sections essentially were dominated by the

presence of a large bedrock outcrop constricting the flow and generating large bedforms. Lamarre *et al.* (2010) performed a discriminant analysis on 68 river sections from which eight variables were measured (slope, pool depth, bar $D_{50}$, bar size, deflection angle, floodplain width, channel width, and floodplain asymmetry), which indicated that the main variables explaining the differences between the alluvial, atypical and typical semialluvial sections are the deflection angle and the pool depth. Hence, there are specific channel morphologies associated with the presence of bedrock outcrops.

Finally, Ebisa-Fola and Rennie (2010) presented the first downstream hydraulic geometry relations for nonalluvial consolidated clay-dominated cohesive-bed river channels. They reported higher values for the depth exponent for those channels than for typical alluvial gravel-bed and sand-bed rivers. Although not from rock-bed channels, their findings highlight some specific hydraulic geometry relations for channels that are laterally constrained.

These studies highlight the role of bedrock outcrop (or cohesive material) on the planform geometry and the migrating pattern of meanders, the morphology of river section, and the downstream hydraulic geometry relations. They thus suggest that there is a "bedrock footprint" that influences river morphodynamics and morphologies in semi-alluvial channels. The presence of moving sediments is crucial in the evolution of rockbed channels but, similarly, the bedrock outcrop may play a distinctive role in the dynamics of the river system and its morphological evolution.

### 31.4.3 Extension of the Channel Types Definition

As alluded to in the previous section, the concepts of constrained and confined rivers might be applied also to channels that exhibit cohesive boundaries. The term semi-alluvial is being used in the literature loosely, but largely to define river sections that have a solid boundary other than natural hard bedrock. As such, it can be suggested that the proposed channel type definitions (Section 31.1) can be extended to define types of semi-alluvial channels. Figure 31.6 presents the two main elements of the definition for semi-alluvial channels. Other than the example of cohesive boundaries depicted in Figure 31.6, confined semi-alluvial configurations can occur in several other settings. The presence of bank protection (Figure 31.7a), roots and woody debris can be seen as confining the river laterally and hence contribute to channel morphodynamics in a similar way to bedrock outcrops. For the constrained semi-alluvial configuration, the presence of marine or lacustrine clay deposits is probably the most frequent configuration observed (Figure 31.7b).

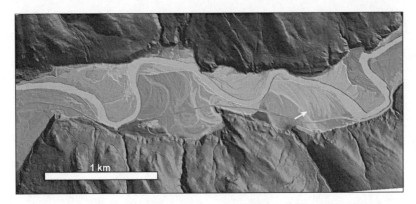

**Figure 31.5**   Confined meanders of the Matane River, Eastern Québec. The LiDAR image reveals the translating migration pattern of meander bends typical of confined meanders (white arrow). (See the color version of this figure in color plate section.)

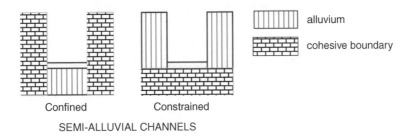

**Figure 31.6**   General semi-alluvial channel types.

Figure 31.8 can be used to discuss the usefulness of such a general semi-alluvial river classification. Figure 31.8 represents the rate of migration for 100 m long river segments along 50 km of the Matane River over the last decade. The Matane River is a highly dynamic gravel-bed river that led to several human interventions to decrease the lateral migration of the river. Locations of bank protection constructed in the last half century are indicated for both sides of the river corridor. The density of bank protections is higher in the downstream (18% of river bank) than in the upstream section where less bank protection is found (4% of river bank). As a consequence, the proportion of eroding banks has decreased in the downstream section (20%) as compared to the upstream section (40%), with the mean migration rate being also smaller in the downstream ($0.8\,\mathrm{m\,a^{-1}}$) than in the upstream section ($1.1\,\mathrm{m\,a^{-1}}$) of the river. This figure shows that the confinement of the Matane River has increased due to human interventions and that the river is now more likely to behave as a confined

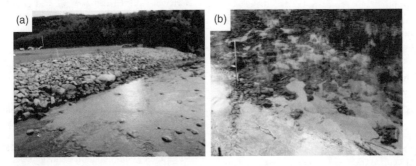

**Figure 31.7**   (a) Bank protection on the Matane River, Québec, that contributes to confining the river; (b) a section of the Ste-Marguerite River, Québec, revealing the Goldthwait marine clay deposit constraining the river.

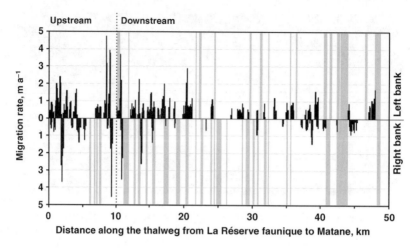

**Figure 31.8**  Migration rate measured on the Matane River for 100 m long river segments. Grey areas indicate locations of bank protection along the distance downstream for both river banks. Left and right banks are separated by the line of zero migration.

semi-alluvial river. Hence, when managing the Matane River system, one has to understand the river in the light of the knowledge that has been gained by work on confined semi-alluvial rivers, whether that constraint is due to a bedrock outcrop or other cohesive boundary. In the same vein, given the plethora of engineering studies into the behaviour of artificially controlled rivers, much can be learnt about natural semi-alluvial rivers by considering the effects of artificial constraints on alluvial rivers.

This extension of definitions is pragmatic and is useful in applied situations, as is shown in the final example (Figure 31.8). However, it is clear that there is a continuum of channel types considered herein from those channels exhibiting boundaries consisting of solid unweathered rock, through to consolidated clays and artificial constraints. Given that some definitions of rock can include soft clays, it remains to be seen whether a morphological distinction needs be drawn between hard rock and clay-bounded river channels. Nevertheless, although Figure 31.1 describes channels at a given time and location rather than specify the controlling processes, we believe that distinctive process domains will dominate in each end-member type such that distinctive dynamics might be elucidated for each member.

## 31.5  ACKNOWLEDGEMENTS

The authors would like to thank Hélène Lamarre, Mathieu Roy, Taylor Olsen and Sylvio Demers for providing unpublished data from posters presented at GBR7 (Lamarre *et al.*, 2010; Olsen *et al.*, 2010) to generate clear illustratations of ideas presented herein.

## 31.6  REFERENCES

Capart, H., Bellal, M., and Young, D-L. 2007. Self-similar evolution of semi-infinite alluvial channels with moving boundaries. *Journal of Sedimentary Research* **7**: 13–22.

Carbonnel, J-P. 1972. *Le Quaternaire Cambodgien. Structure et stratigraphie.* Thesis, University of Paris. Also published (1972) as *Mémoires O.R.S.T.O.M.,* No. 60. [in French].

Carling, P.A. 2009. Geomorphology and Sedimentology of the Lower Mekong River. In Campbell, I.C., editor. *The Mekong: Biophysical Environment of an International River Basin.* New York, Academic Press, pp. 77–111.

Carling, P.A., Tych, W., and Richardson, K. 2005. The hydraulic scaling of step-pool systems. In Parker, G. and Garcia, M.H., editors. *River, Coastal and Estuarine Morphodynamics,* vol. 1. New York, Balkema, Taylor and Francis, pp. 55–63.

Ebisa-Fola, M. and Rennie, C. 2010. Downstream hydraulic geometry of clay-dominated cohesive bed rivers. *Journal of Hydraulic Engineering* **136**: 524–527.

Heritage, G.L., Charlton, M.E., and O'Regan, S. 2001. Morphological classification of fluvial environments: an investigation of the continuum of channel types. *Journal of Geology* **109**: 21–33.

Humphrey, N.F. and Konrad, S.K. 2000. River incision or diversion in response to bedrock uplift. *Geology* **28**: 43–46.

Meshkova, L. V. and Carling, P.A. in press. The geomorphological characteristics of the Mekong River in northern Cambodia: a mixed bedrock-alluvial multi-channel network. *Geomorphology.* doi: 10.1016/j.geomorph.20101.06.041. Published online 27 August, 2011.

Montgomery, D.R. and Buffington, J.M. 1997. Channel-reach morphology in mountain drainage basins. *Bulletin, Geological Society of America* **109**: 596–611.

MRC (Mekong River Commission). 2009. *The Flow of the Mekong.* MRC Management Information Booklet No. 2.

Nicoll, T.J. and Hickin, E.J. 2010. Planform geometry and channel migration of confined meandering rivers on the Canadian Prairies. *Geomorphology* **116**: 37–47.

Schumm, S.A. 2005. *River Variability and Complexity*. Cambridge, Cambridge University Press.

Tooth, S. and McCarthy, T.S. 2004. Anabranching in mixed bedrock-alluvial rivers: the example of the Orange River above Augrabies Falls, Northern Cape Province, South Africa. *Geomorphology* **57**: 235–262.

Turowski, J.M., Hovius, N., Wilson, A., and Horng, M.J. 2008. Hydraulic geometry, river sediment and the definition of bedrock channels. *Geomorphology* **99**: 26–38.

# River Channel Change

# 32

# Changes in Channel Morphology Over Human Time Scales

## John M. Buffington

## 32.1 INTRODUCTION

Rivers are exposed to changing environmental conditions over multiple spatial and temporal scales, with the imposed environmental conditions and response potential of the river modulated to varying degrees by human activity and our exploitation of natural resources. Watershed features that control river morphology include topography (valley slope and channel confinement), discharge (magnitude, frequency, and duration of runoff events), sediment supply (volume, calibre and frequency of sediment delivery), and vegetation (riparian communities (bank strength, roughness) and in-channel wood debris). River stability and response to changing environmental conditions are highly dependent on local context (channel type and associated degrees of freedom; the nature of the imposed sediment, hydrologic, and vegetation regimes; imposed anthropogenic constraints; and the legacy of past natural and anthropogenic disturbances).

Understanding the processes responsible for channel change and assessing river stability has long been of interest to geologists and engineers (Gilbert, 1877; du Boys, 1879; Davis, 1889; Lindley, 1919; Shields, 1936; Lane, 1937; Mackin, 1948; Leopold and Maddock, 1953; Schumm, 1969). Over the last several decades, interest in this topic has grown exponentially as a result of environmental legislation that has spurred greater interdisciplinary collaboration amongst physical and biological scientists studying riverine ecosystems and watershed processes. During this time, considerable progress has been made in understanding channel response and in elucidating biophysical interactions.

For example, progress has been made in understanding textural and structural response of gravel streambeds and consequent effects on bed mobility (Dietrich *et al.*, 1989; Church *et al.*, 1998; Wilcock, 1998; Buffington and

Montgomery, 1999a; Nelson *et al.*, 2009) that, in turn, affect the availability of riparian and aquatic habitats (Lisle, 2005; Burke *et al.*, 2006; May *et al.*, 2009; Moir *et al.*, 2009). Sediment routing models have been developed for examining a wide range of responses, including textural adjustment, reach-scale changes in sediment storage and channel slope, changes in channel width and planform, effects of sediment pulses, and landscape evolution (Hoey and Ferguson, 1994; Nicholas *et al.*, 1995; Benda and Dunne, 1997a, 1997b; Cui and Parker, 2005; Coulthard *et al.*, 2008; Parker *et al.*, 2011; Mosselman, Chapter 9, this volume). In addition, our knowledge of the form and function of rivers has extended beyond traditional studies of sand- and gravel-bed rivers to include a wide variety of channel types and geomorphic settings; in particular, a tremendous amount of work has been done on step-pool channels (Comiti and Mao, Chapter 26, this volume). Numerous recent investigations also document the role of vegetation in affecting channel morphology and response over multiple spatial and temporal scales, including controls on channel width, grain size, bedforms, roughness, sediment transport, alluviation, and rates of landscape lowering (see review by Montgomery *et al.*, 2003). Recent studies also document the role of animals in modulating geomorphic processes and channel characteristics (Rice *et al.*, Chapter 19, this volume). Furthermore, historical studies demonstrate the startling extent of human disturbance to rivers worldwide (Schumm, 1977; Collins *et al.*, 2003; Surian and Rinaldi, 2003; Nilsson *et al.*, 2005; Chin, 2006; Surian, 2006; Walter and Merritts, 2008), fueling the notion that an anthropogenic epoch has emerged (Crutzen, 2002; Meybeck, 2003).

This chapter reviews channel change over human time scales ($10^{-1}$–$10^2$ a), which encompasses small-scale adjustments resulting from seasonal changes in water-

*Gravel-bed Rivers: Processes, Tools, Environments*, First Edition. Edited by Michael Church, Pascale M. Biron and André G. Roy.
© 2012 John Wiley & Sons, Ltd. Published 2012 by John Wiley & Sons, Ltd.

shed inputs to large-scale changes in reach morphology resulting from infrequent floods or decadal to centennial changes in climate (wet/dry cycles). The chapter begins with a review of scales of channel change and the spatial and temporal variability of channel response. This is followed by an examination of the available approaches for predicting channel change which, despite recent advances in the field, are still mainly limited to lowland rivers and assumptions of equilibrium conditions. Transient channel responses are explicitly accounted for in numerical models, but temporal variability of channel condition is typically absent in other quantitative models of channel response. Quantifying temporal variability is critical for assessing channel condition, planning restoration design, and predicting effects of climate change on riverine ecosystems. It is hypothesized that hydroclimate, and its control on both the shape of the hydrograph and the relative size of floods, is a first-order control on the natural variability of channel morphology.

## 32.2   SCALES OF CHANNEL CHANGE

Rivers can exhibit a broad range of responses to changing inputs of water, sediment, and vegetation over human time scales. Channel response may range from small-scale adjustment of channel characteristics (grain size, width, depth) to large-scale alteration of reach morphology and planform pattern.

### 32.2.1   Changes in Channel Characteristics

Successive, overlapping, spatial and temporal scales of morphologic response in alluvial channels include:

(1)   Grain-scale adjustment, comprising:
   (a)   local changes in grain size, packing, protrusion, and friction angle (Fenton and Abbott, 1977; Church, 1978; Buffington et al., 1992; Johnston et al., 1998);
   (b)   development of micro-grain forms (e.g., particle clusters, stone cells; Laronne and Carson, 1976; Brayshaw, 1984; Church et al., 1998; Strom and Papanicolaou, 2008);
   (c)   formation of textural patches (i.e., grain-size facies; Dietrich et al., 1989; 2006; Rice, 1994; Paola and Seal, 1995; Buffington and Montgomery, 1999a; Laronne et al., 2001; Nelson et al., 2009; Yuill et al., 2010).
(2)   Changes in the type, size, and frequency of bed topography, ranging from micro-bed forms (e.g., ripples, bedload sheets; Whiting et al., 1988) to macro-bed forms or channel units (individual bar, pool, step, and riffle topography; Jackson, 1975;

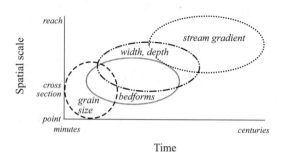

**Figure 32.1**   Spatial and temporal scales of channel response variables in alluvial rivers: grain size (individual grains to textural patches); width, depth (cross-section to subreach variation in average channel geometry); bedforms (micro-forms (e.g., ripples, bedload sheets) to channel units (e.g., bar, pool, step, riffle)); and stream gradient (reach-scale channel aggradation/incision or change in sinuosity). Partly after Knighton (1998).

Lewin, 1978; Bisson et al., 1982; Church and Jones, 1982; Wood-Smith and Buffington, 1996; Halwas and Church, 2002; Hassan et al., 2008).
(3)   Altered channel geometry (changes in local cross-sectional width, depth, and downstream variation of those features; e.g., Trimble, 1997).
(4)   Altered stream gradient due to reach-scale aggradation/incision and changes in channel sinuosity. Here, stream gradient is distinguished from valley gradient, which is not adjustable in the short term.

Larger scales of channel response reflect the cumulative action of smaller-scale processes, particularly sediment transport of bed and bank materials. Hence, a progression of successive scales of response can be envisioned, with grain-size adjustment being the first-order response (Figure 32.1). Furthermore, because alluvial rivers exhibit mutually adjusting channel characteristics, changes in any one parameter can influence all of the others.

The extent of channel change that occurs for a given disturbance depends on the amount of work accomplished by the event (flood magnitude times duration; Wolman and Miller, 1960) and the time needed for a given scale of response to occur. Wolman and Miller's (1960) classic magnitude–frequency argument emphasizes the effectiveness of frequent, moderate-sized events in accomplishing geomorphic work over the long term, but large-scale changes in morphology require large events (Figure 32.2). Similarly, different temporal scales of disturbances (seasonal to centennial) will exhibit characteristic scales of response. Seasonal changes are frequent, typically small-magnitude events that will lead to similarly small degrees of channel change (e.g.,

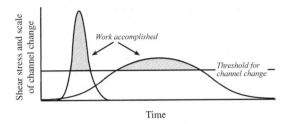

**Figure 32.2** Work and scale of channel change accomplished for flood events of different magnitude and duration (after Costa and O'Connor, 1995). Total work (shaded area) is identical for the events, but the scale of channel change is greater for the high-magnitude event.

bed loosening and changes in grain-size structure and texture as seasonal floods begin; Milhous, 1973), while annual peak floods are typically moderate-sized events that lead to moderate scales of channel change (e.g., altered cross-sectional widths and depths). Over decadal scales, rare infrequent events (e.g., 50–100-year floods or debris flows) may cause significant channel change followed by a period of relaxation from the disturbance (recovery or attainment of some new equilibrium state; Bull, 1991; Simon and Rinaldi, 2006). The duration of the relaxation period depends on the magnitude of the disturbance and the local channel context (i.e., transport capacity relative to sediment supply; Montgomery and Buffington, 1997; 1998). For example, field observations

show that steep, confined channels in central Idaho recover from massive debris-flow inputs within 5–10 years because of high transport capacities and no opportunities for floodplain storage of sediment, while recovery from sediment waves may take decades in lower-gradient, unconfined channels (Megahan *et al.*, 1980; Madej and Ozaki, 1996). Over longer time scales (decades to centuries), wet/dry climate cycles may lead to corresponding cycles of river incision/aggradation (Rumsby and Macklin, 1994), expansion/contraction of channel width (Schumm and Lichty, 1963), and changes in the complexity of bed topography and textural patches. Overall, the sequence of different types and scales of disturbance will influence channel morphology and future responses (Hoey, 1992) with systems potentially showing complex and variable responses over time (Coulthard and Van De Wiel, 2007). Furthermore, the entire fluvial system may be trending toward some new state (i.e., non-stationarity) driven by longer-term changes in climate or by long-term anthropogenic alteration of the basin (Bryan, 1925; Schumm, 1968; 1977; Knox, 1984; Bull, 1991; Brierley and Fryirs, 2005).

The style and extent of channel response will also be limited by channel type and associated degrees of freedom (Table 32.1). In general, bedrock channels have fewer degrees of freedom for morphologic response than alluvial channels. In turn, steep, confined alluvial channels (e.g., step-pool and cascade streams) are less responsive than lower-gradient unconfined channels (e.g., pool-riffle and dune-ripple streams). Furthermore,

**Table 32.1** Reach-scale channel type and degrees of freedom for morphologic change. (+ = likely; p = possible; − = unlikely)[a]

| Channel type | Channel change | | | |
|---|---|---|---|---|
| | Grain size | Width & depth | Bedforms | Stream gradient (sinuosity/elevation)[b] |
| Colluvial | p | p | − | −/p[c] |
| Bedrock | − | − | − | −/− |
| Cascade | p | − | − | −/− |
| Step-pool | p | −/p[d] | p | −/− |
| Plane-bed | + | + | − | −/p |
| Braided | + | + | + | +/+ |
| Pool-riffle | + | + | + | +/+ |
| Dune-ripple | p | + | + | +/+ |

*confined* (Colluvial through Step-pool)
*unconfined* (Plane-bed through Dune-ripple)

[a] Modified from Buffington and Montgomery (1997). Response potential for each channel type is discussed elsewhere (Montgomery and Buffington, 1997; 1998; Buffington *et al.*, 2003).

[b] Changes in stream gradient may occur via altered sinuosity or incision/aggradation that alter the absolute elevation change across a reach. Slashes in the table distinguish these two responses.

[c] Fluvial incision/deposition is possible, depending on the degree of colluvial fill.

[d] Changes in channel depth can occur via pool fill/scour.

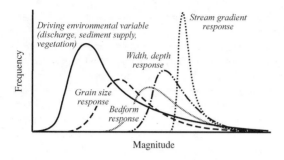

**Figure 32.3** Channel change depends on the overlap between frequency distributions of driving and resisting forces for different scales of morphologic response.

because most geomorphic processes exhibit thresholds for occurrence, channel response will depend on the probability of a given disturbance exceeding the response threshold, the magnitude of which also varies with channel type. Hence, the likelihood of a given channel change will depend on the degree to which the probability distributions of driving environmental conditions (changes in discharge, sediment supply, vegetation) overlap with the probability distributions of process thresholds that lead to changes in channel characteristics (i.e., overlap of driving versus resisting forces; Figure 32.3).

### 32.2.2 Bed Mobility and Channel Type

Bed mobility is a first-order control on channel response and can be indexed by comparing the bankfull Shields (1936) stress ($\tau^*_{bf}$) to the critical value for incipient motion of the median grain size ($\tau^*_{c50}$). The bankfull Shields stress is defined as $\tau^*_{bf} = \rho g h S/[(\rho_s - \rho)gD_{50}]$, wherein $\rho$ and $\rho_s$ are fluid and sediment densities, respectively, $g$ is gravitational acceleration, $h$ is bankfull depth, $S$ is channel slope, and $D_{50}$ is median surface grain size. The critical Shields stress ($\tau^*_{c50}$) for sand- and silt-bed rivers is determined here from the original Shields curve as fit by Brownlie (1981), while for coarse-grained rivers $\tau^*_{c50}$ is defined as a function of channel slope based on recent studies (Lamb et al., 2008; Pitlick et al., 2008); $\tau^*_{c50} = 0.15S^{0.25}$ and $0.36S^{0.46}$, respectively (also see Comiti and Mao, Chapter 26, this volume). Data compiled from rivers around the world show two features regarding $\tau^*_{bf}$ values (Figure 32.4). First, $\tau^*_{bf}$ varies with channel type, with a clear difference in behaviour for sand-bed channels versus coarser-grained rivers (also see Dade and Friend, 1998; García, 2000; Parker et al., 2003; Church, 2006). The sand–gravel transition likely defines the boundary between the two (Figure 32.4; Sambrook Smith and Ferguson, 1995; Parker and Cui, 1998; Ferguson, 2003; Singer, 2008). Multithread channels are

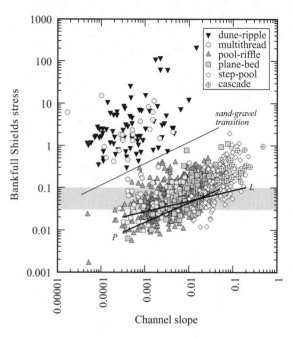

**Figure 32.4** Bankfull Shields stress as a function of channel slope for different reach-scale channel types: dune-ripple (defined by morphology or assumed for single-thread channels with $D_{50} < 2$ mm; $n = 79$), multithread (divided/wandering, braided, and anastomosing channels, $n = 129$), pool-riffle (defined by morphology, or assumed for meandering channels with $D_{50} > 2$ mm; $n = 570$), plane-bed ($n = 185$), step-pool ($n = 168$), and cascade ($n = 23$). Where bankfull information was unavailable, other channel-forming flows were used (e.g., the two-year or mean annual flood). Data sources are reported in Section 32.9, Appendix. An approximate boundary for the sand–gravel transition is shown, as well as curves for critical Shields stress ($\tau^*_{c50}$) reported by Lamb et al. (2008) and Pitlick et al. (2008); $L$ and $P$, respectively, both limited to their respective range of observations. The shaded area indicates the range of $\tau^*_{c50}$ values reported by Shields (1936).

unique in that they span the sand- and gravel-bed domains of $\tau^*_{bf}$. As defined here, this channel type encompasses divided/wandering rivers (Desloges and Church, 1989; Ferguson and Werritty, 1991), braided, and anastomosing channels; a lumped category is used because of inconsistent classification amongst the available data sources. The second feature of Figure 32.4 is that in coarser-grained rivers, $\tau^*_{bf}$ varies systematically with channel slope (Buffington and Montgomery, 2001; Mueller et al., 2005; Pitlick et al., 2008). However, the latter relation is potentially spurious, so it should not be taken as significant, at least on face value. Nevertheless, it is a convenient way to display the $\tau^*_{bf}$ values.

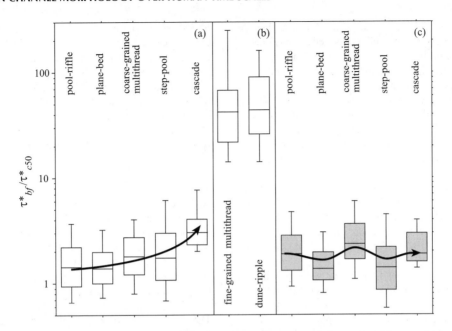

**Figure 32.5** Box plots of excess bankfull Shields stress ($\tau^*_{bf}/\tau^*_{c50}$) for data of Figure 32.4. Here, multithread channels are divided into fine-grained ($D_{50} < 2$ mm, $n = 21$) and coarse-grained classes ($D_{50} \geq 2$ mm, $n = 108$). Values of $\tau^*_{c50}$ are determined from (a) Lamb *et al.* (2008), (b) Shields (1936) and (c) Pitlick *et al.* (2008).

Bed mobility indexed in terms of the excess Shields stress ($\tau^*_{bf}/\tau^*_{c50}$) shows a general increase in the bankfull mobility of $D_{50}$ across different channel types, if the Lamb *et al.* (2008) equation is used to determine the critical Shields stress (Figure 32.5a). The systematic increase in predicted mobility is driven by the fact that the Lamb curve for $\tau^*_{c50}$ has a lower slope than the trend of the $\tau^*_{bf}$ data (Figure 32.4). In contrast, the Pitlick curve for $\tau^*_{c50}$ parallels the $\tau^*_{bf}$ data, predicting that mobility of $D_{50}$ in coarse-grained channels is roughly constant across different channel types (median values of $\tau^*_{bf}/\tau^*_{c50}$ vary from 1.4–2.3, but lack a consistent trend with channel type; Figure 32.5c). Consequently, these two $\tau^*_{c50}$ predictions represent fundamentally different interpretations of bed mobility. Field observations of mobility in different channel types suggest that the Lamb model is the more correct view; however, this issue warrants further investigation. Observed differences in mobility are discussed below in relation to Figures 32.4 and 32.5.

Dune-ripple (sand-bed) rivers are unarmoured and highly mobile, exhibiting large bankfull Shields stresses ($\tau^*_{bf}$ typically $> 0.3$–10; Figure 32.4) and a well-known bedform sequence that adjusts with stage and excess shear stress (Gilbert, 1914; Shields, 1936; Middleton and Southard, 1984). In contrast, pool-riffle and plane-bed channels (gravel-bed rivers) have $\tau^*_{bf}$ values that are several orders of magnitude smaller (typically $> 0.01$–0.4;

Figure 32.4). These channels are commonly armoured and have a near-bankfull threshold for motion of the armour layer (Andrews, 1984; Buffington and Montgomery, 1999a; Ryan *et al.*, 2002; 2005; Whiting and King, 2003; Mueller and Pitlick, 2005; Mueller *et al.*, 2005), with relatively less mobile bedforms, except under extreme conditions (Pitlick, 1992). A near-bankfull threshold is supported by low values of $\tau^*_{bf}/\tau^*_{c50}$ (median of 1.4, Figure 32.5a), while sand-bed channels are highly mobile at bankfull (median $\tau^*_{bf}/\tau^*_{c50} = 44$, Figure 32.5b). In both sand- and gravel-bed rivers, the effective discharge for sediment transport occurs frequently, corresponding with near-bankfull flows in supply-limited systems (Wolman and Miller, 1960; Andrews, 1980; Carling, 1988b; Andrews and Nankervis, 1995; Whiting *et al.*, 1999; Emmett and Wolman, 2001; Crowder and Knapp, 2004; Torizzo and Pitlick, 2004) and with lesser floods in transport-limited rivers (Gomez *et al.*, 2007; Ma *et al.*, 2010). For gravel-bed rivers, the effective discharge and its recurrence interval vary with supply-related armouring of the bed and the resultant slope of the sediment rating curve (Emmett and Wolman, 2001; Barry *et al.*, 2004; Bathurst, 2007). For both sand- and gravel-bed rivers, the effective discharge is a channel maintenance flow, with floods in excess of bankfull required for significant morphologic adjustment, particularly in resistant-boundary rivers (Pickup and Warner, 1976; Nolan *et al.*, 1987;

Carling, 1988b; Gomez et al., 2007). Consequently, multiple levels of geomorphic effectiveness may occur. This is particularly evident in steeper-gradient channels (step-pool, cascade), where movement of boulder-sized structural elements typically requires $20–100^+$-year floods (Hayward, 1980; Grant et al., 1990; Chin, 1998; Lenzi, 2001; Phillips, 2002; Lenzi et al., 2006b; Turowski et al., 2009), while smaller material is mobile annually (Schmidt and Ergenzinger, 1992; Gintz et al., 1996; Lenzi, 2004; Lamarre and Roy, 2008; but see Thompson and Croke, 2008). Greater mobility of $D_{50}$ in step-pool and cascade channels is indicated by large values of both $\tau^*_{bf}$ (typically $> 0.03–1$; Figure 32.4) and $\tau^*_{bf}/\tau^*_{c50}$ (median values of 1.7 and 3, respectively; Figure 32.5a), but these values do not represent the responsiveness of the boulder-sized structural elements of the channel.

The above observations suggest that, while systematic differences in bed mobility occur across different channel types, the mobility of a given grain size (e.g., $D_{50}$) may not be a good indicator of response potential in general. Size-selective transport and multiple levels of geomorphic effectiveness must also be considered, both for sediment transport and larger-scale morphologic adjustment, particularly for boulder-bed channels (Hassan and Zimmermann, Chapter 33, this volume).

Use of excess Shields stress ($\tau^*_{bf}/\tau^*_{c50}$) to interpret bed mobility also requires consideration of sediment supply and channel roughness. High bedload supply will drive textural fining and higher $\tau^*_{bf}$ values (Dietrich et al., 1989; Buffington and Montgomery, 1999b). Similarly, channel roughness (form drag and other losses of momentum) will cause apparent increases in $\tau^*_{bf}$ and $\tau^*_{c50}$ (Buffington and Montgomery, 1997, 2001); in Figures 32.4 and 32.5, both $\tau^*_{bf}$ and $\tau^*_{c50}$ are based on the total boundary shear stress uncorrected for roughness. Correcting boundary shear stress for channel roughness will reduce $\tau^*_{bf}$ and $\tau^*_{c50}$ values by 25–90%, depending on the magnitude and complexity of the roughness (Prestegaard, 1983; Shields and Gippel, 1995; Buffington, 1998; 2001; Buffington and Montgomery, 1999b; Kean and Smith, 2006a; Wilcox et al., 2006; Lamb et al., 2008). This correction is particularly important for steeper-gradient channel morphologies which exhibit systematic declines in: (i) width–depth ratio (greater wall roughness) and (ii) particle submergence (greater particle form drag and spill resistance) with decreasing drainage area (Buffington and Montgomery, 2001). In step-pool channels, the spacing of steps also decreases with slope, further increasing roughness (Judd and Peterson, 1969; Whittaker, 1987; Grant et al., 1990; Chin, 1999b). Systematic changes in channel morphology and associated roughness explain, in part, the observed relation between

Shields stress and channel slope (both for the bankfull and critical values, $\tau^*_{bf}$ and $\tau^*_{c50}$; Figure 32.4), but changes in channel hydraulics with grain emergence at steep slopes may also be important (Armanini and Gregoretti, 2005; Mueller et al., 2005; Vollmer and Kleinhans, 2007; Lamb et al., 2008; Recking, 2009). Even with roughness correction, $\tau^*_{bf}$ and $\tau^*_{bf}/\tau^*_{c50}$ values will likely show relative differences in mobility with channel type (although this hypothesis remains to be tested).

### 32.2.3   Changes in Channel Type

At larger spatial and temporal scales, altered environmental conditions may cause changes in reach-scale channel type (Montgomery and Buffington, 1997) and planform morphology. Potential changes in channel type can be arrayed conceptually in terms of valley slope, confinement, discharge, and sediment supply, and may be associated with specific process domains (Montgomery, 1999). Recent examples are shown in Figure 32.6. The Church (2006) framework (Figure 32.6a) shows changes in alluvial channel type and stability as a function of gradient, sediment supply, and calibre of the sediment load. Figure 32.6b is similar, but also identifies process domains for: (i) the influence of vegetation, (ii) debris flows, and (iii) the occurrence of alluvial, colluvial, and bedrock channels.

Because changes in channel type involve alteration of larger-scale morphologic features, they may take centuries or more to occur (Church, 1995; Dade and Friend, 1998; Bravard, 2010). However, case studies demonstrate that such changes can occur over shorter time scales (years to decades; Schumm, 1977; 2005; Hooke, 1996; Kondolf et al., 2001; Surian and Rinaldi, 2003). For example, severe storms in the 1960s following a period of logging and road construction delivered massive inputs of fine sediment to the South Fork Salmon River in central Idaho. A downstream wave of fine sediment buried gravel pool-riffle channels, converting them to sand-bed dune-ripple channels (e.g., Figure 32.7), with a gradual recovery over the course of several decades (Megahan et al., 1980), but with numerous sand patches and sand stripes (Lisle and Hilton, 1992) persisting to the present day. River networks in central Idaho are particularly susceptible to fine-sediment disturbances because they are underlain by the Idaho Batholith, which produces abundant grus (granitic sands and silts), highlighting the importance of local geology in structuring the types of disturbances and channel responses that may occur.

At basin scales, changes in the abundance and spatial distribution of channel types can affect the availability of aquatic, riparian and hyporheic habitats, the metapopulation dynamics of fish, and the geomorphic function of

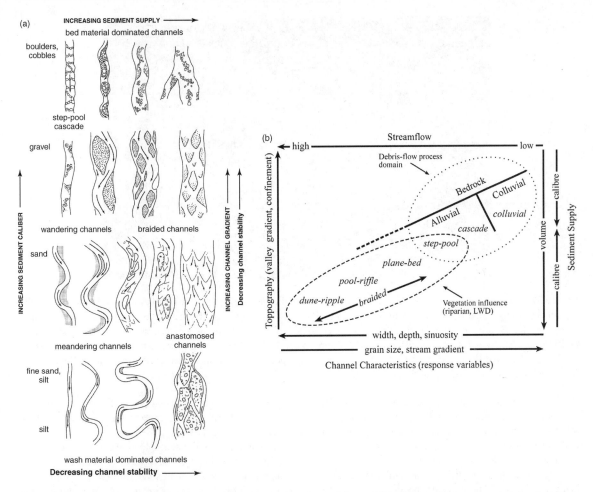

**Figure 32.6** Reach-scale channel morphology as a function of imposed basin conditions (topography (gradient, confinement), discharge, sediment supply (calibre, volume)) as conceptualized by: (a) Church (2006) and (b) Buffington *et al.* (2003). Both approaches are derived from concepts developed by Mollard (1973), Brice (1975), and Schumm (1977; 1985). Panel (a) reproduced, with permission, from Church, M. 2006. Bed material transport and the morphology of alluvial rivers. Annual Review of Earth and Planetary Sciences 34, 325–354. Panel (b) modified from Buffington *et al.* (2003).

the catchment in terms of how disturbances are propagated through the river network. For example, historic effects of logging in the North American Pacific Northwest have likely altered the spatial distribution of channel types and spawning habitats for salmonids at basin scales and could have contributed to the historic decline of salmonids in this region (Buffington *et al.*, 2004a).

## 32.3 SPATIAL AND TEMPORAL VARIABILITY OF CHANNEL CHANGE

Probability distributions of basin inputs that drive channel response (i.e., temporal changes in water, sediment, and vegetation) vary with spatial scale. At the largest scale, physiography and climate set the sediment, hy-

drologic, and vegetation regimes of basins within a given region; for example, determining whether basin hydrology is dominated by snowmelt or rainfall runoff. At smaller scales within a basin, distributions of water, sediment and wood inputs change with position along the river network as a function of: (i) drainage area (Clark *et al.*, 1987; Benda and Dunne, 1997a, 1997b), (ii) process domains (Montgomery, 1999; Brardinoni and Hassan, 2006), and (iii) proximity to tributary confluences that create discontinuities or steps in basin inputs (Rice *et al.*, 2006; 2008). Finally, at the scale of stream reaches and channel units (individual pools, bars, riffles, steps), divergence of channel hydraulics and bedload transport creates patch- and point-scale probability distributions of flow and sediment supply over time

**Figure 32.7** Confluence of the Middle and South Forks of the Payette River, central Idaho, showing a wave of fine sediment forcing a dune-ripple morphology (left channel) in what had previously been a gravel pool-riffle channel similar to that of the South Fork (right channel). Photo courtesy of Carter Borden. Reproduced, with permission, from Buffington, J.M., Woodsmith, R.D., Booth, D.B., Montgomery, D.R., 2003. Fluvial processes in Puget Sound Rivers and the Pacific Northwest. In: Montgomery, D.R., Bolton, S., Booth, D.B., Wall, L. (Eds.), Restoration of Puget Sound Rivers. University of Washington Press, Seattle, WA, pp. 46–78.

(seasons to years). Consequently, the driving disturbance processes and potential channel responses can be represented as a series of nested scales of probability functions that ultimately result in different disturbance–response regimes within and between basins.

Within a basin, the hydrology and sediment supply of headwater areas will be more variable than that of higher-order portions of the river network that have more stable (less variable) supplies of water and sediment due to larger contributing areas (Dunne and Leopold, 1978; Benda and Dunne, 1997a, 1997b; Church, 2002) (Figure 32.8). Furthermore, in headwater streams the magnitude of rare disturbances will be much larger per unit area due to the smaller spatial scale of headwater basins (a higher percentage of the drainage area will contribute to a given event and travel times will be shorter, with little to no opportunity for spatial attenuation of an event or for floodplain dissipation due to channel confinement; Clark *et al.*, 1987; Phillips, 2002; Wohl, 2008; Goode *et al.*, in press). The efficiency of disturbance propagation in headwater areas should also cause larger relative values of disturbance size (i.e., event size relative to mean annual values) and therefore should be more effective geomorphically; this effect is further magnified by channel confinement (Magilligan, 1992). In addition, floods in excess of bankfull are more frequent in headwater areas (Segura and Pitlick, 2010), further increasing potential geomorphic effectiveness. However, headwa-

ter streams have fewer degrees of freedom for channel adjustment (Table 32.1), making them resilient to all but the largest events which, when they occur, will trigger massive changes. For example, rare debris-flow events in headwater basins can cause scour to bedrock or aggradation up to tens of metres that obliterates prior channel morphology. Whether such events cause scour or deposition depends on the run-out path, which is a function of: (i) the debris-flow rheology (water–sediment content, size and sorting of sediment), (ii) channel slope, (iii) downstream changes in confinement, (iv) tributary junction angles, and (v) the presence of large wood debris (Benda and Cundy, 1990; Cenderelli and Kite, 1998; Madej, 2001; Lancaster *et al.*, 2003). In contrast, lower-gradient, unconfined channels have more degrees of freedom (Table 32.1), but experience small perturbations in discharge and sediment supply relative to mean annual values because of their position in the network (larger drainage area) and because they are generally decoupled from hillslopes (Montgomery and Buffington, 1997; Church, 2002). Consequently, channel conditions are expected to be more variable over time in higher-order floodplain channels than in confined headwater portions of a basin, but the magnitude of change, when it occurs, will be larger in headwater channels (Figure 32.8). Wohl (2008) argues that flood disturbances will be most effective midway through a basin, where the relative size of an event remains moderate to large, and where the

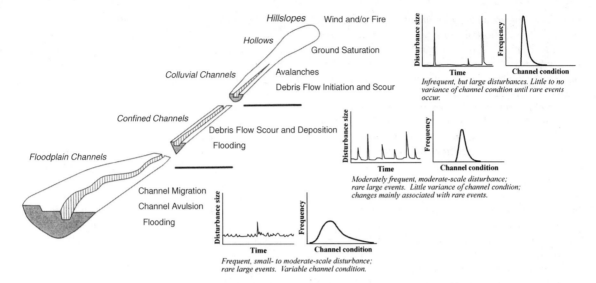

**Figure 32.8** Process domains in mountain rivers, showing disturbance size relative to mean values (first right-hand graph) and variance of channel condition (second right-hand graph) as a function of these disturbances (floods, sediment inputs, changes in vegetation) and degrees of freedom associated with each process domain and channel type (Table 32.1). Modified from Montgomery (1999), and after Benda and Dunne (1997a, 1997b), Church (2002) and Wohl (2008).

more frequent occurrence of moderate-gradient flood-plain channels increases the potential for channel response compared to confined, lower-order channels.

Systematic downstream changes in slope, drainage area, and process domains result in a general progression of channel types and response potentials in mountain basins (Figures 32.6 and 32.8; Schumm, 1977; 2005; Kondolf, 1994; 1995; Montgomery and Buffington, 1997; 1998; Church, 2002). However, this downstream progression can be locally re-set by a variety of factors, including changes in geology (e.g., differences in lithology or structure; Hack, 1957; Rutherford, 1994; Thompson *et al.*, 2006; 2008), changes in geomorphic history (e.g., local glaciation or volcanism; Booth *et al.*, 2003), and tributary confluences of high contrast (producing discontinuities in sediment, water, or wood inputs; Benda *et al.*, 2004a, 2004b; Ferguson *et al.*, 2006; Rice *et al.*, 2006; 2008). Local geologic controls can be particularly important, causing spatial variability in hydrology (Tague *et al.*, 2007; 2008), slope, rock strength, and sediment supply that produce characteristic differences in channel morphology and response potential (Buffington *et al.*, 2003; Montgomery and Bolton, 2003; Brardinoni and Hassan, 2006; Thompson *et al.*, 2006; 2008; Bravard, 2010).

The legacy of past natural disturbances can also affect channel morphology, network structure, and basin function, and may condition rivers for specific responses to future disturbance. In particular, the occurrence of wide valley bottoms and alluvial response reaches along the river network control the propagation of sediment pulses and floods, and their consequent downstream impacts. These features may be glacial, volcanic, structural, or climatic legacies, and are not necessarily correlated with current discharge and sediment regimes. Channel reaches may also be influenced by nested scales of legacies (geologic, climatic, infrequent events (fire, mass wasting, floods/droughts), and seasonal flows), complicating prediction of channel response to future disturbance, and making it difficult to assess causes for observed channel changes. Hence, channel response is likely complex and unique to local basin history (e.g., Carling 1988a).

## 32.4 PREDICTING CHANNEL CHANGE

A large body of research exists for predicting channel change and understanding morphologic stability, particularly for alluvial rivers. The goal of these studies is to predict channel characteristics (grain size, width, depth, slope, sinuosity) as a function of imposed environmental conditions (chiefly discharge and sediment supply) or, conversely, to deduce the discharge and sediment supply associated with a given channel morphology. Most of this work assumes equilibrium conditions; i.e., channel response to a given perturbation results in a stable channel form that exhibits equilibrium transport (equal rates of sediment supply and transport) at reach scales. Unfortunately, channel equilibrium has been described using a variety of terms over the years, causing some potential for confusion. For example, Lindley (1919) described unlined irrigation canals that had attained morphologic equilibrium as being "in regime", meaning the stable morphology for a given discharge and sediment transport regime (Blench 1957). As such, relations for equilibrium channel form are frequently referred to as "regime relations". In contrast, Mackin (1948) used the term "graded" to describe long-term equilibrium of natural rivers, building from observations by Gilbert (1877). The term quasi-equilibrium has also been used to describe the mean statistical state of a channel or group of channels (Blench, 1957; Langbein and Leopold, 1964). Similarly, a channel that actively moves across its floodplain, but retains long-term similarity of channel form on average, is said to be in dynamic equilibrium (Hack, 1960). Studies of channel change that invoke equilibrium conditions can be divided into two broad classes: conceptual and quantitative, each of which is examined in turn below.

### 32.4.1 Conceptual Models for Equilibrium Response

Most conceptual models of channel change relate equilibrium channel form to discharge and sediment supply using empirical or theoretical proportionalities. For example, Gilbert (1877) and du Boys (1879) proposed that channel slope is proportional to bedload discharge, $S \propto Q_b$. They hypothesized that an under-supplied river would erode its bed, decreasing channel slope and bedload transport rates until equilibrium transport and a metastable condition occurred. Conversely, aggradation and increased slope were expected for over-supplied rivers. Gilbert (1917) used this reasoning to explain channel response to massive sediment inputs produced by hydraulic mining in the northern California gold fields. Lane (1955b) later proposed that changes in stream discharge ($Q$) and bedload discharge ($Q_b$) are balanced by changes in channel slope ($S$) and grain size ($D$), $Q_b D \propto QS$. The Lane model is commonly visualized in terms of a scale (or balance) and is frequently invoked as a first-order conceptual model of channel response.

Work by Schumm (1977) broadened these conceptual models to include channel width ($w$), depth ($h$), planform sinuosity ($p$), and meander wavelength ($\lambda$) as functions of stream discharge and bedload transport rate, $Q \propto (wh\lambda)/S$, $Q_b \propto (w\lambda S)/(hp)$, with all terms in the last proportionality influenced by the silt content of the bed and bank material (Schumm, 1960a, 1960b; 1963; 1968). Schumm emphasized that channel morphology is controlled by the calibre of the sediment load and its effects on bank stability (also see Osterkamp and Hedman, 1982).

Combining the above two relations, Schumm (1977) explored potential directions of channel response to

different combinations of altered discharge and sediment load (an approach further developed by Santos-Cayudo and Simons (1972), Petts (1979), Nunnally (1985), and Kellerhals and Church (1989)). These studies emphasize the potential complexity of response in floodplain alluvial channels, given their many degrees of freedom for adjustment (Table 32.1). Furthermore, they demonstrate that a given channel response (e.g., widening) can arise from multiple causes (e.g., increases in $Q$, $Q_b$, or both) and may be modulated by the response of other channel characteristics (e.g., Talbot and Lapointe, 2002a, 2002b). Consequently, it is often difficult to attribute an observed channel change to a specific cause, let alone reconstruct the exact response path, without further information. The reaction path for a given channel change depends on the sequence and magnitude of channel responses that occur during a given perturbation, as well as the history of past disturbances and channel responses to those events (i.e., legacies and pre-conditioning), as discussed above.

A second type of conceptual model involves development of evolutionary phases of channel response (i.e., "stream succession" or genetic models), building from ideas originally introduced by Davis (1889). Genetic models continue to be popular (Nanson and Croke, 1992) and are frequently used for assessing channel condition and restoration potential (Brierley and Fryirs, 2005; Rosgen, 2006). However, the Rosgen (2006) approach has been criticized because of insufficient rigor and uncertainty about using channel form to infer past processes and likely future responses (Simon et al., 2007; 2008).

### 32.4.2 Quantitative Models for Equilibrium Response

Quantitative models of equilibrium channel response use empirical equations, analytical solutions, or numerical routines, allowing more specific predictions of response than those offered by conceptual models.

#### 32.4.2.1 Empirical Equations

Building from work by Kennedy (1895–1896), Lindley (1919) developed empirical regime equations for the design of stable irrigation canals in the Indus River Valley, expressing channel width, depth, and slope as functions of velocity and discharge. Subsequent investigators developed a broad array of empirical regime equations for both canals and natural alluvial rivers (e.g., Lacey, 1929–1930, 1933–1934; Lane, 1937; Inglis, 1949; Blench, 1957; Simons and Albertson, 1963), including the somewhat independent development of downstream hydraulic geometry relations for natural rivers (Leopold and Maddock, 1953): $w = aQ^b$, $h = cQ^f$, $u = kQ^m$, wherein $u$ is mean velocity, $a$, $c$, and $k$ are empirical coefficients, and *b*, *f*, and *m* are empirical exponents. The exponents typically take values of 0.5, 0.4, and 0.1, respectively (Leopold *et al.*, 1964), but may vary regionally (Park, 1977; Wohl, 2004). Although based on different underlying empiricisms, classic regime equations can be reduced to the above hydraulic geometry relations, producing exponents similar to those above, and demonstrating the convergence of the two approaches (Leopold and Maddock, 1953; Blench, 1957; Nixon, 1959). Furthermore, stable irrigation canals and natural rivers are roughly self-similar in terms of downstream hydraulic geometry relations for mean annual discharge (Leopold and Maddock, 1953; Ferguson, 1986; Kellerhals and Church, 1989).

Hydraulic geometry relations continue to be the most popular type of empirical regime equation and have been shown to apply to a broad range of channels, including tidal marshes (Myrick and Leopold, 1963) and supraglacial streams (e.g., Marston, 1983). In mountain rivers, hydraulic geometry equations have recently been applied to bedrock rivers (Montgomery and Gran, 2001; Whipple, 2004; Finnegan *et al.*, 2005) and to headwater channels within the debris-flow process domain (Brummer and Montgomery, 2003; Buffington *et al.*, 2004b; Brardinoni and Hassan, 2007), with results reinforcing the self-similarity of channel dimensions across different channel types, and the general utility of empirical hydraulic geometry relations.

Although hydraulic geometry relations are typically created to characterize current channel morphology, they can also be used to predict changes in equilibrium channel form resulting from altered discharge (Church, 1995), or to predict past discharges from the geometry of palaeochannels (Schumm, 1968; Dury, 1976; Ethridge and Schumm, 1978; O'Connor, 1993). Similitude is commonly invoked to predict changes in channel form by expressing a given hydraulic geometry equation as a ratio of two time periods or two locations (e.g., $w_1/w_2 = a(Q_1/Q_2)^b$; Church, 1995; Griffiths, 2003); the same can be done for Lane's (1955b) proportionality (Clark and Wilcock, 2000). A limitation of this approach is that it assumes that the coefficients and exponents of the hydraulic geometry relations remain constant over time, which is unlikely in basins that undergo fundamental changes in their discharge or sediment regimes (Schumm, 1968; Ethridge and Schumm, 1978; Bray, 1982). In addition, hydraulic geometry relations produce only reconnaissance-level predictions of channel form (Dunne and Leopold, 1978); they are log-log plots with considerable uncertainty (Emmett, 1972), which may suffice for describing average changes in channel form along the downstream course of a river network, but will be inadequate to predict site-specific geometry with any degree of certainty (Buffington *et al.*, 2009). Parker (1982) argues that dimensionless hydraulic geometry relations provide more physical insight and perform better than equivalent dimensional equations (also see Parker, 1979; Andrews, 1984; Parker *et al.*, 2003; 2007), but Rhoads (1992) cautions that spurious results can result depending on the parameters selected for non-dimensionalization.

In retrospect, hydraulic geometry relations are useful first-order predictions of channel form, but they provide little mechanistic insight and, therefore, their value for advancing fluvial geomorphology is questionable (Ferguson, 1986). The self-similarity of channels across orders of magnitude in discharge is remarkable, but at the same time the value of this is suspect, given that we know that reach-scale processes and associated process domains vary along river networks. No insight about these underlying processes and controls on channel morphology are offered by hydraulic geometry relations in-and-of themselves. Eaton and Church (2007) suggest that observed downstream increases in channel width may reflect declining contributions of riparian vegetation to bank strength as the channel depth becomes large relative to typical rooting depths; for a fixed rooting depth, the vegetative cohesion is relatively high in small, shallow channels compared to large, deep rivers. However, downstream increases in channel width occur in poorly vegetated landscapes as well, indicating that vegetation is likely a modulating factor, rather than the primary control on hydraulic geometry.

### 32.4.2.2 *Theoretical Equations*

Theoretical and semi-theoretical equations for predicting channel form include a wide variety of analytical approaches and are sometimes referred to as "rational" (i.e., physically based) regime equations, particularly when written in dimensionless form (Parker, 1979; 1990; Parker *et al.*, 2003; 2007; Eaton and Church, 2007), which is another interpretation of "rational". Ideally, when developing rational solutions, one solves a system of governing equations (e.g., expressions for discharge and equilibrium bedload transport rate) that are written in terms of channel characteristics (slope, width, depth, grain size) so that the imposed watershed conditions (discharge, sediment supply) and the morphologic response variables can be solved simultaneously. The number of channel characteristics that one wishes to predict sets the number of governing equations that are needed. Results highlight that natural channels exhibit a fairly narrow range of forms compared to what is theoretically possible (rational regime equations have numerous solutions of channel form that satisfy continuity of mass and momentum, but only some of these solutions are found in nature; as recently reiterated by Eaton *et al.*, 2004). A variety of extremal hypotheses (initiated by Langbein, 1964) have been developed to explain the narrow range of observed channel forms in terms of optimal conditions (e.g., maximum sediment transporting efficiency, minimum power expenditure, etc.), which are frequently invoked as boundary conditions in solving rational regime relations (see reviews by Ferguson, 1986; Eaton et al., 2004; Huang et al., 2004; Millar, 2005). Extremal approaches have been criticized for their metaphysical nature (offering little process-based insight; Ferguson, 1986), their lack of agreement with observed conditions (Griffiths, 1984), and insensitivity to the particular optimal condition that is invoked (Eaton et al., 2004), suggesting that in those cases the results may be mathematical artifacts of optimization, rather than having physical relevance.

The Holy Grail for rational regime equations is developing a defensible approach for predicting channel width (the most problematic channel characteristic to predict deterministically). Channel width is controlled by the erodibility of the banks which, in turn, is controlled by several variables, including: (i) the stability of cohesionless bank material (a function of grain size, friction angle, and bank slope), (ii) silt and clay content (physical cohesion), (iii) bank vegetation (root strength/biotic cohesion and roughness); (iv) bank height and degree of fluvial undercutting (risk of mass wasting), and (v) armouring by extrinsic factors (e.g., bedrock outcrops, boulders, tree roots, wood debris). Riparian vegetation is particularly important. Palaeo-reconstructions of channel morphology show that braided channels were dominant during the Precambrian to Ordovician periods, but that meandering channels became more common with the rise of terrestrial vegetation during the Late Silurian (~423–408 mya), presumably due to the additional strength and roughness of the banks provided by riparian vegetation (Montgomery et al., 2003). Vegetative bank roughness affects both the magnitude and lateral distribution of boundary shear stress along the bed and banks (Houjou et al., 1990; Kean and Smith, 2006a, 2006b), allowing stabilization of channel width (Parker, 1978) and promotes deposition of sands and silts during overbank flows, further stabilizing channel position and form (Smith, 2004; Allmendinger et al., 2005).

Approaches for predicting channel width can be divided into three broad classes: (i) empirical equations, (ii) numerical models (ASCE, 1998; Mosselman, 1998, and Chapter 9, this volume; Nagata et al., 2000; Parker et al., 2011) and (iii) analytical solutions, including (a) the bankfull threshold channel (Koechlin, 1924; Glover and Florey, 1951; Lane and Carlson, 1953; Lane, 1955a; Henderson, 1963; Parker, 1978; 1979) and (b) extremal hypotheses (i.e., optimality criteria; see recent reviews by Eaton et al., 2004; Huang et al., 2004; Millar, 2005).

None of these approaches is completely satisfying, with the pros and cons of each well discussed by Ferguson (1986) and Piégay et al. (2005). Parker (1978) offers mechanistic insight for the credibility of the bankfull threshold approach, but only gravel- and cobble-bed channels (pool-riffle and plane-bed morphologies) exhibit near-bankfull thresholds for mobility (Figure 32.5a), making this approach applicable only to a subset of channel types.

### 32.4.2.3 State Diagrams

Solutions from rational regime relations are typically presented in terms of "state diagrams" (e.g., Parker, 1990; Buffington et al., 2003; Eaton et al., 2004). For example, Figure 32.9a is a modified version of Parker's (1990) approach, showing unique solutions of equilibrium channel slope ($S$), relative submergence ($h^* = h/D_{50}$), and excess Shields stress ($\tau^*/\tau^*_{c50}$) for given pairs of dimensionless unit discharge ($q^*$) and bedload transport rate ($q_b^*$).

Here, $q^*$ is defined from Parker et al. (2003; 2007) as

$$q^* = \frac{\langle u \rangle h}{\sqrt{g D_{50}} D_{50}} = \frac{\langle u \rangle h^*}{\sqrt{g D_{50}}} \qquad (32.1)$$

wherein $\langle u \rangle$ is the vertically-averaged velocity determined from the law of the wall (Keulegan, 1938) as modified by Wiberg and Smith (1991) to account for particle form drag over non-uniform, rough beds

$$\langle u \rangle = \frac{u^*}{\kappa} \ln\left(\frac{0.48h}{z_0}\right) \qquad (32.2)$$

In Equation (32.2), $u^*$ is the shear velocity ($\sqrt{\tau/\rho} = \sqrt{ghS}$), $\kappa$ is von Kármán's (1930) constant (0.408; Long et al., 1993) and $z_0$ is the height above the bed where the velocity profile goes to zero ($0.1D_{84}$; Whiting and Dietrich, 1990; Wiberg and Smith, 1991), where $D_{84}$ is the surface grain size for which 84% of the sizes are smaller). For a log-normal grain size distribution, $D_{84}$ can be written in terms of $D_{50}$ and the grain-size standard deviation ($\sigma$)

$$D_{84} = 2^{-(\phi_{50}-\sigma_\phi)} = D_{50} 2^{\sigma_\phi} \qquad (32.3)$$

where $\phi_{50}$ is the median grain size in $-\log_2$ phi units (Krumbein, 1936) and $\sigma_\phi$ is the grain-size standard deviation in the same units (set equal to $1.21 \pm 0.01$, which is an average value for rivers with $D_{50} = 8$–256 mm; Buffington, 1999). Although shallow-flow velocity profiles are not logarithmic (Wiberg and Smith, 1991), modified forms of the law of the wall, such as Equation (32.2), can be used to estimate the *average* velocity

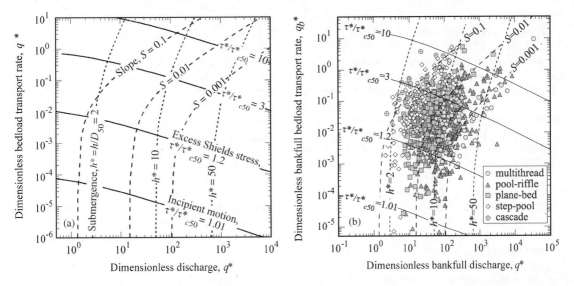

**Figure 32.9** State diagram developed from Equations (32.6) and (32.7), showing: (a) contours of equilibrium channel slope ($S$), relative submergence ($h^* = h/D_{50}$), and excess Shields stress ($\tau^*/\tau^*_{c50}$) as functions of dimensionless discharge ($q^*$) and dimensionless equilibrium bedload transport rate ($q_b^*$), and (b) the same figure populated with field data for different reach-scale channel types evaluated at bankfull stage (data from Figure 32.4). Here, multithread channels have $D_{50} > 2$ mm. The $q^*$ and $q_b^*$ values plotted in (b) are predicted from Equations (32.6) and (32.7). After Parker (1990).

of such flows; determining the full profile and the skin-friction shear stress requires numerical modelling (Wiberg and Smith, 1991). Furthermore, Equation (32.2) does not account for other sources of roughness (e.g., banks, bedforms, wood), potentially overestimating $\langle u \rangle$ in channels with multiple roughness types. Nevertheless, it is a useful first-order prediction in the absence of site-specific channel characteristics needed for more detailed partitioning of shear stress and velocity (Nelson and Smith, 1989; Shields and Gippel, 1995; Buffington, 1998; 2001; Kean and Smith, 2006a; Wilcox et al., 2006). Critical reviews of resistance equations and approaches for determining average velocity are presented by Ferguson (2007; in press).

The dimensionless bedload transport rate is determined here from the Meyer-Peter and Müller (1948) equation as modified by Wong and Parker (2006)

$$q_b^* = 4.93(\tau^* - \tau^*_{c50})^{1.6} \qquad (32.4)$$

However, any suitable bedload transport equation can be used, depending on one's preference and specific goals. In Equation (32.4), the critical Shields stress is predicted as a function of $S$ using the equation of Lamb et al. (2008)

$$\tau^*_{c50} = 0.15S^{0.25} \qquad (32.5)$$

Equation (32.5) predicts $\tau^*_{c50}$ values based on the total boundary shear stress. To be consistent with this definition of $\tau^*_{c50}$, the applied Shields stress in Equation (32.4) is also defined from the total boundary shear stress ($\tau^* = \rho ghS/[(\rho_s - \rho)gD_{50}] = h^*S/R$, wherein $R$ is the submerged specific gravity, $\rho_s/\rho - 1$, with $\rho_s$ and $\rho$ taken as 2650 and 1000 kg m$^{-3}$, respectively). Hence, $\tau^*$ and $\tau^*_{c50}$ are apparent values (uncorrected for roughness). In the Meyer-Peter–Müller equation, $q_b^*$ is defined from the Einstein number $q_b/(\sqrt{RgD_{50}}D_{50})$, where $q_b$ is the volumetric bedload transport rate per unit width.

Inserting the above definitions into Equations (32.1) and (32.4) yields

$$q^* = \frac{\sqrt{h^*S}h^*}{\kappa} ln\left(\frac{4.8h^*}{2^{\sigma_\phi}}\right) \qquad (32.6)$$

$$q_b^* = 4.93(h^*S/R - \tau^*_{c50})^{1.6} = 4.93[(\tau^*/\tau^*_{c50} - 1)\tau^*_{c50}]^{1.6} \qquad (32.7)$$

which expresses the dimensionless discharge ($q^*$) and dimensionless bedload transport rate ($q_b^*$) in terms of three dimensionless channel characteristics: slope ($S$), relative submergence ($h^* = h/D_{50}$), and excess Shields stress ($\tau^*/\tau^*_{c50}$). Analytical solutions are shown as a state diagram (Figure 32.9a), which is similar to those developed by Parker (1990) and Eaton et al. (2004).

The state diagram of Figure 32.9a formalizes Lane's conceptual process–response balance, offering quantitative predictions of changes in equilibrium channel form as a function of altered discharge or sediment supply ($q_b^*$ is a measure of both bedload transport rate and bedload sediment supply for conditions of equilibrium transport). For example, in the framework of Figure 32.9a an increase in sediment supply ($q_b^*$) for a constant discharge ($q^*$) is predicted to cause increases in channel slope ($S$), relative submergence ($h^*$), and excess Shields stress ($\tau^*/\tau^*_{c50}$). This can be explained as follows. The elevated sediment load initially exceeds the channel transport capacity, causing deposition and building of the bed slope, which over time increases the transport capacity of the river (Gilbert, 1877; 1917; du Boys, 1879). Increased sediment volume also leads to textural fining (greater values of both $h^*$ and $\tau^*/\tau^*_{c50}$) that smoothes the bed and promotes increased transport rates (Dietrich et al., 1989; Buffington and Montgomery, 1999b; Eaton and Church, 2009; Madej et al., 2009). The slope and grain-size adjustments proceed until the transport capacity matches the new sediment supply. This response scenario conforms both to Lane's (1955b) conceptual framework and to field and laboratory observations of channel response (Gilbert, 1917; Madej et al., 2009), but the added value of Figure 32.9a is that it allows explicit

quantification of equilibrium changes in $S$, $h^*$, and $\tau^*/\tau^*_{c50}$.

Coupled with digital elevation models (DEMs) and predictions of reach-scale channel type as functions of stream gradient (Buffington et al., 2004a), one can rapidly map the distribution of channels within a basin into state diagrams to examine potential channel responses for different disturbance scenarios (Figure 32.10). Response can be considered in terms of changes in channel characteristics ($S$, $h^*$, and $\tau^*/\tau^*_{c50}$), or changes in reach-scale channel type (e.g., metamorphosis from a pool-riffle channel to a plane-bed morphology). Results can then be mapped back onto the DEM to examine the spatial distribution of potential channel responses within a basin and overlain on other basin resources (e.g., spatial distributions of threatened or endangered aquatic populations and their habitat preferences) to examine the larger biophysical consequences of the predicted changes.

Solutions of equilibrium channel form obtained from state diagrams, such as Figure 32.9a, may be sensitive to how one formulates and parameterizes the governing equations (in this case, $q^*$ and $q_b^*$). In particular, bedload transport equations have notoriously large potential errors if not locally calibrated (Gomez and Church, 1989; Barry et al., 2004; 2007). Furthermore, state diagram

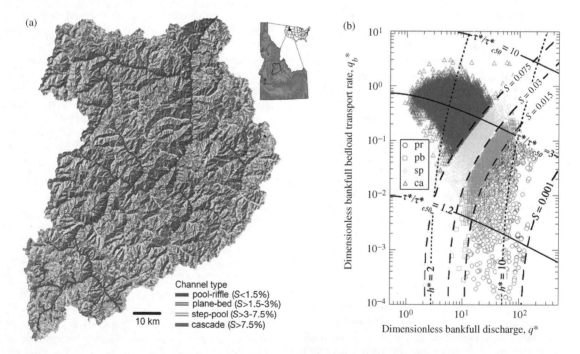

**Figure 32.10** Predicted spatial distributions of: (a) reach-scale channel types in the Middle Fork Salmon River, central Idaho, USA and (b) those data mapped onto the Figure 32.9 regime diagram: pr = pool-riffle ($n = 2616$), pb = plane-bed ($n = 2056$), sp = step-pool ($n = 5983$) and ca = cascade ($n = 50\,135$). (See the color version of this figure in color plate section.)

predictions can be improved if the transport equation is tailored to channel type.

State diagrams have also been developed for predicting channel pattern (i.e., the occurrence of straight, meandering, and braided channels; Parker, 1976), but little work has been done to predict controls on other reach-scale channel types (e.g., the occurrence of pool-riffle, plane-bed, or step-pool channels), except in terms of statistical models (Wohl and Merritt, 2005; Flores *et al.*, 2006; Brardinoni and Hassan, 2007; Altunkayak and Strom, 2009). Morphogenic processes are understood for some of these channel types (Montgomery and Buffington, 1997), and ranges of channel characteristics ($S$, $w/h$, $h^*$) have been empirically determined (Montgomery and Buffington, 1997; Chartrand and Whiting, 2000; Buffington *et al.*, 2003; Wohl and Merritt, 2005; Thompson *et al.*, 2006; Brardinoni and Hassan, 2007; Strom and Papanicolaou, 2009), but rational regime relations have not been developed for predicting specific reach-scale morphologies beyond the basic pattern differences discussed above. Empirically, different reach-scale channel types occupy specific domains of the Figure 32.9b state diagram highlighting two, related, well-known observations: (i) a remarkably similar suite of reach-scale channel morphologies is found across a broad range of physiographic environments and (ii) natural channels exhibit a fairly narrow range of forms compared to what is theoretically possible, with extremal hypotheses invoked to explain the latter observation, as discussed above.

One extremal hypothesis that is currently en vogue is the notion that the stable reach-scale morphology provides the roughness configuration needed for equilibrium transport in alluvial channels (i.e., channel roughness dissipates excess energy beyond that needed for equilibrium transport; Church and Jones 1982; Montgomery and Buffington, 1997; Eaton *et al.*, 2004; Huang *et al.*, 2004; Eaton and Church, 2007). This suggests that roughness is a key parameter in predicting channel change to altered environmental conditions and for understanding the occurrence of characteristic reach-scale morphologies. However, extremal hypotheses are theoretical constructs and limiting factors also need to be considered. For example, step-pool morphology may represent a stable roughness configuration (Whittaker and Jaeggi, 1982; Abrahams *et al.*, 1995; Chin, 2002), but it requires a bimodal supply of both boulder-sized material and finer sediments, which limits the occurrence of this morphology to certain portions of the river network (i.e., steep, confined channels that are coupled to hillslope inputs of boulders, or channels that are within the debris-flow process domain, where boulders can be delivered by debris-flow events). Furthermore, oversupply of boulders will force a cascade morphology, which likely represents a jammed channel (*sensu* Church, 2006), rather than an optimal roughness response.

### 32.4.2.4 Empirical State Diagrams

A number of empirical state diagrams have also been developed that relate channel form to flow and sediment transport parameters, but without formal specification of the governing equations that link the two. For example, empirical state diagrams have been used to: (i) stratify phases of bed topography in sand-bed channels as functions of flow strength, depth, and grain size (Gilbert, 1914; Shields, 1936; Simons and Richardson, 1966; Allen, 1982; Middleton and Southard, 1984), (ii) examine limits on bar formation and pattern in gravel- and sand-bed rivers (Ikeda, 1975; Church and Jones, 1982; Florsheim, 1985), (iii) distinguish controls on straight, meandering, braided, and anastomosed channel patterns as a function of channel slope, discharge, grain size, and bedload transport capacity relative to sediment supply (Lane, 1957; Leopold and Wolman, 1957; Henderson, 1963; Schumm and Khan, 1972; Bray, 1982; Carson, 1984; Ferguson, 1987; Knighton and Nanson, 1993; van den Berg, 1995; Church, 2002), and (iv) delineate physical domains for different channel types (e.g., Chin, 1999a; 2002; Buffington *et al.*, 2003; Wohl and Merritt, 2005; Flores *et al.*, 2006; Brardinoni and Hassan, 2007; Church and Zimmermann, 2007; Altunkayak and Strom, 2009; Zimmermann *et al.*, 2010). The Shields curve has also been used as a state diagram to distinguish the occurrence of different channel types and modes of sediment transport as a function of excess shear stress (Shields, 1936; Dade and Friend, 1998; García, 2000; Parker *et al.*, 2003; Church, 2006; Bunte *et al.*, 2010). These empirical state diagrams can be used to predict channel change, but are not mechanistic process–response models, such as the rational regime relations discussed above.

### 32.4.2.5 Numerical Models

Numerical models can be used to provide quantitative predictions of channel change, but are sensitive to how the models are conceptualized, their complexity (number of dimensions, equations, and parameters), and their scale of application (Piégay *et al.*, 2005). Nevertheless, numerical models have the advantage of being able to quantify transient stages of channel change and specific response trajectories. A full discussion of the available numerical models is beyond the scope of this paper (but see recent reviews by Darby and Van de Wiel, 2003; Pizzuto, 2003; Ferguson, 2008; Mosselman, Chapter 9, this volume).

**Table 32.2** Relative size of floods in different hydroclimates[a]

| Discharge ratio | Snowmelt (Colorado Front Range) | Frontal rainfall (Klamath Mountains, California)[b] | Thunderstorm (Colorado Front Range) |
|---|---|---|---|
| $Q_{ma}/Q_{ma}$[c] | 1 | 1 | 1 |
| $Q_5/Q_{ma}$ | 1.3 | 1.3 | 1.1 |
| $Q_{10}/Q_{ma}$ | 1.4 | 1.9 | 1.9 |
| $Q_{50}/Q_{ma}$ | 1.8 | 3.5 | 4.5 |
| $Q_{100}/Q_{ma}$ | 2 | 4.5 | 8.9 |

[a] Data from Pitlick (1994), based on regional flood frequency curves for mountain basins with roughly comparable ranges of drainage area.

[b] Approximate average value for the three frontal rainfall systems examined by Pitlick (1994).

[c] $Q_{ma}$ = mean annual flood.

## 32.5 CHANNEL STABILITY AND HYDROCLIMATE

The equilibrium concept for channel adjustment is a useful first-order model and a productive means for organizing process–response theory, but it does not address channel stability (temporal variability of channel morphology). For the most part, channels are not in strict, or even quasi, equilibrium, but rather have a mean condition defined by the mode of the work function that they are exposed to (Wolman and Miller, 1960), with some degree of variance about this mean. The degree of variance (or tendency for channel change) depends on the local process domain (Sections 32.2 and 32.3). In addition, regional differences in climate can have a strong influence on basin hydrology (Pitlick, 1994; Poff et al., 2006), with the shape of the hydrograph likely imposing first-order controls on channel morphology and temporal variability of channel conditions (Pickup and Warner, 1976).

For example, rainfall-driven environments are characterized by flashy, peaked hydrographs, and snowmelt-driven environments are characterized by long-duration, low-amplitude hydrographs. These differences affect flood duration and the extent of morphologic adjustment that can occur. For example, ephemeral streams are typically unarmoured and lack well-defined bank and floodplain morphology due to insufficient time for bed and bank adjustments to imposed floods. In these environments, poorly developed armour layers are due to rapid recession of floods and insufficient time for selective transport and winnowing of fine grains needed for armour development (Laronne et al., 1994; Hassan et al., 2006). In contrast, snowmelt streams commonly exhibit well-armoured beds and clearly defined bankfull floodplains due to more frequent and longer-duration flood events.

Furthermore, the size of floods relative to the mean annual flow ($Q_n/Q_{ma}$) differs between hydroclimates,

creating differences in flood variability (Table 32.2). This has several important consequences for channel morphology: (i) the more variable the flow, the more important the higher discharges become in terms of the work they accomplish relative to lower flows (Wolman and Miller, 1960; Pickup and Warner, 1976) and (ii) although the effective discharge for sediment transport occurs at bankfull flow or less in floodplain rivers, larger floods may be needed to alter channel form (Section 32.2). In particular, large floods become increasing important for lateral erosion as bank resistance increases (e.g., banks with greater vegetation, wood armouring, or large-sized sediment; Pickup and Warner, 1976; Carling, 1988b). Stevens et al. (1975) argue that the variance of flood size relative to the mean annual value (Table 32.2) provides an index of channel variability, with equilibrium conditions expected only in cases where $Q_n/Q_{ma}$ does not vary substantially over time. This suggests that channel morphology may be more variable in rainfall environments than in snowmelt-dominated ones because of characteristic differences in relative flood size (Table 32.2). Furthermore, it suggests that climate-driven changes in flood variability may cause corresponding changes in the variability of channel morphology.

## 32.6 CONCLUSION

The potential for channel change varies over space and time as a function of the imposed environmental conditions, the available degrees of freedom for channel response, and the thresholds and time scales for a given response to occur. Consequently, channel response depends on a series of nested scales of probability functions, with unconfined alluvial channels showing the greatest potential for response. Over human time scales, rivers exhibit responses ranging from small-scale adjustments resulting from seasonal changes in watershed inputs to large-scale changes resulting from infrequent floods or decadal to centennial changes in climate (wet/dry cycles). Until recently, our ability to document these changes has been limited to: (i) broad-scale remote sensing (e.g., repeat aerial photography and satellite imagery) that typically provides fairly coarse resolution of channel features or (ii) small-scale, long-term monitoring that provides more detailed information, but only at individual cross-sections or reaches on the order of tens of channel widths in length. However, recent advances in airborne remote sensing (thermal infrared sensors (Torgersen et al., 2001), terrestrial and bathymetric LiDAR (McKean et al., 2008; 2009; Snyder, 2009; Wilkins and Snyder, 2011), and hyperspectral imagery (Marcus et al., 2003)) offer increasingly better resolution of data over multiple spatial scales (Marcus, Chapter 21, this volume).

Our geomorphic tool kit currently includes theoretical and empirical models for predicting channel change, but they are typically over-simplified (e.g., a preponderance of 1-D numerical models and state diagrams that are applicable to a certain class of rivers or a limited range of potential channel responses), or they are capable of providing detailed predictions only over short spatial and temporal scales (as is the case for multidimensional numerical models). Using digital elevation models to stratify the landscape by channel type and process domain offers a means to reduce the sampling effort needed and enables examination of systematic differences in geomorphic condition and response potential within and between basins (Figure 32.10; Buffington et al., 2004a; Benda et al., 2007). However, dynamic response models are needed to couple the identified process domains, and to understand system behaviour and the propagation of disturbances through a watershed.

Disturbance propagation through river networks is understood conceptually (e.g., Schumm, 1977; Montgomery and Buffington, 1997; 1998; Church, 2002), but few mechanistic models have been developed at basin scales (but see reviews by Darby and Van de Wiel (2003), Pizzuto (2003), and Ferguson (2008)). Moreover, an understanding of the legacy of past geologic, climatic, and human disturbances within a basin is essential for accurate prediction of channel response. While the above principles are generally understood, their application remains largely conceptual, and holistic models of basin function (i.e., watershed analyses) are generally lacking, hampering process-based application of river management and restoration (Beechie et al., 2010). In many cases, research and restoration projects are conducted in a piecemeal fashion due to limited, and generally reactive, funding (i.e., addressing perceived problems at a specific location within a basin), perpetuating a myopic focus that does little to advance our understanding of basin function.

In addition, the temporal variability of rivers is frequently under-represented. Geomorphologists and stream restoration practitioners tend to focus on mean conditions (e.g., the bankfull morphology for floodplain alluvial rivers) and to disregard channel variance, or to consider it "noise". Temporal variability is recognized, but mainly from a statistical viewpoint, rather than explicitly quantified and incorporated into our representation of fluvial processes, biophysical condition, and restoration design (i.e., designing for more than the bankfull event; Doyle et al., 2005; Wohl et al., 2005). Accounting for this variability and for non-stationarity of fluvial processes is central to assessing the potential effects of climate change on riverine ecosystems.

Finally, it is worth noting that most channel response models have been developed for alluvial, floodplain rivers, with uncertain application to steeper-gradient, confined, alluvial rivers and bedrock channels. Our understanding of hillslope–channel coupling in these environments also remains rudimentary, although some mechanistic approaches have been proposed (e.g., Whiting and Bradley, 1993; Lancaster et al., 2003). Consequently, further study of fluvial processes, hillslope–channel coupling and channel response potential in steep, confined rivers is warranted, particularly given that more than 80% of the river network in mountain basins is typically composed of steep, boulder-bed channels (Figure 32.10; Stock and Dietrich, 2003; Buffington et al., 2004a).

## 32.7 ACKNOWLEDGEMENTS

James Brasington, Kristin Bunte, Jaime Goode, and Marwan Hassan provided thoughtful reviews of an earlier draft of this paper. I thank Dan Cadol, Marwan Hassan, Victoria Milner, and Paul Mosley (via Mike Church) for graciously providing unpublished data, and I thank Mike Church and Dave Montgomery for providing figures from their work.

## 32.8 REFERENCES

Abrahams, A.D., Li, G., and Atkinson, J.F. 1995. Step-pool streams: Adjustment to maximum flow resistance. *Water Resources Research* **31**: 2593–2602.

Allen, J.R.L. 1982. *Sedimentary Structures: Their Character and Physical Basis*. Amsterdam, Elsevier.

Allmendinger, N.E., Pizzuto, J.E., Potter, N., Johnson, T.E., and Hession, W.C. 2005. The influence of riparian vegetation on stream width, eastern Pennsylvania, USA. *Geological Society of America Bulletin* **117**: 229–243.

Altunkaynak, A. and Strom, K.B. 2009. A predictive model for reach morphology classification in mountain streams using multilayer perceptron methods. *Water Resources Research* **45**: W12501. doi: 10.1029/2009WR008055.

Andrews, E.D. 1980. Effective and bankfull discharges of streams in the Yampa river basin, Colorado and Wyoming. *Journal of Hydrology* **46**: 311–330.

Andrews, E.D. 1984. Bed-material entrainment and hydraulic geometry of gravel-bed rivers in Colorado. *Geological Society of America Bulletin* **95**: 371–378.

Andrews, E.D. and Nankervis, J.M. 1995. Effective discharge and the design of channel maintenance flows for gravel-bed rivers. In Costa, J.E., Miller, A.J., Potter, K.W., and Wilcock, P.R., editors. *Natural and Anthropogenic Influences in Fluvial Geomorphology*. Washington, DC, American Geophysical Union, Geophysical Monograph **89**: 151–164.

Armanini, A. and Gregoretti, C. 2005. Incipient sediment motion at high slopes in uniform flow condition. *Water Resources Research* **41**: W12431. doi: 10.1029/2005WR004001.

ASCE (American Society of Civil Engineers), Task Committee on Hydraulics, Bank Mechanics, and Modeling of River Width Adjustment. 1998. River width adjustment. II. Modeling. *Journal of Hydraulic Engineering* **124**: 903–917.

Barry, J.J., Buffington, J.M., and King, J.G. 2004. A general power equation for predicting bedload transport rates in gravel bed rivers. *Water Resources Research* **40**: W10401. doi: 10.1029/2004WR003190.

Barry, J.J., Buffington, J.M., and King, J.G. 2007. Correction to "A general power equation for predicting bed load transport rates in gravel bed rivers". *Water Resources Research* **43**: W08702. doi: 10.1029/2007WR006103.

Bathurst, J.C. 2007. Effect of coarse surface layer on bed-load transport. *Journal of Hydraulic Engineering* **133**: 1192–1205.

Beechie, T.J., Sear, D.A., Olden, J.D. *et al.* 2010. Process-based principles for restoring river ecosystems. *BioScience* **60**: 209–222.

Benda, L.E. and Cundy, T.W. 1990. Predicting deposition of debris flows in mountain channels. *Canadian Geotechnical Journal* **27**: 409–417.

Benda, L.E. and Dunne, T. 1997a. Stochastic forcing of sediment supply to channel networks from landsliding and debris flow. *Water Resources Research* **33**: 2849–2864.

Benda, L.E. and Dunne, T. 1997b. Stochastic forcing of sediment routing and storage in channel networks. *Water Resources Research* **33**: 2865–2880.

Benda, L.E., Andras, K., Miller, D., and Bigelow, P. 2004a. Confluence effects in rivers: Interactions of basin scale, network geometry, and disturbance regimes. *Water Resources Research* **40**: W05402. doi: 10.1029/2003WR002583.

Benda, L.E., Poff, N.L., Miller, D. *et al.* 2004b. The network dynamics hypothesis: How channel networks structure riverine habitats. *BioScience* **54**: 1–15.

Benda, L.E., Miller, D., Andras, K., Bigelow, P., Reeves, G., and Michael, D. 2007. NetMap: A new tool in support of watershed science and resource management. *Forest Science* **53**: 206–219.

Bisson, P.A., Nielsen, J.L., Palmason, R.A., and Grove, L.E. 1982. A system of naming habitat types in small streams, with examples of habitat utilization by salmonids during low streamflow. In Armantrout, N.B., editor. *Proceedings of a Symposium on Acquisition and Utilization of Aquatic Habitat Inventory Information*. Bethesda, MD, Western Division of the American Fisheries Society, pp. 62–73.

Blench, T. 1957. *Regime Behaviour of Canals and Rivers*. London, Butterworths Scientific Publications.

Booth, D.B., Haugerud, R.A., and Troost, K.G. 2003. The geology of Puget Lowland rivers. In Montgomery, D.R.,

Bolton, S., Booth, D.B. and Wall, L., editors. *Restoration of Puget Sound Rivers*. Seattle, WA, University of Washington Press, pp. 14–45.

Brardinoni, F. and Hassan, M.A. 2006. Glacial erosion, evolution of river long profiles, and the organization of process domains in mountain drainage basins of coastal British Columbia. *Journal of Geophysical Research – Earth Surface* **111**: F01013. doi: 10.1029/2005JF000358.

Brardinoni, F. and Hassan, M.A. 2007. Glacially-induced organization of channel-reach morphology in mountain streams. *Journal of Geophysical Research – Earth Surface* **112**: F03013. doi: 10.1029/2006JF000741.

Bravard, J-P. 2010. Discontinuities in braided patterns: The River Rhône from Geneva to the Camargue delta before river training. *Geomorphology* **117**: 219–233.

Bray, D.I. 1982. Regime equations for gravel-bed rivers. In Hey, R.D., Bathurst, J.C., and Thorne, C.R., editors. *Gravel-bed Rivers*. Chichester, John Wiley & Sons, Ltd, pp. 517–552.

Brayshaw, A.C. 1984. Characteristics and origin of cluster bedforms in coarse-grained alluvial channels. In Koster, E. H. and Steel, R.J., editors. *Sedimentology of Gravels and Conglomerates*. Calgary, Alberta, Canadian Society of Petroleum Geologists, Memoir **10**: 77–85.

Brice, J.C. 1975. *Airphoto Interpretation of the Form and Behavior of Alluvial Rivers*. Final report to the United States Army Research Office, Durham, NC (1 July 1970–31 December 1974). Washington University.

Brierley, G.J. and Fryirs, K.A. 2005. *Geomorphology and River Management*. Oxford, Blackwell.

Brownlie, W.R. 1981. *Prediction of flow depth and sediment discharge in open channels*. Pasadena, CA, California Institute of Technology. WM Keck Laboratory of Hydraulics and Water Resources Report KH-R-43A.

Brummer, C.J. and Montgomery, D.R. 2003. Downstream coarsening in headwater channels. *Water Resources Research* **39**: 1294. doi: 10.1029/2003WR001981.

Bryan, K. 1925. Date of channel trenching (arroyo cutting) in the arid southwest. *Science* **62**: 338–344.

Buffington, J.M. 1998. *The use of streambed texture to interpret physical and biological conditions at watershed, reach, and subreach scales*. Unpublished Ph.D. thesis, University of Washington, Seattle.

Buffington, J.M. 1999. Variability of sediment sorting in coarse-grained rivers: A case of self-similarity. *Eos, Transactions, American Geophysical Union* **80**, Fall Meeting Supplement, Abstract H51A-48: 449.

Buffington, J.M. 2001. Hydraulic roughness and shear stress partitioning in forest gravel-bed rivers. In Nolan, T.J. and Thorne, C.R., editors. *Gravel-Bed Rivers 2000*. Wellington, New Zealand, Special Publication of the New Zealand Hydrological Society, CD-ROM.

Buffington, J.M. and Montgomery, D.R. 1997. A systematic analysis of eight decades of incipient motion studies, with special reference to gravel-bedded rivers. *Water Resources Research* **33**: 1993–2029.

Buffington, J.M. and Montgomery, D.R. 1999a. Effects of hydraulic roughness on surface textures of gravel-bed rivers. *Water Resources Research* **35**: 3507–3522.

Buffington, J.M. and Montgomery, D.R. 1999b. Effects of sediment supply on surface textures of gravel-bed rivers. *Water Resources Research* **35**: 3523–3530.

Buffington, J.M. and Montgomery, D.R. 2001. Reply to comments on "Effects of hydraulic roughness on surface textures of gravel-bed rivers" and "Effects of sediment supply on surface textures of gravel-bed rivers" by John M. Buffington and David R. Montgomery. *Water Resources Research* **37**: 1529–1533.

Buffington, J.M., Dietrich, W.E., and Kirchner, J.W. 1992. Friction angle measurements on a naturally formed gravel streambed: Implications for critical boundary shear stress. *Water Resources Research* **28**: 411–425.

Buffington, J.M., Montgomery, D.R., and Greenberg, H.M. 2004a. Basin-scale availability of salmonid spawning gravel as influenced by channel type and hydraulic roughness in mountain catchments. *Canadian Journal of Fisheries and Aquatic Sciences* **61**: 2085–2096.

Buffington, J.M., Scheidt, N.E., and Welcker, C.W. 2004b. Channel geometry of mountain rivers within the debris-flow process domain of the Idaho Batholith. *Eos, Transactions, American Geophysical Union* **85**: Fall Meeting Supplement, Abstract H41G-01.

Buffington, J.M., Woodsmith, R.D., Booth, D.B., and Montgomery, D.R. 2003. Fluvial processes in Puget Sound Rivers and the Pacific Northwest. In Montgomery, D.R., Bolton, S., Booth, D.B., and Wall, L., editors. *Restoration of Puget Sound Rivers*. Seattle, WA, University of Washington Press, pp. 46–78.

Buffington, J.M., Roper, B.E., Archer, E., and Moyer, C. 2009. Reply to discussion by David L. Rosgen on "The role of observer variation in determining Rosgen stream types in northeastern Oregon mountain streams". *Journal of the American Water Resources Association* **45**: 1298–1312.

Bull, W.B. 1991. *Geomorphic Responses to Climatic Change*. Caldwell, NJ, Blackburn Press.

Bunte, K., Abt, S.R., Swingle, K.W., and Potyondy, J.P. 2010. Bankfull mobile particle size and its prediction from a Shields-type approach. In *Proceedings of the 2nd Joint Federal Interagency Conference (9th Federal Interagency Sedimentation Conference, 4th Federal Interagency Hydrologic Modeling Conference), Las Vegas, NV, 27 June–1 July*. CD-ROM, ISBN 978-0-9779007-3-2, http://acwi.gov/sos/pubs/2ndJFIC/.

Burke, M., Jorde, K., Buffington, J.M., Braatne, J., and Benjankar, R. 2006. Spatial distribution of impacts to channel bed mobility due to flow regulation, Kootenai River, USA. In *Proceedings of the 8th Federal Interagency Sedimentation Conference, Reno, NV, 2–6 April*. US Advisory Committee on Water Information, Subcommittee on Sedimentation, CD-ROM ISBN 0-9779007-1-1. url: http://pubs.usgs.gov/misc/FISC_1947-2006/pdf/1st-7thFISCs-CD/8thFISC/8thFISC.pdf.

Carling, P.A. 1988a. Channel change and sediment transport in regulated U.K. rivers. *Regulated Rivers: Research and Management* **2**: 369–387.

Carling, P.A. 1988b. The concept of dominant discharge applied to two gravel-bed streams in relation to channel stability thresholds. *Earth Surface Processes and Landforms* **13**: 355–367.

Carson, M.A. 1984. Observations on the meandering-braided river transition, the Canterbury Plains, New Zealand: Part two. *New Zealand Geographer* **40**: 89–99.

Cenderelli, D.A. and Kite, S. 1998. Geomorphic effects of large debris flows on channel morphology at North Fork Mountain, eastern West Virginia, USA. *Earth Surface Processes and Landforms* **23**: 1–19.

Chartrand, S.M. and Whiting, P.J. 2000. Alluvial architecture in headwater streams with special emphasis on step-pool topography. *Earth Surface Processes and Landforms* **25**: 583–600.

Chin, A. 1998. On the stability of step-pool mountain streams. *The Journal of Geology* **106**: 59–69.

Chin, A. 1999a. On the origin of step-pool sequences in mountain streams. *Geophysical Research Letters* **26**: 231–234.

Chin, A. 1999b. The morphologic structure of step-pools in mountain streams. *Geomorphology* **27**: 191–204.

Chin, A. 2002. The periodic nature of step-pool mountain streams. *American Journal of Science* **302**: 144–167.

Chin, A. 2006. Urban transformation of river landscapes in a global context. *Geomorphology* **79**: 460–487.

Church, M. 1978. Palaeohydrological reconstructions from a Holocene valley fill. In Miall, A.D., editor. *Fluvial Sedimentology*. Calgary, Alberta, Canadian Society of Petroleum Geologists, *Memoir* **5**: 743–772.

Church, M. 1995. Geomorphic response to river flow regulation: Case studies and time-scales. *Regulated Rivers: Research and Management* **11**: 3–22.

Church, M. 2002. Geomorphic thresholds in riverine landscapes. *Freshwater Biology* **47**: 541–557.

Church, M. 2006. Bed material transport and the morphology of alluvial rivers. *Annual Review of Earth and Planetary Sciences* **34**: 325–354.

Church, M. and Jones, D. 1982. Channel bars in gravel-bed rivers. In Hey, R.D., Bathurst, J.C., and Thorne, C.R., editors. *Gravel-bed Rivers*. Chichester, John Wiley & Sons Ltd, pp. 291–338.

Church, M. and Zimmermann, A. 2007. Form and stability of step-pool channels: Research progress. *Water Resources Research* **43**: W03415. doi: 10.1029/2006WR005037.

Church, M., Hassan, M.A., and Wolcott, J.F. 1998. Stabilizing self-organized structures in gravel-bed stream channels: Field and experimental observations. *Water Resources Research* **34**: 3169–3179.

Clark, G.M., Jacobson, R.B., Kite, J.S., and Linton, R.C. 1987. Storm-induced catastrophic flooding in Virginia and West Virginia, November 1985. In Mayer, L. and Nash, D., editors. *Catastrophic Flooding*. Boston, MA, Allen and Unwin, pp. 355–379.

Clark, J.J. and Wilcock, P.R. 2000. Effects of land-use change on channel morphology in northeastern Puerto Rico. *Geological Society of America Bulletin* **112**: 1763–1777.

Collins, B.D., Montgomery, D.R., and Sheikh, A.J. 2003. Reconstructing the historical riverine landscape of the Puget Lowland. In Montgomery, D.R., Bolton, S., Booth, D.B., and Wall, L., editors. *Restoration of Puget Sound Rivers*. Seattle, WA, University of Washington Press, pp. 79–128.

Costa, J.E. and O'Connor, J.E. 1995. Geomorphically effective floods. In Costa, J.E., Miller, A.J., Potter, K.W., and Wilcock, P.R., editors. *Natural and Anthropogenic Influences in Fluvial Geomorphology*. Washington, DC, American Geophysical Union, Geophysical Monograph **89**: 45–56.

Coulthard, T.J. and Van De Wiel, M.J. 2007. Quantifying fluvial non linearity and finding self organized criticality? Insights from simulations of river basin evolution. *Geomorphology* **91**: 216–235.

Coulthard, T.J., Lewin, J., and Macklin, M.G. 2008. Nonstationarity of basin scale sediment delivery in response to climate change. In Habersack, H., Piégay, H., and Rinaldi, M., editors. *Gravel-Bed Rivers VI: From Process Understanding to River Restoration*. Amsterdam, Elsevier, Developments in Earth Surface Processes **11**: 315–329.

Crowder, D.W. and Knapp, R.A. 2004. Effective discharge recurrence intervals of Illinois streams. *Geomorphology* **64**: 167–184.

Crutzen, P.J. 2002. Geology of mankind. *Nature* **415**: 23.

Cui, Y. and Parker, G. 2005. Numerical model of sediment pulses and sediment-supply disturbances in mountain rivers. *Journal of Hydraulic Engineering* **131**: 646–656.

Dade, W.B. and Friend, P.F. 1998. Grain-size, sediment-transport regime, and channel slope in alluvial rivers. *The Journal of Geology* **106**: 661–675.

Darby, S.E. and Van de Wiel, M.J. 2003. Models in fluvial geomorphology. In Kondolf, G.M. and Piégay, H., editors. *Tools in Fluvial Geomorphology*. Chichester, John Wiley & Sons, Ltd, pp. 503–537.

Davis, W.M. 1889. The rivers and valleys of Pennsylvania. *National Geographic Magazine* **1**: 183–253.

Desloges, J.R. and Church, M.A. 1989. Wandering gravel-bed rivers. *The Canadian Geographer* **33**: 360–364.

Dietrich, W.E., Kirchner, J.W., Ikeda, H., and Iseya, F. 1989. Sediment supply and the development of the coarse surface layer in gravel-bedded rivers. *Nature* **340**: 215–217.

Dietrich, W.E., Nelson, P.A., Yager, E. *et al.* 2006. Sediment patches, sediment supply and channel morphology. In Parker, G. and Garcia, M.H., editors. *River, Coastal and Estuarine: Morphodynamics*. Lisse, the Netherlands, Taylor and Francis/Balkema, pp. 79–90.

Doyle, M.W., Stanley, E.H., Strayer, D.L., Jacobson, R.B., and Schmidt, J.C. 2005. Effective discharge analysis of ecological processes in streams. *Water Resources Research* **41**: W11411. doi: 10.1029/2005WR004222.

du Boys, P. 1879. Le Rhône et les rivièrs a lit affouillable. *Annales des Ponts et Chaussées, Mémoires et Documents, Série* **5**, v.**18**: 141–195 (Anonymous English translation, University of California Berkeley, Water Resources Center Archive.)

Dunne, T. and Leopold, L.B. 1978. *Water in Environmental Planning*. San Francisco, CA, Freeman.

Dury, G.H. 1976. Discharge prediction, present and former, from channel dimensions. *Journal of Hydrology* **30**: 219–245.

Eaton, B.C. and Church, M. 2007. Predicting downstream hydraulic geometry: A test of rational regime theory. *Journal of Geophysical Research-Earth Surface* **112**: F03025. doi: 10.1029/2006JF000734.

Eaton, B.C. and Church, M. 2009. Channel stability in bed load-dominated streams with nonerodible banks: Inferences from experiments in a sinuous flume. *Journal of Geophysical Research – Earth Surface* **114**: F01024. doi: 10.1029/2007JF000902.

Eaton, B.C., Church, M., and Millar, R.G. 2004. Rational regime model of alluvial channel morphology and response. *Earth Surface Processes and Landforms* **29**: 511–529.

Emmett, W.W. 1972. *The Hydraulic Geometry of Some Alaskan Streams South of the Yukon River*. United States Geological Survey, Open-File Report 72-108.

Emmett, W.W. and Wolman, M.G. 2001. Effective discharge and gravel-bed rivers. *Earth Surface Processes and Landforms* **26**: 1369–1380.

Ethridge, F.G. and Schumm, S.A. 1978. Reconstructing paleochannel morphologic and flow characteristics: Methodology, limitations, and assessment. In Miall, A.D., editor. *Fluvial Sedimentology*. Calgary, Alberta, Canadian Society of Petroleum Geologists, Memoir **5**: 703–721.

Fenton, J.D. and Abbott, J.E. 1977. Initial movement of grains on a stream bed: The effect of relative protrusion. *Proceedings of the Royal Society of London* **A**, **352**: 523–537.

Ferguson, R.I. 1986. Hydraulics and hydraulic geometry. *Progress in Physical Geography* **10**: 1–31.

Ferguson, R.I. 1987. Hydraulic and sedimentary controls of channel pattern. In Richards, K.S., editor. *River Channels: Environment and Process*. Oxford, Blackwell, pp. 129–158.

Ferguson, R.I. 2003. Emergence of abrupt gravel to sand transitions along rivers through sorting processes. *Geological Society of America Bulletin* **31**: 159–162.

Ferguson, R.I. 2007. Flow resistance equations for gravel- and boulder-bed streams. *Water Resources Research* **43**: W05427. doi: 10.1029/2006WR005422.

Ferguson, R.I. 2008. Gravel-bed rivers at the reach scale. In Habersack, H., Piégay, H. and Rinaldi, M., editors. *Gravel-Bed Rivers VI: From Process Understanding to River Restoration*. Amsterdam, Elsevier. Developments in Earth Surface Processes **11**: 33–53.

Ferguson, R.I. in press. Reach-scale flow resistance. In Wohl, E. E., editor, *Treatise in Geomorphology, vol. 9*. Fluvial Geomorphology. Amsterdam, Elsevier.

Ferguson, R.I. and Werritty, A. 1991. Channel change and sedimentology in the River Feshie: A wandering gravel-bed river, Scottish Highlands. Werritty, A., editor. In *BGRG and COMTAG Joint International Symposium on Theory in Geomorphology. Field Excursion Guide: Fluvial Processes in Scottish Highland Rivers*. British Geomorphological Research Group and International Geographical Union Commission on Measurement, Theory, and Application in Geomorphology, Universities of Leeds and St. Andrews, UK, pp. 17–36.

Ferguson, R.I., Cudden, J.R., Hoey, T.B., and Rice, S.P. 2006. River system discontinuities due to lateral inputs: Generic styles and controls. *Earth Surface Processes and Landforms* **31**: 1149–1166.

Finnegan, N.J., Roe, G., Montgomery, D.R., and Hallet, B. 2005. Controls on the channel width of rivers: Implications for modeling fluvial incision of bedrock. *Geology* **33**: 229–232.

Flores, A.N., Bledsoe, B.P., Cuhaciyan, C.O., and Wohl, E. 2006. Channel-reach morphology dependence on energy, scale, and hydroclimatic processes with implications for prediction using geospatial data. *Water Resources Research* **42**: W06412. doi: 10.1029/2005WR004226.

Florsheim, J.L. 1985. *Fluvial requirements for gravel bar formation in northwestern California*. Unpublished M.S. thesis, Humboldt State University, Arcata, CA.

García, M.H. 2000. Discussion of "The Legend of A. F. Shields" by J.M. Buffington. *Journal of Hydraulic Engineering* **126**: 718–719.

Gilbert, G.K. 1877. *Report on the Geology of the Henry Mountains*, 1st edition. United States Geographical and Geological Survey of the Rocky Mountain Region, US Government Printing Office.

Gilbert, G.K. 1914. *The Transportation of Débris by Running Water*. United States Geological Survey, Professional Paper 86.

Gilbert, G.K. 1917. *Hydraulic-mining Débris in the Sierra Nevada*. United States Geological Survey, Professional Paper 105.

Gintz, D., Hassan, M.A., and Schmidt, K-H. 1996. Frequency and magnitude of bedload transport in a mountain river. *Earth Surface Processes and Landforms* **21**: 433–445.

Glover, R.E. and Florey, Q.L. 1951. *Stable Channel Profiles*. United States Bureau of Reclamation, Hydraulic Laboratory Report Hyd-325.

Gomez, B. and Church, M. 1989. An assessment of bed load sediment transport formulae for gravel bed rivers. *Water Resources Research* **25**: 1161–1186.

Gomez, B., Coleman, S.E., Sy, V.W.K., Peacock, D.H., and Kent, M. 2007. Channel change, bankfull and effective discharges on a vertically accreting, meandering, gravel-bed river. *Earth Surface Processes and Landforms* **32**: 770–785.

Goode, J.R., Luce, C.H., and Buffington, J.M. in press. Enhanced sediment delivery in a changing climate in semi-arid mountain basins: Implications for water resource management and aquatic habitat in the northern Rocky Mountains. *Geomorphology*.

Grant, G.E., Swanson, F.J., and Wolman, M.G. 1990. Pattern and origin of stepped-bed morphology in high-gradient streams, Western Cascades, Oregon. *Geological Society of America Bulletin* **102**: 340–352.

Griffiths, G.A. 1984. Extremal hypotheses for river regime: An illusion of progress. *Water Resources Research* **20**: 113–118.

Griffiths, G.A. 2003. Downstream hydraulic geometry and hydraulic similitude. *Water Resources Research* **39**: 1094.

Hack, J.T. 1957. *Studies of Longitudinal Stream Profiles in Virginia and Maryland*. United States Geological Survey, Professional Paper 294-B.

Hack, J.T. 1960. Interpretation of erosional topography in humid temperate regions. *American Journal of Science* **258-A**: 80–97.

Halwas, K.L. and Church, M. 2002. Channel units in small high gradient streams on Vancouver Island, British Columbia. *Geomorphology* **43**: 243–256.

Hassan, M.A., Egozi, R., and Parker, G. 2006. Experiments on the effect of hydrograph characteristics on vertical grain sorting in gravel bed rivers. *Water Resources Research* **42**: W09408. doi: 10.1029/2005WR004707.

Hassan, M.A., Smith, B.J., Hogan, D.L. *et al.* 2008. Sediment storage and transport in coarse bed streams: Scale considerations. In Habersack, H., Piégay, H., and Rinaldi, M., editors. *Gravel-bed Rivers VI: From Process Understanding to River Restoration*. Elsevier, Amsterdam, Developments in Earth Surface Processes **11**: 473–497.

Hayward, J.A. 1980. *Hydrology and Stream Sediment from Torlesse Stream Catchment*. Tussock Grasslands and Mountain Lands Institute, Lincoln College, Special Publication 17.

Henderson, F.M. 1963. Stability of alluvial channels. *American Society of Civil Engineers Transactions* **128**: 657–720.

Hoey, T.B. 1992. Temporal variations in bedload transport rates and sediment storage in gravel-bed rivers. *Progress in Physical Geography* **6**: 319–338.

Hoey, T.B. and Ferguson, R.I. 1994. Numerical simulation of downstream fining by selective transport in gravel bed rivers: Model development and illustration. *Water Resources Research* **30**: 2251–2260.

Hooke, J.M. 1996. River responses to decadal-scale changes in discharge regime; the Gila River, SE Arizona. In Branson, J., Brown, A.G., and Gregory, K.J., editors. *Global Continental Changes: The Context of Palaeohydrology*. Geological Society (London), Special Publication 115, pp. 191–204.

Houjou, K., Shimizu, Y., and Ishii, C. 1990. Calculation of boundary shear stress in open channel flow. *Journal of Hydroscience and Hydraulic Engineering* **8**: 21–37.

Huang, H.Q., Chang, H.H., and Nanson, G.C. 2004. Minimum energy as the general form of critical flow and maximum flow efficiency and for explaining variations in river channel pattern. *Water Resources Research* **40**: W04502. doi: 10.1029/2003WR002539.

Ikeda, H. 1975. On the bed configuration in alluvial channels: their types and condition of formation with reference to bars. *Geographical Review of Japan* **48**: 712–730.

Inglis, C.C. 1949. *The Behaviour and Control of Rivers and Canals (with the aid of Models)* Poona, India. Central Waterpower Irrigation and Navigation Research Station, Research Publication 13.

Jackson, R.G. 1975. Hierarchical attributes and a unifying model of bed forms composed of cohesionless material and produced by shearing flow. *Geological Society of America Bulletin* **86**: 1523–1533.

Johnston, C.E., Andrews, E.D., and Pitlick, J. 1998. In situ determination of particle friction angles of fluvial gravels. *Water Resources Research* **34**: 2017–2030.

Judd, H.E. and Peterson, D.F. 1969. *Hydraulics of Large Bed Element Channels*. Logan, UT, Utah State University, Utah Water Research Laboratory Report PRWG 17-6.

Kean, J.W. and Smith, J.D. 2006a. Form drag in rivers due to small-scale natural topographic features: 1. Regular sequences. *Journal of Geophysical Research–Earth Surface* **111**: F04009. doi: 10.1029/2006JF000467.

Kean, J.W. and Smith, J.D. 2006b. Form drag in rivers due to small-scale natural topographic features: 2. Irregular sequences. *Journal of Geophysical Research – Earth Surface* **111**: F04010. doi: 10.1029/2006JF000490.

Kellerhals, R. and Church, M. 1989. The morphology of large rivers: Characterization and management. In Dodge, D.P., editor. *Proceedings of the International Large River Symposium*. Canada Department of Fisheries and Oceans, Canadian Special Publication of Fisheries and Aquatic Sciences 106, pp. 31–48.

Kennedy, R.G. 1895–1996. The prevention of silting in irrigation canals. *Minutes of Proceedings of the Institution of Civil Engineers (Great Britain)* **119**: 281–290.

Keulegan, G.H. 1938. Laws of turbulent flow in open channels. *Journal of Research of the National Bureau of Standards* **21**: 707–741.

Knighton, A.D. and Nanson, G.C. 1993. Anastomosis and the continuum of channel pattern. *Earth Surface Processes and Landforms* **18**: 613–625.

Knighton, A.D. 1998. *Fluvial Forms and Processes*. London, Arnold.

Knox, J.C. 1984. Fluvial responses to small scale climate changes. In Costa, J.E. and Fleisher, P.J., editors. *Developments and Applications of Geomorphology*. Berlin, Springer-Verlag, pp. 318–342.

Koechlin, R. 1924. *Mécanisme de l'eau et principes généraux pour l'établissment d'usines hydro-électriques*. Paris, Béranger.

Kondolf, G.M. 1994. Geomorphic and environmental effects of instream gravel mining. *Landscape and Urban Planning* **28**: 225–243.

Kondolf, G.M. 1995. Geomorphological stream channel classification in aquatic habitat restoration: uses and limitations. *Aquatic Conservation: Marine and Freshwater Ecosystems* **5**: 127–141.

Kondolf, G.M., Smeltzer, M., and Railsback, S.F. 2001. Design and performance of a channel reconstruction project in a coastal California gravel-bed stream. *Environmental Management* **28**: 761–776.

Krumbein, W.C. 1936. Application of logarithmic moments to size frequency distributions of sediments. *Journal of Sedimentary Petrology* **6**: 35–47.

Lacey, G. 1929–1930. Stable channels in alluvium. *Minutes of Proceedings of the Institution of Civil Engineers (Great Britain)* **229**: 259–292.

Lacey, G. 1933–1934. Uniform flow in alluvial rivers and canals. *Minutes of Proceedings of the Institution of Civil Engineers (Great Britain)* **237**: 421–453.

Lamarre, H. and Roy, A.G. 2008. The role of morphology on the displacement of particles in a step-pool river system. *Geomorphology* **99**: 270–279.

Lamb, M.P., Dietrich, W.E., and Venditti, J.G. 2008. Is the critical Shields stress for incipient sediment motion dependent on channel-bed slope? *Journal of Geophysical Research-Earth Surface* **113**: F02008. doi: 10.1029/2007JF000831.

Lancaster, S.T., Hayes, S.K. and Grant, G.E. 2003. Effects of wood on debris flow runout in small mountain watersheds. *Water Resources Research* **39**: 1168. doi: 10.1029/2001WR001227.

Lane, E.W. 1937. Stable channels in erodible material. *American Society of Civil Engineers Transactions* **102**: 123–142.

Lane, E.W. 1955a. The importance of fluvial morphology in hydraulic engineering. *Proceedings of the American Society of Civil Engineers* **81**(745): 1–17.

Lane, E.W. 1955b. Design of stable channels. *American Society of Civil Engineers Transactions* **120**: 1234–1279.

Lane, E.W. 1957. *A Study of the Shape of Channels Formed by Natural Streams Flowing in Erodible Material*. US Army Engineer Division, Missouri River, Corps of Engineers, MRD Sediment Series no. 9, Omaha, NE.

Lane, E.W. and Carlson, E.J. 1953. Some factors affecting the stability of canals constructed in coarse granular materials. In *Proceedings of the Minnesota International Hydraulics Convention, ASCE-IAHR Joint Meeting, Minneapolis, MN, 1-4 September*, pp. 37–48.

Langbein, W.B. 1964. Geometry of river channels. American Society of Civil Engineers, *Journal of the Hydraulics Division* **90**: 301–312.

Langbein, W.B. and Leopold, L.B. 1964. Quasi-equilibrium states in channel morphology. *American Journal of Science* **262**: 782–794.

Laronne, J.B. and Carson, M.A. 1976. Interrelationships between bed morphology and bed-material transport for a small, gravel-bed channel. *Sedimentology* **23**: 67–85.

Laronne, J.B., Reid, I., Yitshak, Y., and Frostick, L.E. 1994. The non-layering of gravel streambeds under ephemeral flood regimes. *Journal of Hydrology* **159**: 353–363.

Laronne, J.B., Garcia, C., and Reid, I. 2001. Mobility of patch sediment in gravel bed streams: Patch character and its implications for bedload. In Mosley, M.P., editor. *Gravel-Bed Rivers V*. Wellington, New Zealand, New Zealand Hydrological Society, pp. 249–280.

Lenzi, M.A. 2001. Step-pool evolution in the Rio Cordon, northeastern Italy. *Earth Surface Processes and Landforms* **26**: 991–1008.

Lenzi, M.A. 2004. Displacement and transport of marked pebbles, cobbles, and boulders during floods in a steep mountain stream. *Hydrological Processes* **18**: 1899–1914.

Lenzi, M.A., Mao, L. and Comiti, F. 2006. Effective discharge for sediment transport in a mountain river: Computational approaches and geomorphic effectiveness. *Journal of Hydrology* **326**: 257–276.

Leopold, L.B. and Maddock, T., Jr 1953. *The Hydraulic Geometry of Stream Channels and Some Physiographic Implications*. United States Geological Survey, Professional Paper 252.

Leopold, L.B. and Wolman, M.G. 1957. *River Channel Patterns: Braided, Meandering, and Straight*. United States Geological Survey, Professional Paper 282-B.

Leopold, L.B., Wolman, M.G., and Miller, J.P. 1964. *Fluvial Processes in Geomorphology*. San Francisco, CA, Freeman.

Lewin, J. 1978. Floodplain geomorphology. *Progress in Physical Geography* **2**: 408–437.

Lindley, E.S. 1919. Regime channels. In *Proceedings of the Punjab Engineering Congress*, pp. 63–74.

Lisle, T.E. 2005. Bed mobility: A key linkage between channel condition and lotic ecosystems. *Eos, Transactions of the American Geophysical Union* **86**: Joint Assembly Supplement, Abstract B44B-01.

Lisle, T.E. and Hilton, S. 1992. The volume of fine sediment in pools: An index of sediment supply in gravel-bed streams. *Water Resources Bulletin* **28**: 371–383.

Long, C.E., Wiberg, P.L., and Nowell, A.R.M. 1993. Evaluation of von Karman's constant from integral flow parameters. *Journal of Hydraulic Engineering* **119**: 1182–1190.

Ma, Y., Huang, H.Q., Xu, J., Brierley, G.J., and Yao, Z. 2010. Variability of effective discharge for suspended sediment transport in a large semi-arid river basin. *Journal of Hydrology* **388**: 357–369.

Mackin, J.H. 1948. Concept of the graded river. *Geological Society of America Bulletin* **59**: 463–512.

Madej, M.A. 2001. Erosion and sediment delivery following removal of forest roads. *Earth Surface Processes and Landforms* **26**: 175–190.

Madej, M.A. and Ozaki, V. 1996. Channel response to sediment wave propagation and movement, Redwood Creek, California, USA. *Earth Surface Processes and Landforms* **21**: 911–927.

Madej, M.A., Sutherland, D.G., Lisle, T.E., and Pryor, B. 2009. Channel responses to varying sediment input: A flume experiment modeled after Redwood Creek, California. *Geomorphology* **103**: 507–519.

Magilligan, F.J. 1992. Thresholds and the spatial variability of flood power during extreme floods. *Geomorphology* **5**: 373–390.

Marcus, W.A., Legleiter, C.J., Aspinall, R.J., Boardman, J.W., and Crabtree, R.L. 2003. High spatial resolution hyperspectral mapping of in-stream habitats, depths, and woody debris in mountain streams. *Geomorphology* **55**: 363–380.

Marston, R.A. 1983. Supraglacial stream dynamics on the Juneau icefield. *Association of American Geographers Annals* **73**: 597–608.

May, C.L., Pryor, B., Lisle, T.E., and Lang, M. 2009. Coupling hydrodynamic modeling and empirical measures of bed mobility to predict the risk of scour and fill of salmon redds in a large regulated river. *Water Resources Research* **45**: W05402. doi: 10.1029/2007WR006498.

McKean, J.A., Isaak, D.J., and Wright, C.W. 2008. Geomorphic controls on salmon nesting patterns described by a new, narrow-beam terrestrial–aquatic lidar. *Frontiers in Ecology* **6**: 125–130.

McKean, J.A., Nagel, D., Tonina, D. *et al.* 2009. Remote sensing of channels and riparian zones with a narrow-beam aquatic-terrestrial LiDAR. *Remote Sensing* **1**: 1065–1096.

Megahan, W.F., Platts, W.S., and Kulesza, B. 1980. Riverbed improves over time: South Fork Salmon. In *Symposium on Watershed Management, Boise, ID, 21–23 July*. New York, American Society of Civil Engineers, pp. 380–395.

Meybeck, M. 2003. Global analysis of river systems: From Earth system controls to Anthropocene syndromes. *Philosophical Transactions of the Royal Society, Biological Sciences* **358**: 1935–1955.

Meyer-Peter, E. and Müller, R. 1948. Formulas for bed-load transport. *Proceedings of the 2nd Meeting of the International Association for Hydraulic Structures Research*. Delft, The Netherlands, International Association for Hydraulics Research, pp. 39–64.

Middleton, G.V. and Southard, J.B. 1984. *Mechanics of Sediment Movement*. Tulsa, OK, Society for Economic Paleontologists and Mineralogists, Short Course 3.

Milhous, R.T. 1973. *Sediment transport in a gravel-bottomed stream*. Unpublished Ph.D. thesis, Oregon State University, Corvallis, OR.

Millar, R.G. 2005. Theoretical regime equations for mobile gravel-bed rivers with stable banks. *Geomorphology* **64**: 207–220.

Moir, H.J., Gibbins, C.N., Buffington, J.M. *et al.* 2009. A new method to identify the fluvial regimes used by spawning salmonids. *Canadian Journal of Fisheries and Aquatic Sciences* **66**: 1404–1408.

Mollard, J.D. 1973. Air photo interpretation of fluvial features. National Research Council of Canada, Ottawa, Ontario, Committee on Geodesy and Geophysics, Subcommittee on Hydrology, *7th Canadian Hydrology Symposium. Fluvial Processes and Sedimentation*, pp. 341–380.

Montgomery, D.R. 1999. Process domains and the river continuum. *Journal of the American Water Resources Association* **35**: 397–410.

Montgomery, D.R. and Bolton, S.M. 2003. Hydrogeomorphic variability and river restoration. In Wissmar, R.C. and Bisson, P.A., editors. *Strategies for Restoring River Ecosystems: Sources of Variability and Uncertainty in Natural Systems.* Bethesda, MD, American Fisheries Society, pp. 39–80.

Montgomery, D.R. and Buffington, J.M. 1997. Channel-reach morphology in mountain drainage basins. *Geological Society of America Bulletin* **109**: 596–611.

Montgomery, D.R. and Buffington, J.M. 1998. Channel processes, classification, and response. In Naiman, R.J. and Bilby, R.E., editors. *River Ecology and Management.* New York, Springer-Verlag, pp. 13–42.

Montgomery, D.R. and Gran, K.B. 2001. Downstream variations in the width of bedrock channels. *Water Resources Research* **37**: 1841–1846.

Montgomery, D.R., Collins, B.D., Buffington, J.M., and Abbe, T.B. 2003. Geomorphic effects of wood in rivers. In Gregory, S., Boyer, K. and Gurnell, A.M., editors. *The Ecology and Management of Wood in World Rivers.* Bethesda, MD, American Fisheries Society, pp. 21–47.

Mosselman, E. 1998. Morphological modelling of rivers with erodible banks. *Hydrological Processes* **12**: 1357–1370.

Mueller, E.R. and Pitlick, J. 2005. Morphologically based model of bed load transport capacity in a headwater stream. *Journal of Geophysical Research – Earth Surface* **100**: F02016. doi: 10.1029/2003JF000117.

Mueller, E.R., Pitlick, J., and Nelson, J.M. 2005. Variation in the reference Shields stress for bed load transport in gravel-bed streams and rivers. *Water Resources Research* **41**: W04006. doi: 10.1029/2004WR003692.

Myrick, R.M. and Leopold, L.B. 1963. *Hydraulic Geometry of a Small Tidal Estuary.* United States Geological Survey, Professional Paper 422-B.

Nagata, N., Hosoda, T. and Muramoto, Y. 2000. Numerical analysis of river channel processes with bank erosion. *Journal of Hydraulic Engineering* **126**: 243–252.

Nanson, G.C. and Croke, J.C. 1992. A genetic classification of floodplains. *Geomorphology* **4**: 459–486.

Nelson, J.M. and Smith, J.D. 1989. Flow in meandering channels with natural topography. In Ikeda, S. and Parker, G., editors. *River Meandering.* Washington, DC, American Geophysical Union, Water Resources Monograph **12**: pp. 69–102.

Nelson, P.A., Venditti, J.G., Dietrich, W.E. *et al.* 2009. Response of bed surface patchiness to reductions in sediment supply. *Journal of Geophysical Research-Earth Surface* **114**: F02005. doi: 10.1029/2008JF001144.

Nicholas, A.P., Ashworth, P.J., Kirkby, M.J., Macklin, M.G. and Murray, T. 1995. Sediment slugs: large-scale fluctuations in fluvial sediment transport rates and storage volumes. *Progress in Physical Geography* **19**: 500–519.

Nilsson, C., Reidy, C.A., Dynesius, M., and Revenga, C. 2005. Fragmentation and flow regulation of the world's large river systems. *Science* **308**: 405–408.

Nixon, M. 1959. A study of bank-full discharges of the rivers of England and Wales. *Proceedings of the Institution of Civil Engineers* **12**: 157–174.

Nolan, K.M., Lisle, T.E., and Kelsey, H.M. 1987. Bankfull discharge and sediment transport in northwestern California. In Beschta, R.L., Blinn, T., Grant, G.E., Ice, G.G., and Swanson, F.J., editors, *Erosion and Sedimentation in the Pacific Rim. Proceedings of the Corvallis Symposium, August, 1987.* International Association of Hydrological Sciences, Publication 165, pp. 439–449.

Nunnally, N.R. 1985. Application of fluvial relationships to planning and designing of channel modifications. *Environmental Management* **9**: 417–426.

O'Connor, J.E. 1993. *Hydrology, Hydraulics and Geomorphology of the Bonneville Flood.* Geological Society of America, Special Paper 274.

Osterkamp, W.R. and Hedman, E.R. 1982. *Perennial-streamflow Characteristics Related to Channel Geometry and Sediment in Missouri River Basin.* United States Geological Survey, Professional Paper 1242.

Paola, C. and Seal, R. 1995. Grain size patchiness as a cause of selective deposition and downstream fining. *Water Resources Research* **31**: 1395–1407.

Park, C.C. 1977. World-wide variations in hydraulic geometry exponents of stream channels: An analysis and some observations. *Journal of Hydrology* **33**: 133–146.

Parker, G. 1976. On the cause and characteristic scales of meandering and braiding in rivers. *Journal of Fluid Mechanics* **76**: 457–480.

Parker, G. 1978. Self-formed straight rivers with equilibrium banks and mobile bed. Part 2. The gravel river. *Journal of Fluid Mechanics* **89**: 127–146.

Parker, G. 1979. Hydraulic geometry of active gravel rivers. American Society of Civil Engineers, *Journal of the Hydraulics Division* **105**: 1185–1201.

Parker, G. 1982. Discussion of "Regime equations for gravel-bed rivers", by D. I. Bray. In Hey, R.D., Bathurst, J.C., and Thorne, C.R., editors. *Gravel-bed Rivers.* Chichester, John Wiley & Sons, Ltd, pp. 542–551.

Parker, G. 1990. Surface-based bedload transport relation for gravel rivers. *Journal of Hydraulic Research* **28**: 417–436.

Parker, G. and Cui, Y. 1998. The arrested gravel front: Stable gravel-sand transitions in rivers, Part 1: Simplified analytical solution. *Journal of Hydraulic Research* **36**: 75–100.

Parker, G., Shimizu, Y., Wilkerson, G.V. *et al.* 2011. A new framework for modeling the migration of meandering rivers. *Earth Surface Processes and Landforms* **36**: 70–86.

Parker, G., Toro-Escobar, C.M., Ramey, M., and Beck, S. 2003. Effect of floodwater extraction on mountain stream morphology. *Journal of Hydraulic Engineering* **129**: 885–895.

Parker, G., Wilcock, P.R., Paola, C., Dietrich, W.E., and Pitlick, J. 2007. Physical basis for quasi-universal relations describing bankfull hydraulic geometry of single-thread gravel bed rivers. *Journal of Geophysical Research – Earth Surface* **112**: F04005. doi: 10.1029/2006JF000549.

Petts, G.E. 1979. Complex response of river channel morphology subsequent to reservoir construction. *Progress in Physical Geography* **3**: 329–362.

Phillips, J.D. 2002. Geomorphic impacts of flash flooding in a forested headwater basin. *Journal of Hydrology* **269**: 236–250.

Pickup, G. and Warner, R.F. 1976. Effects of hydrologic regime on magnitude and frequency of dominant discharge. *Journal of Hydrology* **29**: 51–75.

Piégay, H., Darby, S.E., Mosselman, E., and Surian, N. 2005. A review of techniques available for delimiting the erodible river corridor: A sustainable approach to managing bank erosion. *River Research and Applications* **21**: 773–789.

Pitlick, J. 1992. Flow resistance under conditions of intense gravel transport. *Water Resources Research* **28**: 891–903.

Pitlick, J. 1994. Relation between peak flows, precipitation, and physiography for five mountainous regions in the western USA. *Journal of Hydrology* **158**: 219–240.

Pitlick, J., Mueller, E.R., Segura, C., Cress, R., and Torizzo, M. 2008. Relation between flow, surface-layer armoring and sediment transport in gravel-bed rivers. *Earth Surface Processes and Landforms* **33**: 1192–1209.

Pizzuto, J.E. 2003. Numerical modeling of alluvial landforms. In Kondolf, G.M. and Piégay, H., editors. *Tools in Fluvial Geomorphology*. Chichester, John Wiley & Sons, Ltd, pp. 577–595.

Poff, N.L., Olden, J.D., Pepinm D.M., and Bledsoe, B.P. 2006. Placing global stream flow variability in geographic and geomorphic contexts. *River Research and Applications* **22**: 149–166.

Prestegaard, K.L. 1983. Bar resistance in gravel bed steams at bankfull stage. *Water Resources Research* **19**: 473–476.

Recking, A. 2009. Theoretical development on the effects of changing flow hydraulics on incipient bed load motion. *Water Resources Research* **45**: W04401. doi: 10.1029/2008WR006826.

Rhoads, B.L. 1992. Statistical models of fluvial systems. *Geomorphology* **5**: 433–455.

Rice, S. 1994. Towards a model of changes in bed material texture at the drainage basin scale. In Kirkby, M.J., editor. *Process Models and Theoretical Geomorphology*. Chichester, John Wiley & Sons, Ltd, pp. 160–172.

Rice, S.P., Ferguson, R.I. and Hoey, T.B. 2006. Tributary control of physical heterogeneity and biological diversity at river confluences. *Canadian Journal of Fisheries and Aquatic Sciences* **63**: 2553–2566.

Rice, S.P., Roy, A.G. and Rhoads, B.L. 2008. *River Confluences, Tributaries and the Fluvial Network*. Chichester, John Wiley & Sons, Ltd.

Rosgen, D.L. 2006. *Watershed Assessment of River Stability and Sediment Supply (WARSSS)*. Fort Collins, CO, Wildland Hydrology.

Rumsby, B.T. and Macklin, M.G. 1994. Channel and floodplain response to recent abrupt climate change: The Tyne basin, northern England. *Earth Surface Processes and Landforms* **19**: 499–515.

Rutherford, I.D. 1994. Inherited controls on the form of a large, low energy river: The Murray River, Australia. In Schumm, S.A. and Winkley, B.R., editors. *The Variability of Large Alluvial Rivers*. New York, American Society of Civil Engineers, pp. 177–197.

Ryan, S.E., Porth, L.S., and Troendle, C.A. 2002. Defining phases of bedload transport using piecewise regression. *Earth Surface Processes and Landforms* **27**: 971–990.

Ryan, S.E., Porth, L.S., and Troendle, C.A. 2005. Coarse sediment transport in mountain streams in Colorado and Wyoming, USA. *Earth Surface Processes and Landforms* **30**: 269–288.

Sambrook Smith, G.H. and Ferguson, R.I. 1995. The gravel-sand transition along river channels. *Journal of Sedimentary Research,* **A65**: 423–430.

Santos-Cayudo, J. and Simons, D.B. 1972. River response. In Shen, H.W., editor. *Environmental Impact on Rivers*. Fort Collins, CO, Water Resources Publications, pp. 1–25 (section 1).

Schmidt, K-H. and Ergenzinger, P. 1992. Bedload entrainment, travel lengths, step lengths, rest periods–studied with passive (iron, magnetic) and active (radio) tracer techniques. *Earth Surface Processes and Landforms* **17**: 147–165.

Schumm, S.A. 1960a. The effect of sediment type on the shape and stratification of some modern fluvial deposits. *American Journal of Science* **258**: 177–184.

Schumm, S.A. 1960b. *The Shape of Alluvial Channels in Relation to Sediment Type*. United States Geological Survey, Professional Paper 352-B.

Schumm, S.A. 1963. *A Tentative Classification of Alluvial River Channels*. United States Geological Survey, Circular 477.

Schumm, S.A. 1968. *River Adjustment to Altered Hydrologic Regimen: Murrumbidgee River and Paleochannels, Australia*. United States Geological Survey, Professional Paper 598.

Schumm, S.A. 1969. River metamorphosis. American Society of Civil Engineers, *Journal of the Hydraulics Division* **95**: 255–273.

Schumm, S.A. 1977. *The Fluvial System*. New York, Wiley-Interscience.

Schumm, S.A. 1985. Patterns of alluvial rivers. *Annual Review of Earth and Planetary Sciences* **13**: 5–27.

Schumm, S.A. 2005. *River Variability and Complexity*. Cambridge, Cambridge University Press.

Schumm, S.A. and Lichty, R.W. 1963. *Channel Widening and Floodplain Construction Along Cimarron River in Southwestern Kansas*. United States Geological Survey, Professional Paper 352-D.

Schumm, S.A. and Khan, H.R. 1972. Experimental study of channel patterns. *Geological Society of America Bulletin* **83**: 1755–1770.

Segura, C. and Pitlick, J. 2010. Scaling frequency of channel-forming flows in snowmelt-dominated streams. *Water Resources Research* **46**: W06524. doi: 10.1029/2009WR008336.

Shields, A. 1936. Anwendung der Aehnlichkeitsmechanik und der Turbulenzforschung auf die Geschiebebewegung. Berlin, *Mitteilungen der Preußischen Versuchsanstalt für Wasserbau und Schiffbau* **26**: 1–26.

Shields, F.D. and Gippel, C.J. 1995. Prediction of effects of woody debris removal on flow resistance. *Journal of Hydraulic Engineering* **121**: 341–354.

Simon, A. and Rinaldi, M. 2006. Disturbance, stream incision, and channel evolution: The roles of excess transport capacity and boundary materials in controlling channel response. *Geomorphology* **79**: 361–383.

Simon, A., Doyle, M., Kondolf, M. *et al.* 2007. Critical evaluation of how the Rosgen classification and associated "natural channel design" methods fail to integrate and quantify fluvial processes and channel response. *Journal of the American Water Resources Association* **43**: 1117–1131.

Simon, A., Doyle, M., Kondolf, M. *et al.* 2008. Reply to discussion by Dave Rosgen, "Critical evaluation of how the rosgen classification and associated 'natural channel design' methods fail to integrate and quantify fluvial processes and channel responses". *Journal of the American Water Resources Association* **44**: 793–802.

Simons, D.B. and Albertson, M.L. 1963. Uniform water conveyance channels in alluvial material. *American Society of Civil Engineers Transactions* **128**: 65–167.

Simons, D.B. and Richardson, E.V. 1966. *Resistance to Flow in Alluvial Channels*. United States Geological Survey, Professional Paper 422-J.

Singer, M.B. 2008. Downstream patterns of bed material grain size in a large, lowland alluvial river subject to low sediment supply. *Water Resources Research* **44**: W12202. doi: 10.1029/2008WR007183.

Smith, J.D. 2004. The role of riparian shrubs in preventing floodplain unraveling along the Clark Fork of the Columbia River in the Deer Lodge Valley, Montana. In Bennett, S.J. and Simon, A., editors. *Riparian Vegetation and Fluvial Geomorphology*. Washington, DC, American Geophysical Union, Water Science and Application **8**: 71–85.

Smith, S.M. and Prestegaard, K.L. 2005. Hydraulic performance of a morphology-based stream channel design. *Water Resources Research* **41**: W11413. doi: 10.1029/2004WR003926.

Snyder, N.P. 2009. Studying stream morphology with airborne laser elevation data. *Eos, Transactions, American Geophysical Union* **90**: 45–46.

Stevens, M.A., Simons, D.B. and Richardson, E.V. 1975. Nonequilibrium river form. American Society of Civil Engineers, *Journal of the Hydraulics Division* **101**: 557–566.

Stock, J.D. and Dietrich, W.E. 2003. Valley incision by debris flows: Evidence of a topographic signature. *Water Resources Research* **39**: 1089. doi: 10.1029/2001WR001057.

Strom, K.B. and Papanicolaou, A.N. 2008. Morphological characterization of cluster microforms. *Sedimentology* **55**: 137–153.

Strom, K.B. and Papanicolaou, A.N. 2009. Occurrence of cluster microforms in mountain rivers. *Earth Surface Processes and Landforms* **34**: 88–98.

Surian, N. 2006. Effects of human impacts on braided river morphology: Examples from northern Italy. In Sambrook Smith, G.H., Best, J.L., Bristow, C.S., and Petts, G.E., editors, *Braided Rivers*. Oxford, Blackwell, pp. 327–338.

Surian, N. and Rinaldi, M. 2003. Morphological response to river engineering and management in alluvial channels in Italy. *Geomorphology* **50**: 307–326.

Tague, C., Farrell, M., Grant, G., Lewis, S., and Rey, S. 2007. Hydrogeologic controls on summer stream temperatures in the McKenzie River basin, Oregon. *Hydrological Processes* **21**: 3288–3300.

Tague, C., Grant, G., Farrell, M., Choate, J., and Jefferson, A. 2008. Deep groundwater mediates streamflow response to climate warming in the Oregon Cascades. *Climate Change* **86**: 189–210.

Talbot, T. and Lapointe, M. 2002a. Modes of response of a gravel bed river to meander straightening: The case of the Sainte-Marguerite River, Saguenay Region, Quebec, Canada. *Water Resources Research* **38**(6): doi: 10.1029/2001WR000324.

Talbot, T. and Lapointe, M. 2002b. Numerical modeling of gravel bed river response to meander straightening: The coupling between the evolution of bed pavement and long profile. *Water Resources Research* **38**(6): doi: 10.1029/2001WR000330.

Thompson, C.J. and Croke, J. 2008. Channel flow competence and sediment transport in upland streams in southeast Australia. *Earth Surface Processes and Landforms* **33**: 329–352.

Thompson, C.J., Croke, J., Ogden, R., and Wallbrink, P. 2006. A morpho-statistical classification of mountain stream reach types in southeastern Australia. *Geomorphology* **81**: 43–65.

Thompson, C.J., Croke, J. and Takken, I. 2008. A catchment-scale model of mountain stream channel morphologies. *Geomorphology* **95**: 119–144.

Torgersen, C.E., Faux, R.N., McIntosh, B.A., Poage, N.J., and Norton, D.J. 2001. Airborne thermal remote sensing for water temperature assessment in rivers and streams. *Remote Sensing of Environment* **76**: 386–398.

Torizzo, M. and Pitlick, J. 2004. Magnitude-frequency of bed load transport in mountain streams in Colorado. *Journal of Hydrology* **290**: 137–151.

Trimble, S.W. 1997. Stream channel erosion and change resulting from riparian forests. *Geology* **25**: 467–469.

Turowski, J.M., Yager, E.M., Badoux, A., Rickenmann, D., and Molnar, P. 2009. The impact of exceptional events on erosion, bedload transport and channel stability in a step-pool channel. *Earth Surface Processes and Landforms* **34**: 1661–1673.

van den Berg, J.H. 1995. Prediction of alluvial channel pattern of perennial rivers. *Geomorphology* **12**: 259–279.

Vollmer, S. and Kleinhans, M. 2007. Predicting incipient motion, including the effect of turbulent pressure fluctuations in the bed. *Water Resources Research* **43**: W05410. doi: 10.1029/2006WR004919.

von Kármán, T. 1930. Mechanische Ähnlichkeit und Turbulenz. *Göttingen, (Sonderdrucke aus den) Nachrichten von der Gesellschaft der Wissenschaften Mathematisch-physische Klasse*: 58–76.

Walter, R.C. and Merritts, D.J. 2008. Natural streams and the legacy of water-powered mills. *Science* **319**: 299–304.

Whipple, K.X. 2004. Bedrock rivers and the geomorphology of active orogens. *Annual Review of Earth and Planetary Sciences* **32**: 151–185.

Whiting, P.J. and Dietrich, W.E. 1990. Boundary shear stress and roughness over mobile alluvial beds. *Journal of Hydraulic Engineering* **116**: 1495–1511.

Whiting, P.J. and Bradley, J.B. 1993. A process-based classification system for headwater streams. *Earth Surface Processes and Landforms* **18**: 603–612.

Whiting, P.J. and King, J.G. 2003. Surface particle sizes on armoured gravel streambeds: Effects of supply and hydraulics. *Earth Surface Processes and Landforms* **28**: 1459–1471.

Whiting, P.J., Dietrich, W.E., Leopold, L.B., Drake, T.G., and Shreve, R.L. 1988. Bedload sheets in heterogeneous sediment. *Geology* **16**: 105–108.

Whiting, P.J., Stamm, J.F., Moog, D.B., and Orndorff, R.L. 1999. Sediment transporting flows in headwater streams. *Geological Society of America Bulletin* **111**: 450–466.

Whittaker, J.G. 1987. Sediment transport in step-pool streams. In Thorne, C.R., Bathurst, J.C., and Hey, R.D., editors. *Sediment Transport in Gravel-bed Rivers*. Chichester, John Wiley & Sons Ltd, pp. 545–579.

Whittaker, J.G. and Jaeggi, M.N.R. 1982. Origin of step-pool systems in mountain streams. American Society of Civil Engineers, *Journal of the Hydraulics Division* **108**: 758–773.

Wiberg, P.L. and Smith, J.D. 1991. Velocity distribution and bed roughness in high-gradient streams. *Water Resources Research* **27**: 825–838.

Wilcock, P.R. 1998. Two-fraction model of initial sediment motion in gravel-bed rivers. *Science* **280**: 410–412.

Wilcox, A., Nelson, J.M., and Wohl, E.E. 2006. Flow resistance dynamics in step-pool stream channels: 2. Partitioning between grain, spill, and wood debris resistance. *Water Resources Research* **42**: W05419. doi: 10.1029/2005WR004278.

Wilkins, B.C. and Snyder, N.P. 2011. Geomorphic comparison of two Atlantic coastal rivers: Toward an understanding of physical controls on Atlantic salmon habitat. *River Research and Applications* **27**: 135–156.

Wohl, E.E. 2004. Limits of downstream hydraulic geometry. *Geology* **32**: 897–900.

Wohl, E.E. 2008. Review of effects of large floods in resistant-boundary channels. In Habersack, H., Piégay, H., and Rinaldi, M., editors. *Gravel-Bed Rivers VI: From Process Understanding to River Restoration*. Amsterdam, Elsevier, Developments in Earth Surface Processes **11**: 181–211.

Wohl, E.E. and Merritt, D. 2005. Prediction of mountain stream morphology. *Water Resources Research* **41**: W08419. doi: 10.1029/2004WR003779.

Wohl, E.E., Angermeier, P.L., Bledsoe, B. *et al.* 2005. River restoration. *Water Resources Research* **41**: W10301. doi: 10.1029/2005WR003985.

Wolman, M.G. and Miller, J.P. 1960. Magnitude and frequency of forces in geomorphic processes. *Journal of Geology* **68**: 54–74.

Wong, M. and Parker, G. 2006. Reanalysis and correction of bed-load relation of Meyer-Peter and Müller using their own database. *Journal of Hydraulic Engineering* **132**: 1159–1168.

Wood-Smith, R.D. and Buffington, J.M. 1996. Multivariate geomorphic analysis of forest streams: Implications for assessment of land use impact on channel condition. *Earth Surface Processes and Landforms* **21**: 377–393.

Yuill, B., Nichols, M., and Yager, E. 2010. Coarse bed material patch evolution in low-order, ephemeral channels. *Catena* **81**: 126–136.

Zimmermann, A., Church, M. and Hassan, M.A. 2010. Step-pool stability: Testing the jammed state hypothesis. *Journal of Geophysical Research-Earth Surface* **115**: F02008. doi: 10.1029/2009JF001365.

## 32.9   APPENDIX

Data sources for Figures 32.4, 32.5, and 32.9 are: (1) Addy (2009), (2) Adenlof and Wohl (1994), (3–4) Andrews (1984; 2000), (5*) Andrews and Erman (1986), (6) Ashworth and Ferguson (1989), (**7**) BC Hydro and Power Authority (1975; 1977b; 1983), (**8**) Borland (1973), (9) Bray (1979), a subset of Kellerhals *et al.* (1972), (10) Brush (1961), (11) Buffington (unpublished data for southeast Alaska and central Idaho), (12) Buffington and Montgomery (1999), (13) Buffington *et al.* (2002; unpublished), (14) Bunte *et al.* (2010), (15) Burrows *et al.* (1981), (16) Cadol *et al.* (2009; unpublished), (<u>17</u>) Cant (1978), (18) Charlton *et al.* (1978), (19) Chitale (1970), (20) Cianfrani *et al.* (2009), (21) Clayton and Pitlick (2008), (22) Einstein (1944), (23–24) Emmett (1972; 1975), (25) Florsheim (1985), (26) Haschenburger and Church (1998), (**27**) Galay (1971; 1977), (28) Hassan and Church (2001; unpublished), (29) Hey and Thorne (1986), (30) Higginson and Johnston (1988), (31*) Jones and Seitz (1980), (32) Judd and Peterson (1969), (**33**) Kellerhals (1967), (34) Kellerhals *et al.* (1972), (**35**) Knighton (1974), (36) Lamarre and Roy (2008), (<u>37</u>) Lambeek (1994), (38-39) Lenzi *et al.* (2006a, 2006b), (40) Leopold and Emmett (1997), (41) Leopold and Skibitzke (1967), (**42**) Lisle (1977), (43) Lisle and Madej (1992), (<u>44</u>) McCarthy *et al.* (1991), (**45**) McLean (1980), (46*) Milhous (1973), (47) Miller (1958), (48) Miller *et al.* (2002; unpublished), (49) Milner (2010; unpublished), (50) Moir *et al.* (2006), (<u>51</u>)

Monsalve and Silva (1983), (52) Montgomery and Buffington (1997; unpublished), (53) Montgomery *et al.* (1995; unpublished), (54) Montgomery *et al.* (1996), (<u>55</u>) Morton and Donaldson (1978a, 1978b), (56) Mosley (1981; unpublished), (57) Mueller and Pitlick (2005), (**58**) Neil (1965), (59) Nordin and Beverage (1965), (**60**) Northwest Hydraulic Consultants (1974), (<u>61</u>) Osterkamp (1978), (62) Pitlick and Cress (2002), (63) Powell *et al.* (1998), (<u>66</u>) Rannie (1990), (67) Roper *et al.* (2008; unpublished), (68) Ryan *et al.* (2005), (69) Sear (1993), (70*) Smalley *et al.* (1994), (71) Southerland (2003), (72) Tacconi and Billi (1987), (<u>73</u>) Taylor and Woodyer (1986), (74) Thorne and Lewin (1979), (75) Traylor and Wohl (2000), (76) Weyerhauser (unpublished), (77) Whiting *et al.* (1999), (78) Williams (1978), (<u>79</u>) Winkley (1982), (80) Wohl and Goode (2008), (81) Wohl and Wilcox (2005), (82–83) Wohl *et al.* (1993; 2004) and (**84**) Zimmerman (1975). Bold values indicate sources as cited in Church and Rood (1983), italics indicate channel pattern as defined by Church and Rood (1983), underlining indicates sources as cited by van den Berg (1995), and asterisks indicate sources as cited by Mueller *et al.* (2005).

The data sources used for each channel type are as follows: dune-ripple (**8**, 16, 19, 22–23, 30, 34–**35**, 40, <u>44</u>, <u>55</u>–56, **60**–<u>61</u>, <u>66</u>, 71, <u>73</u>, 78, <u>79</u>), pool-riffle (1, *3*, 5*–6, 9–10, 11–13, 16, 18, 20–21, 23–25, 27–29, 31*, **35**, <u>37</u>, **42**–43, 46*–50, <u>51</u>–54, 56, 62, 64, 67–70*, 71–72, 74, 76–*78*, 82–83), plane-bed (1, 4, 11–12, 14, 25, 32, 47, 49, 52–54, 57, 63, 67–68, 71, 75, 77, 81, 83), multithread (1, *7*, 9, 13, 15, <u>*17*</u>, *18*–19, *23*–*24*, **26**, **33**–34, 41, **45**, 49, 56, **58**–*59*, **60**, 64, 68, *78*, **84**,), step-pool (1–2, 11, 14, 16, 24–25, 32, 36, 38–39, 47, 49–50, 52–53, 67–68, 75–77, 80–81, 83) and cascade (1, 11, 52, 81, 83). Channel types were identified either by the original authors or from photographs, maps, and descriptions provided by a given source. Single-thread channels with $D_{50} < 2$ mm were assumed to be dune-ripple, if no other information was provided. Similarly, meandering, single-thread channels with $D_{50} > 2$ mm were assumed to be pool-riffle.

## 32.10   REFERENCES FOR APPENDIX

Addy, S. 2009. *Hierarchical controls on river channel morphology in montane catchments in the Cairngorms, Scotland*. Unpublished Ph.D. thesis, University of Aberdeen.

Adenlof, K.A. and Wohl, E.E. 1994. Controls on bedload movement in a subalpine stream of the Colorado Rocky Mountains, USA. *Arctic and Alpine Research* **26**: 77–85.

Andrews, E.D. 1984. Bed-material entrainment and hydraulic geometry of gravel-bed rivers in Colorado. *Geological Society of America Bulletin* **95**: 371–378.

Andrews, E.D. 2000. Bed material transport in the Virgin River, Utah. *Water Resources Research* **36**: 585–596.

Ashworth, P.J. and Ferguson, R.I. 1989. Size-selective entrainment of bed load in gravel bed streams. *Water Resources Research* **25**: 627–634.

Bray, D.I. 1979. Estimating average velocity in gravel-bed rivers. American Society of Civil Engineers, *Journal of the Hydraulics Division* **105**: 1103–1122.

Brush, L. 1961. *Drainage Basins, Channels, and Flow Characteristics of Selected Streams in Central Pennsylvania.* United States Geological Survey, Professional Paper 282-F.

Buffington, J.M. and Montgomery, D.R. 1999. Effects of hydraulic roughness on surface textures of gravel-bed rivers. *Water Resources Research* **35**: 3507–3522.

Buffington, J.M., Lisle, T.E., Woodsmith, R.D., and Hilton, S. 2002. Controls on the size and occurrence of pools in coarse-grained forest rivers. *River Research and Applications* **18**: 507–531.

Bunte, K., Abt, S.R., Swingle, K.W., and Potyondy, J.P. 2010. Bankfull mobile particle size and its prediction from a Shields-type approach. In *Proceedings of the 2nd Joint Federal Interagency Conference (9th Federal Interagency Sedimentation Conference, 4th Federal Interagency Hydrologic Modeling Conference).* CD-ROM. ISBN 978-0-9779007-3-2, http://acwi.gov/sos/pubs/2ndJFIC/.

Burrows, R.L., Emmett, W.W., and Parks, B. 1981. *Sediment Transport in the Tanana River Near Fairbanks, Alaska, 1977-79.* United States Geological Survey, Water-Resources Investigations 81-20.

Cadol, D., Wohl, E.E., Goode, J.R., and Jaeger, K.L. 2009. Wood distribution in neotropical forested headwater streams of La Selva, Costa Rica. *Earth Surface Processes and Landforms* **34**: 1198–1215.

Charlton, F.G., Brown, P.M., and Benson, R.W. 1978. *The Hydraulic Geometry of some Gravel Rivers in Britain.* Wallingford, United Kingdom, Hydraulics Research Station Report IT 180.

Chitale, S.V. 1970. River channel patterns. American Society of Civil Engineers, *Journal of the Hydraulics Division* **96**: 201–221.

Church, M. and Rood, M. 1983. *Catalogue of Alluvial River Channel Regime Data.* Vancouver, The University of British Columbia, Department of Geography.

Cianfrani, C.M., Sullivan, S.M.P., Hession, W.C., and Watzin, M.C. 2009. Mixed stream channel morphologies: Implications for fish community diversity. *Aquatic Conservation: Marine and Freshwater Ecosystems* **19**: 147–156.

Clayton, J.A. and Pitlick, J. 2008. Persistence of the surface texture of a gravel-bed river during a large flood. *Earth Surface Processes and Landforms* **33**: 661–673.

Einstein, H.A. 1944. *Bed-load Transportation in Mountain Creek.* United States Department of Agriculture, Soil Conservation Service, Technical Paper SCS-TP-55.

Emmett, W.W. 1972. *The Hydraulic Geometry of Some Alaskan Streams South of the Yukon River.* United States Geological Survey, Open-File Report 72-108.

Emmett, W.W. 1975. *The Channels and Waters of the Upper Salmon River Area, Idaho.* United States Geological Survey, Professional Paper 870-A.

Florsheim, J.L. 1985. *Fluvial requirements for gravel bar formation in northwestern California.* Unpublished M.S. thesis, Humboldt State University, Arcata, CA.

Haschenburger, J.K. and Church, M. 1998. Bed material transport estimated from the virtual velocity of sediment. *Earth Surface Processes and Landforms* **23**: 791–808.

Hassan, M.A. and Church, M. 2001. Sensitivity of bed load transport in Harris Creek: Seasonal and spatial variation over a cobble-gravel bar. *Water Resources Research* **37**: 812–826.

Hey, R.D. and Thorne, C.R. 1986. Stable channels with mobile gravel beds. *Journal of Hydraulic Engineering* **112**: 671–687.

Higginson, N.N.J. and Johnston, H.T. 1988. Estimation of friction factor in natural streams. In White, W.R., editor. *International Conference on River Regime.* Chichester, John Wiley & Sons, Ltd, pp. 251–266.

Judd, H.E. and Peterson, D.F. 1969. *Hydraulics of Large Bed Element Channels.* Logan, UT, Utah State University, Utah Water Research Laboratory Report PRWG 17-6.

Kellerhals, R., Neill, C.R., and Bray, D.I. 1972. *Hydraulic and Geomorphic Characteristics of Rivers in Alberta.* Research Council of Alberta, River Engineering and Surface Hydrology Section, Report 72-1.

Lamarre, H. and Roy, A.G. 2008. The role of morphology on the displacement of particles in a step-pool river system. *Geomorphology* **99**: 270–279.

Lenzi, M.A., Mao, L. and Comiti, F. 2006a. Effective discharge for sediment transport in a mountain river: Computational approaches and geomorphic effectiveness. *Journal of Hydrology* **326**: 257–276.

Lenzi, M.A., Mao, L. and Comiti, F. 2006b. When does bedload transport begin in steep boulder-bed streams? *Hydrological Processes* **20**: 3517–3533.

Leopold, L.B. and Emmett, W.W. 1997. *Bedload and River Hydraulics –Inferences from the East Fork River, Wyoming.* United States Geological Survey, Professional Paper 1583.

Leopold, L.B. and Skibitzke, H.E. 1967. Observations on unmeasured rivers. *Geografiska Annaler* **49A**: 247–255.

Lisle, T.E. and Madej, M.A. 1992. Spatial variation in armouring in a channel with high sediment supply. In Billi, P., Hey, R.D., Thorne, C.R., and Tacconi, P., editors. *Dynamics of Gravel-bed Rivers.* Chichester, John Wiley & Sons, Ltd, pp. 277–293.

Miller, J.P. 1958. *High Mountain Streams: Effects of Geology on Channel Characteristics and Bed Material.* State Bureau of Mines and Mineral Resources, New Mexico Institute of Mining and Technology, Memoir 4.

Miller, S., Glanzman, D., Doran, S. *et al.* 2002. Geomorphology of the Hells Canyon Reach of the Snake River, Technical Report Appendix E.1-2. In *Hells Canyon Complex, FERC No. 1971 License Application.* Idaho Power Company.

Milner, V.S. 2010. *Assessing the performance of morphologically based river typing in Scotland using a geomorphological and ecological approach.* Unpublished Ph.D. thesis, University of Sterling.

Moir, H.J., Gibbins, C.N., Soulsby, C., and Webb, J.H. 2006. Discharge and hydraulic interactions in contrasting channel morphologies and their influence on site utilization by spawning Atlantic salmon (Salmo salar). *Canadian Journal of Fisheries and Aquatic Sciences* **63**: 2567–2585.

Montgomery, D.R. and Buffington, J.M. 1997. Channel-reach morphology in mountain drainage basins. *Geological Society of America Bulletin* **109**: 596–611.

Montgomery, D.R., Buffington, J.M., Smith, R.D., Schmidt, K.M. and Pess, G. 1995. Pool spacing in forest channels. *Water Resources Research* **31**: 1097–1105.

Montgomery, D.R., Buffington, J.M., Peterson, N.P., Schuett-Hames, D. and Quinn, T.P. 1996. Streambed scour, egg burial depths and the influence of salmonid spawning on bed surface mobility and embryo survival. *Canadian Journal of Fisheries and Aquatic Sciences* **53**: 1061–1070.

Mosley, M.P. 1981. Semi-determinate hydraulic geometry of river channels, South Island, New Zealand. *Earth Surface Processes and Landforms* **6**: 127–137.

Mueller, E.R. and Pitlick, J. 2005. Morphologically based model of bed load transport capacity in a headwater stream.

*Journal of Geophysical Research, Earth Surface* **100**: F02016. doi: 10.1029/2003JF000117.

Mueller, E.R., Pitlick, J., and Nelson, J.M. 2005. Variation in the reference Shields stress for bed load transport in gravel-bed streams and rivers. *Water Resources Research* **41**: W04006. doi: 10.1029/2004WR003692.

Nordin, C.F. and Beverage, J.P. 1965. *Sediment Transport in the Rio Grande New Mexico.* United States Geological Survey, Professional Paper 462-F.

Pitlick, J. and Cress, R. 2002. Downstream changes in the channel geometry of a large gravel bed river. *Water Resources Research* **38**: 1216. doi: 10.1029/2001WR000898.

Powell, D.M., Reid, I., Laronne, J.B., and Frostick, L.E. 1998. Cross stream variability of bedload flux in narrow and wider ephemeral channels during desert flash floods. In Klingeman, P.C., Beschta, R.L., Komar, P.D., and Bradley, J.B., editors. *Gravel-bed Rivers in the Environment.* Highlands Ranch, CO, Water Resources Publications, pp. 177–196.

Prestegaard, K.L. 1983. Bar resistance in gravel bed steams at bankfull stage. *Water Resources Research* **19**: 473–476.

Roper, B.B., Buffington, J.M., Archer, E., Moyer, C., and Ward, M. 2008. The role of observer variation in determining Rosgen stream types in northeastern Oregon mountain streams. *Journal of the American Water Resources Association* **44**: 417–427.

Ryan, S.E., Porth, L.S. and Troendle, C.A. 2005. Coarse sediment transport in mountain streams in Colorado and Wyoming, USA. *Earth Surface Processes and Landforms* **30**: 269–288.

Sear, D.A. 1993. Fine sediment infiltration into gravel spawning beds within a regulated river experiencing floods: Ecological implications for salmonids. *Regulated Rivers: Research and Management* **8**: 373–390.

Southerland, W.B. 2003. *Stream geomorphology and classification in glacial-fluvial valleys of the North Cascade mountain range in Washington state.* Unpublished Ph.D. thesis, Washington State University.

Tacconi, P. and Billi, P. 1987. Bed load transport measurements by the vortex-tube trap on Virginio Creek, Italy. In Thorne, C. R., Bathurst, J.C. and Hey, R.D., editors. *Sediment Transport in Gravel-bed Rivers.* Chichester, John Wiley & Sons, Ltd, pp. 583–616.

Thorne, C.R. and Lewin, J. 1979. Bank processes, bed material movement, and planform development in a meandering river. In Rhodes, D.D. and Williams, G.P., editors. *Adjustments of the Fluvial System.* Dubuque, IA, Kendall/Hunt pp. 117–137.

Traylor, C.R. and Wohl, E.E. 2000. Seasonal changes in bed elevation in a step-pool channel, Rocky Mountains, Colorado, USA. *Arctic, Antarctic, and Alpine Research* **32**: 95–103.

van den Berg, J.H. 1995. Prediction of alluvial channel pattern of perennial rivers. *Geomorphology* **12**: 259–279.

Whiting, P.J., Stamm, J.F., Moog, D.B., and Orndorff, R.L. 1999. Sediment transporting flows in headwater streams. *Geological Society of America Bulletin* **111**: 450–466.

Williams, G.P. 1978. Bank-full discharge of rivers. *Water Resources Research* **14**: 1141–1154.

Wohl, E.E. and Goode, J.R. 2008. Wood dynamics in headwater streams of the Colorado Rocky Mountains. *Water Resources Research* **44**: W09429.

Wohl, E.E. and Wilcox, A. 2005. Channel geometry of mountain streams in New Zealand. *Journal of Hydrology* **300**: 252–266.

Wohl, E.E., Vincent, K.R., and Merritts, D.J. 1993. Pool and riffle characteristics in relation to channel gradient. *Geomorphology* **6**: 99–110.

Wohl, E.E., Kuzma, J.N., and Brown, N.E. 2004. Reach-scale channel geometry of a mountain river. *Earth Surface Processes and Landforms* **29**: 969–981.

## 32.11    DISCUSSION

### 32.11.1    *Discussion by Erik Mosselman*

John Buffington provides a rich bibliography on regime relations and hydraulic geometry relations, for which he rightly states channel width to be the most problematic channel characteristic to predict deterministically. However, I missed a discussion on the underlying mechanisms of width adjustment (see ASCE, 1998a). Buffington mentions bank erodibility only briefly as a control of channel width, without mechanistic details, and he does not mention bank accretion at all. Yet we know since Blench (1969) that the Holy Grail of accurate width predictors, be it empirical or rational, cannot be found if we do not consider the mechanisms of bank erosion and bank accretion, because equilibrium width is essentially multivalued and dependent on initial conditions. Moreover, the *a priori* omission of mechanisms of width adjustment produces the false idea that the channel response variables outnumber the available governing equations, and that we should hence search for some mysterious "missing equation". That this missing equation simply corresponds to the omitted equations is often forgotten by invoking extremal hypotheses instead. Objections against the latter include that extremal hypotheses do not fit in modern (Newtonian) scientific paradigms (Nagel, 1979), that they can lead to conclusions incompatible with observations (Griffiths, 1984) and that they do not make any difference with respect to contrasting hypotheses in cases where they do seem to work (Mosselman, 2004). If mechanisms of width adjustment are too difficult to include in practical applications, we may ask ourselves why we would need a single-valued width predictor in the first place. Can't we live with a range of possible widths? In stream restoration, we might either select and fix a specific width from a range of possible values (Wilcock, Chapter 12, this volume) or provide room for natural width fluctuations within certain boundaries.

### 32.11.2    *Discussion by Jens M. Turowski*

Optimization hypotheses as closure relations for regime theories of channel morphology have been debated for several decades. Supporters generally point out the good fit of such models with field data, while sceptics criticise the arbitrariness of optimal closure assumption, and the lack of direct tests for their validity. However, the physicality of such assumptions can be tested by comparing analytical regime models with steady-state solutions of dynamic channel models, when both models are based on the same physical assumptions. This was done for erosional channels by Turowski *et al.* (2009), who showed that both types of models lead to the same scaling relations between channel morphology and forcing parameters.

### 32.11.3 Reply by John M. Buffington

I thank Erik Mosselman for pointing out the lack of discussion regarding mechanisms for channel-width adjustment. In general, processes responsible for bank erosion include fluvial entrainment, mass wasting (frequently triggered by fluvial undercutting), and biogenic activity (e.g., tree throw and animal trampling), while channel narrowing may occur through abandonment of channel branches or bank accretion due to lateral siltation and bar growth. Thorough reviews of the processes and available models for channel-width adjustment are provided by ASCE (1998a; 1998b), Mosselman (1998), Piégay *et al.* (2005) and Rinaldi and Darby (2008).

I did not intend to suggest that width cannot be determined, or that it should be omitted from prediction of channel form. Rather, the governing equation for width is the most problematic. Some of the approaches for predicting width were discussed, but none are completely satisfying (Section 32.4.2.2). For example, uncertainty in the bank strength parameter leads to multiple width solutions in analytical approaches (Eaton *et al.*, 2004). Multiple solutions are perfectly acceptable, particularly if they can be used to represent the expected natural variability of channel conditions over time. However, I would assert that we do not know the range of typical width variations for channels in general, let alone for different channel types and different hydroclimates (Section 32.5). Nor is it clear how to select width ranges in cases where channels are exhibiting transient response to natural or anthropogenic disturbances. Consequently, additional research addressing the above issues is warranted. Fixing a specific, hardened width should be discouraged, particularly for restoration, as it requires perpetual maintenance to retain that single width, which is not a responsible solution, unless required by surrounding infrastructure and human occupation of the river corridor. As suggested, designing for a range of natural width variations may be more productive (e.g., Buffington and Parker, 2005) and will avoid failure of restoration designs based on single-value (i.e., bankfull) flows, as observed in several cases studies (e.g., Kondolf *et al.*, 2001; Smith and Prestegaard, 2005).

I also thank Jens Turowski for his discussion of the credibility of optimization models and for the physical insight offered by comparing the behaviour of analytical versus numerical models (Turowski *et al.*, 2009).

## 32.12 DISCUSSION REFERENCES

ASCE (American Society of Civil Engineers), Task Committee on Hydraulics, Bank Mechanics, and Modeling of River Width Adjustment. 1998a. River width adjustment. I: Processes and mechanisms. *Journal of Hydraulic Engineering* **124**: 881–902.

ASCE (American Society of Civil Engineers), Task Committee on Hydraulics, Bank Mechanics, and Modeling of River Width Adjustment. 1998b. River width adjustment. II: Modeling. *Journal of Hydraulic Engineering* **124**: 903–917.

Blench, T. 1969. *Mobile-bed Fluviology*. Edmonton, University of Alberta Press.

Buffington, J.M. and Parker, G. 2005. Use of geomorphic regime diagrams in channel restoration. *Eos, Transactions, American Geophysical Union* **86**: Fall Meeting Supplement, Abstract H13E-1359.

Eaton, B.C., Church, M., and Millar, R.G. 2004. Rational regime model of alluvial channel morphology and response. *Earth Surface Processes and Landforms* **29**: 511–529.

Griffiths, G.A. 1984. Extremal hypotheses for river regime: An illusion of progress. *Water Resources Research* **20**: 113–118.

Kondolf, G.M., Smeltzer, M., and Railsback, S.F. 2001. Design and performance of a channel reconstruction project in a coastal California gravel-bed stream. *Environmental Management* **28**: 761–776.

Mosselman, E. 2004. Hydraulic geometry of straight alluvial channels and the principle of least action. *Journal of Hydraulic Research* **42**: 219–220, 222.

Mosselman, E. 1998. Morphological modelling of rivers with erodible banks. *Hydrological Processes* **12**: 1357–1370.

Nagel, E. 1979. *The Structure of Science*, 2nd edition. Indianapolis, IN, Hackett.

Piégay, H., Darby, S.E., Mosselman, E., and Surian, N. 2005. A review of techniques available for delimiting the erodible river corridor: A sustainable approach to managing bank erosion. *River Research and Applications* **21**: 773–789.

Rinaldi, M. and Darby, S.E. 2008. Modelling river-bank-erosion processes and mass failure mechanisms: Progress towards fully coupled simulations. In Habersack, H., Piégay, H., and Rinaldi, M., editors. *Gravel-bed Rivers VI: From Process Understanding to River Restoration*. Amsterdam, Elsevier, Developments in Earth Surface Processes **11**: 213–239.

Smith, S.M. and Prestegaard, K.L. 2005. Hydraulic performance of a morphology-based stream channel design. *Water Resources Research* **41**: W11413. doi: 10.1029/2004WR003926.

Turowski, J.M., Lague, D., and Hovius, N. 2009. Response of bedrock channel width to tectonic forcing: Insights from a numerical model, theoretical considerations, and comparison with field data. *Journal of Geophysical Research* **114**: F03016. doi: 10.1029/2008JF001133.

# 33

# Channel Response and Recovery to Changes in Sediment Supply

## Marwan A. Hassan and André E. Zimmermann

## 33.1 INTRODUCTION

Buffington's chapter (Chapter 32, this volume) provides a comprehensive review of changes in channel dynamics of mountain streams over human time scales. One of the topics that the paper discusses is the spatial and temporal variability in channel response to disturbances. The magnitude and frequency of geomorphic processes is key for understanding the dynamics and morphology of alluvial rivers. The importance of magnitude and frequency of flood events for alluvial streams was introduced by Wolman and Miller (1960) who examined the geomorphic work done by rivers in terms of sediment transport rate. They noted that the amount of work done depends on flow magnitude. The magnitude-frequency concept includes two important ideas. The first is that the most morphologically effective flow is often the bankfull flow, while the second idea is that the most effective sediment transporting flow is the flow that moves most of the sediment.

These two flows may be the same in some systems; however, in mountainous environments with relatively stable channel boundaries, the flow that is most geomorphologically effective is unlikely to be the same as the flow that is the most effective sediment transporting flow. In this discussion we focus on steep mountain streams that are dominated by large material that is supplied from adjacent slopes and that moves only during extreme flow events (once every 50 years or so). Some mountain streams have very high rates of sediment supply due to upslope mass wasting processes, and actively re-arrange their bed during modest flood events. Over time mountain streams are apt to move back and forth along a spectrum that has highly mobile and highly stable channels as end points. The movement along this spectrum is in response to sediment supply conditions that may have infrequent return intervals (e.g. landslides,

debris flows, earthquakes) or a consequence of particular (at the human time scale) changes in the watershed (e.g. logging, mining, forest fire, glacial retreat) that affect the amount and calibre of sediment supplied to the channels.

Buffington provides a compelling review of channel dynamics and modelling in the steady-state condition. As he discusses, the steady-state paradigm has been the focus of the majority of past research and is most applicable to lower gradient rivers that are transport limited. In supply-limited streams the channel tends to be highly structured and relatively stable. In contrast to the transport-limited streams from which the magnitude-frequency concept was initially developed, magnitude-frequency and effectiveness of sediment transport are much less well understood for mountain streams. Nevertheless, for supply-limited streams a steady-state condition can, at least theoretically, exist and this is discussed by Buffington. In the following discussion, we will explore the topic of non-equilibrium supply-limited mountain streams. Particular focus will be on response times to changes in supply, and the way in which channels can and do respond.

## 33.2 MAGNITUDE, FREQUENCY, AND EFFECTIVENESS OF SEDIMENT TRANSPORT IN NON-EQUILIBRIUM SYSTEMS

Estimates of sediment transport in streams, and hence the magnitude and frequency of geomorphic processes, have been dominated by the capacity approach. This approach was first developed for sand-bed rivers and might not be suitable for the full range of gravel-bed rivers. In sand-bed rivers most flows can move sediment and there is generally a continuous supply of sediment. Furthermore, the bed surface does not armour or structure, which can

*Gravel-bed Rivers: Processes, Tools, Environments*, First Edition. Edited by Michael Church, Pascale M. Biron and André G. Roy.
© 2012 John Wiley & Sons, Ltd. Published 2012 by John Wiley & Sons, Ltd.

change the mobility threshold of the sediment. Nevertheless, the mobility of the bed can be modified by the presence of bedforms. On the whole, in sand-bed streams, erosion thresholds are low and vary little with time. At the other end of the spectrum, in steep, mountain, gravel-bed streams, time-varying erosional thresholds (due to sediment supply and bed surface structuring) and the effect of the prior sequence of events make it difficult to establish magnitude-frequency relations for geomorphic events. With lower gradient gravel-bed rivers these factors are not as important and the magnitude-frequency concept has been successfully applied using locally calibrated transport relations (e.g., Andrews and Nankervis, 1995; Whiting et al., 1999; Barry et al. 2008).

Episodic sediment supply and bed surface structures associated with gravel-bed streams complicate the prediction of the threshold of sediment transport and result in unstable discharge-sediment transport relations that challenge the magnitude-frequency concept developed on lower-gradient rivers. Mobilization of sediment stored in the channel following an episodic input event depends on flood history (i.e., magnitude, duration, and sequence), sediment characteristics, and the sediment supply history. Consequently, flow events of the same magnitude and duration may produce different channel morphologies, sediment mobility rates and bed surface textures and structures (e.g., Buffington and Montgomery, 1999).

Streams with a relatively large sediment supply, and associated volume of inchannel sediment, typically have texturally finer surfaces, poorly developed surface structures and higher sediment transport rates for a given discharge than channels with the same slope and lower sediment supplies (e.g., Dietrich et al., 1989; Lisle and Madej, 1992; Lisle et al., 1993; Madej et al., 2009). When the sediment supply is low the development of a well-structured, coarse-textured bed significantly reduces the sediment transport rates (Parker et al., 1982; Dietrich et al., 1989; Church et al., 1998; Hassan and Church, 2000; Ryan, 2001; Church and Hassan, 2002; Hassan and Woodsmith, 2004). This raises the problem of different magnitude and effectiveness at the same site of the river. In these streams, large, rare events erode banks and shape the channel. However, medium-size events mobilize most of the small grain-size fractions with little impact on the channel morphology (for example see Pickup and Warner, 1976). Under these conditions, the bed is only partially mobilized and most of the bed material remains immobile for extended periods of time (Wilcock and McArdell, 1993). This implies that there may be a continuum of events, with moderate events that mobilize most of the sediment and rare channel shaping events (Pickup and Warner, 1976).

Thus the flow that is effective at moving most of the volume of the mobilized sediment may not be the same flow that shapes the morphology. This is particularly evident in step-pool cascade channels where the armoured structure of the bed may persist for a number of years, while relatively frequent events move finer material over the structured bed (Yager et al., 2007). Observations from East Creek (for field site description see Oldmeadow and Church, 2006) near Vancouver, British Columbia illustrate that the finer bedload from an upstream lower gradient riffle-pool reach moves through a steeper downstream step-pool stream with little change in grain size. As such, the flow that moves the supplied sediment is not the same flow that would destabilize the channel bed itself.

Conceptually a clear link can be made between the amount of sediment stored in the channel and the nature of sediment transport through a channel. Channels with a large amount of readily mobile sediment are likely to frequently move the sediment that makes up the bed and banks of the channel. In these channels the discharge that moves the annual load is likely to be similar to the discharge that forms the channel. In contrast, channels with little storage are likely to have structured, coarse beds. Under these conditions, flows that are effective at moving the mean annual load are not likely to either mobilize the largest stones or re-organize the channel form. On account of these storage effects, channel storage has been used to forecast transport rates (Lisle and Church, 2002; Yager et al., 2007). The variability associated with how easily the channel boundary is mobilized results in multiple levels of effectiveness for sediment transport and channel morphology (e.g., Pickup and Warner, 1976; Carling, 1988).

Depending on the scale of the storage element and position within the stream network, sediment may be stored for periods ranging from less than a year to decades or even centuries (Dietrich et al., 1982; Swanson et al., 1982; Kelsey et al., 1987; Madej and Ozaki, 1996). The transport capacity of a channel may appear constant at both short (<100 a) and very long timescales (>$10^3$ a), but it is clearly dynamic at intermediate time scales that correspond with the passage of sediment waves that cause fluctuations in channel storage (Lisle and Church, 2002; Lisle and Smith, 2003). At these intermediate timescales, Lisle and Church (2002) asserted that sediment transport capacity responds to changes in sediment supply and storage.

In the preceding discussion it has been emphasized that bed state, sediment supply, and sediment storage play an important role in regulating sediment transport. What remains relatively elusive is the response rate of channels to changes in sediment supply and discharge regime. In the remaining portion of the discussion we will illustrate with a few examples of how channels adjust in response to changes in sediment supply and discharge. These case studies suggest that steep, supply-limited streams may for the most part not have a singular steady state, but rather be continuously evolving.

While the continuously changing state likely dominates most supply-limited rivers, two exceptions to this situation may exist. These two exceptions are the extremes in the sediment supply/discharge function. The first of these may occur when sediment supply rates are very low, but the discharge is able to remove loose grains. During these conditions, a stable channel can form and may exhibit a relatively stable sediment rating curve. Fine sediment, typically sand and gravel, can move over the top of the stable bed without actually modifying the structure of the bed. The second stable sediment transport-discharge curve may occur at the other end of the sediment supply spectrum. If the sediment supply becomes essentially constant after some distance downstream (as the upstream reaches have damped out the initial variability in supply), a stable sediment supply-discharge relation can emerge. During these conditions a wider range of grain sizes can be in transport and the surface of the stream channel can actively exchange sediment with the material in transport, resulting in a variable bed state that maintains an average condition (e.g., mean slope, grain size, roughness, bar spacing). These two stable end states are illustrated with flume data below, while the more common, continuously adapting conditions are illustrated with field cases and flume data.

## 33.3  CASE STUDIES

### 33.3.1  Flume Observations of Stable Sediment Transport States at High and Low Sediment Supply Conditions

Zimmermann (2009) conducted a number of flume experiments that modelled the stability and morphology of step-pool streams. The approach used was designed to allow for the bed to structure and coarsen, and to mimic the variable rates of sediment supply that are likely to occur in nature. To accomplish this, sediment was fed into the flume for one hour at four different times during the armouring/structuring portion of the tests. At the start of each feeding run, the flow was also increased by 20%. At the end of the feeding run, the flow was held constant for an hour, except for the last run, when it was held constant for three hours. Between each feeding test, the flow was also increased by 20% and held constant for an hour. After the last feeding was complete flow was held constant for three hours, then increased 20% and run for another three hours. Information on sediment transport rates and texture was obtained using a light table attached to the end of the flume and a video camera which was used to record shadows of stones passing over the light table (for details see Zimmerman et al., 2008). Another camera was used to record the evolution of the bed surface over the length of the flume. To determine the water and bed surface slope and the development of step-pool structures, a laser profiler with an accuracy of 1 mm was used. These experiments show how the bed of a step-pool channel can respond to feed and changes in discharge, as well as the characteristic response time of the bed, for a flume of a fixed length.

In total, 32 experiments were conducted (see Zimmerman, 2009; Zimmerman et al., 2010). Here, we report data from the last feeding run of Experiment 16 and two subsequent flow increases (Figure 33.1). The grain-size distribution of the feed was the same as the bed material with a $D_{50}$ of 9.8 mm and a $D_{84}$ of 26 mm. The sediment transport rate varied over three orders of magnitude. With the exception of the first 5 to 10 minutes, when the bed was responding to a 20% increase in discharge and the introduction of the sediments, the sediment transport rate out of the flume had a running average near the supply rate. During these conditions the bed was essentially in a stable equilibrium associated with a high rate of sediment supply. Despite this equilibrium the sediment transport rate fluctuated as a result of bed structures (e.g. steps) forming and breaking. Similar patterns of fluctuation in sediment transport have been reported for gravel-sand- and gravel-bed streams (Kuhnle and Southard, 1988; Whiting et al., 1988).

At 760 minutes into the experiment the feeding of sediment was stopped and the discharge was held constant for another three hours. Shortly after the feed rate was stopped, the transport rate began to diminish. By 800 minutes the transport rate had more or less stabilized at a lower rate. A much slower reduction in sediment transport was, however, still occurring. The quasi-stable state illustrated between 800 and 940 minutes characterizes the second equilibrium state that can occur during low sediment-supply conditions. In this case the bed is armoured and there is no more stored sediment in the channel that can be readily mobilized. Furthermore, the structure of the channel remains stable.

The stable equilibrium conditions characterized by stable sediment-supply conditions are characteristic of the classic magnitude-frequency paradigm. With both of these two regimes a relatively stable, albeit different, sediment transport-discharge relation exists. The important difference between the two regimes is that in the one case the surface is actively exchanging grains with the material in transport, while in the other case the sediment in transport is moved over a relatively stable bed. The more challenging, and potentially more common regime for natural channels is to be moving back and forth between these two paradigms. Field examples of such

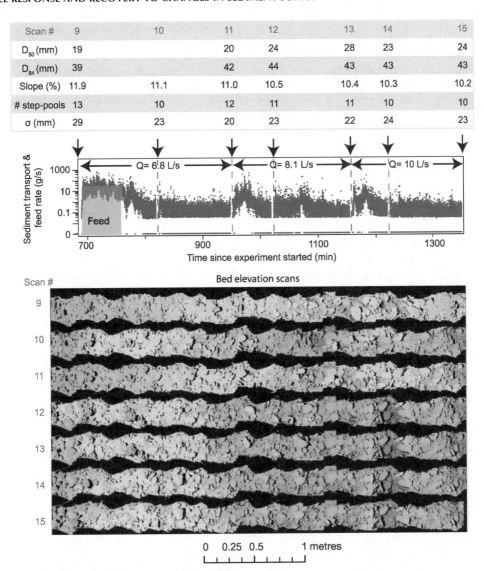

| Scan # | 9 | 10 | 11 | 12 | 13 | 14 | 15 |
|---|---|---|---|---|---|---|---|
| $D_{50}$ (mm) | 19 | | 20 | 24 | 28 | 23 | 24 |
| $D_{84}$ (mm) | 39 | | 42 | 44 | 43 | 43 | 43 |
| Slope (%) | 11.9 | 11.1 | 11.0 | 10.5 | 10.4 | 10.3 | 10.2 |
| # step-pools | 13 | 10 | 12 | 11 | 11 | 10 | 10 |
| $\sigma$ (mm) | 29 | 23 | 20 | 23 | 22 | 24 | 23 |

**Figure 33.1** Sediment transport and bed morphology evolution observed during a portion of Experiment 16 (Zimmermann, 2009). The walls of the flume varied along the length of the channel, hence the variable width shown in the scan. During the first hour, sediment was fed at a constant rate and the sediment transport out of the flume is illustrated in grey points. Reproduced, with permission, from Zimmermann, A. 2009. Experimental investigations of step-pool channel formation and stability. Ph.D thesis, The University of British Columbia, Vancouver, Canada. (See the color version of this figure in color plate section)

conditions are characterized by unsteady sediment transport-discharge relations; these are explored in greater detail in the next section.

To understand the response of streams to changes in supply and/or discharge, we need to understand how fast different stream types can evacuate material from storage, the ability of the channel to change surface grain size, and the ability of the streams to adjust morphology. The flume example shown in Figure 33.1 provides a simplified case of some of these changes and the rates at which they occur. The displayed data record begins after 11 hours of bed conditioning that included three one-hour sessions of feed. No material was fed during the two hours prior to the beginning of the data record (Figure 33.1). During the initial adjustment associated with feeding sediment and a 20% increase in discharge (Figure 33.1) we see that the bed surface became coarser, less steep and less variable (standard deviation ($\sigma$) of local bed elevations decreased). In contrast, in the subsequent runs during which discharge was increased, but no sediment was supplied, the grain size did not increase. Rather the bed tended to degrade to a new stable slope, with a characteristic response time of about 40 minutes. The lack of any significant change in grain size suggests that there may be limits to how much coarsening the bed

can undergo. These limits are presumably a function of the calibre of sediment supplied to a reach and the grain-size distribution of the reach. In terms of the magnitude-frequency concept, the degradation of the channel is indicative of a flow that has the capacity to degrade the bed, not just move the supplied sediment and sediment stored on the surface of the bed.

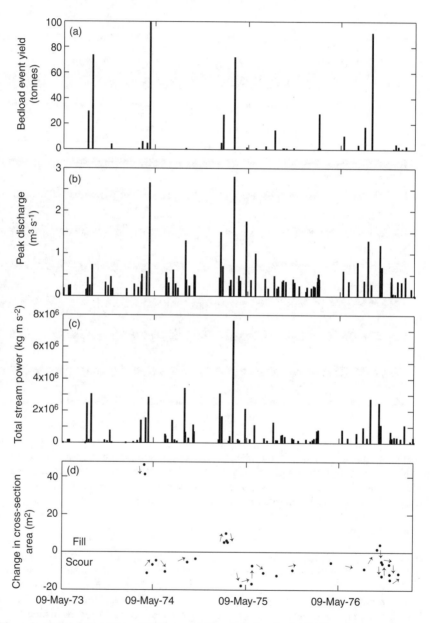

**Figure 33.2** Flow characteristics and event sediment yield versus time in the Torlesse stream: (a) event bedlload, (b) event peak flow, (c) total stream power above threshold for sediment movement as calculated for each flow event, and (d) net change in cross-section area upstream of the sediment monitoring station. Data from Hayward (1980), Appendix VI and Figure 70.

### 33.3.2    Field Examples: Torlesse Creek and Rio Cordon

To explore linkages between sediment supply, bed material transport, event magnitude, and duration we present two examples: Torlesse Creek (Hayward, 1980) in New Zealand and Rio Cordon (Lenzi *et al.*, 2004) in Italy.

Data from Torlesse Creek illustrate the temporal variability and trends of sediment storage and transport based on event sediment yields (e.g., total amount of sediment moved during a flow event) over four flood seasons (1972–1977). Torlesse Creek drains a 3.85 km$^2$ watershed into the Kowai river and thence into the Waimakariri river system in New Zealand (Hayward, 1980). Bed material is mobile during flows that occur several times a year. The basin is steep, with a mean elevation of 1300 m and most of the land surface has slopes ranging between 26 and 35°. The channel morphology is dominated by riffle-pools and boulder steps. At the study site, bed surface slope, channel width, and median particles size are 6.7%, 3 m, and 15 mm, respectively. Sediment transport estimates at this site were derived using a vortex sampler which was installed in 1971–1972. In addition, bed morphology surveys were conducted immediately upstream of the vortex trap to estimate bed stability and within-channel sediment storage.

Event sediment yield estimates are used to illustrate the temporal changes in sediment flux in relation to flood characteristics, including flood magnitude, duration, and sequence. Event sediment yields for the 81 storms in the years 1972–1977 are shown in Figure 33.2, revealing no simple relation between event-scale flood magnitude and bedload yield. Nevertheless, the largest event sediment yields are associated with large flow events. In fact, the six largest hydrological events are the six largest sediment-yielding events. Overall, about 75% of the total bedload yield was mobilized by the six largest hydrological events. Furthermore, the largest event mobilized about 18% of the total sediment yield for the study period. These results demonstrate the relative importance of large events in mobilizing sediment in mountain streams. For a given event magnitude there is, however, a wide variability in event yield. For instance, the event sediment yield varied up to five orders of magnitude for events with about the same flood magnitude. The hydrological ranking of flood magnitude differs from that of the event yield magnitude for all events except for the six largest events. Part of the discordance between flood magnitude and event sediment yield could be explained by the flood characteristics, history of bed structuring, and sediment supply. In the flume example, we see that the bed can quickly stabilize and reduce transport rates; what remains unclear is how fast this can occur in natural rivers.

Information from cross-sectional surveys provides limited insight into the relation between sediment mobility and within-channel sediment storage. Figure 33.2d demonstrates the inconsistency in the relation between event yield and within-channel sediment storage. Hayward (1980) suggests that the observed inconsistencies are a result of the location of the stored sediment relative to the measuring station and the amount of stored sediment. Nevertheless, large amounts of sediment transport are usually associated with significant change in storage at this site (Figure 33.2d). Hayward (1980) described waves of sediment moving downstream between December 1976 and March 1977 and suggested that such sediment waves control channel morphology and sediment yield.

To further explore the relation between flood characteristics and sediment transport, we examined the possible role of flood magnitude and total excess stream power on event sediment yield. Total excess stream power was calculated by summing stream power values that were greater than the critical stream power to initiate the movement of sediment. Peak flow and excess total stream power explained 29% and 48%, respectively, of the variability in event sediment yield. Using peak flow and total stream power together did not improve the relation because they are highly correlated variables. This outcome suggests the importance of flood duration (encapsulated in the summation of excess stream power) and/or sediment supply, in addition to flow magnitude and flood history, and bed surface structures.

Data from the Rio Cordon are available for the period 1987–2004. Rio Cordon drains a 5 km$^2$ watershed. The basin is steep with an elevation range between 1763 and 2748 m, a mean channel gradient of 17%, and step-pool morphology. Sediment transport estimates at this site are derived from observations using a coarse bedload trap and sonic sensors. A key feature of this study is that the trap is designed to collect only material larger than 20 mm, which may be a large proportion of the sediment that is moved in these streams.

Figure 33.3 illustrates the temporal trend in event sediment yield, maximum flood discharge and total excess stream power. Magnitude-frequency analysis highlighted the relative importance of an exceptionally large event that occurred in 1994 (Lenzi *et al.*, 2004). Based on 17 years of data the estimated return period of the 1994 event exceeded 30 years and 50 years, respectively, in terms of sediment yield and flood magnitude. Furthermore, the event sediment yield/effective runoff volume ratio was 34. This ratio may be used to estimate the recovery time following a major sediment supply event. Lenzi *et al.* (2004, their Figure 11) showed that the

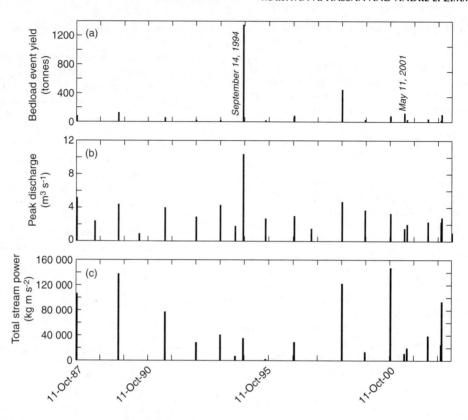

**Figure 33.3**  Flow characteristics and event sediment yield versus time in the Rio Cordon: (a) event bedload, (b) event peak flow, and (c) total stream power above threshold for sediment movement as calculated for each flow events. Data from Lenzi *et al.* (2004), Table 2.

volume of mobilized sediment declines with time due to sediment evacuations. Although the event sediment volume/effective runoff volume was higher for events following 1994, the recovery from the large event of 1994 was relatively fast. The same is true for a small event that occurred on May 11, 2001 (Figure 33.3). Although the largest hydrological event (i.e., 1994) delivered the largest volume of sediment, some of the small events resulted in relatively high sediment yield (e.g., May 11, 2001). Events of about the same peak flows (peak flow ranging between 4.3 and 4.7 m³ s⁻¹) resulted in about two orders of magnitude variability in sediment yield. Like the example of Torlesse Creek, the Rio Cordon data demonstrate the relative importance of the frequent, low-magnitude events on sediment mobilization in small steep channels. Furthermore, the large variability of sediment transport rates highlights the importance of sediment supply and within-channel storage on sediment mobility of coarse bedload material.

In addition to the role of the peak flow, Figure 33.3 shows the relative importance of total stream power on event sediment yield for the Rio Cordon. In spite of the large total stream power, some of the events resulted in relatively low sediment yield. Therefore, we decided to examine the relation between flood magnitude, total stream power, and event sediment yield. For the Rio Cordon, peak flow explains 73% of the event sediment variability. As in the case of the Torlesse Creek study, using both variables (peak flow and total stream power) in the analysis did not improve the relation. For the Rio Cordon data, the peak flow plays a more significant role than total stream power.

The differences between Torlesse Creek and Rio Cordon in terms of the role of the peak flow and total stream power could be attributed to differences in the type of sediment monitoring system used in each study. In the Torlesse, the vortex trap collects all sediment, including sand, while the Rio Cordon trap is limited to material larger than 20 mm. Given that relatively coarse material is collected in the Rio Cordon system, most of the sediment that is collected by the trap is likely to move during high flows, and hence the relatively good relation between peak flow and sediment yield. In the case of the Torlesse, it is likely that total stream power is a better

**Figure 33.4** Changes observed at Healmond Creek, Capilano Watershed, Vancouver, British Columbia, in a newly constructed channel following four winter flood events.

predictor than peak flow because the Torlesse trap collected fine sand as well as coarse bedload. Since fine material is included with the bedload, the movement of sediment, as recorded by the trap, occurs over a wider range of discharge values and as a result duration is also important. Total excess stream power encapsulates both duration and magnitude.

## 33.4 CLOSING REMARKS: A PRACTICAL CASE

The interpretation of relative geomorphic effectiveness of different hydrological events in mountain streams is significantly complicated by the spatial and temporal variability of the magnitude and frequency of the events and their effect. Knowledge regarding the effectiveness of geomorphic events in steep mountain streams could be achieved by studying sediment supply/storage and sediment re-mobilization, while considering temporal and spatial patterns of bed surface arrangements (texture and structure) and their impact on the entrainment of sediment. A key research need is an understanding of how fast changes in grain size, storage, and morphology are apt to occur under different conditions. While an understanding of steady-state processes is useful for a wide range of conditions, there are numerous cases in which the system may not be in equilibrium and estimates of system response rates are required. Such rates include the rate at which the grain size may change, the rate of bar growth or loss, and the rate of aggradation or degradation.

Figure 33.4 illustrates an example of an evolving step-pool/cascade channel. The top panel shows a newly constructed channel with a slope of 18%, while the bottom two panels show the channel after four modest flood events that occurred between November 2009 and January 2010. The four flood events were recorded at a nearby Water Survey of Canada gauge and had an instantaneous peak discharge between 3.8 and $4.1\,\mathrm{m}^3\,\mathrm{s}^{-1}$. For the same gauge the two-year instantaneous peak flow is $5.7\,\mathrm{m}^3\,\mathrm{s}^{-1}$. The new channel was constructed at this location to prevent Healmond Creek from eroding into a silt-rich stream bank and contaminating the downstream water supply. The overall objective of the design was to create a channel that is likely to remain stable over the next few decades, during which debris flows and debris floods will episodically supply large amounts of sediment to the constructed channel. The constructed channel is on a laterally confined alluvial fan just downstream of the fan apex. To determine the dimensions of the excavated channel, it is critical to have an understanding of the aggradation and degradation cycles that are apt to occur. While stable steady-state channel dimensions can be estimated for such systems, building such a channel would be very costly and very difficult as such a channel would require a means of rearranging 2–4 m boulders into a structured channel configuration. Instead an initial unstructured channel was built (Figure 33.4a) with the hope that it would naturally widen, armour and structure into the desired channel configuration (Figure 33.4b and c). In doing so the rate of channel degradation, armouring, and coarsening needed to be estimated. Estimating these rates was very difficult and the design of such channels would be greatly aided by an improved understanding of rates of bed coarsening, erosion, and bed structure development. Such unsteady processes remain a relatively unexplored area of research.

## 33.5  ACKNOWLEDGEMENTS

Research was supported by grants and scholarships from the Natural Sciences and Engineering Research Council of Canada (to Church, Hassan, and Zimmermann). Metro Vancouver provided access to Healmond Creek. Eric Leinberger prepared the figures. We thank John Buffington and Andre Roy for suggestions that significantly improved the chapter.

## 33.6  REFERENCES

Andrews, E.D. and Nankervis, J.M. 1995. Effective discharge and the design of channel maintenance flows for gravel-bed rivers. In Costa, J.E., Miller, A.J., Potter, K.W., and Wilcock, P.R., editors. *Natural and Anthropogenic Influences in Fluvial Geomorphology*. American Geophysical Union, Geophysical Monograph 89, pp. 151–164.

Barry, J.J., Buffington, J.M., Goodwin, P. *et al.* 2008. Performance of bed load transport equations relative to geomorphic significance: predicting effective discharge and its transport rate. *Journal of Hydraulic Engineering* **134**: 601–615.

Buffington, J.M. and Montgomery, D.R. 1999. Effects of supply on surface textures of gravel-bed rivers. *Water Resources Research* **35**: 3523–3530.

Carling, P. 1988. The concept of dominant discharge applied to two gravel-bed streams in relation to channel stability thresholds. *Earth Surface Processes and Landforms* **13**: 355–367.

Church, M. and Hassan, M.A. 2002. Mobility of bed material in Harris Creek. *Water Resources Research* **38**: 1237. doi: 10.1029/2001WR000753.

Church, M., Hassan, M.A., and Wolcott, J.F. 1998. Stabilizing self-organized structures in gravel-bed stream channels: field and experimental observations. *Water Resources Research* **34**: 3169–3179.

Dietrich, W.W., Dunne, T., Humphrey, N.F., and Reid, L.M. 1982. Construction of sediment budgets for drainage basins. In Swanson, F.J., Janda, R.J., Dunne, T., and Swanston, D.N., editors, *Sediment Budgets and Routing in Forested Drainage Basins*. United States Department of Agriculture, Forestry Service, Pacific Northwest Research Station, General Technical Report PNW-141, pp. 5–23.

Dietrich, W.E., Kirchner, J.W., Ikeda, H., and Iseya, F. 1989. Sediment supply and the development of the coarse surface layer in gravel-bedded rivers. *Nature* **340**: 215–217.

Hassan, M. A. and Church, M. 2000. Experiments on surface structure and partial sediment transport on a gravel bed. *Water Resources Research* **36**: 1885–1895.

Hassan, M.A. and Woodsmith, R. 2004. Bedload transport in an obstructed-formed pool in a forested gravel-bed stream. *Geomorphology* **58**: 203–221.

Hayward, J.A. 1980. *Hydrology and Stream Sediments in a Mountain Catchment*. Tussock Grasslands and Mountain

Lands Institutes, Lincoln College, Canterbury, New Zealand, Special Publication 17.

Kelsey, H.M., Lamberson, R., and Madej. M.A. 1987. Stochastic model for long-term transpor of stored sediment in a river channel. *Water Resources Research* **23**: 1738–1750.

Kuhnle, R.A. and Southard, J.B. 1988. Bed load transport fluctuations in a gravel bed laboratory channel. *Water Resources Research* **24**: 247–260.

Lenzi, M.A., Mao, L., and Comiti, F. 2004. Magnitude-frequency analysis of bed load data in an Alpine boulder bed stream. *Water Resources Research* **40**: W07201. doi: 10.1029/2003WR002961.

Lisle, T.E. and Church, M. 2002. Sediment transport-storage for degrading gravel-bed channels. *Water Resources Research* **38**: 1219. doi: 1210.1029/2001WR001086.

Lisle, T.E. and Majej, M.A. 1992. Spatial variation in armouring in a channel with high sediment supply. In Billi, P., Hey, R.D., Thorne, C.R., and Tacconi, P., editors. *Dynamics of Gravel-bed Rivers*. Chichester, John Wiley & Sons, pp. 278–293.

Lisle, T.E. and Smith, B. 2003. Dynamic transport capacity in gravel-bed river systems. In Araya, T., Kuroki, M. and Marutani, T., editors, *Proceedings of the International Workshop for "Source to Sink" Sedimentary Dynamics in Catchment Scale, Hokkaido University, Sapporo, Japan, 16–20 June*, Organizing Committee of the International Workshop for Sedimentary Dynamics, pp. 187–206.

Lisle, T.E., Iseya, F., and Ikeda, H. 1993. Response of a channel with alternate bars to a decrease in supply of mixed-size bed load: a flume experiment. *Water Resources Research* **29**: 3623–3629.

Madej, M. A. and Ozaki, V. 1996. Channel response to sediment wave propagation and movement, Redwood Creek, California, USA. *Earth Surface Processes and Landforms* **21**: 911–927.

Madej, M.A., Sutherland, D.G., Lisle, T.E., and Pryor, B. 2009. Channel responses to varying sediment input: a flume experiment modeled after Redwood Creek, California. *Geomorphology* **103**: 507–519.

Oldmeadow, D.F. and Church, M. 2006. A field experiment on streambed stabilization by gravel structures. *Geomorphology* **78**: 335–350.

Parker, G., Klingeman, P.C., and McLean, D.G. 1982. Bedload and size distribution in paved gravel-bed streams. American Society of Civil Engineers, *Journal of the Hydraulic Division* **108**: 544–571.

Pickup, G. and Warner, R.F. 1976. Effects of hydrological regime on magnitude and frequency of dominant discharge. *Journal of Hydrology* **29**: 51–75.

Ryan, S.E. 2001. The Influence of sediment supply on rates of bed load transport: a case study of three streams on the San Juan National Forest. *Proceedings of the Seventh Federal Interagency Sedimentation Conference, Reno, NV, 25–29 March, Proceedings* **III**: III-48–III-54.

Swanson, F.J., Fredrickson, R.L., and McCorison, F.M. 1982. Material transfer in a western Oregon forested watershed. In Edmonds, R.L., editor, *Analysis of Coniferous Forest Ecosystems in the Western United States*, Stroudsburg, PA, Hutchinson Ross Publishing Co, pp. 233–266.

Whiting, P.J., Dietrich, W.E., Leopold, L.B., Drake, T.G., and Shreve, R.L. 1988. Bedload sheets in heterogeneous sediment. *Geology* **16**: 105–108.

Whiting, P.J., Stamm, J.F., Moog, D.B., and Orndorff, R.L. 1999. Sediment transporting flows in headwater streams. *Geological Society of America Bulletin* **111**: 450–466.

Wilcock, P.R. and McArdell, B.W. 1993. Surface-based fractional transport rates: mobilization thresholds and partial transport of a sand-gravel sediment. *Water Resources Research* **29**: 1297–1312.

Wolman, M.G. and Miller, J.P. 1960. Magnitude and frequency of forces in geomorphic processes. *Journal of Geology* **68**: 54–74.

Yager, E.M., Kirchner, J.W., and Dietrich, W.E. 2007. Calculating bed load transport in steep boulder bed channels. *Water Resources Research* **43**: W07418. doi: 10.1029/2006WR005432.

Zimmermann, A. 2009. *Experimental investigations of step-pool channel formation and stability*. Ph.D thesis, The University of British Columbia, Vancouver, Canada.

Zimmermann, A., Church, M., and Hassan, M.A. 2008. Video-based gravel transport measurements with a flume mounted light table. *Earth Surface Processes and Landforms* **33**: 2285–2296.

Zimmermann, A., Church, M., and Hassan, M.A. 2010. Step-pool stability: testing the jammed state hypothesis. *Journal of Geophysical Research* **115**: F02008. doi: 10.1029/2009JF001365.

# 34

# Alluvial Landscape Evolution: What Do We Know About Metamorphosis of Gravel-bed Meandering and Braided Streams?

François Métivier and Laurie Barrier

*As the science of sediment transportation and deposition develops, it will be possible to predict more and more closely the morphological changes which will take place in a river due to any set of conditions and rate at which they will occur.*
Lane (1955, p.745–746.)

*Often all the modern researcher can do is to quantify the observations of earlier workers.*
Schumm (2005, p. X)

## 34.1  INTRODUCTION

This chapter is an attempt to synthesize a portion of the vast literature concerning the effects of landscape evolution on channel changes in gravel-bed rivers. More precisely, we try to understand how changes in the boundary conditions of an alluvial plain lead to channel metamorphosis as defined by Schumm (1969) between two end-member patterns of rivers: highly sinuous meandering and braided.

To proceed, we consider the problem in its simplest form: two end-member channel patterns, highly sinuous meandering and braided, and their respective landscapes (Figure 34.1). We try to understand what changes in boundary conditions lead to a sustainable change in channel pattern. This fundamental question can be broken into three subquestions: (i) independently of why these different patterns exist, how can one distinguish between the two end-member channel patterns and can the distinction be made quantitatively (Section 34.3); (ii) can one then, after making a clear distinction between these two patterns, quantitatively relate channel

metamorphosis to causative changes in boundary conditions (Sections 34.4 and 34.5); (iii) what record of this history and dynamics are we able to decipher from the stratigraphic record (Section 34.6). As we will see, these questions broadly correspond to the different types of publications we found. But before addressing these questions, we start with a critical look at existing databases, as these are the essential evidence upon which most of our understanding is based (Section 34.2).

Given an exponentially growing body of literature, our strategy was to focus on a somewhat narrower yet more attainable goal. As such, our work strictly applies to alluvial channels. For a comprehensive review of mountain streams, readers are referred to the benchmark works of Montgomery and Buffington (1997) and Wohl (2000). This focus has resulted in us not considering the effect of dead wood on channel morphology, which has an essential influence on mountain streams. For a review of the role of wood in rivers, the reader is referred to Gurnell *et al.* (2002) and Montgomery *et al.* (2003). Finally, we have restricted ourselves to the study of archetypes, hence "pure" meandering and braided streams. As such, we have avoided confrontation with the literature on wandering rivers. The reader is referred to Church (2006) for a discussion.

## 34.2  DATA SOURCES

We first review the main data sets commonly used in the literature. We looked for data sets containing at least information on dependent and independent variables such as discharge, valley slope, and grain size, as well

---

*Gravel-bed Rivers: Processes, Tools, Environments*, First Edition. Edited by Michael Church, Pascale M. Biron and André G. Roy.

**Figure 34.1** Typical examples of meandering and braided gravel-bed streams. Meandering: Seine River near Méry-sur-Seine, France; braided: Bléone River in the French Alps near Dignes-les-Bains. The width of flow is 20–30 m in both cases. Reproduced, with permission, from Google Earth.

as channel width, depth, and sinuosity. Because we do not consider time as a parameter of the problem, we assume that, for a given set of data, fluid discharge, valley slope, grain size, and, when available, sediment transport are independent variables. In contrast, we regard width, depth, and sinuosity (linked to channel slope) as dependent variables.

In this section, we discuss the databases available to us. First, we explain how we filtered these data sets to extract information concerning gravel-bed streams. Then, we analyse the resulting data sets and discuss their advantages and disadvantages. We point out problems and identify needs for future research and data acquisition.

### 34.2.1 Existing Databases and Selection Criteria

#### 34.2.1.1 Hydraulic Geometry and Stream Morphology

The first compendium on river morphology is that of Church and Rood (1983). It contains 500 records in total and the authors made a commendable effort to describe individual data acquisition. Thirty-five single-thread streams have a gravel-bed ($D_{50} \geq 2$ mm), a high ($\geq 1.3$) sinuosity, and sufficient information on discharge, slope, width, and depth. Only six reaches are explicitly referred to as braided and gravel-bed.

More recently, van den Berg (1995) published a complementary database devoted to the study of meandering versus braiding streams that contains 227 records. After filtering, 53 complete records concern gravel-bed meandering streams with a high ($\geq 1.3$) sinuosity and 24 describe gravel-bed braided streams. The van den Berg compendium contains less information

than that of Church and Rood, but it is more recent and therefore contains information acquired after 1983. A small overlap exists between the two databases; however, this remains marginal.

Finally, once both databases are merged and filtered to fit our needs, we end up with a composite data set of 88 highly sinuous meandering gravel-bed streams and 30 gravel-bed braided streams. This composite data set will hereafter be called the CRV data set (data extracted from Church and Rood's and van den Berg's compendia).

The compendia of Parker et al. (2007) and Osterkamp and Hedman (1982) are useful when considering the gravel-bed river regime. No information on sinuosity or vegetation was included because the authors did not address this point in their articles and reports. The channel pattern is not mentioned, however the authors noted whether the streams have a single channel or a single thread.

#### 34.2.1.2 Sediment Transport

Brownlie's (1981) compendium is not suitable for the problems addressed here. Only 82 entries concern gravel-bed streams and no information on river morphology is provided. Few field studies compensate for this. Most published and available data sets concern measurements made at a specific section in order to study bedload transport dynamics (Ashworth et al., 1992; Andrews, 1994; Reid et al., 1995; Meunier et al., 2006; Liu et al., 2008; Milhous, 1973, in Brownlie, 1981). They either do not provide information on the hydraulic geometry and channel planform or they do not make a mass balance calculation that would enable the establishment of annual flux values for bedload to the channel. Very few studies record both a survey of flow and sediment transport over several flow seasons, provide an analysis of channel morphology, and make their data available (see Ryan and Emmett, 2002; King, 2004; Piégay *et al.*, 2004). Among these, the recent compilation for streams in Idaho provided by King *et al.* (2004) proves invaluable because it is at present the only database that together provides classical bankfull geometries and bedload fluxes.

### 34.2.1.3   Vegetation

We used the databases of Andrews (1984) and Hey and Thorne (1986) to examine the effects of vegetation on channel pattern, a topic of much interest today. More than 20 years later, they still remain the best source of information on the relations between river patterns and vegetation. We complemented these data sets with the data sets of Huang and Nanson (1997) on Australian rivers and Rowntree and Dollar (1999) on the Bell River in South Africa.

### 34.2.1.4   Ancient Systems

Finally, we searched for databases containing information similar to that available for modern day rivers (i.e., channel pattern, width, depth, and sinuosity, as well as discharge, slope, grain size, sediment transport, and vegetation cover), but for ancient streams. Many studies have presented quantitative reconstructions of ancient rivers from their deposits and several attempts to synthesize the data produced by these works also exist for sand-bed streams (e.g., Leeder, 1973; Ethridge and Schumm, 1978). However, quantitative studies for gravel-bed rivers are not so common and they still need to be harmonized and synthesized (see Section 34.6.2).

### 34.2.2   Tools

We use simple tools for the analyses in this paper. The use of complex statistical analyses or fitting techniques is inappropriate for two reasons: the data sets are small and the data scatter is large. When needed, we use ordinary least squares fit and linear approximations. We use cumulative distribution functions (CDFs) instead of probability distribution functions (PDFs) to compare distributions visually. CDFs are complemented by quantile–quantile plots (Q–Q plots). Q–Q plots compare the quantiles of two distributions to check whether they are equivalent or significantly different. For instance, to compare the distribution of discharges for a given set of meandering and braided streams, we first calculate the discrete CDFs of the discharges for the two stream types. Each quantile $Q_5, Q_{10}, \ldots, Q_i, \ldots Q_{95}, Q_{100}$ is then compared individually in a plot ($Q_{i,\text{meander}}$, $Q_{i,\text{braided}}$). If the distributions are equal, the plotted points are aligned on the $y = x$ line. If the distributions are similar, but differ in some of their parameters, the points align on another line. If the distributions differ, the points may no longer plot on a line. This is a fast and simple way to visually scan the available databases to find data sets with independent parameter distributions as similar as possible.

### 34.2.3   Relevance of Existing Databases

It is important to identify deficiencies in any given database, first to delineate goals for future field surveys, and second because these may limit the generalizations that can be made from the analysis proposed.

Later, we will discuss what is commonly called hydraulic geometry and regime relations. River regime, or grade, relies on adjusting the dependent variables to a set of three independent parameters: grain size of the particles composing the bed, water discharge, and sediment flux. Figure 34.2 shows the CDF curves and Q–Q plots for the median grain size of the meandering and braided rivers in the CRV data set. It shows that grain-size distributions for braided and meandering streams are similar and, to first order, they follow the same distribution function. However, the range in grain size is limited, as 90% of the streams have $D_{50}$ above 10 mm. Hence, fine gravel-bed streams are not present. Therefore, it can be argued that the studies and analysis used here do not apply to rivers with beds composed of fine gravel.

Figure 34.3 shows the same CDFs and Q–Q plots for the discharges, with quite different results. The discharge distributions do not collapse on the $y = x$ line. First, this means that the statistical distributions of discharges between meandering and braided streams recorded in Church and Rood's and van den Berg's databases are significantly different. Second, the CDFs show a difference of an order of magnitude in the median discharge of the distributions. This means that meandering streams in the CRV data set are "small" rivers, whereas braided streams are much "larger" rivers (in the discharge sense). The issue here is simple: it is impossible to tell whether gravel-bed meandering streams are, on average, smaller streams than braided ones, or if the distributions are biased because the existing databases do not reflect the natural ranges of discharges of both highly sinuous meandering and braided streams.

Strictly speaking, if we wish to compare channel patterns for stream data sets that statistically have the same distribution for both median grain size and discharge, we end up with 32 meandering and 22 braided reaches with a discharge above 100 $\text{m}^3 \text{ s}^{-1}$ (numbers in parentheses in Table 34.1). Figures 34.4 and 34.5 show

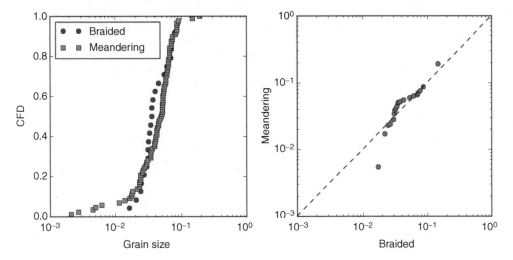

**Figure 34.2**   Left: CDFs of median grain sizes in the existing data on gravel-bed meandering (52 reaches) and braided (30 reaches) streams. Right: Q-Q plot of the same distributions.

the CDFs for the median grain size and discharge of these streams. The grain-size distributions remain similar and the discharge distributions are much closer to the $y = x$ line. At least, they follow a linear relation. This is not perfect, but it approximately fulfils an important criterion: the independent parameters are not equal, but are of the same order of magnitude. Thus, the patterns we observe are not biased by the nature of the data set. We will refer to this stream sub-data-set (gravel-bed, highly meandering and braided streams with discharge above

$100 \, \mathrm{m}^3 \, \mathrm{s}^{-1}$ extracted from Church and Rood's, and van Den Berg's compendia) as the CRV100 data set.

Finally, we calculated the CDFs and Q–Q plot of valley slopes for both meandering and braided streams in the CRV100 data set, when the valley slope was available, either directly or through channel slope and sinuosity (Figure 34.6). The two distributions are not the same, but they probably reflect the same statistical distribution with different parameters because braided streams flow on higher slopes than meandering ones.

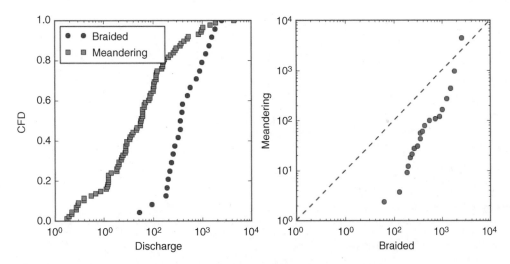

**Figure 34.3**   Left: CDFs of discharges in the existing data on gravel-bed meandering (52 reaches) and braided (30 reaches) streams. Right: Q–Q plot of the same distributions.

**Table 34.1**   Data sources for gravel-bed streams[a]

| Source | NR | NGB | Braided | Sin.-Mean. | Highly sinuous (>1.3) |
|---|---|---|---|---|---|
| Brownlie (1981) | 1764 | 82 | NA | NA | NA |
| Osterkamp and Hedman (1982) | 454 | 123 | NA | NA | NA |
| Church and Rood (1983) | 500 | 430 | 6+(0) | 74 | 35(10) |
| Andrews (1984) | 24 | 24 | 0 | NA | NA |
| Hey and Thorne (1986) | 62 | 62 | 0 | 56 | 14 |
| van den Berg (1995) | 227 | 164 | 24(22) | 53 | 53(22) |
| Rowntree and Dollar (1996) | 10 | 10 | 0 | 10 | 2 |
| Huang and Nanson (1997) | 30 | | 0 | NA | NA |
| King (2004) | 34 | 34 | NA | NA | NA |
| Parker et al. (2007) | 181 | 181 | NA | NA | NA |

[a] Meandering and braided streams were counted when information on discharge, slope, grain size, width, depth, and sinuosity was given. NR: Number of records. NGB: Number of gravel-bed streams. NA: Not applicable. + No information on sinuosity is given for gravel-bed braided streams in the Church and Rood compendium. Numbers in parentheses indicate streams with a bankfull discharge equal to or greater than $100\,\mathrm{m^3\,s^{-1}}$. See text for explanations.

If a conclusion can be drawn from this analysis, it is that further surveys should concentrate on large, gravel-bed meandering streams and small, gravel-bed braided streams to expand existing databases. Furthermore, streams with fine gravel beds should be searched for because they bridge the gap between the more common "gravel-bed" and "sand-bed" rivers. Finally, sediment fluxes, and especially bedload, are unknown for most of the rivers in the databases. Along with morphologic parameters, sediment transport and, especially, bedload (in order to derive long-term fluxes) should be surveyed extensively.

## 34.3   DEFINING MEANDERING AND BRAIDED STREAMS

### 34.3.1   *Planform Definition*

#### 34.3.1.1   Channel and Threads

In this chapter, a channel is considered to be the entire area where flow and sediment transport occur in an alluvial valley, plain, or on a fan. A channel is separated from a potential adjacent floodplain, where flow and sediment transport occur more episodically during the highest flow stages, by banks. These banks correspond to

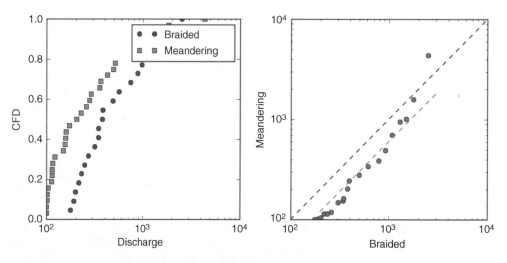

**Figure 34.4**   Left: CDFs of discharges in the existing data on gravel-bed meandering (32 reaches) and braided (22 reaches) streams with a discharge above $100\,\mathrm{m^3\,s^{-1}}$. Right: Q–Q plot of the same distributions.

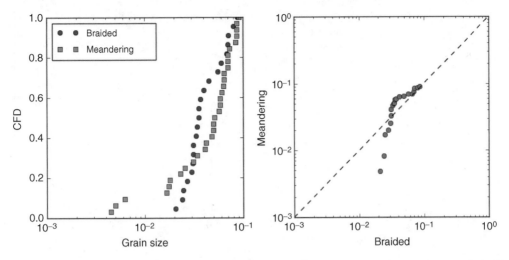

**Figure 34.5** Left: CDFs of the grain size in the existing data on gravel-bed meandering (32 reaches) and braided (22 reaches) streams with a discharge above $100\,\mathrm{m^3\,s^{-1}}$. Right: Q–Q plot of the same distributions.

somewhat sharp topographic steps. A river channel may consist of flow organized in a single thread or in multiple threads within a single channel. A meandering stream is composed of one channel that has one active thread, whereas a braided stream corresponds to one channel with flow divided among several threads. Within and between these active threads, bars or temporary islands usually exist, migrate, and are modified as the threads wander across the channel. These bedforms are part of the channel (Schumm, 1977, 2005). This definition

corresponds to the framework of mechanical stability analyses (Parker, 1976).

### 34.3.1.2 Sinuosity

As in previous studies (e.g., Leopold and Wolman, 1957; Brice, 1975; Rust, 1978a; Friend and Sinha, 1993), sinuosity is defined here as the ratio of the channel length, measured along the stream between two points, to the shortest distance between the same two points.

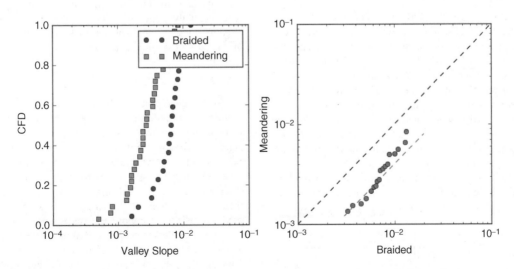

**Figure 34.6** Left: CDFs of valley slopes in the existing data on gravel-bed meandering (32 reaches) and braided (22 reaches) streams with a discharge above $100\,\mathrm{m^3\,s^{-1}}$. Right: Q–Q plot of the same distributions.

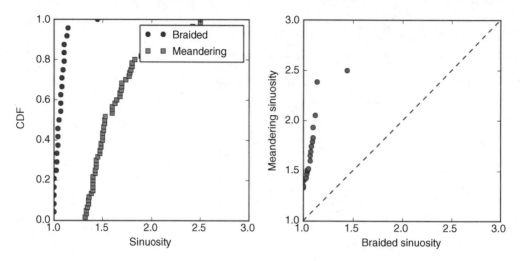

**Figure 34.7** Left: CDFs of the sinuosities in the existing data on gravel-bed meandering (32 reaches) and braided (22 reaches) streams with a discharge above $100\,\mathrm{m}^3\mathrm{s}^{-1}$. Right: Q–Q plot of the same distributions.

Using this definition, a straight channel would have a sinuosity of one. Conversely, meandering channels, which are tortuous channels, have sinuosities greater than one. Meandering streams are highly sinuous when their sinuosity is greater than 1.3 (Schumm, 1977). Individual braided threads may be locally sinuous, but the braided channel as a whole often has a low sinuosity close to one. This can be seen in the CDFs and Q–Q plots of sinuosities for meandering and braided streams for the CRV100 data set (Figure 34.7).

### 34.3.1.3 Type of Sediment Load

In the 1960s and early 1970s, classifications associating channel patterns with sediment transport types were developed based on the study of sand-bed streams (Schumm, 1977, 1987, 2005; Church, 2006). In these classifications, braided streams are defined as being predominantly bedload determined, whereas meandering streams are mostly mixed-load or suspended-load dominated. Highly sinuous meandering streams were always associated with suspended load (Schumm, 1977). These classifications do not hold for meandering in the case of gravel-bed rivers.

The relative contributions of suspended and bed material can be characterized using the dimensionless Rouse number (Vanoni, 1940; Garcia, 2008):

$$Ro = \frac{v_s}{\kappa u_*} = \frac{v_s}{\kappa\sqrt{\tau_b/\rho}} \qquad (34.1)$$

wherein $u_* = \sqrt{\tau_b/\rho}$ is the shear velocity, $\tau_b$ the shear stress exerted on the bed by the flow, $v_s$ the settling

velocity of the sediment composing the bed, and $\kappa = 0.4$ the von Karman constant. For a Rouse number above two, 90% of the sediments are transported in the lower 10% of the flow (Vanoni, 1940) and therefore move as bedload.

We calculated Rouse numbers for the rivers in the CRV100 data set. The values are always much larger than two. This means that the median-size material comprising gravel-bed streambeds moves almost exclusively as bedload. Although a distinction can be made between meandering and braided-stream distributions, there is no clear difference in the material transport mode. Therefore, the distinction between bed, mixed, and suspended load originally proposed by Schumm (1977) for sand-bed streams does not apply when considering the median grain size of gravel-bed streams.

### 34.3.1.4 Aspect Ratio

Lane (1937) was probably the first to cite the importance of the aspect ratio from an engineering point of view. Yet its potential importance as a parameter relevant to characterizing stream morphology was likely cited first by Schumm (1960), who later used it as a fundamental criterion for his stream morphology classification (Schumm, 1963, 1977). It has been widely used since then (e.g., Schumm, 2005; Church, 2006), although a physical basis for its importance was proposed only in the late 1970s by Parker (1976). Based on a linear stability analysis of flow and sediment transport equations, Parker (1976) demonstrated that the aspect ratio was a first-order criterion governing channel morphology. Yet, despite this significant advance, hydraulic geometry

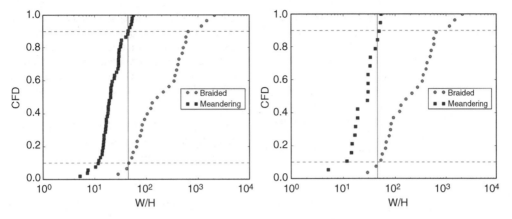

**Figure 34.8** CDFs of the aspect ratios for gravel-bed meandering and braided streams from the CRV data set (left), and CRV100 subdata set (right) of reaches with similar discharges and grain sizes. Dashed lines indicate 10th and 90th percentiles, respectively. The vertical line marks the threshold at $H/W = 45$.

studies have focused on characterizing individual channel width and depth rather than their ratio, and on individual dependant variables rather than their dimensionless ratio. The quantitative importance of the aspect ratio was re-acknowledged less than 10 years ago by Millar (2000) and others from the University of British Columbia (see Chapter 8, this volume).

Figure 34.8 shows the CDFs of the stream aspect ratios for the CRV and CRV100 data sets. They portray the exact same scenario and confirm both Schumm's and Parker's conclusion that meandering and braided streams statistically have very different aspect ratios. Ninety percent of highly sinuous meandering streams from the CRV100 data set have aspect ratios less than 45, whereas 90% of braided streams have aspect ratios above 45. This threshold corresponds closely to the value of 40 proposed by Schumm (Schumm, 1968a, p. 40, Table 5). Thus to first order, aspect ratios of streams seem to be an excellent discriminator between meandering and braided planforms.

### 34.3.2 The Choice of Criteria for Metamorphosis in Channel Patterns

In order to quantify the conditions which induce changes in channel patterns, we must first define objective criteria for these changes. These criteria have been the subject of endless debate since the work of Leopold and Wolman (1957). The criterion they proposed is a threshold slope set by some power function of the discharge, the idea being that meandering streams have slopes less than or equal to the threshold, while braided slopes are above the threshold. This criterion was further developed by Lane (1957) in order to explain observed discrepancies

for the Chippewa River. Similar discrepencies were also discussed by Simpson and Smith (2001). Ultimately, the criterion developed by Leopold and Wolman (1957) and refined by Lane (1957) suggests that slope is an essential parameter for differentiating braided and meandering streams. Discussions of this approach that shed light on its limitations can be found in Carson (1984), van den Berg (1995), and Lewin and Brewer (2001). The main point is that it is basically empirical and it has the drawback that it mixes dependent and independent variables.

Such empirical studies will probably continue to explore the range of possible correlations as databases grow. However, for our purposes, we will use the criterion of Parker (1976), which is the first simple yet physically grounded criterion to appear. Its definition is worthy of discussion because we feel it has been misused. Using a given set of values for discharge, slope, sediment transport, and width for a rectangular channel with non-erodible banks, Parker performed a linear stability analysis of momentum and mass balance equations for both flow and sediment transport. The derived dispersion equation shows that, for a given set of conditions, local instabilities develop on the bed in the form of patterns called braids, which are composed of rows of alternating bars. The number of braids ($m$) dictates the tendency for the stream to evolve into a meandering ($m = 1$) or braided ($m \geq 2$) pattern. Hence, for a given set of boundary conditions and channel sizes, the criterion developed by Parker (1976) reveals how the internal (autogenic) instability of the system leads to its evolution into either a meandering or a braided pattern. Parker proposed that, for meandering or braiding to occur, sediment transport must be non-zero to first order, and that the number of braids (rows of bars) is proportional to a dimensionless ratio $\varepsilon^*$ defined as

$$\varepsilon^* = S_c W / \pi Fr H \qquad (34.2)$$

wherein $S_c$ is the channel bed slope, $W$ the width, $H$ the flow depth, and $Fr$ the flow Froude number. If $\varepsilon^* \ll 1$, then $m = 1$ and the river develops alternate bars and hence evolves into a meandering pattern. If $\varepsilon^* \gg 1$, $m > 1$, then the river develops several rows of alternate bars and evolves into a braided pattern. For $\varepsilon^* \approx 1$, both patterns can co-exist. Parker dropped the $\pi$ value because it is of order one and thus the river braids if $S_c/Fr \gg H/W$, whereas it meanders if $S_c/Fr \ll H/W$. Figure 34.9 analyses the criterion developed by Parker (1976) and applied to the CRV100 data set, showing that the equation works quite well. In a strict sense, not all the rivers comply with the criterion (dotted lines in Figure 34.9). However, it works quite well broadly, as there are few "unpredicted" meandering and braided streams.

As such, we can conclude that, for a given characteristic discharge and channel width, and assuming the bedload is non-zero, natural (autogenic) instabilities will develop, pushing the evolution of a given alluvial stream towards an end member pattern. This agrees with Schumm's empirical findings and classifications and it enables the independent assessment of the external (allogenic) factors controlling the important variables of an alluvial stream ($S_c/Fr$, $W/H$). Parker's criterion, developed more than 30 years ago, therefore seems to be a highly adequate approach to study the consequences of landscape changes on channel metamorphosis.

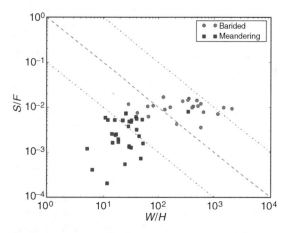

**Figure 34.9** Application of the criterion defined by Parker (1976) to the CRV data set. Dashed lines correspond to $S_c/F = H/W$. Dotted lines correspond to $S_c/F = 0.1H/W$ and $S_c/F = 10H/W$, respectively.

To summarize: both observations and stability analysis lead to the conclusion that the planform dynamic of any thread and bedform is related to the system's internal dynamics and therefore is autogenic. In contrast, thread numbers are controlled by boundary conditions, that is to say allogenic factors.

## 34.4   HYDRAULIC GEOMETRY AND THE RESPECTIVE INFLUENCE OF WATER AND SEDIMENT INPUTS

### 34.4.1   Hydraulic Geometry

The concept of an equilibrium channel with regard to sediment fluxes was introduced by Mackin (1948) and defined as a graded stream (i.e., a stream whose slope is adjusted to transport the sediment input load given an existing water flux and channel form). As pointed out by Mackin, a stable regime channel is at grade. However, the converse is not necessarily true, as the most important feature of a graded stream is its ability to carry the imposed load over long time scales, irrespective of the channel form. Knowing these differences, we will use the term equilibrium channel, regime channel, or graded channel in the most restrictive sense: a stream that has a geometrically stable section and is at grade. The channel, therefore, is defined by its hydraulic geometry.

Although concerns about hydraulic geometry date back to the work of engineers of the British Empire in the late nineteenth century (work reported in Lane, 1937), hydraulic geometry studies likely started with the first series of relations proposed by Leopold and Maddock (1953). They showed that, to first order, certain channel geometry measurements (width, depth, velocity, slope) scale as power-law functions of characteristic discharge, as follows:

$$A = a_A Q^{b_A} \qquad (34.3)$$

wherein $A$ can be any dependant variable of the stream (width $W$, depth $H$, flow velocity $U$, or slope $S_c$), and $Q$ is the fluid discharge. The most intriguing feature of these scaling relations is that the $b_A$ exponents show remarkable constancy.

By far, the most important of these relations is that of the channel width, which turns out to scale approximately as the square root of the discharge, hence:

$$W \propto Q^{1/2} \qquad (34.4)$$

It is important because we are still unable to generally close one of the most important problems in fluvial geomorphology: what sets a river's width?

Considered in more detail, hydraulic geometry equations define the functional dependency of a set of dependant variables that adjust to a set of independent variables constituting the system's boundary conditions, as follows:

$$W, H, S_c = \Phi(Q, Q_b, D, g, \rho, \rho_s) \qquad (34.5)$$

wherein $Q_b$ is the bedload flux, $D$ some characteristic grain sizes, and $g$, $\rho$, and $\rho_s$ are the gravitational acceleration, water density, and sediment density, respectively. As $Q_b$ is usually not known, it has been argued (e.g., Yalin and da Silva, 2001) that Equation (34.5) could be, to first order, reduced to:

$$W, H, S_c = \Phi(Q, D, g, \rho, \rho_s) \qquad (34.6)$$

In order to close the problem for the very simple case of a straight immobile channel, a reliable physical description of the shear stress distribution across any natural channel section is needed (Parker, 1978; Knight, 1981; Diplas, 1990; Shiono and Knight, 1991; Wilcock, 1996; Vigilar and Diplas, 1997; Kean and Smith, 2005). Once this is defined, it becomes possible to ask under what flow conditions the river banks and channel will remain stable. However, just having a stable bank is insufficient because, for a given discharge and grain size, there exists a range of solutions in which the bank is stable, yet only one is selected.

Consequently, predicting hydraulic geometry has been a matter of endless debate. Several researchers have proposed minimizing or maximizing one of the problem's variables. It has long been acknowledged (Gilbert was probably the first to note it) that some of the problem's dependent variables present optimums. It was then argued that the existence of these potential optimum conditions is the missing condition needed to close the problem (for a review, see Yalin and da Silva, 2001; Eaton et al., 2004; Millar, 2005). Indeed, the maximization or minimization of any of the dependent variables makes it possible to select one solution from a set of possible solutions. From a practical point of view, this technique is advantageous as it proposes some simple solutions to the problem.

In an opposite approach, others have considered the minimum number of constraints and equations necessary to define hydraulic geometry relationships (Parker, 1978; Parker et al., 2007). In this case, a physical explanation is found a posteriori for the constraints for which no mechanistic derivation exists.

As often observed in the natural sciences, it is interesting to note that the conclusions are relatively similar, regardless of the method employed. One of the most important conclusions derived from studying the transverse distribution of shear stresses is that an equilibrium stream must have a relatively low maximum shear stress, which is only slightly above critical. Yalin and da Silva (2001) arrive at a seemingly more provocative, yet very similar, conclusion. They conclude that an equilibrium gravel-bed stream is one where the sediment composing the bed is at the threshold of motion. Note that this conclusion is derived for the theoretical case, with no sediment input, whereas the derivations of Parker (1978) and others allow for some bedload transport.

The regime equations proposed by Yalin and da Silva (2001) are interesting because they are provocative. At the very least, they are interesting because, as quoted in Section 34.2, no database exists that contains information on regime morphology and sediment flux. Hence, Yalin and da Silva (2001) conjecture that sediment flux is not necessary because either there is none or it is sufficiently small that it can be neglected to first order. Figure 34.10 shows that this conjecture seems to hold and at least does not contradict Parker and co-authors's recent analysis. We will therefore use Yalin and da Silva's regime equations as they are relatively simple:

$$W = 1.42 \sqrt{\frac{Q}{u_{*cr}}} \qquad (34.7)$$

$$H = \frac{D^{1/7}}{7} \left( \frac{Q}{u_{*cr}} \right)^{3/7} \qquad (34.8)$$

$$S_c = \frac{u_{*cr}^2}{g} \frac{7}{D^{1/7}} \left( \frac{u_{*cr}}{Q} \right)^{3/7} \qquad (34.9)$$

Here, $u_{*cr}$ is the shear velocity corresponding to the inception of motion. For a critical Shield's stress $\theta_c = \rho u_{*cr}^2 / \Delta \rho g D \approx 0.045$ we then have:

$$u_{*cr} = \sqrt{\tau_c / \rho} \approx 0.853 \sqrt{D} \qquad (34.10)$$

Therefore, for a given set of physical parameters (density, gravity, viscosity), dependent variables are solely functions of discharge and some characteristic grain sizes, such as the $D_{50}$ of the bed.

### 34.4.2   The Weak Influence of Discharge

There has been a large effort to understand the effect of discharge on channel width, depth, and slope (or velocity). Since Leopold and Maddock's (1953) work, many researchers have tried to quantify the variability of exponents in equations like (34.3) for different settings and boundary conditions (Huang and Warner, 1995;

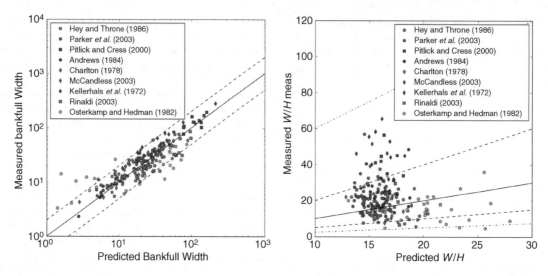

**Figure 34.10** Left: Comparison between measured and predicted bankfull width using Yalin and da Silva's regime equations (2001) for gravel-bed streams. The black line corresponds to perfect agreement $W_{meas} = W_{pred}$, dashed lines correspond to $W_{meas} = 2W_{pred}$ and $W_{meas} = 0.5W_{pred}$. Right: comparison between the measured and predicted aspect ratio using Yalin and da Silva's regime equations (2001) for gravel-bed streams. The black line corresponds to a perfect agreement, dashed lines correspond to an agreement within a factor of two, the dotted line corresponds to an agreement within a factor of four. (See the color version of this figure in color plate section.)

Merigliano, 1997; Blizard and Wohl, 1998; McCandless and Everett, 2002; McCandless, 2003; Wohl, 2004).

No study has really addressed the problem of the influence of discharge on a stream's aspect ratio in spite of its clear importance as a delineator between braided and single thread channels. The study by Eaton *et al.* (2004) is the only one merging a discussion of hydraulic geometry with an analysis of Parker's (1976) stability criterion. Using Parker's criterion, defined from his linear stability analysis and assuming that at regime, the river planform follows Yalin and da Silva's set of regime equations, we end up with the following equations:

$$W\Big/H \approx 10D^{-1/6}Q^{1/14} \tag{34.11}$$

$$S_c\Big/F_r \approx 0.02D^{1/3}Q^{-1/7} \tag{34.12}$$

Figure 34.10 results from Equation (34.11). It works reasonably well, as most streams fall within a factor of 2 of perfect agreement and all the streams fall within a factor of four. The consequences are immediate: given the exponents in Equations (34.11) and (34.12), discharge fluctuations alone cannot drive a change in the channel planform. A 16 000-fold change in discharge would be needed to change the aspect ratio by a factor of two. A reasonable onefold change in discharge would lead to a 1.18 factor change in the aspect ratio and a 0.71 factor

change in friction ($S_c/Fr$). Hence, the influence on channel pattern stability would remain marginal.

To summarize, it is interesting that one of the most important underlying consequences of river regime studies developed during the 50 years since Leopold and Maddock's work is that a change in discharge might not induce a change in the channel pattern from meandering to braided streams or vice versa.

### 34.4.3  The Influence of Bedload

Changes in landscape may induce changes in both grain size and amount of sediment delivered to the channel. As can be seen from Equations (34.11) and (34.12), a onefold change in grain size will mainly affect the friction term in Parkers' stability analysis, by a factor of two. This will affect the aspect ratio by a factor of slightly less than 0.7. Hence, if a change in planform occurs from braided to meandering, or vice versa, it probably will not be because of a change in grain size, provided that the stream retains a gravel bed.

One important assumption embedded in the analyses developed by Schumm (1963, 1977), Yalin and da Silva (2001), and Parker *et al.* (2007) is that sediment transport in stable gravel-bed streams remains small because shear stresses are only slightly above their critical value. Using the CRV100 data set, we can

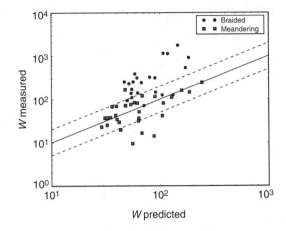

**Figure 34.11** Comparison between measured and predicted bankfull width using Yalin and da Silva's regime equation (2001) for gravel-bed streams. The black line corresponds to perfect agreement $W_{meas} = W_{pred}$; dashed lines correspond to $W_{meas} = 2W_{pred}$ and $W_{meas} = 0.5W_{pred}$.

partially test this assumption and compare the prediction for meandering and braided streams (Figure 34.11). Most highly sinuous meandering streams plot within a factor of two of the 1:1 correlation line, whereas most braided streams plot largely above this line. Measured widths are much larger than predicted ones. For gravel-bed braided streams, the assumption of zero or marginal movement breaks down. This is in agreement with the common perception that braided rivers should not be included in the development of regime geometry relations. However,

this discrepancy can be interpreted in another way (see below).

It is useful to calculate the bankfull/critical shear stress ratio ($\eta = \tau_*/\tau_{*cr}$). Figure 34.12 shows the cumulative distribution functions of $\eta$ for both meandering and braided streams, together with the Q–Q distribution plot. It clearly shows that most meandering streams have shear stresses slightly above the critical shear stress, as predicted by fluid-mechanical studies. Conversely, braided streams have high shear stresses. Note that the shear stress ratio distributions are dissimilar and hence cannot be modelled using the same probability distributions (Paola, 2001). For meandering streams, the median value $\eta_{50} \sim 1.5$, whereas for braided streams, $\eta \sim 3$. For the same grain-size distribution, this results in more than one order of magnitude difference in the sediment flux, confirming the commonly held belief (e.g., Schumm, 2005) that bedload transport is much higher, and probably sustained over a much longer time period, in braided streams than in meandering streams. Figure 34.12 and the analysis it rests upon thus imply that a change in sediment supply transported as bedload might possibly induce a change in planform.

Only one database allows the influence of bedload on hydraulic geometry and, more specifically, on the criterion proposed by Parker (1976) to be checked. This database was published by King et al. (2004). It contains 30 streams for which both $W/H$ and $S_c/Fr$ can be estimated and compared to bedload fluxes at bankfull conditions (we used the bankfull geometry summarized in Mueller and Pitlick (2005), to which we added the values for one stream studied by Ryan and Emmett (2002)). As seen in Figure 34.13, the influence is striking: bedload

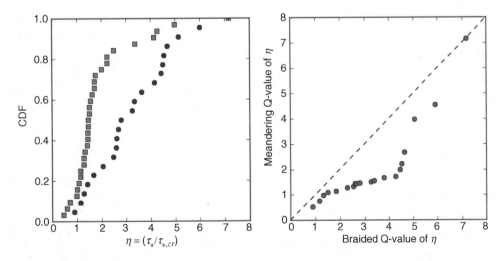

**Figure 34.12** Left: Cumulative distribution functions of $\eta = \tau/\tau_c$ for meandering and braided streams in the CRV data set. Right: Q–Q plot of these distributions.

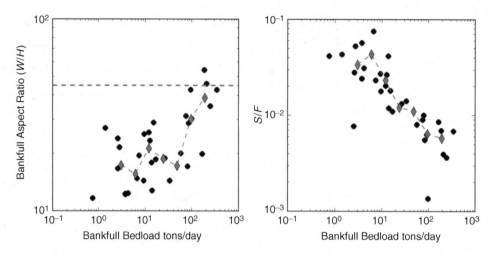

**Figure 34.13**    Influence of bedload transport on the aspect ratio (left) and $S/Fr$ (right) during bankfull flow for gravel-bed streams in Idaho. Data from King *et al.* (2004). We used both values of bankfull bedload fluxes reported by King *et al.* (2004), and Ryan and Emmett (2002), together with bankfull flow condition values reported by Mueller and Pitlick (2005). Black dots: individual streams, grey diamonds: binned averages.

changes alone can induce a fivefold change in the aspect ratio and an order of magnitude change in $S_c/Fr$. However, as the data set is too small and does not contain truely braided streams, a clear and quantified picture does not emerge. Therefore, much remains to be done and bedload flux surveys should be carried out on a much wider scale. Yet our analysis compellingly confirms Mackin's statement (1948) that sediment flux from the drainage basin should be considered a first-order driver of channel planform and metamorphosis, as a change in bedload supply will undoubtedly lead to a substantial change in the parameters controlling channel morphology.

## 34.5   THE ROLE OF SOIL PROPERTIES AND VEGETATION ON BANK STABILITY

The role of bank resistance has long been recognized as a primary control on channel shape (Schumm, 1960; Smith, 1976; Andrews, 1984; Hey and Thorne, 1986; Montgomery and Buffington, 1997; Huang and Nanson, 1998; Rowntree and Dollar, 1999; Millar, 2000; Eaton, 2006). Two factors have been proven to exert a significant control on bank strength and favour its resistance to erosion: soil properties and the riparian vegetation.

The respective influence of soil properties versus vegetation on bank strength remains a debated issue, especially for gravel-bed streams. Schumm (1960) analysed sand-bed rivers in the American Great Plains and demonstrated that clay and silt presence in the bed and banks may critically change bank resistance and therefore control stream aspect ratios. He used this

result to classify alluvial streams (Schumm, 1963; Church, 2006). However, Schumm's analysis rests on data acquired in sand-bed streams. It has therefore been argued that clays and silts may not play such an important role in gravel-bed rivers and that vegetation is probably more important in increasing bank stability (Huang and Nanson, 1997; Rowntree and Dollar, 1999).

Three main issues seem to underlie this debate: (i) is there a well-established connection between channel planform and the cohesive properties of banks; (ii) can one define proxies for bank cohesion using simple soil composition properties or other dependent parameters; (iii) under what conditions does vegetation play a role in bank cohesion (whether positive or negative)?

At first, answering any of these points may seem difficult, both because of the mechanisms involved in bank erosion (i.e., mass failure and fluvial bank erosion) and the difficulties in taking *in situ* measurements of the relevant parameters.

### 34.5.1   Mass Failure

A mass bank failure occurs when a portion of the riverbank collapses along a slab. A bank stability analysis can be conducted to establish a factor of safety, which represents the balance between gravity forces favouring the mass failure of the bank and the bank resistance due to soil cohesion defined by a Coulomb criterion (Millar and Quick, 1998; Simon *et al.*, 2000; Parker *et al.*, 2008). This technique has been applied with some success to different gravel-bed streams

(Darby *et al.*, 2007; Rinaldi *et al.*, 2008; Luppi *et al.*, 2009). An important issue concerns measurement reproducibility for bank shear resistance. The thorough analysis by Parker *et al.* (2008) shows that, in the temperate soils of Goodwin Creek (Mississippi), local variability in effective cohesion, friction angle, and saturated unit weight are such that averages derived from small sample populations can lead to diametrically opposed conclusions regarding bank stability. Averaging over an entire section does not resolve the problem, leading Parker *et al.* (2008) to conclude that, given the natural variability of riverbank geotechnical properties, only a probabilistic assessment of the factor of safety that explicitly includes the distribution functions of effective cohesion can result in realistic and unbiased predictions of bank stability (Darby *et al.*, 2000; El-Ramly *et al.*, 2002; Parker *et al.*, 2008).

These conclusions leave us with two problems. First, the database needed to derive reasonable distribution functions for a range of gravel-bed stream banks does not yet exist. Second, the approach to study ancient rivers seems limited. As diagenesis occurs, the petrophysical properties of former bank deposits are modified and thus are no longer representative of the conditions prevailing when the river was active.

However, a recent reassessment of bank stability may allow for a more simple, yet accurate, assessment of bank resistance. Istanbulluoglu *et al.* (2005) studied the mechanisms by which gullies develop. Starting from a simple geometry, with or without cracks, and assuming a Coulomb friction, they calculated a factor of safety. Assuming the factor of safety was equal to one, they calculated the maximum height a failure block can reach. They then showed that this maximum bank height could be seen as a proxy for cohesion and the internal friction angle. A comparison between measured values of gully bank heights and soil cohesion showed a good correlation. This approach was later adapted by Eaton (2006) to gravel-bed streams in order to constrain a rational regime model using Hey and Thorne's data set.

Although promising, this approach must still be rigorously tested on river data sets in different settings and for different vegetation covers. Furthermore, if the concept proves valid, the maximum height should be a constraint for regime models and not a fitting parameter, as seen in Eaton (2006).

### 34.5.2  *Fluvial Bank Erosion*

The approach delineated above for bank failure through the factor of safety is also limited. Hydraulic erosion at the base of the bank or even directly on the face can be significant, and it is often mentioned as a key process for the mass failure of the entire overlying bank.

Fluvial erosion is modelled using the following equation:

$$\dot{\varepsilon} = k_d(\tau_0 - \tau_c) \qquad (34.13)$$

wherein $\dot{\varepsilon}$ is the erosion rate in volume per unit area per unit time, $k_d$ a detachment rate coefficient called erodibility, $\tau_0$ the boundary shear stress, and $\tau_c$ the critical shear stress required to initiate erosion (e.g., Hanson and Cook, 2004). The only reliable method that exists today to perform field measurements of both $k_d$ and $\tau_c$ relies on using a jet test device (Hanson and Cook, 2004). Hanson and Simon (2001) used jet test measurements to characterize the critical stress of erosion and stream bed erodibility in the Midwestern US. Their results highlight the wide range of critical stresses measured, as well as the erodibility of the material. Hanson and Simon (2001), Simon and Thomas (2002), and Hanson and Hunt (2007) showed a remarkable correlation between erodibility and shear stress, both in the field and in the laboratory.

These important results call for a comparison between such measurements and reach properties. Constantine *et al.* (2009) made a fundamental step in a study on several meandering reaches of the Sacramento River. They compared bank erodibility measured through the jet apparatus technique to the long-term bank erosion coefficient commonly used to calculate meander migration rates. From repeated planform surveys over a 26-year period, they calculated the erosion coefficient for different reaches and compared it to the erodibility coefficient (Figure 6 in Constantine *et al.*, 2009). The correlation is extremely promising. Furthermore, it shows a clear relation between both parameter values (erodibility and bank erosion coefficient) and the soil composition of the Sacramento River reaches. If verified on other streams with different sets of conditions, this approach would represent a very efficient way to relate physically measured and geomorphic parameters. However, as for geotechnical properties, the database still needs to be created.

### 34.5.3  *The Effective Role of Vegetation*

Significant progress has been made in defining bank cohesion, stability, and erodibility, and there are now models integrating all these components (Darby *et al.*, 2007; Rinaldi *et al.*, 2008). Yet, the influence of vegetation on observed bank cohesion is still being debated for three reasons. The first reason for the controversy, as shown in Section 34.4, is that it is possible to derive reasonable first-order hydraulic geometry relations that do not account for vegetation. The second reason comes from the observation that the same vegetation type, in a forest for example, may influence channel planforms in opposing ways, depending on the catchment size (Zimmerman *et al.*, 1967; Hession *et al.*, 2003). Despite evidence that forested reaches may be larger than non-forested ones in small catchments, the vast majority of studies on the effect of riparian vegetation on channel morphology have concentrated on rivers with drainage areas largely above the threshold proposed by Zimmerman *et al.* (1967). Therefore, the role of vegetation on gravel-bed channels is most often associated with increasing bank strength and channel narrowing (Andrews, 1984; Hey and Thorne, 1986; Huang and Nanson, 1997; Millar, 2000; Simon and Collison, 2002; Eaton, 2006; Eaton and Giles, 2009) rather than with widening, erosion, and avulsion. Rivers with dense riparian vegetation are invariably described as being deeper and narrower than their grassy counterparts. This is clear from an analysis of the databases of Andrews (1984), Hey and Thorne (1986), Huang and Nanson (1997, 1998), and Rowntree and Dollar (1999) (Table 34.2). Figure 34.14 shows the CDFs of the aspect ratio for the streams in this database, grouped by the vegetation index according to Hey and Thorne (1986) and Huang and Nanson (1998). The difference is clear and shows that vegetation exerts a strong influence on the aspect ratio of gravel-bed streams. The median aspect ratio can change by a factor of two if, for example, a riparian forest develops on previously poorly vegetated banks (Figure 34.15).

The third reason for controversy comes from the gap between available data and theoretical advances on the role of vegetation. The works of Andrews (1984) and Hey and Thorne (1986) were so important that approximately 25 years after publication, they are still the reference data sets against which all hypotheses are tested. Yet, the gap between these existing data sets and the advances made by researchers on the vegetation-added strength of bank soils is rapidly growing. The vegetation index is not a physical parameter and cannot be directly related to shear strength.

The question then became how to relate vegetation to both shear strength and erodibility. Abernethy and Rutherfurd (2000, 2001) made a first step towards this by adopting techniques and procedures used to assess the role of roots in slope stability analysis. They also developed measurements of root tensile strength on river banks for two riparian species (river red gum and swamp paperback) in Australia. Using individual root tensile strength measurements together with a map of root density by root diameter class and with a simple model, they were able to calculate the resistance added to the banks. The results are highly species-dependent, but the added resistance equals the effective cohesion up to depths of more than 1.7 m below the tree trunks and 0.4 m at a distance of 17 m from the trunks, thus demonstrating the potential influence of vegetation. Others have applied this approach to other species (Simon and Collison, 2002; De Baets *et al.*, 2008) and one hopes to have, in the near future, a compendium of the root-added resistance of a wide variety of species that can be accurately used and applied to model bank resistance and erosion. Many improvements must still be developed to fully understand the mechanical effects of vegetation on river bank stability (Simon and Collison, 2002; Van De Wiel and Darby, 2007). Recent case studies have proven the potential of this approach to precisely assess the relationship between riparian vegetation dynamics, and observed effects on channel bank stability, as well as environmental consequences (Simon *et al.*, 2006; Pollen-Bankhead *et al.*, 2009).

A change in riparian vegetation therefore stands as a first-order driver for changes in stream planform geometry. This result is very similar to both experimental, numerical, and field studies that have shown how and under what conditions woodland and vegetation expansion on a braidplain can induce the progressive abandonment of secondary channels, corralling the flow and driving evolution towards a single thread morphology (e.g., Gran and Paola, 2001; Murray and Paola, 2003; Tal and Paola, 2010). However, if advances are evident and real for "large" streams, the works of Zimmerman *et al.* (1967) and Hession *et al.* (2003) remain important reminders that a large research effort is needed to push our understanding of vegetation effects on smaller first-order streams up to the level reached for larger ones.

**Table 34.2** Average drainage area (km$^2$), average and maximum discharges (m$^3$ s$^{-1}$), and depths (m) recorded in sources containing information on vegetation

| Source | $A$ | $Q_{bf}$ | $H$ | $maxQ_{bf}$ | $maxH_{bf}$ |
|---|---|---|---|---|---|
| Andrews (1984) | 1041 | 44.2? | 0.80 | 255 | 1.85 |
| Hey and Thorne (1986) | 196 | 86.1 | 1.42 | 424 | 3.21 |
| Huang and Nanson (1997) | >20? | 36.5 | 1.47 | 131 | 3.3 |
| Rowntree and Dollar (1999) | 430 | 116.9 | 1.83 | 407.1 | 2.3 |
| Hession *et al.* (2003) | 8.5 | NA | 0.39 | NA | 0.74 |

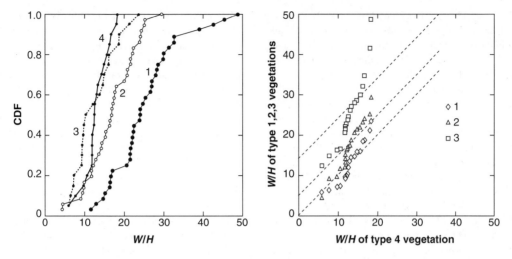

**Figure 34.14**  Left: CDFs of $W/H$ for streams according to Hey and Thorne's classification (1986), revised by Huang and Nanson (1998). Data from Andrews (1984), Hey and Thorne (1986), Huang and Nanson (1997), and Rowntree and Dollar (1999). Right: Q–Q plots of the aspect ratio distributions for vegetation types 1, 2, and 3 versus vegetation type 4. The distributions are similar for types 3 and 4 and tend to become progressively dissimilar as the vegetation contrast increases.

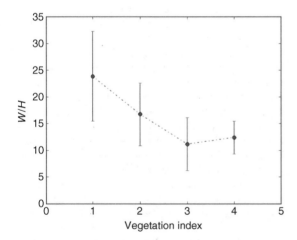

**Figure 34.15**  Average values of $W/H$ as a function of the vegetation index. Data from Andrews (1984), Hey and Thorne (1986), Huang and Nanson (1997), and Rowntree and Dollar (1999). Error bars correspond to $1\sigma$ of the aspect ratio distribution.

## 34.6  THE RECORD OF CHANNEL METAMORPHOSIS

Over long time scales (several thousand to several million years), the only way to study the channel metamorphosis of alluvial rivers is to examine the sedimentary deposits where these changes are recorded.

Deciphering the latter requires the different river channel types to be identified from the remaining sediments. At the minimum, this requires qualitative palaeoenvironmental, and if possible, quantitative paleohydraulic reconstructions.

### 34.6.1  Qualitative Paleoenvironmental Reconstructions

Palaeoenvironmental reconstructions are based on coupled observations of present and past deposits, usually summarized using facies models. A facies model is a conceptual model for the assemblage across space and through time of sedimentary facies (i.e., of sediment bodies characterized by a particular combination of physical, chemical, and biological properties) that are genetically linked to a specific depositional environment (Potter, 1959; Walker, 1979). Sedimentologists have now been working for 50 years to build facies models for sediments from different stream types. At the beginning of this process, they were inspired by the contemporaneous geomorphological advances on channel geometries (e.g., Miall, 1977; Rust, 1978a; Galloway, 1981). Then, they tried establishing ideal facies models for the alluvial deposits associated with the different channel patterns, and rules to recognize them from ancient sediments.

#### 34.6.1.1  Channel Fills

During the 1970s and 1980s, several facies models were provided for gravel-bed braided rivers (e.g., Miall, 1977;

Rust, 1978b, 1979; Steel and Thompson, 1983), as well as for meandering streams with coarse sand and fine gravel loads (e.g., McGowen and Garner, 1970; Bridge and Jarvis, 1976; Jackson, 1976; Nijman and Puigdefá-bregas, 1978). In contrast, works on true gravel-bed meandering rivers remained scarce (Gustavson, 1978; Jackson, 1978; Ori, 1982; Arche, 1983; Forbes, 1983; Massari, 1983). At that time, alluvial facies models were mostly based on the vertical channel-fill sequences associated with the different stream patterns. However, several researchers showed that it is often impossible to distinguish between ancient meandering and braided channel fills from mostly vertical observations and that extensive and 3-D outcrop descriptions must be used instead (Jackson, 1978; Eynon and Walker, 1974; Miall, 1980; Bridge, 1985). Consequently, the use of vertical sedimentary profiles to recognize former meandering and braided streams was progressively abandoned.

The most useful approach to differentiate the various channel fill types is now the architectural element approach. An architectural element is defined as a discrete body of sediments with distinctive facies assemblages, facies geometries, paleocurrent directions, and bounding surfaces, with an emphasis on their 3-D architecture (Allen, 1983; Miall, 1985, 1988, 1996). Genetically, it corresponds to a morphosedimentary unit from a specific depositional environment. In strati-graphic successions, architectural elements of different sizes are all fit together into a hierarchy of sediment bodies of different scales, with each body bound by bedding contacts of various extents, duration, and origin.

Allen (1983) and Ramos and Sopeña (1983) were the first to divide alluvial sediments into architectural elements, thanks to detailed work on large outcrops of ancient sandy and gravelly deposits, respectively. Then, in the late 1980s and early 1990s, Miall (1985, 1988, 1996) asserted general bases to identify architectural elements within alluvial deposits. According to him, only a limited number of basic architectural elements exist (e.g., lateral and downstream accretion bars, thal-weg fills, floodplain deposits) within alluvial systems, regardless of their channel pattern, but these elements combine in different ways depending on the organization and dynamics of the rivers. Thereby, the criterion to determine a channel pattern becomes the manner in which the basic elements are assembled. However, the architectural element approach is more demanding than traditional facies methods. To distinguish the elements and produce reliable palaeoenvironmental reconstruc-tions, it is necessary to work on large exposures, have 3-D controls and acquire plenty of data. Detailed palaeocur-rent analyses are also important to compare the direction of sediment accretion within the architectural elements representing bars and the main orientation of the flow.

Based on previous works, Miall (1985, 1996) illus-trated typical arrangements of architectural elements for several types of stream. He proposed that the channel fill of gravel-bed meandering streams is characterized by gravelly unit bars and gravelly compound bars corre-sponding to point bars that grow mostly by lateral accretion. Conversely, the channel fill of gravel-bed braided rivers would more likely be primarily composed of gravelly unit bars and compound bars that grow mainly by downstream accretion. Within braided chan-nels, point bars can also form associated with the lateral shifting of thalwegs, but they are less numerous than downstream accreting bars. In braided stream sediments, it is also possible to observe thalweg and bar deposits on a larger-scale range than within meandering channel fills (Williams and Rust, 1969; Bristow, 1987; Bridge and Lunt, 2006). Additionally, confluence scours and fills seem to be important architectural elements of braided alluvia (Huggenberger, 1993; Siegenthaler and Huggenberger, 1993).

Despite subsequent discussions (e.g., Brierley and Hickin, 1991; Bridge, 1993, 1995; Miall, 1995), the architectural element approach was widely used to ana-lyse outcrops of ancient gravel-bed stream deposits (e.g., Ramos and Sopeña, 1983; Smith, 1990; DeCelles et al., 1991; Jones et al., 2001). Nevertheless, calibra-tions of the characteristics of architectural elements in modern rivers are needed to help recognize and interpret them in ancient sediments. Yet, in the early 1990s, Smith (1990) noticed that relatively little was known about the structure and dynamics of bars existing in gravel-bed rivers. To fill this gap, many recent studies have focused on the architecture of present-day river bars using aerial and satellite images, topographic surveys, ground-penetrating radar profiles, and core and trench observations (for an outline, see Bridge, 2003; Bridge and Lunt, 2006). However, still relatively few have concentrated on gravel-bed streams (Leclerc and Hickin, 1997; Lunt et al., 2004; Lunt and Bridge, 2004; Wooldridge and Hickin, 2005; Rice et al., 2009). Fur-thermore, these modern works are carried out at the scale of only one or two compound bars, presumably because they are the emergent and accessible places in active channels. The solution to characterize the architecture of whole channels could be studies on frozen river beds or recent channel fills (e.g., Lunt et al., 2004; Lunt and Bridge, 2004; Bersezio et al., 2007; Kostic and Aigner, 2007; Hickin et al., 2009). However, no quan-titative studies have yet been performed on the architec-tural characteristics proposed as diagnostic criteria for channel patterns (e.g., proportion of lateral versus down-stream accretion within channel fills, scale range for embedded thalweg fills and bars, relative amount of preserved deep and shallow deposits). Finally, the works carried out on active streams all deal with deposition over a few decades at the maximum and the problem of sediment preservation over longer time scales remains unresolved.

### 34.6.1.2 Grain Size

Since the 1970s, the number of studies on gravel-bed streams has continually been growing. However, most of the facies models proposed for gravel-bed meandering rivers are based on present-day (e.g., Gustavson, 1978; Jackson, 1978; Arche, 1983; Forbes, 1983; Brierley, 1989, 1991; Smith, 1989; Leclerc and Hickin, 1997) and Quaternary (Maizels, 1983; Campbell and Hendry, 1987; Bersezio et al., 2007; Kostic and Aigner, 2007) channel fills with their planform still visible at the Earth's surface. As far as we know, only two cases of older streams (one Pliocene and one Miocene) were recognized as gravel-bed meandering rivers (Ori, 1982; Massari, 1983; Massari et al., 1993). One may thus wonder why so few rivers of this type are described from stratigraphic records.

As discussed above, it is difficult to unambiguously differentiate meandering and braided channel fills without a detailed analysis of the deposit architecture and palaeocurrents on extensive 3-D outcrops. In addition, with Schumm's classifications in mind, sedimentologists naturally associated gravelly sediments with braided streams (e.g., see Orton and Reading, 1993; Galloway and Hobday, 1996). Similarly, they perceived meandering rivers as mixed-load streams, which typically transport sand and finer sediments. Thus, it can be imagined that some ancient gravels interpreted as braided channel fills were in fact meandering ones.

Nevertheless, the few gravelly meandering channel fills described in the stratigraphic record could also result from either a low occurrence in the past or a low preservation potential in the sedimentary series. Indeed, it is possible that the preservation potential of these rivers is limited because they do not carry much bedload (see Section 34.4.3). Because of this moderate bedload transport, gravel-bed meandering streams are possibly not aggradational rivers and the chance that their deposits are preserved over geologic time scales is much less than their braided counterparts, which form most of the large valley fills and alluvial fans in nearby mountain ranges.

### 34.6.2 Quantitative Palaeohydraulic Reconstructions

Beyond qualitative palaeoenvironmental reconstructions, researchers have also tried extracting quantitative information on ancient streams from their sediments. Palaeohydraulics is thus a discipline that attempts to determine quantitative data linked to hydraulic parameters of former rivers (such as depth, width, width–depth ratio, sinuosity, slope, discharge, sediment supply, etc.) from measurements made on their preserved deposits. A qualitative reconstruction of the stream pattern is usually needed before any reliable quantitative palaeohydraulic analysis. Depending on the observable sediment features, different approaches were then used to reconstruct the geometrical and hydrological characteristics of palaeochannels.

For gravel-bed rivers, the most common approach is based on the principles of sediment transport mechanics. It uses the empirical or theoretical relationships established between the sediment grain size and critical flow conditions necessary to initiate bedload motion (see Church and Gilbert, 1975; Costa, 1983; Williams, 1984, 1988; Maizels, 1989). Workers who attempted palaeohydrological quantifications with this approach suggested that these relations can be used to estimate critical velocities or shear stresses for sediment entrainment from measurements of the gravel size. These measurements can be taken even when the individual bar and channel deposits of ancient gravel-bed rivers are poorly identifiable. However, the local sedimentary structures or regional gradients can be clear enough to allow the assessment of additional parameters such as flow depth or valley slope. Flow depth is usually derived from the size of sedimentary structures produced by the formation and migration of bedforms such as bars or dunes (e.g., Jopling, 1966; Paola and Borgman, 1991; Leclair and Bridge, 2001). The slope is usually derived from terrace gradients. The grain size, together with the depth or slope, is then used to infer the missing parameter at the threshold of motion. Once these three parameters are assessed, some studies then calculate the palaeovelocities and unit discharges. Finally, if the former channels are still visible at the Earth's surface or if their width can be measured by another means, their discharge can be also estimated. With this methodology, palaeohydraulic reconstructions have been performed for present-day floods (Bradley and Mears, 1980; Costa, 1983; Mack et al., 2008), as well as for ancient gravel-bed channels lying on recent terraces (e.g., Birkland, 1968; Malde, 1968; Baker, 1973, 1974; Church, 1978; Maizels, 1983; Ryder and Church, 1986; O'Connor and Baker, 1992) or in valley and basin fills (Allen and Mange-Rajetzky, 1982; Goodwin and Diffendal, 1987; Heller and Paola, 1989; Evans, 1991; Jones and Frostick, 2008; Davidson and Hartley, 2010). One can mention also that Jones and Frostick (2008) recently coupled a study of this kind with a volumetric analysis of gravel bar deposits to assess ancient bedload transport rates.

However, this first approach has limitations. First, there are inherent problems associated with uncertainties in measurements of grain-size distributions, palaeo-depths, and palaeoslopes. Second, this approach assesses instantaneous palaeoflow conditions only from the sediment units sampled, the overall long-term significance of which is hard to judge. The forecast instantaneous conditions are often peak velocities, depths, and discharges, which can be very difficult to relate to the average or bankfull behaviour of the corresponding streams. In addition, flood recurrence intervals most often remain unknown. Consequently, even if reasonable first-order palaeohydrological reconstructions seem possible based on critical motion theories (see Baker and Ritter, 1975; Bridge, 1981; Church et al., 1990; Paola and Mohrrig, 1996), workers must not forget that they are order-of-magnitude exercises (see Church, 1978; Ryder and Church, 1986).

This first approach can be coupled with a second one based on the hydraulic geometry concept (see Section 34.4). It uses the empirical relations established between the channel morphology and controlling factors of some present-day rivers (see Ethridge and Schumm, 1978; Gardner, 1983; Williams, 1984, 1988). Researchers who performed the earliest attempts at palaeohydraulic reconstructions proposed that these semi-empirical relationships can be extrapolated to ancient streams (Dury, 1965; Moody-Stuart, 1966; Schumm, 1968a, 1972; Cotter, 1971). Accordingly, they used these relations to estimate the hydrological characteristics of palaeochannels where one or several of their original dimensions can be identified and measured in map views or cross-sections at the Earth's surface or within stratigraphic successions. From these measurements, parameters such as channel width, depth, cross-sectional area, meander wavelength, or sinuosity can be estimated. These can then be put into the equations established for river morphology and hydrology to calculate width, meander wavelength, or sinuosity (if they cannot be observed), as well as values for mean annual and mean annual flood discharges, channel and valley slopes, mean flow velocities, drainage areas, or stream lengths. This methodology is useful as it deals with the long-term, statistical averages of hydraulic parameters.

However, this approach has mostly been used to perform palaeohydraulic reconstructions for sand-bed streams (e.g., Dury, 1965; Moody-Stuart, 1966; Cotter, 1971; Schumm, 1972; Leeder, 1973; Sylvia and Galloway, 2006), but rarely for gravel-bed rivers (Steer and Abbott, 1984; Eriksson et al., 2006; Davidson and Hartley, 2010). Moreover, like the first palaeohydraulic methodology, it has significant limitations. First, it is not always easy to recognize and measure true individual fills of channels that were active at a single time from the sedimentary series. Furthermore, most palaeohydraulic studies based on hydraulic geometry relations use empirical equations calibrated on specific rivers, which are not necessarily representative of present-day streams around the world, nor of the ancient rivers that have constructed stratigraphic successions. Finally, substituting certain variables (e.g., maximum depth instead of mean depth) or applying equations developed for one system to another one (e.g., relations developed for sand-bed, single-thread or straight streams used for palaeohydraulic reconstructions of finer- and coarser-grained, braided or sinuous channels) can also result in significant errors. Any future improvements to the completeness and consistency of the database on which hydraulic geometry relations are based would therefore make the derived palaeohydraulic reconstructions more efficient.

Using a third approach, Robertson-Rintoul and Richards (1993) proposed that channel planform features are better palaeohydraulic proxies than cross-sectional ones. They determined a braiding intensity index corresponding to the mean density/mean length ratio of threads for channels still visible at terrace surfaces. Using this parameter, along with terrace slopes and grain sizes, they calculated the former mean annual flood discharges. However, this methodology cannot be applied without map views of the ancient rivers. Moreover, even on recent terraces, it is difficult to recognize and measure the threads active at a single time.

While results from palaeohydraulic works performed for sand-bed streams have occasionally been homogenized and compiled (Leeder, 1973; Ethridge and Schumm, 1978), this has not been done for gravel-bed rivers. Even if these estimates only have a first-order value, it would be interesting to compile them in order to compare databases for present-day and ancient channel features. The problem is that palaeohydraulic reconstructions performed for gravel-bed streams lack consistency in how the basic input variables are quantified. For example, although it is often used as a major input parameter, there is no consensus on how to characterize the grain size (e.g., diameter of the largest clast, mean of the diameters of the 10 or 25 largest clasts, $D_{50}$, $D_{84}$, $D_{90}$, or $D_{95}$ of granulometric distributions determined by random counting or sieving). Hence, compiling existing palaeohydraulic data for gravel-bed channels is a difficult task. In fact, it might be necessary to adopt common measurement and assessment procedures before it can be done.

### 34.6.3 Gravel-Bed Channel Metamorphosis

Within stratigraphic successions, many changes in stream patterns from meandering to braided or vice versa have been documented (e.g., Fisk, 1947; Nami and Leeder, 1978; Maizels, 1983; Miall, 1984; Fielding et al., 1993; Ward et al., 2000; Kostic and Aigner, 2007).

However, most of these works concern the metamorphosis of sand-bed channels. Only two studies mention changes of gravel-bed rivers from one pattern to another (Maizels, 1983; Kostic and Aigner, 2007). Furthermore, these changes are not simple channel pattern transformations as they are associated with changes in stream behaviour from aggradation to incision, or vice versa. In fact, the simple metamorphoses involving gravel-bed channels are more often associated with grain-size changes. Indeed, transitions between gravel-bed braided streams and sand-bed meandering streams, with or without sand-bed braided transitional stages, are commonly observed within stratigraphic successions (e.g., Fisk, 1947; Miall, 1984; Huisink, 1997; Nakayama and Ulak, 1999).

In any case, the reasons proposed for such metamorphoses are usually the same, irrespective of the grain size. Workers associate the transformations between braided and meandering streams with modifications in water discharge, sediment supply (amount and grain size), or slope brought on by climatic changes, tectonic uplifts, or sea level rises and falls. They also evoke the influence of terrestrial plants with well-developed root systems (e.g., Schumm, 1968b; Cotter, 1978; Long, 1978; Huisink, 1997; Ward *et al.*, 2000). However, case studies that attempt to quantify the palaeohydraulic factors that change during channel metamorphosis remain scarce (Maizels, 1983).

# 34.7 DISCUSSION AND CONCLUDING REMARKS

We would like to summarize and briefly discuss the problems we have identified from our review of the literature which we believe call for further research in the near future. These fall into three main categories: (i) theoretical approaches; (ii) data acquisition, particularly database development and, more specifically, the problems posed by gravel-bed rivers; (iii) meandering streams.

## 34.7.1  Concepts and Theory

From a theoretical point of view, it seems clear that many major advances have been made since Lane's statement in 1955. Research on bank stability and erosion has led to many advances and we are now in the process of fully integrating vegetation as a component of the physical description of river banks.

Fluid mechanics has been an essential tool in understanding the importance of the shear stress distribution across the flow section and in defining conditions of stability in rivers. There is still much debate among researchers on the conditions that define hydraulic geometry and it probably stems from two main points. First, we still lack a clear understanding of what sets the width of a stream. Second, because boundary fluxes are almost never measured, bedload is considered a dependent variable, although, as nicely stated by Mackin (1948), the river does not decide what bedload it can carry, but rather adapts to carry the imposed load.

In the domain of qualitative palaeoenvironmental reconstructions, the proposed diagnostic criteria to discriminate between deposits of meandering and braided palaeochannels (e.g., ratio of lateral versus downstream accretion, scale ranges of embedded thalweg fills and bars, relative amount of deep and shallow deposits preserved) which have left no visible traces in plan view, still need validation from studies on present gravel-bed and sand-bed rivers. However, if these conceptual advances still lack confirmation through well-defined case studies, it is often because of practical problems of accessibility to whole active reaches occupied by the flow. To get around such a problem, studies on frozen river beds or on recent channel fills seem to be promising.

## 34.7.2  Databases: When Harmony Rules the World

It is the opinion of the authors that databases are the most compelling and urgent problem that the community has to tackle in the near future. For hydraulic geometry and channel pattern, all model tests and applications rely on data that were acquired more than 20 years ago. The van den Berg compendium is not an exception as most of the "new" rivers come from a personal communication from M.P. Mosley. Field surveys have been performed, but are very difficult to find. In recent years, surveys like the ones performed by Ryan and Emmett (2002), McCandless and Everett (2002), McCandless (2003), and King *et al.* (2004) in Wyoming, Maryland, and Idaho should have reached a much wider audience. Reports are often hard to find. The compendium of Parker *et al.* (2007) is a welcome effort, but it does not retain the original data sets in their entirety and it includes references that do not always link to the data, but rather to articles that mention the data. It is the responsibility of journal editors to require that data sets be made available as electronic supplemental material. As a community, it is up to us to define a consistent set of parameters that we then hold ourselves responsible to measure each time we survey a new stream, and to make these data widely available.

From a simple examination of existing databases, it is clear that we lack data on large gravel-bed meandering streams, small braided streams, fine gravel streams, and bedload fluxes. As previously mentioned, until we acknowledge that bedload is not a dependant variable, but an imposed boundary condition, hydraulic geometry relations will be biased because they do not take into account the variable that likely exerts a first-order control on channel pattern. For the same reason, data sets including information on bank strength and vegetation-added strength are urgently needed for a wide range of streams.

As for ancient gravel-bed systems, we lack everything. How can we discuss the existence and form of pristine streams in temperate countries if we do not even know what the channel planforms were during the Quaternary and before humankind? The only databases that report palaeochannel dimensions and potential palaeohydraulic parameters were compiled for sand-bedded streams. At present, as far as we know, there are only a few tens of quantitative studies performed on deposits of ancient gravel-bed streams and they are neither homogenized nor homogenizeable. Finally, trying to harmonize data scattered amongst tens or more articles is a painful experience. Each of us should try to produce one line of normalized information for each new river remains that we study in order to fill in existing data sets.

### 34.7.3   Are Gravel-Bed Meanders Pristine?

In 1963, Schumm made a small comment (see 1963, p.7) regarding small meandering gravel-bed streams in mountain meadows that should be suspended-load channels yet have coarse channel beds. His conclusion was that they are remnants of periods of higher discharge and that the load was not moving most of the time. More recently, Walter and Merritts (2008) even argued that the meandering gravel-bed streams of Pennsylvania, Delaware, and Maryland were not natural, but the result of human pertubation of previously anabranching channels and wetlands.

A review of the stratigraphic literature leads to a converging picture. There are very few gravel-bed meandering channels described within sedimentary series. Several reasons for this have been put forward.

First, it is difficult to unambiguously differentiate between a meandering and a braided channel in the stratigraphic record because this requires extensive 3-D outcrops and detailed analysis on deposit architecture and palaeocurrents.

Second, it is possible that very few deposits of gravel-bed meandering streams are preserved because analysis of the literature persistently leads to the conclusion that these rivers do not carry much bedload. Bedload movement would essentially correspond to internal reworking that maintains dynamic meandering by erosion on outer banks and deposition on downstream bars. Thus, gravel-bed meandering streams seem not to be aggrading rivers and therefore their preservation potential in the geologic record is much less than their braided counterparts, which form most of the large alluvial fans at the piedmonts of mountain ranges.

Third, once again after Schumm, it seems that meandering development is related to the development of vegetation. No meandering streams are recorded before Silurian times, which is when vegetation with well-developed root systems appeared on Earth.

Let us then finish this review by recalling one of the limitations of our work that needs further investigation. We did not go through the literature concerning wandering streams. It may be therefore necessary to look more carefully at these streams as they could represent the natural form of active gravel-bed sinuous streams in vegetated floodplains.

## 34.8   ACKNOWLEDGEMENTS

We are indebted to Michal Tal, Mike Church, and John Pitlick for their patience in reviewing the first draft of the document and their encouragement. Acknowledgments are also due to Sara Mullin for her editorial assistance that helped us to improve the language quality of this article. This research was funded by grant ANR-09-RISK-004/GESTRANS to F. Métivier.

## 34.9   REFERENCES

Abernethy, B. and Rutherfurd, I.D. 2000. The effect of riparian tree roots on the mass-stability of riverbanks. *Earth Surface Processes and Landforms* 25: 921–937.

Abernethy, B. and Rutherfurd, I.D. 2001. The distribution and strength of riparian tree roots in relation to riverbank reinforcement. *Hydrological Processes* 15: 63–79.

Allen, J.R.L. 1983. Studies in fluviatile sedimentation: bars, bar-complexes and sandstone sheets (low-sinuosity braided streams) in the Brownstones (Lower Devonian), Welsh Borders. *Sedimentary Geology* 33: 237–293.

Allen, P.A. and Mange-Rajetzky, M. 1982. Sediment dispersal and paleohydraulics of Oligocene rivers in the eastern Ebro Basin. *Sedimentology* 29: 705–716.

Andrews, E.D. 1984. Bed-material entrainment and hydraulic geometry of gravel-bed rivers in Colorado. *Geological Society of America Bulletin* 95: 371–378.

Andrews, E.D. 1994. Marginal bed load transport in a gravel bed stream, Sagehen Creek, California. *Water Resources Research* 30: 2241–2250.

Arche, A. 1983. Coarse-grained meander lobe deposits in the Jarama River, Madrid, Spain. In Collinson, J.D. and Lewin, J., editors. *Modern and ancient fluvial systems*. International Association of Sedimentologists, *Special Publication* 6: 313–321.

Ashworth, P.J., Freguson, R.I., Ashmore, P.E. *et al.* 1992. Measurements in a braided river chute and lobe 2. Sorting of bed load during entrainment, transport and deposition. *Water Resources Research* 28: 1887–1896.

Baker, V.R. 1973. *Paleohydrology and Sedimentology of Lake Missoula Flooding in Eastern Washington*. Geological Society of America, Special Paper 144.

Baker, V.R. 1974. Paleohydraulic interpretation of Quaternary alluvium near Golden, Colorado. *Quaternary Research* 4: 94–112.

Baker, V.R. and Ritter, D.F. 1975. Competence of rivers to transport coarse bedload material. *Geological Society of America Bulletin* **86**: 975–978.

Bersezio, R., Giudici, M. and Mele, M. 2007. Combining sedimentological and geophysical data for high-resolution 3-D mapping of fluvial architectural elements in the Quaternary Po Plain (Italy). *Sedimentary Geology* **202**: 230–248.

Birkland, P.W. 1968. Mean velocities and boulder tranport during Tahoe-Age floods of the Truckee River, California-Nevada. *Geological Society of America Bulletin* **79**: 137–142.

Blizard, C. and Wohl, E.E. 1998. Relationships between hydraulic variables and bedload transport in a subalpine channel, Colorado Rocky Mountains, U.S.A. *Geomorphology* **22**: 359–371.

Bradley, W.C. and Mears, A.I. 1980. Calculations of flow needed to transport the coarse fraction of Boulder Creek alluvium at boulder, Colorado: Summary. *Geological Society of America Bulletin* **91**: 135–138.

Brice, J.C. 1975. *Air Photo Interpretation of the Form and Behavior of Alluvial Rivers*. Final Report to the United States Army Research Office, Washington, DC. Accession number AD008108.

Bridge, J.S. 1981. Hydraulic interpretation of grain-size distribution using a physical model for bedload transport. *Journal of Sedimentary Petrology* **51**: 1109–1124.

Bridge, J.S. 1985. Paleochannel patterns inferred from alluvial deposits: a critical evaluation. *Journal of Sedimentary Petrology* **55**: 579–589.

Bridge, J.S. 1993. Description and interpretation of fluvial deposits: a critical perspective. *Sedimentology* **40**: 801–810.

Bridge, J.S. 1995. Description and interpretation of fluvial deposits: a critical perspective: reply. *Sedimentology* **42**: 384–389.

Bridge, J.S. 2003. *Rivers and Floodplains*. Oxford, Blackwell.

Bridge, J.S. and Jarvis, J. 1976. Flow and sedimentary processes in the meandering River South Esk, Glen Clova, Scotland. *Earth Surface Processes and Landforms* **1**: 303–336.

Bridge, J.S. and Lunt, I.A. 2006. Depositional models of braided rivers. In Sambrook Smith, G.H., Best, J.L., Bristow, C.S. and Petts, G., editors. *Braided Rivers: Process, Deposits, Ecology and Management*. International Association of Sedimentologists, Special Publication 36, pp. 11–50.

Brierley, G.J. 1989. River planform facies models: the sedimentology of braided, wandering and meandering reaches of the Squamish River, British Columbia. *Sedimentary Geology* **61**: 17–35.

Brierley, G.J. 1991. Bar sedimentology of the Squamish river, British Columbia: definition and application of morphostratigraphic units. *Journal of Sedimentary Petrology* **61**: 211–225.

Brierley, G.J. and Hickin, E.J., 1991. Channel planform as a non-controlling factor in fluvial sedimentology: The case of the Squamish River floodplain, British Columbia. *Sedimentary Geology* **75**: 67–83.

Bristow, C.S. 1987. Brahmaputra river: channel migration and deposition. In Ethridge, F.G., Flores, R.M. and Harvey, M.D., editors. *Recent Developments in Fluvial Sedimentology*. Socíety of Economic Palcontologists and Mineralogists, Special Publication 39, pp. 63–74.

Brownlie, W.R. 1981. *Compilation of Alluvial Channel Data: Laboratory and field*. W.M. Keck Laboratory of Hydraulics and Water Resources, California Intitute of Technology, Pasadena, CA, Technical Report KH-R-43B.

Campbell, J.E. and Hendry, H.E. 1987. Anatomy of a gravelly meander lobe in the Saskatchewan River, near Nipawin, Canada. In Ethridge, F.G., Flores, R.M. and Harvey, M.D., editors. *Recent developments in fluvial sedimentology*. Society of Economic Paleontologists and Mineralogists, *Special Publication* **39**: 179–189.

Carson, M.A. 1984. The meandering-braided river threshold: a reappraisal. *Journal of Hydrology* **73**: 315–334.

Church, M. 1978. Paleohydrological reconstructions from a Holocene valley fill. In Miall, A.D., editor. *Fluvial Sedimentology*. Canadian Society of Petroleum Geologists, Memoir 5, pp. 743–772.

Church, M. 2006. Bed material transport and the morphology of alluvial river channels. *Annual Review of Earth and Planetary Sciences* **34**: 325–354.

Church, M. and Gilbert, R. 1975. Proglacial fluvial and lacustrine environments. In Jopling, A.V. and McDonald, B.C., editors. *Glaciofluvial and Glaciolacustrine Sedimentation*. Society of Economic Paleontologists and Mineralogists, Special Publication 23, pp. 22–100.

Church, M. and Rood, K. 1983. *Catalogue of Alluvial River Channel Regime Data*. The University of British Columbia, Department of Geography, Vancouver.

Church, M., Wolcott, J., and Maizels, J.K., 1990. Paleovelocity: A parsimonious proposal. *Earth Surface Processes and Landforms* **15**: 475–480.

Constantine, C.R., Dunne, T. and Hanson, G.J. 2009. Examining the physical meaning of the bank erosion coefficient used in meander migration modeling. *Geomorphology* **106**: 242–252.

Costa, J.E. 1983. Paleohydraulic reconstruction of flash-flood peaks from boulder deposits in the Colorado Front Range. *Geological Society of America Bulletin* **94**: 986–1004.

Cotter, E. 1971. Paleoflow characteristics of a late cretaceous river in Utha from analysis of sedimentary structures in the Ferron Sandstone. *Journal of Sedimentary Petrology* **41**: 129–138.

Cotter, E. 1978. The evolution of fluvial style, with special reference to the central Appalachian Paleozoic. In Miall, A. D., editor. *Fluvial Sedimentology*. Canadian Society of Petroleum Geologists, Memoir 5, pp. 361–383.

Darby, S.E., Gessler, D., and Thorne, C.R., 2000. Technical communications: computer program for stability analysis of steep, cohesive riverbanks. *Earth Surface Processes and Landforms* **25**: 175–190.

Darby, S.E., Rinaldi, M., and Dapporto, S. 2007. Coupled simulations of fluvial erosion and mass wasting for cohesive river banks. *Journal of Geophysical Research-Earth Surface* **112**: F03022. doi: 10.1029/2006JF000722.

Davidson, S.K. and Hartley, A.J. 2010. Towards a quantitative method for estimating paleohydrology from clast size and comparison with modern rivers. *Journal of Sedimentary Research* **80**; 688–702. http://jsedres.sepmonline.org/cgi/content/abstract/80/7/688.

De Baets, S., Poesen, J., Reubens, B. *et al.* 2008. Root tensile strength and root distribution of typical Mediterranean plant species and their contribution to soil shear strength. *Plant and Soil* **305**: 207–226.

DeCelles, P.G., Gray, M.B., Ridgway, R.B. *et al.* 1991. Controls on synorogenic alluvial-fan architecture, Beartooth Conglomerate (Palaeocene), Wyoming and Montana. *Sedimentology* **38**: 567–590.

Diplas, P. 1990. Characteristics of self-formed straight channels. *Journal of Hydraulic Engineering* **116**: 707–728.

Dury, G.H. 1965. *Theorical Impliations of Underfit Streams*. United States Geological Survey, Professional Paper 452C.

Eaton, B.C. 2006. Bank stability analysis for regime models of vegetated gravel bed rivers. *Earth Surface Processes and Landforms* **31**: 1438–1444.

Eaton, B.C., Church, M., and Millar, R.G. 2004. Rational regime model of alluvial channel morphology and response. *Earth Surface Processes and Landforms* **29**: 511–529.

Eaton, B.C. and Giles, T.R. 2009. Assessing the effect of vegetation-related bank strength on channel morphology and stability in gravel-bed streams using numerical models. *Earth Surface Processes and Landforms* **34**: 712–724.

El-Ramly, H., Morgenstern, N.R., and Cruden, D.M. 2002. Probabilistic slope stability analysis for practice. *Canadian Geotechnical Journal* **39**: 665–683.

Eriksson, P.G., Bumby, A.J., Brümer, J.J., and van der Neut, M. 2006. Precambrian fluvial deposits: enigmatic paleohydrological data from the c. 2-1.9 Ga Waterberg Group, South Africa. *Sedimentary Geology* **190**: 25–46.

Ethridge, F.G. and Schumm, S.A. 1978. Reconstructing paleo-channel morphologic and flow characteristics: methodology, limitations and assessement. In Miall, A.D., editor. *Fluvial Sedimentology*. Canadian Society of Petroleum Geologists, Memoir 5, pp. 703–719.

Evans, J. 1991. Facies relationships, alluvial architecture, and paleohydrology of Paleogene, humid-tropical alluvial-fan system: Chumstick Formation, Washington State, USA. *Journal of Sedimentary Petrology* **61**: 732–755.

Eynon, G. and Walker, R.G. 1974. Facies relationships in Pleistocene outwash gravels, southern Ontario: a model for bar growth in braided rivers. *Sedimentology* **21**: 43–70.

Fielding, C.R., Falkner, A.J., and Scott, S.G., 1993. Fluvial response to foreland basin overfilling; the late Permian Rangal coal measures in the Bowen basin, Queensland, Australia. *Sedimentary Geology* **85**: 475–497.

Fisk, H.N. 1947. *Fine-grained Alluvial Deposits and their Effect on Mississippi River Activity. Final Report*. United States Army Corps of Engineers, Mississippi River Commission, Vicksburg, MS. Accession number ADA950797.

Forbes, D.L., 1983. Morphology and sedimentology of a sinuous gravel-bed channel system: Lower Babbage river, Yukon coastal plain, Canada. In Collinson, J.D. and Lewin, J., editors. *Modern and Ancient Fuvial Systems*. International Association of Sedimentologists, Special Publication 6, 195–206.

Friend, P.F. and Sinha, R. 1993. Braiding and meandering parameters. In Best, J.L. and Bristow, C.S., editors. *Braided Rivers*. Geological Society (London), Special Publication 75, pp. 105–111.

Galloway, W.E. 1981. Depositional architecture of Cenozoic gulf coastal plain fluvial systems. In Ethridge, F.G. and Flores, R.M., editors. *Recent and Ancient Nonmarine Depositional Environments: Models for Exploration*. Society of Economic Paleontologists and Mineralogists, Special Publication 31, pp. 127–155.

Galloway, W.E. and Hobday, D.K. 1996. *Terrigenous Clastic Depositional Systems: Applications to Fossil Fuel and Groundwater Resources*. Berlin, Springer.

Garcia, M.H. 2008. Sediment transport and morphodynamics. In Garcia, M.H., editor. *Sedimentation Engineering: Processes, Management, Modeling, and Practice*. American Society of Civil Engineers, Manual of Practice 110, pp. 21–163.

Gardner, T.W. 1983. Paleohydrology and paleomorphology of a carboniferous, meandering, fluvial sandstone. *Journal of Sedimentary Petrology* **53**: 991–1005.

Goodwin, R.G. and Diffendal, R.F. 1987. Paleohydrology of some Ogallala (Nneogene) stream in the southern panhandle

of Nebraska. In Ethridge, F.G., Flores, R.M. and Harvey, M.D., editors. *Recent Developments in Fluvial Sedimentology*. Society of Economic Paleontologists and Mineralogists, Special Publication 39, pp. 149–157.

Gran, K. and Paola, C. 2001. Riparian vegetation controls on braided stream dynamics. *Water Resources Research* **37**: 3275–3283. doi: 10.1029/2000WR000203.

Gurnell, A.M., Piégay, H., Swanson, F.J., and Gregory, S.V., 2002. Large wood and fluvial processes. *Freshwater Biology* **47**: 601–619.

Gustavson, T.C. 1978. Bed forms and stratification types of modern gravel meander lobes, Nueces River, Texas. *Sedimentology* **25**: 401–426.

Hanson, G.J. and Cook, K. R. 2004. Apparatus, test procedures, and analytical methods to measure soil erodibility in situ. *Applied Engineering in Agriculture* **20**: 455–462.

Hanson, G.J. and Hunt, S.L. 2007. Lessons learned using laboratory jet method to measure soil erodibility of compacted soils. *Applied Engineering in Agriculture* **23**: 305–312.

Hanson, G.J. and Simon, A. 2001. Erodibility of cohesive streambeds in the loess area of the midwestern USA. *Hydrological Processes* **15**: 23–38.

Heller, P.L. and Paola, C. 1989. The paradox of lower Cretaceous gravels and the initiation of thrusting in the Servier orogenic belt, United States western interior. *Geological Society of America Bulletin* **101**: 864–875.

Hession, W.C., Pizzuto, J.E., Johnson, T.E., and Horwitz, R.J. 2003. Influence of bank vegetation on channel morphology in rural and urban watersheds. *Geology* **31**: 147–150.

Hey, R.D. and Thorne, C.R. 1986. Stable channels with mobile gravel beds. *Journal of Hydraulic Engineering* **112**: 671–689.

Hickin, A.S., Kerr, B., Barchyn, T.E., and Paulen, R.C. 2009. Using round-penetrating radar and capacity coupled resistivity to investigate 3-d fluvial architecture and grain-size distribution of a gravel floodplain in northeast British Columbia, Canada. *Journal of Sedimentary Research* **79**: 457–477.

Huang, H.Q. and Nanson, G.C. 1997. Vegetation and channel variation; a case study of four small streams in southeastern Australia. *Geomorphology* **18**: 237–249.

Huang, H.Q. and Nanson, G.C. 1998. The influence of bank strength on channel geometry: an integrated analysis of some observations. *Earth Surface Processes and Landforms* **23**: 865–876.

Huang, H.Q. and Warner, R.F. 1995. The multivariate controls of hydraulic geometry: a causal investigation in terms of boundary shear distribution. *Earth Surface Processes and Landforms* **20**: 115–130.

Huggenberger, P. 1993. Radar facies: recognition of facies patterns and heterogeneities within Pleistocene Rhine gravels, NE Switzerland. In Best, J.L. and Bristow, C.S., editors. *Braided Rivers*. Geological Society (London), Special Publication 75, pp. 163–176.

Huisink, M. 1997. Late-glacial sedimentological and morphological changes in lowland rivers in response to climatic change: the Maas, southern Netherlands. *Journal of Quaternary Science* **12**: 209–223.

Istanbulluoglu, E., Bras, R.L., Flores-Cervantes, H., and Tucker, G.E., 2005. Implications of bank failures and fluvial erosion for gully development: field observations and modeling. *Journal of Geophysical Research – Earth Surface* **110**: F01014. doi: 10.1029/2004JF000145.

Jackson, R.G. 1976. Depositional model of point bar in the lower Wabash River. *Journal of Sedimentary Petrology* **46**: 579–594.

Jackson, R.G. 1978. Preliminary evaluation of lithofacies models for meandering alluvial streams. In Miall, A.D., editor. *Fluvial Sedimentology*. Canadian Society of Petroleum Geologists, Memoir 5, pp. 543–576.

Jones, S.J. and Frostick, L.E. 2008. Inferring bedload transport from stratigraphic successions: examples from Cenozoic and Pleistocene rivers, south central Pyrenees, Spain. In Gallagher, K., Jones, S.J. and Wainwright, J., editors, *Landscape Evolution: Denudation, Climate and Tectonics over Different Time and Space Scales*. Geological Society (London), Special Publication 296, pp. 129–145.

Jones, S.J., Frostick, L.E., and Astin, T. R. 2001. Braided stream and flood plain architecture: the Rio Vero Formation, Spanish Pyrenees. *Sedimentary Geology* **139**: 229–260.

Jopling, A.V. 1966. Some principles and techniques used in reconstructing the hydraulic parameters of paleo-flow regime. *Journal of Sedimentary Petrology* **36**: 5–49.

Kean, J.W. and Smith, J.D. 2005. Generation and verification of theoretical rating curves in the Whitewater River basin, Kansas. *Journal of Geophysical Research* **110**: F04012. doi: 10.1029/2004JF000250.

King, J.G., Emmett, W.W., Whiting, P.J., Kenworthy, R.P., and Barry, J.J. 2004. *Sediment Transport Data and Related Information for Selected Coarse-Bed Streams and Rivers in Idaho*. United States Department of Agriculture, Forest Service, Rocky Mountain Research Station, Fort Collins, CO, General Technical Report RMRS-GTR-131.

Knight, D.W. 1981. Boundary shear in smooth and rough channels. American Society of Civil Engineers, *Journal of the Hydraulics Division* **107**: 839–851.

Kostic, B. and Aigner, T. 2007. Sedimentary architecture and 3-d ground-penetrating radar analysis of gravelly meandering river deposits (Neckar valley, SW Germany). *Sedimentology* **54**: 789–808.

Lane, E.W. 1937. Stable channels in erodible material. *Transactions of the American Society of Civil Engineers* **102**: 123–142.

Lane, E.W. 1955. The importance of fluvial morphology in hydraulic engineering. *American Society of Civil Engineers Proceedings* **81**(745), 1–17.

Lane, E.W. 1957. *A Study of the Shape of Channels Formed by Natural Streams flowing in Erodible Material*. United States Army Corps of Engineers, Missouri River Division, Omaha, NB, Missoouri River Division Sediment Series 9.

Leclair, S.F. and Bridge, J.S. 2001. Quantitative interpretation of sedimentary structures formed by river dunes. *Journal of Sedimentary Research* **71**: 713–716.

Leclerc, R.F. and Hickin, E.J., 1997. The internal structure of scrolled floodplain deposits based on ground-penetrating radar, North Thompson River, British Columbia. *Geomorphology* **21**: 17–38.

Leeder, M.R. 1973. Fluvial fining-upwards cycles and the magnitude of paleochannels. *Geological Magazine* **110**: 265–276.

Leopold, L.B. and Maddock, T. J., Jr 1953. *The Hydraulic Geometry of Stream Channels and some Physiographic Implications*. United States Geological Survey, Professional Paper 252.

Leopold, L.B. and Wolman, M.G. 1957. *River Channel Patterns: Braided, Meandering and Straight*. United States Geological Survey, Professional Paper 282-B.

Lewin, J. and Brewer, P.A., 2001. Predicting channel patterns. *Geomorphology* **40**: 329–339.

Liu, Y., Métivier, F., Lajeunesse, E. *et al.* 2008. Measuring bed load in gravel-bed mountain rivers: averaging methods and sampling strategies. *Geodinamica Acta* **21**: 81–92.

Long, D.G. 1978. Proterozoic stream deposits: some problems of recognition and interpretation of ancient sandy fluvial systems. In Miall, A.D., editor. *Fluvial Sedimentology*. Canadian Society of Petroleum Geologists, Memoir 5, pp. 313–341.

Lunt, I.A. and Bridge, J.S. 2004. Evolution and deposits of a gravelly braid bar, Sagavanirktok River, Alaska. *Sedimentology* **51**: 415–432.

Lunt, I.A., Bridge, J.S., and Tye, R. S. 2004. A quantitative, three-dimentional model of gravelly braided rivers. *Sedimentology* **51**: 377–414.

Luppi, L., Rinaldi, M., Teruggi, L.B., Darby, S.E., and Nardi, L. 2009. Monitoring and numerical modelling of riverbank erosion processes: a case study along the Cecina River (central Italy). *Earth Surface Processes and Landforms* **34**: 530–546.

Mack, G.H., Leeder, M.R., and Carothers-Durr, M. 2008. Modern flood deposition, erosion and fan-channel avulsion on the semiarid Red Canyon and Palomas Canyon alluvial fans in the southern Rio Grande rift, New Mexico, U.S.A. *Journal of Sedimentary Research* **78**: 432–442.

Mackin, J.H. 1948. Concept of the graded river. *Geological Society of America Bulletin* **59**: 463–512.

Maizels, J. 1989. Sedimentology, paleoflow dynamics and flood history of jökulhlaup deposits: paleohydrology of Holocene sediment sequences in southern Iceland sandur deposits. *Journal of Sedimentary Petrology* **59**: 204–223.

Maizels, J.K. 1983. Proglacial channel systems: change and thresholds for change over long, intermediate and short timescales. In Collinson, J.D. and Lewin, J., editors. *Modern and Ancient Fluvial Systems*. International Association of Sedimentologists, Special Publication 6, pp. 251–266.

Malde, H.E. 1968. *The Catastrophic Late Pleistocene Bonneville Flood in the Snake River Plain, Idaho*. United States Geological Survey, Professional Paper 596.

Massari, F. 1983. Tabular cross-bedding in Messinian fluvial channel conglomerates, southern Alps, Italy. In Collinson, J. D. and Lewin, J., editors. *Modern and Ancient Fluvial Systems*. International Association of Sedimentologists, Special Publication 6, pp. 287–300.

Massari, F., Mellere, D., and Doglioni, C. 1993. Cyclicity in non-marine foreland-basin sedimentary fill: The Messinian conglomerate-bearing succession of the Venetian Alps (Italy). In Marzo, M. and Puigdefábregas, C., editors. *Alluvial Sedimentation*. International Association of Sedimentologists, Special Publication 17, pp. 501–520.

McCandless, T.L. 2003. *Maryland Stream Survey: Bankfull Discharge and Channel Characteristics of Streams in the Coastal Plain Hydrologic Region*. United States Department of the Interior, Fish and Wildlife Service, Chesapeake Bay Field Office, Report CBFO-SO2-01.

McCandless, T.L. and Everett, R.A. 2002. *Maryland Stream Survey: Bankfull Discharge and Channel Characteristics of Streams in the Piedmont Hydrologic Region*. United States Fish and Wildlife Service, Chesapeake Bay Field Office, Technical Report CBFO-S03-01.

McGowen, J.H. and Garner, L.E. 1970. Physiographic features and stratification types of coarse-grained point bars: modern and ancient examples. *Sedimentology* **14**: 77–111.

Merigliano, M.F. 1997. Hydraulic geometry and stream channel behavior: an uncertain link 1. *Journal of the American Water Resources Association* **33**: 1327–1336.

Meunier, P., Métivier, F., Lajeunesse, E., Meriaux, A.S., and Faure, J. 2006. Flow pattern and sediment transport in a braided river: the Torrent de St Pierre (French Alps). *Journal of Hydrology* **330**: 496–505.

Miall, A.D. 1977. A review of the braided river depositional environment. *Earth Science Reviews* **13**: 1–62.

Miall, A.D. 1980. Cyclicity and the facies model concept in fluvial deposits. *Bulletin of Canadian Petroleum Geology* **28**: 59–80.

Miall, A.D. 1984. Variations in fluvial style in the lower Cenozoic synorogenic sediments of the Canadian arctic islands. *Sedimentary Geology* **38**: 499–523.

Miall, A.D. 1985. Architectural-element analysis: a new method of facies analysis applied to fluvial deposits. *Earth Science Reviews* **22**: 261–308.

Miall, A.D. 1988. Facies architecture in clastic sedimentary basins. In Kleinspehn, K.L. and Paola, C., editors. *New Perspectives in Basin Analysis*. Berlin, Springer-Verlag, pp. 67–81.

Miall, A.D. 1995. Description and interpretation of fluvial deposits: a critical perspective -discussion. *Sedimentology* **42**: 379–384.

Miall, A.D. 1996. *The Geology of Fluvial Deposits: Sedimentary Facies, Basin Analysis and Petroleum Geology*. Berlin, Springer-Verlag.

Millar, R.G. 2000. Influence of bank vegetation on alluvial channel patterns. *Water Resources Research* **36**: 1109–1118.

Millar, R.G. 2005. Theoretical regime equations for mobile gravel-bed rivers with stable banks. *Geomorphology* **64**: 207–220.

Millar, R.G. and Quick, M.C., 1998. Stable width and depth of gravel-bed rivers with cohesive banks. *Journal of Hydraulic Engineering* **124**: 1005–1013.

Montgomery, D.R. and Buffington, J.M. 1997. Channel-reach morphology in mountain drainage basins. *Geological Society of America Bulletin* **109**: 596–611.

Montgomery, D.R., Collins, B.D., Buffington, J.M., and Abbe, T.B. 2003. Geomorphic effects of wood in rivers. In Gregory, S., Boyer, K.,and Gurnell, A.M., editors. *The Ecology and Management of Wood in World Rivers*. Bethesda, MD, American Fisheries Society, pp. 21–47.

Moody-Stuart, M. 1966. High-and low-sinuosity stream deposits, with examples from the devonian of spitsbergen. *Journal of Sedimentary Petrology* **36**: 1102–1117.

Mueller, E.R. and Pitlick, J. 2005. Morphologically based model of bed load transport capacity in a headwater stream. *Journal of Geophysical Research, Earth Surface* **100**: F02016. doi: 10.1029/2003JF000117.

Murray, A. B. and Paola, C. 2003. Modelling the effect of vegetation on channel pattern in bedload rivers. *Earth Surface Processes and Landforms* **28**: 131–143.

Nakayama, K. and Ulak, P. 1999. Evolution of fluvial style in the Siwalik Group in the foothills of the Nepal Himalaya. *Sedimentary Geology* **125**: 205–224.

Nami, M. and Leeder, M.R. 1978. Changing channel morphology and magnitude in the Scalby Formation (Middle Jurassic) of Yorkshire, England. In Miall, A.D., editor. *Fluvial Sedimentology*. Canadian Society of Petroleum Geologists, Memoir 5, pp. 431–440.

Nijman, W. and Puigdefábregas, C. 1978. Coarse-grained point bar structure in a molasse type fluvial system, Eocene Castisent sandstone formation, South Pyrenean basin. In Miall, A.D., editor. *Fluvial Sedimentology*. Canadian Society of Petroleum Geologists, Memoir 5, pp. 487–510.

O'Connor, J.E. and Baker, V.R. 1992. Magnitudes and implications of peak discharges from glacial Lake Missoula. *Geological Society of America Bulletin* **104**: 267–279.

Ori, G. G. 1982. Braided to meandering channel patterns in humid-region alluvial fan deposits, River Reno, Po plain (northern Italy). *Sedimentary Geology* **31**: 231–248.

Orton, G.J. and Reading, H.G. 1993. Variability of deltaic processes in terms of sediment supply, with particular emphasis on grain size. *Sedimentology* **40**: 475–512.

Osterkamp, W.R. and Hedman, E.R. 1982. *Perennial Streamflow Characteristics Related to Channel Geometry and Sediment in Missouri River Basin*. United States Geological Survey, Professional Paper 1242.

Paola, C. and Borgman, L. 1991. Reconstructing random topography from preserved stratification. *Sedimentology* **38**: 553–565.

Paola, C. 2001. Modelling stream braiding over a range of scales. In Mosley, M.P., editor, *Gravel Bed Rivers V*. Wellington, New Zealand Hydrological Society, pp. 11–46.

Paola, C. and Mohrig, D. 1996. Paleohydraulics revisited: paleoslope estimation in coarse-grained braided rivers. *Basin Research* **8**: 243–254.

Parker, C., Simon, A., and Thorne, C. R. 2008. The effects of variability in bank material properties on riverbank stability: Goodwin Creek, Mississippi. *Geomorphology* **101**: 533–543.

Parker, G. 1976. On the cause and characteristic scales of meandering and braiding in rivers. *Journal of Fluid Mechanics* **76**: 457–480.

Parker, G. 1978. Self-formed straight rivers with equilibrium banks and mobile bed. part 2. The gravel river. *Journal of Fluid Mechanics* **89**: 127–146.

Parker, G., Wilcock, P., Paola, C., Dietrich, W.E., and Pitlick, J. 2007. Physical basis for quasi-universal relations describing bankfull hydraulic geometry of single-thread gravel bed rivers. *Journal of Geophysical Research – Earth Surface* **112**: F04005. doi: 10.1029/2006JF000549.

Piégay, H., Walling, D.E., Landon, N. *et al.* 2004. Contemporary changes in sediment yield in an alpine mountain basin due to afforestation (the upper Drôme in France). *Catena* **55**: 183–212.

Pollen-Bankhead, N., Simon, A., Jaeger, K., and Wohl, E.E. 2009. Destabilization of streambanks by removal of invasive species in Canyon de Chelly National Monument, Arizona. *Geomorphology* **103**: 363–374.

Potter, P.E. 1959. Facies models conference. *Science* **129**: 1292–1294.

Ramos, A. and Sopeña, A. 1983. Gravel bars in low-sinuosity streams (Permian and Triassic, central Spain) In Collinson, J.D. and Lewin, J., editors. *Modern and Ancient Fluvial Systems*. International Association of Sedimentologists, Special Publication 6, pp. 301–312.

Reid, I., Laronne, J.B., and Powell, D.M. 1995. The Nahal Yatir bedload database: sediment dynamics in a gravel-bed ephemeral stream. *Earth Surface Processes and Landforms* **31**: 773–781.

Rice, S.P., Church, M., Wooldridge, C.L., and Hickin, E.J. 2009. Morphology and evolution of bars in a wandering gravel-bed river; lower Fraser River, British Columbia, Canada. *Sedimentology* **56:** 709–736.

Rinaldi, M., Mengoni, B., Luppi, L., Darby, S.E., and Mosselman, E. 2008. Numerical simulation of hydrodynamics and bank erosion in a river bend. *Water Resources Research* **44**: W09428. doi: 10.1029/2008WR007008.

Robertson-Rintoul, M.S.E. and Richards, K.S. 1993. Braided-channel pattern and paleohydrology using an index of total sinuosity. In Best, J.L. and Bristow, C.S., editors. *Braided Rivers*. Geological Society (London), Special Publication 75, pp. 113–118.

Rowntree, K.M. and Dollar, E.S.J. 1996. Controls on channel form and channel change in the Bell River, Eastern Cape, South Africa. *South African Geographical Journal* **78**: 20–28.

Rowntree, K.M. and Dollar, E.S.J. 1999. Vegetation controls on channel stability in the Bell River, Eastern Cape, South Africa. *Earth Surface Processes and Landforms* 24: 127–134.

Rust, B.R. 1978a. A classification of alluvial channel systems. In Miall, A.D., editor. *Fluvial Sedimentology*. Canadian Society of Petroleum Geologists, Memoir 5, pp. 187–198.

Rust, B.R. 1978b. Depositional models for braided alluvium. In Miall, A.D., editor. *Fluvial Sedimentology*. Canadian Society of Petroleum Geologists, Memoir 5, pp. 605–625.

Rust, B.R. 1979. Coarse alluvial deposits. In Walker, R.G., editor. *Facies Models*. Geological Association of Canada, Geosciences Canada Reprint Series 1, pp. 9–21.

Ryan, S.E. and Emmett, W.W. 2002. *The Nature of flow and Sediment Movement in Little Granite Creek near Bondurant, Wyoming*. United States Department of Agriculture, Forest Service, Rocky Mountain Research Station, Ogden, UT, General Technical Report RMRS-GTR-90.

Ryder, J.M. and Church, M. 1986. The Lillooet terraces of Fraser River: a palaeoenvironmental enquiry. *Canadian Journal of Earth Sciences* 23: 869–884.

Schumm, S.A. 1960. *The Shape of Alluvial Channels in Relation to Sediment Type*. United States Geological Survey, Professional Paper 352-B, pp. 17–30.

Schumm, S.A. 1963. *A Tentative Classification of Alluvial River Channels*. United States Geological Survey Circular 477.

Schumm, S.A. 1968a. *River Adjustment to Altered Hydrologic Regimen – Murrumbidgee River and Paleochannels, Australia*. United States Geological Survey, Professional Paper 598.

Schumm, S.A. 1968b. Speculation concerning paleohydrologic controls of terrestrial sedimentation. *Geological Society of America Bulletin* 79: 1573–1588.

Schumm, S.A. 1969. River metamorphosis. American Society of Civil Engineers, *Journal of Hydraulics Division* 95: 255–273.

Schumm, S.A. 1972. Fluvial paleochannels. In Rigby, J.K. and Hamblin, W.K., editors. *Recognition of Ancient Sedimentary Environments*. Society of Economic Paleontologists and Mineralogists, Special Publication 16, pp. 98–107.

Schumm, S.A. 1977. *The fluvial System*. New York, Wiley-Interscience.

Schumm, S.A. 1987. *Experimental fluvial Geomorphology*. New York, John Wiley & Sons, Inc.

Schumm, S.A. 2005. *River Variability and Complexity*. Cambridge, Cambridge University Press.

Shiono, K. and Knight, D.W. 1991. Turbulent open-channel flows with variable depth across the channel. *Journal of Fluid Mechanics* 222: 617–646.

Siegenthaler, C. and Huggenberger, P. 1993. Pleistocene Rhine gravel: deposits of a braided river system with dominant pool preservation. In Best, J.L. and Bristow, C.S., editors. *Braided Rivers*. Geological Society (London), Special Publication 75, pp. 147–162.

Simon, A. and Collison, A.J.C. 2002. Quantifying the mechanical and hydrologic effects of riparian vegetation on streambank stability. *Earth Surface Processes and Landforms* 27: 527–546.

Simon, A. and Thomas, R.E. 2002. Processes and forms of an unstable system with resistant, cohesive streambeds. *Earth Surface Processes and Landforms* 27: 699–718.

Simon, A., Curini, A., Darby, S.E., and Langendoen, E.J. 2000. Bank and near-bank processes in an incised channel. *Geomorphology* 35: 193–217.

Simon, A., Pollen, N., and Langendoen, E. 2006. Influence of two woody riparian species on critical conditions for stream-bank stability: Upper Truckee River, California. *Journal of the American Water Resources Association* 42: 99–113.

Simpson, C.J. and Smith, D.G. 2001. The braided Milk River, northern Montana, fails the Leopold–Wolman discharge-gradient test. *Geomorphology* 41: 337–353.

Smith, D.G. 1976. Effect of vegetation on lateral migration of anastomosed channels of a glacier meltwater river. *Geological Society of America Bulletin* 87: 857–860.

Smith, S.A. 1989. Sedimentation in a meandering gravel-bed river: The River Tywi, South Wales. *Geological Journal* 24: 193–204.

Smith, S.A. 1990. The sedimentology and accretionary styles of an ancient gravel-bed stream: the Budleigh Salterton pebble beds (Lower Triassic), southwest England. *Sedimentary Geology* 67: 199–219.

Steel, R.J. and Thompson, D.B. 1983. Structures and textures in triassic braided stream conglomerates (Bunter pebble beds) in the Sherwood sandstone group, North Staffordshire, England. *Sedimentology* 30: 341–367.

Steer, B.L. and Abbott, P.L. 1984. Paleohydrology of the Eocene Ballena gravels, San Diego County, California. *Sedimentary Geology* 38: 181–216.

Sylvia, D.A. and Galloway, W.E. 2006. Morphology and stratigraphy of the late Quaternary lower Brazos valley: implication for paleo-climate, discharge and sediment delivery. *Sedimentary Geology* 190: 159–175.

Tal, M. and Paola, C. 2010. Effects of vegetation on channel morphodynamics: results and insights from laboratory experiments. *Earth Surface Processes and Landforms* 35: 1014–1028.

Van de Wiel, M.J. and Darby, S.E. 2007. A new model to analyse the impact of woody riparian vegetation on the geotechnical stability of riverbanks. *Earth Surface Processes and Landforms* 32: 2185–2198.

van den Berg, J. H. 1995. Prediction of alluvial channel pattern of perennial rivers. *Geomorphology* 12: 259–279.

Vanoni, V.A. 1940. *Experiments on the transportation of suspended sediment by water*. Ph.D. thesis, California Institute of Technology, Pasadena, CA.

Vigilar, G.G. and Diplas, P. 1997. Stable channels with mobile bed: formulation and numerical solution. *Journal of Hydraulic Engineering* 123: 189–199.

Walker, R.G. 1979. Facies and facies models: General introduction. In Walker, R.G., editor. *Facies models*. Geological Association of Canada, *Geosciences Canada Reprint Series* 1: 1–8.

Walter, R.C. and Merritts, D.J. 2008. Natural streams and the legacy of water-powered mills. *Science* 319: 299–304.

Ward, P.D., Montgomery, D.R., and Smith, R. 2000. Altered river morphology in South Africa related to the Permien-Triassic extinction. *Science* 289: 1740–1735.

Wilcock, P.R. 1996. Estimating local bed shear stress from velocity observations. *Water Resources Research* 32: 3361–3366.

Williams, G.P. 1984. Paleohydrologic equations for rivers. In Costa, J. E. and Fleisher, P.J., editors. *Developments and Applications of Geomorphology*. Berlin, Springer-Verlag, pp. 343–367.

Williams, G.P. 1988. Paleofluvial estimates from dimensions of former channels and meanders. In Baker, V.R., Kochel, R.C. and Patton, P.C., editors. *Flood Geomorphology*. New York, John Wiley & Sons, Ltd, pp. 321–334.

Williams, P.F. and Rust, B.R. 1969. The sedimentology of a braided river. *Journal of Sedimentary Petrology* 39: 649–679.

Wohl, E.E. 2000. *Mountain Rivers*. American Geophysical Union, Water Resources Monograph 14.

Wohl, E.E. 2004. Limits of downstream hydraulic geometry. *Geology* 32: 897–900.

Wooldridge, C.L. and Hickin, E.J., 2005. Radar architecture and evolution of channel bars in wandering gravel-bed rivers: Fraser and Squamish rivers, British Columbia, Canada. *Journal of Sedimentary Research* 75: 844–860.

Yalin, M.S. and da Silva, A.M.F. 2001. *Fluvial Processes*. Delft, International Association of Hydraulic Engineering and Research Monograph.

Zimmerman, R.C., Goodlett, J.C., and Comer, G.H. 1967. The influence of vegetation on channel form of small streams. In *Symposium on River Morphology*. Commission on Surface Waters, International Association of Scientific Hydrology, General Assembly of Bern, Switzerland, 25 September–7 October. Publication 75, pp. 255–275.

## 34.10   DISCUSSION

### 34.10.1   Discussion by R.I. Ferguson

You discuss the possibility that one of the causes of braiding may be a high bedload flux, and quote with approval Mackin's view that the river does not decide what bedload it can carry, but rather adapts to carry the imposed load. Braiding does seem to be associated with high bedload flux, but the causality is very difficult to determine. To take two examples: (i) several authors have attributed local or temporary braiding of otherwise single-channel rivers to increased sediment supply from dune fields (Smith and Smith, 1984), mine waste disposal (Knighton, 1989), or the like. But these cases are open to the alternative interpretation that the immediate effect is a drastic reduction in bed grain size, which causes a big increase in the river's transport capacity (because of lower threshold shear stress) and in turn permits channel widening and braiding; (ii) Schumm and Khan (1972) reported a sequence of stream-table experiments with constant discharge and grain size, but progressively higher gradient. They found that there was a change from single-talweg to braided patterns, and also an increase in bedload flux through the system. But the manipulated variable was slope, not sediment supply, and an increase in gradient with no change in discharge or bed grain size would have caused an increase in bedload flux even if all the channels had stayed straight. It might even have caused more of an increase than was observed, since a braided gravel-bed river with relatively high width–depth ratio is generally less efficient at conveying bedload than is a narrower single channel (e.g. Bettess and White, 1983).

Are you aware of any laboratory experiment in which an equilibrium single channel has become braided after an imposed increase in sediment feed rate? Or in which a series of runs generated equilibrium single channels at low feed rates, but equilibrium braided channels at high feed rates, when all other relevant variables (including slope and discharge) were held constant?

### 34.10.2   Reply by F. Métivier and L. Barrier

The short answer to your question is "no", we are not aware of such an experiment, primarily because it has long proven to be a very difficult task to reproduce experimentally a stable channel that efficiently transports sediments (Paola *et al.*, 2009). Yet it is possible to bring at least a partial answer to your concern.

First, to our knowledge, only one experiment has successfully reproduced channel metamorphosis from a fully braided to a wandering, almost single-thread channel. This experiment was run at the St. Anthony Falls Laboratory (University of Minnesota) by Tal and Paola (2010). Corralling of the flow into a single main thread was obtained by growing vegetation. One of the main outcomes is that the change from a multiple-thread to a single-thread river leads to a significant reduction in sediment transport efficiency. All other parameters held constant this unambiguously shows that a single thread stream is less efficient in transporting sediments than its braided counterpart, in clear contradiction of the statement from Bettess and White that you report.

Second, although sediment fining may provoke a lowering of the critical shear stress, this is not sufficient for channel widening to occur. If no bedload flux is supplied, an excess in shear stress does not lead to widening in the first place, but to incision, as typically exemplified by incision downstream of dams (until a pavement develops that prevents further incision; see Chapter 15 by Grant in this volume). In the case of the Williams River, let us also recall that Smith and Smith (1984) estimate that the input from the Athabasca sand dunes is about 40 times the flux the river carries upstream of the dune field.

Third, let us remind ourselves that the existing stable channel theories for gravel-bed streams (Parker, 1978; Diplas, 1990) all rest on the idea that, for a single-thread stream to remain stable, the maximum shear stress cannot exceed the critical shear stress by more than about 40%. As we have shown, braided rivers are clearly not limited by this constraint. Finally, a recent mechanical analysis performed in the special case of small-scale river models shows that rivers with the same cohesionless material on bed and banks are doomed to braid once they transport sediment (Devauchelle *et al.*, 2007). Hence a poorly vegetated gravel-bed meandering stream can probably not transport much, or it will braid.

## 34.11   DISCUSSION REFERENCES

Bettess, R. and White, W.R. 1983. Meandering and braiding of alluvial channels. *Proceedings of the Institution of Civil Engineers*, part 2 75: 525–538.

Diplas, P. 1990. Characteristics of self-formed straight channels. *Journal of Hydraulic Engineering* **116:** 707–728.

Devauchelle, O., Josserand, C., Lagrée, P.Y., and Zaleski, S. 2007. Morphodynamic modeling of erodible laminar channels. *Physical Review* **E76**: 56318.

Knighton, A.D. 1989. River adjustment to changes in sediment load: the effects of tin mining on the Ringarooma River, Tasmania, 1875–1984. *Earth Surface Processes and Landforms* **14**: 333–359.

Paola, C., Straub, K., Mohrig, D.C., and Reinhardt, L. 2009. The 'unreasonable effectiveness' of stratigraphic and geomorphic experiments. *Earth-Science Reviews* **97**: 1–43.

Parker, G. 1978. Self-formed straight rivers with equilibrium banks and mobile bed. Part 2. The gravel river. *Journal of Fluid Mechanics* **89**: 127–146.

Schumm, S.A. and Khan, H.R. 1972. Experimental study of channel patterns. *Geological Society of America Bulletin* **83**: 1755–1770.

Smith, N.D. and Smith, D.G. 1984. William River: an outstanding example of channel widening and braiding caused by bedload addition. *Geology* **12**: 78–82.

Tal, M. and Paola, C. 2010. Effects of vegetation on channel morphodynamics: results and insights from laboratory experiments. *Earth Surface Processes and Landforms* **35**: 1014–1028.

# 35

# Differences in Sediment Supply to Braided and Single-Thread River Channels: What Do the Data Tell Us?

John Pitlick, Erich R. Mueller, and Catalina Segura

## 35.1 INTRODUCTION

Braided rivers are distinguished from their single-thread counterparts by high channel complexity (multiple bars per active channel width), and wide variations in flow properties and sediment flux. Presumably, braided river dynamics are driven by high rates of sediment supply, which force lateral instability and channel switching (Schumm, 1985; Church, 2006). The key problem highlighted by Métivier and Barrier (Chapter 34, this volume) is that, in most cases, we don't know the sediment supply: *in situ* measurements of sediment loads (bedload and suspended load) are taken at relatively few locations, thus the influence of sediment supply on channel pattern is not well understood. Consequently, the best we can do is to make inferences about the role of sediment supply based on relations between the more easily measured variables, such as discharge, slope, stream power, width–depth ratio and grain size. This approach has a long history, but it does not appear that the distinction between braided and meandering channel patterns is any clearer now than it was when Leopold and Wolman (1957) first defined such a threshold (see Lewin and Brewer, 2001, and subsequent discussion by van den Berg and Bledsoe, 2003).

In order to move forward on this topic, we believe it is essential to incorporate information on sediment supply into the framework for analyzing changes in river channel patterns. It is not likely, however, that we (river scientists) will see an expansion in sediment sampling programs in the near future, thus we will need to develop and test alternative methods for estimating the sediment supply to rivers. In this chapter, we examine the variables governing bed material transport, and ask whether there are important differences in the individual terms – width, depth, slope, and grain size – that would help explain the transition from single-thread to braided channel patterns. We frame the discussion around a bedload transport equation and suggest that such an equation can be applied in the "forward" sense (Church, 2006) to estimate the sediment supply to rivers with different channel patterns. We do not discuss the alternative technique in which the sediment flux is back-calculated from changes in channel morphology – termed the "inverse problem" – as this approach is adequately described in a number of papers (Martin and Church, 1995; Lane *et al.*, 1995; Ashmore and Church, 1998; Church, 2006).

## 35.2 KEY VARIABLES FOR ESTIMATING BEDLOAD TRANSPORT CAPACITY

In the absence of direct measurements, estimates of bedload transport capacity can be made using any one of the commonly available transport relations. This approach has a number of limitations – some more serious than others – but if the location of interest is suitable and care is taken in collecting the necessary data and setting model parameters, then reasonable estimates of transport capacity and sediment yield can be obtained. Applied in this sense, a transport relation is simply a tool for estimating the sediment flux at a particular location. The question addressed here is a bit broader: Can we tell from looking at the different components of a transport relation what processes govern the transition from single-thread to braided channels? In trying to answer this

*Gravel-bed Rivers: Processes, Tools, Environments*, First Edition. Edited by Michael Church, Pascale M. Biron and André G. Roy.
© 2012 John Wiley & Sons, Ltd. Published 2012 by John Wiley & Sons, Ltd.

question we assume that the channels of interest are self-formed and that they transport bedload at capacity. We also assume that instantaneous bedload transport rates can be calculated using a suitable transport equation coupled to values of discharge through relations for flow resistance and channel width. Last we consider the importance of integrating transport rates over time to determine the annual bedload sediment yield.

For the purposes of illustration, we use Parker's (1979) approximation of the Einstein (1950) bedload transport function

$$q^* = 11.2\,\tau^{*1.5}\left(1-\tau_r^*/\tau^*\right)^{4.5} \qquad (35.1)$$

wherein $q^* = q_b/\sqrt{(s-1)gD^3}$ is the Einstein transport parameter, $\tau^* = RS_f/(s-1)D$ is the dimensionless shear stress, $\tau_r^*$ is the reference dimensionless shear stress (analogous to the critical shear stress), $q_b$ is the volumetric transport rate per unit width, $s$ is the specific gravity of sediment, $g$ is the gravitational acceleration, $D$ is the grain size, $R$ is the hydraulic radius, and $S_f$ is the friction slope. Rewriting Equation (35.1) in dimensional form, the width-integrated bedload transport rate is then

$$Q_b = 11.2\,\tau^{*1.5}\left(1-\tau_r^*/\tau^*\right)^{4.5}\sqrt{(s-1)gD^3}\,W \qquad (35.2)$$

wherein $Q_b$ is the volumetric transport rate ($\mathrm{m^3\,s^{-1}}$) averaged over the channel width, $W$. With the bedload function written this way, and taking $s$ and $g$ as constants, it is evident that variations in transport capacity are governed by the interaction of four variables: $\tau^*$, $\tau_r^*$, $D$ and $W$. The question is: are the interactions among these variables sufficiently different in braided and meandering channels to account for the large differences in sediment transport capacity? For example, if the bedload transport capacity was governed by width alone, then wider, braided channels would carry proportionally higher sediment loads than narrower, meandering channels. The effects of width could, in turn, be enhanced or offset by differences in excess shear stress, $\tau^*-\tau_r^*$, or grain size, $D$. In addition, it has been suggested that the characteristic instability of braided rivers is related more to the variations in boundary shear stress than to spatially averaged values (Paola, 1996; Nicholas, 2000; 2003; Bertoldi et al., 2009a), although we have not seen a comparison between shear stress distributions in single-thread and multithread channels. Last, it has been suggested that differences in the frequency of bedload transport may compensate for differences in transport intensity, which may, in turn, lead to a balance in the load carried between high- and low-gradient reaches (Mueller and Pitlick, 2005; Segura and Pitlick, 2010).

## 35.3 WHAT DO THE DATA AND OBSERVATIONS TELL US?

### 35.3.1 Channel Width

The data presented by Métivier and Barrier (Figures 34.9 and 34.10, this volume) indicate that braided rivers have much higher width–depth ratios than meandering rivers, even after pruning the data set to remove the very large braided rivers. As noted by many workers, the constraints on channel width are determined largely by bank stability, parameterized either in terms of a coefficient representing the friction angle of the bank sediment (Millar, 2000, 2005) or a coefficient representing the shear stress in excess of the threshold for motion (Parker, 1979; Parker et al., 2007). Regardless of the approach used in modelling bank stability and channel evolution, it appears that the threshold between meandering and braiding occurs at width–depth ratios of ~50 (Eaton et al., 2010; Métivier and Barrier, Chapter 34, this volume; Millar, Chapter 8, this volume). Above this threshold, the channel is sufficiently wide to allow the growth of mid-channel bars, thus braiding is somewhat of an inevitable consequence of higher width–depth ratios. There is a tradeoff, however, between width and depth that eventually limits bedload transport capacity. For a given discharge and slope, there may be an optimum width and depth for maintaining transport capacity, but that optimum need not be the same for different channel types if one of the other variables in Equation (35.2), e.g. $\tau_r^*$, adjusts in a direction that compensates for differences in width and depth. The question here is: once the braided pattern develops, how do the channel characteristics evolve over time to convey both the water and sediment supplied?

Measurements of channel geometry in braided rivers show that, as the discharge into a reach increases, new threads are activated, and the width of the wetted channel increases very rapidly (Mosley, 1982; Ashmore and Sauks, 2006; Bertoldi et al., 2009b). Hydraulic geometry relations developed from this work indicate that at-a-station exponents for width, $b$, are much higher in braided channels than in single-thread channels. Results from laboratory experiments conducted by Bertoldi et al. (2009b), shown here in Figure 35.1a, indicate that the wetted-perimeter width of braided channels increases as the 0.7 power of discharge. The "active" width of the channel carrying the bedload was always less than the wetted width, but the increase in active width was apparently more rapid than would be expected in single-thread rivers. Ashmore and Sauks (2006) used ground-based orthorectified photographs with field measurements to track channel changes along a 300 m reach of the Sunwapta River in Alberta, Canada. Their results, shown here in Figure 35.1b, suggest that the scaling between active channel width and discharge is approximately linear ($b \approx 1.0$), the implication being that the product of depth and velocity (discharge per unit width) is essentially constant over the range of observed discharges. We can take that a step further and note that if the average slope and grain size likewise remain roughly constant with increasing discharge, then the dimensionless shear stress should also tend towards a constant. Thus, one potential consequence of the rapid change in channel width with discharge in braided rivers is that there may be limited changes in depth, hence potentially small changes in the stress available for bedload transport; this point is illustrated nicely in the experiments conducted by Walter Bertoldi (see Figure 12 in Bertoldi *et al.*, 2009a).

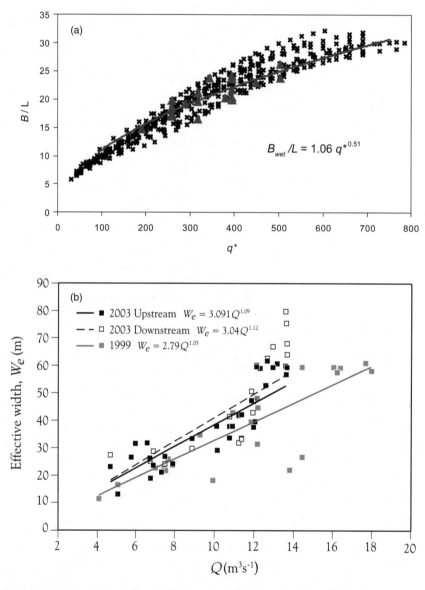

**Figure 35.1** At-a-station hydraulic geometry relations for braided channel width. The upper panel shows results from the laboratory experiments of Bertoldi *et al.* (2009b). Reproduced, with permission, from Bertoldi, W., Zanoni, L., and Tubino, M. 2009b. Planform dynamics of braided streams. *Earth Surface Processes and Landforms* **34**: 547–557; here *B* is the channel width, normalized by a length scale, *L*, and $q^*$ is a dimensionless discharge. The lower panel shows changes in active channel width with discharge based on measurements on the Sunwapta River in Alberta, Canada. From Ashmore and Sauks, 2006.

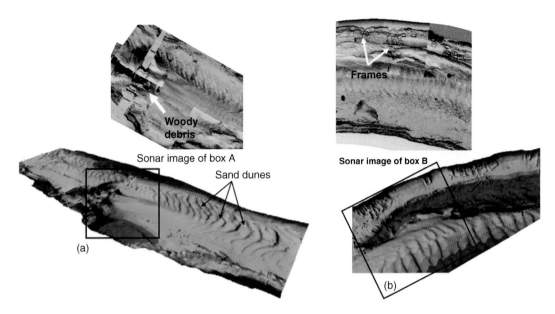

**Plate 17 (Figure 24.10)** MBES bathymetry surface and corresponding sidescan image showing: (a) the location of bridge piling and woody debris; (b) details of frames installed for bank protection.

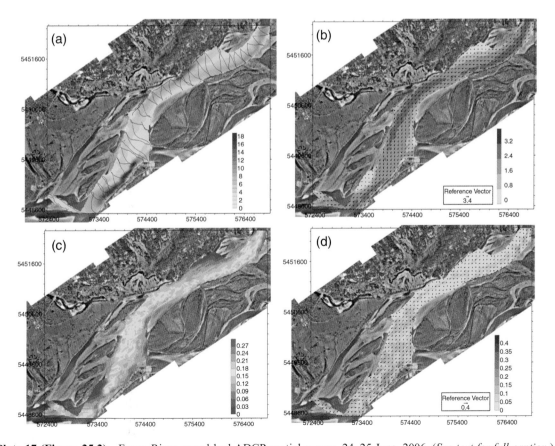

**Plate 17 (Figure 25.2)** Fraser River gravel-bed ADCP spatial survey, 24–25 June, 2006. (*See text for full caption.*)

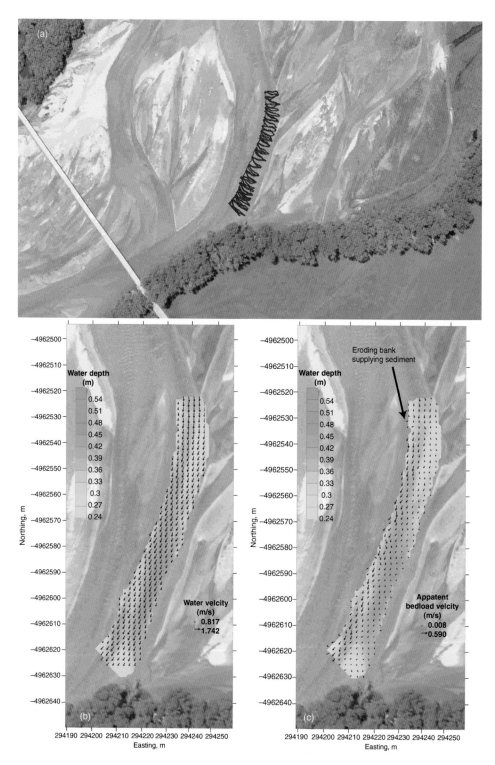

**Plate 18 (Figure 25.3)** Rees River gravel-bed ADCP spatial survey, 13 January, 2010. All distributions interpolated using kriging with 1.1 m grid spacing. Map units are arbitrary coordinates in m: (a) boat track showing positions of ADCP measurements within the braid plain; (b) depth-averaged water velocity (m s$^{-1}$), every second vector in Easting and Northing shown, overlain on water depth (m); (c) apparent bedload velocity (m s$^{-1}$), every second vector in Easting and Northing shown, overlain on water depth (m). Modified from Vericat *et al.* (2010).

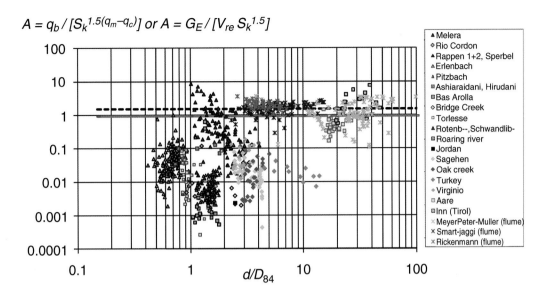

**Plate 19 (Figure 28.1)**   The variable $A$ (coefficient) in the bedload transport Equations (28.14) or (28.17) in combination with Equation (28.15) has been back-calculated from field data given in Rickenmann (2001), and is compared with the flume-based coefficient of Equation (28.14), represented as thick dashed horizontal line, and the coefficient of the Schoklitsch (1962) equation, represented as thick gray horizontal line. The coefficient $A$ is shown versus the relative flow depth ($d/D_{84}$).

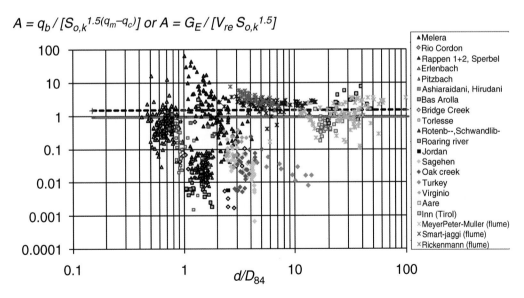

**Plate 19 (Figure 28.2)**   The variable $A$ (coefficient) in the bedload transport Equations (28.14) or (28.17) in combination with Equation (28.15) has been back-calculated from field data given in Rickenmann (2001), and is compared with the flume-based coefficient of Equation (28.14), represented as thick dashed horizontal line, and the coefficient of the Schoklitsch (1962) equation, represented as thick gray horizontal line. In contrast to Figure 28.1, a reduced energy slope $S_o$ has been taken into account additionally, using Equations (28.11) and (28.12). The coefficient $A$ is shown versus the relative flow depth ($d/D_{84}$).

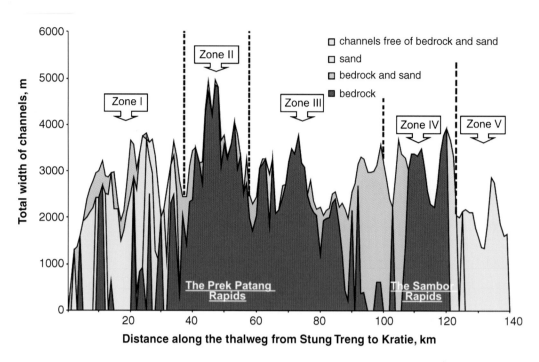

**Plate 20 (Figure 31.3)** Zonation of the channel of the Mekong shown in Figure 31.2 is based in part on the proportion of the channel width occupied by sand fillet over bedrock as shown here. The detail of sand distribution in Zones II and III in particular is complex and is highly simplified here. Modified after Meshkova and Carling, in press. Lightest sections are deep-water with indeterminate bed type.

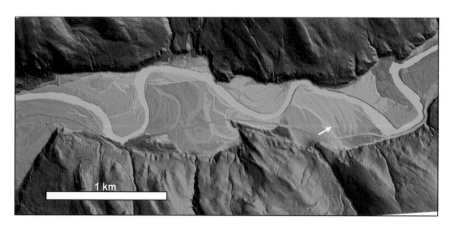

**Plate 20 (Figure 31.5)** Confined meanders of the Matane River, Eastern Québec. The LiDAR image reveals the translating migration pattern of meander bends typical of confined meanders (white arrow).

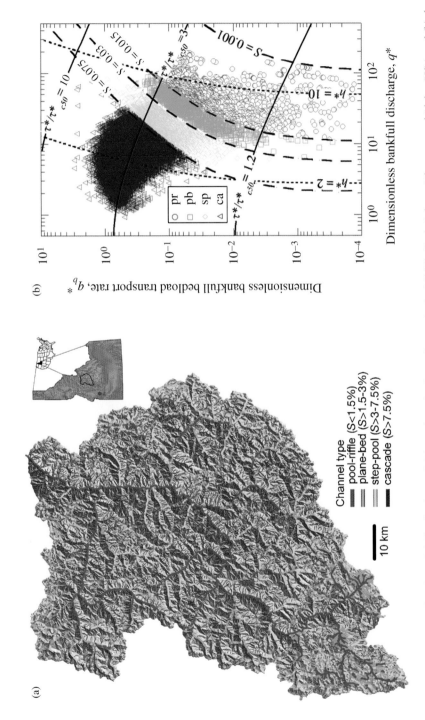

**Plate 21 (Figure 32.10)** Predicted spatial distributions of: (a) reach-scale channel types in the Middle Fork Salmon River, central Idaho, USA and (b) those data mapped onto the Figure 32.9 regime diagram: pr = pool-riffle ($n = 2616$), pb = plane-bed ($n = 2056$), sp = step-pool ($n = 5983$) and ca = cascade ($n = 50\,135$).

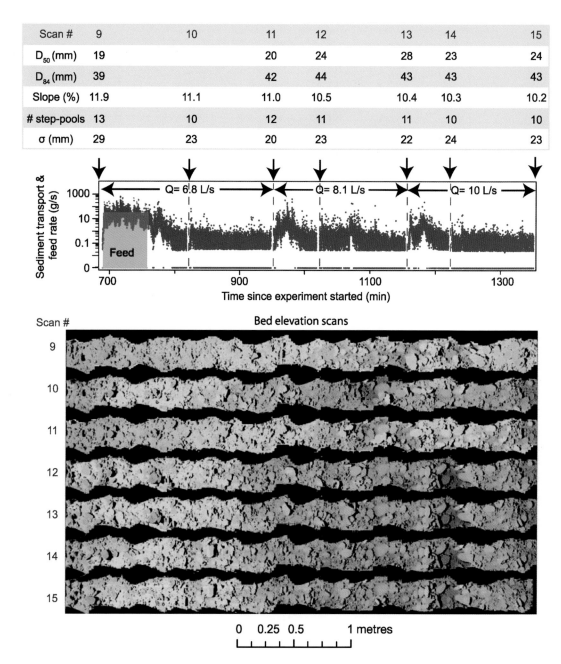

| Scan # | 9 | 10 | 11 | 12 | 13 | 14 | 15 |
|--------|-----|-----|-----|-----|-----|-----|-----|
| $D_{50}$ (mm) | 19 | | 20 | 24 | 28 | 23 | 24 |
| $D_{84}$ (mm) | 39 | | 42 | 44 | 43 | 43 | 43 |
| Slope (%) | 11.9 | 11.1 | 11.0 | 10.5 | 10.4 | 10.3 | 10.2 |
| # step-pools | 13 | 10 | 12 | 11 | 11 | 10 | 10 |
| σ (mm) | 29 | 23 | 20 | 23 | 22 | 24 | 23 |

**Plate 22 (Figure 33.1)**  Sediment transport and bed morphology evolution observed during a portion of Experiment 16 (Zimmermann, 2009). The walls of the flume varied along the length of the channel, hence the variable width shown in the scan. During the first hour, sediment was fed at a constant rate and the sediment transport out of the flume is illustrated in grey points. Reproduced, with permission, from Zimmermann, A. 2009. Experimental investigations of step-pool channel formation and stability. Ph.D thesis, The University of British Columbia, Vancouver, Canada.

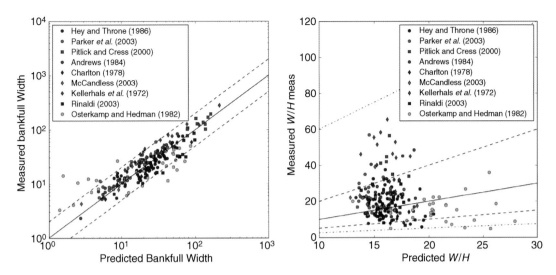

**Plate 23 (Figure 34.10)** Left: Comparison between measured and predicted bankfull width using Yalin and da Silva's regime equations (2001) for gravel-bed streams. The black line corresponds to perfect agreement $W_{meas} = W_{pred}$, dashed lines correspond to $W_{meas} = 2W_{pred}$ and $W_{meas} = 0.5W_{pred}$. Right: comparison between the measured and predicted aspect ratio using Yalin and da Silva's regime equations (2001) for gravel-bed streams. The black line corresponds to a perfect agreement, dashed lines correspond to an agreement within a factor of two, the dotted line corresponds to an agreement within a factor of four

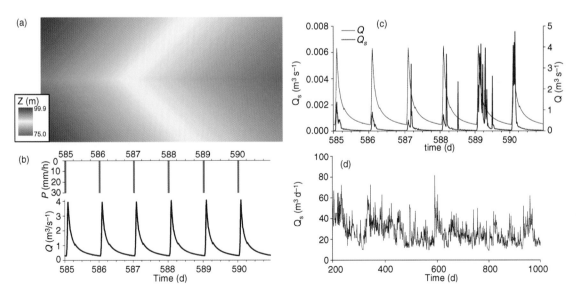

**Plate 23 (Figure 36.1)** Model setup and results for the simulations by Van De Wiel and Coulthard (2010): (a) initial elevations ($Z$) in the idealized rectangular catchment; (b) temporal distribution of rainfall (top, $P$) and simulated discharge at the catchment outlet (bottom, $Q$); (c) intraday bedload yield ($Qs$, red) and flow discharge ($Q$, blue) at the catchment outlet. Sediment yield is highly variable in both time scales, although water discharge is regular and periodic; (d) daily bedload yield, showing significant variability throughout the simulation. Adapted from Van De Wiel and Coulthard, 2010.

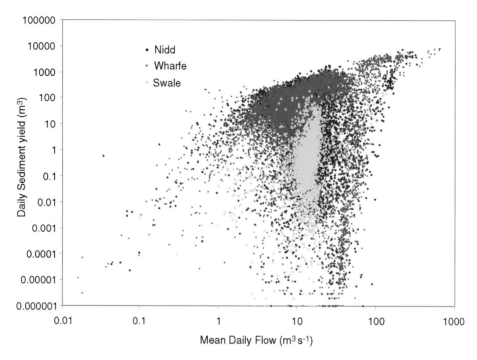

**Plate 24 (Figure 36.6)** $Qs/Qw$ plots for the rivers Swale, Wharfe and Nidd. From Coulthard *et al.*, 2007.

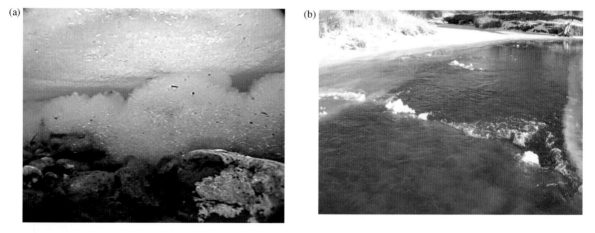

**Plate 24 (Figure 37.3)** (a) Anchor-ice growth on the gravel bed of the Laramie River, Wyoming; (b) an anchor-ice dam formed on a cobble bed in the Laramie River. The anchor ice grew to the water surface, strengthened, and elevated the upstream (foreground) water level.

### 35.3.2 Grain Size

The bed material in braided rivers tends to be more poorly sorted and spatially variable than the bed material in single-thread rivers, and in some braided rivers the bed surface grain-size distribution may approach that of the bulk (subsurface) sediment (Ferguson *et al.*, 1992). The data presented by Métivier and Barrier (Chapter 34, this volume) suggest that there is significant overlap in the median grain size, $D_{50}$, of the bed material in braided and single-thread rivers. It is likely that spatial averaging in the field data obscures important differences in the tails of the distributions, but this first cut suggests that grain sizes are broadly similar. Our measurements of grain size in adjacent reaches of Sunlight Creek, a gravel-bed river in northwest Wyoming, USA, indicate that the bed surface in single-thread reaches is coarser overall than in braided reaches (Figure 35.2), but the difference is not large; $D_{50}$ averages 45 mm in single-thread reaches versus 30 mm in braided reaches. Grain-size distributions of the subsurface sediment suggest that the bulk bed material is proportionally finer in the two types of reaches (Figure 35.2); consequently the ratio of surface to subsurface $D_{50}$ (armoring ratio) is roughly the same, $\sim 2.0$. The similarity in armouring ratios suggests that size-dependent differences in mobility associated with hiding/protrusion effects may not be very large, thus the width-integrated bed transport rates in the two reaches should be approximately the same (which we believe is the case, based on our transport measurements and our observations that the channel shows no obvious signs of aggradation or degradation).

It is not evident in the example discussed above that grain sizes in braided channels are much different from single-thread channels. However, descriptions of braid bar characteristics and depositional features suggest that the bed material in braided rivers is more often sorted into patches where the sediment is predominantly fine- or coarse-grained (e.g., Paola and Seal, 1995). Patches can potentially enhance the mobility of some size fractions while limiting the mobility of others, resulting in highly variable transport rates from one location to another. It seems likely, therefore, that in comparing the bed materials of braided and single-thread channels, we might learn more by looking at the tails of the grain-size distributions, rather than the means.

### 35.3.3 Shear Stress

Equation (35.2) contains two separate terms for the shear stress, one representing the stress available for transport, $\tau^*$, the other representing a reference shear stress, $\tau_r^*$, corresponding to a small but non-negligible transport rate. Transport rates estimated from equations such as (35.2) are very sensitive to the difference between these two terms (or their ratio), hence the potential error associated with a calculation can be very large. In the typical application, estimates of bedload transport rates are based on spatially averaged values of depth, slope, and grain size, which may differ substantially from local values (Paola, 1996; Hoey *et al.*, 2001; Ferguson, 2003; Bertoldi *et al.*, 2009a) (we discuss this point in more detail below). In addition, the first term in Equation (35.2) should be corrected for sources of roughness (boulders, logs, bank irregularities) that do not contribute directly to bedload transport. This is an important consideration, yet most of the data sets used to examine differences in

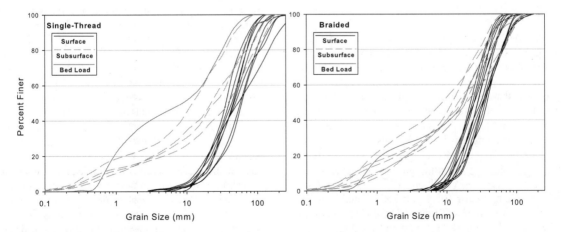

**Figure 35.2**   Grain size distributions of sediment in Sunlight Creek, a relatively small gravel-bed channel that alternates between single-thread and braided channel reaches.

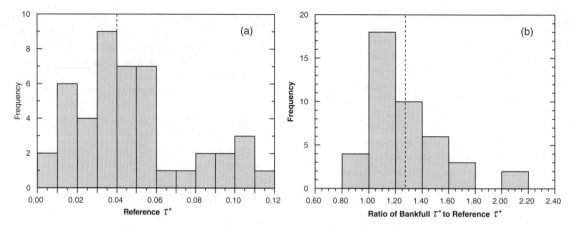

**Figure 35.3** Distributions of shear stress in 43 gravel-bed streams and rivers in the western USA and Canada. Dashed lines indicate the geometric mean of each distribution. Data from Mueller *et al.*, 2005.

channel pattern do not include a correction for form roughness, thus spatially averaged values of shear stress are likely to be greater than the stress causing bedload transport. If the reference shear stress, $\tau_r^*$, is then assigned a constant value, such as 0.030, then the difference between the two stress terms (or their ratio) can be quite large, giving the appearance that reach-average transport intensities are much higher in some types of channels than others. An alternative approach is to allow the reference shear stress to vary in accordance with an empirical relation that accounts for the effects of changes in velocity and increasing roughness in steep channels (Mueller *et al.*, 2005; Lamb *et al.*, 2008). A third and even simpler approach, that gets around the choice of specific values, is to assume that the bankfull Shields stress, $\tau_b^*$, varies in proportion to the reference Shields stress,

$$\langle \tau_b^* \rangle = \tau_r^* \, (1 + \varepsilon) \qquad (35.3)$$

wherein the brackets indicate a section or reach average and $\varepsilon$ is a constant of proportionality representing the excess shear stress at channel-forming flows (Paola, 1996). Based on relatively limited data, Paola (1996) suggested that $\varepsilon \approx 0.2$; using a much larger data set, Parker *et al.* (2007) deduced that $\varepsilon \approx 0.6$. However, in both of these studies, the estimates of $\varepsilon$ were based on assumed values of the reference Shields stress $\tau_r^* = 0.045$ and 0.030, respectively. Recognizing the problems introduced by assigning specific values of shear stress to reference or bankfull conditions, Mueller *et al.* (2005) developed empirical relations for both $\tau_b^*$ and $\tau_r^*$ using coupled measurements of flow and bedload transport in 45 gravel-bed channels in the western USA and Canada. For each site, they formulated a relation between measured bedload transport rates and dimensionless shear

stress, and determined the value of $\tau^*$ corresponding to a small non-zero transport rate. These results, summarized in Figure 35.3, indicate that the reference shear stress for bedload transport in gravel-bed channels ranges from 0.01 to 0.12, with a mean of 0.046. The ratio of $\tau_b^*$ to $\tau_r^*$ ranges from 0.9 to 2.0, with a mean of 1.27 ($\varepsilon = 0.27$).

Nearly all of the data used in the preceding analysis come from relatively stable gravel-bed channels; only a handful of these channels would be classified as meandering, and none of them would be classified as braided (all of the channels are considered to be self-formed, but many of them are located in mountain valleys). Measurements that would allow us to compare transport thresholds in braided rivers with the results shown in Figure 35.3 are limited in number, but nonetheless useful. Table 35.1 lists basic data extracted from several published studies of bedload transport in braided rivers, plus results from our own analyses. The values of $\tau_r^*$ listed in Table 35.1 were inferred either from bedload transport relations presented in the original papers, or from more recent analysis of data obtained through the United States Geological Survey National Water Information System (NWIS). The results listed in Table 35.1 suggest that the range in $\tau_r^*$ in braided rivers (0.010 to 0.087) is similar to single-thread rivers, and the mean $\tau_r^*$ is essentially the same (0.044). Given the small sample size, we do not want to over-interpret this result, and we also recognize that the range in observed values of $\tau_r^*$ in braided rivers could be due to a number of factors, some of which are unrelated to channel planform. A goal of future work, therefore, would be to populate this data set with measurements from a much larger number of braided rivers to determine if thresholds for transport are appreciably different from single-thread rivers.

**Table 35.1**  Basic data of braided rivers in which bedload transport has been measured

| Location | Slope | $D_{50}$ (mm) | $\tau_r^*$ | Data Source |
|----------|-------|---------------|------------|-------------|
| Talkeetna R. | 0.00073 | 41 | 0.010 | USGS-NWIS[a] |
| Susitna R. | 0.00184 | 41 | 0.016 | USGS-NWIS[a] |
| Sunlight Cr. | 0.0095 | 43 | 0.033 | E. R. Mueller, unpubl. data |
| White R. | 0.014 | 73 | 0.047 | Ferguson et al., 1989 |
| River Feshie | 0.0094 | 52 | 0.054 | Ashworth and Ferguson, 1989 |
| Sunwapta R. | 0.0060 | 25 | 0.061 | Ferguson et al., 1992 |
| Lyngsdalselva | 0.022 | 69 | 0.087 | Ashworth and Ferguson, 1989 |

[a]Flow and bedload transport measurements retrieved from the US Geological Survey National Water Information Service (NWIS).

Up to this point, our discussion has focused mostly on differences in spatially averaged properties of channels, the assumption being that we can represent the dynamics of flow and sediment transport with reach-average values of width, depth, shear stress, and grain size. Only recently, with advent of 2-D and 3-D hydrodynamic models, has it been possible to consider the dynamics of more complex cases in which variations in bed topography and channel curvature alter the distribution of shear stress acting on the bed. These effects were recognized long ago, but some of the implications for modelling sediment transport have been discussed only recently. Paola (1996), for example, suggested that, without knowing the precise details of the flow field, bedload transport in braided channels might be modelled more effectively as a spatial stochastic process governed by both the mean and the variance in boundary shear stress. Lacking detailed information on spatial variations of stress in natural channels, he proposed modelling the distribution with a two-parameter gamma probability density function

$$f(\tau) = \frac{\alpha(\tau/\langle\tau_o\rangle)^{\alpha-1}e^{-\alpha(\tau/\langle\tau_o\rangle)}}{\langle\tau_o\rangle\Gamma(\alpha)} \tag{35.4}$$

wherein $\Gamma$ is the standard gamma function, $\tau/\langle\tau_o\rangle$ is the local shear stress, $\tau$, normalized by the reach-average shear stress, $\langle\tau_o\rangle$, and $\alpha$ is a shape parameter, which he estimated from depth and velocity measurements on the Ohau River, New Zealand. Paola compared model results with measurements from flume experiments by Ashmore (1985), and found reasonably good agreement between predicted and measured transport rates by incorporating spatial variations in shear stress; if the stress was set to a reach-average value ($\alpha \rightarrow \infty$), modelled transport rates were consistently too low.

Hoey et al. (2001) used data from their own braided river experiments to formulate probability distributions of shear stress as well as channel width, then applied an equation similar to (35.2) to estimate the total bedload

flux of the channel network. Their results suggest that the stochastic components of shear stress and channel width are both important in predicting the total bedload flux (Hoey et al., 2001). Ferguson (2003) developed a conceptually similar statistical model and concluded that a model that did not include spatial variations in shear stress (or critical shear stress) would under-predict the true transport rate considerably. Nicholas (2000) modified the approach used by Paola (1996) and Hoey et al. (2001) to model the annual bedload sediment yield of the Waimakariri River in New Zealand. In this study, the probability distribution of shear stress was determined from estimates of local flow depths at 36 cross-sections distributed along 45 km of the channel. Nicholas (2000) found that the streamwise patterns of erosion and deposition calculated from the model were broadly consistent with measurements of scour and fill covering the same reach. In a subsequent study, Nicholas (2003) used a 2-D hydraulic model to simulate flow velocity and boundary shear stress in a 470 m reach of the Avoca River in New Zealand. Model parameters were tested on the basis of low-flow measurements of water-surface elevation, flow depth and velocity, and simulations were run for five flows ranging from 5 to 100 m³ s⁻¹. Figure 35.4 compares three of the model-derived distributions of shear stress with fits of the gamma distribution obtained from Equation (35.4) with values of $\alpha$ ranging from ~0.7–1.2. No goodness-of-fit tests were conducted in this case, but it appears that the agreement between the fitted distributions of shear stress and the observed (modelled) values is quite good.

The hypotheses and results presented above motivated us to seek similar relations for flow and shear stress in a single-thread river. In 2004 we initiated research on the Williams Fork River in central Colorado to quantify the effects of channel bed disturbance on benthic organisms, specifically, the accrual of periphyton following spring snowmelt floods. Details of the study are described in Segura et al. (2010). Spatial variations in boundary shear stress were modelled in three separate study reaches

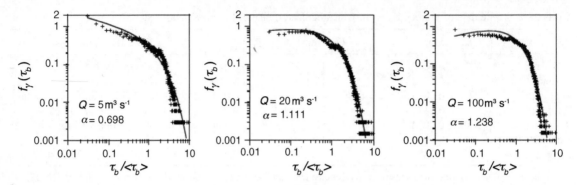

**Figure 35.4** Frequency distributions of boundary shear stress modeled at three discharges, Avoca River, New Zealand. The solid line in each figure indicates a fit of the gamma distribution obtained by adjusting values of the shape parameter, $\alpha$. (from Nicholas, 2003). Reproduced, with permission, from Nicholas, A.P. 2003. Investigation of spatially distributed braided river flows using a two-dimensional hydraulic model. *Earth Surface Processes and Landforms* **28**: 655–674.

using the Multi-Dimensional Surface Water Modeling System (MD-SWMS) developed by the United States Geological Survey (McDonald *et al.*, 2005). Field measurements of water-surface elevations and vertically averaged velocities were used in calibrating model parameters, and the model was run for four flows ranging from 0.3 to 1.0 bankfull. Model output was then used to develop frequency distributions of local flow depth and shear stress, similar to the results presented by Nicholas (2000; 2003). Figure 35.5 shows distributions of the local flow depth, $h$, normalized by the reach average depth,

$<h>$, for four flows in one of the reaches studied by Segura *et al.* (2010). The smooth line in each panel indicates the fit of the gamma distribution, obtained by varying the shape parameter, $\alpha$, to minimize the sum of the differences between observed and fitted values. The agreement between the gamma distribution and the observed values of depth appears to be quite good, however we should note that the best fits were obtained with much higher values of $\alpha$ than those reported by Nicholas (2000). The higher values of $\alpha$ are indicative of a more symmetric, narrowly bounded distribution.

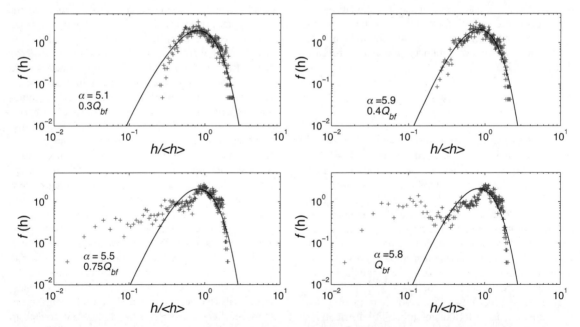

**Figure 35.5** Frequency distributions of depth modeled at four discharges, Williams Fork River, Colorado. The solid line in each figure indicates a fit of the gamma distribution obtained by adjusting values of the shape parameter, $\alpha$.

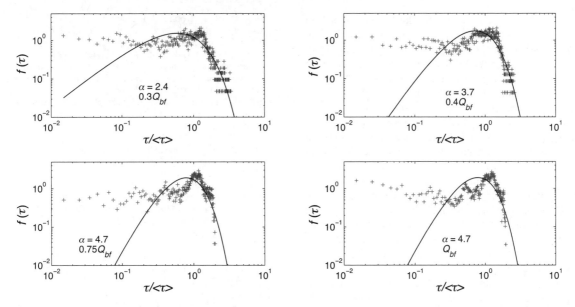

**Figure 35.6** Frequency distributions of boundary shear stress modelled for four discharges, Williams Fork River, Colorado. The solid line in each figure indicates a fit of the gamma distribution obtained by adjusting values of the shape parameter, $\alpha$.

Figure 35.6 shows similar plots comparing frequency distributions of normalized shear stress with the fitted gamma distribution. The agreement here between fitted and observed values of shear stress is not as good as it is for depth, particularly at the two higher flows, where the gamma function over-estimates the higher-than-average stresses by as much as 50%. Perhaps the more important point to note here is that, if we compare the frequency distributions of shear stress in the braided channel with the single-thread channel (Figures 35.4 and 35.6), and if we compare the parameter values used in fitting the distributions, it is evident that the range in shear stress in the braided channel is much higher than it is in the single-thread channel. The results presented by Nicholas (2003) suggest that in braided rivers shear stresses greater than three times the average stress might be relatively common, whereas the results from our work on the Williams Fork River suggest that in single-thread channels these conditions would be rare.

## 35.4   CONCLUSIONS

The challenges of measuring sediment fluxes in natural channels – bedload in particular – have limited us from quantifying the role of sediment supply on channel morphology. We use combinations of easily measured variables, such as discharge, slope, and grain size, as surrogates for sediment supply and transport capacity but, in the end, the number of data sets available for

quantifying explicitly the role of sediment supply in the transition between single-thread and braided channel patterns is relatively small. Our purpose here is to stimulate further discussion and research on the key variables governing this transition, and to suggest that in the absence of comprehensive sediment sampling programmes we can gauge the importance of each of these variables with standard field measurements. Our conclusions can be summarized as follows:

(1)   Braided channels tend to be much wider than single-thread channels; however, as Equation (35.2) indicates, the bedload flux scales linearly with width, hence the total bedload discharge increases, at most, in proportion to the width (and perhaps less if the width of the channel carrying the majority of the bedload is significantly less than the width of the channel carrying the majority of the water). It seems unlikely, therefore, that the seemingly large differences in sediment transport capacity of braided and single-thread channels can be explained simply by differences in channel width.

(2)   The available sediment data suggest that, on average, the bed material in braided rivers is not much finer or coarser than in single-thread rivers. It seems evident, however, that the bed material in braided rivers is much more poorly sorted than in single-thread rivers, and there is some evidence to suggest that, because of differences in channel

dynamics and unsteady flow, the bedload in braided rivers is less likely to be in equilibrium with the local shear stress than it would be in single-thread channels. Further research linking the grain size of the bedload and the bed material to flow conditions would help clarify the influence of sediment properties on planform transitions.

(3) Our analysis of bedload transport thresholds suggests that the range in reference Shields stresses in braided river channels is roughly the same as in single-thread channels. In only a few braided rivers can we make direct comparisons between the bankfull shear stress and the reference shear stress (the stress producing a small bedload transport rate) because the measurements needed to develop bedload transport relations are rarely made in these channels. Bertoldi *et al.* (2009a) developed a 1-D model of flow and bedload transport in braided channels using detailed measurements of channel geometry, and an algorithm for computing lateral variations in unit water discharge and shear stress. They observed that, because of the disproportionate change in active channel width, the local depth and shear stress increased rather slowly with increasing discharge, the main consequence being that the Shields stress increased by less than a factor of two over the range of observed stream powers. They likewise applied the gamma probability density function to fit the distributions of shear stress, but found, in contrast to Nicholas (2003), that the best fits were obtained with values of $\alpha$ much greater than 1.0, implying that the distributions of shear stress in braided channels were potentially much more uniform than proposed in earlier studies. It seems evident, therefore, that additional research aimed at quantifying variations in shear stress and transport intensity would be extremely useful in narrowing the distinction between single-thread and braided river channels.

## 35.5   ACKNOWLEDGEMENTS

The research described here was funded in part by grants from the National Science Foundation (BCS-9986338) and the US Forest Service Stream Systems Technology Center. Comments from an anonymous reviewer were helpful in revising an earlier version of this manuscript.

## 35.6   REFERENCES

Ashmore P.E. 1985. *Process and form in gravel braided streams: laboratory modelling and field observations.* Unpublished Ph.D. Thesis, University of Alberta.

Ashmore P.E. and Church, M. 1998. Sediment transport and river morphology: a paradigm for study. In Klingeman, P.C., Beschta, R.L., Komar, P.D., and Bradley, J.B., editors, *Gravel-Bed Rivers in the Environment.* Highland Ranch, CO, Water Resources Publications, pp. 115–148.

Ashmore, P.E. and Sauks, E. 2006. Prediction of discharge from water surface width in a braided river with implications for at-a-station hydraulic geometry, *Water Resources Research*, **42**, W03406, doi: 10.1029/2005WR003993.

Ashworth, P.E. and Ferguson, R.I. 1989. Size-selective entrainment of bed load in gravel bed streams, *Water Resources Research* **25**: 627–634.

Bertoldi W., Ashmore, P.E., and Tubino, M. 2009a. A method for estimating the mean bed load flux in braided rivers, *Geomorphology* **103**: 330–340. doi: 10.1016/j.geomorph.2008.06.014.

Bertoldi, W., Zanoni, L., and Tubino, M. 2009b. Planform dynamics of braided streams. *Earth Surface Processes and Landforms* **34**: 547–557. doi: 10.1002/esp.1755.

Church, M. 2006. Bed material transport and the morphology of alluvial river channels. *Annual Review of Earth and Planetary Sciences* **34**: 325–354.

Eaton, B.E., Millar, R.G., and Davidson, S. 2010. Channel patterns: braided, anabranching, and single-thread. *Geomorphology* **120**: 353–364.

Einstein, H.A. 1950. *The Bed-load Function for Sediment Transportation in open Channel Flows.* US Department of Agriculture, Soil Conservation Service, Technical Bulletin No. 1026.

Ferguson, R.I. 2003. The missing dimension: effects of lateral variation on 1-D calculations of fluvial bedload transport. *Geomorphology* **56**: 1–14. doi: 10.1016/S0169-555X(03)00042-4.

Ferguson, R.I., Ashmore, P.E., Ashworth, P.J., Paola, C., and Prestegaard, K.L. 1992. Measurements in a braided river chute and lobe: 1. Flow pattern, sediment transport, and channel change. *Water Resources Research* **28**: 1877–1886. doi: 10.1029/92WR00700.

Ferguson, R.I., Prestegaard, K., and Ashworth, P. 1989. Influence of sand on hydraulics and gravel transport in a braided gravel bed river. *Water Resources Research* **25**: 635–643.

Hoey, T., Cudden, J., and Shvidchenko, A. 2001. The consequences of unsteady sediment transport in braided rivers. In Mosley, M.P., editor. *Gravel-Bed Rivers V.* Wellington, New Zealand Hydrological Society, pp. 121–142.

Lamb, M.P., Dietrich, W.E., and Venditti, J.G. 2008. Is the critical Shields stress for incipient sediment motion dependent on channel-bed slope? *Journal of Geophysical Research* **113**: F02008. doi: 10.1029/2007JF000831.

Lane, S., Richards, K., and Chandler, J. 1995. Morphological estimation of the time-integrated bed load transport rate. *Water Resources Research* **31**: 761–772.

Leopold, L.B. and Wolman, M.G. 1957. *River Channel Patterns: Braided, Meandering and Straight.* United States Geological Survey, Professional Paper 282-B.

Lewin, J. and Brewer, P.A. 2001. Predicting channel patterns. *Geomorphology* **40**: 329–339.

Martin Y.E. and Church, M. 1995. Bed material transport estimated from channel surveys: Vedder River, *British Columbia. Earth Surface Processes and Landforms* **20**: 347–361.

McDonald, R.R., Nelson, J.M., and Bennett, J.P. 2005. Multi-dimensional surface-water modeling system user's guide: United States Geological Survey, *Techniques and Methods* Book 6, Section B, Chapter 6.

Millar, R.G. 2000. Influence of bank vegetation on alluvial channel patterns. *Water Resources Research* **36**: 1109–1118.

Millar, R.G. 2005. Theoretical regime relations for mobile gravel-bed rivers with stable banks. *Geomorphology* **64**: 207–220.

Mosley, M.P. 1982. Analysis of the effect of changing discharge on channel morphology and instream uses in a braided river, Ohau River, New Zealand. *Water Resources Research* **18**: 800–812.

Mueller, E.R. and Pitlick, J. 2005. Morphologically based model of bed load transport capacity in a headwater stream. *Journal of Geophysical Research* **110**: F02016. doi: 10.1029/2003JF000117.

Mueller, E.R., Pitlick, J., and Nelson, J.M. 2005. Variation in the reference Shields stress for bed load transport in gravel-bed streams and rivers. *Water Resources Research* **41**: W04006. doi: 10.1029/2004WR003692.

Nicholas, A.P. 2000. Modelling bedload yield in braided gravel bed rivers. *Geomorphology* **36**: 89–106.

Nicholas, A.P. 2003. Investigation of spatially distributed braided river flows using a two-dimensional hydraulic model. *Earth Surface Processes and Landforms* **28**: 655–674.

Paola, C. 1996. Incoherent structures: turbulence as a metaphor for stream braiding. In Ashworth, P.J., Bennett, S.J., Best, J. L., and McLelland, S.J., editors. *Coherent Flow Structures in Open Channels*. Chichester, John Wiley & Sons, Ltd, pp. 706–723.

Paola, C. and Seal, R. 1995. Grain size patchiness as a cause of selective deposition and downstream fining. *Water Resources Research* **31**: 1395–1407.

Parker, G. 1979. Hydraulic geometry of active gravel rivers. American Society of Civil Engineers, *Journal of the Hydraulics Division* **105**: 1185–1201.

Parker, G., Wilcock, P.R., Paola, C., Dietrich, W.E., and Pitlick, J. 2007. Physical basis for quasi-universal relations describing bankfull hydraulic geometry of single-thread gravel bed rivers. *Journal of Geophysical Research* **112**: F04005. doi: 10.1029/2006JF000549.

Schumm, S.A. 1985. Patterns of alluvial rivers. *Annual Review of Earth and Planetary Sciences* **13**: 5–27.

Segura, C. and Pitlick, J. 2010. Scaling frequency of channel-forming flows in snowmelt-dominated streams, *Water Resources Research* **46**: W06524. doi: 10.1029/2009WR008336.

Segura C., McCutchan, J.H., Lewis, W.M., and Pitlick, J. 2010. The influence of channel bed disturbance on algae biomass in a Colorado mountain stream. *Ecohydrology* **4**: 411–421. doi: 10.1002/eco.142.

van den Berg, J.H. and Bledsoe, B.P. 2003. Comment on Lewin and Brewer (2001): "Predicting channel patterns". *Geomorphology* **53**: 333–337.

# Can We Link Cause and Effect in Landscape Evolution?

## Thomas J. Coulthard and Marco J. Van De Wiel

## 36.1 INTRODUCTION

*As the science of sediment transportation and deposition develops, it will be possible to predict more and more closely the morphological changes which will take place in a river due to any set of conditions and rate at which they will occur.*

(Lane, 1955; p. 745–746.)

Geomorphic systems are often examined with three aims in mind: (i) to understand what has happened in the past – often using records or archives of past behaviour; (ii) to develop an understanding of what might control these systems – what may be external or internal controls; (iii) to use the knowledge from (i) and (ii) to develop a way to predict what may happen in the future.

Métivier and Barrier raise these issues with the two questions: Can the metamorphosis of a river be related to causative changes in boundary conditions? And, what record of this history can be deciphered from the stratigraphic record? In effect, is it possible to relate cause to effect? Can we determine how external factors (and of course internal) alter fluvial form, morphology, and stratigraphy? These are the fundamental questions that we wish to explore in this chapter using examples from numerical modelling studies.

The answer to these questions is an unequivocal "yes", if we believe that the fluvial system behaves in a quite straightforward manner, i.e., that there is a direct and simple (e.g., linear) relation that links inputs to outputs. Examining fluvial systems from first principles may lead to some optimism for this outcome, as fluvial geomorphology is at its most basic form simply the study of movement of water and sediment driven by gravity and momentum. For a single particle on a flat bed these are straightforward and simple calculations.

However, natural river systems exhibit heterogeneity on many scales – for example in grain size, particle shape, particle material, cohesive properties, flow turbulence, and history. These heterogeneities and the interactions between them make the relation between input and output, cause and effect, often non-linear (Phillips, 2003, 2006). The process of sediment transport provides an excellent example as, despite its importance for determining fluvial morphology, it rarely – if at all – exhibits a linear relation to shear stress, the main driving force. There are numerous examples of such behaviour. Cudden and Hoey (2003), using bedload and flow measurements from a proglacial stream, show that while there is a relation between point measurements of local shear stress and bedload sediment transport rate, there is a large amount of scatter, of order of magnitude scale. Ashmore (1991) observed "auto-pulses" of internally driven variations of bed-load flux in flume experiments of braided rivers, which have also been observed in the field (e.g. Reid and Frostick, 1986; Goff and Ashmore 1994). Gomez and Church (1989) used 12 different sediment transport relations to predict sediment transport rates for different data sets and found significant data scatter and limited predictive power. These 12 relations were largely empirical, and therefore scatter in outcomes and more general differences between sediment transport models reflect the non-linearity, as found by Cudden and Hoey (2003), as well as larger-scale differences that may occur between different rivers in different parts of the world.

It would appear that this non-linear response is not restricted to short time frames only. When we examine longer time scales, typically greater than 1000 years, many researchers have tried to relate past episodes of fluvial activity to external drivers, such as climate and/or land use (e.g. Macklin and Lewin, 2003; Gilbert *et al.*, 2006; Tomkins *et al.*, 2010). However, such

*Gravel-bed Rivers: Processes, Tools, Environments*, First Edition. Edited by Michael Church, Pascale M. Biron and André G. Roy.
© 2012 John Wiley & Sons, Ltd. Published 2012 by John Wiley & Sons, Ltd.

relations are not clear cut. Interactions amongst catchment processes, intermittency of mass movement processes, and temporary storage of sediments within the catchment disrupt the causal connection between environmental forcing and sediment yield (e.g. Nicholas *et al.*, 1995; Lamoureux, 2002; Wainwright, 2006; Hodder *et al.*, 2007; Temme and Veldkamp, 2009; Van De Wiel and Coulthard, 2010; Chiverell *et al.*, 2010; Jerolmack and Paola, 2010). Furthermore, possible dating and preservation problems, while establishing a chronology of the sedimentary record, may further hamper the relation with past external forces (e.g. Lewin and Macklin, 2003).

In this paper we argue that, since these kinds of uncertainties are an inherent aspect of geomorphological processes themselves, it is unlikely that numerical models will ever overcome them. There is, therefore, a natural limit to the ability of numerical models to predict future geomorphological change, or to unequivocally predict effect from cause.

## 36.2 NON-LINEARITY IN NUMERICAL MODELLING

Numerical modelling has been used to examine non-linearity in river systems, as well as to address the phenomena of self-organized criticality (SOC) that may have important implications for our ability to understand

and to model fluvial systems (e.g. Stølum, 1996; Fonstad and Marcus, 2003; Luo *et al.*, 2006; Bolla-Pittaluga *et al.*, 2009; Blanckaert and De Vriend, 2010).

Investigating SOC and non-linearity, Van De Wiel and Coulthard (2010) recently published work that used a landscape evolution model (CAESAR) to model a very simple $100 \times 200$ cell catchment – shaped like a folded sheet of paper (Figure 36.1a). This DEM had a cell size of 5 m and cross and downstream slopes of 0.02. The CAESAR landscape evolution model (Coulthard *et al.*, 2000; 2002; 2005, Van De Wiel *et al.*, 2007) simulates landscape development by routing water over a regular grid of cells and altering elevations according to erosion and deposition from fluvial and slope processes. CAESAR requires the specification of several parameters or initial conditions, including elevation, grain sizes, and rainfall (catchment mode) or a flow input (reach mode). In theory, CAESAR model operation is simple, where topography drives fluvial and hillslope processes that determine the spatial distribution of erosion and deposition for a given time step. This alters the topography, which becomes the starting point for the next time step. Outputs of the model are elevation and sediment distributions through space and time, and discharges and sediment fluxes at the outlet(s) through time. This very simple model catchment was subjected to regular flood events, i.e., 25 000 daily flood events of 30 mm of rainfall a day, all falling in one hour, which

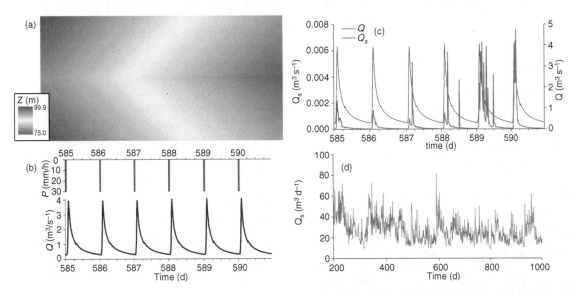

**Figure 36.1** Model setup and results for the simulations by Van De Wiel and Coulthard (2010): (a) initial elevations ($Z$) in the idealized rectangular catchment; (b) temporal distribution of rainfall (top, $P$) and simulated discharge at the catchment outlet (bottom, $Q$); (c) intraday bedload yield ($Qs$, red) and flow discharge ($Q$, blue) at the catchment outlet. Sediment yield is highly variable in both time scales, although water discharge is regular and periodic; (d) daily bedload yield, showing significant variability throughout the simulation. Adapted from Van De Wiel and Coulthard, 2010. (See the color version of this figure in color plate section.)

resulted in corresponding regular flood hydrographs (Figure 36.1b). These floods caused incision along the main channel and the formation of an armoured bed (Van De Wiel and Coulthard, 2010).

The important finding was that, although the flow hydrographs were very regular, the sediment discharge was highly non-linear (Figure 36.1c, d). The rise and fall of sediment transport rates largely follow the water discharge, but are highly irregular, and there are irregular peaks and spikes in the sediment yield (Figure 36.1c). Van De Wiel and Coulthard (2010) suggested that these irregularities may be caused by thresholds within the sediment transport laws and interactions between the multiple grain-sizes.

To investigate whether or not this was the cause, Van De Wiel and Coulthard (2010) divided the catchment into eight different zones with sediment in each zone having a different colour, which acted as a numerical tracer. Analysis of simulated sediment output showed that the sediment is coming from different parts of the catchment at different times. In particular, the experiments showed headward incision following local breaches of the stream bed's armour layer. This provided a cascading erosional mechanism by increasing local shear stresses (by increasing the gradient), which in turn causes erosion of the upstream cell – and so on (Van De Wiel and Coulthard, 2010). For each flood event this cascade can be small (one cell or nothing) or large (as many cells as there are along the length of the channel).

Van De Wiel and Coulthard (2010) suggested that this behaviour could be indicative of a system that exhibits self-organized criticality – made famous by Per Bak's sand-pile experiments (Bak et al., 1987, 1988). Bak et al.'s (1987) theory posited that a system can organize itself into a state or condition whereby a very small disturbance (in this case a flood) can cause either a small or very large reaction (in this case sediment yield). Although there is no strict set of sufficient conditions to define SOC in a system, there a several necessary conditions: (i) non-linear temporal dynamics in the occurrence of disturbance events within the system; (ii) an inverse power-law relation between of the magnitude and frequency of the events; (iii) the existence of a critical state of the system to which the system readjusts after a disturbance; (iv) the existence of a cascading process mechanism by which the same process can initiate both low-magnitude and high-magnitude events.

The implications of a SOC system are significant since the variability in output from SOC systems is not dependant upon the energy inputs, which means that large outputs may come from a small input. Because of this, SOC systems are effectively unpredictable. A second consequence is that SOC limits our ability to link the output from a river (sedimentary record) to the causes of the change. Effectively, SOC removes the link between cause and effect.

However, it should be noted that whilst Van De Wiel and Coulthard's (2010) work showed a mechanism for SOC to operate (the cascading erosion), the magnitude-frequency relation of the outputs was not a negative power law, although they have shown such behaviour in previous studies (Coulthard and Van De Wiel, 2007).

So do the results of Van De Wiel and Coulthard (2010) result in the severing of the link between cause and effect? Certainly they indicate that in a very simple catchment undergoing regular floods there is a high degree of non-linearity, which strongly implies that we may not be able to link cause to effect between the magnitude of rainfall events and corresponding sediment yields. This would have massive implications for fluvial geomorphology and the three aims we established in the first paragraph. However, we must recognize that this is an idealized example and we are only here looking at internal changes. One could legitimately ask if results would be different if we introduce external disturbances (e.g., climate change or tectonic uplift), i.e., if we introduce a cause and look for an effect.

## 36.3   MODEL INVESTIGATIONS

To investigate this latter question we have used the experimental set up of Van De Wiel and Coulthard (2010) with a regular rainfall input. But we introduce a sudden major disturbance: 4 m of uplift for the top 80% of the catchment, 5000 days into the simulation. The uplift is a uniform vertical displacement of the upper catchment and happens instantaneously (between model iterations).

Looking at the time series of sediment yield from the catchment (Figure 36.2), there is a jump in the sediment output when the uplift happens, then sediment yield is elevated for several thousand days as the local gradients increase first at the point of uplift and then as channel incision propagates upstream through the catchment through incision. After several thousand days the incision has returned the long profile of the channel to close to its original gradient and the sediment yields return to pre-disturbance levels. So, in the simple catchment our forcing is clearly recognizable in the signal. However, there is still considerable "noise", similar to the irregular output found by Van De Wiel and Coulthard (2010), and if the amount of uplift were less, the spike caused by uplift could well be masked by this "natural" noise.

Following this experiment, we used the same simulation setup, but added some topographic complexity. The grid was extended beyond the original catchment outlet and a flat floodplain was added, that allowed an alluvial fan to form during our 25 000 floods (Figure 36.3, inset). This is

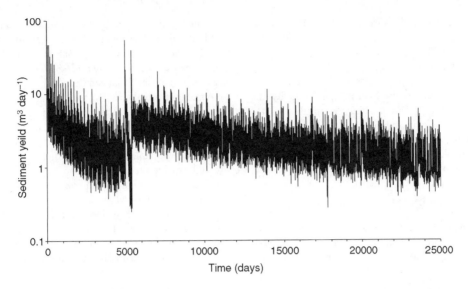

**Figure 36.2** Bedload yield at the outlet of a simple catchment for a simulation with a single 4 m uplift event occurring at day 5000. The impact of the uplift event is clearly noticeable in the sediment yield. The catchment used in this simulation is the same as in Figure 36.1a.

the same catchment set up as used by Coulthard and Van De Wiel (2007) when investigating SOC in alluvial fan systems. Again, we simulated uplift in this catchment after 5000 days, resulting in 4 m of vertical displacement at the break between catchment and floodplain.

This yielded two important results. Firstly, as found by Coulthard and Van De Wiel (2007), allowing an alluvial fan to develop significantly increased the non-linearity or scatter generated for individual flood events. The capability of the fan to be a store, a source, or simply a conduit

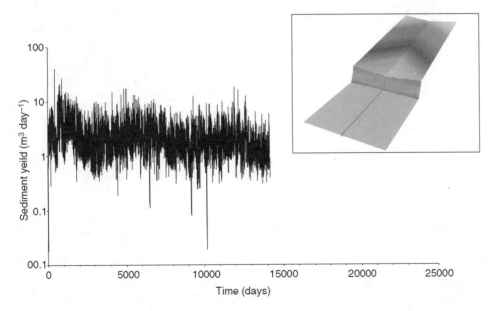

**Figure 36.3** Bedload yield at the outlet of a more complex catchment for a simulation with a single 4 m uplift event occurring at day 5000. The impact of the uplift event is masked, and can not be detected in the sediment yield. The catchment used in this simulation is the similar to that in Figure 36.1a, but it has a floodplain attached in the lower parts (inset).

for sediment enhances the variability seen in the simple catchment experiments. Secondly, no signal from the uplift episode at 5000 days was propagated through to the catchment outlet. The sediment yield signal of the uplift is absorbed, or buffered by sedimentation in the fan, as well as hidden within the "noise" generated by the catchment and the fan (Figure 36.3; the uplift happened after 5000 days). Thus, by adding an alluvial fan, the signal of a major environmental disturbance, i.e. 4 m of uplift, is completely masked. It is, therefore, impossible to link cause to effect in these final simulations.

## 36.4   DISCUSSION

These simulations were deliberately set up to be as parsimonious as possible, and with a very straightforward catchment configuration (Figure 36.1a) the effect of uplift

is quickly transmitted to the catchment sediment yield (Figure 36.2). Yet by adding a relatively simple structure, such as an alluvial fan, the signal from a major tectonic disturbance is masked (Figure 36.3). Clearly, by adding a geomorphic "unit" that can deposit as well as erode, we create a buffer that absorbs the signal and that is capable of generating its own spikes in sediment delivery. How this behaviour manifests itself in more complex catchment configurations is unknown. For example, if we add kilometres of floodplain, tributaries, more alluvial fans this could provide plenty more opportunity for buffering or modulating this signal – but could conversely add some complexity in the sediment response.

Returning to the questions outlined in the introduction: Can we link cause to effect in landscape evolution? What we have presented above implies that in these simulations we cannot assuredly link cause and effect. This has

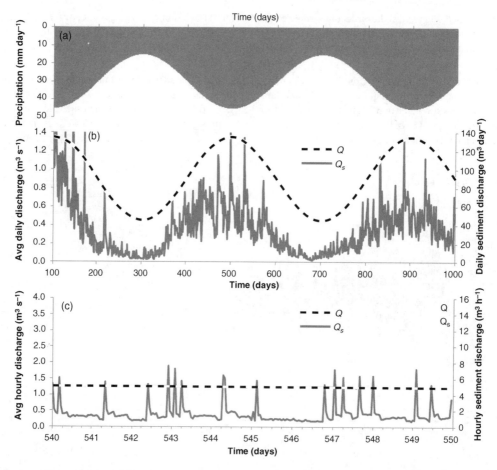

**Figure 36.4**   Results for simulations under large gradual changes in external conditions: (a) rainfall; (b) daily bedload yield (solid line) and flow discharge (dashed); (c) intraday bedload yield (solid) and flow discharge (dashed). Although sediment yield is highly variable over both time scales, the long-term trend of the external conditions can be detected in the daily bedload yield.

severe implications for geomorphology: should we give up trying to predict/understand morphological changes in rivers if we cannot readily link cause to effect? The answer is, of course, "no". But perhaps we should learn to accept that there are some things we cannot predict.

We could look to weather forecasters and climate modellers for some examples of how to deal with non-linear or chaotic systems. Weather dynamics are non-linear, and this has severe impacts on the predictability of future weather patterns. The non-linear interactions in weather systems cause uncertainties and errors to compound, and predictions quickly turn unreliable. Weather forecasts are therefore short term, usually a few days ahead, and maybe up to two weeks at best. For long-term predictions a different approach is taken, focusing on climate prediction rather than on weather forecasting. Climate modellers look at longer-term trends and broader spatial patterns in the weather system. Even though climate changes are equally susceptible to non-linear interactions, this does not mean that climate modelling is futile. The difference is in the detail of what is being modelled. Climate modellers readily accept that there are certain chaotic components of the climate system that restrict what they can predict. For example, we will never be able to predict what the weather will be at a specific time at a specific location in the more distant future. But we can predict broader spatial and temporal trends in climate patterns at regional and global scales. Thus, the expanded time horizon of the predictions comes at the cost of lower spatial and temporal resolution of their detail.

We believe that the issues facing weather and climate modelling are similar to those encountered when modelling fluvial systems. Longer-term simulations are feasible, provided that the metrics of their interpretation are adjusted accordingly. High-resolution predictions are limited to relatively short-term models, maybe up to 10 years or so. Beyond that, the non-linearity of the systems causes errors and uncertainties to accumulate to the extent that the simulations become unreliable. Long-term modelling therefore needs to focus on broader trends, both spatially and temporally. Thus, whilst individual events may go unnoticed, systematic changes, and long-term patterns may be detectable.

To illustrate this, a final experiment was conducted, in which the simple catchment (without the extended flood plain; Figure 36.1a) was subjected to large, but gradual changes in the climate input, i.e., precipitation. Rainfall gradually increased and decreased by 50% (Figure 36.4a), resulting in a corresponding change in the hydrograph (Figure 36.4b). In this case, the long-term trend in sediment yield does appear to reflect the precipitation time series (Figure 36.4b). However, there still is a large irregularity in the short-term sediment yield

signal (Figure 36.4b, c), which cannot be attributed to the external forcing. Thus long-term environmental trends may be detectable in the sediment yield signal, but individual sediment yield events cannot be unequivocally linked to external causes.

These are issues directly addressed by Jerolmack and Paola (2010), who used a simple rice-pile model to represent a geomorphic system. By changing the input of the rice grains into the pile and measuring the size of corresponding avalanches of rice they were able to determine that certain magnitude and period input signals were "shredded" or absorbed by the rice pile and that others persisted.

## 36.5 CONCLUSION

If river systems are non-linear, chaotic, and exhibit self-organized critical behaviour, then the capability to predict may not be governed by technology, model complexity, or level of monitoring resolution, but rather by the non-linear dynamics of the system itself. Therefore, it is important to recognize the limits of our predictive ability, i.e., our capability to link cause and effect, in fluvial systems.

## 36.6 REFERENCES

Ashmore, P. 1991. Channel morphology and bed load pulses in braided, gravel-bed streams. *Geografiska Annaler A* **73**: 37–52.

Bak, P., Tang, C., and Wiesenfeld, K. 1987. Self-organized criticality: an explanation of 1/f noise. *Physical Review Letters* **59**: 381–384.

Bak, P., Tang, C., and Wiesenfeld, K. 1988. Self-organized criticality. *Physical Review A* **38**: 364–374.

Blanckaert, K. and De Vriend, H.J. 2010. Meander dynamics: A nonlinear model without curvature restrictions for flow in open-channel bends. *Journal of Geophysical Research* **115**: F04011. doi: 04010.01029/02009JF001301.

Bolla-Pittaluga, M., Nobile, G., and Seminara, G. 2009. A nonlinear model for river meandering. *Water Resources Research* **45**: W04432. doi: 04410.01029/02008WR007298.

Chiverell, R.C., Foster, G.C., Thomas, G.S.P., and Marshall, P. 2010. Sediment transmission and storage: the implications for reconstructing landform development. *Earth Surface Processes and Landforms* **35**: 4–15.

Coulthard, T.J. and Van De Wiel, M.J. 2007. Quantifying fluvial non-linearity and finding self organized criticality? Insights from simulations of river basin evolution. *Geomorphology* **91**: 216–235.

Coulthard, T.J., Kirkby, M.J., and Macklin, M.G. 2000. Modelling geomorphic response to environmental change in an upland catchment. *Hydrological Processes* **14**: 2031–2045.

Coulthard, T.J., Lewin, J., and Macklin, M.G. 2005. Modelling differential catchment response to environmental change. *Geomorphology* **69**: 222–241.

Coulthard, T.J., Macklin, M.G., and Kirkby, M.J. 2002. A cellular model of Holocene upland river basin and alluvial fan evolution. *Earth Surface Processes and Landforms* **27**: 269–288.

Cudden, J.R. and Hoey, T.B. 2003. The causes of bedload pulses in a gravel channel: the implication of bedload grain-size distributions. *Earth Surface Processes and Landforms* **28**: 1411–1428.

Fonstad, M. and Marcus, W.A. 2003. Self-organized criticality in riverbank systems. *Association of American Geographers Annals* **93**: 281–296.

Gilbert, R., Crookshanks, S., Hodder, K.R., Spagnol, J., and Stull, R.B. 2006. The record of an extreme flood in the sediments of montane Lillooet Lake, British Columbia: implications for paleoenvironmental assessment. *Journal of Paleolimnology* **35**: 737–745.

Goff, J.R. and Ashmore, P. 1994. Gravel transport and morphological change in braided Sunwapta River, Alberta, Canada. *Earth Surface Processes and Landforms* **19**: 195–212.

Gomez, B. and Church, M. 1989. An assessment of bed load sediment transport formulae for gravel bed rivers. *Water Resources Research* **25**: 1161–1186.

Hodder, K.R., Gilbert, R., and Desloges, J.R. 2007. Glaciolacustrine varved sediment as an alpine hydroclimatic proxy. *Journal of Paleolimnology* **38**: 365–394.

Jerolmack, D.J. and Paola, C. 2010. Shredding of environmental signals by sediment transport. *Geophysical Research Letters* **37**: L19401. doi: 19410.11029/12010GL044638.

Lamoureux, S. 2002. Temporal patterns in suspended sediment yield following moderate to extreme hydrological events recorded in varved lacustrine environments. *Earth Surface Processes and Landforms* **27**: 1107–1124.

Lane, E.W. 1955. The importance of fluvial morphology in hydraulic engineering *American Society of Civil Engineers Proceedings* **81** (745), 1–17.

Lewin, J. and Macklin, M.G. 2003. Preservation potential for Late Quaternary river alluvium. *Journal of Quaternary Science* **18**: 107–120. doi: 10.1002/jqs.738.

Luo, W., Peronja, E., Duffin, K., and Stravers, J.A. 2006. Incorporating nonlinear rules in a web-based interactive landform simulation model (WILSIM). *Computers & Geosciences* **32**: 1512–1518.

Macklin, M.G. and Lewin, J. 2003. River sediments, great floods and centennial-scale Holocene climate change. *Journal of Quaternary Science* **18**: 101–105.

Nicholas, A.P., Ashworth, P.J., Kirkby, M.J., Macklin, M.G., and Murray, T. 1995. Sediment slugs: large-scale fluctuations in fluvial sediment transport rates and storage volumes. *Progress in Physical Geography* **19**: 500–519.

Phillips, J.D. 2003. Sources of nonlinearity and complexity in geomorphic systems. *Progress in Physical Geography* **27**: 1–23.

Phillips, J.D. 2006. Evolutionary geomorphology: thresholds and nonlinearity in landform response to environmental change. *Hydrology and Earth System Sciences* **10**: 731–742.

Reid, I. and Frostick, L. 1986. Dynamics of bedload transport in Turkey brook, a coarse-grained alluvial channel. *Earth Surface Processes and Landforms* **11**: 143–155.

Stølum, H.-H. 1996. River meandering as a self-organization process. *Science* **271**: 1710–1713.

Temme, A.J.A.M. and Veldkamp, A. 2009. Multi-process Late Quaternary landscape evolution modelling reveals lags in climate response over small spatial scales. *Earth Surface Processes and Landforms* **34**: 573–589.

Tomkins, J., Lamoureux, S.F., Antoniades, D., and Vincent WF. 2010. Autumn snowfall and hydroclimatic variability during the past millennium inferred from the varved sediments of meromictic Lake A, northern Ellesmere Island, Canada. *Quaternary Research* **74**: 188–198.

Van De Wiel, M.J. and Coulthard, T.J. 2010. Self-organized criticality in river basins: Challenging sedimentary records of environmental change. *Geology* **38**: 87–90.

Van De Wiel, M.J., Coulthard, T.J., Macklin, M.G., and Lewin, J. 2007. Embedding reach-scale fluvial dynamics within the CAESAR cellular automaton landscape evolution model. *Geomorphology* **90**: 283–301.

Wainwright, J. 2006. Degrees of separation: hillslope-channel coupling and the limits of palaeohydrological reconstruction. *Catena* **66**: 93–106.

## 36.7 DISCUSSION

### 36.7.1 Discussion by Jens Turowski

In their discussion of Métivier and Barrier's paper and in two earlier publications (Coulthard and Van De Wiel, 2007; Van De Wiel and Coulthard, 2010), Coulthard and Van De Wiel suggested that chaotic behaviour or self-organized criticality (SOC) could render the sediment yield of catchments essentially unpredictable. Here, as a note of caution, I want to raise a few points on these concepts. I will comment on SOC (1) and chaotic behaviour (2) in general, then I will discuss the particular model set up by the Coulthard and van de Wiel (3), and finally I will point out some known sediment transport behaviour reported in field studies, which suggest a more regular behaviour of catchments (4).

(1) As stated by Coulthard and van de Wiel (2007), a necessary condition for SOC is an inverse power-law scaling between the magnitude and frequency of the events in question. They identified the formation and break up of an armour layer as leading to a suitable cascading mechanism, as required for SOC. However, in the same model, this mechanism sometimes seems to lead to an inverse power-law scaling between the magnitude and frequency of the events (as in the work of Coulthard and Van De Wiel, 2007), and sometimes to exponential scaling (as in the work of Van De Wiel and Coulthard, 2010). It seems unlikely that the same mechanism under some conditions leads to SOC, but not under others. Therefore, for this particular model setup and mechanism, SOC can be excluded. However, chaotic behaviour is still a possible source of the fluctuations.

(2) A deterministic system can show chaotic behaviour when the system output is highly sensitive to the initial system state. Other necessary conditions for chaotic behaviour are so-called topological mixing and dense periodic orbits (Hasselblatt and Katok, 2003). Here, I will focus on the sensitivity to the initial system state. Formally, sensitivity to

the initial system state implies that each point in such a system is arbitrarily close to other points with very different output trajectories. Coulthard and van de Wiel suggest that the formation and break up of an armour layer causes the large observed fluctuations in their model. The local layering of grain sizes, and thus the existence of an armour layer and a lower layer of fine material could be determined in the model landscape, and, at least in principle, also in nature. Whether the system behaves chaotically still needs to be discerned; however, I suggest that our limited predictive ability, both in the model and in nature, is due to an insufficient characterization of the initial state, that is, the knowledge of the existence of an armour layer and of the grain-size distribution of the underlying substrate.

(3) The results of Coulthard and Van De Wiel (2007) and Van De Wiel and Coulthard (2010) rest on simulations with a highly simplified model system focusing on the single process of fluvial sediment transport. The rationale behind this approach was to eliminate complexities and focus on the basic properties and behaviour of the system. However, the complexities of a natural system could also suppress or hide the behaviour observed in such a simplified system. Furthermore, the catchment topography used in the simulations, an inclined V-shape, is highly unrealistic. Such topography will be far away from the equilibrium state of the catchment. Thus, in the simulations, the catchment is in a fast-evolving transient state, which may affect the size and frequency of the fluctuations. The discharges in the experiments of Van De Wiel and Coulthard (2010) range from about $0.25\,\mathrm{m^3\,s^{-1}}$ to $4\,\mathrm{m^3\,s^{-1}}$. These span just over an order of magnitude, much less than what would be observed for many natural streams. The threshold for the onset of bedload transport seems to be around $0.5–1\,\mathrm{m^3\,s^{-1}}$, and the threshold for the break-up of an armour layer can be expected to be factor of 2–10 times larger than this. Thus, the system operates near the threshold for the identified cascading mechanism, the break-up of the armour layer. It can be expected that, for higher transport stages, when all grain-size fractions are fully mobile, the catchment behaves similarly to a system with sediment of a single grain size. As stated by Coulthard and Van De Wiel (2007), such a system does not show strong fluctuations in their model.

(4) Many field data sets show strongly variable transport rates for discharges near the threshold of motion, but less scatter for high transport stages (e.g., Rickenmann, 1997). Furthermore, the sediment volume delivered in a single event shows a good correlation with peak discharge in many streams. In the Erlenbach, a step-pool system with highly active hillslopes and dense vegetation in the Swiss pre-Alps (Turowski *et al.*, 2009), Kendall's $\tau$ (correlation coefficient) between total sediment volume delivered in an event and peak discharge is 0.62 for 279 precipitation-triggered events (Figure 36.5). There clearly is a strong trend for these variables and a more sophisticated analysis

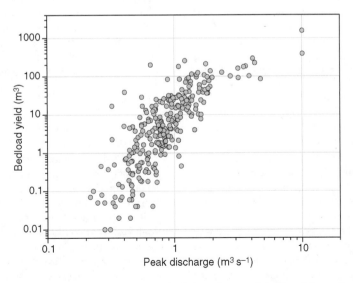

**Figure 36.5** Bedload yield as a function of peak discharge for precipitation-driven floods in the Erlenbach, Swiss Pre-alps.

(for instance including the total water volume delivered throughout the event, the shape of the hydrograph, or soil moisture) can reduce the scatter even further (e.g., Rickenmann, 1997).

In summary, although SOC and chaotic behaviour in catchments is worth pursuing in further study, it is currently unclear if and in how far these concepts apply to real catchments. To clarify these questions, more high-quality field data are needed, especially long-term observation series from catchments with various characteristics.

### 36.7.2  Discussion by Chris Parker

Non-linear dynamics may indeed create variability in a catchment's sediment yield over short-term time scales that is not predictable using known catchment boundary conditions. However, I would hypothesize that all significant changes in the boundary conditions, such as tectonic uplift, should produce a predictable response that is observable in the system. What may cause the response to be unrecognizable at the observation point is adjustment of the channel in between the disturbance and the observation point acting to absorb the effect of the disturbance. By adjusting its own morphology, the channel downstream of the disturbance can both reduce the magnitude and slow the progress of the disturbance signal. Typical dimensions in which the channel will adjust will be cross-section size and shape, channel gradient, channel planform, and bed material size. As a result, the magnitude and timing at which a response is observed at a point downstream depends upon the length of catchment between the disturbance and the observation point, and the ability of the channel to absorb the downstream impact of the disturbance through adjustment. The further away the observation point is from the disturbance, the longer the delay in response will be and the smaller the resultant signal will be. Similarly, the freedom with which the channel can adjust will also have an impact upon the timing and magnitude of the response observed downstream – highly constrained and confined channels will transmit disturbance signals very quickly and effectively; channels with highly malleable boundaries will slow and reduce the disturbance signal. Of course, the disturbance signal can be damped to such an extent by the adjustment of the intervening channel that it is no longer visible beyond the "noise" generated by non-linear driven variability.

Do the authors feel that this process may explain why the modelled example of the tectonic uplift may not have an observable impact on the sediment yield at a distant point downstream? That is, was the distance between the disturbance and the observation point so great, and the channel able to adjust in such an unconstrained manner,

that either the disturbance signal was so damped it was not visible above the non-linear driven variability, or it was so delayed it would have occurred after the end of the simulation? If so, do the authors feel that further research into understanding this type of response is important insofar as it may enable better predictions within non-linear fluvial systems? What do the authors feel is the most suitable method for investigating this aspect of fluvial systems?

### 36.7.3  Reply by Thomas Coulthard and Marco Van De Wiel

Jens Turowski raises five main points, which we will address here in turn. Firstly, Jens comments that in the Van De Wiel and Coulthard (2010) paper we do not show a negative power law for the magnitude frequency of the sediment output. This is correct; it is a log-linear decline in frequency. This is partly due to wishing to be transparent in presentation (these could be binned into logarithmic bins increasing the lower end) as well as having very few smaller sediment values due to the (semi) threshold in the sediment transport law. In effect the threshold restricts very small sediment yields – so whenever you get erosion and deposition you always get a minimum. Figure 2c in Van De Wiel and Coulthard (2010) shows these effects clearly. We would also like to point out that in Coulthard and Van De Wiel (2007) a power-law relation is clear when a variable rainfall is used to drive the model. Our aim in Van De Wiel and Coulthard (2010) was to show that there was a possible *mechanism* for SOC in river catchments which we felt was a far more important indicator than the presence of a power-law relation.

Secondly, in chaotic systems initial conditions are important, but a fundamental facet of SOC systems is that they organize their own initial conditions. In the sand-pile experiments of Bak *et al.* (1987), 1988) and in the rice-pile models of Jerolmack and Paola (2010) the sand and rice organizes itself into a critical state – or angle of repose. In our experiment the model armours its bed and erodes the long profile until it is in the condition where SOC emerges.

Thirdly, does the model set-up, with the simple catchment, help in generating these results by creating a condition that is in a transient state? We have worked backwards to this simple catchment having observed high levels of non-linearity in CAESAR results since Coulthard *et al.* (1998), described and discussed at greater length in Coulthard *et al.* (2007). There, we observed far greater levels of "scatter" or non-linearity in CAESAR models of four real catchments up to 400 km$^2$ in area, running over longer time scales (9000 years) driven by actual rainfall records. From our experience, larger and more complex systems appear to generate more complexity rather than reduce its effect.

Fourthly, and related to the point above regarding catchment sensitivity, we are to a degree using floods to which the catchment is "sensitive", but the catchment has developed this sensitivity through developing a surface armour in response to the magnitude of floods going through it. If we were to introduce larger floods (as we have done in other experiments) and concordant larger grain sizes (to prevent all sediment from simply washing away) then we would expect the same effect. The issue of catchment sensitivity to events of a particular magnitude is an interesting topic and one we have addressed before in Coulthard et al. (2007, where we identified a "sweet spot" of flood discharge in different catchments where there was greater variability (see Figure 36.6). This variability changed according to the size of the catchment, indicating a sensitivity for variation possibly around the threshold for motion.

Finally, we address the question of whether such non-linearity or SOC processes occur in real catchments. It is something that has been found in laboratory experiments (see main text). Yet this is also a question we feel is down to field scientists to address. There is already a large body of data on sediment yields in response to different size flood events – with large amounts of scatter. Maybe it is time to start interrogating these data with a different

perspective – that is, looking for patterns using techniques for analysing non-linear data.

In response to the comments by Chris Parker, we agree that a major disturbance such as 4–5 m of uplift would certainly leave features in the field that would be recognizable, such as prominent river terraces. However, we are only examining the output from the basin here, and over longer time scales this may be the only record we have left from a large drainage basin, as evidence of previous changes may be removed via re-working. We also agree that the length and, more importantly, the "accommodation space" are important in providing space for buffering the system. If we have a drainage basin where the channel is a simple slot, then there will be little or no room for the disturbance to be absorbed – little accommodation space for deposition or buffering. There may well be a hierarchy of efficiency in absorbing these changes amongst different types of depositional feature. For example are alluvial fans better buffers than floodplains?

This raises a further important question – what is the level of buffering required to remove different size disturbances? Furthermore, do these buffers (as the alluvial fan does) introduce more non-linearity than the linear signals they remove? These are issues we intend to address through further numerical modelling, but could also be studied using physical models.

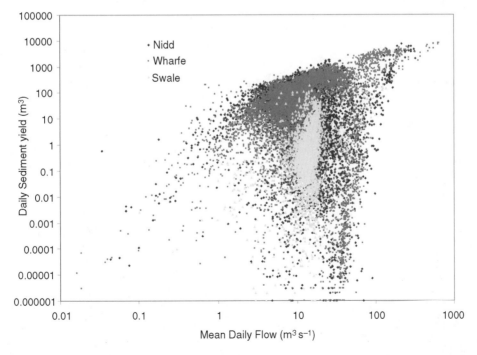

**Figure 36.6** *Qs/Qw* plots for the rivers Swale, Wharfe and Nidd. From Coulthard *et al.*, 2007. (See the color version of this figure in color plate section.)

## 36.8   DISCUSSION REFERENCES

Bak, P., Tang, C., and Wiesenfeld, K. 1987. Self-organized criticality: an explanation of 1/f noise. *Physical Review Letters* **59**: 381–384.

Bak, P., Tang, C., and Wiesenfeld, K. 1988. Self-organized criticality. *Physical Review A* **38**: 364–374.

Coulthard, T.J. and Van De Wiel, M.J. 2007. Quantifying fluvial non linearity and finding self organized criticality? Insights from simulations of river basin evolution. *Geomorphology* **91**: 216–235. doi: 10.1016/j.geomorph.2007.04.011.

Coulthard, T.J., Kirkby, M.J., and Macklin, M.G. 1998. Nonlinearity and spatial resolution in a cellular automaton model of a small upland basin. *Hydrology and Earth System Studies* **2**: 257–264.

Coulthard, T.J., Lewin, J., and Macklin, M.G. 2007. Non-stationarity of basin scale sediment delivery in response to climate change. In Habersack, H., Piegay, H.,and Rinaldi, M., editors *Gravel Bed Rivers VI*. Amsterdam, Elsevier, pp. 315–336.

Hasselblatt, B. and Katok, A. 2003. *A First Course in Dynamics: With a Panorama of Recent Developments*. Cambridge, Cambridge University Press.

Jerolmack, D.J. and Paola, C. 2010. Shredding of environmental signals by sediment transport. *Geophysical Research Letters* **37**: L19401. doi: 19410.11029/12010GL044638.

Rickenmann, D. 1997. Sediment transport in Swiss torrents. *Earth Surface Processes and Landforms* **22**: 937–951.

Turowski, J.M., Yager, E., Badoux, A., Rickenmann, D., and Molnar, P. 2009. The impact of exceptional events on erosion, bedload transport and channel stability in a step-pool channel. *Earth Surface Processes and Landforms* **34**: 1661–1673. doi: 10.1002/esp.1855.

Van De Wiel, M.J. and Coulthard, T.J. 2010. Self-organized criticality in river basins: Challenging sedimentary records of environmental change. *Geology* **38**: 87–90. doi: 10.1130/G30490.1.

# Ice in Gravel-bed Rivers

# River-Ice Effects on Gravel-Bed Channels

## Robert Ettema and Edward W. Kempema

## 37.1 INTRODUCTION

River ice affects flow and bed-material transport in fluvial channels subject to frigid weather conditions. Whether river ice imposes important distinct features or net long-term effects on fluvial channels remains unclear, however. Several ice-related mechanisms increase channel bed and bank erosion, seasonally altering the quantities and rates of sediment and water conveyed, and thereby possibly increasing channel instability. Other river ice processes decrease erosion.

In this chapter, the authors review river-ice effects on gravel-bed channels, offering a broad overview. The review briefly describes the thermal processes attending river ice, describes various forms of river-ice growth and accumulation, and then discusses the relative spatial and temporal scales associated with ice growth and water flow in rivers. The differences in scales influence the characteristics of ice in river channels, the extent to which river ice affects flow, bed-material transport, and the morphologic features of gravel-bed channels. Ice effects on flow distribution and bed-particle transport are described, as are overall channel responses to river ice. Some effects are quite well understood, while others require further research. Practical difficulties with conducting field and laboratory studies investigating ice effects on fluvial channels have caused research progress to be slow. The review concludes by indicating that instrumentation developments and numerical simulation likely will accelerate research during the coming years.

Observations from several rivers, in particular Wyoming's Laramie River, are used by the writers to illustrate river-ice effects on gravel-bed channels. The Laramie River, a small high-plains river (at an average altitude of about 2 200 m) with winter discharges less than $1.5 \, \text{m}^3 \, \text{s}^{-1}$, is an accessible, convenient "field laboratory" for monitoring several ice-related processes. Additional observations from much larger gravel-bed rivers are also presented; ice-related flow and dynamic processes in them occur at substantially different rates and lengths than in the Laramie River.

In the context of the present paper, seasonally cold regions are defined as locations experiencing at least one month per year with average daily temperatures less than $0\,^\circ\text{C}$. These regions normally lie above about latitude 35°N in the northern hemisphere (Figure 37.1) or at high altitudes. At higher latitudes, permafrost, defined as ground that remains below $0\,^\circ\text{C}$ for more than two years, can exert substantial effects on channel morphology. The effects of permafrost on fluvial form and process are not addressed in this paper, but can be found elsewhere (e.g., Gatto, 1995; Best et al., 2005; McNamara and Kane, 2009).

The writers' experience indicates that river-ice effects on flow, bed sediment transport, and fluvial morphology typically are greatest during two seasonal periods: initial ice formation throughout early winter, and ice-cover break-up in spring. Many cold-region rivers are characterized by relatively low water discharge during late autumn and early winter when initial ice covers form. Yet these initial stages of ice formation can be periods marked by significant diurnal surges in coarse sediment transport attributable to direct entrainment of bed material by ice, and by channel constriction by ice accumulation. Far higher discharges normally occur during ice-cover break up; these discharges potentially convey substantial amounts of bed sediment. In some rivers, wintertime operation of hydropower facilities may introduce additional flow periods that affect sediment transport and channel morphology.

Because thermal processes occur at temporal and spatial scales that can differ substantially from those for water flow processes, it is useful to view river-ice effects in terms of the relative scales over which thermal and flow processes occur in channels. Daly (1994) notes that the important length scales in fluvial ice formation, from

*Gravel-bed Rivers: Processes, Tools, Environments*, First Edition. Edited by Michael Church, Pascale M. Biron and André G. Roy.
© 2012 John Wiley & Sons, Ltd. Published 2012 by John Wiley & Sons, Ltd.

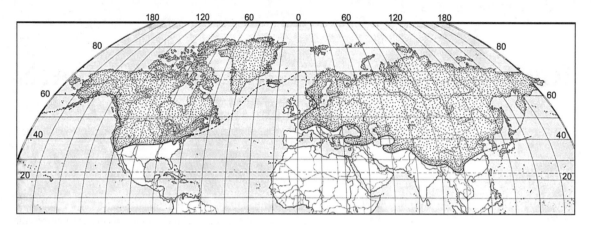

**Figure 37.1**  Region of the northern hemisphere that, for at least one month per year, has an average monthly temperature less than $0\,^{\circ}\mathrm{C}$.

initial frazil seed crystal formation through development of a continuous ice cover, range from $10^{-6}$ to $10^{5}$ m. The writers consider a subset of this range, from about $10^{-3}$ to $10^{3}$ m, which covers the range from frazil disk formation through reach-length effects of ice covers. Ice processes operating over these length scales potentially affect sediment transport and fluvial processes over similar scales, from the transport of individual sand grains through to the modification of entire channel reaches. At very large spatial scales (watershed, region, and greater), frigid weather affects not only modes and extents of river-ice formation, but also the overall quantities of water and sediment to be conveyed by river systems.

## 37.2  THERMAL PROCESSES

Thermal processes during frigid weather can bear significantly upon gravel transport and fluvial morphology in channels. They cause water to cool and solidify as ice, which in turn alters flow boundaries and modifies the forces water exerts on bed material. Heat fluxes strengthen or weaken ice, influence the geotechnical characteristics of channel banks, and control snow melt which regulates rates of water flow in northern rivers.

### 37.2.1  Cooling and Ice Formation

In addition to eventual ice formation, cooling of a river changes the physical characteristics of the water. Ice forms when water attains its freezing temperature and is seeded with ice nuclei. Kinematic viscosity, $\nu$, increases 100% when water cools from 25 to $0\,^{\circ}\mathrm{C}$. Water density, $\rho$, increases about 0.3% when water cools from 25 to $0\,^{\circ}\mathrm{C}$, but attains a maximum at $4\,^{\circ}\mathrm{C}$. Increasing kine-

matic viscosity increases suspended transport of sand (Hong *et al.*, 1984). Evidence exists (e.g., Southard and Boguchwal, 1990) that increased viscosity can change bedform regimes, but it is unlikely to modify gravel-bed morphology, because water viscosity increase negligibly affects gravel entrainment (as per the Shields diagram, e.g., Vanoni, 1975). Ice formation, however, dramatically changes channel hydraulics and introduces mechanisms for moving bed material (Kempema *et al.*, 1986; Ettema, 2008).

Three different types of ice form in turbulent flows when the water column losses enough heat to the atmosphere to begin freezing (Figure 37.2). The most visible ice type is border ice that grows at the water surface. Frazil are millimetre-sized ice disks that grow while suspended in turbulent, supercooled water. The third ice type, anchor ice, is ice that is attached to the river bed. All of these ice types can form simultaneously in a given river reach. The relative abundance of each ice type depends on complex interactions between flow characteristics, heat loss to the atmosphere, number of seed-ice crystals, and bed materials (Tsang, 1982; Ashton, 1986). Each of these ice types can also influence sediment transport, although at different time scales.

Buoyant frazil and supercooled water both resist turbulent mixing and promote stable water-column stratification. Flow- and wind-generated turbulence overcomes this stable stratification and mixes supercooled water and seed ice nuclei from the surface into the stream interior. Owing to differences in buoyancy, there are substantial differences in the rates at which supercooled water and seed ice particles mix into a water body. Supercooled water at, say, $-0.1\,^{\circ}\mathrm{C}$ is more readily advected into the stream interior than ice nuclei because

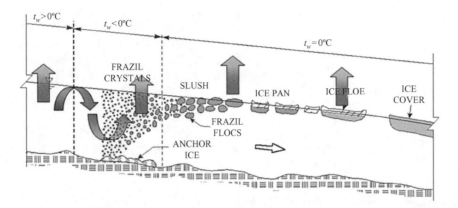

**Figure 37.2** Schematic diagram showing phases of ice formation in water flow along a channel. Vertical arrows represent heat loss from water to atmosphere during ice formation events. During the initial stages of ice formation, the entire water column loses heat to the atmosphere due to turbulent mixing (curved arrows), driving frazil and anchor-ice formation.

it is only 0.01% lighter than water at the freezing point. Ice, in contrast, is about 8.4% lighter than water at $0\,^{\circ}C$. Supercooled water, therefore, is more readily advected down toward the bed by turbulent eddies than are seed ice crystals. An important assumption is that the water body does not cool homogeneously. Water supercools at the surface and turbulent eddies entrain wisps or blobs of this supercooled surface water into the water body interior. Mixing during initial ice formation is important for gravel-bed channels because such mixing leads to a form of ice growth – anchor ice – that establishes a significant mechanism for transporting gravel during winter's onset.

*In situ* growth of anchor ice crystals on a gravel bed occurs because supercooled water reaches the river bed, whereas few seed ice crystals do. Anchor ice crystals are bathed with supercooled water, which absorbs the latent heat of fusion of the growing ice. The growing mass of anchor ice envelops the larger surface bed particles (Figure 37.3a). Initial anchor ice formation comprises scales or balls on coarse gravel and cobbles (Kerr *et al.*, 2002). On relatively warm nights when only small amounts of anchor ice form, it takes the form of 30 to 150 mm diameter balls attached to the bed. On colder nights, the scales and balls coalesce as a more or less continuous anchor ice layer that blankets the bed. In shallow riffles, anchor ice masses often grow to the water surface, creating anchor ice dams (Figure 37.3b). In general, heat loss is greater during colder and windier nights, leading to greater areal coverage and thickness of anchor ice on the bed. On very cold nights, anchor ice can form in subreaches with sand beds, and may be encased by sand ripples and dunes. Kerr *et al.* (2002), Kempema *et al.* (2008) and Stickler and Alfredsen (2009) compre-

hensively review the thermal and flow processes associated with anchor ice formation.

### 37.2.2 Ice Covers, Jams, and Break-Up

Eventually, released anchor ice and frazil agglomerate and rise through the water column, forming drifting slush whose surface freezes over when exposed to the frigid air (Figure 37.2). As the consolidating slush drifts it accumulates as ice masses covering the channel, which gradually freezes over (Figure 37.4a). In sufficiently low-velocity flows, drifting ice masses accumulate to form a more or less uniform cover that thickens by thermal ice growth. In swifter flows, ice accumulates as non-uniform formations termed freeze-up jams and hanging dams, which develop under ice covers (Beltaos, 1995).

Thermal processes may trigger ice growth and movement in rivers, and may result in ice jams, which can be divided into two broad categories:

(1) Freeze-up jams form during the early stages of cover formation as water directly exposed to frigid air cools to form ice.
(2) Break-up jams form during late winter or early spring when thermal processes weaken ice, and increase snow-melt derived flow. Commonly, elevated rainfall during this period also increases flow.

The swifter flows and shallow depths of gravel rivers often complicate the formation of ice covers and result in comparatively large amounts of ice being formed and accumulating in irregular manners. These conditions commonly cause ice accumulations to develop non-uniformly as freeze-up jams that partially block

(a)

(a)

(b)

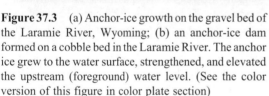

(b)

**Figure 37.4**    (a) Ice cover formation along a gravel-bed channel of the Laramie River. The growing ice cover consists of a mixture of border ice, frazil ice, and released anchor ice; (b) remnant of a large freeze-up jam of frazil and anchor-ice slush accumulated in a gravel-bed reach of the Yellowstone River, Montana.

**Figure 37.3**    (a) Anchor-ice growth on the gravel bed of the Laramie River, Wyoming; (b) an anchor-ice dam formed on a cobble bed in the Laramie River. The anchor ice grew to the water surface, strengthened, and elevated the upstream (foreground) water level. (See the color version of this figure in color plate section)

such channels. Figure 37.4b, for example, illustrates the remnant of a freeze-up jam formed along a gravel-bed reach of the Yellowstone River, Montana. The jam had thickened where water flow was swifter, redistributed the water flow as it formed, then was partially washed out by flow concentration to one side of the channel.

Break-up jams are usually more severe than freeze-up jams because of the larger flow and ice volumes involved. Though caution is needed when generalizing about ice jam occurence, ice jams become more common with increasing latitude (e.g., for the USA, see White *et al.*, 2005). Spring break-up flows and associated ice jams are influenced by the thermal conditions governing ice formation and ice deterioration, snowmelt, and run-off. Figure 37.5 shows how a jam raises the water level above the level that would have prevailed for the same

flow in ice-free conditions. The jam in this illustration is retained by an intact ice sheet, which itself elevates the ice-free flow level. Ice jams are usually retained by channel features such as a constriction, a sharp bend, or a structure like a bridge.

The genesis of flow magnitude and the assemblage of ice in a jam depend strongly on thermal conditions prevailing in a watershed. In this regard, the latitude orientation of flow in a river can affect the severity of ice runs. North-flowing rivers experience more severe ice jams because seasonal melting and ice movement progress from south to north as weather warms. This forces decaying ice from southern reaches onto the still-frozen ice further north in the drainage basins.

## 37.3   AUFEIS

Flows shallower than the potential thickness of a thermally grown ice cover, and of low unit discharge (flow

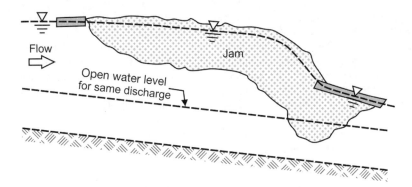

**Figure 37.5**  Sketch showing how an ice jam may affect flow water level.

rate per unit width of channel), may become largely blocked by ice that extends down to the channel bed. The blocked flow then seeps over and freezes as laminations of ice (aufeis) on the ice cover. The resulting spreading and thickening ice growths are called "aufeis" formations. River icings or "naleds" are alternative names for the formations (e.g., Froehlich and Slupak, 1982; Schohl and Ettema, 1986, 1990). Depending on the availability of water flow, they can become several metres thick and are extensively grounded on the channel bed (e.g., Carey, 1973; Harden *et al.*, 1977; Kane, 1981).

Aufeis formations commonly grow in areas of relatively steep topography (Carey, 1973; Harden *et al.*, 1977; Kane, 1981), and therefore commonly occur in braided gravel-bed channels whose shallow winter flows are largely fed by springs. Figure 37.6 shows aufeis in a gravel channel. Once formed, aufeis formations are notably resistant to decay and break-up because they

**Figure 37.6**  Early springtime flow cuts through and exposes a wide aufeis formation (grounded river icing) on a gravel-bed river in western Siberia.

rest on the channel bottom, and usually are thick and strong. Spring and summer flows passing over aufeis formations erode down through them, exposing the channel bed, fragmenting the formations, and eventually washing them from the channel. During cooler and drier summers at some locations, aufeis formations may persist for more than a year. Aufeis presence retards flow, usually dispersing it laterally, thereby reducing flow conveyance of bed material (Carey, 1973).

## 37.4  LENGTH, TIME, AND DYNAMIC SCALES

When discussing ice influences on gravel-bed rivers it is useful to consider the relative magnitudes (or scales) of length and time associated with thermal processes and water flow. The thermal processes associated with ice in rivers generally act over scales that relate strongly to weather conditions and usually much less to factors governing water flow and channel boundary material. However, in the limiting condition of very shallow rivers this statement does not entirely hold, as indicated in Section 37.3 for aufeis formation, a fairly common ice form in gravel-bed rivers.

The essential thermal processes related to ice are those affecting heat loss from water to air, mixing of surface-cooled water into the body of flow, release of latent heat of water fusion, and heat flux through an ice cover. In river flow the time scales for mixing are much faster than those for cooling of water, especially cooling by heat flux through ice (Fischer *et al.*, 1979; Ashton, 1986). Normally, the entire flow depth becomes more-or-less uniformly cooled once an ice cover forms over the flow. When the cover is formed, and then thickens, the rate of heat loss from water to air decreases markedly. Consequently, the maximum thickness of thermally grown ice covers is of the order of 1 m; thicker covers may form by means of jamming, as explained in Section 37.2.2.

The rate of ice seeding during initial ice formation can exert an important effect on the character of ice formation because it regulates, at least initially, the level of super-cooling and the partitioning of frazil and anchor-ice growth. Under conditions of sufficiently frigid weather, relatively low concentration of seed ice, and substantial flow turbulence, extensive areas of a gravel bed can become blanketed by anchor ice, which alters bed roughness and effective elevation (Figures 37.3–37.5). The hydraulic influences of anchor ice formation have yet to be studied.

For a given cumulative heat loss to the air above a river (resulting in a given ice thickness) the importance of ice on channel morphology and bed material transport diminishes as channel depth or hydraulic radius increases. A given ice thickness (for example, 1 m) imposes less influence on flow as the channel depth increases. A 1 m thick ice layer in a 1.5 m deep river has a significant effect on the flow. By contrast, the same 1 m thick ice cover has a relatively small effect on a 10 m deep channel. The effect of the ice cover on the bulk flow is relatively small for a deep channel. However, a large, deep channel may produce more ice, and possibly produce thicker ice jams. Figure 37.7 illustrates that, for the typical range of level cover thickness (nominally of the order of 1 m or less), the relative magnitude of cover thickness to flow depth diminishes with increasing channel scale. This implies that river-ice influences on channel equilibrium diminish as depth increases. For a deep flow, cover thickness affects only a comparatively narrow region near the surface. On the other hand, for a shallow flow an ice cover dramatically increases flow resistance and may divert flow from the channel. The limiting condition in this regard is when aufeis or an ice jam inundates a channel, choking its flow. Reduced flow velocity reduces potential bed material transport.

These considerations suggest that a range of channel depths and ice-cover thicknesses exists for which river ice actively affects channel dynamic equilibrium. Little research has been done to delineate the range quantitatively. Ashton (1986), ASCE (2000), and Ettema (2008) identify parameters for use in this regard.

## 37.5   BED MATERIAL TRANSPORT

The presence of an ice cover can potentially increase or decrease bed material transport. Floating ice covers, ice dams, and ice jams retard flow, thereby reducing hydraulic bed-material transport along a channel. Over the course of the winter, ice can increase bed material transport in two different ways: (i) ice can directly move bed material and (ii) ice can increase local flow velocities, thereby resulting in enhanced hydraulic sediment transport. Direct ice movement of sediment occurs as ice rafting (transporting of sediment by floating ice), and by ice gouging or ice push. Enhanced hydraulic transport can occur at a variety of scales. Local scour can occur at the foot of an anchor-ice dam or ice jam. Reach-length or longer scour can occur when ice-jam release waves ("javes"; Beltaos, 2007) travel downstream. These large-scale events are associated with increased stage and ice runs during breakup, resulting in a combined ice/hydraulic impact on bed material transport. As it is difficult to measure increased bedload transport during ice runs and jams, no quantitative data evidently exist defining rates of transport associated with ice runs. The following sections elaborate river-ice effects on bedload transport.

### 37.5.1   Ice Rafting of Bed Material

Of the three different ice types described in Section 37.2.1, anchor ice is the most important contributor to direct ice entrainment and transport of bed material. Anchor ice forms directly on the river bed, and can "raft" bed material when detaching from the bed. The authors have studied anchor ice formation and ice rafting in the Laramie River, a 15 m wide, ∼1 m deep plains river (here, using the term "plains rivers" as defined by Blench, 1986). The Laramie River is a convenient "natural laboratory" for the study of anchor ice because its riffle-pool morphology contains a variety of slopes, bed materials, and current velocities. Based on published descriptions of anchor-ice formation in other rivers, Kempema and Ettema (2009) conclude that anchor ice formation and ice rafting in the Laramie River is representative of anchor-ice processes in most rivers.

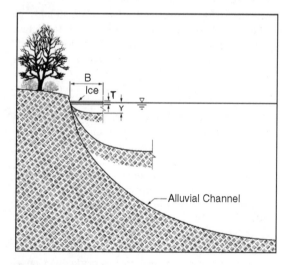

**Figure 37.7**   Length scales associated with an ice cover and channels of varying depths. B: channel width, T: ice thickness, Y: water depth.

Anchor ice, consisting of a combination of largely *in situ* ice growth, with some attached frazil crystals, grows on coarse bed material at night when there is large heat loss from the water surface to the atmosphere (see Tsang, 1982). Growing anchor-ice masses form a dense, porous mat that encapsulates coarse bed material (Figure 37.3a). If the buoyancy of the attached ice overcomes the weight of attached particles, anchor ice may lift off the bed during the night. However, the majority of anchor ice usually remains attached to the bed throughout the night. On clear, frigid, windy nights, anchor-ice masses can grow to very large sizes, covering hundreds of square metres of river bottom. In shallow-water rivers like the Laramie River, anchor ice may grow to the water surface, emerging as small weirs partially backing up flow (Figure 37.3b).

Anchor ice formed at night releases from the bed when incoming solar radiation (insolation) warms the water in the morning (this can occur even when the air temperature remains well below freezing). As insolation weakens the bonds between bed particles and anchor ice, anchor ice lifts off the bed, entraining partially encapsulated bed particles (Figure 37.8) and drifting downstream. Anchor ice forms predominantly on gravel and coarser substrates (Tsang, 1982; Kempema *et al.*, 1986), so its formation and release is a mechanism for coarse-sediment transport.

Anchor-ice formation requires direct contact between the water surface and the atmosphere; it will not form once a surface ice cover has formed over the river. Anchor ice therefore forms in the autumn and spring when there are considerable stretches of open water and when nights are cold enough to drive ice formation. The diurnal processes of night-time anchor-ice formation

**Figure 37.8** Initial release of anchor ice from the bed of the Laramie River. The coarse bed material lifted off the bed by the released anchor ice was ice rafted downstream. The largest clasts in this figure are about 5 cm in diameter.

followed by morning release of anchor ice and entrained sediment produces daily pulses of coarse-grained sediment transport. Ice provides the buoyancy to keep entrained sediment near the top of the water column (Figure 37.8), so ice rafting is capable of moving coarse sediment through low-velocity river reaches. All ice-rafted bed sediment eventually returns to the river bed, but return trajectories can follow three different paths: (i) as insolation continues, the bonds between the ice and the entrained sediment continue to weaken until the sediment drops out of the floating ice back to the bed; (ii) if the released anchor ice mass traverses a shallow riffle, the entrained sediment may be scraped off the bottom of the anchor ice mass and deposited in the riffle; or (iii) the released anchor ice may drift downstream (Figure 37.4a) until reaching the upstream edge of the advancing ice cover, where it, and entrained bed material, become incorporated into the ice cover through thermal ice growth. Bed material included in the ice cover remains there until the ice cover melts in the spring.

The potential significance of anchor-ice rafting has been recognized for a long time. As far back as 1854, Lyell (1854) noted the importance of released anchor ice transporting coarse sediment in northern rivers: "... The power of running water to carry sand, gravel, and fragments of rock to considerable distances is greatly augmented in those regions where, during some part of the year, the frost is of sufficient intensity to convert water, either at the surface or bottom of rivers, into ice." Fluvial anchor-ice formation is common; there are anecdotal observations of anchor-ice rafting from many river systems of varying sizes. However, almost nothing is known about the importance of ice rafting in the overall sediment budget in ice-impacted rivers. Ice rafting impact on channel behaviour is unclear. Preliminary studies suggest that anchor ice and associated ice rafting play an important role in the ecology of gravel-bed channels (Stickler and Alfredsen, 2009).

Kempema and Ettema (2011) review available published data on anchor-ice rafting and find it disconcerting that there have apparently been no detailed studies of fluvial anchor-ice rafting. Their data from the Laramie River indicate that the average released, floating anchor-ice mass contains $22 \pm 25$ kg m$^{-3}$ of sediment (mean $\pm$ standard deviation). Anchor ice rafts gravel, cobbles, and sand in the Laramie River (this observation of the size of anchor-ice-rafted material is confirmed from other studies). The coarsest transported bed material in the Laramie River, with individual clasts weighing up to 9.5 kg, is anchor-ice rafted. This coarse bed material is moved in the winter, when flows are at a minimum. Unfortunately, Kempema and Ettema could not determine an estimate of the total volume of anchor ice formed, so they were unable to determine the overall importance of anchor-ice rafting in the total sediment budget of the stream. However, it appears that ice rafting plays an important role in the sediment dynamics of the Laramie River. Numerous published observations of anchor-ice formation and ice rafting from other rivers show that anchor-ice rafting is a common phenomenon, but its contribution to fluvial sediment dynamics is unclear.

### 37.5.2  Sediment Transport by Water Flow Under Ice Covers

The bedload capacities of prismatic channels with level ice covers align with trends and relations for bed material transport in open water flow through such channels, provided the capacities are considered in terms of shear velocity or shear stress actually exerted at the bed (Ettema and Zabilansky, 2004). To date, detailed comparisons between ice-covered and ice-free flow in channels are based exclusively on laboratory flume data. Essentially, with an adequate estimate of bed shear stress, bedload transport in an ice-covered channel can be estimated using an open-water method.

Variations in cover thickness relative to flow depth and, thereby, alterations in flow distribution, complicate evaluation of ice-cover effects on transport rates for many channels. Few field studies have been conducted to measure rates of sediment transport in ice-covered channels. The studies illustrate the inherent difficulty of obtaining and interpreting such measurements. Lawson et al. (1986), for example, conducted an extensive study of flow and sediment movement in a reach of the Tanana River, Alaska. They obtained measurements of bedload and suspended-load rates at one cross-section, but were unable to conclude much regarding ice effects on bed material transport.

Flow area may be reduced through time as an ice cover forms and thickens. This reduction is caused by reductions in both the width and depth of an ice-covered channel. Flow-width reduction is more difficult to predict than is flow depth change due to ice growth. The formation of subchannels within an ice-covered channel may accentuate narrowing of the flow area, especially if the channel is not prismatic. The subchannels form when accumulations of ice slush or other ice pieces accumulate under the ice cover. In effect, they duct the flow in a manner that significantly alters the flow distribution from that attributable to the imposition of a level ice cover.

The possible imbalance between rate of sediment supply to an ice-covered reach, $q_s$, and the sediment-transport capacity of that reach, $q_{sc}$, involves the complex problem of spatially varied flow and sediment transport, with all its implications for local adjustments of bed slope and channel morphology. If $q_{sc}$ were less than the rate at which sediment load is supplied to the channel, $q_s$, the local bed elevation must rise. Conversely, if $q_{sc} > q_s$, there should be scour and a concurrent drop in local bed level. The former condition usually would prevail for a floating cover, because bulk flow velocity decreases. The latter condition may occur beneath an ice jam (Neill, 1976; Wuebben, 1988a), or when the cover is fixed to a channel bank, because the bulk flow velocity is forced to increase substantially under ice.

### 37.5.3  Erosion Beneath Ice Jams

Ice jams back up flow and may concentrate flow, increasing the magnitude of its velocity and turbulence below the thickest portion of the jam (toe). Localized scour of bed or bank may occur in the vicinity of the jam toe, as illustrated in Figure 37.9. Channel locations recurrently (nominally every year) subject to ice jams may develop substantial scour holes. Tietze (1961) and Newbury (1982), for example, suggest instances of such scour holes at sites of freeze-up jams. Neill (1976), Mercer and Cooper (1977), Wuebben (1988b), and Ziegler

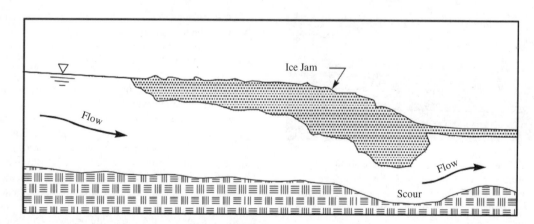

**Figure 37.9**  Local scour of the bed beneath an ice jam.

*et al.* (2005) describe similar jam scour situations. In most circumstances, the scour hole would have no lasting or adverse effect on channel morphology because it soon infills once the jam is released. It is conceivable that, in certain circumstance, localized scour could have a longer-term effect, possibly causing a bar to wash out. Transient erosion events can pose problems for hydraulic structures in channels (e.g., bridges), though.

### 37.5.4   Ice Runs and Ice Gouging

During heavy ice runs resulting from ice cover break-up or ice-jam release, large pieces of ice may gouge and abrade channel banks. Ice runs are reasonably common in gravel channels. Moreover, ice covers in steep, high-velocity flows typically break up fairly dramatically in concert with a sudden rise in flow due to rapid snowmelt and/or rain events. The resultant ice rubble comprises hard, angular blocks of ice that effectively gouge the bed and channel banks.

In situations where an ice run is sluggish, a shear wall of broken ice may fend moving ice from contacting the bank. The shear wall usually is smooth-faced and helps the river pass the ice. Running ice, if sufficiently thick, may still gouge the lower portion of a bank or the river bed.

Ice gouging and abrasion can be severe for channel features protruding into the flow (e.g., bars of various form), and for bank vegetation. In addition, channel locations with a substantial change in channel alignment are especially prone to ice-run gouging and abrasion; e.g., a sharp bend, point bar, and portions of a channel confluence. Figure 37.10 depicts a common, and rather dramatic, ice run along the Athabasca River. The absence

**Figure 37.10**   Ice run along the Athabasca River, Alberta. Reproduced, with permission, from Kowalczyk, T. and Hicks, F. 2003. Observations of dynamic ice jam release on the Athabasca River at Fort McMurray, AB. In Hicks, F., editor. 12th Workshop on River Ice, June, Edmonton, Alberta. Canadian Geophysical Union, Proceedings: 369–392.

of significant bank vegetation reflects the repeated seasonal impact of ice runs along the reach depicted. There is a little information on how ice runs affect the local morphology and vegetation characteristics of these sites. Two features have been observed in gravelly rivers: ice-push ridges and cobble pavements. Ice-push ridges form when a heavy ice run gouges and shoves sediment along the base of banks (e.g., Bird, 1974). Gouged sediment forms ridges beneath the ice run as it comes to rest as a jam. The finer sediments eventually get washed out, leaving the more resistant gravel and boulders in ridges. The ridges usually develop near locations subject to recurrent ice jams.

Cobble pavements may cover bars and the lower portion of banks subject to ice gouging and abrasion. Essentially, an overriding mix of ice and cobbles removes the finer material from the surface of the bars or banks. The resultant surface comprises cobbles whose major axis is aligned parallel to the channel and whose size gradually decreases downstream (Mackay and MacKay, 1977). The resultant cobble pavement may extend for many miles along the banks of large northern rivers, such as the Mackenzie and Yukon (Wentworth, 1932).

## 37.6   CHANNEL RESPONSES TO ICE

In general, the seasonal formation of ice increases channel instability as the flow changes in response to the presence of ice. As indicated in Section 37.4, ice presence induces channel responses over wide ranges of time and length scales. Some responses occur quickly and are localized. A single jam event can trigger change, such as scour beneath the toe of the ice jam, a thalweg shift, or a meander loop cutoff. Other channel morphology responses may occur slowly, not being realized during a single winter, but over a succession of winters.

### 37.6.1   Channel Cross-Section

An ice cover may alter lateral variations in flow depth and boundary shear stress, amplifying variations attributable to the effects of channel curvature, transverse differences in distributions of water flow and bed shear stress, and bed material.

An ice cover may laterally redistribute flow in a channel. Lateral redistribution of flow, though, depends on how the ice cover forms, whether it is attached to the channel banks, and how it thickens. Flow redistribution can be explained using a flow-resistance equation, such as the Darcy–Weisbach equation (Ettema, 2002). The ice cover may laterally redistribute or concentrate flow in accordance with lateral variations in flow depth and/or ice-cover thickness. Ice squeezes or concentrates flow along thalwegs where flow is deeper. If a thalweg were

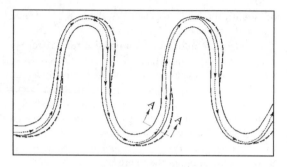

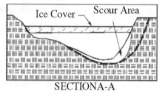

**Figure 37.11**  Ice may concentrate flow to outer bank of bend, possibly triggering bank failure.

close to one side of a channel (e.g., near the outer bank of a bend), such flow concentration may promote thalweg shifting and deepening, as indicated by Figure 37.11. This effect is documented by Ettema and Zabilansky (2004). On the other hand, if a thalweg is located more-or-less centrally in a channel, a fixed cover may deepen or entrench the thalweg. By reducing flow through shallow portions of a cross section, the ice cover may trigger further reductions in conveyance through these shallow areas by promoting local ice accumulation (frazil and anchor-ice slush) and/or bed sediment deposition. Additional flow concentration is possible if the cover is not uniformly thick, if ice is grounded on the channel bed, or if shore-fast/accumulated ice developed from one or both banks.

### 37.6.2  Thalweg Sinuosity

Open-water relations for thalweg sinuosity show it to be sensitive to change in energy gradient (e.g., Schumm and Khan, 1972). For a given flow rate and bed-sediment composition, thalweg sinuosity and channel planform change as channel slope changes. The well-known relation between sinuosity and slope proposed by Schumm and Khan (1972) indicates that, for a given flow rate and bed sediment size, channels lengthen or branch into subchannels as channel slope increases. Considerations of flow energy expenditure can be used to explain how an ice cover reduces the effective gradient for expenditure of flow energy. Therefore, ice-cover formation may trigger a change in thalweg alignment for some channels. An ice-covered flow is effectively equivalent to a deepened and slowed open-water flow (Ettema, 2002).

The ice cover imposes additional flow resistance and thereby increases depth, while decreasing average flow velocity. The channel effectively conveys a deeper, slower flow requiring a lower rate of energy dissipation.

For an alluvial channel, a reduction in energy gradient usually implies an adjustment in planform geometry. Because an ice cover deepens and slows flow, the channel responds as if it were set at a flatter slope. In effect, the channel responds as if it were conveying an equivalent open-water flow with reduced energy gradient. An ice cover, therefore, triggers a shift in thalweg sinuosity and alignment so as to balance flow energy availability and use. For instance, the decrease in effective energy gradient may cause flow in a sinuous-braided channel to concentrate in a single thalweg of greater sinuosity than the open water thalweg. For braided channels, as common in gravel-bed channels, ice-cover presence may concentrate flow into the larger subchannels. Ice-triggered thalweg shifts, however, may not alter overall channel planform.

### 37.6.3  Anabranching, Avulsion, and Cutoff

Channels with tight meander loops or with subchannels around numerous bars or islands are prone to ice-jam formation. Such channels typically have insufficient capacity to convey the incoming ice and water volume. Their morphology may be too narrow, shallow, curved, or irregular to enable passage of drifting ice pieces. Jam formation may greatly constrict flow, causing it to discharge along an alternate, less-resistant course. Dupre and Thompson (1979), Prowse (1993, 2001), and Smith and Pearce (2002) suggest that ice-jam-induced avulsion is common for meandering and braided channels. Zabilansky et al. (2002) studied ice influences on channel conditions along the Fort Peck reach of the Missouri River and documented instances where freeze-up jams led to thalweg shifts in a sinuous-braided reach of a channel, and where jam formation in a tight meander bends resulted in bend cutoff.

An immediate factor triggering altered thalweg alignment is ice accumulation at the entrance to a subchannel, as shown in Figure 37.12. An initial accumulation of drifting ice in one subchannel around a bar may divert ice and flow into a companion subchannel, causing flow to favor subchannel 2, which enlarges. Such adjustments were observed to occur commonly on the Fort Peck reach of the Missouri river (Zabilansky et al., 2002) and in the Laramie River, as depicted in Figure 37.13.

When an ice jam forms at in a meander loop, upstream water levels rise, possibly to the extent that flow proceeds overbank and across the neck of a meander loop. If the meander neck comprises readily erodible sediment, and the flow is of sufficient scouring magnitude, flow

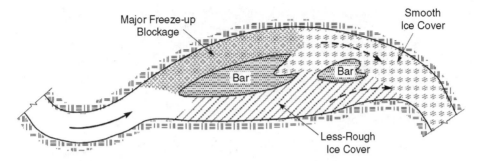

**Figure 37.12** Ice-cover formation in channels with subchannels may alter the location of the major subchannel. An initial accumulation of drifting ice in the upper, dominant subchannel may divert flow into the lower subchannel, which then develops a less rough ice cover. The ice blockage of the upper channel diverts flow to the lower channel, which is scoured and enlarged. Even after melting the lower channel remains dominant.

diverted by the jam may result in a meander-loop neck cut, whereby a new channel forms through the neck and the former channel is left largely cutoff, as Figure 37.14 depicts for the Fort Peck reach of the Missouri River. A meander cutoff shortens and steepens a channel reach, the consequences of which are felt upstream and downstream of the cutoff reach. The net effect of ice jams, in this regard, is to reduce channel sinuosity. MacKay *et al.* (1974) cite examples of such events.

When a meander loop is wide and not easily eroded, over-bank flow resulting from an ice jam may have the opposite effect. Rather than the net consequence being the erosion of channel through the meander loop, over-bank flow may deposit sediment, thus raising bank height and reinforcing the meander loop. Eardley (1938) reports

**Figure 37.13** Sub-channel blockage in the Laramie River on 4 December 2008, viewed from upstream. In 2000, the majority of the flow was through the right channel around the island. By 2005, consistent ice jams in the right channel, as shown here, had shifted the dominant channel to the left side of the island. Increased flow in the channel during freeze-up scoured the left channel, making it dominant.

that ice jams cause substantial sediment deposition on the flood plain of the Yukon River. A similar event is reported for the Fort Peck reach of the Missouri River (Ettema and Zabilansky, 2004). Over-bank deposition of sediment, together with ice-run gouging and sediment erosion from the lower portion of a bank may over-steepen riverbanks.

## 37.7 CHANNEL BANKS

Thermal processes weaken bank material, ice in a channel may gouge and load the channel's banks, and it may significantly reduce vegetation growth along banks. These impacts increase bank susceptibility to erosion, may advance lateral shifting of channels, and increase the local sediment supply to the channel.

Freeze–thaw cycles weaken bank material, as do fluctuations in channel flow depth. Ice cover presence further creates a zone of weakened bank in the vicinity of the ice cover, as indicated in Figure 37.15. The extent of bank freezing depends on bank condition (material, vegetation, snow, etc.), the relative elevations of water table and flow stage, and temperatures of groundwater and river water. The strength of the bankfast ice attachment to a bank depends on the relative elevations of the water table and flow stage, and on the relative water temperatures. Groundwater infiltration into the river will retard border-ice growth and weaken its hold on the bank. The growth of a thick fringe of bankfast ice, though, may affect seepage flow through the bank, possibly constricting it and slightly raising the water table. Higher flow stage raises the water table in a riverbank, and a rapid drop in stage may momentarily reduce bank stability by increasing seepage pressures and, thereby, reduce the shearing resistance of the bank material. Ice-cover formation may raise flow stage, whereas cover break-up may abruptly lower it.

**Figure 37.14** A meander loop cutoff formed by an ice jam in the Fort Peck reach of the Missouri River.

Bankfast ice weakening of banks is significant for steep banks, typically those comprising sufficient clay as to be termed cohesive. It also is likely significant for banks in which the water table declines in elevation away from flow elevation in a channel, because the bankfast ice is less securely anchored into the bank. This erosion

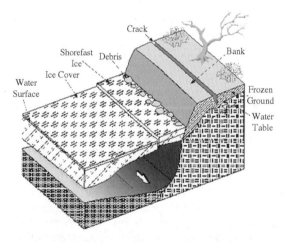

**Figure 37.15** The combined effects of ice may weaken and erode channel banks.

mechanism seems not to have been investigated before, but has been observed; e.g., along the Fort Peck reach of the Missouri River (Zabilansky *et al.*, 2002). As the flow stage in a channel drops, portions of the ice cover attached to a bank may be left cantilevered from the channel's banks. The cantilevered ice soon collapses, wrenching and weakening bank material as it does so. Essentially the same mechanism is termed plucking, which is used with regard to the loss of riprap stones frozen to an ice sheet. Wuebben (1995) extensively discusses plucking concerns in the design of stone riprap for bank protection.

Substantial evidence shows that ice runs affect riverbank morphology (Marusenko, 1956; Smith, 1979; Hamelin, 1979; Uunila, 1997; USACOE, 1983; Doyle, 1988; Wuebben, 1995). The gouging and abrasion of the lower portion of banks, in conjunction with overbank sediment deposition during ice-jam flooding, may produce an elevated ridge or bench feature along some northern rivers. This feature has been dubbed "bechevnik" (a Russian term) for Siberian rivers (Hamelin, 1979). A bechevnik is the marginal strip comprising the lower portion of a riverbank and exposed portion of adjoining river bed that, in days gone by, formed convenient paths for towing boats upstream manually or by horse ("becheva" apparently means tow

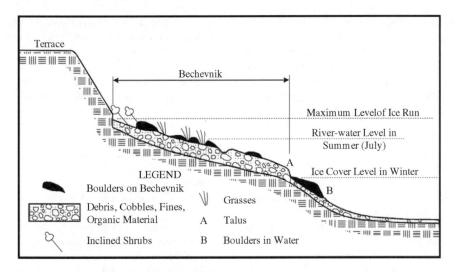

**Figure 37.16**   Ice-gouged low banks along channels, termed bechevnik (tow path in Russian), are cleared of vegetation and usually are cobble or gravel covered (see Figure 37.10).

rope). Figure 37.16 illustrates the main features of a bechevnik, which may form partly from ice abrasion and partly from the deposition of sediment and debris left by the melting of ice rubble stranded after ice runs.

Ice-run gouging and abrasion have an important, though as yet not quantified, effect on riparian vegetation that, in turn, may affect bank erosion and channel shifting. Where ice runs occur with about annual frequency, riparian vegetation communities have difficulty getting established. Ice abrasion and ice-jam flooding may suppress certain vegetation types along banks, as illustrated in Figure 37.16 for a bechevnik. The effect of ice on bank or riparian vegetation requires further study.

## 37.8   DEFINING EFFECTS OF ICE

The foregoing review of fluvial ice influences leads to the question of whether ice has a defining effect upon gravel-channel processes and morphology. Enough evidence exists to venture a tentative answer, though the question has yet to be addressed by means of thorough study. The major geometric parameters of gravel channels (e.g., channel width, hydraulic radius or depth, thalweg sinuosity, and meander radius) are likely not altered significantly by the presence of ice. However, by virtue of the additional erosion mechanisms it introduces, ice increases the frequencies with which channel cross section and thalweg instabilities occur. In this regard, ice also influences vegetation and ecology along gravel-bed channels, and thereby also can affect channel stability.

A single thermal or ice influence may not substantially destabilize a channel equilibrium set by open-water flow conditions. A shift in thalweg alignment or a bank failure, alone, may not destabilize a channel. The channel may adjust back to more or less its stable open-water condition once open-water conditions resume. Besides, a single ice impact may be damped or possibly constrained. For instance, flow concentration along a thalweg may be damped by an increase in bed resistance resulting from surface coarsening of the bed material, an increase in bedform size; or ice-aggravated bank erosion may be damped as bank slope flattens and the channel widens. High banks, which deposit a large mass of sediment into the channel, or scour-resistant strata (e.g., a clay layer or rock outcrop) may constrain thalweg shifting or entrenchment. Nevertheless, the annual cycle of ice formation producing multiple ice-related impacts may amplify the amount of bed material moved by flow through a channel, and increase the difficulties faced by engineering works along the channel; e.g., the performance of water intakes or bridge crossings.

From a study of 24 rivers in Alberta, Smith (1979) proposed that ice covers enlarge channel cross-sections at bankfull stage by as much as 2.6 to 3 times those of comparable-flow rivers not subject to ice runs. He compared the recurrence interval of bankfull flows in the 24 rivers and an empirical relation between the cross-section area and flow rate for bankfull flow. The channel widening effect of ice runs is plausible. However, the extent of widening indicated seems overly large, and requires further confirmation. Kellerhals and Church (1980), in a discussion of Smith (1979), argue against Smith's hypothesis. They suggest that other factors have led to an apparent widening of the channels analysed by Smith; e.g., recent entrenchment of major rivers in Alberta, and ice-jam effects of flow levels. Moreover, it is possible that the banks are somewhat protected by a band of ice forming a shear wall flanking the riverbanks. It is interesting to contrast Smith's proposition with the suggestion mentioned above that ice jams may promote channel narrowing by causing overbank flow (e.g., Uunila, 1997). In accordance with the suggestion, for channels in which the dominant channel-forming flow coincides with ice-cover breakup and jam formation, overbank loss of flow reduces the flow rate accommodated by the channel, which in turn adjusts to handle a smaller bankfull flow. Because river ice is just one of several factors affecting channel morphology, it usually is difficult to attribute a clear morphological relationship to river ice, except for the bechevnik.

Channel forms usually considered less stable at any point in time subject to open-water flow conditions are more likely to be adversely impacted by river ice. Sinuous-point-bar, sinuous-braided, and braided alluvial channels are especially prone to river ice impact, especially if they have steep banks formed of fine, partially cohesive sediments. The thalweg(s) of such channels usually lies close to the outer banks of bends, and the banks themselves are prone to border-ice loading, lack of vegetation cover (typical of eroding banks), and freeze–thaw weakening. The thalweg lies close to the bank, such that the flow continually erodes the bank-toe, thereby keeping the bank steep, and possibly undercutting the bank.

## 37.9   CONCLUDING COMMENTS

Detailed information addressing river-ice effects on alluvial channels is quite sparse, particularly for gravel-bed channels. Until fairly recently, as interests in wintertime fluvial ecology have grown, and as the extent of engineering works has increased in cold regions (such as the design and construction of water intakes and bridges), little attention has been devoted to ice effects on gravel-bed rivers. The prevailing notion, by and large, has been that frigid winters bring flow and bed material transport to a halt. Moreover, logistical difficulties have hampered conduct of detailed field and lab work concerning ice effects on alluvial channels.

Though the general set of questions as to whether river ice affects bed material transport, modifies channel morphology, and reduces or amplifies bank erosion, remains largely unaddressed, there are substantive indications that ice certainly affects bed material transport and channel morphology of gravel-bed channels, doing so over a range of geometry and time scales. Here, the writers have skimmed concisely over the effects, describing them qualitatively and showing that considerable research is needed to fully illuminate and quantify the effects. An important consideration is that river ice does not act alone. In addition to the direct effects of ice on gravel river beds, ice indirectly affects the bed by changing local flow hydraulics leading to differing bed shear stress and associated sediment transport.

Substantial scope exists for further research to better understand river-ice effects. Current developments in instrumentation and numerical simulation hold promise for facilitating new insights by overcoming the difficulties encountered when attempting field work and laboratory experiments. Issues of accessibility, frigid weather, not to mention occasionally dangerous flow conditions, and inadequate equipment performance have hampered field measurement and observation of ice effects on flow and gravel-channel behaviour. Laboratory experiments struggle to replicate the thermal conditions and ice-material properties as they occur in gravel-bed rivers.

In summary, there is an increasing body of research showing how river ice perceptibly affects channel morphology. However, there is no substantial body of evidence showing that ice affects overall channel planform.

## 37.10   REFERENCES

ASCE. 2000. *Hydraulic Modeling: Concepts and Practice*. Reston, VA, American Society of Civil Engineers, Manual of Practice 97.

Ashton, G. editor. 1986. *River and Lake Ice Engineering*. Littleton, CO, Water Resources Publications.

Beltaos, S. 1995. *River Ice Jams*. Highlands Ranch, CO, Water Resources Publications.

Beltaos, S. 2007. The role of waves in ice-jam flooding of the Peace-Athabasca Delta. *Hydrological Processes* **21**: 2548–2559.

Best, H., McNamara, J.P., and Liberty, L. 2005. Association of ice and river channel morphology determined using ground penetrating radar in the Kuparuk River, Alaska. *Arctic, Antarctic, and Alpine Research* **37**: 157–162.

Bird, J.B. 1974. Geomorphic processes in the Arctic. In Ives, J.D. and Barry, R.G. editors, *Arctic and Alpine Environments*. London, Methuen, Chapter 12A, pp. 703–720.

Blench, T. 1986. *Mechanics of Plains Rivers*. Edmonton, University of Alberta.

Carey, K. L. 1973. *Icings Formed from Surface Water and Groundwater*. United States Army Corps of Engineers, Cold Regions Research and Engineering Laboratory, Hanover, NH, Monograph III-D3.

Daly, S.F. editor. 1994. *Report on Frazil Ice*. Prepared by the International Association for Hydraulic Research Working Group on Thermal Regimes. United States Army Corps of Engineers, Cold Regions Research and Engineering Laboratory, Hanover, NH, Special Report SR-43.

Doyle, P.F. 1988. Damage from a sudden river ice breakup. *Canadian Journal of Civil Engineering* **15**: 609–615.

Dupre, W.R. and Thompson, R. 1979. The Yukon Delta: a model for deltaic sedimentation in an ice-dominated environment. *Proceedings of the 11th Annual Offshore Technology Conference, Houston, TX*, pp. 657–664.

Eardley, A.J. 1938. Yukon channel shifting. *Geological Society of America Bulletin* **49**: 343–358.

Ettema, R. 2002. Review of river-channel responses to river ice. *Journal of Cold Regions Engineering* **16**: 191–217.

Ettema, R. 2008. Sediment transport under ice: processes, measurements, modeling, and practice. In Garcia. M., editor, *Sedimentation Engineering*. American Society of Civil Engineers, Manual of Practice 110, pp. 613–648.

Ettema, R. and Zabilansky, L. 2004. Ice Influences on channel stability: insights from Missouri's Fort Peck Reach. *Journal of Hydraulic Engineering* **130**: 279–292.

Fisher, H.B., List, J.E., Koh, R.C., and Imberger, J. 1979. *Mixing in Inland and Coastal Waters*. New York, Academic Press.

Froehlich, W. and Slupik, J. 1982. River icings and fluvial activity in extreme continental climate: Khangai Mountains, Mongolia. In French, H.N., editor, *Proceedings of the 4th Canadian Permafrost Conference, Calgary, Canada*. National Research Council of Canada, Ottawa, pp. 203–211.

Gatto, L. W. 1995. *Soil Freeze-thaw Effects on Bank Erodibility and Stability*. United States Army Corps of Engineers, Cold Regions Research and Engineering Laboratory, Hanover, NH, Special Report 95–24.

Hamelin, L.-E. 1979. The bechevnik: a river bank feature from Siberia. *The Musk Ox* **25**: 70–72.

Harden, D., Barnes, P., and Reimnitz E. 1977. Distribution and character of naleds in northeastern Alaska. *Arctic*. **30**: 28–40.

Hong, R.-J., Karim, F., and Kennedy, J.F. 1984. Low-temperature effects on flow in sand-bed streams. *Journal of Hydraulic Engineering* **110**: 109–125.

Kane, D. 1981. Physical mechanics of aufeis growth. *Canadian Geotechnical Journal* **8**: 186–195.

Kellerhals, R. and Church, M. 1980. Comment on "Effects of channel enlargement by river ice processes on bankfull discharge in Alberta, Canada," by D.G. Smith. *Water Resources Research* **16**: 1131–1134.

Kempema, E.W. and Ettema, R. 2009. Variations in anchor-ice crystal morphology related to river flow characteristics. In Hicks, F. and Warren, S., editors, *15th Workshop on River Ice*. Canadian Geophysical Union, Hydrology Section, Committee on River Ice Processes in the Environment, pp. 159–168.

Kempema, E.W. and Ettema, R. 2011. Anchor ice rafting: observations from the Laramie River. *River Research and Applications* **27**: doi: 10.1002/rra.1450.

Kempema, E., Ettema, R., and McGee, B. 2008. Insights from anchor ice formation in the Laramie River, Wyoming. In *19th International Symposium on Ice, Vancouver, British Columbia, Canada*. International Association for Hydraulic Research, pp. 63–76.

Kempema, E.W., Reimnitz, E., and Hunter, R. E. 1986. *Flume Studies and Field Observations of the Interaction of Frazil Ice and Anchor Ice with Sediments*. United States Geological Survey, Open-File Report 86-515.

Kerr, D. J., Shen, H.T., and Daly, S.F. 2002. Evolution and hydraulic resistance of anchor ice on gravel beds. *Cold Regions Science and Technology* **35**: 101–114.

Kowalczyk, T. and Hicks, F. 2003. Observations of dynamic ice jam release on the Athabasca River at Fort McMurray, AB. In Hicks, F., editor, *Proceedings of the 12th Workshop on River Ice, June, Edmonton, Alberta*. Canadian Geophysical Union, pp. 369–392.

Lawson, D.E., Chacho, E.F., Brockett, B.E. et al. 1986. Morphology, hydraulics and sediment transport of an ice-covered river: field techniques and initial data. United States Army Corps of Engineers, Cold Regions Research and Engineering Laboratory, Hanover, NH, Report 86-11.

Lyell, C. 1854. *Principles of Geology, or The Modern Changes of Earth and Its Inhabitants as Illustrative of Geology*, 2nd (American) edition, New York, D. Appleton and Co.

MacKay, D.K., Sherstone, D.A., and Arnold, K.C. 1974. Channel ice effects and surface water velocities from aerial photography of Mackenzie River break-up. In *Hydrological Aspects of Northern Pipeline Development*. Task Force on Northern Oil Development, Environmental-Social Program, Northern Pipelines, Saskatoon, Saskatchewan, Report 74-12, pp. 71–107.

Mackay, J.R. and MacKay, D.K. 1977. The stability of ice-push features, Mackenzie River, Canada. *Canadian Journal of Earth Sciences* **14**: 2213–2225.

Marusenko, Ya. I. 1956. The action of ice on river banks. *Priroda* **45**(12): 91–93 [in Russian].

McNamara, J.P. and Kane, D.L. 2009. The impact of a shrinking cryosphere on the form of arctic alluvial channels. *Hydrological Processes* **23**: 159–186.

Mercer, A.G. and Cooper, R.H. 1977. River bed scour related to the growth of a major ice jam. *Proceedings of the 3rd National Hydrotechnical Conference, University of Laval, Quebec, 10–11 May*, Canadian Society for Civil Engineering, pp. 291–308.

Neill, C. R. 1976. Scour holes in a wandering gravel river. *Proceedings of the 3rd Annual Conference of the Waterways, Harbors and Coastal Engineering Division, New York, Symposium on Inland Waterways for Navigation, Flood Control, and Water Diversions, Fort Collins, CO, 10–12 August*. American Society of Civil Engineers, pp. 1301–1317.

Newbury, R.W. 1982. *The Nelson River: A Study of Sub-Arctic Processes*. Baltimore, ML, The John Hopkins University Press.

Prowse, T.D. 1993. Suspended sediment concentration during river ice breakup. *Canadian Journal of Civil Engineering* **20**: 872–875.

Prowse, T.D. 2001. River-ice ecology: I: hydrologic, geomorphic, and water-quality effects. *Journal of Cold Regions Engineering* **15**: 1–16.

Schohl, J. and Ettema, R. 1986. Theory and experiments on naled ice growth. *Journal of Glaciology* **32**: 168–177.

Schohl, J. and Ettema, R. 1990. Two dimensional thickening of aufeis. *Journal of Glaciology* **36**: 169–178.

Schumm, S.A. and Khan, H.R. 1972. Experimental study of channel patterns. *Geological Society of America Bulletin* **83**: 1755–1770.

Smith, D.G. 1979. Effects of channel enlargement by river ice processes on bankfull discharge in Alberta, Canada. *Water Resources Research* **15**: 469–475.

Smith, D.G. and Pearce, C.M. 2002. Ice jam-caused fluvial gullies and scour holes on northern river flood plains. *Geomorphology* **42**: 85–95.

Southard, J. B. and Boguchwal, L. A. 1990. Bed configurations in steady unidirectional flows. Part 3. Effects of temperature and gravity. *Journal of Sedimentary Petrology* **60**: 680–686.

Stickler, M. and Alfredsen, K.T. 2009. Anchor ice formation in streams: a field study. *Hydrological Processes* **23**: 2307–2315.

Tietze, W. 1961. Uber die erosion von unter eis fliessendem wasser. *Mainzer geographische studien 1*. Mainz, Georg Westermann, pp. 125–141.

Tsang, G. 1982. *Frazil and Anchor Ice: a Monograph*. Ottawa, National Research Council of Canada, Subcommittee on Hydraulics of Ice Covered Rivers.

Uunila, L.S. 1997. Effects of river ice on bank morphology and riparian vegetation along the Peace River, Clayhurst to Fort Vermilion. *Proceedings of the 9th Workshop on River Ice,*

*Fredericton, New Brunswick, 24–26 September*. Canadian Geophysical Union, pp. 315–334.

USACOE. 1983. *Galena Streambank Protection.* United States Army Corps of Engineers, Alaska District, Anchorage, AK. Galena, Alaska Section 14 Reconnaissance Report.

Vanoni, V. 1975. *Sedimentation Manual.* New York, American Society of Civil Engineers, Manual of Practice 54.

Wentworth, C.K. 1932. The geologic work of ice jams in sub-Arctic river. In Thomas, L.F., editor, *Contributions in Geology and Geography*. St Louis, MO, Washington University, Washington University Studies in Science and Technology 7, pp. 49–82.

White, K., Tuthill, A.M., and Furman, L. 2005. Studies of ice jams in the United States. In: Vasiliev, O.J., van Gelder P.H., Plate, E.J., and Bolgov, M.V., editors, *Extreme Hydrologic Events: New Concepts for Security*. Dordrecht, Springer, NATO Science Series 78, pp. 255–267.

Wuebben, J.L. 1988a. A preliminary study of scour under an ice jam. *Proceedings of the 5th Workshop on Hydraulics of River Ice/Ice Jams, Winnipeg, Manitoba*, pp. 177–190.

Wuebben, J.L. 1988b. Effects of an ice cover on flow in a moveable bed channel, *Proceedings of the Symposium on Ice, Sapporo, Japan*. International Association for Hydraulic Research, pp. 136–147.

Wuebben, J.L. 1995. Ice effects on riprap. In Thorne, C.R., Abt, S., Barends, S.T., and Pilarczyk, K.W., editors. *River, Coastal and Shoreline Protection: Erosion Control Using Riprap and Armourstone*. New York, John Wiley & Sons Ltd, pp. 513–530.

Zabilansky, L.J., Ettema, R. J. Wuebben, J., and Yankielun, N. E. 2002. *Survey of River-ice Influences on Channel Bathymetry along the Fort Peck Reach of the Missouri River, Winter 1998–1999*. United States Army Corps of Engineers, Cold Regions Research and Engineering Laboratory, Hanover NH, Contract Report.

Ziegler, C.K., VanDewalker, H., Slingerland, R., Rodrique, P., and Ashton, G. 2005. Evaluation of sediment transport impacts of the 2003 ice jam in the lower Grasse River. In Daly, S. editor. *13th Canadian River Ice Workshop, Hanover, NH, 15–16 September*. Canadian Geophysical Union. Abstract only.

# 38

# Is There a Northern Signature on Fluvial Form?

James P. McNamara

## 38.1 INTRODUCTION

Ettema and Kempema (Chapter 37, this volume) clearly articulate the processes governing river-ice formation and the potential effects of ice on sediment transport. They suggest that direct and indirect actions by ice can be important geomorphological processes. Their Section 37.5 presents a nice summary of the unique sediment transport processes in ice-dominated channels, and Sections 37.6 and 37.7 document several local geomorphological expressions of the effects of ice. In Section 37.8 they ask an intriguing question that I would like to pursue in this discussion. Does ice have a defining effect upon channel morphology? Ettema and Kempema acknowledge that this question has yet to be addressed appropriately, but speculate that major geometric parameters are likely not altered by ice. I conversely speculate that the form of gravel-bed rivers in cold regions may be adjusted to the actions of ice. Over the last several decades a suite of relatively universal emergent properties has been identified based on the tendency of fluvial systems to minimize energy expenditure as water travels through a catchment (Rigon et al., 1993; Rinaldo et al., 1992; Rodriguez-Iturbe et al., 1992a, 1992b). The fractal dimension of channel networks, the probability distribution of drainage areas in a river basin, the relation between channel length and drainage area, and many other properties have been suggested to possess universalities that cut across physiographic diversity. Yet, local conditions such as bedrock lithology and vegetation can imprint deviations on these apparent universalities. The central question of this discussion is this: Does ice leave a signature on universal geomorphological measures?

Geomorphological patterns arise as a landscape adjusts to competition between driving and resisting forces for mass movement. To consider this question of fluvial form, I first expand on the discussion of driving and resisting forces for sediment entrainment in gravel-bed rivers presented by Ettema and Kempema, then I discuss the concept of geomorphological work in ice-affected rivers, and finally I present some examples of potential ice signatures on fluvial form.

## 38.2 DRIVING AND RESISTING FORCES FOR SEDIMENT ENTRAINMENT IN ICE-AFFECTED RIVERS

The primary driving forces for particle motion and mass movement in northern gravel-bed rivers should not markedly differ from those in other environments. The hydraulic forces imposed by water depth and velocity entrain bed material and erode banks. Ettema and Kempema explained, however, that ice can effect sediment entrainment in gravel-bed rivers directly by such actions as scour and rafting, and indirectly by altering river hydraulics. Numerous studies have documented the geomorphological effects that river ice can have. Walker and Hudson (2003) suggested that most geomorphological work in the Colville River delta, a gravel-bed river in Alaska, occurs from river ice during the spring breakup period. Smith (1979) credited scour by river ice with creating enlarged channels with long return periods of bankfull flow. Kellerhals and Church (1980) agreed that the rivers in Smith's study do have long bankfull flow return periods, but suggested that scouring by ice is not a significant geomorphologic process at more than local scales. An alternative explanation is that ice indirectly impacts channel shape by causing ice jams. Upstream of the jam, flow and erosion occur at stages higher than would occur during ice-free conditions, creating a misleading bankfull stage. The ice-free flow that would fill the channel has a long return period, but the ice-affected flow that shapes the channel is relatively frequent.

*Gravel-bed Rivers: Processes, Tools, Environments*, First Edition. Edited by Michael Church, Pascale M. Biron and André G. Roy.
© 2012 John Wiley & Sons, Ltd. Published 2012 by John Wiley & Sons, Ltd.

Resisting forces include processes and properties that keep material in place such as the cohesiveness and sheltering of bank material, and the weight, shape, packing, and sheltering of bed material. River ice is not commonly considered as a resistive force. However, ice can shelter sediments from streamflow in shallow reaches where bedfast ice occurs. Bedfast ice differs from the more commonly cited anchor ice in that bedfast ice fills the channel, whereas anchor ice refers to submerged ice attached or anchored to the bed surface. Anchor ice can be transient, but can eventually lead to bedfast ice, which remains through the winter into the spring melt period. In this situation the spring snowmelt flows over ice rather than over the streambed, rendering the stream power ineffective (Best *et al.*, 2005; Priesnitz and Schunke, 2002). The effect of bedfast ice depends on the timing of when it melts or lifts from the bed relative to the timing of the flood hydrograph. For example, in the Upper Kuparuk River, Alaska, bedfast ice can persist through the entire snowmelt period in some years, while in other years it leaves the channel near peak flow (McNamara *et al.*, 2008). Priesnitz and Schunke (2002) suggested that sediment transport during snowmelt occurs in three phases in channels with bedfast ice. First, an early phase occurs in which strong flows occur over ice so that no sediment transport occurs. Second, minimal sediment transport occurs as declining flows cut through the ice and gain access to sediments. Third, ice leaves the channel, but minimal sediment transport occurs due to low flows. Forbes (1975) also documented reduced bed-scour due to channel ice and snow during rising flows.

## 38.3 RIVER ICE AND GEOMORPHOLOGIC WORK

A commonly accepted notion proposed by Wolman and Miller (1960) is that the greatest amount of geomorphological work in alluvial channels occurs in high-frequency events of moderate magnitude, i.e., bankfull flow. Wolman and Gerson (1978) further introduced the concept of geomorphological effectiveness, which is the ability of an event to affect the shape of the landscape. This definition takes into account not only the frequency and magnitude of a hydroclimatic event, but also the properties of the landscape (Marren, 2005). In ice-affected rivers, the timing of geomorphological effectiveness is influenced by the thermal dependence of driving and resisting forces (McNamara and Kane, 2009). In large rivers with floating ice, an ice-laden flow rate may be competent to scour banks, whereas the same ice-free flow rate may not. In shallow rivers with bedfast ice an otherwise competent flow may be rendered ineffective as it passes over ice-sheltered sediment.

Figure 38.1 proposes a conceptual model for how ice may affect geomorphologic work in large and small rivers. I must emphasize that Figure 38.1 is presented only as a concept to stimulate discussion. Figure 38.1a is the familiar diagram adapted from Leopold *et al.* (1964). As applied stress increases, the rate of mass movement increases. The frequency of high stress events, however, is low such that the maximum amount of work (curve 3) occurs at some optimum product of curves 1 and 2. In large rivers with a floating ice cover (Figure 38.1b), ice may impose stresses on stream bed and banks that are

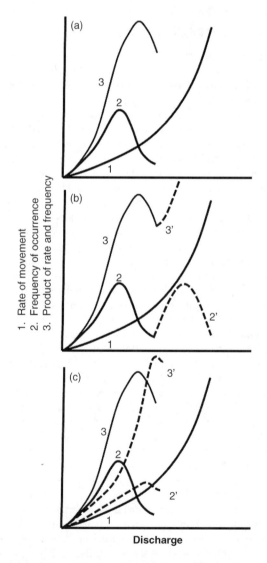

**Figure 38.1** Potential changes (dashed lines with accented numbers) to: (a) Wolman's frequency-work diagram due to (b) floating ice in large rivers, and (c) bedfast ice in small rivers.

higher than the water flow alone would cause (dashed line extending to higher stresses). Of course, the actual stress magnitudes and frequencies of ice-laden flows are unknown, but it seems reasonable that floating ice would impose competent stresses at least annually. If we assume that ice-induced stresses are higher than those associated with ice-free water at equivalent flows, we can expect a bimodal distribution of stresses which, in turn, produces a bimodal distribution of work. In small rivers (Figure 38.1c), the spring breakup period may be rendered ineffective by the influence of bedfast ice. The frequency of competent events is reduced and the greatest amount of work is shifted to the less frequent, large rainstorms that induce competent flow over an ice-free bed. The ideas in Figure 38.1 have not been tested in any empirical or theoretical study, but are presented here to stimulate discussion.

The conflicting roles of ice in large and shallow rivers call into question the relative importance of snowmelt versus rain events. Snowmelt occurs every year with moderate to high magnitudes at times when ice, and possibly permafrost, affects channel stability. Competent rain storms tend to be less frequent, but occur when channels are not affected by ice. Studies investigating the relative importance of rain and snow events do not generally agree. During a five year monitoring period on the Upper Kuparuk River, a gravel-bed river in Alaska, no snowmelt events produced detectable channel change or bedload transport, despite relatively high flows (McNamara et al., 2008). The maximum peak streamflow during the 10 year hydrologic record at the site occurred during an August rain event. This rain event generated a great deal of lateral and vertical channel adjustment. Some channel sections aggraded by more than a metre, others degraded by more than a metre, and banks eroded by up to 10 metres. Bedload measurements are rare in general, and even rarer in ice-affected rivers.

## 38.4 UNIVERSALITY OF FLUVIAL FORM IN ICE-AFFECTED RIVERS

Previous sections made the case that the relation between driving and resisting forces for particle motion in alluvial channels is affected by ice, and that this altered relation impacts the frequency of geomorphologically effective flows. If apparent universalities in fluvial form arise from principles of minimum energy expenditure, and the frequency of geomorphologic work directly effects energy expenditure, and ice affects geomorphologic work, is it reasonable to speculate that ice imprints a signature on universal geomorphologic properties?

Consider hydraulic geometry relations as an example of the impact of ice on fluvial form. The equilibrium channel cross-section is naturally adjusted to efficiently transmit the water and sediment it receives from its catchment. Alluvial rivers that are stable over a period of years tend to possess similar hydraulic geometries that scale with bankfull flow (Millar, 2005). Hydraulic geometry relations are typically modelled as power functions

$$W = aQ^b; \; D = cQ^f; \; S = tQ^{-d}; \; V = kQ^m \quad (38.1)$$

wherein $W$ is the channel width, $D$ is the flow depth, $V$ is average velocity, $S$ is the channel slope, and $Q$ is the bankfull flow. Many studies have shown that the exponents tend towards similar values for rivers worldwide. Most efforts to explain the "universality" of the shape exponents ($b$, $f$, and $d$) relate governing equations describing bedload transport, flow resistance, and bank stability, with so-called extremal hypotheses that quantify some governing mechanism that constrains channel form (Eaton et al., 2004).

Parker et al. (2007) noted that local conditions can cause systematic deviations from universality. For example, rivers in Alberta described by Kellerhals et al. (1972) are systematically wider and shallower than rivers in Britain described by Charlton et al. (1978). Parker et al. (2007) reasoned that the differences are likely due to the role that vegetation plays in bank strength; the well-vegetated banks in British rivers restrict channel widening. It stands to reason that frozen material in the bed and banks will influence channel geometry.

The Kuparuk River, in the continuous permafrost region of northern Alaska, has unusual hydraulic geometry relations (Figure 38.2, Table 38.1) that have been explained as a function of channel ice (McNamara and Kane, 2009). In this example, bankfull flow scales with drainage area by a power function exponent of 0.97 up to a drainage area of approximately 300 km². At greater drainage areas the trend continues with a similar exponent (0.92), however, there is a distinct shift in the coefficient of the power function. This shift is accompanied by a step increase in cross-sectional area which is manifested more in channel width than in channel depth. In the greater drainage areas channel cross-sections are approximately three times larger than would be predicted by the relation for smaller drainage areas. Channels in the smaller drainage areas are relatively narrower and less deep, and, consequently, have smaller-scale cross-sections. However, in larger drainage areas, width increases proportionally less rapidly, while depth appears to increase at the same rate. In the smaller drainage areas channels have an unusually low hydraulic geometry depth exponent. In the larger drainage areas channel depth increases more rapidly than width.

Best et al. (2005) showed that the width anomaly in Figure 38.2 occurs at drainage areas approximately consistent with a transition from predominantly bedfast

**Table 38.1** Hydraulic geometry exponents[a]

|  | b | f | m |
|---|---|---|---|
| Entire Kuparuk River | 0.54 | 0.25 | 0.22 |
| Kuparuk drainage areas smaller than 300 km$^2$ | 0.29 | 0.55 | 0.29 |
| Kuparuk drainage areas greater than 300 km$^2$ | 0.50 | 0.20 | 0.16 |
| "Universal" (Millar, 2005) | 0.45–0.55 | 0.33–0.4 | 0.1 |

[a](see Equation 38.1).

ice to predominantly cap ice. McNamara and Kane (2009) proposed that bedfast ice reduces the frequency of effective flows in shallow channels so that channel change occurs only from infrequent effective summer rain events. Because of the low rate of depth

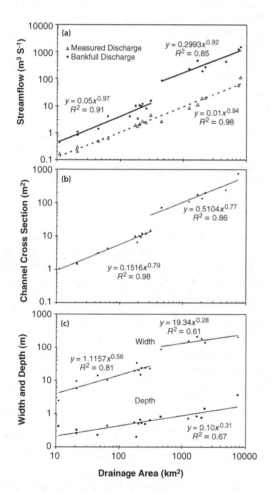

**Figure 38.2** Scaling relations between: (a) streamflow and drainage area, (b) channel cross-sectional area and drainage area, and (c) channel width and depth with drainage area in the Kuparuk River, Alaska. Modified from McNamara and Kane, 2009.

increase and the normal rate of width increase, the average bankfull velocity must increase to maintain continuity. Indeed, the velocity exponent is higher than expected in the smaller channels. The increase in velocity is a condition that cannot be sustained with significant channel adjustment. The response in velocity, rather than width, suggests that the peat-covered banks may enhance bank strength. A transition occurs downstream where channels become deep enough to support cap ice, prompting a new erosional regime. Depth then increases more rapidly, initially accompanied by a very rapid width increase. Beyond this transition the channel capacity may be controlled by other processes, such as downstream ice jams that alter stream hydraulics, or accelerated flow under cap ice. This conceptual model is perhaps more substantiated in the smaller channels than in the larger channels. Indirect observations in many studies cited above support the notion that bedload transport is suppressed by bedfast ice, reducing the frequency of effective flows. The proposed impact on hydraulic geometry in the small channels can be reasonably explained within the traditional framework of geomorphologic effectiveness. However, the anomalous hydraulic geometry of the large channels can be reasonably explained by other processes, including bed and bank material and channel slope. For example, it is possible that the Quaternary and late Tertiary sediments near the coast have been eroded by sea ice and wave action so that base level for the rivers has retrogressed upstream.

## 38.5 CONCLUDING REMARKS

I have attempted to address Ettema and Kempema's comment that major geomorphological measures are not likely affected by ice. It seems reasonable that if ice impacts the timing and magnitude of geomorphologic effectiveness of streamflow, it should indeed impact the equilibrium form of rivers. I present an example of the effects of ice in the Kuparuk River, Alaska. I must point out, however, that the example I provide is only for one geomorphological measure (hydraulic geometry) for one river. The importance of the question demands more field investigations in ice-affected rivers.

Finally, it is difficult to discuss anything about cold-region hydrology or geomorphology without talking about climate change. Processes and patterns in cold-region rivers are adjusted to the presence of ice. If these regions warm to the point where ice is no longer a dominant control, what kind of re-adjustments in fluvial form can we expect?

## 38.6   REFERENCES

Best, H., McNamara, J.P., and Liberty L. 2005. Association of ice and river channel morphology determined using ground penetrating radar in the Kuparuk River, Alaska. *Arctic, Antarctic, and Alpine Research* **37**: 157–162.

Charlton, F.G., Brown, P.M., and Benson, R.W. 1978. *The Hydraulic Geometry of some Gravel Rivers in Britain.* Hydraulics Research Station, Wallingford, United Kingdom Report INT-180.

Eaton, B.C., Church, M., and Millar, R.G. 2004. Rational regime model of alluvial channel morphology and response. *Earth Surface Processes and Landforms* **29**: 511–529.

Forbes, D.L. 1975. *Sedimentary Processes and Sediments, Babbage River Delta, Yukon Coast.* Geological Survey of Canada, Paper 75-1B, pp. 157–160.

Kellerhals, R., Neill, C.R., and Bray, D.I. 1972. *Hydraulic and Geomorphic Characteristics of Rivers in Alberta.* Alberta Research Council, River Engineering and Surface Hydrology Section, Report 72-1.

Kellerhals, R.K. and Church, M. 1980. Comment on 'Effects of channel enlargement by river ice processes on bankfull discharge in Alberta, Canada' by D.G. Smith. *Water Resources Research* **16**: 1131–1134.

Leopold, L.B., Wolman, M.G., and Miller, J.P. 1964. *Fluvial Processes in Geomorphology.* San Francisco, Freeman.

Marren, P.M. 2005. Magnitude and frequency in proglacial rivers: a geomorphological and sedimentological perspective. *Earth-Science Reviews* **70**: 203–251.

McNamara, J.P. and Kane, D.L. 2009. The impact of a shrinking cryosphere on the form of arctic alluvial channels. *Hydrological Processes* **23**: 159–186.

McNamara, J.P., Oatley, J.A., Kane, D.L., and Hinzman, L.D. 2008. Case study of a large summer flood on the North Slope of Alaska: bedload transport. *Hydrology Research* **39**: 299–308.

Millar, R.G. 2005. Theoretical regime equations for mobile gravel-bed rivers with stable banks. *Geomorphology* **64**: 207–220.

Parker, G., Wilcock, P.R., Paola, C., Dietrich, W.E., and Pitlick, J. 2007. Physical basis for quasi-universal relations describing bankfull hydraulic geometry of single-thread gravel bed rivers. *Journal of Geophysical Research* **112**: F04005. doi: 10.1029/2006JF000549.

Priesnitz, K. and Schunke, E. 2002. The fluvial morphodynamics of two small permafrost drainage basins, Richardson Mountains, Northwestern Canada. *Permafrost and Periglacial Processes* **13**: 207–217.

Rigon, R., Rinaldo, A., Rodriguez-Iturbe, I., Bras, R.L., and Ijjasz-Vasquez, E. 1993. Optimal channel networks: a framework for the study of river basin morphology. *Water Resources Research* **29**: 1635–1646.

Rinaldo, A., Rodriguez-Iturbe, I., Rigon, R. *et al.* 1992. Minimum energy and fractal structures of drainage networks. *Water Resources Research* **28**: 2183–2195.

Rodriguez-Iturbe, I., Ijjasz-Vasquez, E.J., Bras, R.L., and Tarboton, D.G. 1992a. Power law distributions of discharge mass and energy in river basins. *Water Resources Research* **28**: 1089–1093.

Rodriguez-Iturbe, I., Rinaldo, A., Rigon, R. *et al.* 1992b. Fractal structures as least energy patterns: the case of river networks *Geophysical Research Letters* **19**: 889–892.

Smith, D.G. 1979. Effects of channel enlargement by river ice processes on bankfull discharge in Alberta, Canada. *Water Resources Research* **15**: 469–475.

Walker, H.J. and Hudson, P.F. 2003. Hydrologic and geomorphic processes in the Colville River delta, Alaska. *Geomorphology* **56**: 291–303.

Wolman, M.G. and Gerson, R. 1978. Relative scales of time and effectiveness of climate in watershed geomorphology. *Earth Surface Processes and Landforms* **3**: 189–208.

Wolman, M.G. and Miller, J.P. 1960. Magnitude and frequency of forces in geomorphic processes. *Journal of Geology* **68**: 54–74.

# 39

# Long-term and Large-scale River-ice Processes in Cold-region Watersheds

**Etienne Boucher, Yves Bégin, Dominique Arseneault, and Taha B.M.J. Ouarda**

## 39.1 INTRODUCTION

Understanding the various spatial and temporal scales to which river ice shapes and alters natural channels is a crucial step towards a better assessment of the full range of physical processes that occur in cold-region watersheds. In Ettema and Kempema's paper on ice effects, the primary focus is on processes that typically occur at the intra-annual time scale and at length scales that are generally equal (and often inferior) to that of the channel reach. Of course, such scales are appropriate to investigate, on one hand, river-ice cover formation and break-up processes, and on the other hand, allow for the study of local sediment transport and ablation, the description of ice-covered hydraulics and the analysis of morphological and geotechnical changes that relate to ice dynamics. However, to establish whether or not river ice, *per se*, can be considered a geomorphologically significant agent in the long term remains to be evaluated on much larger time and spatial scales.

Investigating ice effects at larger spatial and temporal scales in gravel-bed rivers, by definition, implies that the characteristics of the ice regime (frequency, magnitude, duration, moment of occurrence of events) and their variations through time and space need to be taken into account. For example, all of the following questions regarding ice jam dynamics need to be addressed with at least a partial understanding of ice regime characteristics:

- Are natural channels adjusted to local ice dynamics?
- Is the ice regime stable through time and space? If not, what are the main drivers of change at the channel reach and watershed scales?
- Are landforms in a channel reach the product of a single ice jam event or are they maintained by the repeated abrasive action of ice on banks and bed?

- Is ice influence on channel morphology localized or widespread?
- How do landforms change as a function of the spatially varying characteristics of ice regimes?

To date, very few studies have addressed these questions, mostly because spatio-temporally extensive datasets describing river-ice dynamics are extremely rare. Indeed, observations on river ice phenomena are generally scattered, discontinuous and not systematically collected throughout the vast and sparsely populated northern lands. Similarly, when it exists, hydrological information retrieved from gauging stations is often filtered to exclude ice-induced "anomalies" in the hydrographs and may be deliberately positioned in channel reaches that undergo very few ice effects. As a consequence, studies that have reported ice-shaped fluvial landscapes (Dionne, 1974, 1976, 1978; Mackay *et al.*, 1974; Hamelin, 1979; Prowse and Gridley, 1993; Dyke, 2000; Prowse, 2001; Ettema, 2002; Smith and Pearce, 2002; Walker and Hudson, 2003) have usually relied on very little local information on the ice regime. Additionally, the extent of these landforms within watersheds, and most typically their association with the longitudinally varying ice regime characteristics were never assessed quantitatively, owing to the rarity and sparseness of the data.

In the present article, we will explore some issues associated with long-term and large-scale river-ice dynamics (mostly river-ice-jam dynamics). We will review the published literature and bring some illustrative examples from personally collected data on the Necopastic River watershed, located in northern Quebec, Canada. In order to circumvent the previously described difficulty to find spatio-temporally extensive sets of observations within this watershed, we will rely on tree-ring reconstructed ice jam occurrences. These have

*Gravel-bed Rivers: Processes, Tools, Environments*, First Edition. Edited by Michael Church, Pascale M. Biron and André G. Roy.
© 2012 John Wiley & Sons, Ltd. Published 2012 by John Wiley & Sons, Ltd.

the advantage of covering at least the last century in many sites within the Necopastic River watershed. With this data set in hand, we will try to illustrate how ice regime characteristics may have varied through time and space within this cold-region watercourse and examine some of the potential geomorphic responses associated with ice jam dynamics. Although not all studies presented here were conducted on gravel-bed rivers, the fundamental processes and phenomena can easily be generalized to that river type.

## 39.2 THE NECOPASTIC RIVER DATA SET

The Necopastic River watershed ($250 \, \text{km}^2$; $53°73'$ N, $78°28'$ W) is located in the James Bay area in northern Quebec, Canada. The Necopastic River flows in a lithologically homogeneous glacio-fluvial morainic deposit, mainly composed of sands and silts. At bankfull stage, the average discharge is about $25 \, \text{m}^3 \, \text{s}^{-1}$ in the lower reach. The channels are fairly narrow, varying from 5 to 10 m in the upper basin and reaching 20 to 25 m at the outlet. Channel slope and depth (at bankfull) do not depict such a trend. Channel depth is $1.5 \pm 0.5 \, \text{m}$ on average across the basin and the slope is always very low and inferior to 0.001. The Necopastic River is located in the High Boreal zone and thus, riparian vegetation is composed of Black spruce (*Picea mariana* (Mill.) BSP.), Eastern larch (*Larix laricina* (Du Roi) K.Koch) and

occasionally Balsam fir (*Abies balsamea* (L.) Mill.). Ice-scour tolerant shrubs such as Mountain alder (*Alnus viridis* ssp. *crispa* (Ait.) Turrill), Diamondleaf willow (*Salix planifolia* Pursh), and American Dwarf birch (*Betula glandulosa*) are omnipresent along the banks. Many trees living on the Necopastic riverbanks have been injured by floating ice (usually during spring ice jams at these latitudes), especially in mid-basin (Figure 39.1). Such scars can be dendrochronologically dated and extensive ice-jam chronologies can be constructed (Payette, 1980; Smith and Reynolds, 1983; Hupp, 1988; Boucher, 2009a). For additional details on how such chronologies were constructed on the Necopastic, the readers are referred to the work of Boucher *et al.*, 2009a. In the present contribution, we used such chronologies: (i) to detect the presence (or absence) of an ice-jam event at each site and at each year since 1900 and (ii) to evaluate the magnitude of past ice jams within the watershed (calculated using the proportion of sites recording an ice jam within the watershed).

Landforms and processes also were inventoried throughout the watershed using a reconnaissance survey technique (Thorne *et al.*, 1996; Thorne, 1998). In addition to some hydraulic geometry parameters (channel widths, depths, cross-sectional areas, width–depth ratios), bed and bank features, and associated geomorphological processes were systematically described (see Thorne, 1998).

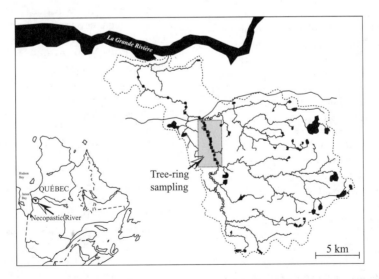

**Figure 39.1** The Necopastic River watershed. Symbols on the map correspond to sampling sites. Open circles represent sites where no ice-jamming activity was found (no ice scars were sampled). Black squares represent sites with an important ice-jam activity (as evidenced by scars on trees) and where an ice-scoured morphology was found (see text for details). Black circles correspond to sites where ice jams occur, though no eroded morphology could be identified. The transition between the upstream (no ice jams) and the downstream portion of the basin corresponds to the passage from white to black symbols (drainage area = $100 \, \text{km}^2$).

## 39.3 SOME PERSPECTIVES ON LONG-TERM AND LARGE-SCALE RIVER-ICE JAM DYNAMICS

### 39.3.1 Ice-Jam Frequency Varies Through Time

Ice-jam frequency [$0 \leq f \leq 1$ event a$^{-1}$] is one of the most important parameters characterizing ice regimes in northern environments and is fundamental to the evaluation of ice-jam risk. Moreover, this parameter is of geomorphological importance for cold-region rivers, as the recurrence of these extreme events may control the rate at which ice-scouring landforms are shaped and maintained along channel reaches.

At its most simple expression, ice-jam frequency is calculated by dividing the number of events recorded by the length of time considered. One of the most striking features that arises when century-long time scales are examined is that ice-jam frequency becomes a highly non-stationary statistic. Ultimately, it designates a value that is very likely to change: (i) through time and (ii) as a function of the time scale used to perform the frequency analysis. Here, we give a few examples taken from the literature, and present some personal data to illustrate the phenomenon.

A few studies focusing on long-term ice-jam dynamics took place in the Peace River Delta, British Columbia, Canada, and have shown that the frequency of these events has considerably evolved over time in this area. Timoney *et al.* (1997) based their analysis of ice jam floods on the perception stage approach (Gerard and Karpuk, 1979) and on an exhaustive analysis of hydrographs and historical documents available in the area. Their results revealed that the 1860–1880 period was characterized by very few ice jam floods in comparison with the 1915–1950 period, when these events were apparently unusually frequent. More particularly, they have shown that, in the Peace-Athabasca Delta, the average ice jam flood frequency is about 1 event in 6.25 years (i.e. $1/6.25 = 0.16$ a$^{-1}$) for the 1826–1995 period. However, Timoney *et al.* (1997) clearly show that this is an average value and that much higher/lower ice-jam flood frequencies could have been obtained if, for example, ice-jam frequencies had been estimated during the 1860–1880 (frequency close to 0) or the 1915–1950 (frequency $> 0.4$ a$^{-1}$) periods, respectively. Another contribution by Timoney *et al.* (1997) was to show that ice-jam floods in the Peace Athabasca delta present a non-random temporal pattern that seems to be strongly associated with the well-known 11 year cycle of solar activity.

Smith (2003) also investigated these changing ice regimes in the Peace River Delta, but focused on the millennial time scale. From a thorough analysis of ice-flood sediments deposited on alluvial levees, Smith (2003) revealed that the average ice flood frequency over the last 1100 years was 0.06 event a$^{-1}$ in the Peace River Delta and showed that this value increased subsequently to oscillate around 0.15 event a$^{-1}$ during the last two centuries. It is interesting to contrast these results with those obtained by Timoney *et al.* (1997) that were evaluated on a shorter time period (and from different proxies). During the common period (the two last centuries), both studies present similar average ice-jam frequencies. However, Smith's data go back much further in time and cover the Little Ice Age, a period of very low ice-flooding activity that probably lowers the average significantly.

On the Necopastic River, the inventory of ice-scoured trees along the banks also revealed such non-stationary ice-jam frequencies. Figure 39.2 depicts, for each site, the temporal variations of ice-jam frequencies. The dark curve represents the variations of these statistics calculated, for each year $t$, with access to only the 20 preceding years (presence/absence data). This moving time-window approach suggests, among other things, that the ice-jam frequency is an estimate that is highly contextual to the period for which it is evaluated. For example, at site 1 (Figure 39.2a), if ice-jam frequencies were estimated during the 1900–1920 period, values around 0.3 events a$^{-1}$ would be expected. This value would be dramatically lower if it was estimated during the 1920–1960 period ($< 0.1$ events a$^{-1}$) and finally would reach unequalled peaks during the recent period (1960–2000; $> 0.4$ events a$^{-1}$). Although they are not always synchronous, similar changes can be observed at all sites within the Necopastic watershed (Figure 39.2b–m).

The length of the time scale itself is also of great importance for the evaluation of ice-jam frequencies. Ideally, and in the light of the preceding discussion, one wishes to estimate these statistics on a time scale that is as long as possible, so that it encompasses at least two (and hopefully more) different ice regimes. In Figure 39.2, the pale gray line represents the evolution of these frequencies, providing that their calculation at year $t$ is based on access to all the preceding years. Thus, the frequency of an ice jam in 1900 is calculated using the period 1880–1900 ($n = 21$), and in 2000, the same frequency is calculated using the period 1880–2000 ($n = 121$). These analyses revealed that the extension of the time scale places the analyst in a better position to describe ice-jam frequencies at the channel reach scale. Again, looking at site 1 (Figure 39.2a), it is easy to see that the incremental addition of the new data is accompanied by a progressively increasing ice-jam frequency that reached more than 0.2 events a$^{-1}$ in 2000, while it was inferior to 0.1 events a$^{-1}$ between 1920 and 1960.

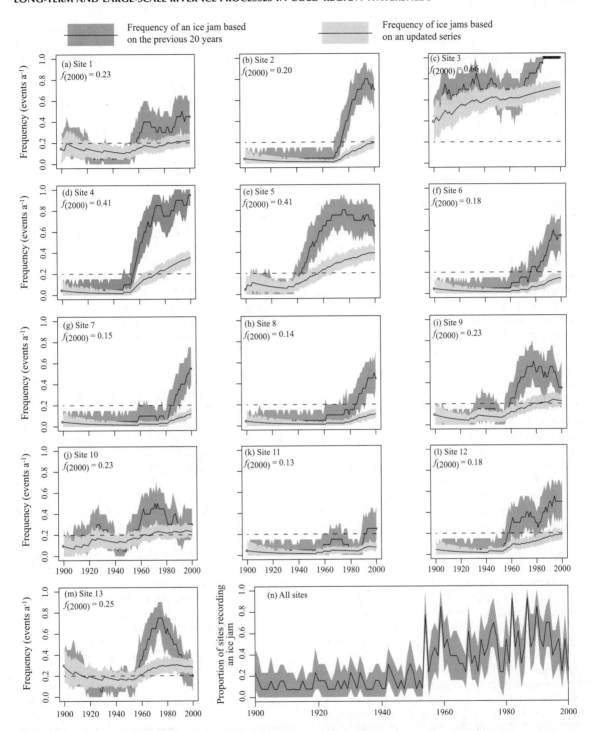

**Figure 39.2** Ice-jam frequency analysis in the Necopastic River watershed. (a) to (m) represent the frequency data (with 90% binomial confidence intervals) for each site where tree-ring data were collected (rectangle in Figure 39.1) and (n) represents the proportion of sites recording an ice jam in the watershed. $f(2000)$ represents the frequency calculated for year AD 2000, using the last 100 years of records.

At the watershed scale, these non-stationarities also exist. Boucher *et al.* (2009a) determined that the magnitude of ice jams within the Necopastic River watershed is best estimated by the proportion of sites that recorded an event. In these conditions, large proportions indicate that hydroclimatic thresholds associated with the triggering of mechanical breakups have been exceeded in many sites. Figure 39.2n presents the evolution of these proportions in the Necopastic watershed. Two very different ice regimes can be observed: a first regime (1900–1950) characterized by relatively rare (proportion < 0.2) ice-jam events, and a second one (1950–2000) when ice jams were much more common (proportion > 0.5). From this dataset, Boucher *et al.* (2009a) demonstrated that the yearly variations in the proportion of sites recording an ice jam, at the watershed scale, are not random, i.e., that they are teleconnected to the Arctic Oscillation (AO) variations. The AO is a major annular mode in the area and during its positive phase, cold and snowy spring conditions prevail. These climatic conditions are thought to help preserve the mechanical integrity of the ice until spring flood occurs.

### 39.3.2　The Frequency of Ice Jams Changes Through Space

Ice-jam frequencies vary between locations in cold-region watersheds. In some sites with a particular configuration (narrow or incurved channels), ice jams can occur almost every year, while in others, these events are very unlikely. These variations are important, since they imply that the risk for ecosystems and riparian populations varies through space accordingly. In order to adequately characterize this downstream (longitudinal) variability, one must rely on multiple ice-jam chronologies that would ideally be evenly distributed within the watershed. However, if it is difficult to find exhaustive and systematic gauge records that allow for an accurate characterization of ice-jam dynamics, it is even harder to replicate these series through space. This is why alternative methods, such as dendrochronology or ground-penetrating radar surveys have proven to be useful to characterize ice-jam dynamics at the watershed scale.

Best *et al.* (2005) have used ground-penetrating radar to estimate the downstream variations of ice thickness in the Kuparuk River basin (Alaska) and related these measurements to ice-jam dynamics. They investigated 10 sites corresponding to a downstream gradient covering 45 to 7465 km$^2$. They found that the section between 300 and 600 km$^2$ corresponded to a transition from bedfast to floating ice. Upstream of this drainage area threshold, the ice possibly remains grounded or attached to the riverbed and its carriage during the spring flood is very unlikely, leading to very few ice jams in this area. By contrast, downstream of this drainage area threshold, the ice appears to float on the water as a consequence of increasing channel depths. River ice is therefore easily mobilized during the spring floods leading to more frequent ice-jam problems. However, Best *et al.* (2005) did not provide any indication of "how frequent" these ice jams were downstream of this drainage area threshold, but based their analysis on observed morphological changes (some of which will be described in the next section) that indicate increasing ice-jamming activity.

In the Necopastic River, the dendrochronological sampling of ice scars on riparian trees allowed for: (i) identification of the drainage area threshold beyond which ice jams become "possible" and (ii) evaluation of downstream changes in ice-jam frequency, where these events occurred. The sampling of trees was performed in channels that drained an area ranging from 5 to 250 km$^2$. The inventory and dating of scars revealed that upstream of 100 km$^2$, ice jams simply cannot occur (no scars were found, systematically, see Figure 39.1). By analogy to the work of Best *et al.* (2005), this property of the Necopastic basin suggests that there probably exists a certain compartmentalization of river-ice processes within cold-region watersheds. In other words, ice jams become possible only when certain hydrological and cryological conditions are met. Such conditions were never quantitatively assessed, but are thought to be "basin specific". In the Necopastic watershed, these conditions are met downstream of the 100 km$^2$ threshold in the absence of significant changes in slope upstream and downstream of this confluence. The 100 km$^2$ threshold corresponds to the confluence of two dendritic subwatersheds (Figure 39.1). Dendritic basins usually produce flashy spring floods, a condition that was identified by Boucher *et al.* (2009a) as being of considerable importance for the triggering of mechanical breakups in this watershed.

Downstream of this 100 km$^2$ threshold, ice-jam frequency varies considerably between sites. Boucher *et al.* (2009b) demonstrated that the average frequency of ice jams was 0.26 event a$^{-1}$, with some sites reaching as much as 0.66 event a$^{-1}$, while others that were less responsive, experienced between 0 and 0.13 event a$^{-1}$ (Figure 39.2a–m). The factors responsible for this variability were not investigated directly in that study and would require further attention, but probably include longitudinal changes in ice density, thickness, and channel form. Nevertheless, an important innovation of this study was to demonstrate that long-term ice-jam chronologies provide the analyst with a better (and also more quantitative) understanding of the spatial variability of these phenomena. Ice-jam dynamics would have been otherwise reduced to a matter of discriminating between the presence and the absence of the phenomenon; an analysis that might lead to over-simplistic conclusions in many situations, especially if one desires to describe environmental impacts associated with ice-jam dynamics.

### 39.3.3 Geomorphological Responses (may) Vary Through Time and Space

Coupling long-term and/or large-scale ice-jam chronologies to geomorphological features can help refine our understanding of the role played by ice in cold-region hydrosystems. More specifically, such an approach allows one to: (i) better evaluate the extent of ice-shaped landforms in fluvial landscapes and (ii) determine whether or not the variations in the ice regime (such as downstream changes in ice-jam frequencies) are accompanied by changes in geomorphological characteristics. Over the last few years, significant advances on these questions have been accomplished by taking advantage of long-term and large-scale datasets.

Smith (1979) first hypothesized that the repeated abrasive action of ice against riverbanks during spring break-up may have resulted in enlarged and higher capacity bankfull channels, in comparison with channels that do not experience significant ice jams. From an analysis of 24 gauging stations in Alberta (Canada), he concluded that mid-sized channels in this area got "enlarged" by a factor of 2.6 to 3. Although this enlargement factor now seems overly large, perhaps one of the most stimulating findings of Smith's (1979) work was to reveal a unique property of cold-region channels: their capacity to adjust in both size and shape to the local ice regime. However, the extent of this adjustment (if there is one) and the underlying processes that control it require further investigation.

Best et al. (2005) came up with some interesting research avenues regarding the processes controlling the adjustment of channels to ice jams in the Kuparuk basin, Alaska. In this basin, a step change exists in the hydraulic geometry relation between channel cross-sectional area and drainage area. The work of Best et al. (2005) suggested that this step change might correspond to a transition from bedfast to floating ice (also described in the preceding section). They used ground-penetrating radar data to survey downstream variations in ice thickness and noticed that enlarged channels correspond to sections that do not freeze to the bottom, a condition that favours ice-jam formation. Therefore, they hypothesized that the frequent ice jams that occur downstream of this transition were responsible for the widespread lateral erosion of river channels in the Kuparuk River basin. This statement is plausible, but needs to be substantiated with additional geomorphological evidence and possibly some additional data on ice-jam dynamics.

In the Necopastic River basin, Boucher et al. (2009b) investigated the downstream geomorphological variability of fluvial landforms and related these variations to changing ice-jam frequencies. This approach allowed them to recognize the particular "signature" of ice-scoured channels in this landscape. This signature was found only downstream of the $100\ km^2$ threshold, and in sites where the ice-jam frequency was equal to or greater than one event occurring every five years ($0.2$ event $a^{-1}$). The particular ice-scoured morphology consists of a two-level bank structure (Figure 39.3). The most important feature of these ice-scoured channels is a steep erosional talus about $0.75\ m$ high and generally found above the bankfull stage. This talus results from the mechanical abrasion of ice against banks. It is thought that ice runs carrying thick and solid ice rafts may increase the shear stress exerted against channel boundaries and therefore locally augment the capacity to perform work (Prowse, 1995). Ice-induced erosion has also excavated tree and shrub roots of ligneous plants living on the higher terrace. These trees are scarred as well and recent alluvia are commonly found at their base, suggesting that ice-jam floods might have resulted in the slow aggradation of these terraces. At the base of this talus, a discontinuous and partly eroded bench ($1.5$ to $2\ m$ wide) is commonly found. This bench is covered with heavily scarred shrubs growing on freshly deposited alluvia, suggesting that this landform could correspond to a genetic floodplain that undergoes significant erosion. Interestingly, where ice jams do not occur, river channels present wide and active floodplains on both sides. Signs of lateral instability are nowhere to be found in this upstream environment.

Similar to Best et al. (2005), Boucher et al. (2009b) have noticed that hydraulic geometry relations did not hold in sites where ice jams are extremely frequent (frequency $> 0.2$ event $a^{-1}$). In fact, relations between drainage area and channel width or cross-sectional area show that sites that experienced frequent ice jams appear as outliers in the graphs of (Figure 39.4a–b). This indicates that sites that undergo significant ice-jam erosion can be enlarged by a factor of $1.5$ to $2$ in the most extreme cases. For example, at mid-basin, sites where very frequent ice jams occur are about $23$–$25\ m$ wide, while those where fewer ice jams occur are narrower ($\sim 14$–$15\ m$).

Whether or not these ice-scoured channels are the product of a single event or the result of several erosion episodes will require further study. But the fact that these two-level channels are found only in sections that experienced frequent ice jams over the last century points to the possibility that the frequency of these events might be

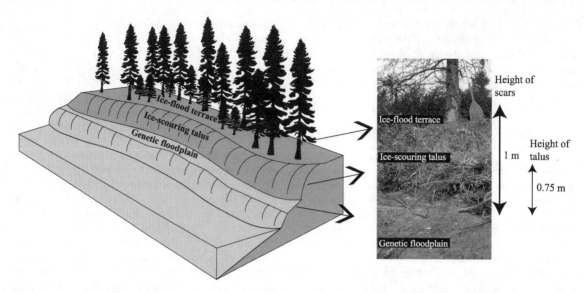

**Figure 39.3**    The geomorphological signature of ice scouring in the Necopastic River watershed; a two-level channel with eroded banks. Note the presence of scarred trees on the top of the ice flood terrace. The cartoon on the left is not to scale with the picture on the right.

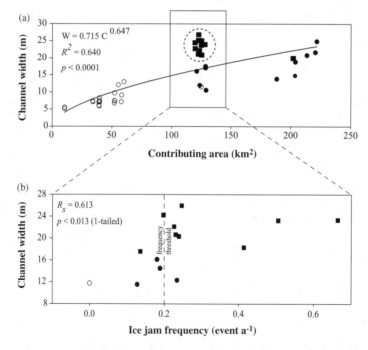

**Figure 39.4**    Relations between channel width and (a) contributing area and (b) ice-jam frequencies in the Necopastic River watershed. Circled points in (a) indicate prominent outliers subject to frequent, damaging ice-jam activity. Symbols correspond to those used in Figure 39.1. Reproduced, with permission, from Boucher, E., Begin, Y., and Arseneault, D. 2009b. Impacts of recurring ice jams on channel geometry and geomorphology in a small-high boreal watershed. Geomorphology 108: 273–281.

an important factor in the long term. The resilience of these environments is thought to be important owing to the numerous ecological (e.g., regeneration of ice-tolerant species), physical (e.g., numerous floods during the ice-free season that re-work sediments) and hydro-meteorological (snowmelt, freeze–thaw cycles) factors that can rapidly mask the damages caused by a single ice jam. Additionally, the impact of the recent rise in ice-jam activity (since the 1950s) must be documented from a geomorphological point of view. Most particularly, a fundamental question remains unanswered: Is this ice-scoured morphology simply a product of the intensification of the erosion over the last 50 years? Boucher et al. (2009b) did not provide a specific answer to that question, but it is clear that without such a long-term and large-scale data set, this question would probably never even have been raised.

## 39.4   CONCLUSIONS

Studying ice-jam dynamics at very large spatial and temporal scales provides hydrologists and geomorphologists with a unique perspective on the evolution of cold-region hydrosystems. However, this perspective is gained at the expense of a more precise evaluation of processes that are otherwise known to govern ice jam dynamics at a finer scale. This is because the proxy records (such as tree-rings) that are used to reconstruct past ice jams do not deliver the information at the precision expected from an analysis based on hydrometric records. For example, documenting past ice jams from tree rings allows for the determination of the presence/ absence of an event for a given year. However, it does not enable precise dating of the moment of its occurrence, measure the duration of the event or determine the exact date of the onset of river ice break-up, release, and jam. In contrast, tree-ring series (and other proxies) cover time scales that are often much longer (often century-long) than those obtained by gauging instruments or other geophysical techniques. Moreover, they provide access to larger spatial scales since they are easily replicable and allow for an intersite comparison of ice-jam dynamics and impacts.

It has been shown that spatio-temporally extensive ice-jam chronologies enable a more representative characterization of ice regimes within cold-region watersheds. In the present discussion, we have shown that ice-jam frequency, a parameter affecting the calculation of ice-jam risk at the local scale, varies through both time and space, and according to the length of the time scale considered. At the scale of recent centuries for example, ice-jam frequency appears like a highly non-stationary statistic. Hence, short-term records would provide biased estimates of ice-jam frequencies (and thus risks) that are highly contextual to the period for which the estimates are calculated. Therefore, it is wise to base the analysis on time scales that are sufficiently long to cover at least more than two different ice regimes.

Some insights into the spatial variations of ice-jam frequencies were also described in the present discussion. Tree rings and ground-penetrating radar data confirm that ice jams do not occur everywhere within basins. A striking feature coming out of these studies is that there probably exists a drainage-area threshold, downstream of which river ice can be mobilized during the spring flood; a necessary condition for the formation of ice jams. These thresholds are likely to vary between regions and watersheds, but their existence suggests that the hydrological, cryological and physical conditions associated with the onset of mechanical breakups can possibly be met only in some more or less specific compartments (or subwatersheds) within basins. Moreover, tree-ring data indicate that even where drainage area thresholds are crossed, ice-jam frequencies can still vary considerably at the local scale. Some sites will experience very frequent ice jams, whilst some other might only record these events once in a century.

Finally, a few long-term and large-scale studies have suggested that ice jams may have a noticeable geomorphological impact within cold-region watersheds. The most striking impact consisted of a possible enlargement of bankfull channels resulting from the abrasive action of ice against riverbanks. A second observation was the appearance of a typical ice-scoured morphology characterized by a pronounced erosion talus located above the genetic floodplain level. It is important to determine whether or not these features are widespread within watersheds. Whilst some studies suggested that these impacts could be widespread beyond a certain drainage-area threshold following mechanical breakups (Smith, 1979, Best et al., 2005), some other works have proposed that the presence of an ice-jam "signature" in the fluvial landscape is only possible if a minimal frequency of events is attained.

Clearly, in order to better understand the role of ice as a geomorphological agent in cold-environment rivers, additional large-scale and long-term studies are required. However, in gravel-bed rivers specifically, these studies should ideally be conducted jointly with other research initiatives focused on understanding the processes occurring at the reach scale (or even at smaller scales). This complementary approach would allow one to embrace a larger spectrum of the complexity found in cold-region rivers and to better understand the imbrication of temporal and spatial scales that characterize river-ice processes in these environments.

## 39.5   REFERENCES

Best, H., McNamara, J.P., and Liberty, L. 2005. Association of ice and river channel morphology determined using ground-penetrating radar in the Kuparuk River, Alaska. *Arctic, Antarctic and Alpine Research* **37**: 157–162.

Boucher, E., Begin, Y., and Arseneault, D. 2009a. Hydro-climatic analysis of mechanical breakups reconstructed from tree-rings, Necopastic watershed, northern Quebec, Canada. *Journal of Hydrology* **375**: 373–382.

Boucher, E., Begin, Y., and Arseneault, D. 2009b. Impacts of recurring ice jams on channel geometry and geomorphology in a small-high boreal watershed. *Geomorphology* **108**: 273–281.

Dionne, J.-C. 1974. How drift-ice shapes the St-Lawrence. *Canadian Geographic Journal* **88**(2): 4–9.

Dionne, J.-C. 1976. Le glaciel de la région de La Grande rivière, Québec subarctique. *Revue de Géographie de Montreal* **30**: 133–153 [in French].

Dionne, J.-C. 1978. Le glaciel en Jamesie et en Hudsonie, Québec subarctique. *Revue de Geographie physique et Quaternaire* **32**: 3–70 [in French].

Dyke, L.D. 2000. Shoreline permafrost along the Mackenzie River. In Dyke, L.D. and Brooks, G.R., editors, *The Physical Environment of the Mackenzie Valley, North-West Territories; A Base Line for the Assessment of Environmental Change*. Ottawa, Geological Survey of Canada, pp. 187–195.

Ettema, R. 2002. Review of alluvial-channel responses to river ice. *Journal of Cold Regions Engineering* **16**: 191–217.

Gerard, R. and Karpuk, E. W. 1979. Probability Analysis of Historical Flood Data. American Society of Civil Engineers, *Journal of the Hydraulics Division* **105**: 1153–1165.

Hamelin, L.E. 1979. The bechevnik: a river bank feature from Siberia. *The Musk Ox* **25**: 70–72.

Hupp, C.R. 1988. Plant ecological aspects of flood geomorphology and paleoflood history. In Baker, V.R., Kochel, R.C., and Patton, P.C., editors, *Flood Geomorphology*. New York, John Wiley & Sons, Inc., pp. 335–356.

Mackay, D.K., Sherstone, D.A., and Arnold, K.C. 1974. Channel ice effects and surface water velocities from aerial photography of Mackenzie River break-up. In *Hydrological Aspects of Northern Pipeline Development*. Task Force on Northern Oil Development, Environmental-Social Program, Northern Pipelines, Saskatoon, Saskatchewan, Report 74-12, pp. 71–107.

Payette, S., 1980. Les grandes crues glacielles de la Rivière aux Feuilles (Nouveau-Québec): une analyse dendrochronologique. *Le Naturaliste Canadien (Canadian Naturalist)* **107**: 215–225 [in French].

Prowse, T.D. 1995. River ice processes. In Beltaos, S., editor, *River Ice Jams*. Highlands Ranch, CO, Water Resources Publications LLC, pp. 29–68.

Prowse, T.D. 2001. River-ice ecology: hydrologic, geomorphic and water-quality aspects. *Journal of Cold Regions Engineering* **15**: 1–16.

Prowse, T.D. and Gridley, N.C. 1993. *Environmental Aspects of River Ice*. National Hydrology Research Institute, Saskatoon, NHRI Science Report 5.

Smith, D.G. 1979. Effects of channel enlargement by river ice processes on bankfull discharge in Alberta, *Canada. Water Resources Research* **15**: 469–475.

Smith, D.G. 2003. 1100 years of ice jam flooding in the Peace River Delta interpreted from flood bed sediments and ice-scarred trees. In Hicks, F., editor, *Proceedings of the 12th Workshop on the Hydraulics of Ice Covered Rivers, Edmonton, 19–20 June*. Canadian Geophysical Union, Hydrological Sciences Section, Committee on River Ice Processes and the Environment, pp. 241–260.

Smith, D.G. and Pearce, C.M. 2002. Ice jams caused fluvial gullies and scour holes on northern river flood plains. *Geomorphology* **42**: 85–95.

Smith, D.G. and Reynolds, D.M. 1983. Tree scars to determine the frequency and stage of high magnitude river ice drives and jams. *Canadian Water Resources Journal* **8**: 77–94.

Thorne, C.R. 1998. *Stream Reconnaissance Handbook: Geomorphological Investigation and Analysis of River Channels*. Chichester, John Wiley & Sons, Ltd.

Thorne, C.R., Allen, R.G., and Simon, A. 1996. Geomorphological river channel reconnaissance for river analysis, engineering and management. *Institute of British Geographers Transactions* **21**: 469–483.

Timoney, K. Peterson, G., Fargey, P. *et al.* 1997. Spring ice jam flooding of the Peace-Athabasca Delta: evidence of a climatic oscillation. *Climatic Change* **35**: 463–483.

Walker, J.H. and Hudson, P.F. 2003. Hydrologic and geomorphic processes in the Colville River delta, Alaska. *Geomorphology* **56**: 291–303.

# Index

accretion bars, in architectural element analysis, 490
acoustic Doppler current profiler (ADCP), 318–9, 325–9
acoustic Doppler velocimeter (ADV), 317
active channel width, in braided channels, 92–3
active layer, 103
  depth, 53
  thickness, 61–3, 104, 106, 120, 175
  size segregation, 63–5
active width of channel, 503
adaptive management, 184
ADCP, 342–9
  and LiDAR, integrated measurements, 296–8
  in gravel-bed rivers, 342–9
  in sand-bed rivers, 342–6
  noise, 344
  principles, 292
  review of applications, 292–3, 295–6
Adda River, Italy, 73
Ain River, France, 128
airborne LiDAR, 323–4
Allt Dubhaig, UK, 57, 60–2
alluvial landscape evolution, 475–94
alluvial overprint, 427
Amazon River, 274
American River, California, 183
anabranching, in ice-affected river, 534
analysis of characteristics, 105
anchor ice, 526–7, 530
  and sediment entrainment, 531
animals as geomorphic agents, 225–9
animals, foraging activity, 228
aquatic habitat, 193–211, 225–6
ArcGIS Bathymetry Toolkit, 278
architectural element analysis, 490
armour, 173–5, 419, 464–5
  armour layer, 514, 518–20
  armour ratio, 61, 505
aspect ratio, *see* width-to-depth ratio

Athabasca River, Alberta, 533
Atlantic salmon (*Salmo salar*), 161, 197, 206–11
Aufeis, 528–9
AVHRR, 263
Avoca River, NZ, 507
avulsion, in ice-affected river, 534

bank accretion, 106–8
bank erodibility coefficient, 108
bank, properties, 107
  model, 107
  shear stress on, 108
bank erosion, 106–8, 162
  hydraulic erosion, 487
  ice gouging, 533
  ice-induced erosion, 535–7, 551
  mass failure, 486–7
  retreat, 107
bank stability, 107
  role of soil properties, 486–7
  role of vegetation, 487–9
  porewater pressure, 107
bar dynamics, field studies, 90–91
  remote sensing, 90–91
barfull stage, 93
bar-pool sequence, 420–1
bars
  alternate, 75–6, 78–80
  analytical models, 72–5
  forced, 74–5
  free, 74
  mid-channel (medial), 76–8
  morphodynamics, 71–85, 90–94, 96–99,
  most probable number, 98
  steady, *see* bars, forced
Bas Arolla, Switzerland, 408
base-level changes, 404
base level, hillslope, 401

bathymetric LiDAR, 272–4
bathymetry
  non-contact mapping, 321, 323–5
  passive method, 325
  photogrammetric methods, 325
  spectral methods, 325
Beatton River, British Columbia, 108
beaver, 227
bechevnik (becevnik), 536–7
bedrock erosion, quarrying, 405
bed, *see* channel bed
bed material, texture, 115
  transport, 502–9
  transport pathway, 349
bed roughness, 103, 364, 440
bed sediment, composition, 105
  deposition, 103–4
  erosion, 103–4
  lateral flux, 126
  lateral storage, 127
bed sediment size, remote sensing measurements,
    276–7
bedfast ice, 542
bedload transport, 39–49
  discrete particle modeling, 119
  full mobility, 42–5
  high resolution process models, 116–20
  in braided channels, 507
  in ice-affected river, 530–2
  in steep channels, 387–92
  prediction, 386–95
  surface processes, 45–9
  Wilcock-Crowe equation, 184
bedload, apparent velocity, 346–8
  fluctuations, 46–47
  flux variability, 512
  sheets, 46–49, 53
bedrock channel, 401, 419–22, 424
  erosion of, 401
  sediment transport in, 401
bedrock confined channel, 424–5
bedrock constrained channel, 424–5
bedrock erosion, 401, 404–7
  by abrasion, 405
  by cavitation, 405
  by shear detachment, 405
  by solution, 405
bedrock footprint, 427
bed-structure sediment load, 104
Beer-Lambert Law, 269
berm, 378
biotope, 153
  mappng using LiDAR, 293–4, 298
Black River, Vermont, 173
Bonaventure River, Quebec, 208, 210
border ice, 526
boundary conditions, upstream, 105
Brahmaputra River, 108
braided channel, 477–82, 502

bedload flux, 500
  braiding intensity, 93
  width scaling, 504
Brazos River,Texas, 269, 332
break-up, mechanical (dynamic), 550
Brenta River, Italy, 92
bridge abutment, 26–7
Brook trout (*Salvelinus fontinalis*), 199
Bull trout (*Salvelinus confluentus*), 199

CAESAR, 513
Camp Creek, Oregon, 217–8
Campbell River, British Columbia, 183, 187
cap ice, 544
Carnation Creek, British Columbia, 57–65
Cascapédia River, Quebec, 219
celerity, of bed level perturbation, 105
CFD modeling, 117–9
channel
  autogenic instability, 481–2
  bedrock confined, 424–5
  bedrock constrained, 424–5
  bedrock exposure, 420–1
  cascade, 356
  gullied, 421–2
  in transient condition, 403, 425
  meandering, 23, 24–5
  non-uniform, *see* non-uniform channel
  response to disturbance, 464ff
  sediment supply-limited, 464
  semi-alluvial, 416, 420-1
  step-pool, 354–9
  threshold, 422
channel bed
  active exchange, 61
  bed material size segregation, 63–5
  changes, 436
  exchange sites, 56–59
  granular changes, 436
  gravel exchange, 56–66
  level, 105
  mobility, 203, 438–40
  passive exchange, 61
  patches, 45
  roughness, 419–20
  scour and fill, 61–3
  structure, 464–5
  surface layer, 56–66
  topography, 106, 228
channel change, 162, 435–51, 475
  bifurcation, 82–4
  conceptual models, 444
  numerical models, 449
  prediction, 443–9
  quantitative models, 444–5
  channel change, scales of, 436–41
  spatial and temporal variability, 441–3
  channel change, state diagrams, 446–9
  theoretical equations, 445–6

channel definition
  by sediment load, 480
  planform, 478–9
  sinuosity, 479–80
  width-to depth ratio, 480–81
channel deformation waves, 96
channel design, *see* stream channel design
channel fill, 489–90
channel geometry, changes, 436
channel metamorphosis, 440–1
channel morphology, ice effects, 537–8
  rock control, 403–11
  substrate control, 404
channel pattern, meandering and braided, 96
  prediction, 81–2
channel planform, in palaeoenvironmental reconstruction, 492
channel planform, mapping by remote sensing, 263–5
channel response, rate, 162
channel stability, 378, 543
  and hydroclimate, 450
  in ice-affected river, 533–4
channel substrate, rock mass strength, 404
channel template, 138
channel transition, meandering to braided, 96–99
channel width, 407–8, 462, 503–4
  active width, 92–3, 503
  and mid-channel bars, 76–8
Chinook salmon (*Oncorhynchus tshawytscha*), 197–8
Clackamas River, Oregon, 173–4
Clearwater River, Washington, 408
coherent flow structures, 13–14, 32, 344
cold-regions drainage basins, river ice effects, 546–53
Coles' wake parameter, 26
Colorado River, USA, 58, 173–7
Columbia River, USA, 198
Colville River, Alaska, 541
concavity index, 407
confluence scour and fill, 490
convective acceleration, 25
Cowlitz River, Washington, 183
crayfish, experiments with, 229–35
crayfish, impact in gravel-bed rivers, 229–35
critical flow, 363
culvert, 162
Cuneo Creek, California, 420
cut-off, in ice-affected river, 534–5

dam breach, 162
dams, geomorphic response, 167–78, 182–7
  analytical approaches to geomorphic response, 169–73
  conceptual model of geomorphic response, 167–8
  downstream degradation, 169
  downstream effects, 169, 182–7
  estimating the trend of geomorphic response,
    170–3
  flushing flows, 176
  geomorphic impacts, 165–7
  global data, 166–7
  gravel introduction, 178

  mitigation of effects, 182ff
  role of tributaries, 175–6
debris floods, 392–5
debris flow, 53, 387, 392–5, 421–2
  transition from fluvial transport, 387, 392–5
Delauney triangulation, 267
DEMs of difference (DoD), 306–11
DEMs, for vertical change detection, 274
Deschutes River, Oregon, 171, 173
design discharge, 141–2
detachment-limited erosion, 405–6
direct numerical simulation (DNS), 104
discharge
  design, 141–2
  ice-laden, 543
  representative formative, 93
discrete particle modeling, 119
disturbance regime, 442
  legacy, 443
DNS, 104
domestic animals, 227
Dora di Veny (river), Italy, 73
Duchesne River, Utah, 173, 176–7
dunes, sand, 103, 344
dynamic equilibrium, 425, 444

EAARL system (LiDAR), 273, 303
echo sounders, 319–21
ecohydraulics, 226
ecological production function, 245
ecology and rivers, 109
ecomorphology, 108–10
ecosystem engineering, 227
ecosystem services, 242–55
  evaluation methods, 243
  final services, 243–5
  indicators, 243–6
  intermediate services, 245
  workshop, 242–55
eddy cascade, 14–15, 32
effective bed shear stress, 103
electromagnetic current meter (ECM), 339–40
energy balance of the mean flow, 6–8
enstrophy balance equations, 9–10
EO-1 hyperspectral sensor, 263
equifinality, 106
equilibrium channel, 138, 482
  conceptual models, 444
equilibrium response
  conceptual models, 444
  quantitative models, 444–5
  state diagrams, 446–9
  theoretical equations, 445–6
Erlenbach stream, Switzerland, 365, 367, 519
erodibility coefficient, bank, 108
erodibility, of channel substrate, 407
erosion
  beneath ice jams, 532–3
  climate-driven, 401

erosion (*Continued*)
  cover-dominated domain, 426
  detachment-limited, 405–6
  ice-induced on stream banks, 551
  of bedrock, 401ff
  parabolic model, 407
  tools-dominated domain, 426
erosion models
  detachment-limited, 406
  hybrid, 406
  saltation-abrasion model, 406–7
  sediment flux-dependent, 406–7
  stream power, 405–8
  transport limited, 406
  undercapacity, 406
erosion rate, 406
erosion threshold, 465
event sediment yield, 469
exchange layer, 104, *see also* active layer
Exner equation, 73, 105, 119

facies models, 489
  and grain size, 491
factor of safety, 486
fish density, and abundance, 218–20
fish habitat, and geomorphology, 216–22
  habitat scales, 216–22
  uncertainty in, 217–8
fish, locally high abundance, 220
  patchiness in habitat relations, 220
flood history, 465
floodplain, 123–132
  deposits, in architectural element analysis, 490
flow concentration, under ice, 534
flow drag, 109
flow regime, tumbling, 354
flow resistance, 379, 384
  and bedload transport, 387–92
  and skimming flow, 388
  base-level resistance, 388
  form resistance, 387
  grain resistance, 387
  Manning-Strickler equation, 389
  modelling, 363–4
  of macro-roughness, 388
  partitioning, 362–3, 387
  variable power equation, 388
flow structures, at confluences, 17
flushing flows, 176
fluvial incision, effects of sediment, 402
fluvial palaeosystems, data sources, 477
formative discharge, representative, 93
Fraser River, British Columbia, 79, 81, 342–7
frazil ice, 526
friction slope, 342
Frio River, Texas, 58
full mobility transport, modeling, 45
  profiles, 42–4
  grain size segregation, 44–5

functional habitat units, 208
fuzzy inference, applied to topographic change, 309–11

Gamma probability density, 507
Gardon River, France, 324
geomorphic gravel augmentation, 183
geomorphic resilience, 160–163
geomorphic work of rivers, 542
geomorphology, and fish habitat, 216–22
GRACE satellite measurements, 274
graded channel, 482
graded state, 444
grain hiding and exposure, 103
grain resistance, 387
grain roughness, detection by terrestrial LiDAR, 293
grain segregation, 103
grain size distribution, 378
grain size, detection by terrestrial LiDAR, 293
grain sorting, 103
granular flow, 40–2
  avalanching, 40
  Bagnold's flow regimes, 40
  profile, 41–2
  rolling, 40
  size segregation, 41
  states of, 40
gravel augmentation, 183
  geomorphic performance, 187
  grain size distribution, 183
gravel exchange, 56–66
  and bar type, 66–7
  exchange depth, 61–3
  exchange probability, 60
  frequency, 59–60
  pathways, 59
  re-exposure, 60
gravel mining, 92
gravel transport, unencumbered, 185
gravel, ecologically appropriate texture, 183
gravel-bed rivers
  and salmonid habitat, 193–211
  channel changes, 475
  data sources, 475–8
  ecosystem services, 242–55
  metamorphosis, 492–3
  modelling with CFD, 117–9
  morphodynamics of bars, 71–85
  process modeling, 116–7
Green River, Colorado, 171, 176–7
Green River, Washington, 183, 187
ground-penetrating radar, 324–5
groyne, 26–7
Gunnison River, Colorado, 58

habitat
  heterogeneity, 207–9
  loss, 161
  rehabilitation, 182

aquatic, 225–6
functional, 153
hanging ice dam, 527
Harris Creek, British Columbia, 57, 59
headcut, 380
Henry Mountains, Utah, 409
hierarchical patch dynamics (HPD), 208
Hondo Creek, Texas, 58
horizontal acoustic Doppler current profiler (HADCP), 317–8
hydraulic environment, remote sensing of, 261–299
hydraulic erosion, 487
hydraulic geometry, 96–99, 138, 185, 386, 403, 482–9
  data sources, 476
  dimensionless, 364, 388
  in palaeoenvironmental reconstruction, 492
  influence of bedload, 484–6
  influence of discharge, 483–4
  of ice-affected rivers, 543–4, 551–2
hydroclimate, 436, 450
Hydropsychids, 228–9
hyporheic flow, 198–203

ice
  anchor, 526–7, 530
  bedfast, 542
  border, 526
  cap ice, 544
  effect on sediment transport, 541
  effects on gravel-bed channels, 525–38
  frazil, 526
  gouging, 533
  jam, freeze-up and break-up, 527–8
  push, 530
  rafting, of sediment, 530
  run, 530, 533
  seeding, 526, 530
ice-jam
  chronology, 550–1
  dynamics, 548–51
  frequency, 548
  magnitude, 550
  threshold (spatial), 550
imbrication, gravel, 231
incision, headward, 514
information systems, for hydraulic data, 332–3
infrastructure scale, 147
instability, autogenic, 481–2
instruments, for hydraulic and morphological measurements,
    315–35
  close-range remote-sensing, 320–5
  acoustic, 316–20
invertebrates, impact in gravel-bed rivers, 228–9
IPS model, 125–6

Jacoby Creek, California, 421
jammed state hypothesis, 378

Kamchatka River, Russia, 200
Kanaka Creek, British Columbia, 228

Kazakhstan debris-flow experiments, 393
kinematic sieving, 41
Kissimmee River, Florida, 325, 327–8
knickpoint, 407
  migration, 405
Kuparuk River, Alaska, 542–3

Lainbach, Germany, 57, 59
Lamar River, Wyoming, 269, 270, 271
Landsat thematic mapper, 263
landscape evolution, cause and effect, 512
  alluvial, 475–94
  modelling, 512–21
landscape modelling, boundary conditions, 520
  error accumulation, 517
Laramie River, Wyoming, 525, 530
large woody debris, 161
legacy of past disturbance, 443
Leonardo da Vinci, 3–4
LES, 25–7
level of detection (LoD), 307
LiDAR, 263
  aerial infrared, 286–91
  airborne, 323–4
  and ADCP, integrated measurements, 296–8
  bathymetric, 272–4, 288, 291, 324
  detection of surface roughness, 263
  intensity of returns, 263
  precision of measurements, 265–6
  terrestrial, 287, 291
  terrestrial, measurement error, 302
linear stability models, 96
Ludwig Prandtl, 3–5
LWD, 161

Mackenzie River, NWT, 533
magnitude and frequency, 436, 464
  of competent events, 542
Manning-Strickler equation, 389
mass failure of stream bank, 486–7
mass flux scaling (MFS), 118
mathematical modeling, 101–12
  analytical solutions, 104–6
  trends in, 101
mean velocity, 342–8
mean vorticity equation, 9
meander model, 107
meandering channel, 23–5, 125–6, 502
meandering river, definition, 478–82
meandering, confined, 427
Mekong River, Cambodia and Laos, 426–8
Merced River, California, 183
Middle Fork John Day River, Oregon, 220
Mississippi River, USA, 274
  Pool 16, 325–9
Missouri River, USA, 17, 343–5, 534–6
mixed bedrock-alluvial system, 424
model
  acceptance criteria, 111

model (*Continued*)
  -benchmark experiments, 111
  calibration, 110–11, 114
    validation, 105, 110–11, 114–5
    verification, 110, 115
    test reaches, 91–2
    testing, 90–94
modelling, data availability, 114
modelling, river habitats, 115
Mokelumne River, California, 183
morphodynamic model, 1-D 184
morphodynamics, mathematical modelling, 101–12,
    123–32
  feedback, 161
  modelling, 116–20
  of multi-thread channels, 78–81
morphological change
  by inverse modeling, 306
  detection, 294–5
  from remote sensing, 303–13
  ground-based measurements, 305–6
  in the wetted channel by remote sensing, 303–6
morphological sediment budget, 184
morphosedimentary unit, 490
multi-beam echo sounder (MBES), 320–1, 329–31

Nahal Hebron, Israel, 57, 59–61
Nahal Og, Israel, 57, 59–60
naled (river icing), 529
natural channel design (NCD), 138, 150, 154, 160
Necopastic River, Quebec, 547–553
channel non-uniformity, 23
non-uniform channel
  curved, 23, 24–5
  local perturbation, 24, 26–7
  varying cross-section, 23, 26
  varying depth, 23, 25–6
  varying width, 23, 26
North Ashburton River, NZ, 268
North River, North Carolina, 229
numerical modelling, 101–12
  1-D, 123–32, 184
  1-D with off-channel storage, 127–32
  planimetric centreline evolution, 124–5
  vegetation, 109
  non-linearity, 513–4

object recognition methods, 339, 341
optimal hypotheses, 462
Orange River, South Africa, 426

palaeocurrent analysis, 490
palaeoenvironmental reconstruction, qualitative, 489–91
    quantitative, 491–2
Parker's channel classification criterion, 481–82
partial mobilization, 465
partial transport, 58–9
particle image velocimetry, large scale (LSPIV),
    321–3

particle travel distance, 406, 417
Payette River, Idaho, 442
Peace River, Alberta, 173
    delta, Alberta, 548
Pedernales River, Texas, 58
Petite Cascapédia River, Quebec, 208, 210
photogrammetry, 265, 267–8
  errors, 267–8
photosieving, for bed sediment size, 276–7
piezoelectric pressure sensor, 339
plane bed, bedrock, 401
planimetric centreline evolution model, 124–5
Platte River, Nebraska, 273
plucking, by ice, 536
pool (in step-pool sequence), 379
pool-riffle, bedrock, 401
pore-fillling sediment load, 104
porosity, of bed sediments, 103
pothole, 401
Prandtl's first kind of secondary flow, 24–7
Prandtl's second kind of secondary flow, 24–7
process domain, 419–22, 442
    debris-flow, 421–2

radar, 263
    ground-penetrating, 324–5
    measuring water surface velocity, 323, 339–41
Raman scattering, 273
RANS, 25–7
Red River, Oklahoma, 173
redd, 227
    Gravels, 228
Redwood Creek, California, 420
Rees River, New Zealand, 346–9
reference shear stress, 505
regime channel, 482
regulated rivers, 165–78
remote sensing of rivers, 261–312
    active imaging, 261
    combined optical and photogrammetric method, 271–2
    confusion of shadow and water, 262–3
    Hydrolight radiative transfer model, 269
    multi-band optical imagery, 270
    of bar dynamics, 90–1
    of bed sediment size, 276–7
    optical imagery, 261
    optical imagery, illumination, 270
    precision, 283–4
    resolution, 283–4
    sequential photography, 264
    vertical change detection, 274–6
Renous River, Quebec, 82
representative discharge, 403–4
representative formative discharge, 93
reservoir, sediment, 125
resilience, geomorphic, 160–3
resistance to flow, dunes, 331
restoration, *see* river restoration
Reynolds averaging, 11

Reynolds equation, 5
Reynolds stress, 25–6
Reynolds-averaged Navier-Stokes equations (RANS), 5–6
Rhine River, Germany, 101–2
Rhine River, Liechtenstein, 73
riffle, artificially constructed, 183
riffle-pool, 28
Rio Cordon, Italy, 57, 59–60, 357, 364–6, 469
Rio Frijoles, Panama, 228
Rio Grande, USA, 173
Rio Torto, Italy, 410
riparian restoration, 160
riparian vegetation, 109
    and bank stability, 487–9
    data sources, 477
    in ice-affected river, 537
River Bain, UK, 231
river bank structure, affected by ice, 551–2
River Bléone, France, 46
River Bollin, UK, 81
River Dane, UK, 77
River Dean, UK, 77
river ecology, 101
river ecosystem services, 242–55
river enhancement, 150
River Feshie, UK, 275, 306–7, 309–11
river ice, effects on gravel-bed channels, 525–53
    and geomorphic work, 542–3
river icing (naled), 529
river metamorphosis, 489–93, 500
    criteria for, 481–2
river modelling, computer technology, 101
river morphodynamics, 90–4
    modelling, 101–14
river morphology and sediment supply, 502–10
river morphology, changes, 435–51
River Rede, UK, 294
river regime, 443
river rehabilitation, 150
river restoration, 150–60
    definition, 150
    engineering design, 151
    form and function, 151–2
    inventory of altered rivers, 152–3
    reference reach, 152
    restoration practice, 226
    social dimension, 153–6
River South Tyne, UK, 293
River Spey, UK, 177
River Spree, Germany, 13
river stability, 435
River Styles, 151, 153
River Tees, UK, 46
River Thames, UK, 153
River Voagris, Greece, 410
River Wharfe, UK, 58, 294, 297–8
River Xerias, Greece, 410
river-ice dynamics, 546
riverine habitat, 193–211

riverscape, and salmonid habitat, 206–11
Rivière Matane, Quebec, 428
Rivière Ste. Marguerite, Quebec, 429
Roaring River, Colorado, 391
rock mass strength, 404
rock-bed river, 424
roughness, 440
    of streambed, 103
    roughness scales, 387–8

Sacramento River, California, 183
Sacramento-San Joaquin river system, 183
salmonid habitat, 193–211
    habitat, and landscape ecology, 207–9
    habitat, complementation, 207–8
    habitat relations, 216–22
    riverscape perspective, 206–11
    watershed controls, 206–7
salmonid spawning habitat, 187, 195–206
    embryo mortality, 196
    fine sediment and hydraulic gradient, 204–6
    hyporheic flow, 198–203
    interregional variability, 200
    redds, 227
    selection, 195–6
    substrate mobility, 203
    substrate texture, 196–7
    testing hypotheses, 201–3
salmonid spawning preferences, 203–6
    factors affecting reproductive success, 197–8
sand dunes, 103, 344
Sandy Creek, Texas, 58
satellite sensors, spatial resolution, 91
scales, in river ice phenomena, length, time, dynamic,
    529–30
Secchi depth, 272
secondary flow, 3–18, 23–8, 31–4
    and channel form, 31–2
    and channel roughness, 32
    and flow resistance, 15
    and mixing, 17–18
    and river morphodynamics, 16–17, 32–4
    and turbulence, 11–15
    effect on sediment motion, 33
    effect on suspended sediment, 33
    energy balance of the mean flow, 6–8
    enstrophy balance equations, 9–10
    in meandering channels, 12–13
    mean vorticity equation, 9
    outer bank circulation cell, 25–1
    Prandtl's first kind, 24–7, 31
    Prandtl's second kind, 24–7, 31–4
    RANS, 5–6
    saturation of curvature, 25
    secondary currents of the first kind, 3–5
    secondary currents of the second kind, 3–5
    separation zone, 27
    skew-induced, 31
    stress-induced, 31–4

secondary flow (*Continued*)
  theoretical framework, 5–10
  turbulent energy balance, 8–9
sediment accommodation space, 521
sediment budget, morphologically based, 184
sediment
  buffering, 516, 521
  continuity, Exner equation, 119
  entrainment, crayfish impact on, 232
  entrainment, in ice-affected rivers, 541–3
  entrainment, spawning impact, 228
  exchange layer, 104 *see also* active layer
  flux, mapping, 342–9
  grain size, in braided and non-braided channels, 505
  gravel augmentation, 183
  load, bed-structure, 104
  load, pore-filling, 104
  patches, 505
  porosity, 103
  preservation, 491
  reservoir, 125–7
  role in semi-alluvial channels, 408–10
  slug, 186
  source, 162
  stage, 419–21
  storage, off-channel, 123–32
  storage, valley-average, 125–6
  stored in channel, 465
sediment supply, 404, 440, 502
  episodic, 465
  estimation, 139–40
sediment transport, 103–4, 512–17
  continuity, 162
  pathway, 349
  stages, 117
  channel capacity, 464
  data sources, 476–7
  equal mobility, 365
  equilibrium, 443
  granular perspective, 39–49
  incipient motion, 364
  modeling, 101–12
  modelling, scale-up, 119–20
  partial mobilization, 465
  partial transport, 58–9
  prediction with high resolution hydraulics, 119
  size segregation, 63–5
  stable state, 466–8
  transport capacity, 419–22
  under ice cover, 532
sediment yield, 469, 502
  variability of, 470
sedimentary link, 220
sediment cover term, 407
sediment cover, and channel dynamics, 410–11
self-organised criticality (SOC), 513–4, 518–20
semi-alluvial channels, 401–12, 416, 430–1, 424–30
shallow flows, 386
shear stress

critical dimensionless, 390
dimensionless, 390
effective, 103
in braided and non-braided channels, 505
shear stress, on river bank, 108
shear velocity, 342–7
Shields parameter, 103, 390, 407, 506
  bankfull, 438
  critical, 364
  excess stress, 439
SHOALS (LiDAR), 273, 303
sidewall effect, 26
Signal crayfish (*Pacifastacus leniusculus*), 229–35
skimming flow, 388
slush, 527
Smart's inclination index, 231, 234
Smoky Hill River, Kansas, 173
Snake River, Oregon, 173
SOC, see Self-organised criticality
Sockeye salmon (*Oncorhynchus nerka*), 227
Soda Butte Creek, Wyoming, 270
soils and bank stability, 486–7
soil cohesion, 486
sonar, 319–21
South Fork Salmon River, Idaho, 440
South Saskatchewan River, Saskatchewan, 275
spawning habitat, salmon, 187, 195–206
spontaneous percolation, 41, 44
spur dyke, 26–7
state diagrams, 446–9
steady state channel, 403, 425
steep channels, 353–95, 464–72
  alluvial, 386ff
  bedload transport rate, 366–8
  definition of, 353–4
  classification, 355–7
  dynamics of, 353–68
  flow resistance, 362–4
  hydrodynamics, 360–2
  morphology, 354–9
  scaling, 355–8
  sediment incipient motion, 364
  sediment storage, 367
  sediment transport, 364–8
step, 354–9, 378–84
  definition, 358–9
  burial, 380
  destruction by impact, 380
  failure, 360, 379–80
  formation, 359–60, 379
  formation, hydraulic control, 359
  formation, stochastic process, 359
  formation, variational approach, 359
  functional concept, 359
  mobility, 382–4
  slump, 380
  spacing, 381–4
  stability, 378, 381–4
  topple, 380

stepped bed, 354, 356
step-pool, 354–9, 378–84, 465
    morphology, 45
    bedrock, 401
strath terrace, 408
stratification, of the water column, 526
stream biota, 225ff
stream channel design, 141
    conceptual basis, 140–1
    decision analysis, 145
    higher order models, 144–5
    sediment continuity, 142–3
    uncertainty, 143–4
    water and sediment supply, 141
stream channel, semi-alluvial, 401–30
stream gradient, changes, 436
stream naturalization, 156
stream power, excess, 469
stream restoration, 137–45, 226
    profession, 139
stream system, response rate, 471
stream velocity, heterogeneity, 344
streambank, *see* bank
streambed, *see* channel bed
streamflow
    and climate, 403–4
    geomorphologically effective, 464
    representative discharge, 403–4
        variability, 404
Strickland River, Papua New Guinea, 125
Strimm Creek, Italy, 354
Stuart-Takla watersheds, British Columbia, 228
sub-resonant regime, 75
supercooled water, 526–7
super-resonant regime, 75
surface layer, 56–65
surface sediment, imbrication, 231
surface sediment, rearrangement, 231, 233
Surface Water and Ocean Topography satellite (SWOT), 284
suspension effect, 407

Tagliamento River, Italy, 79, 81–2, 84, 88, 92
Tectonics, 401, 404
template, channel, 138
terrace, fill, 161
    strath, 408
TerraSAR-X, 263
thalweg fills, in architectural element analysis, 490
thalweg sinuosity, in ice-affected river, 534
thermal processes, and river ice, 526
timber transport, 161
time scale, for bed evolution, 106
TLS, *see* LiDAR, terrestrial
Tollense River, Germany, 13

topographic change, detail versus accuracy, 311–3
    from remote sensing, 303–13
    patchy systematic error, 311
Torlesse Stream, New Zealand, 469
Torrente l'Alpa, Italy, 410
transport layer, 54, 103
transport of non-uniform sediment, 103–4
tread, 379
Tres Arroyos, Chile, 364–5
Trinity River, California, 173, 176–7, 183–7, 274, 324
tumbling flow regime, 362–3
Tuolumne River, California, 187
turbulence anisotropy, 32
turbulence intensity, 32
turbulent energy balance, 8–9
turbulent kinetic energy, in bend flow, 25–6

upscaling of process, 104

vegetation, drag, 109
vegetation, riparian, 108–10, 445
velocity reversal hypothesis, 28
velocity, heterogeneity, 344
velocity-area method (VAM), 323
vertical change detection by remote sensing, 274–6

Waiau River, NZ, 307
Waikato River, NZ, 18
Waimakariri River, NZ, 275, 308, 311, 507
Waioeka River, NZ, 58
Waipoa River, NZ, 58
Wairoa River, NZ, 58
water depth
    by GPR measurements, 274
    by radar measurements, 274
    from remote sensing, 266–74
    optical measurement, 267, 268–70
water flux, mapping, 342–9
water mass by gravitational flux (GRACE measurements), 274
water surface elevation, mapping from remote sensing, 265–6
water surface slope, from remote sensing, 265–6
Wenaha River, Oregon, 217–9
West Fork Smith River, Oregon, 217–8
wetted channel, identification by remote sensing, 262–3
width-to-depth ratio, 32, 97–8, 503
    resonant, 75
Wilcock-Crowe equation, 184
Williams Fork River, Colorado, 507

Yakima River, Washington, 273, 324
Yellowstone River, Montana, 528
Young's modulus, 407
Yukon River, Alaska, 533